H Gen 550

Customs in Common

E. P. Thompson

THE NEW PRESS
NEW YORK

Published in the United States by The New Press, New York
Distributed by W.W. Norton & Company, Inc.
500 Fifth Avenue, New York, NY 10110

Library of Congress Cataloging-in-Publication Data

Thompson, E. P. (Edward Palmer), 1924–
    Customs in common : studies in traditional popular culture / E.P.
Thompson.—1st American ed.
        p.   cm.
    Includes index.
    ISBN 1–56584–074–7
    1. England—Social conditions—18th century.   2. England—
Popular culture—History—18th century.   3. England—Social
life and customs—18th century.   4. Working class—England—
History—18th century.   5. England—Economic conditions—
18th century.   I. Title.
HN398.E5T48   1992
306'.0942'09033—dc20
                                                            92–13039
                                                                CIP

Established in 1990 as a major alternative to the large, commercial
publishing houses, The New Press is the first full-scale nonprofit
American book publisher outside of the university presses. The Press is
operated editorially in the public interest, rather than for private gain; it
is committed to publishing in innovative ways works of educational,
cultural, and community value, which despite their intellectual merits
might not normally be "commercially" viable. The New Press's
editorial offices are located at The City University of New York.

Printed in the United States of America.
10 9 8 7 6 5 4 3 2 1

Contents

to Martin Eve
uncommon customer

List of Illustrations

Preface and Acknowledgements

The studies in this book were intended as a single closely-related argument. This argument is rehearsed in the Introduction. It has, however, taken much longer to complete than I could ever have intended. It commenced — the work on "time" and on "the moral economy" — soon after I published *The Making of the English Working Class* over twenty years ago. Then it was delayed by work on eighteenth-century crime, which resulted in *Whigs and Hunters* and (with colleagues in the University of Warwick's Centre for the Study of Social History) *Albion's Fatal Tree.* Then, in the early eighties, I was turned aside once again, by the emergency of the "second cold war" and by the heavy demands of the peace movement. I do not regret this: I am convinced that the peace movement made a major contribution to dispersing the cold war, which had descended like a polluting cloud on every field of political and intellectual life. These difficulties (as well as ill health) seriously delayed the completion of *Customs in Common.*

I should explain now what I have done to make a consecutive argument. Two chapters are reproduced with no change from earlier publication. These are "Time, Work-Discipline and Industrial Capitalism", first published in *Past and Present*, no. 38, December 1967, and "The Moral Economy of the English Crowd in the Eighteenth Century", *Past and Present*, no. 50, 1971. In the first case, while interesting new work has been done on the question of time, none of it seemed to call for any major revisions to my article. I have left "the moral economy" to stand for a different reason. The thesis has been much discussed, criticised and developed, and at some points overtaken by subsequent research. At first I laboured to revise and to up-date it. But this proved to be a hopeless task. It was a kind of retrospective moving of the goal-posts. I found that I was modifying a text upon which much commentary by other scholars had been hung. I have therefore republished the original study and have written a quite new study, of greater length, "The Moral Economy Reviewed", in which I respond to some critics and reflect upon the issues raised by others.

The other studies in the book have either been extensively revised or appear here for the first time. The "Introduction" and "Patricians and Plebs" include passages which first appeared in "Patrician Society, Plebeian Culture", *Journal of Social History*, Vol. 7, no. 4, summer 1974, and "Eighteenth-century English society: class struggle without class?", *Social History*, Vol. 3, no. 2, May 1978. A shorter version of "Rough Music" appeared as " 'Rough Music': Le Charivari anglais" in *Annales: Économies, Sociétés, Civilisations*, 27e Année, no. 2, Mars-Avril 1972. I am grateful to the editors and journals concerned for allowing me to draw upon this material.

I am grateful also to those institutions and those colleagues who have afforded me hospitality and the opportunity to teach and to keep in touch with the historical profession over this long period. These include several American universities (Pittsburgh, Rutgers, Brown, Dartmouth College), as well as a circuit of Indian universities and the Sir Douglas Robb lectures at the University of Auckland, New Zealand. More recently I am especially grateful to three universities which took the risk of inviting me as a visitor — rusty as I was — and enabled me to rehabilitate myself as a scholar, after the long diversion of the peace movement years. These were, first, Queen's University, Kingston, Ontario (1988); the University of Manchester, which awarded me a Simon Senior Research Fellowship in 1988-89; and Rutgers University, which appointed me as Raoul Wallenberg Distinguished Visiting Professor in 1989-90, working with the Center for Historical Analysis. Without this generous assistance, and the stimulus of congenial colleagues, I might have lost touch with my trade. Finally, my warm thanks are due to the University of Birmingham, for affording to me library and research facilities as a Fellow of the Institute for Advanced Research in the Humanities.

If I were to thank everyone who has sent me references (for example of rough music or of wife sales) this preface would be several pages longer. In some cases I have acknowledged donors in my footnotes. I must beg forgiveness for over-looking others. Among those who have passed on information or who have exchanged views are: John Beattie, the late Kathleen Bumstead, Andrew Charlesworth, Robin Clifton, Penelope Corfield, Anna Davin, Natalie Davis, Isabel Emmett, the late G. Ewart Evans, John Fine, John Fletcher, Vic Gammon, John Gillis, Inge Goodwin, Jack Goody, the late Herbert Gutman, Julian Harber, Brian Harrison, J. F. C. Harrison, Martin Ingram, Joan Lane, Louis Mackay, the late David Morgan, Polly Morris, Bryan Palmer, Alfred Peacock, Iorwerth Prothero, Arnold Rattenbury, Ruth Richardson, John Rule, Raphael Samuel, Peter Searby, Robert Shenton, Paul Slack, Len Smith, Michael Sonenscher, Joan Thirsk, Keith Thomas, Dror Wahrman, John Walsh, E. R. Yarham, Eileen and Stephen Yeo. Very particular thanks are due to the late E. E. Dodd, who undertook many searches for me in the Public Record Office, and to Malcolm Thomas (now Librarian at Friends House, Euston Road) whose gifted services I was once fortunate to have as a research assistant; to Adrian Randall, Wendy Thwaites and John Walter, for acute commentary on my "moral economy" texts; to Douglas Hay and Peter Linebaugh, formerly co-editors of *Albion's Fatal Tree*, for advice on the law, on crime, and on many other matters; to Robert Malcolmson and to Rex Russell, for their generosity in passing on references as to wife sales and agrarian matters; to Roy Palmer, for sharing his inexhaustible and expert knowledge of ballad and broadside literature; to Nicholas Rogers, for keeping me in touch with his outstanding work-in-progress on the London and provincial crowd; and to Jeanette Neeson, whose work on eighteenth-century *Commoners* — soon to be published — will transform the understanding of that century's agrarian and social history, and to whose insights I am deeply indebted. Further particular thanks are due to Eveline King, who has skilfully deciphered and typed my much-corrected manuscript; to two friends over many years, who are also my publishers — in the United States, André Schiffrin, until recently the directing inspiration of Pantheon Books, before this was made impossible by the philistine policies of Random House — and in Britain, Martin Eve of Merlin Press, who has come to my aid in every difficulty. Both have been extraordinarily patient and encouraging in the face of my long delays. Finally, Dorothy Thompson, who has been my fellow-worker and who has shared my interests for more than four decades, has commented on each chapter as it came from the typewriter. Without her help, of many kinds, this book would not have been completed.

My thanks are also due to the libraries and county record offices acknowledged in my footnotes. These include, of course, the British Library, the British Museum Print Room, and the Public Record Office. Transcripts of Crown-Copyright records in the Public Record Office appear by permission of the Controller of H. M. Stationery Office, and my thanks are due for permission to reproduce Plates V and VI. My thanks are also due to the Librarian of Cecil Sharp house; to the marquess of Cholmondeley (for permission to draw upon the Cholmondeley (Houghton) papers, now in the Cambridge University Library); to the Librarian, the William L. Clement Library, Ann Arbor, Michigan, for permission to consult the Shelburne Papers; to the Rt. Hon. the Earl St. Aldwyn (for the papers of Charles Withers); to His Grace, the duke of Marlborough (for the papers of the earl of Sunderland at Blenheim Palace); to Lord Crawford, for permission to reproduce Plates XXIX and XXX, and to all other sources acknowledged in the footnotes and text. The passage (see p. 127) from A. W. B. Simpson, *A History of the Land Law* (Oxford, 2nd edn., 1986) is cited by permission of Oxford University Press. My thanks also go to the British Library and British Museum Print Room for permission to reproduce materials in their collections as illustrations.

Worcester, December 1990

Chapter One

Introduction: Custom
and Culture

All the studies in this book are connected by different paths
with the theme of custom as it was expressed within the
culture of working people in the eighteenth century and into
the nineteenth. It is my thesis that customary consciousness
and customary usages were especially robust in the eighteenth
century: indeed, some "customs" were of recent invention,
and were in truth claims to new "rights". Historians of the
sixteenth and seventeenth centuries have tended to see the
eighteenth century as a time when these customary usages
were in decline, along with magic, witchcraft and kindred
superstitions. The people were subject to pressures to
"reform" popular culture from above, literacy was displacing
oral transmission, and enlightenment (it is supposed) was
seeping down from the superior to the subordinate orders.

But the pressures of "reform" were stubbornly resisted,
and the eighteenth century saw a profound distance opened,
a profound alienation between the culture of patricians and
plebs. Peter Burke, in his illuminating study of *Popular
Culture in Early Modern Europe* (1978) suggests that this
distance was a European-wide phenomenon, and that one
consequence was the emergence of folklore, as sensitive (and
insensitive) observers in the upper ranks of society sent out
exploring parties to inspect the "Little Tradition" of the
plebs, and to record their strange observances and rituals.
Already, as the study of folklore emerged, these usages were
coming to be seen as "antiquities" or survivals, and the great
pioneer of folklore, John Brand, thought it necessary to
preface his *Observations on Popular Antiquities* with an
apology for attending to them at all:

... nothing can be foreign to our enquiry, much less beneath our notice, that concerns the smallest of the Vulgar; of those little Ones who occupy the lowest place, though by no means of the least importance in the political arrangement of human Beings.[1]

Thus folklore at its very origin carried this sense of patronising distance, of subordination (Brand noted that pride and the necessities of civil Polity had "portioned out the human Genus into. . . a variety of different and subordinate Species"), and of customs as survivals. For 150 years the preferred methodology of collectors was to group such survivals as "calendar customs", which found their last refuge in the deepest countryside. As one folklorist wrote at the end of the nineteenth century, his object was to describe:

The old customs which still linger on in the obscure nooks and corners of our native land, or which have survived the march of progress in our busy city's life.[2]

To such collectors we are indebted for careful descriptions of well-dressings or rush-bearings or harvest homes or, indeed, late examples of skimmington ridings. But what was lost, in considering (plural) customs as discrete survivals, was any strong sense of custom in the singular (although with many forms of expression), custom not as post-anything but as *sui generis* — as ambience, *mentalité*, and as a whole vocabulary of discourse, of legitimation and of expectation.

In earlier centuries the term "custom" was used to carry much of what is now carried by the word "culture". Custom was man's "second nature". Francis Bacon wrote of custom as induced and habitual inertial behaviour: "Men Profess, Protest, Engage, Give Great Words, and then Doe just as they have Done before. As if they were Dead Images, and Engines moved onely by the Wheeles of *Custome*." For Bacon, then, the problem was to induce better habits and as early in life as possible:

Since Custom is the principal Magistrate of Man's Life, let Men, by all Means, endeavour to obtain good Customs. . . Custom is most perfect

---

[1] John Brand and Henry Ellis, *Observations on Popular Antiquities* (1813), Vol. I, p. xxi. (Brand's Preface is dated 1795.)
[2] P. H. Ditchfield, *Old English Customs extant at the Present Time* (1896), Preface.

when it beginneth in young Years; This we call Education, which is, in Effect, but an early Custom.

Bacon was not thinking of the labouring people, but one hundred years later Bernard Mandeville, who was quite as convinced as was Bacon of the "Tyranny which Custom usurps over us",[1] was a great deal less well-disposed towards any universal provision of education. It was necessary that "great multitudes of People" should "inure their Bodies to Work" both for themselves and to support the more fortunate in Idleness, Ease and Pleasure:

> To make the Society Happy and People Easy under the meanest Circumstances, it is requisite that great numbers of them should be Ignorant as well as Poor. Knowledge both enlarges and multiplies our Desires. . . The Welfare and Felicity therefore of every State and Kingdom require that the Knowledge of the Working Poor should be confin'd within the Verge of their Occupations and never extended (as to things visible) beyond what relates to their Calling. The more a Shepherd, a Plowman or any other Peasant knows of the World, and the things that are Foreign to his Labour or Employment, the less fit he'll be to go through the Fatigues and Hardships of it with Chearfulness and Content.

Hence for Mandeville reading, writing and arithmetic "are very pernicious to the Poor".[2]

If many of the "poor" were denied education, what else did they have to fall back upon but oral transmission with its heavy freight of "custom". If nineteenth-century folklore, by separating survivals from their context, lost awareness of custom as ambience and *mentalité*, so also it lost sight of the rational functions of many customs within the routines of daily and weekly labour. Many customs were endorsed and sometimes enforced by popular pressure and protest. Custom was certainly a "good" word in the eighteenth century: England had long been priding herself on being Good and Old.[3] It was also an operative word. If, along one path, "custom" carried many of the meanings we assign now to

---

[1] Bernard Mandeville, *The Fable of the Bees* (Harmondsworth, 1970 edn.), p. 191: also p. 334.

[2] *Ibid.*, p. 294.

[3] For an excellent survey of custom, 1700-1880, see Bob Bushaway, *By Rite* (1982). Also R. W. Malcolmson, *Life and Labour in England, 1700-1780* (1981), Chapter 4, "Beliefs, customs and identities".

"culture", along another path custom had close affinities with the common law. This law was derived from the customs, or habitual usages, of the country: usages which might be reduced to rule and precedents, which in some circumstances were codified and might be enforceable at law. This was the case, above all, with *lex loci*, the local customs of the manor. These customs, whose record was sometimes only preserved in the memories of the aged, had legal effect, unless directly voided by statute law.[1] This is discussed more fully in Chapter 3. There were some industrial groups for whom custom was claimed with equal legal force — the Cornish tinners, with their Stannary Court, the free miners of the Forest of Dean with their "Book of Dennis".[2] The rights claimed by the Dean miners could possibly have descended from the thirteenth century, but the "Laws and Customs of the Miners" were codified in an Inquisition of 1610, when 48 free miners recorded their usages (first printed in 1687). Frequently the invocation of the "custom" of a trade or occupation indicated a usage so long exercised that it had taken on the colour of a privilege or right.[3] Thus in 1718 when clothiers in the South-West attempted to lengthen the cloth piece by half a yard, the weavers complained that they were acting "contrary to law, usage and custom from time immemorial". And in 1805 London printers complained that employers were taking advantage of the ignorance of their journeymen by "disputing or denying custom, and by refusing to acknowledge precedents, which have been hitherto the only reference."[4] Many of the classic struggles at the entry to the

---

[1] "A custom or prescription against a statute is void": but an exception was made for local corn measures, where "it is said. . . the custom of the place is to be observed, if it be a custom beyond all memory, and used without any visible interruption": Richard Burn, *The Justice of the Peace and Parish Officer* (14th edition, 1780), vol. I, p. 408.

[2] For the breakdown of custom in the Forest of Dean, see C. Fisher, *Custom, Work and Market Capitalism* (1981). Is it possible that "Dennis" is a corruption of the Statute of De Donis (1285)?

[3] Several of the studies in E. J. Hobsbawm, *Labouring Men* (1964) bear centrally upon custom. See also John Rule, *The Experience of Labour in Eighteenth-Century Industry* (1981), esp. Chapter 8, "Custom, Culture and Consciousness".

[4] John Rule, *op. cit.*, pp. 194, 196.

industrial revolution turned as much on customs as upon wages or conditions of work.

Most of these customs may be described as "visible": they were codified in some form, or they can be accounted for with exactness. But as the plebeian culture became more opaque to gentry inspection, so other customs became less visible. The ceremonies and processionals of the trades, which had once been built into the calendar of the corporate year — under the patronage of Bishop Blaize for the wool-combers, St. Clement for the blacksmiths, St. Crispin for the shoemakers — might still be celebrated on special occasions, such as coronations or anniversaries, in the eighteenth century. But in the nineteenth century such processionals lost their consensual "trade" endorsement, they were feared by employers and corporations as occasions for high spirits and disorder (as indeed they sometimes were),[1] and St. Clement was honoured, not in the streets, but in the trades' club or friendly society meeting in the tavern.[2]

This is symptomatic of the disassociation between patrician and plebeian cultures in the eighteenth and early nineteenth centuries.[3] It is difficult not to see this division in terms of class. A perceptive folklorist, G. L. Gomme, saw folklore as customs, rites and beliefs belonging to the people —

[1] In 1837 a Woolwich shopkeeper complained that on St. Clements Day [November 23rd] "a procession got up by the Blacksmiths' apprentices passed through the principal streets of the Town, attended by a large Mob, some carrying Torches, others discharging fireworks in great abundance in the most reckless manner, by which the horses attached to one of Mr Wheatley's Omnibuses. . . were so terrified as to. . . run the Pole of the Omnibus through your Memorialist's shop window". Memorial of Robert Wollett of Woolwich, 27 November 1837, in PRO HO 73.2.

[2] William Hone, *Every-Day Book* (1826), vol. I, col. 1499; F. E. Sawyer, "Old Clem Celebrations and Blacksmiths Lore", *Folk Lore Journal*, II, 1884, p. 321; G. P. G. Hills, "Notes on Some Blacksmiths' Legends and the Observance of St. Clement's Day", *Proceedings of the Hampshire Field Club*, vol. VIII, 1917-19, pp. 65-82.

[3] For the polarisation of cultures in the seventeenth century, see the editors' introduction to Anthony Fletcher and John Stevenson (eds.), *Order and Disorder in Early Modern England* (Cambridge, 1985); and for the "momentous split" between patrician and plebeian cultures, see Patrick Curry, *Prophecy and Power: Astrology in Early Modern England* (Oxford, 1989), esp. ch. 7.

> And oftentimes in definite antagonism to the accepted customs, rites and beliefs of the State or the nation to which the people and the groups of people belong. These customs, rites and beliefs are mostly kept alive by tradition. . . They owe their preservation partly to the fact that great masses of people do not belong to the civilisation which towers over them and which is never of their own creation.[1]

In the eighteenth century custom was the rhetoric of legitimation for almost any usage, practice, or demanded right. Hence uncodified custom — and even codified — was in continual flux. So far from having the steady permanence suggested by the word "tradition", custom was a field of change and of contest, an arena in which opposing interests made conflicting claims. This is one reason why one must be cautious as to generalisations as to "popular culture". This may suggest, in one anthropological inflexion which has been influential with social historians, an over-consensual view of this culture as "a system of shared meanings, attitudes and values, and the symbolic forms (performances, artifacts) in which they are embodied".[2] But a culture is also a pool of diverse resources, in which traffic passes between the literate and the oral, the superordinate and the subordinate, the village and the metropolis; it is an arena of conflictual elements, which requires some compelling pressure — as, for example, nationalism or prevalent religious orthodoxy or class consciousness — to take form as "system". And, indeed, the very term "culture", with its cosy invocation of consensus, may serve to distract attention from social and cultural contradictions, from the fractures and oppositions within the whole.

At this point generalisations as to the universals of "popular culture" become empty unless they are placed firmly within specific historical contexts. The plebeian culture which clothed itself in the rhetoric of "custom" and which is the central theme of this book was not self-defining or independent of external influences. It had taken form defensively, in opposition to the constraints and controls of

---

[1]G. L. Gomme, *Encyclopaedia of Religion and Ethics* (Edinburgh, 1913), entry on folklore, pp. 57-9, cited in Bushaway, *op. cit.*, pp. 10-11.

[2]P. Burke, *Popular Culture in Early Modern Europe* (1978), Preface, citing A. L. Kroeber and C. Kluckhohn, *Culture: a Critical Review of Concepts and Definitions* (New York, 1952).

the patrician rulers. The confrontations and negotiations between patricians and plebs are explored in Chapter 2, and case studies of the conflict between customary and innovative ("market") *mentalités* follow. In these studies I hope that plebeian culture becomes a more concrete and usable concept, no longer situated in the thin air of "meanings, attitudes and values", but located within a particular equilibrium of social relations, a working environment of exploitation and resistance to exploitation, of relations of power which are masked by the rituals of paternalism and deference. In this way (I hope) "popular culture" is situated within its proper material abode.

Let us resume the characteristic features of the eighteenth-century plebeian culture. As a matter of course it exhibits certain features commonly ascribed to "traditional" cultures. In rural society, but also in thickly populated manufacturing and mining areas (the West of England clothing regions, the Cornish tinners, the Black Country) there is a heavy inheritance of customary definitions and expectations. Apprenticeship as an initiation into adult skills is not confined to its formal industrial expression. It is also the mechanism of inter-generational transmission. The child serves her apprenticeship to household duties, first to her mother (or grandmother), then (often) as a domestic or farm servant. As a young mother, in the mysteries of child-rearing, she is apprentice to the matrons of the community. It is the same in the trades without formal apprenticeship. And with the induction into these particular skills comes an induction into the social experience or common wisdom of the community. Although social life is changing, and although there is much mobility, change has not yet reached that point at which it is assumed that the horizons of each successive generation will be different; nor has that engine of cultural acceleration (and estrangement), formal education, yet interpolated itself significantly into this generational transmission. [1]

---

[1] Two interesting studies of the restraint which custom may impose upon material expectations are: G. M. Foster, "Peasant Society and the Image of Limited Good", *American Anthropologist*, April 1965; Daniel Vickers, "Competency and Competition: Economic Culture in Early

Both practices and norms are reproduced down the generations within the slowly differentiating ambience of custom.
Traditions are perpetuated largely through oral transmission, with its repertoire of anecdote and of narrative
example; where oral tradition is supplemented by growing
literacy, the most widely circulated printed products, such as
chapbooks, almanacs, broadsides, "last dying speeches" and
anecdotal accounts of crime, tend to be subdued to the
expectations of the oral culture rather than challenging it with
alternatives.

This culture transmits vigorously — and perhaps it also
generates — ritualized or stylized performances, whether in
recreation or in forms of protest. It is even possible that
geographic mobility, together with growing literacy, actually
extends the range and distributes such forms more widely:
"setting the price", as the central action of a food riot, moves
across most of the country (Chapter 4); the ritual divorce
known as a "wife sale" appears to have distributed its
incidence throughout the country from some unknown point
of origin (Chapter 7). The evidence of rough music (Chapter
8) suggests that in the more traditional communities — and
these were by no means always ones with a rural profile —
quite powerful self-motivating forces of social and moral
regulation were at work. This evidence may show that while
deviant behaviour might be tolerated up to a point, beyond
that point the community sought to impose upon trans-
gressors its own inherited expectations as to approved marital
roles and sexual conduct. Even here, however, we have to
proceed with caution: this is not *just* "a traditional
culture". The norms so defended are not identical with those
proclaimed by Church or authority; they are defined within
the plebeian culture itself, and the same shaming rituals
which are used against a notorious sexual offender may be
used against the blackleg, or against the squire and his game-
keepers, the excise officer, the JP.

This, then, is a conservative culture in its forms, which
appeal to and seek to reinforce traditional usages. The forms

America", *William and Mary Quarterly*, 3rd series, vol. xlvii, no. 1,
January 1990.

are also non-rational; they do not appeal to "reason" through the pamphlet, sermon or platform; they impose the sanctions of force, ridicule, shame, intimidation. But the content or meanings of this culture cannot so easily be described as conservative. For in social reality labour is becoming, decade by decade, more "free" of traditional manorial, parochial, corporate and paternal controls, and more distanced from direct client dependence upon the gentry. Hence we have a customary culture which is not subject in its daily operations to the ideological domination of the rulers. The gentry's overarching hegemony may define the limits within which the plebeian culture is free to act and grow, but since this hegemony is secular rather than religious or magical it can do little to determine the character of this plebeian culture. The controlling instruments and images of hegemony are those of the Law and not those of the Church or of monarchical charisma. But the Law does not sow pious sisterhoods in cities nor extract the confessions of sinners; its subjects do not tell their rosaries nor go on pilgrimages to the shrines of saints — instead they read broadsides and carouse in taverns and at least some of the Law's victims are regarded, not with horror, but with an ambiguous admiration. The Law may punctuate the limits tolerated by the rulers; it does not, in eighteenth-century England, enter into the cottages, find mention in the widow's prayers, decorate the wall with icons, or inform a view of life.

Hence one characteristic paradox of the century: we have a *rebellious* traditional culture. The conservative culture of the plebs as often as not resists, in the name of custom, those economic rationalizations and innovations (such as enclosure, work-discipline, unregulated "free" markets in grain) which rulers, dealers, or employers seek to impose. Innovation is more evident at the top of society than below, but since this innovation is not some normless and neutral technological/sociological process ("modernization", "rationalization") but is the innovation of capitalist process, it is most often experienced by the plebs in the form of exploitation, or the expropriation of customary use-rights, or the violent disruption of valued patterns of work and leisure (Chapter 6). Hence the plebian culture is rebellious, but rebellious in defence of custom. The customs defended are the people's own, and some of them are in fact based upon rather recent assertions in practice. But when the people search for legitimations for protest, they often turn back to the paternalist regulations of a more authoritarian society, and select from among these those parts most calculated to defend their present interests — food rioters appeal back to the Book of Orders and to legislation against forestallers, etc., artisans appeal back to certain parts (e.g. apprenticeship regulation) of the Tudor labour code.

Nor is the social identity of many working people unambiguous. One can often detect within the same individual alternating identities, one deferential, the other rebellious.[1] This was a problem with which — using different terms — Gramsci concerned himself. He noted the contrast between the "popular morality" of folklore tradition and "official morality". His "man-in-the-mass" might have "two theoretical consciousnesses (or one contradictory consciousness)" — one of praxis, the other "inherited from the past and uncritically absorbed". When discussing ideology in his prison notebooks, Gramsci sees it as resting upon "the spontaneous philosophy which is proper to everybody". This philosophy (he concludes) derives from three sources: first, "language itself, which is a totality of determined notions and concepts, and not just of words, grammatically devoid of content"; second, "common sense"; and, third, popular religion and folklore.[2] Of these three, most Western intellectuals today would unhesitatingly award theoretical primacy to the first (language) as not only the carrier but as the constitutive influence upon consciousness. Indeed, while actual language — for example as dialect — has been little examined,[3] it has become fashionable to assume that the

[1] See Hans Medick, "Plebeian Culture in the Transition to Capitalism", in R. Samuel and G. Stedman Jones (eds.), *Culture, Ideology and Politics* (1982).

[2] See Antonio Gramsci, *Selections from the Prison Notebooks* (1971), pp. 419-25; Bushaway, *op. cit.*, pp. 11-12; T. J. Jackson Lears, "The Concept of Cultural Hegemony: Problems and Possibilities", *American Hist. Rev.*, 90, 1985.

[3] Social historians have made too little use of dialect studies, including Joseph Wright's in *English Dialect Dictionary*, 6 volumes (1898-1905), which is full of clues as to working usages.

plebs were in a sense "spoken" by their linguistic inheritance, which in turn is seen as a *bricolage* of disparate notions derivative from many sources but held in place by patrician categories. The plebs are even seen as captives within a linguistic prison, compelled even in moments of rebellion to move within the parameters of constitutionalism, of "Old England", of deference to patrician leaders and of patriarchy.

We can follow this argument some way. But what it overlooks are Gramsci's alternative sources of "spontaneous philosophy", and in particular "common sense" or praxis. For Gramsci also insisted that this philosophy was not simply the appropriation of an individual but was derived from shared experiences in labour and in social relations, and is "implicit in his activity and which in reality unites him with all his fellow-workers in the practical transformation of the real world. . ." Thus the "two theoretical consciousnesses" can be seen as derivative from two aspects of the same reality: on the one hand, the necessary conformity with the *status quo* if one is to survive, the need to get by in the world as it is in fact ordered, and to play the game according to the rules imposed by employers, overseers of the poor, etc.;[1] on the other hand the "common sense" derived from shared experience with fellow workers and with neighbours of exploitation, hardship and repression, which continually exposes the text of the paternalist theatre to ironic criticism and (less frequently) to revolt.

Another feature of this culture which is of special interest to me is the priority afforded, in certain areas, to "non-economic" over direct monetary sanctions, exchanges and motivations. This feature is now widely discussed as "the moral economy", and is the theme of Chapters 4 and 5. Again and again, when examining the behaviour of working people in the eighteenth century one finds it to be necessary to "de-code" this behaviour and its symbolic modes of expression and to disclose invisible rules unlike those which a historian of subsequent working-class movements has come to expect. In attending to the symbolism of protest, or in

[1] See my "Folklore, Anthropology, and Social History", *Indian Hist. Rev.*, vol. III, no. 2, Jan. 1977, p. 265.

decoding rough music or the sale of wives, one shares some of the preoccupations of historians of the sixteenth and seventeenth centuries of an anthropological orientation. In another sense the problems are different, and perhaps more acute, for capitalist process and non-economic customary behaviour are in active and conscious conflict, as in resistance to new patterns of consumption ("needs"), or in resistance to technical innovations or work-rationalizations which threaten to disrupt customary usage and, sometimes, the familial organization of productive roles.[1] Hence we can read much eighteenth-century social history as a succession of confrontations between an innovative market economy and the customary moral economy of the plebs.

In these confrontations it is possible to see prefigurements of subsequent class formations and consciousness; and the fragmented débris of older patterns are revivified and reintegrated within this emergent class consciousness. In one sense the plebeian culture is the people's own: it is a defence against the intrusions of gentry or clergy; it consolidates those customs which serve their own interests; the taverns are their own, the fairs are their own, rough music is among their own means of self-regulation. This is not *any* "traditional" culture but a rather peculiar one. It is not, for example, fatalistic, offering consolations and defences in the course of a lifetime which is utterly determined and constrained. It is, rather, picaresque, not only in the obvious sense that more people are mobile, go to sea, are carried off to wars, experience the hazards and adventures of the road.[2] In more settled ambiences — in the growing areas of manufacture and of "free" labour — life itself proceeds along a road whose hazards and accidents cannot be prescribed or avoided by forethought: fluctuations in the incidence of mortality, of prices, of unemployment, are experienced as external

---

[1] See, for example, Adrian J. Randall, "Work, Culture and Resistance to Machinery in the West of England Woollen Industry", in Pat Hudson (ed.), *Regions and Industries: a perspective on the Industrial Revolution in Britain* (Cambridge, 1989).

[2] Extreme examples of picaresque livelihoods are in Marcus Rediker, *Between the devil and the deep blue sea* (Cambridge, 1987), and Peter Linebaugh, *The London Hanged* (Harmondsworth, 1991).

accidents beyond any control; in general, the working population has little predictive notation of time — they do not plan "careers", or plan families, or see their lives in a given shape before them, or salt away weeks of high earnings in savings, or plan to buy cottages, or ever in their lives take a "vacation". (A young man, knowing that this will be so, may set off once in a lifetime, upon the road to "see the world".) Hence opportunity is grabbed as occasion arises, with little thought of the consequences, just as the crowd imposes its power in moments of insurgent direct action, knowing that its moment of triumph will last for only a week or a day.

I criticised earlier the term "culture", because of its tendency to nudge us towards over-consensual and holistic notions. And yet I have been driven back to an account of "plebeian culture" which may be open to the same criticisms. This may not much matter if we are using "culture" as a loosely descriptive term. After all, there are other descriptive terms in common currency, such as "society", "politics" and "economy": no doubt these deserve close interrogation from time to time, but if on every occasion that these were employed we had to engage in an exercise of rigorous definition the discourse of knowledge would indeed be cumbersome.

Even so we should not forget that "culture" is a clumpish term, which by gathering up so many activities and attributes into one common bundle may actually confuse or disguise discriminations that should be made between them. We need to take this bundle apart, and examine the components with more care: rites, symbolic modes, the cultural attributes of hegemony, the inter-generational transmission of custom and custom's evolution within historically specific forms of working and social relations. As the anthropologist Gerald Sider has shown in a group of astute studies of Newfoundland fishing villages:

> Customs do things — they are not abstract formulations of, or searches for, meanings, although they may convey meaning. Customs are clearly connected to, and rooted in, the material and social realities of life and work, although they are not simply derivative from, or reexpressions of these realities. Customs may provide a context in which people may do things it would be more difficult to do directly. . . they may keep the need for collective action, collective adjustment of interests, and

collective expression of feelings and emotions within the terrain and domain of the coparticipants in a custom, serving as a boundary to exclude outsiders. [1]

If I were to nominate those components of the bundle which makes up "popular culture" which most require attention today, these would include "needs" and "expectations". The industrial revolution and accompanying demographic revolution were the backgrounds to the greatest transformation in history, in revolutionising "needs" and in destroying the authority of customary expectations. This is what most demarks the "pre-industrial" or the "traditional" from the modern world. Successive generations no longer stand in an apprentice relation to each other. If we need a utilitarian apologia for our historical enquiry into custom — but I think we do not — it might be found in the fact that this transformation, this remodelling of "need" and this raising of the threshold of material expectations (along with the devaluation of traditional cultural satisfactions) continues with irreversible pressure today, accelerated everywhere by universally available means of communication. These pressures are now felt among one billion Chinese, as well as countless millions in Asian and African villages.

It is not simple to discuss these problems from our comfortable perspective to the "North" of the global divide. Any historian of labour is only too well aware of the self-interest and the class-bound apologetics which can always find reasons why the poor should stay poor. To cite Bernard Mandeville once more:

> It is impossible that a Society can long subsist and suffer many of its Members to live in Idleness, and enjoy all the Ease and Pleasure they can invent, without having at the same time great multitudes of People that to make good this effect, will condescend to be quite the Reverse, and by use and patience inure their Bodies to Work for others and themselves besides. [2]

This text has not lost its force today: it is the hidden text of the discourse between North and South. Yet we know also that global expectations are rising like Noah's flood, and that

[1] Gerald M. Sider, *Culture and Class in Anthropology and History* (Cambridge, 1986), p. 940.
[2] Mandeville, *op. cit.*, pp. 292-3.

the readiness of the human species to define its needs and satisfactions in material market terms — and to throw all the globe's resources onto the market — may threaten the species itself (both South and North) with ecological catastrophe. The engineer of this catastrophe will be economic man, whether in classically avaricious capitalist form or in the form of the rebellious economic man of the orthodox Marxist tradition.

As capitalism (or "the market") made over human nature and human need, so political economy and its revolutionary antagonist came to suppose that this economic man was for all time. We stand at the end of a century when this must now be called in doubt. We shall not ever return to pre-capitalist human nature, yet a reminder of its alternative needs, expectations and codes may renew our sense of our nature's range of possibilities. Could it even prepare us for a time when both capitalist and state communist needs and expectations may decompose, and human nature may be made over in a new form? This is, perhaps, to whistle into a typhoon. It is to invoke the rediscovery, in new forms, of a new kind of "customary consciousness", in which once again successive generations stand in apprentice relation to each other, in which material satisfactions remain stable (if more equally distributed) and only cultural satisfactions enlarge, and in which expectations level out into a customary steady state. I do not think that this is likely to happen. But I hope that the studies in this book may illuminate how custom is formed and how complex is its operation.

Chapter Two

The Patricians and the Plebs

"The miserable Circumstance of this Country is now such, that, in short, if it goes on, the Poor will be Rulers over the Rich, and the Servants be Governours of their Masters, the *Plebeij* have almost mobb'd the *Patricij*. . . in a Word, Order is inverted, Subordination ceases, and the World seems to stand with the Bottoim upward."
Daniel Defoe, *The Great Law of Subordination considered or, The Insolence and Insufferable Behaviour of SERVANTS in England duly enquired into* (1724).

I

The relationship which I wish to examine in this chapter is that between "the gentry" and "the labouring poor". Both terms are vague. But we have some notion as to what both stand for. In the first six decades of the eighteenth century one tends to associate the gentry with the land. Land remained the index of influence, the plinth on which power was erected. If one adds to direct landed wealth and status, that part of industry which either directly served the agricultural interest (transport, saddlery, wheelwrights, etc.) or which processed agricultural products (brewing, tanning, milling, the great woollen industry, etc.) one can see where the scales of wealth were tipped. So that, despite the immense growth of London and the growth of Liverpool, Manchester, Bristol, Birmingham, Norwich, Leeds etc., England retained until the 1760s an agrarian profile, and many who earned their wealth in urban, commercial occupations still sought to translate their wealth into gentry status by translating it into land. William Hutton, the Birmingham paper merchant, describes in his memoirs his first purchase of lands (1766): "ever since I was 8 years old, I had shewn a fondness for land. . . and wished to call some my own. This ardent desire after dirt never forsook me."[1]

Yet both "gentlemen" and "the poor" are "gentry-made terms"[2] and both carry a normative freight which can be taken on board uncritically by historians. We are told (for example) that "honour, dignity, integrity, considerateness, courtesy and chivalry were all virtues essential to the character of a gentleman, and they all derived in part from the nature of country life".[3] This suggests a somewhat distanced view of "country life", from which — just as from much eighteenth-century painting of the countryside[4] — the labourers have been subtracted. As for "the poor" this wholly indiscriminate term carries the suggestion that the bulk of the working population were deserving of gentry condescension, and perhaps of charity (and were somehow supported *by* the gentry instead of the direct opposite); and the term puts together paupers and fiercely-independent yeomen, small peasants, farm servants, rural artisans, and so on, in the same gentry-made category.

Vague as the two terms are, yet this chapter will turn upon these two poles and their relation to each other. I shall pass over a great deal of what lies in between: commerce, manu-facture, London's luxury trades, overseas empire. And my emphases will not be those which are popular with most established historians. There is perhaps a reason for this. No-one is more susceptible to the charms of the gentry's life than the historian of the eighteenth century. His major sources are in the archives of the gentry or aristocracy. Perhaps he may even find some of his sources still in the muniments room at an ancient landed seat. The historian can easily identify with his sources: he sees himself riding to hounds, or attending Quarter Sessions, or (if he is less ambitious) he sees himself as at least seated at Parson Woodforde's groaning table. The "labouring poor" did not leave their workhouses stashed with documents for historians to work over nor do they invite

[1] *The Life of William Hutton* (1817), p. 177.
[2] Jeanette Neeson gave me the term "gentry-made" for "the poor".
[3] F. M. L. Thompson, *English Landed Society in the Nineteenth Century* (1963), p. 16.
[4] See John Barrell, *The Dark Side of the Landscape* (Cambridge, 1980).

identification with their back-breaking toil. Nevertheless for the majority of the population the view of life was not that of the gentry. I might phrase it more strongly, but we should attend to the quiet words of M. K. Ashby: "The great house seems to me to have kept its best things to itself, giving, with rare exceptions, neither grace nor leadership to villages, but indeed depressing their manhood and culture."[1]

When I and some colleagues offered, a few years ago, a somewhat sceptical view of the virtues of the Whig great gentry and of their lawyers some part of the historical profession was scandalised.[2] Our threat was beaten off, and a view of eighteenth-century England has been reconstituted which passes over, with a few words, the society's deep contradictions. We are told that it was a thriving "consumer society" (whatever that means) populated by "a polite and commercial people".[3] We are not reminded sharply that this was the century in which the commoners finally lost their land, in which the number of offences carrying the capital penalty multiplied, in which thousands of felons were transported, and in which thousands of lives were lost in imperial wars; a century which ended, despite the agricultural "revolution" and the swelling rent-rolls, in severe rural immiseration. Meanwhile the historical profession maintains a bland view of things: historical conferences on eighteenth-century questions tend to be places where the bland lead the bland. We will attempt a less reassuring reconstruction.

It has been a common complaint that the terms "feudal", "capitalist", or "bourgeois" are too imprecise, and cover phenomena too vast and disparate, to be of serious analytic service. We now, however, find constantly in service a new set of terms such as "pre-industrial", "traditional", "paternalism" and "modernization", which appear to be open to very much the same objections; and whose

[1] M. K. Ashby, *Joseph Ashby of Tysoe* (Cambridge 1961 and London, 1974).

[2] See my *Whigs and Hunters* (London and New York, 1975), and D. Hay, P. Linebaugh and E. P. Thompson (eds.), *Albion's Fatal Tree* (London and New York, 1975).

[3] P. Langford, *A Polite and Commercial People: England 1727-1783* (Oxford, 1989).

theoretical paternity is less certain.

It may be of interest that whereas the first set of terms direct attention to conflict or tension within the social process, the second set appear to nudge one towards a view of society in terms of a self-regulating sociological order. They offer themselves, with a specious scientism, as if they were value-free. They also have an eerie timelessness. My own particular dislike is "pre-industrial", a tent within whose spacious folds there sit beside each other West of England clothiers, Persian silversmiths, Guatemalan shepherds, and Corsican bandits.[1]

However, let us leave them happily in their bazaar, exchanging their surprising cultural products, and look more closely at "paternalism". In some writers the "patriarchal" and the "paternal" appear as interchangeable terms, the one carrying a sterner, the other a somewhat softened implication. The two may indeed run into each other in fact as well as in theory. In Weber's description of "traditional" societies the locus for analysis is posited in the familial relations of the tribal unit or household, and from these are extrapolated relations of domination and dependency which come to characterise a "patriarchal" society as a whole — forms which he relates specifically to ancient and feudal forms of social order. Laslett, who has reminded us urgently as to the social centrality of the economic "household" in the seventeenth century, suggests that this contributed to the reproduction of paternal or of patriarchal attitudes and relations which permeated the whole of society — and which perhaps continued to do so until the moment of "industrialization".[2] Marx, it is true, had tended to see patriarchal attitudes as characteristic of the guild system of the Middle Ages, when:

> The journeymen and apprentices were organised in each craft as it best suited the interest of the masters. The filial relationship in which they stood to their masters gave the latter a double power — on the one hand

[1] "Proto-industrial" introduces new difficulties, but it is a more precise concept than "pre-industrial" and preferable for descriptive purposes.

[2] This impression was given in Peter Laslett's *The World We Have Lost* (1965). For a stricter view of theories of patriarchy, see G. Schochet, *Patriarchalism in Political Thought* (New York, 1975).

because of their influence on the whole life of the journeymen, and on the other because, for the journeymen who worked with the same master, it was a real bond, which held them together against the journeymen of other masters and separated them from these.

Marx argued that in "manufacture" these relations were replaced by "the monetary relation between worker and capitalist"; but this relationship "in the countryside and in small towns retained a patriarchal tinge".[1] This is a large allowance, especially when we recall that at any time before about 1840 the bulk of the British population lived in such conditions.

And so for "a patriarchal tinge" we may substitute the weaker term, "paternalism". It may seem that this magical social quantum, every day refreshed from the innumerable springs of the small workshop, the economic household, the landed estate, was strong enough to inhibit (except here and there, for brief episodes) class confrontation, until industrialisation brought all that in its train. Before this occurred, there was no class-conscious working class; no class-conflict of that kind, but only fragments of proto-conflict; as an historical agent, the working class did not exist, and, since this is so, the exceedingly difficult business of attempting to find out what was the actual consciousness of the inarticulate labouring poor would be tedious and unnecessary. We are invited to think of the consciousness of a Trade rather than of a class, of vertical rather than horizontal divisions. We can even speak of a "one-class" society.

Examine the following accounts of the eighteenth-century landed gentleman. The first —

> The life of a hamlet, a village, a parish, a market town and its hinterland, a whole county, might revolve around the big house in its park. Its reception rooms, gardens, stables and kennels were the centre of local social life; its estate office the exchange for farm tenancies, mining and building leases, and a bank for small savings and investments; its home farm a permanent exhibition of the best available agricultural methods. . .; its law room. . . the first bulwark of law

[1] This is from a very general passage in *The German Ideology* (1845). See Marx and Engels, *Collected Works* (1976), V, pp. 65-7. For the difficulties arising from the appropriation to somewhat different meanings of "patriarchy" in feminist theory, see below, pp. 499-503.

and order; its portrait gallery, music-room and library the headquarters of local culture; its dining-room the fulcrum of local politics.

And here is the second —

> In the course of running his property for his own interests, safety and
> convenience he performed many of the functions of the state. He was
> the judge: he settled disputes among his followers. He was the police: he
> kept order among a large number of people. . . He was the Church: he
> named the chaplain, usually some near relative with or without religious
> training, to care for his people. He was a welfare agency: he took care of
> the sick, the aged, the orphans. He was the army: in case of uprisings. . .
> he armed his kin and retainers as a private militia. Moreover, through
> what became an intricate system of marriages, kinship, and sponsor-
> ship. . . he could appeal for support if need be to a large number of
> relatives in the country or in the towns who possessed property and
> power similar to his own.

These are both acceptable descriptions of the eighteenth-
century landed gentleman. However, it happens that one
describes the aristocracy or great gentry of England, the other
the slave-owners of Colonial Brazil.[1] Both might, equally,
and with the smallest revision, describe a patrician in the
campagna of ancient Rome, one of the landowners in
Gogol's *Dead Souls*, a slave-holder in Virginia,[2] or the
landowners in any society in which economic and social
authority, summary judicial powers, etc., were united in a
single place.

Some difficulties, however, remain. We may call a
concentration of economic and cultural authority "paternalism" if we wish. But if we allow the term, then we must
also allow that it is too large for discriminating analysis. It
tells us little about the nature of power and of the State;
about forms of property-ownership; about ideology and
culture; and it is even too blunt to distinguish between modes
of exploitation, between slave and free labour.

Moreover, it is a description of social relations as they may
be seen from above. This does not invalidate it, but one
should be aware that such a description may be too

---

[1] Harold Perkin, *The Origins of Modern English Society 1780-1800*
(1969), p. 42; Alexander Marchant, "Colonial Brazil", in H. V. Livermore
(ed.), *Portugal and Brazil: an Introduction* (Oxford, 1953), p. 297.
[2] See Eugene D. Genovese, *The World the Slaveholders Made* (New
York, 1969), esp. p. 96.

persuasive. If the first description is the only one that we are offered, then it is only too easy to pass from this to some view of a "one-class society"; the great house is at the apex, and all lines of communication run to its dining-room, estate office or kennels. This is, indeed, an impression easily gained by the student who works among estate papers, quarter sessions records, or the duke of Newcastle's correspondence.

But there might be other ways of describing the society than the one offered by Harold Perkin in the first of our two extracts. The life of a parish might equally well revolve around the weekly market, the summer and winter festivals and fairs, the annual village feast, as about the occasions of the big house. The gossip of poaching, theft, sexual scandal and the behaviour of the overseers of the poor might occupy people's minds rather more than the remote comings and goings up at the park. The majority in the village would have little occasion for savings or investment or for agricultural improvement: they might be more bothered about access to firing, turves and grazing on the common than to crop rotations.[1] The law might appear not as a "bulwark" but as a bully. Above all, there might be a radical disassociation — and at times antagonism — between the culture and even the "politics" of the poor and those of the great.

Few would dispute this. But descriptions of the social order in the first sense, as seen from above, are far more common than are attempts to reconstruct the view from below. And whenever the notion of "paternalism" is introduced, it is the first model which it calls to mind. And the term cannot rid itself of normative implications: it suggests human warmth, in a mutually assenting relationship; the father is conscious of duties and responsibilities towards his son, the son is acquiescent or actively complaisant in his filial station. Even the model of the small economic household carries (despite disclaimers) some sense of emotional cosiness: "time was", Laslett once wrote, "when the whole of life went forward in the family, in a circle of loved, familiar faces, known and fondled objects, all to human size".[2] It

---

[1] They might have been surprised to learn that they belonged to a "consumer society".

[2] See Laslett, *ibid.*, p. 21.

would be unfair to meet this with the reminder that *Wuthering Heights* is presented in exactly such a familial situation. Laslett was reminding us of a relevant aspect of small-scale economic relations, even if the warmth could be of impotent revolt against abject dependency as often as it could be a warmth of mutual respect. In the early years of the industrial revolution workers often harked back to lost paternalist values, Cobbett and Oastler enlarged upon the sense of loss, and Engels endorsed the grievance.

But this raises a further problem. Paternalism as myth or as ideology is nearly always backward-looking. It offers itself in English history less as actuality than as a model of an antique, recently passed, golden age from which present modes and manners are a degeneration. Thus we have Langhorne's *Country Justice* (1774):

> When thy good father held this wide domain,
> The voice of sorrow never mourn'd in vain.
> Sooth'd by his pity, by his bounty fed,
> The sick found medecine, and the aged bread.
> He left their interest to no parish care,
> No bailiff urged his little empire there;
> No village tyrant starved them, or oppress'd;
> He learn'd their wants, and he those wants redress'd. . .
>
> The poor at hand their natural patrons saw,
> And lawgivers were supplements of law!

And so on, to the disclaimer that such relations have any present reality:

> . . . Fashion's boundless sway
> Has borne the guardian magistrate away.
> Save in Augusta's streets, on Gallia's shores,
> The rural patron is beheld no more. . .

But we may take our literary sources where we will. We may move back some sixty or seventy years to Sir Roger de Coverley, a late survivor, a quaint old-fashioned man, both ridiculous and lovable for being so. We may move back another hundred years to *King Lear*, or to Shakespeare's "good old man" Adam; once again, the paternalist values are seen as "antique", they are crumbling before the competitive individualism of the natural man of young capitalism, where "the bond [is] crack'd 'twixt son and father" and where the gods stand up for bastards. Or we may move back another hundred years to Sir Thomas More. Always paternalist actuality appears to be receding into an ever more primitive and idealized past.[1] And the term forces us into confusions of actual and ideological attributes.

To resume: paternalism is a loose descriptive term. It has considerably less historical specificity than such terms as feudalism or capitalism; it tends to offer a model of the social order as it is seen from above; it has implications of warmth and of face-to-face relations which imply notions of value; it confuses the actual and the ideal. This does not mean that the term should be discharged as utterly unfit for service. It has as much and as little value as other generalized terms — authoritarian, democratic, egalitarian — which cannot in themselves, and without substantial additions, be brought to characterize a system of social relations. No thoughtful historian should characterize a whole society as paternalist or patriarchal. But paternalism can, as in Tsarist Russia, in Meiji Japan, or in certain slave-holding societies, be a profoundly important component not only of ideology but of the actual institutional mediation of social relations. How do matters stand in eighteenth-century England?

II

Let us put aside at once one tempting but wholly unprofitable line of investigation: that of attempting to divine the specific gravity of that mysterious fluid, the "patriarchal tinge", in this or that context and at different moments in the century. We commence with impressions: we ornament our hunches with elegant or apt quotations; we end with impressions.

If we look, rather, at the institutional expression of social relations, then this society appears to offer few genuine paternalist features. What one notices about it first of all is the importance of money. The landed gentry are graded less by birth or other marks of status than by rentals: they are worth so many thousand   pounds a year. Among the aristocracy and ambitious gentry, courtship is conducted by fathers and by their lawyers, who guide it carefully towards

[1] See Raymond Williams, *The Country and the City* (Oxford, 1973), *passim*.

its consummation, the well-drawn marriage settlement. Place and office could be bought and sold (provided that the sale did not seriously conflict with the lines of political interest); commissions in the Army; seats in parliament. Use-rights, privileges, liberties, services — all could be translated into an equivalent in money: votes, burgage-rights, immunities from parish office or militia service, the freedom of boroughs, gates on the common. This is the century in which money "beareth all the stroke", in which liberties become properties, and use-rights are reified. A dove-cot on the site of an ancient burgage may be sold, and with it is sold a right to vote; the rubble of an ancient messuage may be bought up in support of a claim for common right and, thereby, of an extra allocation of the common on enclosure.

If use-rights, services, etc., became properties to be marked up at so many £s value, they did not, however, always become commodities open to any purchaser on the free market. The property assumed its value, as often as not, only within a particular structure of political power, influence, interest and dependency, made familiar to us by Namier. Titular offices of prestige (such as Rangers, Keepers, Constables) and such perquisites as came with them might be bought and sold; but these could not be bought or sold by anyone (during Walpole's rule, no Tory or Jacobite peer was likely to succeed in this market); and the holder of an opulent office who incurred the disfavour of politicians or Court might find himself threatened with ejection by legal process.[1] Preferments to the highest and most lucrative offices in the Church, the Law and the Army were in a similar position. The offices came through political influence but, once gained, they normally carried life tenure, and the incumbent must milk them of all possible revenue while he could. The tenure of Court sinecures and of high political office was much more uncertain, although by no means less lucrative: the earl of Ranelagh, the duke of Chandos, Walpole and Henry Fox were among those who founded fortunes upon brief tenures of the office of Paymaster

[1] See the instructive cases of Walpole's entry into Richmond Park, and of General Pepper's eviction from Enfield Chase in my *Whigs and Hunters*, Chapter 8.

General. And on the other hand, the tenure of landed estates, as absolute property, was wholly secure and heritable. It was both the jumping-off point for power and office, and the point to which power and office returned. Rentals might be jacked up by keen stewardship and improving agriculture, but they offered no windfall gains as did sinecure, office, commercial speculation or fortunate marriage. Political influence could do more to maximize profits than could four-course rotations — as, for example, in smoothing the way for private acts, such as enclosure, or in bringing a wad of unearned sinecurist income back to mortgaged estates, in easing the way to a marriage uniting congenial interests, or in gaining preferential access to a new issue of stock.

This was a predatory phase of agrarian and commercial capitalism, and the State was itself among the prime objects of prey. Victory in high politics was followed by the spoils of war, just as victory in war was often followed by the spoils of politics. The successful commanders of Marlborough's wars gained not only public rewards but also huge sums out of military subcontracting, for fodder, transport, ordnance; for Marlborough there was Blenheim Palace, for Cobham and Cadogan the mini-palaces of Stowe and Caversham. The Hanoverian succession brought a new set of courtier-brigands in its train. But the great financial and commercial interests also required access to the State, for charters, privileges, contracts, and for the diplomatic, military and naval strength required to break open the way for trade.[1] Diplomacy gained for the South Sea Company the *assiento*, or licence to trade in slaves in Spanish America; and it was upon the expectations of massive profits from this concession that the South Sea Bubble was blown. Blowing a bubble cannot be done without spit, and the spit in this case took the form of bribes not only to the king's ministers and mistresses, but also (it is probable) to the king.

We are habituated to think of exploitation as something

---

[1] We should not forget that Namier's great enquiry into the character of the parliamentary system originated as a study of "The Imperial Problem during the American Revolution"; see *The Structure of Politics at the Accession of George III*, Preface to first edition (1928).

that occurs at ground level, at the point of production. In the early eighteenth century wealth was created at this lowly level, but it rose rapidly to higher regions, accumulated in great gobbets, and the real killings were to be made in the distribution, cornering and sale of goods or raw materials (wool, grain, meat, sugar, cloth, tea, tobacco, slaves), in the manipulation of credit, and in the seizure of the offices of State. A patrician banditti contested for the spoils of power, and this alone explains the great sums of money they were willing to expend on the purchase of parliamentary seats. Seen from this aspect, the State was less an effective organ of any class than a parasitism upon the backs of that very class (the gentry) who had gained the day in 1688. And it was seen as such, and seen to be intolerable, by many of the small Tory gentry during the first half of the century, whose land tax was transferred by the most patent means to the pockets of courtiers and Whig politicians — to that same aristocratic élite whose great estates were, during these years, being consolidated against the small. An attempt was even made by this oligarchy, in the time of the earl of Sunderland, to make itself institutionally confirmed and self-perpetuating, by the attempted Peerage Bill and by the Septennial Act. That constitutional defences against this oligarchy survived these decades at all is due largely to the stubborn resistance of the largely Tory, sometimes Jacobite, independent country gentry, supported again and again by the vociferous and turbulent crowd.

All this was done in the king's name. It was in the name of the king that successful ministers could purge even the most subordinate officer of State who was not wholly subordinate to their interest. "We have left nothing untry'd, to find out every malignant; and have dismiss'd all of whom we could have the least proof either from their present or pass'd behaviour," wrote the three grovelling Commissioners of Customs in Dublin to the earl of Sunderland in August 1715. It is "our duty not to suffer any subordinate to us to eat His Majesty's Bread, who have not all imaginable zeal & affection for his service & Government."[1] But it was a prime interest among the political predators to confine the

[1] Blenheim MSS (Sunderland), D II, 8.

influence of the king to that of *primus inter predatores*. When George II at his accession seemed to be about to dispense with Walpole, it turned out that he could be bought like any Whig politician, but at a higher price:

> Walpole knew his duty. Never had a sovereign been more generously treated. The King — £800,000 a year down and the surplus of all taxes appropriated to the civil list, reckoned by Hervey at another £100,000: the Queen — £100,000 a year. The rumour ran that Pulteney offered more. If so, his political ineptitude was astounding. No one but Walpole could have hoped to get such grants through the Commons. . . a point which his Sovereign was not slow in grasping. . .
>
> "Consider, Sir Robert," said the King, purring with gratitude as his minister set out for the Commons, "what makes me easy in this matter will prove for your ease too; it is for my life it is to be fixed and it is for your life."[1]

So Walpole's "duty" turns out to be the mutual respect of two safe-breakers raiding the vaults of the same bank. In these decades the noted Whig "jealousy" of the Crown did not rise from any fear that the Hanoverian monarchs would effect a *coup d'état* and trample underfoot the liberties of the subject in assuming absolute power — that rhetoric was strictly for the hustings. It arose from the more realistic fear that an enlightened monarch might find means to elevate himself, as the personification of an "impartial", rationalizing, bureaucratic State power, above and outside the predatory game. The appeal of such a patriot king would have been immense, not only among the lesser gentry, but among great ranges of the populace: it was exactly the appeal of his image as an uncorrupted patriot which carried William Pitt the elder on a flood of popular acclaim to power, despite the hostility of politicians and of Court.[2]

[1] J. H. Plumb, *Sir Robert Walpole* (1960), II, pp. 168-9.

[2] P. Langford, "William Pitt and public opinion, 1757", *English Historical Review*, cccxlvi (1973). But when in power, Pitt's "patriotism" was limited to the right hand of government only. The left hand, Newcastle, "took the treasury, the civil and ecclesiastical patronage, and the disposal of that part of the secret service money which was then employed in bribing members of Parliament. Pitt was Secretary of State, with the direction of war and of foreign affairs. Thus the filth of all the noisome and pestilential sewers of government was poured into one channel. Through the other passed only what was bright and stainless" (T. B. Macaulay, *Critical and Historical Essays* (1880), p. 747.)

"The successors of the old Cavaliers had turned demagogues; the successors of the old Roundheads had turned courtiers." Thus Macaulay; and he continues:

> During many years, a generation of Whigs, whom Sidney would have spurned as slaves, continued to wage deadly war with a generation of Tories whom Jeffreys would have hanged for republicans.[1]

This characterization does not long survive the mid-century. The feud between Whigs and Tories had been greatly softened ten years before the accession of George III, and the ensuing "slaughter of the Pelhamite innocents". The Tory survivors among the great gentry re-entered the commission of peace, regained their political presence in the counties, had hopes of shares in the spoils of power. As manufacture moved up in the scales of wealth against merchanting and speculation, so certain forms of privilege and corruption became obnoxious to moneyed men, who became reconciled to the rationalized "impartial" arena of the free market: killings could now be made without some prior political purchase within the organs of State. The accession of George III changed in many ways the terms of the political game — the opposition got out its old libertarian rhetoric and dusted it, for some (as in the City of London) it assumed a real and revivified content. But the King sadly bungled any attempt to offer himself as an enlightened monarch, an imperial apex to a disinterested bureaucracy. The parasitic functions of the State came under increasing scrutiny and piecemeal attack (the reform of the Excise, attacks on the East India Company, upon places and sinecures, upon the misappropriation of public lands, etc.); but, despite an efficient revenue service, and a serviceable navy and army, the parasitic role of the State survived.

"Old Corruption" is a more serious term of political analysis than is often supposed; for political power throughout most of the eighteenth century may best be understood, not as a direct organ of any class or interest, but as a secondary political formation, a purchasing-point from which other kinds of economic and social power were gained or enhanced; in its primary functions it was costly, grossly

[1] *Ibid.*, p. 746.

inefficient, and it survived the century only because it did not seriously inhibit the actions of those with *de facto* economic or (local) political power. Its greatest source of strength lay precisely in the weakness of the State itself; in the desuetude of its paternal, bureaucratic and protectionist powers; in the licence which it afforded to agrarian, mercantile and manufacturing capitalism to get on with their own self-reproduction; in the fertile soil which it afforded to *laissez-faire*.[1]

It scarcely seems, however, to be a fertile soil for paternalism. We have become used to a rather different view of eighteenth-century politics, presented by historians who have become habituated to seeing this age in terms of the apologetics of its principal actors.[2] If corruption is noted, it can be passed off by noting a precedent; if Whigs were predators, then Tories were predators too. Nothing is out-of-the-way, all is subsumed in the "accepted standards of the age". But the alternative view which I have offered should come with no sense of surprise. It is, after all, the criticism of high politics offered in *Gulliver's Travels* and in *Jonathan Wild*; in part in Pope's satires and in part in *Humphrey*

---

[1] I must emphasise that this is a view of the State as seen from "within". From "without", in its effective military, naval, fiscal, diplomatic and imperial presence, whether directly or indirectly (as in the para-State of the East India Company) it must be seen in a very much more aggressive aspect. John Brewer has helpfully analysed its military strength, and also the efficiency of its fiscal organisation and taxation bureaucracy — Treasury departments and the extensive excise service were comparatively free from the corruption and favours endemic in other government office — in *The Sinews of Power* (1989). This mixture of internal weakness and external strength, and the balance between the two (in "peace" and "war" policies) leads us to most of the real issues of principle thrown up in mid-eighteenth-century high politics. It was when the weaknesses inherent in the internal parasitism wreaked their revenges in external defeat (the loss of Minorca and the ritual sacrifice of Admiral Byng; the American disaster) that elements in the ruling class were shocked out of mere factionalism into a class politics of principle.

[2] But there has been a significant shift in recent historiography, to take more seriously into acccount relations between politicians and the political nation "without doors". See J. H. Plumb, "Political man", in James L. Clifford (ed.), *Man versus Society in Eighteenth-Century Britain* (Cambridge, 1968); John Brewer, *Party Ideology and Popular Politics at the Accession of George III* (Cambridge, 1976); and Linda Colley, *In Defence of Oligarchy: the Tory Party, 1714-1760* (Cambridge, 1982).

Clinker; in Johnson's "Vanity of Human Wishes" and "London" and in Goldsmith's "Traveller". It appears, as political theory, in Mandeville's *Fable of the Bees*, in the polemics of the "country party", with a Tory gloss in Bolingbroke's thought and it reappears, in more fragmentary form, and with a Whiggish gloss, in Burgh's *Political Disquisitions*.[1] In the early decades of the century, the comparison between high politics and the criminal under-world was a common figure of satire:

> I know that if one would be agreeable to men of dignity one must study to imitate them, and I know which way they get Money and places. I cannot wonder that the Talents requisite for a great Statesman are so scarce in the world since so many of those who possess them are every month cut off in the prime of their Age at the Old-Baily.

Thus John Gay, in a private letter, in 1723.[2] The thought was the germ for the *Beggar's Opera*. Historians have commonly dismissed this figure as hyperbole. They should not.

There are, of course, qualifications to be made. One qualification, however, which can *not* be made is that this parasitism was curbed, or jealously watched, by a purposive, cohesive, growing middle class of professional men and of the manufacturing middle class.[3] To be sure, all the elements of such a class were gathering, and recent historical research has emphasised the growth in the wealth, numbers and cultural presence of the commercial, professional, farming and trading sections of society;[4] the occasional assertion of independence in urban politics;[5] the vigorous growth of leisure centres and facilities mainly serving the "middling

---

[1] "In our time the opposition is between a corrupt Court joined by an innumerable multitude of all ranks and stations bought with public money. and the independent part of the nation" (*Political Disquisitions, or an Enquiry into Public Errors, Defects, and Abuses* (1774)). This, of course, is the critique of the old "country" opposition to Walpole also.

[2] C. F. Burgess (ed.), *Letters of John Gay* (Oxford, 1966), p. 45.

[3] But note the relevant discussion in John Cannon, *Parliamentary Reform, 1640-1832* (Cambridge, 1973), p. 49, note 1.

[4] This is a consistent and persuasive theme of Paul Langford, *A Polite and Commercial People, op. cit.*, esp. chapter two.

[5] See Nicholas Rogers, *Whigs and Cities* (Cambridge, 1989).

orders".[1] If in the first decades of the century such groups could be held in place by palpable measures of clientage and dependency,[2] by the mid-century they were numerous enough — certainly in London and also in some large towns — to be no longer dependent upon a few patrons, and to have acquired the independence of the more anonymous market. There is a sense in which a middle class was creating its own shadowy civil society or public sphere.

Nevertheless, all this fell far short of a class with its own institutions and objectives, self-confident enough to challenge the managers of Old Corruption. Such a class did not begin to discover itself (except, perhaps, in London) until the last three decades of the century. For most of the century its potential members were content to submit to a condition of abject dependency. They made little effort (until the Association Movement of the late 1770s) to shake off the chains of electoral bribery and influence; they were consenting adults in their own corruption. After two decades of servile attachment to Walpole, the Dissenters emerged with their reward: £500 p.a. to be allocated to the widows of deserving clergy. Fifty years later, and they had still failed to secure the repeal of the Test and Corporation Acts. As churchmen, the majority fawned for preferment, dined and joked (upon suffrance) at the tables of their patrons, and, like Parson Woodforde, were not above accepting a tip from the squire at a wedding or a christening.[3] As surveyors, attorneys, tutors, stewards, tradesmen, etc., they were contained within the limits of dependency; their deferential letters, soliciting place or favour, are stashed in the

---

[1] See especially P. Corfield, *The Impact of English Towns, 1700-1800* (Oxford, 1982); P. Borsay, *The English Urban Renaissance* (Oxford, 1989); P. Clark (ed.), *The Transformation of English Provincial Towns, 1600-1800* (1984).

[2] Nicholas Rogers, "Aristocratic Clientage, Trade and Independency: Popular Politics in Pre-Radical Westminster", *Past and Present*, 61, 1973.

[3] "April 11 1779. . . There were Coaches at Church. Mr Custance immediately after the Ceremony came to me and desired me to accept a small Present; it was wrapped up in a Piece of white Paper very neat, and on opening of it, I found it contained nothing less than the sum of 4. 4. 0. He gave the Clerk also 0. 10. 6." (*The Diary of a Country Parson* (1963), p. 152).

manuscript collections of the great.[1] (As such, the sources
give a historiographical bias to overemphasize the deferential
element in eighteenth-century society — a man put, perforce,
into the stance of soliciting favours will not reveal his true
mind.) In general, the middle class submitted to a client
relationship. Here and there men of character might break
free, but even the arts remained coloured by dependency
upon the liberality of patrons.[2] The aspirant professional
man or tradesman sought to remedy his sense of grievance
less by social organization than by social mobility (or geo-
graphical mobility to Bengal, or to that European "West" —
the New World). He aimed to purchase immunity from
deference by acquiring the wealth which would give him
"independence", or land and gentry status.[3] The profound
resentments generated by this client status, with its attendant
humiliations and its impediments to the career open to
talents, fuelled much of the intellectual radicalism of the
early 1790s; its embers scorch the foot even in the cool
rationalist periods of Godwin's prose.

Thus for at least the first seven decades of the century we
can find no industrial or professional middle class which
exercises an effective curb upon the operations of predatory
oligarchic power. But if there had been no curbs at all, no
qualifications of parasitic rule, the consequence must have
been anarchy, one faction preying without restraint upon
another. The major qualifications to this rule were four.

First, we have already noted the largely Tory "Country"

---

[1] "The letter-bag of every M.P. with the slightest pretensions to
influence was stuffed with pleas and demands from voters for themselves,
their relations or their dependents. Places in the Customs and Excise, in the
Army and Navy, in the Church, in the East India, Africa and Levant
Companies, in all the departments of state from door-keepers to clerks:
jobs at Court for the real gentry or sinecures in Ireland, the diplomatic
corps, or anywhere else where duties were light and salaries steady" (J. H.
Plumb, "Political man", p. 6).

[2] Hence Blake's angry annotation to Sir Joshua Reynolds: "Liberality!
we want not Liberality. We want a Fair Price & Proportionate Value & a
General Demand for Art" (Geoffrey Keynes (ed.), *The Complete Writings
of William Blake* (1957), p. 446).

[3] For Place's savage comments on deference and independence, see
Mary Thale (ed.), *The Autobiography of Francis Place* (Cambridge, 1972),
pp. 216-18, 250.

tradition of the independent lesser gentry. This tradition is the only one to emerge with much honour from the first half of the century; it re-emerges, in a Whig mantle, with the Association Movement of the 1770s.[1] Secondly, there is the Press: itself a kind of middle-class presence, in advance of other articulated expression — a presence extending in range as literacy extended, and as the Press itself learned how to enlarge and sustain its freedoms.[2] Thirdly, there is "the Law", elevated during this century to a role more prominent than at any other period of our history, and serving as the "impartial", arbitrating authority in place of a weak and unenlightened monarchy, a corrupt bureaucracy and a democracy which offered to the real intrusions of power little more than rhetoric about its ancestry. The civil law afforded to the competing interests both a set of defences to their property and those rules of the game without which all would have fallen into anarchy. The higher institutions of the law were not free from influence and corruption, but they were freer from these than was any other profession. To maintain their credibility, the courts must sometimes find for the small man against the great, the subject against the King. In terms of style, the performance was superb: serene, untainted by influence, remote from the hubbub of affairs, lucid, combining a reverence for the precedents of antiquity with a

---

[1] Although the Country opposition to Walpole had central demands which were democratic in form (annual parliaments, curbs on placemen and corruption, no standing army, etc.), the democracy demanded was of course limited, in general, to the landed gentry (as against the Court and the moneyed interest) as is made clear by continued Tory support for landed property qualifications for MPs. See Quentin Skinner's useful discussion (which, however, neglects the dimension of the political nation "without doors" to which Bolingbroke appealed). "The principles and practice of opposition: the case of Bolingbroke versus Walpole", in Neil McKendrick (ed.), *Historical Perspectives* (1974); H. T. Dickinson, "The eighteenth-century debate on the 'Glorious Revolution'," *History*, vol. lxi, 201 (February 1976), pp. 36-40; and (for the continuity between the platform of old Country party and new radical Whigs), Brewer, *op. cit.*, pp. 19, 253-5. The Hanoverian Whigs also endorsed the high property qualifications for MPs: Cannon, *op. cit.*, p. 36.

[2] See Brewer, *op. cit.*, chapter 8; and, for one example of its provincial extension, John Money, "Taverns, coffee houses and clubs local politics and popular articulacy in the Birmingham area in the age of the American Revolution", *Historical Journal*, (1971), vol. xiv, 1.

flexible assimilation of the present. Money, of course, could buy the best performers, and the longer purse could often exhaust the lesser; but money could never effect an outright purchase of judgement, and on occasion was visibly discomfited. The civil law provided a fair framework within which the predators could fight for some kinds of spoil: for tithes, for claims to timber and common land, over legacies and entails: on occasion their lesser victims could defend themselves in the same medium. But the criminal law, which faced in the main towards the loose and disorderly sort of people, wore an altogether different aspect. Moreover, eighteenth-century law was concerned less with relations between persons than with relations between property, or claims upon property, or what Blackstone called "the Rights of Things" (see below, p. 135).

Fourthly, and finally, there is the ever-present resistance of the crowd: a crowd which stretched at times from small gentry and professional men to the poor (and within whose numbers the first two groups sometimes sought to combine opposition to the system with anonymity), but which appeared to the great, through the haze of verdure surrounding their parks, to be made up of "the loose and disorderly sort". The relation between the gentry and the crowd is the particular concern of this argument.

III

One would not expect paternal responsibilities or filial deference to be vigorous in the predatory regime to which I have gestured. But it is of course possible for a society to be fissured and savagely factional at the top, but to preserve its cohesion below. The military juntas engage in coup and counter-coup, pretenders to the throne exchange places, warlords march and counter-march, but at the base of society the peasantry or plantation-workers remain passive, sometimes submitting to a change of masters, contained by the strength of local paternal institutions, made submissive by the absence of alternative social horizons. Whatever parasitism infested the eighteenth-century State, perhaps the gentry, secure in their counties, threw over the whole of society a paternalist net?

It would not be difficult to find instances of the great

estate or the closed manorial village where this might seem to be so. And we will return to such examples. It would be equally easy to find pasture and forest regions of expanding domestic industry where this is evidently false. The trading of instances will not get us very far. The question we should ask is: What were the institutions, in the eighteenth century, which enabled the rulers to obtain, directly or indirectly, a control over *the whole life* of the labourer, as opposed to the purchase, *seriatim*, of his labour power?

The most substantial fact lies on the other side of the question. This is the century which sees the erosion of half-free forms of labour, the decline of living-in, the final extinction of labour services and the advance of free, mobile, wage labour. This was not an easy or quick transition. Christopher Hill has reminded us of the long resistance made by the free-born Englishman against the pottage of free wage labour. One should note equally the long resistance made by their masters against some of its consequences. These wished devoutly to have the best of both the old world and the new, without the disadvantage of either. They clung to the image of the labourer as an *un*free man, a "servant": a servant in husbandry, in the workshop, in the house. (They clung simultaneously to the image of the free or masterless man as a vagabond, to be disciplined, whipped and compelled to work.) But crops could not be harvested, cloth could not be manufactured, goods could not be transported, houses could not be built and parks enlarged, without labour readily available and mobile, for whom it would be inconvenient or impossible to accept the reciprocities of the master-servant relationship. The masters disclaimed their paternal responsibilities; but they did not cease, for many decades, to complain at the breach of the "great law of subordination", the diminution of deference, that ensued upon their disclaimer:

> The Lab'ring Poor, in spight of double Pay,
> Are saucy, mutinous, and Beggarly.[1]

[1] Defoe, *The Great Law of Subordination Consider'd* (1724), p. 80. See Christopher Hill, "Pottage for Freeborn Englishmen: Attitudes to Wage Labour in Sixteenth and Seventeenth century England", in C. Feinstein (ed.), *Socialism, Capitalism and Economic Growth* (Cambridge, 1964).

The most characteristic complaint throughout the greater part of the century was as to the indiscipline of working people, their irregularity of employment, their lack of economic dependency and their social insubordination. Defoe, who was not a conventional "low wages" theorist, and who could on occasion see merit in higher wages which increased the consuming power of "manufacturers" or of "artificers", stated the full case in his *Great Law of Subordination Consider'd; or, the Insolence and Insufferable Behaviour of Servants in England duly enquir'd into* (1724). He argued that through the insubordination of servants:

> Husbandmen are ruin'd, the Farmers disabled, Manufacturers and Artificers plung'd, to the Destruction of Trade. . . and that no Men who, in the Course of Business, employ Numbers of the Poor, can depend upon any Contracts they make, or perform any thing they undertake, having no Law, no Power. . . to oblige the Poor to perform honestly what they are hir'd to do.

> Under *a stop of Trade*, and a general want of Work, then they are clamorous and mutinous, run from their Families, load the Parishes with their Wives and Children. . . and. . . grow ripe for all manner of mischief, whether publick Insurrection, or private plunder.

> In a *Glut of Trade* they grow saucy, lazy, idle and debauch'd. . . they will Work but two or three Days in the Week.

Paternalist control over the whole life of the labourer was in fact being eroded; wage assessment fell into desuetude; the mobility of labour is manifest; the vigour of eighteenth-century hiring-fairs, "statutes" or "statties", proclaim the right of the rural (as well as urban) labourer to claim if he so wished, a change of master.[1] Moreover, there is evidence (in the very refusal of labourers to submit to the work-discipline demanded of them) of the growth of a newly-won psychology of the free labourer. In one of Defoe's moralistic anecdotes, the JP summons the cloth worker upon a complaint from his employer that his work was being neglected:

[1] See A. Kussmaul, *Servants in Husbandry in Early Modern England* (Cambridge, 1981); R. W. Malcolmson, *Life and Labour in England, 1700-1780* (1981), pp. 71-4; Michael Roberts, " 'Waiting upon Chance': English Hiring Fairs", *Journal of Historical Sociology*, vol. I (1988).

Justice.   Come in Edmund, I have talk'd with your Master.

Edmund.   Not *my Master*, and't please your Worship, I hop I am *my own Master.*

Justice.   Well, your Employer, Mr E —, the Clothier: will the word Employer do?

Edmund.   Yes, yes, and't please your Worship, any thing, but *Master.*[1]

This is a large change in the terms of relations: subordination is becoming (although between grossly unequal parties) negotiation.

The eighteenth century witnessed a qualitative change in labour relations whose nature is obscured if we see it only in terms of an increase in the scale and volume of manufacture and trade. This occurred, of course. But it occurred in such a way that a substantial proportion of the labour force actually became *more* free from discipline in their daily work, more free to choose between employers and between work and leisure, less situated in a position of dependence in their whole way of life, than they had been before or than they were to be in the first decades of the discipline of the factory and of the clock.

This was a transitory phase. One prominent feature was the loss of non-monetary usages or perquisites, or their translation into money payments. Such usages were still extraordinarily pervasive in the early eighteenth century. They favoured paternal social control because they appeared simultaneously as economic and as social relations, as relations between persons not as payments for services or things. Most evidently, to eat at one's employer's board, to lodge in his barn or above his workshop, was to submit to his supervision. In the great house, the servants who were dependent upon "vails" from visitors, the clothing of the mistress, the clandestine perquisites of the surplus of the larder, spent a lifetime ingratiating favours. Even the multiform perquisites within industry, increasingly being redefined as "theft", were more likely to survive where the workers accepted them as favours and submitted to a filial dependency.

On occasion, one catches a glimpse of the extinction of a perquisite or service which must have induced a shock to paternal control out of all proportion to the economic gain to

[1] Defoe, *op. cit.*, p. 97.

the employer. Thus when Sir Jonathan Trelawney, as Bishop of Winchester, was seeking to increase the revenue of his see, he employed as Steward one Heron, a man strongly committed to ruthless economic rationalization. Among accusations brought against Heron, in 1707, by tenants and subordinate officials of the Bishop's Courts were that:

> He breaks old Customes. . . in Minute and Small matters, which are of Small value to your Lordshipp. . . he has denyed to Allow five Shillings at Waltham to the Jury att the Court. . . to drinke your Lordshipps health, a Custome that has beene used time out of Mind. . . he has denyed your Lordshipp's Steward and Officers a small perquisite of haveing theire horses shoo'd att Waltham According to an Antient usage which never Exceeded above Six or Seven Shillings. . . he denied your Lordshipp's Tennants Timber for the repaire of Severall Bridges and Common pounds.

To this Heron replied, somewhat testily:

> I own, I affect sometimes to Intermit those minute Customs as he calls them because I observe that your Predecessor's favours are prescribed for against your Lordship & insisted on as Rights, & then your Lordship is not thanked for them; Besides though they are Minute, yet many Minute Expences. . . amount to a Sume at the end.[1]

In such ways economic rationalization nibbled (and had long been nibbling) through the bonds of paternalism. The other leading feature of this transitional period was of course the enlargement of that sector of the economy which was independent of a client relationship to the gentry. The "subject" economy remained huge: not only the direct retainers of the great house, the chambermaids and footmen, coachmen and grooms and gardeners, the gamekeepers and laundresses, but the further concentric rings of economic clientship — the equestrian trades and luxury trades, the dressmakers and pastry cooks and vintners, the coach makers, the innkeepers and ostlers.

But the century saw a growing area of independence within which the small employers and labourers felt their client relationship to the gentry very little or not at all. These were the people whom the gentry saw as "idle and disorderly", withdrawn from their social control; from among these — the

---

[1] Hants CRO, Eccles. II, 415809, E/B12. See also *Whigs and Hunters*, pp. 126-30.

clothing workers, urban artisans, colliers, bargees and porters, labourers and petty dealers in the food trades — the social rebels, the food or turnpike rioters, were likely to come. They retained many of the attributes commonly ascribed to "pre-industrial labour".[1] Working often in their own cottages, owning or hiring their own tools, usually working for small employers, frequently working irregular hours and at more than one job, they had escaped from the social controls of the manorial village and were not yet subject to the discipline of factory labour.

Many of their economic dealings might be with men and women little higher in the economic hierarchy than themselves. Their "shopping" was not done in emporiums but at market stalls. The poor state of the roads made necessary a multitude of local markets, at which exchanges of products between primary producers might still be unusually direct. In the 1760s,

> Hard-labouring colliers, men and women of Somersetshire and Gloucestershire, travelled to divers neighbouring towns with drifts of horses. . . laden with coals. . . It was common to see such colliers lade or fill a two bushel coal sack with articles of provisions. . . of beef, mutton, large half stript beef bones, stale loaves of bread, and pieces of cheese.[2]

Such markets and, even more, the seasonal fairs provided not only an economic but a cultural nexus, and a major centre for information and exchange of news and gossip.

In many regions, the people had not been shaken alto-

---

[1] Gwyn Williams in *Artisans and Sansculottes* (1968) writes of "the brief, bawdy, violent, colourful, kaleidoscopic, picaresque world of pre-industrial society, when anything from a third to a half of the population lived not only on the subsistence line but outside and sometimes against the law". That is one way of seeing a part of this population: and this is confirmed by several studies in P. Linebaugh, *The London Hanged* (1991). However, another part of this population should not be stereotyped as bawdy, colourful and criminal: upward revisions of the numbers engaged in industry (including rural industries) — see especially P. H. Lindert, "English Occupations, 1670-1811", *J. Econ. Hist.*, 40, (1980) — the rediscovery of the "cottage economy" and of an English peasantry — see David Levine, *Reproducing Families* (Cambridge, 1987) and below p. 176 — and the whole body of work and discussion around "proto-industrialization" have all served to emphasise the substantial and growing sector of the eighteenth-century economy independent of gentry control.

[2] J. Mathews, *Remarks on the Cause and Progress of the Scarcity and Dearness of Cattle* (1797), p. 33.

gether from some sketchy tenure of the land. Since much industrial growth took the form, not of concentration into large units of production, but of the dispersal of petty units and of by-employments (especially spinning) there were additional resources for "independence". This independence was for many never far from mere subsistence: a bountiful harvest might bring momentary affluence, a long wet season might throw people onto the poor rates. But it was possible for many to knit together this subsistence, from the common, from harvest and occasional manual earnings, from by-employments in the cottage, from daughters in service, from poor rates or charity. And undoubtedly some of the poor followed their own predatory economy, like "the abundance of loose, idle and disorderly persons" who were alleged, in the time of George II, to live on the margins of Enfield Chase, and who "infest the same, going in dark nights, with Axes, Saws, Bills, Carts and Horses, and in going and coming Rob honest people of their sheep, lambs and poultry. . ."[1] Such persons appear again and again in criminal records, estate correspondence, pamphlet and press; they appear still, in the 1790s, in the agricultural county surveys; they cannot have been wholly a ruling-class invention.

Thus the independence of labour (and small master) from clientage was fostered on the one hand by the translation of non-monetary "favours" into payments; and on the other by the extension of trade and industry on the basis of the multiplication of many small units of production, with much by-employment (especially spinning) coincident with many continuing forms of petty land tenure (or common right) and many casual demands for manual labour. This is an indiscriminate picture, and deliberately so. Economic historians have made many careful discriminations between different groups of labourers. But these are not relevant to our present enquiry. Nor were these discriminations commonly made by commentators from among the gentry when they considered the general problem of the "insubordination" of labour. Rather, they saw beyond the park gates, beyond the railings of the London mansion, a blur of indiscipline — the "idle

---

[1] Memorial of John Hale, Clerk of Enfield manor court, to George II n.d. Cambridge Univ. Lib., Cholmondeley (Houghton) MSS, 45/40.

and disorderly", "the mob", "the poor", the "populace" — and they deplored —

> their open scoffings at all discipline, religious as well as civil: their contempt of all order, frequent menace to all justice, and extreme promptitude to tumultuous risings from the slightest motives.[1]

It is, as always, an indiscriminate complaint against the populace as a whole. Free labour had brought with it a weakening of the old means of social discipline. So far from a confident patriarchal society, the eighteenth century sees the old paternalism at a point of crisis.

IV

And yet one feels that "crisis" is too strong a term. If the complaint continues throughout the century that the poor were indisciplined, criminal, prone to tumult and riot, one never feels, before the French Revolution, that the rulers of England conceived that their whole social order might be endangered. The insubordination of the poor was an inconvenience; it was not a menace. The styles of politics and of architecture, the rhetoric of the gentry and their decorative arts, all seem to proclaim stability, self-confidence, a habit of managing all threats to their hegemony.

We may of course have overstated the crisis of paternalism. In directing attention to the parasitism of the State at the top, and the erosion of traditional relations by free labour and a monetary economy at the bottom, we have overlooked intermediate levels where the older economic household controls remained strong, and we have perhaps understated the scale of the "subject" or "client" areas of the economy. The control which men of power and money still exercised over the whole life and expectations of those below them remained enormous, and if paternalism was in crisis, the industrial revolution was to show that its crisis must be taken several stages further — as far as Peterloo and the Swing Riots — before it lost all credibility.

[1] *Herald, or Patriot-Proclaimer*, 24 September 1757. Even *within* the park gates the gentry complained of indiscipline. Thus, the servants in the great house were accused of intimidating house-guests by lining the hall on their departure and demanding tips or "vails": see *A Letter from a Gentleman to his Friend, concerning the Custom of Giving and Taking Vails* (1767).

Nevertheless, the analysis allows us to see that ruling-class control in the eighteenth century was located primarily in a cultural hegemony, and only secondarily in an expression of economic or physical (military) power. To say that it was "cultural" is not to say that it was immaterial, too fragile for analysis, insubstantial. To define control in terms of cultural hegemony is not to give up attempts at analysis, but to prepare for analysis at the points at which it should be made: into the images of power and authority, the popular mentalities of subordination.

Defoe's fictional cloth worker, called before the magistrate to account for default, offers a clue: "not *my Master*, and't please your Worship, I hope I am *my own Master*". The deference which he refuses to his employer overflows in the calculated obsequiousness to "your Worship". He wishes to struggle free from the immediate, daily, humiliations of dependency. But the larger outlines of power, station in life, political authority, appear to be as inevitable and irreversible as the earth and the sky. Cultural hegemony of this kind induces exactly such a state of mind in which the established structures of authority and modes of exploitation appear to be in the very course of nature. This does not preclude resentment or even surreptitious acts of protest or revenge; it does preclude affirmative rebellion.

The gentry in eighteenth-century England exercised this kind of hegemony. And they exercised it all the more effectively since the relation of ruler to ruled was very often not face-to-face but indirect. Absentee landowners, and the ever-present mediation of stewards and bailiffs apart, the emergence of the three-tier system of landowner, tenant farmer and landless labourer, meant that the rural labourers, in the mass, did not confront the gentry as employers nor were the gentry seen to be in any direct sense responsible for their conditions of life; for a son or daughter to be taken into service at the great house was seen to be, not a necessity, but a favour.

And in other ways they were withdrawn from the polarities of economic and social antagonism. When the price of food rose, the popular rage fell not on the landowners but upon middlemen, forestallers, millers. The gentry might profit from the sale of wool, but they were not seen to be in a direct exploitive relation to the clothing workers.[1]

In the growing industrial areas, the gentlemen JP frequently lived withdrawn from the main industrial centres, at his country seat, and he was at pains to preserve some image of himself as arbitrator, mediator or even protector of the poor. It was a common view that "whenever a tradesman is made a justice a tyrant is created".[2] The poor laws, if harsh, were not administered directly by the gentry; where there was blame it could fall upon the poor-rate-paring farmers and tradesmen from among whom the overseers came. Langhorne presents the idealized paternalist picture; exhorting the country justice to —

> . . . bend the brow severe
> On the sly, pilfering, cruel overseer;
> The shuffling farmer, faithful to no trust,
> Ruthless as rocks, insatiate as the dust.
> When the poor hind, with length of years decay'd,
> Leans feebly on his once subduing spade,
> Forgot the service of his abler days,
> His profitable toil, and honest praise,
> This slave, whose board his former labours spread![3]

And, once again, at least a ghostly image of paternal responsibilities could be maintained at very little real outlay in effort. The same JP who in his own closed parish aggravated the problems of poverty elsewhere, by refusing settlements and by pulling down the cottages on the common, could at quarter sessions, by granting the occasional appeal against the overseers of other open parishes, or by calling to order the corrupt workhouse master, place himself above the lines of battle.

We have the paradox that the credibility of the gentry as

---

[1] Even in the West of England, where clothiers were becoming gentlemen, a strong sense of distinction was still felt in the first half of the century. An "Englishman" wrote to Lord Harrington in 1738, to complain of "the contrivances and pride of the clothiers, as living in luxury, neglecting their business, trusting servants with the care of their affairs", "beating down the wages of the poor", and paying them in truck. The remedy (he suggested) lay in a commission of enquiry made up of "men of great fortunes", who would be sufficiently independent to attend to the evidence of poor weavers: PRO, SP 36.47.

[2] *Ibid.*

[3] Langhorne, *The Country Justice* (1774).

paternalists arose from the high visibility of certain of their functions, and the low visibility of others. A great part of the gentry's appropriation of the labour value of "the poor" was mediated by their tenantry, by trade or by taxation. Physically they withdrew increasingly from face-to-face relations with the people in village and town. The rage for deer parks and the threat of poachers led to the closure of rights of way across their parks and their encirclement with high palings or walls; landscape gardening, with ornamental waters and fish ponds, menageries and valuable statuary, accentuated their seclusion and the defences of their grounds, which might be entered only through the high wrought-iron gates, watched over by the lodge. The great gentry were defended by their bailiffs from their tenants, and by their coachmen from casual encounters. They met the lower sort of people mainly on their own terms, and when these were clients for their favours; in the formalities of the bench; or on calculated occasions of popular patronage.

But in performing such functions their visibility was formidable, just as their formidable mansions imposed their presence, apart from, but guarding over, the village or town. Their appearances have much of the studied self-conscious- ness of public theatre. The sword was discarded, except for ceremonial purposes; but the elaboration of wig and powder, ornamented clothing and canes, and even the rehearsed patrician gestures and the hauteur of bearing and expression, all were designed to exhibit authority to the plebs and to exact from them deference. And with this went certain significant ritual appearances: the ritual of the hunt; the pomp of assizes (and all the theatrical style of the law courts); the segregated pews, the late entries and early departures, at church. And from time to time there were occasions for an enlarged ceremonial, which had wholly paternalist functions: the celebration of a marriage, a coming-of-age, a national festival (coronation or jubilee or naval victory), the alms- giving to the poor at a funeral.[1]

---

[1] As one example, on the marriage of Sir William Blacket with Lady Barbara Vilers, in 1725, much of Northumberland was enlisted in the celebrations. At Newcastle there were bonfires for two days, and the sounding of bells and guns. The great bell at Hexham burst with the

We have here a studied and elaborate hegemonic style, a theatrical role in which the great were schooled in infancy and which they maintained until death. And if we speak of it as theatre, it is not to diminish its importance. A great part of politics and law is always theatre; once a social system has become "set", it does not need to be endorsed daily by exhibitions of power (although occasional punctuations of force will be made to define the limits of the system's tolerance); what matters more is a continuing theatrical style. What one remarks of the eighteenth century is the elaboration of this style and the self-consciousness with which it was deployed.

The gentry and (in matters of social intercourse) their ladies judged to a nicety the kinds of conspicuous display appropriate to each rank and station: what coach, how many footmen, what table, even what proper reputation for "liberality". The show was so convincing that it has even misled historians; one notices an increasing number of references to the "paternal responsibilities" of the aristocracy, upon which "the whole system rested". But we have so far noted gestures and postures rather than actual responsibilities. The theatre of the great depended not upon constant, day-by-day attention to responsibilities (except in the supreme offices of State, almost every function of the eighteenth-century aristocracy, and many of those of the higher gentry and clergy, was held as a quasi-sinecure, whose duties were farmed out to a subordinate) but upon occasional dramatic interventions: the roasted ox, the prizes offered for some race or sport, the liberal donation to charity in time of dearth, the application for mercy, the proclamation against forestallers. It is as if the illusion of paternalism was too fragile to be risked to more sustained exposure.

The occasions of aristocratic and gentry patronage certainly deserve attention: this social lubricant of gestures could only too easily make the mechanisms of power and exploitation revolve more sweetly. The poor, habituated to their

---

boisterous ringing. At Wellington the crags were illuminated, and a large punchbowl cut in the rock, and filled with liquor, &c, *Newcastle Weekly Courant*, 2 October, 1725.

irrevocable station, have often been made accessories, through their own good nature, to their own oppression: a year of short commons can be compensated for by a liberal Christmas dole. Their rulers were well aware of this. A contributor to the *London Magazine* commented: "Dancing on the Green at Wakes and merry Tides should not only be indulg'd but incourag'd: and little Prizes being allotted for the Maids who excel in a Jig or Hornpipe, would make them return to their daily Labour with a light Heart and grateful Obedience to their Superiors."[1]

But such gestures were calculated to receive a return in deference quite disproportionate to the outlay, and they certainly don't merit the description of "responsibilities". These great agrarian bourgeois evinced little sense of public, or even corporate, responsibility. The century is not noted for the scale of its public buildings but for that of its private mansions; and is as much noted for the misappropriation of the charities of previous centuries as for the founding of new ones.

One public function the gentry assumed wholly as their own: the administration of the law, the maintenance, at times of crisis, of public order. At this point they became magisterially and portentously visible. Responsibility this certainly was, although it was a responsibility, in the first and in the second place, to their own property and authority. With regularity and with awful solemnity the limits of tolerance of the social system were punctuated by London's hanging days; by the corpse rotting on the gibbet beside the highway; by the processional of Assizes. However undesirable the side-effects (the apprentices and servants playing truant from service, the festival of pickpockets, the acclamation of the condemned) the ritual of public execution was a necessary concomitant of a system of social discipline where a great deal depended upon theatre.

In the administration of justice there were gestures also, which partake of the general studied paternalist style. Notably, in the exercise of the prerogative of mercy the aristocracy and great gentry could make evident their degree

---

[1] *London Magazine*, viii, 1738, pp. 139-40. My thanks to Robert Malcolmson.

of interest by furthering or refusing to further intercession for the condemned. And, as Douglas Hay has shown, to share, even indirectly, in the powers of life and death greatly enlarged their hegemonic charisma.[1] The exercise of power of life and death could, on occasion, be arranged to the last detail. The duke of Montagu was writing in 1728 to the duke of Newcastle concerning "my man John Potter", who had been condemned to death for stealing the duke's hangings. Montagu desired that Potter might be transported for life instead of being executed: "I have talked with the Recorder about it, who when the Report is made tomorrow of the Condemned Malefactors at Council, will propose that he may be inserted in the dead warrant, but at the same tyme there may be a Repreeve for him, which he is to know nothing of till the Morning of Execution." Three days later Montagu wrote anxiously to make sure that the letter of reprieve would arrive in time, for if Newcastle were to forget it "he'll be hanged and if he is I had as good be hanged with him, for the Ladys of my famelly give me little rest to save him. . ." The king's role in this exercise of the prerogative of mercy seems to have been fictional.[2]

In any case, one is dubious as to how far it is useful to describe the function of protecting their own property and social order as "paternalist". Certainly, this function exacted little evidence of filial loyalty either from their victims or from the crowds around the gallows.[3] A century which

[1] Douglas Hay, "Property, Authority and the Criminal Law", in Hay *et al., Albion's Fatal Tree* (1975).

[2] Montagu to Newcastle, 19 & 22 March 1727/8, PRO, SP 36.5, fos. 218-9, 230-1.

[3] See Peter Linebaugh, *The London Hanged, op. cit.* Thomas Laqueur's assertion that the authorities had no "authorial" control over the executions is supported by anecdotal evidence of the *Newgate Calendar* kind (examples of cock-ups at Tyburn, sedulously copied in popular chronicles) but not by research into the sources (state papers, legal and military papers, etc.) relevant to such a judgement. Executions were not, as Laqueur supposes, "more risible than solemn", and to present the Tyburn crowd as a "carnival crowd" is both to misunderstand the crowd and to libel "carnival". Hanging days at Tyburn often enacted a conflict between alternative authorial scripts — that of the authorities and that of a resentful or brutalised Tyburn crowd. That sort of execution crowd was *an execution crowd* (and a carnival nothing). It was one of the most brutalised phenomena in history and historians ought to say so: see

added more than one hundred new capital offences to the statute book had a stern (or flippant) view of fatherhood.

V

If the great were withdrawn so much, within their parks and mansions, from public view, it follows that the plebs, in many of their activities, were withdrawn also from them. Effective paternal sway requires not only temporal but also spiritual or psychic authority. It is here that we seem to find the system's weakest link.

It would not be difficult to find, in this parish or in that, eighteenth-century clergy fulfilling, with dedication, paternalist functions. But we know very well that these are not characteristic men. Parson Adams is drawn, not to exemplify the practices of the clergy, but to criticize them; he may be seen, at once, as the Don Quixote of the eighteenth-century Anglican Church. The Church was profoundly Erastian; had it performed an effective, a psychologically compelling paternalist role, the Methodist movement would have been neither necessary nor possible.

All this could no doubt be qualified. But what is central to our purpose is that the "magical" command of the Church and of its rituals over the populace, while still present, was becoming very weak. In the sixteenth and seventeenth centuries, Puritanism had set out to destroy the bonds of idolatry and superstition — the wayside shrines, the gaudy churches, the local miracle cults, the superstitious practices, the confessional priesthood — which, as one may still see in Ireland or in parts of southern Europe today, can hold the common people in awe. The Restoration could not restore a tissue of papist idolatry for which, in any case, England had never been notably disposed. But the Restoration did loosen the new bonds of discipline which Puritanism had brought in its place. There can be little doubt that the early eighteenth century witnessed a great recession in Puritanism, and the

---

Laqueur, "Crowds, carnival and the state of English executions, 1604-1868", in Beier *et al, The First Modern Society* (Cambridge, 1989). At times the crowd could express other kinds of solidarity with the condemned: see Linebaugh, "The Tyburn Riots against the Surgeons", in Hay *et al., op. cit.*

diminution in the size of the popular Puritan following even in those artisan centres which had nourished the Civil War sects. In the result, there was an accession of freedom, although of a negative kind, to the poor — a freedom from the psychic discipline and moral supervision of priesthood or of presbyters.

A priesthood with active pastoral care has usually found ways of co-existing with the pagan or heretical superstitions of its flock. However deplorable such compromises may appear to theologians, the priest learns that many of the beliefs and practices of "folklore" are harmless; if attached to the calendar year of the Church they can be to that degree Christianized, and can serve to reinforce the Church's authority. The forgers of the shackles of Holy Church, Brand — the pioneer of folklore — remarked, "had artfully enough contrived to make them sit easy, by twisting Flowers around them. . . A profusion of childish Rites, Pageants, and Ceremonies diverted the attention of the people from the consideration of their real state, and kept them in humour. . ."[1] What matters most is that the Church should, in its rituals, command the rites of passage of personal life, and attach the popular festivals to its own calendar.

The Anglican Church of the eighteenth century was not a creature of this kind. It was served not by priests but by parsons. It had, except in unusual instances, abandoned the confessional. It recruited few sons of the poor into the priesthood. When so many priests served as temporal magistrates and officered the same law as the gentry, they could scarcely present themselves convincingly as the agents of an alternative spiritual authority. When bishops were political appointments, and when the cousins of the gentry were placed in country livings, where they enlarged their vicarages and adopted the gentry's style of life, it was only too evident from what source the Church's authority was derived.

Above all, the Church lost command over the "leisure" of the poor, their feasts and festivals, and, with this, over a large area of plebeian culture. The term "leisure" is, of course, itself anachronistic. In rural society where small farming and

[1] John Brand and Henry Ellis, *op. cit. ,* Vol. I, p. xvii.

the cottage economy persisted, and in large areas of manufacturing industry, the organization of work was so varied and irregular that it is false to make a sharp distinction between "work" and "leisure". On the one hand, social occasions were intermixed with labour — with marketing, sheep shearing and harvesting, fetching and carrying the materials of work, and so on, throughout the year. On the other hand, enormous emotional capital was invested, not piecemeal in a succession of Saturday nights and Sunday mornings, but in the special feasts and festival occasions. Many weeks of heavy labour and scanty diet were compensated for by the expectation (or reminiscence) of these occasions, when food and drink were abundant, courtship and every kind of social intercourse flourished, and the hardship of life was forgotten. For the young, the sexual cycle of the year turned on these festivals. These occasions were, in an important sense, what men and women lived for; and if the Church had little significant part in their conduct, then it had, to that degree, ceased to engage with the emotional calendar of the poor.

One can see this in a literal sense. While the old saints' days were scattered liberally across the calendar, the Church's ritual calendar concentrated events into the months of light demands upon labour, from the winter to the spring, from Christmas to Easter. While the people still owed tribute to the last two dates, which remained as days of maximum communion, the eighteenth-century calendar of popular festivity coincides closely with the agrarian calendar. The village and town feasts for the dedication of churches — or wakes — had not only moved from the saints' days to the adjacent Sunday, but in most cases they had also been removed (where necessary) from the winter to the summer solstice. In about 1730, the antiquarian, Thomas Hearne, made a note of the feast day of 132 villages or towns in Oxfordshire or on its borders. All fell between May and December; 84 (or more than three-fifths) fell in August and September; no fewer than 43 (or almost one-third) fell in the last week of August and the first week of September (old-style calendar). Apart from a significant group of some twenty, which fell between the end of June and the end of July, and which in a normal year might be expected to fall between the end of the hay harvest and the commencement of the cereal harvest, the weight of the emotional festive calendar fell in the weeks immediately after the harvest was gathered in.[1]

Dr Malcolmson has reconstructed a calendar of feasts for Northamptonshire in the later eighteenth century which shows much the same incidence.[2] Along with the secularization of the calendar goes a secularization of the style and the function of the occasions. If not pagan, then new secular functions were added to old ritual; the publicans, hucksters and entertainers encouraged, with their numerous stalls, the feasts when their customers had uncustomary harvest earnings in their pockets; the village charity and benefit clubs took over the old church ales of Whitsuntide. At Bampton Whit-Monday's club feast included a procession with drum and piper (or fiddler), morris dancers, a clown with a bladder who carried the "treasury" (a money box for contributions), a sword bearer with a cake. There was, of course, no crucifix, no priest or nuns, no images of virgin or saints: their absence is perhaps too little noticed. Not one of the 17 songs or melodies recorded had the least religious association:

> Oh, my Billy, my constant Billy,
> When shall I see my Billy again?
> When the fishes fly over the mountain,
> Then you'll see your Billy again.[3]

Bampton, that living museum of folklore, was not an isolated rural village, but a sturdy centre of the leather industry; just as the Middleton and Ashton of Bamford's boyhood were centres of domestic industry. What is manifest, in many such districts, and in many rural regions also in the eighteenth century, is that one could never for a moment sustain the view which (for example) Paul Bois is able to assert of the eighteenth-century French peasant of the West, that "c'était l'église, a l'ombre de laquelle se nouaient toutes les relations".[4] Of course, the religious and the

---

[1] Bodleian Library, MSS Hearne's diaries, p. 175.
[2] R. W. Malcolmson, "Popular Recreations in English Society, 1700-1850", (Ph. D. thesis, Univ. of Warwick, 1970), pp. 11-17.
[3] P. H. Ditchfield, *Old English Customs* (1896), p. 125.
[4] Paul Bois, *Paysans de l'Ouest* (Paris, 1960), p. 307.

secular (or pagan) had co-existed uneasily, or conflicted, for centuries: the Puritans were concerned to keep morris dancers out of the church, and huckster's stalls out of the church-yard. They complained that church ales were defiled by animal baiting, dancing, and all manner of "lewdness". But there remains a sense in which the Church was the hub around which the spokes of this popular tradition turned; and the Stuart Book of Sports sought to confirm this relationship against Puritan attack. In the eighteenth century, the agrarian seasonal calendar was the hub and the Church provided none of the moving force. It is a difficult change to define but without doubt it was a large one.

The dual experience of the Reformation and of the decline in Puritan presence left a remarkable disassociation between the polite and the plebeian culture in post-Restoration England. Nor should we underestimate the creative culture-forming process from below. Not only the obvious things — folk songs, trades clubs and corn dollies — were made from below, but also interpretations of life, satisfactions and ceremonials. The wife sale, in its crude and perhaps exotic way, performed a function of ritual divorce both more available and more civilized than anything the polite culture could offer. The rituals of rough music, cruel as they might sometimes be, were no more vengeful and really no more exotic than the rituals of a Special Commission of Oyer and Terminer.

The legend of the revival of "merry England" after the Restoration is one which historians have perhaps been too impatient to examine. Even if some of the more sensational claims are discounted (Defoe, as a good accountant, assures us that 6,325 maypoles were erected in the five years after the Restoration)[1] there is no doubt that there was a general and sometimes exuberant revival of popular sports, wakes, rush bearings and rituals. "Help Lord!" exclaimed the Rev. Oliver Heywood, the ejected minister, when recounting the cockfighting, horse racing and stool-ball endemic in the Halifax district in the 1680s: "Oh, what oaths sworn! What wickedness committed!" And recounting the May Day celebrations of 1680 he had lamented: "There never was such

[1] Defoe, *op. cit.*, p. 62.

work in Halifax above fifty years past. Hell is broke loose."[1]

We are more accustomed to analyse the age in terms of its intellectual history, and to think of the decline of hell. But the breaking loose of this hell of a plebeian culture quite beyond their control was the waking nightmare of surviving Puritans such as Heywood and Baxter. Pagan festivals which the Church had attached to its calendar in the middle ages (although with incomplete success) reverted to purely secular festivities in the eighteenth century. Wake nights came to an end; but the feasts of the following day or week became more robust with each decade. The ceremony of strewing rushes in the churches lingered here and there; but the feasts of rush bearings went from strength to strength. Near Halifax again, the incumbent (a Reverend Witter) attempted to prevent these feasts in 1682, at which festivals (Heywood complained) the people make great provision of flesh and ale, come from all parts, "and eat and drink and rant in a barbarous heathenish manner". Mr Witter's doors were broken down and he was abused as a "cobbler".[2] The rush-bearing ceremony continued in this district for at least a further one hundred and fifty years. But, as in most districts, it had lost any sacred significance. The symbols on the richly-decorated carts became bells and painted pots. The picturesque costumes of the men and the white dresses and garlands of the women appear more and more pagan. The pageants pay a mere passing obeisance to Christian symbolism: Adam and Eve, St George and the Dragon, the Virtues, the Vices, Robin Hood and Maid Marian, hobbyhorses, sweeps on pigs, morris dancers. The festivities ended with baitings, wrestling, dancing and drinking, and sometimes with the tour of the houses of the gentry and of wealthy householders for drink, food and money. "I could not suppress these Bacchanals," wrote the Rev. John William de La Flechere of the Shropshire Wakes: "the impotent dyke I opposed only made the torrent swell and foam, without stopping the course." Moreover, the people had found patrons outside the Church: if La Flechere preached against drunkenness, shows and

---

[1] J. Horsfall Turner (ed.), *The Rev. Oliver Heywood, B.A.* (Brighouse, 1881), Vol. II, pp. 294, 271.

[2] *Ibid.*, pp. 264, 294.

bullbaiting, "the publicans and malsters will not forgive me. They think that to preach against drunkenness and to cut their purse strings is the same thing."[1]

But the resurgence of this culture cannot be put down to the commercialization fostered by publicans alone. The gentry had means, through Quarter Sessions, to harry these in their licenses if they had wished. This efflorescence of festivities can scarcely have taken place without a permissive attitude on the part of many of the gentry. In one sense, this was no more than the logic of the times. The materialism of the eighteenth-century rich and the Erastianism of their Church were met by the materialism of the poor. The race meetings of the rich became the poor's popular holidays. The permissive tolerance of the gentry was solicited by the many taverns which — as inn signs still proclaim — sought to put themselves under the patronage of the great. The gentry could make no convincing missionary expeditions to reform the manners and morals of the poor if they were unwilling to reform their own ostentatious and pleasant vices.

But as explanation this is not finally convincing. Only a ruling class which feels itself to be threatened is afraid to flaunt a double standard. Mandeville is only unusual in pressing to the point of satire the argument that private vices were public benefits. In more softened form the same argument, as to the valuable function of luxury in providing employment and spectacle for the poor, was part of the economic cant of the time. Henry Fielding could make the same point without satirical intention:

> To be born for no other Purpose than to consume the Fruits of the Earth is the Privilege. . . of very few. The greater Part of Mankind must sweat hard to produce them, or Society will no longer answer the Purposes for which it was ordained.[2]

---

[1] J. Benson, *Life of the Reverend John William de la Flechere* (1805: 1835 edn.), p. 78, describing Madeley Wake in 1761. (My thanks to Barrie Trinder.)

[2] *An Enquiry into the Causes of the Late Increase of Robbers* (1751), in Henry Fielding, *Complete Works* (1967), Vol. xiii, p. 11. Cf. Bernard Mandeville, *The Fable of the Bees* (Penguin edn. 1970), pp. 257, 292-3.

Indeed, we have seen that the conspicuous display of luxury and "liberality" was part of the theatre of the great. In some areas (wages theory, the poor laws, the criminal code), the materialism of the rich consorted without difficulty with a disciplinary control of the poor. But in other areas — the permissive attitude to the robust, unchristian popular culture, a certain caution and even delicacy in the handling of popular disturbance, even a certain flattery extended to the poor as to their liberties and rights — in these areas we are presented with a problem which demands more subtle analysis. It suggests some reciprocity in the relations between rich and poor; an inhibition upon the use of force against indiscipline and disturbance; a caution (on the part of the rich) against taking measures which would alienate the poor too far, and (on the part of that section of the poor which from time to time rallied behind the cry of "Church and King") a sense that there were tangible advantages to be gained by soliciting the favour of the rich. There is some mutuality of relationship here which it is difficult not to analyse at the level of class relationship.

Of course, no one in the eighteenth century would have thought of describing their own as a "one-class society". There were the rulers and the ruled, the high and the low people, persons of substance and of independent estate and the loose and disorderly sort. In between, where the professional and middle classes, and the substantial yeomanry, should have been, relations of clientage and dependency were so strong that, at least until the 1760s, these groups appear to offer little deflection of the essential polarities. Only someone who was "independent" of the need to defer to patrons could be thought of as having full political identity: so much is a point in favour of the "one-class" view. But class does not define itself in political identity alone. For Fielding, the evident division between the high and the low people, the people of fashion and of no fashion, lay like a cultural fissure across the land:

whilst the people of fashion seized several places to their own use, such as courts, assemblies, operas, balls, &c., the people of no fashion, besides one royal place, called his Majesty's Bear-Garden, have been in constant possession of all hops, fairs, revels, &c. . . . So far from

looking on each other as brethren in the Christian language, they seem
scarce to regard each other as of the same species. [1]

This is a world of patricians and of plebs; it is no accident
that the rulers turned back to ancient Rome for a model of
their own sociological order. But such a polarization of class
relations doesn't thereby deprive the plebs of all political
existence. They are at one side of the necessary equation of
the *res publica*.

A plebs is not, perhaps, a working class. The plebs may
lack a consistency of self-definition, in consciousness; clarity
of objectives; the structuring of class organization. But the
political presence of the plebs, or "mob", or "crowd", is
manifest; it impinged upon high politics at a score of critical
occasions — Sacheverell riots, excise agitation, cider tax,
the patriotic and chauvinistic ebullitions which supported the
career of the older Pitt, and on to Wilkes and the Gordon
Riots and beyond. Even when the beast seemed to be
sleeping, the tetchy sensibilities of a libertarian crowd
defined, in the largest sense, the limits of what was
politically possible. There is a sense in which rulers and
crowd needed each other, watched each other, performed
theatre and countertheatre to each other's auditorium,
moderated each other's political behaviour. This is a more
active and reciprocal relationship than the one normally
brought to mind under the formula "paternalism and
deference".

It is necessary also to go beyond the view that labouring
people, at this time, were confined within the fraternal
loyalties and the "vertical" consciousness of particular
trades; and that this inhibited wider solidarities and
"horizontal" consciousness of class. There is something in
this, certainly. The urban craftsman retained something of a
guild outlook; each trade had its songs (with the implements
of the trade minutely described), its chapbooks and legends.
So the shoemaker's apprentice might be given by his master
*The Delightful, Princely and Entertaining History of the
Gentle-Craft*, and there read:

[1] *Ibid.*, p. 164.

> . . . never yet did any know
> A Shooemaker a Begging go.
> Kind they are one to another,
> Using each Stranger as his Brother.

He read this in 1725, and he would have read much the same in the time of Dekker. At times the distinctions of trades were carried over into festival and social life. Bristol, in the early eighteenth century, saw an annual pugilistic combat on Ash Wednesday between the blacksmiths, and the coopers, carpenters and sailors, with the weavers sometimes joining in on the side of the smiths. And in more substantial ways, when defining their economic interests *as producers*, craftsmen and workers — Thames-side coal heavers, London porters, Spitalfields silk weavers, west of England clothing workers, Lancashire cotton weavers, Newcastle keelmen — organized themselves tightly within their trades, and petitioned the State or corporate authorities for their fading paternalist favours.

Indeed, there is substantial evidence on this side; and the degree to which a guild or "trade" outlook and even vestigial continuity of organization contributed to the early trade unions was understated by the Webbs. Brentano, in 1870, had explored the possibility of continuity of organization and of traditions between the guilds and companies and the early trade unions.[1] But the Webbs, in their weighty *History of Trade Unionism* (1894) decreed decisively against Brentano. They did this, partly by insisting on the distinctively new character of trade unionism (in consequence of a sharp split between the interests of masters and journeymen), and partly by imposing definitions which made much eighteenth-century evidence appear to be suspect or irrelevant — for example, the demand that organization must be continuous and must have national dimensions.[2] Such definitions for a long time discouraged further systematic enquiry, either into collective bargaining by direct action[3] or into local and

[1] L. Brentano, *On the History and Development of Guilds and the Origin of Trade Unions* (1870).
[2] Sidney and Beatrice Webb, *The History of Trade Unionism* (1894/ 1920), chapter 1.
[3] This question was re-opened by E. J. Hobsbawm, "The Machine Breakers", in *Labouring Men* (1964), first published in *Past and Present* in 1952.

regional organization, as of the Newcastle keelmen or west of England clothing workers.

Such studies have multiplied in recent years, and it is now clear that — if there is no record of continuous organization of national unions — there was certainly a continuous tradition of trade union activity throughout the century, and very probably (in clothing districts) continuous local organization and recognised leadership, for actions which sometimes disguised themselves as "rough musics"[1] and sometimes took on the protective masks of friendly societies. Such trade union traditions extend back into the seventeenth century, and I regret that several very helpful recent studies give a contrary impression.[2] Some years ago in the Public Record Office I came upon what may be one of the earliest membership cards of a trade union which has (as yet) been found: it comes from a branch of the journeymen wool-combers at the small town of Alton (Hants) in 1725, although the card is printed in London and the date of formation of the club or "Charity-Stock" is given as 1700. (See plate I.) The woolcombers were being prosecuted (in the court of King's Bench) in consequence of a long-standing dispute extending over several years. Edward and Richard Palmer, clothiers, employed 150 workers in the woollen manu-

---

[1] For local and community trade union organisation, see Adrian Randall, "The Industrial Moral Economy of the Gloucestershire Weavers in the Eighteenth Century", in John G. Rule (ed.), *British Trade Unionism, 1750-1850* (1988), esp. pp. 29-35.

[2] Thus John Rule's helpful collection on *British Trade Unionism: the Formative Years* takes 1750 as the starting date. C. R. Dobson, *Masters and Journeymen: A prehistory of industrial relations* (1980) covers the dates 1717-1800. See also R. W. Malcolmson's valuable essay, "Workers' combinations in eighteenth-century England", in M. and J. Jacob (eds,), *The Origins of Anglo-American Radicalism* (1984), p. 160, note 38, gives a weavers' combination in Bristol in 1707. John Rule discusses the question more closely in *The Experience of Labour in Eighteenth-Century Industry* (1981), esp. pp. 151-4. None of these authors seems to mention the extensive organisation of the Essex weavers in Colchester and region which much preoccupied the Privy Council in 1715. When the mayor of Colchester arrested some of their spokesmen, their fellows effected a rescue and "many hundreds of them Marched into Town, all armed with Pistols, Swords, or Clubs. . ." and also with a clear statement of their grievances and demands: see extensive documentation in PRO, PC 1.14. 101 Parts II and III.

factory. Their woolcombers had formed into a Woolcombers Club, fifteen or twenty of whom met at a public house, the "Five Bells". A strike had been called (of seven combers) to enforce apprenticeship regulations and (in effect also) to enforce a "closed shop". Combers were imported to break the strike, and their workshop was twice broken into, their combs and materials burned. Shortly before these events the common seal which had hitherto been used was replaced by a card or "ticket" which entitled the member "to employment or to receive benefitt in all Clothing Towns where the Woolcombers had formed themselves into Clubbs". Strike pay or benefit for leaving an employer paying under rate (under the "By Laws and Orders" of the Club) was five shillings, with which the member must travel to another town. A blackleg woolcomber imported by the Palmers from Wokingham (Berks) deposed that as he passed along the street in Alton he was "often Affronted and Abused", until at length he left the Palmers' employment. Eight of the combers were duly convicted, and the case was given a little national publicity.[1]

This seems to push the date for trade unionism back at least as far as 1700, and all the recognised features of the craft society are already there — the attempt to make a closed shop, the control of apprenticeship, strike benefit, the tramping system. After all, the elaborate processional display of woolcombers, shoemakers, hatters, weavers, etc., on grand civic occasions (such as the Coronation of George III) did not spring out of nowhere. This was the Manchester order of procession:

The Procession of the Wool-Combers
Two Stewards with white wands. — A man on horseback in white, with a wool wig and sash, beating a pair of kettle drums. — A band of music. — The Arms of Bishop Blaize displayed on a banner. — The Treasurer and Secretary. — A Page Royal, with a white wand. — Bishop Blaze on horseback, attended by ten pages on foot. — The Members, two and two, with wool wigs, sashes, and cockades of the same. — Two Junior Stewards with each a white wand.

[1] Depositions and examinations in PRO, KB 1.3. The offenders, who must have spent some months in prison, were ordered to pay £80 to the prosecutor (their master): *British Journal*, 19 February 1726; *Newcastle Weekly Courant*, 19 February 1726; *Ipswich-Journal*, 7 August 1725, cited by Malcolmson, *op. cit.*, p. 160 (note 39), p. 157.

Bishop Blaize, the patron saint of woolcombers, was supposed to have invented wool-combing and to have been torn to pieces by the sharp-toothed wool "cards". The combers' society on this occasion recited the lines:

> Spectators all that on us now do gaze,
> Behold once more the sons of Bishop Blaze,
> Who here are met in this association,
> To celebrate the King and Queen's C'ronation. . .
> May happy Britain soon enjoy a peace:
> May joy and plenty and our trade increase;
> God save King George the Third; let virtue shine
> Through all the branches of his Royal line.[1]

The Bishop Blaize procession was still being celebrated vigorously in Bradford (Yorks) in 1825. Bishop Blaize is still at the centre of the Kidderminster ticket of 1838 (Plate III).

Such iconography emphasizes an appeal by the early trade unionists to tradition, and an attempt by the journeyman's club or union to take over from the masters' guild or company the representation of the interests of "the Trade". On occasion, the journeymen actually split from the masters' company, as did the hammermen of Glasgow in 1748, who formed their own society, levied contributions, and elected a dean and masters on the pattern of the Masters' Company. There are also several interesting cases of workers' organizations which emerged in close — if antagonistic — relationship to older companies. Perhaps the most consistently militant group of eighteenth-century workers — the Newcastle keelmen — were undoubtedly thoroughly cognisant with the forms of the Company of Hostmen, with whom, indeed, they wrestled for control of their own charitable institutions. The keelmen combined two features not usually found together: on the one hand, they were numerous, subject to a yearly bond, and well-placed to employ the tactics of mass action, strike and intimidation. On the other hand, since a high proportion of their numbers were Scottish, and since the bond did not entitle them to a settlement in Newcastle, it was

---

[1] *A Particular Account of the Processions of the different Trades, in Manchester, on the day of the Coronation of their Majesties, King George the Third and Queen Charlotte* (September 22, 1761), single sheet folio, Manchester Ref. Lib.

in their interests to provide systematically for sickness, injury and old age.[1]

The Webbs may have been right to have demolished some of the romantic myths abroad in the 1880s and 1890s — myths which were fostered by some trade unionists themselves — as to the origin of trade unions in guilds. But what they understated was the notion of "the Trade"; and also the way in which, from the late seventeenth century, the demand for the enforcement of the apprenticeship clauses of the Statute of Artificers became a demand which, increasingly, the journeymen sought to turn to their own advantage, and hence which served as a bridge between the old forms and the new. Brentano was perhaps right when he declared: "trade unions originated with the non-observance of 5 Eliz. c. 4." From the sixteenth century to the early nineteenth century there is evidence of the continuity of these craft and trade traditions in the pottery, friendly society insignia, the emblems and mottos of early unions, and in the chapbooks and verses designed for each trade. This appeal to legitimacy and to precedent (in the Statute of Artificers) can be found in some Essex verses of the late seventeenth century:

> From such as would our rights invade,
> Or would intrude into our trade,
> Or break the law Queen Betty made,
> Libera nos Domine.[2]

They are also found in an "Ode to the Memory of Queen Elizabeth" which prefaces a report of a trial of a cause of apprenticeship involving the London saddlers in 1811:

> Her memory still is dear to journey men,
> For shelter'd by her laws, now they resist
> Infringements, which would else persist:
> Tyrannic masters, innovating fools
> Are check'd, and bounded by her glorious rules.
> Of workmen's rights she's still a guarantee. . .

---

[1] J. M. Fewster, "The Keelmen of Tyneside in the Eighteenth Century", *Durham University Journal*, n.s. Vol. 19, 1957-8.
[2] *HMC Var. Coll.* (1913), p. 581.

And rights of artizans, to fence and guard,
While we, poor helpless wretches, oft must go
And range this liberal nation to and fro.[1]

Indeed, we may have one record of the actual moment of transition from guild to union, in the diary of a Coggeshall weaver, which contains the rules of the Company of Clothiers, Fullers, Baymakers, and New Drapers of Coggeshall (?1659-1698), followed by those transmitted from the Company to a short-lived "Combers' Purse", clearly a local club, formed "that we may show that love we have to our trade, and one to another for trade sake".[2]

The sense of trade solidarities, thus, could be strong. But to suppose that such trade fraternity was necessarily at odds with larger objectives or solidarities is quite false. The trade consciousness of London craftsmen in the 1640s did not inhibit support for John Lilburne. What trade consciousness may inhibit is economic solidarities between different groups of producers as against their employers; but if we lay aside this anachronistic postulate, we will find among eighteenth-century working men and women abundant evidence of horizontal solidarities and consciousness. In the scores of occupational lists which I have examined of food rioters, turnpike rioters, riots over libertarian issues or enclosure of urban commons, it is clear that solidarities were not segregated by trade; in a region where clothing workers, tinners or colliers are predominant, these obviously predominate in the lists of offenders, but not to the exclusion of other working occupations. I hope to have shown, in another place, that all these groups, during food riots, shared a common consciousness — ideology and objectives — as petty consumers of the necessities of life. But these people were consumers also of cultural values, of libertarian rhetoric, of patriotic and xenophobic prejudice; and on these issues they could exhibit solidarities as well. When, in the quiet 1750s, Princess Amelia tried to close access to Richmond New Park, she was opposed by a vigorous horizontal consciousness

---

[1] *Report of the Trial of Alexander Wadsworth against Peter Laurie before Lord Ellenborough, 18 May 1811* (1811), in Columbia Univ. Lib., Seligman Collection, Place Vol. xii.

[2] *HMC Var. Coll.* VIII (1913), pp. 578-584.

which stretched from John Lewis, a wealthy local brewer, to Grub Street pamphleteers, and which embraced the whole local "populace" (pp. 111-114). When, in 1799, the magistrates attempted to put down Shrove Tuesday football in the streets of Kingston, it was "the populace" and "the mob" who assembled and triumphantly defied their orders.[1] The mob may not have been noted for an impeccable consciousness of class; but the rulers of England were in no doubt at all that it was a horizontal sort of beast.

VI

Let us take stock of the argument to this point. It is suggested that, in practice, paternalism was as much theatre and gesture as effective responsibility; that so far from a warm, household, face-to-face relationship we can observe a studied technique of rule. While there was no novelty in the existence of a distinct plebeian culture, with its own rituals, festivals, and superstitions, we have suggested that in the eighteenth century this culture was remarkably robust, greatly distanced from the polite culture, and that it no longer acknowledged, except in perfunctory ways, the hegemony of the Church. As dialect and polite speech drifted apart, so the distance widened.

This plebeian culture was not, to be sure, a revolutionary nor even a proto-revolutionary culture (in the sense of fostering ulterior objectives which called in question the social order); but one should not describe it as a deferential culture either. It bred riots but not rebellions: direct actions but not democratic organizations. One notices the swiftness of the crowd's changes in mood, from passivity to mutiny to cowed obedience. We have this in the satirical ballad of the "Brave Dudley Boys":

[1] Messrs Bytterwood, Cook, and Bradshaw to duke of Portland, 24 February 1799, PRO, HO 42.46. The magistrates complained that the military (at Hampton Court) failed to support them in suppressing the football or in enforcing the Riot Act, the officer-in-command absenting himself (despite prior notice). The duke of Portland annotated the complaint: "These Gent[n] don't appear to have managed this business as well as they might but their credit, as Magistrates, makes it necessary that care sh[d] be taken of them."

We bin marchin' up and deown
Wo boys, wo
Fur to pull the Housen deown
And its O the brave Doodley boys
Wo boys, Wo
It bin O the brave Doodley boys, Wo!

Some gotten sticks, some gotten steavs
Wo boys, wo
Fur to beat all rogues and kne-avs. . .

But the riot reaches its appointed limit, and —

. . . the Dra-gunes they did come,
And twas devil take the hoindmost wum.

We all ran down our pits
Wo boys, wo
We all ran down our pits
Frietened a' most out of our wits
And its O the brave Doodley boys. . .

And thence to the reassertion of deference:

God Bless Lord Dudley Ward
Wo boys, wo
He know'd as times been hard

He called back the sojermen
Wo boys, wo
And we'll never riot again. . .[1]

It is easy to characterise this behaviour as child-like. No doubt, if we insist upon looking at the eighteenth century only through the lens of the nineteenth-century labour movement, we will see only the immature, the pre-political, the infancy of class. And from one aspect, this is not untrue: repeatedly one sees pre-figurements of nineteenth-century class attitudes and organization; fleeting expressions of solidarities, in riots, in strikes, even before the gallows; it is tempting to see eighteenth-century workers as an immanent working class, whose evolution is retarded by a sense of the futility of transcending its situation. But the "to-fro lackeying" of the crowd itself has a history of great antiquity:

[1] I have improperly drawn lines from two different versions: Jon Raven, *The Urban and Industrial Songs of the Black Country and Birmingham* (Wolverhampton, 1977) version (b) p. 50, and Roy Palmer (ed.), *Songs of the Midlands* (Wakefield, 1972), p. 88.

the "primitive rebels" of one age might be seen, from an earlier age, to be the decadent inheritors of yet more primitive ancestors. Too much historical hindsight distracts us from seeing the crowd as it was, *sui generis*, with its own objectives, operating within the complex and delicate polarity of forces of its own context.

I have attempted in chapter 4 to reconstruct these crowd objectives, and the logic of the crowd's behaviour, in one particular case: the food riot. I believe that all other major types of crowd action will, after patient analysis, reveal a similar logic: it is only the short-sighted historian who finds the eruptions of the crowd to be "blind". Here I wish to discuss briefly three characteristics of popular action, and then return once again to the context of gentry-crowd relations in which all took place.

First is the anonymous tradition. The anonymous threat, or even the individual terrorist act, is often found in a society of total clientage and dependency, on the other side of the medal of simulated deference. It is exactly in a rural society, where any open, identified resistance to the ruling power may result in instant retaliation — loss of home, employment, tenancy, if not victimization at law — that one tends to find the acts of darkness: the anonymous letter, arson of the stack or outhouse, houghing of cattle, the shot or brick through the window, the gate off its hinges, the orchard felled, the fish-pond sluices opened at night. The same man who touches his forelock to the squire by day — and who goes down to history as an example of deference — may kill his sheep, snare his pheasants or poison his dogs at night.

I don't offer eighteenth-century England as a theatre of daily terror. But historians have scarcely begun to take the measure of the volume of anonymous violence, usually accompanied by anonymous threatening letters.

What these letters show is that eighteenth-century labouring men were quite capable, in the security of anonymity, of shattering any illusion of deference and of regarding their rulers in a wholly unsentimental and unfilial way. A writer from Witney, in 1767, urged the recipient: "do not suffer such damned wheesing fat guted Rogues to Starve the Poor by such Hellish ways on purpose that they may follow hunting horse racing &c and to maintain their familys in

Pride and extravagance". An inhabitant of Henley-on-Thames, who had seen the volunteers in action against the crowd, addressed himself to "you gentlemen as you are please to call Yourselves — Altho that is your Mistakes — for you are a sett of the most Damnable Rougs that Ever Existed". (An Odiham author, writing on a similar theme in 1800, remarked "we dont care a Dam for them fellows that Call Themselves Gentlemen Soldiers But in our opinion the[y] Look moore like Monkeys riding on Bears".) Sometimes the lack of proper deference comes through merely as a brisk aside: "Lord Buckingham," a handbill writer in Norwich remarked in 1793, "who died the other day had Thirty Thousand Pounds, yeerly For setting his Arse in the House of Lords and doing nothing."[1]

These letters show — and they are dispersed over most parts of England, as well as parts of Wales — that deference could be very brittle indeed, and made up of one part of self-interest, one part of dissimulation, and only one part of the awe of authority. They were part of the countertheatre of the poor. They were intended to chill the spine of gentry and magistrates and mayors, recall them to their duties, enforce from them charity in times of dearth.

This takes us to a second characteristic of popular action, which I have described as countertheatre. Just as the rulers asserted their hegemony by a studied theatrical style, so the plebs asserted their presence by a theatre of threat and sedition. From the time of Wilkes forward the language of crowd symbolism is comparatively "modern" and easy to read: effigy burning, the hanging of a boot from a gallows; the illumination of windows (or the breaking of those without illumination); the untiling of a house which, as Rudé notes, had an almost ritualistic significance. In London the unpopular minister, the popular politician, needed the aid of no pollsters to know their rating with the crowd; they might be pelted with obscenities or chaired in triumph through the streets. When the condemned trod the stage at Tyburn, the audience proclaimed vociferously their assent or disgust with the book.

But as we move backward from 1760 we enter a world of

---

[1] See my essay, "The Crime of Anonymity", in Hay *et al, op. cit.*

theatrical symbolism which is more difficult to interpret: popular political sympathies are expressed in a code quite different from that of the 1640s of of the 1790s. It is a language of ribbons, of bonfires, of oaths and of the refusal of oaths, of toasts, of seditious riddles and ancient prophecies, of oak leaves and of maypoles, of ballads with a political *double-entendre*, even of airs whistled in the streets.[1] We don't yet know enough about popular Jacobitism to assess how much of it was sentiment, how much was substance; but we can certainly say that the plebs on many occasions employed Jacobite symbolism success- fully as theatre, knowing well that it was the script most calculated to enrage and alarm their Hanoverian rulers.[2] In the 1720s, when an intimidated press veils rather than illuminates public opinion, one detects underground moods in the vigour with which rival Hanoverian and Stuart anniversaries were celebrated. The *Norwich Gazette* reported in May 1723 that Tuesday last, being the birthday of King George, was observed in the city "with all the usual demon- strations of joy and loyalty":

And Wednesday being the Anniversary of the Happy Restauration of King Charles II, and with him of the royal family, after a too long and successful usurpation of sanctified tyranny, it was celebrated in this city in an extraordinary manner; for besides ringing of bells, firing of guns, and bonfires, the streets were strown with seggs, oaken boughs set up at the doors, and in some streets garlands and pictures hung out, and

---

[1] For the calendar of popular political symbolism (Jacobite and Hanoverian) see especially Rogers, *Whigs and Cities*, pp. 354-8.

[2] Despite the substantial advances in Jacobite historical studies, the evidence as to the dimensions of popular support remains slippery. An excellent assessment is in Nicholas Rogers, "Riot and Popular Jacobitism in Early Hanoverian England", in Eveline Cruikshanks (ed.), *Ideology and Conspiracy: Aspects of Jacobitism, 1689-1759* (Edinburgh, 1982). Professor Rogers shows that the considerable volume of anti-Hanoverian and Jacobite manifestations (especially between 1714 and 1725) cannot be taken as an indication of organised commitment or of insurrectionary intent but should be considered as symbolic taunting of the Hanoverian rulers — "provocative, defiant, derisory" — and not the less important for that reason. Rogers has developed these insights in *Whigs and Cities, passim*, and he speculates (pp. 378-82) on the reasons for the marked decline in the Jacobite sympathies of English urban crowds between 1715 and 1745.

variety of antick and comick dances. . . (with) bumpers to the Glorious Memory of Charles II.

Manifestly disloyal as this was, not only to the King but also to the Great Man in his own county, it provided no handle to the law officers of the Crown.

This was a war of nerves, now satirical, now menacing. The arrows sometimes found their mark. In 1724 the king's ministers were poring over depositions from Harwich where the loyal Hanoverian caucus had been insulted by a most unsavoury rough music:

> while the Mayor and other Members of the Corporation were assembled in the Town Hall to Commemorate His Majesty's Most happy accession to the Throne by drinking His Majesty's and other most Loyal Healths, he this Deponent. . . did see from a Window. . . a person dressed up with horns on his head attended by a mob.

This "said Infamous Person", John Hart, a fisherman, was being chaired about the town by one or two hundred others of equal infamy. They were "drumming a ridiculous Tune of Roundheaded Cuckolds &c, and [Hart] came to the Mayor's and this Deponent's door and made signs with his hands intimating that We might kiss his Arse".[1]

If some of the crowd's actions can be seen as counter-theatre, this is by no means true of all. For a third characteristic of popular action was the crowd's capacity for swift direct action. To be one of a crowd, or a mob, was another way of being anonymous, whereas to be a member of a continuing organization was bound to expose one to detection and victimization. The eighteenth-century crowd well understood its capacities for action, and its own art of the possible. Its successes must be immediate, or not at all. It must destroy these machines, intimidate these employers or dealers, damage that mill, enforce from their masters a subsidy of bread, untile that house, before troops came on the scene. The mode is so familiar that I need only recall it to mind with one or two citations from the state papers. At Coventry, 1772:

> On Tuesday evening. . . a great Mob to the Number of near 1,000 of the. . . lower class of People. . . assembled by Fife and Beat of Drum on

[1]Examinations and depositions in PRO, SP 44.124, fos. 116-132.

Account, as they pretended, of a Reduction of Wages by. . . one of the principal Ribbon Manufacturers. . . They declared their intention to. . . pull down his House, & to demolish him, if they could meet with him. . . Every gentle Means was made use of. . . to disperse them, but without Effect, and by throwing Stones and breaking his Windows, they began to carry their Purpose into Execution.[1]

In Newcastle-upon-Tyne in 1740, during the triumphant phase of a food riot:

About two on Thursday morning a great number of Colliers and Waggoners, Smiths and other common workmen [the horizontal beast again] came along the Bridge, released the prisoners, and proceeded in great Order through the Town with Bagpipes playing, Drum beating, and Dirty Clothes fixed upon sticks by way of Colours flying. They then increased to some thousands and were in possession of the principal Streets of the Town. The Magistrates met at the Guild Hall and scarce knew what to do.

In the result they panicked, scuffled with the crowd on the Guildhall steps, and fired a volley into it, killing more than one. In retaliation:

Stones flew in among us. . . through the windows like cannon shot. . . at length the mob broke in upon us in the most terrible outrage. They spared our lives indeed but obliged us to quit the place, then fell to plundering and destroying all about 'em. The several benches of justice were immediately and entirely demolished, the Town Clerk's Office was broke open, and all the books, deeds, and records of the town and its courts thrown out of the window.[2]

They broke into the Hutch and took out fifteen hundred pounds, they. . . broke down everything that was ornamental, two very fine capital Pictures of King Charles second and James second. . . they tore, all but the faces. . . and afterwards conducted the Magistrates to their own houses in a kind of Mock Triumph.[3]

Once again, one notes the sense of theatre even in the full flush of rage: the symbolic destruction of the benches of justice, the Clerk's books, the Tory corporation's Stuart portraits, the mock triumph to the magistrates' homes; and

[1] Mayor and Corporation to "My Lord", 7 July, 1772, PRO, WO 40.17.
[2] Mayor of Newcastle-upon-Tyne to duke of Newcastle, 27 June, 1740, PRO, SP 36.51.
[3] Alderman Ridley, "Account of the Riots", Northumberland CRO, 2 RI 27/8.

yet, with this, the order of their processions and the restraint which withheld them (even after they had been fired upon) from taking life.

Of course, the crowd lost its head as often as the magistrates did. But the interesting point is that neither side did this often. So far from being "blind" the crowd was often disciplined, had clear objectives, knew how to negotiate with authority, and above all brought its strength swiftly to bear. The authorities often felt themselves to be faced, literally, with an anonymous multitude. "These men are all tinners," a customs officer wrote from St. Austell in 1766 of local smuggling gangs, "seldom seen above ground in the daytime, and are under no apprehensions of being known by us".[1] Where "ringleaders" were detected, it was often impossible to secure sworn depositions. But solidarity rarely went further than this. If taken, the leaders of the crowd might hope for an immediate rescue, within twenty-four hours; if this moment passed, they could expect to be abandoned.

Other features might be noted: but these three — the anonymous tradition; countertheatre; and swift, evanescent direct action — seem of importance. All direct attention to the unitary context of class relationship. There is a sense in which rulers and crowd needed each other, watched each other, performed theatre and countertheatre in each other's auditorium, moderated each other's political behaviour. Intolerant of the insubordination of free labour, nevertheless the rulers of England showed in practice a surprising degree of licence towards the turbulence of the crowd. Is there some deeply embedded, "structural" reciprocity here?

I find the notion of gentry-crowd reciprocity, of the "paternalism-deference equilibrium" in which both parties to the equation were, in some degree, the prisoners of each other, more helpful than notions of a "one-class society" or of consensus or of a plurality of classes and interests. What must concern us is the polarization of antagonistic interests and the corresponding dialectics of culture. There is very articulate resistance to the ruling ideas and institutions of society in the seventeenth and nineteenth centuries: hence historians expect to analyse these societies in some terms of

[1] PRO, WO 1.989.

social conflict. In the eighteenth century resistance is less articulate, although often very specific, direct and turbulent. One must therefore supply the articulation, in part by de-coding the evidence of behaviour, and in part by turning over the bland concepts of the ruling authorities and looking at their undersides. If we do not do this we are in danger of becoming prisoners of the assumptions and self-image of the rulers: free labourers are seen as the "loose and disorderly sort", riot is seen as spontaneous and "blind", and important kinds of social protest become lost in the category of "crime". But there are few social phenomena which do not reveal a new significance when exposed to this dialectical examination. The ostentatious display, the powdered wigs and the dress of the great must be seen also — as they were intended to be seen — from below, in the auditorium of the theatre of class hegemony and control. Even "liberality" and "charity" may be seen as calculated acts of class appeasement in time of dearth and calculated extortions (under threat of riot) by the crowd: what is (from above) an "act of giving" is (from below) an "act of getting". So simple a category as "theft" may turn out to be, in certain circumstances, evidence of protracted attempts by villagers to defend ancient common right usages, or by labourers to defend customary perquisites. And following each of these clues to the point where they intersect, it becomes possible to reconstruct a customary popular culture, nurtured by experiences quite distinct from those of the polite culture, conveyed by oral traditions, reproduced by example (perhaps, as the century goes on, increasingly by literate means), expressed by symbolism and in ritual, and at a very great distance from the culture of England's rulers.

I would hesitate before I described this as a *class* culture, in the sense that one can speak of a working-class culture, within which children were socialized into a value-system with distinct class notations, in the nineteenth century. But one cannot understand this culture, in its experiential ground, in its resistance to religious homily, in its picaresque flouting of the provident bourgeois virtues, in its ready recourse to disorder, and in its ironic attitudes towards the law, unless one employs the concept of the dialectical antagonisms, adjustments, and (sometimes) reconciliations, of class.

When analysing gentry-plebs relations one finds not so much an uncompromising ding-dong battle between irreconcilable antagonists as a societal "field-of-force". I am thinking of a school experiment (which no doubt I have got wrong) in which an electrical current magnetized a plate covered with iron filings. The filings, which were evenly distributed, arranged themselves at one pole or the other, while in between those filings which remained in place aligned themselves sketchily as if directed towards opposing attractive poles. This is very much how I see eighteenth-century society, with, for many purposes, the crowd at one pole, the aristocracy and gentry at the other, and until late in the century, the professional and trading groups bound down by lines of magnetic dependency to the rulers, or on occasion hiding their faces in common action with the crowd. This metaphor allows one to understand not only the very frequent riot situation (and its management) but also much of what was possible and also the limits of the possible beyond which power did not dare to go.

I am therefore employing the terminology of class conflict while resisting the attribution of identity to *a* class. It seems to me that the metaphor of a field-of-force can co-exist fruitfully with Marx's comment in the *Grundrisse*, that:

> In all forms of society it is a determinate production and its relations which assign every other production and its relations their rank and influence. It is a general illumination in which all other colours are plunged and which modifies their specific tonalities. It is a special ether which defines the specific gravity of everything found in it.[1]

This plebeian culture is, in the end, constrained within the parameters of gentry hegemony: the plebs are ever-conscious of this constraint, aware of the reciprocity of gentry-crowd relations, watchful for points to exert their own advantage. The plebs also take over to their own use some of the gentry's rhetoric. For, once again, this is the century of the advance of "free" labour. And the distinctive feature of the manufacturing system was that, in many kinds of work,

---

[1] For a slightly different translation, see *Grundrisse* (Penguin, 1973), pp. 106-7. Even here, however, Marx's metaphor relates not to class or social forms, but to co-existent dominant and subordinate economic relations.

labourers (taking petty masters, journeymen and their families together) still controlled in some degree their own immediate relations and modes of work, while having very little control over the market for their products or over the prices of raw materials or food. This explains something of the structure of industrial relations and of protest, as well as something of the culture's artefacts and of its cohesiveness and independence of control.[1] It also explains much of the consciousness of the "free-born Englishman", who took to himself some part of the constitutionalist rhetoric of his rulers, and defended stubbornly his rights at law and his rights to white bread and cheap ale. The plebs were aware that a ruling-class that rested its claim to legitimacy upon prescription and law had little authority to over-rule their own customs and rights.

The reciprocity of these relations underlies the importance of the symbolic expressions of hegemony and of protest in the eighteenth century. That is why I have directed so much attention to the notion of theatre. Of course, every society has its own kind of theatre; much in the political life of contemporary societies can be understood only as a contest for symbolic authority. But I am saying more than that the symbolic contests of the eighteenth century were particular to that century and require more study. I think that symbolism, in that century, had a peculiar importance, owing to the weakness of other organs of control: the authority of the Church is departing, and the authority of the schools and the mass media have not yet arrived. The gentry had four major resources of control — a system of influence and preferment which could scarcely contain the unpreferred poor; the majesty and terror of law; the local exercise of favours and charity; and the symbolism of their hegemony. This was, at times, a delicate social equilibrium, in which the rulers were forced to make concessions. Hence the contest for symbolic authority may be seen, not as a way of acting out ulterior "real" contests, but as a real contest in its own right. Plebeian protest, on occasion, had no further objective than to

[1] I am supporting here the argument of Gerald M. Sider, "Christmas mumming and the New Year in Outport Newfoundland", *Past and Present* (May, 1976).

challenge the gentry's hegemonic assurance, strip power of its symbolic mystifications, or even just to blaspheme. It was a contest for "face", but the outcome of the contest might have material consequences — in the way the poor law was administered, in the measures felt by the gentry to be necessary in times of high prices, in whether Wilkes was imprisoned or freed.

At least we must return to the eighteenth century, giving as much attention to the symbolic contests in the streets as to the votes in the House of Commons. These contests appear in all kinds of odd ways and odd places. Sometimes it was a jocular employment of Jacobite or anti-Hanoverian symbolism, a twisting of the gentry's tail. Dr Stratford wrote from Berkshire in 1718:

> Our bumpkins in this country are very waggish and very insolent. Some honest justices met to keep the Coronation day at Wattleton, and towards the evening when their worships were mellow they would have a bonfire. Some bumpkins upon this got a huge turnip and stuck three candles just over Chetwynd's house. . . They came and told their worships that to honour King George's Coronation day a blazing star appeared above Mr Chetwynd's house. Their worships were wise enough to take horse and go and see this wonder, and found, to their no little disappointment, their star to end in a turnip.[1]

The turnip was of course the particular emblem of George I as selected by the Jacobite crowd, when they were in good humour; in ill-humour he was the cuckold king, and horns would do instead of turnips. But other symbolic confrontations in these years could become very angry indeed. In a Somerset village in 1724 an obscure confrontation (one of a number of such affairs) took place over the erection of a maypole. A local land-owner (William Churchey) seems to have taken down "the Old Maypole", newly dressed with flowers and garlands, and then to have sent two men to the bridewell for felling an elm for another pole. In response his apple and cherry orchard was cut down, an ox was killed and dogs poisoned. When the prisoners were released the pole was re-erected and "May Day" was celebrated with "seditious" ballads and derisory libels against the magistrate. Among those dressing the maypole were two labourers, a maltster, a

[1] HMC, *Portland MSS*, pp. vii, 245-6.

carpenter, a blacksmith, a linenweaver, a butcher, a miller, an inn-keeper, a groom and two gentlemen.[1]

As we pass the mid-century the Jacobite symbolism wanes and the occasional genteel offender (perhaps pushing his own interests under the cover of the crowd) disappears with it.[2] The symbolism of popular protest after 1760 sometimes challenges authority very directly. Nor was symbolism employed without calculation or careful forethought. In the great strike of seamen on the Thames in 1768, when some thousands marched upon parliament, the fortunate survival of a document enables us to see this taking place.[3] At the height of the strike (7 May 1768), when the seamen were getting no satisfaction, some of their leaders went into a dock-side pub and asked the publican to write out in a good hand and in proper form a proclamation which they intended posting on all the docks and river-stairs. The publican read their paper and found "many Treasonable & Rebellious Expressions" and at the bottom "No W-, no K-" (i.e. "No Wilkes, No King"). The publican (by his own account) remonstrated with them:

---

[1] PRO, KB 2 (1), Affidavits, Easter 10 G I, relating to Henstridge, Somerset, 1724. On George's accession the common people of Bedford "put the May-pole in mourning" and a military officer cut it down. In August 1725 there was an affray about a maypole in Barford (Wilts.), between the inhabitants and a gentleman who suspected the pole had been stolen from his woods (as it probably was). The gentleman summoned a posse to his aid, but the inhabitants won: for Bedford, *An Account of the Riots, Tumults and other Treasonable Practices since His Majesty's Accession to the Throne* (1715), p. 12; for Barford, *Mist's Weekly Journal*, 28 August, 1725.

[2] However, as the maypole episodes remind us, the Tory tradition of paternalism, which looks backward to the Stuart "Book of Sports", and which extends either patronage or a warm permissiveness to the recreations of the people, remains extremely vigorous even into the nineteenth century. This theme is too large to be taken into this chapter, but see R. W. Malcolmson, *Popular Recreations in English Society, 1700-1850* (Cambridge, 1973); Hugh Cunningham, *Leisure in the Industrial Revolution* (1980), chapters one and two.

[3] William L. Clement Library, Ann Arbor, Michigan, *Shelburne Papers*, vol. 133, "Memorials of Dialogues betwixt several Seamen, a certain Victualler, & a S--l Master in the late Riot".

Publican: "I beg Gentlemen you would not talk of compulsion or be guilty of the least Irregularity."

Seamen: "What do you mean Sir, if we are not speedily redressed there is Ships & Great Guns at Hand which we will use as Occasion shall require in Order to redress Ourselves besides we are determined to unmast every ship in the River & then bid you, & Old England adieu & steer for some other country. . ."

The seamen here were only playing the same game as the legislature with their repeated enactments of capital offences and legislative overkill; both sides to the relation tended to threaten more than they performed. Disappointed by the publican the seamen took their paper to a schoolmaster who undertook this kind of clerical business. Once again the sticking-point was the conclusion to the proclamation — on the right hand "Seamen", on the left hand "No W-, no K-". The schoolmaster had more respect for his own neck than to be the author of such a paper. The following dialogue, by his own account, then ensued, although it is a somewhat unlikely conversation-piece on Shadwell stairs:

Seamen: "You're not a Seaman's Friend."

Schoolmaster: "Gentlemen I am so much Your Friend that I would by no means be an Instrument of doing you the greatest Injury by Proclaiming you Traitors to our Dread Sovereign Lord the King & raisers of Rebellion & Sedition amongst your fellow subjects and this I humbly conceive to be the Contents of Your Paper. . ."

Seamen: "Most of us have ventured our lives in defence of His Majesty's Person, Crown and Dignity and for our native country and on all occasions have attacked the Enemy with courage & Resolution & have been Victorious. But since the conclusion of the War We Seamen have been slighted and our Wages reduced so low & Provisions so Dear that we have been rendered uncapable of procuring the common necessaries of Life for ourselves & Familys, and to be plain with you if our Grievances is not speedily redressed there is Ships & Great Guns enough at Deptford and Woolwich we will kick up such a Dust in the Pool as the Londoners never see before, so when we have given the Merchants a coup de grease [*sic*] we will steer for France where we are well assured we shall meet with a hearty welcome."

Once again the seamen were disappointed; they exeunt on the line, "do you think such a Body of British seamen is to be dictated by an old Fusty School Master?" Somewhere they found themselves a scribe, but even this scribe refused the full commission. The next morning the proclamation duly appeared on the river-stairs, signed at the bottom right "Seamen" and on the left. . . "Liberty & Wilkes for ever!".

The point of this anecdote is that at the very height of the seamen's strike the leaders of the movement spent several hours going from pub to schoolmaster to scribe, in search of a writer willing to set down the biggest affront to authority which they could imagine: "No King". The seamen may not have been in any reflective sense republicans; but this was the biggest symbolic "Great Gun" that they could fire off, and if fired with the seeming support of some thousands of British tars it would have been a great gun indeed.[1]

Contrary to cherished legends, England was of course never without a standing army in the eighteenth century.[2] The maintenance of this army, in Walpole's years, was a particular cause of the Hanoverian Whigs. But for purposes of internal control this was often a small and emergency force. It was, for example, seriously over-stretched and inadequate to the needs of the situation during the riot year 1766. The permanent quartering of troops in populous districts was always impolitic. There was always delay, and often delay for several days, between the onset of disturbance and the arrival of the military. The troops, and equally their officers (whose power to act against civilians could be challenged in the courts) found this service "odious".[3] Jealousy of the Crown, seconded by the avarice of the aristocracy, had led to the weakness of all the effective organs for the enforcement of order. The weakness of the State was expressed in an incapacity to use force swiftly, in an ideological tenderness towards the liberties of the subject,

---

[1] It is not clear whether the seamen who were preparing the handbill were authentic spokesmen for their fellows. Another eye witness of the seamen's demonstrations recorded that "they boasted that they were *for King and Parliament*": P. D. G. Thomas, "The St. George's Fields 'Massacre' on 10 May 1768", *London Journal*, Vol. 4, no. 2, 1978. See also G. Rudé, *Wilkes and Liberty* (Oxford, 1962), p. 50; Brewer, *op. cit.*, p. 190; W. J. Shelton, *English Hunger and Industrial Disorders* (1973), pp. 188, 190.

[2] See John Brewer, *The Sinews of Power, op. cit.*, pp. 44-55.

[3] See Tony Hayter, *The Army and the Crowd in Eighteenth-Century England* (1978), chapters 2 and 3: also pp. 52-3 *et passim*.

and in a sketchy bureaucracy so riddled with sinecurism, parasitism and clientage that it scarcely offered an independent presence.[1]

Thus the price which aristocracy and gentry paid for a limited monarchy and a weak State was, perforce, the licence of the crowd. This is the central structural context of the reciprocity of relations between rulers and ruled. The rulers were, of course, reluctant to pay this price. But it would have been possible to discipline the crowd only if there had been a unified, coherent ruling class, content to divide the spoils of power amicably among themselves, and to govern by means of their immense command over the means of life. Such cohesion did not, at any time before the 1790s, exist, as several generations of distinguished historical scholars have been at pains to show.

The tensions — between court and country, money and and land, factions and families — ran deep. Until 1750 or 1760 the term "gentry" is too undiscriminating for the purposes of our analysis. There is a marked divergence between the Whig and Tory traditions of relations with the crowd. The Whigs, in those decades, were never convincing paternalists.[2] But in the same decades there developed between some Tories and the crowd a more active, consenting alliance. Many small gentry, the victims of land tax and the losers in the consolidation of great estates against the small, hated the courtiers and the moneyed interest as ardently as did the plebs. And from this we see the consolidation of the specific traditions of Tory paternalism — for even in the nineteenth century, when we think of paternalism, it is Tory rather than Whig which we tend to couple with it. At its zenith, during the reigns of the first two Georges, this

---

[1] Despite his persuasive case for the strength of the English "fiscal-military state", John Brewer concedes that "armed force was of very limited value in enforcing authority in England": Brewer, *op. cit.*, p. 63.

[2] Although great care was exercised to limit confrontations with the crowd: see Townshend's correspondence with Vaughan, concerning the West of England weavers' riots in January 1726/7, in PRO, SP 44.81 fos. 454-58: "His Majesty is always desirous that the Mildest Ways shou'd be used to quiet these Disturbances"; the employment of soldiers against the weavers is "very much against the King's inclination", "the King wou'd have no gentle ways omitted. . . [to] bring People to temper" etc.

alliance achieved an ideological expression in the theatrical effects of popular Jacobitism.

By the 'fifties this moment is passing, and with the accession of George III we pass into a different climate. Certain kinds of conflict between court and country had so far softened that it is possible to talk of the calculated paternalist style of the gentry as a whole. In times of disturbance, in handling the crowd, one may now forget the distinction between Whig and Tory — at any rate at the level of the practising JP — and one may see the magistracy as a whole as acting within an established tradition. To maintain a hold over the poor they must show themselves to be neither papists nor puritans. They must, at least in gestures, offer themselves as mediators. During episodes of riot, most JPs, of whatever persuasion, hung back from confrontation, preferred to intervene by moral suasion before summoning force. Indeed, the role of the JP in times of riot might almost be reduced to formula: "I was sure that *one Firm* Magestrate could have any day put an end to the Riot," a Quaker merchant wrote to a friend about a sailors' riot in North Shields in 1792:

> By first speaking to the Sailors as a Majistrate ought to speak on such an Occasion, and, then put on the Man of feeling and Humanity and promise to lay all their grievances before Parliam'. . .[1]

This stance flowed sometimes from an element of active sympathy for the crowd, especially where the gentry felt themselves to be aggrieved at the profit which middlemen were making out of their own and their tenants' corn. A riot in Taunton in 1753 (Newcastle was informed) had been provoked by "one Burcher who has the town mills, & who instead of corn grinds the poor, in short he is generally thought to deserve punishment, in a legal way, for malpractices of this kind. . ."[2] Earl Poulett, the Lord Lieutenant of Somerset, clearly found men like Burcher to be a damned nuisance. They made work for him and for the bench; and, of course, order must be maintained. A general "rising" or state of riot brought other ill consequences in its

---

[1] Friends House Library, Gibson MSS, Vol. ii, p. 113. Henry Taylor to James Phillips, 27 November 1792. My thanks to Malcolm Thomas.

[2] British Library, Newcastle MSS, Add. MSS 32, 732, Poulett to Newcastle, 11 July 1753.

train — the crowd became unmannerly, the locus for disloyal speeches and seditious thoughts, "for they will all follow one another sooner than listen to gentlemen when they are once risen". Indeed, on this occasion "at last some of them came to talk a levelling language, viz. they did not see why some should be rich and others poor". (There were even obscure murmurings about aid from France.)

But the maintenance of order was not a simple matter:

> The Impunity of those Rioters encouraged. . . subsequent ones. Gentlemen in the Commission are affraid to act, nor is it safe for them as their are no troops at Taunton, Ilminster &c &c only a grass guard. . . at Crewkerne without any officer. But it seems to be in general the disposition of those towns & of these gentlemen to let the spirit subside & not to provoke them for fear of the consequences.

The consequences feared were immediate ones: more damage to property, more disorder, perhaps physical threats to the magistracy. Earl Poulett was clearly in two minds on the matter himself. He would, if so advised by your Grace "get some of the principle Ring leaders convicted," but "the disposition of the town, & neighbouring gentlemen (was) against it." There is in any case, neither here nor in hundreds of similar exchanges in 1740, 1753, 1756, the 1760s and later, any sense that the social order as a whole was endangered: what was feared was local "anarchy", the loss of prestige and hegemony in the locality, relaxing social discipline. It is usually assumed that the matter will, in the end, subside, and the degree of severity to be shown — whether a victim or two should or should not swing from the gallows — was a matter of calculated example and effect. We are back in a theatre once more. Poulett apologized to Newcastle for troubling him with these "little disturbances". A Harwich fisherman giving a lewd Jacobite gesture had worried the king's ministers more than many hundreds of men and women marching about the country thirty years later, demolishing mills and seizing grain.

In such situations there was a practised technique of crowd appeasement. The mob, Poulett wrote,

> was appeased. . . by gentlemen going out & desiring to know what they wanted & what they wd have, apprising them of the consequences, & promising them the millers & bakers shd be prosecuted, that they wd

buy up the corn & bring it to market themselves & that they shd have it in small quantitys as they wanted it.[1]

But where the crowd offered a more direct threat to the gentry themselves, then the reaction was more firm. In the same year, 1753, West Yorkshire was disturbed by turnpike riots. Henry Pelham wrote to his brother that Mr Lascelles and his turnpike had been directly attacked: "at the head of his own tenants and followers only". Lascelles had met the rioters and "gallantly thrashed them & took 10 prisoners". The Recorder of Leeds had been threatened, "and all the active part of the magistrates with pulling down their houses, and even taking away their lives". Against this, nothing but a maximum display of ruling-class solidarity would suffice:

> I have endeavoured to persuade the few gentlemen that I have seen to be themselves more active. . . This affair seems to me of such consequence that I am persuaded nothing can entirely get the better of it but the first persons in the country taking an active part in defence of the laws; for if these people see themselves only overpowered by troops, and not convinced that their behaviour is repugnant to the sense of the first people of this country, when the troops are gone, hostilitys will return.[2]

It is a text worth examination. In the first place, it is difficult to recall that it is the Prime Minister of England who is writing, and to the "Home Secretary". What is being discussed appears to be the requisite style of private men of great property in dealing with an offence to their order: the Prime Minister is endeavouring to persuade "the few gentlemen that I have seen" to be more "active". In the second place, the incident illustrates superbly the supremacy of cultural over physical hegemony. Troops afford less security than the reassertion of paternalist authority. Above all, the credibility of the gentry and magistracy must be maintained. At an early stage in disturbance, the plebs should be persuaded *above all* to abandon an insubordinate posture, to couch their demands in legitimate and deferential terms: they should learn that they were likely to get more from a loyal petition than from a riot. But if the authorities failed to persuade the crowd to drop their bludgeons and await redress, then they were willing on occasion to negotiate with

---

[1] *Ibid.*
[2] *Ibid.*, H. Pelham to Newcastle, 7 July 1753.

them under duress; but in such cases it became far more probable that the full and terrible theatre of the Law would later perform its ghastly matinées in the troubled district. Punitive examples must be made, in order to re-establish the credibility of order. Then, once again, the cultural hegemony of the gentry would resume.

VII

This symbolic contest acquires its significance only within a particular equilibrium of social relations. The plebeian culture cannot be analysed independently of this equilibrium; its definitions are, in some part, antitheses to the definitions of the polite culture. What I have been attempting to show, perhaps repetitiously, is that each element of this society, taken separately, may have precedents and successors, but that when all are taken together they add up to a sum which is more than the sum of the parts: it is a structured set of relations, in which the state, the law, the libertarian ideology, the ebullitions and direct actions of the crowd, all perform roles intrinsic to that system, and within limits assigned by that system, which limits are at the same time the limits of what is politically "possible"; and, to a remarkable degree, the limits of what is intellectually and culturally "possible" also. The crowd, at its most advanced, can rarely transcend the libertarian rhetoric of the radical Whig tradition; the poets cannot transcend the sensibility of the humane and generous paternalist.[1] The furious anonymous letters which spring up from society's lower depths blaspheme against the gentry's hegemony but offer no strategy to replace it.

In one sense this is a rather conservative conclusion, for I am endorsing eighteenth-century society's rhetorical self-image — that the Settlement of 1688 defined its form and its characteristic relations. Given that that Settlement

---

[1] I do not doubt that there was a genuine and significant paternalist tradition among the gentry and professional groups. But that is a different theme. My theme here is to define the limits of paternalism, and to present objections to the notion that eighteenth-century social (or class) relations were mediated by paternalism, on paternalism's own terms.

established the form of rule for an agrarian bourgeoisie[1] it seems that it was as much that form of State power as it was that mode of production and productive relations which determined the political and cultural expressions of the next hundred years. Indeed that State, weak as it was in some of its bureaucratic and rationalizing functions, was immensely strong and effective as an auxiliary instrument of production in its own right: in breaking open the paths for commercial imperialism, in imposing enclosure upon the countryside, and in facilitating the accumulation and movement of capital, both through its taxing, banking and funding functions and, more bluntly, through the parasitic extractions of its own officers. It is this specific combination of weakness and of strength which provides the "general illumination" in which all colours of that century are plunged; which assigned to the judges and the magistracy their roles; which made necessary the theatre of cultural hegemony and which wrote its paternalist and libertarian script; which afforded to the crowd its opportunity for protest and for pressures; which laid down the terms of negotiation between authority and plebs, and

---

[1] Professor J. H. Hexter was astonished when I uttered this improper copulation ("agrarian bourgeoisie") at the Davis Center seminar in Princeton in 1976. Perry Anderson was also astonished ten years earlier: "Socialism and pseudo-empiricism", *New Left Review*, xxxv (January-February 1966), p. 8, "A bourgeoisie is based on *towns*; that is what the word means." See also (on my side of the argument), Genovese, *The World the Slaveholders Made*, p. 249; and a judicious commentary on the argument by Richard Johnson, *Working Papers in Cultural Studies*, xi (Birmingham, Spring 1976). My re-statement of this (somewhat conventional) Marxist argument was made in "The peculiarities of the English", *Socialist Register* (1965), esp. p. 318. Here I emphasise not only the economic logic of agrarian capitalism, but the specific amalgam of urban and rural attributes in the life-style of the eighteenth-century gentry: the watering-places; the London or town season; the periodic urban pasage-rites, in education or in the various marriage markets; and other specific attributes of a mixed agrarian-urban culture. The economic arguments (already ably presented by Dobb) have been reinforced by Brenner, "Agrarian class structure and economic development in pre-industrial Europe", *Past and Present*, lxx, February 1976, esp. pp. 62-8. Additional evidence as to the urban facilities available to the gentry is in Peter Borsay, "The English urban renaissance: the development of provincial urban culture, *c.* 1680–*c.* 1760", *Social History*, v (May 1977).

which established the limits beyond which negotiation might not go.

Finally, how far and in what sense do I use the concept of "cultural hegemony"? This can be answered at a practical or at a theoretical level. At a practical level it is evident that the gentry's hegemony over the political life of the nation was effectively imposed until the 1790s. Neither blasphemy nor sporadic episodes of arson call this in question; these do not offer to displace the gentry's rule but only to punish them. The limits of what was politically possible (until the French Revolution) were expressed externally in constitutional forms and, internally, within men's minds, as taboos, limited expectations, and a disposition towards traditional forms of protest, aimed often at recalling the gentry to their paternalist duties.

But it is necessary also to say what this hegemony does *not* entail. It does not entail any acceptance by the poor of the gentry's paternalism upon the gentry's own terms or in their approved self-image. The poor might be willing to award their deference to the gentry, but only for a price. The price was substantial. And the deference was often without the least illusion: it could be seen from below as being one part necessary self-preservation, one part the calculated extraction of whatever could be extracted. Seen in this way, the poor imposed upon the rich some of the duties and functions of paternalism just as much as deference was in turn imposed upon them. Both parties to the question were constrained within a common field-of-force.

In the second place, we must recall once more the immense distance between polite and plebeian cultures, and the vigour of the authentic self-activity of the latter. Whatever this hegemony may have been, it did not envelop the lives of the poor and it did not prevent them from defending their own modes of work and leisure, and forming their own rituals, their own satisfactions and view of life. So that we are warned from this against pressing the notion of hegemony too far and into improper areas.[1] Such

---

[1] In a relevant criticism of certain uses of the concept of hegemony, R. J. Morris notes that it can imply "the near impossibility of the working class or organized sections of that class being able to generate radical. . .

hegemony may have defined the outside limits of what was politically, socially, practicable, and hence influenced the forms of what was practised: it offered the bare architecture of a structure of relations of domination and subordination, but within that architectural tracery many different scenes could be set and different dramas enacted.

Eventually an independent plebeian culture as robust as this might even have nurtured alternative expectations, challenging this hegemony. This is not my reading of what took place, for when the ideological break with paternalism came, in the 1790s, it came in the first place less from the plebeian culture than from the intellectual culture of the dissenting middle class, and from thence it was carried to the urban artisans. But Painite ideas, carried through by such artisans to an ever wider plebeian culture, instantly struck root there; and perhaps the shelter provided by this robust and independent culture enabled them to flourish and propagate themselves, until they gave rise to the great and undeferential popular agitations at the end of the French Wars.

Theoretically I am saying this. The concept of hegemony is immensely valuable, and without it we would be at a loss to understand how eighteenth-century social relations were structured. But while such cultural hegemony may define the limits of what is possible, and inhibit the growth of alternative horizons and expectations, there is nothing determined or automatic about this process. Such hegemony can be sustained by the rulers only by the constant exercise of skill, of theatre and of concession. Second, such hegemony, even when imposed successfully, does not impose an all-embracing view of life; rather, it imposes blinkers, which inhibit vision in certain directions while leaving it clear in others. It can

---

ideas independent of the dominant ideology". The concept implies the need to look to intellectuals for this, while the dominant value system is seen as "an exogenous variable generated independently" of subordinate groups or classes ("Bargaining with hegemony", *Bulletin of the Society for the Study of Labour History*, (Autumn 1977), pp. 62-3). See also Genovese's sharp response to criticisms on this point in *Radical History Review*, Winter 1976-7, p. 98; and T. J. Jackson Lears, "The Concept of Cultural Hegemony", *American Hist. Rev.* xc, 1985.

co-exist (as it did co-exist in eighteenth-century England) with a very vigorous self-activating culture of the people, derived from their own experience and resources. This culture, which may be resistant at many points to any form of exterior domination, constitutes an ever-present threat to official descriptions of reality; given the sharp jostle of experience, the intrusion of "seditious" propagandists, the Church-and-King crowd can become Jacobin or Luddite, the loyal Tsarist navy can become an insurrectionary Bolshevik fleet.

It follows that I cannot accept the view, popular in some structuralist and Marxist circles in Western Europe, that hegemony imposes an all-embracing domination upon the ruled — or upon all those who are not intellectuals — reaching down to the very threshold of their experience, and implanting within their minds at birth categories of subordination which they are powerless to shed and which their experience is powerless to correct. This may perhaps have happened here and there, but not in England, not in the eighteenth century.

VIII

It may now be helpful to restate, and also to qualify, some parts of this argument. When I first proposed it, in the nineteen-seventies, it was taken by some to have set up a more absolute dichotomy between patricians and plebs, with no intermediate forces of any serious influence, than I had intended. And criticism has turned upon the absence, in my analysis, of any role for the middle class. In such a reading, the emergence of a middle-class presence in the 1790s, and the radicalisation of a large section of the intelligentsia, appears as inexplicable, a *deus ex machina*.[1] And critics have complained of the "dualism" and bleak polarisation which ensues, of my failure to admit the middling orders as historical actors and "the neglect of the role of urban

---

[1] See Geoff Eley's helpful critique, "Re-Thinking the Political: Social History and Political Culture in 18th and 19th Century Britain", *Archiv für Sozialgeschichte* (Bonn), Band xxi, 1981. Also Eley, "Edward Thompson, Social History and Political Culture", in Harvey J. Kaye and Keith McClelland (eds.), *E. P. Thompson: Critical Perspectives* (Oxford, 1990).

culture and bourgeois dissidence".[1]

I can agree that my bi-polar model may have more relevance to rural, small town and, especially, manufacturing districts expanding beyond any corporate controls (the locus of "proto-industrialisation") than it does to the larger corporate towns and, certainly, to London. It was no part of my intention to diminish the significance of the growth throughout the century, in numbers, wealth and cultural presence, of the middling orders who came (in the terms of Jürgen Habermas[2]) to create and occupy a "public sphere". These include the groups described by John Brewer:

> . . . lawyers, land agents, apothecaries, and doctors: middlemen in the coal, textile, and grain trades: carters, carriers, and innkeepers: booksellers, printers, schoolteachers, entertainers, and clerks: drapers, grocers, druggists, stationers, ironmongers, shopkeepers of every sort: the small masters in cutlery and toy making, or in all the various luxury trades of the metropolis.[3]

The list could be much extended, and should certainly include the comfortable freeholders and substantial tenant farmers. And it is from such middling groups that Eley sees "the emergence and consolidation of a new and self-conscious bourgeois public":

> Ultimately related to processes of capitalist development and social transformation. . . processes of urban cultural formation, tendentially supportive of an emergent political identity and eventually linked to regional political networks; a new infra-structure of communications, including the press and other forms of literary production. . . and a new universe of voluntary association; and finally, a regenerate parliamentarism. . .[4]

I can assent to all this. But this emergence and consolidation was a complex process, and a very slow one, eventuating over a hundred years and more. As Professor Cannon has noted:

[1] Linda Colley, "The Politics of Eighteenth-Century British History", *Journal of British Studies*, 24, 1986, O. 366.

[2] Jürgen Habermas, "The Public Sphere", *New German Critique*, 3, Fall 1974.

[3] John Brewer, "English Radicalism in the Age of George III", in J. G. A. Pocock (ed.), *Three British Revolutions* (Princeton, N.J., 1980), p. 333.

[4] Eley, "Re-Thinking the Political", *op. cit.*, p. 438.

Though there is much evidence that merchants and financiers, teachers and journalists, lawyers and architects, shopkeepers and industrialists prospered in Hanoverian England, the questions to be explained seem to me to be almost the opposite of Marxist historiography — not how did they come to control government, but why did they not challenge aristocratic domination until towards the end of the century?[1]

The questions seem to me to be located in the actual historical record and not in any variety of historiography. And they continue to perplex historians of many persuasions. Certainly there were many prefigurements of middle-class "emergence" in urban politics. But, as John Brewer argues, middle-class independence was constantly constrained and brought back within the channels of dependency by the powerful controls of clientage:

> The producers of luxury goods — of furniture, carriages, and clothing — retailers of all sorts, those, from prostitutes to dancing masters, who provided services for the rich, all these people (and they constituted a sizeable proportion of the metropolitan workforce) relied for their living on a culture centred upon the Court, Parliament and the London season.[2]

This situation need not induce deference: it could generate resentment and hostility. What it could not do, until the arena of the market became more anonymous, was generate independence.

If we consider the ever-present controls of clientage, of patronage and "interest", we are drawn back to the model of a bi-polar field of force, just as such bi-polar vocabulary was continually in the mouths of the historical actors themselves. Indeed, such a model of the social and political order was an ideological force in its own right. One of the ways in which patricians repelled the admission of the middle class to any share in real power was to refuse their admission to the vocabulary of political discourse. Patrician culture stubbornly resisted any allowance of vitality to the notion of "middle

---

[1] John Cannon, *Aristocratic Century: the Peerage of Eighteenth-Century England* (Cambridge, 1984), p. ix.

[2] Brewer, *op. cit.*, p. 339. See also Brewer, "Commercialization and Politics", in N. McKendrick, John Brewer, and J. Plumb, *The Birth of a Consumer Society* (Bloomington, 1982).

class" until the end of the century.[1] Moreover, it is an error to suppose that the growth in numbers and wealth of the "middling orders" necessarily modified and softened class polarisation in the society as a whole. In some circumstances it diverted hostilities; as we have seen (above pp. 43-46) the middling groups could serve to screen the landowner or great clothier. But so long as so many of the routes to office, preferment and contracts were controlled by the old and corrupt means of patronage, the growth in the numbers of the middling groups could only intensify the competition between them.[2]

Hence my argument has not been about the numbers, wealth or even cultural presence of the middle class, but about its identity as an autonomous, self-motivated political actor, its effective influence upon power, its modification in any serious way of the patrician-plebs equilibrium. I do not wish to retreat from the propositions in this chapter, although I salute the significance of current research into middle-class institutions and into urban political life.

The argument is in part about power, and in part about cultural alienation. (See above, p. 5.) Critics have suggested that I and others of the older generation of "crowd historians", by attending mainly to riots and protests, have excluded from view many other popular manifestations, including loyalist and patriotic ebullience, electoral partisan-ship, and uglier evidences of xenophobia or religious bigotry.[3] I am very willing to grant that these questions have

[1] Paul Langford, *op. cit.*, p. 653 notes the delay in the admission of "middle class" to general usage, and he comments that the middle class "was united in nothing more than in its members' determination to make themselves gentlemen and ladies, thereby identifying themselves with the upper class". I am indebted to Dror Wahrman of Princeton University for a sight of some of his unpublished research into the explicit and politically-motivated resistance to the admission of "middle class" to general usage.

[2] See Linda Colley, *op. cit.*, p. 371: "If sociopolitical antagonisms were becoming sharper in the late eighteenth century (as I believe they were), one would expect to see both an increase in plebeian consciousness and bitterness, and a ruling group that was more avid for office, honors, wealth, and a discrete cultural identity."

[3] For one excellent study see John Walsh, "Methodism and the Mob in the Eighteenth Century", in G. J. Cuming and D. Baker, *Studies in Church History* (Cambridge, 1971), Vol. 8.

not preoccupied me, and I am happy to see these absences being repaired by others.[1] Certainly, a more rounded view of the crowd is becoming available. But one hopes that the view does not become too round. Few generalisations as to the dominant political attitudes of the "plebs" across the eighteenth century are likely to stand, except that the crowd was highly volatile. Eighteenth-century crowds come in great variety, in every shape and size. In the early years of the century there were mughouse gangs, to be turned loose by politicians against their opponents. "I love a mob," said the duke of Newcastle in his later years: "I headed a mob once myself. We owe the Hanoverian succession to a mob."[2] At no time is this volatility more manifest than at the end of the century. Generalisations as to the crowd's political disposition will tell us one thing at the time of the Priestley Riots (1791); another at the height of the popularity of Tom Paine and Reform two or three years later. Revolutionary sentiments can be found in alehouse rhetoric and in anonymous threatening letters between 1797 and 1801 (years of the naval mutinies, the Irish insurrection, years of resistance to taxation and of fierce bread riots) and fervent popular loyalism and anti-Gallicanism can be found between 1803 and 1805 (years of invasion threat, of anger at Napoleon's imperial expansion, which aroused the hostility even of former English "Jacobins", years of mass enlistment in the Volunteers and of Nelson's bitter-sweet victory at Trafalgar).

These swift transitions took place, of course, within individuals as well as within the mood of crowds. Allen Davenport, who came from a labouring family on the Gloucestershire-Wiltshire border, described how he came to Bristol in 1794, at the age of 19:

> I was a bit of a patriot, and thought, at that time, that every thing that was undertaken by England was right, just, and proper; and that every other nation that opposed her was wrong and deserved chastisement. And that France who had just killed her king, exiled her nobles, and

[1] For example, Linda Colley, "The Apotheosis of George III: Loyalty, Royalty and the British Nation, 1760-1820", *Past and Present*, 102, February 1984.
[2] James L. Fitts, "Newcastle's Mob", *Albion*, Vol. 5, no. 1, Spring 1973.

reviled and desecrated the Christian religion, was very wicked indeed; and I shouted "Church and King" as loud and as long as any priest or lord in the kingdom. And believed that England was not only justified, but that it was her bounden duty to put down, and if possible to exterminate such a desperate nation of levellers, blasphemers, and regicides! And that was the feeling of nine tenths of the people of England [in] 1794.[1]

Davenport was to become a leading Spencean, a republican and a Chartist.

The eighteenth-century crowd was protean: now it employed Jacobite symbolism, now it gave full-throated endorsement to Wilkes, now it attacked Dissenting meetinghouses, now it set the price of bread. It is true that certain themes repeat themselves: xenophobia (especially anti-Gallicanism) as well as a fondness for anti-papist and libertarian ("free-born Englishman") rhetoric. But easy generalisations should stop at that point. Perhaps in reaction to overmuch sympathy and defensiveness which was shown by crowd historians of my generation, some younger historians are willing to tell us what the crowd believed, and (it seems) it was always nationalistic and usually loyalist and imperialist in disposition. But not all of these historians have spent much time in searching the archives where the enigmatic and ambivalent evidence will be found, and those of us who have done so are more cautious. Nor can one read off "public opinion" in a direct way from the press, since this was written by and for the middling orders; an enthusiasm for commercial expansion among these readers was not necessarily shared by those who served by land or sea in the wars which promoted this expansion. In contrast to the populist tone of the 1960s it is very much the fashion of our own time for intellectuals to discover that working people were (and are) bigoted, racist, sexist, but/and at heart deeply conservative and loyal to Church and King. But a traditional ("conservative") customary consciousness may in certain conjunctures appear as a rebellious one; it may have its own logic and its own solidarities which cannot be typed in a simple-minded way. "Patriotism" itself may be a rhetorical stratagem which the crowd employs to mount an assault upon

[1] *Life of Allen Davenport* (1845), pp. 18-19.

the corruption of the ruling Hanoverian powers, just as in the next century the Queen Caroline agitation was a stratagem to assault King George IV and his court. When the crowd acclaimed popular admirals it might be a way of getting at Walpole or at Pitt.[1]

We cannot even say how far explicit republican ideas were abroad, especially during the turbulent 1760s. It is a question more often turned aside with a negative than investigated. But we have the *caveat* of Sir John Plumb: "Historians, I feel, never give sufficient emphasis to the prevalence of bitter anti-monarchical, pro-republican senti- ment of the 1760s and 1770s."[2] A similar thought has strayed across the mind of a more excitable historian, Mr J. C. D. Clark, who has quoted John Wesley in 1775, writing to the earl of Dartmouth about the "dangerously dissatisfied" state of the people "all over the nation" "in every city, town, and village where I have been". The people "aim at" the king himself: "they heartily despise His Majesty and hate him with a perfect hatred. They wish to imbrue their hands in his blood; they are full of the spirit of murder and rebellion. . ."[3] One suspects that there are times during the 1760s and 1770s when a part of the English people were more ready to secede from the Crown than were the American colonists, but they had the misfortune not to be protected from it by the Atlantic ocean.

I stand, then, by the patrician/plebs model and the field- of-force metaphor, both for the structuring of power and for the dialectical tug-of-war of ideology. Yet it should not be supposed that these formulae supply an instant analytical resource to unpick the meaning of every action of the crowd. Each crowd action took place in a specific context, was influenced by the local balance of forces, and often found its

[1] Gerald Jordan and Nicholas Rogers, "Admirals as Heroes: Patriotism and Liberty in Hanoverian England", *Journal of British Studies*, Vol. 28, no. 3, July 1989; Kathleen Wilson, "Empire, Trade and Popular Politics in Mid-Hanoverian Britain: the Case of Admiral Vernon", *Past and Present*, 121, 1988.

[2] Plumb, "Political Man", *op. cit.*, p. 15.

[3] J. Telford (ed.), *Letters to the Rev. John Wesley* (1931), Vol. vi, p. 178, cited in J. C. D. Clark, *English Society, 1688-1832* (Cambridge, 1985), p. 236. It is not clear how far Mr Clark endorses Wesley's alarmism.

opportunity and its script from the factional divisions within ruling groups or from issues thrown up in national political discourse. This question has been discussed cogently by Nicholas Rogers in *Whigs and Cities*; he (perhaps unfairly) suspects me of "essentialist" analytical procedures. If so, then Rogers is right and I am wrong, since his command of the material is superb, and his findings are supported by years of research and analysis of the urban crowd.[1] In Rogers's view most urban crowd actions should be seen as taking place on "a terrain in which ideology, culture and power intersect". In the early eighteenth century the rulers themselves, for their own reasons, opened this space for the crowd, allocating to it a client and subaltern role. High-church clergy and civic factionalists enlarged this space. The calendar of political aniversaries and celebrations — processions, illuminations, elections, effigy burnings, carnivalesque ebullitions — all allocated roles to the crowd and enlisted its participation. In this way in the four decades after 1680 "wide sections of the labouring populace" were drawn into the national political discourse:

> Years of acute party strife, in a social context which allowed the common people greater cultural space, had created a dynamic and contentious political culture, centred around royal and national anniversaries, in which the populace itself was a vigorous participant.

It was only under this tutelage that the crowd learned to assert its own autonomy and, on occasion, select its own objectives. The crowd was now a phenomenon that "had to be cultivated, nurtured, and contained", lest it should break out of its subaltern role.[2]

I can accept and applaud Professor Rogers's approach and its execution in his urban studies. It is preferable to a simple reduction to a dual patrician/plebs polarity, and — while it allows to the crowd less autonomy than I find (for example, in provincial food or turnpike or industrial or press-gang or

---

[1] One looks forward eagerly to his forthcoming volume, *Crowds, Politics, and Culture in Eighteenth-Century England*, which promises to replace all previous studies. One also looks forward to Kathleen Wilson's forthcoming, *"The Sense of the People": Urban Political Culture in England, 1715-1785*.

[2] Rogers, *Whigs and Cities*, esp. pp. 351, 368-72.

anti-militia actions) — it replaces urban crowd actions within a more complex political and cultural context. But through all these complexities I still must posit the underlying polarity of power — the forces which pressed to enter upon and occupy any spaces which fell open when ruling groups came into conflict. Even where crowds were clearly managed and subaltern, they were never regarded by the rulers without anxiety. They might always exceed their permit, and the unlicensed crowd would fall back into the "essentialist" polarity, "transforming the official calendar into a carnival of sedition and riot".[1] Underlying all crowd actions one can sense the formation which has been my object of analysis, the patrician/plebs equilibrium.

One component of this, the old pretences of paternalism and deference, were losing force even before the French Revolution, although they saw a temporary revival in the Church-and-King mobs of the early nineties, the military display and anti-Gallicanism of the wars. The Gordon Riots had seen the climax, and also the apotheosis, of plebeian licence; and inflicted a trauma upon the rulers which was registered in a growing disciplinary tone in the eighties. But by then the reciprocal relation between gentry and plebs, tipping now one way, now the other, had lasted for a century. Grossly unequal as this relationship was, the gentry nevertheless needed *some* kind of support from "the poor", and the poor sensed that they were needed. For a hundred years they were not altogether the losers. They maintained their traditional culture; they secured a partial arrest of the work-discipline of early industrialism; they perhaps enlarged the scope of the poor laws; they enforced charities which may have prevented years of dearth from escalating into crises of subsistence; and they enjoyed liberties of pushing about the streets and jostling, gaping and huzzaing, pulling down the houses of obnoxious bakers or Dissenters, and a generally riotous and unpoliced disposition which astonished foreign visitors, and which almost misled them themselves into believing that they were "free". The 1790s expelled that illusion, and in the wake of the experiences of those years the relationship of reciprocity snapped. As it snapped, so, in the

[1] *Ibid.*, p. 372.

same moment, the gentry lost their self-assured cultural hegemony. It suddenly appeared that the world was not, after all, bounded at every point by their rules and overwatched by their power. A man was a man, "for a' that". We move out of the eighteenth-century field-of-force and enter a period in which there is a structural reordering of class relations and of ideology. It is possible, for the first time, to analyse the historical process in terms of nineteenth-century notations of class.

Chapter Three

Custom, Law and Common Right

I

At the interface between law and agrarian practice we find custom. Custom itself *is* the interface, since it may be considered both as praxis and as law. Custom's original lies in praxis; in a treatise on copyhold at the end of the seventeenth century we learn that "customs are to be construed according to vulgar apprehension, because Customs grow generally, and are bred up and brought up amongst the Laygents, therefore are called *Vulgares Consuetudines*'. For Sir Edward Coke (1641) there were "two pillars" for customs — common usage, and time out of mind. For Carter in *Lex Custumaria* (1696) the pillars had become four: antiquity, continuance, certainty and reason:

> For a Custom taketh beginning and groweth to perfection in this manner. When a reasonable Act once done is found to be good, and beneficial to the People, and agreeable to their nature and disposition, then do they use it and practise it again and again, and so by often iteration and multiplication of the Act, it becomes a Custom; and being continued without interruption time out of mind, it obtaineth the force of a Law.

Custom is local, *lex loci*, and may except the locality from common law, as, for example, in "Borough-English" whereby the younger son might inherit. It is "alleged not in the person, but in the manor" (Fisher): "So Custom lies upon

the Land" and "binds the Land" (Carter).[1]
The land upon which custom lay might be a manor, a parish, a stretch of river, oyster beds in an estuary, a park, mountain grazing, or a larger administrative unity like a forest. At one extreme custom was sharply defined, enforceable at law, and (as at enclosure) was a property: this is the business of the court roll, the manorial courts, the recitations of customs, the survey and of village by-laws. In the middle custom was less exact: it depended on the continual renewal of oral traditions, as in the annual or regular perambulation of the bounds of the parish:

> Gervas Knight. . . aged sixty seven yeares and upwards Maketh Oath that ever since he can remember. . . he has known Farming Woods Walk within the Forest of Rockingham. . . and says that ever since he was big enough. . . viz. from about the yeare 1664 until about the yeare 1720 he yearly or every two yeares. . . went with the Vicar and Parishioners of Brigstock to perambulate publickly for the same Parish and thereby make clayme of the Lands thereto belonging and to set forth their bounds. . .[2]

The perambulation followed the ancient watercourses, the hedges of closes, and at each boundary point a cross or mark was made in the ground.[3]
Not only the lord's court but also the church was trustee of the parish memory, and in the early eighteenth century one can still find examples where this trust was vigorously upheld. I have described in *Whigs and Hunters* the remarkable role as

[1] Sir Edward Coke, *The Complete Copy-holder* (1641); S.C. [S. Carter], *Lex Custumaria: or, A Treatise of Copy-hold Estates*, 2nd edn. 1701), ch. 4, which usefully summarises law *c.* 1700. Law relating to custom was of course modified by eighteenth-century judgements, and is usefully summarised *c.* 1800 in R. B. Fisher, *A Practical Treatise on Copyhold Tenure* (1794; 2nd edn. 1803), ch. 6. An authoritative treatise on customary law in the nineteenth century is John Scriven, *A Treatise on the Law of Copy-holds*, (7th edn., 1896). For the later nineteenth century, J. H. Balfour Browne, *The Law of Usages and Customs* (1875), ch. 1.
[2] Deposition of Jarvis Knight, PRO, KB 1.2 Part 2, Trinity 10 Geo. I.
[3] Small boys were sometimes ducked in the ditch or given a clout to imprint the spot upon their memories. Such practices are found everywhere. In Shetland "at a perambulation of the scattald marches of Uist in the year 1818. . . Mr Mowat to make it to be the better remembrd that Tonga was the march, gave Fredman Stickle. . . a crack over the back with his horse-whip": Brian Smith, "What is a Scattald?", in Barbara Crawford (ed.), *Essays in Shetland History* (Lerwick, 1984), p. 104.

recorder of Will Waterson, the vicar of Winkfield in Windsor Forest.[1] The vicar of Richmond led his parishioners in a perambulation which broke down the wall of Richmond Park.[2] An equally active part was played by Mr Henry Goode, the rector of Weldon, a parish which intercommoned with several others in the forest of Rockingham and whose rights were disputed by the parish of Brigstock. In 1724 in one of those disputes over timber rights and lops and tops which can be found in all forest areas, there was a formidable encounter in the forest. In Whitsun week the servants of Lord Gowran of Brigstock felled some trees in Farming Woods Walk and the Gowrans sent their tenants with wagons to carry the timber away. "You are very merry", said a Weldon man: "We will be merry with you." Shortly afterwards more than two hundred Weldon men and women surged into the forest, armed with hatchets, woodbills, pick hafts and staves, "hallowing. . . in a violent riotous and threatning manner and crying out 'Cutt the Waggons, Overthrow the Waggons'. . .", scaring the horses, and carrying off some of the lops and tops. Behind this affray lay further grievances about grazing rights and the impounding by Lord Gowran's orders of Weldon cattle. A deponent said that the rector of Weldon "did on a Sunday in his desk in Church there preach or read something to his Parishioners there that instigated or encouraged the said Riot, and that on the same day that Riot was committed the Bells in the Steeple there were rung backwards or jangled in order to raise or incite the people. . ."[3] Mr Goode continued his campaign twenty years later, with a "Commoner's Letter to his Brethren in Rockingham Forest", in which their precedents and rights were rehearsed. The notion of church guardianship was emphasised by a postscript:

---

[1] E. P. Thompson, *Whigs and Hunters* (1975), esp. pp. 298-300.

[2] Anon., *Two Historical Accounts of the Making of the New Forest and of Richmond New Park* (1751). In 1748 the rector of Bainton (Yorkshire) led his parishioners in breaking down enclosures made by the lord of the manor; the rector, William Territt, ended up at York Assizes: W. E. Tate, *The English Village Community and the Enclosure Movements* (1967), p. 152.

[3] Depositions of Charles Gray and of Richard Collyer in PRO, KB 1.2 Part 2 (1724).

N.B. I desire every Parish, that has any Right of Common in the Forest
of Rockingham, to lay up two of these Letters in the Parish Chest,
which may be a means of instructing their Children, and their Childrens
Children, how to preserve their Right in the Forrest for Ages to come.[1]

Perhaps Henry Goode and Will Waterson strayed a little
beyond a perambulation of the bounds of duty. A recommended Exhortation to be preached in Rogation Week had a
good deal to say about avoiding contention with neighbouring parishes and turning the other cheek. Nevertheless,
explicit commination is visited upon offenders against parish
or common rights: "Accursed be he, said Almighty God by
Moses, who removeth his neighbour's doles and marks":

> They do much provoke the wrath of God upon themselves, which use to
> grind up the doles and marks, which of ancient time were laid for the
> division of meers and balks in the fields, to bring the owners to their
> right. They do wickedly, which do turn up the ancient terries of the
> fields, that old men beforetime⁵ with great pains did tread out; whereby
> the lords' records (which be the tenants' evidence) be perverted and
> translated sometimes to the disheriting of the right owner, to the oppres-
> sion of the poor fatherless, or the poor widow.

And if these exhortations are directed mainly at the petty
malefactor, moving boundary marks in the night or shaving
with his plough a foot off the common balks and walks, yet
the sentence of commination was visited also on the rich and
the great: "So witnesseth Solomon. The Lord will destroy the
house of the proud man: but he will stablish the borders of
the widow." And all farmers were exhorted "to leave behind
some ears of corn for the poor gleaners".[2]

If the memories of the old, perambulation and exhortation
lay towards the centre of custom's interface between law and
praxis, custom passes at the other extreme into areas
altogether indistinct — into unwritten beliefs, sociological
norms, and usages asserted in practice but never enrolled in
any by-law. This area is the most difficult to recover, precisely because it belongs only to practice and to oral tradition. It

---

[1] "A Commoner" [the Rev. Good of Weldon], *A Letter to the
Commoners in Rockingham Forest* (Stamford, 1744), p. 18.
[2] "An Exhortation to be spoken to such Parishes where they use their
Perambulation in Rogation Week", *Certain Sermons and Homilies
appointed to be read in Churches in the Time of Queen Elizabeth* (1851),
pp. 529-30.

may by the area most significant for the livelihood of the poor and the marginal people in the village community. Custumals and by-laws should not be taken to be an exhaustive accounting of the actual practice of common right usages, especially where these bear upon the fringe benefits of common, waste, the herbage of lanesides, to the landless inhabitants or the cottager. For these documentary sources are often partisan briefs drawn up by the lord's steward, or by the substantial landholders on the in-coming of a new lord; or they are the outcome of bargaining and compromise between several propertied parties in the manorial court, in which the cottager or the landless had no voice on the homage. As one learned legal antiquary noted,

> The Entries which are found in the manorial Books or on Manorial Court Rolls, kept in the hands of the Lord's Steward, and purporting to set out the bounds of manors are liable to great suspicion. . . They are always made by Parties having a positive interest in gaining the greatest extent of property possible.[1]

Other rights were of a nature that could never be brought to trial or proved. For example, a King's Bench affidavit of 1721 concerns a woman gleaner who was beaten and driven from the field in Hope-under-Dynemore, Herefordshire. The farmer, in defence, said he "would not suffer her to lease there because she had cursed him".[2] This might indicate only a neighbourhood quarrel, but — the evidence is too scanty for confidence — it might hint at further unwritten custom. A curse, of course, registered something more than a curse would normally register today. Both slander and assault were constant objects of social control. But a curse was more than slander. The Herefordshire case might suggest that a curse was strong enough to unloose the farmer (at least in his own eyes) from the acknowledged bond laid upon the land by custom.

I am suggesting that custom took effect within a context of sociological norms and tolerances. It also took effect within a

---

[1] Stacey Grimaldi, "Report upon the Rights of the Crown in the Forest of Whichwood", 2 vols. (MS in my possession, 1838), i, no pagination, section on "timber and saplings within manors".

[2] PRO, KB 2.1 Part 2, Rex v John Stallard. Elizabeth Blusk miscarried as a result of being beaten by Stallard.

workaday routine of livelihood. It was possible to acknowledge the customary rights of the poor, but place obstacles in the way of their exercise. A petition of the poor inhabitants of Loughton, adjoining Waltham Forest in Essex, claimed the liberty of lopping their firewood from the trees. The lord and lady of the manor had not disputed the right but had limited its exercise to Mondays only, "and if this day prove fair 'tis a loss to them because 'tis the day they generally lett themselves to work with the farmers that employ them for the whole week", whereas formerly they had gathered wood on any wet days when there was no work. Meanwhile (they complained) the lord and lady were felling timber, selling logs, overstocking the forest with cattle, ploughing up the greensward, and setting coney warrens whose rabbits were "eating up their green corn and poysoning their meadows".[1]

Agrarian custom was never fact. It was ambience. It may best be understood with the aid of Bourdieu's concept of "habitus" — a lived environment comprised of practices, inherited expectations, rules which both determined limits to usages and disclosed possibilities, norms and sanctions both of law and neighbourhood pressures.[2] The profile of common right usages will vary from parish to parish according to innumerable variables: the economy of crop and stock, the extent of common and waste, demographic pressures, by-employments, vigilant or absentee landowners, the role of the church, strict or lax court-keeping, the contiguity of forest, fen or chase, the balance of greater and lesser landholders. Within this habitus all parties strove to maximise their own advantages. Each encroached upon the usages of the others. The rich employed their riches, and all the institutions and awe of local authority. The middling farmers, or yeoman sort, influenced local courts and sought to write stricter by-laws as hedges against both large and petty encroachments; they could also employ the discipline of the poor laws against those beneath them, and on occasion they

[1] PRO, C 104.113 Part 1, c. 1720? For the unusually tenacious and ritualised customs of wood in Loughton, see Lord Eversley, *Commons, Forests and Footpaths* (1910), pp. 86ff, 106-8; and below pp. 142-3.

[2] Pierre Bourdieu, *Outline of a Theory of Practice* (Cambridge, 1977), Chap. 4. This is my own gloss upon Bourdieu's stricter concept.

defended their rights against the rich and powerful at law.[1] The peasantry and the poor employed stealth, a knowledge of every bush and by-way, and the force of numbers. It is sentimental to suppose that, until the point of enclosure, the poor were always losers. It is deferential to suppose that the rich and great might not act as law-breakers and predators. A reading of the successive reports on royal forests of the Land Revenue Commissioners will quickly disabuse us on both points.

Forests, chases, great parks and some fisheries were notable arenas, in the eighteenth century, of conflicting claims (and appropriations) of common rights. After a revival in the first decades, the forest courts fell back into disuse, so that the direct invigilation by "the Crown" declined. But the hierarchy of grantees, managers, keepers, forest officers, under-keepers, remained in being, as avaricious as ever, and most of them engaged in the rip-offs which their rank or opportunities of office favoured. The great encroached on the walks, fenced in new hunting lodges, felled acres of timber, or obtained little sweeteners, like the earl of Westmorland who was granted four hundred acres of Whittlewood Forest at one farthing an acre in 1718.[2] In the middle of the hierarchy forest officers and under-keepers, who had long supplemented their petty salaries with perquisites, made inroads into the venison, sold off the brushwood and furze, made private agreements with inn-keepers and pastry-cooks, butchers and tanners.[3] Early in the century Charles Withers, Surveyor-General for Woods and Forests, kept a diary of a tour of several forests. At Wychwood —

This Forest egregiously abused. The timber shrouded and browsed: none coming on in the Knipes or Coppices; cut by Keepers, without assignment, sold to the neighbourhood: especially Burford Town supplied thence. Landlord Nash at the Bull bought this year Ten Load; in short, 'tis scandalous!

[1] This was especially the case where copyhold and customary tenures survived strongly: see C. E. Searle, "Custom, Class Conflict and Agrarian Capitalism: the Cumbrian Customary Economy in the Eighteenth Century", *Past and Present*, 110 (1986), esp. pp. 121-132.

[2] *Commons Journals*, xlvii (1792), p. 193.

[3] P. A. J. Pettit, *The Royal Forests of Northamptonshire, 1558-1714* (Northants. Record Society, 1968), pp. 48-9.

Much the same was found in the New Forest. But, equally, Withers found that the working inhabitants of forest villages and purlieus were continually pressing and enlarging their claims. In the Forest of Dean the colliers were "cutting thriving Timber for their Pits, without assignment. They pretend a custom to demand it, but are now so lawless that they even take it without".[1] And in a Memorial to the Treasury Commissioners in 1729 Withers represented that —

> It is very observable that the Country people everywhere think they have a sort of right to the Wood, & timber in the Forests, and whether the Notion may have been delivered down to them by tradition, from the times these Forests were declared to be such by the Crown, when there were great Struggles and contests about them, he is not able to determine. But it is certain they carefully conceal the Spoyls committed by each other, and are always jealous of everything that is done under the Authority of the Crown.[2]

Disputes over common right in such contexts were not exceptional. They were normal. Already in the thirteenth century common rights were exercised according to "time-hallowed custom",[3] but they were also being disputed in time-hallowed ways. Conflict over "botes" or "estover" (small wood for fencing, repair of buildings, fuel) or "turbary" (turves and peats for fuel) was never-ending; only occasionally did it arise to the high visibility of legal action, or (as with Weldon and Brigstock (p. 99)) to a punch-up between contiguous parishes, or to a confrontation between the powerful rich and the numerous "poor", as in the disputed carrying-away of "lops and tops".[4] But there cannot be a forest or chase in the country which did not have some dramatic episode of conflict over common right in the eighteenth century. It was not only the deer which enraged farmers, by spilling out of the forests and eating their corn. There were also the coney warrens, which became a craze in

---

[1] Earl St Aldwyn's MSS, PPD/7, extracts from journals and diaries, c. 1722, copied in 1830.

[2] Camb. Univ. Lib., C(H) MSS, 62/38/1, Memorial of Charles Withers to Treasury Commissioners, 10 April 1729.

[3] Jean Birrell, "Common Rights in the Medieval Forest", *Past and Present*, 117 (1987), pp. 29ff.

[4] See Alice Holt Forest, for example, in my *Whigs and Hunters*, p. 244.

the early eighteenth century with lords of the manor anxious to improve, not their pastures but their income. In one robust complaint from Charnwood in North Leicestershire, rabbit warrens were identified with Stuart tyranny:

> When Popish Jemmy rul'd this Land
> He rul'd it like a King.
> And bloody Jeffreys went about
> Hanging & Gibbeting.
>
> The Warreners prick'd up their Ears
> That was a Time of Grace,
> Game Laws & Justices were made
> And Rabbets bred apace.
>
> They cover'd all our Common Ground
> Or soon would do, no doubt
> But now, whilst George the Second reigns
> We'l pull the Vermin out. . .

The lines of this "Charnwood Opera" (performed in "The Holly Bush" in the forest) may date from 1753, and refer to episodes three or four years earlier. Lord Stamford, Lord Huntingdon, and three great gentry had planted copious warrens on the commons:

> The Turf is short bitten by Rabbits, And now
> No milk can be stroak'd from ye Old Womans Cow
> Tom Threshers poor Children look sadly, And say
> They must eat Waterporridge, three times in a Day
> Derry down.

In 1749 a great number of inhabitants, men, women and boys of neighbouring villages, including a party of colliers from Cole Orton, converged upon the warrens, marching over the plain "with rustick Noise & laughter. . . the Mobile Clamour mix'd with Threats & Jokes":

> On yonder Hill, See, How They stand
> — with Dogs — and Picks, and Spades in Hand.
> By Mars! A formidable Band!
>   Were they enclin'd to fight
> See! How they troop from ev'ry Town
> To pull these Upstart Warrens down,
> All praying for the Church & Crown
>   And for their Common Right.

In the ensuing encounter the warrens were thrown open. The "rioters" clashed with the Warrener and his party, and one of the rioters was killed. There followed troops of dragoons, wholesale arrests, trials. Right of common was proved for twenty-six neighbouring towns and villages, and Charnwood Forest remained unenclosed for a further half-century.[1]

This serves to remind us that high feeling around common rights, and episodes of disturbance, need not wait upon enclosure. Perhaps enclosure had been the most visible occasion of grievance in the sixteenth and seventeenth centuries.[2] And perhaps in the first six decades of the eighteenth century disputes about deer and other game,[3] about fishing rights, about timber, about the exploitation of quarries, sand-pits and peat, became more frequent and more angry. The notional economy of coincidental use-rights of greater and lesser substance was coming under greater strain. Demographic pressure, together with the growth of by-employments, had made the marginal benefits of turbary, estover etc. of more significance in the package that made up a subsistence-economy for "the poor"; while at the same time the growth of towns and, with this, the growing demand for fuel and building materials enhanced the marketable value of such assets as quarries, gravel- and sand-pits, peat bogs, for the larger landholders and lords of the manor. In a parallel movement, the law was conforming with an age of agricultural "improvement" and was finding claims to coincident use-rights to be untidy. So also did the modernising administrative mind. A survey of Salcey Forest in 1783

[1] The late W. E. Tate was given "The Charnwood Opera" in a mid eighteenth-century hand by a Nottingham bookseller: see Tate, *op. cit.*, plate XIII and p. 214; he kindly sent me a transcript many years ago. The original has been found among Tate's papers in the Reading University Library. See Roy Palmer, *A Ballad History of England* (1979), pp. 59-61; John Nichols, *History and Antiquities of the County of Leicester* (1800), iii, p. 131. The Act to enclose Charnwood Forest was passed in 1808 but not carried into effect until 1829. For other examples of opposition to warrens, see Douglas Hay, "Poaching and the Game Laws on Cannock Chase", in Douglas Hay, Peter Linebaugh and E. P. Thompson, *Albion's Fatal Tree* (1975); Fifth Report of Land Revenue Commissioners (New Forest), *Commons Journals*, xliv (1789), pp. 561, 565. An edition of "The Charnwood Opera" is being prepared for the press by Roy Palmer and John Goodacre.

[2] See Roger Manning, *Village Revolts* (Oxford, 1988).

[3] See my *Whigs and Hunters*, and also John Broad, "Whigs, Deer-Stealers and the Origins of the Black Act", *Past and Present*, 119 (1988).

noted "the ruinous Effects of a Mixture of opposite Interests in the same Property".[1]

If all the agricultural lands of England and Wales had been as open to rip-offs as the royal forests or as beset with disputes as Charnwood, then they might have served as illustrative proofs for the glum theses of Garret Hardin in "The Tragedy of the Commons".[2] It has been Professor Hardin's argument that since resources held in common are not owned and protected by anyone, there is an inexorable economic logic which dooms them to over-exploitation. The argument, in fact, is derived from the English propagandists of parliamentary enclosure, and from a specific Malthusian variant.[3] Despite its commonsense air, what it overlooks is that the commoners themselves were not without commonsense. Over time and over space the users of commons have developed a rich variety of institutions and community sanctions which have effected restraints and stints upon use.[4] If there were signs of ecological crisis in some English forests in the eighteenth century, this was as much for political and legal reasons as for economic or demographic. As the old forest institutions lapsed, so they fell into a vacuum in which political influence, market forces, and popular assertion contested with each other without common rules:

> The present state of the New Forest is little less than absolute anarchy [it was lamented in 1851]. The records are insufficient to ascertain who are entitled to rights; there is no certainty what law, forest or common law, is current; and, consequently, what officers have power, and under what authority to interfere.

At present the forest "has not, and cannot have, an owner. We seem reverting to Eastern and primeval manners". The

---

[1] *Commons Journals*, xlvi (1790-1), p. 101.

[2] *Science*, 162 (1968), pp. 1343-8.

[3] W. F. Lloyd, *Two Lectures on the Checks to Population* (1833), extracts reprinted in G. Hardin and J. Baden (eds.), *Managing the Commons* (San Francisco, 1977).

[4] See Bonnie M. McCoy and James M. Acheson (eds.), *The Question of the Commons* (Tucson, 1987). These studies on the culture and ecology of communal resources turn upon fishing, grazing and forest resources, and do not address the English agrarian context of the eighteenth century, from which W. F. Lloyd's argument is derived.

foresters (including many squatters) supposed, however, that *they* were the owners, improvising rules in informal ways. When a government inspector was sent down to examine the state of the forest in 1848-9, he was burned in effigy off Lyndhurst, the Deputy Warden supplying fuel from the forest for this meritorious purpose.[1]

These were dark places, however, possessed by "savage ignorance and barbarism". Over the rest of agricultural England there was a much stricter governance of common rights, both at common law and in *lex loci*. Common of pasture was stinted by the regulation of the lord's court or by village by-laws, regulations which had sometimes been in continuous evolution for centuries. The orderly village agricultural practices of medieval England disclosed by Warren Ault[2] are far from Garret Hardin's notions of common free-for-all.[3] But stinting could breed its own disputes. The court of Chancery decided, in a case in 1689, that the greater part of the landholders might regulate and stint a common (on grounds of "proper and natural equity") even if "one or two humoursome tenants stand out and will not agree".[4] But "one or two humoursome tenants" was too uncertain a legal term. In 1706 a new case arose from Bishop's Cleeve in Gloucestershire, where the landholders had agreed to stint five thousand acres of common, but the defendant (the rector of the parish) and nine others stood out. Evidently this was more than one or two humoursome fellows, for the court decided that "a right of common cannot be altered without the consent of all parties concerned therein".[5]

---

[1] "The Office of Woods and Forests, Land Revenue, Works and Buildings", *Law Magazine and Quarterly Review of Jurisprudence*, n.s. 14/o.s. 45 (1851), pp. 31-3.

[2] W. O. Ault, *Open-Field Farming in Medieval England: A Study of Village By-Laws* (1972).

[3] Hardin's "Tragedy of the Commons", in Hardin & Baden, *op. cit.*, is historically uninformed and assumes that commons were "pasture open to all. It is to be expected that each herdsman will try to keep as many cattle as possible on the commons".

[4] *Delabeere v Beddingfield* (1689), 2 Vern 103, ER 23, p. 676.

[5] *Bruges et Al' v Curwin et Al'* (1706), 2 Vern 575, ER 23, p. 974. This was revised by 13 Geo. III, c. 81, in 1772, when open field parishes were

One wonders if this might have been at the origin of the parliamentary process of enclosure, which is something of a mystery? For "the first private bill of enclosure ever passed" came up to parliament in February 1710. It concerned Ropley Commons and the old disparked park of Farnham, within the bishopric of Winchester. It was a decidedly unpopular and vigorously contested measure, and it contributed to the ill-will which led to raids on the bishop's deer and eventually to "blacking". It could scarcely have been pushed through in any other way.[1]

Once the private act of enclosure became possible, it was clear that *enclosure* might not take place unless by due parliamentary process if even one humoursome landholder dissented.[2] Until the 1760s (and in some cases later) this could act as a serious disincentive to the landowners. A young gentleman was writing on behalf of his mother to some noble

---

empowered to regulate their agriculture if three-quarters in number and value of the occupiers agreed: Sir W. S. Holdsworth, *A History of English Law*, xi, pp. 454-5. Sheila Lambert, *Bills and Acts* (Cambridge, 1971), p. 143 thinks the act may have been "a dead letter", although Withern-with-Woodthrope (Lincolnshire) was vigorously exercising its provisions in the 1790s (information from Rex Russell).

[1] For Ropley Commons and Farnham Park enclosure (and disturbance) see my *Whigs and Hunters*, pp. 133-41; *Lords Journals*, xix, pp. 50, 65-6, 77, 80, 83, 108, 111; *Commons Journals*, xvi, pp. 374, 381, 385-6, 476, 509. The "first ever private bill" is the description in *Annals of Agriculture*, xxxvii (1801), pp. 226-31, where the Act was reprinted. Lambert, *op. cit.*, pp. 129-30 says that "in 1706 inclosure bills had been almost unknown"; see also E. C. K. Gonner, *Common Land and Inclosure*, 2nd edn. (1966), p. 58. Joan Thirsk (ed.), *The Agrarian History of England and Wales* (Cambridge, 1985), v, pt. 2, p. 380 expresses puzzlement at the reasons for the resort to private act. The Bill passed through the Lords without contest (25 Feb. to 17 Mar. 1710) but ran into opposition in the Commons, with a petition from freeholders, copyholders and leaseholders against it (23 Mar. 1710), and with renewed petitioning next year to repeal the Act, on the grounds of the partial allotment of portions, and the obstruction of highways (3 Feb. 1711). The House referred this and a counter-petition (21 Feb. 1711) to committee, where the matter seems to disappear.

[2] Arthur Young was still complaining in 1798: "what a gross absurdity to bind down in the fetters of custom ten intelligent men willing to adopt the improvements adapted to inclosures, because one stupid fellow is obstinate for the practice of his grandfather": "Of Inclosures", *Annals of Agriculture*, xxi (1798), p. 546.

patron in 1742 about her predicament in the parish of Church
Oakley, Hampshire —

> My Mama has the largest farm there upon her hands, and she finds it a
> very difficult thing to get a Tennant for it, no Person caring to take it
> unless the Parish was inclosed, there being so great a dis-
> agreement amongst the Farmers at Oakly, that in mere spite to each
> other they will not manage the Common Fields so as to make the best
> advantage of them. . .

Enclosure would especially benefit his mother "as she has the
greatest Common there; there are but three freeholders and
the Parsonage, besides herself, they all consent to enclose,
except one person who in crossness sticks out. . .". His
mother begged to ask if the thing could be done, one man not
agreeing to it, without an Act of Parliament "which she
would be sorry to have, not only as it will be a great
Expense, but as she has not any friends in the House. . .".[1]
Historians have noted that the great age of parliamentary
enclosure, between 1760 and 1820, is testimony not only to
the rage for improvement but also to the tenacity with which
"humoursome" or "spiteful" fellows blocked the way to
enclosure by agreement, holding out to the last for the old
customary economy.

So that custom may also be seen as a place of class
conflict, at the interface between agrarian practice and
political power. The customary tenants of Sir William
Lowther in the Cumberland manor of Askham complained in
1803 that "violations of our Antient Custom has always felt
very painfull to us, and embittered many hours of our lives".
And Dr Searle comments:

> Custom, then, was not something fixed and immutable, carrying the
> same body of meaning for both social classes. On the contrary, its
> definition was highly variable in relation to class position, and
> accordingly it became a vehicle for conflict not consensus.[2]

Unequal as were the terms of power in this conflict, yet power
must submit to some constraints, not only because custom

---

[1] Henry Worsley to "Honoured Sir", 8 July 1742, typescript copy in
Earl St Aldwyn MSS. West Oakley was enclosed by agreement, but not
until April 1773.
[2] Searle, *op. cit.*, p. 120.

had juridical endorsement and could itself be a "property", but also because power might bring itself into danger if abuse of customary rights outraged the populace. Charles I's high-handed pursuit of revenue in the royal forests had weakened his throne. Even the most predatory of the Hanoverian Whigs had not forgotten the lesson. George II's consort, Queen Caroline, had "wished to shut up St. James' Park, and asked Sir Robert Walpole what it would cost her to do it. He replied, 'Only a *crown*, Madam' ".[1]

King Charles also set in motion one of the most politically-sensitive contests around common rights, when he enclosed and threw a high wall around Richmond Park. Several parishes were shut out from rights of common, and (Clarendon wrote) "the murmur and noise of the people. . . was too near London not to be the common discourse". The murmur continued in the eighteenth century, and was at its loudest during the rangership of Sir Robert Walpole (through his son), when gates were locked, ladders over the wall were removed, and passengers or carriages were admitted only by ticket. Since the tickets (made of base metal) were easy to counterfeit, they were replaced by paper tickets stamped at the stamp office (6d.) (and the counterfeiting of stamps was then a capital felony). Although the parishioners pulled down the park wall two or three times on their perambulations of parish bounds (see Plate IX), Walpole "pocketed the affront, and built up the wall again".

Walpole's successor as Ranger was Princess Amelia, who was loved no more than Walpole but was more easy to challenge than the great man. The grievances concerned chiefly rights of way through the park, and loss of access to gravel, underwood, furze, and also water rights. In this prosperous neighbourhood those concerned were not only farmers but also gentry, merchants, tradespeople and artisans. Champions of local rights included a stonemason, a brewer, and Timothy Bennett, a shoemaker, whose motto it was that he was "unwilling to leave the world worse than he found it". John Lewis, the brewer, led an agitation in the 1750s which prefigures some of the stratagems of John

---

[1] Horace Walpole, *Memoirs of the Reign of King George the Second* (1847), ii, pp. 220-1.

Wilkes: there were public meetings, memorials in the press
(*London Evening Post*), a widely-signed petition presented to
the King, and finally a series of actions at law.[1] From such
episodes as this one may see the growing confidence of
"civil society".

Cases came up at Surrey Assizes (Kingston) every summer
from 1753 to 1758. Right of highway between Richmond and
Croydon (through the park) was lost (1754), but right of foot-
way (over stiles or ladders) from Richmond to Wimbledon
was won. John Lewis then (1755) forced his way through a
park gate, and sued the gatekeeper (Martha Gray) who
pushed him out, for obstructing three ancient footways, one
between East Sheene and Kingston. Trial was postponed to
the next summer Assizes. At that time supporters of common
right had published and circulated a pamphlet[2] on their side
of the case, and Lord Mansfield — on the grounds that this
could influence the jurors — used this as an excuse to put off
the trial to a subsequent Assizes.

The trial finally came up at Surrey Lent Assizes, 1758,
before Sir Michael Foster, then in his seventieth year. So
many of the forty-eight special jurors who had been summoned to the panel were nervous about trying a cause against the
Princess Amelia that it was necessary to put a talesman on the
jury. Sir Michael promptly fined the absentees £20 a head.
When the prosecution had got through some part of their
evidence, the counsel for the Crown (Sir Richard Lloyd) said
it was "needless for them to go on upon the right, as the
Crown was not prepared to try that", since the obstruction
was charged in the parish of Wimbledon whereas it was in
truth in Mortlake:

---

[1] Anon., *A Tract on the National Interest, and Depravity of the Times*
(1757); E. E. Dodd, "Richmond Park" (typescript, 1963); C. L.
Collenette, *A History of Richmond Park* (1937); my *Whigs and Hunters*,
pp. 181-4; Michael Dodson, *The Life of Sir Michael Foster* (1811),
pp. 84-8; Rev. Gilbert Wakefield, *Memoirs* (1792), who has a good
description of John Lewis's campaign, pp. 243-53; Walpole, *op. cit.*, i,
pp. 401-2, ii, pp. 220-1.

[2] *A Tract on the National Interest.* A copy of this, and also of *German
Cruelty: a Fair Warning to the People of Great-Britain* (1756) is in PRO,
TS 11.347.1083, together with the Crown's brief against Joseph Shepheard,
a Chancery Lane printer.

The judge turned to the jury, and said, he thought they were come there to try a right, which the subject claimed to a way through Richmond Park, and not to cavil about little low objections, which have no relation to that right. . . He thought it below the honour of the Crown, after this business had been depending three assizes, to send one of their select counsel, not to try the right, but to hinge upon so small a point as this.

The judge summed up in favour of the prosecution, and John Lewis won his case. Offered a gate or step-ladders, he chose the latter, as the freer mode of access. (With deer in the park, the gates would be kept closed, and might easily be locked.) When Lewis returned to the court with the complaint that the rungs on the ladders had been set too far apart for children and old men, Sir Michael Foster replied: "I have observed it myself, and I desire, Mr Lewis, that you would see it so constructed, that not only *children and old men*, but OLD WOMEN too, may get up."[1]

The case was a small sensation. For a while it gave the keepers real trouble, since triumphant citizens were clambering the ladders and did not confine themselves to the paths but "ranged & went at their pleasure over the greensward", declaring that "the park was a common & that they had a right to go anywhere. . . they liked". This was to the prejudice of the deer and game and "will greatly interrupt the Royal Family in the use & enjoyment" of the park.[2] Princess Amelia abandoned her Rangership in a paddy. These matters also became part of the discourse of London: the free-born old Englishwoman had triumphed over the royal lady. Such victories, of the humble citizen over the great or the royal, were decidedly infrequent. But even one or two went a long way to give popular legitimacy to the law and to endorse the rhetoric of constitutionalism upon which the

[1] Dodson, *op. cit.*, pp. 86-7; Wakefield, *op. cit.*, pp. 247-8; *Rex v Benjamin Burgess* (1760), 2 Burr. 908, ER 97, pp. 627-8.

[2] Various papers in PRO, TS 11.444.1415, especially "An Historical Account of the Inclosing Richmond New Park", an MS drawn up to brief Crown counsel. Richmond citizens were uncommonly tenacious of their rights of way (or uncommonly obstructed by royalty and aristocracy). In 1806 the iron rails in front of the duke of Queensberry's villa on the Thames were broken down in a "trespass committed by agreement in order to try the right". The jury found a verdict in support of the right and against the duke: *London Chronicle*, 1-3 Apr. 1806.

security of landed property was founded.[1] Even so, we should not forget that the Richmond victory was, in a sense, a victory of bourgeois commoners, who commanded money and resources which the rural commoners rarely did.

II

This chapter is not about enclosure nor about the decline of the peasantry. A novice in agricultural history caught loitering in those areas with intent would quickly be despatched. This is a tangential study of common right usages, and also of law and notions of property-right. But one cannot altogether avoid brushing against the other problems. And one must note that we still have little firm evidence as to the number of landholders who held by copyhold or other forms of customary tenure (such as beneficial leases from the church or from colleges) in the eighteenth century. A scholar with much expertise allows that the question of the proportion of landholders by customary tenures in the late seventeenth century is "almost entirely obscure", but it might have been "as many as one-third".[2] And it remained substantial at the end of the eighteenth — although falling away more rapidly in the last decades. The vigorous operation of the lord's court in the eighteenth century (as many county record offices can testify) is often coincident with some survival of copyhold tenures. There was certainly a substantial peasantry in England in the eighteenth and early nineteenth centuries,[3] and optimistic agricultural historians have sometimes told their story in such a way as to confuse two different totals:

[1] See my comments on "The Rule of Law" in *Whigs and Hunters*, pp. 258-69.

[2] Christopher Clay, in Thirsk (ed.), *Agrarian History*, V, p. 199, and pp. 198-208, and the same author's "Life-leasehold in the Western Counties of England 1650-1750", *Agric. Hist. Rev.*, xxix, 2 (1981).

[3] I welcome Mick Reed's "The Peasantry of Nineteenth-Century England: a Neglected Class", *History Workshop*, 18 (1984), although I am rebuked as a culprit. But what I was arguing ("Land of Our Fathers", *TLS*, 16 Feb. 1967) was that J. D. Chambers and G. E. Mingay were guilty of "statistical dilution", by watering the totals of large employers with the peasantry, hence minimising capitalist agricultural process: "the assimilation of two extremes to provide an impressionistic average does not in fact illuminate either extremity".

the acres and the people.[1] As I remarked in an earlier study, "the economic historian may find that the clues to expanding agrarian process lie in the 'free' [i.e. freehold or rackrent] sector, while the social historian may find that the psychological horizons and expectations of the majority of the farming community lie still within the customary sector".[2]

Secondly, it is now becoming clear that in the long historiographical reaction against those fine historians, Barbara and J. L. Hammond and their classic *The Village Labourer*, there has been a tendency (and in some minds an ideological determination) to seriously undercount the amount of popular protest attending upon loss of common rights or the enclosure of commons (which, as we have already seen, were not the same thing). It is heartening to see that a substantial challenge to the triumphal picture of the social consequences of agricultural improvement is now being made.[3] Even so, we are not going to discover that the eighteenth century was vibrant with major episodes of enclosure protest which have been somehow overlooked. There were more episodes than have been noted, but few of them were major. Resistance was more often sullen than vibrant. For every commoner "Rioutously threatening to kill

[1] Christopher Clay, " 'The Greed of Whig Bishops'?: Church Landlords and their Lessees 1660-1760", *Past and Present*, 87 (1980), exemplifies this kind of confusion: (a) it assumes that the claim that church beneficial leases had equal customary security with copyhold "had no legal validity", although this was precisely the question which was at issue in the 1720s, and (b) by concentrating upon large lay tenants of church lands, the more numerous small customary tenants disappear from view, as they do so often in orthodox agricultural history.

[2] "The Grid of Inheritance", in J. Goody, J. Thirsk and E. P. Thompson (eds.), *Family and Inheritance* (Cambridge, 1976), pp. 328-9.

[3] In the area of common rights, especially J. M. Neeson, "Common Right and Enclosure in Eighteenth-Century Northamptonshire" (Univ. of Warwick Ph.D. thesis, 1978); C. E. Searle, "The Odd Corner of England: Cumbria, *c.* 1700-1914" (Univ. of Essex Ph.D. thesis, 1983). The cogent re-opening of arguments in K. D. M. Snell, *Annals of the Labouring Poor* (Cambridge, 1985), ch. 4, is also welcome. The most devastating critique of the assumptions and the methodology of the "optimists", insofar as these bear upon the small landholder at enclosure, is in J. M. Neeson, "The Disappearance of the English Peasantry, Revisited", in G. Grantham and Carol Leonard (eds.), *Agrarian Organization in the century of Industrialization: Europe, Russia and North America in the Nineteenth Century* (Research in Economic History, Supplement 5) (JAI Press, 1989).

or be killed, that he wd raise 500 people who wd assist in the cutting down & destroying the Mounds and fences. . ."[1] a dozen will be found throwing a gate off its hinges, uprooting some quicksets, or pulling down a notice of enclosure from the church porch.

Yet there was more opposition to enclosure than used to be supposed.[2] The problem of estimating its extent is, in part, one of the appropriate research techniques and the nature of the sources. Enclosure protests were rarely reported in central administrative archives or in London newspapers; they did not take the form of regional "uprisings", highly visible and tumultuous. They will be found (especially before 1760) more often in the exchanges of letters between estate stewards and their absent masters, treated as domestic concerns (like poaching) which could be dealt with by the magistrates' summary powers. Larger affrays might necessitate the aid of neighbours, the levying of loyal tenants and servants, or even the *posse comitatus*. In 1710, when Robert Walpole was Secretary-at-War, he received (in his private capacity) a letter from his steward, John Wrott, describing a major confrontation over common rights on Bedingfield Common. The High Sheriff of Northamptonshire, Lord Cardigan, and other gentry were there with mounted patrols. "The mob began to gather from all corners, some in disguise with masks, and in women's cloakes, and others with axes, spades, pickaxes etc." Even the men whom the Sheriff had summoned to serve in his *posse* sympathised with the mob and helped any prisoners to escape. The crowd was dispersed for the time being, but "they still persist to say the Right of Common is theirs, & next year they hope to see the Hedges demolish't".[3]

---

[1] Thomas Kemp of Leigh, labourer, charged with riot with twelve others unknown, in "obstructing hindring and preventing one John Andrews in marking out the Boundaries of certain. . . Inclosures", Worcs. Lent Assize, 1777, PRO, Assi 4.21. Kemp was imprisoned for six months. The enclosures were of Malvern Link Common, where three years later (Lent Assize, 1780) 21 labourers and one labourer's wife were charged with pulling down 1,100 yards of fence. See also Brian S. Smith, *A History of Malvern* (Leicester, 1964), p. 167.

[2] For a recent record of known disturbances see Andrew Charlesworth (ed.), *An Atlas of Rural Protest* (1983).

[3] Camb. Univ. Lib., C(H) MSS, correspondence, item 608, John Wrott to Walpole, dated Oundle, 31 May 1710; Sir J. H. Plumb, *Sir Robert*

The estate correspondence of one of Walpole's political allies, Lady Diana Fielding in North Wootton (Norfolk), in 1728-9 was much preoccupied with contests between labour- ers and tenants, on one side, and her steward and the parish constable, on the other, concerning the cutting of "whins and flags" on "the Priories", where her ladyship had made new enclosures. Rival parties converged on the common with carts to carry away the whins, "the Mobb" rescued their whins from the steward's carts, threw them about, locked the horses to the cart wheels, "barbrosly used" the steward "& broke 3 of his Ribbs & allmost kill'd him". The mob went on to "break & destroy all the Gates & fences" of the late enclosures. Labourers and tenants shared these actions, but it was easier to discipline the tenants with the threat of loss of their tenancies.[1]

One can turn up other affairs like this in collections of estate papers. Or they may turn up in the press. Three years before, at Stokesby (again in Norfolk), many poor people, men and women, "threw down a new Mill and divers Gates and Fences on the Marsh". Eight or ten of them were carried to Norwich where they were examined: they said they were acting for the "Recovery of their Right", since the Marsh was common until a certain gentleman had taken it away and fenced it in. "Such a beginning had Kett's rebellion", the reporter commented.[2] These offenders were committed to Assizes. And not infrequently Assize records show proceed- ings against offenders who had thrown down fences or demolished enclosures. But such actions need never come to the notice of the law, since commoners claimed (and law cautiously acknowledged) a right to throw down encroach- ments[3] and this "possessioning" was indeed one of the purposes of parish perambulations. There was a fine-drawn

---

Walpole (1972), pp. 157-8. I am not clear why Wrott was at Bedingfield (now Benefield) Common, but the letter suggests ("I hope to receive your orders") that Walpole was personally interested in the enclosure.

[1] Norwich and Norfolk RO, HOW 725, 734 (a).

[2] *Mist's Weekly Journal,* 24 July 1725. See also R. W. Malcolmson, *Life and Labour in England, 1700-1780* (1981), p. 127, and also pp. 23-35.

[3] Since judges did not easily condone direct action, the law on this was cautious and mainly negative: the proper course for aggrieved commoners

line between the assertion of "right" and "riot",[1] and the balance of evidence and also of power might be such as to settle the issue outside the courts. John Lewis, the Richmond brewer, whom we have already noted in his assertion of rights of access to Richmond Park, told a story about another pathway which he found blocked by a locked gate. He passed by with a friend and with some of his men from the

---

should be an action for novel disseisin: see Richard Burn, *The Justice of the Peace and Parish Officer*, 14th edn. (1780), ii, "Forcible Entry". But the right of commoners to take direct action in support of right rested upon ancient law and precedents too strong to over-rule: see the full discussion in *Arlett v Ellis* (1827), 7 B & C 347, ER 108, pp. 752-64, when the Year Book of 15 Henry 7, Brooke's Abridgement and Coke's Institutes were among authorities cited: "If the Lord doth inclose any part, and leave not sufficient common. . . the commoners may break down the whole inclosure". This was affirmed in several cases in the late seventeenth and eighteenth century (e.g. *Mason v Caesar* (Hilary 27/28 Car 2), 2 Mod 65, ER 86), although this did not prevent indictments for riot against commoners who pulled fences down. In the sixteenth and seventeenth centuries, enclosure *riot* could be treason, if more than forty were involved. In the eighteenth century the law supported (feebly) commoners' right to remove nuisances, to pull up fences, and to distrain supernumerary cattle on a stinted common (on which point see *Hall v Harding* (1769), 4 Burr 2425, ER 98, pp. 271ff.). They might not, however, cut down trees nor kill rabbits and dig up coney burrows: this contentious issue much preoccupied the judges in several cases, and the decisive judgement was in *Cooper v Marshall* (1757), 1 Burr 259, ER 97, pp. 303-8, for which see Hay, *op. cit.*, p. 234. Lord Mansfield pronounced that the real issue was not the legality or illegality of the coneys, but "whether the commoner can do himself justice", and it was his decided view that the commoner might not. It was perhaps fortunate for commoners' rights that Lord Mansfield never sat in judgement upon fences. See also Halsbury's *Laws of England*, vi, pp. 250-4, esp. para. 655. Fences might also be removed in pursuance of an order from a manorial court. See Roger B. Manning, *op. cit.*, pp. 40-2.

[1] In 1698 there was an attempt to strengthen and enforce statutes of Edward I and Edward VI against the burning and destroying of enclosures, and a bill was read for the first time: but it met with fierce counter-petitions from Lincolnshire parishes adjoining Epworth Common, and it seems to have been dropped: *Commons Journals*, xii, pp. 38, 47, 96. The Black Act (1723) had ample provisions which might be used against rioters, irrespective of the justice of their cause: see my *Whigs and Hunters, passim.* Parliamentary enclosure was given a new set of teeth, under 9 Geo. III, c. 29, whereby pulling down fences of lands enclosed "in pursuance of any act of parliament" was made felony, with penalty of seven years transportation. I do not recall finding any offender so sentenced under this Act.

brewery the day before "our annual parochial procession at Richmond" —

> 'My lads', says I; 'take care to bring your hatchets with you tomorrow to cut down this gate, for we must go through it to our bounds'. 'Don't speak so loud,' said my friend: 'or you will be heard by the people at the Princess Dowager's.' 'Oh,' I replied, raising my voice: 'I have no objection to be heard. I am John Lewis of Richmond, and mean to knock down this gate tomorrow for a passage according to custom.'

But on the next day "the processioners" found that the gate's lock had been taken off.[1]

In a parish perambulation, some labourers might carry "an axe, a mattock, and an iron crow. . . for the purpose of demolishing any building or fence which had been raised without permission" on the common or waste.[2] This was stubbornly maintained as a lawful assertion of right. But this is also exactly what some offenders are indicted for in Assize records: at Feckenham (Worcestershire) in 1789 for "pulling down, prostrating and destroying with bilhooks, spades, mattocks, axes, saws" etc. fourteen yards of quickset fences;[3] at Culmstock (Devon) in 1807 for coming into a garden and orchard with hatchets, saws, pickaxes, spades and shovels, throwing down the fences, digging up the ground, erecting a tent to keep the owner (or the pretended owner) out of possession;[4] at Porlock (Somerset) in 1774 for entering a garden, throwing down hedges and fences, spoiling and carrying off garden stuff.[5] These could have been little affrays or "riots"[6] or they could have been actions deliberately

---

[1] Wakefield, *op. cit.*, p. 251.

[2] See Bob Bushaway, *op. cit.*, p. 83.

[3] PRO, Assi 4.22, Worcester, Lent 1789. Those charged were a labourer, a husbandman, a butcher, a cordwainer, four yeomen and four needlemakers.

[4] PRO, Assi 24.43, Devon, Summer 1807. Those charged were a spinster ("left the kingdom"), four labourers, and a labourer's wife.

[5] PRO, Assi 24.42, Somerset, Summer 1774: a shopkeeper, a carpenter, a yeoman, and four labourers charged, all found not guilty.

[6] They certainly could stir up strong feeling. When a crowd in the nail-making village of Kingswinford broke down a nailer's fences, pulled up his posts and destroyed his potatoes and beans, one of the crowd (Elizabeth Stevens) threatened to kill two women and "wash her hands in their blood": PRO, Assi 4/22, Worcester, Lent 1789. Three nailers, one nailer's wife, one labourer, two labourers' wives charged.

intended to bring on a case which would try their "right".

Even when riots did occur these need not become visible to historians. Magistrates and gentry were expected to take care of episodes in their own neighbourhood without recourse to troops. When troops were sent to put down rioting "in the new inclosed fields of West Haddon" (Northamptonshire) in 1765, the magistrate was reminded that "until the utmost extent of legal authority shall have been tried, application should not be made for military assistance".[1] In the same year, when forty-odd Banbury rioters were pulling down the fences of a newly-enclosed estate at Warkworth, a company of gentlemen were informed of it at dinner; they instantly were willing to forego their port, mounted their horses, descended on the "levellers" and routed them.[2] Knowledge of a more substantial enclosure riot at Maulden, (Bedfordshire) in 1796, in which two hundred poor people were involved, survives only because a letter about it was preserved in a War Office file of precedents.[3]

But problems and techniques of recovering the evidence is the lesser part of the story. In a study which demands that we review not only our methods but the whole problem, Jeanette Neeson has shown that historians may have been looking in the wrong places and for the wrong things. She presents cogent reasons for supposing that "parliamentary opposition and riot were the least effective, and probably least common, means of opposing enclosure".[4] And re-directing attention to the full length of the enclosure process, from its first promotion to its often-long-delayed imple-mentation, she shows an astonishing volume and a variety of forms of protest — hitherto hidden from view in local records — lobbying, letters, petitions, the mobbing of surveyors, the destruction of records, and on to arson, riot, and fence-breaking, which might continue for years after

[1] PRO, WO 4.172.

[2] *Gentleman's Magazine*, (1765), p. 441.

[3] James Webster, 2 August 1796, in PRO, WO 40.17. I am indebted to Patricia Bell, when Assistant Archivist at the Bedford CRO (in 1968), for discovering more about this riot at which, it seems, the duke of Bedford was present (not, I think, as a rioter): papers then in R box 341.

[4] J. M. Neeson, "The Opponents of Enclosure in Eighteenth-Century Northamptonshire", *Past and Present*, 105 (1984), p. 117.

enclosure was completed. Nor was this stubborn resistance without function. It can be shown to have delayed enclosures, on occasion for decades, and it may sometimes have modified their terms. "If landlords and farmers eventually won the battle for enclosure, rural artisans and agricultural labourers may have had some say in the terms of surrender." [1]

If Dr Neeson's findings for Northamptonshire should be supported by research into other counties, this will change our understanding of eighteenth-century enclosure, and the depth of hostility with which it was regarded by a large part of the rural community. Opposition was in general overcome in the end; open fields were almost without exception enclosed by 1850, and opposition rarely kept commons and wastes open for much longer, except in special circumstances which include large wastes upon which several villages inter-commoned, forest and fenland regions, and commons contiguous to market towns or larger urban centres. Urban protests over common rights were often more formidable and more visible than rural, and while they clearly are not characteristic of agrarian custom they may still afford one point of entry into general questions of common right.

The most obvious reason for urban success is simply that of greater numbers, and the anonymity which numbers supplied to rioters. By no means all the effective urban enclosure riots arose from incorporated boroughs. But the question of incorporation is of real significance, since it distinguishes between prescriptive rights and rights established by custom. Custom is laid upon the land, but prescription "is alledged in the Person": "it is always made in the Name of a Person certain, and his Ancestors, or of those whose Estate he hath", and is normally established by the recitation of the original Grant or Charter. [2] Boroughs incorporated by Charter were legal personalities, whose freemen might therefore plead prescriptive rights more generous than those which law would recognise for custom. In the important decision in Gateward's Case (below, p. 130) it was ruled that

---

[1] Neeson, *op. cit.*, p. 131.
[2] Carter, *Lex Custumaria*, pp. 37-42; Sir W. Blackstone, *Commentaries on the Laws of England* (1765-9), ii, p. 33.

"inhabitants" cannot prescribe to have profit in another's soil, with the reservation "unless they be incorporated".[1] If prescriptive rights to the use of common were granted by charter to a corporation, then the exercise of these rights (and the persons entitled to exercise them) became a matter not for the courts to decide but for the intramural regulation of the corporation.

In fact the often-cited charters from which townsmen derived their rights to the use of town lands are often as ambiguous and as open to various interpretations as rights in manorial villages. We can see this in the case of Coventry. The right was claimed as derived in the first place from a grant of Sir Roger de Montealto (1249) reserving to the "communiariis" "reasonable pasture" for as many beasts "with which they may conveniently plough and carry their arable lands, and which, by reason of those lands, as well of right as of custom, they ought and were wont to have common". This was englished — I suspect by a popular sea-lawyer in the late seventeenth or early eighteenth century — as "saving to all Cottiers reasonable Pasture and Commons for soe many Beasts as they bin abel hereafter to keepe and which they ought and were wont to have as wel by Right as by Customs".[2] As both land and rights became more valuable, attempts to limit these rights or to enclose lands were met with riotous resistance in 1421, 1430, 1469, 1473, 1495, and 1509,[3] while further enclosure was successfully resisted in a

---

[1] *Smith and Gateward* (4 Jac. I), Cro Jac 152, ER 79, p. 133. This was tightened in *Grimstead v Marlowe* (1792), 4 TR 717, ER 100, p. 1263: a tenant or inhabitant claiming prescriptive right may plead only by virtue of an ancient messuage tenure or as a member of a corporation, not *in alieno solo*.

[2] W. Reader, *Some History and Account of the Commons and Lammas and Michaelmas Lands of the City of Coventry* (Coventry, 1879), pt. One, p. 8; Humphrey Wanley, *A Particular and Authentic Account of the Common Grounds of. . . the City of Coventry* (1778), p. 4.

[3] *Victoria County History, Warwickshire*, viii, pp. 202-3. The historian of medieval Coventry is perhaps too dismissive of these small extra-urban matters ("the details do not concern us"): Charles Phythian-Adams, *Desolation of a City* (Cambridge, 1979), p. 183. For Rogation-tide perambulation of the commons in Coventry's calendar, see his "Ceremony and the Citizen", in Peter Clark and Paul Slack (eds.), *Crisis and Order in English Towns, 1500-1700* (1972), pp. 77-8.

major riot in 1525.[1] The definition of who possessed commoners' rights may have hardened only in the seventeenth century. An entry in the Court Leet book in 1663 suggests that all who "inhabit and pay Scot and Lott" had common right (this being a narrower definition than earlier entries suggest).[2] A more popular notion was that the land belonged to the "Mayor, Bailiffs and Commonalty of the City. . . and one Million and others were seized of the said Manor".[3] In 1674 this was clearly defined as freemen enrolled in companies. Throughout the eighteenth century freemen's rights were jealously maintained, especially through the means of apprenticeship; and into the nineteenth century rights in the Lammas Lands were signalled annually (as they were in other towns) by the Lammas riding, when the corporation and freemen rode the boundaries of the fields, trampled any corn grown in them (unless propitiated by supplies of ale and food) and tore down gates and obstructions.[4]

Coventry now in the nineteenth century was hemmed in on all sides by Lammas Lands, which increased the density of the population, and meant that the potential value of the lands as building sites rose annually. Eventually the freemen, after much controversy and a long and crafty negotiation, sold out their rights in exchange for a considerable allocation of these lands. By this time the freeman right had fallen into the hands of a minority (although a large one). Joseph Gutteridge, a ribbon-weaver, felt that the mid-century contest concerned only the rights of a privileged group. But he still regretted the loss of lands which in his youth, in the 1820s, were a "veritable paradise. I would roam over them

---

[1] Phythian-Adams, *Desolation of a City*, pp. 254-7. The riot succeeded in re-opening the enclosures, p. 257. See also R. H. Tawney, *The Agrarian Problem in the Sixteenth Century* (1912; reprint 1967), p. 250 for the city's dispute with the Prior and Convent of St. Mary over sheep commons.

[2] Coventry Leet Book, transcript and summary (compiled by Levi Fox?), Coventry RO, shelf 16.

[3] This rhetorical claim was made by the defendant in *Bennet v Holbech* (22 Charles II), 2 Wms Saund 317, ER 85, pp. 1113-6.

[4] Benjamin Poole, *Coventry: its History and Antiquities* (1879), p. 354.

without let or hindrance. . .".[1]

We have here a mixture of prescriptive right, myth, and assertion by tumultuous numbers. The intramural contest over the exercise of rights arose when the alienation of urban common was undertaken by the Corporation itself, in the name of freeman rights which were themselves becoming more exclusive and corrupt. When the Leicester Corporation enclosed the South Fields in 1753, and let them to three lessees (including two aldermen) riots continued for at least three years, in which the "post and rails and Quick sette. . . set down for the fencing of the said fields" were "Cut Down pulled up and Distroyed by great Numbers. . . in a most riotous and tumultuous manner". The enclosure, first attempted in 1708, was not completed until 1803.[2] In Nottingham where six hundred acres of Lammas Lands and another three hundred and fifty acres of pasture with common right remained open into Victorian times, a witness before the Select Committee on Commons Enclosure (1844) found that this had a most prejudicial effect upon the morals of the people:

> It occasions very great disrespect to the laws of the country generally; as an instance. . . when the day upon which the lands become commonable arrives [usually August 12th]. . . the population issue out, destroy the fences, tear down the gates, and commit a great many other lawless acts, which they certainly have a right to do, in respect of the right of common to which they are entitled. . . the consequence is constant violence and abuse.

The witness explained that the freemen were "all voters, which is a great misfortune, and they are misled with respect to their rights, and the value of them, by parties who have recourse at the periods of election to courses of agitation". They had exercised rights over the Lammas Lands for many years, and "being a very numerous body, and many of the

---

[1] Joseph Gutteridge, *Lights and Shadows on the Life of an Artisan* (Coventry, 1893), pp. 5-6; P. Searby, "Chartists and Freemen in Coventry, 1838-60", *Social History*, 2 (1977).

[2] C. J. Billson, "Open Fields of Leicester", *Trans. Leics. Archaeol. Soc.*, (1925-6), IV, pp. 25-7; Eric Kerridge, *Agrarian Problems in the Sixteenth Century and After* (1969), p. 98; *Records of the Borough of Leicester* v and vi.; A. Temple Patterson, *Radical Leicester* (Leicester, 1953).

body being of a very low class of society, they are enabled to resort to acts of violence which could not be resorted to by an incorporated body. . .".[1] Rights by prescription and rights by the assertion of usage had become altogether indistinct.

Nottingham and other commoners were offered by the printers "No Inclosure!" ballads, perhaps more likely to be read than sung: "You Freemen all of Nottingham come listen to my Song":

> Your Rights and your Liberties I would have you to revere,
> And look unto Posterity I think them always dear;
> To us to our Children by the Charter that prevails,
> So now my Boys united be and have no Posts or Rails. . .
>
> Let's suffer no Encroachments upon our Lane to be,
> But to repel such Tyranny let's ever now agree;
> But let ev'ry brave Freeman enjoy his Right of Land.[2]

The more that one looks, the more that one finds such disputes to be normal, in great towns and in small. They could be massive and very violent, as was the dispute in Sheffield in 1791. A private act had been passed to enclose six thousand acres of common and waste adjacent to the town, compensating the poor with two acres only. This precipitated spectacular riots, which may have influenced the citizens to turn in a Paineite or "Jacobin" direction. The enclosure commissioners were mobbed; the debtors' gaol was broken open and the prisoners released; there were cries of "No King!" and "No Taxes!".[3] Or the affairs could be small and symbolic, as at Streatham Common in 1794 when six men in black drove up in a hackney coach and demolished the duke of Bedford's paled inclosure.[4] London and its environs would have no parks today if commoners had not asserted their rights, and as the nineteenth century drew on rights of

[1] *PP*, 1844, v, pp. 223-6.
[2] *A New Song, entitled No Inclosure! Or, the Twelfth of August* (Tupman, printer, n.d.), in Nottingham Univ. Lib.; my thanks to Roy Palmer.
[3] William Eyre, 30 July 1791, in PRO, HO 42.19; Albert Goodwin, *The Friends of Liberty* (1979), pp. 164-5; John Bohstedt, *Riots and Community Politics in England and Wales* (1983), pp. 199-200.
[4] *Gentleman's Magazine*, (1794), p. 571. At the same time a "mob of poor people" burned the furze on the common because the duke had been selling it for his own profit.

recreation became more important than rights of pasture, and were defended vigilantly by the Commons Preservation Society.[1] We owe to these premature "Greens" such urban lungs as we have.[2] More than that, if it had not been for the stubborn defence by Newbury commoners of their rights to Greenham Common, where on earth could NATO have parked its nukes?[3]

III

Yet we should not press the distinction between prescriptive rights and rights established by custom too far. Although urban commoners might appeal to "chartered rights", when they succeeded it was through the assertion of usage, sheer numbers, political muscle. And the law was open to manipulation. "Prescription" could be a legal fiction, a suppositious (but unrecorded) grant.[4] Perhaps we should

---

[1] A mass of information on the law of commons, with particular relevance to the environs of London, is in G. Shaw-Lefevre (ed.), *Six Essays on Commons Preservation* (1867). The Commons Preservation Society was founded in 1866. Much information on commons, especially surrounding London, is in G. Shaw-Lefevre, *English Commons and Forests* (1894), subsequently revised as Lord Eversley, *Commons, Forests and Footpaths* (1910).

[2] But this could be a double-sided process. Commons contiguous to towns could become marginal zones with "rough" and dubious reputations, and regulated public parks could be a way of extinguishing rights and imposing social discipline: see Raphael Samuel, "Quarry Roughs", in *Village Life and Labour* (1975), esp. pp. 207-27; N. MacMaster, "The Battle for Mousehold Heath", *Past and Present*, no. 127, May 1990.

[3] "A regularly organised mob of many hundreds of the most abandoned and dissolute characters" threw down an encloser's fences "with most terrific hooting and abuse" on Newbury's commons in 1842: "To the Inhabitants of Newbury", 4 page printed broadside, signed R. F. Graham, Greenham, 30 Sept. 1842, in Berks. CRO D/Ex 24123 I.

[4] Late medieval law required that user should be shown since 1189: the fictional doctrine of presumed grant appeared early in the seventeenth century, but was most strongly argued in terms of easements: by *Lewis v Price* (1761) only twenty years enjoyment of use could be evidence of a suppositious grant: see A. W. B. Simpson, *A History of the Land Law*, 2nd edn. (Oxford, 1986), pp. 107-10, 266-7. In the nineteenth century sixty years uncontested user could establish forestal commonage — "the law presumes a grant"; Lord Hobhouse commented, "In plain English, this presumption of grants is a legal fiction resorted to for the purposes of justice": Eversley, *op. cit.*, p. 107.

turn the problem around. In the towns commons were often defended with more success than in the countryside. Does this tell us anything about right, and about property and law?

The tone of some writing on agricultural history suggests that there is little we need to know about law. Even Professor Hoskins, in his sympathetic and informative study of common lands, allows himself to state that "contrary to widespread belief. . . all common land is private property. It belongs to someone, whether an individual or a corporation, and has done so from time immemorial".[1] That might find a legalistic justification — of course Hoskins was simplifying his account — but "belonging", private property in land, is itself a concept which has had a historical evolution. The central concept of feudal custom was not that of property but of reciprocal obligations.[2] An authority on land law suggests that common rights —

> arose as customary rights associated with the communal system of agriculture practised in the primitive village communities. At a very early period such villages would be surrounded with tracts of waste land. . . On such land the villagers as a community would pasture their beasts and from it they would gather wood and turf and so forth. In the course of time, when the increase of population and the reduction in the quantity of uncultivated land started to produce crowding and conflict, their rights would tend to become more clearly defined but would still be communal rights, principally over waste lands regarded as the lands of the community itself. The tenurial system converted the villagers into tenants, and *the theory of the law* placed the freehold of most of the lands of the manor in the lord. Some of his tenants, it is true, will be freeholders, but the majority hold unfreely in villeinage, and the pre-eminence of the lord makes it natural to treat him as the 'owner' of the waste lands. Thus *a theory of individual ownership* supplants earlier more egalitarian notions.[3] (My italics.)

That is not quite "belonging" from "time immemorial". One is reminded of the saying addressed by Russian serfs to their lords: "We are yours, but the land is ours."[4]

It was Tawney's view that, in such matters as common of pasture, "communal aspirations are a matter of feeling and

---

[1] Hoskins, *The Common Lands of England and Wales* (1963), p. 4.

[2] See S. F. C. Milsom, *The Legal Framework of English Feudalism* (Cambridge, 1976).

[3] Simpson, *op. cit.*, p. 108.

[4] J. Blum, *Lord and Peasant in Russia* (Princeton, 1971), p. 469.

custom, not of national law".[1] These "communal aspirations" persist into the eighteenth century where they co-exist
with the most scrupulous regulation of common rights and
stints by village by-laws (and *lex loci* of manorial courts) and
by rigorous definitions of common rights (appendant,
appurtenant, of gross, and by vicinage) at national law. Law
and usages may often seem to be at odds with each other.
Authorities agree that in many parts of England and Wales,
the cottagers and the landless exercised use-rights — of
turbary, estover, and often of pasturage on waste (and sometimes Lammas lands or grazing over the harvested common
fields). Thus Gonner: "Throughout the country it may be
said that often the poor living near the commons, wholly
without question of the occupation of ancient cottages, came
by usage to enjoy the minor rights of common", including
grazing for pigs, geese and sometimes cows.[2] Most authorities go on to state flatly that these minor rights of common
had no basis in law and were illegally exercised or usurped.
And in a self-fulfilling argument the statement is confirmed
by the evidence that they usually received no compensation
for such rights at enclosure. Thus Kerridge: "Occupiers of
poor law and other newly erected cottages, and generally all
squatters on the waste, were not entitled to rights of
common, so no allotment was due to them."[3] And thus
Chambers and Mingay:

> The *occupiers* of common right cottages. . . who enjoyed common right
> by virtue of their *tenancy* of the cottage, received no compensation
> because they were not, of course, the owners of the rights. This was a
> perfectly proper distinction between owner and tenant, and involved no
> fraud or disregard for cottagers on the part of the commissioners.[4]

Yet this is to assume two things: first, the priority of "the
theory of the law" over usages, and, second, the propriety of
splitting off the rights from the user. But these are, precisely,
the questions to be examined. If Coke's definition be
followed — "Customs are defined to be a law or right not

---

[1] Tawney, *op. cit.*, p. 246.
[2] Gonner, *op. cit.*, p. 31.
[3] Kerridge, *op. cit.*, p. 80.
[4] J. D. Chambers and G. E. Mingay, *The Agricultural Revolution,
1750-1880* (1966), p. 97.

written; which, being established by long use and the consent of our ancestors, hath been and is daily practised"[1] — then in many parishes the exercise of minor rights of common might have been proved by antiquity, continuance, certainty and reason as well as those of the landholders and customary tenants. Custom (Coke explained) takes away the common law, yet the common law might correct on such grounds, and especially on the grounds of reason. Kerridge, in one of his intemperate attacks upon Tawney, writes:

> The common law could only allow and confirm customary laws that were reasonable, certain, on good consideration, compulsory, without prejudice to the king, and to the profit of the claimant. Tawney assumed that 'reasonable' in this context was used in a loose or general sense, and that the lord's interests were more likely to seem reasonable to the lawyers than were the customer's; but 'reasonable' and 'unreasonable' are legal terms of art and mean 'compatible', 'consonant', 'consistent', 'reconcilable', or their opposites. A reasonable custom was one that could be reconciled with the other customary laws of that manor and with the common law. Thus to disallow unreasonable customs was, in almost every instance, to reject fraudulent ones.[2]

I cannot in any way accept Kerridge's assurances as to the powers of the common law over custom, which confuse the essential and the trivial, omit the criteria of antiquity and continuous usage, and mistake the true relation between the two.[3] The common law did not sit on high to "only allow and confirm" those customs which it approved; on the contrary, it might only disallow custom if it could fault it on these (and certain other legal) grounds, and only then when a case was referred to the common law courts. Nor, as it happens, can I find that Tawney wrote the opinions which Kerridge puts into his mouth.

"Reasonable" and "unreasonable" may be "legal terms of art" but on a very brief view of case law they were gates through which a large flock of other considerations might

[1] Co. Coph. S. 33.
[2] Kerridge, *op. cit.*, p. 67.
[3] Blackstone, *Commentaries*, i, pp. 76-8, lists as grounds for making custom good: (1) Antiquity ("so long that the memory of man runneth not to the contrary"); (2) Continuity; (3) Peacable user; (4) Must not be unreasonable (at law); (5) Certainty; (6) Compulsory: i.e. not optional; and (7) Consistency.

come baaing and grunting onto the fields of the common law. Perhaps no case was more often cited in its bearing upon the marginal use-rights of the villager that Gateward's Case (1607). This was both a terminus of precedent judgements and the ground upon which many subsequent judgements stood. Defendant had pleaded common right "ratione commorantiae et residentiae suae" in the town of Stixwold in Lincolnshire. This was disallowed because the defendant was occupier of a house in which he had no interest —

> No certain time or estate, but during his inhabitancy, and such manner of interest the law will not suffer, for custom ought to extent to that which hath certainty and continuance.

These are "legal terms of art", although we slide along them from the use-right to the user to his house: "For none can have interest in a common in respect of a house in which he hath no interest." But in disallowing all "inhabitants" or "residents" from the further ground of reasonableness was added that "no improvements can be made in any wastes, if such common should be allowed".[1] The court could not have known that in 350 years time, when the term "improvement" had acquired a new resonance, they had licensed a motorway to carry political economy across the commons.

Gateward's Case was technically brought in restraint of a gentleman who was grazing Stixwold commons, although it seems that in fact Gateward had come forward as a champion of the customary use-rights of the poorer inhabitants also.[2] The cases which came up to the common law courts for a hundred years or more rarely concerned the minor rights of common. They concerned the regulation and adjustment of more substantial landholding interests. Attention was paid to the definition of common appendant and appurtenant: appendant belonged to occupiers of arable land, and carried right to place commonable beasts (those who plough and manure the arable) on the lord's waste. Levancy and

---

[1] *Gateward's Case* (4 Jas I), 6 Co Rep 59b, ER 77, pp. 344-6; *Smith v Gateward* (4 Jas I), Cro Jac 152, ER 79, p. 133. See also my comments in *Family and Inheritance*, pp. 339-41.

[2] For the background to Gateward's Case, see Manning, *Village Revolts*, pp. 83-6.

couchancy stinted the right to the number of beasts that could be wintered on the arable holding. Common appurtenant was attached not to land but to a dominant tenement, and it extended to other stock, such as hogs, goats, geese, and rested upon immemorial usage and prescription. Decisions did not go only one way. On occasion the lord's rights to waste the common, carry off soil, or warren the waste with "coney-boroughs" were restrained. There were even decisions where substantial landholders excluded the lord from parcels of his own waste, under the same levancy and couchancy rule which excluded cottagers. But at least one such judgement against a Suffolk lord of the manor, in 1654, proved ineffectual, not because it was bad law but because it was unenforceable. Sir Francis North, in a learned argument in King's Bench in 1675, observed that it had been —

> A case of small consequence that concerned the lord only for his costs, for he has enjoyed his feeding against that verdict ever since: I can say it upon my own knowledge, for I know the parties and I know the place. . . I may add that this was in popular times, when all things tended to the licentiousness of the common people.[1]

By the mid eighteenth century the law had clearly ruled that levancy and couchancy were incident to common appendant as well as common appurtenant. In 1740, in a case arising from Mark in Somerset concerning the overstocking of Somer Leaze, the court acknowledged that —

> There are indeed some cases in the old books. . . which speak of common sans nombre, and which seem to imply that levancy and couchancy is only necessary in the case of common appurtenant, and not in the case of common appendant. But the notion of common sans nombre, in the latitude in which it was formerly understood, has been long since exploded, and it can have no rational meaning but in contradistinction to stinted common, where a man has a right only to put in such a particular number of cattle.[2]

At the beginning of the century the courts had found a generous interpretation of common appurtenant. A claim of common for cattle levant and couchant on a cottage was

---

[1] *Polter v Sir Henry North* (26 Charles II), 1 Ventris 383, 397, ER 86, pp. 245-54; the place was Elinswell, near Bury St Edmunds.
[2] *Robert Bennett v Robert Reeve* (1740), Willes 227, ER 125, pp. 1144-7.

found good, even if it had no land, since "a cottage contain-
eth a curtilage, & so there may be levancy. . . We will suppose
that a cottage has at least a court to it".[1] The contest around
this swayed back and forth. Did a butcher who kept sheep in
his cellar have levancy and couchancy? The dispute was
finally concluded in the high enclosure years, in 1792, when it
was determined that the cottage must carry sufficient land
for levancy and couchancy.[2]

When minor rights of common acquired a new value,
either in the market (the sale of clay, peats, wood) or in
compensation at enclosure, the courts gave them more
serious attention. Now the decision in Gateward's Case came
into new effect. When it was claimed, in 1741, that the right
of turbary was a custom laid "not only in the tenants but the
occupants" of a Cambridgeshire village, the court found this
"a very great absurdity, for an occupant, who is no more
than a tenant at will, can never have a right to take away the
soil of the lord".[3] In 1772 King's Bench took a more liberal
view of the right to cut rushes, in a case that arose from
Theberton in Suffolk, accepting oral testimony that "everybody in the world may cut rushes on the common".[4] But
this was reversed only two years later in a case arising from
Ludham Waste in Norfolk. It was accepted that copyholders,
occupiers of lands and occupiers of ancient houses might set
up a custom to cut turfs or rushes, but "inhabitants cannot,
because inhabitancy is too vague a description. . .".[5] In
the same tradition the claim — arising from Whaddon,
Buckinghamshire — for "all and every the poor, necessitous
and indigend. . . householders" to gather and break with
woodhooks rotten boughs in two coppices was disallowed
because "there is no limitation. . . the description of poor
householder is too vague and uncertain".[6]

It is not suggested that these decisions were unreasonable,
nor that they denied the "legal terms of art". Most decisions

---

[1] *Emerton v Selby* (2 Anne), 2 Ld Raym. 1015, ER 92, p. 175.
[2] *Scholes v Hargreave* (1792), 5 Term Rep 46, ER 101, p. 26.
[3] *Dean and Chapter of Ely v Warren*, 2 Atk 189-90, ER 26, p. 518.
[4] *Rackham v Joseph and Thompson* (1772), 3 Wils KB 334, ER 95,
pp. 1084-7. A full and interesting report.
[5] *Bean v Bloom* (14 Geo. III), 2 Black W 926, ER 96, pp. 547-9.
[6] *Selby v Robinson* (1788), 2 T R 759, ER 100, p. 409.

arose — at least until the mid eighteenth century — not with the intention of cutting off the petty exercise of minor rights of common, but in disputes between larger operators, with the intention of restraining the exploitation of these rights by interlopers and entrepreneurs. Thus in *Bennett v Reeve*, in 1740, the complainant had taken a ninety-nine year lease of one yard parcel in Old Auster, which carried right of common appendant, and on the basis of this square yard had turned sixty-four sheep onto Somer Leaze. Other cases arose from the exploitation of supposititious rights to sell peats, timber, clay, or (in the case of Norfolk rushes) a blacksmith carrying off rushes by the wagon load. Gateward's Case itself was aimed, not against the poor parishioner's cow or geese, but against a gentleman interloper.

Yet within this rationality there was evolving — as Tawney rightly saw — the ulterior rationality of capitalist definitions of property rights. I will not court an action for trespass into the lands of medieval historians in an attempt to define what, in origin, was meant by "the lord's waste" or "the soil of the lord". But both agrarian and legal historians appear to agree that the notion of the origin of common rights in royal or feudal grants is a fiction. Dr Thirsk has suggested that rights of grazing over pasture and waste were perhaps "the oldest element" in the common field system, descended from "more extensive rights. . . enjoyed from time immemorial", which Anglo-Saxon and Norman monarchs and lords did not graciously institute but, rather, regulated and curtailed.[1] And we have seen that it was "the theory of the law" (above, p. 127) which placed the freehold of the manor in the lord. But this was not in terms of subsequent notions of exclusive "ownership" or property: it was, rather, "in fee simple" and in feudal terms of law. So long as wastes remained extensive and unstinted, landowners and commoners might co-exist without precise definitions of rights. As late as 1620 in a case concerning Holme-on-Spalding Moor a witness deposed that he knew not if a tenement built on the common sixty years before had common by right or "by sufferance or negligence of the freeholder", since

---

[1] Joan Thirsk, "The Common Fields", *Past and Present*, no. 29, December 1964.

at the time it was built "the freeholder made little reckoning of common for so small goods as was then put upon the said common by the said tenants".[1] In a survey of Chilvers Coton (Warwickshire) in 1682 there is a very specific itemisation of freehold and copyhold in the open fields, but the homage becomes vague when it comes to common rights in the waste:

> What beasts sheep or other cattle the Lord of this mannor as such or his ffarmour may keep in Coton or Nuneaton Outwood wee do not precisely know, but the present Lord. . . doth claim a right to keep all manner of cattle but so as not to oppress our Commons.

One notes the phrase "our Commons". As we shall see, in village by-laws common rights in waste land are often expressed in loose or uncertain terms — sometimes all tenants, or copyholders, sometimes "all within this manor", or "inhabitants", or "cottiers", or "parishioners" — *except* when they are referred to the courts. Legal definitions are generally more precise than actual usages, and they may become more so the higher they go up the ladder of law.

There were two occasions which dictated absolute precision: a trial at law and a process of enclosure. And both occasions favoured those with power and purses against the little users. In the late seventeenth century and certainly in the eighteenth the courts increasingly defined (or assumed without argument) that the lord's waste or soil was his personal property, albeit restrained or curtailed by the inconvenient usages of custom. If the lord's access to any part of "his" soil should be restricted "this will be a ready way to enable tenants to withstand all improvements".[2]

Gateward's Case, and successive decisions in this spirit of "improvement", drew an expert knife through the carcass of custom, cutting off the use-right from the user. In one single operation this restrained unlicensed large interlopers, graziers and the like, in the interests of the landholders and customary tenants, and it altogether disqualified indistinct categories of small users, who held neither land nor ancient cottage tenures. While this may not have affected actual village

---

[1] Joan Thirsk, *Tudor Enclosures* (Hist. Assn. 1967), p. 10.
[2] *Polter v Sir Henry North* (26 Charles II), 1 Ventris 397, ER 86, pp. 245-54.

usages much it could leave the landless commoner stripped of any rights if a case came to the courts, or at the point of enclosure. The right of use had been transferred from the user to the house or site of an ancient messuage. It became not a use but a property.

This did not happen instantly nor without ambiguities. The logic of capitalist rationality was delayed by deeply-rooted copyhold and customary tenures.[1] Common appendant could not be detached and sold away from land, although at enclosure it was of course the land's owner and not its user (if farmed by a tenant) who could cash the right. Common appurtenant could be sold with a cottage or with the site of an ancient messuage, carrying so many gates (or grazing rights for beasts) on the common. But this was not a novelty, and legal historians can press us back as far as the twelfth century when certain incorporeal rights (such as church advowsons) began to be treated as properties or "things". Yet this was construed as a right in the "things", not to "own" the thing itself — "a present right" to use or enjoy.

What was happening, from the time of Coke to that of Blackstone, was a hardening and concretion of the notion of property in land, and a re-ification of usages into properties which could be rented, sold or willed. For good reason Blackstone entitled volume two of his *Commentaries*, "Of the Rights of Things" — not because these rights were a novelty (they were an ancient chapter of the law) but because the market in these rights was never more active, or more prolific in tests at law than at this time. Moreover, one might notice that Blackstone referred, not to rights *to* things, but to the rights *of* things. The eighteenth century sees this strange period of mixed law in which usages and rights were attached

---

[1] The lord's right over copyholders' timber was strongly contested, and although it moved in favour of the lord in *Ashmead v Ranger*, decided finally in the House of Lords (1702) by a bare majority of 11 to 10, it was not a decisive victory: see Allan Greenbaum, "Timber Rights, Property Law, and the Twilight of Copyhold", (MS Osgoode Hall Law School, York University, Toronto).

[2] Simpson, *op. cit.*, pp. 103-6; C. B. Macpherson, "Capitalism and the Changing Concept of Property", in Kamenka and Neale (eds.), *Feudalism, Capitalism and Beyond* (1975), p. 110.

to office or to place and then were regarded as if they were things which commanded human rights in their turn. The Rangership of a forest or park could be sold, with the powers, perquisites and rights attached to the office.[1] An ancient messuage (or its site) commanded rights of common, and the thing could be transferred between owners. And in much the same way decisions of the House of Commons in disputed cases tended to re-ify the definition of those who might be electors in boroughs from indistinct categories such as "inhabitants" or the "Commonalty in general" to inhabitants paying scot and lot, and thence to persons inhabiting ancient houses or houses built on ancient foundations (Bridport, 1628 and 1762; Arundel, 1693 and 1715; Bramber, 1715). In Seaford in 1676 the Bailiffs, Jurors and Freemen "had not only voices. . . but also the Election was in the populacy" but in 1761 "the word *populacy*. . . extends only to Inhabitants Housekeepers paying scot and lot", a decision in the same tradition as Gateward's. In Hastings, 1715, electors were confined to "all with estate of inheritance or for life in Burgage Houses or Burgage Lands" within the borough.[2] This led on to the absurdities of the Unreformed House of Commons, where the right of election could lie in dove-cots, pig-styes, a thorn tree or a quarry, and was exercised by the owners of these things by various fictions and stratagems. "The custom of attaching Rights to *place*, or in other words to inanimate matter, instead of to the *person*, independently of place, is too absurd to make any part of a rational argument" — thus spake Tom Paine.[3]

The re-ification — and cashing — of usages as properties came always to a climax at the point of enclosure. The owners of land and not the tenants (unless customary) received land in exchange for the extinguishment of rights. But the law, which disallowed the usages of the many, might allow as properties extinct assets and superordinate rights and offices

---

[1] A good example is Enfield Chase in my *Whigs and Hunters*, pp. 175-81.

[2] These precedents (mostly from *Commons Journals*) were usefully collected in Shelburne Papers (Univ. of Michigan, Ann Arbor), vol. 167, W. Masterman, "Compendium of the Rights and Privileges of Election".

[3] Thomas Paine, *Letter Addressed to the Addressers on the Late Proclamation* (1792), p. 67.

of the few with "interest". When the forest of Delamere was enclosed (1812) half of the eight thousand acres went to the King, together with £200 per annum in rental from the other half. John Arden, as Chief Forester, Bowbearer and Bailiff, with his under-keepers, were amply compensated for their loss of perquisites (including the "pasturage of coneys"), as was Thomas Cholmondeley "as Owner of the dissolved Monastery of Vale Royal, and of divers Messuages, Lands, Tenements and Heriditaments, heretofore parcel of the Possessions of the Abbot and Convent of Vale Royal". All rights of common in the forest were extinguished, save for some "Moss Pits or Turbaries" too wet for pasture and impracticable to be drained: here peats might still be cut. Tenants at rack-rent received no land in lieu of lost rights, although the landowners (who did receive land for their tenants' loss of right of common) were instructed to make them compensation.[1] All of this was proper to law: it follows normal procedures. But it signals a wholesale trans-formation of agrarian practices, in which rights are assigned away from users and in which ancient feudal title is richly compensated in its translation into capitalist property-right.

When Kerridge writes that "to disallow unreasonable customs was, in almost every instance, to reject fraudulent ones" he astonishes one first of all by the claim to omni-science. (Even the great Sir Edward Coke said that "should I go about with a catalogue of several customs, I should with Sysiphus. . . undertake an endless piece of work".) Of course, once the law had detached the right from the user, it could find reasonable grounds for disallowing usages of the greatest antiquity and certainty. The common law allowed "reasons" to be considered which had more to do with the political economy of "improvement" than with a strict atten-tion to the terms of law. Many judges shared the mentalities of improving landowners (reasonable men) and they prided themselves on their intuition into the real intentions of their predecessors and of legislators. As Abbott, C.J. noted, in a case which disallowed (yet again) the claims of "inhabitants",

[1] *An Act for Inclosing the Forest of Delamere* (1812), pp. 23, 27-9, 33.

The meaning of particular words in Acts of Parliament, as well as other instruments, is to be found not so much in a strict etymological propriety of language, nor even in popular use, as in the subject or occasion on which they are used, and the object that is intended to be obtained.[1]

It was tough luck if language's "popular uses" of right seemed unreasonable to a judicial mind. What Kerridge (and other authorities on enclosure)[2] fail to examine is whether, by this re-ification of right and by this introduction of the reasons of "improvement", the law itself may not have been the instrument of class expropriation.

By disqualifying imprecise categories of users — occupiers, inhabitants, residents, "all persons" etc. — Gateward's and successive cases had left to the populace or to inhabitants only the exception of rights of way or easements, "as in a way or causey to church".[3] It was a large allowance. By raising to a reason at law the question of "improvement" it was possible to effect a marriage between "legal terms of art" and the imperatives of capitalist market economy. The decision in 1788 in the Court of Common Pleas against gleaning is familiar, yet it may be of interest to read it once again with an eye to the reasons of law.

Here was certainly a custom which had immemorial sanction and which continued with undiminished vigour into the nineteenth century. The practice was sanctioned by custom, but also regulated by village by-laws.[4] Such

---

[1] *Rex v G. W. Hall* (1822), 1 B & C 136, ER 107, p. 51.

[2] Sadly, W. E. Tate in that fine book, *The Parish Chest* (2nd edn. Cambridge, 1951), p. 289 offered an even more anachronistic imposition of subsequent property categories upon the evidence. He apologised for the lack of allotment of land to the poor at enclosure because "from the legalist point of view. . . any land given to them could only be at the expense of the other proprietors, its legal owners. Open fields and common pastures belonged to the public (so said the lawyers) no more than does say a Co-operative Society, or a limited company, and when the open-field village was liquidated its assets were divided, like those of any other business concern, after satisfying the creditors among the shareholders".

[3] *Smith v Gateward* (4 Jas I), Cro Jac 152, ER 79, p. 133. See also ER 82, p. 157.

[4] For gleaning generally, see David Morgan, *Harvesters and Harvesting* (1982); Bushaway, *op. cit.*, esp. pp. 138-48; P. J. King, "Gleaners, Farmers and the Failure of Legal Sanctions in England, 1780-1850", *Past and Present*, no. 125 (November, 1989).

regulation continues in the eighteenth century, as evidenced by some by-laws, although in other by-laws the practice is assumed, and passed over in silence. In Raunds (Northamptonshire) in 1740 there is a suggestion of tighter controls to exclude foreigners and paupers in receipt of relief: John Adams and family are presented for gleaning without a settlement (1s.), and the by-law is entered: "no certificate person shall either glean in the fields or cutt any furzes from the common".[1] A trial of the general question of right in 1766 in King's Bench was confused. Gleaners, gaoled in Berkshire, had gleaned in an only partly cut field of barley. Lord Mansfield ruled that "stealing, under the colour of leasing or gleaning, is not to be justified". But another learned judge remarked that "the right of leasing does appear in our books. . .".[2] The issue came up to Common Pleas in 1788 from an action for trespass against Mary Houghton, wife of John Houghton, for gleaning in closes at Timworth in Suffolk. The case does not appear to have been argued in terms of custom (perhaps because it would at once have fallen foul of the precedents established by Gateward's Case) but on grounds of the universal recognition of the right at common law. The defendants were "parishioners and inhabitants of the said parish of Timworth, legally settled therein, and being poor and necessitous, and indigent persons. . .". Lord Loughborough found the claim indefinite:

> 1st, I thought it inconsistent with the nature of property which imports exclusive enjoyment.
> 2dly, Destructive of the peace and good order of society, and amounting to a general vagrancy.
> 3dly, Incapable of enjoyment, since nothing which is not inexhaustible, like a perennial stream, can be capable of universal promiscuous enjoyment.

By removing the claim from custom to common law the defence had not removed the difficulty, since "if this custom were part of the common law of the realm, it would prevail in every part of the kingdom, and be of general and uniform practice", whereas in some parts it was unknown and in

[1] Northants CRO, Box 1053/2, Manor of Raunds, Court book, 27 November 1740.
[2] *Rex v John Price* (1766), 4 Burr 1926, ER 98, pp. 1-2.

others variously modified and enjoyed. As for the
defendant's efforts to enlist the law of Moses, "the political
institutions of the Jews cannot be obligatory on us, since even
under the Christian dispensation the relief of the poor is not a
legal obligation, but a religious duty". From this Lord
Loughborough passed to a homily drawn directly from
political economy:

> The consequences which would arise from this custom being established
> as a right, would be injurious to the poor themselves. Their sustenance
> can only arise from the surplus of productive industry; whatever is a
> charge on industry, is a very improvident dimunition of the fund for
> that sustenance; for the profits of the farmer being lessened, he would
> be less able to contribute his share to the rates of the parish; and thus the
> poor, from the exercise of this supposed right in the autumn, would be
> liable to starve in the spring.

Mr Justice Gould gave a directly contrary opinion, with
considerable learning and recitation of precedent. But
Mr Justice Heath and Mr Justice Wilson came to the side of
Lord Loughborough. Heath expressed himself with singular
force: "To sanction this usage would introduce fraud and
rapine, and entail a curse upon the country." He entered even
more largely upon the reasons of political economy:

> The law of Moses is not obligatory on us. It is indeed agreeable to
> Christian charity and common humanity that the rich should provide
> for the impotent poor; but the mode of provision must be of positive
> institution. We have established a nobler fund. We have pledged all the
> landed property of the kingdom for the maintenance of the poor, who
> have in some instances exhausted the source. The inconvenience arising
> from this custom being considered as a right by the poor would be
> infinite. . . It would open the door to fraud, because the labourers
> would be tempted to scatter the corn in order to make a better gleaning
> for their wives, children and neighbours. . . It would raise the insolence
> of the poor. . .

Mr Justice Wilson concurred, but made a little more show of
grounding his opinion in law:

> No right can exist at common law, unless both the subject of it, and they
> who claim it, are certain. In this case both are uncertain. The subject is
> the scattered corn which the farmer chooses to leave on the ground, the
> quantity depends entirely on his pleasure. The soil is his, the seed is his,
> and in natural justice his also are the profits. [1]

[1] *Steel v Houghton et Uxor* (1788), 1 H BL 51, ER 126, pp. 32-9.

It is difficult to think of a purer expression of capitalist rationality, in which both labour and human need have disappeared from view, and the "natural justice" of profits has become a reason at law. In the arguments of *Steele v Houghton et Uxor* we see exposed with unusual clarity the law's complicity with the ideology of political economy, its indifference to the claims of the poor, and its growing impatience with coincident use-rights over the same soil. As Loughborough had it, "the nature of property. . . imports exclusive enjoyment". And how could enjoyment be exclusive if it did not command the power to exclude from property's physical space the insolent lower orders?

In these last few pages we have given a little attention to the law. And we should add a few words to safeguard against possible misunderstanding. The *English Reports* are not packed with cases in which poor commoners challenged their lords or great landowners in the highest courts of the land. On occasion freeholders or customary tenants did so, pledging themselves to each other to share the costs.[1] But taking cases upwards to the courts of Common Pleas or King's Bench was not the cottagers' nor the labourers' "thing". Unless some party with a substantial interest was involved on their side, their rights were liable to be lost silently and without contest.

We may illustrate the point by noticing two cases where the rights of "the poor" were involved. The first is the case of gleaning. In a skilful piece of detective work Peter King has found out more about this case. There were in fact two cases, the first, *Worledge v Manning* (1786), coming up two years before the case of Mary Houghton (1788), but failing to decide the point of law. Both cases came up from the same West Suffolk parish, and the prosecutions were probably supported by subscription among local landholders. Benjamin Manning and John Houghton were both shoe makers, and Dr King suggests that it was only the support of a benevolent Suffolk landowner and magistrate, Capel Lloft, which enabled Houghton to fee counsel. The loss of the cases (and the damages and costs involved) certainly did not

---

[1] An example of such an agreement in Yate (Gloucestershire), 1745, is in Glos. CRO D 2272.

advance the career of either defendant. The Houghtons were forced to mortgage and then to sell their small property. Mary Houghton, the widow of John, is last found in the poor law records, receiving some £6 per annum relief.[1]

For the smallholder, cottager or small commoner the law was always something to avoid. But surely in the nineteenth century — after 1860 at least — small commoners could contest their rights in the courts with the help of powerful philanthropists or the Commons Preservation Society? On occasion this was true. But even in those enlightened years there could be difficulties, which may be illustrated by the case of Mr Willingale. We have already encountered (above, p. 102) the claims to wood of the poor inhabitants of Loughton, adjoining Waltham Forest (itself part of Epping Forest). The right of lopping trees up to a certain height in the winter months was a custom supposed to find its origin in a grant from Queen Elizabeth. Considerable ritual had gathered around its assertion, which must commence on midnight of November 10th, when inhabitants (usually warmed up with ale) perambulated the forest. In the early 1860s the lord of the manor of Loughton enclosed the forest, gave some compensation to tenants, fenced out the public and started felling the trees.

In 1866 "a labouring man named Willingale", with his two sons, broke in upon the fences and made the customary perambulation. All three were convicted of malicious trespass and sentenced to two months hard labour. In prison one of the sons caught pneumonia and died. When Willingale was released the matter was becoming a *cause célèbre* among the Radicals of East London. The Commons Preservation Society had just been founded and it offered to contest the issue, raising a fund of £1,000 for the purpose. A suit was commenced in the name of Willingale, since it could only be pleaded in an inhabitant of Loughton. There was a supporting lobby of Liberal MPs, QCs, editors, and eminent persons including Sir T. Fowell Buxton and John Stuart Mill. Yet despite this support and despite the publicity, Willingale was subjected to the inexorable social control of

[1] P. J. King, "The Origins of the Gleaning Judgement of 1788", forthcoming.

the manorial village. No-one dared employ him in the parish, and it was only with great difficulty that he could find lodging in the village, which he must do to remain an inhabitant. He was privately offered bribes — perhaps as much as £500 — to abandon the suit, but he rejected all offers.

After four years of this, the old man died (1870), hence abating the suit. It was resumed in a new form by the Corporation of London (which had no need to find lodging or employment in the manor). When it gained a qualified victory in 1879, "the whole population of the district turned out at midnight to the number of 5,000 or 6,000" for a last torchlight perambulation. Willingale's surviving son was still championing the common rights of the small occupiers, and his widow was awarded by London Corporation a pension of five shillings a week.[1]

Lord Eversley who records this story, and the part played in it by several philanthropists, appears to have forgotten "old Willingale's" Christian name. What is clear is that, even in mid-Victorian England, it was no easy matter for a labouring man to tangle about common rights with lords or landowners through the forms of law. What chances were there of doing so one hundred years before?

IV

The decision in the Court of Common Pleas in 1788 did not of course extinguish the practice of gleaning, unless perhaps by Mary Houghton and her neighbours in Timworth.[2] Custom remained *lex loci*, and while case law now decided that gleaning could not be claimed as a right in common law, the right might still be claimed as local right, by the custom of the manor or by village by-law. The decision strengthened the

---

[1] Eversley, *op. cit.*, ch. 8. Descriptions of Epping Forest in 1895, with its pollarded hornbeams, are in two letters of William Morris to the *Daily Chronicle*. *Letters of William Morris*, ed. Philip Henderson (1950), pp. 363-7.

[2] A few years after the Common Pleas judgement an observer of the picturesque enthused about the hundred-acre fields covered with gleaners, "while innumerable groups of children are sporting or working around": this was within a few miles of Timworth: S. Pratt, *Gleanings in England* (1801), ii, p. 271.

hands of farmers who wished to check the custom, or to restrict it to the families of their own labourers after enclosure. And enclosure did endanger the right, by removing the harvest from the huge open fields over which the customs of the rural community were habitually exercised, into the severalty of hedged or fenced "closes" with their sense of controlled access and private space. Indeed the decision might have led on to a general repression of gleaning if attempts to do so had not encountered the most stubborn resistance, especially from labouring women who, as Peter King has shown, refused to surrender their "rights" in the face of physical and legal harassment.[1]

No decision in the common law courts had immediate impact on the local practice of custom, although such decisions could stack the hands of the landowners with aces to be cashed for acres when it came to the point of enclosure. Where copyhold and other forms of customary tenure survived — indeed wherever lands survived in a village over which rights of common existed — one may expect to find some form of regulation of use. Some years ago, in my simplicity, I supposed that I had discovered a key to open the door upon the actuality of common right usages in surviving eighteenth-century recitations of customs, and especially in village by-laws still being promulgated in Courts Leet, or in other kinds of parish meeting, with vigour throughout the century. I made a habit then, whenever visiting a County Record Office, to rifle the card index and to collect examples of local regulation. But, alas, when I first came to sketch the present essay and turned this sack of notes onto my study floor, I found myself regarding this pro-miscuous gleaning of ears from several counties with blank dismay.

I learned at least a little humility. For this *lex loci*, which itself is only a partial guide to *praxis loci*, acquires meaning only when placed within the disciplined study of the local context. One must know about the balance of arable and waste, the diffusion or concentration of landholding, about crops and stock, soil fertility, access to markets, population

---

[1] See P. King, "Gleaners, Farmers and the Failure of Legal Sanctions, 1750-1850", *Past and Present*, no. 125 (November 1989).

and poor rates, and all those other matters which the disciplined agricultural historian so patiently puts together.[1] Without this careful provision of context my sack of gleanings turns out to be a sack of chaff. It is not much use to cite the stint for beasts allowed to graze the common per yardland or per cottage unless one can shew who and how many owned or tenanted these cottages and acres.

I might say, in self-defence, that several of the optimistic agrarian historians in the anti-Hammond school appear to have passed over such sources unread. But one is no more entitled to generalise indiscriminately about common right usages over the whole country than about soil, crops, or patterns of landholding. Common right usage, and the oral traditions as to these rights, is as specific and as local as are the geographic features. Perhaps a little may be deduced from such materials, even without contextual discipline. One finds, as one would expect, the tendency to translate rights to pasture on the waste (or gates on the common) into monetary equivalents, a sort of village echo of the re-ification of usages going on all around. Ryton-upon-Dunsmore, Warwickshire, a firmly regulated manor with good records, stipulated in 1735 that "no commons shall be let to no ought tounes [out-town]. . . for no less than 5s a common", whereas parishioners paid only 4s. for the right. There was an attempt to regulate the minor rights of common with unusual tightness: "No parson that is not a parrisoner shall cut any turf upone the common", and furze from the common might be taken only on own backs and only serve firing in own homes.

[1] Works which I have found most valuable in their bearing upon the exercise of common rights include (in addition to work by J. M. Neeson) W. G. Hoskins, *The Midland Peasant* (1957); C. S. and C. S. Orwin, *The Open Fields* (1948); A. C. Chibnall, *Sherington: Fiefs and Fields of a Buckinghamshire Village* (Cambridge, 1965); M. K. Ashby, *The Changing English Village: Bledington* (Kineton, 1974); W. Cunningham, *Common Rights at Cottenham & Stretham in Cambridgeshire* (Royal Hist. Soc., 1910); Joan Thirsk, "Field Systems in the East Midlands", in A. R. H. Baker and R. A. Butlin (eds.), *Studies of Field Systems in the British Isles* (Cambridge, 1973), esp. pp. 246-62; H. E. Hallam, "The Fen Bylaws of Spalding and Pinchbeck", *Lincs. Architectural & Archaeological Society*, (1963), pp. 40-56; R. S. Dilley, "The Cumberland Court Leet and Use of Common Lands", *Trans. Cumberland & Westmorland Antiq. & Archaeological Soc.*, lxvii (1967), pp. 125-51.

Money had made big inroads here:

> The grass hereafter growing in the highways or roads within this manner shall be sold to be mowed and not grazed and the moneys arising annually therefrom to be divided amongst the inhabitants of the said manor according to the rents of their respective livings.

No fewer than forty-seven persons were fined for offences against by-laws in 1735, and forty-eight in each year, 1741 and 1749, and one suspects that an annual exercise in disciplinary control was going on.[1]

My collection (which comes mainly from the Midlands) shows no other example of a manor whose rights had been monetarised to this extent. In some places — East and West Leake (Nottinghamshire) 1730 and Towcester, 1712 — commoners or cottagers received a monetary compensation if they did not exercise a common right.[2] In others the rent for a cow's common is specified, and (as at Harpole, Northamptonshire) the townsmen were permitted to let six cow commons in the heath "to any of the poor inhabitants of Harpole as they. . . shall see necessity or occasion for so doing".[3] In Whilton in the same Hundred a more affirmative by-law is found in 1699: "If any poor person. . . not holding lands or comon in the. . . fields shall at May Day. . . want a cows comon", they can obtain it for 8s. from the fieldsman.[4] Thus in some places rights to pasture could now be hired (but rarely to out-townsmen), in others there was compensation for the non-use of such rights, and sometimes there is a mixture of right and cash. Money is sometimes set aside to pay for the village officers, fieldsearchers, herds etc. or the local improvements; sometimes is redistributed to

---

[1] Warwicks. CRO, MR 19.

[2] Sidney P. Potter, "East and West Leake", *Nottinghamshire Guardian*, 1 Apr. 1933; Northants. CRO, YZ 4289.

[3] Northants. CRO, YZ 6a, Hundred of Norbottle Grove, Court Leet and Baron, "By Laws, Rules and Orders", 12 Oct. 1743. The stint was four cows and breeders for a yardland, but the townsmen could let further rights to any who held only a quartern of land (and therefore right for only one cow), at 8s. a right.

[4] Northants. CRO, YZ 1. M14, Norbottle Court, regulation for Whilton common fields, 1699. See also Hampton-in-Arden, 22 October 1802: "Such poor persons that apply the 1st of March. . . shall have each a Cows commoning", Warwicks. CRO, MR 20.

landholders; sometimes offsets the poor rates. In Hellidon, Northamptonshire, 1744, "any. . . persons that are parishioners and inhabitants of the Parish of Hellidon. . . have Liberty to turn a Horse in the Comonable Places in the ffields. . . at all comonable times. . . paying ten shillings a year to the overseer of the poor".[1]

A uniform concern of all regulations is to exclude interlopers from outside the parish from using the common. This is as old as regulation itself, but nevertheless is often repeated: "It is ordered that the Heardsmen and Shepherds shal not take to keepe any cattle of any other person. . . but onely those of the Inhabitants of this Towne."[2] In manorial villages with extensive copyhold and effective stewardship, rights were adjusted according to levancy and couchancy in a manner that would have satisfied the courts of common law. Rights on the stinted common were assessed in ratio to lands occupied in the open fields. Yet in other parishes indefinite terms abhorrent to the common law — "parishioners", "inhabitants", "any persons" — recur with frequency. Some by-laws pass over in silence usages on the common or waste, being wholly concerned with common of pasture and Lammas grazing; or they may signal practices which in other parishes are so well-known as to need no written rehearsal: "Any man shall have liberty to cut rushes at Xmas & not after Candlemas".[3] Pains are far more frequent upon trespasses in the common field than upon trespassers in the waste. Probably, in parishes with extensive common, the threat was seen as coming less from the cottager or labourer with the odd unlicensed beast than from graziers moving cattle on the hoof, butchers and dealers, or overmighty landholders exceeding their stint. Commons are stinted to establish *maximums* for men of substance.[4]

---

[1] Northants. CRO, D 5.5 (c), draft orders, court leet and baron of Manor of Hellidon, 27 October, 1744.

[2] Cunningham, *op. cit.*, p. 237.

[3] Northants. CRO, F (W.W.) 501/1/1, orders for Wollaston, 1721.

[4] For example, orders in Uphaven (Wiltshire), 1742, PRO, TS 19.3: "That all dealers and jobbers of sheep. . . ought not to keep any more sheep than their Leaze, and not to feed any sheep upon the Common. . . but with the other tenants according to the number of Leazes".

If there was a general place of contest between the farmers (of all shapes and sizes) on the one hand and the cottagers and landless commoners on the other, it can perhaps be detected in the continuing attempts to control the grazing on the marginal herbage in and around the common fields. Gonner tells us that "meers and balks were. . . sometimes fed off by cattle but often of little value", and substantiates this with a citation from an improving pamphleteer of 1773:

> They are literally of no benefit to either the occupier or the Poor; for they are too narrow either to mow, or to graze without a boy to attend each beast with a halter. . .[1]

In this he reports correctly the viewpoint of the improving farmers who have become, perhaps properly, the heroes of much agrarian history. Yet this marginal herbage was viewed very differently by the peasantry, among whom boys (and girls) able to attend on beasts with a halter were plentiful and cheap. In some pasture-hungry Midlands parishes in the early eighteenth century, very considerable efforts were being made by the farmers themselves to increase the acreage in the common fields under greensward by widening joint ways and balks for "flitting grass".[2] If the little people of the village are harassed — and if their stock harasses the large farmers in their turn — it is in this matter of marginal herbage; not only balks, but sykes, the banks of streams, headlands on the fields, tracks under greensward, laneside grazing. Persons are presented "that turne out beasts into the Lanes without a follower".[3] With this go pains against trespass and against

[1] Gonner, *op. cit.*, p. 27.

[2] For an example, see Northants. CRO, YZ 6a, By Laws Rules and Orders for Hundred of Norbottle Grove, 12 October 1743. See also J. M. Neeson, "Common Right and Enclosure in Eighteenth Century Northamptonshire" (Univ. of Warwick Ph.D. thesis, 1978), esp. ch. 2; Baker and Butlin, *op. cit.*, pp. 47-8, 131-2; H. Beecham, "A review of Balks as Strip Boundaries in the Open Fields", *Agric. Hist. Rev.*, iv, (1956), pp. 22-44.

[3] Hants. CRO, 159, 641, Bishop Waltham (Hampshire) presentments, 25 March 1712, and (pain on cows in lanes "without a driver") 2 April 1717. Also Hambledon presentments (159, 613), 29 September 1721. (A readier remedy in most villages was to put such straying beasts in the pound.) A Suffolk phrase for grazing laneside verges was to "feed the Long Meadow", George Ewart Evans, *The Days that We Have Seen* (1975), pp. 50-1.

forking horses on the balks or feeding horses under pretence of making hay.[1] (Horses are great eaters, and once a horse had broken from its tether it could do untold damage to crops.) In tolerant parishes marginal herbage might be grazed provided the beast was not forked or tethered but was led by a halter. A few sheep might be tolerated along the lanes.[2] What Gonner and his pamphleteer see as wasted land use "of little value" was of central importance to the subsistence-economy of "the poor". A correspondent ("Apuleius") in the *Northampton Mercury* in 1726 wrote of —

> Baulks and Borders, and Slades and Bottoms, and other waste Places, in these Common-Fields, which the Farmer is never able to appropriate to himself or his own sole using. . . for there are in most Countries a sort of Cottagers, that have Custom and Right of Commoning, tho' they Rent nothing but their Houses: And if it were a meer Hovel built upon the Waste, who would hinder a poor Man from keeping an Ewe and Lamb, or if he can compass one, a little Heifer? For these can run upon a Green, or among the Lanes and Highways, till the Crop be ended; and then away with them into the common Fields. . . and by this Advantage in some Places divers poor Families are in good Part sustained.

But with enclosure (the correspondent continued) these baulks and borders "become one Staple with the rest. . . in the sole Use and Occupation but of one Person".[3]

The beast led round the margins and along the ridges of a field, or up and down the lanes, by the children or the aged, can be seen in any poor peasant economy to this day. Wordsworth, encountering in his country walks with Beaupuy —

---

[1] "A pain made that no one shall flit with a Tether above Six yds long Excepting on his own Grass. . . A Pain that no one shall flit a Mare in the fields after the foal is a Month old": Atherstone Orders Bylaws and Pains, 1745, Warwicks. CRO, L 2/89. ("Flitting" was to graze a beast on a tether.)

[2] In Horbling (Lincolnshire) the cottagers "buy lambs in April, let them run in the lanes during Summer": *Annals of Agriculture*, xxxvii (1801), p. 522.

[3] *Northampton Mercury*, 17 Oct. 1726. See also Malcolmson, *op. cit.*, pp. 32-3.

> a hunger-bitten Girl,
> Who crept along, fitting her languid self
> Unto a Heifer's motion, by a cord
> Tied to her arm, and picking thus from the lane
> Its sustenance, while the Girl with her two hands
> Was busy knitting. . .

found the image of poverty to be a deep affront, and his friend Beaupuy "in agitation said, 'Tis against *that*/Which we are fighting' ". For Arthur Young, in the *Northern Tour*, it was no less of an affront, and an incitement to the virtues brought by dear times and improvement; when one who "in cheap times, used to bask himself all day in the sun, holding a cow by a line to feed on a balk, in dear ones betakes himself to the pickaxe and the spade".[1]

Levancy and couchancy supposed some land to be levant and couchant upon. The assumption is still there in 31 Eliz., c.7 (1589), prohibiting the erection of cottages without four acres of land. The socio-economic reality of many mid-eighteenth century unenclosed parishes was altogether different. While many small farmers were still to be found, as well as rural craftsmen and craftswomen and traders with a little land, there were in many places a growing number of landless commoners. Their customary rights, if scrutinised by national courts, were nil or — if they were tenants of old cottages — might be attached to the cottage (and its owner) not to the user. Yet it is my impression, from by-laws and literary evidence, that custom as praxis — village usages — generally afforded greater latitude for the exercise of minor rights than will be found in a formal view of the law.

I am not suggesting that poor people could get away with putting a cow or a few sheep on the common without anyone noticing. Everything that anyone did was noticed by someone in the village. Nor need we explain this latitude in terms of "theft", "fraud", or usurpation by the poor; or in terms of the tender paternalist sensibility of landowners. No doubt there are examples of both. But village regulation is often drawn by middle and small farmers, whose reputation for hardheadedness or even meanness is notorious. Yet even in

---

[1] Arthur Young, *A Six Months Tour through the North of England* (1771), i, p. 175.

hardheaded terms there are sound reasons for affording latitude in minor common rights. It is better that a labour force should remain resident and available for the heavy calls of hay and harvest and incidental calls for labour including the extensive women's service in hall, farmhouse and dairy. To afford to the poor subsistence rights, including firing and a cow for the pail, was at the same time a means of holding down poor rates.[1] And to these reasons may be added the reasons of custom and of neighbourhood. Some of those without land were the kin of the farmers; others long-standing neighbours, with skills — thatching, sheep-shearing, hurdle-making, building — involved in the continual exchange of services and favours (without any passage of money) which marks most peasant societies. It is even possible, without sentimentality, to suppose community norms, expectations and senses of neighbourhood obligation, which governed the actual usages of common; and such usages, practised "time out of mind", were fiercely held to be rights.[2]

But we must give way, at this point, before the expertise of the agrarian social historians. Common right is a subtle and sometimes complex vocabulary of usages, of claims to property, of hierarchy and of preferential access to resources, of the adjustment of needs, which, being *lex loci*, must be pursued in each locality and can never be taken as "typical". Alternative assertions of right could be fiercely divisive (for example, in the run-up to enclosure), not only between "rich" and "poor", but between small landholders and landless cottagers, or between cottagers with rights recognised at law and labourers without. I will note a wholly untypical case to conclude this section, not because it can stand for the general

---

[1] Arthur Young himself was of course a belated convert to the advantages of the poor's access to cow commons and cottage gardens, after the high price and dearth years of 1795 and 1800-1: see "An Inquiry into the Propriety of Applying Wastes to the Better Maintenance and Support of the Poor", *Annals of Agriculture*, xxxvi (1801), and also *General Report on Enclosures* (1808; reprinted 1971), esp. pp. 150-70. Snell, *op. cit.*, reviews this evidence, pp. 174-80.

[2] H. Homer, *An Essay upon the Inclosure of Common Fields* (Oxford, 1766), p. 23 speaks of the labourers' "immemorial custom" of enjoying privileges on the common.

case (if anything it is upside-down) but because it may illustrate the way in which various interests articulated their opposition through their claims to common right.

Atherstone in North Warwickshire at the start of the eighteenth century was a small market town. It was the site of a market, deriving from a grant in the time of Henry III, and also a horse fair (with annual races).[1] The town was situated in the midst of a large open field of about seven hundred acres, to which were added Outwoods (135 acres), and a cowpasture of fifteen acres. There are three major players in view in the first half of the century: the lord of the manor, who, in the 1730s, had only five acres in the open field: the landholders, most of whom held by copyhold tenure at the start of the century; and the cottagers, many of them also copyholders, who claimed right of common by prescription.

In 1719 disputes arose between the lord and the copyholders, on the familiar grounds of fines, herriots, and the soke rights of the mill, "to the continuall breach of Christian Amity and freindship". The customers accused the lord's steward of playing both ends against the middle in the Court Leet:

> The Steward. . . putts upon the Jury some poor men who are not Copyholders with whom he can doe what he pleaseth and allthough there is a Hall or Chamber on purpose to keep the Court in, yet the Court is kep in private places and the Jury kep in one Roome, and the Steward doth all his buissines privately in another, and by the antient Customes the Jury ought to be of the best Copyholders and all the buissines used to be done publickly in open Court.[2]

In 1735-8 attempts to enclose Atherstone open field were activated. The parties were now realigned. The copyholders in the field were now enfranchised (by purchase), the lord having been baulked in his efforts to screw up herriots and fines. Lands had been consolidated, and the moving spirit in the enclosure was the major freeholder, Mr Abraham

---

[1] I was first made aware of this case by J. M. Martin, "Warwickshire and the Parliamentary Enclosure Movement" (Birmingham Univ. Ph.D. thesis, 1966). Atherstone is also discussed in the same author's "Village Traders and the Emergence of a Proletariat in South Warwickshire, 1750-1851", *Agric. Hist. Rev.*, 37, pt. 2 (1984), pp. 179-88.

[2] Manorial papers in Warwicks. CRO, MR 9, undated but c. 1719.

Bracebridge (who, however, rented out his land and was "a tradesman & no great farmer").[1] He was now in alliance with the lord of the manor. The opposition was based on the cottagers, 160 of whom claimed rights of common by prescription for two horses and two beasts:

> Tho several of the antient grants & Charters relating to this Town have been search'd. . . the Cottagers have not been able to find there or in any other *writing* the original of this wright of common but can easily prove their wrights by prescription or parole evidence. The freeholders have the general words of wrights of common in their deeds. . .

> Note. Mr Bracebridge some years since, under pretence of his being engaged in a Law Suit relating to the town, obtained the Inspection & custody of all the town books & writings which he now refuses to deliver or shew to the townsmen.

But the town chest remained in the cottagers' possession.[2]

It was the large common field which was at issue, and the unusual feature of this case was that the cottagers claimed more rights to pasture over it than the landholders. They claimed right of common for two horses and two cows each, and the butchers claimed for ten sheep each,[3] for ten months in the year. (The stock was moved around different parts of the common field at different times, but was kept "plentifully supplied with Grass".)[4] The landholders were entitled to common at the rate of four horses and eight cows and twenty sheep per yardland, of which there were $24\frac{1}{4}$ in the open field. By one rough computation, we get:

[1] The Bracebridge family was involved in sugar-refining, banking and jewellery, and Abraham Bracebridge inherited a small estate in Atherstone in 1695. He and his son, Walter, were actively buying up lands in the open field between that time and the 1730s. "The Case of Atherstone concerning Inclosure of the Com. Fields as drawn by Mr. Baxter & Others in January 1738-9", in Warwicks. CRO, Compton Bracebridge MS, HR/35/25; various papers in Warwicks. CRO, MR 9; M. J. Kingman, "Landlord versus Community: the Bracebridge Family and the Enclosure of Atherstone Open Fields", *Warwickshire History*, vii, 4 (1988-9).

[2] Warwicks. CRO, HR/35/25.

[3] A married butcher was allowed ten sheep, a bachelor only five. Sheep placed on the common must be killed before new ones were added. See e.g. "Orders, Bylaws and Pains made by the Jury. . . for the Manor of Atherstone", 3 October 1745, in Warwicks. CRO, L 2/89.

[4] See Martin, "Village Traders", p. 183.

Landholders sheep	500	
Lord of the manor's sheep	20)	
Landholders' beasts	192) =	74 gates
Landholders' horses	96)	
	808	
Cottiers' beasts	320)	
Cottiers' horses	320) =	326 gates
Butchers' sheep	60)	
	700	

There were only six owners of the twenty-four yardlands in the open field, and of these Bracebridge owned nearly eighteen. On the side of the "cottiers" there were 160 who claimed (as "inhabitants", by prescription) "cottagers" rights. [1]

Bracebridge, together with the lord of the manor, the lay tithe-owner, and several landholders, attempted first to enclose the open fields "by agreement", without the assent of the cottagers. When this proved to be more than law would allow, several drafts of enclosure by parliamentary Act were drawn, and the small market town became the scene of covert negotiations and then of furious controversy. [2] Bracebridge offered to the cottagers eighty acres (subsequently raised to one hundred acres) in compensation for the loss of grazing rights over the whole field. One hundred and twenty cottagers and one or two small landholders petitioned against enclosure, on the grounds that it would lessen the value of their houses, diminish population, increase the poor, ruin the market and "lay a fondation for quarrells & contentions about the cottagers rights. . . & at the same time only agrandise & enrich one particular person. . .". [3]

It is evident that the term "cottager" covers several different categories of inhabitant. A few may have been

[1] The figures come from "The Case of Atherstone", drawn by opponents of enclosure, and from a paper drawn by supporters of enclosure in Warwicks. CRO, HR/35/7. There are variations in the count.

[2] It was alleged that a gentleman (Bracebridge?) had been threatened and was obliged to keep a guard on himself and his family. Opponents of enclosure were quick to declare that "we hate Mobs and Mobbish doings as much as he doth": Warwicks. CRO, HR/35/12.

[3] "The Case of Atherstone".

professional persons (from amng whom an eloquent pamphleteer may have come), others shopkeepers, tradesmen, inn-keepers, and butchers (for whom the extensive common rights were a convenience). Another manuscript protest — these sheets were copied in a clear hand and were obviously circulated around the town — suggests that tradesmen had been buying houses in Atherstone because of these rights. The tradesmen "of a lower rank" (it was argued) needed horses for their business, fetching coals, hiring out, or in connection with the local trade in tammy-weaving and felt-making. Other trades which might need horses included "smiths, carpenters, coopers, masons, joyners, wheelwrights".[1] An annotated list of 123 Atherstone copyholders (who may well be the "cottiers" in question) shows among them "the Toyshop", two inn-keepers, and a wheelwright, gardener, shoemaker, bricklayer, weaver, maltster, retired butler, plumber, barber, exciseman and carpenter.[2]

Other cottagers were small peasant farmers, but it seems that a large group were labourers without stock and without other resources. They therefore did not and could not exercise their grazing rights — although in theory the 160 cottiers had rights to graze 320 horses, in fact (the enclosers argued) only eighty horses were grazed, and the land would not carry more.[3] But those cottagers and open field farmers who could graze stock had passed a by-law in the Court Leet to prevent the cottagers who had no stock from letting their gates on the common to others. Although a little "covert" letting still went on, the right was now technically valueless to them, and this was a grievance which Bracebridge and the enclosers tried to exploit. They tried to buy over the poor cottiers by offering to each 20s. per annum compensation for the loss of rights which they could not use. If this attractive bribe could have brought enough poor cottagers to the side of enclosure, then an Act might pass through parliament.

This offer stimulated a reply from the most eloquent of the opposing pamphleteers. "I cannot but observe," he remarked

---

[1] "Some of the Grievances that will result from the Inclosure of the Fields of Atherstone", Warwicks. CRO, HR/35/10.
[2] List of copyholders, n.d., revised and annotated, Warwicks. CRO, HR/35/39.
[3] Warwicks. CRO, HR/35/7.

with heavy sarcasm, "how tender these Gentlemen now seem to be of the rights of the Poor". Bracebridge "seems to be courting the lower and meaner sort and playing them against those in better circumstances. . . Gentlemen become levellers to obtain their own ends". And he reflected upon the historic origin and present function of commons:

> When these Commons in the fields were allotted to the use of the cottagers it was not meant what we call paupers, for in that age their was no such, but different degrees of men superiour and inferiour occupying the Cottages, but it was more the design to prevent poor, or at least to be a security for those whom fortune shou'd frown on, to have recourse for relief, that all might be employ'd in some way or other.

Even if the poor cottagers were unable to buy stock, common usages were intrinsic to their economy:

> By the Harvest work, the men will get 6s p.w. and beer, the women will get 2s till corn harvest then 3s p.w. . . . The gleaning of the fields computed 15s a family in a season. . .

Gleaning was —

> an Injury to no man, although those who make use of this advantage accruing to the Inferior from the beginning of the Harvest being known in the World are at this day by some as Mr [?] call'd thieves. I cannot see in what more than robbing the Fowls of the Air.

To this might be added cutting firewood in the Outwoods, both for use and for sale — 6s. or 8s. per week "hath been known" to be gained by families from this. The men could find occasional labour in husbandry, with the muck cart, trenching and threshing in winter. And this led on to a detailed estimate:

	£ s d
Inferiour Men not stocking their Commons, by their Work by a near Computation including their beer at 5s per week each, they get some weeks more, some less, this being a Medium. . .	13 00 00
Women by their Harvest work, weeding, clotting, Hay Harvest, Reaping which we will allow to employ them Ten Weeks at 2.6d p week	01 05 00
Admitting they have no other work or spining &c they will get by fetching wood 1s 6d p.w.	03 03 00
Allow each Cottager one Boy or Girl able to do anything. . . they will get as much as the Mother	04 03 00

Each Family by their Gleaning or Pikeing in
the Season   00 15 00
                                                        ─────────
                                                        22 06 00
All this does not take into account
spinning and carding. [1]

This forms (the pamphleteer argued) "the Oeconomy of Life for these useful and inferiour people". They can support themselves and live without the aid of "people moving in a superiour sphere, better than the Superiour can without the Inferiour". Since they are "essentially necessary" they should be "indulg'd so far and after the best manner their circumstances will allow; not to be deem'd thieves & trick'd out of their and their Posterity's rights". Enclosure not only would deprive the poor cottager of maintenance, but it would discourage him from trying to gain a competency, and would encourage indolence. The commons right was "a sure foundation whereon he may work, and room for him to advance his fortune as he gets able to buy stock". For these reasons the pamphleteer urged the poor cottagers not to surrender their (latent) rights:

> In case of Inclosure, the Inferiour will be made slaves and oblig'd for what little work will be found to work for what wages those Mercenaries who at present call them Thieves will please to give them.

As for the 20s. per annum offered in compensation, this money will "like the weekly pay be piss'd against the Wall & the Families no better. . .".

It seems that very few of the cottagers were persuaded to accept this 20s. bribe. Nor were those who exercised their grazing rights impressed. They perhaps suspected that the hundred acres compensation offered would be the poorest land in the parish, and they had good reason. [2] The

---

[1] Untitled paper ("We have before us a Paper entitled the Inclosure Vindicated", etc.); the arithmetic seems to be faulty: Warwicks. CRO, HR/35/15. See also HR/35/14. "Clotting" was breaking up clods with a wooden mallet; "piking" could be gleaning, or cleaning the edges of a harvest field: see Joseph Wright, *English Dialect Dictionary*.

[2] A clause drafted for the Act (Warwicks. CRO, HR/35/33) shows that the proposed commons were "very much over run with Gorse Hollies & Thorns and Briers and. . . other parts of it grow Mossey".

proposed Act was withdrawn. Agreement as to enclosure was reached with a majority of the cottagers of a subsequent generation, in 1764, and a letter survives in which a surveyor confided in Bracebridge's grandson details of the hundred acres recommended to be set aside for the cottagers:

> We fixt upon 2 parcels of land which I am sure fourscore Acres is the worst in the fields but as it must be in one piece or two it cannot be done without laying to it about 20 acres [of] as good land as is on the Lower flat.

The surveyor was busy with plans to lay together "Fludgate Nuke" and "Sorry Midsummer", but alas not every bog and quicksand could be included.[1]

The case of Atherstone is not, of course, characteristic of the unenclosed village, any more than was neighbouring Sutton Coldfield where attempts to enclose were rebuffed, to an output of broadsides and songs about "the people's charter'd rights" in 1778, and delayed again in 1805 in part by the opposition of the vicar, John Riland, on the grounds that the town's charter granted rights to —

> *inhabitants, householders*, that is Cottagers, Day Labourers, Shopkeepers, and other little Housekeepers, not Freeholders. The Charter means those, so do I. . .
>
> "I mean the great body of all lower classes of the parish, whose consent has not been obtain'd."[2]

Both Atherstone and Sutton Coldfield claimed their rights and privileges by prescription, from charter and "wright of common", as if the act of writing carried some mysterious power. Villagers in the fenlands in the seventeenth century, in a tithe dispute, paraded "black boxes with writinges with great seales. . . cominge, as they say, from the kinge. . ." In Haxey church a fourteenth-century deed in which the lord, John de Mowbray, pledged to preserve the commons from further improvement was kept in an iron-bound chest (to which the chief freeholders held keys); the chest stood under a window, wherein (icon-like) "was the portraiture of Mowbray set in ancient glass, holding in his hand a writing

[1] Thomas Merler to Bracebridge, 1764, Warwicks. CRO, HR/35.
[2] Rev. W. K. Riland Bedford, *Three Hundred Years of a Family Living, being a History of the Rilands of Sutton Coldfield* (Birmingham, 1889), pp. 131-3.

which was commonly reputed to be an emblem of the deed".[1]

We have seen the role of the church in other cases (above pp. 98-100), and since so much enclosure took place by agreement, or was enrolled in Chancery Decrees, and since it often took a form in which the lord or substantial freeholders surrendered their rights over common and waste in return for licence to enclose their own lands, the memory of these decisions was indeed a source of power.[2] Court books could be "lost" or access to them denied. Oral traditions as to rights might be founded upon some long-forgotten decree. As late as 1880 in a dispute over Wigley Common, near the New Forest, a meeting of the tenants discussed an "old paper" which declared their rights. A copyholder was found to have a heavy box with three locks in his possession, which was known by the tenants as "the monster". Within the box was found an exemplification, under the Great Seal, of a decree in Chancery of 1591, establishing the copyholders' customs. There was subsequently found in the court rolls of the manor some two hundred years later (1783) an order of the homage placing the decree in the custody of three tenants, who each had a key to a lock on the box. "The monster" was, no doubt, a corruption of the Latin *monstravi*. All that the owner recollected of the box was that his grandfather had brought it home after his admission as a tenant, saying: "See, I have brought home the monster!".[3]

V

It was always a problem to explain the commons within capitalist categories. There was something uncomfortable about them. Their very existence prompted questions about the origin of property and about historical title to land.

In the sixteenth and seventeenth centuries landowners had asserted their titles in land against the prerogative of the king,

---

[1] C. Holmes, "Drainers and Fenmen" in A. Fletcher and J. Stevenson (eds.), *Order and Disorder in Early Modern England* (Cambridge, 1985), pp. 192-3. See also Jack Goody, *The Logic of Writing and the Organization of Society* (Cambridge, 1986), pp. 163-5.

[2] See J. A. Yelling, *Common Field and Enclosure in England, 1450-1850* (1977), ch. 5, "Piecemeal and Partial Enclosures".

[3] Eversley, *op. cit.*, pp. 125-8.

and copyholders had asserted their titles and customs against their lords. They therefore had discarded theories of the origin to title in divine right. Yet if they fell back upon Hobbesian violence or on the right of conquest, how could they reply to the telling counter-argument of the Norman Yoke? When Locke sat down to offer an answer, all this was stewing around in his mind. In his First Treatise he dismissed notions of title by succession from Father Adam or from the donation of God. In the Second Treatise his chapter on property commences with an extended metaphor of common right usage. God granted the world to "mankind in common", and the fruits and beasts "are produced by the spontaneous hand of nature". But the common was seen as a negative, not a positive community: it belonged to nobody and was open to any taker.[1] Locke took as a paradigm of the origin of property the mixing of labour (which was man's only original "property", in himself and in his own hands) with the common:

> Whatsoever, then, he removes out of the state that nature hath provided and left it in, he hath mixed his labour with. . . and thereby makes it his property.

"It hath by this labour something annexed to it that excludes the common right of other men":

> Thus the grass my horse has bit, the turfs my servant has cut, and the ore I have dug in any place where I have a right to them in common with others, become my property. . .

It is not clear that Locke has overcome all difficulties — why are the turfs to be his, and not his servant's or, indeed, his horse's? Legal decisions in the eighteenth century introduced arguments from "labour" in terms of the general reasons of "improvement". More often they fell back in the question of custom or *lex loci* upon the legal fiction that customary usages must have been founded upon some original grant, from persons unknown, lost in the mists of antiquity. The law pretended that, somewhere in the year dot, the commons were granted by benevolent Saxon or Norman landowners, so that uses were less of right than by

[1] See Istvan Hont and Michael Ignatieff (eds.), *Wealth and Virtue* (Cambridge, 1983), p. 36.

grace. The fiction was purely ideological: it guarded against the danger that use-rights might be seen as inherent in the users, in which case the successors of Levellers or Diggers might arise and plead their original title.

Locke's property theory was written in terms which two scholars have sternly described as an English "vernacular", as against the stricter European tradition of natural jurisprudence. He "did not follow Grotius's and Pufendorf's restriction of the use of the term 'property' to its modern meaning of exclusive and absolute right of dominion".[1] In the flexible traditions of the English common law the meanings of property remained various — an absolute right, a coincident use-right, a claim to preference, a man's property in his own life or privileges. Undoubtedly C. B. Macpherson was right to show the increasingly absolute definition of property in the seventeenth century, and the triumph of the claim to the "virtually unlimited and saleable rights *to* things" in the eighteenth.[2] This process was not, perhaps, as univocal as Professor Macpherson proposed, and was, indeed, two-sided. For the landowners, landed property was "increasingly becoming subsumed to contract, that is. . . taking on the qualities and functions of capital", through the liquidity of mortgages and the complex forms of marriage settlements, trusts, entail etc. "Yet at the same time, in the name of absolute individual property, the common and use rights of the 'lower orders' were eroded."[3]

Sir William Blackstone had too precise a mind to linger long in speculations, although he endorsed, in passing, the Lockeian view that property in land allows an origin in which in prehistoric times the land "belonged generally to everybody, but particularly to nobody". But his concern was to define the rights to property as he now found them to be justified at law. And he asserted the right of property (and,

---

[1] *Ibid.*, p. 35.
[2] C. B. Macpherson, "Capitalism and the Changing Concept of Property", in E. Kamenka and R. S. Neate (eds.), *Feudalism, Capitalism and Beyond* (1975).
[3] See the overview by G. R. Rubin and David Sugarman (eds.), *Law, Economy and Society* (Abingdon, 1984), esp. pp. 23-42. Also P. S. Atiyah, *The Rise and Fall of Freedom of Contract* (Oxford, 1979), pp. 85-90.

in the case of land, the control of physical space) to be exclusive and unqualified:

> . . . that sole and despotic dominion which one man claims and exercises over the external things of the world, in total exclusion of the right of any other individual in the universe.[1]

This bleak and absolutist definition he then (of course) did go on to qualify. His account of customary rights and copyhold is scrupulous, and on some matters (such as gleaning) he leaned to a liberal view. Yet these customs also were considered less as usages than as properties annexed to *things*. Through the ill-management of history these things were muddled up amongst each other on the land, and it was the business of law to sort each exclusive property out.

Political economy aided and abetted the law. For Adam Smith "property was either 'perfect' and absolute or it was meaningless",[2] and it was the function of government to protect property from the indignation of the poor. As he wrote in *The Wealth of Nations* (1776),

> It is only under the shelter of the civil magistrate that the owner of that valuable property, which is acquired by the labour of many years, or perhaps of many successive generations, can sleep a single night in security.

Somehow the language summons to mind the substantial property, the settled estate, the freehold, while the secure sleep of commoners falls out of view. (After his change-of-heart, Arthur Young reported that poor commoners in a Cambridgeshire village regarded the approach of inclosure "with a sort of terror".)[3] It was Adam Smith's achievement to shift "the terms of analysis from a language of rights to a language of markets", in a "constitutive move in the making of classical political economy".[4]

By the 1780s both law and political economy regarded co-existent properties in the same land with extreme impatience.

---

[1] Blackstone, *op. cit.*, ii, pp. 2, 8.
[2] Hont and Ignatieff, *op. cit.*, p. 25.
[3] *Annals of Agriculture*, xlii (1804), p. 497, describing Morden Guildon, then under enclosure, where the cottagers had been in the habit of keeping cows, wintering them in the farmers' yards at 6d. per week, in summer leading them on balks, etc.
[4] Hont and Ignatieff, *op. cit.*, pp. 24-6.

We recall Lord Loughborough's judgement that "the nature of property. . . imports exclusive enjoyment" (above p. 139). And this was seconded by the immoderate ideological zeal of the propagandists of enclosure. Monotonously, in pamphlet, in the *Annals of Agriculture* and in agricultural surveys, the same impatient tone comes through. Opponents of Lincoln-shire fenland enclosure wish to "live at large, and prey, like pikes, upon one another", or these commoners are "Buccaneers" who "sally out, and drive, or drown or steal, just as suits them".[1] "The appropriation of the forests", Vancouver remarked in the *General View of the Agriculture of Hampshire* (1810),

> Would. . . be the means of producing a number of additional useful hands for agricultural employment, by gradually cutting up and annihilating that nest and conservatory of sloth, idleness and misery, which is uniformly to be witnessed in the vicinity of all commons, waste lands and forests. . .

And the surveyor expressed his earnest wish that "old as he now is, he yet may live to see the day when every species of intercommonable and forest right may be extinguished". The vocabulary — "prey", "buccaneers", "cutting up and annihilating" — reveals a mind-set impervious to alternative definitions; and, as the high tide of enclosure coincided with the political polarisation of the 1790s, so arguments of property and improvement are joined to arguments of class discipline. Parliament and law imposed capitalist definitions to exclusive property in land.

If parliamentarians, landowners, judges and many enclosure commissioners did gross natural injustices in enclosures I do not mean that they were clearly aware of what they were doing. They observed the rules which they them-selves had made. They were so profoundly imbued with pre-conceptions which translated the usages of the poor into the property-rights of the landowners that they really found it difficult to view the matter in any other way. (Although — it is important to note — there were always contrary voices, even among their own ranks.) What may give to this matter a

---

[1] W. Pennington, *Reflections on the various Advantages resulting from the Draining, Inclosing and Allotting of Large Commons and Common Fields* (1769), pp. 32, 37.

greater significance is that this law and this mind-set were not confined in place or in time. The concept of exclusive property in land, as a norm to which other practices must be adjusted, was now extending across the whole globe, like a coinage reducing all things to a common measure.

The concept was carried across the Atlantic, to the Indian sub-continent, and into the South Pacific, by British colonists, administrators, and lawyers, who, while not unaware of the force of local customs and land systems, struggled to construe these within their own measure of property. It is an interesting inversion of the expected sequence of reciprocity between "social being" and "social consciousness" which, in the Marxist tradition, used to be rehearsed in terms of "basis and superstructure". To be sure, capitalist notations of property rights arose out of the long material processes of agrarian change, as land use became loosed from subsistence imperatives and the land was laid open to the market. But now these concepts and this law (or *lex loci* of that part called England of a European island) were transported and imposed upon distant economies in various phases of evolution. Now it was law (or "superstructure") which became the instrument of reorganising (or disorganising) alien agrarian modes of production and, on occasion, for revolutionising the material base.

A global ecological history might be written, one central episode of which turned upon the mis-match between English and alien notions of property in land and the imperialist essays in translation. Even within the main island of Britain, successive emigrations and clearances from the Scottish Highlands were testimony to the decisions of a law which afforded no shelter to a population evicted from lands which they had supposed to be communally owned, from time out of mind, by their clans. But the law could take no cognisance of such a communal personality. Nor could its categories match the communal usages of hunter-gatherer peoples. Locke had ruminated, in his chapter on property, on "the wild Indian. . . who knows no enclosure, and is still a tenant in common". This Indian served as a paradigm for an original state before property became individuated and secure: "In the beginning all the world was America". Locke decided that the American Indian was poor "for want of improving" the land by labour. Since labour (and improvement) constituted the right to property, this made it the more easy for Europeans to dispossess the Indians of their hunting grounds. The Puritan colonists were ready to moralise their appropriation of Indian lands by reference to God's commands, in *Genesis* 1, 28, to "replenish the earth, and subdue it".[1]

Hunting, fishing, and even planting some unfenced patches of corn and squash clearly fell far short of "subduing" the earth. (In any case, the work was left to the women.) It could not be said to be "improvement" and therefore its claim to establish rights of property was slender. The same improving mind-set, whether in Old England or in New, found reprehensible the lack of useful productive labour, whether on the ill-governed forest or waste or in the Indians' hunting grounds. In the English cottager and "the wild Indian" alike there was seen a degrading cultural submission to a picaresque, desultory or vagrant mode of livelihood. "Forests and great Commons", John Bellers wrote, "make the Poor that are upon them too much like the *Indians. . .*". Commons were "a hindrance to Industry, and. . . Nurseries of Idleness and Insolence".[2] Security of property is complete only when commons come to an end.

The same notions of property-right accompanied the earliest British colonists in the South Pacific. In 1770 Cook claimed the east coast of New South Wales for the Crown, not because it was empty of aborigines but because "we never saw one inch of cultivated land in the whole country". Title could therefore rest on "discovery", or *vacuum domicilium*. Title could not be claimed so easily in New Zealand lands, in which both settlement and cultivation was so evident. The trouble was that property rights among the Maori were insufficiently individuated and absolute. James Busby, the British Resident, allowed in 1835 that —

---

[1] An excellent study which brings legal and ecological themes together is William Cronon, *Changes in the Land: Indians, Colonists and the Ecology of New England* (New York, 1983). I am at work on a study of these issues, in relation to the Mohegans of Connecticut, which I hope to conclude shortly.

[2] A. Ruth Fry, *John Bellers, 1654-1725* (1935), p. 128.

> As far as has been ascertained every acre of land in this country is appropriated among the different tribes; and every individual in the tribe has a distinct interest in the property; although his possession may not always be separately defined.[1]

As in New England, setting land loose onto the market was complicated by communal claims upon property. In comparison with their American forerunners, the Maoris were fortunate in that by the time of colonisation the procedures under which the "Pakeha" settlers appropriated land were a little more scrupulous. The Maoris were also numerous and formidable at war. The Treaty of Waitangi (1840) was the most serious attempt made to match capitalist and communal notions of property in land, and the complexity of this task is witnessed by the fact that arguments as to the treaty's interpretation occupy a central place in New Zealand's political life to this day.

But while it was possible for the colonial power to draw up treaties with native nations or tribes (as was done also in many North American cases), it was a different matter when rights to property in land came to be cashed in law. How could land be loosed for the market when even a *hupa*, or sub-tribe, might share among hundreds of persons communal rights in land? A solution must either be political and sociological or it must be legal. As to the first, it was necessary to bring about —

> The detribalization of the Natives — to destroy, if it were possible, the principle of communism which ran through the whole of their institutions. . . and which stood as a barrier in the way of all attempts to amalgamate the Native race into our own social and political system.[2]

As to the second, New Zealand law attempted to deal with it under the Native Land Act of 1865 whose aim was to assimilate native rights to land "as nearly as possible to the ownership of land according to British law". Since British law could never recognise a communist legal personality, section 23 of the Act ordered that communal rights could not

---

[1] Claudia Orange, *The Treaty of Waitangi* (Wellington, 1987), p. 38.
[2] Henry Sewell in *New Zealand Parliamentary Debates*, 9 (1870), p. 361: see Keith Sorrenson, "Maori and Pakeha", in W. H. Oliver (ed.), *The Oxford History of New Zealand* (Oxford, 1981), p. 189.

be vested in more than ten persons. A Maori witness testified: "When the Crown agent was ordered, the Court told us to go outside to arrange whose names should be in. We went outside — perhaps one hundred of us. We picked those who were to be in the grant." This fraudulent device was then pleaded as "according to Maori custom".[1]

The notion of absolute property in land which triumphed in England in the late eighteenth century had both a legal and a political aspect. Property in land required a landowner, improving the land required labour, and therefore subduing the earth required also subduing the labouring poor. As Lord Goderich, the Colonial Secretary, remarked in 1831 (with reference to Upper Canada):

> Without some division of labour, without a class of persons willing to work for wages, how can society be prevented from falling into a state of almost primitive rudeness, and how are the comforts and refinements of civilized life to be procured?[2]

Hence property-plus-improvement required the model of the local property-owner in whose nexus were combined economic, social, and perhaps judicial authority over his labourers, on the model of the English country gentleman (and perhaps JP).

The most ambitious projects to transpose both the law of property and the sociological model of a landowner into an alien context were the succession of land settlements imposed by British administrators upon India. The earliest of these — the Permanent Settlement of Bengal — offers a paradigm of the mind-set which has been my theme. Although the Settlement finally took form in the proclamation of Lord Cornwallis, the Governor General (22 March 1793), it had, as Ranajit Guha has shown, a long prehistory.[3] Proposals of

---

[1] See D. Williams, "The Recognition of 'Native Custom' in Tanganyika and New Zealand — Legal Pluralism or Monocultural Imposition?" in Sack and Minchin (eds.), *Legal Pluralism* (Canberra Law Workshop, VII, ANV, 1985), pp. 139-54: a lucid and helpful study.

[2] Cited by Bryan D. Palmer, in "Social Formation and Class Formation in North America, 1800-1900", *Proletarianization and Family History* (1984).

[3] In the next page or two I have drawn heavily upon Ranajit Guha, *A Rule of Property for Bengal* (Paris, 1963), and also R. B. Ramsbotham, *Studies in the Land Revenue: History of Bengal 1769-87* (Oxford, 1926).

mercantilist, physiocrat and of Smithian political economists alike all agreed in the need to establish security of property, and all converged upon a solution which would vest these permanent property rights in the zemindars. Alexander Dow, the author of *The History of Hindostan* (1768) doubted the supposed zemindary title to property-rights. Land (in his view) was owned by the "Crown" or Moghul emperor, and while granted to the zemindars — who in effect were civil and administrative officers of the empire and collectors and guarantors of revenue — it could not be said to be owned, absolutely and exclusively, by them. In theory at least the grant could be revoked. Nevertheless Dow favoured the settlement of the land upon the zemindars, as an alternative to the corrupt and oppressive system of "farming" out the revenues (which many observers believed had contributed to the terrible famine of 1770). "An established idea of property is the source of all industry among individuals, and, of course, the foundation of public prosperity."

This argument derived title to land from the real or presumed grant from the Moghul power to the East India Company, along with the revenues attached to the land. Philip Francis — perhaps because he felt that this title was insecure — disputed the "erroneous opinion" that in the Moghul empire the governing power had been proprietor of the soil. He preferred to exalt zemindary proprietary rights, and cited as proof "the inheritable quality of the lands". In this he mistook the heritable character of zemindary *office* — to manage the lands and collect their revenue — for the *ownership* of the lands. And if Francis had reflected there were plenty of examples of heritable rights and claims over land, which fell far short of absolute property, acknowledged in English law: the most common being copyhold.

One need not be a specialist in the complexities of South Asian agrarian systems to see that these disputants were trying to compress their features into a modernising — or "improving" — English mask. With the English landowner and JP in his mind, Francis wrote that "zemindars are or ought to be the instruments of government in almost every branch of the civil administration". He even compared the zemindar to the Lord of the Manor. Once a Bengal gentry had been established, then the rest of the desired sociological model could hang from that — "those intermediate gradations of rank, authority and responsibility, by which all great civil societies are held together", and formed into "successive ranks of subordination".[1] This also was a part of the accepted rhetoric of all British parties. Amongst these voices, only that of Warren Hastings and his close circle — the very people whom the improvers indicted as bandits and parasites enriching themselves by farming out the Company's revenues — suggested settling the land upon the ryots, the actual cultivators. It is probable that Hastings was making a debating-point and was not serious.

Charles Cornwallis took up his duties in Bengal just before the French Revolution. It would be interesting to know in what ways he had assembled his notions as to what was proper to the ownership of land. His father had made a fortunate marriage into the Townshend-Walpole clan from whom, no doubt, young Charles had learned not only about turnips but about the patrician arrogation of superordinate rights. A short tenure of office as Chief Justice in Eyre south of the Trent may have taught him to abhor indistinct forest usages. His service in the American Wars will have given him adequate opportunity to meditate on the difference between improved and unimproved lands. "Improvement was a key word which frequently occurred in his minutes and correspondence."[2] In intervals from service his seat was at Culford in Suffolk. Two miles away was Timworth, where, in 1787 — the year after Cornwallis sailed for Bengal — Mary Houghton's flagrant contempt of property-rights occasioned the celebrated judgement against gleaning. Peter King has examined the Cornwallis estate papers, and he has established that the offending Houghtons were indeed within the Cornwallis lands and had given offence to his steward or estate manager, being petty proprietors of a cottage with common rights who had been able to block a cherished plan of enclosure and reorganisation on the Cornwallis lands. It is possible that this could have been the reason for the selection

---

[1] *Ibid.*, pp. 105-22. Philip Francis's plan (which was rejected) was presented in 1776, the same year as the publication of *The Wealth of Nations.*

[2] *Ibid.*, p. 172.

of Mary Houghton for prosecution for gleaning.[1]

Dr King has discovered no reference to the ferocious Mary Houghton in Cornwallis's surviving correspondence. But we need not suppose that the Governor General of Bengal followed every detail of rationalisation on his distant Suffolk estate. He was content to leave mundane decisions to his brother, the bishop of Lichfield. No doubt the brothers shared the same Whiggish, improving outlook. Professor Guha has shown one intellectual origin of the Permanent Settlement in physiocratic thought, but the less theoretical praxis of the Whig patricians was of equal significance.[2] As a historian of my father's generation — in point of fact, my own father — noted: "The same era that saw the English peasant expropriated from his common lands saw the Bengal peasant made a parasite in his own country",[3] and this was done by the same mind-set, the same legal dicta of absolute property-right, and sometimes by the same men.

The immediate motive of the Permanent Settlement was convenience in collecting the revenue and the need to check the abuses of collection. But behind this lay a Whiggish model of class relations, in which — as Locke had written — "subduing or cultivating the earth, and having dominion, we see are joined together". Dominion gave security to exclusive rights in property, and landed property was the proper station not only for planting turnips but also for planting

---

[1] I first suggested a connection between the Mary Houghton case at Timworth and the Cornwallis estates at Culford when I lectured at an Open Meeting of the Past and Present Society on "Law, Use-Rights and Property in Land" in March 1986. This was based on guesswork only. Dr Peter King has now established that there was such a connection, and his thorough examination of "The Origins of the Gleaning Judgement of 1788" is forthcoming.

[2] James Mill in *The History of British India* (1817) voiced the utilitarian reaction when he referred to Cornwallis's "aristocratical prejudices". It is not clear why Dr Guha (*op. cit.*, pp. 170-1) should reprove this as "exaggerated language". It is surely a correct description?

[3] Edward J. Thompson, *The Life of Charles, Lord Metcalfe* (1937), p. 268. "The Permanent Settlement was made in the face of substantial awareness of the facts, in order to clamp down everlasting quietness on these matters of revenue and land possession rights; and it was made by men who could not conceive any better arrangement than that under which England's innumerable Tolpuddles enjoyed such happiness".

political interest. Sir Henry Strachey wrote in 1802 that we are anxious to secure the "assistance of the men of property and influence in preserving the peace throughout the country", but such rights of property should be invested "only in estates of a certain extent":

> There are no gentlemen, in whose honour and probity, in whose spirit and activity, government can repose confidence. There exists not between the common people and the rulers, a middle order, who respect their rulers, or are by them respected; who. . . could. . . exert themselves heartily and effectually, each in his own sphere, for the public good. Such a set of men in the society, is here unknown.[1]

The intention of the Permanent Settlement was to establish a Whig gentry, and the role was given to the greater zemindars, "for preserving order in civil society".[2] The measure "was effected to naturalise the landed institutions of England among the natives of Bengal".[3] It is inadequate to describe the zemindars' true status as that of "hereditary rent-collectors". Even this implies that some direct translation is possible between two radically incompatible systems of land-holding. There simply was no way of converting the practices and customs of Bengal and Bihar or Orissa into a common specie to be exchanged with English practice and common law. As Sir William Hunter was later to write:

> My own investigations point to an infinite gradation in the rights of the various classes interested in the land. In some districts the landholder was almost independent of the Mussulman Viceroy. . . in others he was only a bailiff appointed to receive the rents. In some districts, again, peasant rights were acknowledged, and the old communal system survived as a distinct influence; in others the cultivators were mere serfs. This is the secret of the contradictory objections which were urged against Lord Cornwallis' interpretation of the land-law. . . Those collectors who had to deal with districts in which the landholders were the real owners of the soil, complained that the Permanent Settlement had stripped them of their rights and ruined them; while those who had

---

[1] *Fifth Report from the Select Committee of the House of Commons on the Affairs of the East India Company* (1812), ed. W. K. Firminger (Calcutta, 1917), ii, pp. 609-10.

[2] Cornwallis, cited in Eric Stokes, *The English Utilitarians and India* (Oxford, 1959), p. 5.

[3] Sir Richard Temple, cited in Edward J. Thompson and G. T. Garratt, *Rise and Fulfilment of British Rule in India* (1935), p. 191.

derived their experience from parts of the country in which the Mussulman system had uprooted the ancient houses, objected that Lord Cornwallis had sacrificed the claims of the Government and the rights of the people to elevate a parcel of tax-gatherers and land-stewards into a sham gentry.[1]

This referred to rural Bengal. When Hunter came to consider the subsequent settlement of Orissa (1804),[2] his account was even more nuanced. Taking as his theme "Inchoate Proprietory Rights", he distinguished more clearly between a right of "ownership" vested under the Hindu dynasties in the prince, and a right of "occupancy" vested in the village community or in the cultivators. In between there was a complex hierarchy of tax collectors, land stewards, accountants, down to village heads, whose status was consolidated for the convenience of Moghul revenue and rule:

> A long chain of intermediate holders grew up between the Ruling Power which had the abstract ownership and the Cultivator who enjoyed the actual occupancy. Thus the superior Landholder (zamindar) received the rent from a subordinate Tenure-holder (taluqdar), who gathered it from the Village Heads, who often collected it by means of. . . Village Accountants, who levied it from the individual husbandmen. Each of these had his own separate set of proprietory rights. . . Their rights, from the highest to the lowest, consisted in a title to finger the land-tax and pass it on.[3]

But even this account (Hunter warned) was "clearer and more systematic" than his evidence warranted, "for English words referring to landed rights have acquired a fixity and precision which they could not possess during a period of inchoate growth". What the Permanent Settlement in Orissa attempted to do (following upon the example of Bengal) was to erect the zemindar's "quasi-hereditary, quasi-transferable office of managing the land and transmitting the land-revenue, into a full proprietary tenure". Yet this title to property remained in some sense "abstract", since even

[1] W. W. Hunter, *The Annals of Rural Bengal* (1883), pp. 373-4.
[2] W. W. Hunter, *Orissa* (Calcutta, 1872), "being the second volume of the *Annals of Rural Bengal*", notably ch. 9. The settlement of Orissa was undertaken more scrupulously than that of Bengal, and was procrastinated from 1804 to 1815 to 1836 to 1866 (p. 257).
[3] *Ibid.*, pp. 214, 221-7.

"ownership" could not give to the new "owners" possession or occupancy of the land "as these belonged for the most part to the actual cultivators".[1] In all the debates of the 1770s to 1790s, the Whiggish British mind had largely passed over without consideration the rights of the *ryots* or real possessors of the land.[2] British administrators "defined and consolidated the title of the Landholders, and left the rights of the Cultivators unascertained. The former received a legislative *status*; the latter did not".[3]

Sir Charles Metcalfe saw the Permanent Settlement of Bengal as "the most sweeping act of oppression ever committed in any country, by which the whole landed property of the country had been transferred from the class of people entitled to it, to a set of Baboos, who have made their wealth by bribery and corruption". Lord Cornwallis (he said) was celebrated as "the great creator of private property in land in India". "I should say. . . that he was the creator of private property in the State revenue, and the great destroyer of private property in India, destroying hundreds of thousands of proprietors for every one that he gratuitously created. . ."[4]

Metcalfe argued that

> The real Proprietors of the Land are generally Individuals of the Village Communities who are also, for the most part, the natural occupiers and cultivators of the Land.

The injustice had been done by those who "wishing to advocate the rights of private property, applied English ideas and systems to India", and "classed the cultivators of India, the poor but lawful hereditary possessors of the land, with the labourers of England".[5] What Metcalfe did not see, or say, was that the dispossession of the commoners of England, and the English common law's insistence that "the nature

---

[1] *Ibid.*, pp. 227-8, 255-6, 260-1.

[2] An exception is in the Minutes of the able administrator, John Shore, see Guha, *op. cit.*, pp. 192-4. Also Charles William Boughton Rous, *Dissertation Concerning the Landed Property of Bengal* (1791).

[3] Hunter, *Orissa*, pp. 264-5. Even in the case of Bengal it became belatedly necessary (Act X of 1859) to recognise the "Right of Occupancy" (p. 228).

[4] Thompson, *Metcalfe*, pp. 267-8.

[5] *Ibid.*, esp. pp. 130-40.

of property. . . imports exclusive enjoyment" were the templates for the Settlement of Bengal.

Metcalfe was perhaps the most humane of those whom Eric Stokes described as mounting a paternalist or Burkean romantic reaction to Cornwallis's measures. (Since Burke was an advocate of political economy (below p. 252) and was not noted for defending the rights of commoners, the adjective may be misplaced.) The ideological battles within British ruling groups were fought out upon the Indian land. Subsequent Settlements withdrew from the simplistic Whig model. In Madras and Bombay Munro's *ryotwar* system sought to invest property rights in a yeomanry or middle peasantry.[1] Metcalfe sought even to sustain the communal property of the village. But the administration's inexorable demands for revenue, and its dispossession of defaulters, collapsed all intentions. After these came the utilitarians, a modernising urban liberalism of individualism, money and the market, contemptuous of the landed aristocracy and of "Gothic" or Hindu custom, and (with Bentham and James Mill) eager to impose administrative occidental despotism upon the East. Later again, commencing with Burma and extending in this century to West Africa, there was, in a remarkable series of reversals of Whig ideology, the settlement of extensive lands in the superordinate ownership of the State, combined with measures to inhibit the growth of private property in land.[2]

But all that belongs to a different epoch of imperialism, more preoccupied with the rights of money than with property in land. In Africa colonialism learned how to co-exist with tribal land usages and with customary law, indeed to invent customary law or to codify and institutionalise it in such ways as to create a new and more formal structure of rule.[3] One consequence might be the development of

[1] See Stokes, *op. cit.*, pp. 15, 18-22.

[2] See especially Robert Shenton, *The Development of Capitalism in Northern Nigeria* (Toronto, 1986), ch. 3, for an account of the interlocking pressures of bureaucracy (the expediency of taxation), merchant capital, and "Single Tax" socialist idealism which led to this reversal.

[3] See Terence Ranger, "The Invention of Tradition in Colonial Africa", in Eric Hobsbawm and Terence Ranger (eds.), *The Invention of Tradition* (Cambridge, 1983), esp. pp. 251-62. Even the act of writing

a dual economy and dual regimen, the one "modernised" and fully marketised, the other (indirect rule) sequestered within "custom", where the penetration of market forces was left to loosen labour more gently from the land, and to dissolve traditional forms of communal, or familial property-statute. The processes have not been (and are not) univocal, and there is a growing expert literature on customary law which should signal caution to a novice. Nor should we expect that the history of property in land could be written out in one single overarching theme, such as the triumph of possessive individualism, spanning the continents and centuries. The Permanent Settlement in Bengal was the zenith in the long ascent of the ideology of the patrician Whigs and the great gentry whom I still insist on seeing as an agrarian bourgeoisie. And by its very excess and doctrinaire impracticability it was also that ideology's *reductio ad absurdum.*

VI

This essay has been concerned to explore the interface between, on the one hand, law and ruling ideologies, and, on the other, common right usages and customary consciousness. It does not seek to revive in their old form certain debates, such as the effect of enclosure upon the creation of a proletariat. I am heartened to see that such issues are being addressed once more (in new forms) but my own evidence is not of such a kind as to add much to the discussion.[1]

Custom was a place in which many interests contested for advantage in the eighteenth century. Ultimately, at the point when commons were enclosed, it was a place of unqualified class conflict. The law was employed as an instrument of agrarian capitalism, furthering the "reasons" of

---

custom down could formalise it and expose it to new meanings and manipulation: see Goody, *op. cit.*, pp. 133-56; Don F. McKenzie, "The Sociology of a Text: Oral Culture, Literacy and Print in Early New Zealand", in P. Burke and R. Porter (eds.), *The Social History of Language* (Cambridge, 1987).

[1] The most substantial resistance to the triumphalism of the "agricultural revolution" historians came, not from an agricultural historian, but from Raymond Williams, *The Country and the City.*

improvement. If it is pretended that the law was impartial, deriving its rules from its own self-extrapolating logic, then we must reply that this pretence was class fraud.[1]

The zealous propagandists of enclosure cast as the villains and enemies of "progress" the stubborn cottagers, small-holders, the squatters and the "buccaneers" of forest and fen. But social classes can perform double roles, and these groups have been returning in recent years as the heroes and heroines of a different drama. For these villains can be seen as playing a revolutionary part in the growth of "proto-industrialisation" or of "the cottage economy". Their poverty and the marginality of their access to land was stimulating them to prodigious exertions in developing rural crafts and industrial by-employments on the edges of the commons. And they are flooding back into learned articles, triumphantly spinning or lace-making, carrying milk and poultry and butter and cheese to urban markets, grazing their pack-horses on the waste, introducing stocking-frames and looms, and going out on their depredations on the commons only in the intervals of making shoes or cloth or furniture or nails, and in general exercising every possible proto-industrial virtue.

I don't know what I am mocking — perhaps only the solemnity with which, every decade or two, the historical profession reverses its fashions. For undoubtedly the revision is helpful, and undoubtedly it is in the cottage economy that resources of common right were so important.[2] A Midlands pamphleteer in 1767 wrote that —

> There are some in almost all open parishes, who have houses, and little parcels of land in the field, with a right of common for a cow or three or four sheep, by the assistance of which, with the profits of a little trade or their daily labour, they procure a very comfortable living. Their land

[1] This was clearly expressed in the early working-class movement. The *Poor Man's Guardian* wrote, in 1835, "Property is but the creation of law. Whoever makes the law has the power of appropriating the national wealth. If they did not make the law, they would not have the property"; Malcolm Chase, *'The People's Farm'* (Oxford, 1988), p. 180.

[2] Especially helpful are David Levine, *Reproducing Families* (Cambridge, 1987), and Pat Hudson, "Proto-industrialisation: the Case of the West Riding Wool Textile Industry in the 18th and early 19th Centuries", *History Workshop*, 12 (1981), pp. 38-45.

furnished them with wheat and barley for bread, and, in many places, with beans or peas to feed a hog or two for meat; with the straw they thatch their cottage, and winter their cow, which gives a breakfast and supper of milk nine or ten months in the year for their families. These almost universally disapprove of inclosing.[1]

No doubt some of Atherstone's commoners were such. Others, were more fully occupied in trade: butchers, maltsters, alehouse-keepers, village traders of various kinds, blacksmiths, wheelwrights, masons and builders, those engaged in carpentry, tailoring, shoemaking. J. M. Martin has found such among the commoners disadvantaged by enclosure in South Warwickshire[2] and it was, exactly, in these "mixed agricultural and manufacturing villages" that Neeson has found, in her study of Northamptonshire, the strongest resistance to enclosure.[3]

Indeed, access to an extensive common could be critical to the livelihood of many villagers even if they had no common right, for they could rent upon it grazing for a cow, or parking and some fuel for their essential transport: i.e. grazing for a horse. In Maulden (Bedfordshire) whose extensive common was enclosed in 1797, to the accompaniment of riot (above p. 120) Young was told by a cottager in 1804 that "inclosing would ruin England; it was worse than ten wars. . . I kept four cows before the parish was inclosed, and now I do not keep so much as a goose". In Eaton (Bedfordshire) Arthur Young recorded that "the persons who were most affected and hurt" by the enclosure of 1796 were "higlers — fish, gingerbread, apples, carting for hire, &c; these kept horses, and turned without any right on the commons. . . they complain, but with no right to do it". In March (Cambridgeshire), enclosed in 1793, there were twenty families of dairy-men "who made an entire livelihood, —

---

[1] Anon. [S. Addington?], *An Enquiry into the Reasons for and against Inclosing the Common Fields* (Coventry, 1768). Cf. John Cowper, *An Essay Proving that Inclosing Commons and Common-field-Lands is Contrary to the Interest of the Nation* (1732), p. 8, referring to the loss from enclosure to "Carpenters, Wheelwrights, Millwrights, Smiths, Shoemakers, Taylors, and other Handicraftsmen, as well as to Shopkeepers".

[2] Martin, "Village Traders", *op. cit.*

[3] Neeson, "The Opponents of Enclosure", *op. cit.*

brought up their families decently; — after the enclosure they were reduced to day-labour, or to emigrate. These men were mere hirers and had no common rights themselves".[1] Such persons have eluded the attention of historians since they were neither agriculturalists nor emergent proletarians, and were of no importance to anyone except themselves.

When I first sketched this essay, more than twenty years ago, I rejected the triumphal accounts of improvers and modernisers, but I considered that radical historiography — and notably the Hammonds — had also been at fault in focussing too sharply on parliamentary enclosure, and hence in presenting us with a catastrophic paradigm. But such enclosure was only the last act of several centuries of agrarian capitalism, including extensive enclosure by agreement among the landholders. Relationships in most villages were already monetarised and subjected to market imperatives long before the act of enclosure struck. Common right usages clung by a thread to the customary tree, and many were over-ripe to fall. The wasp was already in them. Copyholders had become tenants at rack-rent, many cottagers had become day labourers, perhaps supplementing their wages with some spinning and a little stock. Grazing rights had been commercialised, and gates on the common could long have been hired. I remember teaching that, by the late eighteenth century, the communal forms of the unenclosed village were only a formal husk, whose kernel had been eaten by money from within.

Yet my own research and that of other scholars has persuaded me to look again. There were many villages where common right usages were a good deal more than form, not least those in which the resources of common and waste, Lammas and laneside grazing, wage-labour at harvest and in busy times, and crafts or by-employments each supplemented each other to make up a subsistence. The subsistence was not any more than meagre, the way of life might be desultory, but it was not subjected from early youth to death to an alien

---

[1] *Annals of Agriculture*, xlii (1804), pp. 27, 39, 323. But Young adds: "Their accounts of advantages, especially when they are gone, are not to be credited".

work-discipline.[1] In some part of their lives "the poor" still felt themselves to be self-determined, and in that sense "free". Indeed "the poor" was a gentry-made term which could sometimes disguise a sturdy peasantry. For John Clare the unenclosed moor was a symbol also of the poor's "freedom":

> Unbounded freedom ruled the wandering scene
> Nor fence of ownership crept in between
> To hide the prospect of the following eye
> Its only bondage was the circling sky. . .[2]

Moreover, even where the communal forms of the un-enclosed village were only an empty husk, form itself is not nothing. Form gave sanction to custom, that habitus, or field of play and possibility, in which interests knew how to co-exist and contend. And it reproduced an oral tradition, a customary consciousness, in which rights were asserted as "ours" rather than as mine or thine. To be sure, this was not some generous and universalistic communist spirit. "Natures wide and common sky"[3] is also the "circling sky": the bounded, circular, jealously possessive consciousness of the parish.[4] The communal economy was parochial and exclusive: if Weldon's rights were "ours", then Brigstock men and women must be kept out (above, p. 99). But for those who "belonged" to the parish, there remained some sense that they "owned" it and had a voice in its regula-tion.[5] In this sense, enclosure, as it came to each village, was experienced as catastrophic to the customary culture. Within the space of a year or two the labourers' world shrank suddenly, from "our" parish to a cottage which might not be their own:

---

[1] Where rural industries developed, they could also be the locus for intensive familial self-exploitation: see J. de Vries, "Labour/Leisure Trade Off", *Peasant Studies*, i (1972).

[2] John Clare, "The Mores".

[3] John Clare, "Emmonsales Heath".

[4] See John Barrell, *The Idea of Landscape and the Sense of Place, 1730-1840: an Approach to the Poetry of John Clare* (Cambridge, 1972).

[5] For the notion of the "real" owners — families with long local presence — see Marilyn Strathern, *Kinship at the Core* (Cambridge, 1981).

Fence now meets fence in owners little bounds
Of field and meadow large as garden grounds
In little parcels little minds to please
With men and flocks imprisoned ill at ease.[1]

Enclosure was announced with the "hated sign" of the private owner, which ordered labourers (like any strangers) not to "trespass" on their own commons.

Despite the long erosion of common right usages and the long pre-history of capitalist penetration into the peasant economy, parliamentary enclosure still "marked a turning-point in the social history of many English villages", a turning-point identified most clearly by Dr Neeson:

> It struck at the roots of the economy of multiple occupations and it taught the small peasantry the new reality of class relations. John Clare's hatred of its symbol — the newly prosperous, socially aspirant farmer — is illustration of the growing separation of classes that enclosure embodied. . . Perhaps this separation was a long time coming. But until enclosure it was masked by other relationships born of customary agricultural regulation and shared use-rights over land. The organization of work in the open field system encouraged co-operation; and defence of common rights required the protection of lesser rights as well as greater. Enclosure tore away the mask not only to reveal more clearly the different interests of small and large landowners but also to profit one at the expense of the other. . . Enclosure had a terrible but instructive visibility.[2]

We are fortunate to have in John Clare's writing a sensitive record of this customary consciousness as it came under agonising strain. It does not matter whether enclosure in Helpston resulted in more or fewer small farmers. The immiseration of the rural workers was not at the centre of Clare's poetic concern (although he did not forget it). What concerned him more was the new instrumental and exploitative stance, not only towards labour ("that necessary tool of wealth and pride") but also towards the natural world. It is not (as some critics suppose) that this peasant poet was more motivated by "aesthetic" than by social protest. Clare may be described, without hindsight, as a poet of ecological protest: he was not writing about man here and

---

[1] John Clare, "The Mores".
[2] Neeson, "Opponents of Enclosure".

nature there, but lamenting a threatened equilibrium in which both were involved:

> Ah cruel foes with plenty blest
> So ankering after more
> To lay the greens and pasture waste
> Which proffited before.[1]

The mutual profit of both greens and pasture and of their farmers is suggested "before"; now these are laid waste for the sole profit of the enclosers.

Helpston was enclosed during Clare's adolescence, and thereafter pre-enclosure Helpston was recalled as an Eden, a world of lost childhood innocence. No doubt his memories were sweetened by the contrast:

> I was never easy but when I was in the fields passing my sabbath and leisure with the shepherds & herdboys as fancys prompted sometimes playing at marbles on the smooth-beaten sheeptracks or leapfrog among the thymy molehills sometimes running among the corn to get the red & blue flowers for cockades to play at soldiers or running into the woods to hunt strawberries or stealing peas in churchtime. . .[2]

This conveys his sense of belonging, since childhood — perhaps especially in childhood — within a shared and "free" communal space, a space which shrank within the fenced bounds of private ownership with enclosure.

We do not have to ask for other evidence to support John Clare, since his poems *are* the evidence of a tormented customary consciousness. If Clare became known as a poet of locality, this also belongs to the customary consciousness. There is a set of customary norms and practices here which go together. There is an economy in which exchanges of services and favours remain significant, of which local features of the landscape are reminders. There is the local idiom of dialect — drawn upon so effectively in Clare's verse — which seems (deceptively) to be a more "social" product than standard-ised English, — dialect which was becoming in the eighteenth century, not the medium of local or regional speech but of regional *plebeian* speech, and which is itself the sign of a

---

[1] John Clare, "The Lamentations of Round-Oak Waters".
[2] *The Prose of John Clare*, ed. J. W. and Anne Tibble (1951), p. 12.

certain kind of customary consciousness.[1] There are local institutions for regulating the occasions of the community, including the poor laws, which might still, in pre-enclosure days be administered with a rough rule-of-thumb neighbourliness, but which in step with "improvement" acquired their end-of-century mix of indignity, dependency and discipline. "The parish", a term which once suggested home and security, was becoming a term ("on the parish") suggestive of meanness and shame. And, finally, there are the forms of customary pastimes and of ritual in which people "lose themselves in recreation in order to recreate themselves as a community".[2]

No doubt we will be warned against sentimentalising this customary pre-enclosure consciousness, which was the vector of its own kinds of narrowness, brutality and superstition. That is true, but it is sometimes the only part of the truth which is now remembered. The commons and wastes shrank, in the nineteenth century, to the village greens (if such survived) and communally-shared custom shrank to the "calendar customs" and survivals collected by the folklorists. I have been trying to recall customary consciousness in a larger sense, in which community was sustained by actual resources and usages. Young Clare was driven to fury by a farmer who actually locked up a public pump —

> To lock up Water — must undoubted stand
> Among the Customs of a Christian Land
> An Action quite Uncommon. . .[3]

No doubt he savoured the double resonance of "Uncommon". The private appropriation of the natural world which enclosure symbolised was (for Clare) an offence to both "nature" and human community, and he identified as

---

[1] I find especially helpful on many of these points Johanne Clare, *John Clare and the Bounds of Circumstance* (Kingston and Montreal, 1987).

[2] See *ibid.*, p. 99; Robert W. Malcolmson, *Popular Recreations in English Society* (Cambridge, 1973), esp. ch. 4 and Hugh Cunningham, *Leisure in the Industrial Revolution* (1980), ch. 2.

[3] John Clare, *The Parish*, ed. Eric Robinson and David Powell, notes p. 90.

enemy to both a logic which is with us still in factory farming and the privatisation of water.

Clare's remarkable enclosure elegies, "The Mores" and "Remembrances", take us back within that conceptual universe before "lawless laws enclosure came". After leading us through childhood memories of play upon the common he comes with startling suddenness upon the gamekeeper's gibbet:

> I see the little mouldiwarps hang sweeing to the wind
> On the only aged willow that in all the field remains
> And nature hides her face while theyre sweeing in their chains
> And in silent murmuring complains
> Here was commons for their hills where they seek for freedom still
> Though every commons gone and though traps are set to kill
> The little homeless miners. . .

These are real moles, but the image is also one of displaced commoners. So close is the mutual ecological imbrication of the human and the natural that each might stand for the other. And Clare strains to convey the strength of feeling of "a rhyming peasant"[1] for a locality whose landmarks are not privately possessed but still (in a shared sense) intensely *owned*!

> By Langley bush I roam but the bush hath left its hill
> On cowper green I stray tis a desert strange and chill
> And spreading lea close oak ere decay had penned its will
> To the axe of the spoiler and self interest fell a prey
> And crossberry way and old round oaks narrow lane
> With its hollow trees like pulpits I shall never see again
> Inclosure like a buonaparte let not a thing remain
> It levelled every bush and tree and levelled every hill
> And hung the moles for traitors — though the brook is running still
> It runs a naked stream cold and chill[2]

The old landmarks of the parish perambulation have gone and that whole universe of custom is now only a memory in the poet's head. The gentry had accomplished the final and most precipitate episode of enclosures during the French

---

[1] Clare wrote that "The Village Minstrel" dissatisfied him because "it does not describe the feelings of a rhyming peasant strongly or localy enough", *Selected Poems and Prose of John Clare*, ed. Eric Robinson and G. Summerfield (Oxford, 1967), p. 67.

[2] John Clare, "Remembrances".

Wars, with the cry that "Bony is coming!", and they had harried their domestic opponents with their Associations for the Protection of Property against Republicans and Levellers. In the word "levelled" Clare turns their world around and reveals its underside of greed and repression. As the Maulden cottager told Arthur Young in 1804 "Inclosing was worse than ten wars". And in the moles, hanged and "sweeing to the wind" there is probably an allusion — for "Remembrances" was written in 1832 — to the Swing riots of 1830 and the victims selected for the gallows.

It is not that John Clare — nor the commoners for whom he spoke — were primitive communists. Viewed from their standpoint, the communal forms expressed an alternative notion of possession, in the petty and particular rights and usages which were transmitted in custom as the *properties* of the poor. Common right, which was in lax terms coterminous with settlement, was *local* right, and hence was also a power to exclude strangers. Enclosure, in taking the commons away from the poor, made them strangers in their own land.

crude "social tension chart" was first put forward in 1948.[1] According to this, we need only bring together an index of unemployment and one of high food prices to be able to chart the course of social disturbance. This contains a self-evident truth (people protest when they are hungry): and in much the same way a "sexual tension chart" would show that the onset of sexual maturity can be correlated with a greater frequency of sexual activity. The objection is that such a chart, if used unwisely, may conclude investigation at the exact point at which it becomes of serious sociological or cultural interest: being hungry (or being sexy), what do people do? How is their behaviour modified by custom, culture, and reason? And (having granted that the primary stimulus of "distress" is present) does their behaviour contribute towards any more complex, culturally-mediated function, which cannot be reduced — however long it is stewed over the fires of statistical analysis — back to stimulus once again?

Too many of our growth historians are guilty of a crass economic reductionism, obliterating the complexities of motive, behaviour, and function, which, if they noted it in the work of their marxist analogues, would make them protest. The weakness which these explanations share is an abbreviated view of economic man. What is perhaps an occasion for surprise is the schizoid intellectual climate, which permits this quantitative historiography to co-exist (in the same places and sometimes in the same minds) with a social anthropology which derives from Durkheim, Weber, or Malinowski. We know all about the delicate tissue of social norms and reciprocities which regulates the life of Trobriand islanders, and the psychic energies involved in the cargo cults of Melanesia; but at some point this infinitely-complex social creature, Melanesian man, becomes (in our histories) the eighteenth-century English collier who claps his hand spasmodically upon his stomach, and responds to elementary economic stimuli.

[1] W. W. Rostow, *British Economy in the Nineteenth Century* (Oxford, 1948), esp. pp. 122-5. Among the more interesting studies which correlate prices, harvests, and popular disturbance are: E. J. Hobsbawm, "Economic Fluctuations and Some Social Movements", in *Labouring Men* (1964) and T. S. Ashton, *Economic Fluctuations in England, 1700-1800* (Oxford, 1959).

To the spasmodic I will oppose my own view.[1] It is possible to detect in almost every eighteenth-century crowd action some legitimising notion. By the notion of legitimation I mean that the men and women in the crowd were informed by the belief that they were defending traditional rights or customs; and, in general, that they were supported by the wider consensus of the community. On occasion this popular consensus was endorsed by some measure of licence afforded by the authorities. More commonly, the consensus was so strong that it overrode motives of fear or deference.

The food riot in eighteenth-century England was a highly complex form of direct popular action, disciplined and with clear objectives. How far these objectives were achieved — that is, how far the food riot was a "successful" form of action — is too intricate a question to tackle within the limits of a chapter; but the question can at least be posed (rather than, as is customary, being dismissed unexamined with a negative), and this cannot be done until the crowd's own objectives are identified. It is of course true that riots were triggered off by soaring prices, by malpractices among dealers, or by hunger. But these grievances operated within a popular consensus as to what were legitimate and what were illegitimate practices in marketing, milling, baking, etc. This in its turn was grounded upon a consistent traditional view of social norms and obligations, of the proper economic functions of several parties within the community, which, taken together, can be said to constitute the moral economy of the poor. An outrage to these moral assumptions, quite as much as actual deprivation, was the usual occasion for direct action.

While this moral economy cannot be described as "political" in any advanced sense, nevertheless it cannot be described as unpolitical either, since it supposed definite, and passionately held, notions of the common weal — notions which, indeed, found some support in the paternalist tradition of the authorities; notions which the people

[1] I have found most helpful the pioneering study by R. B. Rose, "Eighteenth Century Price Riots and Public Policy in England", *International Review of Social History*, vi (1961); and G. Rudé, *The Crowd in History* (New York, 1964).

re-echoed so loudly in their turn that the authorities were, in some measure, the prisoners of the people. Hence this moral economy impinged very generally upon eighteenth-century government and thought, and did not only intrude at moments of disturbance. The word "riot" is too small to encompass all this.

II

As we speak of the cash-nexus which emerged through the industrial revolution, so there is a sense in which we can speak of the eighteenth-century bread-nexus. The conflict between the countryside and the town was mediated by the price of bread. The conflict between traditionalism and the new political economy turned upon the Corn Laws. Economic class-conflict in nineteenth-century England found its characteristic expression in the matter of wages; in eighteenth-century England the working people were most quickly inflamed to action by rising prices.

This highly-sensitive consumer-consciousness co-existed with the great age of agricultural improvement, in the corn belt of the East and South. Those years which brought English agriculture to a new pitch of excellence were punctuated by the riots — or, as contemporaries often described them, the "insurrections" or "risings of the poor" — of 1709, 1740, 1756-7, 1766-7, 1773, 1782, and, above all, 1795 and 1800-1. This buoyant capitalist industry floated upon an irascible market which might at any time dissolve into marauding bands, who scoured the countryside with bludgeons, or rose in the market-place to "set the price" of provisions at the popular level. The fortunes of those most vigorous capitalist classes rested, in the final analysis, upon the sale of cereals, meat, wool; and the first two must be sold, with little intermediary processing, to the millions who were the consumers. Hence the frictions of the market-place take us into a central area of the nation's life.

The labouring people in the eighteenth century did not live by bread alone, but (as the budgets collected by Eden and David Davies show) many of them lived very largely on bread. This bread was not altogether wheaten, although wheaten bread gained ground steadily over other varieties until the early 1790s. In the 1760s Charles Smith estimated that of a supposed population of about six millions in England and Wales, 3,750,000 were wheat-eaters, 888,000 ate rye, 739,000 ate barley, and 623,000 oats.[1] By 1790 we may judge that at least two-thirds of the population were eating wheat.[2] The pattern of consumption reflected, in part, comparative degrees of poverty, and, in part, ecological conditions. Districts with poor soils and upland districts (like the Pennines) where wheat will not ripen, were the strongholds of other cereals. Still, in the 1790s, the Cornish tinners subsisted largely on barley bread. Much oatmeal was consumed in Lancashire and Yorkshire — and not only by the poor.[3] Accounts from Northumberland conflict, but it would seem that Newcastle and many of the surrounding pit villages had by then gone over to wheat, while the countryside and smaller towns subsisted on oatmeal, rye bread, maslin,[4] or a mixture of barley and "gray pease".[5]

Through the century, again, white bread was gaining upon darker wholemeal varieties. This was partly a matter of status-values which became attached to white bread, but by no means wholly so. The problem is most complex, but several aspects may be briefly mentioned. It was to the advantage of bakers and of millers to sell white bread or fine flour, since the profit which might be gained from such sales was, in general, larger. (Ironically, this was in part a consequence of paternalist consumer-protection, since the Assize of Bread was intended to prevent the bakers from taking their profit from the bread of the poor; hence it was in

[1] C. Smith, *Three Tracts on the Corn-Trade and Corn-Laws*, 2nd edn. (1766), pp. 140, 182-5.

[2] See Fitzjohn Brand, *A Determination of the Average Depression of Wheat in War below that of the Preceding Peace etc.* (1800), pp. 62-3, 96.

[3] These generalisations are supported by "replies from towns as to bread in use", returned to the Privy Council in 1796 in PRO, PC 1/33/A.87 and A.88.

[4] For maslin (a mixed bread of several cereals) see Sir William Ashley, *The Bread of our Forefathers* (Oxford, 1928), pp. 16-19.

[5] See Smith, *op. cit.*, p. 194 (for 1765). But the mayor of Newcastle reported (4 May 1796) that rye bread was "much used by the workmen employed in the Coal Trade", and a reporter from Hexham Abbey said that barley, barley and gray pease, or beans, "is the only bread of the labouring poor and farmers' servants and even of many farmers", with rye or maslin in the towns: PRO, PC 1/33/A.88.

the baker's interest to make as little "household" bread as possible, and that little nasty.[1]) In the cities, which were alert to the dangers of adulteration, dark bread was suspect as offering easy concealment for noxious additives. In the last decades of the century many millers adapted their machinery and bolting-cloths, so that they were not in fact able to dress the flour for the intermediary "household" loaf, producing only the finer qualities for the white loaf and the "offal" for a brown loaf which one observer found "so musty, griping, and pernicious as to endanger the constitution".[2] The attempts of the authorities, in times of scarcity, to impose the manufacture of coarser grades (or, as in 1795, the general use of the "household" loaf), were attended by many difficulties, and often resistance by both millers and bakers.[3]

By the end of the century feelings of status were profoundly involved wherever wheaten bread prevailed, and was threatened by a coarser mixture. There is a suggestion that labourers accustomed to wheaten bread actually could not work — suffered from weakness, indigestion, or nausea — if forced to change to rougher mixtures.[4] Even in the face of the outrageous prices of 1795 and 1800-1, the resistance of many of the working people was impermeable.[5] The Guild Stewards of Calne informed the Privy Council in 1796 that

[1] Nathaniel Forster, *An Enquiry into the Cause of the High Price of Provisions* (1767), pp. 144-7.

[2] J. S. Girdler, *Observations on the Pernicious Consequences of Fore-stalling, Regrating and Ingrossing* (1800), p. 88.

[3] The problem was discussed lucidly in [Governor] Pownall, *Considerations on the Scarcity and High Prices of Bread-corn and Bread* (Cambridge, 1795), esp. pp. 25-7. See also Lord John Sheffield, *Remarks on the Deficiency of Grain occasioned by the bad Harvest of 1799* (1800), esp. pp. 105-6 for the evidence that (1795) "there is no household bread made in London". A Honiton correspondent in 1766 described household bread as "a base mixture of fermented Bran ground down and bolted, to which is added the worst kind of meal not rang'd": HMC, *City of Exeter*, series lxxiii (1916), p. 255. On this very complex question see further S. and B. Webb, "The Assize of Bread", *Economic Journal*, xiv (1904), esp. pp. 203-6.

[4] See e.g. Lord Hawkesbury to the duke of Portland, 19 May 1797, in PRO, HO 42/34.

[5] See R. N. Salaman, *The History and Social Influence of the Potato* (Cambridge, 1949), esp. pp. 493-517. Resistance extended from the wheat-eating South and Midlands to the oatmeal-eating North; a correspondent

"creditable" people were using the barley-and-wheat mixture required by authority, and that the manufacturing and labouring poor with large families

> have in general used barley bread alone. The rest, making perhaps something about one-third of the poor manufactures and others, with smaller families (saying they could get nothing *but bread*) have, as before the scarcity, eat nothing but baker's bread, made of wheatmeal called seconds.[1]

The Bailiff of Reigate reported in similar terms:

> . . . as to the poor labourers who have scarce any sustenance but bread, & from the custom of the neighbourhood have always eaten bread made of wheat only; amongst these I have neither urged nor wished a mixture of bread, least they should not be nourished sufficiently to support their labour.

Those few labourers who had tried a mixture "found themselves feeble, hot, & unable to labour with any degree of vigor".[2] When, in December 1800, the government introduced an Act (popularly known as the Brown Bread Act or "Poison Act") which prohibited millers from making any other than wholemeal flour, the response of the people was immediate. At Horsham (Sussex),

> A number of women. . . proceeded to Gosden wind-mill, where, abusing the miller for having served them with brown flour, they seized on the cloth with which he was then dressing meal according to the directions of the Bread Act, and cut it into a thousand pieces; threatening at the same time to serve all similar utensils he might in future attempt to use in the same manner. The amazonian leader of this petticoated cavalcade afterwards regaled her associates with a guinea's worth of liquor at the Crab Tree public-house.

---

from Stockport in 1795 noted that "a very liberal subscription has been entered into for the purpose of distributing oatmeal & other provisions among the poor at reduced prices — This measure, I am sorry to say, gives little satisfaction to the common people, who are still clamorous & insist on having wheaten bread": PRO, WO 1/1094. See also J. L. and B. Hammond, *The Village Labourer* (1966), pp. 119-23.

[1] PRO, PC 1/33/A.88. Compare the return from J. Boucher, vicar of Epsom, 8 Nov. 1800 in HO 42/54: "Our Poor live not only on the finest wheaten bread, but almost on bread alone."

[2] PRO, PC 1/33/A.88.

As a result of such actions, the Act was repealed in less than two months.[1]

When prices were high, more than one-half of the weekly budget of a labourer's family might be spent on bread.[2] How did these cereals pass, from the crops growing in the field, to the labourers' homes? At first sight it appears simple. There is the corn: it is harvested, threshed, taken to market, ground at the mill, baked, and eaten. But at every point within this process there are radiating complexities, opportunities for extortion, flash-points around which riots could arise. And it is scarcely possible to proceed further without sketching out, in a schematic way, the paternalist model of the marketing and manufacturing process — the traditional platonic ideal appealed to in Statute, pamphlet, or protest movement — against which the awkward realities of commerce and consumption were in friction.

The paternalist model existed in an eroded body of Statute law, as well as common law and custom. It was the model which, very often, informed the actions of government in times of emergency until the 1770s; and to which many local magistrates continued to appeal. In this model, marketing should be, so far as possible, *direct*, from the farmer to the consumer. The farmers should bring their corn in bulk to the local pitching market; they should not sell it while standing in the field, nor should they withhold it in the hope of rising prices. The markets should be controlled; no sales should be made before stated times, when a bell would ring; the poor should have the opportunity to buy grain, flour, or meal first, in small parcels, with duly-supervised weights and measures.

---

[1] PRO, PC 1/33/;a.88; *Reading Mercury*, 16 Feb. 1801. Hostility to these changes in milling, which were imposed by an Act of 1800 (41 Geo. III, c.16) was especially strong in Surrey and Sussex. Complainants produced samples of the new bread to a Surrey JP: "They represented it as disagreeable to the taste (as indeed it was), as utterly incompetent to support them under their daily labour, & as productive of bowelly complaints to them and to their children in particular": Thomas Turton to Portland, 7 Feb. 1801, HO 42/61. The Act was repealed in 1801: 42 Geo. III, c.2.

[2] See especially the budgets in D. Davies, *The Case of Labourers in Husbandry* (Bath, 1795); and Sir Frederick Eden, *The State of the Poor* (1797). Also D. J. V. Jones, "The Corn Riots in Wales, 1793-1801", *Welsh Hist. Rev.*, ii, 4 (1965), App. I, p. 347.

At a certain hour, when their needs were satisfied, a second bell would ring, and larger dealers (duly licensed) might make their purchases. Dealers were hedged around with many restrictions, inscribed upon the musty parchments of the laws against forestalling, regrating and engrossing, codified in the reign of Edward VI. They must not buy (and farmers must not sell) by sample. They must not buy standing crops, nor might they purchase to sell again (within three months) in the same market at a profit, or in neighbouring markets, and so on. Indeed, for most of the eighteenth century the middleman remained legally suspect, and his operations were, in theory, severely restricted.[1]

From market-supervision we pass to consumer-protection. Millers and — to a greater degree — bakers were considered as servants of the community, working not for a profit but for a fair allowance. Many of the poor would buy their grain direct in the market (or obtain it as supplement to wages or in gleaning); they would take it to the mill to be ground, where the miller might exact a customary toll, and then would bake their own bread. In London and those large towns where this had long ceased to be the rule, the baker's allowance or profit was calculated strictly according to the Assize of Bread, whereby either the price or the weight of the loaf was ordered in relation to the ruling price of wheat.[2]

This model, of course, parts company at many points with eighteenth-century realities. What is more surprising is to note how far parts of it were still operative. Thus Aikin in 1795 is able to describe the orderly regulation of Preston market:

[1] The best general study of eighteenth-century corn marketing remains R. B. Westerfield, *Middlemen in English Business, 1660-1760* (New Haven, 1915), ch. 2. Also see N. S. B. Gras, *The Evolution of the English Corn Market from the Twelfth to the Eighteenth Century* (Cambridge, Mass., 1915); D. G. Barnes, *A History of the English Corn Laws* (1930); C. R. Fay, *The Corn Laws and Social England* (Cambridge, 1932); E. Lipson, *Economic History of England*, 6th edn. (1956), ii, pp. 419-48; L. W. Moffitt, *England on the Eve of the Industrial Revolution* (1925), ch. 3; G. E. Fussell and C. Goodman, "Traffic in Farm Produce in Eighteenth Century England", *Agricultural History*, xii, 2 (1938); Janet Blackman, "The Food Supply of an Industrial Town (Sheffield)", *Business History*, v (1963).

[2] S. and B. Webb, "The Assize of Bread".

The weekly markets. . . are extremely well regulated to prevent forestalling and regrating. None but the town's-people are permitted to buy during the first hour, which is from eight to nine in the morning: at nine others may purchase: but nothing unsold must be withdrawn from the market till one o'clock, fish excepted. . .[1]

In the same year in the South-West (another area noted for traditionalism) the city authorities at Exeter attempted to control "hucksters, higlers, and retailers" by excluding them from the market between 8 a.m. and noon, at which hours the Guildhall bell would be rung.[2] The Assize of Bread was still effective throughout the eighteenth century in London and in many market towns.[3] If we follow through the case of sale by sample we may observe how dangerous it is to assume prematurely the dissolution of the customary restrictions.

It is often supposed that sale of corn by sample was general by the middle of the seventeenth century, when Best describes the practice in East Yorkshire,[4] and certainly by 1725, when Defoe gave his famous account of the corn trade.[5] But, while many large farmers were no doubt selling by sample in

[1] J. Aikin, *A Description of the Country from thirty to forty Miles round Manchester* (1795), p. 286. One of the best surviving records of a well-regulated market in the eighteenth century is that of Manchester. Here market lookers for fish and flesh, for corn weights and measures, for white meats, for the Assize of Bread, aletasters, and officers to prevent "engrossing, forestalling and regretting" were appointed throughout the century, and fines for short weight and measure, unmarketable meat, etc. were frequent until the 1750s; supervision thereafter was somewhat more perfunctory (although continuing) with a revival of vigilance in the 1790s. Fines were imposed for selling loads of grain before the market bell in 1734, 1737, and 1748 (when William Wyat was fined 20s. "for selling before the Bell rung and declaring he would sell at any Time of the Day in Spite of either Lord of the Mannor or any person else"), and again in 1766. *The Court Leet Records of the Manor of Manchester*, ed. J. P. Earwaker (Manchester, 1888/9), vii, viii and ix, *passim*. For the regulation of forestalling at Manchester, see note 3 on p. 209.

[2] Proclamation by Exeter Town Clerk, 28 March 1795, PRO, HO 42/34.

[3] See S. and B. Webb, *op. cit., passim*; and J. Burnett, "The Baking Industry in the Nineteenth Century", *Business History*, v. (1963), pp. 98-9.

[4] *Rural Economy in Yorkshire in 1641* (Surtees Society, xxxiii, 1857), pp. 99-105.

[5] *The Complete English Tradesman* (1727), ii, pt. 2.

most counties by this date, the old pitching markets were still common, and even survived in the environs of London. In 1718 a pamphleteer described the decline of country markets as having taken place only in recent years:

> One can see little else besides toy-shops and stalls for bawbles and knick-knacks. . . The tolls are sunk to nothing; and where, in the memory of many inhabitants, there us'd to come to town upon a day, one, two, perhaps three, and in some boroughs, four hundred loads of corn, now grass grows in the market-place.

The farmers (he complained) had come to shun the market and to deal with jobbers and other "interlopers" at their doors. Other farmers still brought to market a single load "to make a show of a market, and to have a Price set", but the main business was done in "parcels of corn in a bag or handkerchief which are called *samples*".[1]

This was, indeed, the drift of things. But many smaller farmers continued to pitch their grain in the market as before; and the old model remained in men's minds as a source of resentment. Again and again the new marketing procedures were contested. In 1710 a petition on behalf of the poor people of Stony Stratford (Buckinghamshire) complains that the farmers and dealers were "buying and selling in the farmyards and att their Barne Doores soo that now the poor Inhabitants cannot have a Grist at reasonable rates for our money which is a Great Calamity".[2] In 1733 several boroughs petitioned the House of Commons against the practice: Haslemere (Surrey) complained of millers and meal-men engrossing the trade — they "secretly bought great quantities of corn by small samples, refusing to buy such as hath been pitch'd in open market".[3] There is a suggestion of something underhand in the practice, and of a loss of transparency in the marketing procedure.

As the century advances the complaints do not die down, although they tend to move northwards and westwards. In

---

[1] Anon., *An Essay to prove that Regrators, Engrossers, Forestallers, Hawkers, and Jobbers of Corn, Cattle, and other Marketable Goods are Destructive of Trade, Oppressors to the Poor, and a Common Nuisance to the Kingdom in General* (1719), pp. 13, 18-20.

[2] Bucks. CRO, Quarter Sessions, Michaelmas 1710.

[3] *Commons Journals*, 2 March 1733.

the dearth of 1756 the Privy Council, in addition to setting in motion the old laws against forestalling, issued a proclamation enjoining "all farmers, under severe penalties, to bring their corn to open market, and not to sell by sample at their own dwellings".[1] But the authorities did not like to be pressed on the point too closely: in 1766 (another year of scarcity) the Surrey magistrates enquired whether buying by sample in fact remained a punishable offence, and received a portentously evasive reply — H.M.'s Secretary is not by his office entitled to give interpretation to the Laws.[2]

Two letters give some insight into the spread of new practices towards the West. A correspondent writing to Lord Shelburne in 1766 accused the dealers and millers at Chippenham of "confederacy":

> He himself sent to market for a quarter of wheat, and though there were many loads there, and it soon after the market bell rang, wherever his agent applied, the answer was " 'Tis sold". So that, though. . . to avoid the penalty of the law, they bring it to market, yet the bargain is made before, and the market is but a farce. . .[3]

(Such practices could be the actual occasion of riot: in June 1757 it was reported that "the population rose at Oxford and in a few minutes seized and divided a load of corn that was suspected to have been bought by sample, and only brought to the market to save appearances".[4]) The second letter, from a correspondent in Dorchester in 1772, describes a different practice of market-fixing: he claimed that the great farmers got together to fix the price before the market,

> and many of these men won't sell less than forty bushels, which the poor can't purchase. Therefore the miller, who is no enemy to the farmer, gives the price he asks and the poor must come to his terms.[5]

Paternalists and the poor continued to complain at the extension of market practices which we, looking back, tend

---

[1] PRO, PC 1/6/63.
[2] *Calendar of Home Office Papers* (1879), 1766, pp. 92-4.
[3] *Ibid.*, pp. 91-2.
[4] *Gentleman's Magazine*, xxvii (1757), p. 286.
[5] Anonymous letter in PRO, SP 37/9.

to assume as inevitable and "natural".[1] But what may now appear as inevitable was not, in the eighteenth century necessarily a matter for approval. A characteristic pamphlet (of 1768) exclaimed indignantly against the supposed liberty of every farmer to do as he likes with his own. This would be a "natural", not a "civil" liberty.

> It cannot then be said to be the liberty of a citizen, or of one who lives under the protection of any community; it is rather the liberty of a savage; therefore he who avails himself thereof, deserves not that protection, the power of Society affords.

Attendance of the farmer at market is "a material part of his duty; he should not be suffered to secret or to dispose of his goods elsewhere".[2] But after the 1760s the pitching markets performed so little function in most parts of the South and the Midlands that, in these districts, the complaint against sample-sale is less often heard, although the complaint that the poor cannot buy in small parcels is still being made at the end of the century.[3] In parts of the North it was a different matter. A petition of Leeds labourers in 1795 complains of the "corn factors and the millers and a set of peopul which we call hucksters and mealmen who have got the corn into thare hands that they may hold it up and sell it at thare owne price or they will not sell it." "The farmers carry no corn to market but what they carre in thare pocket for thare sample. . . which cause the poore to groane very

---

[1] Examples, from an abundant literature, will be found in *Gentleman's Magazine*, xxvi (1756), p. 534; Anon. [Ralph Courteville], *The Cries of the Public* (1758), p. 25; Anon. ["C.L."], *A Letter to a Member of Parliament proposing Amendments to the Laws against Forestallers, Ingrossers, and Regraters* (1757), pp. 5-8; *Museum Rusticum et Commerciale*, iv (1765), p. 199; Forster, *op. cit.*, p. 97.

[2] Anon., *An Enquiry into the Price of Wheat, Malt, etc.* (1768), pp. 119-23.

[3] See e.g. Davies (below p. 216). It was reported from Cornwall in 1795 that "many farmers refuse to sell [barley] in small quantities to the poor, which causes a great murmuring": PRO, HO 42/34; and from Essex in 1800 that "in some places no sale takes place excepting at the ordinaries, where buyers and sellers (chiefly Millers and Factors) dine together. . . the benefit of the Market is almost lost to the neighbourhood"; such practices are mentioned "with great indignation by the lower orders": PRO, HO 42/54.

much."[1] So long it took for a process, which is often dated from at least one hundred years earlier, to work its way out.

This example has been followed to illustrate the density and particularity of the detail, the diversity of local practices, and the way in which popular resentment could arise as old market practices changed. The same density, the same diversity, exists throughout the scarcely-charted area of marketing. The paternalist model was, of course, breaking down at many other points. The Assize of Bread, although effective in checking the profits of bakers, simply reflected the ruling price of wheat or flour, and could in no way influence these. The millers were now, in Hertfordshire and the Thames Valley, very substantial entrepreneurs, and sometimes dealers in grain or malt as well as large-scale manufacturers of flour.[2] Outside the main corn-growing districts, urban markets simply could not be supplied without the operation of factors whose activities would have been nullified if legislation against forestallers had been strictly enforced.

How far did the authorities recognise that their model was drifting apart from reality? The answer must change with the authorities concerned and with the advance of the century. But a general answer can be offered: the paternalists did, in their normal practice, recognise much of the change, but they referred back to this model whenever emergency arose. In this they were in part the prisoners of the people, who adopted parts of the model as their right and heritage. There is even an impression that ambiguity was actually welcomed. It gave magistrates in disturbed districts, in time of dearth, some room for manoeuvre, and some endorsement to their attempts to reduce prices by suasion. When the Privy Council authorised (as it did in 1709, 1740, 1756 and 1766) the posting of proclamations in unreadable Gothic type threatening dire penalties against forestallers, badgers, laders, broggers, hucksters, etc., it helped the magistrates to put the fear of God into local millers and dealers. It is true that the legislation against forestallers was repealed in 1772; but the

[1] PRO, HO 42/35.
[2] See F. J. Fisher, "The Development of the London Food Market, 1540-1640", *Econ. Hist. Rev.*, v (1934-5).

repealing act was not well drawn, and during the next major scarcity in 1795 Lord Kenyon, the chief justice, took it upon himself to announce that forestalling remained an indictable offence at common law: "though the act of Edward VI be repealed (whether wisely or unwisely I take not upon me to say) yet it still remains an offence at common law, co-eval with the constitution. . .".[1] The trickle of prosecutions which can be observed throughout the century — usually for petty offences and only in years of scarcity — did not dry up: indeed, there were probably more in 1795 and 1800-1 than at any time in the previous twenty-five years.[2] But it is clear that they were designed for symbolic effect, as demonstrations to the poor that the authorities were acting vigilantly in their interests.

Hence the paternalist model had an ideal existence, and also a fragmentary real existence. In years of good harvests and moderate prices, the authorities lapsed into forgetfulness. But if prices rose and the poor became turbulent, it was revived, at least for symbolic effect.

III

Few intellectual victories have been more overwhelming than that which the proponents of the new political economy won in the matter of the regulation of the internal corn trade. Indeed, so absolute has the victory seemed to some historians that they can scarcely conceal their impatience with the

---

[1] Lord Kenyon's charge to the Grand Jury at Shropshire Assizes, *Annals of Agriculture*, xxv (1795), pp. 110-11. But he was not proclaiming a new view of the law: the 1780 edition of Burn's *Justice*, ii, pp. 213-4 had already stressed that (despite the Acts of 1663 and 1772) "at the common law, all endeavours whatsoever to enhance the common price of any merchandize. . . whether by spreading false rumours, or by buying things in a market before the accustomed hour, or by buying and selling again the same thing in the same market" remained offences.

[2] Girdler, *op. cit.*, pp. 212-60, lists a number of convictions in 1795 and 1800. Private associations were established in several counties to prosecute forestallers: see the Rev. J. Malham, *The Scarcity of Grain Considered* (Salisbury, 1800), pp. 35-44. Forestalling etc. remained offences at common law until 1844: W. Holdsworth, *History of English Law* (1938), xi, p. 472. See also note 2 on pp. 209-10.

defeated party.[1] The model of the new political economy may, with convenience, be taken as that of Adam Smith, although *The Wealth of Nations* may be seen not only as a point of departure but also as a grand central terminus to which many important lines of discussion in the middle of the eighteenth century (some of them, like Charles Smith's lucid *Tracts on the Corn Trade* (1758-9), specifically concerned to demolish the old paternalist market regulation) all run. The debate between 1767 and 1772 which culminated in the repeal of legislation against forestalling, signalled a victory, in this area, for *laissez-faire* four years before Adam Smith's work was published.

This signified less a new model than an anti-model — a direct negative to the disintegrating Tudor policies of "provision". "Let every act that regards the corn laws be repealed", wrote Arbuthnot in 1773; "Let corn flow like water, and it will find its level".[2] The "unlimited, unrestrained freedom of the corn trade" was also the demand of Adam Smith.[3] The new economy entailed a de-moralising of the theory of trade and consumption no less far-reaching than the more widely-debated dissolution of restrictions upon usury.[4] By "de-moralising" it is not suggested that Smith and his colleagues were immoral[5] or were unconcerned for

---

[1] See e.g. Gras, *op. cit.*, p. 241 (". . . as Adam Smith has shown. . ."); M. Olson, *Economics of the Wartime Shortage* (North Carolina, 1963), p. 53 ("People were quick to find a scapegoat").

[2] J. Arbuthnot ("A Farmer"), *An Inquiry into the Connection between the Present Price of Provisions and the Size of Farms* (1773), p. 88.

[3] Adam Smith's "digression concerning the Corn Trade and Corn Laws" is in Book IV, chapter 5 of *The Wealth of Nations*.

[4] R. H. Tawney takes in the question in *Religion and the Rise of Capitalism* (1926), but it is not central to his argument.

[5] The suggestion was made, however, by some of Smith's opponents. One pamphleteer, who claimed to have known him well, alleged that Adam Smith had said to him that "the Christian Religion debased the human mind", and that "Sodomy was a thing in itself indifferent". No wonder that he held heartless views on the corn trade: Anon, *Thoughts of an Old Man of Independent Mind though Dependent Fortune on the Present High Prices of Corn* (1800), p. 4.

the public good.[1] It is meant, rather, that the new political economy was disinfested of intrusive moral imperatives. The old pamphleteers were moralists first and economists second. In the new economic theory questions as to the moral polity of marketing do not enter, unless as preamble and peroration.

In practical terms, the new model worked in this way. The natural operation of supply and demand in the free market would maximise the satisfaction of all parties and establish the common good. The market was never better regulated than when it was left to regulate itself. In the course of a normal year, the price of corn would adjust itself through the market mechanism. Soon after harvest the small farmers, and all those with harvest wages and Michaelmas rents to pay, would thresh out their corn and bring it to market, or release what they had pre-contracted to sell. From September to Christmas low prices might be expected. The middling farmers would hold their corn, in the hope of a rising market, until the early spring; while the most opulent farmers and farming gentry would hold some of theirs until still later — from May to August — in expectation of catching the market at the top. In this way the nation's corn reserves were conveniently rationed, by the price mechanism, over fifty-two weeks, without any intervention by the State. Insofar as middlemen intervened and contracted for the farmers' crops in advance, they performed this service of rationing even more efficiently. In years of dearth the price of grain might advance to uncomfortable heights; but this was providential, since (apart from providing an incentive to the importer) it was again an effective form of rationing, without which all stocks would be consumed in the first nine months of the year, and in the remaining three months dearth would be exchanged for actual famine.

The only way in which this self-adjusting economy might break down was through the meddlesome interference of the

---

[1] On the level of *intention* I see no reason to disagree with Professor A. W. Coats, "The Classical Economists and the Labourer", in E. L. Jones and G. E. Mingay (eds.), *Land, Labour and Population* (1967). But intention is a bad measure of ideological interest and of historical consequences.

State and of popular prejudice.[1] Corn must be left to flow freely from areas of surplus to areas of scarcity. Hence the middleman played a necessary, productive, and laudable role. The prejudices against forestallers Smith dismissed curtly as superstitions on a level with witchcraft. Interference with the natural pattern of trade might induce local famines or discourage farmers from increasing their output. If premature sales were forced, or prices restrained in times of dearth, excessive stocks might be consumed. If farmers did hold back their grain too long, they would be likely to suffer when prices broke. As for the other popular culprits — millers, mealmen, dealers, bakers — much the same logic applied. Their trades were competitive. At the most they could only distort prices from their natural level over short periods, and often to their ultimate discomfiture. When prices began to soar at the end of the century, the remedy was seen not in a return to the regulation of trade, but in more enclosure, tillage of waste lands, improvement.

It should not be necessary to argue that the model of a natural and self-adjusting economy, working providentially for the best good of all, is as much a superstition as the notions which upheld the paternalist model — although, curiously, it is a superstition which some economic historians have been the last to abandon. In some respects Smith's model conformed more closely to eighteenth-century realities than did the paternalist; and in symmetry and scope of intellectual construction it was superior. But one should not overlook the specious air of empirical validation which the model carries. Whereas the first appeals to a moral norm — what *ought* to be men's reciprocal duties — the second appears to say: "this is the way things work, or would work if the State did not interfere". And yet if one considers these sections of *The Wealth of Nations* they impress less as an essay in empirical enquiry than as a superb, self-validating essay in logic.

---

[1] Smith saw the two as going together: "The laws concerning corn may everywhere be compared to the laws concerning religion. The people feel themselves so much interested in what relates either to their subsistence in this life, or to their happiness in a life to come, that government must yield to their prejudices. . .".

When we consider the actual organisation of the eighteenth-century corn trade, empirical verification of neither model is to hand. There has been little detailed investigation of marketing;[1] no major study of that key figure, the miller.[2] Even the first letter of Smith's alphabet — the assumption that high prices were an effective form of rationing — remains no more than an assertion. It is notorious that the demand for corn, or bread, is highly inelastic. When bread is costly, the poor (as one highly-placed observer was once reminded) do not go over to cake. In the view of some observers, when prices rose labourers might eat the same quantity of bread, but cut out other items in their budgets; they might even eat *more* bread to compensate for the loss of other items. Out of one shilling, in a normal year, 6d. might go on bread, 6d. on "coarse meat and plenty of garden stuff"; but in a high-price year the whole shilling would go on bread.[3]

In any event, it is well known that the price movements of grain cannot be accounted for by simple supply-and-demand price mechanisms; and the bounty paid to encourage corn exports distorted matters further. Next to air and water, corn was a prime necessity of life, abnormally sensitive to any

[1] See, however, A. Everitt, "The Marketing of Agricultural Produce", in Joan Thirsk (ed.), *The Agrarian History of England and Wales, 1500-1600*, vol. iv (Cambridge, 1967) and D. Baker, "The Marketing of Corn in the first half of the Eighteenth Century: North-east Kent", *Agric. Hist. Rev.*, xviii (1970).

[2] There is some useful information in R. Bennett and J. Elton, *History of Corn Milling*, 4 vols. (Liverpool, 1898).

[3] Emanuel Collins, *Lying Detected* (Bristol, 1758), pp. 66-7. This seems to be confirmed by the budgets of Davies and Eden (see note 2 on p. 193), and of nineteenth-century observers: see *The Unknown Mayhew*, eds. E. P. Thompson and E. Yeo (1971), App. II. E. H. Phelps Brown and S. V. Hopkins, "Seven Centuries of the Prices of Consumables compared with Builders' Wages rates", *Economica*, xxii (1956), pp. 297-8 allow only 20% of the total household budget to farinaceous food, although the budgets of Davies and Eden (taken in high-price years) show an average of 53%. This again suggests that in such years bread consumption remained stable, but other items were cut out altogether. In London there may already have been a greater diversification of diet by the 1790s. P. Colquhoun wrote to Portland, 9 July 1795, that there was abundance of vegetables at Spitalfields market, especially potatoes, "the great substitute for Bread", carrots and turnips: PRO, PC 1/27/A.54.

deficiency in supply. In 1796 Arthur Young calculated that the overall crop deficiency in wheat was less than 25 per cent; but the price advance was 81 per cent: giving (by his calculation) a profit to the agricultural community of £20 millions over a normal year.[1] Traditionalist writers complained that the farmers and dealers acted from the strength of "monopoly"; they were rebutted in pamphlet after pamphlet, as "too absurd to be seriously treated: what! more than two hundred thousand people. . .!".[2] The point at issue, however, was not whether this farmer or that dealer could act as a "monopolist", but whether the producing and trading interests as a whole were able, with a long-continuing train of favourable circumstances, to take advantage of their command of a prime necessity of life and to enhance the price to the consumer, in much the same way as the advanced industrialised nations today have been able to enhance the price of certain manufactured goods to the less advanced nations.

As the century advanced marketing procedures became less transparent, as the corn passed through the hands of a more complex network of intermediaries. Farmers were selling, not in an open competitive market (which, in a local and regional

---

[1] *Annals of Agriculture*, xxvi (1796), pp. 470, 473. Davenant had estimated in 1699 that a deficiency in the harvest of one-tenth raised the price by three-tenths: Sir C. Whitworth, *The Political and Commercial Works of Charles Davenant* (1771), ii, p. 244. The problem is discussed in W. M. Stern, "The Bread Crisis in Britain, 1795-6", *Economica*, new series, xxxi (1964), and J. D. Gould, "Agricultural Fluctuations and the English Economy in the Eighteenth Century", *Jl. Econ. Hist.*, xxii (1926). Dr Gould puts weight on a point often mentioned in contemporary apologetics for high prices, e.g. *Farmer's Magazine*, ii (1801), p. 81, that the small growers, in a year of scarcity, required their entire crop for seed and for their own consumption: in such factors as this he finds the "chief theoretical explanation of the extreme volatility of grain prices in the early modern period". One would require more investigation of the actual operation of the market before such explanations carry conviction.

[2] Anon. ["A Country Farmer"], *Three Letters to a Member of the House of Commons. . . concerning the Prices of Provisions* (1766), pp. 18-19. For other examples see Lord John Sheffield, *Observations on the Corn Bill* (1791), p. 43; Anon., *Inquiry into the Causes and Remedies of the late and present Scarcity and high Price of Provisions* (1800), p. 33; J. S. Fry, *Letters on the Corn-Trade* (Bristol, 1816), pp. 10-11.

sense, was the aim of the paternalist rather than the *laissez-faire* model) but to dealers or millers who were in a better position to hold stocks and keep the market high. In the last decades of the century, as population rose, so consumption pressed continually upon production, and the producers could more generally command a seller's market. Wartime conditions, while not in fact inhibiting greatly the import of grain during conditions of scarcity, nevertheless accentuated psychological tensions in such years.[1] What mattered in setting the post-harvest price, was the expectation of the harvest yield: and there is evidence in the last decades of the century of the growth of a farming lobby, well aware of the psychological factors involved in post-harvest price levels, assiduously fostering an expectation of shortage.[2] Notoriously, in years of dearth the farmers' faces were wreathed in smiles,[3] while in years of abundant harvest Dame Nature's inconsiderate bounty called forth agricultural cries of "distress". And no matter how bountiful the yield might appear to the eye of the townsman, every harvest was accompanied by talk of mildew, floods, blighted ears which crumbled to powder when threshing commenced.

The free market model supposes a sequence of small to large farmers, bringing their corn to market over the year; but at the end of the century, as high-price year succeeded high-price year, so more small farmers were able to hold back supply until the market rose to their satisfaction. (It was, after all, for them not a matter of routine marketing but of intense, consuming interest: their profit for the year might depend very largely upon the price which three or four corn-stacks might fetch.) If rents had to be paid, the growth in country banking made it easier for the farmer to be

---

[1] See Olson, *Economics of the Wartime Shortage*, ch. 3; W. F. Galpin, *The Grain Supply of England during the Napoleonic Period* (New York, 1925).

[2] See e.g. Anon. ["A West Country Maltster"], *Considerations on the present High Prices of Provisions, and the Necessities of Life* (1764), p. 10.

[3] "I hope", a Yorkshire landowner wrote in 1708, "the dearth of corn which is likely to continue for several years to come will make husbandry very profitable to us, in breaking up and improving all our new land": cited by Beloff, *op. cit.*, p. 57.

accommodated.[1] The September or October riot was often precipitated by the failure of prices to fall after a seemingly plentiful harvest, and indicated a conscious confrontation between reluctant producer and angry consumer.

These comments are offered, not in refutation of Adam Smith, but simply to indicate places where caution should be exercised until our knowledge is greater. We need only say of the *laissez-faire* model that it is empirically unproven; inherently unlikely; and that there is some evidence on the other side. We have recently been reminded that "merchants made money in the eighteenth century", and that grain merchants may have made it "by operating the market".[2] Such operations are occasionally recorded, although rarely as frankly as was noted by a Whittlesford (Cambridgeshire) farmer and corn merchant in his diary in 1802:

> I bought Rey this Time Twelve Month at 50s per Qr. I could have sold it 122s per Qr. The poor had their flower, good rey, for 2s 6d per peck. Parish paid the difference to me, which was 1s 9d per peck. It was a Blessing to the Poor and good to me. I bought 320 Quarters.[3]

The profit on this transaction was above £1,000.

IV

If one can reconstruct clear alternative models behind the policies of traditionalists and of political economists, can one construct the same for the moral economy of the crowd? This is less easy. One is confronted by a complex of rational analysis, prejudice, and traditional patterns of response to dearth. Nor is it possible, at any given moment, clearly to identify the groups which endorsed the theories of the crowd. They comprise articulate and inarticulate, and include men of

---

[1] The point is noted in Anon., *A Letter to the Rt. Hon. William Pitt. . . on the Causes of the High Price of Provisions* (Hereford, 1795), p. 9; Anon. ["A Society of Practical Farmers"], *A Letter to the Rt. Hon. Lord Somerville* (1800), p. 49. Cf. L. S. Pressnell, *Country Banking in the Industrial Revolution* (Oxford, 1956), pp. 346-8.

[2] C. W. J. Grainger and C. M. Elliott, "A Fresh Look at Wheat Prices and Markets in the Eighteenth Century", *Econ. Hist. Rev.*, 2nd series, xx, (1967), p. 252.

[3] E. M. Hampson, *The Treatment of Poverty in Cambridgeshire, 1597-1834* (Cambridge, 1934), p. 211.

education and address. After 1750 each year of scarcity was accompanied by a spate of pamphlets and letters to the press, of unequal value. It was a common complaint of the protagonists of free trade in corn that misguided gentry added fuel to the flames of mob discontent.

There is truth in this. The crowd derived its sense of legitimation, in fact, from the paternalist model. Many gentlemen still resented the middleman as an interloper. Where lords of the manor retained market rights they resented the loss (through sample-sales etc.) of their market tolls. If they were landlord-farmers, who witnessed meat or flour being marketed at prices disproportionately high in relation to their own receipts from the dealers, they resented the profits of these common tradesmen the more. The essayist of 1718 has a title which is a précis of his matter: *An Essay to prove that Regrators, Engrossers, Forestallers, Hawkers and Jobbers of Corn, Cattle, and other Marketable Goods. . . are Destructive of Trade, Oppressors to the Poor, and a Common Nuisance to the Kingdom in General.* All dealers (unless simple drovers or carters, moving provisions from one point to the next) appeared to this not unobservant writer as a "vile and pernicious set of men"; and, in the classic terms of reproval adopted by men of settled estate to the bourgeois,

> they are a vagabond sort of people. . . They carry their all about them, and their. . . stock is no more than a plain riding habit, a good horse, a list of the fairs and markets, and a prodigious quantity of impudence. They have the mark of Cain, and like him wander from place to place, driving an interloping trade between the fair dealer and the honest consumer.[1]

---

[1] Adam Smith noted nearly sixty years later that the "popular odium. . . which attends the corn trade in years of scarcity, the only years in which it can be very profitable, renders people of character and fortune averse to enter into it. It is abandoned to an inferior set of dealers". Twenty-five years later again Earl Fitzwilliam was writing: "Dealers in corn are withdrawing from the trade, afraid to traffic in an article trafficking in which had render'd them liable to so much obloquy & calumny, and to be run at by an ignorant populace, without confidence in protection from those who ought to be more enlighten'd": Fitzwilliam to Portland, 3 Sept. 1800, PRO, HO 42/51. But an examination of the fortunes of such families as the Howards, Frys and Gurneys might call in question such literary evidence.

This hostility to the dealer existed even among many country magistrates, some of whom were noted to be inactive when popular disturbances swept through the areas under their jurisdiction. They were not displeased by attacks on dissenting or Quaker corn factors. A Bristol pamphleteer, who is clearly a corn factor, complained bitterly in 1758 to the JPs of "your law-giving mob", which prevented, in the previous year, the export of corn from the Severn and Wye valleys, and of "many fruitless applications to several Justices of the Peace".[1] Indeed, the conviction grows that a popular hubbub against forestallers was not unwelcome to some in authority. It distracted attention from the farmers and rentiers; while vague Quarter Sessional threats against forestallers gave to the poor a notion that the authorities were attending to their interests. The old laws against forestallers, a dealer complained in 1766,

> are printed in every newspaper, and stuck up in every corner, by order of the justices, to intimidate the engrossers, against whom many murmurings are propagated. The common people are taught to entertain a very high opinion and reverence for these laws. . .

Indeed, he accused the justices of encouraging "the extraordinary pretence, that the power and spirit of the mob is necessary to enforce the laws".[2] But if the laws were actually set in motion, they were directed almost without exception against petty culprits — local wide-boys or market-men, who pocketed small profits on trivial transactions — while the large dealers and millers were unaffected.[3]

[1] Collins, *op. cit.*, pp. 67-74. In 1756 several Quaker meeting-houses were attacked during food riots in the Midlands: *Gentleman's Magazine*, xxvi (1756), p. 408.

[2] Anon., *Reflections on the present High Price of Provisions, and the Complaints and Disturbances arising therefrom* (1766), pp. 26-7, 31.

[3] Contrary to the common assumption, the forestalling legislation had not fallen into desuetude in the first half of the eighteenth century. Prosecutions were infrequent, but sufficiently evident to suggest that they had some effect upon regulating petty dealing in the open market. At Manchester (see note 1 on p. 195) fines for forestalling or regrating took place sometimes annually, sometimes every two or three years, from 1731 to 1759 (seven fines). Commodities involved included butter, cheese, milk, oysters, fish, meat, carrots, pease, potatoes, turnips, cucumbers, apples, beans, gooseberries, currants, cherries, pigeons, fowls, but very rarely oats and wheat. Fines are less frequent after 1760 but include 1766 (wheat and

Thus, to take a late example, an old-fashioned and crusty Middlesex JP, J. S. Girdler, instituted a general campaign of prosecutions against such offenders in 1796 and 1800, with handbills offering rewards for information, letters to the press, etc. Convictions were upheld at several Quarter Sessions, but the amount gained by the speculators amounted only to ten or fifteen shillings. We can guess at the kind of offender whom his prosecutions touched by the literary style of an anonymous letter which he received:

> We no you are an enemy to Farmers, Mealmen and Bakers and our Trade if it had not bene for me and another you you son of a bitch you wold have bene murdurd long ago by offering your blasted rewards and persecuting Our Trade God dam you and blast you you shall never live to see another harvest. . .[1]

---

butter), 1780 (oats and eels), 1785 (meat), and 1796, 1797 and 1799 (all potatoes). Symbolically, the Court Leet officers to prevent forestalling jumped from 3 to 4 appointed annually (1730-1795) to 7 in 1795, 15 in 1796, 16 in 1797. In addition offenders were prosecuted on occasion (as in 1757) at Quarter Sessions. See Earwaker, *Court Leet Records* (cited p. 195), vii, viii and ix and *Constables' Accounts* (p. 212), ii, p. 94. For other examples of offences, see Essex Quarter Sessions, indictments, 2 Sept. 1709, 9 July 1711 (engrossing oats), and also 1711 for cases involving forestallers of fish, wheat, rye, butter, and, again, 13 Jan. 1729/30: Essex CRO, Calendar and Indictments, Q/SR 541, Q/SR 548, Q/SPb b 3; Constables' presentments for forestalling hogs, Oct. 1735 and Oct. 1746: Bury St. Edmunds and West Suffolk CRO, DB/1/8 (5); ditto for forestalling of butter, Nottingham, 6 Jan. 1745/5, *Records of the Borough of Nottingham* (Nottingham, 1914), vi, p. 209; conviction for forestalling of fowls (fine 13s. 4d.) at Atherstone Court Leet and Court Baron, 18 Oct. 1748: Warwicks. CRO, L2/24 23; cautions against the forestalling of butter etc., Woodbridge market, 30 Aug. 1756: Ipswich and East Suffolk CRO, V 5/9/6-3. In most Quarter-Sessional or market records the odd prosecution is to be found, before 1757. The author of *Reflections* (cited p. 209) writing in 1766, says these "almost-forgotten and disregarded statutes" were employed for the prosecution of "some submissive hucksters and indigent or terrified jobbers", and implies that the "principal factors" have despised "these menaces", believing them to be bad law (p. 37). For 1795 and 1800 see note 2, p. 200: the most important cases of the prosecution of large dealers were those of Rushby, for regrating oats (1799): see Barnes, *op. cit.*, pp. 81-3; and of Waddington, convicted for forestalling hops at Worcester Assizes: see *Times*, 4 Aug. 1800 and (for conviction upheld on appeal) I East 143 in *ER*, cii, pp. 56-68.

[1] Girdler, op. cit., pp. 295-6.

Compassionate traditionalists like Girdler were joined by townsmen of various ranks. Most Londoners suspected everyone who had any part in handling grain, flour or bread of every kind of extortion. The urban lobby was, of course, especially powerful in the middle years of the century, pressing for an end to the export bounty, or for the prohibition of all exports in time of dearth. But London and the larger towns harboured inexhaustible reserves of resentment, and some of the wildest accusations came from this milieu. A certain Dr Manning, in the 1750s, published allegations that bread was adulterated not only with alum, chalk, whiting and beanmeal, but also with slaked lime and white lead. Most sensational was his claim that millers turned into their flour "sacks of old ground bones": "the charnel houses of the dead are raked, to add filthiness to the food of the living", or, as another pamphleteer commented, "the present age [is] making hearty meals on the bones of the last".

Manning's accusations went far beyond the bounds of credibility. (A critic computed that if lime was being used on the scale of his allegations, more would be consumed in the London baking than building industry.)[1] Apart from alum, which was widely used to whiten bread, the commonest form of adulteration was probably the admixture of old, spoiled flour with new flour.[2] But the urban population was quick to believe that far more noxious adulterations were practised, and such belief contributed to the "Shude-hill Fight" at Manchester in 1757, where one of the mills attacked was believed to mix "Accorns, Beans, Bones, Whiting, Chopt Straw, and even dried Horse Dung" with its flour, while at another mill the presence of suspicious adulterants near the hoppers (discovered by the crowd) led to the burning of bolters and sieves, and the destruction of

---

[1] Collins, *op. cit.*, pp. 16-37. P. Markham, *Syhoroc* (1758), i, pp. 11-31; *Poison Detected: or Frightful Truths. . . in a Treatise on Bread* (1757), esp. pp. 16-38.

[2] See e.g. John Smith, *An Impartial Relation of Facts Concerning the Malepractices of Bakers* (n.d. [1740?]).

mill-stones and wheels.[1]

There were other, equally sensitive, areas where the complaints of the crowd were fed by the complaints of traditionalists or by those of urban professional people. Indeed, one may suggest that if the rioting or price-setting crowd acted according to any consistent theoretical model, then this model was a selective reconstruction of the paternalist one, taking from it all those features which most favoured the poor and which offered a prospect of cheap corn. It was, however, less generalised than the outlook of the paternalists. The records of the poor show more particularity: it is this miller, this dealer, those farmers hoarding grain, who provoke indignation and action. This particularity was, however, informed by general notions of rights which disclose themselves most clearly only when one examines the crowd in action. For in one respect the moral economy of the crowd broke decisively with that of the paternalists: for the popular ethic sanctioned direct action by the crowd, whereas the values of order underpinning the paternalist model emphatically did not.

The economy of the poor was still local and regional, derivative from a subsistence-economy. Corn should be consumed in the region in which it was grown, especially in times of scarcity. Profound feeling was aroused, and over several centuries, by export in times of dearth. Of an export riot in Suffolk in 1631 a magistrate wrote: "to see their bread thus taken from them and sent to strangers has turned the impatience of the poor into licentious fury and desperation".[2] In a graphic account of a riot in the same county seventy-eight years later (1709), a dealer described how "the Mobb rose, he thinks several hundreds, and said that the corn should not be carried out of town": "of the Mobb some had halberds, some quarter staffs, and some clubbs. . .". When travelling to Norwich, at several places on the way:

---

[1] See J. P. Earwaker, *The Constables' Accounts of the Manor of Manchester* (Manchester, 1891), iii, pp. 359-61; F. Nicholson and E. Axon, "The Hatfield Family of Manchester, and the Food Riots of 1757 and 1812", *Trans. Lancs. and Chesh. Antiq. Soc.*, xxviii (1910/11), pp. 83-90.

[2] *Calendar State Papers, Domestic*, 1631, p. 545.

the Mobb hearing that he was to goe through with corn, told him that it should not go through the Towne, for that he was a Rogue, and Corn-Jobber, and some cry'd out Stone him, some Pull him off his horse, some Knock him down, and be sure you strike sure; that he. . . questioned them what made them rise in such an inhuman manner to the prejudice of themselves and the countrey, but that they still cryed out that he was a Rogue & was going to carry the corn into France. . .[1]

Except in Westminster, in the mountains, or in the great sheep-grazing districts, men were never far from the sight of corn. Manufacturing industry was dispersed in the country-side: the colliers went to their labour by the side of corn-fields; domestic workers left their looms and workshops for the harvest. Sensitivity was not confined to overseas export. Marginal exporting areas were especially sensitive, where little corn was exported in normal years, but where, in times of scarcity, dealers could hope for a windfall price in London, thereby aggravating local dearth.[2] The colliers — Kingswood, the Forest of Dean, Shropshire, the North-East — were especially prone to action at such times. Notoriously the Cornish tinners had an irascible consumer-consciousness, and a readiness to turn out in force. "We had the devil and all of a riot at Padstow", wrote a Bodmin gentleman in 1773, with scarcely-concealed admiration:

Some of the people have run to too great lengths in exporting of corn. . . Seven or eight hundred tinners went thither, who first offered the corn-factors seventeen shillings for 24 gallons of wheat; but being told they should have none, they immediately broke open the cellar doors, and took away all in the place without money or price.[3]

The worst resentment was provoked in the middle years of the century, by foreign exports upon which bounty was paid. The foreigner was seen as receiving corn at prices sometimes below those of the English market, with the aid of a bounty paid out of English taxes. Hence the extreme bitterness sometimes visited upon the exporter, who was seen as a man seeking private, and dishonourable, gain at the expense of his own people. A North Yorkshire factor, who was given a

---

[1] PRO, PC 1/2/165.
[2] See D. G. D. Isaac, "A Study of Popular Disturbance in Britain, 1714-54" (Edinburgh Univ. Ph.D. thesis, 1953), ch. I.
[3] *Calendar of Home Office Papers*, 1773, p. 30.

ducking in the river in 1740, was told that he was "no better than a rebel".[1] In 1783 a notice was affixed to the market-cross in Carlisle, commencing:

> Peter Clemeseson & Moses Luthart this is to give you Warning that you must Quit your unlawfull Dealing or Die and be Damed your buying the Corn to starve the Poor Inhabitants of the City and Soborbs of Carlisle to send to France and get the Bounty Given by the Law for taking the Corn out of the Country but by the Lord God Almighty we will give you Bounty at the Expence of your Lives you Damed Roagues. . .

"And if Eany Publick House in Carlisle [the notice continued] Lets you or Luthart put up. . . Corn at their Houses they shall suffer for it."[2] This feeling revived in the last years of the century, notably in 1795, when rumours flew around the country as to secret exports to France. Moreover, 1795 and 1800 saw the efflorescence of a regional consciousness once more, as vivid as that of one hundred years before. Roads were blockaded to prevent export from the parish. Wagons were intercepted and unloaded in the towns through which they passed. The movement of grain by night-convoy assumed the proportions of a military operation:

> Deep groan the waggons with their pond'rous loads,
> As their dark course they bend along the roads;
> Wheel following wheel, in dread procession slow,
> With half a harvest, to their points they go. . .
> The secret expedition, like the night
> That covers its intents, still shuns the light. . .
> While the poor ploughman, when he leaves his bed,
> Sees the huge barn as empty as his shed.[3]

Threats were made to destroy the canals.[4] Ships were stormed at the ports. The miners at Nook Colliery near Haverfordwest threatened to close the estuary at a narrow point. Even lighters on the Severn and Wye were not

[1] PRO, SP 36/50.
[2] *London Gazette*, March 1783, no. 12422.
[3] S. J. Pratt, *Sympathy and Other Poems* (1807), pp. 222-3.
[4] Some years before Wedgwood had heard it "threatened. . . to destroy our canals and let out the water", because provisions were passing through Staffordshire to Manchester from East Anglia: J. Wedgwood, *Address to the Young Inhabitants of the Pottery* (Newcastle, 1783).

immune from attack.[1]

Indignation might also be inflamed against a dealer whose commitment to an outside market disrupted the customary supplies of the local community. A substantial farmer and publican near Tiverton complained to the War Office in 1795 of riotous assemblies "threatening to pull down or fire his house because he takes in Butter of the neighbouring Farmers & Dairymen, to forward it by the common road waggon, that passes by his door to. . . London".[2] In Chudleigh (Devon) in the same year the crowd destroyed the machinery of a miller who had ceased to supply the local community with flour since he was under contract to the Victualling Department of the Navy for ship's biscuits: this had given rise (he says in a revealing phrase) "to an Idea that ive done much infimy to the Community".[3] Thirty years before a group of London merchants had found it necessary to seek the protection of the military for their cheese-warehouses along the river Trent:

> The warehouses. . . in danger from the riotous colliers are not the property of any monopolizers, but of a numerous body of cheese-mongers, and absolutely necessary for the reception of their cheese, for the conveyance to Hull, there to be ship'd for London.[4]

These grievances are related to the complaint, already noted, of the withdrawal of goods from the open market. As the dealers moved further from London and attended more frequently at provincial markets, so they were able to offer prices and buy in quantities which made the farmers impatient to serve the small orders of the poor. "Now it is out of the course of business", wrote Davies in 1795, "for the farmer to retail corn by the bushel to this or that poor man; except in some particular places, as a matter of favour, to his own labourers". And where the poor shifted their demand from grain to flour, the story was much the same:

[1] PRO, PC 1/27/A.54; A.55-7; HO 42/34; 42/35; 42/36; 42/37; see also Stern, *op. cit.*, and E. P. Thompson, *The Making of the English Working Class* (Penguin, 1968), pp. 70-3.

[2] PRO, WO I/1082, John Ashley, 24 June 1795.

[3] PRO, HO 42/34.

[4] PRO, WO I/986 fo. 69.

Neither the miller nor the mealman will sell the labourer a less quantity than a *sack* of flour under the retail price at shops; and the poor man's pocket will seldom allow of his buying a whole sack at once.[1]

Hence the labourer was driven to the petty retail shop, at which prices were enhanced.[2] The old markets declined, or, where they were kept up, they changed their functions. If a customer attempted to buy a single cheese or half flitch of bacon, Girdler wrote in 1800, "he is sure to be answered by an insult, and he is told that the whole lot has been bought up by some London contractor".[3]

We may take as expressive of these grievances, which sometimes occasioned riot, an anonymous letter dropped in 1795 by the door of the mayor of Salisbury:

> Gentlemen of the Corporation I pray you put a stop to that practice which is made use of in our Markits by Rook and other carriers in your giving them the Liberty to Scower the Market of every thing so as the Inhabitance cannot buy a singel Artickel without going to the Dealers for it and Pay what Extortionat price they think proper and even Domineer over the Peopel as thow they was not Whorthy to Look on them. But their time will soon be at an End as soon as the Solders ear gon out of town.

The corporation is asked to order carriers out of the market until the townspeople have been served, "and stop all the Butchers from sending the meat away by a Carces at a time But make them cut it up in the Markit and sarve the Town first". The letter informs the mayor that upwards of three hundred citizens have "posetively swor to be trow to each other for the Distruction of the Carriers".[4]

Where the working people could buy cereals in small parcels intense feeling could arise over weights and measures. We are exhorted in Luke: "Give, and it shall be given unto you, good measure pressed down, and shaken together, and running over, shall men give unto your bosom." This was

---

[1] Davies, *op. cit.*, pp. 33-4.

[2] "The first principle laid down by a baker, when he comes into a parish, is, to get all the poor in his debt; he then makes their bread of what weight or goodness he pleases. . .": *Gentleman's Magazine*, xxvi (1756), p. 557.

[3] Girdler, *op. cit.*, p. 147.

[4] PRO, HO 42/34.

not, alas, the practice of all farmers and dealers in protestant England. An enactment of Charles II had even given the poor the right to *shake* the measure, so valuable was the poor man's corn that a looseness in the measure might make the difference to him of a day without a loaf. The same Act had attempted, with total lack of success, to enforce the Winchester measure as the national standard. A great variety of measures, varying even within county boundaries from one market-town to the next, gave abundant opportunities for petty profiteering. The old measures were generally larger — sometimes very much larger — than the Winchester; sometimes they were favoured by farmers or dealers, more often they were favoured by the customers. One observer remarked that "the lower orders of people detest it [the Winchester measure], from the smallness of its contents, and the dealers. . . instigate them to this, it being their interest to retain every uncertainty in weights and measures".[1]

Attempts to change the measure often encountered resistance, occasionally riot. A letter from a Clee Hill (Shropshire) miner to a "Brother Sufferer" declared:

> The Parliament for our relief to help to Clem [starve] us Thay are going to lesson our Measure and Wait [weight] to the Lower Standard. We are about Ten Thousand sworn and ready at any time And we wou'd have you get Arms and Cutlasses and swear one another to be true. . . We have but one Life to Loose and we will not clem. . .[2]

Letters to farmers in Northiam (Sussex) warned:

> Gentlemen all ie hope you whill take this as a wharning to you all for you to put the little Bushels bie and take the oald measher [measure] again for if you dont there whill be a large company that shall borne [burn] the little measher when you are all abade and asleep and your cornehouses and cornstacks and you along with them. . .[3]

---

[1] *Annals of Agriculture*, xxvi (1796), p. 327; *Museum Rusticum et Commerciale*, iv (1765), p. 198. The difference in bushels could be very considerable: as against the Winchester bushel of 8 gallons, the Stamford had 16 gallons, the Carlisle 24, and the Chester 32: see J. Houghton, *A Collection for Improvement of Husbandry and Trade* (1727), no. xlvi, 23 June 1693.

[2] *London Gazette*, March 1767, no. 10710.

[3] November 1793, in PRO, HO 42/27. The measures concerned were for malt.

A Hampshire contributor to the *Annals of Agriculture* explained in 1795 that the poor "have erroneously conceived an idea that the price of grain is increased by the late alteration from a nine-gallon bushel to the Winchester, from its happening to take place at a moment of a rising market, by which, the same money was paid for eight as used to be paid for nine gallons". "I confess", he continues,

> I have a decided predeliction for the nine-gallon measure, for the reason that it is the measure which nearest yields a bushel of flour; whence, the poor man is enabled to judge of what he ought to pay for a bushel of flour, which, in the present measure, requires more arithmetic than comes to his share to ascertain. [1]

Even so, the arithmetical notions of the poor may not have been so erroneous. Changes in measures, like changes to decimal currency, tend by some magic to disadvantage the consumer.

If less corn was being bought (at the end of the century) in the open market by the poor, this also indicated the rise to greater importance of the miller. The miller occupies a place in popular folklore, over many centuries, which is both enviable and unenviable. On one hand he was noted as a fabulously successful lecher, whose prowess is still perhaps perpetuated in a vernacular meaning of the word "grinding". Perhaps the convenience of the village mill, tucked around a secluded corner of the stream, to which the village wives and maidens brought their corn for grinding; perhaps also his command over the means of life; perhaps his status in the village, which made him an eligible match — all may have contributed to the legend:

> A brisk young lass so brisk and gay
> She went unto the mill one day. . .
> There's a peck of corn all for to grind
> I can but stay a little time.
>
> Come sit you down my sweet pretty dear
> I cannot grind your corn I fear
> My stones is high and my water low
> I cannot grind for the mill won't go.

---

[1] *Annals of Agriculture*, xxiv (1795), pp. 51-2.

> Then she sat down all on a sack
> They talked of this and they talked of that
> They talked of love, of love proved kind
> She soon found out the mill would grind. . .[1]

On the other hand, the miller's repute was less enviable. "*Loving!*", exclaims Nellie Dean in *Wuthering Heights*: "*Loving!* Did anybody ever hear the like? I might as well talk of loving the miller who comes once a year to buy our corn". If we are to believe all that was written about him in these years, the miller's story had changed little since Chaucer's Reeve's Tale. But where the small country miller was accused of quaintly medieval customs — over-size toll dishes, flour concealed in the casing of the stones, etc. — his larger counterpart was accused of adding new, and greatly more enterprising, peculations:

> For ther-biforn he stal but curteisly,
> But now he was a thief outrageously.

At one extreme we still have the little country mill, exacting toll according to its own custom. The toll might be taken in flour (always from "the best of the meal and from the finer flour that is in the centre of the hopper"); and since the proportion remained the same with whatever fluctuation in price, it was to the miller's advantage if prices were high. Around the small toll-mills (even where toll had been commuted for money payments) grievances multiplied, and there were fitful attempts at their regulation.[2] Since the millers entered increasingly into dealing, and into grinding corn on their own account for the bakers, they had little time for the petty customers (with a sack or two of gleaned corn);

---

[1] James Reeves, *The Idiom of the People* (1958), p. 156. See also Brit. Lib. Place MSS, Add MSS 27825 for "A pretty maid she to the miller would go", verse 2:
> Then the miller he laid her against the mill hopper
> Merry a soul so wantonly
> He pulled up her cloaths, and he put in the stopper
> For says she I'll have my corn ground small and free.

[2] See Markham, *Syhoroc*, ii, p. 15; Bennett and Elton, *op. cit.*, iii, pp. 150-65; information of John Spyry against the Miller of Millbrig Mill, 1740, for taking sometimes 1/6th, sometimes 1/7th, and sometimes 1/8th part as mulcture: West Riding Sessions papers, County Hall, Wakefield.

hence endless delay; hence also, when the flour was returned it might be the product of other, inferior, grain. (It was complained that some millers purchased at half-price damaged corn which they then mixed with the corn of their customers.[1]) As the century wore on, the translation of many mills to industrial purposes gave to the surviving petty corn-mills a more advantageous position. In 1796 these grievances were sufficiently felt to enable Sir Francis Bassett to carry the Miller's Toll Bill, intended to regulate their practices, weights and measures, more strictly.[2]

But these petty millers were, of course, the small fry of the eighteenth century. The great millers of the Thames Valley and of the large towns were a different order of entrepreneurs, who traded extensively in flour and malt. Millers were quite outside the Assize of Bread, and they could immediately pass on any increase in the price of corn to the consumer. England also had its unsung *banalités* in the eighteenth century, including those extraordinary survivals, the soke mills, which exercised an absolute monopoly of the grinding of grain (and the sale of flour) in substantial manufacturing centres, among them Manchester, Bradford, Leeds.[3] In most cases the feoffees who owned the soke rights sold or leased these to private speculators. Most stormy was the history of the School Mills at Manchester, whose soke rights were intended as a charitable endowment to support the grammar school. Two unpopular lessees of the rights inspired, in 1737, Dr Byrom's rhyme:

> *Bone and Skin*, two millers thin,
>   Would starve the town, or near it;
> But be it known, to *Skin and Bone*,
>   That Flesh and Blood can't bear it.

When, in 1757, new lessees sought to prohibit the importation of flour to the growing town, while at the same time managing their mills (it was alleged) with extortion and delay,

---

[1] See Girdler, *op. cit.*, pp. 102-6, 212.

[2] *Annals of Agriculture*, xxiii (1795), pp. 179-91; Bennett and Elton, *op. cit.*, iii, p. 166; 36: Geo III, c.85.

[3] See Bennett and Elton, *op. cit.*, iii, pp. 204 ff; W. Cudworth, "The Bradford Soke", *The Bradford Antiquary* (Bradford, 1888), i, pp. 74ff.

flesh and blood could indeed bear it no longer. In the famous "Shude-hill Fight" of that year at least four men were killed by musketry, but the soke rights were finally broken.[1] But even where no actual soke right obtained, one mill might command a populous community, and could provoke the people to fury by a sudden advance in the price of flour or an evident deterioration in its quality. Mills were the visible, tangible targets of some of the most serious urban riots of the century. The Albion Mills at Blackfriars Bridge (London's first steam mills) were governed by a quasi-philanthropic syndicate; yet when they burned down in 1791 Londoners danced and sang ballads of rejoicing in the streets.[2] The first steam mill at Birmingham (Snow Hill) fared little better, being the target of a massive attack in 1795.

It may appear at first sight as curious that both dealers and millers should continue to be among the objectives of riot at the end of the century, by which time in many parts of the Midlands and South (and certainly in urban areas) working people had become accustomed to buying bread at the baker's shops rather than grain or flour in the market-place. We do not know enough to chart the change-over with accuracy, and certainly much home-baking survived.[3] But even where the change-over was complete, one should not underestimate the sophistication of the situation and of the crowd's objectives. There were, of course, scores of petty riots outside bread shops, and the crowd very often "set the price" of bread. But the baker (whose trade in times of high prices can sacrcely have been an enviable one) was, alone of all those who dealt in the people's necessities (landlord,

[1] See note 1, p. 212 and Bennett and Elton, *op. cit.*, pp. 274ff.
[2] *Ibid.*, iii, pp. 204-6.
[3] Replies from towns to Privy Council enquiry, 1796, in PRO, PC I/33/ A.88: e.g. mayor of York, 16 April 1796, "the poor can get their bread baked at common ovens. . ."; mayor of Lancaster, 10 April, "each family buys their own flour and makes their own bread"; mayor of Leeds, 4 April, it is the custom "to buy corn or meal, and to mix up their own bread, and to bake it themselves or get it baked for hire". A survey of bakers in the hundred of Corby (Northamptonshire) in 1757 shows that out of 31 parishes, one parish (Wilbarston) had four bakers, one had three, three had two, eight had one, and fourteen had no resident baker (four gave no return): Northants. CRO, H (K) 170.

farmer, factor, carrier, miller), in daily contact with the consumer; and he was, more than any of the others, protected by the visible paraphernalia of paternalism. The Assize of Bread clearly and publicly limited their lawful profits (thereby also tending to leave the baking trade in the hands of numerous small traders with little capital), and thus protected them, to some degree, from popular wrath. Even Charles Smith, the able exponent of free trade, thought the continuation of the Assize to be expedient: "in large Towns and Cities it will always be necessary to set the Assize, in order to satisfy the people that the price which the Bakers demand is no more than that what is thought reasonable by the Magistrates".[1]

The psychological effect of the Assize was, therefore, considerable. The baker could hope to enhance his profit beyond the allowance calculated in the Assize only by small stratagems, some of which — short-weight bread, adulteration, the mixing in of cheap and spoiled flour — were subject either to legal redress or to instant crowd retaliation. Indeed, the baker had sometimes to attend to his own public relations, even to the extent of enlisting the crowd on his side: when Hannah Pain of Kettering complained to the justices of short-weight bread, the baker "raised a mob upon her. . . and said she deserved to be whipped, there were enough of such scambling scum of the earth".[2] Many corporations throughout the century, made a great show of supervising weights and measures, and of punishing offenders.[3] Ben Jonson's "Justice Overdo" was still busy in the streets of Reading, Coventry, or London:

[1] Smith, *Three Tracts on the Corn-Trade*, p. 30.
[2] Examination of Hannah Pain, 12 Aug. 1757, Northants. CRO, H (K) 167 (I).
[3] It is notable that punishments for these offences were most frequent in years of dearth, and doubtless these were intended to have symbolic force: thus 6 presentments for false or short weight at Bury St. Edmunds sessions, May 1740: Bury St. Edmunds and West Suffolk CRO, D8/I/8(5); 6 fined for deficient weight in Maidenhead, October 1766: Berks. CRO, M/JMI. At Reading, however, surveillance appears to be fairly constant, in good years as well as bad: Central Public Library, Reading, R/MJ Acc. 167, Court Leet and View of Frankpledge. At Manchester the market officials were vigilant until the 1750s, more casual thereafter, but very active in April 1796: Earwaker, *Court Leet Records*, ix, pp. 113-4.

Marry, go you into every alehouse, and down into every cellar; measure the length of puddings. . . weigh the loaves of bread on his middle finger. . . give the puddings to the poor, the bread to the hungry, the custards to his children.

In this tradition we find a London magistrate in 1795 who, coming on the scene of a riot in Seven Dials where the crowd was already in the act of demolishing the shop of a baker accused of selling light-weight bread, intervened, seized the baker's stock, weighed the loaves, and finding them indeed deficient, distributed the loaves among the crowd.[1]

No doubt the bakers, who knew their customers, sometimes complained of their powerlessness to reduce prices, and diverted the crowd to the mill or the corn-market. "After ransacking many bakers' shops", the miller of Snow Hill, Birmingham, related of the 1795 attack, "they came in great numbers against us. . .".[2] But in many cases the crowd clearly selected its own targets, deliberately by-passing the bakers. Thus in 1740 at Norwich the people "went to every Baker in the City, and affix'd a Note on his Door in these words, Wheat at *Sixteen Shillings a Comb*". In the same year at Wisbech they obliged "the Merchants to sell Wheat at 4d per Bushel. . . not only to them, but also to the Bakers, where they regulated the Weight & Price of Bread".[3]

But it is clear at this point that we are dealing with a far more complex pattern of action than one which can be satisfactorily explained by a face-to-face encounter between the populace and particular millers, dealers or bakers. It is necessary to take a larger view of the actions of the crowd.

---

[1] *Gentleman's Magazine*, lxv (1795), p. 697.

[2] MS notebook of Edward Pickering, Birmingham City Ref. Lib. M 22.11.

[3] *Ipswich Journal*, 12 and 26 July 1740. (I am indebted to Dr R. W. Malcolmson of Queen's University, Ontario, for these references.) The crowd by no means mistook the bakers for their main opponents, and forms of pressure were often of considerable complexity; thus "incendiary" papers set up around Tenterden (1768) incited people to rise and force the farmers to sell their wheat to the millers or the poor at £10 a load, and threatened to destroy the millers who gave to the farmers a higher price: Shelburne, 25 May 1768, PRO, SP 44/199.

V

It has been suggested that the term "riot" is a blunt tool of analysis for so many particular grievances and occasions. It is also an imprecise term for describing popular actions. If we are looking for the characteristic form of direct action, we should take, not squabbles outside London bakeries, nor even the great affrays provoked by discontent with the large millers, but the "risings of the people" (most notably in 1740, 1756, 1766, 1795 and 1800) in which colliers, tinners, weavers and hosiery workers were prominent. What is remarkable about these "insurrections" is, first, their discipline, and, second, the fact that they exhibit a pattern of behaviour for whose origin we must look back several hundreds of years: which becomes more, rather than less, sophisticated in the eighteenth century; which repeats itself, seemingly spontaneously, in different parts of the country and after the passage of many quiet years. The central action in this pattern is not the sack of granaries and the pilfering of grain or flour but the action of "setting the price".

What is extraordinary about this pattern is that it reproduces, sometimes with great precision, the emergency measures in time of scarcity whose operation, in the years between 1580 and 1630, were codified in the *Book of Orders*. These emergency measures were employed in times of scarcity in the last years of Elizabeth, and put into effect, in a somewhat revised form, in the reign of Charles I, in 1630. In Elizabeth's reign the magistrates were required to attend the local markets,

> and where you shall fynde that there is insufficiente quantities broughte to fill and serve the said marketts and speciallie the poorer sorte, you shall thereupon resorte to the houses of the Farmers and others using tyllage. . . and viewe what store and provision of graine theye have remayninge either thrashed or unthrashed. . .

They might then order the farmers to send "convenient quantities" to market to be sold "and that at reasonable price". The justices were further empowered to "sett downe a certen price upon the bushell of everye kynde of graine".[1]

---

[1] "A Coppie of the Councells her[e] for graine delyv[rd] at Bodmyn the xith of May 1586": Bodleian Library, Rawlinson MSS B 285, fos. 66-7.

The queen and her Council opined that high prices were in part due to engrossers, in part to the "greedie desier" of corn-growers who "bee not content wth anie moderate gayne, but seeke & devise waies to kepe up the prices to the manifest oppression of the poorer sort". The Orders were to be enforced "wth out all parciality in sparing anie man".[1]

In essence, then, the *Book of Orders* empowered magistrates (with the aid of local juries) to survey the corn stocks in barns and granaries;[2] to order quantities to be sent to market; and to enforce with severity every part of the marketing, licensing and forestalling legislation. No corn was to be sold except in open market, "unless the same be to some pore handicrafts Men, or Day-Labourers within the parish wherein you doe dwell, that cannot conveniently come to the Market Townes". The Orders of 1630 did not explicitly empower justices to set the price, but ordered them to attend the market and ensure that the poor were "provided of necessary Corne. . . with as much favour in the Prices, as by the earnest Perswasion of the Justices can be obtained". The power to set a price upon grain or flour rested, in emergency, half-way between enforcement and persuasion.[3]

[1] There is some account of the operation of the *Book of Orders* in E. M. Leonard, *Early History of English Poor Relief* (Cambridge, 1900); Gras, *op. cit.*, pp. 236-42; Lipson, *op. cit.*, iii, pp. 440-50; B. E. Supple, *Commercial Crisis and Change in England, 1600-42* (Cambridge, 1964), p. 117. Papers illustrative of their operation are in *Official Papers of Nathaniel Bacon of Stiffkey, Norfolk* (Camden Society, 3rd series, xxvi, 1915), pp. 130-57.

[2] For an example, see *Victoria County History, Oxfordshire*, ed. W. Page (1907), ii, pp. 193-4.

[3] By an Act of 1534 (25 Henry VIII, *c.* 2) the Privy Council had the power to set prices on corn in emergency. In a somewhat misleading note, Gras (*op. cit.*, pp. 132-3) opines that after 1550 the power was never used. It was in any case not forgotten: a proclamation of 1603 appears to set prices (Seligman Collection, Columbia Univ. Lib., Proclamations, James I, 1603); the *Book of Orders* of 1630 concludes with the warning that "if the Corne-masters and other Owners of Victuall. . . shall not willingly performe these Orders", His Majesty will "give Order that reasonable Prices shall be set"; the Privy Council attempted to restrain prices by Proclamation in 1709, Liverpool Papers, Brit. Mus., Add. MS. 38353, fo. 195; and the matter was actively canvassed in 1757 — see Smith, *Three Tracts on the Corn Trade*, pp. 29, 35. And (apart from the Assize of Bread) other price-fixing powers lingered on. In 1681 at Oxford market (controlled by the University) prices were set for butter, cheese, poultry,

This emergency legislation was falling into disrepair during the Civil Wars.[1] But the popular memory, especially in a pre-literate society, is extraordinarily long. There can be little doubt that a direct tradition extends from the *Book of Orders* of 1630 to the actions of clothing workers in East Anglia and the West in the eighteenth century. (The literate had long memories also: the *Book of Orders* itself was republished, unofficially in 1662, and again in 1758, with a prefatory address to the reader referring to the present "wicked combination to make scarcity".)[2]

The Orders were themselves in part a response to the pressure of the poor:

> The Corne is so dear
> I dout mani will starve this yeare —

So ran a doggerel notice affixed in the church porch in the parish of Wye (Kent) in 1630:

> If you see not to this
> Sum of you will speed amis.
> Our souls they are dear,
> For our bodys have sume ceare
> Before we arise
> Less will safise. . .
> You that are set in place
> See that youre profesion you doe not disgrace. . .[3]

---

meat, bacon, candles, oats, and beans: "The Oxford Market", *Collectanea* 2nd ser. (Oxford, 1890), pp. 127-8. It seems that the Assize of Ale lapsed in Middlesex in 1692 (Lipson, *op. cit.*, ii, p. 501), and in 1762 brewers were authorized (by 2 Geo. III, *c.* 14) to raise the price in a reasonable manner; but when in 1773 it was proposed to raise the price by ½d. a quart Sir John Fielding wrote to the earl of Suffolk that the increase "cannot be thought reasonable; nor will the subject submit to it": *Calendar of Home Office Papers*, 1773, pp. 9-14; P. Mathias, *The Brewing Industry in England, 1700-1830* (Cambridge, 1959), p. 360.

[1] See G. D. Ramsay, "Industrial *Laisser-Faire* and the Policy of Cromwell", *Econ. Hist. Rev.*, 1st series, xvi (1946), esp. pp. 103-4; M. James, *Social Problems and Policy during the Puritan Revolution* (1930), pp. 264-71.

[2] *Seasonable Orders Offered from former Precedents Whereby the Price of Corn. . . may be much abated* (1662) — a reprint of the Elizabethan Orders; J. Massie, *Orders Appointed by His Majestie King Charles I* (1758).

[3] *Calendar State Papers, Domestic*, 1630, p. 387.

One hundred and thirty years later (1768) incendiary papers were once again being nailed to church doors (as well as to inn-signs) in parishes within the same lathe of Scray in Kent, inciting the poor to rise.[1] Many similar continuities can be observed, although undoubtedly the pattern of direct action spread to new districts in the eighteenth century. In many actions, especially in the old manufacturing regions of the East and West, the crowd claimed that since the authorities refused to enforce "the laws" they must enforce them for themselves. In 1693 at Banbury and Chipping Norton the crowd "took away the corne by force out of the waggons, as it was carrying away by the ingrossers, saying that they were resolved to put the law in execution, since the magistrates neglected it".[2] During the extensive disorders in the West in 1766 the sheriff of Gloucestershire, a gentleman clothier, could not disguise his respect for the rioters who

> went. . . to a farmhouse and civilly desired that they wou'd thresh out and bring to market their wheat and sell it for five shillings per bushel, which being promised, and some provisions given them unasked for, they departed without the least violence or offence.

If we follow other passages of the sheriff's accounts we may encounter most of the features found in these actions:

> On Friday last a Mobb was rais'd in these parts by the blowing of Horns &c consisting entirely of the lowest of the people such as weavers, mecanicks, labourers, prentices, and boys, &c. . .

"They proceeded to a gristmill near the town. . . cutting open Baggs of Flower and giving & carrying it away & destroying corn &c." They then attended at the main markets, setting the price of grain. Three days later he sent a further report:

> They visited Farmers, Millers, Bakers and Hucksters shops, selling corn, flower, bread, cheese, butter, and bacon, at their own prices. They returned in general the produce [i.e. the money] to the proprietors or in their absence left the money for them; and behaved with great regularity and decency where they were not opposed, with outrage and violence where they was: but pilferd very little, which to prevent, they will not now suffer Women and boys to go with them.

---

[1] *Calendar of Home Office Papers*, 1768, p. 342.
[2] Westerfield, *op. cit.*, p. 148.

After visiting the mills and markets around Gloucester, Stroud and Cirencester, they divided into parties of fifty and a hundred and visited the villages and farms, requesting that corn be brought at fair prices to market, and breaking in on granaries. A large party of them attended on the sheriff himself, downed their cudgels while he addressed them on their misdeameanours, listened with patience, "chearfully shouted God Save the King", and then picked up their cudgels and resumed the good work of setting the price. The movement partook of the character of a general strike of the whole clothing district: "the rioters come into our work-shops. . . and force out all the men willing or unwilling to join them".[1]

This was an unusually large-scale and disciplined action. But the account directs us to features repeatedly encountered. Thus the movement of the crowd from the market-place out-wards to the mills and thence (as in the *Book of Orders*) to farms, where stocks were inspected and the farmers ordered to send grain to market at the price dictated by the crowd — all this is commonly found. This was sometimes accompanied by the traditional round of visits to the houses of the great, for contributions, forced or voluntary. At Norwich in 1740 the crowd, after forcing down prices in the city, and seizing a keel loaded with wheat and rye on the river, solicited contributions from the rich of the city:

> Early on Thursday Morning, by Sound of Horns, they met again; and after a short Confabulation, divided into Parties, and march'd out of Town at different Gates, with a long Streamer carried before them, purposing to visit the Gentlemen and Farmers in the neighbouring Villages, in order to extort Money, Strong Ale, &c, from them. At many places, where the Generosity of People answer'd not their Expectation, 'tis said they shew'd their Resentment by treading down the Corn in the Fields. . .

Perambulating crowds were active in this year, notably in Durham and Northumberland, the West Riding, and several parts of North Wales. Anti-export demonstrators, commenc-ing at Dewsbury (April 1740) were led by a drummer and "a sort of ensign or colours"; they performed a regular circuit of

[1] Letters of W. Dalloway, Brimscomb, 17 and 20 Sept. 1766, in PRO, PC 1/8/41.

the local mills, destroying machinery, cutting sacks, and carrying away grain and meal. In 1766 a perambulating crowd in the Thames Valley called themselves "the Regulators"; a terrified farmer allowed them to sleep in the straw in his yard, and "could hear from his Chamber that they were telling one another whom they had most frightened, & where they had the best success". The pattern continues in the 1790s: at Ellesmere (Shropshire) the crowd stopping the corn as it goes to the mills and threatening the farmers individually; in the Forest of Dean the miners visiting mills and farmers' houses, and exacting money "from persons they meet in the road"; in West Cornwall the tinners visiting farms with a noose in one hand and an agreement to bring corn at reduced prices to market in the other.[1]

It is the restraint, rather than the disorder, which is remarkable; and there can be no doubt that the actions were approved by an overwhelming popular consensus. There is a deeply-felt conviction that prices *ought*, in times of dearth, to be regulated, and that the profiteer put himself outside of society. On occasion the crowd attempted to enlist, by suasion or force a magistrate, parish constable, or some figure of authority to preside over the *taxation populaire*. In 1766 at Drayton (Oxfordshire) members of the crowd went to John Lyford's house "and asked him if he were a Constable — upon his saying 'yes' Cheer said he sho'd go with them to the Cross & receive the money for 3 sacks of flour which they had taken from one Betty Smith and which they w'd sell for 5s a Bushel"; the same crowd enlisted the constable of Abingdon for the same service. The constable of Handborough (also in Oxfordshire) was enlisted in a similar way, in 1795; the crowd set a price — and a substantial one — of 40s a sack upon a wagon of flour which had been inter-

---

[1] Norwich, 1740 — *Ipswich Journal*, 26 July 1740; Dewsbury, 1740 — J. L. Kaye and five magistrates, Wakefield, 30 Apr. 1740, in PRO, SP 36/50; Thames Valley, 1766 — testimony of Bartholomew Freeman of Bisham Farm, 2 Oct. 1766, in PRO, TS 11/995/3707; Ellesmere, 1795 — PRO, WO I/1089, fo. 359; Forest of Dean — John Turner, mayor of Gloucester, 24 June 1795, PRO, WO I/1087; Cornwall — see John G. Rule, "Some Social Aspects of the Cornish Industrial Revolution", in Roger Burt (ed.), *Industry and Society in the South-West* (Exeter, 1970), pp. 90-1.

cepted, and the money for no fewer than fifteen sacks was paid into his hands. In the Isle of Ely, in the same year, "the mob insisted upon buying meat at 4d per lb, & desired Mr Gardner a Magistrate to superintend the sale, as the Mayor had done at Cambridge on Saturday sennight". Again in 1795 there were a number of occasions when militia or regular troops supervised forced sales, sometimes at bayonet-point, their officers looking steadfastly the other way. A combined operation of soldiery and crowd forced the mayor of Chichester to accede in setting the price of bread. At Wells men of the 122nd Regiment began

> by hooting those they term'd forestallers or jobbers of butter, who they hunted in different parts of the town — seized the butter — collected it together — placed sentinels over it — then threw it, & mix't it together in a tub — & afterwards retail'd the same, weighing it in scales, selling it after the rate of 8d per lb. . . though the common price given by the jobbers was rather more than 10d.[1]

It would be foolish to suggest that, when so large a breach was made in the outworks of deference, many did not take the opportunity to carry off goods without payment. But there is abundant evidence the other way, and some of it is striking. There are the Honiton lace-workers, in 1766, who, having taken corn from the farmers and sold it at the popular price in the market, brought back to the farmers not only the money but also the sacks; the Oldham crowd, in 1800, which rationed each purchaser to two pecks a head; and the many occasions when carts were stopped on the roads, their contents sold, and the money entrusted to the carter.[2]

Moreover, in those cases where goods were taken without payment, or where violence was committed, it is wise to

---

[1] Drayton, Oxon — brief against Wm. Denley and three others, in PRO, TS 11/995/3707; Handborough — information of Robert Prior, constable, 6 Aug. 1795, PRO, Assizes 5/116; Isle of Ely — Lord Hardwicke, Wimpole, 27 July 1795, PRO, HO 42/35 and H. Gunning, *Reminiscences of Cambridge* (1854), ii, pp. 5-7; Chichester — duke of Richmond, Goodwood, 14 Apr. 1795, PRO, WO 1/1092; Wells — "Verax", 28 Apr. 1795, PRO, WO 1/1082 and the Rev. J. Turner, 28 Apr., HO 42/34. For an example of a constable who was executed for his part in a tinners' riot in St. Austell, 1729, see Rule, *op. cit.*, p. 90.

[2] See Rose, *op. cit.*, p. 435; Edwin Butterworth, *Historical Sketches of Oldham* (Oldham, 1856), pp. 137-9, 144-5.

enquire whether any particular aggravation of circumstances enters into the case. The distinction is made in an account of an action at Portsea (Hampshire) in 1795. The bakers and butchers were first offered by the crowd the popular price: "those that complied in those demands were paid with exactness". But those who refused had their shops rifled "without receiving any more money than the mob chose to leave". Again, the quarrymen at Port Isaac (Cornwall) in the same year seized barley warehoused for export, paying the reasonably high price of 11s. a bushel, at the same time warning the owner that "if he offer'd to ship the Remainder they would come & take it without making him any recompence". Very often the motive of punishment or revenge comes in. The great riot in Newcastle in 1740, when pitmen and keelmen swept into the Guildhall, destroyed the town books and shared out the town's hutch, and pelted aldermen with mud and stones, came only after two phases of aggravation: first, when an agreement between the pitmen's leaders and the merchants (with an alderman acting as arbitrator) setting the prices of grain had been broken; second, when panicky authorities had fired into the crowd from the Guildhall steps. At one house in Gloucestershire in 1766 shots were fired at the crowd which (writes the sheriff) —

> they highly resented by forceing into the house, and destroying all the furniture, windows, &c and partly untiled it; they have given out since that they greatly repented of this act because 'twas not the master of the house (he being from home) that fired upon them.

In 1795 the tinners mounted an attack upon a Penryn (Cornwall) merchant who was contracted to send them barley, but who had sent them spoiled and sprouting grain. When mills were attacked, and their machinery damaged, it was often in furtherance of a long-standing warning, or as punishment for some notorious practice. [1]

Indeed, if we wish to call in question the unilinear and

[1] Portsea — *Gentleman's Magazine*, lxv (1795), p. 343; Port Isaac — Sir W. Molesworth, 23 March 1795, PRO, HO 42/34; Newcastle — *Gentleman's Magazine*, x (1740), p. 355, and various sources in PRO, SP 36/51, in Northumberland CRO and Newcastle City Archives Office; Gloucestershire, 1766 — PRO, PC 1/8/41; Penryn, 1795 — PRO, HO 42/34.

spasmodic view of food riots, we need only point to this continuing motif of popular intimidation, when men and women near to starvation nevertheless attacked mills and granaries, not to steal the food, but to punish the proprietors. Repeatedly corn or flour was strewn along the roads and hedges; dumped into the river; mill machinery was damaged and mill-dams let off. To examples of such behaviour the authorities reacted both with indignation and astonishment. It was symptomatic (as it seemed to them) of the "frantic" and distempered humours of a people whose brain was inflamed by hunger. In 1795 both the Lord Chief Justice and Arthur Young delivered lectures to the poor, pointing out that the destruction of grain was not the best way to improve the supply of bread. Hannah More added a Half-penny Homily. An anonymous versifier of 1800 gives us a rather more lively example of these admonitions to the lower orders:

> When with your country Friends your hours you pass,
> And take, as oft you're wont, the copious glass,
> When all grow mellow, if perchance you hear
> "That 'tis th' Engrossers make the corn so dear;
> "They must and will have bread; they've had enough
> "Of Rice and Soup, and all such *squashy* stuff:
> "They'll help themselves: and strive by might and main
> "To be reveng'd on all such rogues in grain":
> John swears he'll fight as long as he has breath,
> "'Twere better to be hang'd than starv'd to death:
> "He'll burn Squire Hoardum's garner, so he will,
> "Tuck up old Filchbag, and pull down his mill".
> Now when the Prong and Pitchfork they prepare
> And all the implements of rustick war. . .
> Tell them what ills unlawful deeds attend,
> Deeds, which in wrath begun, and sorrow end,
> That burning barns, and pulling down a mill,
> Will neither corn produce, nor bellies fill. [1]

But were the poor really so silly? One suspects that the millers and dealers, who kept one wary eye on the people and the other on the maximisation of their profits, knew better than the poetasters at their *escritoires*. For the poor had their own sources of information. They worked on the docks. They moved the barges on the canals. They drove the carts

[1] Anon., *Contentment: or Hints to Servants, on the Present Scarcity* (broadsheet, 1800).

and manned the toll-gates. They worked in the granaries and the mills. They often knew the local facts far better than the gentry; in many actions they went unerringly to hidden supplies of grain whose existence the JPs, in good faith, denied. If rumours often grew beyond all bounds, they were always rooted in at least some shallow soil of fact. The poor knew the one way to make the rich yield was to twist their arms.

VI

Initiators of the riots were, very often, the women. In 1693 we learn of a great number of women going to Northampton market, "with knives stuck in their girdles to force corn at their own rates". In an export riot in 1737 at Poole (Dorset) it was reported: "The Numbers consist of so many Women, & the Men supporting them, & Swear, if any one offers to molest any of the Women in their Proceedings they will raise a Great Number of Men & destroy both Ships & Cargoes". The mob was raised in Stockton (Durham) in 1740 by a "Lady with a stick and a horn". At Haverfordwest (Pembroke) in 1795 an old-fashioned JP who attempted, with the help of his curate, to do battle with the colliers, complained that "the women were putting the Men on, & were perfect furies. I had some strokes from some of them on my Back. . .". A Birmingham paper described the Snow Hill riots as the work of "a rabble, urged on by furious women". In dozens of cases it is the same — the women pelting an unpopular dealer with his own potatoes, or cunningly combining fury with the calculation that they had slightly greater immunity than the men from the retaliation of the authorities: "the women told the common men", the Haverfordwest magistrate said of the soldiers, "that they knew they were in their Hearts for them & would do them no hurt".[1]

[1]Northampton — *Calendar State Papers, Domestic*, 1693, p. 397; Poole — memorial of Chitty and Lefebare, merchants, enclosed in Holles Newcastle, 26 May 1737, PRO, SP 41/10; Stockton — Edward Goddard, 24 May 1740, PRO, SP 36/50 ("We met a Lady with a Stick and a horn going towards Norton to raise the people. . . took the horn from her, She using very ill language all the while and followed into the Town, raising all the People she could. . . Ordered the Woman to be taken up. . .

These women appear to have belonged to some pre-history of their sex before its Fall, and to have been unaware that they should have waited for some two hundred years for their Liberation. (Southey could write as a commonplace, in 1807: "Women are more disposed to be mutinous; they stand less in fear of law, partly from ignorance, partly because they presume upon the privilege of their sex, and therefore in all public tumults they are foremost in violence and ferocity".[1]) They were also, of course, those most involved in face-to-face marketing, most sensitive to price significancies, most experienced in detecting short-weight or inferior quality. It is probable that the women most frequently precipitated the spontaneous actions. But other actions were more carefully prepared. Sometimes notices were nailed to church or inn doors. In 1740 "a Mach of Futtball was Cried at Ketring of five Hundred Men of a side, but the design was to Pull Down Lady Betey Jesmaine's Mills". At the end of the century the distribution of hand-written notices may have become more common. From Wakefield (Yorkshire), 1795:

> To Give Notice
> To all Women & inhabitance of Wakefield they are desired to meet at the New Church. . . on Friday next at Nine O'Clock. . . to state the price of corn. . .
> By desire of the inhabitants of Halifax
> Who will meet them there

From Stratton (Cornwall), 1801:

> To all the labouring Men and Tradesmen in the Hundred of Stratton that are willing to save their Wifes and Children from the Dreadfull condition of being STARVED to DEATH by the unfeeling and Griping Farmer. . . Assemble all emeadiately and march in Dreadfull Array to

---

She all the way Crying out, Damn you all, Will You See me Suffer, or be sent to Gaol?"); Haverfordwest — PRO, HO 42/35; Birmingham — J. A. Langford, *A Century of Birmingham Life* (Birmingham, 1868), ii, p. 52.

[1] *Letters from England* (1814), ii, p. 47. The women had other resources than ferocity: a colonel of Volunteers lamented that "the Devil in the shape of Women is now using all his influence to induce the Privates to brake their attachments to their Officers": Lt.-Col. J. Entwisle, Rochdale, 5 Aug. 1795, PRO, WO 1/1086.

the Habitations of the Griping Farmer, and Compell them to sell their Corn in the Market, at a fair and reasonable Price. . .[1]

The small-scale, spontaneous action might develop from a kind of ritualised hooting or groaning outside retailers' shops;[2] from the interception of a wagon of grain or flour passing through a populous centre; or from the mere gathering of a menacing crowd. Very quickly a bargaining-situation would develop: the owner of the provisions knew very well that if he did not comply voluntarily with the price imposed by the crowd (and his compliance made any subsequent prosecution very difficult) he stood in danger of losing his stock altogether. When a wagon with sacks of wheat and flour was intercepted at Handborough (Oxfordshire) in 1795, some women climbed aboard and pitched the sacks on the roadside. "Some of the persons assembled said they would give Forty Shillings a Sack for the Flour, and they would have it at that, and would not give more, and if that would not do, they would have it by force." The owner (a "yeoman") at length agreed: "If that must be the price, it must be the price". The procedure of forced bargaining can be seen equally clearly in the deposition of Thomas Smith, a baker, who rode into Hadstock (Essex) with bread on his panniers (1795). He was stopped in the village street by forty or more women and children. One of the women (a labourer's wife) held his horse

> and having asked whether he had fallen in his price of Bread, he told her, he had no Orders to fall from the Millers, & she then said, "By God if you don't fall you shall not leave any Bread in the Town". . .

Several in the crowd then offered 9d. a quartern loaf, while he demanded 19d. They then "swore that if he would not let them have it at 9d a Loaf, they would take it away, & before

---

[1] Kettering — PRO, SP 36/50: for other examples of the use of football to assemble a crowd, see R. M. Malcolmson, "Popular Recreations in English Society, 1700-1850" (Warwick, Univ. Ph.D. thesis, 1970); Wakefield — PRO, HO 42/35; Stratton — handwritten notice, dated 8 April and signed "Cato", in PRO, HO 42/61 fo. 718.

[2] A correspondent from Rosemary Lane (London), 2 July 1795, complained of being awoken at 5 a.m. "By a most dreadful Groaning (as the Mob call it) but what I should call Squealing": PRO, WO 1/1089 fo. 719.

he could give any other Answer, several Persons then about him took several of the Loaves off his Pads. . .". Only at this point did Smith agree to the sale at 9d. the loaf. The bargaining was well understood on both sides; and retailers, who had to hold on to their customers in the fat years as well as the lean, often capitulated at the first sign of crowd turbulence. [1]

In larger-scale disturbances, once the nucleus of a crowd had been formed, the remainder was often raised by horn or drums. "On Monday last," a letter from a Shropshire magistrate commences in 1756, "the colliers from Broseley &c assembled with horns blowing, & proceeded to Wenlock Market. . .". What was critical was the gathering of the determined nucleus. Not only the "virility" of the colliers, and their particular exposure to consumer-exploitation, explain their prominent role, but also their numbers and the natural discipline of the mining community. "On Thursday morning", John Todd, a pitman at Heaton Colliery, Gateshead, deposed (1740), "at the time of the night shift going on", his fellow pitmen, "about 60 or 80 in number stopped the gin at the pit. . . and it was proposed to come to Newcastle to settle the prices of corn. . .". When they came from Nook Colliery into Haverfordwest in 1795 (the magistrate relates that his curate said: "Doctor, here are the colliers coming. . . I looked up & saw a great crowd of men women & children with oaken bludgeons coming down the street bawling out, 'One & all — one & all' ") the colliers explained later that they had come at the request of the poor townspeople, who had not the morale to set the price on their own. [1]

The occupational make-up of the crowd provides few surprises. It was (it seems) fairly representative of the occupations of the "lower orders" in the rioting areas. At Witney (Oxfordshire) we find informations against a blanket-weaver, a tailor, the wife of a victualler, and a servant; at Saffron Walden (Essex) indictments against two collar-makers, a cordwainer, a bricklayer, a carpenter, a sawyer, a

---

[1] Broseley — T. Whitmore, 11 Nov. 1756, PRO, SP 36/136; Gateshead — information of John Todd in Newcastle City Archives; Haverfordwest — PRO, HO 42/35.

worsted-maker, and nine labourers; in several Devonshire villages (Sampford Peverell, Burlescomb, Culmstock) we find a spinster, two weavers, a woolcomber, a cordwainer, a thatcher, and ten labourers indicted; in the Handborough affair a carpenter, a mason, a sawyer, and seven labourers were mentioned in one information.[1] There were fewer accusations as to the alleged incitement by persons in a superior station in life than Rudé and others have noted in France,[2] although it was more often suggested that the labourers were encouraged by their superiors towards a tone hostile to farmers and middlemen. An observer in the South-West in 1801 argued that the riots were "certainly directed by inferior Tradesmen, Woolcombers, & Dissenters, who keep aloof but by their language & immediate influence govern the lower classes".[3] Occasionally, large employers of labour were alleged to have encouraged their own workers to act.[4]

Another important difference, as compared with France, was the relative inactivity of farm labourers in England as contrasted with the activity of the *vignerons* and petty peasantry. Many cereal farmers, of course, continued the custom of selling cheap grain to their own labourers, while the living-in hired farm servants shared the farmer's board. Rural labourers did participate in riots, when some other groups (like colliers) formed the original nucleus, or where

[1] Witney — information of Thomas Hudson, 10 Aug. 1795, PRO, Assizes 5/116; Saffron Walden — indictments for offences on 27 July 1795, PRO, Assizes 35/236; Devonshire — calendar for Summer Circuit, 1795, PRO, Assizes 24/43; Handborough — information of James Stevens, tythingman, 6 Aug. 1795, PRO, Assizes 5/116. All 13 of the Berkshire rioters of 1766 tried by Special Commission were described as "labourers"; of 66 persons brought before the Special Commission at Gloucester in 1766, 51 were described as "labourers", 10 were wives of "labourers", 3 were spinsters: the descriptions reveal little: *G. B. Deputy Keeper of Public Records, 5th Report* (1844), ii, pp. 198-9, 202-4. For Wales, 1793-1801, see Jones, "Corn Riots in Wales", App. III, p. 350. For Dundee, 1772, see S. G. E. Lythe, "The Tayside Meal Mobs", *Scot. Hist. Rev.*, xlvi (1967), p. 34: a porter, a quarryman, three weavers, and a sailor were indicted.
[2] See Rudé, *The Crowd in History*, p. 38.
[3] Lt.-Gen. J. G. Simcoe, 27 Mar. 1801, PRO, HO 42/61.
[4] Thus in an export riot in Flint (1740) there were allegations that the steward of Sir Thomas Mostyn had found arms for his own colliers: various depositions in PRO, SP 36/51.

some activity brought them together in sufficient numbers. When a large band of labourers toured the Thames Valley in 1766, the action had commenced with gangs at work on a turnpike-road, who said "with one Voice, Come one & all to Newbury in a Body to Make the Bread cheaper". Once in town, they raised further support by parading in the town square and giving three huzzas. In East Anglia in 1795 a similar nucleus was found from among the "bankers" (gangs "employed in cleansing out Drains & in embanking"). The bankers also were less subject to instant identification and punishment, or to the revenges of village paternalism, than were field labourers, being "for the most part strangers from different countries [who] are not so easily quieted as those who live on the spot".[1]

In truth, the food riot did not require a high degree of organisation. It required a consensus of support in the community, and an inherited pattern of action with its own objectives and restraints. And the persistence of this form of action raises an interesting question: how far was it, in any sense, successful? Would it have continued, over so many scores, indeed hundreds, of years, if it had consistently failed to achieve its objectives, and had left nothing but a few ruined mills and victims on the gallows? It is a question peculiarly difficult to answer; but one which must be asked.

VII

In the short-term it would seem probable that riot and price-setting defeated their own objects. Farmers were sometimes intimidated so far that they refused afterwards, for several weeks, to bring goods to market. The interdiction of the movement of grain within the country was likely only to aggravate shortage in other regions. Although instances can be found where riot appeared to result in a fall in prices, and instances can be found of the opposite, and, further, instances can be found where there appears to be little difference in the movement of prices in riot and non-riot markets, none of these instances — however aggregated or averaged — need necessarily disclose the effect of the

[1] Newbury — brief in PRO, TS 11/995/3707; East Anglia — B. Clayton, Boston, 11 Aug. 1795, PRO, HO 42/35.

expectation of riot upon the total market-situation.[1]

We may take an analogy from war. The actual immediate benefits of war are rarely significant, either to victor or defeated. But the benefits which may be gained by the *threat* of war may be considerable: and yet the threat carries no terrors if the sanction of war is never used. If the market-place was as much an arena of class war as the factory and mine became in the industrial revolution, then the threat of riot would affect the entire marketing situation, not only in years of dearth but also in years of moderate harvest, not only in towns notorious for their susceptibility to riot but also in towns where the authorities wished to preserve a tradition of peace. However carefully we quantify the available data these cannot show us to what level prices would have risen if the threat of riot had been altogether removed.

The authorities in riot-prone areas were often cool and competent in handling disturbance. This allows one some-times to forget that riot was a calamity, often resulting in a profound dislocation of social relations in the community, whose results could linger on for years. The provincial magistracy were often in extreme isolation. Troops, if they were sent for, might take two, three or more days to arrive, and the crowd knew this very well. The sheriff of Gloucester-shire could do nothing in the first days of the "rising" of 1766 but attend at Stroud market with his "javelin men". A Suffolk magistrate in 1709 refrained from imprisoning the leaders of the crowd because "the Mob threatened to pull both his house and the Bridewell down if he punished any of their fellows". Another magistrate who led a ragged and unmartial *posse comitatus* through North Yorkshire to Durham in 1740, capturing prisoners on the way, was dismayed to find the citizens of Durham turn out and release two of his prisoners at the gate of the gaol. (Such rescues were common). A Flint grain exporter had an even more un-pleasant experience in the same year. Rioters entered his house, drank the beer and wine in his vaults, and stood —

---

[1] Undoubtedly detailed investigation of short-term price-movements in relation to riot will help to refine the question; but the variables are many, and evidence as to some (*anticipation* of riot, persuasion brought to bear on tenants, dealers, etc., charitable subscriptions, application of poor rates, etc.) if often elusive and difficult to quantify.

with a Drawn Sword pointed upon my Daughter in Laws breast. . . They have a great many Fire Arms, Pikes and Broadswords. Five of the Pikes they declare that four of them shall do to Carry my Four Quarters and the other my head in triumph about with them. . .[1]

The question of order was by no means simple. The inadequacy of civil forces was combined with a reluctance to employ military force. The officers themselves had sufficient humanity, and were surrounded by sufficient ambiguity as to their powers in civil affrays, to show a marked lack of enthusiasm for employment in this "Odious Service".[1] If local magistrates called in the troops, or authorised the use of fire-arms, they had to go on living in the district after the troops had left, incurring the odium of the local population, perhaps receiving threatening letters, and being the victims of broken windows or even arson. Troops billeted in a town quickly became unpopular, even with those who had first called them in. With uncanny regularity requests for the aid of troops are followed, in Home Office or War Office papers, after an interval of five or six weeks, by petitions for their removal. A pitiful petition from the inhabitants of Sunderland in 1800, headed by their Rector, asked for the withdrawal of the 68th Regiment:

> Their principal aim is robbery. Several have been knocked down and plundered of their watches, but always it has been done in the most violent and brutal manner.

One young man had had his skull fractured, another his upper lip cut off. Inhabitants of Wantage, Farringdon and Abingdon petitioned

> in the name of God. . . remove the part of Lord Landaff's regiment from this place, or else Murder must be the consequence, for such a sett of Villains never entered this Town before.

A local magistrate, supporting the petition, added that the "savage behaviour of the military. . . exasperates the populace to the highest degree. The usual intercourse of the husbandmen at fairs and markets is much interrupted."[2]

[1] ". . . a most Odious Service which nothing but Necessity can justify", Viscount Barrington to Weymouth, 18 Apr. 1768, PRO, WO 4/83, fos. 316-7.
[2] Sunderland — petition in PRO, WO 40/17; Wantage and Abingdon — petition to Sir G. Young and C. Dundas, 6 Apr. 1795, *ibid.*

Riot was a calamity. The "order" which might follow after riot could be an even greater calamity. Hence the anxiety of authorities, either to anticipate the event, or to cut it short in its early stages, by personal presence, by exhortation and concession. In a letter of 1773 the mayor of Penryn, besieged by angry tinners, writes that the town was visited by three hundred "of those Banditti, with whom we were forced to beat a Parley and come to an agreement to let them have the Corn for one-third less than the Prime Cost to the Proprietors". Such parleys, more or less reluctant, were common. An experienced Warwickshire magistrate, Sir Roger Newdigate, noted in his diary on 27 September 1766:

> At 11 rode to Nuneaton. . . and with the principal people of the town met the Bedworth colliers and mob who came hallowing and armed with sticks, demanded what they wanted, promised to satisfy all their reasonable demands if they would be peacable and throw away their sticks which all of them then did into the Meadow, then walked with them to all the houses which they expected had engrossed and let 5 or 6 go in search and persuaded the owners to sell what was found of cheese. . .

The colliers then left the town quietly, after Sir Roger Newdigate and two others had each given them half a guinea. They had, in effect, acted according to the *Book of Orders.*[1]

This kind of bargaining, in the first commencement of riot, often secured concessions for the crowd. But we should also note the exertions by magistrates and landowners in anticipation of riot. Thus a Shropshire magistrate in 1756 describes how the colliers "say if the farmers do not bring their corn to the markets, they will go to their houses & thresh for themselves":

> I have sent to my Tenants to order them to take each of them some corn to the market on Saturday as the only means I can think of to prevent greater outrages.

In the same year we may observe magistrates in Devon exerting themselves in a similar way. Riots had occurred at Ottery, farmers' corn seized and sold off at 5s. a bushel, and

[1] Penryn — PRO, WO 40/17; Warwickshire — H. C. Wood, "The Diaries of Sir Roger Newdigate, 1751-1806", *Trans. Birmingham Archaeological Soc.*, lxxviii (1962), p. 43.

several mills attacked. Sir George Yonge sent his servant to affix an admonitory and conciliatory paper in the market-place:

> The mob gather'd, insulted my Servant, and intimidated the Cryer. . . On reading [the paper] they declared It would not do, the Gentlemen need not trouble themselves, for *They* would fix the Price at 4s 9d next Market Day: upon this I rode into the Town yesterday, and told both the Common people and the better sort, that if things were not quiet the military must be sent for. . .

He and two neighbouring gentry had then sent their own corn into the local markets:

> I have ordered mine to be sold at 5s 3d and 5s 6d per bushell to the poorer sort, as we have resolved to keep rather above the Price dictated by the Mob. I shall send to the Millers to know if they can part with any Flour. . .

The mayor of Exeter replied to Yonge that the city authorities had ordered corn to be sold at 5s. 6d.: "Everything was quiet immediately the farmers fell the price. . .". Similar measures were still being taken in Devon in 1801, "some Gentlemen of the most respectable characters in the neighbourhood of Exeter. . . directing. . . their Tenantry to bring Corn to the Market, under the penalty of not having their leases renewed". In 1795 and 1800-1 such orders by traditionalist landowners to their farming tenants were frequent in other counties. The earl of Warwick (an arch-paternalist and an advocate of the legislation against forestallers in its fullest rigour) rode in person around his estates giving such directions to his tenants.[1]

Such pressures as these, in anticipation of riot, may have been more effective than has been proposed: in getting corn to market; in restraining rising prices; and in intimidating certain kinds of profiteering. Moreover, a disposition to riot was certainly effective as a signal to the rich to put the machinery of parish relief and of charity — subsidised corn and bread for the poor — into good repair. In January 1757

---

[1] Shropshire — T. Whitmore, 11 Nov. 1756, PRO, SP 36/136; Devon — HMC, *City of Exeter*, series lxxiii (1916), pp. 255-7; Devon, 1801 — Lt.-Gen. J. G. Simcoe, 27 Mar. 1801, PRO, HO 42/61; Warwick — T. W. Whitley, *The Parliamentary Representation of the City of Coventry* (Coventry, 1894), p. 214.

Reading Corporation agreed:

> that a Subscription be set on foot for Raising money to Buy Bread to be Distributed to the Poor. . . . at a Price to be fixed much below the present price of Bread. . .

The Corporation itself donated £21.[1] Such measures were very commonly followed, the initiative coming sometimes from a corporation, sometimes from individual gentry, sometimes from Quarter Sessions, sometimes from parish authorities, sometimes from employers — especially those who employed a substantial labour-force (such as lead-miners) in isolated districts.

The measures taken in 1795 were especially extensive, various and well-documented. They ranged from direct sub-scriptions to reduce the price of bread (the parishes sometimes sending their own agents direct to the ports to purchase imported grain), through subsidies from the poor rates, to the Speenhamland system. The examination of such measures would take us farther into the history of the poor laws than we intend to go.[2] But the effects were sometimes curious. Subscriptions, while quieting one area, might provoke riot in an adjacent one, through arousing a sharp sense of inequality. An agreement in Newcastle in 1740 to reduce prices, reached between merchants and a deputation of demonstrating pitmen (with aldermen mediating), resulted in "country people" from outlying villages flooding into the city; an unsuccessful attempt was made to limit the sale to persons with a written certificate from "a Fitter, Staithman, Ton Tail Man, or Churchwarden". Participation by soldiers in price-setting riots in 1795 was explained, by the duke of Richmond, as arising from a similar inequality: it was alleged by the soldiers "that while the Country People are relieved by their Parishes and Subscriptions, the Soldiers receive no such Benefit". Moreover, such subscriptions,

---

[1] MS diary of Reading Corporation, Central Public Library, Reading: entry for 24 January 1757. £30 was disbursed "towards the present high price of Bread" on 12 July 1795.

[2] Especially useful are replies from correspondents in *Annals of Agriculture*, xxiv and xxv (1795). See also S. and B. Webb, "The Assize of Bread", *op. cit.*, pp. 208-9; J. L. and B. Hammond, *op. cit.*, ch. vi; W. M. Stern, *op. cit.*, pp. 181-6.

while being intended to buy off riot (actual or potential),
might often have the effect of *raising* the price of bread to
those outside the benefit of subscription.[1] In South Devon,
where the authorities were still acting in 1801 in the tradition
of 1757, the process can be seen. The Exeter crowd demonstrated in the market for wheat at 10s. a bushel:

> The Gentlemen and Farmers met, & the People waited their decision. . .
> They were informed that no Price they shou'd name or fix would be
> agreed to, & principally because the principle of fixing a Price wou'd be
> resisted. The Farmers then agreed at 12s and every Inhabitant to have it
> in proportion to their Families. . .
>   The Arguments of the discontented at Exmouth are very cogent.
> "Give us whatever *quantity* the Stock in Hand will afford, & at a price
> by which we can attain it, & we shall be satisfied; we will not accept any
> Subscription from the Gentry because it enhances the Price, & is a hard-
> ship on them".[2]

The point here is not just that prices, in time of scarcity,
were determined by many other factors than mere market-
forces: anyone with even a scanty knowledge of much-
maligned "literary" sources must be aware of that. It is more
important to note the total socio-economic context within
which the market operated, and the logic of crowd pressure.
One other example, this time from a hitherto riot-free
market, may show this logic at work. The account is that of a
substantial farmer, John Toogood, in Sherborne (Dorset).
The year 1757 commenced with "general complaint" at high
prices, and frequent accounts of riots elsewhere:

> On the 30th of April, being Market-Day, many of our idle and insolent
> Poor Men and Women assembled and begun a Riot in the Market
> House, went to Oborn Mill and brought off several Bags of Flour and
> divided the Spoil here in Triumph.

On the next Monday an anonymous letter, directed to
Toogood's brother (who had just sold ten bushels of wheat at
14s. 10d. — "a great price indeed" — to a miller), was found

---

[1] A point to be watched in any quantified analysis: the price
officially returned from a market in the aftermath of riot might *rise*,
although, as a consequence of riot or threat of riot, the poor might be
receiving corn at subsidised rates.

[2] Newcastle — advertisement 24 June 1740 in City Archives Office;
duke of Richmond, 13 Apr. 1795, PRO, WO 1/1092; Devon — James
Coleridge, 29 Mar. 1801, HO 42/61.

in the abbey: "Sir, If you do not bring your Wheat into the Market, and sell it at a reasonable price, your Barns shall be pulled down. . .".

As Rioting is quite a new Thing in Sherborne. . . and as the neighbouring Parishes seemed ripe for joining in this Sport, I thought there was no Time to be lost, and that it was proper to crush this Evil in it's Bud, in Order to which we took the following Measures.

Having called a Meeting at the Almshouse, it was agreed that Mr. Jeffrey and I should take a Survey of all the most necessitous Families in the Town, this done, We raised about £100 by Subscriptions, and before the next Market Day, our Justice of the Peace and some of the principal Inhabitants made a Procession throughout the Town and published by the Cryer of the Town the following Notice.

"That the Poor Families of this Town will be supplied with a Quantity of Wheat sufficient for their Support every Week 'till Harvest at the Rate of 8s p. Bushel and that if any person whatsoever after this public Notice shall use any threatening Expressions, or commit any Riot or Disorder in this Town, the Offender shall be forthwith committed to Prison."

They then contracted for wheat, at 10s. and 12s. the bushel, supplying it to a "List of the Poor" at 8s. until harvest. (Sixty bushels weekly over this period will have involved a subsidy of between £100 and £200.) "By these Means we restored Peace, and disappointed many loose, disorderly Fellows of the Neighbouring Parishes, who appeared in the Market with their empty Bags, expecting to have had Corn without Money." John Toogood, setting down this account for the guidance of his sons, concluded it with the advice:

If the like Circumstances happen hereafter in your Time and either of you are engaged in Farmering Business, let not a covetous Eye tempt you to be foremost in advancing the Price of Corn, but rather let your Behaviour shew some Compassion and Charity towards the Condition of the Poor. . .[1]

It is within such a context as this that the function of riot may be disclosed. Riot may have been, in the short term, counter-productive, although this has not yet been proved. But, once again, riot was a social calamity, and one to be avoided, even at a high cost. The cost might be to achieve some medium, between a soaring "economic" price in the market, and a traditional "moral" price set by the crowd.

[1] MS diary of John Toogood, Dorset CRO, D 170/1.

That medium might be found by the intervention of paternalists, by the prudential self-restraint of farmers and dealers, or by buying-off a portion of the crowd through charities and subsidies. As Hannah More carolled, in the persona of the sententious Jack Anvil, when dissuading Tom Hod from riot:

> So I'll work the whole day, and on Sundays I'll seek
> At Church how to bear all the wants of the week.
> The gentlefolks, too, will afford us supplies,
> They'll subscribe — and they'll give up their puddings and pies.
>
> *Derry down.* [1]

Derry down, indeed, and even Tra-la-dee-bum-deeay! However, the nature of gentlefolks being what it is, a thundering good riot in the next parish was more likely to oil the wheels of charity than the sight of Jack Anvil on his knees in church. As the doggerel on the *out*side of the church door in Kent had put it succinctly in 1630:

> Before we arise
> Less will safise.

VIII

We have been examining a pattern of social protest which derives from a consensus as to the moral economy of the commonweal in times of dearth. It is not usually helpful to examine it for overt, articulate political intentions, although these sometimes arose through chance coincidence. Rebellious phrases can often be found, usually (one suspects) to chill the blood of the rich with their theatrical effect. It was said that the Newcastle pitmen, flushed with the success of their capture of the Guildhall, "were for putting in practice the old levelling principles"; they did at least tear down the portraits of Charles II and James II and smash their frames. By contrast, bargees at Henley (Oxfordshire) in 1743 called out "Long Live the Pretender"; and someone in Woodbridge (Suffolk) in 1766 nailed up a notice in the market-place which the local magistrate found to be "peculiarly bold and seditious and of high and delicate import": "We are wishing [it said] that our exiled King could come over or send some

---

[1] "The Riot: or, half a loaf is better than no bread, &c", 1795, in Hannah More, *Works* (1830), ii, pp. 86-8.

Officers." Perhaps the same menace was intended, in the South-West in 1753, by threats that "the French w'd be here soon".[1]

Most common are general "levelling" threats, imprecations against the rich. A letter at Witney (1767) assured the bailiffs of the town that the people would not suffer "such damned wheesing fat guted Rogues to Starve the Poor by such Hellish Ways on purpose that they may follow hunting horse-racing etc. and to maintain their familys in Pride and extravagance". A letter on the Gold Cross at Birmingham's Snow Hill (1766), signed "Kidderminster & Stourbridge", was perhaps in the mode of rhyming doggerel —

> . . . there is a small Army of us upwards of three thousand all ready to fight
> & I'll be dam'd if we don't make the King's Army to shite
> If so be the King & Parliament don't order better
> we will turn England into a Litter
> & if so be as things don't get cheaper
> I'll be damd if we don't burn down the Parliament House & make all better. . .

A letter in Colchester in 1772 addressed to all farmers, millers, butchers, shopkeepers and corn merchants, warned all the "damd Rogues" to take care,

> for this is november and we have about two or three hundred bum shells a getting in Readiness for the Mellers [millers] and all no king no parliment nothing but a powder plot all over the nation.

The gentlemen of Fareham (Hampshire) were warned in 1766 to prepare "for a Mob or Sivel war", which would "pull George from his throne beat down the house of rougs [rogues] and destroy the Sets [seats] of the Law makers". "Tis better to Undergo a forrieghn Yoke than to be used thus", wrote a villager near Hereford in the next year. And so on, and from most parts of Britain. It is, in the main, rhetoric, although rhetoric which qualifies in a devastating

---

[1] Newcastle — MS account of riots in City Archives; Henley — Isaac, op. cit., p. 186; Woodbridge — PRO, WO 1/873: 1753 — Newcastle MSS, Brit. Lib. Add MS 32732, fo. 343. Earl Poulet, Lord Lieutenant of Somerset, reported in another letter to the duke of Newcastle that some of the mob "came to talk a Levelling language, viz. they did not see why some sh'd be rich & others poor": ibid., fos. 214-5.

way the rhetoric of historians as to the deference and social solidarities of Georgian England.[1]

Only in 1795 and 1800-1, when a Jacobin tinge is frequent in such letters and handbills, do we have the impression of a genuine undercurrent of articulate political motivation. A trenchant example of these is some doggerel addressed to "the Broth Makers & Flower Risers" which gave a Maldon (Essex) magistrate cause for alarm:

> On Swill & Grains you wish the poor to be fed
> And underneath the Guillintine we could wish to see your heads
> For I think it is a great shame to serve the poor so —
> And I think a few of your heads will make a pretty show.

Scores upon scores of such letters circulated in these years. From Uley (Gloucestershire), "no King but a Constitution down down down O fatall down high caps and proud hats forever down down. . .". At Lewes (Sussex), after several militiamen had been executed for their part in price-setting, a notice was posted: "Soldiers to Arms!"

> Arise and revenge your cause
> On those bloody numskulls, Pitt and George,
> For since they no longer can send you to France
> To be murdered like Swine, or pierc'd by the Lance,
> You are sent for by Express to make a speedy Return
> To be shot like a Crow, or hang'd in your Turn. . .

At Ramsbury (Wiltshire) in 1800 a notice was affixed to a tree:

> Downe with Your Luxzuaras Government both spirital & temperal Or you starve with Hunger. they have stripp you of bread Chees Meate &c &c &c &c. Nay even your Lives have they Taken thousands on their Expeditions let the Burbon Family defend their owne Cause and let us true Britons look to Our Selves let us banish Some to Hanover where they came from Downe with your Constitution Arect a republick Or you and your offsprings are to starve the Remainder of our Days dear Brothers will you lay down and die under Man eaters and Lave your

[1] Witney — *London Gazette*, Nov. 1767, no. 10779; Birmingham — PRO, WO 1/873; Colchester — *London Gazette*, Nov. 1772, no. 11304; Fareham — *ibid.*, Jan. 1767, no. 10690; Hereford — *ibid.*, Apr. 1767, no. 10717.

offspring under that Burden that Blackguard Government which is now eatain you up.
God Save the Poor & down with George III.[1]

But these crisis years of the wars (1800-1) would demand separate treatment. We are coming to the end of one tradition, and the new tradition has scarcely emerged. In these years the alternative form of economic pressure — pressure upon wages — is becoming more vigorous; there is also something more than rhetoric behind the language of sedition — underground union organisation, oaths, the shadowy "United Englishmen". In 1812 traditional food riots overlap with Luddism. In 1816 the East Anglian labourers do not only set the prices, they also demand a minimum wage and an end to Speenhamland relief. They look forward to the very different revolt of labourers in 1830. The older form of action lingers on into the 1840s and even later: it was especially deeply rooted in the South-West.[2] But in the new territories of the industrial revolution it passed by stages into other forms of action. The break in wheat prices after the wars eased the transition. In the northern towns the fight against the corn jobbers gave way to the fight against the Corn Laws.

There was another reason why 1795 and 1800-1 bring us into different historical territory. The forms of action which we have been examining depended upon a particular set of social relations, a particular equilibrium between paternalist authority and the crowd. This equilibrium was dislodged in the wars, for two reasons. First, the acute anti-Jacobinism of the gentry led to a new fear of any form of popular self-activity; magistrates were willing to see signs of sedition in price-setting actions even where no such sedition existed; the fear of invasion raised the Volunteers, and thus gave to the

---

[1] Maldon — PRO, WO 40/17; Uley — W. G. Baker, Oct. 1795, HO 42/36; Lewes — HO 42/35; Ramsbury — enclosure in the Rev. E. Meyrick, 12 June 1800, HO 42/50.

[2] See A. Rowe, "The Food Riots of the Forties in Cornwall", *Report of Royal Cornwall Polytechnic Society* (1942), pp. 51-67. There were food riots in the Scottish Highlands in 1847; in Teignmouth and Exeter in November 1867; and in Norwich a curious episode (the "Battle of Ham Run") as late as 1886.

civil powers much more immediate means for meeting the crowd, not with parley and concession, but with repression.[1] Second, such repression was legitimised, in the minds of central and of many local authorities, by the triumph of the new ideology of political economy.

Of this celestial triumph, the Home Secretary, the duke of Portland, served as Temporal Deputy. He displayed, in 1800-1, a quite new firmness, not only in handling disturbance, but in overruling and remonstrating with those local authorities who still espoused the old paternalism. In September 1800 a significant episode occurred in Oxford. There had been some affair of setting the price of butter in the market, and cavalry appeared in the town (at the request — as it transpired — of the Vice-Chancellor). The Town Clerk, on the direction of the mayor and magistrates, wrote to the Secretary at War, expressing their "surprise that a military body of horse soldiers should have made their appearance early this morning":

> It is with great pleasure I inform you that the people of Oxford have hitherto shewn no disposition to be riotous except the bringing into the market [of] some hampers of butter and selling it at a shilling a pound and accounting for the money to the owner of the butter be reckoned of that description. . .

"Notwithstanding the extreme pressure of the times", the City authorities were of "the decided opinion" that there was "no occasion in this City for the presence of a regular Soldiery", especially since the magistrates were being most active in suppressing "what they conceive to be one of the principal causes of the dearness, the offences of forestalling, ingrossing, and regrating. . .".

The Town Clerk's letter was passed over to the duke of Portland, and drew from him a weighty reproof:

> His Grace. . . desires you to inform the Mayor and Magistrates, that as his official situation enables him in a more particular manner to appreciate the extent of the publick mischief which must inevitably ensue from a continuance of the riotous proceedings which have taken place in several parts of the Kingdom in consequence of the present

---

[1] See J. R. Western, "The Volunteer Movement as an Anti-Revolutionary Force, 1793-1801", *Eng. Hist. Rev.*, lxxi (1956).

scarcity of Provisions, so he considers himself to be more immediately called upon to exercise his own judgement and discretion in directing adequate measures to be taken for the immediate and effectual suppression of such dangerous proceedings. For greatly as His Grace laments the cause of these Riots, nothing is more certain than that they can be productive of no other effect than to increase the evil beyond all power of calculation. His Grace, therefore, cannot allow himself to pass over in silence that part of your letter which states "that the People of Oxford have hitherto shewn no disposition to be riotous, except the bringing into Market some Hampers of Butter, and selling it at a Shilling a pound, and accounting for the money to the Owner of the Butter, can be reckoned of that description".

So far from considering this circumstance, in the trivial light in which it is represented in your letter (even supposing it to stand unconnected with others of a similar and a still more dangerous nature, which it is to be feared is not the case) His Grace sees it in the view of a violent and unjustifiable attack on property pregnant with the most fatal consequences to the City of Oxford and to it's Inhabitants of every description; and which His Grace takes it for granted the Mayor and Magistrates must have thought it their bounden duty to suppress and punish by the immediate apprehension and committal of the Offenders.[1]

Throughout 1800 and 1801 the duke of Portland busied himself enforcing the same doctrines. The remedy for disturbance was the military or Volunteers; even liberal subscriptions for cheap corn were to be discouraged, as exhausting stocks; persuasion upon farmers or dealers to lower prices was an offence against political economy. In April 1801 he wrote to Earl Mount Edgcumbe,

Your Lordship must excuse the liberty I take in not passing unnoticed the agreement you mention to have been voluntarily entered into by the Farmers in Cornwall to supply the Markets with Corn and other Articles of Provision at reduced Prices. . .

The duke had information that the farmers had been subjected to pressure by the county authorities:

. . . the experience I have. . . calls upon me to say that every undertaking of the kind cannot in the nature of things be justified and must unavoidably and shortly add to and aggravate the distress which it

[1] W. Taunton, 6 Sept. 1800; I. King to Taunton, 7 Sept. 1800: PRO, WO 40/17 and HO 43/12. In private letters Portland exerted himself even more forcefully, writing to Dr Hughes of Jesus College, Oxford (12 Sept.) of the "unjust & injudicious proceedings of your foolish Corporation": Univ. of Nottingham, Portland MSS, PwV III.

pretends to alleviate, and I will venture also to assert that the more general it could be rendered the more injurious must be the consequences by which it could not fail to be attended because it necessarily prevents the Employment of Capital in the Farming Line. . .[1]

The "nature of things" which had once made imperative, in times of dearth, at least some symbolic solidarity between the rulers and the poor, now dictated solidarity between the rulers and "the Employment of Capital". It is, perhaps, appropriate that it was the ideologist who synthesized an hysteric anti-Jacobinism with the new political economy who signed the death-warrant of that paternalism of which, in his more specious passages of rhetoric, he was the celebrant. "The Labouring *Poor*", exclaimed Burke: "Let compassion be shewn in action",

> . . . but let there be no lamentation of their condition. It is no relief to their miserable circumstances; it is only an insult to their miserable understandings. . . Patience, labour, sobriety, frugality, and religion, should be recommended to them; all the rest is downright *fraud*.[2]

Against that tone the notice at Ramsbury was the only possible reply.

IX

I hope that a somewhat different picture has emerged from this account than the customary one. I have tried to describe, not an involuntary spasm, but a pattern of behaviour of which a Trobriand islander need not have been ashamed.

It is difficult to re-imagine the moral assumptions of another social configuration. It is not easy for us to conceive

---

[1] Portland, 25 Apr. 1801, PRO, HO 43/13, pp. 24-7. On 4 October 1800 Portland wrote to the Vice-Chancellor of Oxford University (Dr Marlow) as to the dangers of the people "giving way to the notion of their difficulties being imputable to the avarice and rapacity of those, who instead of being denominated Engrossers are correctly speaking the purveyors and provident Stewards of the Public": Univ. of Nottingham, Portland MSS, PwV III.

[2] E. Burke, *Thoughts and Details on Scarcity, originally presented to the Rt. Hon. William Pitt in. . . November, 1795* (1800), p. 4. Undoubtedly this pamphlet was influential with both Pitt and Portland, and may have contributed to the tougher policies of 1800.

that there may have been a time, within a smaller and more integrated community, when it appeared to be "unnatural" that any man should profit from the necessities of others, and when it was assumed that, in time of dearth, prices of "necessities" should remain at a customary level, even though there might be less all round.

"The economy of the mediaeval borough", wrote R. H. Tawney, "was one in which consumption held somewhat the same primacy in the public mind, as the undisputed arbiter of economic effort, as the nineteenth century attached to profits".[1] These assumptions were under strong challenge, of course, long before the eighteenth century. But too often in our histories we foreshorten the great transitions. We leave forestalling and the doctrine of a fair price in the seventeenth century. We take up the story of the free market economy in the nineteenth. But the death of the old moral economy of provision was as long-drawn-out as the death of paternalist intervention in industry and trade. The consumer defended his old notions of right as stubbornly as (perhaps the same man in another role) he defended his craft status as an artisan.

These notions of right were clearly articulated. They carried for a long time the church's imprimatur. The *Book of Orders* of 1630 envisaged moral precept and example as an integral part of emergency measures:

> That all good Means and Perswasions bee used by the Justices in their severall Divisions, and by Admonitions and Exhortations in Sermons in the Churches. . . that the Poore may bee served of Corne at convenient and charitable Prices. And to the furtherance thereof, that the richer Sort bee earnestly mooved by Christian Charitie, to cause their Graine to be sold under the common Prices of the Market to the poorer sort: A deed of mercy, that will doubtlesse be rewarded of Almighty God.

At least one such sermon, delivered at Bodmin and Fowey (Cornwall) before the Sessions in 1630 by the Rev. Charles Fitz-Geffrey, was still known to eighteenth-century readers. Hoarders of corn were denounced as

> these Man-haters, opposite to the Common good, as if the world were made onely for them, would appropriate the earth, and the fruits thereof, wholly to themselves. . . As Quailes grow fat with

[1] R. H. Tawney, *Religion and the Rise of Capitalism* (1926), p. 33.

Hemlocke, which is poison to other creatures, so these grow full by Dearth. . .

They were "enemies both to God and man, opposite both to Grace and Nature". As for the dealer, exporting corn in time of scarcity, "the savour of lucre is sweet to him, though raked out of the puddle of the most filthy profession in Europe. . .".[1]

As the seventeenth century drew on, this kind of exhortation became muted, especially among the Puritans. With Baxter one part of moral precept is diluted with one part of casuistry and one part of business prudence: "charity must be exercised as well as justice", and, while goods might be withheld in the expectation of rising prices, this must not be done "to the hurt of the Commonwealth, as if. . . keeping it in be the cause of the dearth".[2] The old moral teaching became, increasingly, divided between the paternalist gentry on one hand, and the rebellious plebs on the other. There is an epitaph in the church at Stoneleigh (Warwickshire) to Humphrey How, the porter to Lady Leigh, who died in 1688:

> Here Lyes a Faithful Friend unto the Poore
> Who dealt Large Almes out of his Lord[ps] Store
> Weepe Not Poore People Tho' Y[e] Servat's Dead
> The Lord himselfe Will Give You Dayly Breade
> If Markets Rise Raile Not Against Theire Rates
> The Price is Stil the Same at Stone Leigh Gates.[3]

The old precepts resounded throughout the eighteenth century. Occasionally they might still be heard from the pulpit:

> Exaction of any kind is base; but this in the Matter of Corn is of the basest Kind. It falls heaviest upon the Poor, It is robbing them because they are so. . . It is murdering *them* outright whom they find half dead, and plundering the wreck'd Vessel. . . These are the Murderers accused by the Son of *Sirach*, where he saith, *The Bread of the Needy is their Life: he that defraudeth them thereof is a Man of Blood.* . . Justly may

---

[1] C. Fitz-Geffrey, *God's Blessing upon the Providers of Corne: and God's Curse upon the Hoarders* (1631; reprint 1648), pp. 7, 8, 13.

[2] Tawney, *op. cit.*, p. 222. See also C. Hill, *Society and Puritanism in Pre-Revolutionary England* (1964), esp. pp. 277-8.

[3] I am indebted to Professor David Montgomery for this evidence.

such Oppressors be called *'Men of Blood'*; and surely will the Blood of those, who thus perish by their means, be required at their Hands.[1]

More often they were heard in pamphlet or newspaper:

> To keep up the Price of the very Staff of Life at such an extravagent Sale, as that the Poor. . . cannot purchase it, is the greatest Iniquity any Man can be guilty of; it is no less than Murder, nay, the most cruel Murder.[2]

Sometimes in broadsheet and ballad:

> Go now you hard-hearted rich men,
>   In your miseries, weep and howl,
> Your canker'd gold will rise against you,
>   And Witness be against your souls. . .[3]

and frequently in anonymous letters. "Donte make a god of your mony", the gentlemen of Newbury were warned in 1772:

> but think of the por you great men do you think of gohing to heaven or hell. think of the Sarmon which preach on 15 of March for dam we if we dont make you do you think to starve the pore quite you dam sons of wors [whores]. . .[4]

"Averishes Woman!", a corn-hoarder in Cornwall was addressed in 1795 by Cornish tinners: "We are. . . determined to assemble and immediately to march till we come to your Idol, or your God or your Mows [Moses?], whome you esteem as such and pull it down and likewise your House. . .".[5]

Today we shrug off the extortionate mechanisms of an unregulated market economy because it causes most of us only inconvenience, unostentatious hardships. In the eighteenth century this was not the case. Dearths were real dearths. High prices meant swollen bellies and sick children whose food was

---

[1] Anon. ["A Clergyman in the Country"], *Artificial Dearth: or, the Iniquity and Danger of Withholding Corn* (1756), pp. 20-1.

[2] Letter to *Sherborne Mercury*, 5 Sept. 1757.

[3] "A Serious Call to the Gentlemen Farmers, on the present exorbitant Prices of Provisions", broadside, n.d., in Seligman Collection (Broadsides — Prices), Columbia Univ.

[4] *London Gazette*, Mar. 1772, no. 11233.

[5] Letter from "Captins Audacious, Fortitude, Presumption and dread not", dated 28 Dec. 1795, "Polgooth and other mines", and addressed to Mrs Herring, *ibid.*, 1796, p. 45.

coarse bread made up from stale flour. No evidence has yet been published to show anything like a classic *crise des subsistances* in England in the eighteenth century:[1] the mortality of 1795 certainly did not approach that in France in the same year. But there was what the gentry described as a distress that was "truly painful": rising prices (wrote one) "have stript the cloaths from their backs, torn the shoes and stockings from their feet, and snatched the food from their mouths".[2] The risings of the Cornish tinners were preceded by harrowing scenes: men fainted at their work and had to be carried home by their fellows in scarcely better state. The dearth was accompanied by an epidemic described as "Yellow Fever", very possibly the jaundice associated with near-starvation.[3] In such a year Wordsworth's "pedlar" wandered among the cottages and saw

> The hardships of that season; many rich
> Sank down as in a dream among the poor,
> And of the poor did many cease to be,
> And their place knew them not. . .[4]

But if the market was the point at which working people most often felt their exposure to exploitation, it was also the point — especially in rural or dispersed manufacturing districts — at which they could most easily become organised. Marketing (or "shopping") becomes in mature industrial society increasingly impersonal. In eighteenth-century Britain or France (and in parts of southern Italy or Haiti or rural India or Africa today) the market remained a social as well as an economic nexus. It was the place where one-hundred-and-one social and personal transactions went on; where news was passed, rumour and gossip flew around, politics was (if ever) discussed in the inns or wine-shops round the market-square. The market was the place where the people, because they

---

[1] This is *not* to argue that such evidence may not be soon forthcoming as to local or regional demographic crisis.

[2] *Annals of Agriculture*, xxiv (1795), p. 159 (evidence from Dunmow, Essex).

[3] Letter of 24 June 1795 in PRO, PC 1/27/A.54; various letters, esp. 29 Mar. 1795, HO 42/34.

[4] W. Wordsworth, *Poetical Works*, ed. E. de Selincourt and Helen Darbishire (Oxford, 1959), v, p. 391.

were numerous, felt for a moment that they were strong.[1]

The confrontations of the market in a "pre-industrial" society are of course more universal than any national experience. And the elementary moral precepts of the "reasonable price" are equally universal. Indeed, one may suggest in Britain the survival of a pagan imagery which reaches to levels more obscure than Christian symbolism. Few folk rituals survived with such vigour to the end of the eighteenth century as all the paraphernalia of the harvest-home, with its charms and suppers, its fairs and festivals. Even in manufacturing areas the year still turned to the rhythm of the seasons and not to that of the banks. Dearth always comes to such communities as a profound psychic shock. When it is accompanied by the knowledge of inequalities, and the suspicion of manipulated scarcity, shock passes into fury.

One is struck, as the new century opens, by the growing symbolism of blood, and by its assimilation to the demand for bread. In Nottingham in 1812 the women paraded with a loaf upon a pole, streaked with red and tied with black crepe, emblematic of "bleeding famine decked in Sackecloth". At Yeovil (Somerset) in 1816 there was an anonymous letter, "Blood and Blood and Blood, a General Revolution their mus be. . .", the letter signed with a crude heart dripping blood. In the East Anglian riots of the same year such phrases as, "We will have blood before dinner". In Plymouth "a *Loaf* which had been *dipped in blood*, with a heart by it, was found in the streets". In the great Merthyr riots of 1831 a calf was sacrificed and a loaf soaked in its blood, impaled on a flagpole, served as emblem of revolt.[2]

This fury for corn is a curious culmination of the age of agricultural improvement. In the 1790s the gentry themselves were somewhat perplexed. Sometimes crippled by

---

[1] See Sidney Mintz, "Internal Market Systems as Mechanisms of Social Articulation", *Intermediate Societies, Social Mobility and Communication* (American Ethnological Society, 1959); and the same author's "Peasant Markets", *Scientific American*, cciii (1960), pp. 112-22.

[2] Nottingham — J. F. Sutton, *The Date-book of Nottingham* (Nottingham 1880), p. 286; Yeovil — PRO, HO 42/150; East Anglia — A. J. Peacock, *Bread or Blood* (1965), *passim*; Merthyr — G. A. Williams, "The Insurrection at Merthyr Tydfil in 1831", *Trans. Hon. Soc. of Cymmrodorion*, 2, (Session 1965), pp. 227-8.

an excess of rich food,[1] the magistrates from time to time put aside their industrious compilation of archives for the disciples of Sir Lewis Namier, and peered down from their parklands at the corn-fields in which their labourers hungered. (More than one magistrate wrote in to the Home Office, at this critical juncture, describing the measures which he would take against the rioters if only he were not confined to his house by gout.) The country will not be secure at harvest, wrote the Lord Lieutenant of Cambridgeshire, "without some soldiers, as he had heard that the People intended to help themselves when the Corn was ripe". He found this "a very serious apprehension indeed" and "in this open country most likely to be effected, at least by stealth".[2]

"Thou shalt not muzzle the ox that treadeth out the corn." The breakthrough of the new political economy of the free market was also the breakdown of the old moral economy of provision. After the wars all that was left of it was charity — and Speenhamland. The moral economy of the crowd took longer to die: it is picked up by the early co-operative flour mills, by some Owenite socialists, and it lingered on for years somewhere in the bowels of the Co-operative Wholesale Society. One symptom of its final demise is that we have been able to accept for so long an abbreviated and "economistic" picture of the food riot, as a direct, spasmodic, irrational response to hunger — a picture which is itself a product of a political economy which diminished human reciprocities to the wages-nexus. More generous, but also more authoritative, was the assessment of the sheriff of Gloucestershire in 1766. The mobs of that year (he wrote) had committed many acts of violence,

> some of wantoness and excess; and in other instances some acts of courage, prudence, justice, and a consistency towards that which they profess to obtain.[3]

[1] In 1795, when subsidised brown bread was being given to the poor of his own parish, Parson Woodforde did not flinch before his continuing duty to his own dinner: March 6th, ". . . for Dinner a Couple of boiled Chicken and Pigs Face, very good Peas Soup, a boiled Rump of Beef very fine, a prodigious fine, large and very fat Cock-Turkey rosted, Maccaroni, Batter Custard Pudding", etc.: James Woodforde, *Diary of a Country Parson*, ed. J. Beresford (World's Classics, 1963), pp. 483, 485.

[2] Lord Hardwicke, 27 July 1795, PRO, HO 42/35.

[3] W. Dalloway, 20 Sept. 1766, PRO, PC 1/8/41.

Chapter Five

The Moral Economy Reviewed

I

The foregoing chapter was first published as an article in *Past and Present* in 1971. I have republished it without revision. I see no reason to retreat from its findings. And it has now entered into the stream of subsequent historical scholarship — it has been criticised and extensions of its theses have been proposed. It would confuse the record if I were to alter a text upon which commentary depends.

But some comment on my commentators is required. And also upon significant work which approaches the same problems, with little or no reference to my own. This is not a simple matter. For the "market" turns out to be a junction-point between social, economic and intellectual histories, and a sensitive metaphor for many kinds of exchange. The "moral economy" leads us not into a single argument but into a concourse of arguments, and it will not be possible to do justice to every voice.

A word first about my essay. Although first published in 1971 I commenced work on it in 1963 while awaiting proofs of *The Making of the English Working Class*. The project started then, for a joint study of British and French grain riots in the 1790s, in collaboration with Richard Cobb whose fine *Terreur et Subsistances, 1793-1795* came out in 1964. He was then in Leeds and I was in Halifax and Gwyn A. Williams (then in Aberystwyth) was also enlisted as a collaborator in the project. I don't remember how or when the project fell through, except that each member of the triumvirate moved in a different direction, Richard Cobb to Oxford, Gwyn Williams to York and myself to the University of Warwick. By 1970, when Cobb published his *The Police and the People*, our plan had certainly been dropped. There need be no regret for the failure of my part in that project to come to a conclusion, since Roger Wells has now explored every aspect of food and its mediations in England in the 1790s in copious detail in his *Wretched Faces* (1988).

But this explanation serves to place my essay, which was an enterprise not marginal but central to my research interests for nearly ten years. My files bulge with material collected on mills and marketing and meal mobs, etc., but since much of this repeats the evidence adduced in my article, it need not now be deployed. But a lot of work underlay my findings, and I may be forgiven if I am impatient with trivial objections.

II

It may be necessary to restate what my essay was about. It was not about *all* kinds of crowd, and a reader would have to be unusually thick-headed who supposed so.[1] It was about the crowd's "moral economy" in a context which the article defines. Nor was it about English and Welsh food riots in the eighteenth century — their where, why and when? — although it was certainly concerned with these. My object of analysis was the *mentalité*, or, as I would prefer, the political culture, the expectations, traditions, and, indeed, superstitions of the working population most frequently involved in actions in the market; and the relations — sometimes negotiations — between crowd and rulers which go under the unsatisfactory term of "riot". My method was to reconstruct a paternalist model of food marketing, with protective institutional expression and with emergency

---

[1] Mark Harrison reprimands me for applying the term "crowd" to what was "a very specific category of mass formation": *Crowds and History: Mass Phenomena in English Towns, 1790-1835* (Cambridge, 1988), p. 13. I followed George Rudé and Eric Hobsbawm in preferring the term "crowd" to the pejorative "mob" which some previous historians had used. No-one ever supposed that all crowds were riotous, although Harrison's attention to their variety is helpful. Harrison also pronounces that my article "has a number of shortcomings, which will be examined more fully in chapter 6". Since chapter 6 does not mention my article, and the shortcomings are identified nowhere else in his book, I am still waiting for the blow to fall.

routines in time of dearth, which derived in part from earlier Edwardian and Tudor policies of provision and market-regulation; to contrast this with the new political economy of the free market in grain, associated above all with *The Wealth of Nations*; and to show how, in times of high prices and of hardship, the crowd might enforce, with a robust direct action, protective market-control and the regulation of prices, sometimes claiming a legitimacy derived from the paternalist model.

To understand the actions of any particular crowd may require attention to particular market-places and particular practices in dealing. But to understand the "political" space in which the crowd might act and might negotiate with the authorities must attend upon a larger analysis of the relations between the two. The findings in "The Moral Economy" cannot be taken straight across to any "peasant market" nor to all proto-industrial market-places nor to Revolutionary France in the Years II and II nor to nineteenth-century Madras. Some of the encounters between growers, dealers and consumers were markedly similar, but I have described them as they were worked out within the given field-of-force of eighteenth-century English relations.

My essay did not offer a comprehensive overview of food riots in England in that century; it did not (for example) correlate the incidence of riots with price movements, nor explain why riot was more common in some regions than in others, nor attempt to chart a dozen other variables. Abundant new evidence on such questions has been brought forward in recent years, and much of it has been helpfully brought under examination in Andrew Charlesworth's *An Atlas of Rural Protest in Britain, 1548-1900* (1983). Dr John Stevenson complains that "The Moral Economy" tells us "virtually nothing about why some places were almost perennially subject to disturbances, whilst others remained almost completely undisturbed",[1] but this was not the

---

[1] J. Stevenson, "Food Riots in England, 1792-1818", in R. Quinault and J. Stevenson (eds.), *Popular Protest and Public Order* (London, 1974), p. 67. Also J. Stevenson, "The 'Moral Economy' of the English Crowd: Myth and Reality", in Anthony Fletcher and J. Stevenson (eds.), *Order and Disorder in Early Modern England* (Cambridge, 1985) — an essay which adds little to the discussion.

essay's theme. Nor is there any sense in which the findings of scholars (such as Dr Stevenson) who have been addressing such themes must necessarily contradict or compete with my own. Economic and social historians are not engaged in rival party-political performances, although one might sometimes suppose so. The study of wages and prices and the study of norms and expectations can complement each other.

There are still a few ineducable positivists lingering about who do not so much disagree with the findings of social historians as they wish to disallow their questions. They propose that only one set of directly economic explanations of food riots — questions relating to the grain trade, harvests, market prices, etc., is needed or is even proper to be asked. An odd example is a short essay published by Dale Williams in 1976 entitled "Were 'Hunger' Rioters Really Hungry?".[1] In this he described my "moral economy" as intended as "a replacement" for an economic or quantitative approach. He had somehow got it into his head that riots must *either* be about hunger *or* about "social issues involving local usages and traditional rights". But it will be recalled that I warn against precisely this confusion at the outset of my essay, using the analogy of a sexual tension chart: "the objection is that such a chart, if used unwisely, may conclude investigation at the exact point at which it becomes of serious sociological or cultural interest: being hungry (or being sexy), what do people do?" (p. 187). *Of course* food rioters were hungry — and on occasion coming close to starvation. But this does not tell us how their behaviour is "modified by custom, culture and reason".

Nevertheless, this illustrates one point which we take far too easily for granted. Comparative study of food riots has been, inevitably, into the history of nations which *had* riots. There has been less comparative reflection upon national histories which afford evidence — and sometimes evidence sadly plentiful — of dearth passing into famine without passing through any phase in which riots of the West-European kind have been noted. Famines have been suffered in the past (as in Ireland and in India) and are suffered today

[1] *Past and Present*, no. 71, May 1976.

in several parts of Africa, as our television screens reveal, with a fatalism sometimes mistaken for apathy or resignation. It is not only that beyond a certain point the undernourished have no physical or emotional resources for riot. (For this reason riot must take place *before* people are so weakened, and it may presuppose a watchful estimate of future supply and of market prices.) It is also that riot is a group, community, or class response to crisis; it is not within the power of a few individuals to riot. Nor need it be the only or the most obvious form of collective action — there may be alternatives such as the mass-petitioning of the authorities, fast days, sacrifices and prayer; perambulation of the houses of the rich; or the migration of whole villages.

Riot need not be favoured within the culture of the poor. It might provoke the gods (who had already sent dearth as a "Judgement"), and it could certainly alienate the governors or the rich from whom alone some small relief might come. An oncoming harvest failure would be watched with fear and awe. "Hunger employs its own outriders. Those who have already experienced it can see it announced, not only in the sky, but in the fields, scrutinized each year with increasing anxiety, week by week during the hot summer months. . ."[1] In the eighteenth century Britain was only emerging from the "demographic *ancien régime*", with its periodical visitations of famine and of plague, and dearth revived age-old memories and fears. Famine could place the whole social order on the rack, and the rulers were tested by their response to it. Indeed, by visible and well-advertised exertions the rulers might actually strengthen their authority during dearth, as John Walter and Keith Wrightson have argued from seventeenth-century examples. Central government, by issuing proclamations, invoking the successive regulations which became known as the *Book of Orders*, and proclaiming national days of fast, and the local authorities by a flurry of highly-visible activity against petty offenders ranging from badgers, forestallers and regrators to drunkards, swearers, sabbath-breakers, gamblers and rogues, might actually gain

---

[1] R. C. Cobb, *The Police and the People* (Oxford, 1970), p. 323. For a comparative overview, see David Arnold, *Famine: Social Crisis and Historical Change* (Oxford, 1988).

credibility among that part of the population persuaded that dearth was a judgement of God.[1] At the least, the authorities made a public display of their concern. At the best, they might restrain rising prices or persuade farmers to release stocks to the open market.

Riot may even be a signal that the *ancien régime* is ending, since there is food in barns or granaries or barges to be seized or to be got to market, and some bargaining to be done about its price. True famine (where there really is no stock of food) is not often attended with riot, since there are few rational targets for the rioters. In the pastoral North-West of England as late as the 1590s and 1620s the population appears to have suffered from famine mortality. But "the poor. . . starved to death quietly, & created no problems of order for their governors".[2] In the Irish famine of 1845-7 there were a few anti-export riots in the early stages,[3] but the Irish people could be congratulated in the Queen's speech in 1847 for having suffered with "patience and resignation". Riot is

---

[1] John Walter and Keith Wrightson, "Dearth and the Social Order in Early Modern England", *Past and Present*, 71 (1976). See also (for a sharper assertion of authority) John Walter, "Grain Riots and Popular Attitudes to the Law: Maldon and the Crisis of 1629" in John Brewer and John Styles (eds.), *An Ungovernable People* (1980). For the *Book of Orders*, see A. Everitt, "The Marketing of Agricultural Produce", in J. Thirsk (ed.), *The Agrarian History of England and Wales*, vol. iv, *1500-1640* (Cambridge, 1967), pp. 581-6; P. Slack, "The Book of Orders: The Making of English Social Policy, 1577-1631", *TRHS*, xxx (1980); R. B. Outhwaite, "Food Crisis in Early Modern England: Patterns of Public Response", *Proceedings of the Seventh International Economic History Congress* (Edinburgh, 1978), pp. 367-74; R. B. Outhwaite, "Dearth and Government Intervention in English Grain Markets, 1590-1700", *Econ. Hist. Rev.*, xxxiii, 3 (1981); and Buchanan Sharp, "Popular Protest in 17th-Century England", in Barry Reay (ed.), *Popular Culture in 17th-Century England* (1985), esp. pp. 274-289. Sharp argues (p. 279) that seventeenth century food riots "were often attempts to enforce officially-sanctioned market regulations and can be regarded, in many instances, not as attacks upon established order but as efforts to reinforce it".

[2] Sharp, *op. cit.*, p. 275; A. B. Appleby, in the classic account of famine mortality in Cumberland and Westmorland in the late sixteenth and early seventeenth centuries, reports no disturbances: see *Famine in Tudor and Stuart England* (Liverpool, 1978).

[3] Cecil Woodham Smith, *The Great Hunger* (1970), pp. 120-1; James S. Donnelly, Jr., *The Land and the People of Nineteenth-Century Cork* (1975), pp. 89-91.

usually a rational response, and it takes place, not among helpless or hopeless people, but among those groups who sense that they have a little power to help themselves, as prices soar, employment fails, and they can see their staple food supply being exported from the district.

The passivity of the victims of famine is noted also in Asia. Under the *ancien régime* of famine in the East (as in the terrible Orissa famine of 1770) districts were depopulated by deaths and fugitives. The ryots fled the land to which they were tied. "Day and night a torrent of famished and disease-stricken wretches poured into the great cities." Those who stayed on the land

> Sold their cattle; they sold their implements of agriculture; they devoured their seed-grain; they sold their sons and daughters, till at length no buyer of children could be found; they ate the leaves of the trees and the grass of the field. . .

But they did not (in the sense that we have been using) riot. Nor did they riot in the Bengal famine of 1866, when "many a rural household starved slowly to death without uttering a complaint or making a sign", just as there are tales of the West of Ireland in 1847 where whole families walled themselves up in their cabins to die.[1]

In the Bengal famine of 1873-4, the people turned to government as the only possible provider. Over 400,000 settled down along the lines of relief roads, pleading for relief and work: "they dreaded quitting the road, which they imagined to be the only place where subsistence could be obtained". At one place the line of carts bringing in the famine-struck from the villages stretched for twenty miles. At first there was screaming from the women and children, and begging for coin or grain. Later, the people were "seated on the ground, row after row, thousand upon thousand, in silence. . .".[2]

[1] W. H. Hunter, *The Annals of Rural Bengal* (1883), i, pp. 26-27. Many of the poor in the western counties of Ireland were overcome by fever in their own homes: see Sir W. P. MacArthur, "Medical History of the Famine", in R. D. Edwards and T. D. Williams (eds.), *The Great Famine* (Dublin, 1956), esp. pp. 270-89.

[2] Sir Richard Temple, Lieutenant-Governor of Bengal, memorandum on the scarcity of 1873-4, *Extra Supplement of the Gazette of India*, 26 Feb. 1875, pp. 25, 56-7.

There is not one simple, "animal", response to hunger. Even in Bengal the evidence is contradictory and difficult to interpret. There is some evidence of the male heads of household abandoning their families (below p. 347), and other accounts of intense familial solidarities and of self-abnegation. A relief worker in rural Bengal in 1915 gives us a common story:

> At noon I sat down at the foot of a tree to eat my bit of lunch. . . The people spotted me and long before I had finished there was a crowd of starving people around me. I did not finish it. I had a loaf of bread with me and. . . I gave the rest to the children. One little chap took his share and immediately broke it up into four pieces for his mother, two sisters and himself, leaving by far the smallest portion for himself.[1]

This is a learned response to hunger, which even the small children know. Begging, in which the children again are assigned their roles, is another learned response, or strategy. So also may be threats to the wealthy, or the theft of foodstuffs.[2]

"Riot" — itself a clumsy term which may conceal more than it reveals — is not a "natural" or "obvious" response to hunger but a sophisticated pattern of collective behaviour, a collective alternative to individualistic and familial strategies of survival. Of course hunger rioters were hungry, but hunger does not dictate that they must riot nor does it determine riot's forms.

In 1984 Dale E. Williams launched a direct assault on "The Moral Economy" in an article in *Past and Present* under the title "Morals, Markets and the English Crowd in 1766".[3] The article draws a little upon his own substantial doctoral thesis on "English Hunger Riots in 1766" presented in 1978. But its intent is mainly polemical, and it is tedious to find that, after nearly two decades, one is invited to return to square one and to argue everything through again.

Andrew Charlesworth and Adrian Randall have been kind enough to correct the record and to point out Williams's

---

[1] J. Mitchell, *Bankura Wesleyan College Magazine*, January 1916.
[2] Much curious and contradictory evidence as to responses to famine is in Robert Dirks, "Social Response during Severe Food Shortages and Famines", *Current Anthropology*, xxi (1980), pp. 21-44.
[3] *Past and Present*, 104 (1984).

self-contradictions.[1] To their critique I will only add that several of his sallies appear to be directed against his own findings in his doctoral thesis. So far from refuting my account of norms and behaviour, the crowds in Williams's thesis conform to the account in "The Moral Economy". Given high prices and the advance signals of dearth, the West of England clothing workers inhibited further exports of grain from the district, regulated markets with unusual discipline, forcibly persuaded farmers to send supplies to market, made certain of the authorities — including Mr Dalloway, the High Sheriff of Gloucestershire — for a time the "prisoners" of their demands, stimulated local measures of charity and relief, and (if I read Dr Williams aright) may have prevented dearth from passing into famine. And if Dale Williams wants examples of the crowd being informed by concern for "local usages and traditional rights" he need only turn to Dale Williams's thesis where he will find sufficient examples, such as the crowd punishing millers by destroying their bolting machinery, as well as an Appendix of anonymous letters full of threats against broggers, forestallers, regrators, corn hoarders, sample sales, and the rest.[2]

Dr Williams has brought no issues of principle into debate, he is simply confused as to the questions which he is asking. There may also be a little ideological pressure behind his polemic. When I first published "The Moral Economy", "the market" was not flying as high in the ideological firmament as it is today. In the 1970s something called "modernisation theory" swept through some undefended minds in Western academies, and subsequently the celebration of "the market economy" has become triumphal and almost universal. This renewed confidence in "the market" can be found in

[1] A. Charlesworth and Adrian Randall, "Morals, Markets and the English Crowd in 1766", *Past and Present*, 114 (1987), pp. 200-13. On the 1766 riots see also A. J. Randall, "The Gloucestershire Food Riots in 1766", *Midland History*, x (1985); W. J. Shelton, *English Hunger & Industrial Disorder* (1973), and reviews of Shelton by myself in *Econ. Hist. Rev.*, 2nd series, xxvii (1974), pp. 480-4 and by Peter Linebaugh in *Bull. Soc. Lab. Hist.*, 28 (1974), pp. 57-61.

[2] Univ. of Wales Ph.D. thesis, 1978. Dale Williams's excellent article on "Midland Hunger Riots in 1766" in *Midland History*, iii, 4 (1976), might even have been written in illustration of the moral economy thesis. What happened between 1976 and 1984 to change the events of 1766?

Dr Williams's article, where I am rebuked for failing to pay "sufficient attention to the *systems* which produce wealth". "The riot groups of 1766 were. . . all participants in a capitalist market system which, by the 1760s, was developed to a pitch of refinement unmatched elsewhere in the world." "The Moral Economy" has become suspect because it explored with sympathy alternative economic imperatives to those of the capitalist market "system". . . and offered one or two sceptical comments as to the infallibility of Adam Smith.

Similar questions worried more courteous critics shortly after "The Moral Economy" was published: Professors A. W. Coats and Elizabeth Fox-Genovese. I did not reply to either comment, since the arrows flew past my ear. Professor Coats[1] devoted his comment to rehearsing Smithian doctrine on the internal trade in grain, in terms of its logical consistency (but without recourse to empirical confirmation), and he repeated uncritically the statement that "high prices resulted mainly from physical shortages", as if this explanation of price movements suffices for all cases. But, as we shall see (pp. 283-7), it does not. Then Coats debated my notion as to the "de-moralizing of the theory of trade and consumption" implicit in the model of the new political economy. What I say (above, pp. 201-2) is this:

> By 'de-moralising' it is not suggested that Smith and his colleagues were immoral or were unconcerned for the public good. It is meant, rather, that the new political economy was disinfested of intrusive moral imperatives. The old pamphleteers were moralists first and economists second. In the new economic theory questions as to the moral polity of marketing do not enter, unless as preamble and peroration.

Coats takes this to imply an acceptance on my part of the credentials of "positive" economics, as a science purged of norms, and he reminds me of the "moral background and implications of Smith's economic analysis". But I had not forgotten that Smith was also author of the *Theory of Moral Sentiments* (1759). I had supposed that Coats's point had been met in a footnote (above p. 202) in which I had allowed Smith's intention to serve the public good but had added that "intention is a bad measure of ideological interest and of

---

[1] A. W. Coats, "Contrary Moralities: Plebs, Paternalists and Political Economists", *Past and Present*, 54 (1972), pp. 130-3.

historical consequences". It is perfectly possible that *laissez-faire* doctrines as to the food trade could have been *both* normative in intent (i.e. Adam Smith believed they would encourage cheap and abundant food) *and* ideological in outcome (i.e. in the result their supposedly de-moralised scientism was used to mask and to apologise for other self-interested operations).

I would have thought that my views were commonplace. The Tudor policies of "provision" cannot be seen, in a modern sense, as an "economic" strategy only: they depended also on theories of the State, of the reciprocal obligations and duties of governors and governed in times of dearth, and of paternalist social control; they still, in the early seventeenth century, had strong religious or magical components. In the period 1700-1760, with the dominance of mercantilist theory, we are in a kind of middle passage of theory. The magical components of the Tudor theory became much weaker. And the social location of the theory became more ambiguous; while some traditionalist gentry and magistrates invoked it in times of dearth, the authority of the theory was fast eroding as any acceptable account of normal marketing practice. The paternal obligations of "provision" were at odds with the mercantilist imperative to maximise the export of grain. At the same time there was a certain migration of the theory from the rulers to the crowd.

Nevertheless, the form of much economic argument remained (on all sides) moralistic: it validated itself at most points with reference to moral imperatives (what obligations the state, or the landowners, or the dealers *ought* to obey). Such imperatives permeated economic thinking very generally, and this is familiar to any student of economic thought. One historian has written that

> Economic theory owes its present development to the fact that some men, in thinking of economic phenomena, forcefully suspended all judgments of theology, morality, and justice, were willing to consider the economy as nothing more than an intricate mechanism, refraining for the while from asking whether the mechanism worked for good or evil.[1]

[1] W. Letwin, *The Origins of Scientific Economics* (1963), pp. 147-8. See however Joyce Appleby, *Economic Thought and Ideology in Seventeenth-Century England* (Princeton, 1978), pp. 258-9 for qualifications.

Joyce Appleby has shown the moral economy "in retreat" in the mid-seventeenth century, but the tension between norms and "mechanism" once again became marked in the eighteenth. A *locus classicus* is the scandal provoked by Mandeville's *Fable of the Bees*, which, by its equation private vices = public benefits, sought exactly to divorce moral imperatives on the one hand and economic process on the other. This was felt by some to be an outrage to official morality; by demystifying economic process it would strip authority of its paternal legitimacy; and the book was presented, in 1723, by the Grand Jury of Middlesex as a public nuisance.

Thus the notion of "economics" as a non-normative object of study, with objective mechanism independent of moral imperatives, was separating itself off from traditionalist theory during the mercantilist period, and with great difficulty: in some areas it did this with less difficulty (national book-keeping, arguments about trade and bullion), but in areas which related to internal distribution of the prime necessities of life the difficulties were immense. For if the rulers were to deny their own duties and functions in protecting the poor in time of dearth, then they might devalue the legitimacy of their rule. So tenaciously and strongly was this view held that as late as 1800 the Lord Chief Justice, Lord Kenyon, pronounced that the fact that forestalling remained an offence at Common Law "is a thing most essential to the existence of the country". "When the people knew there was a law to resort to, it composed their minds" and removed the threat of "insurrection".[1] This is an argument, not from economics and not even from law, but from the highest reasons of State.

The "morality" of Adam Smith was never the matter at issue, but — in relation to the internal trade in grain — the terms and the vocabulary, indeed the problematic of that argument. "The market economy created new moral problems", Professor Atiyah has written, and "it may not have been so obvious then, as it became later, that this was not so much to separate morality and economics, as to adopt

[1] Douglas Hay, "The State and the Market: Lord Kenyon and Mr. Waddington", *Past and Present* (forthcoming).

a particular type of morality in the interests of a particular type of economy".[1] Perhaps I might have made it more clear that "preamble and peroration" had real significance in the intentions of the classical political economists: these were something more than rhetorical devices. Professor Coats's reminder that Smithian economics "were securely grounded in the liberal-moral philosophy of the eighteenth-century enlightenment" has in recent years become a centre for intense academic interest and we will return to it.

Maybe the trouble lies with the word "moral". "Moral" is a signal which brings on a rush of polemical blood to the academic head. Nothing has made my critics angrier than the notion that a food rioter might have been more "moral" than a disciple of Dr Adam Smith. But that was not my meaning (whatever the judgement might have been in the eye of God). I was discriminating between two different sets of assumptions, two differing discourses, and the evidence for the difference is abundant. I wrote of "a consistent traditional view of social norms and obligations, of the proper economic functions of several parties within the community, which, taken together, can be said to constitute the moral economy of the poor" (above p. 188). To this were added a dense tissue of precedents and of practices in the sequence of food marketing. I could perhaps have called this "a sociological economy", and an economy in its original meaning (*oeconomy*) as the due organisation of a household, in which each part is related to the whole and each member acknowledges her/his several duties and obligations. That, indeed, is as much, or more, "political" than is "political economy", but by usage the classical economists have carried off the term.

Elizabeth Fox-Genovese's arrow flies past my ear for much the same reason.[2] She finds that both traditional and classical economics can be said to be "moral" (at least in their own self-image) and also that both were "part of larger ruling class ideologies". There is not much here that conflicts with,

[1] P. S. Atiyah, *The Rise and Fall of Freedom of Contract* (Oxford, 1979), p. 84.

[2] Elizabeth Fox-Genovese, "The Many Faces of Moral Economy", *Past and Present*, 58 (1973).

or even engages with, my arguments, and perhaps Fox-Genovese's real difference of emphasis lies in her feeling that I "lean towards a romantic view of the traditionalists". My tendency "to favour the paternalists" leads me to overlook that "if the rise of a market society brought indisputable horrors, it also brought an emphasis on individual freedom of choice, the right to self-betterment, eventually the opportunity to political participation".

That is also what we are assured — or used to be assured — by the modernisation theorists. And *of course* the rioters were already deeply involved, in some part of their lives, in a market economy's exchanges of labour, services, and of goods. (I will refrain from mentioning those critics who have put up the fat-headed notion that there has been proposed an absolute segregation between a moral and a market economy, to save their blushes.[1]) But before we go on to consider all these undoubted human goods we should delay with the market as dispenser of subsistence in time of dearth, which alone is relevant to my theme. For despite all the discourse that goes on about "the market" or "market relations", historiographical interest in the actual marketing of grain, flour or bread is little more evident today than it was in 1971.[2]

[1] One is reminded of David Thorner's wise caveat: "We are sure to go astray, if we try to conceive of peasant economies as exclusively 'subsistence' oriented and to suspect capitalism wherever the peasants show evidence of being 'market' oriented. It is much sounder to take it for granted, as a starting point, that for ages peasant economies have had a double orientation towards both. In this way, much fruitless discussion about the nature of so-called 'subsistence' economies can be avoided". Would that the same warning was borne in mind in discussions of "proto-industrial" economies! See "Peasant Economy as a Category in History", in Teodor Shanin (ed.), *Peasants and Peasant Societies*, 2nd ed. (Oxford, 1987), p. 65.

[2] The outstanding exception is Wendy Thwaites, "The Marketing of Agricultural Produce in Eighteenth Century Oxfordshire" (Univ. of Birmingham Ph.D. thesis, 1980). See also the same author's "Dearth and the Marketing of Agricultural Produce: Oxfordshire, c. 1750-1800", *Agric, Hist. Rev.*, xxxiii (1985), pt. ii; John Chartres, "Markets and Marketing in Metropolitan Western England in the late Seventeenth and Eighteenth Centuries", in Michael Havinden (ed.), *Husbandry and Marketing in the South-West* (Exeter, 1973), pp. 63-74, and John Chartres, "The Marketing of Agricultural Produce", in Joan Thirsk (ed.), *The Agrarian History of England and Wales*, vol. v, pt. 2 (Cambridge, 1985), ch. 17. The silence as

Is market *a* market or is market a metaphor? Of course it can be both, but too often discourse about "the market" conveys the sense of something definite — a space or institution of exchange (perhaps London's Corn Exchange at Mark Lane?) — when in fact, sometimes unknown to the term's user, it is being employed as a metaphor of economic process, or an idealisation or abstraction from that process. Perhaps to acknowledge this second usage, Burke sometimes employed the word without the definite article:

> Market is the meeting and conference of the *consumer* and *producer*, when they mutually discover each other's wants. Nobody, I believe, has observed with any reflection what market is, without being astonished at the truth, the correctness, the civility, the general equity, with which the balance of wants is settled. . . The moment that government appears at market, all the principles of market will be subverted.[1]

That is loop-language: it is wholly self-fulfilling. And much the same feedback loop-language is being used today in the higher theorising of market relations. Political economy has its sophisticated intellectual genealogies, and the history of political economy is a vigorous academic discourse with its own journals and its controversies and conferences, in which changes are rung on approved themes: Pufendorf, Virtue, natural law, Pocock, Grotius, the Physiocrats, Pocock, Adam Smith. These chimes have fascination, and for the bell-ringers it is an admirable mental exercise, but the peal can become so compelling that it drowns out other sounds. Intellectual history, like economic history before it, becomes imperialist and seeks to over-run all social life. It is necessary to pause, from time to time, to recall that how people thought their times need not have been the same as how those times eventuated. And how some people thought "market" does not prove that market took place in that way. Because Adam Smith offered "a clear analytical demonstration of

---

to corn milling has at last broken by John Orbell, "The Corn Milling Industry, 1750-1820", in C. H. Feinstein and S. Pollard (eds.), *Studies in Capital Formation in the United Kingdom* (Oxford, 1988), which shows (p. 162) the rapidly rising rate of annual capital investment in milling, from 1761 rising to a peak in the dearth (and riot) year of 1801.

[1] Edmund Burke, "Thoughts and Details on Scarcity" (1795), in *Works* (1801), vii, pp. 348-51.

how markets in subsistence goods and labour could balance themselves out in a manner consistent with strict justice and the natural law of humanity"[1] this does not show that any empirically observable market worked out in that way. Nor does it tell us how strict justice to the rights of property could balance with natural humanity to labouring people.

Messrs Hont and Ignatieff, in the course of a prestigious research project into "Political Economy and Society, 1750-1850" at King's College, Cambridge, have fallen across my "Moral Economy" article and they rebuke it for failing to conform to the parameters of Cambridge political thought:

> By recovering the moral economy of the poor and the regulatory system to which they made appeal, Thompson has set the iconoclasm of the Smithian position in sharp relief, crediting him with the first theory to revoke the traditional social responsibility attached to property. Yet the antinomy — moral economy versus political economy — caricatures both positions. The one becomes a vestigial, traditional moralism, the other a science 'disinfested of intrusive moral imperatives'. To the extent that favouring an adequate subsistence for the poor can be called a moral imperative, it was one shared by paternalists and political economists alike. . . On the other hand, to call the moral economy traditionalist is to portray it simply as a set of vestigial moral preferences innocent of substantive argument about the working of markets. In fact, so-called traditionalists were quite capable of arguing their position on the same terrain as their political economist opponents. Indeed, and this is the crucial point, debate over market or 'police' strategies for providing subsistence for the poor divided philosophers and political economists among themselves no less deeply than it divided the crowd for Smith. Indeed, it makes no sense to take Smith as typical of the range of opinion within the European Enlightenment camp. This becomes apparent if one moves beyond the English context, to which Thompson confines his discussion, and considers the debate in its full European setting. The crucial context for Smith's 'Digression on Grain' was not the encounter with the English or Scottish crowd, but the French debates over the liberalization of the internal trade in 1764-6, which occurred. . . when Smith himself was in France.[2]

There are some wilful confusions here. The first point to make about this passage is that, just as much as with the ineducable positivists, it is not so much offering to debate my

[1] Istvan Hont and Michael Ignatieff, "Needs and Justice in *The Wealth of Nations*", in I. Hont and M. Ignatieff (eds.), *Wealth and Virtue* (Cambridge, 1983), p. 43.

[2] *Ibid.*, pp. 14-15.

views as to disallow my questions. Hont and Ignatieff prefer to operate in a detached discipline of political ideas and rhetoric. They do not wish to know how ideas presented themselves as actors in the market-place, between producers, middlemen and consumers, and they imply that this is an improper light in which to view them. It may be "the crucial point" for Hont and Ignatieff that debate over market strategies divided philosophers among themselves no less deeply than it divided the crowd from Smith, but my essay is about the crowd and not about philosophers. Hont and Ignatieff are rebuking me for writing an essay in social history and in popular culture instead of in approved Cambridge themes. I ought to have grabbed a bell-rope and pealed out Quesnay along with Pufendorf, Pocock, Grotius, Hume and the rest.

Even so, Hont and Ignatieff's censures are sloppier than the case calls for. So far from "crediting" Adam Smith "with the first theory to revoke the traditional social responsibility attached to property" (their words, not mine) I am at pains to note the opposite, describing the *Wealth of Nations* "not only as a point of departure but also as a grand central terminus to which many important lines of discussion in the middle of the eighteenth century. . . all run". (Above p. 201.) It is in fact Hont and Ignatieff, and not Thompson, who write that "by 1776, Smith remained the only standard-bearer for 'natural liberty' in grain",[1] a spectacular mis-statement which they reach by confusing the British context with the French context in the aftermath of the *guerre des farines*. As for portraying the "moral economy" as "a set of vestigial moral preferences innocent of substantive argument about the working of markets", the trouble is, once again, the vulgarity of the crowd. They were not philosophers. They did, as my essay shows, have substantive and knowledgeable arguments about the working of markets, but about actual markets rather than theorised market relations. I am not persuaded that Hont and Ignatieff have read very far in the pamphlets and newspapers — let alone in the crowd relations — where these arguments will be found and I do not know what business they have to put me, or the crowd, down.

[1] *Ibid.*, p. 18.

I did not, of course, take Smith as "typical of the range of opinion within the European Enlightenment camp". I took Smith's "Digression Concerning the Corn Trade" in Book Four, Chapter 5, of *The Wealth of Nations* as being the most lucid expression in English of the standpoint of the new political economy upon market relations in subsistence foodstuffs. As such it was profoundly influential within British governmental circles, and few chapters can have had a more palpable influence upon policies or have been used more extensively to justify policies which were already being enacted. Pitt and Grenville read it together in the 1780s and became wholly converted; when Pitt wavered in the crisis year 1800 Grenville called him back to their old faith.[1] Burke was an ardent adherent and had reached similar positions independently; he had been, in 1772, a prime mover in the repeal of the ancient forestalling legislation, and he was to moralise the "laws" of political economy and nominate them to be divine.[2] In the nineteenth century class after class of administrators were sent out to India, fully indoctrinated at Haileybury College in Smith's "Digression", and ready to respond to the vast exigencies of Indian famine by resolutely resisting any improper interventions in the free operation of the market. T. R. Malthus, appointed Professor of Political Economy at Haileybury in 1805, was an early and apt instructor.

Hont and Ignatieff know that "the crucial context" for Smith's digression "was not the encounter with the English or Scottish crowd, but the French debates over the liberalization of the internal trade in 1764-6". I wonder how they know? A French philosophic influence is more reputable than an English or Scottish crowd, and of course Adam Smith was profoundly influenced by physiocratic thought. The influence of "the French debates" may be guessed at, but is not evident in the few pages of Smith's digression. The debate about the liberalisation of trade had proceeded in England

[1] See Roger Wells, *Wretched Faces* (Gloucester, 1988), p. 88.
[2] See Douglas Hay, "The State and the Market", *op. cit.*,; C. B. Macpherson, *Burke* (Oxford, 1980), *passim*; Burke, "Thoughts and Details on Scarcity", p. 354: "the laws of commerce, which are the laws of nature, and consequently the laws of God".

No. 3

From ALTON in *Hampſhire* *Aprill* the *10th* 17 2 5

THeſe are to Certifie, That the Bearer hereof *Joseph Wilkinson* hath given into this Charity-Stock

Alexander Rake

Wm Gates
Sam. Briſtow
⎱ TRUSTEES.

Printed by *J. Clarr in Bow* Church-Yard, *London.*

Plate I. One of the earliest surviving trade union cards, which was filed among the Crown's affidavits when woolcombers were prosecuted in 1725 in Alton, Hants. (See p. 59.) Note that the union (or "Charity") has a London printer and claims to have been founded in 1700. Bishop Blaize, the patron of the woolcombers, is in the centre.

Plate II. The ticket of the Amicable Society of Woolstaplers, 1785, invokes associations with trade and with pastoral life rather than with industry.

Plate III. This woolcombers' union card of 1838 still has the figure of
Bishop Blaize at top centre.

THE
PILLORY
IN ITS
GLORY,
With the Eloquent Speech it made foon after WILLIAMS had left it.
To which is added, an Antient Prophecy of MERLIN's
On the JACK-BOOT.

We hear that WILLIAM's Pillory (fuppofed to be made of the Defcendants of the Oaks of
Dodona, which formerly fpoke Prophetic) made a Speech as foon as he had left it to the
following Purport:

GENTLEMEN,

" THE very favourible Treatment I have juft now met with from you calls immediate
Thanks. I have been accuftomed to Ufage of a very different nature : for feldom have
I fhewn 'my Face but Filth of every kind hath been thrown againft it.--But fuch is the prefent
Occafion, and fuch your juft Opinion of it, that now you have been pleafed to decorate me with
Laurels, and honour me with your Acclamations.   Such univerfal Applaufe makes me fome-
thing proud of myfelf and induces me to think I am not unwortny of having Perfons of higher
Rank ftand upon me.   Perhaps I foon may, as Matters go on ; And I muft own to you, I
fhould be glad to experience your Behaviour towards me, when Criminals of a fuperior Station
peep thro' my wooden Windows.   Indeed I heartily wifh they foon may: fuch with Gentlemen
is no Libel; nor can the DOUBLE FEED Advocate by all his Art in Inuendo's, make it fo.   Why
fhould not great Villains ftand upon me as well as little ones? If any Lawer, in that place I
now look upon, fhould dare to attempt to pervert the Laws of this Land, and undermine the
Liberties of the People, why fhould not I expofe him to your View and Contempt? or if any
Perfon fhould take a private Bribe to betray a public Truft , why fhould not I lift up the Rafcal
to your Refentment? I would have every Man meet with his due Reward: or if he deferves
Halters or Axes let them have them: or, if any fhall merit only a Poft upon me, your grateful
Servant is very ready to exalt them, tho' loads of Dirt and rotten Eggs, inftead of Laurels and
Acclamations fhould be my Lot."

An antient Prophecy of MERLIN's.

WHEN from the North a cruel Bird call'd ----,
  Shall fly o'er ENGLAND and devour its Fruit,
Shall o'er this Land his baneful Pinions fpread.
And from their Months fhall take the Children's Bread ;
Shall, Cuckoo-like, make other Nefts his own,
And caft his filthy Eggs behind the ----
Then Magna Charta to Excife fhall turn;
The Apple be caft off, the Merchant mourn ;
Then fhall pack'd Juries try the Fact alone,
And under J---- the Bench fhall groan,
Then Pillories into Repute fhall come,
And the Prefs, ENGLAND's Bulwark, be ftruck dumb,

Plate IV. This broadside combines visual and literary forms with the
old oral form of rhyming "prophecies". Williams, a bookseller, was
sentenced to the pillory for republishing Wilkes's *North Briton*,
no. 45. He was cheered by the crowd, which "erected a gallows of
ladders, on which they hung a jack-boot [symbol of the King's
favourite, the Earl of Bute], an axe and a Scotch bonnet which
articles, after a while, were taken down, the top of the boot cut off
with the axe, and then both boot and bonnet thrown into a large
bonfire". (Thomas Wright, *Caricature History of the Georges*
London, 1867, p. 300).

ANTICIPATION
OF THE
Death-bed Confession.
OF A
NOTORIOUS SINNER.

MY Father was a celebrated Cocker, my Mother the Daughter of a Fiddler, and previous to her Marriage, had employed her Charms to fome advantage. By thefe laudible means my Parents were poffeffed of fome wealth : no expence was fpared to give me an Education, and the accomplifhment of a Gentleman; but alas, my fteril nature was never able to abide the firft rudiments of a fcholar, and all my attempts at gentility only ferved to make me rediculous.

How I have fulfilled the duties of the cloth, my Charity towards the poor Cottagers will evince, and having obtained the rank of a Magiftrate, I unblufhingly firft exercifed my authority in convicting and fending to prifon a poor honeft man, the father of a large family, for felling ale without a licence; though all my neighbours knew it was through my influence alone that a licence had been refufed him; I was induced to commit this act of meannefs and wanton cruelty, only becaufe he was the Tenant of a refpectable gentleman, richer and more refpectable than myfelf, whom I hated for obliging me ftrictly to obferve the pious duties I had undertaken, and was amply paid for, but had no inclination to perform.

Manifold have been my Sins, and at the awful moment of diffolution their horrid deformity prefents itfelf to my difturbed mind. I humbly afk forgivenefs of the numbers I have oppreffed, and hope thefe my laft words may be publifhed as a warning to thofe of mean extraction, who, like me, may become poffeffed of fome little power, and employ it to the injury of their fellow-creatures.

A Penitent SINNER.

Plate V. A lampoon on a clerical magistrate (see p. 519). Two Staffordshire gentlemen were feuding in 1796-1800, John Gough, Esq., and the Reverend Thomas Lane, JP, Rector of Handsworth, to whom are attributed these last dying words. John Gough was trying to enlist his tenants in the feud, and skilfully combined visual lampoon with the most popular literary form, the "last dying words" of the condemned.

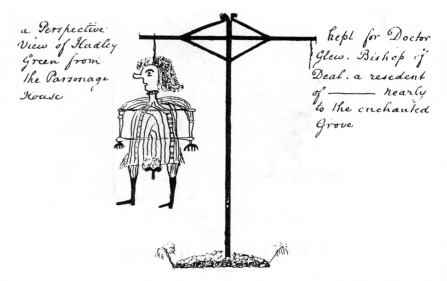

a Perspective View of Hadley Green from the Parsonage House

kept for Doctor Glew. Bishop of Deal. a resedent of —— nearly to the enchanted Grove

Bretheren . Bretheren behold my exalted Station . Planted amongst elegant trees . Shrubs and sweet flowers, but all appear to me Piss a beds . Nettles and Brambles . I feel the Sting of my Consience . O yea I repent from ever been Parson Just Ass and so forth . O what a miserable. Shitting . Stinking Dogmatick Prig of an April fool I do appear , all over Filth . from such filth of Body and Consience Good Lord diliver Me . and from this high Promotion I beseech thee. to encline my Heart to do Iestice that I may walk in Peace before all Men . Women and Children , Amen

Plate VI. Isaac Emmerton, a nurseryman, was prosecuted in 1800 for such lampoons and for erecting a ten-foot-high gibbet with an effigy ridiculing the Reverend C. J. Cottrell, JP., the Rector of Handley, Middlesex, the chairman of the local Commissioners of Tax (see p. 481).

THE PLURALIST AND OLD SOLDIER

A Soldier once and in the Beggar's list
Did thus addreſs a well-fed Pluralist.

Soldier.

At Guardalupe my Leg, and Thigh I lost;
No Pension have I, tho' its right I boast.
Your Rev.ce please, some Charity bestow.
Heav'n will pay double, when you're there, you know.

Pluralist.

Heav'n pay me double —! Vagrant; know that I
Ne'er give to Strolers, they're so apt to lie:
Your Parish, and some work would you become,
So haste away — or Constable's your doom.

Soldier.

May't please your Rev.ce hear my case, and then,
You'll say I'm poorer than the most of Men.
When Marlbro Sieged Lisle I first drew breath,
And there my father met untimely Death;
My Mother follow'd of a broken heart;
So I've no friend, or Parish for my part.

Pluralist.

I say begone — with that he loudly knocks
And Timber-toe, begun to smell the Stocks:
Away he stumps — but in a Rood or two
Thrice clear'd his Wezon, and his tho.te broke thro

Soldier.

`Thus tis to beg of those who (Sometimes) Preach
Up Charity, and all the Virtues teach:
But their disguise, to Common-Sense is thin,
A Pocket button'd —. Hypocrite within _.
Send me kind Heav'n the well-tann'd Cap.te Face.
Who gives me Twelvepence, and a Curse with Grace
But let me not, in House, or Lane, or Street
These Treble-pension'd Parsons ever meet:
And when I die, may I still number'd be
With the rough Soldier to eternity.

Plate VII. This 1766 broadside by John Collier (or "Tim Bobbin"),
the celebrated Lancashire caricaturist, combines the popular appeal
to patriotism with popular hostility to pluralist clergy.

Plate VIII. J. Penkethman, *Artachthos:*
Authentic Accounts of the History and Price
of Wheat, Bread, Malt &c was published in
1638 and republished in 1765. This
frontespiece carries below: "From the Original
Tables, formerly in the Treasury, of the
King's Exchequer at Westminster and late in
the Possession of the Right Honourable
Edward Earl of Oxford." This shows the
careful regulation of weights and measures
of wheat and the punishment in the stocks
of forestallers and regrators.

Richmond Park.

Plate IX. Parishioners, led by their vicar, beat the bounds of their parish, and assert their right of way into Richmond Park by breaking down the wall (see p. 111).

Plate X. As prices began to fall in 1801, caricaturists mocked corn hoarders who had supplies left on their hands. The agricultural labourer is shown (right) as innocent.

Plate XI. Based on an incident in Bishop's-Clyst, Devon, in August 1800. There was a long tradition in Devon of crowds scouring the countryside and visiting farmers reputed to be hoarding corn, and threatening them with rope. Women are shown to be prominent in this action.

Plate XII. "A Legal Method of Thrashing Out Grain" — a tribute to Lord Chief Justice Kenyon, who had presided over the trial and conviction of Rusby, a corn factor, for regrating oats (July 1800), and who sought to revive the old laws against forestalling, &c., on the grounds that — despite their repeal — they remained recognised by the common law.

Plate XIII. During the grain crisis of 1800-01 the Home Secretary, the duke of Portland, actively supported *laissez-faire*, and in March 1801 he issued a circular letter to Lords Lieutenant deploring those local authorities who had been reviving the old laws against sale by sample.

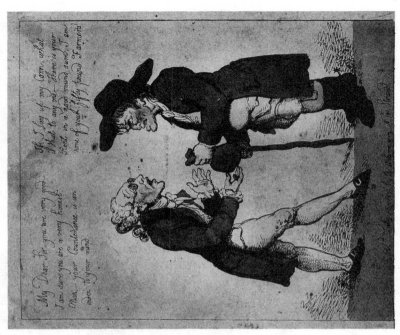

Plate XIV. An urban view of landlord and farmer conspiring
with each other to raise prices during the grain crisis of 1801.

Plate XV. Monopolizers are
left with unsold corn, May
1801. The Mayor is setting the
Assize of Bread. The
agricultural labourer looks
through the window and says,
"Dang I, if I did not think
it would come to this at last!"

Plate XVI. Prices reilly do fall in the autumn of 1801.

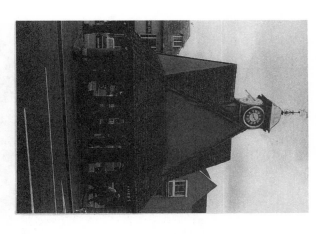

Plate XVIIa (left). The Butter Cross at Witney, Oxon, was built in 1683 and repaired in 1811. Many market buildings were built in the seventeenth century and still provide evidence of the vigour of market controls. Plate XVIIb (right). The Corn Market at Ledbury, Herefordshire, was built shortly after 1617. Corn storage chambers were added above, some fifty years later, where any unsold grain was held until the next market day. As corn came to be sold by sample in the next century, the chambers were hired out, and a poultry and butter market continued below.

Plate XVIII. Time, work and mortality are invoked at the Neptune Yard, Walker, Newcastle-upon-Tyne.

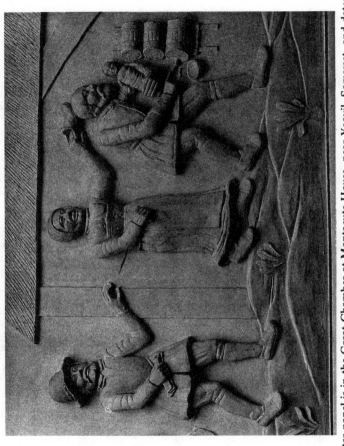

Plate XIX. This plaster panel is in the Great Chamber at Montacute House, near Yeovil, Somerset, and dates from *circa* 1601. The husband, who had been left in charge of the baby, is surprised by his wife while he is surreptitiously drawing beer. She hits him over the head with a shoe, and this is witnessed by a neighbour (rear).

Plate XX. On the right of this Montacute panel, either the husband or a proxy is made to ride a pole. This is described often as riding Skimmington, but a "true" Skimmington has two riders, one impersonating the wife who belabours the husband, who rides facing the horse's or donkey's tail. (See Hogarth's Skimmington, plate XXII.) The Montacute riding might equally well be Riding the Stang (North of England) or cool-staffing in the West Country.

Plate XXI. Hogarth's illustration from "Hudibras" of burning the rumps at Temple Bar shows the street theatre of London politics, and the preparation of effigies for the bonfire.

Plate XXII. Hogarth's illustration from "Hudibras" of a Skimmington.

Drawn by Rowlandson.

D.ᴿ SYNTAX WITH THE SKIMERTON RIDERS.

Plate XXIII. Rowlandson's "Skimerton" (from illustrations to "Dr. Syntax") shows all the symbolism and paraphernalia of a carnival of cuckoldry, and shows a more active participation by the women than does Hogarth.

A GENERAL SUMMONS

TO ALL THE HORNIFIED FUMBLERS,

To assemble at Horn Fair October 18,

Printed and sold by T. Batchelar, 115, Long Alley, Moorfields, London.

Plate XXIV. A summons to Horn Fair at Charlton (north of Blackheath). Claiming great antiquity, in the eighteenth century this carnival of cuckoldry was patronised by many genteel young people, masked and in drag, and with horns plentifully in evidence.

A New SUMMONS from
St Nicholas Terrible, Captain General of
FORKED ORDER
17 24

Ye Hornifi'd Husbands who come once a Year,
With Baskets, Pickaxes, & Spades to HORN-FAIR
To level a Path for your Waggish-taild Wives,
If e'er you expect to lead peaceable Lives
Make the best of your Bargain, & think it no scorn
That Fortune has doom'd you to wearing the Horn,
For 'twas worn by OLD NICK, before you were begot
And will be so, after you're all dead and rotten,
Make him but ye Captain to fight for your Cause
And then you'll have nothing to fear, my brave Boys
Sold by the Printsellers &c. Price 6 Pence.

Plate XXV. The printer, T. Batchelar, used these premises between
1817 and 1828 (information from Roy Palmer) so that this
"Summons" extends the iconography of cuckoldry and skimmingtons
well into the nineteenth century.

Plate XXVI. This diabolic mask, known as the "Ooser", was held at a farm in Melbury Osmond, Dorset, but it is now lost. The lower jaw was moveable and was worked with a string; in its last years it was supposedly used to frighten unruly children.

CHAPTER VIII.

OLD SHOPS, OLD HOUSES, AND OLD INHABITANTS.

As a picture of the past, and one that had never
been altered for many long years, I shall now endeavour to bring before the eye the trades and shops,
odd characters, and old houses, ancient lanes, yards,
and 'twitchells,' in some such order as they stood,
and with the old names by which the trades were

Plate XXVII. This reconstruction of riding the stang comes from a local
history of Grimsby, published in 1857. A proxy (or neighbour?) is
being ridden, in some comfort, while the victim watches apprehensively
out of the window.

Plate XXVIII. The last days of rough music: a "lewbelling" in a
Warwickshire village (Brailes) in 1909. The band parades before the
effigies of "the erring pair", which are set up in front of the woman's
house. After three nights the dummies are burned. Notice that this
band is wholly male, and the "historic instruments" have given way to
kettles, milk churns and corrugated iron.

JOHN HOBBS, JOHN HOBBS.

Sung by Mr. LOVEGROVE, with unbounded Applause, in " Any Thing New," at the Lyceum Theatre, Strand.

A JOLLY shoe-maker, John Hobbs, John Hobbs,
A jolly shoe-maker, John Hobbs;
   He married Jane Carter,
   No damsel look'd smarter,
   But he caught a Tartar,
John Hobbs, John Hobbs,
Yes, he caught a Tartar, John Hobbs.

He tied a rope to her, John Hobbs, John Hobbs,
He tied a rope to her, John Hobbs:
   To 'scape from hot water
   To Smithfield he brought her,
   But nobody bought her,
Jane Hobbs, Jane Hobbs,
They all were afraid of Jane Hobbs.

Oh, who'll buy a wife? says Hobbs, John Hobbs,
A sweet pretty wife, says Hobbs;
   But somehow they tell us,
   The wife-dealing fellows
   Were all of them *sellers*,
John Hobbs, John Hobbs,
And none of 'em wanted Jane Hobbs.

The rope it was ready, John Hobbs, John Hobbs,
Come, give me the rope, says Hobbs,
   I won't stand to wrangle,
   Myself I will strangle,
   And hang dingle dangle,
John Hobbs, John Hobbs,
He hung dingle daugle, John Hobbs.

But down his wife cut him, John Hobbs, John Hobbs,
But down his wife cut him, John Hobbs;
   With a few hubble bubbles
   They settled their troubles,
   Like most married couples,
John Hobbs, John Hobbs,
Oh, happy shoe-maker John Hobbs.

Plate XXIX. John Hobbs: like much standard ballad-vendor's stock,
this is intended to amuse, and has no evidential value whatsoever.

A FULL ACCOUNT of the EXTRAORDINARY CIRCUMSTANCE OF

A MAN

SELLING HIS WIFE

In the Market-place, Thetford,

On Saturday last, for the sum of £5. together with a true and laughable Dialogue which took place between the man & his wife after she was sold, when she was retiring with her new husband.

On Saturday last the Market-place of Thetford was thrown into a state of excitement, seldom witnessed there, by a man about forty years of age, in a shabby-genteel dress; leading a smart-looking woman, with a handkerchief round her neck, and shouting with a loud voice, "who'll buy a wife?" After arriving at the centre of the Market, he mounted a chair, and offered her for sale. "She was good looking, but that was all he could say for her." A young man of plausible appearance offered 10s. for her; but he was immediately opposed by an old gentleman bidding 5s. more. Afterwards the young man became the purchaser for £5. The money was paid down and the husband on handing over the handkerchief to the purchaser, began to dance and sing, declaring he had got rid of a troublesome noisy wife, which caused much merriment in the crowd. The young woman turned sharply round and said, you know you old rascal you are jealous—you are no man, and have no need of a young wife, and that is the reason you sold me, you useless old dog. Here the laugh was turned against him, and the women began to clap their hands at him. He then said she was a gormandizing woman, and would eat any man's substance up; and declared if he had kept her another year, she would have eaten him out of house and harbour. Here the woman looked blue, but soon turned round, nothing daunted, and said, "swallow your substance indeed, that might soon be swallowed by any lady present for what there is of it. Only think, he wished half a pound of sugar and one ounce of tea to serve us both the whole blessed week; and as for dinners, fresh meat we never saw, but a half-penny worth of onions and a small quantity of bread & cheese were our dinners for days together." Here the women became uproarous, but he walked off singing, "I fairly got rid of her." The fortunate purchaser led her away in loud huzzas. The seller's name is John Simpson, of Brandenham, and the purchaser's name is John Hart, of whom he had been jealous, having lodged in his house.

You married men and women too,
 Of every degree,
If you wish to live contented,
 Pray be advis'd by me ;
Take caution from this man and wife,
 Who did in Brandenham dwell—
And what between them did take place
 I unto you will tell

CHORUS.

So men look out what you are about,
 For your wives do all you can,
For a woman is a blessing,
 And a comfort to a man.

It happened in that neighbourhood,
 Upon the other day,
A man resov'd to sell his wife,
 Through jealousy they say;
To part it was agreed it seems,
 To Thetford market they went.

And for five pounds he sold her,
 And half-a-crown was spent,

This man was worth some money.
 And a miser did appear,
He kept his wife on bread and cheese,
 With allowance of small beer ;
Besides he kept her from her tea,
 Woman's comfort and delight,
Likewise he was so jealous,
 He lay grunting every night.

Oh, jealousy is a cruel thing,
 I'd have you push it out,
It is worse than Itch, Stitch, Palsy,
 The Rheumatism or Gout;
So you that feel those cruel pains,
 Think on this man and wife,
Be sure you have convincing proof,
 Before you blame your wife.

Printed for, and Sold by Joseph Bamfylde, Thetford.

Plate XXX. This locally-printed Thetford wife sale broadside was probably based on a real incident, touched up for entertainment.

nerai à observer qu'une coutume aussi infâme s'est conservée sans interruption, qu'elle est mise chaque jour à exécution ; que si quelques magistrats des comtés, informés que de sem—blables marchés allaient se faire, ont cherché à les empêcher en envoyant sur les lieux des constables ou huissiers, la populace les a tou—jours dispersés, et qu'elle a maintenu ce qu'elle considère comme son droit.

Plate XXXI. This vignette concludes an account of the sale of wives in London in a French travel book which like many others exaggerates the prevalence of the custom ("qu'elle est mise chaque jour à exécution").

Plate XXXII. *Punch's* "physiology of courtship": it is intended to typify the English manner of courtship as conceived by the French and Germans. The scene is Smithfield market: on the right "Lord the Honourable Sir Brown (eldest son of the Lord Mayor) is making in the cold and formal fashion of his compatriots, a declaration of his sentiments to a young miss, daughter of a duke. . ." On the left "may be perceived a church dignitary in a fit of the spleen disposing of his wife, for ready cash, to a field-marshal — sad, but only too frequent Result, of our insular Incompatability of Temper".

and Scotland also, and had become more heated at the time of the dearth of 1756-7, when many English local authorities had symbolically enforced some of the old protective legislation.[1] As it happens the only authority cited by Smith in his digression is not a French physiocrat but Charles Smith, whose *Three Tracts on the Corn Trade* date from 1758 (above p. 201). Adam Smith is likely to have been influenced in his market theories by Scottish experience as well as French, but the digression is argued almost wholly in terms of English practices and laws.[2]

My essay was taken by some to be derogatory both to Adam Smith and to the "free market", which is a very great personage these days. But my comments were deferential, mild and agnostic. They were offered

> Not in refutation of Adam Smith, but simply to indicate places where caution should be exercised until our knowledge is greater. We need say only of the *laissez-faire* model that it is empirically unproven; inherently unlikely; and that there is some evidence on the other side (p. 207).

There is no final historical verdict after more than two hundred years, because Adam Smith theorised a state of perfect competition and the world is still waiting for this state to arrive.

But, even if we were to suppose market conditions more perfect, there are peculiarities in the market for the necessities of subsistence which raise their own theoretical

---

[1] Adam Smith's "real contact" with the French thinkers came during his visit to Paris, December 1765 to October 1766: see Adam Smith, *An Inquiry into the Nature and Causes of the Wealth of Nations*, ed. R. H. Campbell and A. S. Skinner (Oxford, 1976), i, pp. 22-3, note 8. He will therefore have been absent from Britain during the height of the 1766 rioting. But Smith himself insisted that his views of *laissez-faire* were already formed in 1749: see Jacob Viner, *The Long View and the Short* (Glencoe, Illinois, 1958), p. 215.

[2] Even Smith's famous comparison of the popular prejudices against forestallers to belief in "witchcraft" might have been borrowed from an earlier pamphleteer: see *Reflections on the Present High Price of Provisions; and the complaints and disturbances arising therefrom* (1766), p. 39, which refers also to witchcraft and notes that in the Commission for the appointment of magistrates "inchantments, sorceries, arts of magic, forestalling, regratings, and ingrossings are ranged together, as offences of a similar nature, because they were committed by wicked persons, in a manner both amazing and unknown".

problems. The question is not whether, in the long run, it is not advantageous to all parties for communications to be improved and for national and, in the end, international markets in grain or in rice to be formed. As soon as that question is proposed the answer is self-evident. . . and we are into a feedback loop. Direct obstruction of this flow, whether by local authorities or by the crowd, could be plainly reactionary. But dearth and famine are always in the short run and not the long. And Adam Smith has only long-run remedies (such as high prices encouraging the breaking-up of more acres for grain) for short-run crisis. By 1776, when *The Wealth of Nations* was published, the desirability of a more fluent national commerce in grain had become a truism. What were disputed (in France as in England), were the measures the authorities might or should take in times of high prices and dearth. Here there were wide disagreements, not only between traditionalists (and of course the crowd) and political economists, but also — as Hont and Ignatieff very helpfully show — within the ranks of the political economists. [1]

Adam Smith took a sterner and more doctrinaire position on the inviolability of *laissez-faire* even during times of dearth than did many of his colleagues. He insisted that the interests of dealers (inland) and the "great body of the people" were "exactly the same", "*even in years of the greatest scarcity*". "The unlimited, unrestricted freedom of the corn trade, as it is the only effectual preventive of the miseries of a famine so it is the best palliative of the inconvenience of a dearth." [2] Smith was not, "the only standard-bearer for 'natural liberty' in grain" but he was one of the more extreme standard-bearers for this liberty to remain uncontrolled even in times of great scarcity. And he must have known very well that it was exactly this point of emergency measures in time of dearth that was most controversial. His notable forerunner in developing *Political Oeconomy*, Sir James Steuart, had refused this fence, and

---

[1] Hont and Ignatieff, *op. cit.*, pp. 16-19.
[2] These passages are selected for emphasis by Salim Rashid in "The Policy of *Laissez-faire* during Scarcities", *Economic Journal*, 90 (1980), pp. 493-503.

was an advocate of the stockpiling of grain in public granaries for sale in time of dearth.[1] Smith's successor and biographer, Dugald Stewart, was a true executor when he lectured in unqualified terms on the "unlimited liberty of the corn trade" right through the crisis year of 1800.[2] On this question Adam Smith was neither "vulgarised" nor "misunderstood".

It is not (as some accounts imply) the total theoretical structure of *The Wealth of Nations* which is at issue, but the few pages of Smith's digression on the corn trade in that treatise. These pages acquired oracular authority, and in each episode of scarcity — in Britain in 1795 and 1800, in Ireland, India and the Colonial Empire through much of the nineteenth century — these were the arguments which politicians and administrators rehearsed. In Britain in the 1790s both Government and Foxite opposition endorsed these arguments, and when the Home Secretary, the duke of Portland, harried traditionalist Lords Lieutenant, magistrates and local authorities with homilies on political economy and instructions to preserve the freedom of markets, he was not vulgarising the views of Dr Smith but enforcing these strictly.

Thus when the Nottingham Corporation endorsed the crowd's imposition of price ceilings and brought pressure onto local farmers to supply the market at these rates, Portland insisted, in Smithian terms, that

> Whenever any reduction in the price of a Commodity has been effected by intimidation it has never been of any duration, and besides, by having things out of their natural and orderly courses, it almost necessarily happens that the evil, instead of being remedied returns with increased violence.[3]

To this Portland added, but with his own special vehemence, the Smithian theme of natural justice to the rights of property: there should be a "religious observance of the respect. . . due to private property", and the Lord

[1] Sir James Steuart, "A dissertation on the policy of grain", in *Works* (1805; reprint 1967), v, pp. 347-77. Steuart's proposal was first made in 1757, but was maintained in subsequent years.

[2] Dugald Stewart, *Lectures on Political Economy* (Edinburgh, 1855; reprint 1968), ii, p. 52.

[3] Wells, *Wretched Faces*, p. 238.

Lieutenant of Oxfordshire, the duke of Marlborough — a traditionalist and paternalist — was instructed that:

> If the employment of Property is not secure, if every Man does not feel that he has power to retain what he possesses so long as he pleases and dispense it at the time, in the manner and for the Price he chuses to fix upon it, there must be an end of Confidence in Industry and of all valuable and virtuous Exertions of all descriptions. . . the whole Order of things must be overturned and destroyed.

All must "maintain the Principle of perfect Freedom of Property".[1]

It was the same principle and the same authority that was appealed to during famine conditions in Western India in 1812. The judge and magistrate of Kaira had urged the government to intervene by importing grain and selling it to retailers at little over its cost price. The proposal was rejected:

> The Right Honourable the Governor in Council is disposed to think. . . that those approved and recognised principles. . . which prescribe an entire and unrestricted freedom in the grain trade, as best adapted to the relief of any existing scarcity and to the prevention of famine, are particularly applicable to the dealers in grain in the province of Goozerat. . . The digression of the celebrated author of the *Wealth of Nations* concerning the Corn-Trade. . . particularly as far as respects the *inland Trader*, is forcibly and irresistibly applicable to every state of society where merchants, or dealers, in grain may be established.[2]

Similar homilies were expressed in orders of the Madras Government in 1833 which argued that high prices constitute the best security against famine: "The interference of Government in such emergencies. . . disturbs the natural current (by which, where trade is free, the demands of any commodity is sure to meet, as far as circumstances will allow, with a corresponding supply) and has a tendency to convert a

---

[1] Roger Wells, "The Grain Crisis in England, 1794-96, 1799-1801" (Univ. of York Ph.D. thesis, 1978), pp. 472-3. Also Wells, *Wretched Faces*, pp. 238-9.

[2] Srinivasa Ambirajan, "Economic Ideas and Indian Economic Policies in the 19th Century" (Manchester Univ. Ph.D. thesis, 1964), pp. 363-4. A similar circular, quoting almost verbatim from *The Wealth of Nations*, originated from the Board of Revenue in Madras in 1811: Arnold, *Famine*, p. 113. See also Ambirajan, S., *Classical Political Economy and British Policy in India* (Cambridge, 1978).

season of scarcity into one of absolute famine".[1]

Despite the appalling example of the great Irish famine, Smithian imperatives continued to inform policies in India during the famines of the 1860s and 1870s. Baird Smith, reporting on the famine of 1860-1, applauded the non-interventionist principles of *The Wealth of Nations* and advised that the remedy for dearth be left to "the order of nature [which] if it occasionally produces dire sufferings, does also provide generally the most effective means for their mitigation".[2] (In Orissa alone, in 1860, famine deaths were estimated at 1,364,529.[3]) It has been suggested that some administrators were fortified in policies of non-interference by literal-minded assent to Malthusian doctrines.[4] The magistrate at Patna was advised by the Governor-General that, while it was "beyond the power. . . of the public authorities to remedy the unfortunate dearth of grain", yet the magistrates may "effect much to soften the distress and calm the irritation of the people":

[1] *Ibid.*, p. 366. The view that famines were always the consequence of well-intentioned interventions by the authorities which disrupted the "natural" flow of trade is one of Adam Smith's least well-supported assertions: "Whoever examines, with attention, the history of the dearths and famines which have afflicted any part of Europe during either the course of the present, or that of the two preceding centuries" will find that dearths arise in a few cases from the waste of war but in the greatest number of cases "by the fault of the seasons; and that *a famine has never arisen from any other cause but the violence of government attempting, by improper means, to remedy the inconvenience of dearth*". (My italics.) Upon this pretence to omniscience, Smith and his disciples could denounce protective measures as iniquitous. Smith also asserted that "the drought in Bengal, a few years ago, might probably have occasioned a very great dearth. Some improper regulations, some injudicious restraints, imposed by the servants of the East India Company upon the rice trade, contributed, perhaps, to turn that dearth into a famine." This assertion has been challenged by H. Sur, "The Bihar Famine of 1770", *Indian Econ. & Social Hist. Review*, xiii, 4 (1976), who finds a better explanation in the collapse of the traditional Moghul administration and the ensuing vacuum.

[2] B. M. Bhatia, *Famines in India* (Bombay, 1967), p. 105.

[3] Ambirajan, thesis, p. 367.

[4] See S. Ambirajan, "Malthusian Population Theory and Indian Famine Policy in the 19th Century", *Population Studies*, xxx, 1 (1976).

> By manifesting a sympathy in their sufferings, by a humane, patient and indulgent hearing of their complaints, by encouraging them to look forward to the approaching harvest. . . they may be persuaded to bear with resignation the inevitable calamities under which they labour.[1]

This throws one back, not only to Smith and to Malthus, but also to Edmund Burke's *Thoughts on Scarcity*.

What political economy forbade was any "violent interferences with the course of trade", including the prosecution of profiteers or hoarders, the fixing of maximum prices, and government intervention in grain or rice dealing.[2] Relief exercises must take the form of distributing a pittance of purchase money (at whatever height "the order of nature" had brought prices to) to those whose need passed the examination of labour on public relief works.[3] These policies, or negatives in the place of policies, were based upon theories which — however elaborated by other authors — rested upon the few pages of Adam Smith's digression.

These pages, then, were among the most influential writings in history, with a global influence which was sometimes baneful. Their arguments discredited or disallowed traditional protective interventions in time of dearth, could be used to justify profiteering and hoarding, and could serve as apologetics to soothe the troubled consciences of the authorities by commending inactivity as correct political economy. Two Indian economists who have had the temerity to question their profession's habitual complacency about Smith's views on the grain trade receive a lofty rebuke from Hont and Ignatieff: they have "overlooked" "the traditional theory of justice framing Smith's discourse of free trade in subsistence goods during dearth and famines". And they cite this passage of the digression:

> To hinder. . . the farmer from sending his goods at all times to the best market, is evidently to sacrifice the ordinary laws of justice to an idea of publick utility, to a sort of reasons of state — an act of legislative

---

[1] Ambirajan, thesis, pp. 366-7.
[2] See Bhatia, *op. cit.*, p. 105.
[3] The absolutes of political economy were modified by the Famine Code of 1880, although the general principle of non-intervention in the grain trade "remained inviolate until the Second World War": Arnold, *op. cit.*, p. 114.

authority which ought to be exercised only, which can be pardoned only, in cases of the most urgent necessity.

And somehow or other Hont and Ignatieff find this passage endorsement of their conclusion that "Smith's discourse was not about the conditions of actual famines, which belonged to the discourse on grave necessity which 'breaks all laws' ". But one may search in vain in the digression or anywhere in *The Wealth of Nations* for any such "discourse on grave necessity". What is pretentiously named as a "discourse" is, at most, a brief saving clause (measures "which can be pardoned only in cases of the most urgent necessity") and a prolonged silence as to what these measures might be.[1]

As for "the traditional theory of justice framing Smith's discourse of free trade", the justice is to the rights of property. As Hont and Ignatieff acknowledge elsewhere, Smith "insisted on the all but absolute priority of the property rights of grain merchants and farmers over the claims of need made by poor labourers". This position was more extreme than that of many contemporary political economists and physiocrats; indeed, Diderot considered the privileging of private property above need in times of famine to be a "cannibal principle".[2]

My argument is not (as it happens) intended to show that Dr Adam Smith was a cannibal. Smithian advocacy of free trade in grain had evident virtues in the long run but had only negative relevance in times of crisis, since his remedies — such as increasing cereal production — were long-run remedies or — such as very high prices — were not remedies at all. Among the deficiencies of Smithian doctrine were 1) that it *was* doctrinaire and counter-empirical. It did not want to know how actual markets worked, any more than its disciples do today. As dogma it could serve as an apologia for inactivity, as exemplified in several Irish and Indian disasters. 2) It promoted the notion that high prices were a (painful) remedy for dearth, in drawing supplies to the afflicted region

[1] Hont and Ignatieff, *op. cit.*, p. 20. Adam Smith in *The Theory of Moral Sentiments*, ed. D. D. Raphael and A. L. Macfie (Oxford, 1976), p. 27, found "violent hunger" to be an offence against "propriety". Though sometimes "unavoidable" it "is always indecent".

[2] *Ibid.*, p. 22.

of scarcity. But what draws supply are not high prices but people with sufficient money in their purses to pay high prices. A characteristic phenomenon in times of dearth is that it generates unemployment and empty purses; in purchasing necessities at inflated prices people cease to be able to buy inessentials, and the shoemaker, the weaver, the stockinger, the fisherman, the barber, the transport worker, and many others fall on hard times.[1] Hence the number of those able to pay the inflated prices declines in the afflicted regions, and food may be exported to neighbouring, less afflicted, regions where employment is holding up and consumers still have money with which to pay. In this sequence, high prices can actually withdraw supply from the most afflicted. A leading authority on recent famines, Dr Amartya Sen, notes that in a slump hunger and even starvation have "little market pull" and in many famines food was exported from the famine-stricken country or region. This was notoriously the case in Ireland in the 1840s and was observed in Indian famines also:

> Adam Smith's proposition is, in fact, concerned with efficiency in meeting a market demand, but it says nothing on meeting a need that has not been translated into effective demand because of lack of market-based entitlement and shortage of purchasing power.[2]

3) The most unhappy error flows from Smith's metaphor of price as a means of rationing. Smith argues that high prices discourage consumption, putting "everybody more or less, but particularly the inferior ranks of people, upon thrift and good management". By comparing the dealer who raises prices to the "prudent master of a vessel" rationing his crew, there is a persuasive suggestion of a fair distribution of limited resources. These resources will be rationed not only between individual consumers but also over time, dividing "the inconveniences" of scarcity "as equally as possible

[1] Thus in Bengal in 1873 the first to starve were "non-agricultural classes" — weavers, metal workers, carpenters, fishermen, menials. The field labourers and small cultivators followed: *Extra Supplement to the Gazette of India*, 26 Feb. 1875, p. 33.
[2] Amartya Sen, *Poverty and Famines* (Oxford, 1981), pp. 161-2. "Food being *exported* from famine-stricken areas may be a 'natural' characteristic of the market, which respects entitlement rather than needs."

through all the different months and weeks and days of the year.

However persuasive the metaphor, there is an elision of the real relationships assigned by price, which suggests — for the argument has been repeated ever since and may still be heard today — ideological sleight-of-mind. Rationing by price does not allocate resources equally among those in need; it reserves the supply to those who can pay the price and excludes those who can't. Perhaps one-fifth or one-quarter of the English population in the eighteenth century rubbed along on the edge of bare subsistence, and was in danger of falling below this whenever prices rose. In a recent authoritative study it is shown that

> In hard years perhaps 20 per cent of the population could not, unaided, have bought sufficient bread even if they had been able to eliminate all other expenditure; and. . . in a very hard year, 45 per cent of the entire population could be thrown into such destitution.[1]

What Hay finds for eighteenth-century England, Sir William Hunter and other observers found for nineteenth-century India. Even in normal years one-fifth of the population "went through life on insufficient food".[2] The raising of prices during dearth could "ration" them out of the market altogether.

This is something one must hold steadily in view. High prices of bread mattered little to the rich, were inconvenient to the middling sort, were painful to steadily-employed labourers, but could threaten the survival of the poor. That is why they were at once a matter of "politics". It was against this socially-unequal "rationing" by purse that the food riot was a protest and perhaps a remedy.

This may remind us that the world has not done yet with dearth or with famine. The problem occupies many able minds and, as one might expect, some of the most relevant work comes from Indian economists and historians, for whom famine is not so distant a problem and yet who share with Britain some common histories of administration, law, and ideology. One arresting approach is that of Amartya Sen,

[1] Douglas Hay, "War, Dearth and Theft in the Eighteenth Century", *Past and Present*, 95 (1982), p. 132.
[2] See Bhatia, *op. cit.*, p. 39.

in his *Poverty and Famines* (1981), which employs "entitlement theory" and also an advanced statistical apparatus. "Entitlement" indicates all the various means by which people gain access to essential food supply, whether this is through direct subsistence farming or through the provision by an employer or master (in his household) or by purchase in the market. A famine is triggered by the breakdown of such entitlements and the merit of this approach is that it does not only tell us that there has been a decline in the amount of food available but it also examines "why some groups had to starve while others could feed themselves. . . What allows one group rather than another to get hold of the food that is there?".[1]

Dr Sen examines twentieth-century famines in Asia and Africa, for which the statistical data is more reliable than any we have for the eighteenth century, and he concludes that, in the greater number of cases examined, famine cannot be simply attributed to "food availability decline". Where there had been a crop failure, "a moderate short-fall in *production*" was "translated into an exceptional short-fall in *market release*". The market cannot be isolated and abstracted from the network of political, social and legal relations in which it is situated. Once the downward spiral of famine is entered, the process can become cumulative, and "no matter how a famine is *caused*, methods of *breaking* it call for a large supply of food in the public distribution system".[2]

This approach is relevant to dearth in eighteenth-century Europe also,[3] and is preferable to the one most commonly adopted, which focuses on harvest failures as if these could supply not only necessary but also sufficient explanation of all that followed. Dr Sen argues that this "FAD" (food availability decline) approach

> Gives little clue to the causal mechanism of starvation, since it does not go into the *relationship* of people to food. Whatever may be the

[1] Sen, *op. cit.*, p. 154.
[2] *Ibid.*, pp. 75, 79.
[3] See Louise Tilly, "Food Entitlement, Famine, and Conflict", in R. I. Rotberg and Theodore K. Rabb (eds.), *Hunger and History* (Cambridge, 1985), pp. 135-152.

oracular power of the FAD view, it is certainly Delphic in its reticence.[1]

In general the eighteenth-century English poor were sheltered by poor laws and charity from outright starvation, but Dr Sen's argument remains valid. Smithian and Malthusian explanations of years of dearth rest heavily upon crop failures (FAD) and remain "Delphic" as to the relationship of people to food and the socially-differential entitlements that obtained.

The "relationship of people to food" involves systems of power, property and law. Conflict over entitlement to food in the market might be seen as a forum of class struggle, if most historians were not too prissy nowadays to use the term. It may also be seen as a forum for the conflict of interests, "Town" versus "Country", as manufacturing workers, woollen workers, or colliers, confronted farmers and dealers.

Both forms of conflict can be observed in England during the high-price years of the Napoleonic Wars, and as government intervened with doctrine and with armed force in support of the unfettered operation of agrarian capitalism there can be no doubt which classes and interests were winners. Professor Mingay has estimated that, in areas which he has investigated, rents rose between 40 per cent and 50 per cent between 1750 and 1790; and between 1790 and 1815 rents rose by a further 80 per cent to 90 per cent.[2] At the same time (as the substantial farm buildings of that period remain to witness) the middling and larger farmers were well able to pay these enhanced rentals and were rising in prosperity and in assumptions of social status. Rent was the means by which the landowners clawed back their share of farming profits. These rentals indicated a very considerable rise in the wealth of the agrarian capitalist classes (in which affluence the agricultural labourers had no share), and this was supported in its turn by the sale of food — and especially cereals — to the consumers of the "Town". The wealth of the landowners

---

[1] See Sen, *op. cit.*, p. 154. And see A. K. Ghose, "Food Supply and Starvation: a Study of Famines with reference to the Indian Sub-Continent", *Oxford Economic Papers*, xxxiv (1982).

[2] G. E. Mingay, "The Course of Rents in the Age of Malthus", in Michael Turner (ed.), *Malthus in his Time* (Basingstoke, 1986), pp. 90-1.

was further supported by enclosures, which reached a peak in the war years when three million acres, or 9 per cent of the land area of England, came under parliamentary enclosure, much of this coming under the plough for cereal crops.[1]

This prosperity did not pass unnoticed among the woollen workers, colliers and "proto-industrial" manufacturers who lived adjacent to prospering farming areas. It is in this context that the confrontations of 1795-96 and 1800-1 must be seen. Dr Roger Wells's *Wretched Faces* (1988) is the most copiously documented study of every aspect of these years of dearth that we have or are ever likely to have, and one must express gratitude to him for his archival industry and for the illumination that flows from many of his pages. Yet certain of his conclusions seem to be to be wrong-headed and to be contradicted by his own evidence, and this may be because even Dr Wells has been unduly influenced by the seeming common-sense of the Smithian (FAD) approach.

There were of course serious harvest short-falls in these years, and the country might have faced real famine conditions if there had not been considerable foreign imports.[2] But when Roger Wells writes that the implementation of "the moral economy" was "a recipe for disaster"[3] he is taking too narrow a view of the question. His case against "the moral economy" — a catch-all term which he uses throughout his major study to indicate *any* measures taken by the authorities or imposed by the crowd to protect the consumer, to regulate markets or to control price — is at times as alarmist as that of Edmund Burke or the duke of Portland. He argues that market disturbances "decimated

<hr />

[1] Michael Turner, "Corn Crises in Britain in the Age of Malthus", in Turner, *op. cit.*, p. 120.

[2] Adam Smith's doctrine of non-interference in the grain trade was limited, in his digression, to the *inland* trader. Wells is mistaken when he supposes (e.g. *Wretched Faces*, p. 7) that vigorous governmental exercises in the import of corn during a time of shortage was in breach of Smithian precepts. But (in Smith's doctrine) government must not then intervene in the internal market by selling off imports beneath the self-regulating market rate, and this was generally avoided in the 1790s by selling off the cargo immediately at the port of arrival, at which sales representatives from inland towns and parishes often attended.

[3] Roger Wells, "The Revolt of the South-West, 1800-01", *Social History*, 6 (1977), p. 743; Wells, *Wretched Faces*, p. 230.

future supplies and then accelerated inflation", that "price controls aggravated the impact of violence", that "havoc followed where the Assize of Bread operated", and that the moral economy "directly stimulated violent populist intervention while simultaneously weakening community resolve to contain disorder".[1] And he conjures up visions of a vicious circle with "riot deterring supplies, empty markets stimulating renewed violence, and further disturbances annihilating commercial confidence":

> Ultimately, from a global perspective, the entire country would be affected. In this context the 'positive' aspects of popular intervention, discouraging mercantile malpractice, militating against maximum exploitation, rivetting public attention on the poor's plight and galvanising greater relief measures, pale in significance. For these latter characteristics of protest, however important, were essentially localised. The historian's assessment of riot must also adopt governmental criteria. Macro, as opposed to micro economic examination of the grain trade reveals the dangers of protest to national subsistence in general, and the consumption centres in particular. Staving off starvation in the most vulnerable locations necessitated the speediest suppression of riot.[2]

The trouble is that hunger is usually "localised" (in the stomach). Deaths from starvation appear as localised microdots. Roger Wells has been reading too many state papers of Pitt's war administration and has been drawn into their feedback loops. Moreover in his over-coloured language ("disaster", "decimated", "violence", "violent populist intervention", "annihilating") we have moved a long way from the self-disciplined and often bloodless direct actions of the crowd, with its "protocol" and "orderly disorder"[3] which recent historiography has disclosed and which Dr Wells's own researches confirm, and have moved back to the bad old school when every crowd was recorded as a violent gullible "mob".

There is something in Wells's case, and it is strongest when he cites — especially in the summer of 1795 — the widespread crowd blockades of the passage of grain by water or

---

[1] *Ibid.*, pp. 178-181, 230-6.
[2] *Ibid.*, p. 181.
[3] John Bohstedt, *Riots and Community Politics in England and Wales, 1790-1810* (Cambridge, Mass., 1983), p. 27.

by road. This embargo could have precipitated disaster in large centres of consumption such as Birmingham, Nottingham and Leicester, although it did not. In other matters Wells (uncharacteristically) offers thin and uncertain evidence. His few examples do not persuade that price regulation always "decimated" the future supply of those markets. Where towns or manufacturing districts depended upon a local food supply, the farmers also depended upon their local custom; and the crowd might visit the farmers with threats to requisition supplies. In the end the farmers must go back to the market and there was a complexity of influences upon their behaviour: relationships with the consumers, with their landlords, with their own consciences.

Roger Wells's assertion that "havoc" followed where the Assize of Bread operated" is supported by a single anecdote from Oxfordshire in 1800. But as it happens Oxford is the one centre for which we have a careful study of the operation of the Assize in the eighteenth century, and this by no means supports the ascription of "havoc". Dr Wendy Thwaites's research suggests that the operation of the Assize may have marginally raised the price of bread in Oxford in normal years but restrained the rise in years of dearth. It afforded to the market authorities, the bakers and the consumers "a sense of security in relation to each other",[1] and it should in any case be seen not in isolation but as part of a wider regulation which included weight and quality control. London also set an Assize of Bread throughout the eighteenth century, and so far from "havoc" food riots in the capital were rare.[2]

Roger Wells draws too one-sided a balance. It is true that Pickard, Birmingham's biggest merchant-miller, was forced out of business by the hostility of the crowd in September 1800.[3] But this did not leave Birmingham provisionless. There was another steam mill, the "Union Mill", although

[1] W. Thwaites, "The Assize of Bread in 18th-Century Oxfordshire", *Oxoniensia*, li (1986), pp. 171-81.

[2] Differing explanations for the rarity of food riots in London are to be found in George Rudé, *Paris and London in the 18th Century* (1970), pp. 55-7; John Stevenson, *Popular Disturbances in England, 1700-1870* (1979), pp. 99-100; Bohstedt, *op. cit.*, pp. 208-9. Undoubtedly securing the provisioning of London was a priority of State.

[3] See Wells, *Wretched Faces*, pp. 180-1.

this mainly supplied bread to its numerous tradesmen and operative subscribers, and at prime cost — perhaps a translation of "moral economy" principles into early co-operation.[1] And Pickard's mill was not closed: it was rented to a new company, as an emergency measure, to ensure the continued supply of the town. Pickard's son, Edward, recorded the erratic fluctuations in the fortunes of this emergency Company of "benevolent gentlemen":

> One of the gentlemen was at Hull soon after the first term [of six month's rental] commenced, and having left Birmingham under a fearful impression that the town would be really without a supply of food, ventured to make a very large purchase of wheat. . . which had just arrived from the Baltic, and sent it to Birmingham on account of this new Company. How the wheat was paid for or by whom I know not: I presume their banker accomodated them with the money. . . Exorbitant as was the price of wheat at that time, it unexpectedly rose considerably higher: and although the Company was thus enabled to provide a large quantity of flour weekly to the poor at a lower rate than the general dealers, yet at the end of the first six months, they found their profits so large, that they feared some popular indignation on the exhibition of their accounts. They therefore applied to my father to prolong their term, which he did, to enable them, as they said, to make some diminution in their gains, and thus present to the public a more satisfactory statement. About the period of the renewal of the term, the price of wheat began to give way, and continued falling into the end of it: in consequence of which, and also from losses sustained on other large purchases again made early in their last term, these benevolent men sunk not only all their first six months profits, but also lost all the capital they had advanced.[2]

This story conforms to the properties of neither Smithian nor "moral economy" doctrine. It suggests that in these eccentric wartime conditions all parties in the grain market were playing blind man's buff. In any case, generalisations as to the characteristics and functions of food riots are risky if taken only from these war years, since they are a special case:

[1] Anon., "A Record of the Staff of Life from 1796 to 1900: at the Old Mill of the City", *Birmingham Magazine of Arts and Industries*, iii (1899). See also J. Tann, "Co-operative Corn Milling; Self-help during the grain crises of the Napoleonic Wars", *Agric. Hist. Rev.*, 28 (1980), p. 52; the Union Mill was founded in 1796 with 1360 subscribers, principally labouring workmen.

[2] MS notebook of Edward Pickard, Birmingham Reference Library, MS 22/11.

both the climax and the terminus of the riot tradition, in a context of war and invasion fears, with the gentry and their retainers under arms (as Yeomanry) and in a state of anti-Jacobin panic. These last years of the eighteenth century were also a watershed in marketing constituencies and practices, mid-way between the locally-supplied markets where consumers and farmers, magistrates and dealers, all knew something of each other, might come face to face with each other, and could "negotiate" prices, even by "riot"; and the more impersonal relations of the large urban markets which farmers rarely visited, supplied by dealers who purchased in distant markets.[1] Moreover the 1790s experience is further complicated by the deep inner divisions within the ruling authorities, with central government imposing *laissez-faire* dogmas but with some local authorities and traditionalist landowners attempting to control prices by persuasion, and giving a nod and a wink to the crowd. In such confused conditions we are likely to come up with contradictory findings, and with some examples of "havoc".

It is over the long view through the seventeenth and eighteenth centuries that the strongest case can be made for riot's "success". Two historians of the seventeenth century conclude that riots were "invariably successful in stimulating authoritative actions to alleviate grievances".[2] This is true in general of the eighteenth century also. Price regulation might even succeed, and the most persuasive analysis of the crowd's success will be found in John Bohstedt's chapter on "Devon's Classic Food Riots" in his *Riots and Community Politics in England and Wales, 1790-1810* (1983). He shows the small or medium-sized market town to be the classic site of crowd direct action (supported by the visitation of farmers in the neighbourhood), and suggests that such actions were supported by both horizontal and vertical networks of relationship within communities which had their own traditions and remembered their own precedents. In the

---

[1] These points are developed by Bohstedt, *op. cit., passim*, especially in his contrast between Manchester and Devon's markets. Still in 1800 the Birmingham Union Mill normally obtained their supply in Birmingham market or within a radius of twenty miles: J. Tann, *op. cit.*, p. 54.

[2] Walter and Wrightson, *op. cit.*, p. 41.

vertical relationships he suggests that "social patronage" may be a more helpful term than "paternalism", a patronage which however entailed reciprocal duties and obligations. While riot, or direct action to bring down prices, was by no means legitimate, yet both the authorities and the crowd abided by a recognised "protocol". Rioters "did not challenge directly the whole system of property and power", and so long as this was so, and violence was avoided, the authorities were sometimes accomplices to price-fixing, recognising that "social peace was more important than absolute property rights or, rather, profit rights". Hence rioters "modified the property rights of farmers and food dealers. . . and their exertion of force at the margin of legitimacy and illegality was a real if limited exercise of political power". Indeed, "riots were a dynamic constituent moment in the system of property and power".[1]

John Bohstedt claims with confidence the Devon rioters' success: "riot would have been neither so frequent nor so orderly had there been no payoff". Food rioting of course appears in other national histories also, first in Europe and China,[2] subsequently in India and elsewhere. There is some suggestion that it marks a transitional phase between the

[1] Bohstedt, *op. cit.*, esp. chs. 2 and 9 and pp. 54, 202, 220-1. Cf. Thwaites, thesis, pp. 522-7, for an estimate of riot's effectiveness in prompting consumer protection.

[2] China provides an example of successful bureaucratic management of food supplies, during the Qing dynasty in the eighteenth century. The Chinese state undertook far-reaching measures to feed the people during times of scarcity; these included public granaries, the provision of loans, discouragement of hoarders, encouragement of circulation by canals and roads. This was supported by a "Confucian" value-system which endorsed the imperative of "benevolence", and by the popular belief that any regime which presided over disasters such as famine and flood had "lost the mandate of heaven". Hence everything to do with the distribution of food in time of scarcity was of highly-sensitive political import. The Chinese peasant did not beg for charity, he demanded relief and saw the bureaucracy as bound by its office to provide this, and the rich as bound by duty. Many actions of Chinese food rioters closely resembled European riots — blockading transport, attacking hoarders, lobbying bureaucrats and the rich — and riot was a recognised way of putting the state measures of relief in motion: Lillian M. Li, "Introduction: Food, Famine and the Chinese State"; R. Bin Wong, "Food Riots in the Qing dynasty"; Paul R. Greenough, "Comment"; all in *Journal of Asian Studies*, August 1982.

locally-based demographic *ancien régime* of absolute subsistence crises and the "modern" national "free market"
regulated by price and by police alone.[1] Riot is unlikely to
have had so universal an emergence if there had not been
some "payoff", some space in which direct action was a
protection from the newly-liberated appetites of agrarian
interests, a warning to speculators and profiteers and an
alarm signal to the authorities to set emergency measures and
charities into motion. Such action could (and can) take many
forms, from humble petitions to threatening letters and
arson,[2] or to blockades and attacks on mills, but it was
always a profoundly political as well as economic event.

Riot, as "a dynamic constituent moment in the system of
property and power", has obviously taken different forms
and significance in different national histories, and in the
English case must be seen within the particular structure of
patrician/plebeian relations which we have examined (chapter
two), with its limits and its space for licence. But let us
read back from the Indian and Irish evidence to the English.
In a lucid study David Arnold has looked into the emergence
of a food riot tradition in India, perhaps commencing in the
Madras Presidency in 1876. Some 120 incidents swept South
India in 1918-19, with similar characteristics and objectives to
their counterparts in eighteenth-century England and France:
the prevention of exports, forcing down of prices, and pressing local officials to take measures to ensure provision. Just
as in England two centuries before, the "looting" of food
shops did not result usually in the theft but in the spoiling of
goods, and its intention was to humiliate dealers whom the
crowd held to be guilty of profiteering and hoarding at a time
of extreme hardship. Thus one function of riot was to
moderate the appetite for profit unleashed by the developing
"free market", and Arnold relates its assertiveness to the

---

[1] For the interplay of other factors in different national histories, see
Charles Tilly, "Food Supply and Public Order in Modern Europe", in
C. Tilly (ed.), *The Formation of National States in Europe* (Princeton,
1975), pp. 380-455; and Louise Tilly in Rotberg and Rabb (eds.), *Hunger
and History*, pp. 143-8.

[2] For threatening letters, see my "The Crime of Anonymity", in
Douglas Hay *et. al., Albion's Fatal Tree*, pp. 325-41. For arson, see Wells,
Wretched Faces, pp. 165-7.

transitional moment between locally-based markets and an emergent national grain market — a transition accompanied by sudden fluctuations of price, by the export of grain from areas affected by dearth, and ruptures of the customary channels of communication. He also suggests that, at least in the short term, riot was successful, in terms of its own objectives.[1] What this may suggest is that riot is functional, and may be expected to show itself at the same transitional moment in many national histories.

Why, then, does it not assert itself in Irish history? There were severe episodes of famine in Ireland in the eighteenth and early nineteenth century, long before the "Great Hunger". But the Irish case is not as clear as it has sometimes been made to seem. It is often stated that there is not a tradition of food rioting in Ireland.[2] Yet during the serious famine of 1740-1, the Dublin paper, *Pue's Occurrences*, reported bakers' and mealmen's shops broken open by the Dublin mob, and the boarding of a ship on the Liffey (June 1740), an anti-export riot in Galway quelled by the army (August), anti-export and price-setting riots in Youghal and generally in Munster (December), shops in Limerick broken into (March 1741), and a boat loaded with oats for Waterford stopped on the river at Carrick-on-Suir, with troops firing on the crowd (April 1741).[3] That does not sound like a nation with no food riot tradition. Women were reported as rioters in Wexford in 1757[4] and in 1758 John Wesley found "the mob" busy in Sligo harbour, unloading a Dutch ship of corn bought up by forestallers "to starve the poor" — the mob brought it all to the market and "sold it for the owners at the common price. And this they did with all the calmness and composure imaginable, and without striking or hurting anyone".[5]

Thus the "classical" food riot was certainly known to the

---

[1] David Arnold, "Looting, Grain Riots and Government Policy in South India, 1918", *Past and Present*, 84 (1979).

[2] See for example George Rudé, *Protest and Punishment* (Oxford, 1978), p. 57, who says that food riot "played little part" before 1829-31.

[3] These examples were collected in a pamphlet published by the Foreign Office and Irish Office, *Famine in Ireland, 1740-41* (1847).

[4] *Gentleman's Magazine*, May (1757).

[5] Wesley's *Journal*, 27 May 1758.

eighteenth-century Irish, and it may be under-reported in general histories. If food riot failed to prevent exports and to relieve famine (as in 1740-1) this might account for a weakening of the tradition as the century wore on.[1] And one can only speculate as to the reasons for the divergent national traditions. Perhaps food rioters had less "political" clout in Ireland, since they did not threaten in the same direct way the stability and "face" of a resident governing gentry. Nor (in the absence of poor laws) did they stimulate in the same way an apparatus of relief, nor even (despite some examples) of gentry charity.[2]

Thus in Ireland food riots did not "work", partly because there was no political space (as in England) within which the plebs could exert pressure on their rulers. Arguing backwards from these cases we may pass the English evidence under review once more. Twenty years ago the notion that food riots could have served any positive function could scarcely gain the attention of historians. Smithian doctrine saw them as examples of social malfunction, while also postulating harvest short-fall (FAD) as sufficient explanation for most surges in the price of grain. What one scholar has called "an anachronistic reading of early modern society as a market society marked by the triumph of economic individualism", has given credibility to "a Malthusian model of social and economic change", which proposes an unproblematic and un-mediated relationship between harvest, price, and (until the seventeenth century) mortality.[3]

But recent advances in historical demography are now showing us a more complex set of events. A. B. Appleby clearly identified regional famine in the north-west in 1596-7 and 1622-3, and raised in interesting ways the question as to

[1] But food riots are reported in 1792, Samuel Clark and J. S. Donnelly (eds.), *Irish Peasants* (Manchester, 1983), p. 55; and in 1793, C. H. E. Philpin (ed.), *Nationalism and Popular Protest in Ireland* (Cambridge, 1987), p. 196 (counties Cork and Waterford).
[2] See L. M. Cullen and T. C. Smout, *Comparative Aspects of Scottish and Irish Economic and Social History* (Edinburgh, 1977), p. 10 and ch. 2.
[3] John Walter, "The Social Economy of Dearth in Early Modern England", in John Walter and Roger Schofield (eds.), *Famine, Disease, and the Social Order in Early Modern Society* (Cambridge, 1989), pp. 82, 121.

why the rest of England had managed to escape starvation. Several cogent reasons have been proposed for the difference in the "ecology of famine" between the north-west and the south. And to these may be added the differential effectiveness of measures of relief, which ensured that what little surplus grain was available was brought to market or transferred at subsidised rates to those in most need. The *Book of Orders* may have had more than symbolic functions and (with the aid of poor relief and charities) have mitigated the effects of dearth in the south, whereas the north-western region was not only pastoral and corn-poor, it also lacked the administrative and financial structures to set the *Book of Orders* in motion.[1]

Wrigley and Schofield's important *Population History of England* enables us to pursue these arguments further. While it is usually argued that the threat of famine had passed from England by 1650, a weak relation between grain prices and mortality can be shown until 1745. A weak relation (when generalised across the nation) might mask sharp local crises, or differential mortality in which the excess deaths fell chiefly among "the poor", or certain exposed groups. Moreover, the threat of famine had not moved far away. Wrigley and Schofield examine a sample of 404 parishes between 1541 and 1871 for years in which the death rate in many parishes was markedly above trend; 1727-9 and 1741-2, which are dearth and riot years, appear high on the table (with death rates from 30 to 40 per cent above trend), although other riot years — 1709, 1757, and 1795 — do not.[2] But these cannot be confidently identified as local subsistence crises, since epidemics may have caused the high mortality.[3]

These are complex questions. For the purposes of our argument it is sufficient to note that local crises persist into the eighteenth century, that harvest shortfall or high prices have a differential impact upon different (even neighbouring) communities, and that insignificant movements in national

[1] John Walter and Roger Schofield, "Famine, Disease and Crisis Mortality in Early Modern Society", in *ibid.*, p. 47.
[2] E. A. Wrigley and R. S. Schofield, *The Population of England, 1541-1871* (Cambridge, Mass., 1981), p. 653. The riot years 1766-7 show a death rate 10.4% above trend.
[3] See *ibid.*, pp. 668-9.

statistical series may mask very sharp local suffering. More-over, "by far the highest overall incidence of [local] crisis mortality occurred in the south-west, in an area extending from south Gloucestershire and west Wiltshire through Dorset to Devon": i.e. precisely one of the strongest food riot areas in the eighteenth century. [1]

This suggests that rioters had good reasons for concern, and for actions in self-defence. And that in high-price years they were pressed close to a margin, so that even small modifications of their market situation might make a mortal difference. There were many ways of obtaining subsistence, not all of which depended upon the market, [2] and in emergency "the poor" were not altogether without resources. A correspondent writing from "a manufacturing neighbour-hood" in the West at a time of low employment and high prices (1741), concluded:

> The poor every month grow poorer, for their clothes apparently wear into rags and they are in no capacity of buying new ones. They have sold almost all their little superfluities already, or perhaps one had a gold ring, another two or three pewter dishes, a third a brass pot or kettle; these they have been disposing of to buy bread for themselves and families. . .[3]

That is not (yet) a crisis of subsistence, but it is the context for chronic malnutrition.

One should not misread "entitlement theory" to conclude that there were no such things as failures of grain supply, and that every dearth is man-made. What Sen shows is that, given a shortfall in harvest, the way in which the supply is distri-buted between social groups is decidedly man-made, and depends upon choices between means of allocation, of which market price is only one among many. Even in times of dearth there was always some supply, and the problem was how to squeeze this surplus out of granaries and barns and

---

[1] *Ibid.*, p. 692.

[2] See John Walter, "The Social Economy of Dearth", a good deal of which still applies in the early eighteenth century.

[3] "Philo-Georgius" to duke of Newcastle, 7 Dec. 1741, Brit. Lib. Add MS 32, 698, f. 496.

direct it to those in most need.[1] The measures comprised in
the *Book of Orders* worked reasonably well, and it is not
clear why they lapsed after 1630. In a clearly-argued essay,
Dr Outhwaite has suggested that the complexity and inefficiency of their operation resulted in "disenchantment".[2]
But interest and ideology might also be awarded a role, as the
market oriented, cereal-growing landed classes became more
influential in the state. For long periods after 1660 the
problem was not dearth but abundant production, low prices
and rent arrears, and mercantilist theory was preoccupied
with cereal export (and bounties). In such conditions the
Tudor measures of provision lay dormant, although they
were not forgotten in high-price years. In 1693 in Oxfordshire
the crowd took the corn "as it was carrying away by the
ingrossers, saying they were resolved to put the law in
execution since the magistrates neglected it".[3] "Some of our
rioters" (a dealer wrote in 1766) "have been so infatuated as
to think they were only assisting the execution of wholesome
laws. . ."[4]

What may have eased the abrogation of the *Book of
Orders* was the growing effectiveness of the poor laws in
providing an institutional safety-net for those with a settlement. The responsibility which the central authorities refused
was taken back to the parish or to the urban corporation.
And alongside this limited relief, in times of dearth the local
traditions of charity had more vitality than they are sometimes credited with. In a sense the Tudor practices of "house-
keeping" and of hospitality were extended into the
eighteenth-century landed gentleman's contest, through large

---

[1] Professor Sen continues to lay great stress on the *political* context of
famine in the twentieth century. Governments which are accountable to
public opinion are more likely to exert themselves in relief measures than
those which are not, and "it is hard to find a case in which a famine has
occurred in a country with a free press and an active opposition within a
democratic system": Amartya Sen, "Individual Freedom as a Social
Commitment", *New York Review of Books*, 14 June, 1990.

[2] Outhwaite, "Dearth and Government Intervention", p. 404.

[3] *The Life and Times of Anthony Wood, Antiquary of Oxford, 1632-
95*, ed. A. Clark, cited in W. Thwaites, "The Corn Market and Economic
Change: Oxford in the 18th Century", *Midland History* (forthcoming).

[4] *Reflections on the Present High Price of Provisions*, p. 27.

gestures of "liberality", for local influence.[1]

In every high-price year — at least until the 1760s — substantial landowners came forward in most parts of the country, sending corn at reduced rates to market as an example to others, selling off cheap grain at their gates, ordering their tenants to supply the market at moderate rates, entering into county agreements to reduce prices and to prosecute those who sold by sample, forestallers, etc., and so on. (By the 1780s and 1790s opinion was more divided, and those — like the earl of Warwick — who continued the old charitable gestures, tended to mark themselves out as traditional "Tory" paternalists.) This tradition of highly-visible charity may in part be ascribed to humanitarian motives and to an approved self-image of the gentry as protectors of the poor against heartless employers, mean parish overseers and grasping middlemen. But it was also a calculated stance in the culturally-constructed alliance between patricians and plebs against the middling orders, and it distracted attention from the landowners' prosperity to point to prominent Dissenters and Quakers among the profiteering food dealers.[2]

Viewed from this aspect, poor laws and emergency charities were constituent components of the system of property and power. Indeed, subsidies and subscriptions can often be seen as direct moves to buy off riot, or even as a reward for not rioting.[3] John Bohstedt has warned us:

[1] Much of what John Walter writes about seventeenth-century charities in time of dearth applies equally to the first seven decades of the eighteenth century: Walter, "Social Economy of Dearth".

[2] So widespread was the abuse of Quaker dealers that the Friends issued a public statement in 1800: "The Society of Friends. . . having been for some time calumniated as oppressors of the laborious and indigent classes of the community, by combining to monopolize those necessary articles of life, Corn and Flour, think themselves called upon to vindicate their own innocence and integrity. . .": *Meetings for Sufferings*, xl, pp. 404-6, 6 October 1800 (Friends House Library, London). My thanks to the Librarian, Malcolm Thomas.

[3] In 1766 local gentry raised a subscription in Melksham "in consideration of the poor not having joined in the late riots which occurred all round the town", and beef was distributed to over 1,600 poor persons. But the beef was given in November, months after the height of the crisis had passed. Dr Randall suggests that the riotous poor of Chippenham,

It is not historically useful to separate the undoubted humanitarian-ism of these charities from their function in preserving class rule. Plebeian misery assaulted the conscience of the wealthy and challenged their capacity for remedy, just as it threatened to assault their property and challenge the legitimacy of their political monopoly.

In the 1790s "a waning 'paternalism'. . . was merely thinly-disguised self-preservation".[1]

From the 1790s this was the case, and the supposed threat of "Jacobinism" provided an additional spur. But in earlier decades one can perceive a kind of social bargain, less calculating and more unconscious — a kind of obligatory dues paid for the everyday exercise of hegemony. It gave a character of liberality to some country gentry which allows one to forgive them other sins. "In this sense", John Walter has written, "years of dearth continued to provide an arena in which the nature of social responsibilities between the poor and their betters could be continually re-negotiated". But over the longer course, what had been once perceived as reciprocal duties (and by the labourers as rights) became re-defined as "discriminatory and discretionary charity". If "the poor" escaped "vulnerability to crises of sub-subsistence" it was at the cost of becoming "enmeshed in a web of deference and dependence".[2] Yet if this is true of rural England — and perhaps of some towns — the record of food riot shows an alternative.

In any case, relief measures cannot be shrugged off as only a matter of gestures or as an exercise in social control. There is reason to suppose that they may have mitigated crises of subsistence. If the margin between a poor subsistence and (for groups at risk) famine was small, then marginal

---

Stroud, Frome or Bradford (Wiltshire) might have done better: A. J. Randall, "Labour and the Industrial Revolution in the West of England Woollen Industry" (Univ. of Birmingham Ph.D. thesis, 1979), p. 166.

[1] Bohstedt, *op. cit.*, pp. 96-7, 48. See also Peter Mandler's discussion of the conversion of the landed gentry in these years from a weak pater-nalism which acknowledged the customary rights of the poor to a language of the "natural order" (as defined by Smith and by Malthus) in which "the only true natural right" is that of property: "The Making of the New Poor Law *Redivivus*", *Past and Present*, 117 (November 1987).

[2] Walter, "Social Economy of Dearth", pp. 127-8; Walter and Schofield, "Famine, Disease and Crisis Mortality", p. 48.

redistribution to those in most need may have mattered enough to have shifted a demographic digit. Even between neighbouring towns the different profile of riot/relief might have influenced mortality. The patchwork of poor laws, charities, subsidies — even petty measures like limits upon malting, banning hair-powder, or commending austere diets to the deferential middling orders — might have added their mite to someone's survival.

This is simply to rehearse that food supply (and indeed demography) have their own kind of politics, in which riot may be seen as a rational and effective agent. If there had been no food riots then this whole elaborate patchwork of protection might never have come into being. If we say, with Roger Wells, that "staving off starvation in the most vulnerable locations necessitated the speediest suppression of riot", then we are taking a short-term view of the need, in emergency, to force the traffic in grain through a popular blockade. Over the longer-term view of two centuries and more, riot and the threat of riot may have staved off starvation, sometimes by actually forcing prices down, and more generally by forcing Government to attend to the plight of the poor, and by stimulating parish relief and local charity. The thesis then must be that the solidarities and collective actions of the urban working people, and in the manufacturing and mining districts, did something to bring the crisis of subsistence to an end. And conversely — but as a more tentative hypothesis — it might be that the comparative *absence* of riot in nineteenth-century Ireland and India was one factor (among others) which allowed dearth to pass into famine. And if this is the case, then the best thing that we, in our affluence, can do to help the hungry nations is to send them experts in the promotion of riot.[1]

[1] Wendy Thwaites, who kindly read these pages in manuscript, has very sensibly rebuked me for even making this joke. She points out that the resources of modernised hungry nations have advanced since the eighteenth century, and (citing Nigel Twose, *Cultivating Hunger* (Oxfam, 1984)) describes a vehicle developed to deter rioters in the Dominican Republic or Haiti: "the AMAC-1 has nineteen weapon points, four multiple grenade launchers, a water cannon, an infra-red video camera for surveillance, and its bodywork can be electrified with a 7,000 volt charge". She concludes that for riot to work there "have to be certain constraints on

I say this only partly in jest, for what are at issue are the community defences and the political influence of the working people. At the very least, rulers are likely to be more busy with the relief of the poor if they fear that otherwise their rule may be endangered by riot. I don't, of course, suppose that there was (and is) one alternative and universal set of remedies, "the moral economy", for the successful overcoming of dearth and the prevention of famine. It is exactly against such universalist dogma (the "free market") that I have been arguing. Perhaps all that can be expected in times of crisis is energetic improvisation, using whatever resources and options lie to hand. If political economy rests upon persuasive but misleading metaphors (such as "rationing"), the moral economy nourished its own irrationalisms and superstitions, such as the popular conviction that every dearth was the consequence of hoarding and speculation, "artificial scarcity", or even some malevolent *pacte de famine*.

A case can always be made on both sides of the question. The exemplary punishment of profiteers[1] or fraudulent dealers has sometimes had a beneficent effect upon prices, but the draconian imposition of price maximums has on occasion summoned forth a black market or a producers' strike (the peasants withholding supply) with consequences

---

how far the authorities will go in repression". I have left my jest in because it enables me also to include her thoughtful caution.

[1] Adam Smith in his digression took a benign view of profiteers, since (a) the high profits of years of scarcity compensated dealers for the modest returns of normal years, and (b) the excessive profits of a few might be the inevitable price to pay for the market's functions for the general public. In any case, hoarders and profiteers (if they misjudged the market) would be caught out when prices fell. No-one has as yet succeeded in finding a way to study systematically the question of hoarding and profiteering in eighteenth-century high-price years, nor is it easy to see how it could be done. But that is no reason for the widely-held dogma that its effect (if it happened at all) was insignificant, and that no case can be made for excessive prices (in a seller's market, shored up by Corn Laws) which transferred wealth from the petty consumers to the grain-growing interests. Some scholars show great expertise in such matters as the behaviour of rats and fleas, or in the ratios of seed-corn to available harvest surplus, while stubbornly refusing to acknowledge rather large factors such as human greed.

no less baneful than those of doctrinaire *laissez-faire*. The mentality of urban revolutionaries has sometimes been profoundly hostile to the peasantry, and in the twentieth century collectivist states have precipitated famines as appalling as those presided over by complacent political economy. Some theorists today are interested in remembering the first, and in forgetting the second, which are tidied away as unmentionable in little exercises of political thought. For that reason I have redressed the account, to show that rioters had their reasons.

And (in conclusion) more caution might be proper in the use of the term, "market". I return to my earlier question: is market an actual market or is it a metaphor? One hears on every side these days talk of "a market economy". When this is contrasted with the centralised direction of old-style collectivist states one understands what is being described. And, very certainly, the "market" here is beneficial and can also be democratic, in stimulating variety and in expressing consumer choice. But I cannot clearly say what was "a market economy" in eighteenth-century England; or, rather, I cannot find a non-market-economy to contrast it with. One cannot think of an economy without a market; and even the most zealous food rioters, such as Cornish tinners or Kingswood miners or West of England clothing workers,[1] were inextricably committed to the market, both as producers and as consumers. How could they have existed for a month or a week without it? What we can find are different ways of regulating the market or of manipulating exchanges between producers and consumers, to the advantage of one party or the other. It is with the special case of the marketing of "necessities" in time of dearth that we have been concerned,

[1]We are fortunate in having excellent studies of these groups of workers, both in their capacities as (hard-bargaining) producers and (riotous) consumers. Even "custom" was not pre-market or non-market but a particular community consensus as to the regulation of wages and prices. See J. G. Rule, "The Labouring Miner in Cornwall, c. 1740-1820", (Univ. of Warwick Ph.D. thesis, 1971), esp. pp. 116-80; R. W. Malcolmson, "A Set of Ungovernable People", in J. Brewer and J. Styles (eds.), *An Ungovernable People* (1980) (the mining population of Kingswood); A. J. Randall, "Labour and the Industrial Revolution in the West of England Woollen Industry" (Univ. of Birmingham Ph.D. thesis, 1979).

and the crowd's preferred model was precisely the "open market" in which the petty producers freely competed, rather than the closed market when large dealers conducted private bargains over samples in the back parlours of inns.[1]

The "market economy", I suspect, is often a metaphor (or mask) for capitalist process. It may even be employed as myth. The most ideologically-compelling form of the myth lies in the notion of the market as some supposedly-neutral but (by accident) beneficent entity; or, if not an entity (since it can be found in no space but the head) then an energising spirit — of differentiation, social mobility, individualisation, innovation, growth, freedom — like a kind of postal sorting-station with magical magnifying powers, which transforms each letter into a package and each package into a parcel. This "market" may be projected as a benign consensual force, which involuntarily maximises the best interests of the nation. It may even seem that it is the "market system" which has "produced" the nation's wealth — perhaps "the market" grew all that grain?

Market is indeed a superb and mystifying metaphor for the energies released and the new needs (and choices) opened up by capitalist forms of exchange, with all conflicts and contradictions withdrawn from view. Market is (when viewed from this aspect) a mask worn by particular interests, which are not coincident with those of "the nation" or "the community", but which are interested, above all, in being mistaken to be so. Historians who suppose that such a market really could be found must show it to us in the records. A metaphor, no matter how grand its intellectual pedigree, is not enough.

III

Let us next take the question of the role of women in food riots. In 1982 Jennifer Grimmett and M. I. Thomis published a helpful chapter on the theme,[2] in which they raised but left

---

[1] *Mist's Weekly Journal*, 12 March 1726 reported that the mob rose on market days in Northampton, Kettering, Oundle, Wellingborough, Stony Stratford, because farmers would not bring corn to the market-place "but kept it in the Inns". At Towcester a riot was prevented by the Cryer giving notice that corn must be brought "into open market".

[2] Malcolm I. Thomis and Jennifer Grimmett, *Women in Protest, 1800-1850* (1982), ch. 2. This is based on a survey of published sources and some use of newspapers in 1800 and 1812.

unanswered the question as to which sex was the more prominent. Kenneth Logue, in a study of "meal mobs" in Scotland found that women were very active, although they comprised only 28 per cent of those charged before the courts. But this was possibly because "they were less likely to be prosecuted than their male colleagues", so that, again, the question is left open.[1] In 1988 John Bohstedt sought to bring a conclusive answer in a substantial article which purports to demolish "the myth of the feminine food riot".[2]

Bohstedt's conclusions are as follows:

> Women did not dominate food riots; food riots were not a distinctly feminine province. . . Women typically joined men in food riots. . . Women's co-operation with men is much more significant than the monopoly suggested by the older view. Women were significant partners to men as bread rioters partly because they were essential partners as bread-winners in the household economies of pre-industrial society and partly because bread riots were still effective politics in stable small-to-medium-sized traditional towns.

These conclusions are sustained in two ways. First, John Bohstedt presents what purport to be refined statistics of all riots in England and Wales between 1790 and 1810. Second, he introduces some pages of speculation as to gender roles in the proto-industrial household economy.

I have already expressed my admiration for Bohstedt's major study of riot. And there is interesting material in this new article. But the piece obscures as much as it reveals. The first difficulty is that there is no "myth of the feminine food riot" to demolish. No-one, no historian, has ever suggested that food riots were a "monopoly" of women or were pre-dominantly feminine, and Bohstedt can show none. The best that he can do is hold up to censure Barbara and J. L. Hammond for writing (in 1911) of the crisis year of 1795 as the year of "the revolt of the housewives", because of "the conspicuous part taken by women" in the food riots.[3] That

---

[1] Kenneth J. Logue, *Popular Disturbances in Scotland, 1780-1815* (Edinburgh, 1979), pp. 199, 202-3.

[2] John Bohstedt, "Gender, Household and Community Politics: Women in English Riots, 1790-1810", *Past and Present*, no. 120 (August 1988), pp. 88-122. The claim to have demolished "the myth of the feminine food riot" is at pp. 90, 93.

[3] *Ibid.*, p. 88. J. L. and B. Hammond, *The Village Labourer* (1911; reprint 1966), pp. 116-8.

does not constitute a "myth", so that we are being led into a spurious polemic. Previous historians have, perhaps, not always given enough attention to women's part in riots, but most have agreed that women were highly visible rioters and were frequently involved. Since all historians show riots in which men also were highly visible, or in which men and women acted together, no-one has suggested that food riots were "a distinctly feminine province".

In his eagerness to drive this mythical opponent from the field, Bohstedt introduces his tables. He has with great industry assembled a "sample" of 617 riots between 1790 and 1810 and he drills this sample through various statistical manoeuvres. Now I don't know what to say to this. There are times when his figures are helpful — for example, in showing a rough division between different occasions for riot. And Bohstedt is a careful scholar who sometimes remembers the limitations of his evidence. But in general his history becomes less credible the more he surrenders to his own figures and the further he gets away from "literary" and contextual sources. This is because much of the evidence is too "soft" to be introduced to the hard definitions of a table. And when one looks at some of John Bohstedt's counting, the points at issue may seem absurd. Of his 617 riots he is able to identify 240 as food riots. These are further refined as:

A. Women dominant	B. Women and men	C. Men only	D. Gender unknown
35	42	81	82

If one deducts D, and puts A and B together, then 77 out of 158, or 49 per cent of these food riots had female participation and 51 per cent did not. So that if one wished to claim that women took part in "most" food riots, one would be at fault by 2 per cent. But, putting B and C together, one would discover that 123 out of 158, or 78 per cent had male participation — which could be a step on the way to a myth of a male food riot, to be demolished by a subsequent generation of computers.

When Bohstedt offers to drill these figures through more refined manoeuvres (such as violence and disorder quotients), he must make anyone laugh who is familiar with the source material which he is using. Let me explain some of the difficulties. There are, first of all, the difficulties in gathering any reliable count. These are familiar, and have often been discussed.[1] Bohstedt's sample is drawn from the *Annual Register*, two London newspapers, and the in-letters to the Home Office concerning disorders (HO 42). This is a wide survey, but the provincial coverage of the London press was patchy, JPs might not always wish to report their local affairs to the central authorities, the sample tends to over-report dramatic or violent affrays and under-report quieter episodes (hence possibly under-reporting women's participation), and so on. When compared to regional studies which draw upon local sources, Bohstedt's sample shows a serious under-count. A most thorough study, by Alan Booth, of food riots in the north-west of England in the same years, lists forty-six disturbances of which only twelve are in Bohstedt's sample. Booth adds that "in most riots where sexual composition was recorded women appear to have been both more numerous and particularly active", and he goes on to cite thirteen examples. Hence Booth's examples (which he does not suggest are exhaustive) exceed the total of Bohstedt's count of food riots in all categories, which *must* undercount the feminine presence.[2]

Next, we must consider the nature of the evidence which is being used. How does it come about that in eighty-two cases (or more than one third of the sample) the sex of the rioters is unknown, and how hard or soft is the evidence in the eighty-one cases of men only? The evidence often comes in a sexually-indeterminate vocabulary: "rioters", "the mob", "the poor", "the inhabitants", "the populace". Let us take a letter of 12 July 1740 from Norwich, published in the *Ipswich Journal*, which describes a riot by "the common People", "the meanest of the People", "the Multitude,":

> About Eight in the Evening the Mayor committed three of four dis-
> orderly Fellows to Prison; which Act so incens'd the Mob, that they
> broke open the Prison, releas'd their Companions, and have scarce left

[1] The best comment is Roger Wells, "Counting riots in eighteenth-century England", *Bulletin of Lab. Hist. Soc.*, 37 (1978), pp. 68-72. Alan Booth discusses successive errors in estimates in his excellent and dense study, "Food Riots in the North-West of England, 1790-1801", *Past and Present*, 77 (1977), esp. pp. 89-90.

[2] Bohstedt, *Riots and Community Politics*, pp. 11-14, 230-1; Booth, *op. cit.*, pp. 98-9.

a Pane of Glass in the whole Prison. . . Upon this Outrage of the Mob, an unthinking Gentleman is said to have taken a Musket out of the Hands of a Dragoon, and shot a Man thro' the Head. You will imagine how this enrag'd the Populace; and the Consequence of that Evening's Work was, three Men, a Boy, and two Women, were shot. . .[1]

This report commences as indeterminate (D), becomes male (C) at "disorderly Fellows", and moves sharply across to (B) — women and men — only when the dragoons, by firing point-blank into the crowd, take a random sample. Amongst all the indeterminate ("mob", "populace") and male vocabulary, the first mention of women, in a long report, is when two of them are shot. A similar sexually-indeterminate crowd, in 1757, descended on a Hereford miller, and insisted on searching his house and mill for grain. The miller refused:

Yet they persisted in having another search, saying that if he had no grain he had some money, upon which declaration there was necessity for fireing on them in which four women and two men were wounded, which occasioned the rest to disperse.[2]

Again and again reports of "mobs" leave them sexually indeterminate until the moment of some action or arrests make individuals visible. Nor is this any indication of sexist bias in the reporter. The bias (if there is one) is more likely to be in the mind of the twentieth-century historian or reader whose expectations, when he reads of "mobs", are of crowds composed of men, and who reads the accounts accordingly. Perhaps, in the later nineteenth century, "the mob" became a male noun? But the image called to the eighteenth-century mind by these collective nouns was very different — for them a "mob" suggested women, men and (often) older children, especially boys. I think it probable that Bohstedt's table is misleading, and that many riots in column (D) (gender unknown) and some in (C) (men only) were mixed affairs.

Moreover, these figures which enter the tables, whether derived from the press or from a letter to the Home Office, normally report a particular moment of riot — perhaps its

[1] *Ipswich Journal*, 26 July 1740. I am indebted to Robert Malcolmson for this.
[2] *Bristol Journal*, 11 June 1757, cited in Jeremy N. Caple, "Popular Protest and Public Order in 18th-century England: the Food Riots of 1756-7" (Queens Univ. Ontario, M.A. thesis, 1978), p. 102.

crisis — and they rarely describe its evolution. Yet a riot may pass through phases, for example it might commence with actions by women, be joined by men, and end with men alone. In my view there are two situations in which we may expect to find a predominantly male crowd. First, when disciplined male working groups, accustomed to acting together, spearhead the riot: such may be the case with coal miners, keelmen, Cornish tinners, and seamen. In the second case, when heavy conflict is expected with the authorities, the women sometimes seem to fall back — or perhaps are asked by the men to do so.

Yet the evidence is not as tidy as that. Miners and tinners were archetypical male rioters, yet also it is notorious that the whole communities shared in their movements. The Kingswood "mob" is usually thought of as masculine, for example in its destruction of turnpikes and toll-gates. But on occasion its resistance to authority was more like a rising of the whole district. During riots against the cider tax of 1738 the excise officers were "resisted by that savage Crew by Fire Armes": "there are now in the Forest not less than 1000 Men, Women and Boys in Armes, destroying all before them. . .".[1] In 1740 the Kingswood colliers marched into Bristol and demonstrated against the price of corn at the Council House, leaving behind "their usual Armour of Clubs and Staffs", but accompanied by "some weavers, colliers' wives and abundance of other women".[2] Both the absence of "armour" and the presence of women suggests (on that occasion) a commitment to peaceable courses.

In 1740 the north-east was swept with food riots, which culminated in the sacking of the Newcastle Guildhall. (See above p. 70 & p. 231.) Pitmen and keelmen were prominent in this, and at a superficial view this might appear as a male riot. But a longer and closer view will show an alternation of male and female presence. The regional actions against export were first raised in Stockton by "a Lady with a Stick and a horn". (See above p. 233.) Women as well as men took part in boarding vessels loaded with corn, and forcing them

---

[1] G. Blenkinsop, 14 Oct. 1738 in PRO, T 1/299(15).
[2] *Northampton Mercury*, 6 Oct. 1740; R. Malcolmson in Brewer and Styles, *op. cit.*, p. 117.

to off-load to the crowd on shore.[1] When — after three weeks of popular export embargo — the Sheriff raised the *posse comitatus* against them, the people of Stockton, to the number of three thousand, "sent for the Colliers of Ederly and Caterhorn".[2] Meanwhile there had been small disturbances in Newcastle-on-Tyne, involving a group of women "incited by a leader calling herself 'General' or Jane Bogey, ringing bells and impeding the passage of horses carrying grain through the town".[3] After five women had been committed,[4] the troubles in Newcastle died down, only to resume on a much greater scale in mid-June, with the involvement of keelmen and pitmen (who struck their pits). In the first phase, "a body of 3 or 4 hundred men women and children" came into the city and demanded corn at a low rate; granaries were broken into, and the crowd marched about the streets in triumph, huzzaing and blowing horns. The magistrates then summoned and armed the Watch and Ward and seized some prisoners; the crowd then appears in accounts as increasingly male, with "Colliers, Wagoners, Smiths and other common workmen", well armed with cudgels, breaking open the keep and releasing the prisoners, and marching in great discipline through the town with drum, bagpipes and mock colours.[5]

Other episodes were to follow, including the firing on the crowd and the attack on the Guildhall. My point is to illustrate the evolution of a food rioting crowd, which may now be incited by women, may then become of assorted sexes and ages, and may then (when rescue and confrontation are the object) become predominantly male. But none of this should be stereotyped. The most careful historian of the affair observes that the role of women and children was under-

[1] Edward Goddard, 24 May 1740 in PRO, SP 36/50/431 and miscellaneous depositions in SP 36/51.

[2] J. J. Williamson, Sheriff of Durham, 10 June 1740 in PRO, SP 36/51.

[3] Joyce Ellis, "Urban Conflict and Popular Violence: the Guildhall Riots of 1740 in Newcastle-upon-Tyne", *Int. Rev. Social Hist.*, xxv, 3 (1980).

[4] They were discharged at the Sessions a few days later.

[5] "Account of the Riots" by Alderman Ridley in Northumberland CRO, 2R1 27/8.

stated in subsequent investigations, and that of pitmen over-stated. Women contributed to both physical and verbal episodes of violence, breaking into granaries and one woman going down on her knees in front of the magistrates and crying out "Blood for blood!".[1] The authorities came down most heavily upon the women who had unloaded wheat from a boat at Stockton,[2] whereas in Newcastle they selected the pitmen for indictment and passed over the women.

This shows whole communities in action, with one sex or the other coming into prominence as each assumes a different part. The episode might fall into any one of John Bohstedt's categories according to the moment at which it was reported. It also shows that the crowd might be made up of different elements, consciously playing different parts in co-operation with each other. There are other occasions when it is reported that the "people" sent for the miners to help them. In anti-export riots in St Asaph (Flint) in 1740 it was said that "men, women and boys" were joined by "Severall Colliers and Miners"; not only so, but it was alleged that the colliers "belonging" to Sir Thomas Mostyn were deliberately laid off, given cudgels, and encouraged to take part. In the event they completely dominated the affair, marching together under Mostyn colours and crying out "a Mostyn!".[3] In Coventry (1756) the poor — presumably of both sexes — "patted the colliers on the back and urged them to go thro with what they had begun".[4] And at Nottingham in the same year, the colliers negotiated an agreement with the mayor, and then, as they were leaving the town "a number of women. . . gave them money to come back, and showed them to a Wind-mill. . . having French stones". The colliers obligingly destroyed several mills in the vicinity.[5] In the anti-export

---

[1] Ellis, *op. cit.*, pp. 341-6.

[2] At Durham Assizes Anne Withy, Hannah Crone and William Young were transported for seven years for taking a large quantity of wheat out of a ship at Stockton. Three more women and one man were tried and acquitted: *Newcastle Journal*, 9 Aug. 1740. My thanks to Robert Malcolmson again.

[3] William Price, 13 June 1740 in PRO, SP 36/51, and various depositions in SP 36/50 and 36/51.

[4] PRO, SP 36/135.

[5] Caple, *op. cit.*, p. 82.

riots in Poole (Dorset) in 1737 (by contrast) the women took action, with the men supporting them and swearing that "if any one offers to molest any of the Women in their Proceedings" they would raise a great number of men and destroy both ships and cargoes" (above p. 233).[1]

Two unusual examples of supportive gender actions come from Scotland. In January 1813 in Montrose the magistrates tried to bully the town carters into loading grain onto ships, and the carters reluctantly promised to do so; but (surprise!) on their return to their homes they found that they could not, because their wives had locked the stables or sent the horses away. In 1801 in Errol the Volunteers were called out for possible action against a "meal mob". "As they were going to parade, some of the women, mainly the wives and mothers of the Volunteers, took their guns from them, but immediately gave them back." The crowd then stoned an inn with impunity, and, Kenneth Logue suggests, "It may be that women simply removed part of the firing mechanisms, rendering the weapons useless and relieving the Volunteers of the unhappy task of shooting at their own townspeople".[2]

A more elaborate series of actions was described in Exeter in 1757:

Last Market-Day some Farmers demanded 11s. per Bushel for Wheat, and were agreeing among themselves to bring it to 15s. and then make a stand. But the Graecians (as the Inhabitants of St. Sidwell's are called) hearing of this Complot, sent their wives in great Numbers to Market, resolving to give no more than 6s. per Bushel, and, if they would not sell it at that Price, to take it by Force; and such wives, as did not stand by this Agreement, were to be well flogg'd by their Comrades. Having thus determined, they marched to the Corn-Market, and harangued the Farmers in such a Manner, that they lowered their price to 8s. 6d. The Bakers came, and would have carried off all at that Price, but the Amazonians swore, that they would carry the first man who attempted it before the Mayor, upon which the Farmers swore they would bring no more to Market; and the sanguine Females threatened the Farmers, that, if they did not, they would come and take it by Force out of their

---

[1] Holles Newcastle to Secretary at War, 26 May 1737, PRO, SP 41/10.
[2] Logue, *op. cit.*, pp. 21. 44.

Ricks. The Farmers submitted and sold it for 6s. on which the poor weavers and woolcombers were content.[1]

One doubts whether the male "Graecians" could have "sent their wives" on such a skilfully exercised sequence of actions, unless they had mutually agreed upon their gender roles: which (in this case) left the action and the thinking to the women, and only the eating to the men.

A further (and insurmountable) difficulty is that evidence taken from the years 1790-1810, however skilfully it is counted, cannot support generalisations as to the feminine presence in food riots which extended over a period of well over two hundred years. After 1812 food riots in most parts of the country gave way to other kinds of (political, trade union) protest. So that John Bohstedt's quantities are taken from the last stages of the traditional riot, in which — as he himself argues — the role of women may have been changing. At the least, generalisations would have to be supported by a review of the evidence across the seventeenth and eighteenth centuries.[2]

Instead of attempting this, John Bohstedt leaps across to another line of argument altogether. He raises doubts as to whether women had a significant place in the market at all. Indeed, pursuing the rather fashionable ploy in the Western academy of offering oneself as more-feminist-than-thou, he suggests that those who offer women as marketers are pedlars of sexist stereotypes. I am one target of his scorn, since in my essay I had, while drawing particular attention to the very active part played by women, suggested that one reason for this might be that they were "those most involved in face-to-face marketing, most sensitive to price significancies, most experienced in detecting short-weight or inferior quality" (p. 234). Bohstedt challenges this: "It is an anachronistic mistake to assume that women's role in food riots grew out of some special female role as the shopper of the family. Nowhere is there evidence for the frequent assumption that in

[1] R. W. Malcolmson, *Life and Labour in England, 1700-1780* (1981), p. 118.

[2] Wendy Thwaites has found women present in Oxfordshire food riots in 1693, 1713, 1757, 1766 and 1795: Thwaites, thesis, table p. 472 (for 1795), pp. 485-6.

this period women were the primary shoppers. . .". "Plebeian women were income producers and earners, not unwaged housewives and shoppers confined by gender to the more modern role of 'home-making'."[1] Indeed, he waxes indignant at the stereotype of his own invention: "Women were not simply housewife furies, drying their hands and heading off to the market or igniting there as a crowd of shoppers". He does not attempt to show who did the purchasing of provisions, or how,[2] but he develops instead hypotheses as to the "nearly coequal" relations between women and men in the proto-industrial household economy.

I agree that "housewives" and "shopping" are (in their current usage) anachronistic terms, although I used neither of them. I have a little difficulty, in that I don't regard skills in marketing or home-making as unimportant and inferior, although it is true that male-dominated cultures may make them seem so, and may then try to confine women to "inferior" roles. But there are really two questions here: an empirical question — who did the marketing and how? — and a theoretical question about the proto-industrial household economy, and we will take them in that order.

There is no single source to which one can go to establish gender roles in the market-place. Women were certainly present as sellers of food, although few were licensed dealers.[3] One might expect to find, in a market-town, a large throng of sellers of poultry, eggs, butter, vegetables, fruit and other locally-grown produce, and most of these were women: the wives, daughters and servants of local farmers,

[1] Thomas and Grimmett, op. cit., p. 10, also accuse me, on the same grounds, of placing women "firmly in the market-place, if not exactly beside the kitchen sink"; and they also throw no light on how marketing was done.

[2] Bohstedt is strangely inconsistent. He suggests that men did the marketing (p. 116). But women (who did not normally do so and hence were confined to the household?) were nevertheless somehow knitting the networks of neighbourhood, and he commends a French study for noting that housework "overflowed into communal co-operation" in "fetching water and *provisions*, for example" (p. 98, my italics).

[3] See Wendy Thwaites' excellent study, "Women in the Market Place: Oxfordshire c. 1690-1800", *Midland History*, ix (1984), pp. 23-42, and, for the earlier tradition, Rodney Hilton, "Women Traders in Medieval England", in *Class Conflict and the Crisis of Feudalism* (1985), p. 213.

while others would be petty dealers from the labouring class. In a strictly governed market some of these might pay toll for stands — for example, at the Butter Cross (see Plate XVIIa) — but more commonly they would set out their wares on the periphery.[1] In 1816 a local historian described Bicester market —

> I have heard many of the aged inhabitants say that they have formerly seen the whole market-hill covered with sacks of corn etc; the avenues leading to it crowded by the farmers' wives with their baskets of butter, eggs and poultry. . .[2]

In fact the poultry, fruit and vegetable market was sometimes known as "the women's market". An experienced dealer, looking back to the 1760s, described the prosperous tourist market of Bath, where "the farmer, his wife, daughter, or servant", trudged there with "the best milk butter, whey butter, cheeses. . . roasting pigs. . . fattened bacon. . . black and white pudding, abundance of lard, chitterlings nicely cleaned, and made up by the hand of a neat dairy maid; variety of poultry. . . fresh eggs. . . fruits, flowers, herbs, honey, and the honey combs, &c, &c, &c.".[3] By the 1790s this trade was being taken over by "jobbers, higlers, &c.",[4] and as farmers became more prosperous it was the common complaint that farmers were "purchasing piano fortes for their daughters, instead of bringing their butter and eggs to market".[5]

It is less easy to identify the purchasers, although they were certainly of both sexes. Oxford, a well-regulated corn market

[1] In the early eighteenth century Lord of the Market of Woodbridge (Suffolk) was threatening to prosecute "persons who come to this town with fish, fowl, fruits, butter, cheese, eggs" on market days, and who carry these things from house to house, instead of taking a stand or stall in the market: Ipswich and East Suffolk CRO, V 5/9/6 - 3 (3). Perhaps similar attempts at control were behind a rash of prosecutions of petty dealers (garden stuff, fruit, fish) for regrating in Oxford in 1712: of 24 persons prosecuted, 21 were women: Thwaites, p. 30.

[2] J. Dunkin cited in *ibid.*, p. 29.

[3] J. Mathews, *Remarks on the Cause and Progress of the Scarcity and Dearness of Cattle*. . . (1797), pp. 9-10.

[4] *Ibid.*, pp. 70-71.

[5] J. Malham (Vicar of Helton, Dorset, and Ordinary of the Wiltshire County Gaol), *The Scarcity of Grain Considered* (Salisbury, 1800), p. 43.

in the eighteenth century, has very little record of petty purchases, and the records show the main buyers to be bakers, millers and dealers. But petty purchases may have gone unrecorded. Or perhaps working people did not often buy a sack of wheat of a bushel of flour.[1] An inquest on Ruth Pierce, who died in bizarre circumstances in Devizes market in 1753, shows that she had clubbed together with three other women to buy one sack of wheat from a farmer.[2] Regions had differing practices, but by the mid-century in many parts of the South and Midlands working people were buying flour or bread, not wheat.[3] Five cases involving Assize of Bread offences (short-weight, etc.) came up at Oxfordshire Quarter Sessions, Epiphany 1758, from Ploughley Hundred, and four of the purchasers whose oaths were taken were women.[4] The Crown brief in 1766 against Hester Pitt and Jane Pitt shows that they stopped Mary Cooke in Ruscombe, near Stroud, as she was on horseback loaded with sixteen dozen of bread, pushed her off the horse and took the bread.[5] This reminds us that in the second half of the century, bakers' and hucksters' shops were increasingly common, that bread might be brought around by horse, or horse-and-cart, and that riot could be by women against women.

The evidence suggests to me that working people were not, by the 1790s, buying wheat, flour or bread in the market on market day, but getting it elsewhere, at inns, shops, or bakeries. Catherine Phillips tells us in 1792 that "it was formerly the custom of the wives of labourers and artificers to purchase, on market days, two or three gallons of malt, which would perhaps brew tolerable good table beer for the week", but they were now ceasing to do so since the malt tax

---

[1] Thwaites, thesis, i, pp. 208-21, discusses the question with care.

[2] "Inquisition on Ruth Pierce", *Wiltshire Archaeological and Natural History Magazine*, xii (1870), pp. 256-7. My thanks to Mary Prior.

[3] "A Person in Business", *Two Letters on the Flour Trade* (London, 1757, 1766), pp. 7-8; the author is writing from Hampshire. See also Wendy Thwaites, "Dearth and the Marketing of Agricultural Produce: Oxfordshire", *Agric. Hist. Rev.*, xxxiii (1985), p. 121.

[4] Thwaites, "Women in the Market Place", p. 37.

[5] PRO, TS 11/1138/5956: Special Commission, Gloucester, 14 Nov. 1766, Crown Brief.

had raised the price too high.[1] Where people came in to the urban market from a little distance, they perhaps got hold of some transport, and women, men and older children piled on together; no doubt husband and wife often went round the market together. An observer in 1800 noted a man and wife coming to an inn to buy a peck of wheat, and "after the wheat was measured, the woman says to her husband, 'John I want some money to go to the grocer's for some tea, sugar, butter' ".[2] In this division of gender roles, hers was to finish off the shopping and his (no doubt) was to stay at the inn and drink.

All ages, shapes, sizes and sexes would throng together in a busy market. The genteel were falling away as the century wore on; they did not like to be squashed in the plebeian press and they sent their servants instead. (They are more likely to have sent the cook or kitchen maid to buy provisions than the footman.) The wives and daughters of cottagers might stay on to spend their small takings from selling eggs or cherries on cloth or ribbons or houseware. (Money earned from such produce belonged to "the distaff side" of the family budget.) Some farmers would stay on, get drunk, and have to be collected by their wives.[3] There would be carters and ostlers, ballad-mongers, perhaps a fiddler or two, and a card-sharper. There would be wide-eyed children, hoping to scrump an apple. There would be courting couples, on the only day out when they saw each other. Bakers and millers, higglers and jobbers, market officials. And a throng of purchasers, very many of whom were women. As a rule it was the woman's role to bake, brew and cook — Mary Collier, the washer-woman, eloquently disclosed woman's dual roles as wage-earner and house-worker, in 1739[4] — and it has long been assumed that women had the major role in purchasing provisions. The point has not been fully proven,

[1] Catherine Phillips, *Considerations on the Causes of the High Price of Grain. . .* (1792), p. 7.

[2] William Brooks, *The True Causes of our present Distress for Provisions* (1800), pp. 29-30. My thanks to Dr Thwaites.

[3] F. W. Steer (ed.), "The Memoirs of James Spershott", *The Chichester Papers*, 30 (Chichester, 1962).

[4] See Mary Collier, *The Woman's Labour*, ed. Marian Sugden and E. P. Thompson (1989).

but if research is directed at it then I have little doubt as to its results.

The market was, in any case, a great occasion of sociability. Dare one suggest that market day could actually be fun? If women played so important a part in networking households into a community how could it happen that they should not take part in so important an occasion for community social-ising (and gossip) as the market? Bohstedt offers us no evidence, but suggests that both the family income and necessary purchases were "probably collected by the man on ᵗthe weekly trip to the warehouse and the market". He is thinking of a "proto-industrial" clothing worker or nail-maker, who works in his own household economy, but must collect raw materials and deliver the finished product to the putter-out. But the day for delivering his "piece" was not often the same as market day. And in a majority of house-holds spinning was the mainstay of women's work until the 1790s or later, and the women (wives or spinsters) would have to visit their own putter-out, or the shopkeeper who acted as agent, as frequently. A 1741 pamphlet shows women in Hampshire, Wiltshire and Dorset coming in to market on farmers' wagons, taking their spun yarn to the clothiers: "then they get the few things they want, and return to the Inn to be carried home again". (There might be as many as three or four hundred poor people, chiefly women, in the market doing this.[1]) A well-informed observer, in 1794, wrote of the dismay of a labourer, "whose wife and children return home from the next market town with the sad tidings that the Wool-man puts out no more handwork. . .".[2]

If women usually did the cooking in the household economy and if some (but not all) women's food riots had targets in the market-place, common-sense suggests that women knew a lot about food marketing. It often seems so from the reports. In 1740 in Newport Pagnell (at a time when the crowd was blocking exports) farmers sold two wagons of wheat to factors. The wheat was disguised by being packed

---

[1] Alice Clark, *Working Life of Women in the Seventeenth Century* (1919; reprint 1982), pp. 108-9.

[2] "A.B.", *Observations on the detriment that is supposed must arise to the family of every cottager. . . from the loss of woollen spinning. . .* (1794).

like cheese, but "some cunning old women" suspected the deception, stopped the wagons, and (joined by three hundred more women) entered into a long and successful engagement with the farmers.[1] John Bohstedt wishes to play down this female role in the market because he wants to emphasise the productive role of women in the proto-industrial household, which made them "virtually equal to men in the communal economy and polity". Women took part in riots, "not as housewives but as full-fledged contributors to the family income". "They should be seen as proto-citizens and constituents of the local polity and economy, nearly coequal to men in claiming their rights to affordable bread."

I don't wish to dispute the importance of the women's labour in the clothing or metal-working household. But there is no reason why they should not also have been the main food marketers just as the men may have dealt most often with the tools and materials of the trade. What may be misleading are the notions of "equality" and status brought to bear upon them from our own status-conscious and contractual society. These women (and these men) were for themselves and not for us: they were proto-nothing. They were not bugged by notions of equality, in a competitive sense, since they were deeply habituated to the acceptance that men's and women's roles were different, and that neither was the more nor the less for that. There were certainly places of overlap, and also occasions when each sex (the women more often than the men) would take part in the other's work. But Bohstedt goes too far, in his commendable attempt to emphasise the women's independent position, in suggesting that the roles of men and women in the household or cottage economy were almost indistinguishable.[2]

On the contrary, different gender roles were firmly demarked, perhaps the more firmly in that each sex's sphere of responsibility held the other's respect. One emphatically

---

[1] *Ipswich Journal*, 7 June 1740.
[2] Bohstedt may be drawing too far upon the suggestions of Hans Medick on "The proto-industrial family economy", in Peter Kriedte, H. Medick and Schlumbohm, *Industrialization before Industrialization* (Cambridge, 1987), pp. 60-3.

literary source is the poem "descriptive of the manners of the clothiers" in the West Riding of Yorkshire, *circa* 1730. It is, exactly, a comedy of manners about gender roles in a "proto-industrial" household, although one of small master rather than journeyman status. In this the food is certainly cooked by the Mistress, with the help of "prentice Bess": in includes broth, oaten cakes, mutton, bread (home baked), "dumplins", and home-brewed ale. The "Maister" oversees the needs of the weaving trade; he or his sons (or apprentices) will get wool from the Wolds, take it out to the spinners, get size, dye, and so on. The Mistress must oversee getting yeast (perhaps from a neighbour), malt and hops for brewing, soap and "blue". She and Bess must also "sit at t'bobbin wheel", dye, do the washing (and washing-up), get the children to and from school, and oversee the work folk when the master is away. And a dozen other things.[1]

It was exactly the extent and manifest importance of the woman's role, and her manifold responsibilities, each calling for specialised skills, which gave to her authority in the household and respect in the community. Her work was indispensable and she well knew it. It is pointless to try to grade the feminine and masculine spheres of work in terms of degrees of "near equality". Certainly in the public sphere of law and religion and property the woman was in a subject position. But in the household economy the terms which we need are "authority", "worth" and "respect": perhaps the parity and mutual interdependence of unlikes.[2]

If women were especially prominent in food riots in regions where the manufacturing household economy was strong, such as clothing districts, this was in part because their role in this economy gave them authority and self-confidence. But this was not because gender roles were almost indistinguishable. The female sphere of authority probably took in most marketing for provisions, and within

[1] The full text is in *Publications of the Thoresby Society*, xli, pt. 3, p. 95 (1947). Extracts are in H. Heaton, *Yorkshire Woollen and Worsted Industries* (1920), pp. 344-7; Thompson, *The Making of the English Working Class*, pp. 300-1.

[2] See Dorothy Thompson, "Women, Work and Politics in Nineteenth-Century England: the Problem of Authority", in Jane Randall (ed.), *Equal or Different* (Oxford, 1987), pp. 61-3.

the household the women had responsibility for baking, brewing, and seeing that the household was fed. They were therefore especially sensitive to price and quality, and were the first to have to work out economies and strategies of survival when dearth threatened. This role made them as much guardians of the household's survival as were the men, who might earn the greater part of the family income. They would discuss their problems, anger or anxieties with other women, not only on market day but daily on their neighbourhood occasions. This favoured — Alice Clark wrote long ago — "the formation of a feminine public opinion on current events". Thus households would be bonded and the nucleus for direct actions prepared.[1]

By downplaying this role and by fastening his analysis upon women's role as income-earners in the manufacturing household, Bohstedt — quite against his own intentions — gives an almost patronising account of women as rioters: "Women typically *joined* men in food riots" (above p. 306, my italics). The suggestion is conveyed that women expressed their solidarity *with* men, as their "near coequals". But the evidence does not feel like that. On these matters the women were often the leaders of community opinion, and the initiators of actions; sometimes they were the sole executors of actions, and the men joined in in solidarity with them as often as they joined the men.

In 1766 and afterwards there were fewer spontaneous crowd actions in the market-place because less grain was being sold there. Sales were removing to inns, and the open market was in some places coming to an end. Working people in the south and midlands were increasingly buying bread. This might fluctuate in price, or (if the priced loaf remained steady) in weight, which was more difficult to judge. In the high-price years of the 1790s, the huge quartern or half-quartern loaves normally baked in many towns went out of reach of "the poor", who "were obliged to buy fragments of bread, with several surfaces exposed to the sun, air, flies,

---

[1] Clark, *op. cit.*, p. 51. See also Maxine Berg's suggestion as to networks in *The Age of Manufactures* (1985), pp. 164-7, and the excellent survey of women's work in the family economy in Bridget Hill, *Women, Work, and Sexual Politics in Eighteenth-Century England* (Oxford, 1989), chapters 3 and 4.

dust, and all the contingencies of a huckster's shop".[1] But the end product in a huckster's shop was a futile target for those who wished to bring down the price of grain. Hence the crowd had to plan more carefully, and to select targets, often outside the market-place, such as inns, canals, wharfs, granaries, farms, mills, wagons on the road. These actions around wheat or flour must have followed upon discussions (and rumours of hoarding or speculation) within the working community.

Spontaneous actions by women in the market-place were more frequent in the first half of the century, because wheat and flour were still in the open market. Thus in Oxford in 1693 we find women in the market "pelting millers, mealmen, bakers etc with stones";[2] in 1740 most of the riots were against export, but market-place riots are also reported, such as that at Peterborough where "a number of women rose in a tumultous manner on the market day, rioted the farmers out of their sacks & strow'd their corn in the street".[3] Similar market-place actions by women are reported in 1757 in Bewdley, Worcester, Taunton, Newcastle-under-Lyme, and Salisbury, while in 1766 in Kidderminster, when some poor women were bidding in the corn market for a bag of wheat, and a baker offered more, "the people immediately became riotous".[4] If that sort of affair then fell away, women might (and did) still initiate spontaneous actions in the market-place about other foodstuffs, such as potatoes or meat. In Ashby-de-la-Zouche in 1766, when a farmer put up his butter by 2d. a pound, "an old woman clapped one hand around the nape of his neck and with the other smeared his face with butter".[5]

It is not a significant matter whether women took part in

---

[1] Thomas Parsons, *Letters to an M.P. on the absurdity of popular prejudices. . .* (Bath, 1800).

[2] Thwaites, thesis, ii, pp. 468-9.

[3] *Gloucester Journal*, 24 June 1740.

[4] Bewdley — *Northampton Mercury*, 6 June 1757; Worcester — *Worcester Journal*, 19 May 1757; Taunton, Newcastle-under-Lyme, Salisbury, Kidderminster — all in R. W. Malcolmson, *Life and Labour in England, 1700-1780* (1981), pp. 117-8.

[5] Dale E. Williams, "Midland Hunger Riots in 1766", *Midland History*, iii, 4 (1976).

more or less than 50 per cent of the recorded riots. What remains significant — and indeed remarkable — is the extensive evidence of women's active part in food riots over a period of more than two hundred years, and in many parts of Great Britain.[1] No other issue commanded women's support so wholeheartedly and consistently, at least in England.[2] On a review of indictments in the Western and Oxford Assize circuits in the second half of the eighteenth century, there are a few cases of what appear to be the community's defence of trade practices (but not of formal trade unionism), of resistance to enclosures, of rough music, and of civic politics in old clothing towns, all of which appear to have significant female involvement. But food riots are the indictments where the women are most often to be found. There are some all-male indictments,[3] just as there are some all-female ones.[4] There are indictments where there seems to be the selection of a token woman,[5] just as there seem to be token men.[6] There are other cases where the prosecution

[1] John Walter in Charlesworth (ed.), *An Atlas of Rural Protest* (1983), shows women present in riots in Kent (1595), Essex (1596), and unloading a ship at Southampton (1608).

[2] In Scotland at the end of the eighteenth century, the issue which occasioned the highest participation of women in direct action "was opposition to the exercise of church patronage by lay patrons against the popular wishes of the congregation". Food riots came second. Logue, *op. cit.*, pp. 199-204.

[3] PRO, Assi 24/42, Devon, Winter 1767: 21 men (17 weavers, 2 woolcombers, 2 labourers, 1 cordwainer) for attacking a boulting mill; *ibid.*, 9 men of Ottery St Mary for pulling down a water mill (and the two following cases); *ibid.*, Somerset 1766, cheese riot, Wellington (13 woolcombers, weavers, etc. indicted); *ibid.*, Somerset, Summer 1767, cheese riot, 7 labourers of Trowbridge indicted (but no true bill found); *ibid.*, Wiltshire, Winter 1767, 8 men indicted (5 broadweavers, 2 scribblers, 1 labourer).

[4] PRO, Assi 4/22, Shropshire, Summer 1767, 5 women of Culmington, for cutting sacks and throwing grain on the floor. Assi 4/20, Worcestershire, Summer 1768, 7 women for carrying away 60 bushels of wheat. Assi 4/21, Worcestershire, Lent 1775, 7 women from Old Swinford (1 widow, 2 spinsters, 2 colliers' wives and 2 labourers' wives) for a flour riot in which 200 took part. Assi 24/43, Somerset, Lent 1801, 4 women for compelling the sale of bread under market price.

[5] PRO, Assi 24/43, Devon, Summer 1801, 5 labourers and 1 single-woman, for compelling the sale of barley under the market price.

[6] PRO, Assi 24/42, Somerset, Summer 1767, butter riot, 5 women and 1 labourer indicted.

appears to be even-handed in serving out indictments.[1] But the indictments testify to the vigorous presence of women.

There is room for further research into this, for as yet no-one appears to have interrogated the legal records systematically over a long period of time. Nor should we expect that uniform answers will be forthcoming. John Bohstedt notes that of fifty-four rioters committed for trial in Devon in 1795 and 1801, only seven were women; but that at Manchester in 1795, of twelve persons charged for food rioting, nine were women.[2] My own searches into Assize records show a similar discrepancy between the Western circuit (taking in Devon, Wiltshire, Dorset and Somerset riots in 1765-72) with 114 men and only fourteen women indicted; and the Oxford circuit (taking in food rioters indicted in Herefordshire, Worcestershire and Shropshire in 1767 to 1774), where there are twenty women and only five men.[3] Do these figures indicate differential gender behaviour or differential practices in policing and prosecution?[4]

We do not know how far the authorities were as willing to prosecute women as men, or whether women must have committed particular "outrages" before they were indicted.[5] There is a little evidence to suggest that in the deeply traditional West of England, where food rioting was almost a tolerated mode of "negotiation", the authorities found the indictment of female rioters to be distasteful. In 1765

[1] For a Bicester (Oxfordshire) wheat riot in 1757, 4 men and 4 women were tried, of whom 1 man and 1 woman were sentenced to 7 years transportation; for a riot involving beans, 2 men were transported, and 1 woman was branded: Thwaites, thesis, pp. 471, 473.

[2] Bohstedt, "Gender, Household and Community Politics", p. 120, note 116.

[3] PRO, Assi 24/42, 24/43, 4/20, 4/21, 4/22. I have only counted cases of riot related explicitly to food.

[4] Douglas Hay has found women leading food riots in Staffordshire in 1740, 1757, 1783 and 1800: "Crime, Authority and the Criminal Laws in Staffordshire 1750-1800" (Univ. of Warwick Ph.D. thesis, 1975), p. 265, and private communication.

[5] In 1795 miners from the Forest of Dean searched a trow at Awre on the Severn. Finding wheat and flour, 100 men, women and children came down from the Forest with horses and asses and carried off 500 bushels. According to a witness "the women were more riotous than the men". But 5 miners were arrested, of whom 2 were hanged for stealing flour; PRO, Assi 5/116; *London Chronicle*, 17-19 Nov. 1795.

Tiverton was convulsed by community-and-trade riots
against the Mayor and Corporation, in which (according to
literary evidence) the women were most prominent, dashing
in upon the Mayor through the windows of an inn, pulling
off his wig and threatening to kill him if he did not sign a
paper. But of twenty-six indicted for these riots, only six were
women.[1] But, then, what was the function of prosecution?
In the Western circuit the prosecution of food rioters seems
to have been a haphazard and often a lenient process. It was
often difficult to persuade the grand jury to find a true bill
against food rioters, and (once found) the petty jury might
not convict. For a Devon attack on a bolting-mill in 1767,
twenty-one were discharged and in two cases a bill could "not
be found" by the grand jury, and for another attack on a mill
all of eighteen indicted in Ottery St Mary were "not to be
found".[2] And so on. A little more zeal was shown in 1795
and 1800-1, but a Devon forced sale in 1801 resulted in the
acquittal of five men charged and no process against the only
woman, while the prosecution was abandoned of two men
indicted for terrorising a farmer (with a rope about his neck)
to sign a paper. On the other hand four women from
Montacute (Somerset) were indicted for grand larceny for
compelling Elizabeth Hopkins to sell seventy-two loaves at a
lower rate than she was willing, and Mary Gard and Sarah
Baker were convicted.[3]

In several other cases in both Western and Oxford circuits
the offenders were bound over with one shilling fine, or were
discharged as "paupers".[4] This suggests that the function of
prosecution was to inspire momentary terror until order
could be restored, and that the accused would be brought to a
due state of contrition by the anxiety and nuisance of the trial

[1] PRO, Assi 24/42, Devon, Summer 1765; F. J. Snell, *The Chronicles
of Twyford* (Tiverton, 1893), pp. 192-201.

[2] PRO, Assi 24/42. Those whose indictments were "not to be found"
by the grand jury in Ottery St Mary included 4 carpenters, 4 woolcombers,
3 husbandmen, 2 tailors, 2 labourers, 2 cordwainers, 1 thatcher.

[3] PRO, Assi 24/43.

[4] In a Taunton cheese riot, 11 men and 6 women were indicted. All
were found "paupers" and discharged. The "paupers" included 3 woolcombers, 2 serge weavers, 2 cordwainers, 2 labourers, 1 whitesmith,
1 fuller: and 3 spinsters, the wives of a cordwainer, a labourer and a serge
weaver; PRO, Assi 24/42, Somerset, Winter 1767.

itself. Prosecution was attended with difficulties — the selection of offenders, the drilling of reluctant witnesses, the odium attaching to the prosecutor — and local magistrates (notoriously in the West) were reluctant to set the process in motion.[1] Since prosecution was both selective and uncertain — that is, it was undertaken to provide an "example" but had no necessary direct relation to the incidence of riot — it cannot be assumed that it was gender-blind. Except in cases where women were manifestly predominant in riots, the authorities might have found it to be more convenient to make an example of men.

There might even have been a hierarchy of levels of prosecution, with differing gender ratios at each level. At the top of the hierarchy would be the Special Commissions of Oyer and Terminer which government instituted in late 1766 with the aim of making "examples" in the disturbed districts. Those brought to trial here were predominantly male: thirteen men in Berkshire, and no women; fifteen men in Wiltshire, and four women; and in Gloucestershire fifty-four men and twelve women.[2] There may have been some reluctance to launch women into a process which might end in their execution,[3] but once so launched it is difficult to say whether they received any preferential treatment from the courts.[4] Of the Wiltshire women, Priscilla Jenkins was sentenced to death for stealing in a dwelling-house (commuted to life transportation), Elizabeth Moody and Mary

[1] See Wells, *Wretched Faces*, ch. 16, "The Role of the Courts".

[2] These are the formal returns in Baga de Secretis, *G.B. Deputy Keeper of Public Records, 5th Report* (1844), Appendix II, pp. 198-204. But some prisoners were held over for subsequent trial or their cases were dismissed. The *Gloucester Journal*, 15 Dec. 1766, reported that 96 rioters were then in prison, of whom 16 were women: see also Williams, thesis, pp. 162-3. But other records suggest that as many as 22 women were committed: cases against one or two were dropped, and another turned evidence against her fellows; crown brief, PRO, TS 11/1188/5956, and "A Calendar of the Criminal Prisoners in the Castle Gaol of Gloucester", 13 Dec. 1766 (annotated) in TS 11/995/3707.

[3] This is suggested by John Beattie in his authoritative article, "The Criminality of Women in Eighteenth-Century England", *Journal of Soc. Hist.*, viii, (1975), p. 113, note 57. Also Beattie, *Crime and the Courts in England, 1660-1800* (Oxford, 1986), pp. 436-9.

[4] Booth, *op. cit.*, p. 106 finds that in the courts in Lancashire 1790-1801 "no differentiation seems to have been made between the sexes".

Nash were transported for seven years for stealing to the value of 1s. 7d. in a dwelling-house, and Sarah Pane, a widow, found guilty of stealing flour to the value of 6d., was privately whipped and discharged. This seems severe enough. But these were the counts upon which juries had been willing to convict. On a closer view it seems that they had been selected for trial because all except Sarah Pane, went beyond "food riot" to theft from the homes of farmers or traders. Priscilla Jenkins was supposed to have taken off a gammon of bacon, a pair of boots, a bundle of things on her head tied up in a handkerchief. . . and a gun. Elizabeth Moody and Mary Nash were not such desperate felons, but they were accused of breaking into a house, smashing the windows and some of the furniture, and carrying off the family's clothes.[1]

A little more can be worked out about the Gloucestershire accused.[2] The Special Commission at Gloucester was restrained by a grand jury which refused to act as a rubber-stamp and perhaps by a reluctant petty jury. Of twenty-one women who were being prepared for trial, one was not indicted, presumably as *feme covert*. More than one-half of the remainder were either acquitted (eight) or the grand jury found "ignoramus" (three). Of seventy-five male prisoners, about the same proportion got off, with eighteen acquittals and twenty "no true bills". And there is no great difference in the conviction rate: seven out of twenty-one women as against thirty-five out of seventy-five men. The marked difference is in the severity of the convictions and sentencing. Sixteen of the men were convicted of felonies, nineteen of misdemeanours, whereas only two of the women were found felons and five were found guilty of misdemeanours. Nine rioters were sentenced to death — all men, although in six cases the condemned were reprieved — and nine were

[1] Crown briefs in PRO, TS 11/1116/5728. Elizabeth Moody and Mary Nash were both pregnant, giving birth immediately after their trials, Mary Nash with twins: it is not clear whether their sentences were enforced. See Williams, *op. cit.*, pp. 167, 170.

[2] Some of the following deductions depend upon rough annotations to the Gaol Calendar in PRO, TS 11/995/3707. On *feme covert*, see Blackstone, *op. cit.*, iv, pp. 26-7 and John Beattie, *op. cit.*, p. 238, note 71. *op. cit.*; *Gloucester Journal*, 22 Dec. 1766; Gloucester CRO, Q/SG 1767-70, Gloucester Gaol Calendar, 13 Jan. 1767.

sentenced to seven years' transportation, of whom two were women.

A closer view of the cases does not tell us much. Six of the female acquittals were for a cheese riot at Farmer Collett's, for which one man was also acquitted and one other man convicted. Mary Hillier ran after the mob in Minchinhampton and "told them Mr Butt was come home & had fired a gun and killed 2 children and desired them to come back and pull down the House". The grand jury found no true bill. Elizabeth Rackley and Elizabeth Witts, both sentenced to transportation, were convicted of stealing 10d. worth of flour, but as part of several night-time break-ins of the mill of Richard Norris. It was the night-time breaking and entering which made the offence felony.[1] The clearest case of gender discrimination concerned John Franklyn and Sarah Franklyn, his wife, jointly committed for entering a shop in Stroud and carrying off in their laps soap, glue and other things. But Sarah was not indicted, presumably because while acting with her husband she was, according to the legal doctrine of *feme couvert*, not responsible for her actions. That was fortunate for her, since John Franklyn was found guilty of grand larceny and was transported for seven years.[2]

This suggests that the heavier exercises of the courts might fall a little less heavily on women. But the lighter exercises need not show the same gender inflection. Summary committals to Bridewells or convictions for minor public order offences were used by magistrates to cool off a crowd, without respect for differences of sex. For example, a letter from Lincolnshire in 1740 notes that "we have had a Disturbance by the Mobb at Bourn they Cutt Some Sacks of Wheat in the Boat & Obstructed its passage to Spalding for a time, but was Quel'd seasonably by the Officers of the Town & 5 Women Committed to the House of Correction".[3] Such episodes are unlikely to have left traces in national records,

---

[1] Elizabeth Rackley was later pardoned.

[2] Gaol Calendar in PRO, TS 11/995/3707. On *feme couvert*, see Blackstone, *op. cit.*, iv, pp. 26-7 and John Beattie, *op. cit.*, p. 238, note 71.

[3] Letter of John Halford, 1 July 1740, in Lincs., Archives Office, 3 Anc. 7/4/14.

although after the 1760s they were more likely to be brought to Quarter Sessions.[1]

John Bohstedt tells us that "repression did not know gender", and he is right that troops were frequently ordered to fire into mixed crowds. From Anne Carter of Maldon, Essex, in 1629 to Hannah Smith of Manchester in 1812, a trickle of victims or heroines were sent to the gallows, while others were sentenced to transportation.[2] Yet I am undecided; it remains possible that, while "examples" were made from time to time, the examples made of women were fewer, that they sometimes enjoyed the "privilege of their sex", and that much depended upon place, time and the temper of the authorities.

If the central authorities insisted that examples had to be made, then gender did not matter. In 1766 government and law officers were pressing hard for capital offenders to be selected, and the Treasury Solicitor regretted that "at Leicester, the Evidence is very slight, against a Woman for throwing Cheese out of a Waggon to the Mob, which if not a Highway Robbery, is not Capital".[3] (Hannah Smith was convicted of highway robbery nearly fifty years later, for selling off butter cheaply to the crowd.) In the end, no women were hanged for the riots of 1766, although Sarah Hemmings was capitally convicted for her part in a riot in Wolverhampton: the town petitioned for her life, and the sentence was commuted to life transportation.[4] In 1800 *The Times* correspondent lamented from Nottingham and its environs that "there is not even a prospect of the riot

[1] Ann Welford and Barbara Mason were sentenced to six months hard labour at Northampton Quarter Sessions in 1796 for trying, with a great number of persons, "principally women", to stop a market wagon: *Northampton Mercury*, 9 Apr. 1796. My thanks to Jeanette Neeson.

[2] For Anne Carter, see John Walter, "Grain Riots and Popular Attitudes to the Law: Maldon and the Crisis of 1629", in Brewer and Styles (eds.), *An Ungovernable People*, pp. 47-84, an excellent study which follows the rioters back into the local records. For Hannah Smith, see Thomis and Grimmett, *op. cit.*, pp. 43-44.

[3] Memorandum as to the state of evidence against food rioters (1766) from Treasury Solicitor in Shelburne Papers, Vol. 132, William L. Clements Library, University of Michigan, Ann Arbor; see also PRO, SP Dom 44/141.

[4] Williams, "Midland Hunger Riots in 1766", p. 277.

subsiding", owing to the non-arrest of the women, who were "the principal aggressors".[1] In the sixteenth and early seventeenth centuries, women rioters had been liminal people with an "ambivalent legal status at the margins of the law's competence". They claimed, in enclosure riots, "that women were lawlesse, and not subject to the lawes of the realme as men are but might. . . offend without drede or punishment of law".[2] If the sex had been disabused of that illusion in the eighteenth century, yet perhaps some notion of "privilege", both among offenders and prosecutors, lingered on in such regions as the West.

Were there other peculiarities of the feminine input into food riots? I doubt the value of tabulating disorder and violence according to gender, partly because of the imperfect nature of the evidence, partly because all riot must involve disorder and violence of some kind. When an affair involved outright confrontation, with cudgels against fire-arms — the attack on a mill, the break-in to a keep to rescue prisoners — the predominant sex would be male. The women are more commonly reported as throwing missiles — stones or potatoes — and on one occasion, in the Midlands in 1766 "planted in rows five or six deep", defending a bridge with stones and brickbats against horsemen.[3] Whatever conclusions we reach as to the gender reciprocities and respect between women and men in these communities, it would be foolish to suppose that these dissolved sexual differences. Without doubt the physical confrontation of men and women, of soldiers and crowd, aroused sexual tensions, perhaps expressed by the women in robust ribaldry, by the male forces of "order" in a contest between the inhibition of violence and sexually-excited aggression.[4] On occasion the military affected contempt for the women. The commander of troops sent to deal with a riot in Bromsgrove in 1795

[1] Wells, *op. cit.*, p. 121.

[2] John Walter in *An Ungovernable People*, p. 63; see also Roger B. Manning, *Village Revolts* (Oxford, 1988), pp. 96, 116.

[3] Williams, *op. cit.*, pp. 273-4.

[4] After "repeated solicitations" from a Captain of marines, the constable of Brentwood reluctantly arrested two women, in "The Ship" alehouse, who had been "singing a song in Brentwood Street reflecting on the military": Essex CRO, Q/SBb 352/55 (Aug. 1793).

complained loftily that they found the cause was "a parcel of old women. . . as in all pretended riots in this part of the country". But this parcel of women (not all of whom were old) had given a good account of themselves, some seventy of them stopping a wagon and six horses, and carrying off twenty-nine sacks of wheaten flour.[1]

When women rioted they made no attempt to disguise their sex or to apologise for it. In my view there was very little cross-dressing in food riots, although once or twice there are unconfirmed reports of men in women's clothes.[2] These "rites of inversion" or, maybe, simple exercises in the most available disguise, were more commonly encountered in turnpike riots, in "carnival" protests, and, later, in Luddism.[3] But inversion, whether intentional or not, was exactly what the women did *not* wish to achieve. So far from wishing to present an ominous androgynous image, they sought to present their particular right, according to tradition and gender role, as guardians of the children, of the household, of the livelihood of the community. That symbolism — the blood-stained loaves on poles, the banging of kitchen ware — belonged especially to the women's protests. They evinced what Temma Kaplan has called "female consciousness" rather than feminist, which rested upon "their acceptance of the sexual division of labor" which is one which "assigns women the responsibility of preserving life". "Experiencing reciprocity among themselves and competence in preserving

---

[1] PRO, WO 1/1091, 5 and 8 Aug. 1795; Assi 2/26 and 5/116.

[2] *Jackson's Oxford Journal*, 28 May 1757 reports a wagon of wheat taken away in Bath by a mob in women's clothes. I have not found any eighteenth-century indictment for such an offence in a food riot.

[3] See Natalie Davis, "Women on Top", in *Society and Culture in Early Modern France* (Stanford, 1975). I think Professor Davis overlooks the fact that a woman's gown was the most readily-available garment to disguise a collier or a cottager. Some of the upside-down symbolic effects (which she describes so well) were consequence rather than intention. Attacks on turnpikes had more military symbolism: "Deponent saith. . . they heard the Noise of Horns blowing. . . and soon after a great Number of Persons armed with Guns & Axes, some of them disguised with black'd faces and Womens Cloathes. . .". This was an attack on a turnpike gate in Ledbury, Herefordshire. James Baylis, labourer, who was apprehended said that he had blacked his face with a burnt cork, and that the gown, apron and straw hat which he wore were his wife's: informations in PRO, TS 11/1122/5824, 4 Nov. 1735.

life instills women with a sense of their collective right to administer daily life, even if they must confront authority to do so.[1]

Nothing pleased female rioters more than the humiliation of pompous male "aggro". In a Tiverton riot in 1754 a certain Lieutenant Suttie attracted the crowd's notice by his zeal; he was heard to say to a JP, "Give me leave sir, to order the men to fire, and you shall see the fellows hop like peas". The troopers were unleashed upon the crowd and they "rode through the streets hacking with their broad-swords and stabbing with their bayonets":

> While the troopers were dashing about in the execution of their orders, some women seized Lieutenant Suttie by the collar and took away his sword, which he never recovered. This was a sore blow to his pride, and a favourite subject of banter on the part of his friends, who, very cruelly, would not allow him to forget his skirmish with the women and the inglorious loss of his weapon.[2]

Not for the first or last time, disarming symbolised emasculation.

Men in authority still feared the violence and the incitement of the female tongue (see below pp. 501-2), and women could sometimes attain their ends by mockery, insult, or by shaming farmers or dealers by their expostulations. Susannah Soons was convicted in Norwich in 1767 for "uttering several scandalous and inflammatory speeches", and Mary Watts in Leicester for "assaulting" the magistrates "with indecent and opprobrious Language and Gestures".[3] In Montrose in 1812, when the Riot Act was being read and the military were deployed to disperse the crowd, Elizabeth Beattie called out, "Will no person take that paper out of his hand?" and tried to snatch the Act from the magistrate.[4]

Elizabeth Beattie knew what she was doing. But so did Anne Carter, in 1629. She clearly despised the pomp of the local authorities, calling one of Maldon's chief magistrates in 1622 "bloud sucker and. . . many other unseemely tearmes".

---

[1] Temma Kaplan, "Female Consciousness and Collective Action: The Case of Barcelona, 1910-1918", *Signs*, vii, 3 (1982), pp. 545, 560, 565.

[2] Snell, *The Chronicles of Twyford*, pp. 194-5. This was an election riot.

[3] Williams, thesis, pp. 203, note 2, and p. 279.

[4] Logue, *op. cit.*, p. 22.

When the bailiff had questioned her about her absence from church, she had answered back: "that yf he woold prouid [provide] wone to doe hir worke shee would goe". In the riots she described herself as "Captain", calling out: "Come, my brave lads of Maldon, I will be your leader for we will not starve."[1] "General Jane Bogey" in Newcastle in 1740 knew what she was doing, and so did "Lady Ludd", the title claimed by leaders of riots in 1812 in both Nottingham and Leeds.[2] So too did fifty-four-year-old Hannah Smith who "headed up the mob" for some days in Manchester in the same year, bringing down the prices of potatoes, butter and milk, and boasting that she could raise a crowd in a minute.[3] It was lack of deference as much as rioting which got Anne Carter and Hannah Smith hanged. What clergyman was likely to give a character reference, what nobleman to intercede, on behalf of such viragos?

The women's riots may not have been precisely of the same violence quotient as the men's, but they were not shrinking, demure affairs. Frequently they came to a climax when women led off the fore-horses, climbed aboard the wagons and threw down the sacks to their fellows, sometimes took the horses out of the shafts and pulled the wagon back themselves to a place for convenient distribution of its load.[4] In the engagement at Newport Pagnell in 1740 (above pp. 319-20), the women fought with the farmers for a considerable time, declaring that they were "unwilling that so much Wheat should go out of the Kingdom, while they wanted bread, [and] swore they would lose their lives before they would part with it". At length "with great acclamations of joy the waggons were unloaded". The reporter of the *Northampton Mercury* found that the affair merited a little comment:

[1] Walter, *op. cit.*, pp. 58, 72.
[2] Ellis, *op. cit.*, p. 340; Thomis and Grimmett, *op. cit.*, p. 31.
[3] *Ibid.*, pp. 43-5.
[4] For examples, see *Derby Mercury*, 10 July 1740 (Derby 1740). Elizabeth Beer and Elizabeth Bell were each sentenced to 7 years transportation for their part in this riot. Information of Thos. Higgins against Ann Burdon, who stopped his wagon in Long Handborough in August 1795, took the horse out of the shafts, and got into the shafts to prevent the horses being put back in: PRO, Assi 5/116.

The Conquerors are now holding a Grand Council to consider what to do with it among themselves. Such uncommon Bravery and Resolution appearing in the soft & tender Sex is a Matter of Surprize to those who stile themselves their despotick Sovereigns, & the Lords of Creation.[1]

Such bravery was not uncommon. Repeatedly women faced troops and were fired upon. In one of the only letters that survives from a food rioter, he wrote of a great riot in Nottingham (1800): "your hearts would have ached to have seen the women Calling for Bread and Declaring they would fight till they died Before they would be used so any longer. . . the conduct of the people. . . who stood the fire from the yeomanry with such undaunted courage that astonished the gentlemen for they poured such showers of stones on them in all directions that they could load their pieces no more after they had fired them. . .".[2]

Perhaps the poor of both sexes partnered each other better in bad times than we suppose. Maybe men were more prominent in food riots than women, and maybe not.[3] But if one adds up all that is already known (and there is much still to find out) there were an awful lot of women involved in food riots, sometimes on their own, more often in mixed affairs in which there was a loyal gender partnership.

For two hundred and more years these food riots were the most visible and public expressions of working women's lack of deference and their contestation with authority. As such these evidences contest, in their turn, the stereotypes of feminine submission, timidity, or confinement to the private world of the household. Robert Southey (p. 234) may not have been so silly after all. Indeed, when once aroused the women may have been more passionate than men in their eloquence, less heedful of the consequences, and, in their role

[1] *Northampton Mercury*, 2 June 1740; *Ipswich Journal*, 7 June 1740.
[2] Intercepted letter of J. and L. Golby to "Dear Brother and Sister", dated Nottingham 7 Sept. 1800, in PRO, HO 42/51. Extracts of the letter are in Quinault and Stevenson (eds.), *op. cit.*, pp. 58-9 and in Wells, *Wretched Faces*, pp. 120-2.
[3] Or maybe the answer differed according to place and time. Walter, *op. cit.*, p. 62 writes that "women were present in almost every food riot in the period [i.e. early seventeenth century] and some riots were exclusively feminine affairs".

as guardians of the family, more determined to get quick results.[1] Perhaps — as John Bohstedt suggests — many women were more immersed than were men "in the moral, less in the market, economy", and they were among the last to give the practices of the moral economy up.[2]

That is not the whole truth about women and authority, but food riots provide an important and weighty chunk of evidence, which must not be tidied away. It may enlarge our sense of the possibilities of feminine "nature". The more difficult question may be, not why women sometimes rioted, but why, in the mid nineteenth century, the tradition of public protest became so much weaker and women's presence retreated into a serial world of private households.[3] Perhaps (in contrast to what came after) a "myth of the feminine food riot" should be rehabilitated after all?

IV

I do not know how far back one must go to find the origin of the term, "moral economy". I think that it comes from the late eighteenth century, but I cannot now find references. It

[1] Tom Wedgwood wrote to his father, Josiah, describing "the mob" in the Potteries in March 1783: "The women were much worse than the men, as for example, Parson Sneyd got about 30 men to follow him. . . but a woman cried: 'Nay, nay, that wunna do, that wunna do', and so they turned back again, and it was agreed that the corn taken [in] the boat should be sold at a fair price": *The Wedgwood Letters*, ed. Ann Finer and G. Savage (1965), p. 268. My thanks to Douglas Hay.

[2] Women and miners were prominent in traditional price-setting in south-west England in 1847, and women and fishermen in north-east Scotland: A. Rowe, "Food Riots of the Forties in Cornwall", *Royal Cornwall Polytechnic Society* (1942); E. Richards, *The Last Scottish Food Riots, Past and Present Supplement* (1981). See also Roger E. Swift, "Food Riots in Mid-Victorian Exeter, 1847-67", *Southern History*, 2 (1980). Robert Storch, in a most interesting study, shows how in 1867 in Devon and Oxfordshire, traditions of food riot, of rough music, and of "Guy Fawkes" carnival came together, with the women and the disguised "bonfire boys" playing the leading roles: "Popular Festivity and Consumer Protest: Food Price Disturbances in the Southwest and Oxfordshire in 1867", *Albion*, 14, 3-4 (1982). Although women were often the most active in these events, few of the women were arrested or brought to trial. See Storch, p. 233, note 41.

[3] Dorothy Thompson, "Women and Nineteenth-Century Radical Politics: a Lost Dimension", in Juliet Mitchell and Ann Oakley (eds.), *The Rights and Wrongs of Women* (Harmondsworth, 1976), pp. 112-138.

was certainly around in the 1830s,[1] and it was used by Bronterre O'Brien, the Chartist, in 1837 in a polemic against political economists:

> True political economy is like true domestic economy; it does not consist solely in slaving and saving; there is a moral economy as well as political. . . These quacks would make wreck of the affections, in exchange for incessant production and accumulation. . . It is, indeed, the MORAL ECONOMY that they always keep out of sight. When they talk about the tendency of large masses of capital, and the division of labour, to increase production and cheapen commodities, they do not tell us of the inferior human being which a single and fixed occupation must necessarily produce.[2]

This directly anti-capitalist usage is close to that which I introduce into *The Making of the English Working Class*, when I referred to food riots as being "legitimized by the assumptions of an older moral economy, which taught the immorality of. . . profiteering upon the necessities of the people". And I went on to describe the food riots of 1795 as "a last desperate effort" to re-impose the "old paternalist moral economy" as against the economy of the free market.[3]

I subsequently defined more carefully the term, the practices associated with it, and the contradictory components of paternalist control and crowd rebellion. The reason for this retrospective enquiry is that the theory of a moral economy has now taken off in more than one direction and in several fields of specialist study, and my essay is sometimes cited as authority. But while the term is available for every development which can be justified, my own usage has in general been confined to confrontations in the market-place over access (or entitlement) to "necessities" — essential food. It is not only that there is an identifiable

---

[1] Thus Robert Southey was claiming to espouse "MORAL versus political economy", see David Eastwood, "Robert Southey and the Intellectual Origins of Romantic Conservatism", *Eng. Hist. Rev.*, civ (1989), p. 323. The "moral economy of the factory system" was employed in a very different sense by Dr Andrew Ure in *The Philosophy of Manufactures* (1835).

[2] *Bronterre's National Reformer*, 21 Jan. 1837. I am indebted to Dorothy Thompson for this reference.

[3] (Penguin, 1968), pp. 67-73.

bundle of beliefs, usages and forms associated with the marketing of food in time of dearth, which it is convenient to bind together in a common term, but the deep emotions stirred by dearth, the claims which the crowd made upon the authorities in such crises, and the outrage provoked by profiteering in life-threatening emergencies, imparted a particular "moral" charge to protest. All of this, taken together, is what I understand by moral economy.[1]

If the term is to be extended to other contexts, then it must be redefined or there will be some loss of focus. Adrian Randall has so redefined it, in applying it to "The Industrial Moral Economy of the Gloucestershire Weavers" in the eighteenth century.[2] The same weaving communities that were involved in food riots (1766) were involved in industrial actions (1756); these were informed by the same values, showed the same community solidarities and sanctions (such as rough music against those who broke the norms of the trade), a similar appeal to custom and to Tudor and Stuart statute law (when this protected their own interests), and a similar insistence that, where the community's economic well-being was concerned, market forces and the profits of individuals should be subdued to custom. Moreover, Randall

---

[1] Similar "moral economy" themes have been examined in different national histories — notably (France) Louise Tilly, "The Food Riot as a Form of Political Conflict in France", *Journal of Interdisciplinary History*, i (1971), pp. 23-57, and Cynthia A. Bouton, "L' 'économie morale' et la Guerre des farines de 1775", and also the editors' "Introduction" in Florence Gauthier and Guy-Robert Ikni (eds.), *La Guerre du Blé au XVIIIe Siècle* (Paris, 1988); Laura Rodriguez, "The Spanish Riots of 1766", *Past and Present*, 59 (1973); Barbara Clark Smith, "Food Rioters in the American Revolution", in Alfred F. Young, (ed.), *Beyond the American Revolution* (Urbana, forthcoming); John Rogers, "The 1866 Grain Riots in Sri Lanka", *Comparative Studies in Society and History*, xxix, 3 (1987).

[2] A. J. Randall in John Rule (ed.), *British Trade Unionism, 1750-1850* (1988), pp. 29-51. See also Charlesworth and Randall, "Morals, Markets and the English Crowd", pp. 206-9. Professor Charles Tilly, in a private communication, has suggested a further definition: "The term 'moral economy' makes sense when claimants to a commodity can invoke non-monetary rights to that commodity, and third parties will act to support *these* claims — when, for example, community membership supersedes price as a basis of entitlement. To the extent that moral economy comes merely to mean tradition, custom, or exchange outside the established market, it loses its conceptual force.".

shows that the industrial crowd also would seek to press the gentry into the role of conciliators and arbitrators, so that "the moral economy was the obverse of the paternalist model".

I am more than half persuaded by this argument. In those West of England clothing towns there was a dense texture of trade rituals and customary usages, endorsed by community sanctions, which may be seen as the stubborn plebeian underside to mercantilist industry. Of course these workers were habituated to an economy with markets, but markets conducted within customary norms; in times of conflict they affirmed the priorities of "the Trade", or they elevated the defence of the interests of the working community above those of the profits of the few, and if the term "moral economy" helps us to identify these norms and practices, then let it be used. It certainly helps us to see the strongly defensive, and, in that sense, conservative nature of this plebeian culture.

But where are we to draw the line? Pirates had strongly-transmitted usages and customs: did they have a moral economy.[1] Keith Snell suggests that the poor's right to a settlement "formed a consistent part of those 'moral economy' values" which I have analysed. And he extends the list of candidates for inclusion in this moral economy to the poor laws generally, to yearly hirings and "fair wages", and even to "popular consumption, fashion [and] leisure activities". *Then* he turns around and gives me a dressing-down for "the amorphous character" of my moral economy.[2]

I admire Dr Snell's work, but on this occasion I am perplexed, because I can see little evidence that he knows much about the tensions around the nexus of food in time of dearth. What is "amorphous" is his own extension of the term's use, and this stems from the error of supposing that what are at issue are "moral economy *values*". But if values, on their own, make a moral *economy* then we will be turning up moral economies everywhere. My own notion of the moral

[1] Marcus Rediker, *Between the Devil and the Deep Blue Sea* (Cambridge, 1987), ch. 6.

[2] K. D. M. Snell, *Annals of the Labouring Poor* (Cambridge, 1985), pp. 99-199, 103.

economy of the crowd in the food market includes ideal models or ideology (just as political economy does), which assigns economic roles and which endorses customary practices (an alternative "economics"), in a particular balance of class or social forces. It is by taking "values" or "moral attitudes" out of the context of a particular historical formation that Snell gets his amorphous results.

However, I have no right to patent the term. Some historians prefer a more descriptive and looser use. No other term seems to offer itself to describe the way in which, in peasant and in early industrial communities, many "economic" relations are regulated according to non-monetary norms. These exist as a tissue of customs and usages until they are theatened by monetary rationalisations and are made self-conscious *as* a "moral economy". In this sense, the moral economy is summoned into being in resistance to the economy of the "free market".[1] As Charlesworth and Randall have argued, "The basis of the moral economy was that very sense of community which a common experience of capitalist industry generated".[2] The rationalisations or "modernisations" of the capitalist market offended against community norms and continually called into being a "moral" antagonist.

This is an extension which is further generalised by William Reddy in *The Rise of Market Culture*, for whom the moral economy is "a set of values and moral standards that were violated by technical and commercial change":

Defence of such moral standards need not have been motivated by memory of the past. The inadequacy of market language was constantly being brought to the laborer's attention by the very conditions of work.

And Reddy concludes that "something like a moral economy is bound to surface anywhere that industrial capitalism

---

[1] The great British miners' strike of 1984 was a late example of such a confrontation, although "free market" forces appeared in the guise of every resource of the State.

[2] Charlesworth and Randall, "Morals, Markets and the English Crowd", p. 213.

spreads".[1] This has the advantage of discarding the notion that "moral economy" must always be traditional, "backward-looking", etc.; on the contrary, it is continuously regenerating itself as anti-capitalist critique, as a resistance movement.[2] We are close to the language of Bronterre O'Brien. But what this gains in breadth it loses in focus, and in inexpert hands may bleed off the edge into uncontextual moralistic rhetoric.[3]

There is less danger of this in the alert theoretical discussions in the field of peasant studies, where a "moral economy theory" is now at the centre of controversy. This is thanks to James C. Scott whose *The Moral Economy of the Peasant* (1976) generalised an argument derived from studies in Lower Burma and Vietnam. The term is drawn from my own essay but it is now brought to bear upon "peasant conceptions of social justice, of rights and obligations, of reciprocity". But what distinguishes Scott's use is that it goes much further than descriptive accounts of "values" or "moral attitudes". Since for the peasantry, subsistence depends upon access to land, customs of land use and of entitlement to its produce are now at the centre of analysis rather than the marketing of food. And custom is seen (against a background of memories of famine) as perpetuating subsistence imperatives, and usages which insure the community against risk. These imperatives are also expressed in protective landlord-tenant (or patron-client) relations, and in resistances to technical innovations and to market rationalisations, where these might entail risks in the event of crisis. Scott analyses village redistributive institutions and religious charitable obligations, and shows that "there is good reason for viewing both the norm of reciprocity and the

---

[1] William Reddy, *The Rise of Market Culture* (Cambridge, Mass., 1984), pp. 331-4.

[2] Carl Gersuny and Gladys Kaufman, "Seniority and the Moral Economy of U.S. Automobile Workers, 1934-46", *Journal of Social History*, xviii (1985), extend the notion into non-"economic" trade union defences.

[3] A danger which Reddy himself does not wholly avoid in his sequel, *Money and Liberty in Modern Europe* (Cambridge, 1987), in which "asymmetrical monetary exchange" is made the key to all modern history, wherein "honour" and "money" enact an unequal contest.

right to subsistence as genuine moral components of the 'little tradition'. . ." — that is, in peasant culture universally. The threat to these institutions and norms associated with European expansion and with market rationalisations has often provoked the peasantry to participation in revolutionary movements.[1]

There is some likeness here to the moral economy of the eighteenth-century English crowd, although Scott does not elaborate the comparison and he is in fact more interested in patron-client relations in the village rather than in those confrontations or negotiations which mark the European tradition of food riot.[2] Predictably his theories have been vigorously contested by protagonists of "market forces", and Samuel L. Popkin delivered a polemic against what were presented as "the moral economists" in *The Rational Peasant* (1979). This offered the characteristic peasant as a rational actor, shrewdly adjusting to the market economy in a satisfactorily self-interested and normless manner. So that the old debate between moral and political economists seemed likely to re-enact itself over the paddy fields of South-East Asia — a debate into which it would be foolish for me to enter, although my sympathies are certainly with James Scott.

However, Professor Scott has moved the debate forwards (and sideways) in his *Weapons of the Weak*, and onto territory where comparisons may be explored with advantage. This territory is not only that of the tenacious forms of resistance to power of the weak and of the poor: "in ridicule, in truculence, in irony, in petty acts of non-compliance, in dissimulation. . . in the disbelief in elite homilies, in the steady and grinding efforts to hold one's own

[1] James C. Scott, *The Moral Economy of the Peasant: Rebellion and Subsistence in Southeast Asia* (New Haven, 1976). See also James M. Polachek, "The Moral Economy of the Kiangsi Soviet", *Journal of Asian Studies*, xlii, 4 (1983), p. 825.

[2] For constructive criticism, see David Hunt, "From the Millenium to the Everyday: James Scott's Search for the Essence of Peasant Politics", *Radical Hist. Rev.*, 42 (1988), pp. 155-72; Michael Adas, " 'Moral Economy' or 'Contest State'?", *Journal of Social History*, xiii, 4 (1980).

against overwhelming odds".[1] It is also, and at the same time, into the limits which the weak can impose upon power. As Barrington Moore has argued in *Injustice*:

> In any stratified society. . . there is a set of limits on what both rulers and subjects, dominant and subordinate groups can do. There is also a set of mutual obligations that bind the two together. Such limits and obligations are not set down in formal written constitutions or contracts. . .

There is (rather) "an unverbalized set of mutual understandings", and "what takes place is a continual probing on the part of rulers and subjects to find out what they can get away with, to test and *discover* the limits of obedience and disobedience". This takes us, by way of the concept of social reciprocity, or, as Moore prefers, mutual obligation ("a term that does *not* imply equality of burdens or obligations"),[2] back to the "moral economy", in the sense of the equilibrium or "field of force" which I examined in Chapter I and in the bargaining between unequal social forces in which the weaker still has acknowledged claims upon the greater. Of those who have recently developed these ideas I find a particular sympathy with Michael Watts, whose *Silent Violence* examines food and famine among the Hausa in northern Nigeria. He sees the norms and practices of an imperative collective subsistence ethic as permeating the peasant universe, but he sees this without sentimentality:

> The moral economy was not especially moral and the Caliphate was certainly no Rousseauian universe of peasant welfare and benevolent patrons. Rather, the moral economy was necessary to the survival of ruler and ruled, and the price was paid by prevailing power blocs for the maintenance and reproduction of the social relations of production replete with its exploitative relations and class struggles.

---

[1] James C. Scott, *Weapons of the Weak: Everyday Forms of Peasant Resistance* (New Haven, 1985), p. 350. See also the editors' contributions in Andrew Turton and Shigeharu Tanabe (eds.), *History and Peasant Consciousness in South East Asia* (Osaka, 1984), and the special issue of the *Journals of Peasant Studies*, xiii, 2 (1986).

[2] Barrington Moore Jr, *Injustice: The Social Bases of Obedience and Revolt* (1978), pp. 18, 506.

"There is no need to saddle the moral economy with the legacy of Durkheim, Rousseau, and Ruskin."[1]

Much of the very interesting discussion which is now extending under the rubric of "moral economy" from African and Asian to Latin American[2] or to Irish studies has little to do with my (1971) usage but is concerned with the social dialectic of unequal mutuality (need and obligation) which lies at the centre of most societies. The term "moral economy" has won acceptance because it is less cumbersome than other terms (such as "dialectical asymmetrical reciprocity") which we might otherwise be clobbered with. When an Irish historian writes of "moral economy", he is writing of eighteenth-century paternalism, deference, and non-economic (i.e. unprofitable) "easygoing farming practices" such as low rents and tolerance of arrears.[3] A scholar (Paul Greenough) writing on the Bengal famine of 1943-44 has an even more extended definition:

> By 'moral economy' I mean the cluster of relations of exchange between social groups, and between persons, in which the welfare and the merit of both parties to the exchange takes precedence over other considerations such as the profit of the one or the other.[4]

These capacious definitions will certainly allow in most things we might wish to introduce, and if the term will encourage historians to discover and write about all those areas of human exchange to which orthodox economics was once blind, then this is a gain.

If we employ the terminology of class, then "moral economy" in this definition may be concerned with the way in which class relations are negotiated. It shows how

[1] Michael Watts, *Silent Violence: Food, Famine and Peasantry in Northern Nigeria* (Berkeley, 1983), pp. 106, 146.

[2] Leslie Anderson, "From Quiescence to Rebellion: Peasant Political Activity in Costa Rica and Pre-Revolutionary Nicaragua" (Univ. of Michigan Ph.D. thesis, 1987; Erick D. Langer, "Labor Strikes and Reciprocity on Chuquisaca Haciendas", *Hispanic American History Review*, lxv, 2, 1985.

[3] Thomas Bartlett, "An End to Moral Economy: The Irish Militia Disturbances of 1793", in C. H. E. Philpin (ed.), *Nationalism and Popular Protest in Ireland* (Cambridge, 1987).

[4] Paul R. Greenough, "Indian Famines and Peasant Victims: The Case of Bengal in 1943-44", *Modern Asian Studies*, xiv, 2 (1980), p. 207.

hegemony is not just imposed (or contested) but is articulated in the everyday intercourse of a community, and can be sustained only by concession and patronage (in good times), by at least the gestures of protection in bad.[1] Of the two parts of the term, the "economy" can probably now look after itself, since it will be defined in each scholar's practice. It is the "moral" part which may now require more attention. One benefit that has accrued from the term's transportation into peasant studies is that it can be viewed in operation within cultures whose moral premises are not identical with those of a Judeo-Christian inheritance.[2]

No-one has made this more explicit than has Professor Greenough in his study of Bengal famine, and he has done this on the directly comparative ground of the crisis of subsistence. Greenough presents a conspectus of the Bengali peasants' value-system,[3] and he derives this, not (as does Scott) from remembered scarcity and from risk-avoiding strategies, but, on the contrary, from a Bengal tradition of abundance. At the centre of this value-system is *Laksmi*, both a conception of order and abundance and a benevolent goddess of prosperity. Prosperity flows down from above, from *Laksmi*, or from "kings", patrons or parents. In its simplest form there are two situations only: the givers and the receivers of rice, and in time of crisis the peasant's reflex is to seek refuge in the patron-client relationship, to search for new patrons, or to wait in patience for *Laksmi's* gifts to be restored. Greenough also finds "an unyielding Bengali antipathy to individual assertion":

> Temple art, learned texts, and folk apothegms reiterate that whatever success one has comes only through a superior's benevolence. . . There is no widely accepted creed of commercial accumulation.[4]

[1] See Scott, *Weapons of the Weak*, ch. 8 — an excellent discussion of "hegemony" in this everyday sense.

[2] See also Charles F. Keyes, "Economic Action and Buddhist Morality in a Thai Village", *Journal of Asian Studies*, xlii, 4 (1983).

[3] Paul R. Greenough, *Prosperity and Misery in Modern Bengal* (Oxford, 1982), esp. ch. 1. Greenough derives his account from Hindu cosmology and is silent as to any differences between Hindu and Moslem villagers.

[4] Paul R. Greenough, "Indulgence and Abundance as Asian Peasant Values: a Bengali Case in Point", *Journal of Asian Studies*, xlii, 4 (1983), p. 842.

This brief summary will serve if it leaves us with the expectation that "giving" and beseeching "protection" are critical to the peasantry's discourse of crisis, rather than "duties" or "rights". Greenough finds in this an explanation for the Bengali response to famine. In the appalling conditions of 1943-44 attacks on granaries or shops were rare. "Food of all sorts lay before their eyes", while people were starving on the streets of Calcutta, "but no one attempted to seize it by force". The attitude of the people was one of "complete resignation", and "they attribute their misery to fate or *karma* alone. . .". An English medical officer contrasted this with the Punjab or the United Provinces where "you would have had terrific riots", and:

> The husbands and brothers would have had those food shops opened, but in Bengal they died in front of bulging food shops.
> Q. Bulging with grain?
> A. Yes, they died in the streets in front of shops bulging with grain.
> Q. Because they could not buy?
> A. Yes, and it was due to the passive, fatalistic attitude of those people that there were no riots. . .[1]

A leading Bengali Communist wrote with admiration of these villagers, "saturated with the love of peace and honesty", turning away from the path of looting, and with "unbounded fortitude. . . standing in the queue of death".[2] And, regarding this evidence, Greenough concludes that this behaviour represented "the continued acceptance in a crisis of the very values which hitherto had sustained the victims":

> Abandoned victims could do no more than to dramatize their helplessness in the hope of re-stimulating a flow of benevolence. Mendicancy, cries and wails, imploring gestures, the exhibition of dead or dying children — all were part of the destitutes' attempts to evoke charity and to transfer responsibility for their nurture to new 'destined providers'.[3]

Professor Greenough's intervention is most welcome. But it does present certain difficulties. One set of difficulties arises from his interpretation of complex evidence. His reconstruction of the value-system of Bengali peasants bears

[1] Greenough, *Prosperity and Misery*, pp. 266-7.
[2] *Ibid.*, p. 268.
[3] *Ibid.*, p. 271.

the mark of a certain school of holistic anthropology and allows no space for variety and contradiction. This is most evident in his discussion of the demoralisation induced by prolonged dearth, the break-up of families, and the abandonment of wives and children by the father. Greenough concludes that "familial disintegration did not occur randomly but seems to have been a result of the intentional exclusion of less-valued family members from domestic subsistence". Such exclusion was "desperate but not reprehensible" and was "explicable in terms of Bengali moral conceptions". The most favoured member of the family (in this account) is the male family head, who might — even if he should be the only survivor — reconstitute the familial lineage. So deeply are these patriarchal values internalised that the abandoned passively assent to their own abandonment.[1]

This may be true, or may be part of the truth.[2] But Greenough hangs his interpretive apparatus upon slender evidence — a few accounts of the "banishment" of wives or desertion of families — and alternative interpretations are not tested.[3] And he affirms his conclusions in increasingly confident form, as if they were incontestible findings. What were "desperate" measures on one page becomes, fifty pages

[1] *Ibid.*, pp. 215-25 and "Indian Famines and Peasant Victims", pp. 225-33.

[2] Megan Vaughan in "Famine Analysis and Family Relations: 1949 in Nyasaland", *Past and Present*, 108 (1985), has similar disturbing evidence of the aged, the young and the disabled being abandoned, and of husbands abandoning their families: and M. Vaughan, *The Story of an African Famine. Gender and Famine in Twentieth-Century Malawi* (1987).

[3] Some men may have left their families in the hope of finding work (and sending remittances) or in the expectation that in their absence the wife's kin or village charities would support the family. Wives might have been encouraged to go begging as the ultimate recourse against starvation. Similarly, the sale of children may have been an ultimate strategy to secure their survival. (Greenough assumes that "the dominant motive" for selling children was to secure cash for the parents' food, or else to "relieve themselves of the intolerable clamoring of their children for food"! *Prosperity and Misery*, p. 221.) Greenough's account of age-differential mortality during famine (*ibid.*, ch. 6) makes no attempt to relate this to the findings of historical demography as to trends commonly encountered during subsistence crisis. Indeed his treatment of historical and demographic studies is cavalier: see David Arnold, *Famine*, pp. 89-90.

later, the sweeping assertion that "authority figures in peasant households abandoned numerous dependents deemed inessential for the reconstitution of family and society in the post-crisis period".[1] What is found in extremity is now offered as if it were the norm: "husbands and heads of families appropriated domestic assets and abandoned their spouses, and parents sold children for cash".[2]

We must leave these questions to specialists in Bengali culture. But they strongly influence Greenough's comparative findings as to riot:

> This pattern of victimization has nothing in common with European traditions of rage and revolt. In Europe famine violence was turned 'outward' and 'upward' against offending landlords, merchants, and officials; in Bengal the tradition was to turn violence 'inward' and 'downward' against clients and dependents. This was the cold violence of abandonment, of ceasing to nourish, rather than the hot violence of bloodshed and tumult.[3]

The comparison would be more convincing if Greenough had not misread the European evidence in such a way as to accentuate the violence of that tradition. He prefers an exciteable letter from the Abbé Raynal, in which European food rioters in the 1780s are shown as pursuing each other with daggers in their hands, "massacring each other", "tearing and devouring their own limbs", etc., to the less sensational conclusions of historians of riot.[4] This rigging of the evidence, in which submissive sufferers are contrasted with "enraged looters", devalues his comparative study.

There remains, however, the significant interrogation of "moral" premises, in relation to subsistence, in differing cultures. In criticising *The Moral Economy of the Peasant*, Greenough argues that:

> Scott's model of the moral economy. . . is essentially legal in nature. Scott says that peasants everywhere assert a *right* to subsistence, that

---

[1] *Prosperity and Misery*, pp. 215 and 264. Cf. Greenough, "Indulgence and Abundance", pp. 832-3: heads of households "coolly abandon" their dependents; in "an extreme realization of core patriarchal values. . . it becomes acceptable to channel threats of extinction toward less essential actors like clients, women and children".

[2] "Indulgence and Abundance", p. 847.

[3] *Ibid.*, p. 847; *Prosperity and Misery*, pp. 270-1.

[4] *Ibid.*, p. 268.

this assertion is felt to be *just*, and that it arises from a *norm* of reciprocity; further, it is the *duty* of elites to subsist their peasants, and any failure to do so entails a loss of their *legitimacy*. This Latinate terminology is derived from study of the numerous food riots that erupted in Western Europe in the seventeenth through nineteenth centuries; its appropriateness in explaining Bengali conditions is doubtful. Bengalis in crisis have spoken of their needs for "boons" (*bar*), "help" (*sahajya*), and "gifts" (*dan*), but rarely of their "rights"; of "indulgence" rather than "reciprocity"; of kingly *dharma*. . . but rarely of an enforceable class "duty".

This is not just "a narrow matter of terminology, but of the cognitive structures and customary paths for action that are conjured by the use of such terms".[1]

This is partly an academic language-game which, unfortunately, is rigged once more in order to score points off Scott. For Greenough has confused the language (and cognitive structures) of the historical subjects and of the academic interpreter. Neither English food rioters nor Burmese peasants acted with a vocabulary of "norms", "reciprocity" or "legitimacy" on their lips, and, equally, Professor Greenough's interpretive terminology ("cosmology", "hierarchical", "anthropomorphized") can be as Latinate (or Hellenic), as Scott's and, perhaps, even less likely to be found on the lips of a Bengal peasant.

But let us forgive him his polemical zeal. For he has reminded us of two important things. The first is that even extreme hunger, and even the simplest act of preparing food, may have differential cultural expression: "to cultivate, cook, share, and eat rice in Bengal is to perform a series of rituals. . . To dissect out an area of economic activity and label it 'subsistence' is to sever the social, sacral and even cosmic links" that food preparation and commensality may represent. For these reasons Greenough suspects that "the moral economy of rice in much of Asia is more truly moral, more pregnant with implication, than economic and political historians have been ready to admit".[2] But there is no reason to confine these thoughts to Asia or to rice. Bread, which is "the staff of life", features in the Lord's Prayer, bread and salt are the gifts with which European peasants

---

[1] "Indulgence and Abundance", p. 846.
[2] *Ibid.*, p. 848.

once welcomed visitors, and the wafer of the sacrament of Eucharist was unleavened bread.

We are also reminded that we are always in danger of confusing the historical evidence with the terms of interpretation which we have ourselves introduced. Food rioters did sometimes appeal to justice (or "fair" prices) and they certainly protested against unfair practices; but the language of "duties", "obligations", "reciprocity" and even of "rights" is mostly our own. Rioters abused those accused of sharp practices in marketing as "rogues", and, in the theatre of confrontation, anonymous letter-writers elaborated a rhetoric of threat — murder, arson, even revolt.[1] Yet if we were to find ways of interrogating the cognitive structure of food rioters, we might find certain essential premises, whether expressed in the simplest biblical terms of "love" and "charity", or whether in terms of notions of what humans "owe" to each other in time of need, notions which may have little to do with any Christian instruction but which arise from the elementary exchanges of material life.

There was a plebeian "discourse" here, almost beneath the level of articulacy, appealing to solidarities so deeply assumed that they were almost nameless, and only occasionally finding expression in the (very imperfect) record which we have. Walter Stephens, indicted for riot before the Gloucestershire Special Commission in December 1766, was alleged to have declared that "what the Mob had done was right and justifiable, and that for all the Justices' acting they would have it all on a Level before it were long".[2] That certainly is not reputable political thought, and it will not be allowed to pass by King's College, Cambridge. But Walter Stephens said this at a time when he stood in danger of being tried for his life for these opinions (which, at the present moment, is not

---

[1] See my essay, "The Crime of Anonymity", in Hay, Linebaugh and Thompson, *Albion's Fatal Tree*, esp. the "Sampler of Letters", pp. 326-43. But even these letters are studied and "literary" productions.

[2] Crown brief in PRO, TS 11/1188/5956. I cannot find out what happened to Walter Stephens. His name does not appear on the Calendar of Prisoners in TS 11/995/3707. The case against him may have been dropped, or he might have been the Thomas Stephens committed for riot and diverse outrages and felonies, who appears in the Calendar with an annotation "acquitted".

— so far as I know — the case with any Fellow of King's) and his meanings deserve our respect.

Comparative enquiry into what is "the moral" (whether as norm or as cognitive structure) will help us to understand these meanings. It is an agenda for forward research. It would be a shame to leave future historians with nothing to do. In any case, if I did father the term "moral economy" upon current academic discourse, the term has long forgotten its paternity. I will not disown it, but it has come of age and I am no longer answerable for its actions. It will be interesting to see how it goes on.

Chapter Six

Time, Work-Discipline and Industrial Capitalism

We kept an old Servant whose name was *Wright*, in constant Work, though paid by the Week, he was a Wheel-wright by Trade. . . It happen'd one Morning that a Cart being Broken-down upon the Road. . . the old Man was fetch'd to repair it where it lay; while he was busy at his Work, comes by a Countryman that knew him, and salutes him with the usual Compliment, *Good-Morrow Father Wright, God speed your Labour*; the old Fellow looks up at him. . . and with a kind of pleasant Surlyness, answer'd, *I don't care whether he does or no, 'tis Day-Work.*

> D. Defoe, *The Great Law of Subordination Considered; or the Insolence and Insufferable Behaviour of SERVANTS in England duly enquired into* (1724)

To the upper Part of Mankind Time is an Enemy, and. . . their chief Labour is to kill it; whereas with the others, Time and Money are almost synonymous.

> Henry Fielding, *An Enquiry into the Causes of the late Increase of Robbers* (1751)

Tess. . . started on her way up the dark and crooked lane or street not made for hasty progress; a street laid out before inches of land had value, and when one-handed clocks sufficiently subdivided the day.

> *Thomas Hardy*

I

It is commonplace that the years between 1300 and 1650 saw within the intellectual culture of Western Europe important changes in the apprehension of time.[1] In the *Canterbury*

[1] Lewis Mumford makes suggestive claims in *Technics and Civilization* (1934), esp. pp. 12-18, 196-9: see also S. de Grazia, *Of Time, Work, and Leisure* (New York, 1962), Carlo M. Cipolla, *Clocks and Culture 1300-1700* (1967), and Edward T. Hall, *The Silent Language* (New York, 1959).

Tales the cock still figures in his immemorial role as nature's timepiece: Chauntecleer —

> Caste up his eyen to the brighte sonne,
> That in the signe of Taurus hadde yronne
> Twenty degrees and oon, and somwhat moore,
> He knew by kynde, and by noon oother loore
> That it was pryme, and crew with blisful stevene. . .

But although "By nature knew he ech ascensioun/Of the equynoxial in thilke toun", the contrast between "nature's" time and clock time is pointed in the image —

> Wel sikerer was his crowyng in his logge
> Than is a clokke, or an abbey orlogge.

This is a very early clock: Chaucer (unlike Chauntecleer) was a Londoner, and was aware of the times of Court, of urban organisation and of that "merchant's time" which Jacques Le Goff, in a suggestive article in *Annales*, has opposed to the time of the medieval church.[1]

I do not wish to argue how far the change was due to the spread of clocks from the fourteenth century onwards, how far this was itself a symptom of a new Puritan discipline and bourgeois exactitude. However we see it, the change is certainly there. The clock steps on to the Elizabethan stage, turning Faustus's last soliloquy into a dialogue with time: "the stars move still, time runs, the clock will strike". Sidereal time, which has been present since literature began, has now moved at one step from the heavens into the home. Mortality and love are both felt to be more poignant as the "Snayly motion of the mooving hand"[2] crosses the dial. When the watch is worn about the neck it lies in proximity to the less regular beating of the heart. The conventional Elizabethan images of time as a devourer, a defacer, a bloody

---

[1] J. Le Goff, "Au Moyen Age: Temps de L'Eglise et temps du marchand", *Annals E.S.C.*, xv (1960); and the same author's "Le temps du travail dans le 'crise' du XIVᵉ Siècle: du temps médiéval au temps moderne", *Le Moyen Age*, lxix (1963).

[2] M. Drayton, "Of his Ladies not Comming to London", *Works*, ed. J. W. Hebel (Oxford, 1932), iii, p. 204.

tyrant, a scytheman, are old enough, but there is a new immediacy and insistence.[1]

As the seventeenth century moves on the image of clockwork extends, until, with Newton, it has engrossed the universe. And by the middle of the eighteenth century (if we are to trust Sterne) the clock had penetrated to more intimate levels. For Tristram Shandy's father — "one of the most regular men in everything he did. . . that ever lived" — "had made it a rule for many years of his life, — on the first Sunday night of every month. . . to wind up a large house-clock, which we had standing on the back-stairs head". "He had likewise gradually brought some other little family concernments to the same period", and this enabled Tristram to date his conception very exactly. It also provoked *The Clockmakers Outcry against the Author*:

> The directions I had for making several clocks for the country are countermanded; because no modest lady now dares to mention a word about winding-up a clock, without exposing herself to the sly leers and jokes of the family. . . Nay, the common expression of street-walkers is, "Sir, will you have your clock wound up?"

Virtuous matrons (the "clockmaker" complained) are consigning their clocks to lumber rooms as "exciting to acts of carnality".[2]

However, this gross impressionism is unlikely to advance the present enquiry: how far, and in what ways, did this shift in time-sense affect labour discipline, and how far did it influence the inward apprehension of time of working people? If the transition to mature industrial society entailed a severe restructuring of working habits — new disciplines, new incentives, and a new human nature upon which these incentives could bite effectively — how far is this related to changes in the inward notation of time?

---

[1] The change is discussed in Cipolla, *op. cit.*; Erwin Sturzl, "Der Zeitbegriff in der Elisabethanischen Literatur", *Wiener Beitrage zur Englischen Philologie*, lxix (1965); Alberto Tenenti, Il Senso della Morte e l'amore della vita nel rinascimento (Milan, 1957).

[2] Anon., *The Clockmaker's Outcry against the Author of. . . Tristram Shandy* (1760), pp. 42-3.

II

It is well known that among primitive peoples the measurement of time is commonly related to familiar processes in the cycle of work or of domestic chores. Evans-Pritchard has analysed the time-sense of the Nuer:

> The daily timepiece is the cattle clock, the round of pastoral tasks, and the time of day and the passage of time through a day are to a Nuer primarily the succession of these tasks and their relation to one another.

Among the Nandi an occupational definition of time evolved covering not only each hour, but half hours of the day — at 5.30 in the morning the oxen have gone to the grazing-ground, at 6 the sheep have been unfastened, at 6.30 the sun has grown, at 7 it has become warm, at 7.30 the goats have gone to the grazing-ground, etc. — an uncommonly well-regulated economy. In a similar way terms evolve for the measurement of time intervals. In Madagascar time might be measured by "a rice-cooking" (about half an hour) or "the frying of a locust" (a moment). The Cross River natives were reported as saying "the man died in less than the time in which maize is not yet completely roasted" (less than fifteen minutes).[1]

It is not difficult to find examples of this nearer to us in cultural time. Thus in seventeenth-century Chile time was often measured in "credos": an earthquake was described in 1647 as lasting for the period of two credos; while the cooking time of an egg could be judged by an Ave Maria said aloud. In Burma in recent times monks rose at daybreak

---

[1] E. E. Evans-Pritchard, *The Nuer* (Oxford, 1940), pp. 100-4; M. P. Nilsson, *Primitive Time Reckoning* (Lund, 1920), pp. 32-3; P. A. Sorokin and R. K. Merton, "Social Time: a Methodological and Functional Analysis", *Amer. Jl. Sociol.*, xlii (1937); A. I. Hallowell, "Temporal Orientation in Western Civilization and in a Pre-Literate Society", *Amer. Anthrop.*, new series, xxxix (1937). Other sources for primitive time reckoning are cited in H. G. Alexander, *Time as Dimension and History* (Albuquerque, 1945), p. 26, and Beate R. Salz, "The Human Element in Industrialization", *Econ. Devel. and Cult. Change*, iv (1955), esp. pp. 94-114.

"when there is light enough to see the veins in the hand".[1]
The Oxford English Dictionary gives us English examples —
"pater noster wyle", "miserere whyle" (1450), and (in the
New English Dictionary but not the Oxford English
Dictionary) "pissing while" — a somewhat arbitrary
measurement.

Pierre Bourdieu has explored more closely the attitudes
towards time of the Kaabyle peasant (in Algeria) in recent
years: "An attitude of submission and of nonchalant
indifference to the passage of time which no one dreams of
mastering, using up, or saving. . . Haste is seen as a lack of
decorum combined with diabolical ambition". The clock is
sometimes known as "the devil's mill"; there are no precise
meal-times; "the notion of an exact appointment is unknown; they agree only to meet 'at the next market' ". A
popular song runs:

> It is useless to pursue the world, No one will ever overtake it.[2]

Synge, in his well-observed account of the Aran Islands,
gives us a classic example:

> While I am walking with Michael someone often comes to me to ask the
> time of day. Few of the people, however, are sufficiently used to
> modern time to understand in more than a vague way the convention of
> the hours and when I tell them what o'clock it is by my watch they are
> not satisfied, and ask how long is left them before the twilight.[3]

> The general knowledge of time on the island depends, curiously enough,
> upon the direction of the wind. Nearly all the cottages are built. . . with
> two doors opposite each other, the more sheltered of which lies open all
> day to give light to the interior. If the wind is northerly the south door is
> opened, and the shadow of the door-post moving across the kitchen
> floor indicates the hour; as soon, however, as the wind changes to the

---

[1] E. P. Salas, "L'Evolution de la notion du temps et les horlogers à
l'époque coloniale au Chili", *Annales E.S.C.*, xxi (1966), p. 146; *Cultural
Patterns and Technical Change*, ed. M. Mead (New York, UNESCO,
1953), p. 75.
[2] P. Bourdieu, "The attitude of the Algerian peasant toward time", in
Mediterranean Countrymen, ed. J. Pitt-Rivers (Paris, 1963), pp. 55-72.
[3] Cf. *ibid.*, p. 179: "Spanish Americans do not regulate their lives by the
clock as Anglos do. Both rural and urban people, when asked when they
plan to do something, gives answers like: 'Right now, about two or four
o'clock' ".

south the other door is opened, and the people, who never think of putting up a primitive dial, are at a loss. . .

When the wind is from the north the old woman manages my meals with fair regularity; but on the other days she often makes my tea at three o'clock instead of six. . .[1]

Such a disregard for clock time could of course only be possible in a crofting and fishing community whose framework of marketing and administration is minimal, and in which the day's tasks (which might vary from fishing to farming, building, mending of nets, thatching, making a cradle or a coffin) seem to disclose themselves, by the logic of need, before the crofter's eyes.[2] But his account will serve to emphasise the essential conditioning in differing notations of time provided by different work-situations and their relation to "natural" rhythms. Clearly hunters must employ certain hours of the night to set their snares. Fishing and seafaring people must integrate their lives with the tides. A petition from Sunderland in 1800 includes the words "considering that this is a seaport in which many people are obliged to be up at all hours of the night to attend the tides and their affairs upon the river".[3] The operative phrase is "attend the tides": the patterning of social time in the seaport follows *upon* the rhythms of the sea; and this appears to be natural and comprehensible to fishermen or seamen: the compulsion is nature's own.

In a similar way labour from dawn to dusk can appear to be "natural" in a farming community, especially in the harvest months: nature demands that the grain be harvested

[1] J. M. Synge, *Plays, Poems, and Prose* (Everyman edn., 1941), p. 257.

[2] The most important event in the relation of the islands to an external economy in Synge's time was the arrival of the steamer, whose times might be greatly affected by tide and weather. See Synge, *The Aran Islands* (Dublin, 1907), pp. 115-6.

[3] PRO, WO 40/17. It is of interest to note other examples of the recognition that seafaring time conflicted with urban routines: the Court of Admiralty was held to be always open, "for strangers and merchants, and sea-faring men, must take the opportunity of tides and winds, and cannot, without ruin and great prejudice attend the solemnity of courts and dilatory pleadings", see E. Vansittart Neale, *Feasts and Fasts* (1845), p. 249, while in some Sabbatarian legislation an exception was made for fishermen who sighted a shoal off-shore on the Sabbath day.

before the thunderstorms set in. And we may note similar "natural" work-rhythms which attend other rural or industrial occupations: sheep must be attended at lambing time and guarded from predators; cows must be milked; the charcoal fire must be attended and not burn away through the turfs (and the charcoal burners must sleep beside it); once iron is in the making, the furnaces must not be allowed to fail.

The notation of time which arises in such contexts has been described as task-orientation. It is perhaps the most effective orientation in peasant societies, and it remains important in village and domestic industries. It has by no means lost all relevance in rural parts of Britain today. Three points may be proposed about task-orientation. First, there is a sense in which it is more humanly comprehensible than timed labour. The peasant or labourer appears to attend upon what is an observed necessity. Second, a community in which task-orientation is common appears to show least demarcation between "work" and "life". Social intercourse and labour are intermingled — the working day lengthens or contracts according to the task — and there is no great sense of conflict between labour and "passing the time of day". Third, to men accustomed to labour timed by the clock, this attitude to labour appears to be wasteful and lacking in urgency.[1]

Such a clear distinction supposes, of course, the independent peasant or craftsman as referent. But the question of task-orientation becomes greatly more complex at the point where labour is employed. The entire family economy of the small farmer may be task-orientated; but within it there may be a division of labour, and allocation of roles, and the discipline of an employer-employed relationship between the farmer and his children. Even here time is beginning to become money, the employer's money. As soon as actual

---

[1] Henri Lefebvre, *Critique de la Vie Quotidienne* (Paris, 1958), ii, pp. 52-6, prefers a distinction between "cyclical time" — arising from changing seasonal occupations in agriculture — and the "linear time" of urban, industrial organisation. More suggestive is Lucien Febvre's distinction between "Le temps vécu et le temps-mesure", *La Problème de L'Incroyance en XVIe Siècle* (Paris, 1947), p. 431. A somewhat schematic examination of the organisation of tasks in primitive economies is in Stanley H. Udy, *Organisation of Work* (New Haven, 1959), ch. 2.

hands are employed the shift from task-orientation to timed labour is marked. It is true that the timing of work can be done independently of any time-piece — and indeed precedes the diffusion of the clock. Still, in the mid seventeenth century substantial farmers calculated their expectations of employed labour (as did Henry Best) in "dayworks" — "the Cunnigarth, with its bottomes, is 4 large dayworkes for a good mower", "the Spellowe is 4 indifferent dayworkes", etc.;[1] and what Best did for his own farm, Markham attempted to present in general form:

> A man. . . may mow of Corn, as Barley and Oats, if it be thick, loggy and beaten down to the earth, making fair work, and not cutting off the heads of the ears, and leaving the straw still growing one acre and a half in a day: but if it be good thick and fair standing corn, then he may mow two acres, or two acres and a half in a day; but if the corn be short and thin, then he may mow three, and sometimes four Acres in a day, and not be overlaboured. . .[2]

The computation is difficult, and dependent upon many variables. Clearly, a straightforward time-measurement was more convenient.[3]

This measurement embodies a simple relationship. Those who are employed experience a distinction between their employer's time and their "own" time. And the employer must *use* the time of his labour, and see it is not wasted: not the task but the value of time when reduced to money is dominant. Time is now currency: it is not passed but spent.

---

[1] *Rural Economy in Yorkshire in 1641. . . Farming and Account Books of Henry Best*, ed. C. B. Robinson (Surtees Society, xxxiii, 1857), pp. 38-9.

[2] G.M., *The Inrichment of the Weald of Kent*, 10th edn. (1660), ch. xii: "A generall computation of men, and cattel's labours: what each may do without hurt daily", pp. 112-8.

[3] Wage-assessments still, of course, assumed the statute dawn-to-dusk day, defined, as late as 1725, in a Lancashire assessment: "They shall work from five in the morning till betwixt seven and eight at the night, from the midst of March to the middle of September" — and thereafter "from the spring of day till night", with two half hours for drinking, and one hour for dinner and (in summer only) one half hour for sleep: "else, for every hour's absence to defaulk a penny": *Annals of Agriculture*, xxv (1796).

We may observe something of this contrast, in attitudes towards both time and work, in two passages from Stephen Duck's poem, "The Thresher's Labour".[1] The first describes a work-situation which we have come to regard as the norm in the nineteenth and twentieth centuries:

> From the strong Planks our Crab-Tree Staves rebound,
> And echoing Barns return the rattling Sound.
> Now in the Air our knotty Weapons Fly;
> And now with equal Force descend from high:
> Down one, one up, so well they keep the Time,
> The *Cyclops* Hammers could not truer chime. . .
> In briny Streams our Sweat descends apace,
> Drops from our Locks, or trickles down our Face.
> No intermission in our Works we know;
> The noisy Threshall must for ever go.
> Their Master absent, others safely play;
> The sleeping Threshall doth itself betray.
> Nor yet the tedious Labour to beguile,
> And make the passing Minutes sweetly smile,
> Can we, like Shepherds, tell a merry Tale?
> The Voice is lost, drown'd by the noisy Flail. . .
>
> Week after Week we this dull Task pursue,
> Unless when winnowing Days produce a new;
> A new indeed, but frequently a worse,
> The Threshall yields but to the Master's Curse:
> He counts the Bushels, counts how much a Day,
> Then swears we've idled half our Time away.
> Why look ye, Rogues! D'ye think that this will do?
> Your Neighbours thresh as much again as you.

This would appear to describe the monotony, alienation from pleasure in labour, and antagonism of interests commonly ascribed to the factory system. The second passage describes the harvesting:

> At length in Rows stands up the well-dry'd Corn,
> A grateful Scene, and ready for the Barn.
> Our well-pleas'd Master views the Sight with joy,
> And we for carrying all our Force employ.
> Confusion soon o'er all the Field appears,
> And stunning Clamours fill the Workmens Ears;
> The Bells, and clashing Whips, alternate sound,
> And rattling Waggons thunder o'er the Ground.

---

[1] "The Threshers Labour", ed. E. P. Thompson and Marian Sugden (1989).

The Wheat got in, the Pease, and other Grain,
Share the same Fate, and soon leave bare the Plain:
In noisy Triumph the last Load moves on,
And loud Huzza's proclaim the Harvest done.

This is, of course, an obligatory set-piece in eighteenth-century farming poetry. And it is also true that the good morale of the labourers was sustained by their high harvest earnings. But it would be an error to see the harvest situation in terms of direct responses to economic stimuli. It is also a moment at which the older collective rhythms break through the new, and a weight of folklore and of rural custom could be called as supporting evidence as to the psychic satisfaction and ritual functions — for example, the momentary obliteration of social distinctions — of the harvest-home. "How few now know", M. K. Ashby writes, "what it was ninety years ago to get in a harvest! Though the disinherited had no great part of the fruits, still they shared in the achievement, the deep involvement and joy of it".[1]

III

It is by no means clear how far the availability of precise clock time extended at the time of the industrial revolution. From the fourteenth century onwards church clocks and public clocks were erected in the cities and large market towns. The majority of English parishes must have possessed church clocks by the end of the sixteenth century.[2] But the accuracy of these clocks is a matter of dispute; and the sundial remained in use (partly to set the clock) in the seventeenth, eighteenth and nineteenth centuries.[3]

[1] M. K. Ashby, *Joseph Ashby of Tysoe* (Cambridge, 1961), p. 24.
[2] For the early evolution of clocks, see Cipolla, *op. cit., passim*; A. P. Usher, *A History of Mechanical Inventions*, rev. edn. (Cambridge, Mass., 1962), ch. vii; Charles Singer *et al* (eds.), *A History of Technology* (Oxford, 1956), iii, ch. xxiv; R. W. Symonds, *A History of English Clocks* (Penguin, 1947), pp. 10-16, 33; E. L. Edwards, *Weight-driven Chamber Clocks of the Middle Ages and Renaissance* (Alrincham, 1965).
[3] See M. Gatty, *The Book of Sun-diales*, rev. edn. (1900). For an example of a treatise explaining in detail how to set time-pieces by the sundial, see John Smith, *Horological Dialogues* (1675). For examples of benefactions for sundials, see C. F. C. Beeson, *Clockmaking in Oxfordshire* (Banbury Hist. Assn., 1962), pp. 76-8; A. J. Hawkes, *The Clockmakers and Watchmakers of Wigan, 1650-1850* (Wigan, 1950), p. 27.

Charitable donations continued to be made in the seventeenth century (sometimes laid out in "clockland", "ding dong land", or "curfew bell land") for the ringing of early morning bells and curfew bells.[1] Thus Richard Palmer of Wokingham (Berkshire) gave, in 1664, lands in trust to pay the sexton to ring the great bell for half an hour every evening at eight o'clock and every morning at four o'clock, or as near to those hours as might be, from the 10th September to the 11th March in each year

> not only that as many as might live within the sound might be thereby induced to a timely going to rest in the evening, and early arising in the morning to the labours and duties of their several callings, (things ordinarily attended and rewarded with thrift and proficiency). . .

but also so that strangers and others within sound of the bell on winter nights "might be informed of the time of night, and receive some guidance into their right way". These "rational ends", he conceived, "could not but be well liked by any discreet person, the same being done and well approved of in most of the cities and market-towns, and many other places in the kingdom. . .". The bell would also remind men of their passing, and of resurrection and judgement.[2] Sound served better than sight, especially in growing manufacturing districts. In the clothing districts of the West Riding, in the Potteries, (and probably in other districts) the horn was still used to awaken people in the mornings.[3] The farmer aroused his own labourers, on occasion, from their cottages; and no doubt the knocker-up will have started with the earliest mills.

[1] Since many early church clocks did not strike the hour, they were supplemented by a bell-ringer.

[2] *Charity Commissioners Reports* (1837/8), xxxii, pt. 1, p. 224; see also H. Edwards, *A Collection of Old English Customs* (1842), esp. pp. 223-7; S. O. Addy, *Household Tales* (1895), pp. 129-39; *County Folk-lore, East Riding of Yorkshire*, ed. Mrs Gutch (1912), pp. 150-1; *Leicestershire and Rutland*, ed. C. J. Billson (1895), pp. 120-1; C. F. C. Beeson, *op.cit.*, p. 36; A. Gatty, *The Bell* (1848), p. 20; P. H. Ditchfield, *Old English Customs* (1896), pp. 232-41.

[3] H. Heaton, *The Yorkshire Woollen and Worsted Industries* (Oxford, 1965), p. 347. Wedgwood seems to have been the first to replace the horn by the bell in the Potteries: E. Meteyard, *Life of Josiah Wedgwood* (1865), i, pp. 329-30.

A great advance in the accuracy of household clocks came with the application of the pendulum after 1658. Grandfather clocks began to spread more widely from the 1660s, but clocks with minute hands (as well as hour hands) only became common well after this time.[1] As regards more portable time, the pocket watch was of dubious accuracy until improvements were made in the escapement and the spiral balance-spring was applied after 1674.[2] Ornate and rich design was still preferred to plain serviceability. A Sussex diarist notes in 1688:

> bought. . . a silver-cased watch, w[eh] cost me 3*1i*. . . . This watch shewes ye hour of ye day, ye month of ye year, ye age of ye moon, and ye ebbing and flowing of ye water; and will goe 30 hours with one winding up.[3]

Professor Cipolla suggests 1680 as the date at which English clock- and watch-making took precedence (for nearly a century) over European competitors.[4] Clock-making had emerged from the skills of the blacksmith,[5] and the affinity can still be seen in the many hundreds of independent clock-makers, working to local orders in their own shops, dispersed through the market-towns and even the large villages of England, Scotland and Wales in the eighteenth century.[6]

---

[1] W. I. Milham, *Time and Timekeepers* (1923), pp. 142-9; F. J. Britten, *Old Clocks and Watches and Their Makers*, 6th edn. (1932), p. 543; E. Burton, *The Longcase Clock* (1964), ch. ix.

[2] Milham, *op. cit.*, pp. 214-26; C. Clutton and G. Daniels, *Watches* (1965); F. A. B. Ward, *Handbook of the Collections illustrating Time Measurement*(1947), p. 29; Cipolla, *op. cit.*, p. 139.

[3] Edward Turner, "Extracts from the Diary of Richard Stapley", *Sussex Archaeol. Coll.*, ii (1899), p. 113.

[4] See the admirable survey of the origin of the English industry in Cipolla, *op. cit.*, pp. 65-9.

[5] As late as 1697 in London the Blacksmith's Company was contesting the monopoly of the Clockmakers (founded in 1631) on the grounds that "it is well known that they are the originall and proper makers of clocks &c. and have full skill and knowledge therein. . .": S. E. Atkins and W. H. Overall, *Some Account of the Worshipful Company of Clockmakers of the City of London* (1881), p. 118. For a village blacksmith/clock-maker see J. A. Daniell, "The Making of Clocks and Watches in Leicestershire and Rutland", *Trans. Leics. Archaeol. Soc.*, xxvii (1951), p. 32.

[6] Lists of such clock-makers are in Britten, *op. cit.*; John Smith, *Old Scottish Clockmakers* (Edinburgh, 1921); and I. C. Peate, *Clock and Watch Makers in Wales* (Cardiff, 1945).

While many of these aspired to nothing more fancy than the work-a-day farmhouse longcase clock, craftsmen of genius were among their numbers. Thus John Harrison, clock-maker and former carpenter of Barton-on-Humber (Lincoln-shire), perfected a marine chronometer, and in 1730 could claim to have

> brought a Clock to go nearer the truth, than can be well imagin'd, considering the vast Number of seconds of Time there is in a Month, in which space of time it does not vary above one second. . . I am sure I can bring it to the nicety of 2 or 3 seconds in a year.[1]

And John Tibbot, a clock-maker in Newtown (Montgomery-shire), had perfected a clock in 1810 which (he claimed) seldom varied more than a second over two years.[2] In between these extremes were those numerous, shrewd, and highly-capable craftsmen who played a critically important role in technical innovation in the early stages of the industrial revolution. The point, indeed, was not left for historians to discover: it was argued forcibly in petitions of the clock- and watch-makers against the assessed taxes in February 1798. Thus the petition from Carlisle:

> . . . the cotton and woollen manufactories are entirely indebted for the state of perfection to which the machinery used therein is now brought to the clock and watch makers, great numbers of whom have, for several years past. . . been employed in inventing and constructing as well as superintending such machinery. . .[3]

Small-town clock-making survived into the eighteenth century, although from the early years of that century it became common for the local clock-maker to buy his parts ready-made from Birmingham, and to assemble these in his own workshop. By contrast, watch-making, from the early years of the eighteenth century, was concentrated in a few centres, of which the most important were London,

---

[1] Records of the Clockmaker's Company, London Guildhall Archives, 6026/1. See (for Harrison's chronometer) Ward, *op. cit.*, p. 32.

[2] I. C. Peate, "John Tibbot, Clock and Watch Maker", *Montgomery-shire Collections*, xlviii, pt. 2 (Welshpool, 1944), p. 178.

[3] *Commons Journals*, liii, p. 251. The witnesses from Lancashire and Derby gave similar testimonies: *ibid.*, pp. 331, 335.

Coventry, Prescot and Liverpool.[1] A minute subdivision of labour took place in the industry early, facilitating large-scale production and a reduction in prices: the annual output of the industry at its peak (1796) was variously estimated at 120,000 and 191,678, a substantial part of which was for the export market.[2] Pitt's ill-judged attempt to tax clocks and watches, although it lasted only from July 1797 to March 1798, marked a turning-point in the fortunes of the industry. Already, in 1796, the trade was complaining at the competition of French and Swiss watches; the complaints continue to grow in the early years of the nineteenth century. The Clockmakers' Company alleged in 1813 that the smuggling of cheap gold watches had assumed major proportions, and that these were sold by jewellers, haberdashers, milliners, dressmakers, French toy-shops, perfumers, etc., "almost entirely for the use of *the upper classes of society*". At the same time, some cheap smuggled goods, sold by pawnbrokers or travelling salesmen, must have been reaching the poorer classes.[3]

It is clear that there were plenty of watches and clocks around by 1800. But it is not so clear who owned them.

[1] Centres of the clock- and watch-making trade petitioning against the tax in 1798 were: London, Bristol, Coventry, Leicester, Prescot, Newcastle, Edinburgh, Liverpool, Carlisle, and Derby: *Commons Journals*, liii, pp. 158, 167, 174, 178, 230, 232, 239, 247, 251, 316. It was claimed that 20,000 were engaged in the trade in London alone, 7,000 of these in Clerkenwell. But in Bristol only 150 to 200 were engaged. For London, see M. D. George, *London Life in the Eighteenth Century* (1925), pp. 173-6; Atkins and Overall, *op. cit.*, p. 269; *Morning Chronicle*, 19 Dec. 1797; *Commons Journals*, liii, p. 158. For Bristol, *ibid.*, p. 332. For Lancashire, *Victoria County History, Lancashire.*

[2] The lower estimate was given by a witness before the committee on watch-makers' petitions (1798): *Commons Journals*, liii, p. 328 — estimated annual home consumption 50,000, export 70,000. See also a similar estimate (clocks and watches) for 1813, Atkins and Overall, *op. cit.*, p. 276. The higher estimate is for watch-cases marked at Goldsmiths Hall — silver cases, 185,102 in 1796, declining to 91,346 in 1816 — and is in the *Report of the Select Committee on the Petitions of Watchmakers*, PP, 1817, vi and 1818, ix, p. 1, 12.

[3] Atkins and Overall, *op. cit.*, pp. 302, 308 — estimating (excessively?) 25,000 gold and 10,000 silver watches imported, mostly illegally, per annum; and Anon., *Observations on the Art and Trade of Clock and Watchmaking* (1812), pp. 16-20.

Dr Dorothy George, writing of the mid eighteenth century, suggests that "labouring men, as well as artisans, frequently possessed silver watches", but the statement is indefinite as to date and only slightly documented.[1] The average price of plain longcase clocks made locally in Wrexham between 1755 and 1774 ran between £2 and £2 15s. 0d.; a Leicester price-list for new clocks, without cases, in 1795 runs between £3 and £5. A well-made watch would certainly cost no less.[2] On the face of it, no labourer whose budget was recorded by Eden or David Davies could have meditated such prices, and only the best-paid urban artisan. Recorded time (one suspects) belonged in the mid-century still to the gentry, the masters, the farmers and the tradesmen; and perhaps the intricacy of design, and the preference for precious metal, were in deliberate accentuation of their symbolism of status.

But, equally, it would appear that the situation was changing in the last decades of the century. The debate provoked by the attempt to impose a tax on all clocks and watches in 1797-8 offers a little evidence. It was perhaps the most unpopular and it was certainly the most unsuccessful of all of Pitt's assessed taxes:

> If your Money he take — why your Breeches remain;
> And the flaps of your Shirts, if your Breeches he gain;
> And your Skin, if your Shirts; and if Shoes, your bare feet.
> Then, never mind TAXES — *We've beat the Dutch fleet!*[3]

The taxes were of 2s. 6d. upon each silver or metal watch; 10s. upon each gold one; and 5s. upon each clock. In debates upon the tax, the statements of ministers were remarkable only for their contradictions. Pitt declared that he expected the tax to produce £200,000 per annum:

---

[1] George, *op. cit.*, p. 70. Various means of time-telling were of course employed without clocks: the engraving of the wool-comber in *The Book of English Trades* (1818), p. 438 shows him with an hour-glass on his bench; threshers measured time as the light from the door moved across the barn floor; and Cornish tinners measured it underground by candles (information from J. G. Rule).

[2] I. C. Peate, "Two Montgomeryshire Craftsmen", *Montgomeryshire Collections*, xlviii, pt. 1 (Welshpool, 1944), p. 5; Daniell, *op. cit.*, p. 39. The average price of watches exported in 1792 was £4: *PP*, 1818, ix, p. 1.

[3] "A loyal Song", *Morning Chronicle*, 18 Dec. 1797.

In fact, he thought, that as the number of houses paying taxes is 700,000 and that in every house there is probably one person who wears a watch, the tax upon watches only would produce that sum.

At the same time, in response to criticism, ministers maintained that the ownership of clocks and watches was a mark of luxury. The Chancellor of the Exchequer faced both ways: watches and clocks "were certainly articles of convenience, but they were also articles of luxury. . . generally kept by persons who would be pretty well able to pay. . .". "He meant, however, to exempt Clocks of the meaner sort that were most commonly kept by the poorer classes."[1] The Chancellor clearly regarded the tax as a sort of Lucky Bag; his guess was more than three times that of the Pilot:

GUESSWORK TABLE

Articles	Tax	Chancellor's estimate	Would mean
Silver and metal watches	2s. 6d.	£100,000	800,000 watches
Gold watches	10s. 0d.	£200,000	400,000 watches
Clocks	5s. 0d.	£3 or £400,000	c. 1,400,000 clocks

His eyes glittering at the prospect of enhanced revenue, Pitt revised his definitions: a *single* watch (or dog) might be owned as an article of convenience — more than this were "tests of affluence".[2]

Unfortunately for the quantifiers of economic growth, one matter was left out of account. The tax was impossible to collect.[3] All householders were ordered, upon dire pains, to return lists of clocks and watches within their houses. Assessments were to be quarterly:

[1] The exemptions in the Act (37 Geo. III, c. 108, cl., xii, xxii and xxiv) were (a) for one clock or watch for any householder exempted from window and house tax (i.e. cottager), (b) for clocks "made of wood, or fixed upon wood, and which clocks are usually sold by the respective makers thereof at a price not exceeding the sum of 20s. . .", (c) Servants in husbandry.

[2] *Morning Chronicle*, 1 July 1797; *Craftsman*, 8 July 1779; *Parl. Hist.*, xxxiii, *passim*.

[3] In the year ending 5 April 1798 (three weeks after repeal) the tax had raised £2,600: *PP*, ciii, Accounts and Papers (1797-98), xlv, pp. 933 (2) and 933 (3).

Mr. Pitt has very proper ideas of the remaining finances of the country. The *half-crown* tax upon watches is appointed to be collected *quarterly*. This is grand and dignified. It gives a man an air of consequence to pay *sevenpence halfpenny* to support *religion, property*, and *social order*.[1]

In fact, the tax was regarded as folly; as setting up a system of espionage; and as a blow against the middle class.[2] There was a buyer's strike. Owners of gold watches melted down the covers and exchanged them for silver or metal.[3] The centres of the trade were plunged into crisis and depression.[4] Repealing the Act in March 1798, Pitt said sadly that the tax *would* have been productive much beyond the calculation originally made; but it is not clear whether it was his own calculation (£200,000) or the Chancellor of the Exchequer's (£700,000) which he had in mind.[5]

We remain (but in the best of company) in ignorance. There were a lot of timepieces about in the 1790s: emphasis is shifting from "luxury" to "convenience"; even cottagers may have wooden clocks costing less than twenty shillings. Indeed, a general diffusion of clocks and watches is occurring (as one would expect) at the exact moment when the industrial revolution demanded a greater synchronisation of labour.

Although some very cheap — and shoddy — time-pieces were beginning to appear, the prices of efficient ones remained for several decades beyond the normal reach of the artisan.[6] But we should not allow normal economic

[1] *Morning Chronicle*, 26 July, 1797.

[2] One indication may be seen in the sluggardly collection of arrears. Taxes imposed, July 1797: receipts, year ending Jan. 1798 — £300. Taxes repealed, March 1798: arrears received, year ending Jan. 1799, £35,420; year ending Jan. 1800, £14,966. *PP*, cix, Accounts and Papers (1799-1800), li, pp. 1009 (2) and 1013 (2).

[3] *Morning Chronicle*, 16 Mar. 1798; *Commons Journals*, liii, p. 328.

[4] See petitions, cited in note 1 on p. 365; *Commons Journals*, liii, pp. 327-33; *Morning Chronicle*, 13 Mar. 1798. Two-thirds of Coventry watchmakers were said to be unemployed: *ibid.*, 8 Dec. 1797.

[5] *Craftsman*, 17 Mar. 1798. The one achievement of the Act was to bring into existence — in taverns and public places — the "Act of Parliament Clock".

[6] Imported watches were quoted at a price as low as 5s. in 1813: Atkins and Overall, *op. cit.*, p. 292. See also note 1 on p. 367. The price of an efficient British silver pocket watch was quoted in 1817 (*Committee on*

preferences to mislead us. The small instrument which regulated the new rhythms of industrial life was at the same time one of the more urgent of the new needs which industrial capitalism called forth to energise its advance. A clock or watch was not only useful; it conferred prestige upon its owner, and a man might be willing to stretch his resources to obtain one. There were various sources, various occasions. For decades a trickle of sound but cheap watches found their way from the pickpocket to the receiver, the pawnbroker, the public house.[1] Even labourers, once or twice in their lives, might have an unexpected windfall, and blow it on a watch: the militia bounty,[2] harvest earnings, or the yearly wages of the servant.[3] In some parts of the country Clock and Watch Clubs were set up — collective hire-purchase.[4] Moreover, the time-piece was the poor man's bank, an investment of

---

Petitions of Watchmakers, PP, 1817, vi) at two to three guineas; by the 1830s an effective metal watch could be had for £1: D. Lardner, *Cabinet Cyclopaedia* (1834), iii, p. 297.

[1] Many watches must have changed hands in London's underworld: legislation in 1754 (27 Geo. II, c. 7) was directed at receivers of stolen watches. The pickpockets of course continued their trade undeterred: see, e.g. *Minutes of Select Committee to Inquire into the State of the Police of the Metropolis* (1816), p. 437 — "take watches could get rid of them as readily as anything else. . . It must be a very good patent silver watch that fetched £2; a gold one £5 or £6". Receivers of stolen watches in Glasgow are said to have sold them in quantities in country districts in Ireland (1834): see J. E. Handley, *The Irish in Scotland, 1798-1845* (Cork, 1943), p. 253.

[2] "Winchester being one of the general rendezvous for the militia volunteers, has been a scene of riot, dissipation and absurd extravagence. It is supposed that nine-tenths of the bounties paid to these men, amounting to at least £20,000 were all spent on the spot among the public houses, milliners, watch-makers, hatters, &c. In mere wantonness Bank notes were actually eaten between slices of bread and butter": *Monthly Magazine*, Sept. 1799.

[3] Witnesses before the Select Committee of 1817 complained that inferior wares (sometimes known as "Jew watches") were touted in country fairs and sold to the gullible at mock aucfions: *PP*, 1817, vi, pp. 15-16.

[4] Benjamin Smith, *Twenty-four Letters from Labourers in America to their Friends in England* (1829), p. 48: the reference is to parts of Sussex — twenty people clubbed together (as in a Cow Club) paying 5s. each for twenty successive weeks, drawing lots each for one £5 time-piece.

savings: it could, in bad times, be sold or put in hock.[1] "This 'ere ticker", said one Cockney compositor in the 1820s, "cost me but a five-pun note ven I bort it fust, and I've popped it more than twenty times, and had more than forty poun' on it altogether. It's a garjian haingel to a fellar, is a good votch, ven you're hard up".[2]

Whenever any group of workers passed into a phase of improving living standards, the acquisition of time-pieces was one of the first things noted by observers. In Radcliffe's well-known account of the golden age of the Lancashire hand-loom weavers in the 1790s the men had "each a watch in his pocket" and every house was "well furnished with a clock in elegant mahogany or fancy case".[3] In Manchester fifty years later the same point caught a reporter's eye:

> No Manchester operative will be without one a moment longer than he can help. You see, here and there, in the better class of houses, one of the old-fashioned, metallic-faced eight-day clocks; but by far the most common article is the little Dutch machine, with its busy pendulum swinging openly and candidly before all the world.[4]

Thirty years later again it was the gold double watch-chain which was the symbol of the successful Lib-Lab trade union leader; and for fifty years of disciplined servitude to work, the enlightened employer gave to his employee an engraved gold watch.

IV

Let us return from the time-piece to the task. Attention to time in labour depends in large degree upon the need for the synchronisation of labour. But in so far as manufacturing industry remained conducted upon a domestic or small workshop scale, without intricate subdivision of processes,

[1] *PP*, 1817, vi, pp. 19, 22.
[2] [C. M. Smith], *The Working Man's Way in the World* (1853), pp. 67-8.
[3] W. Radcliffe, *The Origin of Power Loom Weaving* (Stockport, 1828), p. 167.
[4] *Morning Chronicle*, 25 Oct. 1849. But J. R. Porter, *The Progress of the Nation* (1843), iii, p. 5 still saw the possession of a clock as "the certain indication of prosperity and of personal respectability on the part of the working man".

the degree of synchronisation demanded was slight, and task-orientation was still prevalent.[1] The putting-out system demanded much fetching, carrying, waiting for materials. Bad weather could disrupt not only agriculture, building and transport, but also weaving, where the finished pieces had to be stretched on the tenters to dry. As we get closer to each task, we are surprised to find the multiplicity of subsidiary tasks which the same worker or family group must do in one cottage or workshop. Even in larger workshops men sometimes continued to work at distinct tasks at their own benches or looms, and — except where the fear of the embezzlement of materials imposed stricter supervision — could show some flexibility in coming and going.

Hence we get the characteristic irregularity of labour patterns before the coming of large-scale machine-powered industry. Within the general demands of the week's or fortnight's tasks — the piece of cloth, so many nails or pairs of shoes — the working day might be lengthened or shortened. Moreover, in the early development of manufacturing industry, and of mining, many mixed occupations survived: Cornish tinners who also took a hand in the pilchard fishing; Northern lead-miners who were also smallholders; the village craftsmen who turned their hands to various jobs, in building, carting, joining; the domestic workers who left their work for the harvest; the Pennine small-farmer/weaver.

It is in the nature of such work that accurate and representative time-budgets will not survive. But some extracts from the diary of one methodical farming weaver in 1782-83

---

[1] For some of the problems discussed in this and the following section, see especially Keith Thomas, "Work and Leisure in Pre-Industrial Societies", *Past and Present*, 29 (1964). Also C. Hill, "The Uses of Sabbatarianism", in *Society and Puritanism in Pre-Revolutionary England* (1964); E. S. Furniss, *The Position of the Laborer in a System of Nationalism* (Boston, 1920; reprint 1965); D. C. Coleman, "Labour in the English Economy of the Seventeenth Century", *Econ. Hist. Rev.*, 2nd series, viii (1955-6); S. Pollard, "Factory Discipline in the Industrial Revolution", *Econ. Hist. Rev.*, 2nd series, xvi (1963-4); T. S. Ashton, *An Economic History of England in the Eighteenth Century* (1955), ch. vii; W. E. Moore, *Industrialization and Labor* (New York, 1952); and B. F. Hoselitz and W. E. Moore, *Industrialization and Society* (UNESCO, 1963).

may give us an indication of the variety of tasks. In October 1782 he was still employed in harvesting, and threshing, alongside his weaving. On a rainy day he might weave $8\frac{1}{2}$ or 9 yards; on October 14th he carried his finished piece, and so wove only $4\frac{3}{4}$ yards; on the 23rd he "worked out" till 3 o'clock, wove two yards before sunset, "clouted [mended] my coat in the evening". On December 24th "wove 2 yards before 11 o'clock. I was laying up the coal heap, sweeping the roof and walls of the kitchen and laying the muck [midden?] till 10 o'clock at night." Apart from harvesting and threshing, churning, ditching and gardening, we have these entries:

January 18, 1783:   "I was employed in preparing a Calf stall & Fetching the Tops of three Plain Trees home which grew in the Lane and was that day cut down & sold to john Blagbrough."

January 21st: "Wove $2\frac{3}{4}$ yards the Cow having calved she required much attendance." (On the next day he walked to Halifax to buy medicine for the cow.)

On January 25th he wove 2 yards, walked to a nearby village, and did "sundry jobs about the lathe and in the yard & wrote a letter in the evening". Other occupations include jobbing with a horse and cart, picking cherries, working on a mill dam, attending a Baptist association and a public hanging.[1]

This general irregularity must be placed within the irregular cycle of the working week (and indeed of the working year) which provoked so much lament from moralists and mercantilists in the seventeenth centuries. A

[1] MS diaries of Cornelius Ashworth of Wheatley, in Halifax Ref. Lib.; see also T. W. Hanson, "The Diary of a Grandfather", *Trans. Halifax Antiq. Soc.* (1916). M. Sturge Henderson, *Three Centuries in North Oxfordshire* (Oxford, 1902), pp. 133-46, 103, quotes similar passages (weaving, pig-killing, felling wood, marketing) from the diary of a Charlbury weaver, 1784. It is interesting to compare time-budgets from more primitive peasant economies, e.g. Sol Tax, *Penny Capitalism — a Guatemalan Indian Economy* (Washington, 1953), pp. 104-5; George M. Foster, *A Primitive Mexican Economy* (New York, 1942), pp. 35-8; M. J. Herskovits, *The Economic Life of Primitive Peoples* (New York, 1940), pp. 72-9; Raymond Firth, *Malay Fishermen* (1946), pp. 93-7.

rhyme printed in 1639 gives us a satirical version:

> You know that Munday is Sundayes brother;
> Tuesday is such another;
> Wednesday you must go to Church and pray;
> Thursday is half-holiday;
> On Friday it is too late to begin to spin;
> The Saturday is half-holiday again.[1]

John Houghton, in 1681, gives us the indignant version:

> When the framework knitters or makers of silk stockings had a great price for their work, they have been observed seldom to work on Mondays and Tuesdays but to spend most of their time at the ale-house or nine-pins. . . The weavers, 'tis common with them to be drunk on Monday, have their head-ache on Tuesday, and their tools out of order on Wednesday. As for the shoemakers, they'll rather be hanged than not remember St. Crispin on Monday. . . and it commonly holds as long as they have a penny of money or pennyworth of credit.[2]

The work pattern was one of alternate bouts of intense labour and of idleness, wherever men were in control of their own working lives. (The pattern persists among some self-employed — artists, writers, small farmers, and perhaps also with students — today, and provokes the question whether it is not a "natural" human work-rhythm.) On Monday or Tuesday, according to tradition, the hand-loom went to the slow chant of *Plen-ty of Time, Plen-ty of Time*: On Thursday and Friday, *A day t'lat, A day t'lat.*[3] The temptation to lie in an extra hour in the morning pushed work into the evening, candle-lit hours.[4] There are few trades which are not described as honouring Saint Monday: shoemakers, tailors, colliers, printing workers, potters, weavers, hosiery workers, cutlers, all Cockneys. Despite the full employment

---

[1] *Divers Crab-Tree Lectures* (1639), p. 126, cited in John Brand, *Observations on Popular Antiquities* (1813), i, pp. 459-60. H. Bourne, *Antiquitates Vulgares* (Newcastle, 1725), pp. 115 ff. declares that on Saturday afternoons in country places and villages "the Labours of the Plough Ceast, and Refreshment and Ease are over all the Village".

[2] J. Houghton, *Collection of Letters* (1683), p. 177, cited in Furniss, *op. cit.*, p. 121.

[3] Hanson, *op. cit.*, p. 234.

[4] J. Clayton, *Friendly Advice to the Poor* (Manchester, 1755), p. 36.

of many London trades during the Napoleonic Wars, a
witness complained that "we see Saint Monday so religiously
kept in this great city. . . in general followed by a Saint
Tuesday also".[1] If we are to believe "The Jovial Cutlers", a
Sheffield song of the late eighteenth century, its observance
was not without domestic tension:

> How upon a good Saint Monday,
> Sitting by the smithy fire,
> Telling what's been done o't Sunday,
> And in cheerful mirth conspire,
>> Soon I hear the trap-door rise up,
>> On the ladder stands my wife:
>> "Damn thee, Jack, I'll dust they eyes up,
>> Thou leads a plaguy drunken life;
>> Here thou sits instead of working,
>> Wi' thy pitcher on thy knee;
>> Curse thee, thou'd be always lurking.
>> And I may slave myself for thee".

The wife proceeds, speaking "with motion quicker/Than my
boring stick at a Friday's pace", to demonstrate effective
consumer demand:

> "See thee, look what stays I've gotten,
> See thee, what a pair o' shoes;
> Gown and petticoat half rotten,
> Ne'er a whole stitch in my hose. . ."

and to serve notice of a general strike:

> "Thou knows I hate to broil and quarrel,
> But I've neither soap nor tea;
> Od burn thee, Jack, forsake thy barrel,
> Or nevermore thou'st lie wi' me".[2]

---

[1] *Report of the Trial of Alexander Wadsworth against Peter Laurie*
(1811), p. 21. The complaint is particularly directed against the Saddlers.

[2] *The Songs of Joseph Mather* (Sheffield, 1862), pp. 88-90. The theme
appears to have been popular with ballad-makers. A Birmingham example,
"Fuddling Day, or Saint Monday" (for which I am indebted to the late
Charles Parker) runs:

> Saint Monday brings more ills about,
>> For when the money's spent,
> The children's clothes go up the spout,
>> Which causes discontent;
> And when at night he staggers home,
>> He knows not what to say,
> A fool is more a man than he
>> Upon a fuddling day.

Saint Monday, indeed, appears to have been honoured almost universally wherever small-scale, domestic, and out-work industries existed; was generally found in the pits; and sometimes continued in manufacturing and heavy industry.[1] It was perpetuated, in England, into the nineteenth — and, indeed, into the twentieth[2] — century for complex economic and social reasons. In some trades, the small masters themselves accepted the institution, and employed Monday in taking-in or giving-out work. In Sheffield, where the cutlers had for centuries tenaciously honoured the Saint, it had become "a settled habit and custom" which the steel-mills themselves honoured (1874):

> This Monday idleness is, in some cases, enforced by the fact that Monday is the day that is taken for repairs to the machinery of the great steelworks.[3]

Where the custom was deeply-established, Monday was the day set aside for marketing and personal business. Also, as Duveau suggests of French workers, "le dimanche est le jour de la famille, le lundi celui de l'amitié"; and as the

---

[1] It was honoured by Mexican weavers in 1800: see Jan Bazant, "Evolution of the textile industry of Puebla, 1544-1845", *Comparative Studies in Society and History*, viii (1964), p. 65. Valuable accounts of the custom in France in the 1850s and 1860s are in George Duveau, *La Vie Ouvrière en France sous le Second Empire* (Paris, 1946), pp. 242-8, and P. Pierrard, *La Vie Ouvrière à Lille sous le Second Empire* (Paris, 1965), pp. 165-6. Edward Young, conducting a survey of labour conditions in Europe, with the assistance of U.S. consuls, mentions the custom in France, Belgium, Prussia, Stockholm, etc. in the 1870s: E. Young, *Labour in Europe and America* (Washington, 1875), pp. 576, 661, 674, 685, etc.

[2] Notably in the pits. An old Yorkshire miner informs me that in his youth it was a custom on a bright Monday morning to toss a coin in order to decide whether or not to work. I have also been told that "Saint Monday" is still honoured in its pristine purity by a few coopers in Burton-on-Trent.

[3] E. Young, *op. cit.*, pp. 408-9 (Report of U.S. Consul). Similarly, in some mining districts, "Pay Monday" was recognised by the employers and the pits were only kept open for repairs: on Monday, only "dead work is going on", *Report of the Select Committee on the Scarcity and Dearness of Coal, PP*, 1873, x, QQ 177, 201-7.

nineteenth century advanced, its celebration was something of a privilege of status of the better-paid artisan.[1]

It is, in fact, in an account by "An Old Potter" published as late as 1903 that we have some of the most perceptive observations on the irregular work-rhythms which continued on the older pot-banks until the mid-century. The potters (in the 1830s and 1840s) "had a devout regard for Saint Monday". Although the custom of annual hiring prevailed, the actual weekly earnings were at piece-rates, the skilled male potters employing the children, and working, with little supervision, at their own pace. The children and women came to work on Monday and Tuesday, but a "holiday feeling" prevailed and the day's work was shorter than usual, since the potters were away a good part of the time, drinking their earnings of the previous week. The children, however, had to prepare work for the potter (for example, handles for pots which he would throw), and all suffered from the exceptionally long hours (fourteen and sometimes sixteen hours a day) which were worked from Wednesday to Saturday:

> I have since thought that but for the reliefs at the beginning of the week for the women and boys all through the pot-works, the deadly stress of the last four days could not have been maintained.

"An Old Potter", a Methodist lay preacher of Liberal-Radical views, saw these customs (which he deplored) as a consequence of the lack of mechanisation of the pot-banks; and he urged that the same indiscipline in daily work influenced the entire way of life and the working-class organisations of the Potteries. "Machinery means discipline in industrial operations":

> If a steam-engine had started every Monday morning at six o'clock, the workers would have been disciplined to the habit of regular and continuous industry. . . I have noticed, too, that machinery seems to lead to habits of calculation. The Pottery workers were woefully deficient in this matter; they lived like children, without any

---

[1] Duveau, op. cit., p. 247. "A Journeyman Engineer" (T. Wright) devotes a whole chapter to "Saint Monday" in his Some Habits and Customs of the Working Classes (1867), esp. pp. 112-6, under the mistaken impression that the institution was "comparatively recent", and consequent upon steam power giving rise to "a numerous body of highly skilled and highly paid workmen" — notably engineers!

calculating forecast of their work or its result. In some of the more northern counties this habit of calculation has made them keenly shrewd in many conspicuous ways. Their great co-operative societies would never have arisen to such immense and fruitful development but for the calculating induced by the use of machinery. A machine worked so many hours in the week would produce so much length of yarn or cloth. Minutes were felt to be factors in these results, whereas in the Potteries hours, or even days at times, were hardly felt to be such factors. There were always the mornings and nights of the last days of the week, and these were always trusted to make up the loss of the week's early neglect.[1]

This irregular working rhythm is commonly associated with heavy week-end drinking: Saint Monday is a target in many Victorian temperance tracts. But even the most sober and self-disciplined artisan might feel the necessity for such alternations. "I know not how to describe the sickening aversion which at times steals over the working man and utterly disables him for a longer or shorter period, from following his usual occupation", Francis Place wrote in 1829; and he added a footnote of personal testimony:

> For nearly six years, whilst working, when I had work to do, from twelve to eighteen hours a day, when no longer able, from the cause mentioned, to continue working, I used to run from it, and go as rapidly as I could to Highgate, Hampstead, Muswell-hill, or Norwood, and then "return to my vomit". . . This is the case with every workman I have ever known; and in proportion as a man's case is hopeless will such fits more frequently occur and be of longer duration.[2]

We may, finally, note that the irregularity of working day and week were framed, until the first decades of the

---

[1] "An Old Potter", *When I was a Child* (1903), pp. 16, 47-9, 52-4, 57-8, 71, 74-5, 81, 185-6, 191. Mr W. Sokol, of the University of Wisconsin, has directed my attention to many cases reported in the *Staffordshire Potteries Telegraph* in 1853-4, where the employers succeeded in fining or imprisoning workers who neglected work, often on Mondays and Tuesdays. These actions were taken on the pretext of breach of contract (the annual hiring), for which see Daphne Simon, "Master and Servant", in *Democracy and the Labour Movement*, ed. J. Saville (1954). Despite this campaign of prosecutions, the custom of keeping Saint Monday is still noted in the *Report of the Children's Employment Commission, PP*, 1863, xviii, pp. xxvii-xxviii.

[2] F. Place, *Improvement of the Working People* (1834), pp. 13-15: Brit. Mus. Add MS 27825. See also John Wade, *History of the Middle and Working Classes*, 3rd edn. (1835), pp. 124-5.

nineteenth century, within the larger irregularity of the working year, punctuated by its traditional holidays, and fairs. Still, despite the triumph of the Sabbath over the ancient saints' days in the seventeenth century,[1] the people clung tenaciously to their customary wakes and feasts, and may even have enlarged them both in vigour and extent.[2]

How far can this argument be extended from manufacturing industry to the rural labourers? On the face of it, there would seem to be unrelenting daily and weekly labour here: the field labourer had no Saint Monday. But a close discrimination of different work-situations is still required. The eighteenth- (and nineteenth-) century village had its own self-employed artisans, as well as many employed on irregular task work.[3] Moreover, in the unenclosed countryside, the classical case against open field and common was in its inefficiency and wastefulness of time, for the small farmer or cottager:

> . . . if you offer them work, they will tell you that they must go to look up their sheep, cut furzes, get their cow out of the pound, or, perhaps, say they must take their horse to be shod, that he may carry them to a horse-race or cricket-match (Arbuthnot, 1773.)

> In sauntering after his cattle, he acquires a habit of indolence. Quarter, half, and occasionally whole days are imperceptibly lost. Day labour becomes disgusting. . . (Report on Somerset, 1795.)

> Whenalabourerbecomespossessedofmorelandthanheandhis family can cultivate in the evenings. . . the farmer can no longer depend on him for constant work. . . (*Commercial & Agricultural Magazine*, 1800.)[4]

[1] See Hill, *op. cit.*
[2] Clayton, *op. cit.*, p. 13, claimed that "common custom has established so many Holy-days, that few of our manufacturing work-folks are closely and regularly employed above two-third parts of their time". See also Furniss, *op. cit.*, pp. 44-5, and the abstract of my paper in the *Bulletin of the Society for the Study of Labour History*, 9 (1964).
[3] "We have four or five little farmers. . . we have a bricklayer, a carpenter, a blacksmith, and a miller, all of whom. . . are in a very frequent habit of drinking the King's health. . . Their employment is unequal; sometimes they are full of business, and sometimes they have none; generally they have many leisure hours, because. . . the hardest part [of their work] devolves to some men whom they hire. . .", "A Farmer", describing his own village (see note 3 on p. 380), in 1798.
[4] Cited in J. L. and B. Hammond, *The Village Labourer* (1920), p. 13; E. P. Thompson, *The Making of the English Working Class* (1963), p. 220.

To this we should add the frequent complaints of agricultural improvers as to the time wasted, both at seasonal fairs, and (before the arrival of the village shop) on weekly market days.[1]

The farm servant, or the regular wage-earning field labourer, who worked, unremittingly, the full statute hours or longer, who had no common rights or land, and who (if not living-in) lived in a tied cottage, was undoubtedly subject to an intense labour discipline, whether in the seventeenth or the nineteenth century. The day of a ploughman (living-in) was described with relish by Markham in 1636:

> . . . the Plowman shall rise before four of the clock in the morning, and after thanks given to God for his rest, & prayer for the success of his labours, he shall go into his stable. . .

After cleansing the stable, grooming his horses, feeding them, and preparing his tackle, he might breakfast (6-6.30 a.m.), he should plough until 2 p.m. or 3 p.m., take half an hour for dinner; attend to his horses etc. until 6.30 p.m., when he might come in for supper:

> . . . and after supper, hee shall either by the fire side mend shooes both for himselfe and their Family, or beat and knock Hemp or Flax, or picke and stamp Apples or Crabs, for Cyder or Verdjuyce, or else grind malt on the quernes, pick candle rushes, or doe some Husbandly office within doors till it be full eight a clock. . .

Then he must once again attend to his cattle and ("giving God thanks for benefits received that day") he might retire.[2]

Even so, we are entitled to show a certain scepticism. There are obvious difficulties in the nature of the occupation. Ploughing is not an all-the-year-round task. Hours and tasks must fluctuate with the weather. The horses (if not the men) must be rested. There is the difficulty of supervision: Robert Loder's accounts indicate that servants (when out of sight) were not always employed upon their knees thanking God for their benefits: "men can worke yf they list & soe they can

[1] See e.g. *Annals of Agriculture*, xxvi (1796), p. 370 n.

[2] G. Markham, *The Inrichment of the Weald of Kent*, 10th edn. (1660), pp. 115-7.

loyter".[1] The farmer himself must work exceptional hours if
he was to keep all his labourers always employed.[2] And the
farm servant could assert his annual right to move on if he
disliked his employment.

Thus enclosure and agricultural improvement were both,
in some sense, concerned with the efficient husbandry of the
time of the labour-force. Enclosure and the growing labour-
surplus at the end of the eighteenth century tightened the
screw for those who were in regular employment; they were
faced with the alternatives of partial employment and the
poor law, or submission to a more exacting labour discipline.
It is a question, not of new techniques, but of a greater sense
of time-thrift among the improving capitalist employers. This
reveals itself in the debate between advocates of regularly-
employed wage-labour and advocates of "taken-work" (i.e.
labourers employed for particular tasks at piece-rates). In the
1790s Sir Mordaunt Martin censured recourse to taken-work

> which people agree to, to save themselves the trouble of watching their
> workmen: the consequence is, the work is ill done, the workmen boast
> at the ale-house what they can spend in "a waste against the wall", and
> make men at moderate wages discontented.

"A Farmer" countered with the argument that taken-work
and regular wage-labour might be judiciously intermixed:

> Two labourers engage to cut down a piece of grass at two shillings or
> half-a-crown an acre; I send, with their scythes, two of my domestic
> farm-servants into the field; I can depend upon it, that their
> companions will keep them up to their work; and thus I gain. . . the
> same additional hours of labour from my domestic servants, which are
> voluntarily devoted to it by my hired servants.[3]

---

[1] Attempting to account for a deficiency in his stocks of wheat in 1617,
Loder notes: "What should be the cause herof I know not, but it was in
that yeare when R. Pearce & Alce were my servants, & then in great love (as
it appeared too well) whether he gave it my horses. . . or how it went away,
God onely knoweth". *Robert Loder's Farm Accounts*, ed. G. E. Fussell
(Camden Society, 3rd series, liii, 1936), pp. 59, 127.

[2] For an account of an active farmer's day, see William Howitt,
Rural Life of England (1862), pp. 110-1.

[3] Sir Mordaunt Martin in *Bath and West and Southern Counties
Society, Letters and Papers* (Bath, 1795), vii, p. 109; "A Farmer",
"Observations on Taken-Work and Labour", *Monthly Magazine*, Sept.
1798, May 1799.

In the nineteenth century the debate was largely resolved in favour of weekly wage-labour, supplemented by task-work as occasion rose. The Wiltshire labourer's day, as described by Richard Jefferies in the 1870s, was scarcely less long than that described by Markham. Perhaps in resistance to this unremitting toil he was distinguished by the "clumsiness of his walk" and "the deadened slowness which seems to pervade everything he does".[1]

The most arduous and prolonged work of all was that of the labourer's wife in the rural economy. One part of this — especially the care of infants — was the most task-orientated of all. Another part was in the fields, from which she must return to renewed domestic tasks. As Mary Collier complained in a sharp rejoinder to Stephen Duck:

> . . . when we Home are come,
> Alas! we find our Work but just begun;
> So many Things for our Attendance call,
> Has we ten Hands, we could employ them all.
> Our Children put to Bed, with greatest Care
> We all Things for your coming Home prepare:
> You sup, and go to Bed without delay,
> And rest yourselves till the ensuing day;
> While we, alas! but little Sleep can have,
> Because our froward Children cry and rave. . .
>
> In ev'ry Work (we) take our proper Share;
> And from the Time that Harvest doth begin
> Until the Corn be cut and carry'd in,
> Our Toil and Labour's daily so extreme,
> That we have hardly ever *Time to dream.*[2]

Such hours were endurable only because one part of the work, with the children and in the home, disclosed itself as necessary and inevitable, rather than as an external imposition. This remains true to this day, and, despite school times and television times, the rhythms of women's work in the home are not wholly attuned to the measurement of the clock. The mother of young children has an imperfect sense

[1] J. R. Jefferies, *The Toilers of the Field* (1892), pp. 84-8, 211-2.

[2] Mary Collier, now a Washer-woman, at Petersfield in Hampshire, *The Woman's Labour: an Epistle to Mr. Stephen Duck; in Answer to his late Poem, called The Thresher's Labour* (1739), pp. 10-11, reprinted (1989).

of time and attends to other human tides. She has not yet altogether moved out of the conventions of "pre-industrial" society.

V

I have placed "pre-industrial" in inverted commas: and for a reason. It is true that the transition to mature industrial society demands analysis in sociological as well as economic terms. Concepts such as "time-preference" and the "backward sloping labour supply curve" are, too often, cumbersome attempts to find economic terms to describe sociological problems. But, equally, the attempt to provide simple models for one single, supposedly-neutral, technologically-determined, process known as "industrialisation" is also suspect.[1] It is not only that the highly-developed and technically-alert manufacturing industries (and the way of life supported by them) of France or England in the eighteenth century can only by semantic torture be described as "pre-industrial". (And such a description opens the door to endless false analogies between societies at greatly differing economic levels.) It is also that there has never been any single type of "the transition". The stress of the transition falls upon the whole culture: resistance to change and assent to change arise from the whole culture. And this culture expresses the systems of power, property-relations, religious institutions, etc., inattention to which merely flattens phenomena and trivialises analysis. Above all, the transition is not to "industrialism" *tout court* but to industrial capitalism or (in the twentieth century) to alternative systems whose features are still indistinct. What we are examining here are not only changes in manufacturing technique which demand greater synchronisation of labour and a greater exactitude in time-routines in *any* society; but also these changes as they were lived through in the society of nascent industrial capitalism. We are concerned simultaneously with time-sense in its technological conditioning, and with time-measurement as a means of labour exploitation.

[1] See the valuable critique by André Gunder Frank, "Sociology of Development and Underdevelopment of Sociology", *Catalyst* (Buffalo, Summer 1967).

There are reasons why the transition was peculiarly protracted and fraught with conflict in England: among those which are often noted, England's was the first industrial revolution, and there were no Cadillacs, steel mills, or television sets to serve as demonstrations as to the object of the operation. Moreover, the preliminaries to the industrial revolution were so long that, in the manufacturing districts in the early eighteenth century, a vigorous and licensed popular culture had evolved, which the propagandists of discipline regarded with dismay. Josiah Tucker, the dean of Gloucester, declared in 1745 that "the *lower* class of people" were utterly degenerated. Foreigners (he sermonised) found "the *common people* of our *populous cities* to be the most *abandoned*, and *licentious* wretches on earth":

> Such brutality and insolence, such debauchery and extravagance, such idleness, irreligion, cursing and swearing, and contempt of all rule and authority. . . Our people are *drunk with the cup of liberty*.[1]

The irregular labour rhythms described in the previous section help us to understand the severity of mercantilist doctrines as to the necessity for holding down wages as a preventative against idleness, and it would seem to be not until the second half of the eighteenth century that "normal" capitalist wage incentives begin to become widely effective.[2] The confrontations over discipline have already been examined by others.[3] My intention here is to touch upon several points which concern time-discipline more particularly. The first is found in the extraordinary Law Book of the Crowley Iron Works. Here, at the very birth of the large-scale unit in manufacturing industry, the old autocrat, Crowley, found it necessary to design an entire civil and penal code, running to more than 100,000 words, to govern and regulate his refractory labour-force. The preambles to Orders Number 40

---

[1] J. Tucker, *Six Sermons* (Bristol, 1772), pp. 70-1.

[2] The change is perhaps signalled at the same time in the ideology of the more enlightened employers: see A. W. Coats, "Changing attitudes to labour in the mid-eighteenth century", *Econ. Hist. Rev.*, 2nd series, xi (1958-9).

[3] See Pollard, *op. cit.*; N. McKendrick, "Josiah Wedgwood and Factory Discipline", *Hist. Journal*, iv (1961); also Thompson, *op. cit.*, pp. 356-74.

(the Warden at the Mill) and 103 (Monitor) strike the prevailing note of morally-righteous invigilation. From Order 40:

I having by sundry people working by the day with the connivence of the clerks been horribly cheated and paid for much more time than in good conscience I ought and such hath been the baseness & treachery of sundry clerks that they have concealed the sloath & negligence of those paid by the day. . .

And from Order 103:

Some have pretended a sort of right to loyter, thinking by their readiness and ability to do sufficient in less time than others. Others have been so foolish to think bare attendance without being employed in business is sufficient. . . Others so impudent as to glory in their villany and upbrade others for their diligence. . .

To the end that sloath and villany should be detected and the just and diligent rewarded, I have thought meet to create an account of time by a Monitor, and do order and it is hereby ordered and declared from 5 to 8 and from 7 to 10 is fifteen hours, out of which take $1\frac{1}{2}$ for breakfast, dinner, etc. There will then be thirteen hours and a half neat service. . .

This service must be calculated "after all deductions for being at taverns, alehouses, coffee houses, breakfast, dinner, playing, sleeping, smoaking, singing, reading of news history, quarelling, contention, disputes or anything foreign to my business, any way loytering".

The Monitor and Warden of the Mill were ordered to keep for each day employee a time-sheet, entered to the minute, with "Come" and "Run". In the Monitor's Order, verse 31 (a later addition) declares:

And whereas I have been informed that sundry clerks have been so unjust as to reckon by clocks going the fastest and the bell ringing before the hour for their going from business, and clocks going too slow and the bell ringing after the hour for their coming to business, and those two black traitors Fowell and Skellerne have knowingly allowed the same; it is therefore ordered that no person upon the account doth reckon by any other clock, bell, watch or dyall but the Monitor's, which clock is never to be altered but by the clock-keeper. . .

The Warden of the Mill was ordered to keep the watch "so locked up that it may not be in the power of any person to alter the same". His duties also were defined in verse 8:

Every morning at 5 a clock the Warden is to ring the bell for beginning to work, at eight a clock for breakfast, at half an hour after for work again, at twelve a clock for dinner, at one to work and at eight to ring for leaving work and all to be lock'd up.

His book of the account of time was to be delivered in every Tuesday with the following affidavit:

This account of time is done without favour or affection, ill-will or hatred, & do really believe the persons above mentioned have worked in the service of John Crowley Esq the hours above charged.[1]

We are entering here, already in 1700, the familiar landscape of disciplined industrial capitalism, with the time-sheet, the time-keeper, the informers and the fines. Some seventy years later the same discipline was to be imposed in the early cotton mills (although the machinery itself was a powerful supplement to the time-keeper). Lacking the aid of machinery to regulate the pace of work on the pot-bank, that supposedly-formidable disciplinarian, Josiah Wedgwood, was reduced to enforcing discipline upon the potters in surprisingly muted terms. The duties of the Clerk of the Manufactory were:

To be at the works the first in the morning, & settle the people to their business as they come in, — to encourage those who come regularly to their time, letting them know that their regularity is properly noticed, & distinguishing them by repeated marks of approbation, from the less orderly part of the workpeople, by presents or other marks suitable to their ages, &c.

Those who come later than the hour appointed should be noticed, and if after repeated marks of disapprobation they do not come in due time, an account of the time they are deficient in should be taken, and so much of their wages stopt as the time comes to if they work by wages, and if they work by the piece they should after frequent notice be sent back to breakfast-time.[2]

---

[1] Order 103 is reproduced in full in *The Law Book of the Crowley Ironworks*, ed. M. W. Flinn (Surtees Society, clxvii, 1957). See also Law Number 16, "Reckonings". Order Number 40 is in the "Law Book", Brit. Lib. Add MS 34555.

[2] MS instructions, *circa* 1780, in Wedgwood MSS (Barlaston), 26.19114.

These regulations were later tightened somewhat:

> Any of the workmen forceing their way through the Lodge after the
> time alow'd by the Master forfeits 2/-d.[1]

and McKendrick has shown how Wedgwood wrestled with
the problem of Etruria and introduced the first recorded
system of clocking-in.[2] But it would seem that once the
strong presence of Josiah himself was withdrawn the
incorrigible potters returned to many of their older ways.

It is too easy, however, to see this only as a matter of
factory or workshop discipline, and we may glance briefly at
the attempt to impose "time-thrift" in the domestic manufacturing districts, and its impingement upon social and
domestic life. Almost all that the masters *wished* to see
imposed may be found in the bounds of a single pamphlet,
the Rev. J. Clayton's *Friendly Advice to the Poor*, "written
and publish'd at the Request of the late and present Officers
of the Town of Manchester" in 1755. "If the *sluggard hides
his hands* in his bosom, rather than applies them to work; if
he spends his Time in sauntring, impairs his Constitution by
Laziness, and dulls his Spirit by Indolence. . ." then he can
expect only poverty as his reward. The labourer must not
loiter idly in the market-place or waste time in marketing.
Clayton complains that "the Churches and Streets [are]
crowded with Numbers of Spectators" at weddings and
funerals, "who in spight of the Miseries of their Starving
Condition. . . make no Scruple of wasting the best Hours in
the Day, for the sake of gazing. . .". The tea-table is "this
shameful devourer of Time and Money". So also are wakes
and holidays and the annual feasts of friendly societies. So
also is "that slothful spending the Morning in Bed":

[1] "Some regulations and rules for this manufactory more than 30 years
back", dated *circa* 1810, in Wedgwood MSS (Keele University),
4045.5.

[2] A "tell-tale" clock is preserved at Barlaston, but these "tell-tales"
(manufactured by John Whitehurst of Derby from about 1750) served only
to ensure the regular patrol and attendance of night-watchmen, etc. The
first printing time-recorders were made by Bundy in the U.S.A. in 1885.
Ward, *op. cit.*, p. 49; also T. Thomson's *Annals of Philosophy*, vi (1815),
pp. 418-9 and vii (1816), p. 160; Charles Babbage, *On the Economy of
Machinery and Manufacturers* (1835), pp. 28, 40; Bruton, *op. cit.*,
pp. 95-6.

The necessity of early rising would reduce the poor to a necessity of going to Bed betime; and thereby prevent the Danger of Midnight revels.

Early rising would also "introduce an exact Regularity into their Families, a wonderful Order into their Oeconomy".

The catalogue is familiar, and might equally well be taken from Baxter in the previous century. If we can trust Bamford's *Early Days*, Clayton failed to make many converts from their old way of life among the weavers. Nevertheless, the long dawn chorus of moralists is prelude to the quite sharp attack upon popular customs, sports, and holidays which was made in the last years of the eighteenth century and the first years of the nineteenth.

One other non-industrial institution lay to hand which might be used to inculcate "time-thrift": the school. Clayton complained that the streets of Manchester were full of "idle ragged children; who are not only losing their Time, but learning habits of gaming", etc. He praised charity schools as teaching Industry, Frugality, Order and Regularity: "the Scholars here are obliged to rise betimes and to observe Hours with great Punctuality".[1] William Temple, when advocating, in 1770, that poor children be sent at the age of four to work-houses where they should be employed in manufactures and given two hours' schooling a day, was explicit about the socialising influence of the process:

There is considerable use in their being, somehow or other, constantly employed at least twelve hours a day, whether they earn their living or not; for by these means, we hope that the rising generation will be so habituated to constant employment that it would at length prove agreeable and entertaining to them. . .[2]

Powell, in 1772, also saw education as a training in the "habit of industry"; by the time the child reached six or seven it should become "habituated, not to say naturalized to Labour and Fatigue".[3] The Rev. William Turner, writing from Newcastle in 1786, recommended Raikes' schools as "a spectacle of order and regularity", and quoted a manufacturer of hemp and flax in Gloucester as affirming that the

[1] Clayton, *loc. cit.*, pp. 19, 42-3.
[2] Cited in Furniss, *op. cit.*, p. 114.
[3] Anon. [Powell], *A View of Real Grievances* (1772), p. 90.

schools had effected an extraordinary change: "they are. . . become more tractable and obedient, and less quarrelsome and revengeful".[1] Exhortations to punctuality and regularity are written into the rules of all the early schools:

> Every scholar must be in the school-room on Sundays, at nine o'clock in the morning, and at half-past one in the afternoon, or she shall lose her place the next Sunday, and walk last.[2]

Once within the school gates, the child entered the new universe of disciplined time. At the Methodist Sunday Schools in York the teachers were fined for unpunctuality. The first rule to be learned by the scholars was:

> I am to be present at the School. . . a few minutes before half-past nine o'clock. . .

Once in attendance, they were under military rule:

> The Superintendent shall again ring, — when, on a motion of his hand, the whole School rise at once from their seats; — on a second motion, the Scholars turn; — on a third, slowly and silently move to the place appointed to repeat their lessons, — he then pronounces the word "Begin". . .[3]

The onslaught, from so many directions, upon the people's old working habits was not, of course, uncontested. In the first stage, we find simple resistance.[4] But, in the next stage, as the new time-discipline is imposed, so the workers begin to fight, not against time, but about it. The evidence here is not wholly clear. But in the better-organised artisan trades, especially in London, there is no doubt that hours were progressively shortened in the eighteenth century as combination advanced. Lipson cites the case of the London tailors

[1] W. Turner, *Sunday Schools Recommended* (Newcastle, 1786), pp. 23, 42.

[2] *Rules for the Methodist School of Industry at Pocklington, for the instruction of Poor Girls in Reading, Sewing, Knitting, and Marking* (York, 1819), p. 12.

[3] *Rules for the Government, Superintendence, and Teaching of the Wesleyan Methodist Sunday Schools* (York, 1833). See also Harold Silver, *The Concept of Popular Education* (1965), pp. 32-42; David Owen, *English Philanthrophy, 1660-1960* (Cambridge, Mass., 1965), pp. 23-7.

[4] The best account of the employers' problem is in S. Pollard, *The Genesis of Modern Management* (1965), ch. v, "The Adaptation of the Labour Force".

whose hours were shortened in 1721, and again in 1768: on both occasions the mid-day intervals allowed for dinner and drinking were also shortened — the day was compressed.[1] By the end of the eighteenth century there is some evidence that some favoured trades had gained something like a ten-hour day.

Such a situation could only persist in exceptional trades and in a favourable labour market. A reference in a pamphlet of 1827 to "the English system of working from 6 o'clock in the morning to 6 in the evening"[2] may be a more reliable indication of the general expectation as to hours of the mechanic and artisan outside London in the 1820s. In the dishonourable trades and outwork industries hours (when work was available) were probably moving the other way.

It was exactly in those industries — the textile mills and the engineering workshops — where the new time-discipline was most rigorously imposed that the contest over time became more intense. At first some of the worst masters attempted to expropriate the workers of all knowledge of time. "I worked at Mr. Braid's mill", declared one witness:

> There we worked as long as we could see in summer time, and I could not say at what hour it was that we stopped. There was nobody but the master and the master's son who had a watch, and we did not know the time. There was one man who had a watch. . . It was taken from him and given into the master's custody because he had told the men the time of day. . .[3]

A Dundee witness offers much the same evidence:

> . . . in reality there were no regular hours: masters and managers did with us as they liked. The clocks at the factories were often put forward in the morning and back at night, and instead of being instruments for the measurement of time, they were used as cloaks for cheatery and oppression. Though this was known amongst the hands, all were afraid

---

[1] E. Lipson, *The Economic History of England*, 6th edn. (1956), iii, pp. 404-6. See e.g. J. L. Ferri, *Londres et les Anglais* (Paris, An xii), pp. 163-4. Some of the evidence as to hours is discussed in G. Langenfelt, *The Historic Origin of the Eight Hours Day* (Stockholm, 1954).

[2] *A Letter on the Present State of the Labouring Classes in America*, by an intelligent Emigrant at Philadelphia (Bury, 1827).

[3] Alfred [S. Kydd], *History of the Factory Movement*. . . (1857), i, p. 283, quoted in P. Mantoux, *The Industrial Revolution in the Eighteenth Century* (1948), p. 427.

to speak, and a workman then was afraid to carry a watch, as it was no uncommon event to dismiss any one who presumed to know too much about the science of horology.[1]

Petty devices were used to shorten the dinner hour and to lengthen the day. "Every manufacturer wants to be a gentleman at once", said a witness before Sadler's Committee:

and they want to nip every corner that they can, so that the bell will ring to leave off when it is half a minute past time, and they will have them in about two minutes before time. . . If the clock is as it used to be, the minute hand is at the weight, so that as soon as it passes the point of gravity, it drops three minutes all at once, so that it leaves them only twenty-seven minutes, instead of thirty.[2]

A strike-placard of about the same period from Todmorden put it more bluntly: "if that piece of dirty suet, 'old Robertshaw's engine-tenter', do not mind his own business, and let ours alone, we will shortly ask him how long it is since he received a gill of ale for running 10 minutes over time".[3] The first generation of factory workers were taught by their masters the importance of time; the second generation formed their short-time committees in the ten-hour movement; the third generation struck for overtime or time-and-a-half. They had accepted the categories of their employers and learned to fight back within them. They had learned their lesson, that time is money, only too well.[4]

VI

We have seen, so far, something of the external pressures which enforced this discipline. But what of the internalisation of this discipline? How far was it imposed, how far assumed? We should, perhaps, turn the problem around once again, and place it within the evolution of the Puritan ethic. One cannot claim that there was anything radically new in the

[1] Anon., *Chapters in the Life of a Dundee Factory Boy* (Dundee, 1887), p. 10.

[2] *PP*, 1831-32, xv, pp. 177-8. See also the example from the Factory Commission (1833), in Mantoux, *op. cit.*, p. 427.

[3] Placard in my possession.

[4] For a discussion of the next stage, when the workers had learned "the rules of the game", see E. J. Hobsbawm, *Labouring Men* (1964), ch. xvii, "Custom, Wages and Work-load".

preaching of industry or in the moral critique of idleness. But there is perhaps a new insistence, a firmer accent, as those moralists who had accepted this new discipline for themselves enjoined it upon the working people. Long before the pocket watch had come within the reach of the artisan, Baxter and his fellows were offering to each man his own interior moral time-piece.[1] Thus Baxter, in his *Christian Directory*, plays many variations on the theme of Redeeming the Time: "use wholly in the way of duty". The imagery of time as currency is strongly marked, but Baxter would seem to have an audience of merchants and of tradesmen in his mind's eye:

> Remember how gainful the Redeeming of Time is. . . in Merchandize, or any trading; in husbandry or any gaining course, we use to say of a man that hath grown rich by it, that he hath made use of his Time.[2]

Oliver Heywood, in *Youth's Monitor* (1689), is addressing the same audience:

> Observe exchange-time, look to your markets; there are some special seasons, that will favour you in expediting your business with facility and success; there are nicks of time, in which, if your actions fall, they may set you forward apace: seasons of doing or receiving good last not always; the fair continues not all the year. . .[3]

The moral rhetoric passes swiftly between two poles. On the one hand, apostrophes to the brevity of the mortal span, when placed beside the certainty of Judgement. Thus Heywood's *Meetness for Heaven* (1690):

> Time lasts not, but floats away apace; but what is everlasting depends upon it. In this world we either win or lose eternal felicity. The great weight of eternity hangs on the small and brittle thread of life. . . This is our working day, our market time. . . O Sirs, sleep now, and awake in hell, whence there is no redemption.

---

[1] John Preston used the image of clock-work in 1628: "In this curious clocke-worke of religion, every pin and wheel that is amise distempers all": *Sermons Preached before His Majestie* (1630), p. 18. Cf. R. Baxter, *A Christian Directory* (1673), i, p. 285: "A wise and well skilled Christian should bring his matters into such order, that every ordinary duty should know his place, and all should be. . . as the parts of a Clock or other Engine, which must be all conjunct, and each right placed".

[2] *Ibid.*, i, pp. 274-5, 277.

[3] *The Whole Works of the Rev. Oliver Heywood* (Idle, 1826), v, p. 575.

Or, from *Youth's Monitor* again: time "is too precious a commodity to be undervalued. . . This is the golden chain on which hangs a massy eternity; the loss of time is unsufferable, because irrecoverable".[1] Or from Baxter's *Directory*:

> O where are the brains of those men, and of what metal are their hardened hearts made, that can idle and play away that Time, that little Time, that only Time, which is given them for the everlasting saving of their souls?[2]

On the other hand, we have the bluntest and most mundane admonitions on the husbandry of time. Thus Baxter, in *The Poor Man's Family Book* advises: "Let the time of your Sleep be so much only as health requireth; For precious time is not to be wasted in unnecessary sluggishness": "quickly dress you"; "and follow your labours with constant diligence".[3] Both traditions were extended, by way of Law's *Serious Call*, to John Wesley. The very name of "the Methodists" emphasises this husbandry of time. In Wesley also we have these two extremes — the jabbing at the nerve of mortality, the practical homily. It was the first (and not hell-fire terrors) which sometimes gave an hysterical edge to his sermons, and brought converts to a sudden sense of sin. He also continues the time-as-currency imagery, but less explicitly as merchant or market-time:

> See that ye walk circumspectly, says the Apostle. . . redeeming the time; saving all the time you can for the best purposes; buying up every fleeting moment out of the hands of sin and Satan, out of the hands of sloth, ease, pleasure, worldly business. . .

Wesley, who never spared himself, and until the age of eighty rose every day at 4 a.m. (he ordered that the boys at Kingswood School must do the same), published in 1786 as a tract his sermon on *The Duty and Advantage of Early Rising*: "By *soaking*. . . so long between warm sheets, the flesh is as it were parboiled, and becomes soft and flabby. The nerves, in the mean time, are quite unstrung". This reminds us of the voice of Isaac Watts' Sluggard. Wherever Watts looked in nature, the "busy little bee" or the sun rising at his "proper

[1] *Ibid.*, v, pp. 386-7; see also p. 562.
[2] Baxter, *op. cit.*, i, p. 276.
[3] R. Baxter, *The Poor Man's Family Book*, 6th edn. (1697), pp. 290-1;

hour", he read the same lesson for unregenerate man.[1] Alongside the Methodists, the Evangelicals took up the theme. Hannah More contributed her own imperishable lines on "Early Rising":

> Thou silent murderer, Sloth, no more
> My mind imprison'd keep;
> Nor let me waste another hour
> With thee, thou felon Sleep.[2]

In one of her tracts, *The Two Wealthy Farmers*, she succeeds in bringing the imagery of time-as-currency into the labour-market:

> When I call in my labourers on a Saturday night to pay them, it often brings to my mind the great and general day of account, when I, and you, and all of us, shall be called to our grand and awful reckoning. . . When I see that one of my men has failed of the wages he should have received, because he has been idling at a fair; another has lost a day by a drinking-bout. . . I cannot help saying to myself, Night is come; Saturday night is come. No repentance or diligence on the part of these poor men can now make a bad week's work good. This week is gone into eternity.[3]

Long before the time of Hannah More, however, the theme of the zealous husbandry of time had ceased to be particular to the Puritan, Wesleyan, or Evangelical traditions. It was Benjamin Franklin, who had a life-long technical interest in clocks and who numbered among his acquaintances John Whitehurst of Derby, the inventor of the "tell-tale" clock, who gave it its most unambiguous secular expression:

> Since our Time is reduced to a Standard, and the Bullion of the Day minted out into Hours, the Industrious know how to employ every Piece of Time to a real Advantage in their different Professions: And he that is prodigal of his Hours, is, in effct, a Squanderer of Money. I remember a notable Woman, who was fully sensible of the intrinsic Value of *Time*. Her Husband was a Shoemaker, and an excellent Craftsman, but never minded how the Minutes passed. In vain did she inculcate to him, *That Time is Money*. He had too much Wit to

[1] *Poetical Works of Isaac Watts, D.D.* (Cooke's Pocket Edn., [1802]), pp. 224, 227, 232. The theme is not new, of course: Chaucer's Parson said. "Sleepinge longe in quiete is eek a great norice to Lecherie".

[2] H. More, *Works* (1830), ii, p. 42. See also p. 35, "Time".

[3] *Ibid.*, iii, p. 167.

apprehend her, and it prov'd his Ruin. When at the Alehouse among his idle Companions, if one remark'd that the Clock struck Eleven, *What is that*, says he, *among us all?* If she sent him Word by the Boy, that it had struck Twelve; *Tell her to be easy, it can never be more.* If, that it had struck One, *Bid her be comforted, for it can never be less.* [1]

The reminiscence comes directly out of London (one suspects) where Franklin worked as a printer in the 1720s — but never, he reassures us in his *Autobiography*, following the example of his fellow-workers in keeping Saint Monday. It is, in some sense, appropriate that the ideologist who provided Weber with his central text in illustration of the capitalist ethic [2] should come, not from that Old World, but from the New — the world which was to invent the time-recorder, was to pioneer time-and-motion study, and was to reach its apogee with Henry Ford. [3]

VII

In all these ways — by the division of labour; the supervision of labour; fines; bells and clocks; money incentives; preachings and schoolings; the suppression of fairs and sports — new labour habits were formed, and a new time-discipline was imposed. It sometimes took several generations (as in the Potteries), and we may doubt how far it was ever fully accomplished: irregular labour rhythms were perpetuated (and even institutionalised) into the present century, notably in London and in the great ports. [4]

[1] *Poor Richard's Almanac*, Jan. 1751, in *The Papers of Benjamin Franklin*, ed. L. W. Labaree and W. J. Bell (New Haven, 1961), iv, pp. 86-7.

[2] Max Weber, *The Protestant Ethic and the Spirit of Capitalism* (1930), pp. 48-50 and *passim*.

[3] Ford commenced his career repairing watches: since there was a difference between local time and standard railroad time, he made a watch, with two dials, which kept both times — an ominous beginning: H. Ford, *My Life and Work* (1923), p. 24.

[4] There is an abundant literature of nineteenth-century dockland which illustrates this. However, in recent years the casual labourer in the ports has ceased to be a "casualty" of the labour market (as Mayhew saw him) and is marked by his preference for high earnings over security: see K. J. W. Alexander, "Casual Labour and Labour Casualties", *Trans. Inst. of Engineers and Shipbuilders in Scotland* (Glasgow, 1964). I have not touched in this paper on the new occupational time-tables introduced in

Throughout the nineteenth century the propaganda of time-thrift continued to be directed at the working people, the rhetoric becoming more debased, the apostrophes to eternity becoming more shop-soiled, the homilies more mean and banal. In early Victorian tracts and reading-matter aimed at the masses one is choked by the quantity of the stuff. But eternity has become those never-ending accounts of pious death-beds (or sinners struck by lightning), while the homilies have become little Smilesian snippets about humble men who by early rising and diligence made good. The leisured classes began to discover the "problem" (about which we hear a good deal today) of the leisure of the masses. A considerable proportion of manual workers (one moralist was alarmed to discover) after concluding their work were left with

> several hours in the day to be spent nearly as they please. And in what manner. . . is this precious time expended by those of no mental cultivation?. . . We shall often see them just simply annihilating those portions of time. They will for an hour, or for hours together. . . sit on a bench, or lie down on a bank or hillock. . . yielded up to utter vacancy and torpor. . . or collected in groups by the road side, in readiness to find in whatever passes there occasions for gross jocularity; practising some impertinence, or uttering some jeering scurrility, at the expense of persons going by. . .[1]

This, clearly, was worse than Bingo: non-productivity, compounded with impertinence. In mature capitalist society all time must be consumed, marketed, put to *use*; it is offensive for the labour force merely to "pass the time".

But how far did this propaganda really succeed? How far are we entitled to speak of any radical restructuring of man's social nature and working habits? I have given elsewhere some reasons for supposing that this discipline was indeed internalised, and that we may see in the Methodist sects of the early nineteenth century a figuration of the psychic crisis

---

industrial society — notably night-shift workers (pits, railways, etc.): see the observations by "A Journeyman Engineer" [T. Wright], *The Great Unwashed* (1868), pp. 188-200; M. A. Pollock (ed.), *Working Days* (1926), pp. 17-28; Tom Nairn, *New Left Review* 34 (1965), p. 38.

[1] John Foster, *An Essay on the Evils of Popular Ignorance* (1821), pp. 180-5.

entailed.[1] Just as the new time-sense of the merchants and gentry in the Renaisance appears to find one expression in the heightened awareness of mortality, so, one might argue, the extension of this sense to the working people during the industrial revolution (together with the hazard and high mortality of the time) helps to explain the obsessive emphasis upon death in sermons and tracts whose consumers were among the working-class. Or (from a positive stand-point) one may note that as the industrial revolution proceeds, wage incentives and expanding consumer drives — the palpable rewards for the productive consumption of time and the evidence of new "predictive" attitudes to the future[2] are evidently effective. By the 1830s and 1840s it was commonly observed that the English industrial worker was marked off from his fellow Irish worker, not by a greater capacity for hard work, but by his regularity, his methodical paying-out of energy, and perhaps also by a repression, not of enjoyments, but of the capacity to relax in the old, uninhibited ways.

There is no way in which we can quantify the time-sense of one, or of a million, workers. But it is possible to offer one check of a comparative kind. For what was said by the mercantilist moralists as to the failures of the eighteenth-century English poor to respond to incentives and disciplines is often repeated, by observers and by theorists of economic growth, of the peoples of developing countries today. Thus Mexican paeons in the early years of this century were regarded as an "indolent and child-like people". The Mexican mineworker had the custom of returning to his village for corn planting and harvest:

> His lack of initiative, inability to save, absences while celebrating too many holidays, willingness to work only three or four days a week if that paid for necessities, insatiable desire for alchohol — all were pointed out as proof of a natural inferiority.

---

[1] Thompson, *op. cit.*, chs. xi and xii.
[2] See the important discussion of forecasting and predictive attitudes and their influence upon social and economic behaviour, in Bourdieu, *op. cit.*

He failed to respond to direct day-wage incentives, and (like the eighteenth-century English collier or tinner) responded better to contract and sub-contract systems:

> Given a contract and the assurance that he will get so much money for each ton he mines, and that it doesn't matter how long he makes doing it, or how often he sits down to contemplate life, he will work with a vigour which is remarkable.[1]

In generalisations supported by another study of Mexican labour conditions, Wilbert Moore remarks: "Work is almost always task-orientated in non-industrial societies. . . and. . . it may be appropriate to tie wages to tasks and not directly to time in newly developing areas".[2]

The problem recurs in a dozen forms in the literature of "industrialisation". For the engineer of economic growth, it may appear as the problem of absenteeism — how is the Company to deal with the unrepentant labourer on the Cameroons plantation who declares: "How man fit work so, any day, any day, weh'e no take absen'? No be 'e go die?" ("How could a man work like that, day after day, without being absent? Would he not die?")[3]

> . . . the whole mores of African life, make a high and sustained level of effort in a given length of working day a greater burden both physically and psychologically than in Europe.[4]

> Time commitments in the Middle East or in Latin America are often treated somewhat casually by European standards; new industrial workers only gradually become accustomed to regular hours, regular attendance, and a regular pace of work; transportation schedules or the delivery of materials are not always reliable. . .[5]

The problem may appear as one of adapting the seasonal rhythms of the countryside, with its festivals and religious holidays, to the needs of industrial production:

[1] Cited in M. D. Bernstein, *The Mexican Mining Industry, 1890-1950* (New York, 1964), ch. vii; see also Mead, *op. cit.*, pp. 179-82.

[2] W. E. Moore, *Industrialization and Labor* (Ithaca, 1951), p. 310, and pp. 44-7, 114-22.

[3] F. A. Wells and W. A. Warmington, *Studies in Industrialization: Nigeria and the Cameroons* (1962), p. 128.

[4] *Ibid.*, p. 170. See also pp. 183, 198, 214.

[5] Edwin J. Cohn, "Social and Cultural Factors affecting the Emergence of Innovations", in *Social Aspects of Economic Development* (Economic and Social Studies Conference, Istanbul, 1964), pp. 105-6.

The work year of the factory is necessarily in accord with the workers' demands, rather than an ideal one from the point of view of most efficient production. Several attempts by the managers to alter the work pattern have come to nil. The factory comes back to a schedule acceptable to the Cantelano. [1]

Or it may appear as it did in the early years of the Bombay cotton-mills, as one of maintaining a labour force at the cost of perpetuating inefficient methods of production — elastic time-schedules, irregular breaks and meal-times, etc. Most commonly, in countries where the link between the new factory proletariat and their relatives (and perhaps land-holdings or rights to land) in the villages are much closer — and are maintained for much longer — than in the English experience, it appears as one of disciplining a labour force which is only partially and temporarily "committed" to the industrial way of life. [2]

The evidence is plentiful, and, by the method of contrast, it reminds us how far we have become habituated to different disciplines. Mature industrial societies of all varieties are marked by time-thrift and by a clear demarcation between

---

[1] Manning Nash, "The Recruitment of Wage Labor in the Development of New Skills", *Annals of the American Academy*, cccv (1956), pp. 27-8. See also Manning Nash, "The Reaction of a Civil-Religious Hierarchy to a Factory in Guatemala", *Human Organization*, xiii (1955), pp. 26-8, and Salz, *op. cit.*, (note 1 on p. 355), pp. 94-114.

[2] W. E. Moore and A. S. Feldman (eds.), *Labor Commitment and Social Change in Developing Areas* (New York, 1960). Useful studies of adaptation and of absenteeism include W. Elkan, *An African Labour Force* (Kampala, 1956), esp. chs. ii and iii; and F. H. Harbison and I. A. Ibrahim, "Some Labor Problems of Industrialization in Egypt", *Annals of the American Academy*, cccv (1956), pp. 114-29. M. D. Morris, *The Emergence of an Industrial Labor Force in India* (Berkeley, 1965) discounts the seriousness of the problems of discipline, absenteeism, seasonal fluctuations in employment, etc. in the Bombay cotton-mills in the late nineteenth century, but at many points his arguments appear to be at odds with his own evidence: see pp. 85, 97, 102; see also C. A. Myers, *Labour Problems in the Industrialization of India* (Cambridge, Mass., 1958), ch. iii, and S. D. Mehta, "Professor Morris on Textile Labour Supply", *Indian Economic Journal*, i, 3 (1954), pp. 333-40. Useful studies of an only partially "committed" labour force are G. V. Rimlinger, "Autocracy and the early Rusian Factory System", *Jl. Econ. Hist.*, xx (1960) and T. V. von Laue, "Russian Peasants in the Factory", *ibid.*, xxi (1961).

"work" and "life".[1] But, having taken the problem so far, we may be permitted to moralise a little, in the eighteenth-century manner, ourselves. The point at issue is not that of the "standard-of-living". If the theorists of growth wish us to say so, then we may agree that the older popular culture was in many ways otiose, intellectually vacant, devoid of quickening, and plain bloody poor. Without time-discipline we could not have the insistent energies of industrial man; and whether this discipline comes in the forms of Methodism, or of Stalinism, or of nationalism, it will come to the developing world.

What needs to be said is not that one way of life is better than the other, but this is a place of the most far-reaching conflict; that the historical record is not a simple one of neutral and inevitable technological change, but is also one of exploitation and of resistance to exploitation; and that values stand to be lost as well as gained. The rapidly-growing literature of the sociology of industrialisation is like a landscape which has been blasted by years of moral drought: one must travel through many tens of thousands of words of parched a-historical abstraction between each oasis of human actuality. Too many of the Western engineers of growth appear altogether too smug as to the gifts of character-formation which they bring in their hands to their backward brethren. The "structuring of a labour force", Kerr and Siegel tell us:

> . . . involves the setting of rules on times to work and not work, on method and amount of pay, on movement into and out of work and from one position to another. It involves rules pertaining to the maintenance of continuity in the work process. . . the attempted minimization of individual or organized revolt, the provision of view of the world, of ideological orientations, of beliefs. . .[2]

Wilbert Moore has even drawn up a shopping-list of the "pervasive values and normative orientations of high relevance to the goal of social development" — "these

[1] See G. Friedmann, "Leisure and Technological Civilization", *Int. Soc. Science Jour.*, xii (1960), pp. 509-21.
[2] C. Kerr and A. Siegel, "The Structuring of the Labor Force in Industrial Society: New Dimensions and New Questions", *Industrial and Labor Relations Review*, ii (1955), p. 163.

changes in attitude and belief are 'necessary' if rapid economic and social development is to be achieved":

> Impersonality: judgement of merit and performance, not social background or irrelevant qualities.
> Specificity of relations in terms of both context and limits of interaction.
> Rationality and problem-solving.
> Punctuality.
> Recognition of individually limited but systematically linked interdependence.
> Discipline, deference to legitimate authority.
> Respect for property rights. . .

These, with "achievement and mobility aspirations", are not, Professor Moore reassures us,

> suggested as a comprehensive list of the merits of modern man. . . The "whole man" will also love his family, worship his God, and express his aesthetic capacities, But he will keep each of these other orientations "in their place".[1]

It need cause no surprise that such "provision of ideological orientations" by the Baxters of the twentieth century should have been welcome to the Ford Foundation. That they should so often have appeared in publications sponsored by UNESCO is less easily explained.

VIII

It is a problem which the peoples of the developing world must live through and grow through. One hopes that they will be wary of pat, manipulative models, which present the working masses only as an inert labour force. And there is a sense, also, within the advanced industrial countries, in which this has ceased to be a problem placed in the past. For we are now at a point where sociologists are discussing the "problem" of leisure. And a part of the problem is: how did it come to be a problem? Puritanism, in its marriage of convenience with industrial capitalism, was the agent which converted people to new valuations of time; which taught children even in their infancy to improve each shining hour; and which saturated peoples' minds with the equation, time is

---

[1] E. de Vries and J. M. Echavarria (eds.), *Social Aspects of Economic Development in Latin America* (UNESCO, 1963), p. 237.

money.[1] One recurrent form of revolt within Western industrial capitalism, whether bohemian or beatnik, has often taken the form of flouting the urgency of respectable time-values. And the interesting question arises: if Puritanism was a necessary part of the work-ethos which enabled the industrialised world to break out of the poverty-stricken economies of the past, will the Puritan valuation of time begin to decompose as the pressures of poverty relax? Is it decomposing already? Will people begin to lose that restless urgency, that desire to consume time purposively, which most people carry just as they carry a watch on their wrists?

If we are to have enlarged leisure, in an automated future, the problem is not "how are people going to be able to *consume* all these additional time-units of leisure?" but "what will be the capacity of experience of the people who have this undirected time to live?" If we maintain a Puritan time-valuation, a commodity-valuation, then it is a question of how this time is put to *use*, or how it is exploited by the leisure industries. But if the purposive notation of time-use becomes less compulsive, then people might have to re-learn some of the arts of living lost in the industrial revolution: how to fill the interstices of their day with enriched, more leisurely, personal and social relations; how to break down once more the barriers between work and life. And hence would stem a novel dialectic in which some of the old aggressive energies and disciplines migrate to the newly-industrialising nations, while the old industrialised nations seek to rediscover modes of experience forgotten before written history begins:

> . . . the Nuer have no expression equivalent to "time" in our language, and they cannot, therefore, as we can, speak of time as though it were something actual, which passes, can be wasted, can be saved, and so forth. I do not think that they ever experience the same feeling of fighting against time or of having to co-ordinate activities with an abstract passage of time because their points of reference are mainly the activities themselves, which are generally of a leisurely character. Events

[1] Suggestive comments on this equation are in Lewis Mumford and S. de Grazia, cited note 1 on p. 352; Paul Diesing, *Reason in Society* (Urbana, 1962), pp. 24-8; Hans Meyerhoff, *Time in Literature* (Univ. of California, 1955), pp. 106-19.

follow a logical order, but they are not controlled by an abstract system, there being no autonomous points of reference to which activities have to conform with precision. Nuer are fortunate.[1]

Of course, no culture re-appears in the same form. If people are to meet both the demands of a highly-synchronised automated industry, and of greatly enlarged areas of "free time", they must somehow combine in a new synthesis elements of the old and of the new, finding an imagery based neither upon the seasons nor upon the market but upon human occasions. Punctuality in working hours would express respect for one's fellow workers. And unpurposive passing of time would be behaviour which the culture approved.

It can scarcely find approval among those who see the history of "industrialisation" in seemingly-neutral but, in fact, profoundly value-loaded terms, as one of increasing rationalisation in the service of economic growth. The argument is at least as old as the industrial revolution. Dickens saw the emblem of Thomas Gradgrind ("ready to weigh and measure any parcel of human nature, and tell you exactly what it comes to") as the "deadly statistical clock" in his observatory, "which measured every second with a beat like a rap upon a coffin-lid". But rationalism has grown new sociological dimensions since Gradgrind's time. It was Werner Sombart who — using the same favourite image of the Clockmaker — replaced the God of mechanical materialism by the Entrepreneur:

> If modern economic rationalism is like the mechanism of a clock, someone must be there to wind it up.[2]

The universities of the West are today thronged with academic clocksmiths, anxious to patent new keys. But few have, as yet, advanced as far as Thomas Wedgwood, the son of Josiah, who designed a plan for taking the time and work-discipline of Etruria into the very workshops of the child's formative consciousness:

---

[1] Evans-Pritchard, *op. cit.*, p. 103.
[2] "Capitalism", *Encyclopaedia of the Social Sciences* (New York, 1953), iii, p. 205.

My aim is high — I have been endeavouring some master stroke which should anticipate a century or two upon the large-paced progress of human improvement. Almost every prior step of its advance may be traced to the influence of superior characters. Now, it is my opinion, that in the education of the greatest of these characters, not more than one hour in ten has been made to contribute to the formation of those qualities upon which this influence has depended. Let us suppose ourselves in possession of a detailed statement of the first twenty years of the life of some extraordinary genius; what a chaos of perceptions!. . . How many hours, days, months have been prodigally wasted in unproductive occupations! What a host of half formed impressions & abortive conceptions blended into a mass of confusion. . .

In the best regulated mind of the present day, had not there been, & is not there some hours every day passed in reverie, thought ungoverned, undirected?[1]

Wedgwood's plan was to design a new, rigorous, rational, closeted system of education: Wordsworth was proposed as one possible superintendent. His response was to write *The Prelude* — an essay in the growth of a poet's consciousness which was, at the same time, a polemic against —

> The Guides, the Wardens of our faculties,
> And Stewards of our labour, watchful men
> And skilful in the usury of time,
> Sages, who in their prescience would controul
> All accidents, and to the very road
> Which they have fashion'd would confine us down,
> Like engines. . .[2]

For there is no such thing as economic growth which is not, at the same time, growth or change of a culture; and the growth of social consciousness, like the growth of a poet's mind, can never, in the last analysis, be planned.

---

[1] Thomas Wedgwood to William Godwin, 31 July 1797, published in David Erdman's important article, "Coleridge, Wordsworth and the Wedgwood Fund", *Bulletin of the New York Public Library*, lx (1956).

[2] *The Prelude* (1805), book v, lines 377-83. See also draft in *Poetical Works of William Wordsworth*, ed. E. de Selincourt and Helen Darbishire (Oxford, 1959), v, p. 346.

Chapter Seven

The Sale of Wives

I

Until a few years ago the historical memory of the sale of wives in England might better be described as amnesia. Who would want to remember practices of such barbarity? By the 1850s nearly all commentators were committed to the view that the practice was (a) exceedingly rare, and (b) utterly offensive to morality (although some folklorists began to toy apologetically with the notion of pagan survival).

The tone of Chambers's *The Book of Days* (1878) is representative. The picture "is simply an outrage upon decency. . . It can only be considered as a proof of the besotted ignorance and brutal feelings of a portion of our rural population". And it was the more important to disclaim and denounce the practice because Britain's "continental neighbours" had noticed the "occasional instances of wife-sale" and they "seriously believe that it is a habit of all classes of our people, and constantly cite it as evidence of our low civilization".[1] The French, with their habitual rancorous levity, were the worst offenders in this: Milord John Bull was portrayed, booted and spurred, in Smithfield Market, crying *"à quinze livres ma femme!"*, while Milady stood haltered in a pen.[2]

---

[1] *The Book of Days*, ed. R. Chambers (1878), i, pp. 487-8.

[2] Interesting comments on the practice appear as early as 1776, *Courrier de L'Europe* (26 Nov.). Thereafter the French press often carried examples with appropriate comment. See also [J. E. Jouy], *L'Hermite de Londres* (Paris, 1821), ii, p. 324; Anon., *Six mois à Londres* (Paris, 1817); and Piliet, note 1, p. 438 below. Many examples are cited in J. W. von Achenholtz, *Annals*, v (1790), pp. 329-30, ix (1796), pp. 187-8.

The Book of Days was able to gather only eight cases, between 1815 and 1839, and these cases, with three or four more, were circulated with little further enquiry for fifty or more years in antiquarian or journalistic accounts. As enlightenment waxed, so curiosity waned. For the first half of this century historical memory was generally satisfied with occasional throwaway references in popular accounts of eighteenth-century popular mores. These were commonly offered as a colourful element within an antithetical liturgy contrasting the animalistic culture of the poor (Gin Lane, Tyburn and Mother Proctor's Pews, bull-baiting, fireworks tied to animals, pugilism with nailed boots, naked races, wife sales) with whatever forms of enlightenment was supposed to have displaced these.[1]

Against this indifference, one powerful influence was asserted: the careful reconstruction of the sale of a wife, in a credible human context, taking a significant place in the structure of the plot of a major novel, *The Mayor of Casterbridge*. Thomas Hardy was a superbly perceptive observer of folk customs, and his touch is rarely more sure than in this novel. But in the episode of Michael Henchard's sale of his wife, Susan, in a wayside fair to a passing sailor, Hardy appears to have relied, not upon observation (or direct oral tradition) but on newspaper sources. These sources (as we shall see) are usually enigmatic and opaque. And the episode, as drawn in the novel, in its seemingly casual provenance and in its brutal expression, does not conform to more "typical" evidence. The auction of Susan Henchard lacks ritual features; the purchaser arrives fortuitously and bids on impulse. Hardy succeeds admirably, in his reconstruction of the episode and in his disclosure of its consequences, in presenting the general popular consensus as to the legitimacy of the transaction and as to its irrevocable character — a conviction certainly shared by Susan

---

[1] Thus wife sales find mention in J. Wesley Bready, *England Before and After Wesley* (1938), under a section headed: "Immorality as Sport".

Henchard.[1] But in the last analysis Hardy's presentation still fell within the same stereotype as that of *The Book of Days*. "For my part", the drunken Henchard says,

> I don't see why men who have got wives and don't want 'em, shouldn't get rid of 'em as these gipsey fellows do their old horses. . . Why shouldn't they put 'em up and sell 'em by auction to men who are in need of such articles?

The assumption underlying both accounts is that the wife sale was a direct chattel purchase. And once this stereotype has become established, it is only too easy to read the evidence through it. It can then be assumed that the wife was auctioned like a beast or chattel, perhaps against her will, either because the husband wished to be rid of her or for merely mercenary motives. As such, the custom disallowed any scrupulous examination. It could be taken as a melancholy example of abject feminine oppression, or an illustration of the levity with which marriage was regarded among the male poor.

But it is this stereotype — and not the fact that wives were on occasion sold — which requires interrogation. In any case, it seemed advisable to collect some evidence before offering confident explanations. In the 1960s I commenced — with much assistance from friends and correspondents — to build up files on "ritual" sales in the eighteenth and nineteenth centuries; and in the late 1960s and through the 1970s I inflicted drafts of this chapter upon many seminars and audiences in Britain and the United States. By 1977 I had some three hundred cases on my index cards, although at least fifty of these are too vague or dubious to be taken as evidence. Meanwhile I delayed publication of my findings, although these were briefly reported in other scholars' work.[2] Further delay resulted in my research being overtaken, and in

---

[1] Hardy attributes Susan's conviction to "the extreme simplicity of her intellect": by the sale, her purchaser "had acquired a morally real and justifiable right to her. . . though the exact bearings and legal limits of that right were vague".

[2] I reported some conclusions in "Folklore, Anthropology, and Social History", *Indian Historical Review*, iii, 2 (1978). For other reports, see J. Weeks, *Sex, Politics and Society* (1981) and Robert W. Malcolmson, *Life and Labour in England, 1700-1780* (1981), pp. 103-4.

1981 there was published a substantial volume, *Wives for Sale*, by Samuel Pyeatt Menefee.

Mr Menefee's ethnographic study was undertaken as a dissertation in the Department of Social Anthropology at Oxford University, and the subject had perhaps come to the notice of this Department when I gave a paper on this theme to one of its seminars. I could claim no proprietorship in the topic, and, indeed, my intention had been to arouse historical and anthropological interest. Nevertheless, my first response was to regard my own work as having been made redundant. Mr Menefee had pursued the theme with great industry; had circulated many libraries and record offices; had assembled much curious and some relevant material; and had over-passed my own count, with an Appendix of 387 cases. More-over, he shared my redefinition of the ritual by subtitling his volume, "An Ethnographic Study of British Popular Divorce". With a little sadness — for the theme had preoccupied me for some years — I laid my paper aside.

It is revived now, and presented tardily to the public, because I do not think, after all, that Mr Menefee and I duplicate each other or are pursuing the same questions. Mr Menefee wrote as an apprentice ethnographer, and his knowledge of British social history and its disciplines was elementary. As a result he has little understanding of social context, few criteria for distinguishing between sound and corrupt evidence, and his fascinating examples appear in a jumble of irrelevant material and contradictory inter-pretations. We may be grateful for his book, which is immensely painstaking and carefully documented. But it cannot be taken as the final word on the sale of wives.

The ritual may be of only marginal interest, and may have little general relevance to sexual behaviour or marital norms. It offers only a small window upon these questions. Yet there are not many such windows, and we will never have a full view until every window is uncurtained and the perspectives intersect. From this fragmentary and enigmatic evidence we must tease out what insights we can into the norms and sensibility of a lost culture, and into the interior crises of the poor.

II

The quantitative evidence as to wife sales and their frequency is, in most respects, the least satisfactory to be offered in this chapter, so we will commence with this. I have collected some three hundred cases, of which I have disallowed fifty as dubious. Menefee lists 387 cases, but this includes many vague and dubious cases, frequent double-counting of the same case, and cases which are not "true" ritual sales. Let us say that I have two hundred and fifty authentic cases and Menefee has three hundred. But about one hundred and fifty cases appear in both lists — cases collected from such obvious sources as *Notes and Queries*, the indexes to *The Times*, folklore collections, etc. Thus together we have collected some four hundred examples.

Even so, I have felt it necessary to prune this material, especially in the earlier (pre-1760) years and those later than 1880. The sale or exchange of a wife, for sexual or domestic services, appears to have taken place, on occasion, in most places and at most times. It may be only an aberrant trans-action, with or without a pretended contractual basis — it is recorded sometimes today. Unfortunately, some of the earlier examples afford almost no evidence as to the nature of the practice recorded. Thus a local historian's record "from an old document relating to Bilston" — "November, 1692. John, ye son of Nathan Whitehouse, of Tipton, sold his wife to Mr. Bracegirdle", cannot arise, without further evidence to the dignity of being counted as a ritual wife sale.[1] But some of the later examples, although better documented, also present difficulties. Thus a young married woman gave evidence in a Leeds police court in 1913 (in a maintenance case) that she had been sold for £1 by her husband to a work-mate who lived in the next street. Her child was fathered by the second man: he acknowledged it for six weeks and then told her to drown it. But this man was already married, and he subsequently returned to his wife.[2] If this was a wife sale then the custom was in an advanced stage of decomposition and the practice departs from previously-accepted usage.

[1] F. W. Hackwood, *Staffordshire Customs, Superstititions and Folk-lore* (1924), p. 70.
[2] *Leeds Weekly Citizen*, 6 June 1913.

There are some cases before 1760 and after 1880 which provide better evidence. But for the purpose of counting I decided to leave pre-1760 cases to historians better qualified to read the evidence, and to ignore those after 1880. This reduced me to 218 cases which I can accept as authentic between 1760 and 1880:[1]

Wife Sales: Visible Cases

1760-1800	42
1800-1840	121
1840-1880	55

Cases have come to hand from every region of England, but I have only one case in this period from Scotland and very few cases from Wales. Counties with ten or more examples are: Derbyshire (10), Devon (12), Kent (10), Lancashire (12), Lincolnshire (14), Middlesex and London (19), Nottinghamshire (13), Staffordshire (16), Warwickshire (10), and (high at the top of the table) Yorkshire (44).

These figures show little, except that the practice certainly occurred, and in most parts of England. The numbers are of *visible* cases, and visibility must be taken in at least three senses. First, these are events whose trace happens to have become visible to me. While Menefee and I offer the same general profile, we have both been dependent in some degree on what caught the notice of folklorists or was copied by metropolitan newspapers. There are no sources from which one could extract a systematic sample, and only a scanning of provincial newspapers in every region could pretend to such a sample.[2] Second, these were events which had to acquire a certain notoriety to leave any traces in the records at all. A ritual sale in the market-place of a large town might do this, but a private sale in a public house might not, unless some unusual circumstance attended it. Since the second form was

[1] The quantities reported here are based upon my study as it stood in 1977. I have not attempted the difficult task of checking and conflating with the examples in the Appendix of S. P. Menefee, *Wives for Sale* (Oxford, 1981), (cited hereafter as Menefee), nor have I added cases which have come to hand since its publication.

[2] My collection probably gives too much weight to Yorkshire (where I used to live and where A. J. Peacock kindly collected samples) and to Lincolnshire (where Rex Russell kindly did the same), and it may give too little weight to the West of England.

favoured in some districts, and displaced the first form generally after 1830 or 1840, we can never hope to recover any accurate quantities.

But it is visibility in a third sense which is of most importance, which offers the largest qualification to any quantities, and which illustrates the slippery nature of the evidence which we must handle. For when did a wife sale become visible to a genteel or middle-class public and hence become worthy of a note in public print? The answer must relate to indistinct changes in social awareness, in moral standards, and in news values. The practice became a matter for more frequent report and comment early in the nineteenth century. But through much of the eighteenth century newspapers were not vehicles for social or domestic comment of this kind. There is good reason to suppose that wife sales were widely practised well before 1790. The custom was little reported because it was not considered worthy of report, unless some additional circumstance (humorous, dramatic, tragic, scandalous) gave it interest. This silence might have been for several reasons: polite ignorance (the distance between the cultures of the newspaper public and of the poor), indifference to a custom so commonplace that it required no comment, or distaste. Wife sales became newsworthy contemporaneously with the evangelical revival, which, by raising the threshold of middle-class tolerance, redefined a matter of popular "ignorance" into one of public scandal.

This has unfortunate consequences. For although the practice is reported after 1790 on occasion as comedy or human interest, it is more often reported in a tone of moral disapproval so strong as to obliterate that evidence which only objectivity could have brought. Wife sales showed that a "system of trading in human flesh" was "not confined to the shores of Africa"; the rope in which the wife was haltered might be better employed in hanging or whipping the parties to the transaction; and (commonly) it was "a most disgusting and disgraceful scene" (Smithfield, 1832), "one of those disgusting scenes which are a disgrace to civilized society" (Norwich, 1823), "an indecent and degrading transaction" (York, 1820). The husband who sold his wife was "a brute in human shape" (Nottingham, 1844), and the wife herself was

either an "impudent hussy" or an object of maudlin pity.
This makes enquiry difficult. A decadal count of visible
cases between 1800-60 shows: 1800-09, 22; 1810-19, 32;
1820-29, 33; 1830-39, 47; 1840-49, 22; 1850-59, 14.[1] If
plotted on a graph this would show a rising curve of sales,
reaching a peak in the early 1830s (9 sales in 1833) and then
falling off sharply. But a graph of actual sales might run
counter to a graph of visible sales. For the latter graph is not
one of sales but of the moral outrage provoked by sales. This
outrage was accompanied by increasing action against sales
by magistrates, constables, market officials and moralists. It
was also associated with a rising current of disapproval within
the popular culture itself, fed from evangelical, rationalist
and radical or trade unionist sources. It is quite possible that
actual sales could have come to a peak at some point in the
eighteenth or very early nineteenth century, and publicity
given to sales between 1820 and 1850 may have been given to
late and somewhat shame-faced survivals of a practice
already in decline. This publicity, in its turn, may have helped
to drive the wife sale out of the public market-place and into
more secretive forms.

Some literary evidence supports this suggestion. Thus there
is a clear description of ritual wife sale, with public auction
and with delivery in a halter, in a workmanlike legal treatise
on *The Laws Respecting Women As They Regard Their
Natural Rights*, published in 1777. Neither I nor Menefee
have many cases before 1777 which clearly indicate a ritual
sale, yet the author of this practical treatise can have had no
motive for inventing the matter. John Brand also, in his
Observations on Popular Antiquities, reports the practice in
terms which suggest survival from a more vigorous tradition:

> A remarkable Superstition still prevails among the lowest of our Vulgar,
> that a Man may lawfully sell his Wife to another, provided he deliver her
> over with a Halter about her Neck.[2]

[1] Menefee (Appendix) has: 1800-09, 32; 1810-19, 45; 1820-29, 47;
1830-39, 48; 1840-49, 20; 1850-59, 18.
[2] John Brand, *Observations on Popular Antiquities*, arranged and
revised by Henry Ellis (1813), ii, p. 37, which adds: "It is painful to observe
that instances of this occur frequently in our Newspapers".

From these references we might assume that the ritual wife sale was commonplace in 1777, and scarcely worthy of comment, and had been so for a century or more. I think this improbable, and the tone of reports in the press suggests a different evolution. Thus an Oxford case in 1789 is noted as "the vulgar mode of *Divorce* lately adopted"; in 1790 a Derbyshire report noted the delivery of the wife in a halter "in the usual way which has been lately practised", and in the same year newspapers in both Derby and Birmingham found it necessary to note that, "as instances of the sale of wives have of late frequently occurred among the lower class of people", such sales were "illegal and void".[1] This could suggest that the wife sale, in its ritual form of market-place auction and halter, while prevalent in some parts of the country in 1777 was only slowly spreading to others.[2] By the 1800s newspapers can refer to sales "in the usual style" and to "disgraceful scenes which have of late become too common".[3] But the evidence as to this evolution is uncertain, and the question must be left open.

It is always uncertain whether the cases reported are the tip of an iceberg or a true index of frequency.[4] At any time before

[1] *Jackson's Oxford Journal*, 12 Dec. 1789; *Northampton Mercury*, 19 Dec. 1789; *Derby Mercury*, 4 and 25 Feb. 1790; *Birmingham Gazette*, 1 Mar. 1790.

[2] Cornwall may have been slow to adopt a practice widespread in Devon. A sale in 1819 in Redruth was reported as "the first of its kind" there: *West Briton*, 17 Dec. 1819.

[3] For examples, *Norfolk Chronicle*, 9 Feb. 1805; W. Andrews, *Bygone England* (1892), p. 203.

[4] Lawrence Stone is over-confident when he concludes (*Road to Divorce*, Oxford 1990, p. 148) that "fewer than three hundred cases of wife-sale occurred in all England during the peak seventy years from 1780 to 1850". If this were so, it would be highly improbable that both Menefee and I should have recovered almost that number from a somewhat random sample of printed sources. In my view many sales, especially before 1820, will not have been recorded at all. Professor Stone underestimates the opacity of the plebeian culture to polite inspection (including his own): he is right, however, to say that wife sales were "very infrequent" as compared with the number of (male) desertions and of elopements: see *ibid.*, pp. 142, 148.

1790 and 1830 visibility cannot be taken to indicate the exceptional nature of the event. When the rector of Clipsham in Rutland indicted a parishioner in 1819 for purchasing a wife, it was noted that "the purchaser was selected for punishment, as the most opulent, and fittest to make an example of" — yet Clipsham at that time contained only 33 houses and 173 inhabitants.[1] By the 1830s and 1840s, however, there is more suggestion that the visible cases were regarded as unusual or as survivals. In 1839 a sale at Witney was noted as "one of those disgraceful occurrences, happily not. . . frequent"; while a sale at Bridlington in the previous year was compared to "a similar transaction" in the same town ten years before.[2]

The consensus of mid nineteenth-century enlightened opinion was that the practice existed only amongst the lowest stratum of the labourers, especially in the remote countryside: as Brand had expressed it, "the lowest of our Vulgar". This may be tested against occupations attributed to either the husband or the purchaser in my sample. While the nature of the reports is not such as to ensure accuracy, attributions of occupation are given in 158 cases:

Wife Sales: Attributed Occupation of Husband or Purchaser

15 Labourers
8 Colliers (including pitmen and miners)
7 Navvies (including ditchers and bankers)
6 Coachmen (including postillions and ostlers)
5 Blacksmiths : Farmers : Farm labourers or "countrymen" : Shoe-makers : Soldiers : Tailors
4 Chimney-sweeps : Gardeners
3 Bricklayers : Brickmakers : Butchers : Carpenters or joiners : Factory workers : Horse or cattle dealers : Nailmakers : Tinkers
2 Bakers : Clerks : Donkey-drivers : Dustmen : Gentlemen : Graziers : Grinders : Ironworkers : Sailors : Stockingers : Watermen : Weavers

---

[1] *The Times*, 2 Feb. 1819. The case from Rutland Quarter Sessions (Oakham) and perhaps an example was being looked for from the whole county? See also Roy Palmer, *The Folklore of Leicestershire and Rutland* (Wymondham, 1985), pp. 58-9.

[2] *Jackson's Oxford Journal*, 4 May 1839; *York Herald & General Advertiser*, 27 Oct. 1838; *Hull Advertiser*, cited in *Operative*, 4 Nov. 1838.

1 Basket-maker : Blanket-hawker : Breeches-maker : Button-maker :
Carter : Cinder-burner : Cloth worker : Coal dealer : Delver : Fell-
monger : Gingerbread Hawker : Hatter : Hay salesman : Hog driver :
Lighterman : Mason : Mattress-maker : Officer : Painter : Publican :
Rag merchant : Sand carrier : Sawyer : Steel-burner : Stone-cutter :
Straw-cutter : Tradesman : Woodward
Designated by office, circumstance, etc., rather than by occupation:
Pauper (2) : Pensioner (2) : Returned from transportation (2) : Poacher
(1) : and Henry Brydges, 2nd duke of Chandos.

One should add to this general (but imprecise) suggestions
that wife selling was prevalent among certain occupational
groups, such as railway navvies, bargees, and tinkers or
travellers. But highly picaresque occupations, with great
mobility and many accidents of fortune, seem — as with
sailors and soldiers — to have encouraged different notations
of "marriage", which was seen on both sides to be a more
transient arrangement.

This table of occupations carries (the duke of Chandos
apart) few surprises.[1] There is a large group (19) engaged in
some way in the livestock and transport trades, and likely to
frequent cattle markets. Another group (14) come from the
building trades, which shared with navvying a high mobility.
The odd men out are those of higher social status. Of the two
reputed gentlemen, one purchased the wife of a clothworker
in Midsomer Norton, Somerset, in 1766 for six guineas: no
public ritual is mentioned, the sale was by private contract,
and, by her own account, the wife was not consulted (see
below p. 431). In the other case, at Plymouth in 1822, the
gentleman was the husband and intending seller: we will
return to this unusually well-documented case (below
pp. 440-1). A further case, at Smithfield in 1815, attracted

---

[1] It is probable that the duke of Chandos did buy his second wife,
Maria, from an ostler in Newbury *circa* 1740, since the story clung to him
persistently with circumstantial additions. But I am not convinced that
Maria was sold in an inn-yard in a halter, nor that Chandos's presence at
the sale was a matter of chance: this detail rests on oral transmission across
130 years, see *N & Q*, 4th series, vi (1870), p. 179. See also Menefee, p. 214
(Case 15).

attention precisely because of the wealth and status of the parties: the husband was a cattle grazier, the purchaser a "celebrated horse-dealer", the purchase price high (fifty guineas and "a valuable horse upon which the purchaser was mounted"), and "the lady (the object of the sale), young, beautiful, and elegantly dressed, was brought to market in a coach, and exposed to the view of her purchaser with a silk halter round her shoulders, which were covered with a rich white lace veil". It was noted reprovingly in the press that "hitherto we have only seen those moving in the lowest classes of society thus degrading themselves". [1]

The occupational profile suggested by this sample is not that of the luxury trades nor of the skilled artisans, but of the older plebeian culture that preceded these and long co-existed with them. Workers in the staple productive industry, textiles, are greatly under-represented; although Yorkshire provides more examples than any other county, it shows colliers and unskilled trades, but no croppers or wool-combers, and only two weavers. In the sample there are blacksmiths but no engineers or instrument-makers; navvies but no shipwrights; and only three mill-hands or factory operatives. The women, being wives, are described by their looks, deportment or supposed moral conduct, but very rarely by occupation. But we do know that there were two pit-lasses; at least two were paupers sold off to save parish poor rates; one was a factory operative and another a winder in a mill.

It would be futile (for reasons that will become apparent) to quantify the rising or falling cost of buying wives. At the top of the list (an unsatisfactory case) a Wolverhampton coal-dealer was supposed to have sold his wife in 1865 to an American sailor at £100, plus £25 each for two children. [2] At the other extreme wives were given free, or for a glass of ale; the lowest sum of money exchanged was three-farthings. Perhaps two shillings and sixpence to five shillings was the median range, although many examples fall above or below this. But the husband frequently exacted a bowl of punch or a

---

[1] John Ashton, *Social England under the Regency* (1890), i, pp. 374-5.
[2] *Wolverhampton Chronicle* cited in *Yorkshire Gazette*, 28 Jan. 1865.

gallon of beer on top of the purchase price, and sometimes some other article — a watch, some cloth, some tobacco. A Westminster donkey-driver sold his wife to another driver for thirteen shillings and a donkey. In a much-cited case in Carlisle (1832) a farmer, renting 42 acres, sold his wife to a pensioner for twenty shillings and a large Newfoundland dog. He slipped the straw-halter, in which he had led his wife to market, off her neck and put it around the neck of his new acquisition, betaking himself to the nearest inn.[1]

III

This is all very well for those who enjoy quantitative gossip, but we must now get to serious work and enquire: what is the significance of the form of behaviour which we have been trying to count? The material appears in the press, most often, in an abbreviated — or occasionally a sensational — form, opaque to investigation. The report may be of the briefest:

> On Tuesday, February 25th, one Hudson brought his wife into Stafford market-place and disposed of her by public auction, after many biddings, at five shillings and five pence.[2]

> A fellow named Jackson sold his wife for 10s. 6d. at Retford, last week, in the public market.[3]

Or a report may carry a more jocular tone:

> Monday last Jonathan Heard, gardener at Witham, sold his wife and child, a fowl and eleven pigs, for six guineas to a bricklayer of the same place. He this day made a demand of them and received them with open arms amidst a prodigious concourse of people. The knowing ones think the bricklayer has a very hard bargain.[4]

Or the report may be somewhat fuller. The *Derby Mercury* in 1841 described a "disgraceful scene" in Stafford market:

---

[1] This much-reprinted example seems to derive from the *Lancaster Herald*, reaching *The Times*, 26 Apr. 1832, and the *Annual Register* for 1832. The colourful report was perhaps dressed up by the reporter: see *Chambers's Journal*, 19 Oct. 1861.

[2] *Monthly Magazine*, ix (1800), p. 304.

[3] *Derby Mercury*, 18 Aug. 1841.

[4] *Chelmsford Chronicle*, 18 July 1777, in A. J. Brown (ed.), *English History from Essex Sources* (Chelmsford, 1952), p. 203.

A labouring man, of idle and dissolute habits, called Rodney Hall, residing at Dunstone Heath near Penkridge led his wife into the town with a halter round her body, for the purpose of disposing of her in the public market to the best bidder. Having taken her into the market-place and paid toll he led her twice round the market, when he was met by a man named Barlow, of the same class of life, who purchased her for eighteen pence and a quart of ale, and she was formally delivered over to the purchaser. The parties then went to the 'Blue Posts Inn' to ratify the transfer. . .[1]

A further example concerns Barton-upon-Humber (Lincolnshire), 1847:

On Wednesday. . . it was announced by the cryer that the wife of Geo. Wray, of Barrow. . . would be offered for sale by auction in the Barton market-place at 11 o'clock;. . . punctually to the time the salesman made his appearance with the lady, the latter having a new halter tied round her waist. Amidst the shouts of the lookers on, the lot was put up, and. . . knocked down to Wm. Harwood, waterman, for the sum of one shilling, three-halfpence to be returned 'for luck'. Harwood walked off arm in arm with his smiling bargain, with as much coolness as if he had purchased a new coat or hat.[2]

This is, usually, all the material that we have. Only in a very few cases — for example, when some case arises in the courts — do we obtain more information. But the material is not worthless, and as one works over it certain patterns emerge. The sale of a wife was by no means a casual, and rarely a comic, affair. It was highly ritualised; it should be performed in public and with accepted ceremony. It is possible that there were two forms of wife sale, favoured in different parts of the country, which overlapped with each other and which confuse the picture: 1) a form requiring publicity in the market-place and the use of the halter; I call this the "true" ritual wife sale; 2) a form involving a paper contract of sale, with witnesses, and some abbreviated ritual of "delivery" in a public bar. Of my 218 cases, a market-place

---

[1] *Derby Mercury*, 18 Aug. 1841.
[2] *Stamford Mercury*, 12 Mar. 1847. For a sequel, see *ibid.*, 25 May 1849: Harwood refused to acknowledge (in county court) a debt contracted by his "wife" before purchase, "inasmuch as at the time he bought the woman, he did not take her debts along with her. The Judge (with astonishment): 'What do you mean by buying the woman?' The lady alluded to here stepped forward, and said she was purchased in the usual way. . . His Honour seemed to be dumfounded".

sale is indicated in 121, a sale inside an inn (before witnesses) in 10 cases, and a private paper contract (with no mention of an inn) in 5 cases. The halter is mentioned in 108 cases, usually in the market-place but on occasion inside the inn. There is no evidence as to the form (market, inn or halter) in the remaining 82 cases.

In the true wife sale, ritual prescribed some of the following forms, although there were regional variations and not every one of the forms discussed below need, in any one case, be observed.

a) The sale must take place in an acknowledged market-place or similar nexus of exchange. Antiquity or familiarity influenced the choice. Frequently the parties took their station before the old market "cross" or some outstanding feature: at Preston (1817) the obelisk, at Bolton (1835) the new "gas pillar".[1] If the sale took place in a large village without a market, then the parties would perform the ceremony in front of the main inn or wherever public transactions customarily took place. But such village sales seem to have been rare, and even from large villages the parties usually proceeded to the market-town, walking miles to their objective.[2]

On occasion the scene of the sale was some other public mart or exchange: at Dartmouth (1817) the public quay,[3] or, as in Hardy's novel, a fair. Popular opinion seems to have been uncertain as to the legitimacy of such transactions. In a confusing case in Bath market-place (1833) a "dashingly attired" lady in a silk halter was put up for sale, although she had been sold earlier in the week, for 2s. 6d., at Lansdown Fair, "but the bargain was not considered legal; first because the sale was not held in a public market-place, and secondly because the purchaser had a wife already".[4] The second reason was probably the more weighty of the two, since sales

---

[1] *Preston Chronicle*, 3 May 1817; *Bolton Chronicle*, cited in *British Whig* (Kingston, Ontario), 8 May 1835.

[2] "This day a woman sold in the Market for 4/- the parties came from Stoke Golding": Anon., "Memorandum Book of Occurences at Nuneaton" (typescript in Warwicks. CRO of original in Nuneaton Public Library), entry for 1 June 1816.

[3] *The Times*, 12 Apr. 1817.

[4] *Ibid.*, 27 Aug. 1833 and *Man*, 1 Sept. 1833, citing *Bath Chronicle*.

at other fairs certainly took place.[1]

b) The sale was sometimes preceded by some public announcement or advertisement. The town cryer or bell-man might be employed, or the husband might carry a notice of intending sale through the market. Baring-Gould records the story of a Devonshire publican who posted a —

NOTICE

This here be to hinform the publick as how James Cole be dispozed to sell his wife by Auction. Her be a dacent, clanely woman, and be of age twenty-five ears. The sale be to take place in the New Inn, Thursday next, at seven o'clock.

One is unhappy with this story (and its self-consciously comic orthography), even though Baring-Gould insisted upon it and claimed that the woman was still living at the time of writing (1908).[2] But undoubtedly some advance announcements took place.

c) The halter was central to the ritual. The wife was brought to market in a halter, usually around her neck, sometimes around her waist. It was usually of rope and was new (costing about 6d.), but there were silk halters, halters decorated with ribbons, straw plaitings and mere "penny slips".

The symbolism of the halter may have undergone some evolution. The critical term may be "delivery". Some early reports suggest that on occasion the husband and the purchaser first came to an agreement of sale (which might then be drawn up as a paper) and that the wife was then, on the next day or following week, publicly "delivered" to the purchaser in a halter. In a late example (Stockport, 1831) we have the actual form of words. The husband made an agreement to sell his wife to a butcher, Booth Milward:

---

[1] For example, Market Drayton Fair, *Shrewsbury Chronicle*, 27 June 1817; Bakewell Fair, *Derby and Chesterfield Reporter*, 14 June 1838; Horsham colt fair, 1820, 1825, and 1844, Henry Burstow, *Reminiscences of Horsham* (1911), pp. 73-4; Headley fair, W. W. Capes, *Scenes of Rural Life in Hampshire* (1901), p. 302. Also Menefee, ch. 3.

[2] Sabine Baring-Gould, *Devonshire Characters and Strange Events* (1908), p. 61.

I, Booth Milward, bought of William Clayton, his wife for five shillings, to be delivered on the 25th of March, 1831, to be delivered in a alter, at Mr. Jn. Lomax's house.

The agreement, drawn in a beershop, was signed by the husband and three witnesses.[1]

But "delivered" had not yet acquired the casual sense of delivering groceries or a message. In its common usage before 1800 it signified more "to free, to give up entirely, to surrender, to hand over to another's possession or keeping" (OED). Hence delivery in a halter symbolised the surrender of the wife into another's possession, and the importance of the ritual lay exactly in its public demonstration that the husband was a willing (or resigned) party to the surrender. This publicity was also essential because it displayed the wife's consent — or enabled her to repudiate a contract entered into between her husband and another without her consent.

However and whenever the ritual of the halter originated, by the end of the eighteenth century it was regarded in many parts of the country as an essential constituent of a "lawful" transfer. At Thame the re-sale of a wife took place in 1789: a man who had sold his wife two or three years before for half a guinea was told by his neighbours that "the bargain would not stand good, as she was not sold in public Market". He therefore "led her seven Miles in a String to Thame Market, and there sold her for Two Shillings and Six Pence, and paid *Four-Pence Toll*".[2]

The wife might be led into market in a halter, or the halter could be produced at the moment of sale. (If the woman was bashful, she might prefer to be haltered beneath her clothes, around her waist, keeping the spare rope in her pocket: when the auction commenced the husband took hold of the halter's end.) And ritual of this kind tends to breed its own local refinements and superstitions. In some cases it was held necessary to lead her around the market a magical three times.[3] In other cases the wife was led in a halter all the way

---

[1] *The Times*, 6 Apr. 1831.

[2] *Northampton Mercury*, 2 Jan. 1790.

[3] At a sale in Witney in 1839 it was reported that the woman was led three times around the market-place followed by hundreds of people, "the

to market from her home, and then led back in the same way
to her new home.[1] The symbolism was obviously derived
from the beast market, and here and there more elaborate
forms were devised to sustain the pretence that the wife was a
beast. Perhaps this was, in an old folk mode, a play at out-
witting the devil (or God)? The most frequent additional
business was to tie the wife to market railings, to fasten her in
a sheep-pen, to take her through turnpike gates (sometimes
again the magical three), and, most often, to pay to the
market officials the toll for a beast sale. And it seems to have
been accepted practice in some markets — including, for a
time, Smithfield — for the officials to receive the toll.[2]

d) In the market someone must perform the office of
auctioneer, and there must be at least the semblance of an
open auction. In most cases the husband auctioned his own
wife, but on occasion someone of official status — a market
official, poor law officer, auctioneer or drover — performed
the part.

Considerable ingenuity was shown in adopting the style of
a qualified auctioneer. At its most dismal we have the
recollections of an old Gloucester annalist who, when a boy
in 1838, was hanging around the beast market when he and
his companions saw a countryman leading a "fatigued, dust-
covered woman by a halter":

> A facetious old pig dealer exclaimed, 'Hallo, old 'un. What's up? What
> bist a gwain to do wee the old ooman, to drown her, hang her, or what?'
> 'No, I be gwain to sell her,' was the reply. There was a chorus of
> laughter at this. 'Who be her?' the pig dealer asked. 'Her be my wife,'
> the countryman answered, soberly, 'and as tidy, sober, industrious,
> hard-working a creetur as was ever meyud. Her be as clean and tidy as a
> pink, and wud skin a flint to save a saxpuns; but her a got such a
> tongue, and kips on nagging from monnin' to midnite. I can't have a
> moment's peace for her tongue, so we have agreed to part, and her have
> agreed to go to the highest bidder in the Market. . .' 'Be you willin' to be

woman waving a blue handkerchief" and exhibiting "a most barefaced and
disgusting effrontery": *Jackson's Oxford Journal*, 4 May 1839.

[1] A husband took his wife one mile out of town before bringing her
back in a halter to Arundel market, "he having been told that he must put
the rope on at that distance, or the sale would not be legal": *The Times*,
25 Dec. 1824.

[2] I have at least 14 cases of tolls paid and accepted, and other cases of
commissions to auctioneers or drovers, Menefee has others.

sold, missus?' enquired one. 'Iss, I be,' she replied very tartly. 'Now then', said the man, 'how much for her?' There was a pause, when an old cow-banger, with a ground-ash stick, bawled out 'Saxpuns for her!' The husband, holding the halter in one hand and raising the other, cried out in the stereotyped style 'Gwain at saxpuns; who ses a shillin?' There was another prolonged pause, when I, a vivacious youth. . . imprudently exclaimed 'A shilling!' 'Gwain, gwain at a shillin. Have ee all done?' called the husband. . . The bystanders laughed and chaffed, one exclaiming 'Here's a go, youngster! Her'll be knocked down to thee!' I perspired with apprehension. . . With renewed earnestness the vendor again cried: 'Who'll bid eighteen pence, vor her be a capital ooman as ever baked a batch o' bread or made a happle dumplin.' To my intense relief a tidy, respectable-looking man made the bid, and the husband, striking his hands together, exclaimed, 'Her be thine, man. Thee'st got a bargain and a good ooman, all but her tongue. Be good to her.' The vendee took the end of the halter, having paid the eighteen pence, and led the woman away.[1]

The account arouses suspicions, with its verbatim recall of fifty-years-past conversations. No doubt it is embellished in the telling. But the episode does include ritual features found in most sales: the wife's public consent ("Be you willin' to be sold, missus?", "Iss, I be"), the formal auction, the transfer of the halter. The husband passes over the frivolous bid from the boy, but closes instantly with a serious bid (which may possibly have come from an expected quarter).

The auctioneer's elaborate encomiums on the desirability of the article for sale ("her be as clean and tidy as a pink") was also expected by the crowd. It is a highly-theatrical transaction, and the husband sometimes acted up to this with jocular bravado, entertaining the audience with a patter which was in part traditional, in part carefully rehearsed. (This was, perhaps, one way of braving through a situation of public exposure.) Little reliance can be placed on newspaper accounts embellished for the readers,[2] and less on the wife

---

[1] Frank W. Sterry, *"H.Y.J.T."* [H. Y. J. Taylor] (Gloucester, 1909).

[2] Most often cited is the supposed patter of a small farmer, Joseph Thompson, at Carlisle in 1832, who is supposed to have cautioned the crowd against "troublesome wives. . . Avoid them the same as you would a mad dog, a roaring lion, a loaded pistol, cholera morbus, Mount Etna", etc. But then he went on to recommend Mary Anne — "she can read novels, and milk cows. . . make butter and scold the maid; she can sing Moore's Melodies, and plait her frills and caps; she cannot make rum, gin or whiskey, but she is a good judge of the quality from long experience in

sale ballads and broadsheets, which were standard printers'
stock.[1] But 'Samuel Lett', a ballad from Bilston (Staffordshire), gives at least an authentic sense of the humorous
expectations — a jocular alternation of praise and denigra-
tion — provoked by an auction:

> This is ter gie notice
> That bandy legged Lett
> Will sell his wife Sally
> For what he can get.
>
> At 12 o'clock sertin
> The sale'll begin.
> So all yer gay fellers
> Be there wi' yur tin.
>
> For Sally's good lookin'
> And sound as a bell,
> If you'n ony once heerd her
> You'n know that quite well.
>
> Her bakes bread quite handy
> An' eats it all up;
> Brews beer, like a good 'un,
> An' drinks every cup.[2]

A public auction, then, was central to the ritual, but the
form allowed for improvisations and variety. And it was by
no means always good-humoured. It could be degrading for
all parties and most of all for the wife.

e) Ritual demanded the passage of some money. This was
generally one shilling or above, although less was sometimes
given. The purchaser commonly agreed to pay for a quantity
of drink in addition to the purchase price, and sometimes an
additional sum was added for the halter. The husband

---

tasting them" etc. (See below p. 416, note 1.) I think this speech (but not
the sale) is a journalist's invention.

[1] Roy Palmer, with great generosity, has passed on to me many
examples of these. Some are spurious or are mere excuses for sexual
innuendo (listing the tools of each trade — "the cobbler bristled up his wife
with two big balls of wax"). See also Menefee, ch. 11.

[2] Jon Raven found this ballad in G. T. Lawley's notes in Bilston
Central Library. He recorded it to his own tune on his record *Kate of
Coalbrookdale* (Argo ZFB29). See also Jon Raven, *The Urban and
Industrial Songs of the Black Country and Birmingham* (Wolverhampton,
1977), pp. 143-4, 253.

frequently returned a small portion of the purchase money to the purchaser "for luck": in this the parties followed the old — and still vigorous — form of the horse and cattle markets, the return of "luck money".

f) The actual moment of the transfer of the halter was sometimes solemnised by an exchange of pledges analogous to a marriage ceremony: " 'Be you willing Missis to have me, and take me for better or worse?' 'I be willing,' says she. 'And be you willing to sell her for what I bid maister?' 'I be,' said he, 'and will give you the rope into the bargain'." [1] On occasion the report notes that the wife returned her old ring to her husband and received a new one from her purchaser. The passing of the end of the rope from seller to purchaser might also be accompanied by a public declaration by the former that he was renouncing his wife, and would no longer be responsible for her debts or actions. It could also be a moment for sentimental adieus, as in a record from Spalding (Lincolnshire) in 1786:

> Hand [took] a halter and put [it] upon her, and delivered her to Hardy, pronouncing the following words: — 'I now, my dear, deliver you into the hands of Thomas Hardy, praying the blessings of God to attend you both, with all happiness.' Hardy replied: 'I now, my dear, receive you with the blessings of God, praying for happiness,' Etc. and took off the halter, saying, 'Come, my dear, I receive you with a kiss; and you, Hand, shall have a kiss at parting. [2]

The transfer and exchange might be the end of the matter, the newly-linked couple departing hurriedly from the scene. But the ceremony was also sometimes followed by the adjournment of all three parties, with witnesses and friends, to the nearest inn, where the sale might be "ratified" by the signing of papers. It would also, of course, be pledged in drink (which, as we have seen, was sometimes included in the purchase money or returned by the seller for "luck").

Where the exchange was pre-arranged this part of the proceedings would presumably depend on the amount of good-will or ill-will in the air. Where bad feeling was

[1] Recollections of a "Nonagenarian" in *Hereford Times*, 21 May 1876; E. M. Leather, *The Folk-Lore of Herefordshire* (Hereford, 1912; reprint 1970), p. 118.
[2] Menefee, p. 100.

dominant, but a "paper" was required, this might be drawn prior to the public auction and at the sale the parties would split up for ever. Where goodwill was ascendant all parties would drink and draw up a paper together. A number of examples of such "contracts" survive, the most frequently cited being an entry in the toll-book at the Bell Inn, Edgbaston Street, Birmingham:

> August 31, 1773. Samuel Whitehouse, of the parish of Willenhall. . . this day sold his wife, Mary Whitehouse, in open market, to Thomas Griffiths, of Birmingham, value, one shilling. To take her with all her faults.

The signature of Samuel and Mary Whitehouse and of a witness followed.[1] Some eighty years later we have a Worcester example:

> Thomas Middleton delivered up his wife Mary Middleton to Philip Rostins for one shilling and a quart of ale; and parted wholly and solely for life, never to trouble one another.

Witness.	Thomas **X** Middleton, his mark
Witness.	Mary Middleton, his wife
Witness.	Philip **X** Rostins, his mark
Witness.	S. H. Stone, Crown Inn, Friar St.[2]

Presumably S. H. Stone was the publican where the paper was drawn up. It is of interest that of the three parties only Mary Middleton could sign her name.

Such papers were safeguarded, like "marriage lines", as a proof of respectability. Thus a Mrs Dunn of Ripon was quoted in 1881 as saying: "Yes, I *was* married to another man, but he sold me to Dunn for 25 shillings, and I have it to show in black and white, with a receipt stamp on it, as I did not want people to say I was living in adultery".[3] So convinced were people as to the legality of the procedure that they would attempt to secure an attorney's aid in drawing such papers, or would endorse them with official stamps. In Bolton (1833), after the market-place auction had taken place, the three parties adjourned to the "One Horse Shoe" where "the purchase money was paid after a stamped receipt

[1] *Annual Register*, 1773.
[2] *Worcester Chronicle*, 22 July 1857.
[3] *N & Q*, 6th series, iv (1881), p. 133.

had been given" and the wife was then "duly delivered". "The party afterwards partook of beefsteaks together, as a parting meal, and paid for two quarts of ale. . ."[1] Husband and wife had come into Bolton from a village five miles away, and the purchaser was a neighbour from the same place. What might have seemed, from a briefer or more sensational report, to be an unstructured and open auction can now be seen to have been carefully arranged.

This covers the main features of the "true" ritual wife sale: the open market, publicity, the halter, the form of auction, the passage of money, the solemn transfer, and on occasion ratification by paper. Elaborations or more exotic forms (such as literally stepping into the first husband's shoes) are sometimes found.[2] But the only significant alternative form which has left clear evidence was that of a more private transaction in the public bar of an inn. Although this took place before witnesses it was a form which avoided the full glare of publicity of the open market sale, and hence it may be seriously under-reported.[3] Cases most often came to light when some other matter (poor law settlement or custody of children) brought them before the authorities.

In 1828 the three parties to such a sale were brought before the West Kent Quarter Sessions, charged with a misdemeanour, and the court proceedings throw a little light on the form and how it was regarded. The three shared a parish (poor law) cottage in Speldhurst, and they agreed to meet at the "George and Dragon" in nearby Tonbridge. The publican deposed:

> Skinner came first, and asked for a pot of beer; he sat in the kitchen; his wife then came in, and shortly after Savage entered; they all drank together, and in a little time Savage went out; he soon returned, and Skinner then said to him, "Will you buy my wife?" He replied, "What will you have for her?" Skinner said, "A shilling and a pot of beer." Savage then tendered him half a crown, and Skinner delivered his wife to him; they drank together, and then went away; there were about four persons present; before they went, the woman took a handkerchief

[1] *Bolton Chronicle*, cited in *British Whig*, 8 May 1835.
[2] *Birmingham Daily Mail*, 29 Mar. 1871.
[3] It may have been the form most favoured in Kent, where I have several examples; and for a sale outside a pub in East London, see below, p. 455.

from her pocket-hole, which appeared to have been round her waist, and Skinner taking it, said, "I've now nothing more to do with you, and you may go with Savage."

We also know, on this occasion, a little about the reasons for the sale. Rumour was rife in the village that Mrs Skinner had taken Savage as her lover. As a result the overseers of the poor (who owned the cottage) ordered Skinner to turn Savage out, or he would be turned out as well. In their simplicity the three seem to have supposed that by a sale (or act of divorce and re-marriage) the parish authorities would permit Savage and the new Mrs Savage to remain in undisturbed tenancy of the cottage. But the Tonbridge Vestry was not so easily placated. Perhaps all three were evicted as soon as the sale came to light. Or perhaps Skinner took his solitary way from the "George and Dragon" to the parish workhouse, where he was resident at the time of the court proceedings.

Passing sentence on all three the "very learned" Chairman of the Bench allowed himself to indulge in a little dry wit ("the lady certainly did not rate her own value very highly, for a pot of beer and a shilling was the only consideration given for that valuable commodity") before passing on to higher levels of invigilatory moral exhortation. The practice of wife sales was "highly immoral and illegal" and "had a tendency to bring the holy estate of matrimony into contempt". But "the crime" would have been greater if it had been committed in open market. Taking also into consideration the fact that the offence was committed "in a state of ignorance", he thought a sentence of one month's imprisonment for each of them was sufficient. It is not recorded whether the accommodation at the local gaol was more, or less, salubrious than that at the local workhouse. The convicted felons had almost nothing to offer in their defence. Mrs Skinner said, "My husband did not go on to my wishes, and that was the reason I wished to part" [a laugh].[1]

IV

It is now clear — although it was not so in the 1960s when I commenced to collect this evidence — that we must remove the wife sale from the category of brutal chattel purchase and

[1] *Morning Chronicle*, 25 July 1828.

place it within that of divorce and re-marriage. This still may arouse inappropriate expectations, since what is involved is the exchange of a woman between two men in a ritual which humiliates the woman as a beast. Yet the symbolism cannot be read only in that way, for the importance of the publicity of the public market-place and of "delivery" in a halter lay also in the evidence thus provided that all three parties concurred in the exchange. The consent of the wife is a necessary condition for the sale. This is not to say that her consent may not have been extracted under duress — after all, a husband who wanted (or threatened) to sell a wife was not much of a consort. A wife who was sold in Redruth (1820) and who was brought, with her purchaser, before the Quarter Sessions in Truro, "stated her husband had ill-treated her so frequently and expressed his determination of selling her, that she was induced to submit to the exposure to get rid of him". This must have been true of some cases. But not, perhaps, the whole truth in this Redruth case, for the wife went on to admit "that she had lived with. . . her purchaser before she was publicly sold to him".[1] In many sales, even where there was a semblance of an open auction and public bidding, the purchaser was pre-arranged and was already the wife's lover.

To recover the "truth" about any marital history is not easy: to attempt to recover it, from newspaper snippets, after 150 years have passed is to go on a fool's errand. Even where direct assertions are made as to the wife's "misconduct" prior to the sale, all that we are given is the evidence of gossip or scandal. Yet this evidence does not tell us exactly nothing — let us take three cases, all from the year 1837.

The first concerns a sale in the butter market at Bradford (West Yorkshire). The report notes: "The alleged ground of the separation was the incontinence of the wife, whose affections were stated to have been alienated by an old delver, who had occasionally got his dinner at their house." When the husband commenced the auction "the first and only *bona fide* bid" was a sovereign from the delver. This "was immediately accepted, and, the money being paid, the couple

---

[1] *West Briton*, 14 Apr. 1820.

walked off amidst the execrations of the crowd".[1]

The second took place in Walsall market. Here a man led in his wife by a halter from a village eight or nine miles away, and sold her in a few minutes for 2s. 6d. The purchaser was a nailer, who had come in from the same village. All parties were reported to be satisfied. The wife had in fact been living with the purchaser for the previous three years.[2]

The third case took place in Wirksworth, Derbyshire. The wife of John Allen had eloped with James Taylor the previous summer. The "injured husband", learning that the couple were at Whaley Bridge, went and found them together in lodgings. "He demanded £3 for her clothes, which Taylor said he would pay on condition that he would accompany them to Wirksworth on the market day, and deliver her, as he called it, according to the law." Here we have a clear case of "delivery": Allen passed over the end of the halter to Taylor, and made a formal statement.

> 'I, John Allen, was bereaved of my wife by James Taylor, of Shottle, on the 11th of July last. I have brought her here to sell her for 3s 6d. Will you buy her, James?' James answered: 'I will, here is the money, and you are witness, Thomas Riley' — calling to a potman who was appointed for the purpose.
> The ring was delivered to Allen with three sovereigns and 3s 6d, when he shook hands with his wife and her paramour, wishing them all the good luck in the world.[3]

It could be argued that the first example offers no more than gossip; but the second and third cannot be passed over so easily. A purchaser does not happen to arrive from the same village, eight miles away, at the moment of sale: this was pre-arranged. Nor is a reporter likely to have invented the story of prior elopement and co-habitation. Indeed, the frequency of cases in which the wife was sold to a man with whom she was living already — and had been so living in some cases for three, four or five years[4] — raises a quite different question: why, if elopement and desertion was

---

[1] *Halifax Express*, cited in *The Times*, 9 Feb. 1837.
[2] *Wolverhampton Chronicle*, cited in *Globe*, 27 Oct. 1837.
[3] *Derbyshire Courier*, cited in *The Times*, 22 Aug. 1837.
[4] *See e.g. Derby Mercury*, 3 Jan. 1844; Nottingham case in *The Times*, 23 Sept. 1834; Menefee, p. 279 note 32; *London City Mission Magazine*, Aug. 1861, p. 189.

possible, on occasion, on the wife's part as well as on the husband's, did the parties still feel it necessary to undergo the public (and shaming) ritual of a sale?

I will come back to this searching question, although the answer may in the end be found only in the inaccessible personal history of each case. The difficulty with this material is not only that the evidence is so unsatisfactory but also that one can not conclusively show any one case to be "representative". Today's obligatory methodological imperative is to quantify, but the complexities of personal relationships are especially resistant to this exercise. And the "typical" short newspaper report gives no information at all on the motives of the parties — it is no more than a bleak report of a sale.

However, I have attempted to press the evidence into rude classifications, with this result:

Sales and Attempted Sales, 1760-1880: Consent of Wife

No information	123
Wife consenting	41
Wife sold to lover	40
Arranged divorce	10
Wife not consenting	4
	218

Since "no information" means no information on the point whatsoever, this shows 91 cases which signify the wife's assent or active participation as against 4 non-consents. If we look at sales between 1831 and 1850 (at which time the news reports tend to be fullest), we find:

Sales, 1831-50: Consent of Wife

No information	27
Wife consenting	10
Wife sold to lover	19
Arranged divorce	4
Wife not consenting	—
	60

I regard these quantities as literary and impressionistic evidence, as contrasted with the "hard" evidence in this chapter, which is the close interrogation of texts and contexts. The classifications are not finely-aimed. Let us examine each in its turn.

Wife not consenting. Moralistic notices at the time, as well as much subsequent historical commentary, imply that the wife was a passive chattel or unwilling party to the transaction. In fact, three of the four cases in the first table did not result in sales. In each of these cases we are told that a bargain was made privately between the husband and a purchaser, but was subsequently disowned by the wife.

The exception rests upon a letter addressed by Ann Parsons to a Somerset magistrate, 9 January 1768:

> I am the daughter of Ann Collier that lived at the bottom of Rush Hill and in the Early part of Life to my Great Mortification I was Married to a Man who had no Regard for himself or for the Support of Me and My Children. At the Commencement of the last Warr he Entered into the Kings service and Sir I Can't relate to you the tenth part of the abuses that I received from Him before his admission and Since his Return from the Army, at last for the Support of his Extravagancy He made Sale of me and Sold me for Six pound and Six Shillings and I was not in the least acquainted until he told me what he had done. At the same time He requested of me to keep the younges child. . .

In support of this account she enclosed a bill of sale drawn between her husband, John Parsons of Midsomer Norton, clothworker, and John Tooker of the same parish, gentleman: this asigned and set over Ann Parsons "with all right Property Claim Services and demand whatsoever" to John Tooker.

This is clear enough. But Ann Parsons went on to complain — not that the sale had taken place — but that her husband had not honoured the treaty. Three months after the sale (which took place on 24 October 1766) her husband "Visited me and Demanded Mor Money and abused me and the Man that he sold me too violently forcing open the door Swearing he would be Death to us both", and continuing this harassment until she applied for protection to a magistrate, who committed John Parsons to the Bridewell in Shepton Mallet. Committal had taken place the previous Michaelmas, and Ann Parsons was now afraid of the vengeance he might take when set at liberty. Her reason for petitioning the magistrate was to ensure her husband's continued detention.

It is not easy to know what to make of this story. Ann Parsons may (as she testified) have been sold without her knowledge and consent; or she may have thought this to be the best story to tell to the JP from whom she was seeking protection. Once sold — and (note) to a man of higher social status — it is certain that she wished the contract to be honoured, and she was pursuing her ex-marital revenge with skill and success.[1]

In the other cases of non-consent there is less to go on. In one case (North Bovey, Devon, *circa* 1866) it is said that the husband made a private agreement with a purchaser to sell his wife for a quart of beer. She repudiated the agreement, took her two children to Exeter, and returned to North Bovey only for her husband's funeral.[2] Another case came to light in a trial for bigamy in Birmingham in 1823. John Homer, an ex-soldier, was alleged to have treated his wife brutally and to have finally sold her against her will in a halter in the market. But the purchaser was her own brother, who for three shillings was "buying her out" of the marriage or "redeeming" her. (One does not know whether this case should be classified as non-consent or as an arranged divorce.) Homer then supposed that he was free to marry again and made the error of going through a formal church ceremony. He was convicted of bigamy and sentenced to seven years transportation.[3] In the other case, at Swindon Fair in 1775, it was said that an "eminent shoemaker" of Wootton Bassett came to a formal agreement with a cattle dealer to sell his wife to him for £50, and to "deliver her upon demand the next morning" —

> Agreeable to this bargain the purchaser set out in a post-chaise accompanied by many of his friends, decked in white cockades, in order to demand his purchase, when to their disappointment neither Crispin nor Crispiana. . . were to be met with.[4]

These cases do not contradict the rule, which was noted by some contemporaries, that the wife's consent was essential.

[1] Brit. Lib. Add MSS 32, 084 ff. pp. 14-15. My thanks to Douglas Hay for the transcription.

[2] *Devon N & Q*, iv (1906-7), p. 54.

[3] *Birmingham Chronicle*, 7 Aug. 1823.

[4] *Jackson's Oxford Journal*, 23 Dec. 1775.

This is confirmed by occasions when the wife repudiated with vigour an attempted sale. A visitor to Smithfield market in 1817 saw a man struggling to place a halter around the neck of a young woman of remarkable beauty. In the midst of a large and growing crowd, the wife resisted the attempt with all her strength. Crowd and constables intervened and the couple were taken before a magistrate. The husband explained that his wife had been unfaithful and he was therefore asserting a right to sell her.[1] In the wife's resistance to the halter we have confirmation that both halter and her consent were essential to confer legitimacy on the transaction. Even where the purchaser was not pre-arranged and where there was a genuine auction with open bidding, the wife was able to exercise a veto. Thus a report from Manchester (1824) says that "after several biddings she was knocked down for 5s; but not liking the purchaser, she was put up again for 3s and a quart of ale".[2] In a more dubious Bristol case (1823) the wife was "quite satisfied" with her purchaser, who, however, then re-sold her to another; "the lady. . . not liking the transfer, made off with her mother" and refused to be claimed by the second purchaser unless "by order of a magistrate, who dismissed the case".[3]

There must have been cases of forcible wife sale, in which the wife was terrified into consent or was too simple-minded or friendless to resist.[4] And there must have been other affairs in taverns which were drunken muddles. William Hutton, in a poem, "The Pleasures of Matrimony", reconstructed one of these which might have been a model

---

[1] *L'Hermite de Londres, ou Observations sur les Moeurs et Usages des Anglais au Commencement du XIX Siècle* (Paris, 1821), ii, pp. 318 ff.

[2] *The Times*, 29 June 1824.

[3] See Menefee, p. 68.

[4] Menefee, pp. 115 and 117 suggests examples, but those I have consulted are inconclusive. In a Grassington case, 1807, the wife "refused to be delivered": *Annual Register*, 1807, p. 378. In the case of a woman supposedly sold in the Grass Market, Edinburgh (1828), a broadside gives a lurid account of seven hundred women stoning and attacking the husband "in consequence of the insult the fair sex had received": W. Boag, printer, Newcastle, *Bibliotheca Lindesiana* (1898), no. 1656. However an identical story, with the same seven hundred women, is found in a broadside in the Madden Collection (no. 1872), but is there attributed not to Edinburgh but to Liverpool. See also Menefee, Case 215, p. 239.

for the sale in *The Mayor of Casterbridge*. The wife called into the ale-house to get her husband to come home to help with "the infant flock"; the husband was beside himself with anger (even though "he spent the money which she earn'd") and sold her to a fellow-drinker — William Martin, a young stockinger — for a pint of ale:

> The pint was order'd, bargain struck,
> And nothing back return'd for luck.
> The parties of a halter thought,
> But this they found would cost a groat.
>
> The halter scheme was instant lost,
> As being twice what Hannah cost,
> For that same reason neither would
> Pay fourpence that she might be toll'd.

But a deed of sale was drawn and signed between the two men, with the two children of the marriage divided — the child on its feet to the father, the babe-in-arms to the mother. Throughout all this the wife is described as a non-consenting party. But she does go off with the young stockinger, tramps with him from Hinckley to Loughborough: they fall in love with each other, live happily for a year, and are devastated when the husband repents and sends the Hinckley overseers to bring her back —

> She follow'd, but in anguish cried,
> O that the knot could be untied! [1]

The poem is not evidence, but it is not altogether fiction either, since it was based on the poet's own experiences as a stockinger's apprentice in the 1740s, and the purchaser, William Martin, was his own friend. Yet the poem had been written (or re-written) in 1793, and was no doubt reinvented from distant recollections. [2] I am suggesting, not that wives

[1] William Hutton, *Poems: chiefly Tales* (1804). Menefee, pp. 194-5 is quoting Hutton by way of a cutting of an article by G. T. Lawley (possibly "In the Good Old Days", *County Advertiser for Staffordshire and Worcestershire*, 7 Aug. 1921): both get the poem a bit wrong and delete Hannah's opposition to the sale (which she subsequently accepts).

[2] Hutton's *Poems* were in part reconstituted from manuscripts of thirty or more years earlier, burned with his premises in the Birmingham Riots of 1791. For William Martin, see Llewellyn Jewitt, *The Life of William*

were not sometimes sold under duress, but that if they
distinctly repudiated the transaction then the sale was not
held to be good according to customary lore and sanction.
The alternative view, of the wife sale as a chattel purchase
against the wife's will, presents very serious difficulties. For
that would have offended against law on a number of counts,
and very probably an action could lie for rape. Some wives
might be too ignorant to take recourse to law and have no
kin to come to their defence. But even in the eighteenth-
century village people knew how to make their way to the
magistrate's, parson's or parish officer's door; and it is
beyond all probability that no such case should ever have
occurred. If any such case had ever come before the courts,
then the courts — at any time after 1815 — would have
administered exemplary punishment and with the maximum
of publicity, for polite opinion had come to abhor the
practice, and JPs and constables often sought to intervene
and prevent it. But no record of any action of that kind, on
the wife's application, or on the part of her kin or friends,
has come to light.

Wife Consenting. This is the least satisfactory category.
The evidence is derived from some explicit reference to
consent in the source, or else to some such phrase as the wife
departed with her purchaser "in high glee", seemed "very
happy", "much pleased", or "eager". A few other cases are
included in which the indications of consent are so strong that
they allow of no other inference: as, for example, where the
first marriage was in common law only and where the sale
was followed immediately by a second marriage in church or
registry, or cases where the husband immediately regretted
the sale, tried to get his wife to return to him, but she
refused.

No Information. In these cases the sources afford no
information as to the wife's consent. But the reading has been
strict. In a number of cases it could be possible to infer her
assent from circumstantial evidence: thus, when all three
parties come to a market-town from a village several miles

Hutton (1872), pp. 144-6; Catherine Hutton, *The Life of William Hutton*
(1817), p. 128.

distant; where the wife is a signatory to a paper sale; where the wife is sold to a lodger or neighbour; cases where the husband sells (or gives) his stock or implements of trade with his wife (thus implying that he is leaving the new couple in possession of his livelihood); cases where the husband evinces acute jealousy, or where he evinces a show of unusual generosity to the new couple; or a handful of cases recorded by local historians who go on to add that the second marriage was happy and long-lasting. I am satisfied in my own mind that in many of these cases the wife was an active party to the exchange, but, since the evidence is slender, I have resisted the temptation to remove them from this group.

Arranged Divorce. This small group includes four cases in which the wife was sold to her own kin — to her brother, to her mother, and (two cases) to her brother-in-law. What this indicates is that a sale might not only be an exchange between husbands; it might also be a device by means of which a wife could annul or be "bought out of" her existing marriage. Both parties might then feel free to take a new consort. If the husband was making life unbearable for the wife she might agree to a sale and make her own arrangements for her "purchase".[1] In at least one case she is named as her own purchaser, and how this could be possible we will see in a notorious case at Plymouth (below p. 440). It also seems that the purchaser (in open auction) need not be the man whom the wife expected to end up living with, for the sale could be made to an "agent" acting on that man's behalf (or even on her own behalf).[2] Finally, this group includes two cases in which we are simply told that the sale was by a "previous

---

[1] See e.g. *Yorkshire Gazette*, 3 Aug. 1833 (Halifax case of sale to own mother); *Derby & Chesterfield Reporter*, 12 Feb. 1835; *Birmingham Chronicle*, 7 Aug. 1823 (wife sold to her own mother).

[2] Macclesfield case, reported in *Lincoln, Rutford & Stamford Mercury*, 7 Nov. 1817. Also Oxford case in J. R. Green, "Oxford During the Eighteenth Century", in C. L. Stainer (ed.), *Studies in Oxford History*, xl (1901), pp. 218-9, which suggests that the purchaser may have been acting as agent for the Woodward of Bagley. In the only oral record of a wife sale which I have collected, the family tradition — as recounted by the wife's grandson — is that the husband married her to get hold of her house, and then tried to sell her off. But "neighbours bought her in" and took her back to her parents' home: account of the late Bob Hiscox (then aged 84) of Pilton, Somerset, given to me in 1975; the sale was in Shepton Mallet

arrangement". And in three cases the wife was sold off by poor law officials.[1]

In one of these cases, which was brought to light in the *Second Annual Report of the Poor Law Commissioners* (1836) one sees official institutions (workhouse, overseers of the poor, vestry, church) co-existing with unofficial rites. In 1814 Henry Cook, a pauper whose settlement was in Effingham, Surrey, was "apprehended by the parish officers of Slinford, in Sussex, as the father of an illegitimate child" of a Slinford woman. "In accordance with the old system, a forced marriage was contracted", but one infers that the couple did not live together, for six months later Mrs Cook and her child were in Effingham workhouse. The master of the workhouse, who farmed his office for a fixed annual sum, complained at the expense of the newcomers. The overseers of the poor accordingly told the workhouse master to take Mrs Cook (with Henry Cook's agreement) to Croydon, where she was duly sold in the market in a halter to John Earl, from the parish of Dorking, Surrey. It is not said whether Earl was Mrs Cook's lover or not, nor how and why he came into the picture; all that we know is that the one shilling purchase price paid by Earl was given to him by the Effingham workhouse master, who was evidently most anxious to get these charges off his hands. A receipt was drawn up over a 5s. stamp and the workhouse master was a witness to the document. The new couple were then brought back to Effingham workhouse for the first night of their honeymoon, before being sent on the next day to Dorking where (after due publication of banns) they went through the marriage ceremony in church: "the parish officers of Effingham on this occasion provided them with a leg of mutton as a wedding dinner". All the expenses of these transactions were entered in the parish accounts and "regularly passed at a parish vestry". The story, which

---

and was perhaps the case reported in the *Castle Cary Visitor* of September or October 1848 in which the husband was roughly handled by the crowd (information from John Fletcher, who introduced me to Bob Hiscox).

[1] A young woman of Swadlincote whose husband had "some time since absconded" leaving her chargeable on the parish, sold in market by parish officer: *Derby Mercury*, 4 Feb. 1790.

started unhappily, ended in the same way, with Mrs Earl (now with seven or eight children) deserted by Earl (who had "ascertained" that his marriage was "not valid", presumably because Mrs Cook-Earl had been forced by these august conspirators — overseers, workhouse master and vestry — into bigamy?) and removed back to Effingham and the mercies of its poor law officials.

One really can not make out anything of the inwardness of this affair. Was Cook falsely sworn as father of the first child? Was Earl Mrs Cook's lover? All that is certain is that the marital history of the three was heavily influenced by economy-minded officials; and that, in 1814-15, the legitimacy of ritual wife sale went unquestioned in the parishes of Effingham and Dorking.

Wife sold to lover. None have been included in this group unless there is an explicit allegation to this effect in the source. No doubt many more could be added from the categories of "consent" and "no information". This can be supported by some literary evidence. One of the fullest accounts of the custom is from a Major-General Pillet, who travelled widely in England as a prisoner-of-war (on parole of honour) during the French Wars. His chapter on the subject is entitled "Divorces among the common people", and in his account the sale was always with the wife's consent, and generally followed upon her "misconduct". The purchaser must be single, and "is generally a lover of the commodity sold, and is well acquainted with it. She is only brought into the market place for the sake of form." [1] In any case, the sale only took place — as a Devon folklorist noted — "when the course of matrimony has arrived at a crisis". [2]

[1] R. Pillet, *L'Angleterre vue à Londres et dans ses provinces* (Paris, 1815), translated as *Views of England, during a Residence of 10 Years, 6 of them as a Prisoner-of-War* (Boston, Mass., 1818), ch. 33.

[2] *Devon N & Q*, iv (1906-7), p. 54. "Generally the affair was a pre-arranged one between the buyer, the seller, and the sold, who seem to have salved their consciences by going through the ceremony of a mock-auction": "Better-Half Barter", *Chambers's Journal*, 19 Feb. 1870. *The Laws Respecting Women, as they regard their Natural Rights* (1777), p. 55, described sale as "a method of dissolving marriage" among the common people, when "a husband and wife find themselves heartily tired of each other, and agree to part, if the man has a mind to authenticate the intended

How such crises arrived. . . at this point we must abandon
all search for the typical. I have not come upon any case in
which the evidence allows us to reconstruct a detailed marital
history. But there are two cases in which, for accidental
reasons, some information survives. In the first, there was a
settlement dispute between the Somerset parishes of Spaxton
and Stogumber. In 1745, when he was fifteen, William Bacon
obtained a settlement in Stogumber by hiring himself for a
year's service. Three years later (1748) he was "taken up" as
the father of a bastard child with which Mary Gadd, of the
same parish, was then pregnant. The couple were forced into
marriage, although William Bacon later testified that he
knew of his own marriage only by hearsay since he was
"carried to Stogumber Church by the officers of the parish",
and "being very high in Liquor he doesn't know whether he
was married or not". The couple never lived together: William
left Mary in Stogumber and found work in Bridgewater, a few
miles away. Mary gave birth to their child, Betty, in December
1748 (in William's absence); several years later she was living
with Robert Jones, with whom she had ten more children
between 1757 and 1775. In the years that followed, William
lived with another woman, by whom he had several children.

All this had gone on without any ritual of wife sale until
1784, when both William and Mary will have been in their
early fifties. Then the Stogumber poor law officers intervened in their marital (or extra-marital) affairs once more.
William Bacon had improved his position a little, becoming
the lessee of some grist mills in the parish of Spaxton, at
sixteen guineas a year. Thus this became his parish of settlement. Meanwhile Mary and her four youngest children
looked as if they might at some time in the future become
paupers, and one of them — young Mary — was "big with
child". She was about twenty, and her pregnancy was the
reason for the parish officers of Stogumber applying for a
removal order, "not to suffer her to have Child in the parish,
which would have been a Bastard". On the 18th December
1784 William Bacon was hauled in and examined as to his

---

separation by making it a matter of public notoriety". "A purchaser is
generally provided beforehand on these occasions."

settlement before two magistrates. The removal order had been drawn, not only for young Mary, but also for her mother and three siblings, although none of them were then chargeable. The administrative despotism of the poor laws was about to fall upon both families. Mary (the mother) and her four younger children were to be separated from Robert Jones (the children's father) and sent off to be supported by the miller and his family in Spaxton — and this after the passage of thirty-six years! Two days later (20th December) William Bacon came to Stogumber market-place to sell Mary and the children; he asked five shillings for them (that is, one shilling a-piece) and Robert Jones "accepted them at the price". This happened on the same day as the removal order — to expel all five to Spaxton — had been made, and the sale was used by both families as a device to defy the move.[1]

That case is typical of nothing, unless of the exceeding meanness of which poor law officials were capable. It seems that neither William nor Mary had felt any need for any ritual "divorce" until the overseers tried to break up their actual (if not legal) homes. (Possibly the wife sale was a fairly recent innovation in Somerset?) The other case comes from Plymouth in 1822 and it attracted unusual attention owing to the wealth and status of the parties. Here we are able to add a few details, as to which the husband and wife corroborated — or did not contradict — each other. Notice was given that a young and handsome lady, who would soon succeed to £600, would ride to town on her own horse, for sale in the cattle market. She arrived punctually, accompanied by the ostler of the "Lord Exmouth" inn, was met by her husband, and the auction had reached the sum of £3 (a bid from the ostler) when constables intervened, and husband and wife were taken to the Guildhall before the mayor.

Interrogated, the husband said he did not think there was "any harm" in doing it. He and his wife had not lived together for a considerable time; they had been married about two and a half years, and she brought him a child three

---

[1] Somerset CRO, D/P/Stogm, 13/3/6 (Settlement appeals). My thanks to Dr Polly Morris, and to Mr R. J. E. Bush, Somerset Deputy County Archivist. See also L. G. Mead, "What am I bid?", *The Greenwood Tree*, vol. 10, Autumn 1985 for a careful inspection of parish registers.

weeks after marriage, a child which (the innocence suggested here is surprising) "until after it was born he never knew anything about". The baby died shortly afterwards —

> He got a coffin for it, paid the expenses of the funeral, and put it comfortably out of the way, without ever reproaching his wife with her conduct; but all would not do. She soon deserted him. . .

— went to live with another man, by whom she had had one child since and was expecting another. The sale had been arranged at her instance: she said that someone was ready to give £20 for her — £3 in hand and £17 at Christmas. He had advertised the sale in Modbury on three separate market days, and had come to Plymouth by her appointment. The wife confirmed his account, adding that, since she had some doubt as to whether her lover would honour his promise to buy her at the auction, she had employed the ostler of the "Lord Exmouth" to buy her out of the marriage with her own money, provided that the price did not exceed £20. Both assumed the legitimacy of the ritual. The husband said "many people in the country told him he could do it", and the wife added "she had been told by different persons that the thing could be done, by public sale in the market place on a market day". "There was nothing below board in it", said the husband.[1]

The case is quite untypical. The vocabulary of ritual sale could be turned to many purposes. But the case illustrates the vocabulary clearly, and the general popular endorsement of its legitimacy. It is an interesting example of the dis-association of co-existing cultures, which allowed many people to accede to some of the forms and sanctions of Law and Church, but nevertheless to endorse customs which on occasion over-rode them. "Lor' bless yer honours", a West Country man said to the Reverend Baring-Gould, "you may ask any one if that ain't marriage, good, sound, and Christian, and everyone will tell you it is".[2]

---

[1] *Public Ledger*, 23 Dec. 1822; *The Times*, 23 Dec. 1822; H. F. Whitfield, *Plymouth and Devonport* (Plymouth, 1900), pp. 296-7.

[2] Baring-Gould, *op. cit.*, pp. 59-60. In some cases the actors may have genuinely assimilated their ritual sale and Christian marriage forms. The *Glouster Journal*, 24 Nov. 1766, reported that a husband in Thorne (Yorkshire) had sold his "old" wife in a halter for 5s. to a neighbour. Both

V

The ritual wife sale was probably an "invented traditon".[1] It may not have been invented until the late seventeenth century and possibly even later. Certainly there were instances of wives being sold before 1660, but I know of none before the eighteenth century which affords clear evidence of the public auction and the halter.[2]

The symbolism was derived from the market, but not necessarily (at first) from the beast market. Several early cases are of sale by weight, the best-documented (which rests on churchwardens' presentments) being from Chinnor (Oxfordshire) in 1696, where Thomas Heath, a maltster, was presented (and did penance) for selling his wife at "2d.q." the lb.[3] This suggests that the transaction at first borrowed the forms of the malt, cheese or butter market, and subsequently (halter, auction, turnpike gates, tolls, the pens) those of the cattle market or horse fair.

This suggests, not an ancient custom of forgotten origin transmitted down the centuries, but the pressure of new needs seeking for a ritual as outlet. An explanation suggested by nineteenth-century observers was that wife selling was a

---

men then went to Doncaster for a marriage licence, and at the ceremony the first husband gave the bride away to her new husband. (The minister officiating knew nothing of the circumstances.)

[1] See Eric Hobsbawm's introduction to Eric Hobsbawm and Terence Ranger (eds.), *The Invention of Tradition* (Cambridge, 1983).

[2] Sir Keith Thomas, Martin Ingram and other correspondents have with great kindness passed on to me early examples of allegations of the sale of a wife. These appear to be private transactions which follow no one particular form. Dr Ingram, who is an authority on sixteenth- and seventeenth-century church court records, has encouraged me in my view that wife selling in its ritual fform is a creation of the very late seventeenth and the eighteenth centuries: see Martin Ingram, *Church Courts, Sex and Marriage in England, 1570-1640* (Cambridge, 1987), p. 207.

[3] S. A. Peyton, *The Churchwarden's Presentments in the Oxfordshire Peculiars of Dorchester, Thame and Banbury* (Oxford, 1928), pp. 184-5. Other cases: Wife sold for 3/4d. a lb (but in fact by "guess" at 7s. 6d.), *Aris's Birmingham Gazette*, 11 Mar. 1745; wife sold at Rowley (Staffordshire) for 1 lb 6 oz of bread by husband who is now "gone for a soldier", *ibid.*, 18 Mar. 1745; Case 33 in Menefee, p. 216, from Newmarket, 1770 of wife sold at $5\frac{1}{2}$d. a lb.

consequence of wars, with the separations and the new attachments that resulted. This was especially noted at the end of the French Wars:

> In the manufacturing districts in 1815 and 1816 hardly a market day passed without such sales month after month. The authorities shut their eyes at the time, and the people were confirmed in the perfect legality of the proceedings. [1]

There is some evidence as to sales of this kind, when a long-absent (or supposedly-dead) husband returned from the sea or from the wars to find his wife with a new husband and family. [2] The French Wars, when multitudes were uprooted from their parishes, will have multiplied these occasions. Many wives, like Margaret in Wordsworth's "The Ruined Cottage", will have been left behind without news —

> She had learned
> No tidings of her husband; if he lived,
> She knew not that he lived; if he were dead,
> She knew not he was dead. [3]

But such cases count for only a small minority of our collection. The majority of wife sales were not occasioned by wars.

They were occasioned by the breakdown of marriages, and were a device to enable a public divorce and re-marriage by the exchange of a wife (not any woman) between two men. For such a device to be effective required certain conditions: the decline in the punitive invigilation over sexual conduct of the church and its courts: the assent of the community, and a measure of autonomy of plebeian culture from the polite: a distanced, inattentive or tolerant civil authority. These

---

[1] *N & Q*, 3rd series, iv (1863), p. 450.

[2] E.g. *Sherborne Mercury*, 13 Sept. 1784 and *Aris's Birmingham Gazette*, 6 Sept. 1784 (Worcester case of husband returning from "some years abroad"); *Jackson's Oxford Journal*, 20 Aug. 1785 (returned sailor, Liverpool); *Independent Whig*, 28 May 1815 (soldier returned after ten years); *The Times*, 10 Nov. 1838 (Dulverton, Devon — husband returned from transportation). In a famous Halifax case, the returned soldier sold his wife to the father of her three children, who was able to marry her only 25 years later, when the first husband had died. She was given away by her grandson: William Andrews, *Curiosities of the Church* (1890), pp. 177-8.

[3] W. Wordsworth, *Poetical Works* (Oxford, 1959), v, p. 35.

conditions were met in England through much of the eighteenth century, in which the ritual struck root and became established.

One scarcely needs to explain that marriages break down and that some form of divorce is a convenience. There was, of course, no such divorce available to the English or Welsh people at this time. The alternative might be informal exchanges and cohabitations. In practice the absence of forms had usually favoured the male partner, who could — as poor law and Sessional records testify — far more easily desert his wife and children than she could desert them. The man might be able to take with him some trade; once hidden in the city from the pursuit of the overseers of the poor he might set up with a new "common law" partner. The wife's outlet from an impossible or violent marriage was normally to the home of her parents or kin — unless she had already found herself a new lover.

There were suggestions among historians of fifty years ago that a great part of the labouring people in the eighteenth century lived in normless and formless animal promiscuity, and although this lampoon has been a good deal revised, some echoes of it still survive. The wife sale has sometimes been offered as an exemplar of this brutalism. But, of course, this is exactly what it is not. If sexual behaviour and marital norms were unstructured, where would have been the need for this high-profile public rite of exchange? The wife sale was invented in a plebeian culture which was sometimes credulous or superstitious, but which had a high regard for rituals and forms.

We have noted already the strongholds of this kind of culture — those communities, sometimes described as proto-industrial, tightly-knit by bonds of both kinship and economic activity: colliers, cutlers, framework knitters and stockingers, the iron workers of the Black Country, weavers, those who served the markets and transport. It does not matter much whether church or common-law marriages were most in favour in this community or that,[1] nor whether

[1] The best overview is John R. Gillis, *For Better, For Worse: British Marriages, 1600 to the Present* (Oxford, 1985); also R. B. Outhwaite (ed.), *Marriage and Society* (1981).

bastardy and pre-nuptial conception rates were rising. These indices do not tell us all that we might wish to know about the marital norms, expectations, reciprocities and roles of couples when once committed to a household and to children. A marriage (whether formal or common law) engages compulsions of kin, of neighbours, of work-fellows; it involves far more emotional interests than those of the two persons primarily concerned. We shall see, when we come to consider "rough music", that the expectations of the community penetrated into the family home, directing and sometimes constraining marital conduct. The watchful eyes of kin and of neighbours meant that marital offences were unlikely to go unknown in the wider community. Marital disputes were often taken out of doors and acted out as street-theatre, with a voluble appeal to the neighbours as an audience of jurors.

This was not a Puritan culture, and Methodists and evangelical reformers were shocked by the licence which they imputed to it, and especially by the sexual laxity of the young and unmarried. But there is abundant evidence that the consensus of such communities was such as to impose certain proprieties and norms, and to defend the institution of marriage itself, or of the family household.

This household was an "economic" as well as a domestic unit; indeed, it is impossible to show where "economic" relations ended and "personal" relations began, for both were imbricated in the same total context. When lovers courted each other they were "sweethearts", but when they were settled in the new unit they were each others' "help-meets", a word which carries sentiment and domestic function or economic role in equal measure. It is wrong to suppose that, because men and women had a need for each other's economic support, or for the support of their children in the daily work of the home, this necessarily excluded affection and gave rise to a callous instrumentalism. "Feeling may be more, rather than less, tender or intense because relations are 'economic' and critical to mutual survival".[1]

[1] See my "Happy Families", *New Society*, 8 Sept. 1977; H. Medick and D. Sabean, *Interest and Emotion* (Cambridge, 1984), pp. 9-27.

Within such communities it was impossible to change marriage partners — and to move into a new household in the next street or the next village — without it being a cause for daily, continuing scandal. Separation, especially if children were involved, made a rent in the kinship netting and disturbed the working neighbourhood.[1] It might seem to threaten other households. But the new couple might not be able to take the easy way out, by migrating to the nearest city and its more tolerant "anonymity", simply because it was not easy. The trade (nail-making, frame-work knitting, colliery) might be local, no other employer might be on offer, no other cottage to rent. If they stayed in their own community, some ritual which acknowledged the transaction must be found.

I concur with the most careful historian of British popular marriage — John Gillis — that the wife sale was most strongly supported in these plebeian or proto-industrial communities; that in general it was not a peasant custom and "the rite itself was not meant to deal with marriages in which property was involved";[2] and that it declined in frequency in the large cities, "where people could separate and remarry without anyone knowing or caring" — an overstatement, since in any urban street people knew or made it their business to find out. In short, we have moved from a land-usage to a money economy: a marriage with household is set up from the joint savings of bride and bridegroom (perhaps as servants or apprentices) and not from dower or land-rights. But we are still in a communal world of a known working neighbourhood with its market nexus. And if the community is knit together by kinship and common work it also has strands of common culture, made up of strong oral traditions (which are essential to transmit folk rituals) and an inheritance of custom and anecdote which is often encoded in the dialect speech of the people.

One further reason why, in such communities, a rite which signalled divorce might have been necessary could lead us

---

[1] When children are mentioned in reports of wife sales, it is generally assumed that babies-in-arms and toddlers stay with the mother: occasionally a family is split, and the older (working age?) children go with the father.

[2] Gillis, *op. cit.*, p. 218.

further into the psychic resources of those men and women than we are able to follow. But one may hazard that even when a couple had changed partners and removed to some other district, the more "simple" minded (as Hardy described Susan Henchard) would continue to feel acute mental discomfort if there had been no rite which unloosed them from their previous allegiance or oath. An oath could have a terrifying sanction, an inexorable obligation, upon men and women of this time; and the marriage vow carried with it a whole freight of traditional lore.

All this argues the need for some rite, and the rite itself has been sufficiently described. It can be seen as a bleak transaction, or as street-theatre, or as a shaming ritual. The nearest that we can get to a thick description of the whole affair is in a reconstitution by an observant journalist, who saw it as a comedy of manners of the Black Country (Appendix pp. 463-6). But the form was flexible enough to carry many different messages, according to the cases involved and the judgement of the public.

This can be illustrated by the function of money paid in the exchange. The sum passed varied from the merest formality to substantial damages. Here are some examples as they arise from my notes. In Stowmarket in 1787 a farmer sold his wife for five guineas. Then he presented her with a guinea to buy a new gown, and ordered the bells to be rung for the occasion.[1] At Sheffield in 1796 a husband sold his wife for 6d. He then paid a guinea for a coach to take her and her purchaser to Manchester.[2] In Hull in 1806 a man sold his wife for twenty guineas to a man who had lodged with them for four years: this looks like punitive damages.[3] At Smithfield in 1832 the wife was sold for 10s. with 2s. commission to the drover. The wife was then released from the pens opposite to the "Half Moon" public house, which the three parties then entered, where the late husband spent the greater part of the purchase money in brandy and water.[4]

---

[1] *Ipswich Journal*, 28 Jan. 1787, cited in J. Glyde, *New Suffolk Garland* (Ipswich, 1866), p. 286.

[2] *The Times*, 30 Mar. 1796, citing *Sheffield Register*.

[3] *Annual Register*, 1806.

[4] *The Times*, 25 Feb. 1832.

At Boston (Lincolnshire), 1821, a price of 1s., the husband returning 11d. to the purchaser "for luck".[1] But at the same place in 1817 a wife had been sold for three-farthings, and the husband "delivered into the bargain her paraphernalia, a shoulder of mutton, basket, &c.".[2]

That it was a shaming ritual for the wife is explicit in the symbolism. Most wives (like "Rough Moey's" in the Appendix) were at some point in tears. But because a wife is reported as "scarcely to be sustained from fainting" as she was being "dragged" in a halter to sale (Dartmouth, 1817) we cannot necessarily infer that she was an unwilling party to the exchange; we know, in this case, that she was sold to "her first sweetheart", and her reluctance might equally have come from the shame of the public exposure.[3] The humiliation might also extend to the husband who was acknowledging that he had been cuckolded. If the report can be trusted, Jonathan Jowett, a farmer near Rotherham (1775), braved his way through the transaction with a "ludicrous piece of business". He agreed to sell his wife for twenty-one guineas to William Taylor, a potter, whom he suspected of being her lover, and he duly delivered her in a "regular procession":

> Jowett went first, having his head ornamented, by his own desire, with a large pair of ram's horns gilded, on the front of which the following sentence was wrote in gold letters, 'cornuted by William Taylor'; a broad collar was fixed about his neck by which a ring and a cord being fastened thereto, one of his neighbours led him. And the wife with a halter about her neck was led by her husband to the place appointed amidst the shouts of upwards of one thousand spectators — Jowett returned the purchaser a guinea for luck and both sides seemed pleased with the bargain.[4]

The affair was being performed in the public eye. Just as the condemned before execution, the parties were acting up to expected roles. But they were given licence to improvise their own lines. For the husband the theatre provided opportunities for saving face. He could ridicule and humiliate

---

[1] *Hull Advertiser*, 2 Feb. and 23 Mar. 1821.
[2] *Stamford Mercury*, 7 Nov. 1817.
[3] *The Times*, 12 Apr. 1817.
[4] *Sherborne Journal*, 24 Aug. 1775. It was reported of a sale in Witney in 1848 that the wife was led by a halter to the market by her husband who wore a huge pair of horns: *Gazette des Tribunaux*, 22 June 1848.

his wife in the patter of an auctioneer; or he could suggest
good-riddance by asking a derisory price; or he could court a
reputation for generosity, showing his goodwill by causing
the bells to be rung, showering gifts on the new couple, or
hiring a coach; or he could, like "Rough Moey", signify
a comic resignation — "We all on us know how the matter
stands. It cawn't be helped, so we needn't be so savige
about it."

Not all partings were smooth. In a few cases the husband
is reported as evincing anger or jealousy towards his rival. In
other cases he "repented" the sale and harassed the new
couple. A stocking-weaver in Ansty (Leicestershire) in 1829
sold his wife to another stockinger. A few weeks later he
passed the new couple's house and "saw her at work in a
stocking frame, apparently very contentedly". This sight of
his former helpmeet now helping his rival enraged his
jealousy, he came back with a loaded gun and was aiming it
at her through the window when a passer-by intervened.[1]
Another case which ended in an unhappy parting took place
in Goole market (1849). Here a waterman named Ashton had
been an in-patient in Hull Infirmary with an infected knee;
meanwhile (according to the report) his wife eloped with a
paramour, taking with them a great part of the husband's
effects. On his release from the Infirmary Ashton tracked the
couple down and a sale was agreed. The wife was made to
mount a chair in the market-place with a halter around her
waist. After a little "spirited" bidding,

> The woman was eventually knocked down to her paramour for five and
> ninepence, when, snapping her fingers in her husband's face, she
> exclaimed: 'There, good for nought, that's more than thee would fetch,'
> and departed, apparently in high glee, with her new lord and master, the
> husband as they were passing him holding out his hand to her and
> saying, 'Give us a wag of thy hand, old lass, before we part'.[2]

But that is not all that "savige", and by no means as savage
as things which commonly have gone on in twentieth-
century divorce courts. Indeed, it is the language of
moralistic reporters which sometimes seems more savage than
the behaviour reported. As an instance here is a Yorkshire

[1] *Morning Chronicle*, 9 Feb. 1828.
[2] *Doncaster, Nottingham & Lincoln Gazette*, 14 Dec. 1849.

newspaper in 1829:

> According to the usual custom [the husband] purchased a new halter, for which he gave sixpence, and having tied it round his wife's neck, paraded her along the street, the impudent hussey being nothing loth to this public display of her attractions. A purchaser soon appeared, who bid eighteen pence for the woman and the rope, and her husband soon came to terms. A bargain was struck and the shameless parties retired amid the jeers of the assembled crowd, to a public house, where the money was spent, and the former owner of the slut drank to the luck of the purchaser, and the jade declared she was quite satisfied with the transfer, for she had 'got the lad she loved'.[1]

Beneath this crippled language one can detect humour, generosity and independent minds.

When this was street-theatre, what was the role of the audience? The crowds were sometimes large — sometimes "many hundreds" were reported — but more commonly the usual market day throng. So far as one can infer the response of the crowd was dictated by their views as to the rights and wrongs of the particular marital case enacted before them. Where the husband was known to have ill-treated his wife, the new couple might be cheered on their way; where the husband was popular and it was thought that he had been betrayed by his wife and her lover, they might witness the scene with hisses and execrations. At Ferrybridge (Yorkshire) in 1815 the purchaser and wife were pelted with snow and mud.[2] A North Yorkshire case, where an old man was held to have been betrayed by his young wife, resulted in the new couple being burned in effigy on the village green.[3] And there are other cases of the rough musicking of the new

---

[1] *York Courant*, 30 June 1829

[2] *N & Q*, 2nd series, i (1856), pp. 420-1. In Norwich when it was learned that the purchaser was already married and that he had turned his own wife out of door, he was hustled by the crowd: *Norfolk Chronicle*, 3 May 1823. Another pelting at Glastonbury, *Sherborne & Yeovil Mercury*, 21 Oct. 1833; *Western Flying Post*, 21 Oct. 1833.

[3] *N & Q*, 6th series, v (1882), signed A.J.M. —. This is A. J. Munby, whose MS Diary (Trinity College Library, Cambridge), iv, 27 February 1860, has the original story as told to him by "J.W. & Rev. J.S.". Munby ends the account in his diary: "Such is the influence of modern refinement that the whole village are indignant, and have even burnt the pair in effigy on the Green. Poor things!". (My thanks to Anna Davin for this reference.)

couple, most of them after 1850, when the rite was falling into disuse.[1] On other occasions the crowd appears to have defended the right of the parties to proceed with a sale. General Pillet witnessed an occasion at Ashburn (Derbyshire) during the French Wars, when a JP tried to prevent a sale and the constables were mobbed and pelted by the crowd. The crowd protected the sale from intervention in a similar way at Bolton (1835).[2]

It is one's impression that, until the early nineteenth century, neither lay nor clerical authorities were over-zealous in rebuking any of the parties. Some rural clergy and magistrates were well aware of the practice, and entries in baptismal registers can be found: "Amie Daughter of Moses Stebbing by a bought wife delivered to him in a Halter" (Perleigh, Essex, 1782).[3] The magistrate who tried, unsuccessfully, to intervene at Ashburn, confessed to General Pillet that the grounds of his action were uncertain. He could act against the parties for disturbing the peace ("coming to the market in a sort of tumult"), but "as to the act of selling itself, I do not think I have a right to prevent it. . . because it rests upon a custom preserved by the people, of which perhaps it would be dangerous to deprive them".[4] A disciplinary tone becomes more evident after the Wars, with heavy and indignant censures from the courts and press, the break-up of sales by constables, and the parties haled into

[1] For an angry episode, see *Bury Times*, 12 Nov. 1870. The wife had "transferred her affections" to a neighbour on the other side of the street, whose own wife died five weeks before the sale. The wife had eight children, four of whom ("in the receipt of wages") she took with her on her sale. After the sale first the wife was burnt in effigy in front of her new home, and the next day her purchaser; the report implies that women took the leading part in this rough music. Menefee has other good examples, pp. 117, 126.

[2] *Preston Pilot*, 7 Feb. 1835, citing *Bolton Chronicle*.

[3] See Menefee, Case 47, and pp. 270 and 198 note 16. Also entry in Formby Catholic Register for 9 April 1799 of birth of a child to James Wright and Mary Johnson: "This Mary Johnson was sold by her husband at formby Cross and purchased by Jas Wright for 15s and a crown bowl of Punch", Lancs. CRO, RCFO I (1799), p. 7. My thanks to Robert Malcolmson.

[4] See note 1 on p. 438.

court.[1] But it was not altogether clear what the courts could do with them.[2] For in the eyes of the law the rite of wife sale was a non-event. (If it had been accepted as an event, this would have entailed bigamy.) Legally, the parties might have been taking part in a pantomime. Indeed, when a dispute between two parishes about the maintenance of three children came before the sessions at Boston (Lincolnshire) in 1819, it was held that at law the paternity *must* be with the wife's lawful husband, John Forman, even though he had sold her to another man, Joseph Holmes, seventeen years before, had ceased then to cohabit with her, and two of the three children (the eldest of which was twelve) had been entered in the baptismal register as sons of Joseph and Prudence Holmes. Counsel argued that the sale of a wife was "a scandalous action", that children born in wedlock must be taken to be those of their legal parents, and that "it would be monstrous to admit of a husband's coming forward to bastardize the issue of his own wife". The court upheld these views.[3]

Since all agreed that wife sales were "monstrous" and "scandalous" the courts could proceed for misdemeanours, although not felonies. We have already followed the fate of the unfortunate Charles and Mary Skinner and John Savage, as they took their way from poor law cottage or workhouse via the tap-room of the "George and Dragon" at Tonbridge to prison (above pp. 426-7). They were conducted there by a very grand indictment, drawn (*vi et armis*) in the manner of Kings Bench —

> Being persons of wicked and depraved minds, and wholly lost to a due sense of decency, morality, and religion. . . did, with force of arms, at

---

[1] A man was sentenced at Manchester to three months imprisonment and to the pillory in 1815 for selling his wife: *Derby Mercury*, 3 Aug. 1815. Judge Edward Christian in his *Charges to Grand Juries* (1819), p. 93, called for prosecutions against the "shameful and scandalous practice" then so prevalent, and suggested that seller and purchaser might be sent to the pillory. Since the pillory was abolished in 1816 (Geo. III, c. 178) this charge was presumably delivered in 1815 or before.

[2] The practices were described as "mere pretences to sanction the crime of adultery" in the *Birmingham Gazette*, 1 Mar. 1790.

[3] *Stamford Mercury*, 12 Feb. 1819. For a similar decision at Warwick Quarter Sessions, see *Warwick Advertiser*, 15 Apr. 1809.

combine, confederate and agree together to bring into contempt the holy estate of matrimony. . . and to corrupt the morals of his Majesty's liege subjects, and to encourage a state of adultery, wickedness and debauchery. . . di da di da di da. . . sold all his marital rights. . . di da di da. . . for a certain valuable consideration, (to wit,) the sum of one shilling and a pot of beer. . . di da tiddely pom. . . to the great displeasure of Almighty God, to the great scandal and subversion of the holy estate of matrimony, and of religion, morality, decency and good order, in contempt of our Lord the King, &c.[1]

These monstrous miscreants were especially privileged in their indictment. A Rutland purchaser had to be content with being indicted as "a person of most wicked lewd lascivious depraved and abandoned mind and disposition and wholly lost to all sense of decency Morality and Religion", for which he was fined one shilling.[2] It was less common for the wives to be harrassed by the courts, since the law supposed them to be acting under the cover or control of their husbands. As Menefee has shown, the matter only entered the standard magistrates' reference books in the 1830s, at which time sentences of imprisonment (one, three, and even six months) were imposed.[3]

This may have done something to "put wife sales down", although it is more likely to have driven them out of the market-place and into the pub. More influential, in the decline of the ritual, will have been the decline in its legitimacy within the popular consensus — the old plebeian culture was fast losing its hold, faced with criticism from within, and uncertainty as to its own sanctions and codes. The Radical and Chartist press viewed the practice as scandalous.[4] Even Eliza Sharples, the "moral" (i.e. common-law) wife of Richard Carlile, who acknowledged the sale's function as divorce, found the practice offensive and brutal: "How much better would a quiet separation have

[1] *Sunday Herald*, 27 July 1828.
[2] Palmer, *The Folklore of Leicestershire and Rutland*, p. 58.
[3] See Menefee, ch. 8, and (for sentences) p. 299, note 24 and p. 300, notes 25 and 27.
[4] See e.g. *Northern Star*, 3 Mar. 1838. But the *Destructive and Poor Man's Conservative*, 13 July 1833, while finding wife sales "an outrage", added that "there should be some immediate cheap method of separation provided by the Legislature for the humbler classes. . .". Such a law would "put an end to such scenes".

been, and each left to a new and free choice. While women will consent to be treated as inferior to men, so long may we expect men to be brutes."[1]

By the mid-century, in the agitation which led up to the Matrimonial Causes Act of 1857 (which first established secular divorce procedures) there were more frequent comments on the double standards which permitted a difficult and costly divorce procedure to the rich, through the Ecclesiastical Courts and the House of Lords, but which denied these to the poor. Although — as *Punch* pointed out — the same procedure was free to the poor also:

> At the Central Court, one Stephen Cummins, painter, is found guilty of bigamy. He sells his wife for six shillings, and 'one shilling to drink health.' That the transaction may be in due form, Cummins gives a receipt. The Recorder, sentencing Cummins to imprisonment and hard labour for one year, says, 'Under any circumstances, it were a great public offence for a man to go through the ceremony of marriage with another woman, while his wife was living.' But then the poor are so depraved — are so illiterate! They will *not* go to the Ecclesiastical Court — they will *not* appeal to the House of Lords. A legal separation, conveying the right of future marriage, is always to be had on proper evidence given, — and yet the poor will not purchase their remedy.[2]

Caroline Norton made the same point in equally angry terms: since the time of Henry VIII, the English method of divorce "has remained an indulgence sacred to the aristocracy":

> The poorer classes have no form of divorce amongst them. The rich man makes a new marriage, having divorced his wife in the House of Lords: his new marriage is legal; his children are legitimate. . . The poor man makes a new marriage, *not* having divorced his wife in the House of Lords; his new marriage is null; his children are bastards; and he himself is liable to be put on his trial for bigamy. . . Not always offending knowingly, — for nothing can exceed the ignorance of the poor on this subject; they believe a Magistrate can divorce them; that an absence of seven years constitutes a nullity of the marriage tie; or that they can give each other reciprocal permission to divorce: and among some of the rural populations, the grosser belief prevails, that a man may legally *sell* his wife, and so break the bond of union! They believe anything, rather than what is the fact, — viz. that *they* cannot do legally that which they know is done legally in the classes above them. . .[3]

[1] *Isis*, 5 May 1832.
[2] *Punch*, xvii (1849), p. 129.
[3] The Hon. Mrs Norton, *A Letter to the Queen on Lord Chancellor Cranworth's Marriage and Divorce Bill* (1855), pp. 14-15.

By the 1850s the wife sale was a survival, in pockets where the old "plebeian" culture still endured. There is a late case, in Bradford (Yorkshire) in 1858, which suggests a moment of cultural insecurity, as the oral transmission of the forms is breaking down. Hartley Thompson offered his wife, "of prepossessing appearance", for sale in front of a beerhouse in a Bradford suburb. By one account the couple, both factory workers, "had become mutually tired of each other, and, it is said, had been mutually unfaithful to their marriage vow". A sale had taken place (it is not explained in what form) to the wife's lover, Ike Duncan, also a factory worker. "However, it was afterwards discovered that some formality, considered essential, had been overlooked." On the present occasion every possible formality was carried through. The bell-man was sent around to announce the sale. The wife appeared in a new halter, decorated with red, white, and blue streamers. An auctioneer was prepared on horseback. A large crowd assembled. But the owners of the factory in which they were employed prevented the sale by threatening to sack anyone who took part. Ike Duncan was kept in at work and the wife declared that "she would not be sold to any person. . . but Ike". The sale was called off. [1]

From the 1850s onwards the practice retreated into the more secretive forms of paper contracts witnessed in the public bar. The latest case in my collection which specifically mentions a halter is Hucknall Torkard, near Sheffield, 1889, where "a leading member of the Salvation Army" sold his wife to a friend for a shilling and led her by a halter to his house. [2] Paper contracts come to light more frequently: one Lincolnshire villager called at the Barton-on-Humber stamp-office to get a stamp on his. [3] The exchanges were sad and sometimes furtive affairs, outside or inside the pubs. One witness recalled a sale outside a pub in Whitechapel: the husband "a wretched-looking fellow", the wife "a respectably dressed woman, aged about thirty"; the landlord as auctioneer, and a young man who "it was understood would be the highest bidder". The newly-united pair walked

---

[1] *Bradford Observer*, 25 Nov. 1858; *Stamford Mercury*, 26 Nov. 1858.
[2] *Yorkshire Gazette*, 11 May 1889.
[3] *Stamford Mercury*, 22 Aug. 1856.

off, "the man with an air of bravado, and the woman with a sniff in the air", while the ex-husband "looked glum, and [his] neighbours manifested neither sympathy nor approval".[1] In the Midlands and the North it was said that sales took place among navvies, some colliers, bargees, some labourers. All that ritual now seemed to demand was publicity. The press reported (1882) a woman sold by her husband for a glass of ale in a pub in Alfreton on a Saturday night. "Before a room full of men he offered to sell her for a glass of ale, and the offer being accepted by the young man, she readily agreed, took off her wedding-ring, and from that time considered herself the property of the purchaser.[2]

Folklorists and journalists in the 1870s and 1880s indicate that the sense of the legitimacy of the practice endured. The *Standard* in a leading article in 1881 claimed that sales still took place in pubs in the Potteries, in certain mining districts, and in Sheffield amongst steel workers. The halter was rarely used. "The seller", wrote the editorialist, "the 'chattel', and the buyer all firmly believe that they are taking part in a strictly legal act of divorce and re-marriage".[3] On the same day the Home Secretary, Sir William Harcourt, was questioned about the matter in the House of Commons by an Irish Nationalist MP. His reply was curt:

> Everyone knows that no such practice exists. ["Oh!"] Well, Sir, if hon. Gentlemen from Ireland know the case to be different with reference to that country, I have nothing to say. . .

But in the view of the Home Secretary in England the practice was "unknown".[4]

VI

Wife sales have served to inspire eloquent exercises in moralism. In the nineteenth century the French, and other Continental neighbours, used them against the English in

---

[1] S. C. Hall, *Retrospect of a Long Life* (1883), i, pp. 43-4. This could, however, refer to a sale before 1850. Menefee (Case 245) suggests 1833.

[2] *South Wales Daily News*, 2 May 1882.

[3] *Standard*, 30 May 1881. Later cases are cited in *Daily Mail*, 1 Mar. 1899, *Globe*, 16 Nov. 1903, and A. R. Wright, *English Folklore* (1928).

[4] *Parliamentary Debates*, 261, col. 1646-7, 30 May 1881.

indignation or in jest. Americans also (wrote the feminist, Caroline Dall) "are anxious to understand this outrage. Is it possible that a government which forbids the sale of a negro cannot forbid the sale of a Saxon wife?".[1] Even the Anglo-Indian or "Eurasian" community, resentful of their twilight racial status, brought the matter up accusingly.[2] The polite classes in England — as we have seen abundantly — in their turn accused the brutalised labouring poor.

Since the scanty evidence did not exactly "feel" like that, I commenced my research, and in due course took the makings of this chapter around as an occasional lecture. By the late 1970s I was regretting my choice, and I would have stopped giving it as a lecture anyway, even if I had not been distracted by other matters. For it was decided by some feminists that my lecture was a male reading of the evidence and was offensive to correct views of "women's history". American feminists in the tradition of Caroline Dall voiced this criticism most strongly. At one university which has a little reputation (Yale) a faculty member shouted out as I left the lecture-room that my lecture had been "a con trick". On another occasion I was taken to task very forcibly by a scholar whom I greatly respect for suppressing the fact that the wife, when sold, was being cheated of her dower and attendant rights. But the evidence for this has not yet come my way.[3]

In short, it got about that I was taking around an anti-feminist lecture, and welcome parties were prepared. While British audiences were more good-humoured, I became weary

[1] Caroline H. Dall, *"Woman's Right to Labour" or Low Wages and Hard Work* (Boston, Mass., 1860), pp. 44-6.

[2] Herbert Alick Stark, *Hostages to India* (Calcutta, 1936), p. 78.

[3] We know too little about the decline of dower among working people, although see Alan Macfarlane, *Marriage and Love in England, 1300-1840* (Oxford, 1986), ch. 12. In a few cases wives sold in rural districts might have lost cottage property with common rights: see Bob Hiscox, above p. 436, note 2. J. F. Howson, rector of Guisely and Archdeacon of Craven (Yorkshire) recalled in the 1930s talking with an old man in his parish, who said: "A grandmother o' mine wur sold that road, she were that. 'Ave 'eered my father tell abaht it many a time. They put an 'alter rahnd 'er neck, tha' knaws, 'appen to maake it legal like. . . And worst of it wur. . . 'at we lost two cottages along of it, we did an' all". (Private communication to me from E. R. Yarham.)

of the hostile tone of questions — as if I was trying to pass some fraud over on the audience — and also a little hurt, since I had supposed myself to be on the side of women's rights (a supposition as to which my questioners were anxious to disabuse me). So I put the lecture away. This kind of intellectual charivari is only to be expected after generations of masculine-inflected history; it is merited; and it is a small price to pay for the rapid advance in feminine readings and definitions.

What I had done was to arouse certain expectations and then disappoint them. My title, "The Sale of Wives", had led the audience to expect a scholarly disquisition on yet one more example of the miserable oppression of women. But my matter did not (and does not) exactly conform to that stereo-type. Indeed, my intention was to decode behaviour (and even inter-personal relationships) which had been stereotyped by middle-class moralists (mostly male). The matter of feminine oppression was a subordinate theme.

Perhaps too much so. Perhaps in this chapter it has been too much taken for granted. One cannot always be reiterating the elemental organisation of a society and its gender relations, just as, if one is always parsing the parts of speech, one cannot listen to what a sentence is saying. If all that one can find in the relations between men and women is patriarchy, then one may be missing something else of importance — and of importance to women as well as to men. The wife sale is certainly telling us something about male-domination, but something which we already know. What we could not know, without research, is the small space for personal assertion which it might afford to the wife.

Let us agree, without any reservation, that the wife sale took place in a society in which the law, the church, economy and custom placed women in an inferior or (formally) powerless position. We may call this patriarchy if we wish, although a man did not have to be head of a household to be privileged over most women (of his own class). Men of all classes used a vocabulary of authority, and of ownership, with respect to their wives and children, and church and law encouraged this. The wife sale, then, appears as an extreme instance of the general case. The wife is sold like a chattel and the ritual, which casts her as a mare or cow, is degrading and was intended to degrade. She was exposed, in her sexual nature, to the inspection and coarse jests of a casual crowd. Although sold with her own assent, it was a profoundly humiliating experience which sometimes provoked her fellow women to anger[1] and sometimes called forth their sympathy: "Neer mind, Sal, keep yer pecker up, and never say die!" (below, p. 464).

Even if we redefine the wife sale as divorce-with-consent it was an exchange of a woman between two men[2] and not of a man between two women. (There are, in fact, records of husband sales, but they could be counted on the fingers of one hand.)[3] The fact that the ritual took place within the forms and vocabulary of a society in which gender relations were structured in superordinate/subordinate ways is not in doubt.

Yet there was something at work within the form, which sometimes contradicted its intention. Sales need not take place to the husband's advantage. Nor should we suppose that the norms of these working people were identical to those prescribed by church and law — that gives rise to serious mis-readings. In these "proto-industrial" working communities the relations between the sexes were undergoing some change. It is not yet appropriate to use a vocabulary of "rights"; perhaps "worth" or "respect" are the terms we need. The worth of women in these hard-working households was substantial, as was their responsibility, and it brought an area of corresponding authority and independence. I shall suggest, when we come to consider rough music, that male

[1] See Menefee, p. 124.

[2] Even this must be qualified, since (as anthropologists warn us) what is exchanged is not "a woman" but rights over a woman: see J. R. Goody, "Marriage Prestations, Inheritance and Descent in Pre-Industrial Societies", *Journal of Comparative Family Studies*, p. 40.

[3] There is a cryptic report of the sale of a husband in a halter at Dewsbury market cross, *Cambridge Gazette*, 26 Aug. 1815, *Warwick Advertiser*, 19 Aug. 1815. Another (1814?) in Drogheda was widely cited: e.g. Pillet, *op. cit.*, p. 185. A broadside (*Bibliotheca Lindesiana*, no. 1631) has a circumstantial account of the sale of a shoemaker by his wife in Totnes, Devon, 1824, but I doubt this case, which looks like confected printer's copy. There are a few *bona fide* cases of private contractual sales, for example of a husband who had left his wife to go to Australia: *Birmingham Daily Post*, 12 Jan. 1888.

insecurity in the face of this growing independence may explain some of the "skimmingtons" in the traditional West, with their obsession with cuckoldry and fear of women "on top". And the robust women whom we have seen in the front of food riots scarcely fall into the role of abject victims — a role ascribed to them a few years ago in the orthodoxy of certain campus feminists.

To read the history of women as one of unrelieved victimhood, as if anything before 1970 was feminine pre-history, can make for good polemics. But it is scarcely flattering to women. I was disabused of this early in my career as an adult tutor when I was talking to a Workers' Educational Association day school in a market-town in North Lincolnshire, and was waxing into condescending eloquence about women's oppression. An elderly self-educated villager, with a keen weather-beaten face, became tense, and at length burst out: "We women knew our rights, you know. We knew what was our due". And I realised with embarrassment that my callow emphasis on feminine victim-hood had been received by her and other members of the audience as an insult. They instructed me that working women had made their own cultural spaces, had means of enforcing their norms, and saw to it that they received their "dues". Their dues might not have been today's "rights", but they were not history's passive subjects.

Many years later I was at a conference somewhere in New England, when a speaker had been denouncing with great vivacity, and much applause, the sins of the author of *The Making of the English Working Class* "brackets male" and was indicating my omissions. It was all fair stuff, but my friend, the late Herbert Gutman, felt I needed some reassurance and whispered into my ear: "You know, these people are making the same mistake as some of the historians of the blacks did. They always wanted to show their subjects as victims. They denied them their self-activity."[1] Since Herb's whisper was more like a growl, his comment upset five or six rows before and behind us. Never mind, he was right.

---

[1] In one sense Herbert G. Gutman, *The Black Family in Slavery & Freedom* (New York, 1976), is a massive correction of acounts of slavery which have understated the slaves' cultural identity.

The wife sale was one possible (if extreme) move available in the politics of the personal of eighteenth-century working people. Yes, the rules of these politics were male-dominative, although the women in the community were the particular guardians of the institutions of the family. But it would seem that the women had the skill, on occasion, to turn the moves to their own advantage. I can see no reason why anyone should have supposed this to be an "anti-feminist" conclusion.

There are certainly victims among those sold wives,[1] but far more often the reports suggest their independence and their sexual vitality. The women are described as "fine-looking", "buxom", "of good appearance", "a comely-looking country girl", or as "enjoying the fun and frolic heartily".[2] Sally, in the Bilston ballad of "Samuel Lett", gives us the folk type of the sort of wife who might get sold:

> Her wears men's breeches
> So all the folks say;
> But Lett shouldna let her
> Have all her own way.
>
> Her swears like a trooper
> And fights like a cock,
> And has gin her old feller
> Many a hard knock.[3]

And we may identify at least one wife sold (in Hereford market very early in the nineteenth century) who lives up to this type —

> That was the woman who carried the bloody loaf in the bread riots. I saw it all. I saw her head the women to seize the load of grain. Old Dr Symonds told her to take the garter off her right leg and tie it to the

---

[1] One wife who was sold at Spilsby (Lincolnshire) in 1821 was committed to the house of correction the next week for threatening to set fire to her former husband's premises: *Stamford Mercury*, 7 Dec. 1821. There is a fierce denunciation of the husband who had sold her, published by Martha Barnard in a wall poster in Cambridge, July 1841: reproduced in Philip Ward, *Cambridge Street Literature* (Cambridge, 1978), p. 48.

[2] Among many examples, *British Whig*, 8 May 1835; *Leeds Times*, 10 Aug. 1844; *Derby Mercury*, 11 Oct. 1848; John Hewitt, *History and Topography of the Parish of Wakefield* (1963). Also Menefee, p. 276 note 10.

[3] See p. 423, note 2.

fore horse, and let the team go, and they did. . . They made a fine song about them all, beginning with —

> Have you not heard of our Herefordshire women?
> How they ran and left their spinning —
> How they ran without hat or feather
> To fight for bread, 'twas through all weather —
> Oh, our brave Herefordshire women![1]

We are not told whether she was sold before or after this affray.[2] But she does not sound like someone who could have been sold unless she had wanted that.

Another wife, who was sold in Wenlock market for 2s. 6d. in the 1830s, was quite decided about the matter. When her husband got to "market-place 'e turned shy, and tried to get out of the business, but Mattie mad' un stick to it. 'Er flipt her apern in 'er gude man's face, and said, 'Let be, yer rogue. I wull be sold. I wants a change' ".[3]

[1] "Nonagenarian" in *Hereford Times*, 15 Apr. 1876.

[2] The food riots were probably those of 1800. A wife was reported as being sold in Hereford in 1802 by a butcher for £1. 4s. and a bowl of punch: *Morning Herald*, 16 Apr. 1802.

[3] C. M. Gaskell, "Old Wenlock and its Folklore", *Nineteenth Century*, (1894).

APPENDIX

The account below is from Frederick W. Hackwood, *Staffordshire Customs, Superstitions and Folklore* (Lichfield, 1924), pp. 71-3. He describes it as "a descriptive account of a wife sale at Wednesbury, upwards of a century ago, written and published by a spectator", but no further details are given of the source.

"The town-crier, taking his stand before a low tavern, rings his bell to attract attention, and then gives notice in slow, deliberate phrases, that 'a woman —and her little baby — will be offered — for sale — in the Market Place — this afternoon — at four o'clock — by her husband — Moses Maggs'."

The announcement was received by roars of laughter, followed by loud "hurrahs," for the worthy named was one of the most notorious characters in the town, and commonly known as Rough Moey. He was a stout, burly fellow of about forty-five; his face had once been deeply pitted by smallpox, but the impress of the disease had been literally ploughed out by deep-blue furrows, the result of a pit explosion. He had lost one eye, and the place of one leg was supplied by a wooden stump. Neither in feature nor in figure was he prepossessing.

Shopkeepers came to their doors to pass remarks on the bell-man's announcement, and women with arms akimbo stood about the street in groups of two or three to gossip on the same subject. Other interested loafers adjourned the discussion to the nearest taproom. The crier moved away to repeat his announcement elsewhere, followed by a crowd of ragged urchins.

Just before the specified time a crowd gathered in the Market Place, in front of the White Lion, a well-frequented tavern, where four tall fellows, armed with cudgels, cleared a space, and kept back the eager sightseers from crushing upon a man, a woman, and an infant — the lions of the day.

The woman was younger than the man, probably about twenty-three, with as many good looks as was compatible with her situation in life, married, or "leased" to such a man as her mate. In her arms she carried a child about twelve months old, which was quite undisturbed by the uproar around. The woman was evidently in her best attire, her face was freshly washed, her hair was gathered behind in a bob and tied by a bit of blue ribbon, the ends of which floated behind in gallant streamers, no doubt in honour of the occasion.

Though a common hempen halter hung loosely round her neck, the end of which was held by her husband and master, she did not — to judge by her appearance — find the situation trying or unpleasant; and to such encouraging cries as "Ne'er mind, Sal, keep yer pecker up, and never say die!" she replied with a merry laugh, and such remarks as assured her hearers that she'd be glad to get rid of the old rascal, and that it served her right for marrying such an old vagabond.

Then some sort of order having been obtained, some ale was sent for, two tubs were brought out into the space and up-ended by the four stout fellows, on one of which the woman and her child were mounted, and on the other the man took his stand. While the ale was being consumed by the principals, a fiddler was brought in to enliven the proceedings with a merry tune or two.

During the interlude, inquiries among the crowd by the recording inspector, elicited these facts. That Rough Moey had given a sturdy pit wench, about half his own age, a new gown and other articles of dress, with a fortnight's treat, to marry him. That after a time she had transferred her affections to a good looking young collier; upon which the husband naturally became jealous and took to beating her. This, instead of curing her, only awakened thoughts of retaliation; and, as Moey often came home at night in a state of helpless intoxication, she would gently unstrap the wooden leg of the sleeping drunkard and thrash him with it to her heart's content. At last, tiring of this state of affairs, the discomfited husband had resolved to put an end to it by the only means known to him, that of making a "lawful" transfer of an undesired wife, by selling her to her admirer in open market.

The fiddling having ceased, the attention of the crowd was concentrated on the principal actors in the scene. The man, holding the halter in his left hand, raised aloft a quart jug full of ale in the other, and with a sly wink of his single eye, said in a loud throaty voice, "Laerdies an' gentlemin, 'ere's all yoar good 'ealths!" — and taking a long, long draught, finished with a long sigh of satisfaction, "Ah-h-h!" while inverting the jug to show that it was empty. A number of his friends (or "butties", as he called them) responded with "Thank thee, Moey"; while some of the women shouted at him, "Well done, old lad!"

Near to the woman stood a stalwart young fellow, evidently the intending purchaser, who supplied her with ale. She was keeping up a running fire of wordy exchanges with the women around; but notwithstanding this attitude of bravado, her eyes were seen presently to fill with tears, and her bosom began to heave as if her heart were beating fiercely under the strain of suppressed excitement. Then her voice faltered, and hurriedly handing the child to the young man, she sat down on the tub, buried her face in her hands, and wept bitterly. Instantly all laughing ceased, the clamour was hushed, and a look of indignation spread over every woman's countenance. Even some of the men seemed unable to suppress a sense of outrage, expression to which was given by the expectant purchaser, who hissed out in a savage voice, "Come, now, o'l chap, ha' done with this foolery; and get on wi' it!"

So old Rough Moey got on in this strain: "Laerdies an' gentlemin," he said, "we all on us know how the matter stands. It cawn't be helped, so we needn't be so savige about it." Then fortifying himself with another drink, and winking hideously with his remaining eye, he continued: "Laerdies an' gentlemin, I ax lafe to oppose to yer notice, a very handsome young ooman, and a nice little baby wot either belongs to me or to somebody else." Here there was a general laugh, good humour again gaining the ascendant among the onlookers.

"Her's a good cratur," went on the amateur auctioneer, "an' goos pritty well in harness, wi' a little flogging. Her con cook a sheep's yed like a Christian, and mak broth as good as Lord Dartmouth. Her con carry a hundred and a 'alf o' coals from the pit for three good miles; her con sell it well, and put it down her throat in less ner three minits."

This sally raised another laugh, and the orator was rewarded with more drink. Thus refreshed, Moey proceeded: "Now, my lads, roll up, and bid spirited. It's all right, accordin' to law. I brought her through the turnpike, and paid the mon the toll for her. I brought her wi' a halter, and had her cried; so everythin's right accordin' to law, and there's nothin' to pay. Come on wi' yer bids, and if yer gies me a good price fer the ooman, I'll gie yer the young kid inter the bargain. Now, gentlemin, who bids? Gooin', gooin', gooin'! I cawn't delay — as the octioneer sez, I cawn't dwell on this lot!"

The orator ceased, and a cheer rewarded his efforts. A voice from the crowd shouted "Eighteenpence".

"Eighteenpence," repeated Moey, "on'y eighteenpence for a strong and full-growed young ooman! Why, yo'd ha' to pay the parson seven and six for marryin' yer, an' here's a wife ready made to yer honds — an' on'y eighteenpence bid!"

"I'll gie thee half-a-crown, o'd Rough Un," came from the young man whom all knew would be the purchaser.

"I'll tell thee wot, Jack," said Moey, "if thee't mak it up three gallons o' drink, her's thine, I'll ax thee naught fer the babby, an' the halter's worth a quart. Come, say six shillins!"

After a little chaffering the young man agreed to pay for three gallons of ale, which it was stipulated should be forthcoming at once, so that his newly-bought wife, himself, and a few chosen "butties", not forgetting the obliging fiddler, should participate in the ratifying pledge-cup.

The bargain being thus concluded, the halter was placed in the young man's hand, and the young woman received the congratulations of numerous dingy matrons. She wiped her eyes and smiled cheerfully; her new husband planted a sharp barking kiss on her rounded cheek by way of ratification, and as the new wedding party moved away the crowd broke up and slowly dispersed. The tragi-comedy of rude Black Country life was terminated.

Chapter Eight

Rough Music

I

"Rough music" is the term which has been generally used in England since the end of the seventeenth century to denote a rude cacophony, with or without more elaborate ritual, which usually directed mockery or hostility against individuals who offended against certain community norms.[1]

It appears to correspond, on the whole, to *charivari* in France, to the Italian *scampanate*, and to several German customs — *haberfeld-treiben, thierjagen* and *katzenmusik*.[2] There is, indeed, a family of ritual forms here, which is European-wide, and of great antiquity, but the degree of kinship within this family is open to enquiry.[3]

In international scholarship *charivari* has won acceptance as the term descriptive of the whole genus. In 1972 I followed this example by entitling a study published in

[1] OED offers an early use of "rough music" in 1708, but it is noted as "the harmony of tinging kettles and frying pans" in R. Cotgrave, *A Dictionarie of the French and English Tongues* (1611). Regional terms such as "skimmington", "lowbelling", "hussiting" and "riding the stang" were probably more generally used, for which see Joseph Wright, *The English Dialect Dictionary*, 6 vols. (1896-1905).

[2] For French sources see the bibliography in Jacques le Goff and Jean Claude Schmitt (eds.), *Le Charivari* (École des Hautes Études en Sciences Sociales, Paris, 1981), pp. 435-42. This is cited hereafter as *Le Charivari*. For Italy, A. del Vecchio, *Le Seconde Nozze* (Firenze, 1885), esp. pp. 290-301. For Germany, E. Hoffman-Krayer and H. Bachtold-Staubli, *Handworterbuch des Deutschen Aberglaubens* (Berlin, 1931-2), entries under "Katzenmusik", "Haberfeldtreiben", "Thierjagen", etc; George Phillips, *Ueber den Urspring der Katzenmusiken* (Freiburg im Breisgau, 1849), and the contributions of Ian Farr and Ernst Hinrichs in *Le Charivari*.

[3] See Violet Alford, "Rough Music or Charivari", *Folklore*, lxx (1959), p. 507; H. Usener, "Italische Volksjustiz", *Rheinisches Museum für Philologie*, lxi (1901), and the section of contributions in *Le Charivari* on

France " 'Rough Music': Le Charivari anglais".[1] The difficulty of this assimilation soon became apparent. For the very term "charivari" arouses inapposite expectations and constructs the subject according to a French problematic, with its strong emphasis upon charivari as occasioned by second marriages, and also upon the role of unmarried youths. When a learned round table on charivari was convened in Paris in 1977, some visitors from Britain, Germany and Italy had reason to feel that the terms of discourse were "francocentric" and inapposite to their own national evidence. Yet there is no other generic term of international scope, and to say that a French typology has become dominant outside of France's own borders — and is exported with the word — is also to pay tribute to France's strong traditions in folklore, ethnology and anthropology.[2] One could not imagine, in the 1970s, a round table of international scholars convening in a British university to discuss rough music, and one should applaud the French intellectual initiative.

But, while applauding, one should resist inappropriate constructions. Perhaps one should resist, for most purposes, the term "charivari" altogether (unless one is working on French materials), and should stick to "rough music" for English materials?

"Rough music" is also a generic term, and even within the British islands, the ritual forms were so various that it is possible to view them as distinct species. Yet beneath all the

---

ancient and medieval Europe. P. Saintyves, "Le charivari de l'adultère et les courses à corps nus", *L'Ethnographie* (1935), pp. 7-36 offers a wide-ranging survey of penalties and humiliations for adultery, but one must agree with Lévi-Strauss that, so far as the rituals of charivari are concerned, most of his examples are not relevant. There are, however, striking similarities in rituals cited in Persia and Northern India (Saintyves pp. 22 and 28), and also in the brutally-sadistic ritual witnessed by Gorki in the Crimea: see A. Bricteux, "Le Châtiment Populaire de l'infidélité conjugale", *Revue Anthropologique*, xxxii (1922), pp. 323-8. For Hungary, see Tekle Dömötör in *Acta Ethnographica Academice Scientarum Hungaricae*, (Pest, 1958), pp. 73-89.

[1] *Annales E.S.C.*, (1972). Some passages in that article reappear in this chapter.

[2] See the summary of discussion in *Le Charivari*, pp. 401-3.

elaborations of ritual certain basic human properties can be found: raucous, ear-shattering noise, unpitying laughter, and the mimicking of obscenities. It was supported, in Thomas Hardy's description, by "the din of cleavers, tongs, tambourines, kits, crouds, humstrums, serpents, ram's horns, and other historical kinds of music".[1] But if such "historical" instruments were not to hand, the rolling of stones in a tin kettle — or any improvisation of draw-tins and shovels — would do. In a Lincolnshire dialect glossary (1877) the definition runs: "Clashing of pots and pans. Sometimes played when any very unpopular person is leaving the village or being sent to prison."[2]

It is not *just* the noise, however, although satiric noise (whether light or savage) is always present. The noise formed part of a ritualised expression of hostility, even if in the (perhaps debased?) forms recorded in late nineteenth-century examples the ritual was attenuated to a few scraps of doggerel or to the repetition of the "music" on successive nights. In other cases the ritual could be elaborate, and might include the riding of the victim (or a proxy) upon a pole or a donkey; masking and dancing; elaborate recitatives; rough mime or street drama upon a cart or platform; the miming of a ritual hunt; or (frequently) the parading and burning of effigies; or, indeed, various combinations of all of these.

In Britain the rituals extended across the spectrum from the good-humoured chaffing of the newly-wed to satire of the greatest brutality. Cornish "shallals" might only be a light

[1] See Thomas Hardy's admirably-observed novel, *The Mayor of Casterbridge* (1884). A Leicestershire dialect dictionary adds: "Pokers and tongs, marrow-bones and cleavers, warming-pans and tin kettles, cherry-clacks and whistles, constables' rattles, and blacders with peas in them, cow's horns and tea-trays" as well as "yells and hisses": A. B. and S. Evans, *Leicestershire Words, Phrases and Proverbs* (1881). Compare Diderot et d'Alembert, *Encyclopédie* (Paris, 1753), p. 208: "bruit de dérision, qu'on fait le nuit avec des poëles, des bassins, des chauderons, &c."; A. Van Gennep, *Manuel de Folklore Francais Contemporain* (Paris, 1946), i, pt. 2, p. 616: "chaudrons, casseroles, sonnettes, cloches à vaches, grelots de cheveaux ou de mulets, faux, morceaux de fer et de zinc, trompes en corne", etc. Compare for Italy, G. Gabrieli, "La 'Scampanata' o 'Cocciata' nelle nozze della Vedova", *Lares*, ii (1931), pp. 58-61.

[2] E. Peacock, *A Glossary of Words used in. . . Manley and Corringham, Lincs.* (English Dialect Society, 1887), p. 208.

community comment on bride or bridegroom — on their previous sexual reputation, and on whether they were held to be well- or ill-assorted.[1] Such affairs, not unlike Saxony *polter-abends*,[2] migrated across the Atlantic, and long survived in parts of the United States in the form of "shivarees".[3]

At the other end of the spectrum, perhaps one of the most psychologically-brutal rituals was that of the Devon stag-hunt. In this, a youth dressed in horns (and sometimes skins) would act as proxy for the victim. He would, by pre-arrangement, be "discovered", perhaps in a wood near the village, and be hunted by the "hounds" (the village youths) through the streets, backyards, across the gardens, run to earth and flushed out of alleys and stables. The hunt would continue for an hour or more, and, with a sadistic psychological refinement, the "stag" would avoid, until a final kill, approaching too close to the house of the intended victim. Eventually the kill took place — slow, brutal, and realistic. The "stag" was run to earth on the door-step of the victim, and a bladder of bullock's blood which he carried on

[1] See M. A. Courtney, "Cornish Folk-Lore", *Folk-lore Journal*, v (1887), pp. 216-7; A. L. Rowse, *A Cornish Childhood* (1942), pp. 8-9.

[2] For a good description of this ritual, when crockery was smashed against the door of newly-weds, see Henry Mayhew, *German Life and Manners as Seen in Saxony at the Present Day* (1864), i, p. 457.

[3] See Alice T. Chase in *American Notes and Queries*, i, p. 263, (September 1888); W. S. Walsh, *Curiosities of Popular Custom* (Philadelphia, 1914). "Shivarees" were reported as widely distributed in Ohio, Indiana, Illinois, Kansas and Nebraska. All married couples might expect a "shivaree", which could be bought off only by drink and hospitality to the crowd. For this, and also for more robust (and sometimes violent) affairs, see Bryan Palmer's fine study of "Discordant Music: Charivaris and Whitecapping in Nineteenth-Century North America", *Labour/Le Travailleur*, iii (1978); Alfred D. Young, "English Plebeian Culture and Eighteenth-Century American Radicalism", in Margaret and James Jacob (eds.), *The Origins of Anglo-American Radicalism* (1984); and Bertram Wyatt-Brown, "Charivari and Lynch Law", in his *South Honor: Ethics and Behaviour in the Old South* (New York, 1982), ch. 16. Good-humoured rough music to celebrate weddings also migrated to New Zealand, in the form of "tin-canning", and is occasionally practised at this day. I was kindly shown much oral reminiscence of "tin-kettling" when lecturing at the University of Auckland in 1988. This material is now held by Professor R. C. J. Stone.

his breast was pierced by a hunter's knife and spilled upon the stones outside the victim's house.[1]

One notes here the ritual hunt with diabolic undertones.[2] The manifestation of "wooset-hunting" still to be found in nineteenth-century Wiltshire carried a similar symbolism. An observer in a Wiltshire village in the 1830s encountered a procession, accompanied by the beating of frying-pans, the shaking of kettles with stones, the blowing of sheeps' horns and the sounding of sheep bells. Four men carried on long sticks hollowed turnips, with candles inside:

> Those were followed by a person bearing a cross of wood. . . seven feet high; on the arms of which was placed a chemise, and on the head of it a horse's skull, to the sides of which were fixed a pair of deer's horns, as if they grew there; and to the lower part of the horse's skull the under jaw bones were so affixed, that by pulling a string, the jaws knocked together as if the skull were champing the bit; and this was done to make a snapping noise during pauses in the music.

The procession, "got up by the village lads", went past the house or houses of the victims for three successive nights, on three successive occasions, with intermissions between each triplet: that is, for nine nights in all. It was (says the observer) employed against "conjugal infidelity".[3]

Other refined regional rituals could be cited. But we may say that most of the other forms fall into four groups, although these may overlap and borrow features from each other. These groups are: a) the *ceffyl pren* (Welsh for "wooden horse") associated with "Rebecca riots" in several parts of Wales); b) "riding the stang", widely distributed in

---

[1] Sabine Baring-Gould, *The Red Spider* (1887), ii, pp. 78, 109; Theo Brown, "The 'Stag-Hunt' in Devon", *Folklore*, xliii (1952), pp. 104-9. Cf. Carlo Ginzburg on "Charivari, associations juveniles, chasse sauvage" in *Le Charivari*, pp. 131-40.

[2] Until recently a frightening and diabolic horned mask used in such rituals survived in Dorset: see H. S. L. Dewar, "The Dorset Ooser" (Dorchester, 1968). (Plate XXVI).

[3] F. A. Carrington, "Of Certain Wiltshire Customs", *Wilts. Archaeological Magazine*, i (1854), pp. 88-9.

the Scottish Lowlands and northern England; c) "skim-mington" or "skimmety" riding, entrenched still, in the nineteenth century, in the West Country, but surviving elsewhere in the South; and d) plain rough music, un-accompanied by any riding, although very often accom-panied by the burning of the victims in effigy, found almost everywhere, and commonly in the Midlands and the South. Indeed, it is not clear whether unadorned rough music is a distinct form, or is simply the vestigial ritual still surviving into the nineteenth and early twentieth centuries after the elaborations of older ritual had fallen away. Thus in Cambridgeshire in the first decade of this century, the banging of tins and shaking of kettles is all of the ritual that is left.[1]

We will return to the *ceffyl pren*. The forms of plain rough music (d) will become sufficiently evident when we describe particular occasions. "Riding the stang" (b) and the "skimmington" (c) require some formal description.

In "riding the stang" either the offender, or a proxy (sometimes a near neighbour, sometimes a youth) repre-senting him, was carried on a long pole, or stang, attended by a rough band, or a "swarm of children, huzzaing and throw-ing all manner of filth".[2] If the victim was ridden in person, the procession might end by tipping him into a duck-pond or watery ditch.[3] Sometimes a ladder or a donkey might be substituted for the "stang"; more often an effigy in a cart.[4] If the riding was by proxy, a traditional recitative or "nominy" was shouted at different parts of the town or village:

---

[1] Enid Porter, *Cambridgeshire Customs and Folklore* (1969), pp. 9-10.

[2] J. T. Brockett, *A Glossary of North Country Words in Use* (Newcastle-on-Tyne, 1829).

[3] S. O. Addy, *A Glossary of Words Used in the Neighbourhood of Sheffield* (1888), pp. 185-6; Thomas Wright, *The Archaeological Album* (1845), pp. 54-6.

[4] W. E. A. Axon, *Cheshire Gleanings* (Manchester, 1884), pp. 300-1; Mrs Gutch, *County Folk-lore: East Riding of Yorkshire* (1912), pp. 130-3.

Here we cum, wiv a ran a dan dan;
It's neather fo' mah cause nor tha cause
    that Ah ride this stang
But it is fo' Jack Nelson, that Roman-nooased man.
Cum all you good people that live i' this raw,
Ah'd he' ya tak wahnin, for this is oor law;
If onny o' you husbans your gud wives do bang
Let em cum to uz, an we'll ride em the stang.
He beat her, he bang'd her, he bang'd her indeed;
He bang'd her afooar sha ivver stood need.
He bang'd her wi neather stick, steean, iron nor
    stower,
But he up wiv a three-legged stool an knockt her
    backwards ower.
        Upstairs aback o' bed
        Sike a racket there they led.
        Doon stairs, aback o' door
        He buncht her whahl he meead her sweear.
Noo if this good man dizzant mend his manners,
The skin of his hide sal gan ti the tanner's,
An if the tanner dizzant tan it well,
He sal ride upon a gate spell;
An if the spell sud happen to crack,
He sal ride upon the devil's back;
An if the devil sud happen ti run,
We'll shut him wiv a wahld-goose gun;
An if the gun sud happen ti missfire,
Ah'll bid y good neet, for Ah's ommast tired.[1]

The procedure was repeated, sometimes in several parishes, sometimes on three nights. If an effigy was carried, it was shot at, buried, or, most commonly burned.

This rhyme or "nominy" — the example is from Hedon in

---

[1] Mrs Gutch, *op. cit.* Other examples of such recitatives or "nominys" are in A. Easther and T. Lees, *A Glossary of the Dialect of Almondbury and Huddersfield* (1883), pp. 128-9; R. Blakeborough, *Character, Folklore and Custom of the North Riding of Yorkshire* (1898), p. 89; George Ratcliffe, *Sixty Years of It* (London and Hull, n.d. [c. 1935]), p. 2; G. Oliver, *Y Byrde of Gryme* (Grimsby, 1866), pp. 207-8; Thomas Miller, *Our Old Town* (1857), p. 198; Axon, *op. cit.*, p. 301; E. Cooper, *Muker: the Story of a Yorkshire Parish* (Clapham, 1948), p. 84; *Yorkshire Notes and Queries*, ed. C. F. Forshaw (Bradford, i, 1905), p. 209; *N & Q*, 9th series, i (11 June 1898), p. 479; *Folk-lore Journal*, i (1883), pp. 394-6.

the East Riding of Yorkshire — allowed for improvisations to be added, to suit the victim and the occasion.[1] The name of the offender might be shouted, although in some regions it was concealed to avoid an action for defamation,[2] or lightly disguised in a pun. When a husband called Lamb was beaten by his wife, he was ridden by proxy with a "nominy" similar to Hedon's, whose third line ran "But it is for the awde Yowe that threshest poor Lamb".[3] Variants of the rhymes have a wide geographic dispersal over the North and the Midlands. In Grassington,

> He neither took stick staff nor stoure
> But he up with his fist and he knocked her owre
> He struck so hard and it sank so deep
> The blood ran down like a new sticked sheep.[4]

The essentials of the "nominy" seem to have been as indelibly memorised as children's rhymes, and collectors have found elderly informants to be word-perfect in them. The words preserved in printed folklore collections may perhaps be a little bowdlerised, either by collectors or by their informants. An American collector, fifty years ago, preserved a version of the last two lines which is more credible (and also rhymes better) than the Hedon version preserved by that excellent collector, Mrs Gutch:

> If the gun should happen to miss,
> We'll scale him to death with a barrel o' red-hot piss.[5]

[1] The "nominy" (traditional doggerel accompanying the riding) is not the same as lampoons or rhymes made for the occasion, which Martin Ingram treats together with rough music in "Riding, Rough Music and Mocking Rhymes in Early Modern England", in Barry Reay (ed.), *Popular Culture in Seventeenth-Century England* (1985).

[2] Edwin Grey, *Cottage Life in a Hertfordshire Village* (St. Albans, n.d.), pp. 160-2.

[3] James Hardy (ed.), *The Denham Tracts* (1895), ii, p. 5.

[4] Robert White Collection, Newcastle University Library, Bell/White 3. My thanks to Dave Harker.

[5] James M. Carpenter was collecting in the late 1920s and early 1930s. My thanks to Roy Palmer and to Malcolm Taylor (librarian) for copies of records at Cecil Sharp House: the originals are in the Library of Congress. For the late Victorian and Edwardian collectors' censorship of the bawdy from folksong, see Vic Gamman, "Folk Song Collecting in Sussex and Surrey, 1843-1914", *History Workshop Journal*, 10 (1980), and "Song, Sex and Society in England, 1600-1850", *Folk Music Journal* (1982), pp. 219-20.

When a friend of mine, a village schoolmistress in North Yorkshire, recorded an account of the "stang", her informant — a man of about sixty — refused to repeat the words to her, and would only put them on her typewriter when she had left the room.

The "stang" merges its form almost imperceptibly with the "skimmington", and in parts of the Midlands it is scarcely useful to distinguish between the two. The "nominys" used in the East Riding "stang" (above) and in a West Somerset "skimmity" are clearly of common derivation:

> Now Jimsy Hart, if thee disn mend thy manners,
> The skin of thy ass we'll send to the tanner's;
> And if the tanner, he on't tan un well,
> We'll hang un 'pon a naail in hell;
> And if the naail beginth to crack,
> We'll hang un 'pon the devil's back;
> And if the devil urnth away,
> We'll hang un there another day.[1]

Some folklore accounts of the "stang" seem much like "skimmingtons", such as this one from Northenden in Cheshire. In about 1790 Alice Evans the wife of a weaver, and a powerful athletic woman "chastised her own lord and master for some act of intemperance and neglect of work" —

> This conduct (of hers) the neighbouring lords of creation were determined to punish, fearing their own spouses might assume the same authority. They therefore mounted one of their body, dressed in female apparel, on the back of an old donkey, the man holding a spinning wheel on his lap, and his back towards the donkey's head. Two men led the animal through the neighbourhood, followed by scores of boys and idle men, tinkling kettles and frying pans, roaring with cows' horns, and making a most hideous hullabaloo, stopping every now and then while the exhibitioner on the donkey made the following proclamation:
> > Ran a dan, ran a dan, ran a dan,
> > Mrs Alice Evans has beat her good man;
> > It was neither with sword, spear, pistol, or knife
> > But with a pair of tongs she vowed to take his life. . .[2]

The "skimmington", as it survived into the nineteenth century in the West Country, was distinguished by two

[1] Joseph Wright, *English Dialect Dictionary* (1903), v, entry under "Skimmington".

[2] Axon, *op. cit.*, pp. 330-1, citing Charles Hulbert, *History and Description of the County of Salop* (1828).

features: the elaboration of the ritual, and the frequency with which the victims satirised remained (as had been the case two or three centuries earlier)[1] the woman at odds with the values of a patriarchal society: the scold, the husband-beater, the shrew. Wiltshire Quarter Sessions records of 1618 give us an idea of the possible elaboration:

> About noon came again from Calne to Quemerford another drummer. . . and with him three or four hundred men, some like soldiers armed with pieces and other weapons, and a man riding upon a horse, having a white night cap upon his head, two shoeing horns hanging by his ears, a counterfeit beard upon his chin made of a deer's tail, a smock upon the top of his garments, and he rode upon a red horse with a pair of pots under him, and in them some quantity of brewing grains. . .

Coming to the victims' house (Thomas Mills, a cutler, and his wife, Agnes), the gunners shot off their pieces, "pipes and horns were sounded, together with lowbells and other smaller bells. . . and rams' horns and bucks' horns. . .". The doors and windows of the house were stoned, Agnes was dragged out of her chamber, thrown in the mud, beaten, and threatened with being carried off to Calne to the cucking-stool.[2]

Two centuries and more after this, "skimmingtons" were still being recorded in the West Country, if not on the same scale yet requiring elaborate preparation. In Uphill (Somerset) in 1888, 270 years after Agnes Mills was victimised in Quemerford, a wagon was drawn through the streets at dusk:

> Preceding it was a band of motley musicians, beating a fearsome tattoo on old buckets, frying pans, kettles, and tin cans. Mounted on horses, and riding with mock solemnity beside the waggon, was a body-guard of six grotesquely attired cavaliers. Erected on a platform on the waggon were two effigies.

[1] See especially Martin Ingram, "Ridings, Rough Music and the 'Reform of Popular Culture' in Early Modern England", *Past and Present*, 105 (1984), and David Underdown, *Revel, Riot and Rebellion* (Oxford, 1985), *passim*.

[2] See Ingram, "Ridings", p. 82, whose transcription corrects that in *Folklore*, xli (1930), pp. 287-90.

The procession went round the village, and then turned into a field where the effigies were burned to the accompaniment of the "Dead March".[1]

The ritual had many variants and allowed for much improvisation, invention and dressing-up. Where the victim satirised was a masterful woman or a husband-beater, two proxy performers might be seated in a cart or face-to-face on a donkey, beating each other furiously with culinary weapons, or back-to-back, with the man holding the beast's tail.[2] Where the reputed infidelity of the wife was the occasion, a petticoat or shift would be carried in the procession, along with horns, brewing grains and other symbols of cuckoldry. (Plate XXIII.)[3] On one occasion, recorded in Dorset as late as 1884, three character were satirised, one male, two female: both the females rode on donkey-back, while one of them "was represented as having an extraordinarily long tongue, which was tied back to the neck, whilst in one hand she held some note-paper, and in the other pen and holder".[4]

So much for the forms. More could be said. And more has been said. Unfortunately, those nineteenth-century folk-lorists to whom we are indebted for many of the best accounts of these rituals were interested, in the main, in the forms themselves; and, if they went further, it was most often to speculate upon their origin and relationship, to classify the forms according to a sort of human botany. Admirably-observed accounts of the form may include only the most casual, throw-away, allusion to the occasion for the event: the status of the victims, their supposed offence, the consequence of the rough music.

Nevertheless, before proceeding, let us see what evidence is offered to us from the forms themselves.

---

[1] *Somerset County Herald*, 24 Aug. 1946; also 23, 30 Aug. 1952. My thanks to John Fletcher for directing me to this and other sources.

[2] G. Roberts, *The History and Antiquities of Lyme Regis and Charmouth* (1834), pp. 256-61.

[3] See e.g. *N & Q*, 4th series, xi (1873), p. 455, referring to an occasion in Bermondsey (London) "about thirty years ago".

[4] J. S. Udal, *Dorsetshire Folklore* (Hertford, 1922), pp. 195-6, citing the *Bridport News*, Nov. 1884.

1) The forms are dramatic: they are a kind of "street theatre". As such, they are immediately adapted to the function of publicising scandal. Moreover, the dramatic forms are usually processional. Perhaps one should say, indeed, that they are *anti*-processional, in the sense that horsemen, drummers, banners, lantern-carriers, effigies in carts, etc., mock, in a kind of conscious antiphony, the ceremonial of the processionals of state, of law, of civic ceremonial, of the guild and of the church.

But they do not *only* mock. The relationship between the satirical forms of rough music and the dignified forms of the host society is by no means simple. In one sense the processional may seek to assert the legitimacy of authority. And in certain cases this reminder may be remarkably direct. For the forms of rough music and of charivari are part of the expressive symbolic vocabulary of a certain kind of society — a vocabulary available to all and in which many different sentences may be pronounced. It is a discourse which (while often coincident with literacy) derives its resources from oral transmission, within a society which regulates many of its occasions — of authority and moral conduct — through such theatrical forms as the solemn procession, the pageant, the public exhibition of justice or of charity, public punishment. the display of emblems and favours, etc. [1]

The formal continuities are sometimes startling. The naked parade or "carting" of lewd women or of prostitutes was a punishment which had once been imposed by ecclesiastical and civil authorities. Thus, in the Lincoln diocese in 1556 Emma Kerkebie, found guilty of adultery, was sentenced to the public penance: "That the said Emme shal ride through the city and market in a cart, and be ronge out with basons": i.e. rough musicked. [2] A similar punishment was inflicted by officers of the Parliamentary forces in 1642 upon "a whore,

---

[1] See C. Phythian-Adams, "Ceremony and the Citizen: the Communal Year at Coventry, 1500-1700", in Peter Clark and Paul Slack (eds.), *Crisis and Order in English Towns, 1500-1700* (1972).

[2] J. Strype, *Ecclesiastical Memorials relating chiefly to Religion and the Reformation* (1822), iii, p. 409. Riding backwards with the face to the horse's tail was a punishment inflicted for perjury, corruption, etc. by courts in London and by the Star Chamber in the sixteenth and early seventeenth centuries: see Ingram, "Riding, Rough Music and Mocking Rhymes".

which had followed our camp from London". She was "first led about the city, then set in the pillory, after in the cage, then duckt in a river, and at the last banisht the City".[1] And riding upon a pole or a "wooden horse" was a recognised military punishment, and was inflicted upon soldiers whose behaviour (assaults, petty thefts) endangered relations with the civil populace. Thus in 1686 a court martial sentenced an offending soldier accused of the theft of two silver cups "to ride the wooden horse the next market day in the public market place. . . for the space of two hours with a paper on his breast signifying his offence".[2] The punishment humiliated the offender in front of the populace, and hence it supposedly repaired the damage done to military-civil relations.[3]

The punishment could still be inflicted under Army regulations until the early nineteenth century. In 1845, at Yeovil, the same punishment had become an informal institution, it being reported that —

> The almost obsolete punishment of "riding the stang", or wooden horse, was revived in this town last Thursday by a number of builders who, suspecting that one of their number had made free with his comrades' dinners, pinioned him and paraded him through the streets upon a piece of wood with the words "the thif" chalked on his back. The Lynchers had contrived to refine the cruelty of the punishment by sharpening to a point the rafter on which the unfortunate fellow rode, and by jagging it in several places. He was taken home to Bradford Abbas in a cart on Friday, being so much injured as to be unable to walk.[4]

[1] Letters of Nehemiah Wharton, *Archaeologia*, xxxv (1853), pp. 310-34.

[2] PRO, WO 30/17, pp. 68-9. See also Young, *op. cit.*, p. 190 for the use of this military punishment at Louisbourg (1746) and Boston Common (1764). Black soldiers still received this punishment in the American Civil War: Bell I. Wiley, *Southern Negroes 1861-1865* (New Haven, 1965), pp. 317-8.

[3] The wooden horse may have been a permanent civil piece of punitive machinery in some places, along with pillory and stocks. An action in Newcastle-under-Tyne in 1654 turned on a man libelling another as "a base beggarly rascal, and hath cozened the Parliament a hundred times, and deserves to ride the wooden horse, standing on the Sandhill": *Tompkins v Clark* (1654), Style 422, ER 82, p. 829.

[4] *Sherborne, Dorchester and Taunton Journal* (1845) reported in *Somerset County Herald*, 23 Aug. 1952.

I do not know whether the formal (legal) and the informal (customary) infliction of such punishments coincided in late medieval and early modern times or whether popular, self-regulating forms (which were often initiated independently of any persons in authority, and which were sometimes conducted in such a way as to ridicule them) took over to new uses forms which the authorities were ceasing to employ. The answer may be "both". Until the early nineteenth century, publicity was of the essence of punishment. It was intended, for lesser offences, to humiliate the offender before her or his neighbours, and in more serious offences to serve as example. The symbolism of public execution irradiated popular culture in the eighteenth century and contributed much to the vocabulary of rough music.[1] The elaborate effigies of the offenders which were carted or ridden through the community always ended up with a hanging or a burning — which recalled the burning of heretics. In extreme cases a mock funeral service was conducted over the effigy before a "burial". One would be mistaken to see this as only a grotesque jest. To burn, bury or read the funeral service over someone still living was a terrible community judgement, in which the victim was made into an outcast, one considered to be already dead.[2] It was the ultimate in excommunication.

Effigy burning does not belong only with rough music. It can often be found in Britain and in North America detached from other forms of rough music and of course it has been

---

[1] See Douglas Hay, Peter Linebaugh and E. P. Thompson, *Albion's Fatal Tree* (1975). Compare Natalie Z. Davis, "The Rites of Violence", *Society and Culture in Early Modern France* (Stanford, 1975).

[2] Among examples of burial: *Leicester Herald*, 17 Apr. 1833 (an unpopular employer is rough musicked by framework knitters, his effigy is carried around on a gallows, executed by gunfire, placed in a grave, and then burned); *Hampshire and Berkshire Gazette*, 4 Feb. 1882 (a man who has jilted a woman whom he has been courting for several years — his effigy is carried through the village, the funeral knell is tolled, the effigy is hanged, cut down, shot at and burned); *Gloucester Standard*, 8 Oct. 1892 (the "Dead March" is played during the rough musicking of "scabs" in a boot and shoemakers dispute).

and remains central to Guy Fawkes Day.[1] November 5th was
a day when effigy burning and rough music ran into each
other, and local or public scores were often paid off.[2] And
effigies were appropriated to every kind of political and
religious demonstration. They were simply one (effective and
enduring) component of the available symbolic vocabulary,
which could be employed in combination with other
components (noise, lampoons, obscenities), or could be
detached from these altogether. Innumerable examples —
political, industrial, private grievances — can be found in any
locality.

With growing literacy, effigies, verse lampoon and
anonymous letters or papers posted on the church doors or
gates could all be used together. The Reverend Charles
Jeffrys Cottrell, JP, the Rector of Hadley in Middlesex, was
driven in 1800 to take legal action when he received in the
post a portrait of a gibbeted parson with his genitals exposed,
inscribed "O what a miserable Shitting Stinking Dogmatick
Prig of an April fool I do appear". (Plate VI.) It seems,
from the accompanying depositions, that the prime mover in
the campaign against him was Isaac Emmerton, a nurseryman and seedsman, who had also erected on his own land,
overlooking the Great North Road, a ten-foot-high gibbet
from which was suspended an effigy in a black coat which he
had got from a local undertaker. Cottrell was chairman of
the local Commissioners of Tax against whom Emmerton
had a grievance. But clearly this "Parson and Just Ass"
was generally unpopular and people in nearby Barnet were
enjoying similar "ludicrous drawings", which were being

[1] Alfred Young, "Pope's Day, Tar and Feathers and Cornet Joyce,
Jun", (forthcoming), discusses both American and English sources; C. S.
Burne, "Guy Fawkes Day", *Folk-lore*, xxiii, 4 (1912).

[2] Rough music often flourished on November 5th, when it was the
custom to make effigies of "any evil doer, bad liver, or unpopular
person" in the village and burn these before their homes (example, an
unmarried couple): *Trans. Devon Assoc.*, lxvi (1934). See the excellent
essay " 'Please to Remember the Fifth of November': Conflict, Solidarity
and Public Order in Southern England, 1815-1900", in Robert E. Storch,
Popular Culture and Custom in Nineteenth-Century England (1982),
esp. pp. 82-4. John Fletcher, a famous wizard in Pilton, has collected many
examples of Guy Fawkes rough musickings in nineteenth-century
Somerset, Glastonbury, Wells and Bridgwater being especially ebullient.

passed around. Isaac Emmerton explained, very reasonably, that the effigy was a scarecrow to protect some "curious seeds" and that for this purpose "none but a black coat would answer".[1]

This has taken us a little out of our way. But the consideration of even such a commonplace part of the symbolic vocabulary as the effigy enforces the point that the symbolism owes much to authority's pomp of awe and justice, and that rough music may be ambivalent and move between the mockery of authority and its endorsement, the appeal to tradition and the threat of rebellion. By the eighteenth century rough music was normally — but not always — initiated independently of any persons in authority or of gentry status, and was sometimes conducted in opposition to them. Since the church courts in England were in decline from the late seventeenth century, and were exercising less effectively their powers to inflict penalties for domestic and sexual offences, it is tempting to suggest that the vigour of eighteenth-century rough music indicated a shift from ecclesiastical regulation to community self-regulation in such cases. But this hypothesis has not been seriously tested. Or, if one sees an antiphony between the forms of authority and of the populace, one might ask whether, as ritual and processional declined in Protestant England, so the satiric anti-processional element in popular forms declined in ratio? In Catholic societies which maintained the processions and festivals of church and state with more vigour, did the mock processionals of charivari maintain for longer their elaboration?

2) The forms are pliant. Indeed, they have great flexibility. Even in the same region similar forms can be used to express a good-humoured jest or to invoke inexorable community antagonism. "Skimmingtons" of great elaboration were sometimes mounted as community jokes — for example, in Exeter in 1817 a riding with horsemen, a band, twenty-four donkeys, and much paraphernalia was laid on to ridicule the second marriage of a local saddler who had made himself

---

[1] Depositions and letter in PRO, King's Bench Affidavits, KB 1.30 (Easter 40 Geo. III, no. 2). For anonymous threatening letters, see my "The Crime of Anonymity", in Hay, Linebaugh and Thompson, *op. cit.*

obnoxious as a braggart and ostentatious patriot during the French Wars.[1] In Barnsley in 1844 the marriage of two local characters thought for some reason to be comic was "published" by an elaborate procession of power-loom weavers. Two led, one dressed in a skin, the other with a flag "Haste to the Wedding"; next a cart drawn by a mule with a fiddler astride it, and with whistles and tin cans played by the cart's occupants.[2] Jests of this kind might easily turn sour. When a butcher on the Isle of Wight, at Newport, married "an elderly maiden lady of good fortune" (1782) his fellow butchers attended to celebrate the event with marrowbones and cleavers. The bridegroom lost his temper and ordered them to go away:

> They had been expecting to be treated instead of being threatened with prison as a riotous mob. They returned, each with a pair of rams' horns fixed on their heads, and a drummer which they had hired. . . beating the cuckolds march. Outraged, the bridegroom fired at them, killing one and wounding two.[3]

The "skimmington" could also, in one variant, be used to establish what was known as a "horn fair" — in Devon if a "skimmington" or "skivetton" rode uncontested through a town, and nailed a pair of horns to the church door, then the claim to establish a cattle fair was made (and upheld).[4] "In consequence of some Woman in Calstock having beat her Husband", a correspondent wrote to the duke of Portland in 1800, "the Miners have made a Procession thro' the Neighbourhood & several Market Towns, in order, as they say, to establish an Horn or Cuckold's Fair at Calstock Town; the first of which Fairs is to be held there on Tuesday next". "Riotous Consequences" were apprehended, as "several very notorious bad Fellows" were among them.[5] The most famous Horn Fair might have had some such origin, and was held at Charlton on the Kentish edge of

[1] *Exeter Flying Post*, 2 Oct. 1817; U. Radford, "The Loyal Saddler of Exeter", *Trans. Devon Assoc.*, lxv (1933), pp. 227-35.

[2] *Halifax Guardian*, 20 Jan. 1844. Thanks to Dorothy Thompson.

[3] *Hampshire Chronicle*, 11 Feb. 1782. Thanks to John Rule.

[4] J. R. Chanter, "North Devon Customs", *Trans. Devon Assoc.*, ii (1867-8), pp. 38-42.

[5] J. P. Carpenter to Portland, 22 June 1800, PRO, HO 42.50.

London. By the seventeenth century it had become an annual carnival, held on St. Luke's day. In the eighteenth century it was proclaimed by printed summonses (Plate XXIV), and consisted of "a riotous mob, who. . . meet at Cuckold's Point, near Deptford, and march from thence in procession, through the town and Greenwich, to Charlton, with horns of different kinds upon their heads; and at the fair. . . even the gingerbread figures have horns".[1] Attendance at this supposedly licentious and bacchanalian event was not confined to the plebs — young patricians also might come, masked and in transvestite disguise — and all the symbolic vocabulary of "skimmingtons" and cuckoldry was kept vigorously alive (Plate XV).[2]

The more one examines the diversity of the evidence, the more difficult it is to define exactly what a rough music was. Sometimes we have nothing more than a boozy, jocular row outside the cottage on a couple's first wedding-night — although rarely without a satirical accent — by the unmarried young men of the community.[3] Some forms were also employed as games on festivals or as initiations into trades.[4] In the North-East in the eighteenth and early nineteenth centuries when a pitman married he was made to "ride the

[1] Francis Grose, *A Classical Dictionary of the Vulgar Tongue*, 2nd edn. (1788).

[2] John Brand, *Observations on Popular Antiquities* (1813), ii, p. 112; William Hone, *The Every-Day Book* (1826), i, cols. 1386-8; Robert W. Malcolmson, *Popular Recreations in English Society* (Cambridge, 1973), pp. 77-8.

[3] The late Mr G Ewart Evans kindly loaned to me a tape of an account given to him by Mrs Flack of Depden Green, near Bury St Edmunds in 1964, who described such "music" as very common until 1920 at weddings. People of "all sorts" gathered, and were asked in for drinks. She recalled only one occasion where it was used against supposed offenders. In London and elsewhere butchers' men made up bands, with marrowbones beating on cleavers (ground to the production of notes like a peal of bells), and attended wedding parties until paid off with money or beer: R. Chambers, *The Book of Days* (1878), i, p. 360.

[4] See Ingram, "Riding, Rough Music and Mocking Rhymes", pp. 94-6. "Wooset" or "hooset" hunting seems to be a cousin to Christmas and animal-guising customs, such as the hooden horse in East Kent and souling in Cheshire: see P. Maylam, *The Hooden Horse, an East Kent Christmas Custom* (Canterbury, 1909), ch. 4; Violet Alford, *The Hobby Horse and other Animal Masks* (1978).

stang", and was carried on a pole by his fellow pitmen to a
pub where he was expected to treat his mates to drinks:

> They myed me ride the stang, as suin
> As aw show'd fyece at wark agyen.[1]

This was a good-humoured custom whose only function was
as a ransom for drink. But in the same region in the same
period "riding the stang" was a severe, and on occasion
mutilating, punishment inflicted by pitmen and seamen upon
blacklegs during a strike or upon informers or crimps.[2]

3) Even when rough music was expressive of the most
absolute community hostility, and its intention was to
ostracise or drive out an offender, the ritual element may be
seen as channelling and controlling this hostility. There seems
to have been a progressive distancing from direct physical
violence, although the evidence is inconclusive. Dr Martin
Ingram shows us seventeenth-century next-door-neighbours
serving as proxies for the ridings, just as proxies are
frequently found in the nineteenth century. But just as Agnes
Mills of Quemerford was physically assaulted and thrown in
the mud in 1618, so examples of such assaults — or of "stang
ridings" ending in the midden or the duck-pond — can be
found two hundred years later.[3] And the "stang", as we

---

[1] Thomas Wilson, *The Pitman's Pay, and other poems* (Gateshead,
1843), pp. 56-63.

[2] *Newcastle Chronicle*, 7 and 21 May 1785, 4 Nov. 1792; *Sunderland
Herald*, 12 Feb. 1851; W. Henderson, *Notes on the Folk-lore of the
Northern Counties of England and the Borders* (1879), p. 30. In February
1783 at the close of the first American war sailors got shore leave and
revenged themselves upon informers who had betrayed them to the press-
gang by "stanging" them through the streets: the women "bedaubed them
plentifully with rotten eggs, soap suds, mud, &c.". One was treated so
severely on the "stang" that he subsequently died: "The Press Gang in the
Northern Counties", *Monthly Chronicle of North Country Lore and
Legend*, v, 47 (1891).

[3] This was especially the case with blacklegs, and also with sexual
offenders if taken *flagrante delicto*: W. Woodman, "Old Customs of
Morpeth", *History of the Berwickshire Naturalists' Club*, xiv (1894),
p. 127. There are infrequent cases of running a victim out of town in
nineteenth-century England (e.g. R. L. Tongue, *Somerset Folklore* (1965),
p. 181 for a "wicked" old woman run out on a hurdle with tin cans tied
round it accompanied by a rough band — a practice more common in the
New World).

have seen, could be employed as a mutilating instrument. In Galloway wife-beaters were ridden to a "nominy",

> Ocht yt's richt'll no be wrang,
> Lick the wife an ride the stang.
> At the words 'wife' and 'stang' they liftit it as heich as they could, an then loot it suddenly fa' again; and he cam doon wi' a thud every time on some o' the ens o' the brenches yt had been left sticking oot for his benefit, an the scraichs o' him wus fearfu.
> The stang wus through atween his legs, ye ken.[1]

So any generalisation must be qualified. A "skimmington" or "stang riding" could get out of hand, and if the person victimised offered resistance, or was so unwise as to rush out of the house when a proxy or effigy was displayed before it, some violence was likely to ensue. But at the same time a rough music was a licensed way of releasing hostilities which might otherwise have burst beyond any bounds of control. A scholar who has studied both charivaris and lynchings in the Old South of the United States suggests that "ritual only half-loosens social controls; it circumscribes just how far the participants should go, thus upholding stability and order".[2] In contrast to a lynching party this may be so, although the Ku Klux Klan ritualised lynching as well.

The argument that rough music rituals were a form of *displacement* of violence — its acting out, not upon the person of the victim, but in symbolic form — has some truth. It is my impression that in nineteenth-century England the proxy and the effigy usually stood in for the offender.[3] Rough music did not only give expression to a conflict within a community, it also regulated that conflict within forms which established limits and imposed restraints. It is (again) my impression that where the ritual forms still had a vigorous life in oral tradition, the disorder of rough music was most "orderly", whereas when they migrated across the Atlantic and were re-enacted with uncertainty in a society with general

---

[1] R. de B. Trotter, *Galloway Gossip: the Stewartry* (Dumfries, 1901), p. 442. My thanks to Roy Palmer.

[2] Wyatt-Brown, *op. cit.*, p. 447.

[3] Firmer law enforcement and heavier policing may have contributed to this.

access to firearms, the outcome was more often violent.[1]
Even the softened "shivaree", which in Canada may have
owed more to French than to British influence, and which
was frequently employed on the occasion of re-marriage,
could with little change of form assume a more brutal
expression. One author described a charivari supported by
"some of the young gentlemen in the town" on the occasion
of the marriage of a runaway negro (a barber) to an Irish
woman. Clearly, racism added a vicious tone to the ritual.
The young man was dragged from his bed and ridden on a
rail, almost naked, on a winter night, and he died under this
treatment.[2]

4) What is announced — when the stag collapses with his
pierced bladder of blood on the doorstep, when the effigies
are burned before the cottage, when the rough band parades
night after night while the victim listens within — is the total
publicity of disgrace. It is true that the forms of rough music
are sometimes ritualised to the point of anonymity or
impersonality: occasionally the performers are masked or
disguised: more often they come at night. But this does not
mitigate in any way the disgrace: indeed, it announces
disgrace, not as a contingent quarrel with neighbours, but as
judgement of the community. What had before been gossip
or hostile glances becomes common, overt, stripped of the
disguises which, however flimsy and artificial, are part of the
currency of everyday intercourse.

Perhaps we are sheltered from each other more by artifice
than we realise. Two parties to a social pretence, even when
each knows perfectly well that the other is pretending, are
none the less enabled by that artifice to co-exist. Even

---

[1] See Palmer, *op. cit.*, and Wyatt-Brown. Canada had vigorous
traditions of charivari, derived from both English and French traditions
and applied to many purposes. See also Bryan Palmer, *Working-Class
Experience* (Toronto, 1983), pp. 41-5. Charivaris accompanied the
rebellion in Lower Canada in 1837, and they were often supported by
patrician young men, with elaborate masking and masquerading. As late
as 1846 the first by-law passed by the city of Kingston, Ontario, was to
"suppress the useless and foolish custom, called the Charivari"
(Minutes in Kingston City Archives).

[2] Susanna Moodie, *Roughing It in the Bush; or Life in Canada*
(1852), i, pp. 230-1. My thanks to Robert Malcolmson.

hypocrisy is a kind of mist which blurs the hard radiance of mutual hostility. But rough music is a public naming of what has been named before only in private. After that, there is no more mist. The victim must go out into the community the next morning, knowing that in the eyes of every neighbour and of every child he or she is seen as a person disgraced.

It is therefore not surprising that rough music, except in its lightest forms, attached to the victim a lasting stigma. Observers often noted this. The intention of rough music, especially when it was repeated night after night, was, exactly, to "drum out" the victim(s) from the neighbourhood. "A Skimmington riding makes many laugh," an observer noted, "but the parties for whom they ride never lose the ridicule and disgrace which it attaches." [1] "As a rule", noted another observer of "riding the stang", "the guilty parties could not afterwards endure the odium thus cast upon them, but made a 'moonlight flit', i.e. left the neighbourhood clandestinely". [2] Of rough music at Woking (Surrey) it was noted that it "carried with it local ostracism":

> In more than one case the culprit was refused regular employment, and it was not unusual for shopkeepers and others to decline their business. [3]

On occasion, rough music could lead on to death, through humiliation (as Hardy suggests in the *Mayor of Casterbridge*) or from suicide. [4]

Not all, and perhaps not the majority of cases suffered from rough music as brutal as this; common nineteenth-century targets, the quarrelsome couple or the wife-beater, were usually treated somewhat more lightly. For some offences, once the offenders had paid the penalty of being humiliated they might be held to have expiated their

---

[1] Roberts, *op. cit.*, p. 260.

[2] *N & Q*, 5th series, v (1876).

[3] A. C. Bickley, "Some Notes on a Custom at Woking Surrey", *Home Counties Magazine*, iv (1902), p. 28.

[4] For suicide resulting from rough music, see *Caledonian Mercury*, 29 Mar. 1736 (occasion: wife-beating); *Northampton Herald*, 16 Apr. 1853 — attempted suicide of married labourer who had fathered the child of an unmarried young woman.

offence and subsequently be left alone.[1] But some kinds of sexual offenders were not forgiven; and for these one must suggest that they were subjected to a hostility of magical dimensions, a ritual hunt. The community defined the boundaries of permitted behaviour by expelling the hunted from its protection.

One is thinking here of the village or small town community or the compact urban neighbourhood. For not only individuals or families but also communities have reputations to maintain. There are villages or streets which acquire the reputation of being "rough".[2] Neighbours within a community may be rebuked for their behaviour — "They'll think we're all savages." Such a community may meet any enquiry from outsiders with extreme reticence, protecting its "own". Even intolerable behaviour is tolerated, or kept hidden from outside view,[3] — until and unless the offence is so grave that it is signalled by rough music, which signifies that the offenders are extruded and their neighbours (and perhaps even their kin) don't "own" them any more.[4]

5) There is a suggestion in some accounts that rough music was performed in the execution of some actual deliberative judgement, however shadowy, in the local community. "The *Vehm-Gericht* is self-constituted, sits in the tavern, and passes its sentence without summons and hearing of the accused" — thus an observer on the Devon stag-hunt.[5] At a Staffordshire village "a committee is formed to examine into the case. Then the village poet is employed to give a history of the occurrence in verse".[6] In

---

[1] Cf. Nicole Belmont, "Fonction de la derision et symbolisme du bruit dans le charivari", *Le Charivari*, p. 18.

[2] See M. K. Ashby, *Joseph Ashby of Tysoe* (1974), pp. 150-1.

[3] Folklore collectors often found this reticence quite impenetrable, especially on sexual matters. They were not only outsiders geographically but also (being genteel or middle class) socially. I have been asked by informants not to mention names or details of persons rough musicked fifty or more years ago, because children or grandchildren still live in the village. Other enquirers have told me of the same resistance.

[4] "Own" still has this meaning in Yorkshire. See Wright's *English Dialect Dictionary* for "own-born parish" and for the meaning of "own" as "to recognize, identify; to acknowledge an acquaintanceship".

[5] Baring-Gould, *op. cit.*, ii, p. 78.

[6] *N & Q*, 1st series, ix, 17 June (1854), p. 578.

parts of South Wales there was a "Coolstrin" court, which
sometimes summoned offenders before it, and whose chairman was crowned with the collar-bone of a horse. At Woking
(Surrey), where rough music appears to have been institutionalised in unusual strength, there was known to be a village
"court" that was "put into shape at an alehouse. . . but
when, who by, and how, was kept a profound secret".[1]
Thomas Hardy suggests such a court in the "Peter's Finger"
inn, where "ex-poachers and ex-gamekeepers, whom squires
had persecuted without a cause, sat elbowing each other".[2]
In less formal senses, the support of the community was
assumed: the women loaned their kitchen utensils, the men
clubbed together their pennies for beer for the band.[3]

Even where no "court" of judgement existed, the essential
attribute of rough music appears to be that it only works *if* it
works: that is, if (first) the victim is sufficiently "of" the
community to be vulnerable to disgrace, to *suffer* from it:
and (second) if the music does indeed express the consensus
of the community[4] — or at least of a sufficiently large and
dominant part of the community (supported, as was nearly
always the case, by the boys who found in a riding a superb
occasion for legitimised excitement and aggression, directed

---

[1] Bickley, *op. cit.* The same author, in a novel, *Midst Surrey Hills: a
Rural Stay* (1890), devotes a chapter to a reconstruction of such a tave rn
"court". For a consultation at the smithy, see Hardy (ed.), *The Denham
Tracts*, ii, p. 4. For the "Coolstrin" court in South Wales, see W. Sikes,
British Goblins: Welsh folklore &c (1880) and John Gillis, *For Better,
For Worse* (Oxford, 1985), p. 133.

[2] See Hardy, *The Mayor of Casterbridge*, ch. 36.

[3] See e.g. *N & Q*, 2nd series, x (1860), p. 477. An elderly informant,
Mr Gustavus Pettit of Leamington Spa, who witnessed a rough music when
he was a child in the last years of the last century, told me that he overheard
adult labourers planning the affair in a communal wash-house attached to
a group of cottages: see also *Coventry Evening Telegraph*, 10 Sept. 1970.

[4] Some categorise a charivari as a "ritual of degradation" or reversal.
To be effective it must carry the force of an impersonal or community
judgement: "The denouncer must so identify himself to the witnesses that
during the denunciation they regard him not as a private but as a publicly
known person. He must not portray himself as acting according to his
personal, unique experience. He must rather be regarded as acting in his
capacity as a public figure, drawing upon communally entertained and
verified experience." H. Garfinkel, "Conditions of Successful Degradation
Ceremonies", *Amer. Jour. of Sociology*, vol. 61, March 1965, p. 423.

against adults) to cow or to silence those others who — while perhaps disapproving of the ritual — shared in some degree the same disapproval of its victim.

Hardy shows this point superbly in the *Mayor of Caster-bridge* . There are some, like Longways, who hearing rumours of the impending "skimmety" feel "'tis too rough a joke, and apt to wake riots in towns". But no energetic steps are taken to prevent it, and, on the day, the authorities are not fore-warned, the constables hide from the crowd in an alley and stuff their staves into a water-pipe, discreet citizens stay indoors. When authority at length arrives on the scene, no-one has seen the "skimmety", no-one will inform on any other who has taken part. In the street, where only minutes before the procession had blared its raucous way, "the lamp flames waved, the Walk trees soughed, a few loungers stood about with their hands in their pockets. . . Effigies, donkey, lanterns, band, all had disappeared like the crew of *Comus*".

II

And, like the crew of *Comus*, they disappeared also from written British history in the twentieth century, to return only in the past decade.[1] If we are to interrogate rough music and its functions, we must turn back to nineteenth-century folk-lorists and observers, who themselves may have been pater-nalists, observing the "popular antiquities" of an alien culture across a wide social distance.

Their comments on rough music were often reticent and contradictory. Thus, of the Devon stag-hunt, one observer

---

[1] In Britain some interest continued among folklorists. However, English academic disciplines have shown until recently considerable hostility towards folklore, as "a mixture of scholarly curio-collecting and crack-pot fantasy": *TLS*, 16 Sept. 1969. Even Keith Thomas's path-breaking *Religion and the Decline of Magic* (1971) has only one passing reference to rough music. The revival of scholarly interest came from across the Channel, with Claude Lévi-Strauss, *Mythologiques I. Le Cru et le Cuit* (Paris, 1964), and with Natalie Z. Davis's important article, "The Reasons of Misrule", *Past and Present*, 50 (1971). My own first attempt at this chapter appeared in France but not in Britain, in *Annales E.S.C.* in 1972. The phenomena have since been visible in more and more studies, on both sides of the Atlantic, and became momentarily fashionable: see Edward Shorter, *The Making of the Modern Family* (New York, 1975), pp. 218-27.

tells us that it could be held "only when *two married* people
were known to be guilty". In another part of Devon it "did
not apply to married people" but to youths "guilty of grave
moral offence"; in yet another the victim was "a male
pervert". A further witness gives us yet another definition:

> The stag hunt takes place either on the wedding-night of a man who has
> married a girl of light character, or when a wife is suspected of having
> played her husband false.[1]

A similar conflict of evidence arises with the "skimmington"
and "riding the stang". Some observers assumed that the
"skimmington" had one target only: "to put to shame
households where the mistress had got the whip-hand of the
master"; others emphasise adultery as the occasion; yet
others discriminate between two variant forms — the
"skimmington" and "skimmerton" — applied to different
purposes.[2]

The most helpful definitions are, perhaps, those which are
least exact and which suggest a fluidity of function. Thus
Roberts identified several occasions for "riding the skimmerton": 1) when a man and his wife quarrel, and he gives up to
her; 2) when a woman is unfaithful to her husband, and
he submits patiently, without resenting her conduct; 3) any
grossly licentious conduct on the part of married persons.[3]
With "riding the stang", where there is a similar conflict of
evidence, Brockett's observation is useful: the ritual was —

> inflicted upon fornicators, adulterers, severe husbands, and such
> persons as follow their occupations during particular festivals or
> holidays, or at prohibited times, when there is a stand or combination
> among workmen.[4]

Another account is equally flexible: the ritual "set forth the
public reprobation of certain disgraceful actions, e.g. sins
against the seventh commandment, cruelty to women,
especially the beating of wives by their husbands,

[1] Brown, *op. cit.*, pp. 104-7; Baring-Gould, *op. cit.*, ii, p. 78; Baring-
Gould, *A Book of Folklore* (1913), pp. 251-2.
[2] *N & Q*, 4th series, iii, 26 June (1868), p. 608; *ibid.*, 4th series, xi, 15
March (1873), p. 225; *ibid.*, 4th series, iii, 5 June (1869), p. 529; Tongue,
op. cit., p. 181.
[3] Roberts, *op. cit.*, pp. 256-7.
[4] Brockett, *op. cit.*, entry for "Riding the Stang".

unfaithfulness of workmen to their fellows when on strike, and dishonest tricks in trade".[1]

It is useful, if arbitrary, to divide these occasions into two groups, which may be described as "domestic" and "public", and to examine each separately. We will examine the "public" group later. Of the "domestic" group, from many occasions, we may attempt a preliminary sub-division of the offences which occasioned rough music.

1) Specific offences against a patriarchal notation of marital roles. These include wives who beat or assault their husbands; the virago, or scold, or the "masterful" or nagging wife and the submissive husband; notorious quarrelsomeness in a married couple; and the complaisant cuckold or *mari complaisant*. In all these cases, although the woman may have occasioned the offence, both parties were satirised in the public disgrace, since the husband had failed to establish his patriarchal authority.

2) Rough music — although sometimes of a somewhat lighter character — might be enacted against the re-marriage of widows or widowers; and against marriages held by the community to be in some sense ill-assorted, grotesque, founded upon avarice, displaying a great disparity in ages, or even sizes or in which at least one party to the marriage had a lively pre-marital sexual reputation.

3) A number of sexual offences could occasion rough music. Unfortunately contemporary definition of the offence is usually evasive and lacking in specificity. Most often, the occasion appears to have been adultery between two married persons. A noted seducer of young women (especially if himself married) could be victimised. On occasion homosexuality or other "nameless" behaviour, regarded as perversion, was the object. A broken marriage or the sale of a wife could (but usually did not) bring rough music as a sequel.

4) Wife-beating or other ill-treatment of the wife by the husband; and cruelty to children.

Before examining these occasions further, it will be of interest to note the findings of other studies, based not upon

---

[1] W. Henderson, *Notes of the Folk-lore of the Northern Counties of England and the Borders* (1879), p. 29.

British but upon French and European materials. Violet Alford, who claimed to have more than 250 examples of charivari "under her hand" offered this break-down:

77 The re-marriage of widows or widowers.
49 Wives beating husbands.
35 Adultery.
24 For newly-married couples.
89 "Other causes" (some of which might be in my category of "public").

Her examples are of interest, but since they are derived from South, Central, and Western Europe, and are culled from perhaps eight centuries, they necessarily lack specificity of context.[1]

The learned French folklorist, Arnold Van Gennep, attempted no tabulation of his findings, but suggested that the main occasion for charivari in France over several centuries was for the marriage of widow or widower. Charivari has been directed also —

> aux maris battus par leur femme; aux avares, notamment dès la période enfantine, aux parrains et marraines chiches de dregées et de sous; aux étrangers qui, venus s'installer aux même de passage, ne paient pas le *bienvenue*; aux filles folles de leur corps; aux femmes adultères; aux ivrognes invétérés, brutaux et tapageurs; aux dénonciateurs et calomnieteurs; aux maris qui courent trop le guilledon; bref, à tous ceux qui, d'une manière ou d'une autre, excitent contre eux l'opinion publique de la communiaute locale.[2]

To the sexual occasions may be added girls who turn down a suitor of repute in the community for another who is richer, too old, or foreign; pregnant brides who marry in white; a youth who "sells" himself to a woman for her money; marriages which do not respect the prohibited degrees of kinship; girls who take a married man as their lover; *maris complaisants*, or husbands who "se conduisant dans leur ménage d'une manière plutôt féminine que masculine".[3] All these offenders (if we except certain cases which might fall into the "public" category) appear to fall within my divisions

[1] Alford, "Rough Music or Charivari", *op. cit.*
[2] Van Gennep, *op. cit.*, i, p. 202.
[3] *Ibid.*, i, pt. 2, pp. 614-28.

1), 2) and 3). Van Gennep appears to cite only one case of wife-beating.[1]

Lévi-Strauss, on the basis of unpublished findings by P. Fortier-Beaulieu, affirmed that 92.5 per cent of the cases under examination are occasioned by re-marriage, accompanied by disparity in age or wealth; or between individuals who are old; or after improper conduct during widowhood.[2] Unfortunately, these findings were based on a survey conducted in 1937, into (precisely) manifestations on the occasion of the re-marriage of a widow or widower, and hence had an inbuilt tendency to endorse Lévi-Strauss's theorisation of charivari as signalling a fracture in "la continuité idéale de la chaîne des alliances matrimoniales".[3]

In her important study Natalie Davis examined some aspects of charivari in sixteenth-century France. Her findings suggest that the overwhelming majority of cases fell within categories 1) and 2), and that re-marriage was a primary target for the rituals. The most frequent occasion for charivari in villages (she writes):

> was in connection with second marriages, especially when there was a gross disparity in age between the bride and groom. Then the masked youth with their pots, tambourines, bells, rattles and horns might make their clamor for a week outside the house of their victims, until they settled and paid a fine.

In an urban context she detects a shift; second marriages receive less attention, while the husband-beating wife and the beaten husband receive more, "for according to the provision of divine and civil law, the wife is subject to the husband; and if husbands suffer themselves to be governed by their wives, they might as well be led out to pasture". Adulteries, it would seem, received attention, and miscellaneous "faits vicieux" —

---

[1] A case is cited in Franche-Comté, *ibid.*, p. 619, note 2. In Diderot et d'Alambert, *Encyclopédie* (Paris, 1753, edn.), p. 208, it is assumed that charivari is occasioned by "personnes qui convolent en secondes, en troisièmes noces; & meme de celles qui épousent des personnes d'un âge fort inégal au leur".

[2] Lévi-Strauss, *op. cit.*, pp. 293-5. See also P. Fortier-Beaulieu, *Mariages et Noces Campagnardes dans. . . le Department de la Loire* (Paris, 1937).

[3] See Appendix II.

thefts, murders, bizarre marriages, seductions; but wife-beating scarcely at all.[1]

Subsequent research, by Davis and others, has refined these views and has added new occasions, but has not seriously revised them.[2] Martin Ingram's work on rough music in early modern England suggests both parallels and divergences. The institutional or quasi-institutional role of young unmarried men, or of the French youth "abbeys", has not yet been proved to have been found in England.[3] Ingram finds that "domestic situations, especially female domination, were the most usual occasions for charivaris in early modern England", just as they could occasion charivaris in seventeenth-century Lyons or Geneva.[4] An impression is formed that British rough music, over several centuries, may have been more abrasive and retributive than French charivari; although it is not impossible that, until recently, charivari has been a little softened and made picturesque in the French *folklorique* tradition.[5] Nineteenth- and twentieth-century collectors had been familiar with colourful parties investing a wedding and serenading the couple until paid off with money or drinks:

[1] N. Z. Davis, "The Reasons of Misrule: Youth Groups and Charivaris in Sixteenth-Century France", *Past and Present*, 50 (1971). The author cites one case only occasioned by wife-beating, at Dijon in the month of May, 1583: see p. 45, note 13.

[2] See especially the contributions of André Burguière and Nicole Castan in *Le Charivari*.

[3] However Bernard Capp, "English Youth Groups and *The Pinder of Wakefield*", in Paul Slack (ed.), *Rebellion, Popular Protest and the Social Order in Early Modern England* (Cambridge, 1984) offers some suggestive evidence.

[4] Ingram, "Riding, Rough Music and Mocking Rhymes", p. 169 and "Ridings", pp. 90-91; Natalie Zemon Davis, "Charivari, honneur et communauté à Lyon et à Genève au XVIIᵉ siecle", *Le Charivari*, pp. 221-8.

[5] The account of suicides and vendettas associated with charivari which is hinted at by Alford, "Rough Music or Charivari", pp. 510 and 513-4 contrasts with more romantic accounts by some popular authors. Compare the psychic violence of the "el vito" as described by J. A. Pitt Rivers, *The People of the Sierra* (1954), pp. 169 ff.

Dis donc vielle carcasse
Veux-tu pas nous payer
La dime de tes noces
Aux enfants du quartier.
Si tu fais la rebelle
On vient t'avertir,
Que pendant la semaine
On battre Charivari![1]

This had become, in expectation, what a charivari *was* and the ritual was theorised accordingly. And the paradigm of charivari was seen to be in the serenading of the re-marriage of the widow or the widower.

But the evidence available from Germany, some parts of Central and Eastern Europe, and North America does not give the same priority to second marriages. In Bavaria the punitive *haberfeldtreiben* passed through phases, but was primarily directed at offenders against sexual norms,[2] while the occasions for *katzenmusik* in Western Germany seem to have been as various as occasions for "skimmingtons" and "stangs".[3] Re-marriage rarely is mentioned among these, nor does it feature in Roumania, where other attributes of rough music — noisy, masked demonstrations with effigies and obscene verses — are found.[4] Nor, indeed, in Hungary, which had, until recently, a group of colourful, and sometimes vindictive, practices involving rough music (with ploughshares tied together and caterwauling), animal guising, mock marriage ceremonies, shadowy courts of popular law (as in Bavaria) and lampoons.[5] Re-marriage does turn up as an occasion for charivaris in North America, especially in regions of strong French influence, but the evidence is as various as the British.[6]

Let us content ourselves, for the moment, with saying that the evidence is untidy, and does not even show us whether

---

[1] Musée national des Arts et Traditions populaires, Paris, MS B 19, song from Thônes (Haute Savoie). See Shorter, *op. cit.*, p. 221 for a variant.

[2] See Ian Farr and Ernst Hinrichs in *Le Charivari*.

[3] Hoffman-Krayer and Bachtold-Staubli, *op. cit.*, entry under "Katzenmusik".

[4] See Dominique Lesourd in *Le Charivari*.

[5] Tekle Dömötör, *op. cit.*

[6] See especially Bryan Palmer, "Discordant Music".

French charivari or English rough music is the mutant from some common European stock; or, indeed, whether in their simplest components of noise and ridicule, both may not be universal.

Re-marriage of a widow or widower may have occasioned rough music in England, if accompanied by other circumstances, such as a disparity of ages or the imputed avarice of a young bride for a wealthy old widower. But examples are few. Rough music — and especially the "skimmington" — was directed until the nineteenth century against those who had offended against male-dominative norms and imperatives (group 1). A "skimmington" —

> Is but a riding, used of course
> When the grey mare's the better horse;
> When o'er the breeches greedy women
> Fight, to extend their vast dominion.[1]

Or in Andrew Marvell's *Last Instructions to a Painter*:

> A Punishment invented first to awe
> Masculine Wives, transgressing Natures Law.
> Where when the brawny Female disobeys,
> And beats the Husband till for peace he prays;
> No concern'd *Jury* for him Damage finds,
> No partial *Justice* her Behaviour binds;
> But the just Street does the next House invade,
> Mounting the neighbour Couple on lean Jade.
> The Distaff knocks, the Grains from Kettle fly,
> And Boys and Girls in Troops run houting by. . .

---

[1] From the fullest literary account of a "skimmington riding", in Samuel Butler, *Hudibras*, Second Part, Canto II, ed. J. Wilders (Oxford, 1967), pp. 142-9. The Second Part of this poem was first published in 1663. This section continues:

> When *Wives* their Sexes shift, like *Hares*,
> And ride their *Husbands*, like *Night-mares*,
> And they in mortal *Battle* vanquish'd,
> Are of their *Charter* dis-enfranchizd,
> And by the Right of *War* like *Gills* (a)
> Condemn'd to *Distaff, Horns* (b), and *Wheels* (c);
> For when Men by their *Wives* are Cow'd,
> Their *Horns* of course are understood.

(a) *Gills* — wenches, girls; (b) *Horns* — the symbol of the cuckold; (c) *Wheels* — spinning-wheels (like distaffs) are symbols of women's work and feminine roles.

Still, in the eighteenth century and, in some regions, in the nineteenth, the "patriarchal" humiliation of unruly women remains a predominant theme; or of those families in which (as the phrase is) "the grey mare is the better horse".[1] When Henri Misson met in the London streets a woman carrying a straw effigy crowned with a fine pair of horns, "preceded by a Drum, and follow'd by a Mob, making a most grating Noise with Tongs, Grid-irons, Frying-pans, &c.", he was told that "a Woman had given her Husband a sound beating for accusing her of making him a Cuckold, and that upon such Occasions some kind Neighbour of the *poor innocent injur'd Creature* [la pauvre Calomniéel] generally perform'd this Ceremony".[2] This was, presumably, London's attenuated "skimmington", and the mockery was being directed quite as much against the husband as the wife. But as late as 1838 Mrs Gaskell (a reliable observer) was writing to Mary Howitt of "Riding Stang" as "a custom all over Cheshire", and in its older male-dominative form:

> When any woman, a wife more particularly, has been scolding, beating or otherwise abusing the other sex, and is publicly known, she is made to ride stang. A crowd of people assemble towards evening after work hours, with an old, shabby, broken down horse. They hunt out the delinquent. . . and mount her on their Rozinante. . . astride with her face to the tail. So they parade her through the nearest village or town; drowning her scolding and clamour with the noise of frying pans &c, just as you would scare a swarm of bees. And though I have known this done in many instances, I never knew the woman seek any redress, or the avengers proceed to any more disorderly conduct after they had once made the guilty one "ride stang".[3]

I have placed "patriarchal" in inverted commas, because the term can involve us in difficulties. Feminist theorists, who allocate a central place to patriarchy, are rarely historians and they are sometimes impatient with historians' objections. As a result "patriarchy" is invoked indiscriminately, to cover

[1] Robert W. Malcolmson, *Life and Labour in England, 1700-1780* (1981), p. 105.
[2] Henri Misson de Valbourg, *Memoirs et Observations Faites par un Voyageur en Angleterre* (Paris, 1698), p. 70, and H. Misson, *Memoirs and Observations in his Travels over England* (1719), p. 129.
[3] J. A. V. Chapple and Arthur Pollard (eds.), *The Letters of Mrs. Gaskell* (Manchester, 1966), pp. 29-31. My thanks to David Englander.

every situation and institution of male-domination. The "trouble with patriarchy" (as Sheila Rowbotham warned long ago) is not only that it generalises a very specific set of theories and institutions where the monarch or the head of the household commanded authority over subjects, wife, children, apprentices, servants, etc. — theories and institutions under challenge in the seventeenth century and beginning to decompose — but also that the term is so undiscriminating that it offers no vocabulary to express differences in degree and even in quality of male-domination. As Rowbotham warned:

> "Patriarchy" implies a structure which is fixed, rather than the kaleidoscope of forms within which women and men have encountered one another. It does not carry any notion of how women might act to transform their situation as a sex. Nor does it even convey a sense of how women have resolutely manoeuvred for a better position within the general context of subordination. . .

Moreover, "some aspects of male-female relationships are evidently not simply oppressive, but include varying degrees of mutual aid. The concept of 'patriarchy' has no room for such subtleties." " 'Patriarchy' suggests a fatalistic sub-mission which allows no space for the complexities of women's defiance",[1] and if this is so — and in widespread ideological usage it is so — it does not illuminate women's history but obscures and even confiscates some part of it.

Male-domination is not at issue, but this may take place through brothers, neighbours, employers, the structures of law or of religion, as much as through the household-head implicit in Filmer's patriarchal theory.[2] Moreover, "patriarchy" gives us a poor vocabulary to express large modifications in the forms of male-domination and control, gender alienation or (on occasion) gender partnership. Both sexes might find themselves committed to the house of correction for no more explicit an offence than being "loose

---

[1] Sheila Rowbotham, "The Trouble with 'Patriarchy' ", *New States-man*, 21-28 Dec. 1979, reprinted in Rowbotham, *Dreams and Dilemmas* (1983), pp. 207-14.
[2] See G. Schochet, *Patriarchalism in Political Thought* (New York, 1975).

and disorderly persons".[1] But in backward or "traditional" areas, women might be presumed to be "loose and disorderly" if they were working people and if they had no male structure of control and protection. These assumptions find clear expression in an affidavit (1704) by Thomas Sexton, a Suffolk husbandman, who was defending himself against a charge of assault brought by Joanna Box, spinster:

> The said Joanna & Mary Box are two lusty young wenches & fare well & plentifully, & will not go to service, but live with their said mother, in a little house & occupy no land, nor having any visible estate or stock to live upon in an honest way, except Spining wch is a miserable trade now since the wars; no man nor woman living with them, except when some men of no very good fame haunt & frequent their company.[2]

Joanna and Mary's mother was married to a chimney sweep but they had split up. This Suffolk husbandman presumed that he could insinuate that any such masterless women were whores.

Such truly "patriarchal" attitudes persist into the nineteenth (and indeed twentieth) centuries. The ducking-stool is still employed against scolds (almost always against the feminine tongue) in the eighteenth century,[3] and there are even instances of the use of the vicious scold's bridle in the early nineteenth century. There is a remarkable

---

[1] Examples can be found in most CROs, especially in the committals to bridewells or houses of correction. For plentiful "loose and disorderly" committals (both sexes) see e.g. Hants. CRO, QS B/xvib/2/5, Calendars of prisoners in House of Correction, April, July and October 1723. Or in the 1760s an unusually zealous magistrate in Cirencester (Thomas Bush) was frequently committing persons for swearing (usually men), for disobedience to their masters (apprentices), for being "rogues and vagabonds" and (Ann Rundle, committed 28 July 1766) for "Being a Very Lewd Idle and Disorderly Person and Refusing to Give Security for her Good Behaviour". Gloucester CRO, Q/SG 1763-6. All this was normal; see Joanna Innes, "Prisons for the poor: English bridewells, 1555-1800", in Francis Snyder and Douglas Hay, *Labour and Crime* (1987), esp. pp. 84-5, 99, 114 n 21.

[2] PRO, KB 2.1 (Part One), Affidavits, Anne (Misc.): *Regina v William Copsey.*

[3] "Mary the wife of John Morris of Gosport being convicted upon her own Confession & pleading guilty to. . . being a comon scold & disturber of the peace of her neighbours doe undergo the punishment of the ducking Stoole at the city of Winchester. . ." Hants. CRO, QM/5, Minute Book, 6 October 1724.

reminiscence of this from the deeply-traditional little town of
Wenlock in Shropshire. Public punishments — whippings,
the stocks, the shrew's bridle — were inflicted on Mondays,
which were market days:

> Often have I seen poor Judy Cookson walked round the town in the
> shrew's bridle. 'Er was said to be the best abuser in the borough, and 'er
> wud go and curse anybody for three-ha'pence — that was the fee.

The bridle "punished a Christian terrible", "the poor
Creature's face streamed with blood" and two teeth fell out
in removing the bridle:

> Judy used to abuse Sir Watkins agent something terrible, 'im as they
> called 'King Collins', for 'e did what 'e listed and none durst say 'im
> nay. She was a fearsome pelrollick, it is true, was Judy, but I never
> knowed the bridle did 'er any good. It makes me swimmy-headed. . .
> only to think of those Mondays, with the relatives all cursing and crying,
> the lads laughing and jesting, and lawyer men looking on to see as *their*
> law was carried out.[1]

I could not restrain myself from working in this remarkable reminiscence, which throws new light on the functions of
scolding and cursing — an intrepid "pelrollick" such as Judy
was assuming a function as advocate of the intimidated
majority. From the same source I must also cite another
reminiscence, which illustrates how the traditional controls
on sexual conduct could (indeed, always did) bear most
hardly on women. Until well into the nineteenth century the
most traditionalist clergy inflicted upon members of the
congregation accused of sexual offences (including the
conception of children in advance of marriage) the penance
of standing in the church porch in a white sheet. In Wenlock
this was inflicted especially upon girls who "lost their good
name". One day a neighbour met Betty Beaman at the village
pump:

> As I was holding the pail, she was a-pumping in. 'Er burst into tears, for
> 'er was a-thinking, poor crittur, of 'er young days. 'Er said, "Sally I
> bain't what I was, and never shall be, afore I paid penance. That's many
> a year agone, but standing' up in that there white sheet a' took

---

[1] C. M. Gaskell, "Old Wenlock and its Folklore", *The Nineteenth
Century* (Feb. 1894).

something out of me that'll never come back. The spirit left me, and
even sin', though I can eat my wittles regler, somehow I 'ave a-lived like
in the dust.[1]

The punishment for bastardy was always more flagrantly
sexist. Unmarried mothers, especially if they were
"repeaters", could be confined to a house of correction for a
year, on a diet of bread and water. A reforming magistrate
reported that —

> A woman. . . committed. . . on account of her first child within a month
> after it was born — asked me pertinently, 'Why the man who had
> seduced her was not to be imprisoned as well as herself?' I could only
> answer, 'Because women were not legislators and men were parish
> officers.'[2]

I am happy to call these controls "patriarchal", although
the term is unhelpful: these offences and humiliations were
inflicted, not by "patriarchs", but by neighbours,
magistrates, poor law officials, estate bailiffs, officious
clergy. But one was unlikely to find such practices as the
scold's bridle, the ducking-stool and the penance surviving in
eighteenth-century Manchester or Leeds or Gloucester.[3]
And this can be of real significance if we are to interpret the
meaning of rough music and of "skimmingtons". In an
important essay David Underdown has drawn attention to a
general sense of insecurity in gender relations between 1560
and 1660, finding expression in witchcraft accusations, in the

[1] *Ibid.* See also John Gillis, *op. cit.*, p. 131.

[2] Sir G. O. Paul, *Address to His Majesty's Justices of the Peace for the
County of Gloucester, Epiphany General Quarter Sessions 1809*
(Gloucester, 1809), pp. 129, 135. However, although form and theory
allowed this sexist discrimination, late eighteenth-century practice was
more lenient. Paul collected figures to show the number of "criminal
offenders" in county gaols and bridewells in the sixteen years ending in
1807: these showed 241 males imprisoned for "bastardy" (presumably for
failing to pay the affiliation orders sworn against them) and 39 females.
There were also 213 imprisoned for leaving their families chargeable on the
parish (presumably all male). The sexist laws remained available to
vindictive magistrates and poor law officials, but were being used less
often. It had also been accepted that the public whipping of women was
"an offence against the common decency" and by 32 Geo. III, c. 45 (1792)
this could no longer be inflicted on women convicted as rogues and
vagabonds: see *ibid.*, pp. 8, 35.

[3] Or so I suppose. The matter has not yet been fully researched.

more vigorous punishment of the scold, and in the elaboration and practice of forms of rough music.[1] And he has
noted that these phenomena are to be found, in the West of
England, not so much in the arable farming villages as in the
woodland and pasture districts — the regions in which dairying and the clothing industry were based. Both industries
afforded employment and (with dairying) responsible roles
for women, and Underdown suggests that the harassment of
the "women on top" (by both official shaming rituals —
ducking-stool and scold's bridle — and unofficial ones —
"skimmingtons") need not simply be ascribed to the
"traditionalism" of the West Country, but may, rather, be
expressive of growing male insecurity as women in fact were
becoming more independent and assertive.[2] This may have
been found, precisely, in those "communities most subject to
the destabilising effects of economic change".[3] And when
we come to the later seventeenth century and eighteenth
century we must also take account of the supposed move
towards more egalitarian gender relations in proto-industrial
regions (of which the West Country woollen industry was
one). We have already discussed this in relation to women's
role in food riots (above p. 320-2). Certainly we need a
vocabulary more flexible than "patriarchy" to explore the
contradictions and to analyse the fluctuations and modifications in gender relations in changing occupations and

[1] See Keith Thomas, op. cit., pp. 528-31; D. E. Underdown, "The
Taming of the Scold: the Enforcement of Patriarchal Authority in Early
Modern England", in Anthony Fletcher and John Stevenson (eds.),
Order and Disorder in Early Modern England (Cambridge, 1985).

[2] An example of this feminine presence and self-confidence may be
taken from Coronation Day celebrations for Queen Anne in the lace-
making and clothing town of Honiton (23 April 1702): three hundred
women and girls in good order, two and two, with three women
drummers, and a guard of twenty-five young men on horseback, marched
up and down the town from 10 a.m. to 8 p.m., hurrahing and weaving long
white rods with tassels of white and blue ribbon (the Queen's colours) and
bone lace: F. N. Poynter (ed.), The Journal of James Yonge (1962), p. 210.
Similar processionals with wands sometimes marked the anniversaries of
female benefit societies, and Thomas Hardy, in the second chapter of Tess
of the D'Urbervilles, may have been right to say that the club "had walked
for hundreds of years".

[3] Underdown, op. cit., p. 135. See also David Underdown, Revel,
Riot and Rebellion (Oxford, 1985), esp. pp. 102-3.

communities. Rough music against wife-beaters was enforcing different norms and values than were "skimmingtons" against women who "wore the breeches". If we try to bring both within the categories of patriarchy, then we are still left with everything to be explained.

Many examples could be given of rough music occasioned by offences in groups 2) and 3). Satire upon ill-assorted marriages is recorded. The marriage of a man in his seventies to a girl of eighteen occasioned at Charing Cross in London in 1737 "a grand Hudibrastic Skymmington, composed of the chairmen and others of that class".[1] Rough music is still from time to time recorded in the nineteenth century against scolds as well as against husband-beaters.[2] And against adulterers, seducers of young women, and other kinds of (usually nameless) sexual offenders, it continues.[3] Ironical rough musics welcome back runaway couples or married partners who have split up and come back together, and wife sales, when they affront neighbourhood opinion in some particular way, can ensue in effigy burning and ran-tanning (above p. 450).[4] There is, however, one significant shift in occasions in the early years of the nineteenth century: the rapid rise to predominance of offenders in group 4), the wife-beaters. If a similar rise took place in other parts of Europe, it has not yet been recorded.

So large was this shift that the majority of contributors to *Notes and Queries* from the 1850s, and of commentators and editors of regional folklore collections and dialect glossaries

---

[1] *Read's Weekly Journal*, 16 Apr. 1737.

[2] *N & Q*, 4th series, iv (1869), p. 105 (Somerset, 1826); *ibid.*, 5th series, v (1876), p. 253 (Lancashire, late eighteenth century?); *ibid.*, 2nd series, x (1860), p. 363.

[3] Conjugal infidelity — both parties tied back to back on a donkey, W. H. K. Wright (ed.), *The Western Antiquary* (Plymouth, 1882), p. 31; against a coal-dealer with "loose notions on the privileges of married life" at Market Rasen, Lincolnshire, 1872, *Stamford Mercury*, 19 Jan. 1872; against an ostler who had proved unfaithful to his newly-wedded bride at Northallerton (Yorkshire) in 1887, *York Herald*, 1 Mar. 1887; against a young man who had jilted his mistress in a Hampshire village in 1882, *Hants and Berks Gazette*, 4 Feb. 1882; and many others.

[4] S. P. Menefee, *Wives for Sale* (Oxford, 1981), pp. 117, 126-7, 183; *Northern Standard*, 4 Nov. 1882; *Bury Times*, 12 Nov. 1870; Katharine M. Briggs, *The Folklore of the Cotswolds* (1974), pp. 116-7.

in the same years, assume that the inhibition of wife-beating is the primary function of rough music. There is ample evidence to assure us that this was not an invention of folklorists; and some of their accounts suggest accurate observation. From a village in Surrey or Sussex (1840s?):

> As soon as it was dark a procession was formed. First came two men with huge cow horns; then another with a large old fish-kettle round his neck. . . Then came the orator of the party, and then a motley assembly with hand-bells, gongs, cow horns, whistles, tin kettles, rattles, bones, frying pans. . . At a given signal they halted, and the orator began to recite a lot of doggerel verses. . . beginning:
> 'There is a man in this place
> Has beat his wife!! (*forte*: a pause)
> Has beat his wife!! (*fortissimo*)
> It is a very great shame and disgrace
> To all who live in this place,
> It is indeed upon my life!!'

The rough band then broke out with every instrument, accompanied by howling and hooting. "A bonfire was then lighted, round which the whole party danced as if they were crazy." The noise could be heard two miles away. After half an hour, silence was proclaimed, and the orator advanced once more towards the house, and expressed the hope that he would not have to return, urging upon the husband a moral reformation.[1]

Newspaper reports or legal documents enable one to look a little more closely into such incidents. At a substantial rough musicking at Waddesdon (Buckinghamshire) in 1878, when more than two hundred men, women, and children serenaded one Joseph Fowler on at least two occasions, Fowler explained (in court) that "the cause of the row was that he had an illegitimate child, and he did not think it was well used, and in consequence gave his wife three stripes".[2] One should note that this suggests not just an event (wife-beating), but an event with a *history*, well-known to the community. The victim (Fowler) appears to be a man who was held to have mis-used his wife in more than one way, and over a period; although she had accepted his illegitimate child into

---

[1] *N & Q*, 2nd series, x (1860), p. 477.

[2] *Bucks Herald*, 27 July 1878. It was a tenaciously held popular belief that the husband had the right to chastise his wife with three blows, and no more, and with a stick no thicker than his own thumb.

the home, he continued to abuse her.

In a Berkshire case of 1839 we have rather more detail. The immediate history of the event is as follows. The victim, William Goble, was a small farmer, occupying a cottage and a few acres; he was a tenant of Mr John Walter, but his farm lay in the midst of the estate of a neighbouring landowner, Mr Simmonds. On Saturday August 17th he and his wife had a quarrel, which "ended in blows". On Monday, the 19th, Mrs Goble was "very unwell", and a surgeon was called in from Wokingham. That evening there was the first occasion of rough music, with sixteen or eighteen men and boys with flags, horns, etc., parading before his house. The music was repeated, by larger numbers, on no fewer than eight occasions. On the sixth occasion Mr Walter's son (that is, the landlord's son), his gardener, and several other servants, came to Goble's aid, and there was a scuffle between the parties, which resulted in legal action.

In most respects this appears as characteristic rough musicking. The adults most frequently involved included eight labourers, two carpenters, one sawyer, one blacksmith, one shoemaker, one bricklayer, as well as the groom, coachman, gamekeeper and miller to Mr Simmonds. The unusual element in the case is the involvement in the affair of the households of two rival landowners' estates; and in subsequent litigation it appeared plausible that Mr Simmonds was aiding and encouraging the rough music (protracted over an unusual number of days) in the hope of driving Goble (whose lands intruded inconveniently into his estate) out of his tenancy. And beneath the rivalry of the two gentlemen we find a further layer of rivalry again, between the households and the young men attached to the Walter estate (Bearwood) and the Simmonds estate (Aborfield). During the course of the affair the Bearwood gardener (who was among the party which came to Goble's aid) received an anonymous letter, accusing the Bearwood men of being "licktrenchers", and comparing the Bearwood butler to "a tom tit upon a round of Beef". The letter concluded: "If I was your wife you should not have a bit of Sugar in your tea I would put a turd in to see if that would sweeten it. . .".[1]

[1] Miscellaneous documents in Berks. CRO, D/EW1, L.3. My thanks to John Fine who directed me to them.

An unsatisfactory case; but if one knew more of any case, it might well prove to be equally unsatisfactory. It emphasises that context is generally thicker and more complex than is disclosed by any superficial view. Wife-beating is a simple explanation: but in any community both wife and husband, and their marital history, are known to the neighbours; and even the most "domestic" of incidents takes place within the context of other tensions and allegiances. Thus in this case we appear to have a marital episode provoking the traditional response among some, and serving as a pretext for others. The victim is, in a sense, an "alien" on a boundary: his lands lie within another estate. And his offence touches off a rivalry between two neighbouring gentry, and also between the households and youth of two adjacent rural communities.

A third example must suffice: from Cambridgeshire in 1904. In this case rough music was directed against a man whom a girl of the local village had married when she was in service in London:

> The marriage had not been a success, so the girl had returned to her home, to which she was, after a time, traced by her husband, a heavy drinker. Rumours began to spread that he was ill-treating his wife, who often appeared in the village with a black eye or a cut on her face. Then, one winter's night, he came home drunk, dragged her out of bed and threw her out of the house.

Two neighbours came to her aid, beat up the husband and trussed him with rope. For some time after this he was quiet. Then he resumed his drinking, and his ill usage of his wife. Finally, the rough music took place: two hours of hubbub on tin kettles and pans, with shouts of "clear out! clear out!". On the next morning the husband left for London.[1] The incident, once again, emphasises that we are dealing not with an isolated episode but with an event whose history was well-known; and, once again, we have the element of a local community closing against an "alien".

It is not as simple to decipher the significance of these rough musics as may at first appear. Even classic charivari on re-marriage continues to inspire conflicting (but persuasive) explanations. The diversity of the forms and occasions for rough music should discourage any attempt to propose any

[1] Porter, *op. cit.*, pp. 9-10.

single function as *the* function for the "skimmington" or
"stang". These forms were, as I have suggested, part of the
symbolic vocabulary of the time, capable of being expressed
in sentences with different meanings. But it was not just *any*
vocabulary, for each symbol was evocative of meaning in its
own right: the man sitting mutely with a distaff in his hands,
being belaboured by a man in woman's clothes; the
symbolism of effigies and gallows; the metaphors of the
hunt. If we are right to resist a structuralist analysis in which
the mythic constituents from which charivari may have been
derived assume ascendancy over the social process and
replace it by formal logic, so also we must guard against
disintegrating the mythic properties into a plastic empiricism
of one case after another, defined only by their manifest
functions. Between myth, on one hand, and function, on the
other, there is — Carlo Ginzburg has reminded us — the
intermediacy of rehearsed and transmitted *rites.*[1] Those
who enact these rites may have long forgotten their mythic
origins. Yet the rites themselves powerfully evoke mythic
meanings, even if only fragmentarily and half-consciously
understood. Rough music is a vocabulary which brushes the
carnival at one extreme and the gallows at the other; which is
about crossing forbidden frontiers or mixing alien categories;
which traffics in transvestism and inversion; whose flaring
bonfires may recall heretics or even hell whose horned master
brings to mind the cuckold who is mocked. Still, in the early
years of this century, a boy (whom I later knew as a vigorous
man) witnessed a rough music in industrial Yorkshire, and
said it was "like devil's madjic". (See p. 532.)

But this vocabulary was not re-enacted involuntarily by
village yokels as if they were somnambulists in the possession
of a "folk memory". If we are always to discard the meanings
given to an event by the participants themselves, and search
instead for an ulterior meaning more in conformity to the

[1] See Carlo Ginzburg, "Charivari, associations juveniles, chasse
sauvage", in *Le Charivari*. In my article in *Annales E.S.C.* I took issue with
the formalist structuralism of Lévi-Strauss's interpretation of charivari in
Le Cru et le Cuit. Ginzburg criticises me in turn for formless empiricism
and obsession with manifest functions, and seeks to show common ground
between our positions in the forms *and* functions of rites. I can accept his
correction.

structure of myth, then this is to diminish the rationality and stature of the actors and underestimate the self-awareness of illiterate people. They may not have read *Mythologiques*, but they had their own notions as to what they were turning out about.

This "folk" was not perfect nor pretty nor was it empty of all norms. They employed the inherited vocabulary selectively, for their own reasons. The importance of rough music to the historian may lie not in any single function or group of functions, but in the fact that the episodes are — if only we can get inside the motives of the actors — a most sensitive indicator of changing notations of sexual norms or marital roles. It is evidence, also, of the ways in which even the most private or "personal" relationship is conditioned by norms and roles imposed by the society in which the couple acts, quarrels, or loves. The society is the host, but the couple are hostages to its opinion. The wife who is beaten, or whose husband is faithless, is perhaps also a daughter, a niece, a sister, a cousin, to others in the community. The wife who scolds and brow-beats her husband, who takes his financial and business affairs into her hands, threatens by her un-reproved example the marital equilibrium of her neighbours. A participant in a riding in Suffolk in 1604, directed against a wife who had beaten her husband, explained that the object was that "not only the woman which had offended might be shamed. . . but other women also by her shame might be admonished [not] to offend in like sort".[1] The rites may be less interesting in themselves than as tools to prize open the secrets of a community's moral code. For vigorous rough music can show us the border between the tolerated and the intolerable.

The shift to wife-beaters as prime targets for rough music in Britain in the nineteenth century could be an index of profound changes in gender relations. It suggests, with the corresponding dying-away of "skimmingtons", some decomposition of the older "patriarchal" framework. And while such rough musics were generally led by men or

[1] Cited by Ingram, "Riding, Rough Music and Mocking Rhymes", p. 174.

youths,[1] with children (often of both sexes) as followers, there are a few pieces of evidence to suggest that women were on occasion leading the actions or turning them to their own account.[2]

In Glamorgan in the early nineteenth century there is an account of the women in one community refusing to support a rough music procession aimed at a couple where the wife had beaten her husband. They remained indoors and "mocked at [the men] through the windows", while some "collected to scoff" at the house of the victims and "poured out a din of hoots and yells" to drown the rough music band.[3] One wonders if other communities witnessed a similar turning of the tide? In one (half-remembered?) Lincolnshire variant on the "stang nominy", the women are incited to deal with the husband-beater in their own way:

[1] The evidence as to who took part is inconclusive, and varied according to the offence. While men would carry a "stang" or "ride skimmington", women often turned out to hoot and bang pans (see Plate XXIII). When cases came to the courts, those indicted were nearly always male: thus a case at Burton (Oxfordshire) in 1803, where 15 labourers were indicted and 5 imprisoned: Oxfordshire CRO, QSM I/7; in a Warwickshire case, 1811, those indicted were two wheelwrights, one husbandman, one farmer, one labourer, one shoemaker, and one tallow chandler: Warwicks. CRO, QS 32/3, bundle 3.

[2] Women sometimes led rough musics in the eighteenth century: in 1747 at Billingshurst a husband who was ill-treating and starving his wife was rung out of his house by women, who put him in a blanket and ducked him in the pond (cited in *Sussex Agricultural Express*, 28 Oct. 1848). An Islington tradesman in 1748 whipped his wife with rods "till the Blood ran down her Heels": she "had a Warrant against him, and carrying him to a Justice of the Peace, he was. . . sent to Prison, to which Place he was conducted through the Pelting, and Hissing, and Blows of two Thirds of the Women in the Town": *Northampton Mercury*, 11 July 1748. In parts of the Scottish Lowlands it was reported that women "rode the stang" on wife-beaters, seizing the offender with their own hands: R. Forsyth, *The Beauties of Scotland* (Edinburgh, 1806), iii, p. 157.

[3] Charles Redwood, *The Vale of Glamorgan* (1839), p. 289-95, cited in Gillis, *op. cit.*, esp. pp. 133-4. But "patriarchal" rough music long continued in parts of mid and North Wales: see Julius Rodenberg, *An Autumn in Wales* (1856), translated and ed. by William Linnard (Cowbridge, 1985).

Ran, tan, tan!
The sign of the old tin kettle, and the old tin pan.

Old Abram Higback has been paying his good woman;
But he neither paid her for what or for why,
But he up with his fist, and blacked her eye.

Now all ye old women, and old women kind,
Get together, and be in a mind;
Collar him, and take him to the shit-house,
And shove him over head.

Now if that does not mend his manners,
The skin of his arse must go to the tanners;
And if that does not mend his manners,
Take him and hing him on a nail in Hell.

And if the nail happens to crack,
Down with your flaps, and at him piss. [1]

We can see in these charming verses the evidence of refinement and "modernisation".

So it is possible that the rough musicking of wife-beaters
indicates some "reform" of popular manners or amelioration
of the lot of wives. But I cannot share the confidence of
Edward Shorter, who, citing my own earlier article, argued
that the evidence confirms "the early modernization of
domestic relationships in England":

> As egalitarian relationships between husband and wife diffused, the
> community began to perceive as intolerable such vestiges of earlier
> patriarchal authority as the right to slam one's wife about; and so it
> moved to rebuke wife-beaters. [2]

I do not know firm evidence that "egalitarian relationships" between husband and wife were becoming diffused in
England by 1850. Some historians have noted a decline in the
respect afforded to women during the industrial revolution. I
repeat my earlier warning: the increase in rough music against
wife-beaters could with equal reason be read as an index to
the increasing brutality with which some wives were being
treated, or as to their loss of other "traditional" defences in
this situation. It is not even clear that "patriarchal
authority" in the older tradition included approval for

[1] From Sturton by Stowe, in the James M. Carpenter collection in
Cecil Sharp House.
[2] Shorter, *op. cit.*, p. 235.

husbands who "slammed their wives about", for, in an older masculine code of honour and shame, women could be sheltered from male violence by the notion that such assaults were "unmanly". In most traditional societies, the defence of the maltreated wife is the responsibility of her male kin, and in the first place of her brothers. This defence might be supplemented by the intervention of the priest. In England, between 1800 and 1850, various factors could have operated to bring about a new kind of crisis. Geographic mobility could have removed more wives from the protection of their kin. The English clergy had no confessional and rather little pastoral role — they were not frequent visitors to labourers' homes. The law afforded little protection to the wife treated with brutality. Is it possible that there were more frequent instances of the inhibitions upon male marital violence — inhibitions which in the older community would have been upheld by neighbourhood opinion or kin — breaking down? In such circumstances the community may have turned the old forms of rough music to new account.

In any case, rough music was not automatic and was not always visited upon an offence. We do not have a "pre-industrial society" in which "community norms imposed themselves with steely force", as if acting out an inherited cultural programming, until "modernization" brought enlightenment.[1] Not all wife-beaters were ran-tanned or burned in effigy, and in certain cases rough music may have been an excuse for "a little innocent amusement" or a pretext to "satiate. . . personal malice or revenge" arising from a history of conflicts:

> Some perhaps may entertain a notion that they are rendering their aid to protect the weak and defenceless. . . [but] it too frequently happens that they are unconsciously lending themselves as the instruments of gratifying private pique. . .[2]

It is the same when sexual offenders are the target. Because certain adulterers were rough musicked, it cannot be assumed that we are observing a community of pagan puritans, for whom marital fidelity was an imperative. To be sure, the

[1] *Ibid.*, p. 218.
[2] This is from a brief on behalf of a victim of rough music, Berks. CRO, D/EW1.L3.

rituals emphasise that the working people did not live in casual, unstructured promiscuity. Even where the marriage rites of the church were ignored, or where there was a large tolerance of pre-marital intercourse, the society maintained distinct norms of sexual behaviour.

These norms, however, should not be set up as absolutes. On the contrary, I suspect that each occasion when adulterers and similar offenders were subjected to rough music had a known history; that more evidence would lead us to particular aggravations of an offence which, in other cases, might pass unnoticed — or noticed only by gossip. It need not have been adultery as such which invoked public disgrace, but the way in which particular adulterers (perhaps already unpopular for other reasons) "carried on".

Where adultery was the evident target, it is possible that the community was incensed to this degree, not so much by the fact, as by the "flagrancy" with which it was committed and which might threaten the institution of marriage itself, as when a married person eloped with another married partner,[1] or when two couples (or two partners) attempted to change spouses and to remain living within the same small community.[2] or a *ménage-à-trois*.[3] In the village of "Lark Rise" illegitimate children were accepted, but adultery between a labourer's wife and a lodger, in the labourer's own house, called down rough music which expelled all three from the parish.[4]

The rites of rough music were part of the resources of what it is now obligatory to call the "discourse" of a society. They were employed with intelligence and wit on occasion, and on other occasions with prejudice (against innovators, "deviants", outsiders) and rancour.[5] The rites are like a

---

[1] *N & Q*, 6th series, vi (1882); *ibid.*, 5th series, v (1876).

[2] See Appendix I.

[3] At Gorton, Manchester, "riding the stang" was administered when "it was discovered that a painter was living harmoniously with two women in one house", *N & Q*, 5th series, v (1876).

[4] Flora Thompson, *Lark Rise to Candleford* (Oxford, 1954), pp. 145-6.

[5] A vindictive "skimmerton riding" was visited on a gardener and his wife and the wife's brother in Oakhill (Somerset) in 1900: the wife and her brother were German, and the villagers refused to believe that he was her brother: *Shepton Mallet Journal*, 31 Aug. 1900.

keyboard that can be played lightly, satirically, or struck brutally. Rough music may be employed in factional conflicts in a community. There is nothing automatic about the process; much depends on the balance of forces within a community, the family networks, personal histories, the wit or stupidity of natural leaders.

The decisive factor may be whether offenders are already unpopular for other reasons. I was told by an informant in Somerset of a man who had been rough musicked because he had been detected in keeping a very young woman (whom he had met at a fair) as his secret mistress. But this did not demonstrate that all such liaisons, in this industrial village, called forth rough music. For this offender was unpopular for other reasons: he lived in an isolated cottage, and was a professing Methodist and teetotaller, who earned his living by delivering cider to public houses. He was held to be an outsider and a censorious hypocrite. No doubt the rough music was planned in the local pub, whose customers enjoyed publicising their teetotal opponent's scandal. [1]

Hence the compilation of occasions for rough music is not enough. We need, even more, a detailed inner history of even a few particular incidents, and the recovery of their contexts. That is why David Rollison's remarkable study of a "groaning" in the Gloucestershire village of Westonbirt in 1716 is such an important addition to our understanding. [2] This "groaning" was a piece of street theatre, to which all and sundry were invited, savagely mocking a substantial farmer and bailiff accused of sodomy; it employed elements in rough music's vocabulary — transvestism, blasphemy, obscenity and drama. But it does not prove that all homosexuals were visited with rough music. In Rollison's recovery of the episode he is aided by an unusually rich archive of letters passing between the village and its absentee (but vigilant)

[1] Information of the late Bob Hiscox of Pilton, Somerset, given to me in 1975 and referring to events *circa* 1910.
[2] David Rollison, "Property, Ideology and Popular Culture in a Gloucestershire Village, 1660-1740", *Past and Present*, 93 (1981), reprinted in Slack (ed.), *op. cit.* For another well-documented (but enigmatic) case, see Joan R. Kent, "Folk Justice and Royal Justice in early 17th-century England: a 'Charivari' in the Midlands", *Midland History*, viii (1983).

landowner, who felt himself to be scandalised, and good order and established religion to be mocked in the insult to his bailiff. The episode arose out of a history, and the supposed offender was decisively unpopular for other reasons. The "groaning" enlarges in meaning and is enriched in complexity when placed in this context, and at the same time it floods this context with its eccentric and eerie light. It is an exemplary study, which may be set beside the "skimmington" in Hardy's *Mayor of Casterbridge* — which also acquired its meaning in a context and from a history.

III

Plastic in "domestic" contexts, the forms could be adapted also to "public occasions — and perhaps always had been: a leader of the "Rising in the West" in 1628-31 was supposed to go under the name of "Lady Skimmington".[1] Rough music was applied to a score of purposes. Petty theft from one's neighbours appears to have been one occasion. In 1691 in a Warwickshire village two offenders were musicked by the smith (dressed as an old woman) and a farmer (wearing buck's horns) at the head of a hundred others who "tumultuously and riotously led a dance forwards and backwards across the town. . . for the space of three hours", shouting in chorus outside the victims' house: 'Pay for the timber, you rogue, you cuckoldy dog, you stole', and 'pay for the clocking [chickens] and ducks, you whore".[2] But it could, equally be used in a different direction altogether, "to mark disapproval of a magisterial decision",[3] or of an officious or severe prosecution. The prosecutor of a boy (who had been stealing eggs) at Iver (Buckinghamshire) in 1878 brought rough music down upon his own head: his effigy was burned to the accompaniment of shouts of "quack,

---

[1] D. G. Allan, "The Rising in the West, 1628-31", *Econ. Hist. Rev.*, 2nd series, v, i (1952-3); Buchanan Sharp, *In Contempt of All Authority* (Univ. of California, 1980), who argues (p. 105) that there was never any one "leader" who was "Skimmington", just as there was never any General Ludd or Rebecca.

[2] *Warwickshire Quarter-Sessions Proceedings*, ed. H. C. Johnson and N. J. Williams (Warwick, 1964), pp. xiii-xiv.

[3] J. H. Bloom, *Folklore, Old Customs and Superstitions in Shakespeare Land* (1930), p. 53.

quack".[1] More serious and sustained was an outbreak at Ampthill (Bedfordshire) in 1817, following upon the conviction and execution of a local man for rape. As many as two hundred people assembled on successive nights before the house of the prosecutrix, exhibiting obscene effigies of herself and of her father and mother, stoning the house, and "hallooing and charging the family with having hung the man". The trouble was ended only when four of the actors were imprisoned.[2]

Rough music was also employed against unpopular officials. In 1797 a tallow chandler, a yeoman and five labourers were indicted for their part in an affair at Belchamp St. Paul's (Essex); they had mounted the effigy of a resident excise officer on an ass, paraded it before his house, fired guns at it, and burned the effigy at a stake on the green — on three occasions.[3] Instances can be found of rough music employed against the police;[4] against informers;[5] against body snatchers;[6] against crimps; against unpopular preachers[7] and Mormons;[8] against the unfair dismissal of a servant, eviction from a tied cottage, and against game-keepers. In a well-reported cast at Chilton (Buckingham-shire) in 1878 a crowd of some twenty or thirty men and

[1] *Bucks Herald*, 13 July 1878. A Warwickshire woman was rough musicked for prosecuting her own son for taking 6s. 9d. from her purse: *Leamington Chronicle*, 16 July 1870. My thanks to Chris Ryan.

[2] Bedfordshire CRO, QSR 23, 1817, pp. 230-1.

[3] PRO, KB 11.59.

[4] See e.g. W. E. Haigh, *A New Glossary of the Dialect of the Huddersfield District* (Oxford, 1928), p. 118; John Bland, *Bygone Days in Market Harborough* (Market Harborough, 1924), pp. 102-3.

[5] A. Boyer, *Political State of Great Britain*, LIII, 1737, p. 116.

[6] See, for example, Ruth Richardson, *Death, Dissection and the Destitute* (1987), p. 138.

[7] Against a "cobler" preaching at Towcester, 1767, Northants. CRO, Quarter Sessions Grand File, 1767. Early Methodist history provides many examples of the rough musicking of preachers and noted members: information from John Walsh. The rector of Fillingham was ran-tanned and his effigy was "ridden the stang" before being burned: *Stamford Mercury*, 23 May 1884.

[8] In Soham (Cambridgeshire) on April Fool's Day, 1853, there were mock Mormon weddings outside the homes of local believers, in which seven "brides" on donkeys were married to a single "husband": *Millenial Star*, xv (1853), p. 269. My thanks to J. F. C. Harrison.

boys rough musicked (for the third time) Mr Augustus Campbell of Chilton House, his gamekeeper, and his coachman. It is clear that the villagers believed that the gamekeeper, on Campbell's orders, was shooting or poisoning their dogs if they strayed onto the estate. The music had been got up on this occasion by a farmer whose land was adjacent to Campbell's and two of whose puppies had been involved in an incident the previous day. But the landowner and his servants may have been unpopular for other reasons. Campbell was an in-comer from Berkshire, and the crowd sang before his door: "the meanest, measliest, lowest man that e'er in Berkshire stood". Outside the coachman's house they shouted, "Who stole the dogs?" and "Blackbird!". Outside the gamekeeper's they called "go home, gipsy keeper" and "gipsy king!".[1]

Still, in the nineteenth century, rough music and forms of ridicule could be employed by people of substance against each other, sometimes putting up more humble people to do the actual business and hiding behind them. In 1805 a carter in Tewkesbury was employed to carry certain ridiculous effigies in a "procession" through the town in a cart; he claimed that he didn't realise that the figures represented the surveyor and inspector of the taxes.[2] In the 1790s a long and bitter feud developed between two neighbouring landowners near Handsworth (Staffordshire). The hostilities, which involved disputes about game but which extended to a dozen other issues, also drew in the brother-in-law of one landowner, the Rev. Thomas Lane, the rector of Handsworth. He was clearly unpopular, since he had been involved in pulling down cottages and closing down alehouses. His opponent visited him with the vocabulary of rough music, persuading his own tenants in Handsworth to display offensive effigies and handbills. (See Plate V.)[3] But gentry involvement was

---

[1] *Bucks. Herald*, 19 Oct. 1878.

[2] PRO, KB 1.33 (Part One), *Rex v James Attwood, John Sashand and Henry Rickett*: affidavit of James Attwood.

[3] Handbill in KB 1.30 (Part Two), Mich. 41 Geo. III, no. 1: affidavit of Joseph Storrer (1800), and papers in file 41. For the background to this case, see Douglas Hay, "Crime, Authority and the Criminal Laws in Staffordshire, 1750-1800" (Univ. of Warwick Ph.D. thesis, 1975), pp. 309-14.

now becoming uncommon and rough music was regarded as plebeian and, for that reason, potentially subversive.

In Woking rough music was used for upholding common rights, and employed against those who overstocked the common or cut excessive turfs and faggots.[1] And if we are to assume that effigy burnings belong to the same family of rituals (and most of them were accompanied by raucous noise and processional) the list could be extended indefinitely: against a tithe-proctor for herrings, against a landlord over-zealous to extend his fishing rights, against enclosure, and against any person riding rough-shod over local custom. Parson Woodforde records a dispute between Justice Creed and his churchwardens about the gallery in the church, which the justice wanted to take down and which the singers wanted to keep. The dispute escalated by way of a brawl in church to a court case, and the magistrate's effigy,

> Was had through the streets of Castle Cary. . . upon the Engine, and then had into the Park and burnt in a bonfire immediately before the Justice's house. . . The whole Parish are against the Justice.[2]

Any historians with full notebooks could compile their own lists. Rough music was commonly adapted to industrial conflict. The "cool-staffing" (or cowl-staffing) of blacklegs by West Country weavers was a riding of them to a duck pond on a pole,[3] just as the "stang" was used in the same way by pitmen and seamen in the North-East. The usage was especially widespread in the West, the heartland of the "skimmington", and the ritual vocabulary was also employed

---

[1] See Bickley, *op. cit.*

[2] James Woodforde, *The Diary of a Country Parson* (1949), p. 53. For an Oxfordshire case arising from a church dispute, see J. C. Cox, *Churchwardens' Accounts* (1913), p. 53.

[3] W. E. Minchinton, "The Beginnings of Trade Unionism in the Gloucestershire Woollen Industry", *Trans. Bristol & Gloucs. Arch. Soc.* (1951), pp. 134-5; Adrian Randall, "Labour and the Industrial Revolution in the West of England Woollen Industry" (Univ. of Birmingham Ph.D. thesis, 1979), esp. pp. 300-1, 541; F. J. Snell, *The Chronicles of Twyford* (Tiverton, 1893), pp. 186-7, 191-2, 232-2. For Banbury shag-weavers, see John Money, *Experience and Identity, Birmingham and the West Midlands, 1760-1800* (Manchester, 1977), pp. 240-1; Robert Spillman, 25/26 August 1793 in PRO, HO 42/26.

in actions against workhouses and turnpikes.[1] In London a
wheel-barrow could take the place of a "stang": it was used
in this way in 1696 against a journeyman hatter working
beneath the rates.[2] Southwark hat-dyers, in 1770 —

> took one of their brother journeymen into custody, whom they charged
> with working over hours without any more pay, and for taking under
> price. They obliged him to mount an ass, and ride through all the parts
> of the Borough where hatters were employed. . . a label was carried on a
> pole before him, denoting his offence; and a number of boys
> attended with shovels, playing the rough music. At all shops they came
> to in their way of business, they obliged the men to strike, in order to
> have their wages raised.[3]

A similar case of "donkeying" took place in Coventry in
1818, during a strike of ribbon-weavers, but on this occasion
the victim on parade was an elderly ribbon manufacturer.[4]
Rough music on various occasions was being employed in
London — notably Kentish London — until the end of the
nineteenth century. It was employed in Woolwich in 1870
with great ceremony against a waterman convicted of carrying more fares than he was licensed to carry; in this case, his
effigy was paraded by fellow watermen accompanied by a
rough band, placed in a barge, set to float on the Thames,
fired at, and ultimately burned.[5]

One might cite many other examples. These were commonplace of industrial conflict, at least until the early
nineteenth century, and the "ran-tanning" of blacklegs

[1] In May 1725 over a hundred men and women (broadweavers?)
assembled in Stroud to pull down the workhouse, carried an overseer
around the parish on a stick, and threatened to put one of "the gentlemen"
on the stick if they met him: PRO, Assi 5.44 (i). For a turnpike episode,
also in Stroud, see SP 36.32.

[2] S. and B. Webb, *The History of Trade Unionism* (1920), p. 28. A
case was reported in 1743 of an unapprenticed hatter being "stanged" with
such violence in Southwark that he died: *Sherborne Mercury*, 18 Oct. 1743.

[3] *Annual Register* (1770), p. 74.

[4] "Donkeying" was vigorous in the Coventry silk industry, and was
used against both workers and employers who defied the regulations of
"the Trade"; *The Times*, 20 Aug. 1819; *Report of the Trial of the Prisoners
Charged with Rioting and Destroying the Machinery of Josiah Beck*
(Coventry, 1832), p. 3; *PP*, 1835, xxv, p. 1834; information from Peter
Searby.

[5] *Greenwich & Deptford Chronicle*, 12 Mar. 1870. My thanks to
Geoffrey Crossick.

continues into the twentieth century. But there appears to have been only one occasion in Britain when ritual forms were deeply involved with activity of mass dimensions. These occur in the early nineteenth century in Wales, and are associated with the *ceffyl pren.*

The form of this ritual corresponded closely to that of "riding the stang":

> a figure of a horse is carried at night in the midst of a mob with their faces blackened, and torches in their hands, to the door of any person whose domestic conduct may have exposed him to the censure of his neighbours, or who may have rendered himself unpopular by informing against another, and by contributing to enforce the law. On the horse is mounted some-one who, when the procession makes a halt opposite the residence. . . addresses the mob on the cause of their assembling. . .

When the exhibition was directed against "domestic" offenders it was accompanied "with the grossest indecency". In the 1820s and 1830s in parts of South Wales the *ceffyl pren* was increasingly brought into use against "public" offenders — in agrarian grievances, against prosecutors in cases of petty theft, against unpopular municipal officials, etc. The translation of the ritual from the private to the public domain was viewed by the authorities with anxiety:

> The right which is thus arrogated of judging. . . another man's domestic conduct, is certainly characteristic of a rude state of society; when the same measures are applied to. . . thwarting the operation of the laws of the land, they become of much more serious import. The principle is perfectly Irish, and. . . contains the germ of resistance to legal order.[1]

This last observation was borne out by the use of the *ceffyl pren* in the "Rebecca riots" against the turnpike tolls in South Wales in the 1840s. The "Scotch Cattle" disturbances in the mining areas of the early 1820s (mainly in Monmouthshire) had already evinced ritualistic elements: men, with blackened faces, dressed as women; animal-guising with horns, skins, and masks; the blowing of horns, lowing,

---

[1]*First Report of the Constabulary Commissioners* (1839), pp. 83-4; PRO 52.35 and 73.4 (memorandum of Sir E. Head); J. C. Davies, *Folklore of West and Mid-Wales* (Aberystwyth, 1911), p. 85.

rattling of chains, and firing of guns outside the homes of blacklegs or informers.[1]

In the 1830s and into the 1840s the practices of the *ceffyl pren* extended through Carmarthenshire, until the "laws of the land" gave way to the law of "Rebecca", the mythical leader (as well as the *nom-de-plume*) of the agrarian rebels.[2] At the height of the disturbances, "Rebecca" extended her authority simultaneously over the private and public realms. Her followers delivered children to the doors of their putative fathers, threatened young men who refused to marry the girls they had "betrayed", warned husbands to stop beating their wives, and forcibly reconciled the astonished vicar of Bangor Teify to his separated wife, while at the same time pursuing the campaign against turnpikes, articulating agrarian grievances, and intimidating informers against her rule.

Some of her actions were curious, but also deeply revealing. Some three years earlier a young labourer, returning in a "drunken frolic" from a wedding, had met an unmarried lady landowner in the road and had kissed her. For this offence — far more against status than honour — he had been fined twenty shillings. Now the followers of "Rebecca" demanded the return of the fine; when the money was refused they damaged the plantations of both the offending magistrate who had inflicted the fine and of the offended lady. "This shows", commented another local gentleman,

> that the public is perverted in its notions of justice, which in a political point of view is a thing much more difficult to be dealt with than a mere marauding Banditti.

It shows, one would add, the fuel on which popular grievances were fed, and the length of time that the embers could burn. It shows also that for a brief few months even the poorest and most despised of the people of Carmarthenshire had a glimpse of an ideal of truly popular justice. Two weeks later the same gentleman wrote that "a poor idiotic girl" had

---

[1] See D. J. V. Jones, "Popular Disturbances in Wales, 1792-1832" (Univ. of Wales, Aberystwyth, Ph.D. thesis, 1965), esp. pp. 217, 195ff.

[2] See D. Williams, *The Rebecca Riots* (Cardiff, 1955). Professor Williams writes (p. 56): "it can. . . be said with complete certainty that the Rebecca Riots were an extension of the practice of the *ceffyl pren*"; See also D. J. V. Jones, *Rebecca's Children* (Oxford, 1989), esp. ch. 6.

come to his door begging. When he refused her, and told her to go to the hated officials of the poor law, "she quietly said she would tell 'Becca":

> I told her that if she did not behave well & continued to use that threat she wd be sent to prison — her only reply was murmured out (in Welsh) "I'll tell 'Becca." [1]

In the end "Rebecca" ceded her temporal authority, but undoubtedly her spiritual dictatorship survived for much longer, and in ways which only a Welsh-speaking historian will be able to disclose. There is a report as late as 1898 from Llanbister in Radnorshire, describing the descent of a "Rebecca" gang, with blackened faces, upon the (separate) houses of a man and woman who had made some "breach of the laws of morality". Both in a nearly naked state (it was January) were forced to walk backwards and forwards in a stream for twenty minutes, and then to run up and down the fields while they were beaten with straps and sticks. They were then taken back to the man's house, where "Rebecca" sat in judgement. They were condemned to undergo further flogging, and to march up and down the fields hand in hand. Their hair was cut off, and they were threatened with tar and feathers (which was not in the end used).[2] The incident reminds us that the rituals of rough music and charivari, transposed across the Atlantic, contributed not only to the good-humoured "shivaree" but may also have given something to lynch law and the Ku Klux Klan.[3] And it suggests, finally, that we might look again at certain

---

[1] These accounts are based on PRO, HO 45.454 (i) and (ii), and especially the reports of Edward Lloyd Hall, the gentleman cited above, in (ii), fos. 521-3, 664ff; H. T. Evans, *Rebecca and Her Daughters* (Cardiff, 1910); "Rebecca in West Wales", *West Wales Hist. Records*, VII (1917-18).

[2] *Hull and North Lincs. Times*, 15 Jan. 1898.

[3] See Wyatt-Brown, *op. cit.*, pp. 435-561. "Carting", tarring and feathering, and riding on a pole were frequent in eighteenth- and nineteenth-century North America, and were sometimes used against "public" offenders, sometimes against domestic offenders, including wife-beaters: see J. E. Cutler, *Lynch-Law: an Investigation into the History of Lynching in the United States* (1905), esp. pp. 46-7, 60-71, 63-7, 92, 103; R. B. Morris, *Government and Labor in Early America* (New York, 1965), p. 147; H. D. Graham and T. R. Gurr (eds.), *The History of Violence in America* (New York, 1969), p. 70.

manifestations of popular retribution in the twentieth century, to see whether similar ritual elements might not be present also in these: to the public humiliation after the liberation of European countries of women who had kept company with members of the occupying forces during World War II, or to the rites of public humiliation practised during the Cultural Revolution in China.

IV

"Public" rough music presents few analytical problems. In its industrial forms it is clear enough what offences blacklegs had committed and whose popular "law" was being enforced. As more becomes known about the popular dimension of eighteenth-century politics in London and the cities, so elements in the vocabulary of rough music — mocking, obscenities and the emblems of cuckoldry — turn out to be everywhere. They are employed by Tories, Whigs, the followers of Wilkes, and the ungoverned "mob" alike. It would be foolish even to begin to cite examples, since such symbols were the medium of discourse, and sometimes of negotiation, between the plebs and the patricians. Crowd actions were sometimes little other than the manipulation of these symbols, in the endeavour to demystify authority or to ridicule political opponents (see pp. 68-9 and Plate XXI).[1]

One doubts whether it is useful to debate whether rough music belonged to a plebeian, as contrasted with a consensual, tradition. Certainly, until late in the eighteenth century the vocabulary was well enough understood among all social classes. Domestic rough music was socially conservative, in the sense that it defended custom and male-dominative tradition, and Ingram has argued that the élite saw little threat in it and were casual in their attempts to put the practices down. On the other hand, rough music was always potentially subversive, with its rites of inversion, its blasphemies and obscenities, and, as Rollison has shown in

---

[1] See Nicholas Rogers, "Popular Protest in Early Hanoverian London", in Slack (ed.), *op. cit.*; Peter Burke, "Popular Culture in Seventeenth-Century London", in Reay (ed.), *op. cit.*; John Brewer, *Party Ideology and Popular Politics at the Accession of George III* (Cambridge, 1976), *passim*.

his study of the "groaning" at Westonbirt, it could rapidly acquire a polemical social meaning. In the eighteenth century, as the distance widened between the culture of the patricians and that of the plebs, so rough music became more distinctively a plebeian form. It thrived, as a means of self-regulation, above all in certain kinds of "peasant" and of proto-industrial community.[1] Yet rough music cannot be claimed as a "working-class" tradition, for the forms were imperfectly integrated into the early organised labour movement. Luddism depended for its success upon the swift movements of small groups of men in silence; the oaths and ceremonies of illegal trade unions grew out of a different group of rituals. And thereafter it appears to be true that the more sophisticated, organised, and politically-conscious the movement, the less indebtedness it shows to traditional forms of folk violence. The Chartists of Monmouthshire put behind them the forms of the "Scotch Cattle".[2]

The burning of effigies, accompanied by tumult or processional, might appear to offer an exception to this generalisation. This continued in vigorous use into the present century (it is by no means extinct today), and it was often employed by the "radicals". It was employed (among many examples) by the English "Jacobin" reformers of the 1790s; against the magistrates and yeomanry after "Peterloo" in 1819; during the agitations for the Reform Bill of 1832; and against unpopular landowners or farmers during the labourers' agitation of the 1870s in the Eastern Counties.

But effigy burning is not a noted method of the Chartists, nor of reform and trade union agitations generally. This may have been because reformers sensed, in the very forms, a disposition to favour the traditional — or even atavistic — mood of the people. For it was a form which was used, very consciously, by traditionalists against reformers or out-groups. After Guy Fawkes, the most burned-in-effigy man in

[1] Gerald M. Sider argues convincingly that groups which maintained the self-regulation of their working economy also upheld certain rituals: "Christmas Mumming in Outport Newfoundland", *Past and Present*, 71 (1976).

[2] On the decline of folk violence, see Dorothy Thompson, *The Early Chartists* (1971), pp. 16-17, and "Chartism as a Historical Subject", *Bull. Soc. Lab. Hist.*, 20 (1970), p. 12.

British history was without any doubt Tom Paine. The number and distribution of the officially-inspired "Church and King" Paine-burnings, especially in 1790-93, has never been counted. But it was immense, taking in almost every township and many villages in England. Undoubtedly many of these affairs drew upon the rituals of rough music. In Heckmondwike (Yorkshire) a man impersonating Tom Paine was "discovered" among some coal-pits, reading *Rights of Man*. He was seized, his face was covered with a frightful mask, and he was led by a rope through the market place. The mask was then deftly transferred to a straw effigy, which was placed against a lamp-post and shot at, to the accompaniment of tremendous hootings and cries of "Church and King".[1]

There were a few cities where the reformers were strong enough to respond in kind. Bishop Horsley received a well-merited burning-in-effigy in his own cathedral city of Rochester after he had said, in the House of Lords, that "the mass of the people have nothing to do with the laws, but to obey them".[2] But reformers were more often the targets of such affairs, and they formed a dislike for their "mob" characteristics. Where the rites of rough music survive after 1815 they appear to have an increasingly socially-conservative character.

So much is easy to set down: and it may mean less than it seems to mean. For it is by no means easy to identify the kind of nineteenth-century community in which rough music survived longest. While the elaborated forms of the ritual were clearly a folklorist's delight, while such forms as "wooset-hunting" and the stag-hunt were recorded in isolated West Country villages with names like Ogburne St. George, Whitechurch Canonicorum and Okeford Fitzpaine, and can be seen as animated ethnological vestiges, exotic

---

[1] Frank Peel, *Spen Valley: Past and Present* (Heckmondwike, 1893), pp. 307-8.

[2] *Parliamentary Register*, xliii, pp. 351-4. The duke of Brunswick (in effigy) was given a ceremonial hanging and burning on Kensington Common on November 5th, 1792: letter from London in *Pittsburgh Gazette*, 2 Feb. 1793. In Norwich in 1796 bonfires were preceded by a mock procession in which effigies of Pitt, Windham and the bishop of Rochester were carted with ropes around their necks.

blow-flies in rural amber, at the same time good old-fashioned rough music continued vigorously in an urban and industrial context. We have noted it in Kentish London; it was vigorous in mid nineteenth-century Huddersfield or Pudsey in the West Yorkshire industrial belt;[1] and in Gorton, near Manchester, when a married surgeon who had eloped with a patient's wife was the object, Gorton cotton mills were closed for half a day in order that eight hundred factory hands could take part.[2]

There is, even in such cases, a sense that rough music belonged in some way to the "older", "rougher" parts of the town; but it is difficult to detect exactly what such descriptions imply, unless the tautology that where rough music persisted must be rough. Thomas Hardy suggests that his "skimmington" emerged from the district of Mixen Lane —

> the Adullam of all the surrounding villages. It was the hiding-place of those who were in distress, and in debt, and trouble of every kind. Farm-labourers and other peasants, who combined a little poaching with farming, and a little brawling and bibbing with their poaching, found themselves sooner or later in Mixen Lane. Rural mechanics too idle to mechanize, rural servants too rebellious to serve, drifted or were forced into Mixen Lane.

But the evidence does not altogether confirm Hardy's characterisation. The vigorous rough music described in Appendix 1 took place early in this century in Siddal, a district of Halifax dominated by one large woollen mill, and with some mining, quarrying and brick-making. Decidedly working-class and traditional, yet Siddal was also one of the first places where (in 1892) I.L.P. councillors were elected. It is clear that the "old culture" of rough music could survive with great tenacity alongside more "modern" forms, and could co-exist with these. Yet this does not happen everywhere, and one must look for additional explanations for this co-existence. Munby found, in the 1860s, old forms surviving as a set in the Surrey of Ripley:

---

[1] See e.g. Easther and Lees, *op. cit.*, pp. 128-9; J. Lawson, *Letters to the Young on Progress in Pudsey* (Stanningley, 1887), p. 66.

[2] *N & Q*, 5th series, v (1876), p. 253.

They still play football in the street on Shrove Tuesday, and turn out on Guy Faux Day in a long procession of masks and mummers: they still pursue every cruel husband with the Nemesis of marrowbones and cleavers.

On May Day young girls in muslin still carried little Maypoles wreathed with flowers from house to house. But Munby could suggest no reason for these survivals other than the village's isolation — six miles from a railway and no intercourse with London other than a weekly carrier's cart.[1]

In the same year that Munby visited Ripley, rough music was a little discouraged by a legal decision that a stag-hunt was "a game" within the meaning of 5 & 6 Will. IV, c. 50, and hence prohibited in the streets.[2] It was widely argued thereafter that all rough music in the streets were prohibited "games". It is doubtful whether this had much influence on rough music's decline, which was inexorable but very slow. In 1930 it was reported in the *Evening Standard* that —

Grey-haired women, their hair streaming in the breeze, clasped hands and danced solemnly round a bonfire where the effigies of three people were in flames. No smile was on their faces, and from their lips fell curses on a young husband. All around them were a host of men, women and children, chanting monotonously and beating tin cans, old kettles and cracked bells.

This "hussitting" in the Berkshire village of Woodley was directed at a man who had been summoned by his wife for cruelty, and against his mother and sister who had sided against the wife: "It is 30 years since we gave anyone 'rough music' ", one of the oldest villagers said. "Then it was a married man who had been annoying girls."[3]

I would hazard that there may be a relation between the continuity of rough music and the continuity of local dialect. (The *ceffyl pren* persisted most vigorously in Welsh-speaking regions, such as Carmarthen.) The rites belong in an orally-

---

[1] Munby diaries in Trinity College, Cambridge, vols. xvii, p. 241, 4 March 1863; xix, pp. 4-5, 7, 13, 2 May 1863. My thanks to Anna Davin.

[2] See *Pappin v Maynard*, in *Law Times*, 21 Nov. 1863. Decisions in King's Bench in the late seventeenth century had defined "riding skimmington" as riot, see Ingram, *op. cit.*, p. 101.

[3] *Evening Standard*, 3 Oct. 1930.

transmitted culture, and the strength of dialect signals also the tenacity of a traditional consciousness, upheld (perhaps) in such villages as Ripley and Woodley by closely-knitted kinship. Both dialect and customs can reproduce themselves together, and can long persist into mature industrial society. But at a certain point those engines of cultural acceleration, literacy and schooling, combine with increasing in-migration and general mobility, to "saturate" the old culture, to disperse it as a living practice, to break down the old sensibility, leaving nothing but antiquarian survivals.

What then may survive, in pockets in urban districts and, more often, in the remote countryside, are certain old traditions maintained sometimes by particular occupational groups who are at odds with the politer modern norms and who are seen by their neighbours as "rough" or "ruffians" (i.e. "rough 'uns"). In the North Yorkshire village of Kirkby Malzeard "stang riding" still was being practised at the end of the last century, with a variant of the old "nominy". It always originated in the pub. "Everything originated in the pub in them days. They'd all be 'leaders' ", recalled an informant in 1971. The initiators were a small group of men: building workers, a blacksmith, itinerant labourers who worked at various jobs, working on estates, at fair grounds, hedging and dyking in the winter; "they were rough types", poachers, heavy drinkers — "if they thought they could get a glass of beer they'd bray owt". But they were also the people who kept alive the "Plough Stots" and the complex Sword Dance of Kirkby Malzeard, and who performed it for money or drink at fairs and at flower shows:

> These sort used to go sword dancing — but they always used to spend the money on beer, and sleep out in the woods. . . But the Stang was different. They did that because working class people are more faithful to their wives than are t'nobs. And anyone as beats 'is wife up or a child is a bad 'un. They really had to feel very, very strongly about this carry-on. Then it was a big disgrace, it brought it out in the open. They didn't do it just for a lark.

The last time the "stang" was ridden in Kirkby Malzeard was because a labourer had been beating his wife:

> He'd a houseful of kids — ten or a dozen children. It had got out that he'd been braying his wife — coming home from the pub, she'd be there with a houseful of kids, and then he'd start in and bashed her about.

They got a big effigy which they fastened on a hand-cart, "and these big brawling chaps they went to the house and bumped on the door". As they went down the village street they rang a big bell and reeled off "the ditty". "They used to make such a din and commotion people would pay anything to get them away." [1]

This sounds folksy and even reassuring. But rough music could also be an excuse for a drunken orgy or for blackmail. It could legitimise the aggression of youths, and (if one may whisper it) youths are not always, in every historical context, protagonists of rationality or of change. I make the point strongly, arguing in a sense with part of myself, for I find much that attracts me in rough music. It is a property of a society in which justice is not wholly delegated or bureau-criticised, but is enacted by and within the community. Where it is enacted upon an evident malefactor — some officious public figure or a brutal wife-beater — one is tempted to lament the passing of the rites. But the victims were not all of this order. They might equally be some lonely sexual non-conformist, some Sue Bridehead and Jude Fawley living together out of holy wedlock. And the psychic terrorism which could be brought to bear upon them was truly terrifying: the flaring and lifelike effigies, with their ancient associations with heretic-burning and the maiming of images — the magical or daemonic suggestiveness of masking and of animal-guising — the flaunting of obscenities — the driving out of evil spirits with noise.

Rough music belongs to a mode of life in which some part of the law belongs still to the community and is theirs to enforce. To this one may assent. It indicates modes of social self-control and the disciplining of certain kinds of violence and anti-social offence (insults to women, child abuse, wife-beating) which in today's cities may be breaking down. But, when we consider the societies which have been under our examination, one must add a rider. Because law belongs to people, and is not alienated, or delegated, it is not thereby made necessarily more "nice" and tolerant, more cosy and folksy. It is only as nice and as tolerant as the prejudices and norms of the folk allow. Some forms of rough music

---

[1] Accounts collected by the late Kathleen Bumstead in 1971.

disappeared from history in shadowy complicity with bigotry, jingoism and worse. In Sussex rough music was visited upon "pro-Boers", including William Morris's close friend, Georgie Burne-Jones. In Bavaria the last manifestations of *haberfeldtreiben* were linked to mafia-like blackmail, anti-semitism and, in the final stage, to ascendant Nazism.[1] For some of its victims, the coming of a distanced (if alienated) Law and a bureaucratised police must have been felt as a liberation from the tyranny of one's "own".

[1] See *Le Charivari*, pp. 294, 306.

APPENDIX I

The late Mr Hanson Halstead was born in Siddal, Halifax at the end of the last century. He was for some years an engineer, active trade unionist and socialist, and member of the NCLC; but he seemed more like a countryman, was a strong dialect speaker, and in his later years took on a smallholding with pig-keeping. At the end of his life, in the early 1960s, he started jotting down reminiscences in a Boots diary (which he gave to me). The episode below is undated, but probably dates from the earliest years of the present century.

The Burning of the Shrew

When Mary came hoam from her wark she war full o news. She said, 'Has ta heard, Bill, 'at Jack so and so has gorn a living wi Misis so and so in Jubilee Road?' 'Well, I'll be damned. Them 'at haven't trouble seem to make some for the'sens.' 'Aye, but I haven't told thee all yet.' 'Well, what else is ther to tell?' 'Well, to-morn neet they are goin to burn them up.' 'So there is goin to be some fun, eh?' 'Aye, sum on 'em is making two big dummies, stuffed wi' sawdust, and pariffin oil, and they are going to be facing one another on a long pole, and there is going to be a procession around the village and to end in Jubilee Road.'

A lott were all looking for'ard to it, a lott 'at wor no better theirselves. On the night, as it became dusk they went and fetched out the dummies, and it was like some devil's madjic. They sett off around the village, and the procession grew and grew — folk wi' bells and draw tins, cake tins, owt 'at would make a noise; and it was nearly as good a noise as a jazz band ont wireless reckons to make with £2,000 worth of instruments. It went around the village, and landed in Jubilee Road. Talk about advertising! The police was there, and, Hell, they had to get a lott to break a way through, for the dummeys. There were a lott more people packed in Jubilee Road than lived in Siddal and no advertising. Well, the dummeys went through. The police tried to get it, but women danced in front of them and sat down in the street in front of them to stop them. But it went on, and up Scarhall stepps and back darn Backhold Lane around to Jubilee Road. Then they sett them on fire, and when they got in front of the house, and it was blazing like hell, the police was protecting the door. Then it was thrown on top of them. Two days later they removed, and they drummed them out unceremoniously with cake-tins and draw-tins. But that crowd! you could have walked on their heads. There will never be a crowd like that in Jubilee Road again, and no advertising. (A little bit of savagery.) Don't think I am making out Siddal to be a reight good moral place: I am not. It was like any other place, as the Parson's egg.

(One or two modifications to spelling and also to punctuation.)

APPENDIX II

It has been noted (see p. 495 above) that Lévi-Strauss cited in *Mythologiques I. Le Cru et le Cuit* an unpublished survey of the practice of charivari carried out by P. Fortier-Beaulieu, from which he derived the conclusion that in 92.5 per cent of the examined cases, the occasion for charivari was re-marriage.

Some extracts from Fortier-Beaulieu's survey were published in *Revue de folklore francaise et de folklore colonial*, xi (1940). The original replies to his questionnaire remain in the archives of the Musée National des Arts et Traditions Populaires (see MS B 19, 1 a 620, et MS 44,390) and I am greatly indebted to M. le Conservateur, and to the staff of the Musée for their courtesy and assistance in permitting me to consult these archives.

The survey took place between June and August 1937, and took the form of a questionnaire submitted to Mairies by P. Fortier-Beaulieu, at that time Secrétaire à la Propaganda of the Folklore Society. The questionnaire, in fact, makes no reference to charivari, but is headed simply "Manifestation à l'occasion du remariage d'un veuf ou d'une veuve"; a reply was called for urgently, to enable Fortier-Beaulieu to prepare a report on "Veuvage et le Remariage" at the forthcoming International Congress of Folklore.

Thus the enquiry was not conducted into the practice of charivari as such, but into any type of manifestation at re-marriage. It is therefore surprising, not that 92.5 per cent of the responses cite re-marriage as the occasion for charivari, but that the number falls short of 100 per cent. But the responses are not, in any case, of a kind which may be submitted to a serious exercise in quantification. Of 307 responses, 123 signalled manifestations of some kind upon re-marriage (usually charivari), 113 signalled no manifestations, 42 signalled that such manifestations no longer occurred, and 29 signalled "néant". Of the 123 affirmative replies, perhaps one half were perfunctory and completed in haste ("oui", "non"), while some thirty or forty were answered scrupulously and in detail. Except in a few cases, where the mayor passed the questionnaire over to a local folklorist or historian, the respondents had no special qualifications to answer the questions. One deduces that often the form was passed over to a secretary in the Mairie, while on a few fortunate occasions the mayor was a man of wide local knowledge and observation, and took pleasure in a task unfamiliar among routine business.

Thus the value of the survey lies not in any quantitative deductions, of even the most elementary kind, but in the materials presented in some thirty of the more conscientious replies. Before attending to these, we must offer a caution. The survey, in 1937, is dealing not with a custom in its vigour, but with vestiges and survivals. Hence we may not properly deduce from it functions which belong to the custom in its maturity. "A l'heure actuelle cette coutume qui n'existe que dans les campagnes est une plaisanterie et un divertissement pour la jeunese" (Rodez, Aveyron); it survived, if at all, as a good-humoured form of blackmail, to raise a few sous *pour boire.*

Insofar as such vestiges can offer evidence, there are replies which give support to most of the hypotheses debated by students of charivari. From Brive (Corrèze): "La veuve qui se remarie n'est guère bien considérée comme devenant infidèle à la mémoire du mari défunt"; or, again, "parce que le mariage est considéré comme un sacrement et que les conjoints n'ont pas moralement le droit de le rompre même après la mort" (Castillon, Ariège). A few replies indicate in some manner the representation of the spirit of the dead spouse at the charivari: "on évoque la vie passée des époux, leurs moeurs, leur vie galante, quelquefois c'est bien corsé" (Donzers, Drôme). Sexual ridicule of the aged, and in particular of disparity of ages, is frequently mentioned. An explanation which is offered only once is "pour chasser les mauvais esprits" (Aups, Var). The theory of a limited "pool of eligibles" also appears — if the second marriage should "enlève une possibilité du moins du choix pour les autres" (Séez, Savoie). The jealousy of friends, neighbours, parents (or of the parents of the dead spouse), and of children is more often mentioned. A charivari at Hyères (Var) had been organised by the grown-up son of the widower. The function was to protect "les intérêts des enfants du premier lit" (Remiremont, Vosges); "les enfants d'un premier lit ayant souvent à pâtir du second mariage — d'où le péjoratif:

marâtre" (Cahors, Lot). The relationship of charivari to differing inheritance customs is not a question which, to my knowledge, has yet been adequately pursued.

While most of the responses assume that the promoters of charivari were "des jeunes gens", a few replies suggest more particularity: the initiators are described, in one, as "les voisins ennemis et plus particulièrement les parents mécontents par l'union" (Uzès, Gard). Whoever were the initators, the charivari was supported — as most replies make clear — by "un peu tout le monde de la basse classe" (Burzet, Ardèche); although in some regions there was some distinction among the actors:

> Dans certains cas où la différence d'âge est trop accentuée (vieillard contractant union avec jeune fille) les femmes manifestant plus que les hommes — Dégoût, peut-être, plus souvent jalousie si l'homme est fortuné.
>
> (Castillon, Ariège)

It is clear that re-marriage *as such* rarely provoked charivari; there was normally some other attendant circumstance. In certain regions, it is true, there was a marked disposition to disapprove of re-marriage and (correspondingly) to honour widowhood:

> La veuve qui respecte son veuvage est très bien vue dans le village. Les voisins l'aident dans son ménage et les hommes font le Dimanche matin les corvées volontaires pour lui couper son bois, lui faucher ses prés et labourer ses champs.
>
> (Castillon, Ariège).

In other regions, on the contrary, as one perceptive respondent noted, re-marriage was made essential by the economic nature of the household. Thus there were no manifestations against re-marriage in Nibelle-St. Sauveur (Loiret), a commune —

> composée pour sa grande majorité de petits propriétaires ruraux exploitant eux-mêmes, la vie en ménage est une nécessité. En conséquence, les veufs et veuves. . . se remarient généralement en un court délai. . .

Perhaps the most thoughtful reply came from Dax (Landes).* "Calhibari" was occasioned frequently by

---

*From Dr Aparisi-Serres, secrétaire général de la Société de "Borda": See *Revue de folklore. . .*, xi (1940), pp. 17-19.

remarriage, "mais il faut en outre une circonstance qui rende le remariage grotesque, odieux ou antipathique". Such a circumstance might be in 1) the difference in ages of the couple, 2) the difference in their social position, as when "un propriétaire 'monsieur' qui épouse une jeune paysanne", 3) a difference in fortune which suggested that one of the spouses was marrying for money, 4) the infirmity of the widow or widower, "ce qui suppose toujours la *vente* de soi-même", 5) the antecedent sexual conduct of either party, as for example "si l'on soupconne qu'ils étaient *bien* ensemble du vivant du mort ou de la morte" (this could occasion the bravest charivaris), 6) if both parties were old.

The suggestion that some aggravation of circumstances was necessary is present in many replies: "quand elle s'ajoute à la disproportion d'âge" (Moulins, Allier); "quand les futurs époux — veufs ou veuves — prêtent un peu le flanc à la critique et au ridicule" (Burzet, Ardèche); "plutôt à la veuve de mauvaise conduite qui se remarie" (Ruffec, Charente); "un vieux riche épousant une jeunesse pauvre. . . surtout s'il y a des enfants déjà grands d'un premier lit" (Brioude, Haute Loire). Without such aggravation, it was possible for the remarried to avoid the compliment of charivari even in a district where it was endemic. The respondent from Vico (Corse) replied in an unexpectedly personal sense:

> On tient plutôt compte de situations particulières: l'auteur de ces renseignements est un veuf remarié qui n'a pas eu l'honneur du campanaccio [charivari] parce que Instituteur dans la Commune, épousant une Institutrice.

One reply afforded a valuable case-history of such particularity. The most recent charivari in Abzac (Gironde) "s'adressait à un homme d'âge mûr qui allait épouser une jeune fille que l'on savait enceinte et qui avait une conduite plus que douteuse". A procession was held, in which were three wagons drawn by donkeys. In the first was a goat, with the slogan: "Viande à bas prix", in the second "un vieillard complètement perclus"; in the third, "un jeune homme déguisé en nourrice faisait le simulacre d'allaiter un énorme poupon et au moyen d'une paille de seigle fendue imitait les cris du nouveau-né". When charivari could attain such heights in the 1930s, there is no cause for surprise that its occasional outcome in violence was signalled in some 16 per cent of the replies: e.g. Dax (Landes), Thèze (Basses Pyrénées), Conques (Aveyron), Remiremont (Vosges). One wonders what the percentage would have been in 1837?

So much for re-marriage. What of the 7.5 per cent of cases which (it would seem) fell outside this category? This must indicate simply that handful of replies where the respondent went beyond the enquiries of the questionnaire, and added unsolicited information. From Conques: "quand une femme a blessé son mari au visage, on conduit tous les ânes ou mulets de la contrée, en procession dans les rues de la localité". Charivaris had been held in Echire (Deux-Sèvres) when one of the engaged "avait eu certaines atteintes au point de vue galanteries, enfant naturel, etc.". From Dampniet (Corrèze) there came a valuable case-history:

> Au village de la Jubertie une famille composée du père, de la mère et du fils, vivait dans une petite aisance. Une femme sexagénaire survint qui troubla ce bonheur paisible. Le père en devint toqué. Mais ne pouvant lui-même épouser 'la belle' il voulut la donner pour femme à son propre fils âgé de 26 ans et d'esprit un peu simple. Celui-ci accepte d'épouser la sexagénaire.

This charivari had violent and tragic tones: the father tried to drown himself, and (failing) committed arson against one of its organisers. The matter no doubt forced itself upon the page, although not falling within the terms of the questionnaire, since it had occurred only two months previously — in April 1937 — and had caused the mayor much concern.

One further reply deserves quotation — a reply thrown in, perhaps, as an afterthought:

> Le 'callabari' se fait quelquefois à d'autres personnes que des veufs et des veuves — par exemple à des curés, des maîtres d'école, des fonctionnaires en résidence dans les villages lorsque la population devait se plaindre d'eux.
>
> (Tarbes, Hautes Pyrénées).

This evidence demolishes the supposed statistic of "92.5 per cent".

Index of Names and Places

AMERICAN LITERATURE
TRADITION AND INNOVATION

4 HENRY ADAMS
TO THE PRESENT

EDITED BY

Harrison T. Meserole
Pennsylvania State University

Walter Sutton
Syracuse University

Brom Weber
University of California, Davis

D. C. HEATH AND COMPANY
Lexington, Massachusetts Toronto London

Cover illustration courtesy of the Print Department, Boston Public Library.

Illustrated by Michael Tulysewski.

1974 Edition in four volumes.

Copyright © 1969 by D. C. Heath and Company.

Printed in the United States of America.

International Standard Book Number: 0-669-95976-6

Library of Congress Catalog Card Number: 74-15672

Preface

Imaginative literature is one of the richest expressions of the human mind, and among the literatures of the modern world American literature is today recognized as perhaps the most dynamic and productive, one of the great artistic achievements of Western civilization. It becomes a pleasure, therefore, as well as a humanistic responsibility to read and to read about this literature, to seek its origins in the writings of the first settlers to colonize the Eastern seaboard of the continent, and to follow its progress and development over the three and a half centuries of its history.

This is the principal purpose of *American Literature: Tradition and Innovation:* to provide for the modern student a representative selection of the best and most significant American prose and poetry from the beginnings to the present day.

The very richness of our literary heritage creates for editors the special problem of selection. We have tried to solve this problem by establishing strict criteria for inclusion of texts within these volumes. First, since it is our aim to present a freshly considered anthology to represent the range and power of American literature as literature, we have given first attention to major writers, those men and women whose creative imaginations have been the predominant force in shaping the American literary tradition. Second, we have given generous representation to those minor writers who made significant contribution to the literary history of their particular period or in the development of a particular genre in American letters. And finally, to provide fullest indication of the scope and variety of our literature, we have included several "gatherings" of important works by lesser known writers.

The editors have organized these writings into sections, using chronological sequence of authors as the basic pattern but with occasional departure from strict date sequence to achieve thematic unity or in recognition of a basic similarity of approach or response to a current of emphasis among writers of different generations. Thus Jonathan Edwards is placed with Puritan prose writers Roger Williams, Michael Wigglesworth, and Cotton Mather instead of with his chronological contemporary Benjamin Franklin. Titles of sections further underline this principle of organization: Walt Whitman and Emily Dickinson, for example, are grouped as "Pioneers of the Modern," and Ezra Pound, T. S. Eliot, Theodore Dreiser, Gertrude Stein, and Sherwood Anderson form a unit representing the early twentieth-century "Revolution in the Arts."

The editorial apparatus is designed to encourage a variety of approaches to the literature and to permit optimum use of class time. A brief introductory essay for each section suggests relationships between elements within the section, and the headnote for each author, and for each "gathering" of authors, contains background material the student needs for informed reading of the texts. Each headnote concludes with a brief bibliography of essential books, often with annotative comment. Fuller bibliographical assistance is given in the selective lists of sources included at the end of the anthology. Annotation has been kept to a minimum, while at the same time providing sufficient information to save the student the time of leafing through dictionaries of allusions, quotations, biography, mythology, and the like.

The editors have taken full advantage of recent textual and bibliographical scholarship in their effort to provide what is in their best judgment an accurate and authoritative text. When the original version of a text, as in some Colonial writings and dialect pieces, seemed to present untoward obstacles to comprehension, punctuation has been added and more liberal use of annotation employed to clarify meaning. We have not, however, "modernized" the text nor have we altered the language of the original, preferring to retain in all its richness and individuality the original writing as it was published in the author's lifetime.

In its plan and in the integration of the large number and variety of texts, this anthology represents the joint labor and judgment of the three editors; but Professor Meserole has assumed principal responsibility for the Colonial Period; Professor Weber for the Nineteenth Century; and Professor Sutton for the Twentieth Century. In the preparation of textual materials, Professor Meserole was assisted by Mrs. Sara B. Chase, and has benefited from the critical advice of several colleagues, particularly Professor Richard B. Gidez of The Pennsylvania State University. Professor Sutton was assisted by Delia K. Clarke and Catherine B. Sutton; he is also especially indebted for counsel and criticism to Professor A. Grove Day of the University of Hawaii. Professor Weber's assistants were Mrs. Gerry Baker and Mrs. Charlotte Honeywell; he would particularly wish to thank for their efforts in his behalf Professors David S. Wilson, Everett Carter and Robert A. Wiggins, all of the University of California at Davis. All the editors are grateful to Dean Darwin T. Turner of the Agricultural and Technical College of North Carolina.

Any good anthology reflects not only the training and experience of its editors but also, necessarily, their viewpoints. Perhaps not all teachers of American literature will agree with our choices or interpretations. Accordingly, we have tried to maintain balance throughout the anthology, guarding against both eccentricity and excessive reliance upon traditional opinion while providing adequate factual and critical information in our essays, headnotes and annotations. We have also tried to represent the forces of innovation and the relation between past and present without imposing on the selections printed here any arbitrary historical, philosophical, sociological, or aesthetic prejudices which might contravene the prerogatives of the teacher or block the student from coming to terms, on his own, with the living works of American literature.

Harrison T. Meserole

Walter Sutton

Brom Weber

Dates following selections indicate first book publication. Two dates appear when a large amount of time has elapsed between first printed appearance and book publication. The appearance of a dashed rule in the text of a selection indicates an omission in the text.

Contents

* Indicates material printed here is excerpted.

Tradition and Modernity

All times are times of transition, but at the beginning of the twentieth century the accelerating impetus of the industrial, scientific, and cultural revolutions was catapulting western civilization into a wholly new era of the machine and the laboratory. Men and women who matured in the nineteenth century and lived on into the twentieth had to try to come to terms with an alien social and intellectual environment. The changes required an adjustment to the quickening tempo and the social pressures of an industrial society. They also called for an effort to absorb the cultural implications of a relatively short period of intellectual history in which the ideas of Darwin, Marx, Freud, and Einstein (and others) drastically altered man's conception of himself, his society, and the physical universe. It is not to be expected that a generation or even two or three generations could accommodate themselves fully to a cultural upheaval that demanded a reexamination and revision of ingrained customs, attitudes, and values. But among writers and other artists, the "antennae of the race," as Ezra Pound called them, there was a heightened sensitivity and response to the process of change.

In the years following the Civil War, the mere physical fact of the shift of population from the farm to the cities gave rise to problems. From the late

Paris Exhibition: View from the Pont Alexandre by Will B. Anderson from a photo by Neurden Fréres, Paris. Courtesy of Historical Pictures Services, Chicago.

nineteenth century into the mid-twentieth, the urbanization that Jefferson and Franklin feared developed new social pressures as successive immigrant groups and religious and racial minorities struggled to gain acceptance and fuller opportunity in an expanding economy. With the appearance of Stephen Crane's *Maggie: A Girl of the Streets* (1893; 1896), a new type of fiction, the city novel, emerged. More fully developed by other authors like Theodore Dreiser, it was to become a focus for the treatment of the problems of urban life in America by protesters, reformers, and writers in the naturalistic tradition through the Depression-ridden thirties into the present period of acute crisis in the cities.

Revolutionary changes in scientific and economic theory from the latter half of the nineteenth century had profound consequences. The Darwinian concept of evolution helped to undermine orthodox religious faith and to replace the garden world of the Romantics with the naturalistic image of the jungle. "Hard Darwinism" provided a rationalization for an unrestricted laissez-faire struggle for the survival of the fittest in the economic realm. In literature the biological determinism of evolutionary theory contributed greatly to the pessimistic determinism of the naturalistic tradition, with Theodore Dreiser as an early American representative.

Marxist economic theory, which originated in the same period, had a deep and lasting effect. Although Marxism, with its emphasis on the force of environment complemented the biological determinism of Darwinism, it also encouraged protest and reform through its call for a revolutionary change in the economic organization of society. In America its influence was strongest during the period of unrest that preceded World War I and during the Depression years of the 1930's. In both these periods, however, its effect was not so much to foment revolution (although some adherents worked to that end) as to advance the cause of greater economic democracy of the kind desired by Whitman in *Democratic Vistas* (1871). Although the direct influence of Marxism on American literature is most apparent in the Utopian protest fiction of the late nineteenth century and in the proletarian fiction of the 1930's (especially in that of John Dos Passos and John Steinbeck), Marxist attitudes and ideas also affected the work of novelists of the 1920's, like F. Scott Fitzgerald, and of the post-World War-II period.

With the turn of the century the theories of Sigmund Freud and Albert Einstein produced further shifts in man's conception of his own nature and of the physical universe in which he exists. Freudian psychology, which stressed the power of the unconscious mind, not only reinforced the biological determinism of the naturalists; through its popularization of the imagery of dreams, it also stimulated a renewal of the symbolist tradition in literature and contributed to avant-garde aesthetic movements like Dadaism and Surrealism. In literary criticism, the ideas of pioneers like Freud and Carl Jung resulted in the development of psychoanalytical and of myth and archetype criticism.

Although less clearly traceable, the effects of Einstein's imperfectly understood theory of relativity have been no less pervasive. In society at large, the idea has worked to undermine the claims of absolutism and to encourage a relativism of values. In literature and the arts, new ways of thinking about time and about the relation of time and space affected artists' ideas about their world and their work, and stimulated experimentation in multidimensional forms. In poetry the idea of relativity fostered organic rather than traditional theories of form and contributed to such ideas about the temporal and typographical spacing of verses as those associated with William Carlos Williams' "variable foot."

Although some of these new ideas and influences have by now been at work over the space of nearly a hundred years, their impact was greatest upon those whose mature lives bridged the last and present centuries. Of nineteenth century writers who lived long enough to observe and comment upon the implications of the modern revolution, the greatest span of time and change occurred during the lifetime of Henry Adams, which began in 1838, in the day of the stagecoach and steamboat, when the population of the twenty-six states was a mere seventeen million. It ended in 1918, when America, a nation of more than a hundred million, emerged from the first great war of the twentieth century as a leading world power. It is not easy to "place" a man like Adams, who by birth and the term of his active life was a man of the nineteenth century and a close contemporary of Mark Twain (1835–1910) and Henry James (1843–1916). As a professional historian and an intellectual, Adams was aware of the process of change in which he and his contemporaries were involved; he consciously attempted to analyze it and adjust his viewpoint to it. His later work was shaped by twentieth century thought and focused on conflicts of tradition and modernity in his own ideas and values.

The problems in which he was most deeply involved were social and religious. There was from the beginning the question of his public role: As the descendant of presidents of the early Republic and as heir to a family tradition of public service, he had to accept the bitter fact that there was no place for him in the power structure of the Washington to which he returned in the gilded years following the Civil War. Political impotence remained a frustration throughout his life. Philosophically and religiously he was torn between his recognition of the "multiplistic" world predicted by the science of his time and his temperamental need for a unifying principle. Adams turned to a tradition of religious mysticism and, idealizing the culture of the middle ages, contrasted "thirteenth century unity" and "twentieth century multiplicity" in his *Mont-Saint-Michel and Chartres* (1904; 1913) and *The Education of Henry Adams* (1909; 1918). The latter title carries a burden of irony, for Adams was all too conscious of the fact that his nineteenth-century background and training had not and could not prepare him for intellectual life in the twentieth century.

Other conflicts, stemming from the same process of cultural change, mark the work of younger writers who came of age before the end of the nineteenth century. Some, like Edwin Arlington Robinson, shared with Adams and the English Victorians the problem of conflicting faith and doubt. For others, like Henry James and the younger Edith Wharton and Willa Cather, the relativity of social mores and values became a central theme, especially as these were revealed through contrasting cultures (European and American), classes (the old- and newly-rich), and periods (the old and new America).

It remained for still younger writers like Ezra Pound and T. S. Eliot to accomplish the modern revolution in verse and prose and to contribute American leadership to international literary movements in London and Paris. The boundaries of the generations are not hard and fast, however. In the foremost rank of the rising moderns was Gertrude Stein, who, although a close contemporary of Edith Wharton and Willa Cather, was educated under conditions that made her more fully receptive and responsive to the influences of the new age.

Henry Adams   *1838–1918*

Great grandson and grandson of presidents (John Adams and John Quincy Adams), Henry Brooks Adams was not to achieve distinction in the life of politics and public service shared by so many other members of his famous Massachusetts family. After graduation from Harvard in 1858 he studied law without enthusiasm in Berlin and in Dresden (1859–1860). He remained abroad during the Civil War, serving as secretary to his father, Charles Francis Adams, United States minister to England during the administrations of Lincoln and Johnson (1861–1869). Returning to Washington in 1868, Adams was struck by the dynamic strength, the crudeness, and the corruptness of postwar American social and political life. He accepted an appointment as assistant professor of history at Harvard, where he remained for seven years (1870–1877), contributing to the development of the University's history program as an admired and respected teacher and scholar—although he characteristically regarded his academic career as a failure. Moving to Washington, Adams settled down as an observer of the political scene and a friend (or, in his words, "stable-companion") to statesmen. In 1880 he anonymously published *Democracy*, a disillusioned and satiric inside view of Washington politics and society; it was followed by *Esther* (1884), a pseudonymous novel of New York society. Following the tragic death by suicide of his wife in 1885, he traveled to the South Seas and Japan in company with his friend John LaFarge, the painter. Upon returning, he completed his monumental *History of the United States During the Administrations of Jefferson and Madison* (9 vols., 1889–1891). In his later years, Adams became preoccupied with the contrast between medieval Christian culture, unified (it seemed to him) by the worship of the Virgin as a source of creative power, and the pluralistic culture of science-conditioned modern society, symbolized by the efficient but inhuman dynamo. The books in which he discussed these different periods and the relation between them are *Mont-Saint-Michel and Chartres: A Study of*

Thirteenth-Century Unity ([privately printed, 1904;]1913) and *The Education of Henry Adams: A Study of Twentieth-Century Multiplicity* ([1907;] 1918). In these works he attempted to develop a "dynamic" theory of history based on the idea of the acceleration of force. Ironic and skeptical in tone, the *Education* is perhaps less interesting as a contribution to historical theory than as an expression of its nineteenth century author's resistance to—as well as his effort to understand—the new age that was dawning as his life declined. Other books by Adams include *The Life of Albert Gallatin* (1879), *John Randolph* (1882), *Memoirs of Marau Taaroa, Last Queen of Tahiti* (1893; rev. 1901), *The Life of George Cabot Lodge* (1911), and *The Degradation of the Democratic Dogma* (1920).

Adams' voluminous published correspondence includes *A Cycle of Adams Letters, 1861–1865*, ed. W. C. Ford, 2 vols. (Boston, 1920); *Letters of Henry Adams, 1858–1918*, ed. W. L. Ford, 2 vols. (Boston, 1930–1938); *Henry Adams and His Friends: A Collection of His Unpublished Letters*, ed. H. D. Cater (Boston, 1947); and *The Selected Letters of Henry Adams*, ed. Newton Arvin (New York, 1951). Among numerous biographies of Adams and critiques of his work, two useful recent studies are J. C. Levenson, *The Mind and Art of Henry Adams* (Boston, 1957), and George Hochfield, *Henry Adams: An Interpretation and Introduction* (New York, 1962).

The text of "The Virgin and the Dynamo" is that of *The Education of Henry Adams* (New York, 1918), Chapter 25.

The Dynamo and the Virgin (1900)

Until the Great Exposition of 1900[1] closed its doors in November, Adams haunted it, aching to absorb knowledge, and helpless to find it. He would have liked to know how much of it could have been grasped by the best-informed man in the world. While he was thus meditating chaos, Langley[2] came by, and showed it to him. At Langley's behest, the Exhibition dropped its superfluous rags and stripped itself to the skin, for Langley knew what to study, and why, and how; while Adams might as well have stood outside in the night, staring at the Milky Way. Yet Langley said nothing new, and taught nothing that one might not have learned from Lord Bacon,[3] three hundred years before; but though one should have known the "Advancement of Science" as well as one knew the "Comedy of Errors," the literary knowledge counted for nothing until some teacher should show how to apply it. Bacon took a vast deal of trouble in teaching King James I and his subjects, American or other, towards the year 1620, that true

[1] The Paris Exposition of 1900.

[2] Samuel Pierpont Langley (1834–1906), American astronomer and secretary of the Smithsonian Institution (1887–1906) who pioneered in the measurement of solar and lunar radiation and in airplane aviation.

[3] Francis Bacon (1561–1626), whose *Advancement of Learning* (1605) and *Novum Organum* (1620) helped lay the foundation of modern inductive science.

science was the development or economy of forces; yet an elderly American in 1900 knew neither the formula nor the forces; or even so much as to say to himself that his historical business in the Exposition concerned only the economies or developments of force since 1893, when he began the study at Chicago.[4]

Nothing in education is so astonishing as the amount of ignorance it accumulates in the form of inert facts. Adams had looked at most of the accumulations of art in the storehouses called Art Museums; yet he did not know how to look at the art exhibits of 1900. He had studied Karl Marx and his doctrines of history[5] with profound attention, yet he could not apply them at Paris. Langley, with the ease of a great master of experiment, threw out of the field every exhibit that did not reveal a new application of force, and naturally threw out, to begin with, almost the whole art exhibit. Equally, he ignored almost the whole industrial exhibit. He led his pupil directly to the forces. His chief interest was in new motors to make his airship feasible, and he taught Adams the astonishing complexities of the new Daimler[6] motor, and of the automobile, which, since 1893, had become a nightmare at a hundred kilometres an hour, almost as destructive as the electric tram which was only ten years older; and threatening to become as terrible as the locomotive steam-engine itself, which was almost exactly Adams's own age.

Then he showed his scholar the great hall of dynamos, and explained how little he knew about electricity or force of any kind, even of his own special sun, which spouted heat in inconceivable volume, but which, as far as he knew, might spout less or more, at any time, for all the certainty he felt in it. To him, the dynamo itself was but an ingenious channel for conveying somewhere the heat latent in a few tons of poor coal hidden in a dirty engine-house carefully kept out of sight; but to Adams the dynamo became a symbol of infinity. As he grew accustomed to the great gallery of machines, he began to feel the forty-foot dynamos as a moral force, much as the early Christians felt the Cross. The planet itself seemed less impressive, in its old-fashioned, deliberate, annual or daily revolution, than this huge wheel, revolving within arm's-length at some vertiginous speed, and barely murmuring — scarcely humming an audible warning to stand a hair's-breadth further for respect of power — while it would not wake the baby lying close against its frame. Before the end, one began to pray to it; inherited instinct taught the natural expression of man before silent and infinite force. Among the thousand symbols of ultimate energy, the dynamo

---

[4] Adams' interest in modern power had been awakened by the dynamos exhibited at the Columbian Exposition of 1893 in Chicago.

[5] As set forth in *Das Kapital* of Karl Marx (1818–1883).

[6] Gottlieb Daimler (1834–1890), inventor and developer of internal combustion engines for automobiles.

was not so human as some, but it was the most expressive.

Yet the dynamo, next to the steam-engine, was the most familiar of exhibits. For Adams's objects its value lay chiefly in its occult mechanism. Between the dynamo in the gallery of machines and the engine-house outside, the break of continuity amounted to abysmal fracture for a historian's objects. No more relation could he discover between the steam and the electric current than between the Cross and the cathedral. The forces were interchangeable if not reversible, but he could see only an absolute *fiat* in electricity as in faith. Langley could not help him. Indeed, Langley seemed to be worried by the same trouble, for he constantly repeated that the new forces were anarchical, and specially that he was not responsible for the new rays, that were little short of parricidal in their wicked spirit towards science. His own rays, with which he had doubled the solar spectrum, were altogether harmless and beneficent; but Radium denied its God—or, what was to Langley the same thing, denied the truths of his Science.[7] The force was wholly new.

A historian who asked only to learn enough to be as futile as Langley or Kelvin made rapid progress under this teaching, and mixed himself up in the tangle of ideas until he achieved a sort of Paradise of ignorance vastly consoling to his fatigued senses. He wrapped himself in vibrations and rays which were new, and he would have hugged Marconi[8] and Branly[9] had he met them, as he hugged the dynamo; while he lost his arithmetic in trying to figure out the equation between the discoveries and the economies of force. The economies, like the discoveries, were absolute, supersensual, occult; incapable of expression in horse-power. What mathematical equivalent could he suggest as the value of a Branly coherer? Frozen air, or the electric furnace, had some scale of measurement, no doubt, if somebody could invent a thermometer adequate to the purpose; but X-rays had played no part whatever in man's consciousness, and the atom itself had figured only as a fiction of thought. In these seven years man had translated himself into a new universe which had no common scale of measurement with the old. He had entered a supersensual world, in which he could measure nothing except by chance collisions of movements imperceptible to his senses, perhaps even imperceptible to his instruments, but perceptible to each other, and so to some known ray at the end of the scale. Langley seemed prepared for anything, even for an indeterminable number of universes interfused—physics stark mad in metaphysics.

Historians undertake to arrange sequences,—called stories, or histories—assuming in silence a relation of cause and effect. These

<hr>

[7] Because its disintegration was an apparent contradiction of the principle of the conservation of matter and energy.

[8] Guglielmo Marconi (1874–1934), inventor of radio-telegraphy.

[9] Edward Branly (1846–1940), inventor of a detector for radio waves.

assumptions, hidden in the depths of dusty libraries, have been astounding, but commonly unconscious and childlike; so much so, that if any captious critic were to drag them to light, historians would probably reply, with one voice, that they had never supposed themselves required to know what they were talking about. Adams, for one, had toiled in vain to find out what he meant. He had even published a dozen volumes of American history for no other purpose than to satisfy himself whether, by the severest process of stating, with the least possible comment, such facts as seemed sure, in such order as seemed rigorously consequent, he could fix for a familiar moment a necessary sequence of human movement. The result had satisfied him as little as at Harvard College. Where he saw sequence, other men saw something quite different, and no one saw the same unit of measure. He cared little about his experiments and less about his statesmen, who seemed to him quite as ignorant as himself and, as a rule, no more honest; but he insisted on a relation of sequence, and if he could not reach it by one method, he would try as many methods as science knew. Satisfied that the sequence of men led to nothing and that the sequence of their society could lead no further, while the mere sequence of time was artificial, and the sequence of thought was chaos, he turned at last to the sequence of force; and thus it happened that, after ten years' pursuit, he found himself lying in the Gallery of Machines at the Great Exposition of 1900, his historical neck broken by the sudden irruption of forces totally new.

Since no one else showed much concern, an elderly person without other cares had no need to betray alarm. The year 1900 was not the first to upset schoolmasters. Copernicus and Galileo[10] had broken many professorial necks about 1600; Columbus had stood the world on its head towards 1500; but the nearest approach to the revolution of 1900 was that of 310, when Constantine set up the Cross.[11] The rays that Langley disowned, as well as those which he fathered, were occult, supersensual, irrational; they were a revelation of mysterious energy like that of the Cross; they were what, in terms of mediæval science, were called immediate modes of the divine substance.

The historian was thus reduced to his last resources. Clearly if he was bound to reduce all these forces to a common value, this common value could have no measure but that of their attraction on his own mind. He must treat them as they had been felt; as convertible, reversible, interchangeable attractions on thought. He made up his mind to venture it; he would risk translating rays into faith. Such a reversible process would vastly amuse a chemist, but the chemist could not deny

[10] The effect of the studies of both Copernicus (1473 – 1543) and Galileo (1564 – 1642) was to establish the revolutionary concept of a heliocentric solar system.
[11] Constantine I (280? – 337) was the first Christian emperor of Rome.

that he, or some of his fellow physicists, could feel the force of both. When Adams was a boy in Boston, the best chemist in the place had probably never heard of Venus except by way of scandal, or of the Virgin except as idolatry; neither had he heard of dynamos or automobiles or radium; yet his mind was ready to feel the force of all, though the rays were unborn and the women were dead.

Here opened another totally new education, which promised to be by far the most hazardous of all. The knife-edge along which he must crawl, like Sir Lancelot in the twelfth century,[12] divided two kingdoms of force which had nothing in common but attraction. They were as different as a magnet is from gravitation, supposing one knew what a magnet was, or gravitation, or love. The force of the Virgin was still felt at Lourdes,[13] and seemed to be as potent as X-rays; but in America neither Venus nor Virgin ever had value as force—at most as sentiment. No American had ever been truly afraid of either.

This problem in dynamics gravely perplexed an American historian. The Woman had once been supreme; in France she still seemed potent, not merely as a sentiment, but as a force. Why was she unknown in America? For evidently America was ashamed of her, and she was ashamed of herself, otherwise they would not have strewn fig-leaves so profusely all over her. When she was a true force, she was ignorant of fig-leaves, but the monthly-magazine-made American female had not a feature that would have been recognized by Adam. The trait was notorious, and often humorous, but any one brought up among Puritans knew that sex was sin. In any previous age, sex was strength. Neither art nor beauty was needed. Every one, even among Puritans, knew that neither Diana of the Ephesians nor any of the Oriental goddesses was worshipped for her beauty. She was goddess because of her force; she was the animated dynamo; she was reproduction—the greatest and most mysterious of all energies; all she needed was to be fecund. Singularly enough, not one of Adams's many schools of education had ever drawn his attention to the opening lines of Lucretius, though they were perhaps the finest in all Latin literature, where the poet invoked Venus exactly as Dante invoked the Virgin:—

"Quae quoniam rerum naturam *sola* gubernas."[14]

The Venus of Epicurean philosophy survived in the Virgin of the Schools:—

"Donna, sei tanto grande, e tanto vali,

[12] An allusion to a test imposed upon Lancelot in Chrétien de Troyes' *Chevalier de la Charratte*.
[13] Lourdes, a pilgrimage center for Roman Catholics, is famous for the healing powers of a spring associated with the Virgin.
[14] "Thou, since thou alone governest the nature of things" (*De Rerum Naturam*, I, 21, by Titus Lucretius Carus [99?–55 B.C.]).

Che qual vuol grazia, e a te non ricorre,
Sua disianza vuol volar senz' ali."[15]

All this was to American thought as though it had never existed. The true American knew something of the facts, but nothing of the feelings; he read the letter, but he never felt the law. Before this historical chasm, a mind like that of Adams felt itself helpless; he turned from the Virgin to the Dynamo as though he were a Branly coherer. On one side, at the Louvre and at Chartres, as he knew by the record of work actually done and still before his eyes, was the highest energy ever known to man, the creator of four-fifths of his noblest art, exercising vastly more attraction over the human mind than all the steam-engines and dynamos ever dreamed of; and yet this energy was unknown to the American mind. An American Virgin would never dare command; an American Venus would never dare exist.

The question, which to any plain American of the nineteenth century seemed as remote as it did to Adams, drew him almost violently to study, once it was posed; and on this point Langleys were as useless as though they were Herbert Spencers[16] or dynamos. The idea survived only as art. There one turned as naturally as though the artist were himself a woman. Adams began to ponder, asking himself whether he knew of any American artist who had ever insisted on the power of sex, as every classic had always done; but he could think only of Walt Whitman; Bret Harte, as far as the magazines would let him venture; and one or two painters, for the flesh-tones. All the rest had used sex for sentiment, never for force; to them, Eve was a tender flower, and Herodias[17] an unfeminine horror. American art, like the American language and American education, was as far as possible sexless. Society regarded this victory over sex as its greatest triumph, and the historian readily admitted it, since the moral issue, for the moment, did not concern one who was studying the relations of unmoral force. He cared nothing for the sex of the dynamo until he could measure its energy.

Vaguely seeking a clue, he wandered through the art exhibit, and, in his stroll, stopped almost every day before St. Gaudens's General Sherman,[18] which had been given the central post of honor. St. Gaudens himself was in Paris, putting on the work his usual interminable last touches, and listening to the usual contradictory suggestions of

---

[15] "Lady, thou art so great, and so much art thou worth, / That he who wishes grace and does not turn to thee, / Would have his wish fly upward without wings" (Dante, *Paradiso*, XXXIII, 13–15).

[16] Herbert Spencer (1820–1903), the founder of evolutionary philosophy, for whom the idea of the "persistence of force" was a basic principle, acknowledged the ultimate inscrutability of the universe.

[17] Wife of King Herod, Herodias was responsible for the death of John the Baptist.

[18] Equestrian statue by Augustus Saint-Gaudens (1848–1907), Irish-born American sculptor.

brother sculptors. Of all the American artists who gave to American art whatever life it breathed in the seventies, St. Gaudens was perhaps the most sympathetic, but certainly the most inarticulate. General Grant or Don Cameron[19] had scarcely less instinct of rhetoric than he. All the others—the Hunts, Richardson, John La Farge, Stanford White[20] —were exuberant; only St. Gaudens could never discuss or dilate on an emotion, or suggest artistic arguments for giving to his work the forms that he felt. He never laid down the law, or affected the despot, or became brutalized like Whistler[21] by the brutalities of his world. He required no incense; he was no egoist; his simplicity of thought was excessive; he could not imitate, or give any form but his own to the creations of his hand. No one felt more strongly than he the strength of other men, but the idea that they could affect him never stirred an image in his mind.

This summer his health was poor and his spirits were low. For such a temper, Adams was not the best companion, since his own gaiety was not *folle;* but he risked going now and then to the studio on Mont Parnasse to draw him out for a stroll in the Bois de Boulogne, or dinner as pleased his moods, and in return St. Gaudens sometimes let Adams go about in his company.

Once St. Gaudens took him down to Amiens, with a party of Frenchmen, to see the cathedral. Not until they found themselves actually studying the sculpture of the western portal, did it dawn on Adams's mind that, for his purposes, St. Gaudens on that spot had more interest to him than the cathedral itself. Great men before great monuments express great truths, provided they are not taken too solemnly. Adams never tired of quoting the supreme phrase of his idol Gibbon, before the Gothic cathedrals: "I darted a contemptuous look on the stately monuments of superstition."[22] Even in the footnotes of his history, Gibbon had never inserted a bit of humor more human than this, and one would have paid largely for a photograph of the fat little historian, on the background of Notre Dame of Amiens, trying to persuade his readers—perhaps himself—that he was darting a contemptuous look on the stately monument, for which he felt in fact the respect which every man of his vast study and active mind always feels before objects worthy of it; but besides the humor, one felt also the relation.

---

[19] James Donald Cameron (1833–1918), Republican politician and capitalist.
[20] William Morris Hunt (1824–1879), painter and brother of Richard Morris Hunt (1827–1895), a well-known architect. John La Farge (1835–1910), a painter and friend of Henry Adams, whom he accompanied on a journey to Japan and the South Seas. Henry Hobson Richardson (1838–1886) and Stanford White (1853–1906) were leading American architects.
[21] James A. McNeill Whistler (1834–1903), American painter known also for his combativeness and satiric wit.
[22] Edward Gibbon (1737–1794), author of *History of the Decline and Fall of the Roman Empire* (1776–1788).

Gibbon ignored the Virgin, because in 1789 religious monuments were out of fashion. In 1900 his remark sounded fresh and simple as the green fields to ears that had heard a hundred years of other remarks, mostly no more fresh and certainly less simple. Without malice, one might find it more instructive than a whole lecture of Ruskin.[23] One sees what one brings, and at that moment Gibbon brought the French Revolution. Ruskin brought reaction against the Revolution. St. Gaudens had passed beyond all. He liked the stately monuments much more than he liked Gibbon or Ruskin; he loved their dignity; their unity; their scale; their lines; their lights and shadows; their decorative sculpture; but he was even less conscious than they of the force that created it all — the Virgin, the Woman — by whose genius "the stately monuments of superstition" were built, through which she was expressed. He would have seen more meaning in Isis with the cow's horns, at Edfoo,[24] who expressed the same thought. The art remained, but the energy was lost even upon the artist.

Yet in mind and person St. Gaudens was a survival of the 1500's; he bore the stamp of the Renaissance, and should have carried an image of the Virgin round his neck, or stuck in his hat, like Louis XI.[25] In mere time he was a lost soul that had strayed by chance into the twentieth century, and forgotten where it came from. He writhed and cursed at his ignorance, much as Adams did at his own, but in the opposite sense. St. Gaudens was a child of Benvenuto Cellini,[26] smothered in an American cradle. Adams was a quintessence of Boston, devoured by curiosity to think like Benvenuto. St. Gaudens's art was starved from birth, and Adams's instinct was blighted from babyhood. Each had but half of a nature, and when they came together before the Virgin of Amiens they ought both to have felt in her the force that made them one; but it was not so. To Adams she became more than ever a channel of force; to St Gaudens she remained as before a channel of taste.

For a symbol of power, St. Gaudens instinctively preferred the horse, as was plain in his horse and Victory of the Sherman monument. Doubtless Sherman also felt it so. The attitude was so American that, for at least forty years, Adams had never realized that any other could be in sound taste. How many years had he taken to admit a notion of what Michael Angelo and Rubens[27] were driving at? He could not say; but he knew that only since 1895 had he begun to feel the Virgin or Venus as force, and not everywhere even so. At Chartres — perhaps at

[23] John Ruskin (1819–1900), the author of *The Stones of Venice* (1851–1853), was, unlike Gibbon, an admirer of Gothic architecture.
[24] Isis, Egyptian fertility goddess; Edfoo, or Edfu, a city on the upper Nile.
[25] Louis XI, King of France (1423–1483).
[26] Cellini (1500–1571), Italian metal worker and sculptor, who expressed his passionate nature in his art and his personal life, as described in his *Autobiography*.
[27] Michelangelo Buonarroti (1475–1564) of Italy; Peter Paul Rubens (1577–1640), the Flemish painter of sensuous nudes.

Lourdes—possibly at Cnidos if one could still find there the divinely naked Aphrodite of Praxiteles[28]—but otherwise one must look for force to the goddesses of Indian mythology. The idea died out long ago in the German and English stock. St. Gaudens at Amiens was hardly less sensitive to the force of the female energy than Matthew Arnold at the Grande Chartreuse.[29] Neither of them felt goddesses as power—only as reflected emotion, human expression, beauty, purity, taste, scarcely even as sympathy. They felt a railway train as power; yet they, and all other artists, constantly complained that the power embodied in a railway train could never be embodied in art. All the steam in the world could not, like the Virgin, build Chartres.[30]

Yet in mechanics, whatever the mechanicians might think, both energies acted as interchangeable forces on man, and by action on man all known force may be measured. Indeed, few men of science measured force in any other way. After once admitting that a straight line was the shortest distance between two points, no serious mathematician cared to deny anything that suited his convenience, and rejected no symbol, unproved or unproveable, that helped him to accomplish work. The symbol was force, as a compass-needle or a triangle was force, as the mechanist might prove by losing it, and nothing could be gained by ignoring their value. Symbol or energy, the Virgin had acted as the greatest force the Western world ever felt, and had drawn man's activities to herself more strongly than any other power, natural or supernatural, had ever done; the historian's business was to follow the track of the energy; to find where it came from and where it went to; its complex source and shifting channels; its values, equivalents, conversions. It could scarcely be more complex than radium; it could hardly be deflected, diverted, polarized, absorbed more perplexingly than other radiant matter. Adams knew nothing about any of them, but as a mathematical problem of influence on human progress, though all were occult, all reacted on his mind, and he rather inclined to think the Virgin easiest to handle.

The pursuit turned out to be long and tortuous, leading at last into the vast forests of scholastic science. From Zeno to Descartes,[31] hand in hand with Thomas Aquinas, Montaigne, and Pascal,[32] one stumbled as stupidly as though one were still a German student of 1860. Only

[28] Greek sculptor of the 4th century B.C.
[29] See "Stanzas from the Grande Chartreuse" in *Poems, Second Series* (1855), by Matthew Arnold (1822–1888).
[30] Adams had celebrated cultural unity represented by the cathedral at Chartres in *Mont-Saint-Michel and Chartres* ([1904;] 1913).
[31] Zeno, Greek Eleatic philosopher (5th century B.C.); René Descartes (1596–1650), French philosopher and mathematician.
[32] St. Thomas Aquinas (1225?–1274), Italian scholastic philosopher; Michel Eyquem de Montaigne (1533–1592), the urbane and skeptical essayist; Blaise Pascal (1623–1662), French mathematician and moralist, known for his *Pensées* (1670), intended as a defense of the Christian religion.

with the instinct of despair could one force one's self into this old thicket of ignorance after having been repulsed at a score of entrances more promising and more popular. Thus far, no path had led anywhere, unless perhaps to an exceedingly modest living. Forty-five years of study had proved to be quite futile for the pursuit of power; one controlled no more force in 1900 than in 1850, although the amount of force controlled by society had enormously increased. The secret of education still hid itself somewhere behind ignorance, and one fumbled over it as feebly as ever. In such labyrinths, the staff is a force almost more necessary than the legs; the pen becomes a sort of blind-man's dog, to keep him from falling into the gutters. The pen works for itself, and acts like a hand, modelling the plastic material over and over again to the form that suits it best. The form is never arbitrary, but is a sort of growth like crystallization, as any artist knows too well; for often the pencil or pen runs into side-paths and shapelessness, loses its relations, stops or is bogged. Then it has to return on its trail, and recover, if it can, its line of force. The result of a year's work depends more on what is struck out than on what is left in; on the sequence of the main lines of thought, than on their play or variety. Compelled once more to lean heavily on this support, Adams covered more thousands of pages with figures as formal as though they were algebra, laboriously striking out, altering, burning, experimenting, until the year had expired, the Exposition had long been closed, and winter drawing to its end, before he sailed from Cherbourg, on January 19, 1901, for home.

1918

Edwin Arlington Robinson   1869–1935

A remote descendant of the Puritan poet Anne Bradstreet, Edwin Arlington Robinson was born in Head Tide, Maine, and grew up in Gardiner, the original of his fictive Tilbury Town. His lonely youthful struggle to master the craft of poetry impressed him with the ironic contrast (which was to provide a common theme of his work) between the conventional success standards of society and the individualistic requirements of the artist for an achievement too often ignored by his fellows. At twenty-two, Robinson entered Harvard for two years of special study. After his return to Gardiner in the panic year of 1893, personal illness and disappointment, the lingering death of his mother, and family misfortunes deepened his ingrained sensitivity to suffering and his pessimism about the human condition—qualities reflected in his early poems, with their ironic psychological analysis and their revelation of the frustrations and warping influences of New England village life. In 1896 he moved to New York, where he eked out a precarious living in temporary jobs including a stint as an inspector of subway construction. His first two books of verse—*The Torrent and the Night Before* (1896) and *The Children of the Night* (1897)—were printed at his own expense. Although they were favorably noticed, neither they nor his third book, *Captain Craig* (1902), brought financial relief.

In 1905, when his work was brought to the attention of President Theodore Roosevelt by his son Kermit, Robinson's fortunes changed for the better. Through Roosevelt's friendly influence, the poet secured a leading publisher for his next book, *The Town Down the River* (1910), and a clerical position in the New York Custom House. From 1911 onward he spent his summers at the MacDowell Colony in Peterborough, New Hampshire, working in leisurely solitude on the transitional poems of *The Man Against the Sky* (1916) and on the much longer philosophical and narrative poems of his later years. After a brief excursion into playwriting—*Van Zorn* (1914), *The Porcupine* (1915)—Robinson began the blank verse narratives of his

Arthurian trilogy: *Merlin* (1917), *Lancelot* (1920), and *Tristram* (1927). These and other successful poems of the same period brought Robinson a measure of affluence and popular recognition in the form of three Pulitzer prizes—for *Collected Poems* (1921) and *The Man Who Died Twice* (1924), as well as for *Tristram*.

In his last years Robinson published a number of poems focused on the problems of modern life: *Cavender's House* (1929), *The Glory of the Nightingales* (1930), *Matthias at the Door* (1931), and *Amaranth* (1934). The posthumously published *King Jasper* (1935) reflects Robinson's concern for contemporary economic and social problems as well as his continuing preoccupation with the problem of values, as it represents both the death of capitalism (in the person of the title character) and the persistence of the creative life force. The response of readers over the years since his death suggests that Robinson may be remembered more for the finely crafted poems of his Tilbury Town period than for the more ambitious and extended philosophical poems. Like his younger contemporary Frost, Robinson brings together in his work traditional metrics and a modern sensibility, with its skepticism, pessimism, and irony. But unlike Frost, the more thorough skeptic, Robinson never entirely abandoned the transcendentalist optimism of his New England heritage which persists, for all the darkness of his vision, in the image of the intuited glimmer of saving light in his early but never surrendered "Credo." The prevailing pessimism of his earlier poems is also relieved by a vein of native humor—usually ironic, as in "New England"; sometimes gentle, as in "Mr. Flood's Party"; sometimes self-satirical, as in "Miniver Cheevy."

The standard edition of Robinson's work is *Collected Poems of Edwin Arlington Robinson* (New York, 1937). Useful shorter collections include *Tilbury Town: Selected Poems of Edwin Arlington Robinson*, ed. Lawrance Thompson (New York, 1953) and *Edwin Arlington Robinson: Selected Early Poems and Letters,* ed. C. T. Davis (New York, 1960). Volumes of published correspondence are *Selected Letters of Edwin Arlington Robinson*, ed. Ridgely Torrence (New York, 1940); *Letters of Edwin Arlington Robinson to Howard George Schmitt*, ed. C. J. Weber (Waterville, Me., 1945); and *Untriangulated Stars: Letters of Edwin Arlington Robinson to Harry de Forest Smith, 1890–1905,* ed. Denham Sutcliffe (Cambridge, Mass., 1947). The standard biographies are Hermann Hagedorn, *Edwin Arlington Robinson: A Biography* (New York, 1938) and Emery Neff, *Edwin Arlington Robinson* (New York, 1948). The most interesting and useful of numerous critiques of Robinson's work include Yvor Winters, *Edwin Arlington Robinson* (Norfolk, Conn., 1946); Ellsworth Barnard, *Edwin Arlington Robinson: A Critical Study* (New York, 1952); and E. S. Fussell, *Edwin Arlington Robinson: The Literary Background of a Traditional Poet* (Berkeley, Calif., 1954). A descriptive bibliography of the work published during Robinson's lifetime is C. B. Hogan, *A Bibliography of Edwin Arlington Robinson* (New Haven, Conn., 1936).

The text of "The Children of the Night" is from the volume of the same title (New York, 1897); other selections are from *Collected Poems of Edwin Arlington Robinson* (New York, 1937).

The Children of the Night

For those that never know the light,
　　The darkness is a sullen thing;
And they, the Children of the Night,
　　Seem lost in Fortune's winnowing.

But some are strong and some are weak,—
　　And there's the story. House and home
Are shut from countless hearts that seek
　　World-refuge that will never come.

And if there be no other life,
　　And if there be no other chance   10
To weigh their sorrow and their strife
　　Than in the scales of circumstance,

'T were better, ere the sun go down
　　Upon the first day we embark,
In life's imbittered sea to drown,
　　Than sail forever in the dark.

But if there be a soul on earth
　　So blinded with its own misuse
Of man's revealed, incessant worth,
　　Or worn with anguish, that it views   20

No light but for a mortal eye,
　　No rest but of a mortal sleep,
No God but in a prophet's lie,
　　No faith for "honest doubt" to keep;

If there be nothing, good or bad,
　　But chaos for a soul to trust,—
God counts it for a soul gone mad,
　　And if God be God, He is just.

And if God be God, He is Love;
　　And though the Dawn be still so dim,   30
It shows us we have played enough
　　With creeds that make a fiend of Him.

There is one creed, and only one,
　　That glorifies God's excellence;
So cherish, that His will be done,
　　The common creed of common sense.

It is the crimson, not the gray,
　　That charms the twilight of all time;

It is the promise of the day
    That makes the starry sky sublime;   40

It is the faith within the fear
    That holds us to the life we curse;—
So let us in ourselves revere
    The Self which is the Universe!

Let us, the Children of the Night,
    Put off the cloak that hides the scar!
Let us be Children of the Light,
    And tell the ages what we are!

1896

Credo

I cannot find my way: there is no star
In all the shrouded heavens anywhere;
And there is not a whisper in the air
Of any living voice but one so far
That I can hear it only as a bar
Of lost, imperial music, played when fair
And angel fingers wove, and unaware,
Dead leaves to garlands where no roses are.

No, there is not a glimmer, nor a call,
For one that welcomes, welcomes when he fears,   10
The black and awful chaos of the night;
For through it all—above, beyond it all—
I know the far-sent message of the years,
I feel the coming glory of the Light.

1896

Cliff Klingenhagen

Cliff Klingenhagen had me in to dine
With him one day; and after soup and meat,
And all the other things there were to eat,
Cliff took two glasses and filled one with wine
And one with wormwood. Then, without a sign
For me to choose at all, he took the draught
Of bitterness himself, and lightly quaffed
It off, and said the other one was mine.

And when I asked him what the deuce he meant
By doing that, he only looked at me   10
And smiled, and said it was a way of his.

And though I know the fellow, I have spent
Long time a-wondering when I shall be
As happy as Cliff Klingenhagen is.

1897

Richard Cory

Whenever Richard Cory went down town,
We people on the pavement looked at him:
He was a gentleman from sole to crown,
Clean favored, and imperially slim.

And he was always quietly arrayed,
And he was always human when he talked;
But still he fluttered pulses when he said,
"Good-morning," and he glittered when he walked.

And he was rich — yes, richer than a king —
And admirably schooled in every grace: 10
In fine, we thought that he was everything
To make us wish that we were in his place.

So on we worked, and waited for the light,
And went without the meat, and cursed the bread;
And Richard Cory, one calm summer night,
Went home and put a bullet through his head.

1897

Luke Havergal

Go to the western gate, Luke Havergal,
There where the vines cling crimson on the wall,
And in the twilight wait for what will come.
The leaves will whisper there of her, and some,
Like flying words, will strike you as they fall;
But go, and if you listen she will call.
Go to the western gate, Luke Havergal —
Luke Havergal.

No, there is not a dawn in eastern skies
To rift the fiery night that's in your eyes;   10
But there, where western glooms are gathering,
The dark will end the dark, if anything:
God slays Himself with every leaf that flies,
And hell is more than half of paradise.
No, there is not a dawn in eastern skies —
In eastern skies.

Out of a grave I come to tell you this,
Out of a grave I come to quench the kiss
That flames upon your forehead with a glow
That blinds you to the way that you must go.   20
Yes, there is yet one way to where she is,
Bitter, but one that faith may never miss.
Out of a grave I come to tell you this —
To tell you this.

There is the western gate, Luke Havergal,
There are the crimson leaves upon the wall.
Go, for the winds are tearing them away, —
Nor think to riddle the dead words they say,
Nor any more to feel them as they fall;
But go, and if you trust her she will call.   30
There is the western gate, Luke Havergal —
Luke Havergal.

1896

George Crabbe [1]

Give him the darkest inch your shelf allows,
Hide him in lonely garrets, if you will, —
But his hard, human pulse is throbbing still
With the sure strength that fearless truth endows.
In spite of all fine science disavows,
Of his plain excellence and stubborn skill
There yet remains what fashion cannot kill,
Though years have thinned the laurel from his brows.

Whether or not we read him, we can feel
From time to time the vigor of his name   10
Against us like a finger for the shame
And emptiness of what our souls reveal
In books that are as altars where we kneel
To consecrate the flicker, not the flame.

1896

For a Dead Lady

No more with overflowing light
Shall fill the eyes that now are faded,
Nor shall another's fringe with night
Their woman-hidden world as they did.

---

[1] The English poet (1754 – 1832), whose work, including *The Village* (1783), was marked by realism and occasional grim humor.

No more shall quiver down the days
The flowing wonder of her ways,
Whereof no language may requite
The shifting and the many-shaded.

The grace, divine, definitive,
Clings only as a faint forestalling;   10
The laugh that love could not forgive
Is hushed, and answers to no calling;
The forehead and the little ears
Have gone where Saturn keeps the years;
The breast where roses could not live
Has done with rising and with falling.

The beauty, shattered by the laws
That have creation in their keeping,
No longer trembles at applause,
Or over children that are sleeping;   20
And we who delve in beauty's lore
Know all that we have known before
Of what inexorable cause
Makes Time so vicious in his reaping.

1910

Miniver Cheevy

Miniver Cheevy, child of scorn,
      Grew lean while he assailed the seasons;
He wept that he was ever born,
      And he had reasons.

Miniver loved the days of old
      When swords were bright and steeds were prancing;
The vision of a warrior bold
      Would set him dancing.

Miniver sighed for what was not,
      And dreamed, and rested from his labors;   10
He dreamed of Thebes and Camelot,
      And Priam's neighbors.

Miniver mourned the ripe renown
      That made so many a name so fragrant;
He mourned Romance, now on the town,
      And Art, a vagrant.

Miniver loved the Medici,
      Albeit he had never seen one;

He would have sinned incessantly
 Could he have been one.

    20

Miniver cursed the commonplace
 And eyed a khaki suit with loathing;
He missed the mediæval grace
 Of iron clothing.

Miniver scorned the gold he sought,
 But sore annoyed was he without it;
Miniver thought, and thought, and thought,
 And thought about it.

Miniver Cheevy, born too late,
 Scratched his head and kept on thinking;
    30
Miniver coughed, and called it fate,
 And kept on drinking.

       1910

Eros Turannos [1]

She fears him, and will always ask
 What fated her to choose him;
She meets in his engaging mask
 All reasons to refuse him;
But what she meets and what she fears
Are less than are the downward years,
Drawn slowly to the foamless weirs
 Of age, were she to lose him.

Between a blurred sagacity
 That once had power to sound him,
    10
And Love, that will not let him be
 The Judas that she found him,
Her pride assuages her almost,
As if it were alone the cost. —
He sees that he will not be lost,
 And waits and looks around him.

A sense of ocean and old trees
 Envelops and allures him;
Tradition, touching all he sees,
 Beguiles and reassures him;
    20
And all her doubts of what he says
Are dimmed with what she knows of days—
Till even prejudice delays
 And fades, and she secures him.

[1] "Love, the Tyrant" in Greek.

The falling leaf inaugurates
      The reign of her confusion;
The pounding wave reverberates
      The dirge of her illusion;
And home, where passion lived and died,
Becomes a place where she can hide,   30
While all the town and harbor side
      Vibrate with her seclusion.

We tell you, tapping on our brows,
      The story as it should be, —
As if the story of a house
      Were told, or ever could be;
We'll have no kindly veil between
Her visions and those we have seen, —
As if we guessed what hers have been,
      Or what they are or would be.   40

Meanwhile we do no harm; for they
      That with a god have striven,
Not hearing much of what we say,
      Take what the god has given;
Though like waves breaking it may be
Or like a changed familiar tree,
Or like a stairway to the sea
      Where down the blind are driven.

1916

Mr. Flood's Party

Old Eben Flood, climbing alone one night
Over the hill between the town below
And the forsaken upland hermitage
That held as much as he should ever know
On earth again of home, paused warily.
The road was his with not a native near;
And Eben, having leisure, said aloud,
For no man else in Tilbury Town to hear:

"Well, Mr. Flood, we have the harvest moon
Again, and we may not have many more;   10
The bird is on the wing, the poet says,[1]
And you and I have said it here before.
Drink to the bird." He raised up to the light
The jug that he had gone so far to fill,

[1] An allusion to Stanza 7 of FitzGerald's *The Rubáiyát of Omar Khayyám*: "Come, fill the Cup, and in the fire of Spring / Your winter-garment of Repentance fling: / The Bird of Time has but a little way / To flutter — and the Bird is on the Wing."

And answered huskily: "Well, Mr. Flood,
Since you propose it, I believe I will."

Alone, as if enduring to the end
A valiant armor of scarred hopes outworn,
He stood there in the middle of the road
Like Roland's ghost winding a silent horn.[2]   20
Below him, in the town among the trees,
Where friends of other days had honored him,
A phantom salutation of the dead
Rang thinly till old Eben's eyes were dim.

Then, as a mother lays her sleeping child
Down tenderly, fearing it may awake,
He set the jug down slowly at his feet
With trembling care, knowing that most things break;
And only when assured that on firm earth
It stood, as the uncertain lives of men   30
Assuredly did not, he paced away,
And with his hand extended paused again:

"Well, Mr. Flood, we have not met like this
In a long time; and many a change has come
To both of us, I fear, since last it was
We had a drop together. Welcome home!"
Convivially returning with himself,
Again he raised the jug up to the light;
And with an acquiescent quaver said:
"Well, Mr. Flood, if you insist, I might.   40

"Only a very little, Mr. Flood—
For auld lang syne. No more, sir; that will do."
So, for the time, apparently it did,
And Eben evidently thought so too;
For soon amid the silver loneliness
Of night he lifted up his voice and sang,
Secure, with only two moons listening,
Until the whole harmonious landscape rang—

"For auld lang syne." The weary throat gave out,
The last word wavered, and the song was done.   50
He raised again the jug regretfully
And shook his head, and was again alone.
There was not much that was ahead of him,
And there was nothing in the town below—
Where strangers would have shut the many doors
That many friends had opened long ago.

                                                       1921

[2] An allusion to the hero of the medieval French *Chanson de Roland* who pridefully
delayed sounding his horn for aid in battle until it was too late for help to reach him.

Karma [1]

Christmas was in the air and all was well
With him, but for a few confusing flaws
In divers of God's images. Because
A friend of his would neither buy nor sell,
Was he to answer for the axe that fell?
He pondered; and the reason for it was,
Partly, a slowly freezing Santa Claus
Upon the corner, with his beard and bell.

Acknowledging an improvident surprise,
He magnified a fancy that he wished   10
The friend whom he had wrecked were here again.
Not sure of that, he found a compromise;
And from the fulness of his heart he fished
A dime for Jesus who had died for men.

1925

New England

Here where the wind is always north-north-east
And children learn to walk on frozen toes,
Wonder begets an envy of all those
Who boil elsewhere with such a lyric yeast
Of love that you will hear them at a feast
Where demons would appeal for some repose,
Still clamoring where the chalice overflows
And crying wildest who have drunk the least.

Passion is here a soilure of the wits,
We're told, and Love a cross for them to bear;   10
Joy shivers in the corner where she knits
And Conscience always has the rocking-chair,
Cheerful as when she tortured into fits
The first cat that was ever killed by Care.

1925

[1] Sanskrit for "deed" or "act." The reference here is to causality or fate in Buddhistic or
Hindu thought.

William Vaughn Moody   *1869–1910*

Born in Spencer, Indiana, William Vaughn Moody grew up in the Ohio
River town of New Albany. The death of his parents, when he was in his
early teens, threw him upon his own resources. In his effort to support and
educate himself, he taught, beginning at the age of sixteen, in various
schools in Indiana and New York State. At twenty he entered Harvard on a
scholarship and completed the B.A. degree program in three years. After
graduate study and teaching at Harvard, he accepted a position in English at
the University of Chicago in 1895. Besides writing and publishing the verse
he had collected in *Poems* (1901), Moody was actively engaged in teaching
and scholarship. He wrote a history of English literature in collaboration
with his friend and colleague Robert Morss Lovett. Because he became
increasingly interested in drama, Moody left his teaching position in Chicago after a few years to give full time to his writing. His most ambitious
project in drama was a projected trilogy of philosophical verse plays: *The
Fire Bringer* (1904) celebrated Prometheus as a symbol of man's necessary
rebellion against God and of his aspiration. *The Masque of Judgment*
(1900), the first written but second in order, attacked the Puritan idea of
man's depravity and revealed the destructiveness of the idea of sin. The
uncompleted third play, *The Death of Eve*, was to show the triumph of the
principle of love over hatred and the sense of sin. Moody also wrote two
prose plays which were produced, unlike the verse drama, on the New York
stage in 1909: they were *The Great Divide*—originally published as *A Sabine
Woman* (1906)— and *The Faith Healer*. Moody was the most liberal and
intellectual of American poets of his generation. Reflecting as it does a
mature and consciously-formulated philosophic outlook, his writing also
reveals his sympathy with the oppressed and his shame and indignation
(shared by other writers, including Mark Twain) about his country's role in
the Spanish-American War. Moody died on the eve of the modern revolution
in poetry. Written in the traditional metrical patterns he favored, his poems

have an admirable lyric élan, but their language seems sometimes rhyme-ridden. One wonders what work Moody might have produced, with his unusual gifts of intelligence and sensibility, had he lived to write in freer forms.

The standard edition of Moody's work is *The Poems and Plays of William Vaughn Moody*, ed. J. M. Manly, 2 vols. (Boston, 1912). *Selected Poems of William Vaughn Moody*, ed. R. M. Lovett (Boston, 1931), has a substantial biographical and critical introduction by its editor, Moody's old friend. Published correspondence includes *Some Letters of William Vaughn Moody*, ed. D. G. Mason (Boston, 1913), and *Letters to Harriet,* ed. Percy MacKaye (Boston, 1935). Among the few substantial biographical and critical studies are D. D. Henry, *William Vaughn Moody: A Study* (Boston, 1934), which includes a bibliography, and the more recent work by Martin Halpern: *William Vaughn Moody* (New York, 1964).

The text used here is that of William Vaughn Moody, *Poems* (Boston, 1901).

Gloucester Moors

A mile behind is Gloucester town
Where the fishing fleets put in,
A mile ahead the land dips down
And the woods and farms begin.
Here, where the moors stretch free
In the high blue afternoon,
Are the marching sun and talking sea,
And the racing winds that wheel and flee
On the flying heels of June.

Jill-o'er-the-ground is purple blue,   10
Blue is the quaker-maid,
The wild geranium holds its dew
Long in the boulder's shade.
Wax-red hangs the cup
From the huckleberry boughs,
In barberry bells the grey moths sup,
Or where the choke-cherry lifts high up
Sweet bowls for their carouse.

Over the shelf of the sandy cove
Beach-peas blossom late.   20
By copse and cliff the swallows rove
Each calling to his mate.
Seaward the sea-gulls go,
And the land-birds all are here;
That green-gold flash was a vireo,
And yonder flame where the marsh-flags grow
Was a scarlet tanager.

This earth is not the steadfast place
We landsmen build upon;
From deep to deep she varies pace,   30
And while she comes is gone.
Beneath my feet I feel
Her smooth bulk heave and dip;
With velvet plunge and soft upreel
She swings and steadies to her keel
Like a gallant, gallant ship.

These summer clouds she sets for sail,
The sun is her masthead light,
She tows the moon like a pinnace frail
Where her phosphor wake churns bright.   40
Now hid, now looming clear,
On the face of the dangerous blue
The star fleets tack and wheel and veer,
But on, but on does the old earth steer
As if her port she knew.

God, dear God! Does she know her port,
Though she goes so far about?
Or blind astray, does she make her sport
To brazen and chance it out?
I watched when her captains passed: 50
She were better captainless.
Men in the cabin, before the mast,
But some were reckless and some aghast,
And some sat gorged at mess.

By her battened hatch I leaned and caught
Sounds from the noisome hold,—
Cursing and sighing of souls distraught
And cries too sad to be told.
Then I strove to go down and see;
But they said, "Thou art not of us!"   60
I turned to those on the deck with me
And cried, "Give help!" But they said, "Let be:
Our ship sails faster thus."

Jill-o'-er-the-ground is purple blue,
Blue is the quaker-maid,
The alder-clump where the brook comes through
Breeds cresses in its shade.
To be out of the moiling street
With its swelter and its sin!
Who has given to me this sweet,   70
And given my brother dust to eat?
And when will his wage come in?

Scattering wide or blown in ranks,
Yellow and white and brown,
Boats and boats from the fishing banks
Come home to Gloucester town.
There is cash to purse and spend,
There are wives to be embraced,
Hearts to borrow and hearts to lend,
And hearts to take and keep to the end, —   80
O little sails, make haste!

But thou, vast outbound ship of souls,
What harbor town for thee?
What shapes, when thy arriving tolls,
Shall crowd the banks to see?
Shall all the happy shipmates then
Stand singing brotherly?
Or shall a haggard ruthless few
Warp her over and bring her to,
While the many broken souls of men   90
Fester down in the slaver's pen,
And nothing to say or do?

1901

On a Soldier Fallen in the Philippines

Streets of the roaring town,
Hush for him, hush, be still!
He comes, who was stricken down
Doing the word of our will.
Hush! Let him have his state,
Give him his soldier's crown.
The grists of trade can wait
Their grinding at the mill,
But he cannot wait for his honor, now the trumpet has been
    blown.
Wreathe pride now for his granite brow, lay love on his breast of
    stone.   10

Toll! Let the great bells toll
Till the clashing air is dim.
Did we wrong this parted soul?
We will make it up to him.
Toll! Let him never guess
What work we set him to.
Laurel, laurel, yes;
He did what we bade him do.
Praise, and never a whispered hint but the fight he fought was
    good;

Never a word that the blood on his sword was his country's own
heart's-blood.   20

A flag for the soldier's bier
Who dies that his land may live;
O, banners, banners here,
That he doubt not nor misgive!
That he heed not from the tomb
The evil days draw near
When the nation, robed in gloom,
With its faithless past shall strive.
Let him never dream that his bullet's scream went wide of its
island mark,
Home to the heart of his darling land where she stumbled and
sinned in the dark.   30

1901

The Menagerie

Thank God my brain is not inclined to cut
Such capers every day! I'm just about
Mellow, but then— There goes the tent-flap shut.
Rain's in the wind. I thought so: every snout
Was twitching when the keeper turned me out.

That screaming parrot makes my blood run cold.
Gabriel's trump! the big bull elephant
Squeals "Rain!" to the parched herd. The monkeys scold,
And jabber that it's rain water they want.
(It makes me sick to see a monkey pant.)   10

I'll foot it home, to try and make believe
I'm sober. After this I stick to beer,
And drop the circus when the sane folks leave.
A man's a fool to look at things too near:
They look back, and begin to cut up queer.

Beasts do, at any rate; especially
Wild devils caged. They have the coolest way
Of being something else than what you see:
You pass a sleek young zebra nosing hay,
A nylghau looking bored and distingué,—   20

And think you've seen a donkey and a bird.
Not on your life! Just glance back, if you dare.
The zebra chews, the nylghau hasn't stirred;
But something's happened, Heaven knows what or where,
To freeze your scalp and pompadour your hair.

I'm not precisely an æolian lute
Hung in the wandering winds of sentiment,
But drown me if the ugliest, meanest brute
Grunting and fretting in that sultry tent
Didn't just floor me with embarrassment!   30

'Twas like a thunder-clap from out the clear,—
One minute they were circus beasts, some grand,
Some ugly, some amusing, and some queer:
Rival attractions to the hobo band,
The flying jenny, and the peanut stand.

Next minute they were old hearth-mates of mine!
Lost people, eyeing me with such a stare!
Patient, satiric, devilish, divine;
A gaze of hopeless envy, squalid care,
Hatred, and thwarted love, and dim despair.   40

Within my blood my ancient kindred spoke,—
Grotesque and monstrous voices, heard afar
Down ocean caves when behemoth awoke,
Or through fern forests roared the plesiosaur
Locked with the giant-bat in ghastly war.

And suddenly, as in a flash of light,
I saw great Nature working out her plan;
Through all her shapes from mastodon to mite
Forever groping, testing, passing on
To find at last the shape and soul of Man.   50

Till in the fullness of accomplished time,
Comes brother Forepaugh,[1] upon business bent,
Tracks her through frozen and through torrid clime,
And shows us, neatly labeled in a tent,
The stages of her huge experiment;

Blabbing aloud her shy and reticent hours;
Dragging to light her blinking, slothful moods;
Publishing fretful seasons when her powers
Worked wild and sullen in her solitudes,
Or when her mordant laughter shook the woods.   60

Here, round about me, were her vagrant births;
Sick dreams she had, fierce projects she essayed;
Her qualms, her fiery prides, her crazy mirths;
The troublings of her spirit as she strayed,
Cringed, gloated, mocked, was lordly, was afraid,

[1] Adam Forepaugh (1831–1890), showman and circus owner, Barnum's chief rival in the late 19th century.

On that long road she went to seek mankind;
Here were the darkling coverts that she beat
To find the Hider she was sent to find;
Here the distracted footprints of her feet
Whereby her soul's Desire she came to greet.   70

But why should they, her botch-work, turn about
And stare disdain at me, her finished job?
Why was the place one vast suspended shout
Of laughter? Why did all the daylight throb
With soundless guffaw and dumb-stricken sob?

Helpless I stood among those awful cages;
The beasts were walking loose, and I was bagged!
I, I, last product of the toiling ages,
Goal of heroic feet that never lagged, —
A little man in trousers, slightly jagged.   80

Deliver me from such another jury!
The Judgment-day will be a picnic to 't.
Their satire was more dreadful than their fury,
And worst of all was just a kind of brute
Disgust, and giving up, and sinking mute.

Survival of the fittest, adaptation,
And all their other evolution terms,
Seem to omit one small consideration,
To wit, that tumblebugs and angleworms
Have souls: there's soul in everything that squirms.   90

And souls are restless, plagued, impatient things,
All dream and unaccountable desire;
Crawling, but pestered with the thought of wings;
Spreading through every inch of earth's old mire
Mystical hanker after something higher.

Wishes *are* horses, as I understand.
I guess a wistful polyp that has strokes
Of feeling faint to gallivant on land
Will come to be a scandal to his folks;
Legs he will sprout, in spite of threats and jokes.   100

And at the core of every life that crawls
Or runs or flies or swims or vegetates —
Churning the mammoth's heart-blood, in the galls
Of shark and tiger planting gorgeous hates,
Lighting the love of eagles for their mates;

Yes, in the dim brain of the jellied fish
That is and is not living — moved and stirred

From the beginning a mysterious wish,
A vision, a command, a fatal Word:
The name of Man was uttered, and they heard.   110

Upward along the æons of old war
They sought him: wing and shank-bone, claw and bill
Were fashioned and rejected; wide and far
They roamed the twilight jungles of their will;
But still they sought him, and desired him still.

Man they desired, but mind you, Perfect Man,
The radiant and the loving, yet to be!
I hardly wonder, when they came to scan
The upshot of their strenuosity,
They gazed with mixed emotions upon *me*.   120

Well, my advice to you is, Face the creatures,
Or spot them sideways with your weather eye,
Just to keep tab on their expansive features;
It isn't pleasant when you're stepping high
To catch a giraffe smiling on the sly.

If nature made you graceful, don't get gay
Back-to before the hippopotamus;
If meek and godly, find some place to play
Besides right where three mad hyenas fuss:
You may hear language that we won't discuss.   130

If you're a sweet thing in a flower-bed hat,
Or her best fellow with your tie tucked in,
Don't squander love's bright springtime girding at
An old chimpanzee with an Irish chin:
There may be hidden meaning in his grin.

                                                       1901

The Bracelet of Grass

The opal heart of afternoon
Was clouding on to throbs of storm,
Ashen within the ardent west
The lips of thunder muttered harm,
And as a bubble like to break
Hung heaven's trembling amethyst,
When with the sedge-grass by the lake
I braceleted her wrist.

And when the ribbon grass was tied,
Sad with the happiness we planned,   10

Palm linked in palm we stood awhile
And watched the raindrops dot the sand;
Until the anger of the breeze
Chid all the lake's bright breathing down,
And ravished all the radiancies
From her deep eyes of brown.

We gazed from shelter on the storm,
And through our hearts swept ghostly pain
To see the shards of day sweep past,
Broken, and none might mend again.   20

Broken, that none shall ever mend;
Loosened, that none shall ever tie.
O the wind and the wind, will it never end?
O the sweeping past of the ruined sky!

1901

A Grey Day

Grey drizzling mists the moorlands drape,
Rain whitens the dead sea,
From headland dim to sullen cape
Grey sails creep wearily.
I know not how that merchantman
Has found the heart; but 't is her plan
Seaward her endless course to shape.

Unreal as insects that appall
A drunkard's peevish brain,
O'er the grey deep the dories crawl,   10
Four-legged, with rowers twain:
Midgets and minims of the earth,
Across old ocean's vasty girth
Toiling — heroic, comical!

I wonder how that merchant's crew
Have ever found the will!
I wonder what the fishers do
To keep them toiling still!
I wonder how the heart of man
Has patience to live out its span,   20
Or wait until its dreams come true.

1901

Robert Frost   *1874–1963*

Although Robert Frost was born in San Francisco, his name and his poetry are wholly identified with the New England to which he was transported, at the age of eleven, by his widowed mother. His only formal education beyond high school consisted of a fleeting residence at Dartmouth College and two years of study at Harvard when he was in his mid-twenties. After working at a succession of odd jobs, Frost bought a farm in New Hampshire in 1900 and began a prolonged struggle to support his growing family by farming and teaching and to find acceptance as a poet in the face of editorial indifference. It was not until 1912, when he took his family to England, where the renaissance of modern poetry had already begun under the aegis of Ezra Pound, T. E. Hulme, and their Imagist associates, that Frost found a publisher for his poems of New England. *A Boy's Will* (1913), with its title taken from Longfellow, and *North of Boston* (1914) won praise for their naturalness of language and fidelity to experience. When Frost returned to America in 1915 and settled again on a New Hampshire farm, he assumed a solid and commanding position in American letters—a position from which he exerted a continuing influence on several generations of younger poets. As a visiting professor and poet in residence at various colleges and universities, he became widely known as a reader and representative of poetry at a time when the poet had not yet become a familiar figure on the American campus. His reputation grew steadily with the appearance of successive books of poems: *Mountain Interval* (1916), *New Hampshire* (1923), *West-Running Brook* (1928), *Collected Poems* (1930; 1939), *A Further Range* (1936), *A Witness Tree* (1942), and *Steeple Bush* (1947). *A Masque of Reason* (1945) and *A Masque of Mercy* (1947) are dramatic disquisitions on moral and religious problems. The only volume to follow *Complete Poems* (1949) was the collection of later lyrics, *In the Clearing* (1962).

Despite his skeptical modern outlook, Frost was, like Robinson, conservative in his choice of metrical patterns: his only concession to innovation was his introduction into the traditional forms of his lyrics and longer blank verse poems of the counterpoint of idiomatic New England speech rhythms. But his work does have affinities with the theories of the Imagists and other modern poets. There is in his poems a concern for the evocative image that releases "an intellectual and emotional complex" within a concentrated span, if not an "instant" of time. This quality, which Frost stressed in his description of himself as a "synecdochist" who uses a part to suggest the whole, can be seen in such shorter poems as "The Pasture" and "Spring Pools." In these a disarming simplicity conceals from the too-casual reader the extent to which the poet has charged his language with complex metaphorical implications. Frost is less modern, however, in the didacticism of his description of the poem as an experience which "begins in delight and ends in wisdom."

The standard editions of Frost's poetry are *Complete Poems of Robert Frost, 1949* (New York, 1949) and *In the Clearing* (New York, 1962). The fullest collection of his correspondence is *Selected Letters of Robert Frost,* ed. Lawrance Thompson (New York, 1964). Among numerous biographies the most definitive is Lawrance Thompson, *Robert Frost: The Early Years, 1874–1915* (New York, 1966), the first volume of a work in progress. A helpful introduction to representative criticism of Frost's work is J. M. Cox, ed., *Robert Frost: A Collection of Critical Essays* (Englewood Cliffs, N. J., 1962). The most complete bibliography is Louis and Esther Mertins, *The Intervals of Robert Frost: A Critical Bibliography* (Berkeley, Calif., 1947).

The text used here is that of *Complete Poems of Robert Frost, 1949* (New York, 1949).

The Pasture

I'm going out to clean the pasture spring;
I'll only stop to rake the leaves away
(And wait to watch the water clear, I may):
I sha'n't be gone long. — You come too.

I'm going out to fetch the little calf
That's standing by the mother. It's so young
It totters when she licks it with her tongue.
I sha'n't be gone long. — You come too.

1914

The Tuft of Flowers

I went to turn the grass once after one
Who mowed it in the dew before the sun.

The dew was gone that made his blade so keen
Before I came to view the leveled scene.

I looked for him behind an isle of trees;
I listened for his whetstone on the breeze.

But he had gone his way, the grass all mown,
And I must be, as he had been,—alone,

'As all must be,' I said within my heart,
'Whether they work together or apart.'   10

But as I said it, swift there passed me by
On noiseless wing a bewildered butterfly,

Seeking with memories grown dim o'er night
Some resting flower of yesterday's delight.

And once I marked his flight go round and round,
As where some flower lay withering on the ground.

And then he flew as far as eye could see,
And then on tremulous wing came back to me.

I thought of questions that have no reply,
And would have turned to toss the grass to dry;   20

But he turned first, and led my eye to look
At a tall tuft of flowers beside a brook,

A leaping tongue of bloom the scythe had spared
Beside a reedy brook the scythe had bared.

The mower in the dew had loved them thus,
By leaving them to flourish, not for us,

Nor yet to draw one thought of ours to him,
But from sheer morning gladness at the brim.

The butterfly and I had lit upon,
Nevertheless, a message from the dawn,   30

That made me hear the wakening birds around,
And hear his long scythe whispering to the ground,

And feel a spirit kindred to my own;
So that henceforth I worked no more alone;

But glad with him, I worked as with his aid,
And weary, sought at noon with him the shade;

And dreaming, as it were, held brotherly speech
With one whose thought I had not hoped to reach.

'Men work together,' I told him from the heart,
'Whether they work together or apart.'   40

1913

After Apple-Picking

My long two-pointed ladder's sticking through a tree
Toward heaven still,
And there's a barrel that I didn't fill
Beside it, and there may be two or three
Apples I didn't pick upon some bough.
But I am done with apple-picking now.
Essence of winter sleep is on the night,
The scent of apples: I am drowsing off.
I cannot rub the strangeness from my sight
I got from looking through a pane of glass   10
I skimmed this morning from the drinking trough
And held against the world of hoary grass.
It melted, and I let it fall and break.
But I was well
Upon my way to sleep before it fell,
And I could tell
What form my dreaming was about to take.
Magnified apples appear and disappear,
Stem end and blossom end,
And every fleck of russet showing clear.   20
My instep arch not only keeps the ache,
It keeps the pressure of a ladder-round.
I feel the ladder sway as the boughs bend.
And I keep hearing from the cellar bin
The rumbling sound
Of load on load of apples coming in.
For I have had too much
Of apple-picking: I am overtired
Of the great harvest I myself desired.
There were ten thousand thousand fruit to touch,   30
Cherish in hand, lift down, and not let fall.
For all
That struck the earth,
No matter if not bruised or spiked with stubble,
Went surely to the cider-apple heap
As of no worth.
One can see what will trouble
This sleep of mine, whatever sleep it is.
Were he not gone,
The woodchuck could say whether it's like his   40
Long sleep, as I describe its coming on,
Or just some human sleep.

1914

Mending Wall

Something there is that doesn't love a wall,
That sends the frozen-ground-swell under it,
And spills the upper boulders in the sun;
And makes gaps even two can pass abreast.
The work of hunters is another thing:
I have come after them and made repair
Where they have left not one stone on a stone,
But they would have the rabbit out of hiding,
To please the yelping dogs. The gaps I mean,
No one has seen them made or heard them made,   10
But at spring mending-time we find them there.
I let my neighbor know beyond the hill;
And on a day we meet to walk the line
And set the wall between us once again.
We keep the wall between us as we go.
To each the boulders that have fallen to each.
And some are loaves and some so nearly balls
We have to use a spell to make them balance:
'Stay where you are until our backs are turned!'
We wear our fingers rough with handling them.   20
Oh, just another kind of outdoor game,
One on a side. It comes to little more:
There where it is we do not need the wall:
He is all pine and I am apple orchard.
My apple trees will never get across
And eat the cones under his pines, I tell him.
He only says, 'Good fences make good neighbors.'
Spring is the mischief in me, and I wonder
If I could put a notion in his head:
'*Why* do they make good neighbors? Isn't it   30
Where there are cows? But here there are no cows.
Before I built a wall I'd ask to know
What I was walling in or walling out,
And to whom I was like to give offense.
Something there is that doesn't love a wall,
That wants it down.' I could say 'Elves' to him,
But it's not elves exactly, and I'd rather
He said it for himself. I see him there
Bringing a stone grasped firmly by the top
In each hand, like an old-stone savage armed.   40
He moves in darkness as it seems to me,
Not of woods only and the shade of trees.
He will not go behind his father's saying,
And he likes having thought of it so well
He says again, 'Good fences make good neighbors.'

                                                    1914

Home Burial

He saw her from the bottom of the stairs
Before she saw him. She was starting down,
Looking back over her shoulder at some fear.
She took a doubtful step and then undid it
To raise herself and look again. He spoke
Advancing toward her: 'What is it you see
From up there always—for I want to know.'
She turned and sank upon her skirts at that,
And her face changed from terrified to dull.
He said to gain time: 'What is it you see,'   10
Mounting until she cowered under him.
'I will find out now—you must tell me, dear.'
She, in her place, refused him any help
With the least stiffening of her neck and silence.
She let him look, sure that he wouldn't see,
Blind creature; and awhile he didn't see.
But at last he murmured, 'Oh,' and again, 'Oh.'

'What is it—what?' she said.

                          'Just that I see.'

'You don't,' she challenged. 'Tell me what it is.'   20

'The wonder is I didn't see at once.
I never noticed it from here before.
I must be wonted to it—that's the reason.
The little graveyard where my people are!
So small the window frames the whole of it.
Not so much larger than a bedroom, is it?
There are three stones of slate and one of marble,
Broad-shouldered little slabs there in the sunlight
On the sidehill. We haven't to mind *those*.
But I understand: it is not the stones,   30
But the child's mound—'

                          'Don't, don't, don't, don't,' she cried.

She withdrew shrinking from beneath his arm
That rested on the bannister, and slid downstairs;
And turned on him with such a daunting look,
He said twice over before he knew himself:
'Can't a man speak of his own child he's lost?'

'Not you! Oh, where's my hat? Oh, I don't need it!
I must get out of here. I must get air.
I don't know rightly whether any man can.'   40

'Amy! Don't go to someone else this time.
Listen to me. I won't come down the stairs.'
He sat and fixed his chin between his fists.
'There's something I should like to ask you, dear.'

'You don't know how to ask it.'

                                'Help me, then.'

Her fingers moved the latch for all reply.

'My words are nearly always an offense.
I don't know how to speak of anything
So as to please you. But I might be taught   50
I should suppose. I can't say I see how.
A man must partly give up being a man
With women-folk. We could have some arrangement
By which I'd bind myself to keep hands off
Anything special you're a-mind to name.
Though I don't like such things 'twixt those that love.
Two that don't love can't live together without them.
But two that do can't live together with them.'
She moved the latch a little. 'Don't — don't go.
Don't carry it to someone else this time.   60
Tell me about it if it's something human.
Let me into your grief. I'm not so much
Unlike other folks as your standing there
Apart would make me out. Give me my chance.
I do think, though, you overdo it a little.
What was it brought you up to think it the thing
To take your mother-loss of a first child
So inconsolably — in the face of love.
You'd think his memory might be satisfied —'

'There you go sneering now!'   70

                        'I'm not, I'm not!
You make me angry. I'll come down to you.
God, what a woman! And it's come to this,
A man can't speak of his own child that's dead.'

'You can't because you don't know how to speak.
If you had any feelings, you that dug
With your own hand — how could you? — his little grave;
I saw you from that very window there,
Making the gravel leap and leap in air,
Leap up, like that, like that, and land so lightly   80
And roll back down the mound beside the hole.
I thought, Who is that man? I didn't know you.

And I crept down the stairs and up the stairs
To look again, and still your spade kept lifting.
Then you came in. I heard your rumbling voice
Out in the kitchen, and I don't know why,
But I went near to see with my own eyes.
You could sit there with the stains on your shoes
Of the fresh earth from your own baby's grave
And talk about your everyday concerns.   90
You had stood the spade up against the wall
Outside there in the entry, for I saw it.'

'I shall laugh the worst laugh I ever laughed.
I'm cursed. God, if I don't believe I'm cursed.'

'I can repeat the very words you were saying.
"Three foggy mornings and one rainy day
Will rot the best birch fence a man can build."
Think of it, talk like that at such a time!
What had how long it takes a birch to rot
To do with what was in the darkened parlor.   100
You *couldn't* care! The nearest friends can go
With anyone to death, comes so far short
They might as well not try to go at all.
No, from the time when one is sick to death,
One is alone, and he dies more alone.
Friends make pretense of following to the grave,
But before one is in it, their minds are turned
And making the best of their way back to life
And living people, and things they understand.
But the world's evil. I won't have grief so   110
If I can change it. Oh, I won't, I won't!'

'There, you have said it all and you feel better.
You won't go now. You're crying. Close the door.
The heart's gone out of it: why keep it up.
Amy! There's someone coming down the road!'

'*You* — oh, you think the talk is all. I must go —
Somewhere out of this house. How can I make you —'

'If — you — do!' She was opening the door wider.
'Where do you mean to go? First tell me that.
I'll follow and bring you back by force. I *will!* —'   120

1914

Birches

When I see birches bend to left and right
Across the lines of straighter darker trees,
I like to think some boy's been swinging them.
But swinging doesn't bend them down to stay
As ice-storms do. Often you must have seen them
Loaded with ice a sunny winter morning
After a rain. They click upon themselves
As the breeze rises, and turn many-colored
As the stir cracks and crazes their enamel.
Soon the sun's warmth makes them shed crystal shells   10
Shattering and avalanching on the snow-crust —
Such heaps of broken glass to sweep away
You'd think the inner dome of heaven had fallen.
They are dragged to the withered bracken by the load,
And they seem not to break; though once they are bowed
So low for long, they never right themselves:
You may see their trunks arching in the woods
Years afterwards, trailing their leaves on the ground
Like girls on hands and knees that throw their hair
Before them over their heads to dry in the sun.   20
But I was going to say when Truth broke in
With all her matter-of-fact about the ice-storm
I should prefer to have some boy bend them
As he went out and in to fetch the cows —
Some boy too far from town to learn baseball,
Whose only play was what he found himself,
Summer or winter, and could play alone.
One by one he subdued his father's trees
By riding them down over and over again
Until he took the stiffness out of them,   30
And not one but hung limp, not one was left
For him to conquer. He learned all there was
To learn about not launching out too soon
And so not carrying the tree away
Clear to the ground. He always kept his poise
To the top branches, climbing carefully
With the same pains you use to fill a cup
Up to the brim, and even above the brim.
Then he flung outward, feet first, with a swish,
Kicking his way down through the air to the ground.   40
So was I once myself a swinger of birches.
And so I dream of going back to be.
It's when I'm weary of considerations,
And life is too much like a pathless wood
Where your face burns and tickles with the cobwebs
Broken across it, and one eye is weeping
From a twig's having lashed across it open.

I'd like to get away from earth awhile
And then come back to it and begin over.
May no fate willfully misunderstand me   50
And half grant what I wish and snatch me away
Not to return. Earth's the right place for love:
I don't know where it's likely to go better.
I'd like to go by climbing a birch tree,
And climb black branches up a snow-white trunk
Toward heaven, till the tree could bear no more,
But dipped its top and set me down again.
That would be good both going and coming back.
One could do worse than be a swinger of birches.

1916

The Road Not Taken

Two roads diverged in a yellow wood,
And sorry I could not travel both
And be one traveler, long I stood
And looked down one as far as I could
To where it bent in the undergrowth;

Then took the other, as just as fair,
And having perhaps the better claim,
Because it was grassy and wanted wear;
Though as for that the passing there
Had worn them really about the same,   10

And both that morning equally lay
In leaves no step had trodden black.
Oh, I kept the first for another day!
Yet knowing how way leads on to way,
I doubted if I should ever come back.

I shall be telling this with a sigh
Somewhere ages and ages hence:
Two roads diverged in a wood, and I —
I took the one less traveled by,
And that has made all the difference.   20

1916

The Oven Bird

There is a singer everyone has heard,
Loud, a mid-summer and a mid-wood bird,
Who makes the solid tree trunks sound again.

He says that leaves are old and that for flowers
Mid-summer is to spring as one to ten.
He says the early petal-fall is past
When pear and cherry bloom went down in showers
On sunny days a moment overcast;
And comes that other fall we name the fall.
He says the highway dust is over all.   10
The bird would cease and be as other birds
But that he knows in singing not to sing.
The question that he frames in all but words
Is what to make of a diminished thing.

1916

To Earthward

Love at the lips was touch
As sweet as I could bear;
And once that seemed too much;
I lived on air

That crossed me from sweet things
The flow of—was it musk
From hidden grapevine springs
Down hill at dusk?

I had the swirl and ache
From sprays of honeysuckle   10
That when they're gathered shake
Dew on the knuckle.

I craved strong sweets, but those
Seemed strong when I was young;
The petal of the rose
It was that stung.

Now no joy but lacks salt
That is not dashed with pain
And weariness and fault;
I crave the stain   20

Of tears, the aftermark
Of almost too much love,
The sweet of bitter bark
And burning clove.

When stiff and sore and scarred
I take away my hand
From leaning on it hard
In grass and sand,

The hurt is not enough:
I long for weight and strength
To feel the earth as rough
To all my length.

30

1923

Nothing Gold Can Stay

Nature's first green is gold,
Her hardest hue to hold.
Her early leaf's a flower;
But only so an hour.
Then leaf subsides to leaf.
So Eden sank to grief,
So dawn goes down to day.
Nothing gold can stay.

1923

Fragmentary Blue

Why make so much of fragmentary blue
In here and there a bird, or butterfly,
Or flower, or wearing-stone, or open eye,
When heaven presents in sheets the solid hue?

Since earth is earth, perhaps, not heaven (as yet)—
Though some savants make earth include the sky;
And blue so far above us comes so high,
It only gives our wish for blue a whet.

1923

Stopping by Woods on a Snowy Evening

Whose woods these are I think I know.
His house is in the village though;
He will not see me stopping here
To watch his woods fill up with snow.

My little horse must think it queer
To stop without a farmhouse near
Between the woods and frozen lake
The darkest evening of the year.

He gives his harness bells a shake
To ask if there is some mistake.

10

The only other sound's the sweep
Of easy wind and downy flake.

The woods are lovely, dark and deep,
But I have promises to keep,
And miles to go before I sleep,
And miles to go before I sleep.

1923

Fire and Ice

Some say the world will end in fire,
Some say in ice.
From what I've tasted of desire
I hold with those who favor fire.
But if it had to perish twice,
I think I know enough of hate
To say that for destruction ice
Is also great
And would suffice

1923

Spring Pools

These pools that, though in forests, still reflect
The total sky almost without defect,
And like the flowers beside them, chill and shiver,
Will like the flowers beside them soon be gone,
And yet not out by any brook or river,
But up by roots to bring dark foliage on.

The trees that have it in their pent-up buds
To darken nature and be summer woods—
Let them think twice before they use their powers
To blot out and drink up and sweep away   10
These flowery waters and these watery flowers
From snow that melted only yesterday.

1928

Two Tramps in Mud Time

Out of the mud two strangers came
And caught me splitting wood in the yard.
And one of them put me off my aim
By hailing cheerily 'Hit them hard!'

I knew pretty well why he dropped behind
And let the other go on a way.
I knew pretty well what he had in mind:
He wanted to take my job for pay.

Good blocks of oak it was I split,
As large around as the chopping block;   10
And every piece I squarely hit
Fell splinterless as a cloven rock.
The blows that a life of self-control
Spares to strike for the common good
That day, giving a loose to my soul,
I spent on the unimportant wood.

The sun was warm but the wind was chill.
You know how it is with an April day
When the sun is out and the wind is still,
You're one month on in the middle of May.   20
But if you so much as dare to speak,
A cloud comes over the sunlit arch,
A wind comes off a frozen peak,
And you're two months back in the middle of March.

A bluebird comes tenderly up to alight
And turns to the wind to unruffle a plume
His song so pitched as not to excite
A single flower as yet to bloom.
It is snowing a flake: and he half knew
Winter was only playing possum.   30
Except in color he isn't blue,
But he wouldn't advise a thing to blossom.

The water for which we may have to look
In summertime with a witching-wand,
In every wheelrut's now a brook,
In every print of a hoof a pond.
Be glad of water, but don't forget
The lurking frost in the earth beneath
That will steal forth after the sun is set
And show on the water its crystal teeth.   40

The time when most I loved my task
These two must make me love it more
By coming with what they came to ask.
You'd think I never had felt before
The weight of an ax-head poised aloft,
The grip on earth of outspread feet.
The life of muscles rocking soft
And smooth and moist in vernal heat.

Out of the woods two hulking tramps
(From sleeping God knows where last night,   50
But not long since in the lumber camps).
They thought all chopping was theirs of right.
Men of the woods and lumberjacks,
They judged me by their appropriate tool.
Except as a fellow handled an ax,
They had no way of knowing a fool.

Nothing on either side was said.
They knew they had but to stay their stay
And all their logic would fill my head:
As that I had no right to play   60
With what was another man's work for gain.
My right might be love but theirs was need.
And where the two exist in twain
Theirs was the better right—agreed.

But yield who will to their separation,
My object in living is to unite
My avocation and my vocation
As my two eyes make one in sight.
Only where love and need are one,
And the work is play for mortal stakes,   70
Is the deed ever really done
For Heaven and the future's sakes.

                                                        1936

Desert Places

Snow falling and night falling fast, oh, fast
In a field I looked into going past,
And the ground almost covered smooth in snow,
But a few weeds and stubble showing last.

The woods around it have it—it is theirs.
All animals are smothered in their lairs.
I am too absent-spirited to count;
The loneliness includes me unawares.

And lonely as it is that loneliness
Will be more lonely ere it will be less—   10
A blanker whiteness of benighted snow
With no expression, nothing to express.

They cannot scare me with their empty spaces
Between stars—on stars where no human race is.
I have it in me so much nearer home
To scare myself with my own desert places.

                                                        1936

Provide, Provide

The witch that came (the withered hag)
To wash the steps with pail and rag,
Was once the beauty Abishag,

The picture pride of Hollywood.
Too many fall from great and good
For you to doubt the likelihood.

Die early and avoid the fate.
Or if predestined to die late,
Make up your mind to die in state.

Make the whole stock exchange your own!   10
If need be occupy a throne,
Where nobody can call *you* crone.

Some have relied on what they knew;
Others on being simply true.
What worked for them might work for you.

No memory of having starred
Atones for later disregard,
Or keeps the end from being hard.

Better to go down dignified
With boughten friendship at your side   20
Than none at all. Provide, provide!

                                        1936

The Gift Outright

The land was ours before we were the land's.
She was our land more than a hundred years
Before we were her people. She was ours
In Massachusetts, in Virginia,
But we were England's, still colonials,
Possessing what we still were unpossessed by,
Possessed by what we now no more possessed.
Something we were withholding made us weak
Until we found out that it was ourselves
We were withholding from our land of living,   10
And forthwith found salvation in surrender.
Such as we were we gave ourselves outright
(The deed of gift was many deeds of war)
To the land vaguely realizing westward,
But still unstoried, artless, unenhanced,
Such as she was, such as she would become.

                                        1942

Choose Something Like a Star

O Star (the fairest one in sight),
We grant your loftiness the right
To some obscurity of cloud —
It will not do to say of night,
Since dark is what brings out your light.
Some mystery becomes the proud.
But to be wholly taciturn
In your reserve is not allowed.
Say something to us we can learn
By heart and when alone repeat.   10
Say something! And it says, 'I burn.'
But say with what degree of heat.
Talk Fahrenheit, talk Centigrade.
Use language we can comprehend.
Tell us what elements you blend.
It gives us strangely little aid,
But does tell something in the end.
And steadfast as Keats' Eremite,
Not even stooping from its sphere,
It asks a little of us here.   20
It asks of us a certain height,
So when at times the mob is swayed
To carry praise or blame too far,
We may choose something like a star
To stay our minds on and be staid.

1943

Edith Wharton *1862–1937*

Edith Newbold Jones was born into a New York family of wealth and social prominence and grew up near the Washington Square of Henry James's youth. Privately educated at home and abroad, she began writing at an early age, and in 1878, when she was sixteen, privately printed her first book, a collection of poems. At twenty-three she married Edward Wharton, a wealthy Bostonian. His precarious health caused them to travel and live abroad. In 1907 they settled in France, which was to remain Edith Wharton's home for the rest of her life, although her marriage ended in divorce in 1913. A prolific writer, Mrs. Wharton produced more than fifty books, most of them in the form of short fiction and novels. *The Greater Inclination* (1899) was the first of her collections of stories. *The House of Mirth* (1905), the best of her early novels, typically deals with the conflict between the rigid conventions of society and the emotional needs of its heroine, Lily Bart. Although, like James, Mrs. Wharton drew upon her international experience for much of her writing, her deepest concern was not so much for the clash of values of differing cultures as for the conflict between the mores of the class of the very rich and the will of individuals who either belong or aspire to it. In this respect she is perhaps closer in her interests to the younger F. Scott Fitzgerald than to her older friend Henry James. But she did also write powerfully of New England rural and small town decadence and frustration in *Ethan Frome* (1911) and *Summer* (1917). Most of Mrs. Wharton's carefully-written stories analyze ironically, with an insider's intimate knowledge, the predicament of an individual (usually an imperfect hero or heroine) in conflict with the repressive conventions of his society. The character's defeat is often achieved through a kind of trick (as in "Roman Fever") which may represent either human deceit or circumstance or a combination of the two. Mrs. Wharton's collections of short stories include *The Descent of Man* (1904), *The Hermit and the Wild Woman and Other Stories* (1908), *Xingu and Other Stories* (1916), and *The World Over*

(1936). *Tales of Men and Ghosts* (1910) is a collection of psychological stories of neurotic projection of the kind perfected by Henry James in *The Turn of the Screw*. Among later novels, *The Age of Innocence* (1920) impressively depicts the unmanning effect of genteel conventions upon its hero, Newland Archer. *Hudson River Bracketed* (1929), which contrasts the cultures of the raw Midwest and the effete East, has its sequel in *The Gods Arrive* (1932), which extends the contrast to Europe. Edith Wharton gives the fullest statement of her theory of her art in *The Writing of Fiction* (1925). *A Backward Glance* (1934) is her autobiography.

There is no collected edition of Edith Wharton's works. A selected edition of her shorter fiction is *Best Short Stories of Edith Wharton*, ed. Wayne Andrews (New York, 1958). Among useful biographical and critical studies are Blake Nevius, *Edith Wharton: A Study of Her Fiction* (Berkeley, Calif., 1953); M. L. Lyde, *Edith Wharton: Convention and Morality in the Work of a Novelist* (Norman, Okla., 1959); Millicent Bell, *Edith Wharton and Henry James: The Story of Their Friendship* (New York, 1965); and Grace Kellog, *The Two Lives of Edith Wharton: The Woman and Her Work* (New York, 1965). The most recent and complete bibliography is V. J. Brenni, *Edith Wharton: A Bibliography* (Morgantown, W. Va., 1966).

The text of "Roman Fever" is that of *The World Over* (New York, 1936).

Roman Fever

1

From the table at which they had been lunching two American ladies of ripe but well-cared-for middle age moved across the lofty terrace of the Roman restaurant and, leaning on its parapet, looked first at each other, and then down on the outspread glories of the Palatine and the Forum, with the same expression of vague but benevolent approval.

As they leaned there a girlish voice echoed up gaily from the stairs leading to the court below. "Well, come along, then," it cried, not to them but to an invisible companion, "and let's leave the young things to their knitting"; and a voice as fresh laughed back: "Oh, look here, Babs, not actually *knitting* — " "Well, I mean figuratively," rejoined the first. "After all, we haven't left our poor parents much else to do. . ." and at that point the turn of the stairs engulfed the dialogue.

The two ladies looked at each other again, this time with a tinge of smiling embarrassment, and the smaller and paler one shook her head and coloured slightly.

"Barbara!" she murmured, sending an unheard rebuke after the mocking voice in the stairway.

The other lady, who was fuller, and higher in colour, with a small determined nose supported by vigorous black eyebrows, gave a good-humoured laugh. "That's what our daughters think of us!"

Her companion replied by a deprecating gesture. "Not of us individually. We must remember that. It's just the collective modern idea of Mothers. And you see—" Half guiltily she drew from her handsomely mounted black hand-bag a twist of crimson silk run through by two fine knitting needles. "One never knows," she murmured. "The new system has certainly given us a good deal of time to kill; and sometimes I get tired just looking—even at this." Her gesture was now addressed to the stupendous scene at their feet.

The dark lady laughed again, and they both relapsed upon the view, contemplating it in silence, with a sort of diffused serenity which might have been borrowed from the spring effulgence of the Roman skies. The luncheon-hour was long past, and the two had their end of the vast terrace to themselves. At its opposite extremity a few groups, detained by a lingering look at the outspread city, were gathering up guide-books and fumbling for tips. The last of them scattered, and the two ladies were alone on the air-washed height.

"Well, I don't see why we shouldn't just stay here," said Mrs. Slade, the lady of the high colour and energetic brows. Two derelict basket-chairs stood near, and she pushed them into the angle of the parapet, and settled herself in one, her gaze upon the Palatine. "After all, it's still the most beautiful view in the world."

"It always will be, to me," assented her friend Mrs. Ansley, with so slight a stress on the "me" that Mrs. Slade, though she noticed it, wondered if it were not merely accidental, like the random underlinings of old-fashioned letter-writers.

"Grace Ansley was always old-fashioned," she thought; and added aloud, with a retrospective smile: "It's a view we've both been familiar with for a good many years. When we first met here we were younger than our girls are now. You remember?"

"Oh, yes, I remember," murmured Mrs. Ansley, with the same undefinable stress.— "There's that head-waiter wondering," she interpolated. She was evidently far less sure than her companion of herself and of her rights in the world.

"I'll cure him of wondering," said Mrs. Slade, stretching her hand toward a bag as discreetly opulent-looking as Mrs. Ansley's. Signing to the head-waiter, she explained that she and her friend were old lovers of Rome, and would like to spend the end of the afternoon looking down on the view—that is, if it did not disturb the service? The head-waiter, bowing over her gratuity, assured her that the ladies were most welcome, and would be still more so if they would condescend to remain for dinner. A full moon night, they would remember. . . .

Mrs. Slade's black brows drew together, as though references to the moon were out-of-place and even unwelcome. But she smiled away her frown as the head-waiter retreated. "Well, why not? We might do

worse. There's no knowing, I suppose, when the girls will be back. Do
you even know back from *where*? I don't!"

Mrs. Ansley again coloured slightly. "I think those young Italian
aviators we met at the Embassy invited them to fly to Tarquinia for tea.
I suppose they'll want to wait and fly back by moonlight."

"Moonlight — moonlight! What a part it still plays. Do you suppose they're as sentimental as we were?"

"I've come to the conclusion that I don't in the least know what
they are," said Mrs. Ansley. "And perhaps we didn't know much more
about each other."

"No; perhaps we didn't."

Her friend gave her a shy glance. "I never should have supposed
you were sentimental, Alida."

"Well, perhaps I wasn't." Mrs. Slade drew her lids together in
retrospect; and for a few moments the two ladies, who had been intimate since childhood, reflected how little they knew each other. Each
one, of course, had a label ready to attach to the other's name; Mrs.
Delphin Slade, for instance, would have told herself, or any one who
asked her, that Mrs. Horace Ansley, twenty-five years ago, had been
exquisitely lovely — no, you wouldn't believe it, would you? . . .
though, of course, still charming, distinguished. . . Well, as a girl
she had been exquisite; far more beautiful than her daughter Barbara,
though certainly Babs, according to the new standards at any rate,
was more effective — had more *edge*, as they say. Funny where she
got it, with those two nullities as parents. Yes; Horace Ansley was —
well, just the duplicate of his wife. Museum specimens of old New
York. Good-looking, irreproachable, exemplary. Mrs. Slade and Mrs.
Ansley had lived opposite each other — actually as well as figuratively
— for years. When the drawing-room curtains in No. 20 East 73rd
Street were renewed, No. 23, across the way, was always aware of it.
And of all the movings, buyings, travels, anniversaries, illnesses — the
tame chronicle of an estimable pair. Little of it escaped Mrs. Slade. But
she had grown bored with it by the time her husband made his big *coup*
in Wall Street, and when they bought in upper Park Avenue had already begun to think, "I'd rather live opposite a speak-easy for a
change; at least one might see it raided." The idea of seeing Grace
raided was so amusing that (before the move) she launched it at a
woman's lunch. It made a hit, and went the rounds — she sometimes
wondered if it had crossed the street, and reached Mrs. Ansley. She
hoped not, but didn't much mind. Those were the days when respectability was at a discount, and it did the irreproachable no harm to laugh
at them a little.

A few years later, and not many months apart, both ladies lost
their husbands. There was an appropriate exchange of wreaths and
condolences, and a brief renewal of intimacy in the half-shadow of their

mourning; and now, after another interval, they had run across each other in Rome, at the same hotel, each of them the modest appendage of a salient daughter. The similarity of their lot had again drawn them together, lending itself to mild jokes, and the mutual confession that, if in old days it must have been tiring to "keep up" with daughters, it was now, at times, a little dull not to.

No doubt, Mrs. Slade reflected, she felt her unemployment more than poor Grace ever would. It was a big drop from being the wife of Delphin Slade to being his widow. She had always regarded herself (with a certain conjugal pride) as his equal in social gifts, as contributing her full share to the making of the exceptional couple they were: but the difference after his death was irremediable. As the wife of the famous corporation lawyer, always with an international case or two on hand, every day brought its exciting and unexpected obligation: the impromptu entertaining of eminent colleagues from abroad, the hurried dashes on legal business to London, Paris or Rome, where the entertaining was so handsomely reciprocated; the amusement of hearing in her wake: "What, that handsome woman with the good clothes and the eyes is Mrs. Slade—*the* Slade's wife? Really? Generally the wives of celebrities are such frumps."

Yes; being *the* Slade's widow was a dullish business after that. In living up to such a husband all her faculties had been engaged; now she had only her daughter to live up to, for the son who seemed to have inherited his father's gifts had died suddenly in boyhood. She had fought through that agony because her husband was there, to be helped and to help; now, after the father's death, the thought of the boy had become unbearable. There was nothing left but to mother her daughter; and dear Jenny was such a perfect daughter that she needed no excessive mothering. "Now with Babs Ansley I don't know that I *should* be so quiet," Mrs. Slade sometimes half-enviously reflected; but Jenny, who was younger than her brilliant friend, was that rare accident, an extremely pretty girl who somehow made youth and prettiness seem as safe as their absence. It was all perplexing—and to Mrs. Slade a little boring. She wished that Jenny would fall in love—with the wrong man, even; that she might have to be watched, out-manoeuvred, rescued. And instead, it was Jenny who watched her mother, kept her out of draughts, made sure that she had taken her tonic. . .

Mrs. Ansley was much less articulate than her friend, and her mental portrait of Mrs. Slade was slighter, and drawn with fainter touches. "Alida Slade's awfully brilliant; but not as brilliant as she thinks," would have summed it up; though she would have added, for the enlightenment of strangers, that Mrs. Slade had been an extremely dashing girl; much more so than her daughter, who was pretty, of course, and clever in a way, but had none of her mother's—well, "vividness," some one had once called it. Mrs. Ansley would take up current words like this, and cite them in quotation marks, as unheard-of audacities. No; Jenny was not like her mother. Sometimes Mrs. Ansley thought Alida Slade was disappointed; on the whole she had had a sad life. Full of failures and mistakes; Mrs. Ansley had always been rather sorry for her. . .

So these two ladies visualized each other, each through the wrong end of her little telescope.

2

For a long time they continued to sit side by side without speaking. It seemed as though, to both, there was a relief in laying down their somewhat futile activities in the presence of the vast Memento Mori which faced them. Mrs. Slade sat quite still, her eyes fixed on the golden slope of the Palace of the Cæsars, and after a while Mrs. Ansley ceased to fidget with her bag, and she too sank into meditation. Like many intimate friends, the two ladies had never before had occasion to be silent together, and Mrs. Ansley was slightly embarrassed by what seemed, after so many years, a new stage in their intimacy, and one with which she did not yet know how to deal.

Suddenly the air was full of that deep clangour of bells which periodically covers Rome with a roof of silver. Mrs. Slade glanced at her wrist-watch. "Five o'clock already," she said, as though surprised.

Mrs. Ansley suggested interrogatively: "There's bridge at the Embassy at five." For a long time Mrs. Slade did not answer. She appeared to be lost in contemplation, and Mrs. Ansley thought the remark had escaped her. But after a while she said, as if speaking out of a dream: "Bridge, did you say? Not unless you want to. . . But I don't think I will, you know."

"Oh, no," Mrs. Ansley hastened to assure her. "I don't care to at all. It's so lovely here; and so full of old memories, as you say." She settled herself in her chair, and almost furtively drew forth her knitting. Mrs. Slade took sideway note of this activity, but her own beautifully cared-for hands remained motionless on her knee.

"I was just thinking," she said slowly, "what different things Rome stands for to each generation of travellers. To our grandmothers, Roman fever; to our mothers, sentimental dangers — how we used to be guarded! — to our daughters, no more dangers than the middle of Main Street. They don't know it — but how much they're missing!"

The long golden light was beginning to pale, and Mrs. Ansley lifted her knitting a little closer to her eyes. "Yes; how we were guarded!"

"I always used to think," Mrs. Slade continued, "that our mothers had a much more difficult job than our grandmothers. When Roman fever stalked the streets it must have been comparatively easy to gather in the girls at the danger hour; but when you and I were young, with such beauty calling us, and the spice of disobedience thrown in, and no worse risk than catching cold during the cool hour after sunset, the mothers used to be put to it to keep us in — didn't they?"

She turned again toward Mrs. Ansley, but the latter had reached a delicate point in her knitting. "One, two, three — slip two; yes, they must have been," she assented, without looking up.

Mrs. Slade's eyes rested on her with a deepened attention. "She can knit — in the face of *this*! How like her. . ."

Mrs. Slade leaned back, brooding, her eyes ranging from the ruins which faced her to the long green hollow of the Forum, the fading glow of the church fronts beyond it, and the outlying immensity of the Colosseum. Suddenly she thought: "It's all very well to say that our girls have done away with sentiment and moonlight. But if Babs Ansley isn't out to catch that young aviator — the one who's a Marchese — then I don't know anything. And Jenny has no chance beside her. I know that too. I wonder if that's why Grace Ansley likes the two girls to go everywhere together? My poor Jenny as a foil — !" Mrs. Slade gave a hardly audible laugh, and at the sound Mrs. Ansley dropped her knitting.

"Yes — ?"

"I — oh, nothing. I was only thinking how your Babs carries everything before her. That Campolieri boy is one of the best matches in Rome. Don't look so innocent, my dear — you know he is. And I was wondering, ever so respectfully, you understand . . . wondering how two such exemplary characters as you and Horace had managed to produce anything quite so dynamic." Mrs. Slade laughed again, with a touch of asperity.

Mrs. Ansley's hands lay inert across her needles. She looked straight out at the great accumulated wreckage of passion and splendour at her feet. But her small profile was almost expressionless. At length she said: "I think you overrate Babs, my dear."

Mrs. Slade's tone grew easier. "No; I don't. I appreciate her. And perhaps envy you. Oh, my girl's perfect; if I were a chronic invalid I'd — well, I think I'd rather be in Jenny's hands. There must be times . . . but there! I always wanted a brilliant daughter . . . and never quite understood why I got an angel instead."

Mrs. Ansley echoed her laugh in a faint murmur. "Babs is an angel too."

"Of course — of course! But she's got rainbow wings. Well, they're wandering by the sea with their young men; and here we sit . . . and it all brings back the past a little too acutely."

Mrs. Ansley had resumed her knitting. One might almost have imagined (if one had known her less well, Mrs. Slade reflected) that, for her also, too many memories rose from the lengthening shadows of those august ruins. But no; she was simply absorbed in her work. What was there for her to worry about? She knew that Babs would almost certainly come back engaged to the extremely eligible Campolieri. "And she'll sell the New York house, and settle down near them in Rome, and never be in their way . . . she's much too tactful. But she'll have an excellent cook, and just the right people in for bridge and cocktails . . . and a perfectly peaceful old age among her grand-children."

Mrs. Slade broke off this prophetic flight with a recoil of self-disgust. There was no one of whom she had less right to think unkindly than of Grace Ansley. Would she never cure herself of envying her? Perhaps she had begun too long ago.

She stood up and leaned against the parapet, filling her troubled eyes with the tranquillizing magic of the hour. But instead of tranquillizing her the sight seemed to increase her exasperation. Her gaze turned toward the Colosseum. Already its golden flank was drowned in purple shadow, and above it the sky curved crystal clear, without light or colour. It was the moment when afternoon and evening hang balanced in mid-heaven.

Mrs. Slade turned back and laid her hand on her friend's arm. The gesture was so abrupt that Mrs. Ansley looked up, startled.

"The sun's set. You're not afraid, my dear?"

"Afraid — ?"

"Of Roman fever or pneumonia? I remember how ill you were that winter. As a girl you had a very delicate throat, hadn't you?"

"Oh, we're all right up here. Down below, in the Forum, it does get deathly cold, all of a sudden . . . but not here."

"Ah, of course you know because you had to be so careful." Mrs. Slade turned back to the parapet. She thought: "I must make one more effort not to hate her." Aloud she said: "Whenever I look at the Forum from up here, I remember that story about a great-aunt of yours, wasn't she? A dreadfully wicked great-aunt?"

"Oh, yes; Great-aunt Harriet. The one who was supposed to have sent her young sister out to the Forum after sunset to gather a night-blooming flower for her album. All our great-aunts and grand-mothers used to have albums of dried flowers."

Mrs. Slade nodded. "But she really sent her because they were in love with the same man — "

"Well, that was the family tradition. They said Aunt Harriet confessed it years afterward. At any rate, the poor little sister caught the fever and died. Mother used to frighten us with the story when we were children."

"And you frightened *me* with it, that winter when you and I were here as girls. The winter I was engaged to Delphin."

Mrs. Ansley gave a faint laugh. "Oh, did I? Really frightened you? I don't believe you're easily frightened."

"Not often; but I was then. I was easily frightened because I was too happy. I wonder if you know what that means?"

"I—yes . . ." Mrs. Ansley faltered.

"Well, I suppose that was why the story of your wicked aunt made such an impression on me. And I thought: 'There's no more Roman fever, but the Forum is deathly cold after sunset—especially after a hot day. And the Colosseum's even colder and damper.'"

"The Colosseum—?"

"Yes. It wasn't easy to get in, after the gates were locked for the night. Far from easy. Still, in those days it could be managed; it *was* managed, often. Lovers met there who couldn't meet elsewhere. You knew that?"

"I—I daresay. I don't remember."

"You don't remember? You don't remember going to visit some ruins or other one evening, just after dark, and catching a bad chill? You were supposed to have gone to see the moon rise. People always said that expedition was what caused your illness."

There was a moment's silence; then Mrs. Ansley rejoined: "Did they? It was all so long ago."

"Yes. And you got well again—so it didn't matter. But I suppose it struck your friends—the reason given for your illness, I mean—because everybody knew you were so prudent on account of your throat, and your mother took such care of you. . . You *had* been out late sight-seeing, hadn't you, that night?"

"Perhaps I had. The most prudent girls aren't always prudent. What made you think of it now?"

Mrs. Slade seemed to have no answer ready. But after a moment she broke out: "Because I simply can't bear it any longer—!"

Mrs. Ansley lifted her head quickly. Her eyes were wide and very pale. "Can't bear what?"

"Why—your not knowing that I've always known why you went."

"Why I went—?"

"Yes. You think I'm bluffing, don't you? Well, you went to meet the man I was engaged to—and I can repeat every word of the letter that took you there."

While Mrs. Slade spoke Mrs. Ansley had risen unsteadily to her feet. Her bag, her knitting and gloves, slid in a panic-stricken heap to the ground. She looked at Mrs. Slade as though she were looking at a ghost.

"No, no—don't," she faltered out.

"Why not? Listen, if you don't believe me. 'My one darling, things can't go on like this. I must see you alone. Come to the Colosseum immediately after dark tomorrow. There will be somebody to let you in. No one whom you need fear will suspect'—but perhaps you've forgotten what the letter said?"

Mrs. Ansley met the challenge with an unexpected composure. Steadying herself against the chair she looked at her friend, and replied: "No; I know it by heart too."

"And the signature? 'Only *your* D.S.' Was that it? I'm right, am I? That was the letter that took you out that evening after dark?"

Mrs. Ansley was still looking at her. It seemed to Mrs. Slade that a slow struggle was going on behind the voluntarily controlled mask of her small quiet face. "I shouldn't have thought she had herself so well in hand," Mrs. Slade reflected, almost resentfully. But at this moment Mrs. Ansley spoke. "I don't know how you knew. I burnt that letter at once."

"Yes; you would, naturally — you're so prudent!" The sneer was open now. "And if you burnt the letter you're wondering how on earth I know what was in it. That's it, isn't it?"

Mrs. Slade waited, but Mrs. Ansley did not speak.

"Well, my dear, I know what was in that letter because I wrote it!"

"You wrote it?"

"Yes."

The two women stood for a minute staring at each other in the last golden light. Then Mrs. Ansley dropped back into her chair. "Oh," she murmured, and covered her face with her hands.

Mrs. Slade waited nervously for another word or movement. None came, and at length she broke out: "I horrify you."

Mrs. Ansley's hands dropped to her knee. The face they uncovered was streaked with tears. "I wasn't thinking of you. I was thinking — it was the only letter I ever had from him!"

"And I wrote it. Yes; I wrote it! But I was the girl he was engaged to. Did you happen to remember that?"

Mrs. Ansley's head drooped again. "I'm not trying to excuse myself. . . I remembered. . ."

"And still you went?"

"Still I went."

Mrs. Slade stood looking down on the small bowed figure at her side. The flame of her wrath had already sunk, and she wondered why she had ever thought there would be any satisfaction in inflicting so purposeless a wound on her friend. But she had to justify herself.

"You do understand? I'd found out — and I hated you, hated you. I knew you were in love with Delphin — and I was afraid; afraid of you, of your quiet ways, your sweetness . . . your . . . well, I wanted you out of the way, that's all. Just for a few weeks; just till I was sure of him. So in a blind fury I wrote that letter. . . I don't know why I'm telling you now."

"I suppose," said Mrs. Ansley slowly, "it's because you've always gone on hating me."

"Perhaps. Or because I wanted to get the whole thing off my mind." She paused. "I'm glad you destroyed the letter. Of course I never thought you'd die."

Mrs. Ansley relapsed into silence, and Mrs. Slade, leaning above her, was conscious of a strange sense of isolation, of being cut off from the warm current of human communion. "You think me a monster!"

"I don't know. . . It was the only letter I had, and you say he didn't write it?"

"Ah, how you care for him still!"

"I cared for that memory," said Mrs. Ansley.

Mrs. Slade continued to look down on her. She seemed physically reduced by the blow—as if, when she got up, the wind might scatter her like a puff of dust. Mrs. Slade's jealousy suddenly leapt up again at the sight. All these years the woman had been living on that letter. How she must have loved him, to treasure the mere memory of its ashes! The letter of the man her friend was engaged to. Wasn't it she who was the monster?

"You tried your best to get him away from me, didn't you? But you failed; and I kept him. That's all."

"Yes. That's all."

"I wish now I hadn't told you. I'd no idea you'd feel about it as you do; I thought you'd be amused. It all happened so long ago, as you say; and you must do me the justice to remember that I had no reason to think you'd ever taken it seriously. How could I, when you were married to Horace Ansley two months afterward? As soon as you could get out of bed your mother rushed you off to Florence and married you. People were rather surprised—they wondered at its being done so quickly; but I thought I knew. I had an idea you did it out of *pique*—to be able to say you'd got ahead of Delphin and me. Girls have such silly reasons for doing the most serious things. And your marrying so soon convinced me that you'd never really cared."

"Yes. I suppose it would," Mrs. Ansley assented.

The clear heaven overhead was emptied of all its gold. Dusk spread over it, abruptly darkening the Seven Hills. Here and there lights began to twinkle through the foliage at their feet. Steps were coming and going on the deserted terrace—waiters looking out of the doorway at the head of the stairs, then reappearing with trays and napkins and flasks of wine. Tables were moved, chairs straightened. A feeble string of electric lights flickered out. Some vases of faded flowers were carried away, and brought back replenished. A stout lady in a dust-coat suddenly appeared, asking in broken Italian if any one had seen the elastic band which held together her tattered Baedeker. She poked with her stick under the table at which she had lunched, the waiters assisting.

The corner where Mrs. Slade and Mrs. Ansley sat was still shadowy and deserted. For a long time neither of them spoke. At length Mrs. Slade began again: "I suppose I did it as a sort of joke—"

"A joke?"

"Well, girls are ferocious sometimes, you know. Girls in love especially. And I remember laughing to myself all that evening at the idea that you were waiting around there in the dark, dodging out of sight, listening for every sound, trying to get in—. Of course I was upset when I heard you were so ill afterward."

Mrs. Ansley had not moved for a long time. But now she turned slowly toward her companion. "But I didn't wait. He'd arranged everything. He was there. We were let in at once," she said.

Mrs. Slade sprang up from her leaning position. "Delphin there? They let you in?— Ah, now you're lying!" she burst out with violence.

Mrs. Ansley's voice grew clearer, and full of surprise. "But of course he was there. Naturally he came—"

"Came? How did he know he'd find you there? You must be raving!"

Mrs. Ansley hesitated, as though reflecting. "But I answered the letter. I told him I'd be there. So he came."

Mrs. Slade flung her hands up to her face. "Oh God—you answered! I never thought of your answering. . ."

"It's odd you never thought of it, if you wrote the letter."

"Yes. I was blind with rage."

Mrs. Ansley rose, and drew her fur scarf about her. "It is cold here. We'd better go. . . I'm sorry for you," she said, as she clasped the fur about her throat.

The unexpected words sent a pang through Mrs. Slade. "Yes; we'd better go." She gathered up her bag and cloak. "I don't know why you should be sorry for me," she muttered.

Mrs. Ansley stood looking away from her toward the dusky secret mass of the Colosseum. "Well—because I didn't have to wait that night."

Mrs. Slade gave an unquiet laugh. "Yes; I was beaten there. But I oughtn't to begrudge it to you, I suppose. At the end of all these years. After all, I had everything; I had him for twenty-five years. And you had nothing but that one letter that he didn't write."

Mrs. Ansley was again silent. At length she turned toward the door of the terrace. She took a step, and turned back, facing her companion.

"I had Barbara," she said, and began to move ahead of Mrs. Slade toward the stairway.

1936

Willa Cather   *1873–1947*

Born on a farm near Winchester, Virginia, Willa Sibert Cather moved with her family in 1883 to the prairie country of Nebraska, where she grew up among the northern and central European immigrants whose lives she portrayed in her fiction. After schooling that gave her a grounding in the classics and in music, as well as in the usual subjects, she entered the University of Nebraska, from which she graduated in 1895. For several years she worked on newspapers and taught high school in the East. From 1906 to 1912 she was on the staff of *McClure's Magazine*, where several of her early stories appeared. Her first book was a well-received collection of poems, *April Twilights* (1903; enlarged ed., 1933). *The Troll Garden* (1905) was a collection of her early short stories. After the appearance of her first novel, *Alexander's Bridge* (1912), Miss Cather turned — perhaps under the influence of her admired friend, Sarah Orne Jewett, the Maine regionalist — to the pioneering life she had known on the Nebraska prairies. Her best and most characteristic work portrays the heroic struggle of creative individuals to find fulfillment in a challenging and often harsh environment. Alexandra Bergson, the heroine of *O Pioneers!* (1913), with its title from Whitman, persists in her efforts to build a life on the prairie farm she must manage after the death of her father. In *The Song of the Lark* (1915) Thea Kronberg finally wins recognition as a singer after much striving to justify her vocation as an artist. *My Ántonia* (1918) is a celebration of the vitality and courage of its Bohemian-American heroine, recognized by Miss Cather's narrator, Jim Burden, as "a rich mine of life, like the founders of early races." In these qualities Ántonia is a true fictional daughter of the Bohemian hero of "Neighbour Rosicky" (1930), one of three short novels collected in *Obscure Destinies* (1932). Like Hamlin Garland and Sherwood Anderson, Miss Cather recognized the meanness and repressive materialism of American life in stories like "The Sculptor's Funeral" (1905). *Youth and the Bright Medusa* (1920) is a collection of stories dealing with problems of the artist's life. *The*

Professor's House (1925) is somewhat atypical in its depiction of a crisis of middle age in its academic hero. After her conversion to the Protestant Episcopal faith in 1922, Miss Cather turned to the more distant past in two novels dealing sympathetically with the early history of the Roman Catholic church in America: *Death Comes for the Archbishop* (1927) is a story of New Mexico in the period of the Mexican War; *Shadows on the Rock* (1931) is set in seventeenth century Quebec. In one of her last novels, *Sapphira and the Slave Girl* (1940), Miss Cather chose for her subject memories of the Virginia of her early childhood. *Not Under Forty* (1936) is a collection of essays telling of the author's literary theories and associations.

The standard edition of Miss Cather's work is *The Novels and Stories of Willa Cather*, 13 vols. (Boston, 1937–1941). A comprehensive collection of her early stories is *Willa Cather's Collected Short Fiction, 1892–1912*, ed. M. R. Bennett (Lincoln, Nebr., 1965). The most complete biography is E. K. Brown, *Willa Cather, a Critical Biography*, completed by Leon Edel (New York, 1953). Helpful brief critiques include David Daiches, *Willa Cather, a Critical Introduction* (Ithaca, N.Y., 1951), and Dorothy Van Ghent, *Willa Cather* (Minneapolis, Minn., 1964).

The text of "The Sculptor's Funeral" is that of *Youth and the Bright Medusa* (Boston, 1920); "Neighbour Rosicky" is from *Obscure Destinies* (1932).

The Sculptor's Funeral

A group of the townspeople stood on the station siding of a little Kansas town, awaiting the coming of the night train, which was already twenty minutes overdue. The snow had fallen thick over everything; in the pale starlight the line of bluffs across the wide, white meadows south of the town made soft, smoke-coloured curves against the clear sky. The men on the siding stood first on one foot and then on the other, their hands thrust deep into their trousers pockets, their overcoats open (they never buttoned them), their shoulders screwed up with the cold; and they glanced from time to time toward the southeast, where the railroad track wound along the river shore. They conversed in low tones and moved about restlessly, seeming uncertain as to what was expected of them. There was but one of the company who looked as if he knew exactly why he was there, and he kept conspicuously apart; walking to the far end of the platform, returning to the station door, then pacing up the track again, his chin sunk in the high collar of his overcoat, his burly shoulders drooping forward, his gait heavy and dogged. Presently he was approached by a tall, spare, grizzled man clad in a faded Grand Army suit, who shuffled out from the group and advanced with a certain deference, craning his neck forward until his back made the angle of a jack-knife three-quarters open.

'I reckon she's a-goin' to be pretty late ag'in tonight, Jim,' he remarked in a squeaky falsetto. 'S'pose it's the snow?'

'I don't know,' responded the other man with a shade of annoyance, speaking from out an astonishing cataract of red beard that grew fiercely and thickly in all directions.

The spare man shifted the quill toothpick he was chewing to the other side of his mouth. 'It ain't likely that anybody from the East will come with the corpse, I s'pose,' he went on reflectively.

'I don't know,' responded the other, more curtly than before.

'It's too bad he didn't belong to some lodge or other. I like an order funeral myself. They seem more appropriate for people of some repytation,' the spare man continued, with an ingratiating concession in his shrill voice, as he carefully placed his toothpick in his vest pocket. He always carried the flag at the G.A.R. funerals in the town.

The heavy man turned on his heel, without replying, and walked up the siding. The spare man rejoined the uneasy group. 'Jim's ez full ez a tick, ez ushel,' he commented commiseratingly.

Just then a distant whistle sounded, and there was a shuffling of feet on the platform. A number of lanky boys, of all ages, appeared as suddenly and slimily as eels wakened by the crack of thunder; some came from the waiting-room, where they had been warming themselves by the red stove, or half asleep on the slat benches; others uncoiled themselves from baggage trucks or slid out of express wagons. Two clambered down from the driver's seat of a hearse that stood backed up against the siding. They straightened their stooping shoulders and lifted their heads, and a flash of momentary animation kindled their dull eyes at that cold, vibrant scream. It stirred them like the note of a trumpet; just as it had often, in his boyhood, stirred the man who was coming home to-night.

The night express shot, red as a rocket, from out the eastward marsh lands and wound along the river shore under the long lines of shivering poplars that sentinelled the meadows, the escaping steam hanging in grey masses against the pale sky and blotting out the Milky Way. In a moment the red glare from the headlight streamed up the snow-covered track before the siding and glittered on the wet, black rails. The burly man with the dishevelled red beard walked swiftly up the platform toward the approaching train, uncovering his head as he went. The group of men behind him hesitated, glanced questioningly at one another, and awkwardly followed his example. The train stopped, and the crowd shuffled up to the express car just as the door was thrown open, the man in the G.A.R. suit thrusting his head forward with curiosity. The express messenger appeared in the doorway, accompanied by a young man in a long ulster and travelling-cap.

'Are Mr. Merrick's friends here?' enquired the young man.

The group on the platform swayed uneasily. Philip Phelps, the banker, responded with dignity: 'We have come to take charge of the remains. Mr. Merrick's father is very feeble and can't be about.'

'Send the agent out here,' growled the express messenger, 'and tell the operator to lend a hand.'

The coffin was got out of its rough box and down on the snowy platform. The townspeople drew back enough to make room for it and then formed a close semi-circle about it, looking curiously at the palm leaf which lay across the black cover. No one said anything. The baggageman stood by his truck, waiting to get at the trunks. The engine panted heavily, and the fireman dodged in and out among the wheels with his yellow torch and long oil-can, snapping the spindle boxes. The young stranger, one of the dead sculptor's pupils who had come with the body, looked about him helplessly. He turned to the banker, the only one of that black uneasy stoop-shouldered group who seemed enough of an individual to be addressed.

'None of Mr. Merrick's brothers are here?' he asked uncertainly.

The man with the red beard for the first time stepped up and joined the others. 'No, they have not come yet; the family is scattered. The body will be taken directly to the house.' He stooped and took hold of one of the handles of the coffin.

'Take the long hill road up, Thompson, it will be easier on the horses,' called the liveryman as the undertaker snapped the door of the hearse and prepared to mount to the driver's seat.

Laird, the red-bearded lawyer, turned again to the stranger: 'We didn't know whether there would be anyone with him or not,' he explained. 'It's a long walk, so you'd better go up in the hack.' He pointed to a single battered conveyance, but the young man replied stiffly: 'Thank you, but I think I will go up with the hearse. If you don't object,' turning to the undertaker, 'I'll ride with you.'

They clambered up over the wheels and drove off in the starlight up the long, white hill toward the town. The lamps in the still village were shining from under the low, snow-burdened roofs, and beyond, on every side, the plains reached out into emptiness, peaceful and wide as the soft sky itself, and wrapped in a tangible, white silence.

When the hearse backed up to a wooden sidewalk before a naked, weather-beaten frame house, the same composite, ill-defined group that had stood upon the station siding was huddled about the gate. The front yard was an icy swamp, and a couple of warped planks, extending from the sidewalk to the door, made a sort of rickety footbridge. The gate hung on one hinge, and was opened wide with difficulty. Steavens, the young stranger, noticed that something black was tied to the knob of the front door.

The grating sound made by the coffin, as it was drawn from the hearse, was answered by a scream from the house; the front door was wrenched open, and a tall, corpulent woman rushed out bareheaded into the snow and flung herself upon the coffin, shrieking, 'My boy, my boy! And this is how you've come home to me!'

As Steavens turned away and closed his eyes with a shudder of unutterable repulsion, another woman, also tall, but flat and angular, dressed entirely in black, darted out of the house and caught Mrs. Merrick by the shoulders, crying sharply: 'Come, come, Mother; you mustn't go on like this!' Her tone changed to one of obsequious solemnity as she turned to the banker: 'The parlour is ready, Mr. Phelps.'

The bearers carried the coffin along the narrow boards, while the undertaker ran ahead with the coffin-rests. They bore it into a large, unheated room that smelled of dampness and disuse and furniture polish, and set it down under a hanging lamp ornamented with jingling glass prisms and before a 'Rogers group' of John Alden and Priscilla, wreathed with smilax. Henry Steavens stared about him with the sickening conviction that there had been a mistake, and that he had somehow arrived at the wrong destination. He looked at the clover-green Brussels, the fat plush upholstery, among the hand-painted china plaques and panels and vases, for some mark of identification — for something that might once conceivably have belonged to Harvey Merrick. It was not until he recognized his friend in the crayon portrait of a little boy in kilts and curls, hanging above the piano, that he felt willing to let any of these people approach the coffin.

'Take the lid off, Mr. Thompson; let me see my boy's face,' wailed the elder woman between her sobs. This time Steavens looked fearfully, almost beseechingly into her face, red and swollen under its masses of strong, black, shiny hair. He flushed, dropped his eyes, and then, almost incredulously, looked again. There was a kind of power about her face — a kind of brutal handsomeness, even; but it was scarred and furrowed by violence, and so coloured and coarsened by fiercer passions that grief seemed never to have laid a gentle finger there. The long nose was distended and knobbed at the end, and there were deep lines on either side of it; her heavy, black brows almost met across her forehead, her teeth were large and square, and set far apart — teeth that could tear. She filled the room; the men were obliterated, seemed tossed about like twigs in an angry water, and even Steavens felt himself being drawn into the whirlpool.

The daughter — the tall, raw-boned woman in crêpe, with a mourning-comb in her hair which curiously lengthened her long face — sat stiffly upon the sofa, her hands folded in her lap, her mouth and eyes drawn down, solemnly awaiting the opening of the coffin. Near the door stood a mulatto woman, evidently a servant in the house, with a timid bearing and an emaciated face pitifully sad and gentle. She was weeping silently, the corner of her calico apron lifted to her eyes, occasionally suppressing a long, quivering sob. Steavens walked over and stood beside her.

Feeble steps were heard on the stairs, and an old man, tall and frail, odorous of pipe smoke, with shaggy, unkempt grey hair and a dingy beard, tobacco-stained about the mouth, entered uncertainly. He went slowly up to the coffin and stood rolling a blue cotton handkerchief between his hands, seeming so pained and embarrassed by his wife's behaviour that he had no consciousness of anything else.

'There, there, Annie, dear, don't take on so,' he quavered timidly, putting out a shaking hand and awkwardly patting her elbow. She turned and sank upon his shoulder with such violence that he tottered a little. He did not even glance toward the coffin, but continued to look at her with a dull, frightened, appealing expression, as a spaniel looks at the whip. His sunken cheeks slowly reddened and burned with miserable shame. When his wife rushed from the room, her daughter strode after her with set lips. The servant stole up to the coffin, bent over it for a moment, and then slipped away to the kitchen, leaving Steavens, the lawyer, and the father to themselves.

The old man stood looking down at his dead son's face. The sculptor's splendid head seemed even more noble in its rigid stillness than in life. The dark hair had crept down upon the wide forehead; the face seemed strangely long, but in it there was not that repose we expect to find in the faces of the dead. The brows were so drawn that there were two deep lines above the beaked nose, and the chin was thrust forward defiantly. It was as though the strain of life had been so sharp and bitter that death could not at once relax the tension and smooth the countenance into perfect peace—as though he were still guarding something precious, which   might even yet be wrested from him.

The old man's lips were working under his stained beard. He turned to the lawyer with timid deference: 'Phelps and the rest are comin' back to set up with Harve, ain't they?' he asked. 'Thank 'ee, Jim, thank 'ee.' He brushed the hair back gently from his son's forehead. 'He was a good boy, Jim; always a good boy. He was ez gentle ez a child and the kindest of 'em all—only we didn't none of us just onderstand him.' The tears trickled slowly down his beard and dropped upon the sculptor's coat.

'Martin, Martin! Oh, Martin! come here,' his wife wailed from the top of the stairs. The old man started timorously: 'Yes, Annie, I'm coming.' He turned away, hesitated, stood for a moment in miserable indecision; then reached back and patted the dead man's hair softly, and stumbled from the room.

'Poor old man, I didn't think he had any tears left. Seems as if his eyes would have gone dry long ago. At his age nothing cuts very deep,' remarked the lawyer.

Something in his tone made Steavens glance up. While the mother had been in the room, the young man had scarcely seen anyone else; but now, from the moment he first glanced into Jim Laird's florid face and bloodshot eyes, he knew that he had found what he had been heartsick at not finding before—the feeling, the understanding, that must exist in someone, even here.

The man was red as his beard, with features swollen and blurred by dissipation, and a hot, blazing blue eye. His face was strained—that of a man who is controlling himself with difficulty—and he kept plucking at his beard with a sort of fierce resentment. Steavens, sitting by the window, watched him turn down the glaring lamp, still its jangling pendants with an angry gesture, and then stand with his hands locked behind him, staring down at the sculptor's face. He could not help wondering what link there had been between the porcelain vessel and so sooty a lump of potter's clay.

From the kitchen an uproar was sounding; when the dining-room door opened, the import of it was clear. The mother was abusing the maid for having forgotten to make the dressing for the chicken salad which had been prepared for the watchers. Steavens had never heard anything in the least like it; it was injured, emotional, dramatic abuse, unique and masterly in its excruciating cruelty, as violent and unrestrained as had been her grief of twenty minutes before. With a shudder of disgust the lawyer went into the dining-room and closed the door into the kitchen.

'Poor Roxy's getting it now,' he remarked when he came back. 'The Merricks took her out of the poor-house years ago; and if her loyalty would let her, I guess the poor old thing could tell tales that would curdle your blood. She's the mulatto woman who was standing in here a while ago, with her apron to her eyes. The old woman is a fury; there never was anybody like her. She made Harvey's life a hell for him when he lived at home; he was so sick ashamed of it. I never could see how he kept himself sweet.'

'He was wonderful,' said Steavens slowly, 'wonderful; but until to-night I have never known how wonderful.'

'That is the eternal wonder of it, anyway; that it can come even from such a dung-heap as this,' the lawyer cried, with a sweeping gesture which seemed to indicate much more than the four walls within which they stood.

'I think I'll see whether I can get a little air. The room is so close I am beginning to feel rather faint,' murmured Steavens, struggling with one of the windows. The sash was stuck, however, and would not yield, so he sat down dejectedly and began pulling at his collar. The lawyer came over, loosened the sash with one blow of his red fist and sent the window up a few inches. Steavens thanked him, but the nausea which had been gradually climbing into his throat for the last half-hour left him with but one desire—a desperate feeling that he must get away from this place with what was left of Harvey Merrick.

Once when Merrick returned from a visit home, he brought with him a singularly suggestive bas-relief of a thin, faded old woman, sitting and sewing something pinned to her knee; while a full-lipped, full-blooded little urchin, his trousers held up by a single gallows, stood beside her, impatiently twitching her gown to call her attention to a butterfly he had caught. Steavens, impressed by the tender and delicate modelling of the woman's face, had asked him if it were his mother. He remembered the dull flush that had burned up in the sculptor's face.

The lawyer was sitting in a rocking-chair beside the coffin, his head thrown back and his eyes closed. Steavens looked at him earnestly, puzzled at the line of the chin, and wondering why a man should conceal a feature of such distinction under that disfiguring shock of beard. Suddenly, as though he felt the young sculptor's keen glance, Jim Laird opened his eyes.

'Was he always a good deal of an oyster?' he asked abruptly. 'He was terribly shy as a boy.'

'Yes, he was an oyster, since you put it so,' rejoined Steavens. 'Although he could be very fond of people, he always gave one the impression of being detached. He disliked violent emotion; he was reflective, and rather distrustful of himself—except, of course, as regarded his work. He was sure enough there. He distrusted men pretty thoroughly and women even more, yet somehow without believing ill of them. He was determined, indeed, to believe the best; but he seemed afraid to investigate.'

'A burnt dog dreads the fire,' said the lawyer grimly, and closed his eyes.

Steavens went on and on, reconstructing that whole miserable boyhood. All this raw, biting ugliness had been the portion of the man whose mind was to become an exhaustless gallery of beautiful impressions—so sensitive that the mere shadow of a poplar leaf flickering against a sunny wall would be etched and held there forever. Surely, if ever a man had the magic word in his finger-tips, it was Merrick. Whatever he touched, he revealed its holiest secret.

Steavens understood now the real tragedy of his master's life; neither love nor wine, as many had conjectured; but a blow which had fallen earlier and cut deeper than anything else could have done—a shame not his, and yet so unescapably his, to hide in his heart from his very boyhood. And without—the frontier warfare; the yearning of a boy, cast ashore upon a desert of newness and ugliness and sordidness, for all that is chastened and old, and noble with traditions.

At eleven o'clock the tall, flat woman in black announced that the watchers were arriving, and asked them to 'step into the dining-room.' As Steavens rose, the lawyer said dryly:

'You go on—it'll be a good experience for you. I'm not equal to that crowd to-night; I've had twenty years of them.'

As Steavens closed the door after him, he glanced back at the lawyer, sitting by the coffin in the dim light, with his chin resting on his hand.

The same misty group that had stood before the door of the express car shuffled into the dining-room. In the light of the kerosene lamp they separated and became individuals. The minister, a pale, feeble-looking man with white hair and blond chin-whiskers, took his seat beside a small side table and placed his Bible upon it. The Grand Army man sat down behind the stove and tilted his chair back comfortably against the wall, fishing his quill toothpick from his waistcoat pocket. The two bankers, Phelps and Elder, sat off in a corner behind the dinner-table, where they could finish their discussion of the new usury law and its effect on chattel security loans. The real estate agent, an old man with a smiling, hypocritical face, soon joined them. The coal and lumber dealer and the cattle shipper sat on opposite sides of the hard-coal burner, their feet on the nickel-work. Steavens took a book from his pocket and began to read. The talk around him ranged through various topics of local interest while the house was quieting down. When it was clear that the members of the family were in bed, the Grand Army man hitched his shoulders and, untangling his long legs, caught his heels on the rounds of his chair.

'S'pose there'll be a will, Phelps?' he queried in his weak falsetto.

The banker laughed disagreeably, and began trimming his nails with a pearl-handled pocket-knife.

'There'll scarcely be any need for one, will there?' he queried in his turn.

The restless Grand Army man shifted his position again, getting his knees still nearer his chin.

'Why, the ole man says Harve's done right well lately,' he chirped.

The other banker spoke up. 'I reckon he means by that Harve ain't asked him to mortgage any more farms lately, so as he could go on with his education.'

'Seems like my mind don't reach back to a time when Harve wasn't bein' edycated,' tittered the Grand Army man.

There was a general chuckle. The minister took out his handkerchief and blew his nose sonorously.

Banker Phelps closed his knife with a snap. 'It's too bad the old man's sons didn't turn out better,' he remarked with reflective authority. 'They never hung together. He spent money enough on Harve to stock a cattle ranch, and he might as well have poured it into Sand Creek. If Harve had stayed at home and helped nurse what little they had, and gone into stock on the old man's bottom farm, they might all have been well fixed. But the old man had to trust everything to tenants and was cheated right and left.'

'Harve never could have handled stock none,' interposed the cattleman. 'He hadn't it in him to be sharp. Do you remember when he bought Sander's mules for eight-year-olds, when everybody in town knew that Sander's father-in-law give 'em to his wife for a wedding present eighteen years before, an' they was full-grown mules then?"'

The company laughed discreetly, and the Grand Army man rubbed his knees with a spasm of childish delight.

'Harve never was much account for anything practical, and he shore was never fond of work,' began the coal and lumber dealer. 'I mind the last time he was home; the day he left, when the old man was out to the barn helpin' his hand hitch up to take Harve to the train, and Cal Moots was patchin' up the fence; Harve, he come out on the step and sings out, in his ladylike voice: "Cal Moots, Cal Moots! please come cord my trunk."'

'That's Harve for you,' approved the Grand Army man. 'I kin hear him howlin' yet, when he was a big feller in long pants and his mother used to whale him with a rawhide in the barn for lettin' the cows git foundered in the cornfield when he was drivin' 'em home from pasture. He killed a cow of mine that-a-way onct—a pure Jersey and the best milker I had, an' the ole man had to put up for her. Harve, he was watchin' the sun set acrost the marshes when the anamile got away.'

'Where the old man made his mistake was in sending the boy East to school,' said Phelps, stroking his goatee and speaking in a deliberate, judicial tone. 'There was where he got his head full of nonsense. What Harve needed, of all people, was a course in some first-class Kansas City business college.'

The letters were swimming before Steavens's eyes. Was it possible that these men did not understand, that the palm on the coffin meant nothing to them? The very name of their town would have remained forever buried in the postal guide had it not been now and again mentioned in the world in connection with Harvey Merrick's. He remembered what his master had said to him on the day of his death, after the congestion of both lungs had shut off any probability of recovery, and the sculptor had asked his pupil to send his body home. 'It's not a pleasant place to be lying while the world is moving and doing and bettering,' he had said with a feeble smile, 'but it rather seems as though we ought to go back to the place we came from, in the end. The townspeople will come in for a look at me; and after they have had their say, I shan't have much to fear from the judgment of God!'

The cattleman took up the comment. "Forty's young for a Merrick to cash in; they usually hang on pretty well. Probably he helped it along with whiskey.'

'His mother's people were not long-lived, and Harvey never had a robust constitution,' said the minister mildly. He would have liked to say more. He had been the boy's Sunday-School teacher, and had been fond of him; but he felt that he was not in a position to speak. His own sons had turned out badly, and it was not a year since one of them had made his last trip home in the express car, shot in a gambling-house in the Black Hills.

'Nevertheless, there is no disputin' that Harve frequently looked upon the wine when it was red, and it shore made an oncommon fool of him,' moralized the cattleman.

Just then the door leading into the parlour rattled loudly and everyone started involuntarily, looking relieved when only Jim Laird came out. The Grand Army man ducked his head when he saw the spark in his blue, bloodshot eye. They were all afraid of Jim; he was a drunkard, but he could twist the law to suit his client's needs as no other man in all western Kansas could do, and there were many who tried. The lawyer closed the door behind him, leaned back against it and folded his arms, cocking his head a little to one side. When he assumed this attitude in the courtroom, ears were always pricked up, as it usually foretold a flood of withering sarcasm.

'I've been with you gentlemen before,' he began in a dry, even tone, 'when you've sat by the coffins of boys born and raised in this town; and, if I remember rightly, you were never any too well satisfied when you checked them up. What's the matter, anyhow? Why is it that reputable young men are as scarce as millionaires in Sand City? It might almost seem to a stranger that there was someway something the matter with your progressive town. Why did Reuben Sayer, the brightest young lawyer you ever turned out, after he had come home from the university as straight as a die, take to drinking and forge a cheque and shoot himself? Why did Bill Merrit's son die of the shakes in a saloon in Omaha? Why was Mr. Thomas's son, here, shot in a gambling-house? Why, did young Adams burn his mill to beat the insurance companies and go to the pen?'

The lawyer paused and unfolded his arms, laying one clenched fist quietly on the table. 'I'll tell you why. Because you drummed nothing but money and knavery into their ears from the time they wore knickerbockers; because you carped away at them as you've been carping here to-night, holding our friends Phelps and Elder up to them for their models, as our grandfathers held up George Washington and John Adams. But the boys were young, and raw at the business you put them to, and how could they match coppers with such artists as Phelps and Elder? You wanted them to be successful rascals; they were only unsuccessful ones — that's all the difference. There was only one boy ever raised in this borderland between ruffianism and civilization who didn't come to grief, and you hated Harvey Merrick more for winning out than you hated all the other boys who got under the wheels. Lord, Lord, how you did hate him! Phelps, here, is fond of saying that he could buy and sell us all out anytime he's a mind to; but he knew Harve wouldn't have given a tinker's damn for his bank and all his cattle farms put together. A lack of appreciation, that way, goes hard with Phelps.

'Old Nimrod thinks Harve drank too much; and this from such as Nimrod and me!

'Brother Elder says Harve was too free with the old man's money—fell short in filial consideration, maybe. Well, we can all remember the very tone in which brother Elder swore his own father was a liar, in the county court; and we all know that the old man came out of that partnership with his son as bare as a sheared lamb. But maybe I'm getting personal, and I'd better be driving ahead at what I want to say.'

The lawyer paused a moment, squared his heavy shoulders, and went on: 'Harvey Merrick and I went to school together, back East. We were dead in earnest, and we wanted you all to be proud of us some day. We meant to be great men. Even I—and I haven't lost my sense of humour, gentlemen—I meant to be a great man. I came back here to practise, and I found you didn't in the least want me to be a great man. You wanted me to be a shrewd lawyer—oh, yes! Our veteran here wanted me to get him an increase of pension, because he had dyspepsia; Phelps wanted a new county survey that would put the widow Wilson's little bottom farm inside his south line; Elder wanted to lend money at five per cent a month, and get it collected; and Stark here wanted to wheedle old women up in Vermont into investing in real-estate mortgages that are not worth the paper they are written on. Oh, you needed me hard enough, and you'll go on needing me!

'Well, I came back here and became the damned shyster you wanted me to be. You pretend to have some sort of respect for me; and yet you'll stand up and throw mud at Harvey Merrick, whose soul you couldn't dirty and whose hands you couldn't tie. Oh, you're a discriminating lot of Christians! There have been times when the sight of Harvey's name in some Eastern paper has made me hang my head like a whipped dog. And again, times when I liked to think of him off there in the world, away from all this hog-wallow, climbing the clean up-grade he'd set for himself.

'And we? Now that we've fought and lied and sweated and stolen, and hated as only the disappointed strugglers in a bitter, dead little Western town know how to do, what have we got to show for it? It's not for me to say why, in the inscrutable wisdom of God, a man like Harvey should ever have been called from this place of hatred and bitter waters; but I want this Boston man to know that the drivel he's been hearing here to-night is the only tribute any truly great man could have from such a lot of sick, side-tracked, burnt-dog, land-poor sharks as the here-present financiers of Sand City—upon which town may God have mercy!'

The lawyer thrust out his hand to Steavens as he passed him, caught up his overcoat in the hall, and had left the house before the

Grand Army man had had time to lift his ducked head and crane his long neck about at his fellows.

Next day Jim Laird was drunk and unable to attend the funeral services. Steavens called twice at his office, but was compelled to start East without seeing him. He had a presentiment that he would hear from him again, and left his address on the lawyer's table; but if Laird found it, he never acknowledged it. The thing in him that Harvey Merrick had loved must have gone underground with Harvey Merrick's coffin; for it never spoke again, and Jim got the cold he died of driving across the Colorado mountains to defend one of Phelps's sons who had got into trouble out there by cutting Government timber.

1905

Neighbour Rosicky

1

When Doctor Burleigh told neighbour Rosicky he had a bad heart, Rosicky protested.

"So? No, I guess my heart was always pretty good. I got a little asthma, maybe. Just a awful short breath when I was pitchin' hay last summer, dat's all."

"Well now, Rosicky, if you know more about it than I do, what did you come to me for? It's your heart that makes you short of breath, I tell you. You're sixty-five years old, and you've always worked hard, and your heart's tired. You've got to be careful from now on, and you can't do heavy work any more. You've got five boys at home to do it for you."

The old farmer looked up at the Doctor with a gleam of amusement in his queer triangular-shaped eyes. His eyes were large and lively, but the lids were caught up in the middle in a curious way, so that they formed a triangle. He did not look like a sick man. His brown face was creased but not wrinkled, he had a ruddy colour in his smooth-shaven cheeks and in his lips, under his long brown moustache. His hair was thin and ragged around his ears, but very little grey. His forehead, naturally high and crossed by deep parallel lines, now ran all the way up to his pointed crown. Rosicky's face had the habit of looking interested, — suggested a contented disposition and a reflective quality that was gay rather than grave. This gave him a certain detachment, the easy manner of an onlooker and observer.

"Well, I guess you ain't got no pills fur a bad heart, Doctor Ed. I guess the only thing is fur me to git me a new one."

Doctor Burleigh swung round in his desk-chair and frowned at the old farmer. "I think if I were you I'd take a little care of the old one, Rosicky."

Rosicky shrugged. "Maybe I don't know how. I expect you mean fur me not to drink my coffee no more."

"I wouldn't, in your place. But you'll do as you choose about that. I've never yet been able to separate a Bohemian from his coffee or his pipe. I've quit trying. But the sure thing is you've got to cut out farm work. You can feed the stock and do chores about the barn, but you can't do anything in the fields that makes you short of breath."

"How about shelling corn?"

"Of course not!"

Rosicky considered with puckered brows.

"I can't make my heart go no longer'n it wants to, can I, Doctor Ed?"

"I think it's good for five or six years yet, maybe more, if you'll take the strain off it. Sit around the house and help Mary. If I had a good wife like yours, I'd want to stay around the house."

His patient chuckled. "It ain't no place fur a man. I don't like no old man hanging round the kitchen too much. An' my wife, she's a awful hard worker her own self."

"That's it; you can help her a little. My Lord, Rosicky, you are one of the few men I know who has a family he can get some comfort out of; happy dispositions, never quarrel among themselves, and they treat you right. I want to see you live a few years and enjoy them."

"Oh, they're good kids, all right," Rosicky assented.

The Doctor wrote him a prescription and asked him how his oldest son, Rudolph, who had married in the spring, was getting on. Rudolph had struck out for himself, on rented land. "And how's Polly? I was afraid Mary mightn't like an American daughter-in-law, but it seems to be working out all right."

"Yes, she's a fine girl. Dat widder woman bring her daughters up very nice. Polly got lots of spunk, an' she got some style, too. Da's nice, for young folks to have some style." Rosicky inclined his head gallantly. His voice and his twinkly smile were an affectionate compliment to his daughter-in-law.

"It looks like a storm, and you'd better be getting home before it comes. In town in the car?" Doctor Burleigh rose.

"No, I'm in de wagon. When you got five boys, you ain't got much chance to ride round in de Ford. I ain't much for cars, noway."

"Well, it's a good road out to your place; but I don't want you bumping around in a wagon much. And never again on a hay-rake, remember!"

Rosicky placed the Doctor's fee delicately behind the desk-telephone, looking the other way, as if this were an absent-minded gesture. He put on his plush cap and his corduroy jacket with a sheepskin collar, and went out.

The Doctor picked up his stethoscope and frowned at it as if he were seriously annoyed with the instrument. He wished it had been telling tales about some other man's heart, some old man who didn't look the Doctor in the eye so knowingly, or hold out such a warm brown hand when he said good-bye. Doctor Burleigh had been a poor boy in the country before he went away to medical school; he had known Rosicky almost ever since he could remember, and he had a deep affection for Mrs. Rosicky.

Only last winter he had had such a good breakfast at Rosicky's, and that when he needed it. He had been out all night on a long, hard confinement case at Tom Marshall's, — a big rich farm where there was plenty of stock and plenty of feed and a great deal of expensive farm machinery of the newest model, and no comfort whatever. The woman had too many children and too much work, and she was no manager. When the baby was born at last, and handed over to the assisting neighbour woman, and the mother was properly attended to, Burleigh refused any breakfast in that slovenly house, and drove his buggy — the snow was too deep for a car — eight miles to Anton Rosicky's place. He didn't know another farm-house where a man could get such a warm welcome, and such good strong coffee with rich cream. No wonder the old chap didn't want to give up his coffee!

He had driven in just when the boys had come back from the barn and were washing up for breakfast. The long table, covered with a bright oilcloth, was set out with dishes waiting for them, and the warm kitchen was full of the smell of coffee and hot biscuit and sausage. Five big handsome boys, running from twenty to twelve, all with what Burleigh called natural good manners, — they hadn't a bit of the painful self-consciousness he himself had to struggle with when he was a lad. One ran to put his horse away, another helped him off with his fur coat and hung it up, and Josephine, the youngest child and the only daughter, quickly set another place under her mother's direction.

With Mary, to feed creatures was the natural expression of affection, — her chickens, the calves, her big hungry boys. It was a rare pleasure to feed a young man whom she seldom saw and of whom she was as proud as if he belonged to her. Some country housekeepers would have stopped to spread a white cloth over the oilcloth, to change the thick cups and plates for their best china, and the wooden-handled knives for plated ones. But not Mary.

"You must take us as you find us, Doctor Ed. I'd be glad to put out my good things for you if you was expected, but I'm glad to get you any way at all."

He knew she was glad, — she threw back her head and spoke out as if she were announcing him to the whole prairie. Rosicky hadn't said anything at all; he merely smiled his twinkling smile, put some more coal on the fire, and went into his own room to pour the Doctor a little drink in a medicine glass. When they were all seated, he watched his wife's face from his end of the table and spoke to her in Czech. Then, with the instinct of politeness which seldom failed him, he turned to the Doctor and said slyly: "I was just tellin' her not to ask you no questions about Mrs. Marshall till you eat some breakfast. My wife, she's terrible fur to ask questions."

The boys laughed, and so did Mary. She watched the Doctor devour her biscuit and sausage, too much excited to eat anything herself. She drank her coffee and sat taking in everything about her visitor. She had known him when he was a poor country boy, and was boastfully proud of his success, always saying: "What do people go to Omaha for, to see a doctor, when we got the best one in the State right here?" If Mary liked people at all, she felt physical pleasure in the sight of them, personal exultation in any good fortune that came to them. Burleigh didn't know many women like that, but he knew she was like that.

When his hunger was satisfied, he did, of course, have to tell them about Mrs. Marshall, and he noticed what a friendly interest the boys took in the matter.

Rudolph, the oldest one (he was still living at home then), said: "The last time I was over there, she was lifting them big heavy milk-cans, and I knew she oughtn't to be doing it."

"Yes, Rudolph told me about that when he come home, and I said it wasn't right," Mary put in warmly. "It was all right for me to do them things up to the last, for I was terrible strong, but that woman's weakly. And do you think she'll be able to nurse it, Ed?" She sometimes forgot to give him the title she was so proud of. "And to think of your being up all night and then not able to get a decent breakfast! I don't know what's the matter with such people."

"Why, Mother," said one of the boys, "if Doctor Ed had got breakfast there, we wouldn't have him here. So you ought to be glad."

"He knows I'm glad to have him, John, any time. But I'm sorry for that poor woman, how bad she'll feel the Doctor had to go away in the cold without his breakfast."

"I wish I'd been in practice when these were getting born." The doctor looked down the row of close-clipped heads. "I missed some good breakfasts by not being."

The boys began to laugh at their mother because she flushed so red, but she stood her ground and threw up her head. "I don't care, you wouldn't have got away from this house without breakfast. No doctor ever did. I'd have had something ready fixed that Anton could warm up for you."

The boys laughed harder than ever, and exclaimed at her: "I'll bet you would!" "She would, that!"

"Father, did you get breakfast for the doctor when we were born?"

"Yes, and he used to bring me my breakfast, too, mighty nice. I was always awful hungry!" Mary admitted with a guilty laugh.

While the boys were getting the Doctor's horse, he went to the window to examine the house plants. "What do you do to your geraniums to keep them blooming all winter, Mary? I never pass this house that from the road I don't see your windows full of flowers."

She snapped off a dark red one, and a ruffled new green leaf, and put them in his buttonhole. "There, that looks better. You look too solemn for a young man, Ed. Why don't you git married? I'm worried about you. Settin' at breakfast, I looked at you real hard, and I seen you've got some grey hairs already."

"Oh, yes! They're coming. Maybe they'd come faster if I married."

"Don't talk so. You'll ruin your health eating at the hotel. I could send your wife a nice loaf of nut bread, if you only had one. I don't like to see a young man getting grey. I'll tell you something, Ed; you make some strong black tea and keep it handy in a bowl, and every morning just brush it into your hair, an' it'll keep the grey from showin' much. That's the way I do!"

Sometimes the Doctor heard the gossipers in the drug-store wondering why Rosicky didn't get on faster. He was industrious, and so were his boys, but they were rather free and easy, weren't pushers, and they didn't always show good judgment. They were comfortable, they were out of debt, but they didn't get much ahead. Maybe, Doctor Burleigh reflected, people as generous and warm-hearted and affectionate as the Rosickys never got ahead much; maybe you couldn't enjoy your life and put it into the bank, too.

2

When Rosicky left Doctor Burleigh's office he went into the farm-implement store to light his pipe and put on his glasses and read over the list Mary had given him. Then he went into the general merchandise place next door and stood about until the pretty girl with the plucked eyebrows, who always waited on him, was free. Those eyebrows, two thin India-ink strokes, amused him, because he remembered how they used to be. Rosicky always prolonged his shopping by a little joking; the girl knew the old fellow admired her, and she liked to chaff with him.

"Seems to me about every other week you buy ticking, Mr. Rosicky, and always the best quality," she remarked as she measured off the heavy bolt with red stripes.

"You see, my wife is always makin' goose-fedder pillows, an' de thin stuff don't hold in dem little down-fedders."

"You must have lots of pillows at your house."

"Sure. She makes quilts of dem, too. We sleeps easy. Now she's makin' a fedder quilt for my son's wife. You know Polly, that married my Rudolph. How much my bill, Miss Pearl?"

"Eight eighty-five."

"Chust make it nine, and put in some candy fur de women."

"As usual. I never did see a man buy so much candy for his wife. First thing you know, she'll be getting too fat."

"I'd like dat. I ain't much fur all dem slim women like what de style is now."

"That's one for me, I suppose, Mr. Bohunk!" Pearl sniffed and elevated her India-ink strokes.

When Rosicky went out to his wagon, it was beginning to snow,—the first snow of the season, and he was glad to see it. He rattled out of town and along the highway through a wonderfully rich stretch of country, the finest farms in the county. He admired this High Prairie, as it was called, and always liked to drive through it. His own place lay in a rougher territory, where there was some clay in the soil and it was not so productive. When he bought his land, he hadn't the money to buy on High Prairie; so he told his boys, when they grumbled, that if their land hadn't some clay in it, they wouldn't own it at all. All the same, he enjoyed looking at these fine farms, as he enjoyed looking at a prize bull.

After he had gone eight miles, he came to the graveyard, which lay just at the edge of his own hay-land. There he stopped his horses and sat still on his wagon seat, looking about at the snowfall. Over yonder on the hill he could see his own house, crouching low, with the clump of orchard behind and the windmill before, and all down the gentle hill-slope the rows of pale gold cornstalks stood out against the white field. The snow was falling over the cornfield and the pasture and the hay-land, steadily, with very little wind,—a nice dry snow. The graveyard had only a light wire fence about it and was all overgrown with long red grass. The fine snow, settling into this red grass and upon the few little evergreens and the headstones, looked very pretty.

It was a nice graveyard, Rosicky reflected, sort of snug and homelike, not cramped or mournful,—a big sweep all round it. A man could lie down in the long grass and see the complete arch of the sky over him, hear the wagons go by; in summer the mowing-machine rattled right up to the wire fence. And it was so near home. Over there across the cornstalks his own roof and windmill looked so good to him that he promised himself to mind the Doctor and take care of himself. He was awful fond of his place, he admitted. He wasn't anxious to leave it. And it was a comfort to think that he would never have to go farther than the edge of his own hayfield. The snow, falling over his barnyard and the graveyard, seemed to draw things together like. And they were all old neighbours in the graveyard, most of them friends; there was nothing to feel awkward or embarrassed about. Embarrassment was the most disagreeable feeling Rosicky knew. He didn't often have it, — only with certain people whom he didn't understand at all.

Well, it was a nice snowstorm; a fine sight to see the snow falling so quietly and graciously over so much open country. On his cap and shoulders, on the horses' backs and manes, light, delicate, mysterious it fell; and with it a dry cool fragrance was released into the air. It meant rest for vegetation and men and beasts, for the ground itself; a season of long nights for sleep, leisurely breakfasts, peace by the fire. This and much more went through Rosicky's mind, but he merely told himself that winter was coming, clucked to his horses, and drove on.

When he reached home, John, the youngest boy, ran out to put away his team for him, and he met Mary coming up from the outside cellar with her apron full of carrots. They went into the house together. On the table, covered with oilcloth figured with clusters of blue grapes, a place was set, and he smelled hot coffee-cake of some kind. Anton never lunched in town; he thought that extravagant, and anyhow he didn't like the food. So Mary always had something ready for him when he got home.

After he was settled in his chair, stirring his coffee in a big cup, Mary took out of the oven a pan of *kolache* stuffed with apricots, examined them anxiously to see whether they had got too dry, put them beside his plate, and then sat down opposite him.

Rosicky asked her in Czech if she wasn't going to have any coffee.

She replied in English, as being somehow the right language for transacting business: "Now what did Doctor Ed say, Anton? You tell me just what."

"He said I was to tell you some compliments, but I forgot 'em." Rosicky's eyes twinkled.

"About you, I mean. What did he say about your asthma?"

"He says I ain't got no asthma." Rosicky took one of the little rolls in his broad brown fingers. The thickened nail of his right thumb told the story of his past.

"Well, what is the matter? And don't try to put me off."

"He don't say nothing much, only I'm a little older, and my heart ain't so good like it used to be."

Mary started and brushed her hair back from her temples with both hands as if she were a little out of her mind. From the way she glared, she might have been in a rage with him.

"He says there's something the matter with your heart? Doctor Ed says so?"

"Now don't yell at me like I was a hog in de garden, Mary. You know I always did like to hear a woman talk soft. He didn't say anything de matter wid my heart, only it ain't so young like it used to be, an' he tell me not to pitch hay or run de corn-sheller."

Mary wanted to jump up, but she sat still. She admired the way he never under any circumstances raised his voice or spoke roughly. He was city-bred, and she was country-bred; she often said she wanted her boys to have their papa's nice ways.

"You never have no pain there, do you? It's your breathing and your stomach that's been wrong. I wouldn't believe nobody but Doctor Ed about it. I guess I'll go see him myself. Didn't he give you no advice?"

"Chust to take it easy like, an' stay round de house dis winter. I guess you got some carpenter work for me to do. I kin make some new shelves for you, and I want dis long time to build a closet in de boys' room and make dem two little fellers keep dere clo'es hung up."

Rosicky drank his coffee from time to time, while he considered. His moustache was of the soft long variety and came down over his mouth like the teeth of a buggy-rake over a bundle of hay. Each time he put down his cup, he ran his blue handkerchief over his lips. When he took a drink of water, he managed very neatly with the back of his hand.

Mary sat watching him intently, trying to find any change in his face. It is hard to see anyone who has become like your own body to you. Yes, his hair had got thin, and his high forehead had deep lines running from left to right. But his neck, always clean shaved except in the busiest seasons, was not loose or baggy. It was burned a dark reddish brown, and there were deep creases in it, but it looked firm and full of blood. His cheeks had a good colour. On either side of his mouth there was a half-moon down the length of his cheek, not wrinkles, but two lines that had come there from his habitual expression. He was shorter and broader than when she married him; his back had grown broad and curved, a good deal like the shell of an old turtle, and his arms and legs were short.

He was fifteen years older than Mary, but she had hardly ever thought about it before. He was her man, and the kind of man she liked. She was rough, and he was gentle,—city-bred, as she always said. They had been shipmates on a rough voyage and had stood by each other in trying times. Life had gone well with them because, at bottom, they had the same ideas about life. They agreed, without discussion, as to what was most important and what was secondary. They didn't often exchange opinions, even in Czech,—it was as if they had thought the same thought together. A good deal had to be sacrificed and thrown overboard in a hard life like theirs, and they had never disagreed as to the things that could go. It had been a hard life, and a soft life, too. There wasn't anything brutal in the short, broad-backed man with the three-cornered eyes and the forehead that went on to the top of his skull. He was a city man, a gentle man, and though he had married a rough farm girl, he had never touched her without gentleness.

They had been at one accord not to hurry through life, not to be always skimping and saving. They saw their neighbours buy more land and feed more stock than they did, without discontent. Once when the creamery agent came to the Rosickys to persuade them to sell him their cream, he told them how much money the Fasslers, their nearest neighbours, had made on their cream last year.

"Yes," said Mary, "and look at them Fassler children! Pale, pinched little things, they look like skimmed milk. I'd rather put some colour into my children's faces than put money into the bank."

The agent shrugged and turned to Anton.

"I guess we'll do like she says," said Rosicky.

3

Mary very soon got into town to see Doctor Ed, and then she had a talk with her boys and set a guard over Rosicky. Even John, the youngest, had his father on his mind. If Rosicky went to throw hay down from the loft, one of the boys ran up the ladder and took the fork from him. He sometimes complained that though he was getting to be an old man, he wasn't an old woman yet.

That winter he stayed in the house in the afternoons and carpentered, or sat in the chair between the window full of plants and the wooden bench where the two pails of drinking-water stood. This spot was called "Father's corner," though it was not a corner at all. He had a shelf there, where he kept his Bohemian papers and his pipes and tobacco, and his shears and needles and thread and tailor's thimble. Having been a tailor in his youth, he couldn't bear to see a woman patching at his clothes, or at the boys'. He liked tailoring, and always patched all the overalls and jackets and work shirts. Occasionally he made over a pair of pants one of the older boys had outgrown, for the little fellow.

While he sewed, he let his mind run back over his life. He had a good deal to remember, really; life in three countries. The only part of his youth he didn't like to remember was the two years he had spent in London, in Cheapside, working for a German tailor who was wretchedly poor. Those days, when he was nearly always hungry, when his clothes were dropping off him for dirt, and the sound of a strange language kept him in continual bewilderment, had left a sore spot in his mind that wouldn't bear touching.

He was twenty when he landed at Castle Garden in New York, and he had a protector who got him work in a tailor shop in Vesey Street, down near the Washington Market. He looked upon that part of his life as very happy. He became a good workman, he was industrious, and his wages were increased from time to time. He minded his own business and envied nobody's good fortune. He went to night school and learned to read English. He often did overtime work and was well paid for it, but somehow he never saved anything. He couldn't refuse a loan to a friend, and he was self-indulgent. He liked a good dinner, and a little went for beer, a little for tobacco; a good deal went to the girls. He often stood through an opera on Saturday nights; he could get standing-room for a dollar. Those were the great days of opera in New York, and it gave a fellow something to think about for the rest of the week. Rosicky had a quick ear, and a childish love of all the stage splendour; the scenery, the costumes, the ballet. He usually went with a chum, and after the performance they had beer and maybe some oysters somewhere. It was a fine life; for the first five years or so it satisfied him completely. He was never hungry or cold or dirty, and everything amused him: a fire, a dog fight, a parade, a storm, a ferry ride. He thought New York the finest, richest, friendliest city in the world.

Moreover, he had what he called a happy home life. Very near the tailor shop was a small furniture-factory, where an old Austrian, Loeffler, employed a few skilled men and made unusual furniture, most of it to order, for the rich German housewives up-town. The top floor of Loeffler's five-storey factory was a loft, where he kept his choice lumber and stored the odd pieces of furniture left on his hands. One of the young workmen he employed was a Czech, and he and Rosicky became fast friends. They persuaded Loeffler to let them have a sleeping-room in one corner of the loft. They bought good beds and bedding and had their pick of the furniture kept up there. The loft was low-pitched, but light and airy, full of windows, and good-smelling by reason of the fine lumber put up there to season. Old Loeffler used to go down to the docks and buy wood from South America and the East from the sea captains. The young men were as foolish about their house as a bridal pair. Zichec, the young cabinet-maker, devised every sort of convenience, and Rosicky kept their clothes in order. At night and on Sundays, when the quiver of machinery underneath was still, it was the quietest place in the world, and on summer nights all the sea winds blew in. Zichec often practised on his flute in the evening. They were both fond of music and went to the opera together. Rosicky thought he wanted to live like that for ever.

But as the years passed, all alike, he began to get a little restless. When spring came round, he would begin to feel fretted, and he got to drinking. He was likely to drink too much of a Saturday night. On Sunday he was languid and heavy, getting over his spree. On Monday he plunged into work again. So he never had time to figure out what ailed him, though he knew something did. When the grass turned green in Park Place, and the lilac hedge at the back of Trinity churchyard put out its blossoms, he was tormented by a longing to run away. That was why he drank too much; to get a temporary illusion of freedom and wide horizons.

Rosicky, the old Rosicky, could remember as if it were yesterday the day when the young Rosicky found out what was the matter with him. It was on a Fourth of July afternoon, and he was sitting in Park Place in the sun. The lower part of New York was empty. Wall Street, Liberty Street, Broadway, all empty. So much stone and asphalt with nothing going on, so many empty windows. The emptiness was intense, like the stillness in a great factory when the machinery stops and the belts and bands cease running. It was too great a change, it took all the strength out of one. Those blank buildings, without the stream of life pouring through them, were like empty jails. It struck young Rosicky that this was the trouble with big cities; they built you in from the earth itself, cemented you away from any contact with the ground. You lived in an unnatural world, like the fish in an aquarium, who were probably much more comfortable than they ever were in the sea.

On that very day he began to think seriously about the articles he had read in the Bohemian papers, describing prosperous Czech farming communities in the West. He believed he would like to go out there as a farm hand; it was hardly possible that he could ever have land of his own. His people had always been workmen; his father and grandfather had worked in shops. His mother's parents had lived in the country, but they rented their farm and had a hard time to get along. Nobody in his family had ever owned any land, — that belonged to a different station of life altogether. Anton's mother died when he was little, and he was sent into the country to her parents. He stayed with them until he was twelve, and formed those ties with the earth and the farm animals and growing things which are never made at all unless they are made early. After his grandfather died, he went ?back to live with his father and stepmother, but she was very hard on him, and his father helped him to get passage to London.

After that Fourth of July day in Park Place, the desire to return to the country never left him. To work on another man's farm would be all he asked; to see the sun rise and set and to plant things and watch them grow. He was a very simple man. He was like a tree that has not many roots, but one tap-root that goes down deep. He subscribed for a Bohemian paper printed in Chicago, then for one printed in Omaha. His mind got farther and farther west. He began to save a little money to buy his liberty. When he was thirty-five, there was a great meeting in New York of Bohemian athletic societies, and Rosicky left the tailor shop and went home with the Omaha delegates to try his fortune in another part of the world.

4

Perhaps the fact that his own youth was well over before he

began to have a family was one reason why Rosicky was so fond of his boys. He had almost a grandfather's indulgence for them. He had never had to worry about any of them — except, just now, a little about Rudolph.

On Saturday night the boys always piled into the Ford, took little Josephine, and went to town to the moving-picture show. One Saturday morning they were talking at the breakfast table about starting early that evening, so that they would have an hour or so to see the Christmas things in the stores before the show began. Rosicky looked down the table.

"I hope you boys ain't disappointed, but I want you to let me have de car tonight. Maybe some of you can go in with de neighbours."

Their faces fell. They worked hard all week, and they were still like children. A new jackknife or a box of candy pleased the older ones as much as the little fellow.

"If you and Mother are going to town," Frank said, "maybe you could take a couple of us along with you, anyway."

"No, I want to take de car down to Rudolph's, and let him an' Polly go in to de show. She don't git into town enough, an' I'm afraid she's gettin' lonesome, an' he can't afford no car yet."

That settled it. The boys were a good deal dashed. Their father took another piece of apple-cake and went on: "Maybe next Saturday night de two little fellers can go along wid dem."

"Oh, is Rudolph going to have the car every Saturday night?"

Rosicky did not reply at once; then he began to speak seriously: "Listen, boys; Polly ain't lookin' so good. I don't like to see nobody lookin' sad. It comes hard fur a town girl to be a farmer's wife. I don't want no trouble to start in Rudolph's family. When it starts, it ain't so easy to stop. An American girl don't git used to our ways all at once. I like to tell Polly she and Rudolph can have the car every Saturday night till after New Year's, if it's all right with you boys."

"Sure it's all right, Papa," Mary cut in. "And it's good you thought about that. Town girls is used to more than country girls. I lay awake nights, scared she'll make Rudolph discontented with the farm."

The boys put as good a face on it as they could. They surely looked forward to their Saturday nights in town. That evening Rosicky drove the car the half-mile down to Rudolph's new, bare little house.

Polly was in a short-sleeved gingham dress, clearing away the supper dishes. She was a trim, slim little thing, with blue eyes and shingled yellow hair, and her eyebrows were reduced to a mere brushstroke, like Miss Pearl's.

"Good evening, Mr. Rosicky. Rudolph's at the barn, I guess." She never called him father, or Mary mother. She was sensitive about having married a foreigner. She never in the world would have done it if Rudolph hadn't been such a handsome, persuasive fellow and such a gallant lover. He had graduated in her class in the high school in town, and their friendship began in the ninth grade.

Rosicky went in, though he wasn't exactly asked. "My boys ain't goin' to town tonight, an' I brought de car over fur you two to go in to de picture show."

Polly, carrying dishes to the sink, looked over her shoulder at him. "Thank you. But I'm late with my work tonight, and pretty tired. Maybe Rudolph would like to go in with you."

"Oh, I don't go to de shows! I'm too old-fashioned. You won't feel so tired after you ride in de air a ways. It's a nice clear night, an' it ain't cold. You go an' fix yourself up, Polly, an' I'll wash de dishes an' leave everything nice fur you."

Polly blushed and tossed her bob. "I couldn't let you do that, Mr. Rosicky. I wouldn't think of it."

Rosicky said nothing. He found a bib apron on a nail behind the kitchen door. He slipped it over his head and then took Polly by her two elbows and pushed her gently toward the door of her own room. "I washed up de kitchen many times for my wife, when de babies was sick or somethin'. You go an' make yourself look nice. I like you to look prettier'n any of dem town girls when you go in. De young folks must have some fun, an' I'm goin' to look out fur you, Polly."

That kind, reassuring grip on her elbows, the old man's funny bright eyes, made Polly want to drop her head on his shoulder for a second. She restrained herself, but she lingered in his grasp at the door of her room, murmuring tearfully: "You always lived in the city when you were young, didn't you? Don't you ever get lonesome out here?"

As she turned round to him, her hand fell naturally into his, and he stood holding it and smiling into her face with his peculiar, knowing, indulgent smile without a shadow of reproach in it. "Dem big cities is all right fur de rich, but dey is terrible hard fur de poor."

"I don't know. Sometimes I think I'd like to take a chance. You lived in New York, didn't you?"

"An' London. Da's bigger still. I learned my trade dere. Here's Rudolph comin', you better hurry."

"Will you tell me about London some time?"

"Maybe. Only I ain't no talker, Polly. Run an' dress yourself up."

The bedroom door closed behind her, and Rudolph came in from the outside, looking anxious. He had seen the car and was sorry any of his family should come just then. Supper hadn't been a very pleasant occasion. Halting in the doorway, he saw his father in a kitchen apron, carrying dishes to the sink. He flushed crimson and something flashed in his eye. Rosicky held up a warning finger.

"I brought de car over fur you an' Polly to go to de picture show, an' I made her let me finish here so you won't be late. You go put on a clean shirt, quick!"

"But don't the boys want the car, Father?"

"Not tonight dey don't." Rosicky fumbled under his apron and found his pants pocket. He took out a silver dollar and said in a hurried whisper: "You go an' buy dat girl some ice cream an' candy tonight, like you was courtin'. She's awful good friends wid me."

Rudolph was very short of cash, but he took the money as if it hurt him. There had been a crop failure all over the county. He had more than once been sorry he'd married this year.

In a few minutes the young people came out, looking clean and a little stiff. Rosicky hurried them off, and then he took his own time with the dishes. He scoured the pots and pans and put away the milk and swept the kitchen. He put some coal in the stove and shut off the draughts, so the place would be warm for them when they got home late at night. Then he sat down and had a pipe and listened to the clock tick.

Generally speaking, marrying an American girl was certainly a risk. A Czech should marry a Czech. It was lucky that Polly was the daughter of a poor widow woman; Rudolph was proud, and if she had a prosperous family to throw up at him, they could never make it go. Polly was one of four sisters, and they all worked; one was book-keeper in the bank, one taught music, and Polly and her younger sister had been clerks, like Miss Pearl. All four of them were musical, had pretty voices, and sang in the Methodist choir, which the eldest sister directed.

Polly missed the sociability of a store position. She missed the choir, and the company of her sisters. She didn't dislike housework, but she disliked so much of it. Rosicky was a little anxious about this pair. He was afraid Polly would grow so discontented that Rudy would quit the farm and take a factory job in Omaha. He had worked for a winter up there, two years ago, to get money to marry on. He had done very well, and they would always take him back at the stockyards. But to Rosicky that meant the end of everything for his son. To be a landless man was to be a wage-earner, a slave, all your life; to have nothing, to be nothing.

Rosicky thought he would come over and do a little carpentering for Polly after the New Year. He guessed she needed jollying. Rudolph was a serious sort of chap, serious in love and serious about his work.

Rosicky shook out his pipe and walked home across the fields. Ahead of him the lamplight shone from his kitchen windows. Suppose he were still in a tailor shop on Vesey Street, with a bunch of pale, narrow-chested sons working on machines, all coming home tired and sullen to eat supper in a kitchen that was a parlour also; with another crowded, angry family quarrelling just across the dumb-waiter shaft, and squeaking pulleys at the windows where dirty washings hung on dirty lines above a court full of old brooms and mops and ash-cans. . . .

He stopped by the windmill to look up at the frosty winter stars and draw a long breath before he went inside. That kitchen with the shining windows was dear to him; but the sleeping fields and bright stars and the noble darkness were dearer still.

5

On the day before Christmas the weather set in very cold; no snow, but a bitter, biting wind that whistled and sang over the flat land and lashed one's face like fine wires. There was baking going on in the Rosicky kitchen all day, and Rosicky sat inside, making over a coat that Albert had outgrown into an overcoat for John. Mary had a big red geranium in bloom for Christmas, and a row of Jerusalem cherry trees, full of berries. It was the first year she had ever grown these; Doctor Ed brought her the seeds from Omaha when he went to some medical convention. They reminded Rosicky of plants he had seen in England; and all afternoon, as he stitched, he sat thinking about those two years in London, which his mind usually shrank from even after all this while.

He was a lad of eighteen when he dropped down into London, with no money and no connexions except the address of a cousin who was supposed to be working at a confectioner's. When he went to the pastry shop, however, he found that the cousin had gone to America. Anton tramped the streets for several days, sleeping in doorways and on the Embankment, until he was in utter despair. He knew no English, and the sound of the strange language all about him confused him. By chance he met a poor German tailor who had learned his trade in Vienna, and could speak a little Czech. This tailor, Lifschnitz, kept a repair shop in a Cheapside basement, underneath a cobbler. He didn't much need an apprentice, but he was sorry for the boy and took him in for no wages but his keep and what he could pick up. The pickings were supposed to be coppers given you when you took work home to a customer. But most of the customers called for their clothes themselves, and the coppers that came Anton's way were very few. He had, however, a place to sleep. The tailor's family lived upstairs in three rooms; a kitchen, a bedroom, where Lifschnitz and his wife and five children slept, and a living-room. Two corners of this living-room were curtained off for lodgers; in one Rosicky slept on an old horsehair sofa, with a feather quilt to wrap himself in. The other corner was rented to a wretched, dirty boy, who was studying the violin. He actually practised there. Rosicky was dirty, too. There was no way to be anything else. Mrs. Lifschnitz got the water she cooked and washed with from a pump in a brick court, four flights down. There were bugs in the place, and multitudes of fleas, though the poor woman did the best she could. Rosicky knew she often went empty to give another potato or a spoonful of dripping to the two hungry, sad-eyed boys who lodged with her. He used to think he would never get out of there, never get a clean shirt to his back again. What would he do, he wondered, when his clothes actually dropped to pieces and the worn cloth wouldn't hold patches any longer?

It was still early when the old farmer put aside his sewing and his recollections. The sky had been a dark grey all day, with not a gleam of sun, and the light failed at four o'clock. He went to shave and change his shirt while the turkey was roasting. Rudolph and Polly were coming over for supper.

After supper they sat round in the kitchen, and the younger boys were saying how sorry they were it hadn't snowed. Everybody was sorry. They wanted a deep snow that would lie long and keep the wheat warm, and leave the ground soaked when it melted.

"Yes, sir!" Rudolph broke out fiercely; "if we have another dry year like last year, there's going to be hard times in this country."

Rosicky filled his pipe. "You boys don't know what hard times is. You don't owe nobody, you got plenty to eat an' keep warm, an' plenty water to keep clean. When you got them, you can't have it very hard."

Rudolph frowned, opened and shut his big right hand, and dropped it clenched upon his knee. "I've got to have a good deal more than that, Father, or I'll quit this farming gamble. I can always make good wages railroading, or at the packing house, and be sure of my money."

"Maybe so," his father answered dryly.

Mary, who had just come in from the pantry and was wiping her hands on the roller towel, thought Rudy and his father were getting too serious. She brought her darning-basket and sat down in the middle of the group.

"I ain't much afraid of hard times, Rudy," she said heartily. "We've had a plenty, but we've always come through. Your father wouldn't never take nothing very hard, not even hard times. I got a mind to tell you a story on him. Maybe you boys can't hardly remember the year we had that terrible hot wind, that burned everything up on the Fourth of July? All the corn an' the gardens. An' that was in the days when we didn't have alfalfa yet, — I guess it wasn't invented.

"Well, that very day your father was out cultivatin' corn, and I was here in the kitchen makin' plum preserves. We had bushels of plums that year. I noticed it was terrible hot, but it's always hot in the kitchen when you're preservin', an' I was too busy with my plums to mind. Anton come in from the field about three o'clock, an' I asked him what was the matter.

"'Nothin',' he says, 'but it's pretty hot, an' I think I won't work no more today.' He stood round for a few minutes, an' then he says: 'Ain't you near through? I want you should get up a nice supper for us tonight. It's Fourth of July.'

"I told him to git along, that I was right in the middle of preservin', but the plums would taste good on hot biscuit. 'I'm goin' to have fried chicken, too,' he says, and he went off an' killed a couple. You three oldest boys was little fellers, playin' round outside, real hot an' sweaty, an' your father took you to the horse tank down by the windmill an' took off your clothes an' put you in. Them two box-elder trees was little then, but they made shade over the tank. Then he took off all his own clothes, an' got in with you. While he was playin' in the water with you, the Methodist preacher drove into our place to say how all the neighbours was goin' to meet at the schoolhouse that night, to pray for rain. He drove right to the windmill, of course, and there was your father and you three with no clothes on. I was in the kitchen door, an' I had to laugh, for the preacher acted like he ain't never seen a naked man before. He surely was embarrassed, an' your father couldn't git to his clothes; they was all hangin' up on the windmill to let the sweat dry out of 'em. So he laid in the tank where he was, an' put one of you boys on top of him to cover him up a little, an' talked to the preacher.

"When you got through playin' in the water, he put clean clothes on you and a clean shirt on himself, an' by that time I'd begun to get supper. He says: 'It's too hot in here to eat comfortable. Let's have a picnic in the orchard. We'll eat our supper behind the mulberry hedge, under them linden trees.'

"So he carried our supper down, an' a bottle of my wild-grape wine, an' everything tasted good, I can tell you. The wind got cooler as the sun was goin' down, and it turned out pleasant, only I noticed how the leaves was curled up on the linden trees. That made me think, an' I asked your father if that hot wind all day hadn't been terrible hard on the gardens an' the corn.

"'Corn,' he says, 'there ain't no corn.'

"'What you talkin' about?' I said. 'Ain't we got forty acres?'

"'We ain't got an ear,' he says, 'nor nobody else ain't got none. All the corn in this country was cooked by three o'clock today, like you'd roasted it in an oven.'

"'You mean you won't get no crop at all?' I asked him. I couldn't believe it, after he'd worked so hard.

"'No crop this year,' he says. 'That's why we're havin' a picnic. We might as well enjoy what we got.'

"An' that's how your father behaved, when all the neighbours was so discouraged they couldn't look you in the face. An' we enjoyed ourselves that year, poor as we was, an' our neighbours wasn't a bit better off for bein' miserable. Some of 'em grieved till they got poor digestions and couldn't relish what they did have."

The younger boys said they thought their father had the best of it. But Rudolph was thinking that, all the same, the neighbours had managed to get ahead more, in the fifteen years since that time. There must be something wrong about his father's way of doing things. He wished he knew what was going on in the back of Polly's mind. He knew she liked his father, but he knew, too, that she was afraid of something. When his mother sent over coffee-cake or prune tarts or a loaf of fresh bread, Polly seemed to regard them with a certain suspicion. When she observed to him that his brothers had nice manners, her tone implied that it was remarkable they should have. With his mother she was stiff and on her guard. Mary's hearty frankness and gusts of good humour irritated her. Polly was afraid of being unusual or conspicuous in any way, of being "ordinary," as she said!

When Mary had finished her story, Rosicky laid aside his pipe.

"You boys like me to tell you about some of dem hard times I been through in London?" Warmly encouraged, he sat rubbing his forehead along the deep creases. It was bothersome to tell a long story in English (he nearly always talked to the boys in Czech), but he wanted Polly to hear this one.

"Well, you know about dat tailor shop I worked in in London? I had one Christmas dere I ain't never forgot. Times was awful bad before Christmas; de boss ain't got much work, an' have it awful hard to pay his rent. It ain't so much fun, bein' poor in a big city like London, I'll say! All de windows is full of good t'ings to eat, an' all de pushcarts in de streets is full, an' you smell 'em all de time, an' you ain't got no money,—not a damn bit. I didn't mind de cold so much, though I didn't have no overcoat, chust a short jacket I'd outgrowed so it wouldn't meet on me, an' my hands was chapped raw. But I always had a good appetite, like you all know, an' de sight of dem pork pies in de windows was awful fur me!

"Day before Christmas was terrible foggy dat year, an' dat fog gits into your bones and makes you all damp like. Mrs. Lifschnitz didn't give us nothin' but a little bread an' drippin' for supper, because she was savin' to try for to give us a good dinner on Christmas Day. After supper de boss say I can go an' enjoy myself, so I went into de streets to listen to de Christmas singers. Dey sing old songs an' make very nice music, an' I run round after dem a good ways, till I got awful hungry. I t'ink maybe if I go home, I can sleep till morning an' forgit my belly.

"I went into my corner real quiet, and roll up in my fedder quilt. But I ain't got my head down, till I smell somet'ing good. Seem like it git stronger an' stronger, an' I can't git to sleep noway. I can't understand dat smell. Dere was a gas light in a hall across de court, dat always shine in at my window a little. I got up an' look round. I got a little wooden box in my corner fur a stool, 'cause I ain't got no chair. I picks up dat box, and under it dere is a roast goose on a platter! I can't believe my eyes. I carry it to de window where de light comes in, an' touch it and smell it to find out, an' den I taste it to be sure. I say, I will eat chust one little bite of dat goose, so I can go to sleep, and tomorrow

I won't eat none at all. But I tell you, boys, when I stop, one half of dat goose was gone!"

The narrator bowed his head, and the boys shouted. But little Josephine slipped behind his chair and kissed him on the neck beneath his ear.

"Poor little Papa, I don't want him to be hungry!"

"Da's long ago, child. I ain't never been hungry since I had your mudder to cook fur me."

"Go on and tell us the rest, please," said Polly.

"Well, when I come to realize what I done, of course, I felt terrible. I felt better in de stomach, but very bad in de heart. I set on my bed wid dat platter on my knees, an' it all come to me; how hard dat poor woman save to buy dat goose, and how she get some neighbour to cook it dat got more fire, an' how she put it in my corner to keep it away from dem hungry children. Dey was a old carpet hung up to shut my corner off, an' de children wasn't allowed to go in dere. An' I know she put it in my corner because she trust me more'n she did de violin boy. I can't stand it to face her after I spoil de Christmas. So I put on my shoes and go out into de city. I tell myself I better throw myself in de river; but I guess I ain't dat kind of a boy.

"It was after twelve o'clock, an' terrible cold, an' I start out to walk about London all night. I walk along de river awhile, but dey was lots of drunks all along; men, and women too. I chust move along to keep away from de police. I git onto de Strand, an' den over to New Oxford Street, where dere was a big German restaurant on de ground floor, wid big windows all fixed up fine, an' I could see de people havin' parties inside. While I was lookin' in, two men and two ladies come out, laughin' and talkin' and feelin' happy about all dey been eatin' an' drinkin', and dey was speakin' Czech, — not like de Austrians, but like de home folks talk it.

"I guess I went crazy, an' I done what I ain't never done before nor since. I went right up to dem gay people an' begun to beg dem: 'Fellow-countrymen, for God's sake give me money enough to buy a goose!'

"Dey laugh, of course, but de ladies speak awful kind to me, an' dey take me back into de restaurant and give me hot coffee and cakes, an' make me tell all about how I happened to come to London, an' what I was doin' dere. Dey take my name and where I work down on paper, an' both of dem ladies give me ten shillings.

"De big market at Covent Garden ain't very far away, an' by dat time it was open. I go dere an' buy a big goose an' some pork pies, an' potatoes and onions, an' cakes an' oranges fur de children, — all I could carry! When I git home, everybody is still asleep. I pile all I bought on de kitchen table, an' go in an' lay down on my bed, an' I ain't waken up till I hear dat woman scream when she come out into her kitchen. My goodness, but she was surprise! She laugh an' cry at de same time, an' hug me and waken all de children. She ain't stop fur no breakfast; she git de Christmas dinner ready dat morning, and we all sit down an' eat all we can hold. I ain't never seen dat violin boy have all he can hold before.

"Two three days after dat, de two men come to hunt me up, an' dey ask my boss, and he give me a good report an' tell dem I was a steady boy all right. One of dem Bohemians was very smart an' run a Bohemian newspaper in New York, an' de odder was a rich man, in de importing business, an' dey been travelling togedder. Dey told me how t'ings was easier in New York, an' offered to pay my passage when dey was goin' home soon on a boat. My boss say to me: 'You go. You ain't got no chance here, an' I like to see you git ahead, fur you always been a good boy to my woman, and fur dat fine Christmas dinner you give us all.' An' da's how I got to New York."

That night when Rudolph and Polly, arm in arm, were running home across the fields with the bitter wind at their backs, his heart leaped for joy when she said she thought they might have his family come over for supper on New Year's Eve. "Let's get up a nice supper, and not let your mother help at all; make her be company for once."

"That would be lovely of you, Polly," he said humbly. He was a very simple, modest boy, and he, too, felt vaguely that Polly and her sisters were more experienced and worldly than his people.

6

The winter turned out badly for farmers. It was bitterly cold, and after the first light snows before Christmas there was no snow at all, —and no rain. March was as bitter as February. On those days when the wind fairly punished the country, Rosicky sat by his window. In the fall he and the boys had put in a big wheat planting, and now the seed had frozen in the ground. All that land would have to be ploughed up and planted over again, planted in corn. It had happened before, but he was younger then, and he never worried about what had to be. He was sure of himself and of Mary; he knew they could bear what they had to bear, that they would always pull through somehow. But he was not so sure about the young ones, and he felt troubled because Rudolph and Polly were having such a hard start.

Sitting beside his flowering window while the panes rattled and the wind blew in under the door, Rosicky gave himself to reflection as he had not done since those Sundays in the loft of the furniture-factory in New York, long ago. Then he was trying to find what he wanted in life for himself; now he was trying to find what he wanted for his boys, and why it was he so hungered to feel sure they would be here, working this very land, after he was gone.

They would have to work hard on the farm, and probably they

would never do much more than make a living. But if he could think of them as staying here on the land, he wouldn't have to fear any great unkindness for them. Hardships, certainly; it was a hardship to have the wheat freeze in the ground when seed was so high; and to have to sell your stock because you had no feed. But there would be other years when everything came along right, and you caught up. And what you had was your own. You didn't have to choose between bosses and strikers, and go wrong either way. You didn't have to do with dishonest and cruel people. They were the only things in his experience he had found terrifying and horrible; the look in the eyes of a dishonest and crafty man, of a scheming and rapacious woman.

In the country, if you had a mean neighbour, you could keep off his land and make him keep off yours. But in the city, all the foulness and misery and brutality of your neighbours was part of your life. The worst things he had come upon in his journey through the world were human,—depraved and poisonous specimens of man. To this day he could recall certain terrible faces in the London streets. There were mean people everywhere, to be sure, even in their own country town here. But they weren't tempered, hardened, sharpened, like the treacherous people in cities who live by grinding or cheating or poisoning their fellow-men. He had helped to bury two of his fellow-workmen in the tailoring trade, and he was distrustful of the organized industries that see one out of the world in big cities. Here, if you were sick, you had Doctor Ed to look after you; and if you died, fat Mr. Haycock, the kindest man in the world, buried you.

It seemed to Rosicky that for good, honest boys like his, the worst they could do on the farm was better than the best they would be likely to do in the city. If he'd had a mean boy, now, one who was crooked and sharp and tried to put anything over on his brothers, then town would be the place for him. But he had no such boy. As for Rudolph, the discontented one, he would give the shirt off his back to anyone who touched his heart. What Rosicky really hoped for his boys was that they could get through the world without ever knowing much about the cruelty of human beings. "Their mother and me ain't prepared them for that," he sometimes said to himself.

These thoughts brought him back to a grateful consideration of his own case. What an escape he had had, to be sure! He, too, in his time, had had to take money for repair work from the hand of a hungry child who let it go so wistfully; because it was money due his boss. And now, in all these years, he had never had to take a cent from anyone in bitter need,—never had to look at the face of a woman become like a wolf's from struggle and famine. When he thought of these things, Rosicky would put on his cap and jacket and slip down to the barn and give his work-horses a little extra oats, letting them eat it out of his hand in their slobbery fashion. It was his way of expressing what he felt, and made him chuckle with pleasure.

The spring came warm, with blue skies,—but dry, dry as a bone. The boys began ploughing up the wheat-fields to plant them over in corn. Rosicky would stand at the fence corner and watch them, and the earth was so dry it blew up in clouds of brown dust that hid the horses and the sulky plough and the driver. It was a bad outlook.

The big alfalfa-field that lay between the home place and Rudolph's came up green, but Rosicky was worried because during that open windy winter a great many Russian thistle plants had blown in there and lodged. He kept asking the boys to rake them out; he was afraid their seed would root and "take the alfalfa." Rudolph said that was nonsense. The boys were working so hard planting corn, their father felt he couldn't insist about the thistles, but he set great store by that big alfalfa field. It was a feed you could depend on,—and there was some deeper reason, vague, but strong. The peculiar green of that clover woke early memories in old Rosicky, went back to something in his childhood in the old world. When he was a little boy, he had played in fields of that strong blue-green colour.

One morning, when Rudolph had gone to town in the car, leaving a work-team idle in his barn, Rosicky went over to his son's place, put the horses to the buggy-rake, and set about quietly raking up those thistles. He behaved with guilty caution, and rather enjoyed stealing a march on Doctor Ed, who was just then taking his first vacation in seven years of practice and was attending a clinic in Chicago. Rosicky got the thistles raked up, but did not stop to burn them. That would take some time, and his breath was pretty short, so he thought he had better get the horses back to the barn.

He got them into the barn and to their stalls, but the pain had come on so sharp in his chest that he didn't try to take the harness off. He started for the house, bending lower with every step. The cramp in his chest was shutting him up like a jack-knife. When he reached the windmill, he swayed and caught at the ladder. He saw Polly coming down the hill, running with the swiftness of a slim greyhound. In a flash she had her shoulder under his armpit.

"Lean on me, Father, hard! Don't be afraid. We can get to the house all right."

Somehow they did, though Rosicky became blind with pain; he could keep on his legs, but he couldn't steer his course. The next thing he was conscious of was lying on Polly's bed, and Polly bending over him wringing out bath towels in hot water and putting them on his chest. She stopped only to throw coal into the stove, and she kept the tea-kettle and the black pot going. She put these hot applications on him for nearly an hour, she told him afterwards, and all that time he was drawn up stiff and blue, with the sweat pouring off him.

As the pain gradually loosed its grip, the stiffness went out of his jaws, the black circles round his eyes disappeared, and a little of his natural colour came back. When his daughter-in-law buttoned his shirt over his chest at last, he sighed.

"Da's fine, de way I feel now, Polly. It was a awful bad spell, an' I was so sorry it all come on you like it did."

Polly was flushed and excited. "Is the pain really gone? Can I leave you long enough to telephone over to your place?"

Rosicky's eyelids fluttered. "Don't telephone, Polly. It ain't no use to scare my wife. It's nice and quiet here, an' if I ain't too much trouble to you, just let me lay still till I feel like myself. I ain't got no pain now. It's nice here."

Polly bent over him and wiped the moisture from his face. "Oh, I'm so glad it's over!" she broke out impulsively. "It just broke my heart to see you suffer so, Father."

Rosicky motioned her to sit down on the chair where the tea-kettle had been, and looked up at her with that lively affectionate gleam in his eyes. "You was awful good to me, I won't never forgit dat. I hate it to be sick on you like dis. Down at de barn I say to myself, dat young girl ain't had much experience in sickness, I don't want to scare her, an' maybe she's got a baby comin' or somet'ing."

Polly took his hand. He was looking at her so intently and affectionately and confidingly; his eyes seemed to caress her face, to regard it with pleasure. She frowned with her funny streaks of eyebrows, and then smiled back at him.

"I guess maybe there is something of that kind going to happen. But I haven't told anyone yet, not my mother or Rudolph. You'll be the first to know."

His hand pressed hers. She noticed that it was warm again. The twinkle in his yellow-brown eyes seemed to come nearer.

"I like mighty well to see dat little child, Polly," was all he said. Then he closed his eyes and lay half-smiling. But Polly sat still, thinking hard. She had a sudden feeling that nobody in the world, not her mother, not Rudolph, or anyone, really loved her as much as old Rosicky did. It perplexed her. She sat frowning and trying to puzzle it out. It was as if Rosicky had a special gift for loving people, something that was like an ear for music or an eye for colour. It was quiet, unobtrusive; it was merely there. You saw it in his eyes,—perhaps that was why they were merry. You felt it in his hands, too. After he dropped off to sleep, she sat holding his warm, broad, flexible brown hand. She had never seen another in the least like it. She wondered if it wasn't a kind of gypsy hand, it was so alive and quick and light in its communications,—very strange in a farmer. Nearly all the farmers she knew had huge lumps of fists, like mauls, or they were knotty and bony and uncomfortable-looking, with stiff fingers. But Rosicky's was like quicksilver, flexible, muscular, about the colour of a pale cigar, with deep,

deep creases across the palm. It wasn't nervous, it wasn't a stupid lump; it was a warm brown human hand, with some cleverness in it, a great deal of generosity, and something else which Polly could only call "gypsy-like,"—something nimble and lively and sure, in the way that animals are.

Polly remembered that hour long afterwards; it had been like an awakening to her. It seemed to her that she had never learned so much about life from anything as from old Rosicky's hand. It brought her to herself; it communicated some direct and untranslatable message.

When she heard Rudolph coming in the car, she ran out to meet him.

"Oh, Rudy, your father's been awful sick! He raked up those thistles he's been worrying about, and afterwards he could hardly get to the house. He suffered so I was afraid he was going to die."

Rudolph jumped to the ground. "Where is he now?"

"On the bed. He's asleep. I was terribly scared, because, you know, I'm so fond of your father." She slipped her arm through his and they went into the house. That afternoon they took Rosicky home and put him to bed, though he protested that he was quite well again.

The next morning he got up and dressed and sat down to breakfast with his family. He told Mary that his coffee tasted better than usual to him, and he warned the boys not to bear any tales to Doctor Ed when he got home. After breakfast he sat down by his window to do some patching and asked Mary to thread several needles for him before she went to feed her chickens,—her eyes were better than his, and her hands steadier. He lit his pipe and took up John's overalls. Mary had been watching him anxiously all morning, and as she went out of the door with her bucket of scraps, she saw that he was smiling. He was thinking, indeed, about Polly, and how he might never have known what a tender heart she had if he hadn't got sick over there. Girls nowadays didn't wear their heart on their sleeve. But now he knew Polly would make a fine woman after the foolishness wore off. Either a woman had that sweetness at her heart or she hadn't. You couldn't always tell by the look of them; but if they had that, everything came out right in the end.

After he had taken a few stitches, the cramp began in his chest, like yesterday. He put his pipe cautiously down on the window-sill and bent over to ease the pull. No use,—he had better try to get to his bed if he could. He rose and groped his way across the familiar floor, which was rising and falling like the deck of a ship. At the door he fell. When Mary came in, she found him lying there, and the moment she touched him she knew that he was gone.

Doctor Ed was away when Rosicky died, and for the first few weeks after he got home he was hard driven. Every day he said to himself that he must get out to see that family that had lost their father. One soft, warm moonlight night in early summer he started for the farm. His mind was on other things, and not until his road ran by the graveyard did he realize that Rosicky wasn't over there on the hill where the red lamplight shone, but here, in the moonlight. He stopped his car, shut off the engine, and sat there for a while.

A sudden hush had fallen on his soul. Everything here seemed strangely moving and significant, though signifying what, he did not know. Close by the wire fence stood Rosicky's mowing-machine, where one of the boys had been cutting hay that afternoon; his own work-horses had been going up and down there. The new-cut hay perfumed all the night air. The moonlight silvered the long, billowy grass that grew over the graves and hid the fence; the few little evergreens stood out black in it, like shadows in a pool. The sky was very blue and soft, the stars rather faint because the moon was full.

For the first time it struck Doctor Ed that this was really a beautiful graveyard. He thought of city cemeteries; acres of shrubbery and heavy stone, so arranged and lonely and unlike anything in the living world. Cities of the dead, indeed; cities of the forgotten, of the "put away." But this was open and free, this little square of long grass which the wind for ever stirred. Nothing but the sky overhead, and the many-coloured fields running on until they met that sky. The horses worked here in summer; the neighbours passed on their way to town; and over yonder, in the cornfield, Rosicky's own cattle would be eating fodder as winter came on. Nothing could be more undeathlike than this place; nothing could be more right for a man who had helped to do the work of great cities and had always longed for the open country and had got to it at last. Rosicky's life seemed to him complete and beautiful.

1932

The Revolution in the Arts

The modern revolution in the arts which erupted in the first decade of the new century, first in painting and sculpture and then literature, was both a reaction to contemporary change and a renewal of the romantic revolution of the early nineteenth century.

The period of the First World War was a time of cleavage between old and new in aesthetic and social conventions. The world was being transformed by developments in science and technology as well as in politics. The investigations of Freud and the new psychologists were undermining established ideas of human nature, while the old certainties of time and space were dissolving in the universe projected by the new physics, which no longer permitted even the solace of a simple materialism. Concurrently, progress in technology speeded the building of a new machine world by modern man as Promethean engineer. Reacting to their rapidly changing environment, the arts produced a succession of intense and short-lived revolutionary programs—Futurism, Imagism, Vorticism, Dadaism, Surrealism. Each had its day and declined, but all contributed to the development of new aesthetic theories and new techniques.

Nude Descending A Staircase, No. 11, 1912, by Marcel Duchamp
Philadelphia Museum of Art: The Louise and Walter Arensberg Collection

On the eve of the war, the international Imagist movement inaugurated by Ezra Pound and the English critic T. E. Hulme announced specifications for a new poetry distinguished by objectivity, economy of language, and freedom of form. The "tenets" of Imagism, first published in *Poetry: A Magazine of Verse* in March, 1913, deserve to be memorized as a capsulated aesthetic for modern poetry:

      I. Direct treatment of the "thing," whether subjective or objective.

      II. To use absolutely no word that does not contribute to the presentation.

      III. As regarding rhythm: to compose in sequence of the musical phrase, not in sequence of the metronome.

The Imagists insisted upon a hardness and precision to counter the difuseness and verbosity of much Victorian poetry; they rejected the confines of traditional rhyme and meter, substituting the free "sequence of the musical phrase" for a mechanically measured "metronome" rhythm. Their rebellion against outworn Victorian conventions was much like the rebellion of the earlier Romantics against the conventions of Neoclassicism, and their principles of poetic form were a further development of the theory of organic form inaugurated by the Romantics and defined, in America, by Emerson and Whitman. The concept of organicism developed by the Romantics and carried forward by the Imagists and other twentieth century theorists underlies the modern revolution in all the arts.

The importance and influence of Ezra Pound as a crusader in breaking the mold of old forms, pioneering in new ones, and advocating a rigorous discipline for both the critic and the poet cannot easily be overemphasized. He was a tireless promoter of the arts and leader of causes. In the early essay "Vorticism" (1914), he tells the story of the Imagist and Vorticist movements.

His efforts in criticism were supported and extended by T. S. Eliot, whose first prose work, *The Sacred Wood, Essays on Poetry and Criticism,* appeared in 1920, when writers and critics were in general rebellion against prevailing standards in art and taste. Objecting to both impressionism and moralism, Eliot stimulated by precept and example a "technical" criticism concerned with the structural principles of literature—a criticism which he and his followers regarded as "classical" in its traditionalism and its emphasis on impersonality.

Developments in various intellectual disciplines, especially the new science of psychology, also contributed to the modern movement. Gertrude Stein, a decade older than Pound, had been exposed to psychological theory since her student days at Radcliffe in the 1890's, when she studied under William James. Her own experimental writing reflects the influence of both James's idea of the stream of consciousness and Sigmund Freud's theory of the unconscious. Freud's ideas also contributed to Dadaism, that anarchic postwar movement of artists and writers that would accept no conventional restraints upon spontaneous individual expression. (Malcolm Cowley has given an entertaining account of Dada in Paris in his *Exile's Return: A Literary Odyssey of the 1920's* [rev. ed., 1951].) Gertrude Stein's early interest in automatic writing reveals her to be a forerunner and fellow traveler of the Dadaists. Dadaism was supplanted by Surrealism, which has remained an influence.

The looming presence of Theodore Dreiser as a novelist who stayed close to his native American experience and paid little attention to the ideas of the avant-garde is a reminder that the modern movement involved not only new techniques but new attitudes and a new outlook. The iconoclasm and scorn for convention of Dreiser (nourished by nineteenth century mechanistic and nihilistic thought) is typical of the moderns' wholesale rejection of their immediate past. In his pessimism and even cynicism, Dreiser was attuned to the spirit of his times. Disillusionment with tarnished shibboleths was typical of "debunking" social critics and historians at home

The Rude Descending A Staircase (Rush Hour at the Subway), cartoon satirizing the 1913 Armory Show (Boston Museum of Fine Arts).

and of exiled writers of the "lost generation." Their negativism led to positive results, however, as it contributed to the struggle of the American writer and his society for greater freedom from genteel restraints.

The first fruits of the modern movement in literature appeared during the decade of the war as Pound and Eliot and their contemporaries laid the foundations for the new poetry. In fiction, Sherwood Anderson's *Winesburg, Ohio* (1919), which reveals the author's intuitive responses to new developments in technique and outlook, became established as a native classic and inspiration to younger writers. Without the groundbreaking efforts of these pioneers of the modern, it is not likely that America would have achieved the phenomenal production of new poetry and distinguished fiction in the years between the wars.

Ezra Pound   *1885–1972*

The most fiery leader of the modern revolution in poetry, Ezra Loomis Pound was born in Hailey, Idaho, and grew up in a suburb of Philadelphia, where his father was an official in the U.S. Mint. He went to the University of Pennsylvania, where as a sophomore he formed a life-long friendship with a young medical student from Rutherford, New Jersey, William Carlos Williams. Transferring to Hamilton College in 1903, he graduated in 1905 and returned to Pennsylvania for graduate study in Romance literature (M.A., 1906). After a brief stint as an instructor at Wabash College, where he was regarded as too Bohemian and "advanced" for Crawfordsville, Indiana, Pound left the "half-savage country" of his birth for the more cultured atmosphere of Europe. Stopping in Venice, where he arranged for the printing of his first volume of poems, *A Lume Spento* (1908), he proceeded to London, which was to be his home for more than a decade. Here Pound found a publisher for his first commercially-issued books of verse, *Personae* and *Exultations* (1909). During these productive early years Pound, always a tireless promoter, gave generous encouragement and practical aid to other as yet unestablished writers, including Robert Frost, James Joyce, and T. S. Eliot. He was active in such revolutionary movements as Imagism and Vorticism—both chronicled in his early essay, "Vorticism" (1914). He edited the first Imagist anthology, *Des Imagistes*(1914), and acted as foreign editor and chief talent scout for *Poetry*, Harriette Monroe's Chicago magazine of verse. He also kept up a copious correspondence, maintaining contact with old friends like Williams and giving advice to the first of several generations of younger poets.

Pound's long career as a poet and critic embraces three successive phases or stages of development: The first, a period of apprenticeship, during which he devoted himself largely to translations and imitations in traditional forms of earlier Italian and Provençal poets, especially the wandering troubadours, ended about 1912, as Pound became involved in the modernist revolution and began writing in free, or organic, verse. This newer tendency, represented by the published tenets of Imagism, can be seen in many of the poems of *Ripostes* (1913) and in the imagistic and highly effective Chinese poems of *Cathay* (1915), which, although traditional in subject and based on translations from older Chinese poets. like Li-Po, are yet "modern" in tone and technique. What Pound himself came to view as the too-pure aestheticism of his Imagist period altered with his growing social and historical consciousness. Like others of his generation, Pound was deeply shocked and disillusioned by the First World War. The poetic record of this disillusionment and of the poet's view of his own career is given in *Hugh Selwyn Mauberley* (1920), which Pound also described as his farewell to England. Leaving London for the Continent, he spent four years in Paris as a member of the expatriate colony that included Gertrude Stein, Ford Madox Ford, and Hemingway, and then moved on to the Italian Riviera, settling in Rapallo for a long residence. From this time forward, Pound devoted most of his energies to the writing of the *Cantos,* the historically oriented "tale of the tribe," in which the poet, in the role of an Odyssean voyager, undertook the ambitious task of exploring western civilization from the classical past, through the medieval period and the Renaissance, to the modern age, and of prescribing remedies for its cultural ills. The first substantial unit of the larger work, *A Draft of XVI Cantos* (1925), was followed by *A Draft of XXX Cantos* (1930), *Eleven New Cantos: XXXI–XLI* (1934), *The Fifth Decad of Cantos* (1937), and *Cantos LII–LXXI* (1940).

In 1945 Pound, who had been indicted for treason for speaking against the American war effort on radio Rome, was arrested in Genoa by the U. S. Army and sent to a military prison camp near Pisa, where he spent three weeks in solitary confinement in a steel cage before being granted less inhumane treatment. *The Pisan Cantos* (1948), which received the Bollingen Prize for Poetry (and precipitated a famous critical controversy), are based on this prison experience. Following his transfer to Washington, where he was adjudged incompetent to stand trial, Pound was remanded to St. Elizabeth's Hospital. Released in 1958, he returned to Italy. Two subsequent groups of cantos, *Section Rock Drill* (1957) and *Thrones: 96–109 de los Cantares* (1959), are less impressive than *The Pisan Cantos*, which, as the most personal and immediate part of the work, seems a fitting climax and culmination of all that had gone before. At Pisa, Pound had also been working on a favorite long-term project in translation, *The Unwobbling Pivot and the Great Digest of Confucius* (1947).

In addition to his achievement as a poet, Pound's criticism, beginning with his early work *The Spirit of Romance* (1910), has been an important force in twentieth century literature. As a prime mover and shaper of the modernist revolution, Pound disseminated his ideas about the nature and function of poetry (and such other arts as music, sculpture, and painting) and about the relation of the arts to their cultural and economic environment through a multitude of essays and books including *Pavannes and Divisions* (1918), *Instigations* (1920), *How to Read* (1931), *ABC of Economics* (1933), *ABC of Reading* (1934), *Make It New* (1934), *Guide to Kulchur* (1938; American ed. entitled *Culture*), *Patria Mia* (1950), *Money Pamphlets by* £(6 vols., 1950–52), and *Impact: Essays on Ignorance and the Decline of American Civilization* (1960).

Standard editions are *Personae* (New York, 1926), collected poetry exclusive of the Cantos; *The Cantos of Ezra Pound, 1–95* (New York, 1965); *Literary Essays of Ezra Pound*, ed. T. S. Eliot (New York, 1954); and *The Letters of Ezra Pound, 1907–1941*, ed. D. D. Paige (New York, 1950). Useful general introductions to Pound's work include M. L. Rosenthal, *A Primer of Ezra Pound* (New York, 1960) and Walter Sutton, ed., *Ezra Pound: A Collection of Critical Essays* (Englewood Cliffs, N. J., 1963). Helpful aids for the study of individual works are J. H. Edwards and William Vasse, *Annotated Index to* The Cantos *of Ezra Pound* (Berkeley and Los Angeles, 1957); J. J. Espey, *Ezra Pound's* Mauberley: *A Study in Composition* (Berkeley and Los Angeles, 1955); and L. S. Dembo, *The Confucian Odes: A Critical Study* (Berkeley and Los Angeles, 1963). Among many other more general critical studies are Hugh Kenner, *The Poetry of Ezra Pound* (Norfolk, Conn., 1951); Donald Davie, *Ezra Pound: Poet as Sculptor* (London, 1963); and Noel Stock, *Poet in Exile: Ezra Pound* (London, 1964). The only documented biography is Charles Norman, *Ezra Pound* (New York, 1960). The fullest bibliography of Pound's work is Donald Gallup, *A Bibliography of Ezra Pound* (London, 1963).

The text of the poems given here, exclusive of *The Cantos*, is that of *Personae* (New York, 1926). Selections from *The Cantos* are from *The Cantos of Ezra Pound, 1–95* (New York, 1965). The text of "Vorticism" is that of *Fortnightly Review*, XCVI (September 1, 1914), 461–471.

Vorticism

"It is no more ridiculous that a person should receive or convey an emotion by means of an arrangement of shapes, or planes, or colours, than that they should receive or convey such emotion by an arrangement of musical notes."

I suppose this proposition is self-evident. Whistler said as much, some years ago, and Pater proclaimed that "All arts approach the conditions of music."[1]

Whenever I say this I am greeted with a storm of "Yes, but . . . ." "But why isn't this art futurism?" "Why isn't?" "Why don't?" and above all: "What, in Heaven's name, has it got to do with your Imagiste poetry?"

Let me explain at leisure, and in nice, orderly, old-fashioned prose.

We are all futurists to the extent of believing with Guillaume Appollonaire that "On ne peut pas porter *partout* avec soi le cadavre de son père."[2] But "futurism," when it gets into art, is, for the most part, a descendant of impressionism. It is a sort of accelerated impressionism.

---

[1] James Abbot McNeill Whistler (1834–1903), American painter who settled in London in 1863; Walter Pater (1839–1894), English critic and art historian.

[2] "One cannot carry everywhere with one the body of one's father."

There is another artistic descent *via* Picasso and Kandinsky;[3] *via* cubism and expressionism. One does not complain of neo-impression or of accelerated impressionism and "simultaneity," but one is not wholly satisfied by them. One has perhaps other needs.

It is very difficult to make generalities about three arts at once. I shall be, perhaps, more lucid if I give, briefly, the history of the vorticist art with which I am most intimately connected, that is to say, vorticist poetry. Vorticism has been announced as including such and such painting and sculpture and "Imagisme" in verse. I shall explain "Imagisme," and then proceed to show its inner relation to certain modern paintings and sculpture.

Imagisme, in so far as it has been known at all, has been known chiefly as a stylistic movement, as a movement of criticism rather than of creation. This is natural, for, despite all possible celerity of publication, the public is always, and of necessity, some years behind the artists' actual thought. Nearly anyone is ready to accept "Imagisme" as a department of poetry, just as one accepts "lyricism" as a department of poetry.

There is a sort of poetry where music, sheer melody, seems as if it were just bursting into speech.

There is another sort of poetry where painting or sculpture seems as if it were "just coming over into speech."

The first sort of poetry has long been called "lyric." One is accustomed to distinguish easily between "lyric" and "epic" and "didactic." One is capable of finding the "lyric" passages in a drama or in a long poem not otherwise "lyric." This division is in the grammars and school books, and one has been brought up to it.

The other sort of poetry is as old as the lyric and as honourable, but, until recently, no one had named it. Ibycus and Liu Ch'e[4] presented the "Image." Dante is a great poet by reason of this faculty, and Milton is a wind-bag because of his lack of it. The "image" is the furthest possible remove from rhetoric. Rhetoric is the art of dressing up some unimportant matter so as to fool the audience for the time being. So much for the general category. Even Aristotle distinguishes between rhetoric, "which is persuasion," and the analytical examination of truth. As a "critical" movement, the "Imagisme" of 1912 to '14 set out "to bring poetry up to the level of prose." No one is so quixotic as to believe that contemporary poetry holds any such position. . . . Stendhal formulated the need in his *De L'Amour*: —

"La poésie avec ses comparaisons obligées, sa mythologie que ne croit pas le poète, sa dignité de style à la Louis XIV, et tout l'attirail de ses ornements

---

[3] Pablo Picasso (1884–1973) and Wassily Kandinsky (1866–1944), leaders of the modern revolution in painting.
[4] Ibycus (5th century B.C.), Greek lyric poet; Liu Chi, a 14th-century Chinese poet and painter.

appelé poétique, est bien au dessous de la prose dès qu'il s'agit de donner une idée claire et précise des mouvements du cœur, or dans ce genre on n'émeut que par la clarté."[5]

Flaubert and De Maupassant lifted prose to the rank of a finer art, and one has no patience with contemporary poets who escape from all the difficulties of the infinitely difficult art of good prose by pouring themselves into loose verses.

The tenets of the Imagiste faith were published in March, 1913,[6] as follows: —

I. Direct treatment of the "thing," whether subjective or objective.

II. To use absolutely no word that does not contribute to the presentation.

III. As regarding rhythm: to compose in sequence of the musical phrase, not in sequence of the metronome.

There followed a series of about forty cautions to beginners, which need not concern us here.

The arts have indeed "some sort of common bond, some inter-recognition." Yet certain emotions or subjects find their most appropriate expression in some one particular art. The work of art which is most "worth while" is the work which would need a hundred works of any other kind of art to explain it. A fine statue is the core of a hundred poems. A fine poem is a score of symphonies. There is music which would need a hundred paintings to express it. There is no synonym for the *Victory of Samothrace*[7] or for Mr. Epstein's flemites.[8] There is no painting of Villon's *Frères Humains*. Such works are what we call works of the "first intensity."

A given subject or emotion belongs to that artist, or to that sort of artist who must know it most intimately and most intensely before he can render it adequately in his art. A painter must know much more about a sunset than a writer, if he is to put it on canvas. But when the poet speaks of "Dawn in russet mantle clad," he presents something which the painter cannot present.

I said in the preface to my *Guido Cavalcanti*[9] that I believed in an absolute rhythm. I believe that every emotion and every phase of emotion has some toneless phrase, some rhythm-phrase to express it.

(This belief leads to *vers libre* and to experiments in quantitative verse.)

[5] "Poetry, with its necessary comparisons, its mythology that the poet does not believe, its elevation of style à la Louis XIV, and all the paraphernalia of its ornaments, called poetic, is much inferior to prose when it struggles to present a clear and precise idea of the impulses of the heart, but in this genre (prose) one does not arouse except by clarity."

[6] In *Poetry: A Magazine of Verse* (Chicago), together with the definition of the image given below in note 13.

[7] Classical Greek sculpture in the Louvre in Paris; also known as the *Winged Victory*.

[8] Sculptures by Jacob Epstein (1880–1959), New York-born English sculptor.

[9] *The Sonnets and Ballate of Guido Cavalcanti* (Boston, 1912).

To hold a like belief in a sort of permanent metaphor is, as I understand it, "symbolism" in its profounder sense. It is not necessarily a belief in a permanent world, but it is a belief in that direction.

Imagisme is not symbolism. The symbolists dealt in "association," that is, in a sort of allusion, almost of allegory. They degraded the symbol to the status of a word. They made it a form of metonomy. One can be grossly "symbolic," for example, by using the term "cross" to mean "trial." The symbolist's *symbols* have a fixed value, like numbers in arithmetic, like 1, 2, and 7. The imagiste's images have a variable significance, like the signs *a*, *b*, and *x* in algebra.

Moreover, one does not want to be called a symbolist, because symbolism has usually been associated with mushy technique.

On the other hand, Imagisme is not Impressionism, though one borrows, or could borrow, much from the impressionist method of presentation. But this is only negative definition. If I am to give a psychological or philosophical definition "from the inside," I can only do so autobiographically. The precise statement of such a matter must be based on one's own experience.

In the "search for oneself," in the search for "sincere self-expression," one gropes, one finds some seeming verity. One says "I am" this, that, or the other, and with the words scarcely uttered one ceases to be that thing.

I began this search for the real in a book called *Personæ*,[10] casting off, as it were, complete masks of the self in each poem. I continued in long series of translations, which were but more elaborate masks.

Secondly, I made poems like "The Return," which is an objective reality and has a complicated sort of significance, like Mr. Epstein's "Sun God," or Mr. Brzeska's "Boy with a Coney."[11] Thirdly, I have written "Heather," which represents a state of consciousness, or "implies," or "implicates" it.

A Russian correspondent, after having called it a symbolist poem, and having been convinced that it was not symbolism, said slowly: "I see, you wish to give people new eyes, not to make them see some new particular thing."

These two latter sorts of poems are impersonal, and that fact brings us back to what I said about absolute metaphor. They are Imagisme, and in so far as they are Imagisme, they fall in with the new pictures and the new sculpture.

Whistler said somewhere in the *Gentle Art*[12]: "The picture is interesting not because it is Trotty Veg, but because it is an arrange-

---

[10] *Personae* (London, 1909), Pound's first commercially published book of poems. He used the same title for the collected edition (1926) of his poems other than the Cantos.

[11] Sculpture by Henri Gaudier-Brzeska (1891–1915), French-born sculptor and close friend of Pound during his early years in London. See Pound's poem "The Return" below.

[12] *The Gentle Art of Making Enemies* (London, 1890).

ment in colour." The minute you have admitted that, you let in the jungle, you let in nature and truth and abundance and cubism and Kandinsky, and the lot of us. Whistler and Kandinsky and some cubists were set to getting extraneous matter out of their art; they were ousting literary values. The Flaubertians talk a good deal about "constatation." "The 'nineties" saw a movement against rhetoric. I think all these things move together, though they do not, of course, move in step.

The painters realise that what matters is form and colour. Musicians long ago learned that programme music was not the ultimate music. Almost anyone can realise that to use a symbol *with an ascribed or intended meaning* is, usually, to produce very bad art. We all remember crowns, and crosses, and rainbows, and what not in atrociously mumbled colour.

The Image is the poet's pigment.[13] The painter should use his colour because he sees it or feels it. I don't much care whether he is representative or non-representative. He should *depend*, of course, on the creative, not upon the mimetic or representational part in his work. It is the same in writing poems, the author must use his *image* because he sees it or feels it, *not* because he thinks he can use it to back up some creed or some system of ethics or economics.

An *image*, in our sense, is real because we know it directly. If it have an age-old traditional meaning this may serve as proof to the professional student of symbology that we have stood in the deathless light, or that we have walked in some particular arbour of his traditional paradiso, but that is not our affair. It is our affair to render the *image* as we have perceived or conceived it.

Browning's "Sordello"[14] is one of the finest *masks* ever presented. Dante's "Paradiso" is the most wonderful *image*. By that I do not mean that it is a perseveringly imagistic performance. The permanent part is Imagisme, the rest, the discourses with the calendar of saints and the discussions about the nature of the moon, are philology. The form of sphere above sphere, the varying reaches of light, the minutiæ of pearls upon foreheads, all these are parts of the Image. The image is the poet's pigment; with that in mind you can go ahead and apply Kandinsky, you can transpose his chapter on the language of form and colour and apply it to the writing of verse. As I cannot rely on your having read Kandinsky's *Ueber das Geistige in der Kunst*,[15] I must go on with my autobiography.

Three years ago in Paris I got out of a "metro" train at La Concorde, and saw suddenly a beautiful face, and then another and another,

---

[13] The Image has been defined as "that which presents an intellectual and emotional complex in an instant of time" (E. P.). See note 6 above.

[14] *Sordello* (1840), a long narrative poem based on legendary stories of the life of the title character, a 12th-century Provençal poet.

[15] *Concerning the Spiritual in Art.*

and then a beautiful child's face, and then another beautiful woman, and I tried all that day to find words for what this had meant to me, and I could not find any words that seemed to me worthy, or as lovely as that sudden emotion. And that evening, as I went home along the Rue Raynouard, I was still trying, and I found, suddenly, the expression. I do not mean that I found words, but there came an equation . . . not in speech, but in little splotches of colour. It was just that — a "pattern," or hardly a pattern, if by "pattern" you mean something with a "repeat" in it. But it was a word, the beginning, for me, of a language in colour. I do not mean that I was unfamiliar with the kindergarten stories about colours being like tones in music. I think that sort of thing is nonsense. If you try to make notes permanently correspond with particular colours, it is like tying narrow meanings to symbols.

That evening, in the Rue Raynouard, I realised quite vividly that if I were a painter, or if I had, often, *that kind* of emotion, or even if I had the energy to get paints and brushes and keep at it, I might found a new school of painting, of "non-representative" painting, a painting that would speak only by arrangements in colour.

And so, when I came to read Kandinsky's chapter on the language of form and colour, I found little that was new to me. I only felt that someone else understood what I understood, and had written it out very clearly. It seems quite natural to me that an artist should have just as much pleasure in an arrangement of planes or in a pattern of figures, as in painting portraits of fine ladies, or in portraying the Mother of God as the symbolists bid us.

When I find people ridiculing the new arts, or making fun of the clumsy odd terms that we use in trying to talk of them amongst ourselves; when they laugh at our talking about the "ice-block quality" in Picasso, I think it is only because they do not know what thought is like, and that they are familiar only with argument and gibe and opinion. That is to say, they can only enjoy what they have been brought up to consider enjoyable, or what some essayist has talked about in mellifluous phrases. They think only "the shells of thought," as De Gourmont[16] calls them; the thoughts that have been already thought out by others.

Any mind that is worth calling a mind must have needs beyond the existing categories of language, just as a painter must have pigments or shades more numerous than the existing names of the colours.

Perhaps this is enough to explain the words in my "Vortex": —

"Every concept, every emotion, presents itself to the vivid consciousness in some primary form. It belongs to the art of this form."[17]

[16] Remy de Gourmont (d. 1915), French critic and editor of the influential journal *Mercure de France.*
[17] Appearing in the July number of *Blast* (E. P.), the Vorticist little magazine edited by Percy Wyndham Lewis, (1884 – 1957), painter and novelist.

That is to say, my experience in Paris should have gone into paint. If instead of colour I had perceived sound or planes in relation, I should have expressed it in music or in sculpture. Colour was, in that instance, the "primary pigment"; I mean that it was the first adequate equation that came into consciousness. The Vorticist uses the "primary pigment." Vorticism is art before it has spread itself into flaccidity, into elaboration and secondary applications.

What I have said of one vorticist art can be transposed for another vorticist art. But let me go on then with my own branch of vorticism, about which I can probably speak with greater clarity. All poetic language is the language of exploration. Since the beginning of bad writing, writers have used images as ornaments. The point of Imagisme is that it does not use images *as ornaments*. The image is itself the speech. The image is the word beyond formulated language.

I once saw a small child go to an electric light switch and say, "Mamma, can I *open* the light?" She was using the age-old language of exploration, the language of art. It was a sort of metaphor, but she was not using it as ornamentation.

One is tired of ornamentations, they are all a trick, and any sharp person can learn them.

The Japanese have had the sense of exploration. They have understood the beauty of this sort of knowing. A Chinaman said long ago that if a man can't say what he has to say in twelve lines he had better keep quiet. The Japanese have evolved the still shorter form of the *hokku*.

> "The fallen blossom flies back to its branch:
> A butterfly."

That is the substance of a very well-known *hokku*. Victor Plarr[18] tells me that once, when he was walking over snow with a Japanese naval officer, they came to a place where a cat had crossed the path, and the officer said, "Stop, I am making a poem." Which poem was, roughly, as follows: —

> "The footsteps of the cat upon the snow:
> (are like) plum-blossoms."

The words "are like" would not occur in the original, but I add them for clarity.

The "one image poem" is a form of super-position, that is to say it is one idea set on top of another. I found it useful in getting out of the impasse in which I had been left by my metro emotion. I wrote a thirty-line poem, and destroyed it because it was what we call work "of second intensity." Six months later I made a poem half that length; a year later I made the following *hokku*-like sentence: —

---

[18] See Pound's treatment of Victor Plarr in *Mauberley*. (note 24).

> "The apparition of these faces in the crowd:
> Petals, on a wet, black bough."

I dare say it is meaningless unless one has drifted into a certain vein of thought.[19] In a poem of this sort one is trying to record the precise ⟵ instant when a thing outward and objective transforms itself, or darts into a thing inward and subjective.

This particular sort of consciousness has not been identified with impressionist art. I think it is worthy of attention.

The logical end of impressionist art is the cinematograph. The state of mind of the impressionist tends to become cinematographical. Or, to put it another way, the cinematograph does away with the need of a lot of impressionist art.

There are two opposed ways of thinking of a man; firstly, you may think of him as that toward which perception moves, as the toy of circumstance, as the plastic substance *receiving* impressions; secondly, you may think of him as directing a certain fluid force against circumstance, as *conceiving* instead of merely reflecting and observing. One does not claim that one way is better than the other, one notes a diversity of the temperament. The two camps always exist. In the 'eighties there were symbolists opposed to impressionists, now you have vorticism, which is, roughly speaking, expressionism, neo-cubism, and imagism gathered together in one camp and futurism in the other. Futurism is descended from impressionism. It is, in so far as it is an art movement, a kind of accelerated impressionism. It is a spreading, or surface art, as opposed to vorticism, which is intensive.

The vorticist has not this curious tic for destroying past glories. I have no doubt that Italy needed Mr. Marinetti,[20] but he did not set on the egg that hatched me, and as I am wholly opposed to his æsthetic principles I see no reason why I, and various men who agree with me, should be expected to call ourselves futurists. We do not desire to evade comparison with the past. We prefer that the comparison be made by some intelligent person whose idea of "the tradition" is not limited by the conventional taste of four or five centuries and one continent.

Vorticism is an intensive art. I mean by this, that one is concerned with the relative intensity, or relative significance, of different sorts of expression. One desires the most intense, for certain forms of expression *are* "more intense" than others. They are more dynamic. I do not mean they are more emphatic, or that they are yelled louder. I can explain my meaning best by mathematics.

There are four different intensities of mathematical expression

[19] Mr. Flint and Mr. Rodker have made longer poems depending on a similar presentation of matter. So also have Richard Aldington, in his *In Via Sestina*, and "H. D." in her *Oread*, which latter poems express much stronger emotions than that in my lines here given (E. P.).
[20] Filippo Tomaso Marinetti, Italian poet and propagandist for the Futurist movement.

known to the ordinarily intelligent undergraduate, namely: the arithmetical, the algebraic, the geometrical, and that of analytical geometry.

For instance, you can write

$$3 \times 3 + 4 \times 4 = 5 \times 5,$$
or, differently, $3^2 + 4^2 = 5^2$.

That is merely conversation or "ordinary common sense." It is a simple statement of one fact, and does not implicate any other.

Secondly, it is true that

$$3^2 + 4^2 = 5^2, 6^2 + 8^2 = 10^2, 9^2 + 12^2 = 15^2, 39^2 + 52^2 = 65^2.$$

These are all separate facts, one may wish to mention their underlying similarity; it is a bore to speak about each one in turn. One expresses their "algebraic relation" as

$$a^2 + b^2 = c^2.$$

That is the language of philosophy. IT MAKES NO PICTURE. This kind of statement applies to a lot of facts, but it does not grip hold of Heaven.

Thirdly, when one studies Euclid one finds that the relation of $a^2 + b^2 = c^2$ applies to the ratio between the squares on the two sides of a right-angled triangle and the square on the hypotenuse. One still writes it $a^2 + b^2 = c^2$, but one has begun to talk about form. Another property or quality of life has crept into one's matter. Until then one had dealt only with numbers. But even this statement does not *create* form. The picture is given you in the proposition about the square on the hypotenuse of the right-angled triangle being equal to the sum of the squares on the two other sides. Statements in plane or descriptive geometry are like talk about art. They are a criticism of the form. The form is not created by them.

Fourthly, we come to Descartian or "analytical geometry." Space is conceived as separated by two or by three axes (depending on whether one is treating form in one or more planes). One refers points to these axes by a series of coefficients. Given the idiom, one is able *actually to create*.

Thus, we learn that the equation $(x - a)^2 + (y - b)^2 = r^2$ governs the circle. It is the circle. It is not a particular circle, it is any circle and all circles. It is nothing that is not a circle. It is the circle free of space and time limits. It is the universal, existing in perfection, in freedom from space and time. Mathematics is dull as ditchwater until one reaches analytics. But in analytics we come upon a new way of dealing with form. It is in this way that art handles life. The difference between art and analytical geometry is the difference of subject-matter only. Art is more interesting in proportion as life and the human consciousness are more complex and more interesting than forms and numbers.

This statement does not interfere in the least with "spontaneity" and "intuition," or with their function in art. I passed my last *exam.* in mathematics on sheer intuition. I saw where the line *had* to go, as clearly as I ever saw an image, or felt *caelestem intus vigorem*.[21]

The statements of "analytics" are "lords" over fact. They are the thrones and dominations that rule over form and recurrence. And in like manner are great works of art lords over fact, over race-long recurrent moods, and over to-morrow.

Great works of art contain this fourth sort of equation. They cause form to come into being. By the "image" I mean such an equation; not an equation of mathematics, not something about *a*, *b*, and *c*, having something to do with form, but about *sea*, *cliffs*, *night*, having something to do with mood.

The image is not an idea. It is a radiant node or cluster; it is what I can, and must perforce, call a VORTEX, from which, and through which, and into which, ideas are constantly rushing. In decency one can ⟵ only call it a VORTEX. And from this necessity came the name "vorticism." *Nomina sunt consequentia rerum*,[22] and never was that statement of Aquinas more true than in the case of the vorticist movement.

It is as true for the painting and the sculpture as it is for the poetry. Mr. Wadsworth and Mr. Lewis are not using words,[23] they are using shape and colour. Mr. Brzeska and Mr. Epstein are using "planes in relation," they are dealing with a relation of planes different from the sort of relation of planes dealt with in geometry, hence what is called "the need of organic forms in sculpture."

I trust I have made clear what I mean by an "intensive art." The vorticist movement is not a movement of mystification, though I dare say many people "of good will" have been considerably bewildered.

The organisation of forms is a much more energetic and creative action than the copying or imitating of light on a haystack.

There is undoubtedly a language of form and colour. It is not a symbolical or allegorical language depending on certain meanings having been ascribed, in books, to certain signs and colours.

Certain artists working in different media have managed to understand each other. They know the good and bad in each other's work, which they could not know unless there were a common speech.

As for the excellence of certain contemporary artists, all I can do is to stand up for my own beliefs. I believe that Mr. Wyndham Lewis is a very great master of design; that he has brought into our art new units of design and new manners of organisation. I think that his series "Timon" is a great work. I think he is the most articulate expression of my own decade. If you ask me what his "Timon" means, I can reply by asking you what the old play means. For me his designs are a creation on the same *motif*. That *motif* is the fury of intelligence baffled and shut

---

[21] "Divine energy within."
[22] "Names are the consequence of things."
[23] Edward Wadsworth, (1889 – 1949), English painter; for Wyndham Lewis, see above, note 17.

in by circumjacent stupidity. It is an emotional *motif*. Mr. Lewis's painting is nearly always emotional.

Mr. Wadsworth's work gives me pleasure, sometimes like the pleasure I have received from Chinese and Japanese prints and painting; for example, I derive such pleasure from Mr. Wadsworth's "Khaki." Sometimes his work gives me a pleasure which I can only compare to the pleasure I have in music, in music as it was in Mozart's time. If an outsider wishes swiftly to understand this new work, he can do worse than approach it in the spirit wherein he approaches music.

"Lewis is Bach." No, it is incorrect to say that "Lewis is Bach," but our feeling is that certain works of Picasso and certain works of Lewis have in them something which is to painting what certain qualities of Bach are to music. Music was vorticist in the Bach-Mozart period, before it went off into romance and sentiment and description. A new vorticist music would come from a new computation of the mathematics of harmony, not from a mimetic representation of dead cats in a fog-horn, alias noise-tuners.

Mr. Epstein is too well known to need presentation in this article. Mr. Brzeska's sculpture is so generally recognised in all camps that one does not need to bring in a brief concerning it. Mr. Brzeska has defined sculptural feeling as "the appreciation of masses in relation," and sculptural ability as "the defining of these masses by planes." There comes a time when one is more deeply moved by that form of intelligence which can present "masses in relation" than by that combination of patience and trickery which can make marble chains with free links and spin out bronze until it copies the feathers on a general's hat. Mr. Etchells still remains more or less of a mystery.[24] He is on his travels, whence he has sent back a few excellent drawings. It cannot be made too clear that the work of the vorticists and the "feeling of inner need" existed before the general noise about vorticism. We worked separately, we found an underlying agreement, we decided to stand together.[25]

1914

---

[24] Pound's statement still holds.

[25] I am often asked whether there can be a long imagiste or vorticist poem. The Japanese, who evolved the hokku, evolved also the Noh plays. In the best "Noh" the whole play may consist of one image. I mean it is gathered about one image. Its unity consists in one image, enforced by movement and music. I see nothing against a long vorticist poem.

On the other hand, no artist can possibly get a vortex into every poem or picture he does. One would like to do so, but it is beyond one. Certain things seem to demand metrical expression, or expression in a rhythm more agitated than the rhythms acceptable to prose, and these subjects, though they do not contain a vortex, may have some interest, an interest as "criticism of life" or of art. It is natural to express these things, and a vorticist or imagiste writer may be justified in presenting a certain amount of work which is not vorticism or imagisme, just as he might be justified in printing a purely didactic prose article. Unfinished sketches and drawings have a similar interest; they are trials and attempts toward a vortex (E. P.).

The Seafarer [1]

(FROM THE ANGLO-SAXON)

May I for my own self song's truth reckon,
Journey's jargon, how I in harsh days
Hardship endured oft.
Bitter breast-cares have I abided,
Known on my keel many a care's hold,
And dire sea-surge, and there I oft spent
Narrow nightwatch nigh the ship's head
While she tossed close to cliffs. Coldly afflicted,
My feet were by frost benumbed.
Chill its chains are; chafing sighs   10
Hew my heart round and hunger begot
Mere-weary mood. Lest man know not
That he on dry land loveliest liveth,
List how I, care-wretched, on ice-cold sea,
Weathered the winter, wretched outcast
Deprived of my kinsmen;
Hung with hard ice-flakes, where hail-scur flew,
There I heard naught save the harsh sea
And ice-cold wave, at whiles the swan cries,
Did for my games the gannet's clamour,   20
Sea-fowls' loudness was for me laughter,
The mews' singing all my mead-drink.
Storms, on the stone-cliffs beaten, fell on the stern
In icy feathers; full oft the eagle screamed
With spray on his pinion.
                              Not any protector
May make merry man faring needy.
This he little believes, who aye in winsome life
Abides 'mid burghers some heavy business,
Wealthy and wine-flushed, how I weary oft   30
Must bide above brine.
Neareth nightshade, snoweth from north,
Frost froze the land, hail fell on earth then,
Corn of the coldest. Nathless there knocketh now
The heart's thought that I on high streams
The salt-wavy tumult traverse alone.
Moaneth alway my mind's lust
That I fare forth, that I afar hence
Seek out a foreign fastness.
For this there's no mood-lofty man over earth's midst,   40
Not though he be given his good, but will have in his youth greed;
Nor his deed to the daring, nor his king to the faithful

---

[1] "The Seafarer" (author and date of composition unknown) is perhaps the finest surviving Old English lyric poem. Pound's translation slightly reduces the 108 lines of the original poem.

But shall have his sorrow for sea-fare
Whatever his lord will.
He hath not heart for harping, nor in ring-having
Nor winsomeness to wife, nor world's delight
Nor any whit else save the wave's slash,
Yet longing comes upon him to fare forth on the water.
Bosque taketh blossom, cometh beauty of berries,
Fields to fairness, land fares brisker,   50
All this admonisheth man eager of mood,
The heart turns to travel so that he then thinks
On flood-ways to be far departing.
Cuckoo calleth with gloomy crying,
He singeth summerward, bodeth sorrow,
The bitter heart's blood. Burgher knows not —
He the prosperous man — what some perform
Where wandering them widest draweth.
So that but now my heart burst from my breastlock,
My mood 'mid the mere-flood,   60
Over the whale's acre, would wander wide.
On earth's shelter cometh oft to me,
Eager and ready, the crying lone-flyer,
Whets for the whale-path the heart irresistibly,
O'er tracks of ocean; seeing that anyhow
My lord deems to me this dead life
On loan and on land, I believe not
That any earth-weal eternal standeth
Save there be somewhat calamitous
That, ere a man's tide go, turn it to twain.   70
Disease or oldness or sword-hate
Beats out the breath from doom-gripped body.
And for this, every earl whatever, for those speaking after —
Laud of the living, boasteth some last word,
That he will work ere he pass onward,
Frame on the fair earth 'gainst foes his malice,
Daring ado, . . .
So that all men shall honour him after
And his laud beyond them remain 'mid the English,
Aye, for ever, a lasting life's-blast,   80
Delight 'mid the doughty.
                              Days little durable,
And all arrogance of earthen riches,
There come now no kings nor Cæsars
Nor gold-giving lords like those gone.
Howe'er in mirth most magnified,
Whoe'er lived in life most lordliest,
Drear all this excellence, delights undurable!
Waneth the watch, but the world holdeth.
Tomb hideth trouble. The blade is layed low.   90
Earthly glory ageth and seareth.

No man at all going the earth's gait,
But age fares against him, his face paleth,
Grey-haired he groaneth, knows gone companions,
Lordly men, are to earth o'ergiven,
Nor may he then the flesh-cover, whose life ceaseth,
Nor eat the sweet nor feel the sorry,
Nor stir hand nor think in mid heart,
And though he strew the grave with gold,
His born brothers, their buried bodies   100
Be an unlikely treasure hoard.

1912

The Return

See, they return; ah, see the tentative
Movements, and the slow feet,
The trouble in the pace and the uncertain
Wavering!

See, they return, one, and by one,
With fear, as half-awakened;
As if the snow should hesitate
And murmur in the wind,
   and half turn back;
These were the "Wing'd-with-Awe,"   10
  Inviolable.

Gods of the wingèd shoe!
With them the silver hounds,
   sniffing the trace of air!

Haie! Haie!
  These were the swift to harry;
These the keen-scented;
These were the souls of blood.

Slow on the leash,
   pallid the leash-men!   20
1912

The River-Merchant's Wife: A Letter

While my hair was still cut straight across my forehead
I played about the front gate, pulling flowers.
You came by on bamboo stilts, playing horse,
You walked about my seat, playing with blue plums.

And we went on living in the village of Chokan:
Two small people, without dislike or suspicion.

At fourteen I married My Lord you.
I never laughed, being bashful.
Lowering my head, I looked at the wall.
Called to, a thousand times, I never looked back.   10

At fifteen I stopped scowling,
I desired my dust to be mingled with yours
Forever and forever and forever.
Why should I climb the look out?

At sixteen you departed,
You went into far Ku-to-yen, by the river of swirling eddies,
And you have been gone five months.
The monkeys make sorrowful noise overhead.
You dragged your feet when you went out.
By the gate now, the moss is grown, the different mosses,   20
Too deep to clear them away!
The leaves fall early this autumn, in wind.
The paired butterflies are already yellow with August
Over the grass in the West garden;
They hurt me. I grow older.
If you are coming down through the narrows of the river Kiang,
Please let me know beforehand,
And I will come out to meet you   30
      As far as Cho-fu-Sa.

                       By Rihaku[1]

                       1915

Taking Leave of a Friend

Blue mountains to the north of the walls,
White river winding about them;
Here we must make separation
And go out through a thousand miles of dead grass.

Mind like a floating wide cloud,
Sunset like the parting of old acquaintances
Who bow over their clasped hands at a distance.
Our horses neigh to each other
      as we are departing.

                       By Rihaku

                       1915

---

[1] Rihaku is the Japanese form of the name of the Chinese poet Li Po (701–762).

In a Station of the Metro[1]

The apparition of these faces in the crowd:
Petals on a wet, black bough.

1916

Hugh Selwyn Mauberley

LIFE AND CONTACTS

I

E. P. Ode Pour L'Election De Son Sepulchre[1]

For three years, out of key with his time,
He strove to resuscitate the dead art
Of poetry; to maintain "the sublime"
In the old sense. Wrong from the start —

No, hardly, but seeing he had been born
In a half savage country, out of date;
Bent resolutely on wringing lilies from the acorn;
Capaneus;[2] trout for factitious bait;

Ἴδμεν γάρ τοι πάνθ᾽, ὅσ᾽ ἐνὶ Τροίῃ[3]
Caught in the unstopped ear;
Giving the rocks small lee-way   10
The chopped seas held him, therefore, that year.

His true Penelope was Flaubert,
He fished by obstinate isles;
Observed the elegance of Circe's hair
Rather than the mottoes on sun-dials.

Unaffected by "the march of events,"
He passed from men's memory in *l'an trentiesme*
De son eage;[4] the case presents
No adjunct to the Muses' diadem.   20

---

[1] The "Metro" is the Paris subway. Although this *haiku*-like poem was not printed in a collection until its appearance in *Lustra* (1916), Pound earlier described the circumstances of its composition in his essay "Vorticism" (1914).

[1] "E. P. Ode on the Selection of His Tomb." The title is borrowed from an ode ("L'Election de son sépulchre") by Pierre de Ronsard (1524–1585).

[2] In Aeschylus' *The Seven Against Thebes*, Capaneus was struck dead by Zeus for swearing that he would defy him by forcing entrance into Thebes.

[3] "For we know everything which is in Troy," from the Sirens' song in the *Odyssey* (Book XII, 1. 189).

[4] "In the thirtieth year of his age," a slightly altered version of the first line of "The Testament" of François Villon (b. 1431).

adjunct-not essential   diadem-crown, authority   Muse- artistic inspiration goddesses of the arts

II

The age demanded an image
Of its accelerated grimace,
Something for the modern stage,
Not, at any rate, an Attic grace;

Not, not certainly, the obscure reveries
Of the inward gaze;
Better mendacities
Than the classics in paraphrase!

The "age demanded" chiefly a mould in plaster,
Made with no loss of time,   10
A prose kinema, not, not assuredly, alabaster
Or the "sculpture" of rhyme.

* motion in the abstract

III

The tea-rose tea-gown, etc.
Supplants the mousseline of Cos,[5]
The pianola "replaces"
Sappho's barbitos.

Christ follows Dionysus,
Phallic and ambrosial
Made way for macerations; - grow thin/soften
Caliban casts out Ariel.[6]

All things are a flowing.
Sage Heracleitus[7] says;   10
But a tawdry cheapness
Shall outlast our days.

Even the Christian beauty
Defects — after Samothrace;[8]
We see τὸ καλόν[9]
Decreed in the market place.

Faun's flesh is not to us,
Nor the saint's vision.
We have the press for wafer;
Franchise for circumcision.   20

[5] Cos, an Aegean island.
[6] An allusion to the gross and earthy Caliban and the ethereal Ariel of Shakespeare's *The Tempest*.
[7] Heraclitus (6th century, B.C.), the philosopher of flux.
[8] An Aegean island; the allusion may be to the sculpture known as the Winged Victory of Samothrace.
[9] "The beautiful."

reverie- fanciful dream   mendacities~lies

All men, in law, are equals.
Free of Pisistratus,[10]
We choose a knave or an eunuch
To rule over us.

O bright Apollo,
τίν' ἄνδρα, τίν' ἥρωα, τίνα θεόν,[11]
What god, man, or hero
Shall I place a tin wreath upon!

IV

Anti-war (WW I)

These fought in any case,
and some believing,
　　　　　pro domo,[12] in any case . . .

Some quick to arm,
some for adventure,
some from fear of weakness,
some from fear of censure,
some for love of slaughter, in imagination,
learning later . . .
some in fear, learning love of slaughter;

10

Died some, pro patria,
　　　　　non "dulce" non "et decor" . . .[13]
walked eye-deep in hell
believing in old men's lies, then unbelieving
came home, home to a lie,
home to many deceits,
home to old lies and new infamy;
<u>usury</u> age-old and age-thick
and liars in public places.

Pound hated usury, a new feudalism, - and the non-productive money earning class.

Daring as never before, wastage as never before.
Young blood and high blood,
fair cheeks, and fine bodies;

20

fortitude as never before

frankness as never before,
disillusions as never told in the old days,
hysterias, trench confessions,
laughter out of dead bellies.

---

[10] Pisistratus, an Athenian dictator of the 6th century B.C. *also intellectual leader*
[11] "What man, what hero, what god," an altered version of a verse (1. 2) from Pindar's "Second Olympian Ode." The English *tin* echoes the Greek τίν'.
[12] "For home."
[13] An ironic allusion to the line from Horace (*Odes*, III, ii, 13): *"Dulce et decorum est pro patria mori"* ("It is sweet and fitting to die for one's country").

V

There died a myriad,
And of the best, among them,
For an old bitch gone in the teeth,
For a botched civilization,

Charm, smiling at the good mouth,
Quick eyes gone under earth's lid,

For two gross of broken statues,
For a few thousand battered books.

Yeux Glauques[14]

Gladstone[15] was still respected,
When John Ruskin produced
"King's Treasuries";[16] Swinburne
And Rossetti still abused.

Fœtid Buchanan[17] lifted up his voice
When that faun's head of hers[18]
Became a pastime for
Painters and adulterers.

The Burne-Jones cartons[19]
Have preserved her eyes;   10
Still, at the Tate, they teach
Cophetua to rhapsodize;[20]

Thin like brook-water,
With a vacant gaze.
The English Rubaiyat was still-born
In those days.[21]

[14] "Glaucous [or blue-green] Eyes." Pound may have borrowed the phrase, which is probably meant to suggest the color of the sea (and not glaucoma), from Théophile Gautier (1811–1872) or Gustave Flaubert (1821–1880).
[15] William E. Gladstone (1809–1898), Victorian political leader, Liberal Member of Parliament and Prime Minister.
[16] "Sesame: of Kings' Treasuries" is the opening essay (originally a lecture) in John Ruskin's *Sesame and Lilies* (1865).
[17] An allusion to "The Fleshly School of Poetry" (1871), an essay in which Robert Buchanan (1841–1901) attacked Dante Gabriel Rossetti (1828–1882) and other Pre-Raphaelite poets for their presumed sensuality.
[18] The reference is to Elizabeth Siddal (d. 1862), model for the Pre-Raphaelite painters and later the wife of D. G. Rossetti.
[19] *Carton* is the French form of *cartoon*, a full-size preliminary drawing or design.
[20] Elizabeth Siddal was the model of Sir E. C. Burne-Jones's uncompleted painting, "King Cophetua and the Beggar's Daughter," which hangs in the Tate Gallery in London.
[21] Pound's comment on the early neglect of Edward Fitzgerald's translation of *The Rubáiyát of Omar Khayyám* (1859).

The thin, clear gaze, the same
Still darts out faun-like from the half-ruin'd face,
Questing and passive. . . .
"Ah, poor Jenny's case" . . .[22]

20

Bewildered that a world
Shows no surprise
At her last maquero's
Adulteries.

"Siena Mi Fe'; Disfecemi Maremma"[23]

Among the pickled fœtuses and bottled bones,
Engaged in perfecting the catalogue,
I found the last scion of the
Senatorial families of Strasbourg, Monsieur Verog.[24]

For two hours he talked of Gallifet;[25]
Of Dowson; of the Rhymers' Club;
Told me how Johnson (Lionel)[26] died
By falling from a high stool in a pub . . .

But showed no trace of alcohol
At the autopsy, privately performed —
Tissue preserved — the pure mind
Arose toward Newman[27] as the whiskey warmed.

10

Dowson found harlots cheaper than hotels;
Headlam for uplift; Image[28] impartially imbued
With raptures for Bacchus, Terpsichore and the Church.
So spoke the author of "The Dorian Mood,"
M. Verog, out of step with the decade,
Detached from his contemporaries,
Neglected by the young,
Because of these reveries.

20

[22] Pound is identifying Elizabeth Siddal with the prostitute title character of Rossetti's "Jenny," a poem attacked by Buchanan.
[23] "Siena made me; Maremma undid me" (Dante, *Purgatorio*, V, 135), spoken by the spirit of a Sienese woman whose husband had sent her to Maremma to be murdered.
[24] The name fits Victor Gustave Plarr (1863–1929), Librarian of the Royal College of Surgeons, author of a book of poems entitled *In the Dorian Mood* (1896), and biographer of the poet Ernest Dowson (1867–1900).
[25] Possibly a reference to a French general, Marquis de Galliffet, who led a cavalry charge at Sedan in the Franco-Prussian War.
[26] Lionel Pigot Johnson (1867–1902), poet and critic, who became a convert to Roman Catholicism.
[27] John Henry Cardinal Newman (1801–1890), converted to Roman Catholicism in 1845, became a proselytizer of the faith among English intellectuals.
[28] The Reverend Stewart Headlam (1847–1924), a friend of Dowson; Selwyn Image (1849–1930), a designer in several of the arts, associated with a magazine of design, *The Century Guild Hobby-Horse*.

Brennbaum

The sky-like limpid eyes,
The circular infant's face,
The stiffness from spats to collar
Never relaxing into grace;
The heavy memories of Horeb, Sinai and the forty years,
Showed only when the daylight fell
Level across the face
Of Brennbaum "The Impeccable."[29]

Mr. Nixon

In the cream gilded cabin of his steam yacht
Mr. Nixon[30] advised me kindly, to advance with fewer
Dangers of delay. "Consider
    "Carefully the reviewer.

"I was as poor as you are;
"When I began I got, of course,
"Advance on royalties, fifty at first," said Mr. Nixon,
"Follow me, and take a column,
"Even if you have to work free.

"Butter reviewers. From fifty to three hundred
"I rose in eighteen months;   10
"The hardest nut I had to crack
"Was Dr. Dundas.[31]

"I never mentioned a man but with the view
"Of selling my own works.
"The tip's a good one, as for literature
"It gives no man a sinecure. — *office that pays wage for little work (church)*

"And no one knows, at sight, a masterpiece.
"And give up verse, my boy,
"There's nothing in it."

    . . . . . .

---

[29] The epithet and the physical description suggest Max Beerbohm (1872–1956), satiric essayist and caricaturist, who was called the "incomparable Max." But the allusion to Jewish tradition does not fit Beerbohm, who was a Gentile.

[30] Mr. Nixon, sometimes thought to have been modeled on Arnold Bennett (1867–1931), is presented as the type of the self-seeking writer, a false artist, in contrast to the stylist of the poem following.

[31] An apparently fictional character representing the influential critic-reviewer.

Likewise a friend of Bloughram's[32] once advised me: 20
Don't kick against the pricks,
Accept opinion. The "Nineties" tried your game
And died, there's nothing in it.

X

Beneath the sagging roof
The stylist[33] has taken shelter,
Unpaid, uncelebrated,
At last from the world's welter

Nature receives him;
With a placid and uneducated mistress
He exercises his talents
And the soil meets his distress.

The haven from sophistications and contentions
Leaks through its thatch;   10
He offers succulent cooking;
The door has a creaking latch.

XI

"Conservatrix of Milésien"[34]
Habits of mind and feeling,
Possibly. But in Ealing[35]
With the most bank-clerkly of Englishmen?

No, "Milésian" is an exaggeration.
No instinct has survived in her
Older than those her grandmother
Told her would fit her station.

XII

"Daphne with her thighs in bark
Stretches toward me her leafy hands," — [36]
Subjectively. In the stuffed-satin drawing-room
I await The Lady Valentine's commands,

[32] Pound has identified this character with the title character of Browning's "Bishop Bloughram's Apology," despite the difference in spelling.
[33] The circumstances of the stylist are those of the English novelist and close friend of Pound, Ford Madox Ford (1873–1939), who farmed for a few years after returning from service in the first World War.
[34] *Milésien*, which appears in both its French and English form in this satiric portrait, is probably intended to suggest the high culture of the ancient Ionian city of Miletus.
[35] A suburb of London.
[36] The nymph Daphne was transformed into a laurel tree while being pursued by Apollo. The quotation is Pound's translation of lines from "*Le Château du souvenir*" by Théophile Gautier (1811–1872).

Knowing my coat has never been
Of precisely the fashion
To stimulate, in her,
A durable passion;

Doubtful, somewhat, of the value
Of well-gowned approbation   10
Of literary effort,
But never of The Lady Valentine's vocation:

Poetry, her border of ideas,
The edge, uncertain, but a means of blending
With other strata
Where the lower and higher have ending;

A hook to catch the Lady Jane's attention,
A modulation toward the theatre,
Also, in the case of revolution,
A possible friend and comforter.   20

    .   .   .   .   .

Conduct, on the other hand, the soul
"Which the highest cultures have nourished"
To Fleet St. where
Dr. Johnson flourished;[37]

Beside this thoroughfare
The sale of half-hose has
Long since superseded the cultivation
Of Pierian roses.[38]

Envoi (1919)

Go, dumb-born book,
Tell her that sang me once that song of Lawes:[39]
Hadst thou but song
As thou hast subjects known,
Then were there cause in thee that should condone
Even my faults that heavy upon me lie,
And build her glories their longevity.

Tell her that sheds
Such treasure in the air,
Recking naught else but that her graces give   10
Life to the moment,

---

[37] Fleet Street was closely identified with literary activity in the time of Dr. Samuel Johnson (1709–1784).
[38] Pieria in ancient Macedonia was noted for the worship of the Muses.
[39] The first verse and the poem that follows are in the tradition of the well known "Go, Lovely Rose" of Edmund Waller (1606–1687). The composer Henry Lawes (1596–1662) set it and other poems by Waller to music.

I would bid them live
As roses might, in magic amber laid,
Red overwrought with orange and all made
One substance and one colour
Braving time.

Tell her that goes
With song upon her lips
But sings not out the song, nor knows
The maker of it, some other mouth,
May be as fair as hers,   20
Might, in new ages, gain her worshippers,
When our two dusts with Waller's shall be laid,
Siftings on siftings in oblivion,
Till change hath broken down
All things save Beauty alone.

Mauberley (1920)

"Vacuos exercet aera morsus."[40]

I

Turned from the "eau-forte
Par Jaquemart"[41]
To the strait head
Of Messalina:[42]

"His true Penelope
Was Flaubert,"[43]
And his tool
The engraver's.

Firmness,
Not the full smile,
His art, but an art   10
In profile;

Colourless
Pier Francesca,
Pisanello lacking the skill
To forge Achaia.[44]

---

[40] "He bites emptily at the air."   [41] "Etching by Jaquemart," a 19th-century French artist.
[42] Profligate wife of the Roman emperor Claudius.
[43] See above, E. P. Ode Pour L'Election de Son Sépulchre, l. 13.
[44] Piero della Francesca, 15th-century Italian painter; Vittore Pisano, 15th-century Veronese
medalist and painter; Achaia is a province of ancient Greece and an old name for the country.

II

*"Qu'est ce qu'ils savent de l'amour, et qu'est ce qu'ils peuvent
comprendre?*
    *S'ils ne comprennent pas la poésie, s'ils ne sentent pas la
musique, qu'est ce qu'ils peuvent comprendre de cette passion en
comparaison avec laquelle la rose est grossière et le parfum des
violettes un tonnerre?"*   Caid Ali[45]

For three years, diabolus in the scale,[46]
He drank ambrosia,
All passes, ANANGKE[47] prevails,
Came end, at last, to that Arcadia.

He had moved amid her phantasmagoria,
Amid her galaxies,
NUKTIS 'AGALMA[48]

.   .   .   .
Drifted . . . drifted precipitate,
Asking time to be rid of . . .
Of his bewilderment; to designate   10
His new found orchid. . . .

To be certain . . . certain . . .
(Amid ærial flowers) . . . time for arrangements —
Drifted on
To the final estrangement;

Unable in the supervening blankness
To sift TO AGATHON[49] from the chaff
Until he found his sieve . . .
Ultimately, his seismograph:

— Given that is his "fundamental passion,"   20
This urge to convey the relation
Of eye-lid and cheek-bone
By verbal manifestations;

To present the series
Of curious heads in medallion —

[45] "What do they know of love and what are they able to understand? If they do not
understand poetry, if they do not feel music, what are they able to understand of that
passion in comparison with which the rose is gross and the scent of violets a thunderbolt?"
Caid Ali is a name invented by Pound.
[46] J. J. Espey explains "the devil in the (musical) scale" as the "augmented fourth, which
gave the medieval musicians great difficulty" (*Ezra Pound's Mauberley* [Berkeley and Los
Angeles, 1955], p. 76 n).
[47] "Fate."
[48] "Night's ornament."
[49] "The good."

He had passed, inconscient, full gaze,
The wide-banded irides[50]
And botticellian sprays implied
In their diastasis;

Which anæsthesis, noted a year late,
And weighed, revealed his great affect,
(Orchid), mandate
Of Eros, a retrospect.

. . . . . .
Mouths biting empty air,[51]
The still stone dogs,
Caught in metamorphosis, were
Left him as epilogues.

"The Age Demanded"

For this agility chance found
Him of all men, unfit
As the red-beaked steeds of
The Cytheræan[52] for a chain bit.

The glow of porcelain
Brought no reforming sense
To his perception
Of the social inconsequence.

Thus, if her colour
Came against his gaze,
Tempered as if
It were through a perfect glaze

He made no immediate application
Of this to relation of the state
To the individual, the month was more temperate
Because this beauty had been.

The coral isle, the lion-coloured sand
Burst in upon the porcelain revery:
Impetuous troubling
Of his imagery.

Mildness, amid the neo-Nietzschean clatter,
His sense of graduations,
Quite out of place amid
Resistance to current exacerbations,

30

10

20

[50] Irises.   [51] See the Latin epigraph to *Mauberley, 1920.*
[52] Aphrodite.

Invitation, mere invitation to perceptivity
Gradually led him to the isolation
Which these presents place
Under a more tolerant, perhaps, examination.

By constant elimination
The manifest universe   30
Yielded an armour
Against utter consternation,

A Minoan undulation,
Seen, we admit, amid ambrosial circumstances
Strengthened him against
The discouraging doctrine of chances,

And his desire for survival,
Faint in the most strenuous moods,
Became an Olympian *apathein*[53]
In the presence of selected perceptions.   40

A pale gold, in the aforesaid pattern,
The unexpected palms
Destroying, certainly, the artist's urge,
Left him delighted with the imaginary
Audition of the phantasmal sea-surge,

Incapable of the least utterance or composition,
Emendation, conservation of the "better tradition,"
Refinement of medium, elimination of superfluities,
August attraction or concentration.

Nothing, in brief, but maudlin confession,   50
Irresponse to human aggression,
Amid the precipitation, down-float
Of insubstantial manna,
Lifting the faint susurrus
Of his subjective hosannah.

Ultimate affronts to
Human redundancies;

Non-esteem of self-styled "his betters"
Leading, as he well knew,
To his final   60
Exclusion from the world of letters.

[53] Absence of emotion.

IV

Scattered Moluccas[54]
Not knowing, day to day,
The first day's end, in the next noon;
The placid water
Unbroken by the Simoon;[55]

Thick foliage
Placid beneath warm suns,
Tawn fore-shores
Washed in the cobalt of oblivions;

Or through dawn-mist   10
The grey and rose
Of the juridical
Flamingoes;

A consciousness disjunct,
Being but this overblotted
Series
Of intermittences;

Coracle of Pacific voyages,
The unforecasted beach;
Then on an oar[56]   20
Read this:

"I was
And I no more exist;
Here drifted
An hedonist."

Medallion

Luini[57] in porcelain!
The grand piano
Utters a profane
Protest with her clear soprano.

The sleek head emerges
From the gold-yellow frock

---

[54] The Spice Islands of the Netherlands Indies, here a symbol of sensuous abandon.
[55] The simoom, a hot, violent desert wind.
[56] Compare the request of Elpenor in Canto I, 11, below, lines 54–57.
[57] Bernardino Luini, early 16th-century Milanese painter.

As Anadyomene[58] in the opening
Pages of Reinach.[59]

Honey-red, closing the face-oval,
A basket-work of braids which seem as if they were   10
Spun in King Minos'[60] hall
From metal, or intractable amber;

The face-oval beneath the glaze,
Bright in its suave bounding-line, as,
Beneath half-watt rays,
The eyes turn topaz.

Canto I [1]

english version of Latin translation of Homar
structure of Cantos is modern intellectual epic.

And then went down to the ship,
Set keel to breakers, forth on the godly sea, and
We set up mast and sail on that swart ship,
Bore sheep aboard her, and our bodies also
Heavy with weeping, and winds from sternward
Bore us out onward with bellying canvas,
Circe's this craft, the trim-coifed goddess.
Then sat we amidships, wind jamming the tiller,
Thus with stretched sail, we went over sea till day's end.
Sun to his slumber, shadows o'er all the ocean,   10
Came we then to the bounds of deepest water,
To the Kimmerian lands,[2] and peopled cities
Covered with close-webbed mist, unpierced ever
With glitter of sun-rays
Nor with stars stretched, nor looking back from heaven
Swartest night stretched over wretched men there.
The ocean flowing backward, came we then to the place
Aforesaid by Circe.
Here did they rites, Perimedes and Eurylochus,
And drawing sword from my hip   20
I dug the ell-square pitkin;
Poured we libations unto each the dead,

---

[58] Aphrodite as the "sea-born" goddess.
[59] Salomon Reinach (1858–1932), French archaeologist and author of *Apollo* (1904), a volume of essays on art.
[60] Legendary king of Crete for whom Daedalus built the labyrinth.
[1] Although Pound had begun drafting *The Cantos* during the years of the first World War, this first canto was not collected in its present form until the appearance of *A Draft of XVI Cantos* (1925). The canto tells the story of Odysseus' visit to the underworld in Book XI of the *Odyssey*. Pound's translation is not from the Greek text, however, but from the Latin translation by Andreas Divas published in 1538 (see note 6 below). The speaker is Odysseus.
[2] The Cimmerians were a mythical people whose land was a region of perpetual mist and darkness.

First mead and then sweet wine, water mixed with white flour.
Then prayed I many a prayer to the sickly death's-heads;
As set in Ithaca, sterile bulls of the best
For sacrifice, heaping the pyre with goods,
A sheep to Tiresias[3] only, black and a bell-sheep.
Dark blood flowed in the fosse,
Souls out of Erebus, cadaverous dead, of brides
Of youths and of the old who had borne much;   30
Souls stained with recent tears, girls tender,
Men many, mauled with bronze lance heads,
Battle spoil, bearing yet dreory[4] arms,
These many crowded about me; with shouting,
Pallor upon me, cried to my men for more beasts;
Slaughtered the herds, sheep slain of bronze;
Poured ointment, cried to the gods,
To Pluto the strong, and praised Proserpine;
Unsheathed the narrow sword,
I sat to keep off the impetuous impotent dead,   40
Till I should hear Tiresias.
But first Elpenor came, our friend Elpenor,
Unburied, cast on the wide earth,
Limbs that we left in the house of Circe,
Unwept, unwrapped in sepulchre, since toils urged other.
Pitiful spirit. And I cried in hurried speech:
"Elpenor, how art thou come to this dark coast?
"Cam'st thou afoot, outstripping seamen?"
       And he in heavy speech:
"Ill fate and abundant wine. I slept in Circe's ingle.   50
"Going down the long ladder unguarded,
"I fell against the buttress,
"Shattered the nape-nerve, the soul sought Avernus.
"But thou, O King, I bid remember me, unwept, unburied,
"Heap up mine arms, be tomb by sea-bord, and inscribed:
"A man of no fortune, and with a name to come.
"And set my oar up, that I swung mid fellows."

And Anticlea[5] came, whom I beat off, and then Tiresias Theban,
Holding his golden wand, knew me, and spoke first:
"A second time? why? man of ill star,   60
"Facing the sunless dead and this joyless region?
"Stand from the fosse, leave me my bloody bever
"For soothsay."
       And I stepped back,
And he strong with the blood, said then: "Odysseus

---

[3] Tiresias was the blind prophet of Thebes who figures in Sophocles' *Oedipus Rex* and in other works. Compare Eliot's use of the figure of Tiresias in *The Waste Land*.
[4] An Anglo Saxon word for "bloody."
[5] Anticlea was the mother of Odysseus, but he had been instructed to hold her spirit away from the blood until that of Tiresias had drunk and gained strength to prophesy.

"Shalt return through spiteful Neptune, over dark seas,
"Lose all companions." And then Anticlea came.
Lie quiet Divus.[6] I mean, that is Andreas Divus,
In officina Wecheli, 1538,[7] out of Homer.
And he sailed, by Sirens and thence outward and away
And unto Circe.
        Venerandam,[8]
In the Cretan's phrase, with the golden crown, Aphrodite,
Cypri munimenta sortita est,[9] mirthful, oricalchi,[10] with golden
Girdles and breast bands, thou with dark eyelids
Bearing the golden bough of Argicida.[11] So that:[12]

                                                    1925

Canto XLV

With *Usura*   usury

With usura hath no man a house of good stone
each block cut smooth and well fitting
that design might cover their face,
with usura
hath no man a painted paradise on his church wall
harpes et luthes
or where virgin receiveth message
and halo projects from incision,
with usura   10
seeth no man Gonzaga[1] his heirs and his concubines
no picture is made to endure nor to live with
but it is made to sell and sell quickly
with usura, sin against nature,
is thy bread ever more of stale rags
is thy bread dry as paper,
with no mountain wheat, no strong flour
with usura the line grows thick
with usura is no clear demarcation

[6] At this point the poet begins speaking in the first person, addressing the translator he has been following and referring to Odysseus as "he."
[7] "In the workshop of Wechel" and the date 1538 are from the imprint of the translation by Divus used by Pound.
[8] "Compelling adoration," a phrase relating to Aphrodite.
[9] "The citadels of Cyprus were her realm," from the second Homeric hymn to Aphrodite, translated into Latin by Georgius Dartona Cretensis, the Cretan mentioned in the preceding line.
[10] In Latin *orichalchi* means "of the copper." The term apparently refers to a votive gift to Aphrodite.
[11] A name for the messenger god Hermes as the "slayer of Argus." The golden bough which Aeneas carried to the underworld as a talisman seems to be identified with the caduceus of Hermes, who conducted the souls of the dead to Hades.
[12] "So that:" An introduction to the continuing "voyage" of *The Cantos*.
[1] The allusion is obscure, but J. H. Edwards and W. W. Vasse suggest that it may be to Cardinal Ercole Gonzaga (1505–1563), a patron of the arts in Mantua (*Annotated Index to the Cantos* [Berkeley and Los Angeles, 1957], p. 80).

and no man can find site for his dwelling.   20
Stone cutter is kept from his stone
weaver is kept from his loom
WITH USURA
wool comes not to market
sheep bringeth no gain with usura
Usura is a murrain, usura
blunteth the needle in the maid's hand
and stoppeth the spinner's cunning. Pietro Lombardo[2]
came not by usura
Duccio[3] came not by usura   30
nor Pier della Francesca; Zuan Bellin'[4] not by usura
nor was 'La Calunnia' painted.[5]
Came not by usura Angelico;[6] came not Ambrogio Praedis,[7]
Came no church of cut stone signed: *Adamo me fecit.*[8]
Not by usura St Trophime
Not by usura Saint Hilaire,[9]
Usura rusteth the chisel
It rusteth the craft and the craftsman
It gnaweth the thread in the loom
None learneth to weave gold in her pattern;   40
Azure hath a canker by usura; cramoisi[10] is unbroidered
Emerald findeth no Memling[11]
Usura slayeth the child in the womb
It stayeth the young man's courting
It hath brought palsey to bed, lyeth
between the young bride and her bridegroom
               CONTRA NATURAM
They have brought whores for Eleusis[12]
Corpses are set to banquet
at behest of usura.   50

1937

From *Canto LXXXI*

What thou lovest well remains,
                 the rest is dross

[2] Italian architect and sculptor (1435–1515)
[3] Duccio di Buoninsegna (1278–1319), Italian painter.
[4] Piero dei Francheschi and Giovanni Bellini, 15th-century Italian painters.
[5] A painting by Sandro Botticelli (1444–1510) of Florence.
[6] Fra Angelico (1387–1455), Florentine painter.
[7] Ambroglio de Predis, 15th-century Milanese painter.
[8] "Adam made me"—the signature of the architect of the Zeno Maggiore, the Veronese basilica.
[9] Medieval churches in Arles and Poitiers.
[10] Crimson cloth.
[11] Hans Memling, 15th-century Flemish painter.
[12] A city in ancient Greece famous for its religious celebrations (rooted in fertility rites) of the Eleusinian mysteries of Demeter and Persephone.

What thou lov'st well shall not be reft from thee
What thou lov'st well is thy true heritage
Whose world, or mine or theirs
                              or is it of none?
First came the seen, then thus the palpable
        Elysium, though it were in the halls of hell,
What thou lovest well is thy true heritage

The ant's a centaur in his dragon world.   10
Pull down thy vanity, it is not man
Made courage, or made order, or made grace,
        Pull down thy vanity, I say pull down.
Learn of the green world what can be thy place
In scaled invention or true artistry,
Pull down thy vanity,
                        Paquin¹pull down!
The green casque has outdone your elegance.

"Master thyself, then others shall thee beare"
        Pull down thy vanity   20
Thou art a beaten dog beneath the hail,
A swollen magpie in a fitful sun,
Half black half white
Nor knowst'ou wing from tail
Pull down thy vanity
        How mean thy hates
Fostered in falsity,
        Pull down thy vanity,
Rathe to destroy, niggard in charity,
Pull down thy vanity,   30
        I say pull down.

But to have done instead of not doing
                this is not vanity
To have, with decency, knocked
That a Blunt² should open
        To have gathered from the air a live tradition
or from a fine old eye the unconquered flame
This is not vanity.
        Here error is all in the not done,
all in the diffidence that faltered,   40

                                        1948

¹ A Parisian dress designer.
² Probably Wilfrid Scawen Blunt (1840–1922), English poet and political writer, an un- •
compromising champion of Irish, Egyptian, and Indian nationalism.

T. S. Eliot   *1888–1965*

In August, 1914, when T. S. Eliot arrived in England at the age of twenty-six, he was a student of philosophy (and an unpublished poet) whose plans to continue his graduate work in Germany had suddenly been aborted by the outbreak of war. Quickly "discovered" by Ezra Pound, who was already established in London as a leader of the literary avant-garde, Eliot began to devote his full energies to poetry and criticism, supporting himself precariously by free-lance reviewing and teaching. The appearance of *Prufrock and Other Observations* (1917), *Poems* (1920), and *The Sacred Wood: Essays on Poetry and Criticism* (1920) launched the career which was to make him the most influential single poet and critic writing in English during the years between the wars.

Thomas Stearns Eliot was born in 1888 in St. Louis, Missouri, the son of a successful businessman and grandson of a crusading Unitarian preacher and community leader who had gone west from his native Massachusetts a half century before. Eliot went east to Harvard, where he became acquainted with the French symbolist poets, especially Jules Laforgue, whose witty and ironic verse influenced "Prufrock" and other of his early poems. After earning his M.A. degree in 1910, Eliot studied at the Sorbonne and at Oxford and then returned to Harvard as an assistant in philosophy. In 1914 he received the traveling fellowship for study in Germany that was to lead him instead to England and a new career. The early years in London were difficult. Newly married and pressed for funds, Eliot sought the dubious security of a clerical position in Lloyd's Bank. Like Pound, Eliot was deeply disillusioned by the war, which seemed to portend, not progress, but the cataclysmic breakdown of western culture. His major poem, *The Waste Land* (1922), worked into final form with the editorial assistance of Pound, expresses the sense of oppression, confusion, and despair that Eliot found in himself and his society. The poem also established the poet's reputation and set the dominant tone and temper of much of the poetry of the 1920's. *Poems, 1909–1925* (1925), which included "The Hollow Men," was followed, a decade later, by *Poems, 1909–1935* (1936).

For Eliot, the postwar years were a period of deepening conservatism and orthodoxy. In 1925 he joined the publishing house that was soon to be known as Faber & Faber and settled, somewhat prematurely, into the role of elder statesman and mentor of the modern literary establishment. In 1927 he became a British citizen and entered the Church of England. A year later he characterized himself, in *For Lancelot Andrewes* (1928), as "a royalist in politics, a classicist in literature, and an Anglo-Catholic in religion." His continuing preoccupation with the conflict of faith and doubt and with the problem of personal salvation infused his later poetry, from *Ash Wednesday* (1930) through the *Four Quartets* (1943), with a mystical impulse toward a transcendent spiritual reality not unlike that sought, each in his own way, by the earlier New England puritan Jonathan Edwards and the New England transcendentalist Emerson. In these closely crafted, interrelated poems, inspired in part, according to Eliot, by the formal organization of Beethoven's later quartets, one of the most striking images of the time out of time toward which the poet strains is the "still point of the turning world" in "Burnt Norton" (1935), the first of the *Quartets*.

All Eliot's poetry was shaped in accordance with conscious critical principles set forth in the essays of *The Sacred Wood* and in later lectures and essays including those written for *The Criterion*, the literary review he edited from 1922 to 1939. Cumulatively this body of criticism, which influenced a generation of poets and critics, paid special regard to the traditions and methods of the Elizabethan and Jacobean dramatists, the seventeenth century metaphysical poets, and the nineteenth century French symbolists. Central to Eliot's own poetry and criticism was the "impersonal theory of poetry" defined in "Tradition and the Individual Talent" (1919) and reinforced by the idea of the "objective correlative," in "Hamlet and His Problems" (1919), as "a set of objects, a situation, a chain of events which shall be the formula" of the particular emotion the poet wishes to express. Among Eliot's numerous books of criticism are *Ezra Pound: His Metric and Poetry* (1917), *Homage to John Dryden* (1924), *Selected Essays, 1917–1932* (1932). *The Use of Poetry and the Use of Criticism* (1933), *Essays Ancient and Modern* (1936), *Selected Essays* (1950), *The Three Voices of Poetry* (1953), *The Frontiers of Criticism* (1950), and *On Poetry and Poets* (1957). Volumes of social criticism, which set forth Eliot's extremely conservative opinions, include *After Strange Gods, A Primer of Modern Heresy* (1934), *The Idea of a Christian Society* (1940), and *Notes towards the Definition of Culture* (1948).

In view of his admiration of John Dryden and earlier English dramatists, it is not surprising that Eliot attempted to develop a verse drama appropriate to the modern theater. These efforts produced *Murder in the Cathedral* (1935), a morality play based on the assassination of St. Thomas à Becket, and four later plays dealing with moral and religious problems in contemporary settings: *The Family Reunion* (1939), *The Cocktail Party* (1950), *The Confidential Clerk* (1954), and *The Elder Statesman* (1959).

Eliot's reputation has suffered a decline in the years since World War II among younger poets who have reacted against the orthodoxies of the academic literary establishment and who have found greater inspiration in the more secular viewpoints and the more open poetic forms of Ezra Pound and William Carlos Williams.

Standard editions of Eliot's writings include *Selected Essays, New Edition* (New York, 1950; 1960), *Collected Plays* (New York, 1962), and *Collected Poems, 1909–1962* (New York, 1963). Although superseded by the last two of these, *The Complete Poems and Plays* (New York, 1952) is still a useful source. Helpful general introductions are F. O. Matthiessen, *The Achievement of T. S. Eliot*, 3rd ed. (New York, 1958), and Hugh Kenner, ed., *T. S. Eliot: A Collection of Critical Essays* (Englewood Cliffs, N. J., 1962). Closer analyses are provided by Grover Smith, *T. S. Eliot's Poetry and Plays: A Study in Sources and Meaning* (Chicago, 1956), and George Williamson, *A Reader's Guide to T. S. Eliot* (New York, 1953). Other more general critiques are Elizabeth Drew, *T. S. Eliot: The Design of His Poetry* (New York, 1949), and Hugh Kenner, *The Invisible Poet: T. S. Eliot* (New York, 1959). Valuable information about Eliot's family background and early associations can be found in Herbert Howarth, *Notes on Some Figures Behind T. S. Eliot* (Boston, 1964). Donald Gallup, *T. S. Eliot, A Bibliography* (New York, 1953), provides a complete listing of Eliot's publications to 1950.

The text of the poems given here is that of *Collected Poems, 1909–1962* (New York, 1963). "Tradition and the Individual Talent" is from *Selected Essays, New Edition* (New York, 1960).

The Love Song of J. Alfred Prufrock

S'io credesse che mia risposta fosse
A persona che mai tornasse al mondo,
Questa fiamma staria senza piu scosse.
Ma perciocche giammai di questo fondo
Non torno vivo alcun, s'i'odo il vero,
Senza tema d'infamia ti rispondo.[1]

[handwritten: speaking from hell?]

Let us go then, you and I,
When the evening is spread out against the sky
Like a patient etherised upon a table;
Let us go, through certain half-deserted streets,
The muttering retreats
Of restless nights in one-night cheap hotels
And sawdust restaurants with oyster-shells:
Streets that follow like a tedious argument
Of insidious intent
To lead you to an overwhelming question. . .   10

[1] "If I believed that my answer were being made to one who could ever return to the world, this flame would shake no more. But since, if what I hear is true, never from this depth did man return alive, I answer you without fear of infamy." In Dante's *Inferno* (XXVII, 61–66), these words are addressed to the poet by the spirit of Guido da Montefeltro.

Oh, do not ask, "What is it?"
Let us go and make our visit.

In the room the women come and go
Talking of Michelangelo.

*superficiality
of socialites
against boldness of
Michelangelo*

The yellow fog that rubs its back upon the window-panes,
The yellow smoke that rubs its muzzle on the window-panes
Licked its tongue into the corners of the evening,
Lingered upon the pools that stand in drains,
Let fall upon its back the soot that falls from chimneys,
Slipped by the terrace, made a sudden leap,   20
And seeing that it was a soft October night,
Curled once about the house, and fell asleep.

And indeed there will be time
For the yellow smoke that slides along the street,
Rubbing its back upon the window-panes;
There will be time, there will be time
To prepare a face to meet the faces that you meet;
There will be time to murder and create,
And time for all the works and days of hands
That lift and drop a question on your plate;   30
Time for you and time for me,
And time yet for a hundred indecisions,
And for a hundred visions and revisions,
Before the taking of a toast and tea.

In the room the women come and go
Talking of Michelangelo.

And indeed there will be time
To wonder, "Do I dare?" and, "Do I dare?"
Time to turn back and descend the stair,
With a bald spot in the middle of my hair—   40
[They will say: "How his hair is growing thin!"]
My morning coat, my collar mounting firmly to the chin,
My necktie rich and modest, but asserted by a simple pin—
[They will say: "But how his arms and legs are thin!"]
Do I dare
Disturb the universe?
In a minute there is time
For decisions and revisions which a minute will reverse.

For I have known them all already, known them all:—
Have known the evenings, mornings, afternoons,   50
I have measured out my life with coffee spoons;

I know the voices dying with a dying fall[2]
Beneath the music from a farther room.
　　So how should I presume?

　　And I have known the eyes already, known them all—
The eyes that fix you in a formulated phrase,
And when I am formulated, sprawling on a pin,
When I am pinned and wriggling on the wall,
Then how should I begin
To spit out all the butt-ends of my days and ways?　　　　　　　60
　　And how should I presume?

　　And I have known the arms already, known them all—
Arms that are braceleted and white and bare
[But in the lamplight, downed with light brown hair!]
Is it perfume from a dress
That makes me so digress?
Arms that lie along a table, or wrap about a shawl.
　　And should I then presume?
　　And how should I begin?

　　.　　.　　.　　.　　.

Shall I say, I have gone at dusk through narrow streets　　　　70
And watched the smoke that rises from the pipes
Of lonely men in shirt-sleeves, leaning out of windows? . . .

　　I should have been a pair of ragged claws
Scuttling across the floors of silent seas.

　　.　　.　　.　　.　　.

And the afternoon, the evening, sleeps so peacefully!
Smoothed by long fingers,
Asleep . . . tired . . . or it malingers,
Stretched on the floor, here beside you and me.
Should I, after tea and cakes and ices,
Have the strength to force the moment to its crisis?　　　　　80
But though I have wept and fasted, wept and prayed,
Though I have seen my head [grown slightly bald] brought in
　　upon a platter,[3]
I am no prophet—and here's no great matter;
I have seen the moment of my greatness flicker,
— And I have seen the eternal Footman hold my coat, and snicker,
And in short, I was afraid.

　　And would it have been worth it, after all,
After the cups, the marmalade, the tea,

[2] An echo of Shakespeare's "That strain again! it had a dying fall," from the opening of
Twelfth Night (I, i, 4).
[3] An allusion to the fate of John the Baptist (*Matthew* 14: 3–11).

Among the porcelain, among some talk of you and me,
Would it have been worth while,   90
To have bitten off the matter with a smile,
To have squeezed the universe into a ball
To roll it toward some overwhelming question,
To say: "I am Lazarus, come from the dead,
Come back to tell you all, I shall tell you all"— [4]
If one, settling a pillow by her head,
        Should say: "That is not what I meant at all.
        That is not it, at all."

        And would it have been worth it, after all,
Would it have been worth while,   100
After the sunsets and the dooryards and the sprinkled streets,
After the novels, after the teacups, after the skirts that trail along
        the floor—
And this, and so much more?—
It is impossible to say just what I mean!
But as if a magic lantern threw the nerves in patterns on a screen:
Would it have been worth while
If one, settling a pillow or throwing off a shawl,
And turning toward the window, should say:
        "That is not it at all,   *the woman wants no*
        That is not what I meant, at all."   *emotional commitment* 110

        .   .   .   .
No! I am not Prince Hamlet, nor was meant to be;
Am an attendant lord, one that will do
To swell a progress, start a scene or two,
Advise the prince; no doubt, an easy tool,
Deferential, glad to be of use,
Politic, cautious, and meticulous;
Full of high sentence, but a bit obtuse;
At times, indeed, almost ridiculous—
Almost, at times, the Fool. [5]

        I grow old . . . I grow old . . .   120
I shall wear the bottoms of my trousers rolled.

        Shall I part my hair behind? Do I dare to eat a peach?
I shall wear white flannel trousers, and walk upon the beach.
I have heard the mermaids singing, each to each. [6]

        I do not think that they will sing to me.

        I have seen them riding seaward on the waves

[4] For the story of Lazarus, see *John* 11: 1–44.
[5] The characterization is especially suggestive of Polonius.
[6] In this context the mermaids symbolize passion.

Combing the white hair of the waves blown back
When the wind blows the water white and black.

We have lingered in the chambers of the sea
By sea-girls wreathed with seaweed red and brown
Till human voices wake us, and we drown.

Prufrock's dream world – fear of reality 130

1917

Geronion[1]

> *Thou hast nor youth nor age*
> *But as it were an after dinner sleep*
> *Dreaming of both.*[2]

linked with Henry Adams' "Education"

Here I am, an old man in a dry month,
Being read to by a boy, waiting for rain.
I was neither at the hot gates[3]
Nor fought in the warm rain
Nor knee deep in the salt marsh, heaving a cutlass,
Bitten by flies, fought.
My house is a decayed house,
And the jew squats on the window sill, the owner,
Spawned in some estaminet of Antwerp,
Blistered in Brussels, patched and peeled in London.
The goat coughs at night in the field overhead; 10
Rocks, moss, stonecrop, iron, merds.[4]
The woman keeps the kitchen, makes tea,
Sneezes at evening, poking the peevish gutter.
                        I an old man,
A dull head among windy spaces.

Signs are taken for wonders. "We would see a sign!"
The word within a word, unable to speak a word,
Swaddled with darkness. In the juvescence of the year
Came Christ the tiger[5] 20

In depraved May, dogwood and chestnut, flowering judas,[6]
To be eaten, to be divided, to be drunk
Among whispers; by Mr. Silvero

---

[1] Eliot bases the name of his title character on the Greek *geron*, "an old man."
[2] Shakespeare, *Measure for Measure* (III, i, 32–34).
[3] An allusion to the Battle of Thermopylae (literally "hot gates"), in which the Spartans defeated the Persians in 480 B.C.
[4] Turds.
[5] These lines, beginning with "Signs are taken . . . ," are loaded with echoes of the Gospels. See especially *John* 1:1, 4:48 and *Matthew* 12:38. "Christ the tiger," which echoes the language of prophecy, also points to the primitive origins of the Christian myth, which Eliot recognizes, here as in *The Waste Land*, as descended from ancient fertility rites.
[6] "Flowering judas" is a reminder of the betrayal of Jesus.

With caressing hands, at Limoges
Who walked all night in the next room;

    By Hakagawa, bowing among the Titians;
By Madame de Tornquist, in the dark room
Shifting the candles; Fräulein von Kulp[7]
Who turned in the hall, one hand on the door.
            Vacant shuttles   30
Weave the wind. I have no ghosts,
An old man in a draughty house
Under a windy knob.

    After such knowledge, what forgiveness? Think now
History has many cunning passages, contrived corridors   *Paris peace—*
And issues, deceives with whispering ambitions,   *Polish corridor?*
Guides us by vanities. Think now
She gives when our attention is distracted
And what she gives, gives with such supple confusions
That the giving famishes the craving. Gives too late   40
What's not believed in, or if still believed,
In memory only, reconsidered passion. Gives too soon
Into weak hands, what's thought can be dispensed with
Till the refusal propagates a fear. Think
Neither fear nor courage saves us. Unnatural vices
Are fathered by our heroism. Virtues
Are forced upon us by our impudent crimes.
These tears are shaken from the wrath-bearing tree.[8]

    The tiger springs in the new year.[9] Us he devours. Think at
    last
We have not reached conclusion, when I   50
Stiffen in a rented house. Think at last
I have not made this show purposelessly
And it is not by any concitation[10]
Of the backward devils.
I would meet you upon this honestly.
I that was near your heart was removed therefrom
To lose beauty in terror, terror in inquisition.
I have lost my passion: why should I need to keep it
Since what is kept must be adulterated?
I have lost my sight, smell, hearing, taste and touch: 60
How should I use them for your closer contact?

[7] These fictional names collectively represent the fragmented cosmopolitan culture of
Gerontion's world.
[8] The "wrath-bearing tree" most obviously suggests the tree in the Garden of Eden. See
Genesis 2:16 – 17, 3:1 – 19.
[9] See note 5 above.
[10] Excitation.

These with a thousand small deliberations
Protract the profit of their chilled delirium,
Excite the membrane, when the sense has cooled,
With pungent sauces, multiply variety
In a wilderness of mirrors. What will the spider do,
Suspend its operations, will the weevil
Delay? De Bailhache, Fresca, Mrs. Cammel,[11] whirled
Beyond the circuit of the shuddering Bear[12]
In fractured atoms. Gull against the wind, in the windy straits   70
Of Belle Isle,[13] or running on the Horn,[14]
White feathers in the snow, the Gulf claims,
And an old man driven by the Trades[15]
To a sleepy corner.

Tenants of the house,
Thoughts of a dry brain in a dry season.

1920

Sweeney Among the Nightingales[1]

ὤμοι, πέπληγμαι καιρίαν πληγὴν ἔσω.[2]

Apeneck Sweeney spreads his knees
Letting his arms hang down to laugh,
The zebra stripes along his jaw
Swelling to maculate giraffe.

The circles of the stormy moon
Slide westward toward the River Plate,[3]
Death and the Raven drift above
And Sweeney guards the hornèd gate.[4]

---

[11] See note 7 above.
[12] The constellation known also as the Great Dipper, which seems to revolve about the North Star.
[13] Between Newfoundland and Labrador.
[14] Cape Horn.
[15] Most obviously the trade winds, with the further suggestion of commerce as a debilitating influence in the modern world.

[1] Since the setting is a dive, if not actually a brothel, "nightingales" suggests prostitution in its modern context, as well as passion in its older classical and Christian contexts. Eliot once said that all he intended to create in this poem was a "sense of foreboding" (F. O. Matthiessen, *The Achievement of T. S. Eliot* [New York, 1947], p. 129). But the plot against Sweeney in the brothel seems to be developed as an ironic modern analogue to the fatal plot against Agamemnon by the faithless Clytemnestra and her lover Aegisthus.
[2] "Alas, I have been struck deep with a deadly blow" (Aeschylus, *Agamemnon*, 1. 1343).
[3] The Rio de la Plata in South America.
[4] The gate of horn is described as the gate of true dreams in Virgil's *Aeneid*, Book VI. In this context the image may also suggest death.

Gloomy Orion and the Dog[5]
Are veiled; and hushed the shrunken seas;
The person in the Spanish cape
Tries to sit on Sweeney's knees

Slips and pulls the table cloth
Overturns a coffee-cup,   10
Reorganized upon the floor
She yawns and draws a stocking up;

The silent man in mocha brown
Sprawls at the window-sill and gapes;
The waiter brings in oranges
Bananas figs and hothouse grapes;

The silent vertebrate in brown
Contracts and concentrates, withdraws;
Rachel *née* Rabinovitch
Tears at the grapes with murderous paws;   20

She and the lady in the cape
Are suspect, thought to be in league;
Therefore the man with heavy eyes
Declines the gambit, shows fatigue,

Leaves the room and reappears
Outside the window, leaning in,
Branches of wistaria
Circumscribe a golden grin;

The host with someone indistinct
Converses at the door apart,   30
The nightingales are singing near
The Convent of the Sacred Heart,

And sang within the bloody wood
When Agamemnon cried aloud,
And let their liquid siftings fall
To stain the stiff dishonoured shroud.

1920

---

[5] Constellations. The Raven may also refer to a constellation (Corvus).

1 gambit opening in which a pawn
is sacraficed to get an advantage
in position

The Waste Land [1]

"Nam Sibyllam quidem Cumis ego ipse oculis meis vidi
in ampulla pendere, et cum illi pueri dicerent: Σίβυλλα
τί θέλεις; respondebat illa: ἀποθανεῖν θέλω." [2]

For Ezra Pound
il miglior fabbro. [3]

I

The Burial of the Dead [4]

April is the cruellest month, breeding
Lilacs out of the dead land, mixing
Memory and desire, stirring
Dull roots with spring rain.   displaced aristocracy
Winter kept us warm, covering
Earth in forgetful snow, feeding
A little life with dried tubers.
Summer surprised us, coming over the Starnbergersee [5]
With a shower of rain; we stopped in the colonnade,
And went on in sunlight, into the Hofgarten, [6]   10
And drank coffee, and talked for an hour.
Bin gar keine Russin, stamm' aus Litauen, echt deutsch. [7]
And when we were children, staying at the archduke's,
My cousin's, he took me out on a sled,
And I was frightened. He said, Marie,
Marie, hold on tight. And down we went.
In the mountains, there you feel free.
I read, much of the night, and go south in the winter.

What are the roots that clutch, what branches grow
Out of this stony rubbish? Son of man, [8]   20

---

[1] In order to preserve the original format of *The Waste Land*, Eliot's notes are given in full, following the text of the poem. They are supplemented by the present editors' numbered footnotes, which accompany the text. The footnotes also refer to Eliot's notes by citing his initials and the line numbers which introduce his notes: "TSE, 1. 20." Especially important are Eliot's first introductory notes on the general plan and symbolism of the poem, his note on the Tarot cards (TSE, 1. 46), and his note on Tiresias (TSE, 1. 218).

[2] "For I myself saw, with my own eyes, the Sibyl of Cumae hanging in a cage, and when the boys called out to her, 'Sibyl, what do you want?' she answered, 'I want to die.'" (Petronius, *Satyricon*, Ch. 48.)

[3] "The better craftsman" (Dante, *Purgatorio*, XXVI, 117).

[4] The title of the funeral service in *The Book of Common Prayer*.

[5] A resort lake near Munich.

[6] An outdoor cafe in a park or garden.

[7] "I am no Russian—come from Lithuania, pure German."

[8] TSE, 1. 20.

You cannot say, or guess, for you know only
A heap of broken images, where the sun beats,
And the dead tree gives no shelter, the cricket no relief,[9]
And the dry stone no sound of water. Only
There is shadow under this red rock,
(Come in under the shadow of this red rock),
And I will show you something different from either
Your shadow at morning striding behind you
Or your shadow at evening rising to meet you;
I will show you fear in a handful of dust.   30

>   *Frisch weht der Wind*
>   *Der Heimat zu*
>   *Mein Irisch Kind,*
>   *Wo weilest du?*[10]

"You gave me hyacinths first a year ago;
"They called me the hyacinth girl."
— Yet when we came back, late, from the Hyacinth garden,[11]
Your arms full, and your hair wet, I could not
Speak, and my eyes failed, I was neither
Living nor dead, and I knew nothing,   40
Looking into the heart of light, the silence.
Oed' und leer das Meer.[12]   ← missed opportunity for love

Madame Sosostris, famous clairvoyante,
Had a bad cold, nevertheless
Is known to be the wisest woman in Europe,
With a wicked pack of cards.[13] Here, said she,
Is your card, the drowned Phoenician Sailor,
(Those are pearls that were his eyes.[14] Look!)
Here is Belladonna, the Lady of the Rocks,
The lady of situations.   50
Here is the man with three staves, and here the Wheel,
And here is the one-eyed merchant, and this card,
Which is blank, is something he carries on his back,
Which I am forbidden to see. I do not find
The Hanged Man.[15] Fear death by water.   water - salvation?
I see crowds of people, walking round in a ring.   death?
Thank you. If you see dear Mrs. Equitone,   birth?

[9] TSE, 1. 23.
[10] "Fresh blows the wind / toward the homeland; / my Irish child, / where are you lingering?" (TSE, 1. 31).
[11] The pattern of the death and rebirth process is suggested by the reference to Hyacinth.
[12] "Desolate and empty the sea" (TSE, 1. 42).
[13] TSE, 1. 46.
[14] From Ariel's song in Shakespeare, *The Tempest* (I, ii, 398).
[15] An allusion to the sacrificial figure in primitive fertility rites and (by extension) in later religious myths.

Tell her I bring the horoscope myself:
One must be so careful these days.

Unreal City,[16]   60
Under the brown fog of a winter dawn,
A crowd flowed over London Bridge, so many,
I had not thought death had undone so many.[17]
Sighs, short and infrequent, were exhaled,[18]
And each man fixed his eyes before his feet.   *modern London/*
Flowed up the hill and down King William Street,   *Dante's hell*
To where Saint Mary Woolnoth kept the hours
With a dead sound on the final stroke of nine.[19]
There I saw one I knew, and stopped him, crying: "Stetson!
"You who were with me in the ships at Mylae![20]   70
"That corpse you planted last year in your garden,
"Has it begun to sprout? Will it bloom this year?
"Or has the sudden frost disturbed its bed?
"Oh keep the Dog far hence, that's friend to men,
"Or with his nails he'll dig it up again![21]
"You! hypocrite lecteur!—mon semblable,—mon frère!"[22]

II

A Game of Chess

The Chair she sat in, like a burnished throne,[23]
Glowed on the marble, where the glass
Held up by standards wrought with fruited vines
From which a golden Cupidon peeped out   80
(Another hid his eyes behind his wing)
Doubled the flames of sevenbranched candelabra
Reflecting light upon the table as
The glitter of her jewels rose to meet it,
From satin cases poured in rich profusion;
In vials of ivory and coloured glass
Unstoppered, lurked her strange synthetic perfumes,
Unguent, powdered, or liquid—troubled, confused

---

[16] Eliot cites Baudelaire's poetic description of Paris in *Les Fleurs du Mal*: "Swarming city, full of dreams, / Where the ghost in broad daylight hails the passerby" (TSE, 1. 60).

[17] Eliot's version of the following lines from Dante's *Inferno*: "So long a train of people, I should never have believed that death had undone so many" (TSE, 1. 63).

[18] Eliot cites Dante: "Here was no complaint that could be heard, except of sighs, that made the eternal air tremble" (TSE, 1. 64).

[19] A reference to the bell of the 18th-century London church (TSE, 1. 68).

[20] Despite the reference to the naval battle of Mylae (260 B.C.), Stetson would seem to be hailed as a World War I comrade.

[21] These lines echo John Webster's *The White Devil* (V, iv, 97–98): "But keep the wolf far thence, that's foe to men, / For with his nails he'll dig them up again" (TSE, 1, 74).

[22] "Hypocrite reader!—my likeness,—my brother!" (TSE, 1.76).

[23] These lines echo Enobarbus' famous description of Cleopatra's barge in Shakespeare's *Antony and Cleopatra* (TSE, 1. 77).

And drowned the sense in odours; stirred by the air
That freshened from the window, these ascended   90
In fattening the prolonged candle-flames,
Flung their smoke into the laquearia,[24]
Stirring the pattern on the coffered ceiling.
Huge sea-wood fed with copper
Burned green and orange, framed by the coloured stone,
In which sad light a carvèd dolphin swam.
Above the antique mantel was displayed
As though a window gave upon the sylvan scene
The change of Philomel,[25] by the barbarous king
So rudely forced;[26] yet there the nightingale   100
Filled all the desert with inviolable voice
And still she cried, and still the world pursues,
"Jug Jug" to dirty ears.
And other withered stumps of time
Were told upon the walls; staring forms
Leaned out, leaning, hushing the room enclosed.
Footsteps shuffled on the stair.
Under the firelight, under the brush, her hair
Spread out in fiery points
Glowed into words, then would be savagely still.   110

    "My nerves are bad to-night. Yes, bad. Stay with me.
"Speak to me. Why do you never speak. Speak.
      "What are you thinking of? What thinking? What?
"I never know what you are thinking. Think."

    I think we are in rats' alley[27]
Where the dead men lost their bones.

    "What is that noise?"
                The wind under the door.[28]
"What is that noise now? What is the wind doing?"
                Nothing again nothing.   120

                            "Do
"You know nothing? Do you see nothing? Do you remember
"Nothing?"

    I remember
Those are pearls that were his eyes.[29]
"Are you alive, or not? Is there nothing in your head?"
                                But

---

[24] "Fretted ceiling" — Eliot cites Virgil's *Aeneid*: "lighted lamps hang from the golden fretted ceiling, and flaming torches banish the night" (TSE, 1. 92).
[25] An allusion to Ovid's story of the rape of Philomel by her brother-in-law King Tereus and of her metamorphosis into a nightingale by the gods (TSE, 1. 99).
[26] TSE, 1. 100.   [27] TSE, 1. 115.   [28] TSE, 1. 118.   [29] See note 14 above.

O O O O that Shakespeherian Rag—
It's so elegant
So intelligent
"What shall I do now? What shall I do?"   130
"I shall rush out as I am, and walk the street
"With my hair down, so. What shall we do to-morrow?
"What shall we ever do?"
                              The hot water at ten.
And if it rains, a closed car at four.
And we shall play a game of chess,
Pressing lidless eyes and waiting for a knock upon the door.[30]

          When Lil's husband got demobbed,[31] I said—
I didn't mince my words, I said to her myself,   140
HURRY UP PLEASE ITS TIME[32]
Now Albert's coming back, make yourself a bit smart.
He'll want to know what you done with that money he gave you
To get yourself some teeth. He did, I was there.
You have them all out, Lil, and get a nice set,
He said, I swear, I can't bear to look at you.
And no more can't I, I said, and think of poor Albert,
He's been in the army four years, he wants a good time,
And if you don't give it him, there's others will, I said.
Oh is there, she said. Something o' that, I said.   150
Then I'll know who to thank, she said, and give me a straight
          look.
HURRY UP PLEASE ITS TIME
If you don't like it you can get on with it, I said.
Others can pick and choose if you can't.
But if Albert makes off, it won't be for lack of telling.
You ought to be ashamed, I said, to look so antique.
(And her only thirty-one.)
I can't help it, she said, pulling a long face,
It's them pills I took, to bring it off, she said.
(She's had five already, and nearly died of young George.)   160
The chemist[33] said it would be all right, but I've never been the
          same.
You are a proper fool, I said.
Well, if Albert won't leave you alone, there it is, I said,
What you get married for if you don't want children?
HURRY UP PLEASE ITS TIME
Well, that Sunday Albert was home, they had a hot gammon,
And they asked me in to dinner, to get the beauty of it hot—
HURRY UP PLEASE ITS TIME

---

[30] TSE, 1. 138.
[31] "Demobilized." The scene has shifted from the drawing room to a pub.
[32] The pubkeeper's warning that the legal closing hour is near.
[33] British for "pharmacist."

HURRY UP PLEASE ITS TIME
Goonight Bill. Goonight Lou. Goonight May. Goonight.   170
Ta ta. Goonight. Goonight.
Good night, ladies, good night, sweet ladies, good night,
    good night.[34]

III

The Fire Sermon

The river's tent is broken: the last fingers of leaf
Clutch and sink into the wet bank. The wind
Crosses the brown land, unheard. The nymphs are departed.
Sweet Thames, run softly, till I end my song.[35]
The river bears no empty bottles, sandwich papers,
Silk handkerchiefs, cardboard boxes, cigarette ends
Or other testimony of summer nights. The nymphs are departed.
And their friends, the loitering heirs of city directors;   180
Departed, have left no addresses.
By the waters of Leman I sat down and wept . . .[36]
Sweet Thames, run softly till I end my song,
Sweet Thames, run softly, for I speak not loud or long.
But at my back in a cold blast I hear[37]
The rattle of the bones, and chuckle spread from ear to ear.
A rat crept softly through the vegetation
Dragging its slimy belly on the bank
While I was fishing in the dull canal
On a winter evening round behind the gashouse   190
Musing upon the king my brother's wreck
And on the king my father's death before him.[38]
White bodies naked on the low damp ground
And bones cast in a little low dry garret,
Rattled by the rat's foot only, year to year.
But at my back from time to time I hear[39]
The sound of horns and motors, which shall bring
Sweeney to Mrs. Porter in the spring.[40]
O the moon shone bright on Mrs. Porter[41]
And on her daughter   200
They wash their feet in soda water
Et O ces voix d'enfants, chantant dans la coupole![42]

    Twit twit twit
Jug jug jug jug jug jug

---

[34] Ophelia's words at the end of her mad scene in Shakespeare's *Hamlet* (IV, v, 72–74).
[35] The refrain of Edmund Spenser's "Prothalamion" (TSE, 1. 179).
[36] The line echoes "by the rivers of Babylon" of Psalm 137; "Leman" is Lake Geneva in Switzerland.
[37] See note 39 below.
[38] TSE, 1. 192.   [39] TSE, 1. 196.   [40] TSE, 1. 197.   [41] TSE, 1. 199.
[42] "And, oh, those children's voices, singing in the cupola!" (TSE, 1. 202).

So rudely forc'd.
Tereu[43]

Unreal City
Under the brown fog of a winter noon
Mr. Eugenides, the Smyrna merchant
Unshaven, with a pocket full of currants
C.i.f. London: documents at sight,[44]   210
Asked me in demotic French
To luncheon at the Cannon Street Hotel
Followed by a weekend at the Metropole.

At the violet hour, when the eyes and back
Turn upward from the desk, when the human engine waits
Like a taxi throbbing waiting,
I Tiresias, though blind, throbbing between two lives.[45]
Old man with wrinkled female breasts, can see
At the violet hour, the evening hour that strives   220
Homeward, and brings the sailor home from sea,[46]
The typist home at teatime, clears her breakfast, lights
Her stove, and lays out food in tins.
Out of the window perilously spread
Her drying combinations touched by the sun's last rays,
On the divan are piled (at night her bed)
Stockings, slippers, camisoles, and stays.
I Tiresias, old man with wrinkled dugs
Perceived the scene, and foretold the rest —
I too awaited the expected guest.   230
He, the young man carbuncular, arrives,
A small house agent's clerk, with one bold stare,
One of the low on whom assurance sits

[43] With "jug, jug . . . ," a representation of the nightingale's song and a reminder of Philomel.

[44] TSE, 1. 210.

[45] See Eliot's note on Tiresias (TSE, 1. 218), in which he quotes a relevant passage from Ovid's *Metamorphoses* (III, 320–338) which has been translated as follows: ". . . Jove, they say, was happy / And feeling pretty good (with wine) forgetting / Anxiety and care, and killing time / Joking with Juno. 'I maintain,' he told her, / 'You females get more pleasure out of loving / Than we poor males do, ever.' She denied it, / So they decided to refer the question / To wise Tiresias' judgment: he should know / What love was like from either point of view. / Once he had come upon two serpents mating / In the green woods, and struck them from each other, / And thereupon, from man was turned to woman, / And was a woman seven years, and saw / The serpents once again, and once more struck them / Apart, remarking: 'If there is such magic / In giving you blows, that man is turned to woman, / It may be woman is turned to man. Worth trying.' / And so he was a man again; as umpire, / He took the side of Jove. And Juno / Was a bad loser, and she said that umpires / Were always blind, and made him so forever. / No god can overrule another's action, / But the Almighty Father, out of pity, in compensation, gave Tiresias power / To know the future, so there was some honor / Along with punishment." (*Metamorphoses*, tr. Rolfe Humphries [Bloomington, Ind., 1955], p. 67.)

[46] Eliot cites "Sappho's lines," probably from the fragment (CXLIX) addressed to Hesperus, the Evening Star (TSE, 1. 221), but readers are more likely to be reminded of R. L. Stevenson's "Requiem": "Home is the sailor, home from the sea."

As a silk hat on a Bradford millionaire.[47]
The time is now propitious, as he guesses,
The meal is ended, she is bored and tired,
Endeavours to engage her in caresses
Which still are unreproved, if undesired.
Flushed and decided, he assaults at once;
Exploring hands encounter no defence;   240
His vanity requires no response,
And makes a welcome of indifference.
(And I Tiresias have foresuffered all
Enacted on this same divan or bed;
I who have sat by Thebes below the wall
And walked among the lowest of the dead.)[48]
Bestows one final patronising kiss,
And gropes his way, finding the stairs unlit . . .
    She turns and looks a moment in the glass,
Hardly aware of her departed lover;   250
Her brain allows one half-formed thought to pass:
"Well now that's done: and I'm glad it's over."
When lovely woman stoops to folly and
Paces about her room again, alone,
She smoothes her hair with automatic hand,
And puts a record on the gramophone.[49]

    "This music crept by me upon the waters"[50]
And along the Strand,[51] up Queen Victoria Street.
O City city, I can sometimes hear
Beside a public bar in Lower Thames Street,   260
The pleasant whining of a mandoline
And a clatter and a chatter from within
Where fishmen lounge at noon: where the walls
Of Magnus Martyr hold[52]
Inexplicable splendour of Ionian white and gold.

        The river sweats[53]
    Oil and tar
    The barges drift
    With the turning tide
    Red sails   270

[47] The phrase suggests a newly-rich vulgarian. Bradford is an English industrial city.
[48] Tiresias prophesied in Thebes, for Oedipus among others, and in Hades, for Odysseus (see Ezra Pound, *Canto I*).
[49] These lines are Eliot's ironic modern variation on Goldsmith's well-known poem "Woman," which begins: "When lovely woman stoops to folly, / And finds too late that men betray, / What charm can soothe her melancholy? / What art can wash her tears away?" (TSE, 1. 253).
[50] TSE, 1. 257.   [51] A London street.   [52] TSE, 1. 264.
[53] For the beginning of this song of the Thames-daughters (TSE, 1. 266), Eliot borrows the refrain (11. 278–279, 290–291) of Wagner's song of the Rhine-daughters.

Wide
To leeward, swing on the heavy spar.
The barges wash
Drifting logs
Down Greenwich reach[54]
Past the Isle of Dogs.[55]
> Weialala leia
> Wallala leialala

> Elizabeth and Leicester[56]
Beating oars   280
The stern was formed
A gilded shell
Red and gold
The brisk swell
Rippled both shores
Southwest wind
Carried down stream
The peal of bells
White towers
> Weialala leia   290
> Wallala leialala

"Trams and dusty trees.
Highbury bore me. Richmond and Kew
Undid me.[57] By Richmond I raised my knees
Supine on the floor of a narrow canoe."

"My feet are at Moorgate, and my heart
Under my feet. After the event
He wept. He promised 'a new start.'
I made no comment. What should I resent?"

"On Margate Sands.[58]   300
I can connect
Nothing with nothing.
The broken fingernails of dirty hands.
My people humble people who expect
Nothing."
> la la

---

[54] A stretch of the Thames at Greenwich.

[55] A peninsula in the river.

[56] The idealized river excursion of Queen Elizabeth and her lover (suggestive of the noble passion of Antony and Cleopatra) is contrasted with the sordid experiences of the modern working class Thames daughters (TSE, 1. 279).

[57] Eliot cites the lines from Dante he echoes here: "Remember me, who am La Pia. / Siena made me; Maremma undid me" (TSE, 1. 293). Pound made use of the same quotation for the title of one of his Mauberley poems (see above).

[58] Moorgate is a lower class section of London; Margate Sands is a seashore resort.

To Carthage then I came[59]

Burning burning burning burning[60]
O Lord Thou pluckest me out[61]
O Lord Thou pluckest   310

burning

IV

Death by Water [62]

Phlebas the Phoenician, a fortnight dead,
Forgot the cry of gulls, and the deep sea swell
And the profit and loss.
                        A current under sea
Picked his bones in whispers. As he rose and fell
He passed the stages of his age and youth
Entering the whirlpool.
                        Gentile or Jew
O you who turn the wheel and look to windward,   320
Consider Phlebas, who was once handsome and tall as you.

V

What the Thunder Said [63]

After the torchlight red on sweaty faces[64]
After the frosty silence in the gardens
After the agony in stony places
The shouting and the crying
Prison and palace and reverberation
Of thunder of spring over distant mountains
He who was living is now dead
We who were living are now dying
With a little patience   330

Here is no water but only rock
Rock and no water and the sandy road
The road winding above among the mountains
Which are mountains of rock without water
If there were water we should stop and drink

---

[59] TSE, 1. 307.   [60] TSE, 1. 308.   [61] TSE, 1. 309.
[62] The "death by water" of the sailor Phlebas is an ironic reminder of the death of the sacrificial figure in the fertility rites. For Phlebas, who was a materialistic trader rather than a spiritual quester, there is no suggestion of a rebirth.
[63] See Eliot's general note for this part of the poem.
[64] These lines (322–330) combine the atmosphere of modern revolution with allusions to the passion and death of Christ.

Amongst the rock one cannot stop or think
Sweat is dry and feet are in the sand
If there were only water amongst the rock
Dead mountain mouth of carious teeth that cannot spit
Here one can neither stand nor lie nor sit   340
There is not even silence in the mountains
But dry sterile thunder without rain
There is not even solitude in the mountains
But red sullen faces sneer and snarl
From doors of mudcracked houses
          If there were water
    And no rock
    If there were rock
    And also water
    And water   350
    A spring
    A pool among the rock
    If there were the sound of water only
    Not the cicada
    And dry grass singing
    But sound of water over a rock
    Where the hermit-thrush sings in the pine trees[65]
    Drip drop drip drop drop drop drop
    But there is no water

       Who is the third who walks always beside you?[66]   360
When I count, there are only you and I together
But when I look ahead up the white road
There is always another one walking beside you
Gliding wrapt in a brown mantle, hooded
I do not know whether a man or a woman
— But who is that on the other side of you?

       What is that sound high in the air[67]
Murmur of maternal lamentation
Who are those hooded hordes swarming
Over endless plains, stumbling in cracked earth   370
Ringed by the flat horizon only
What is the city over the mountains
Cracks and reforms and bursts in the violet air
Falling towers
Jerusalem Athens Alexandria

---

[65] TSE, 1. 357.   [66] TSE. 1. 360. See also *Luke* 24:13–34.
[67] As background for these lines (TSE, 367–377), Eliot cites a German text by Hermann Hesse, which reads, in English: "Already half of Europe, already at least half of East Europe, is on the road to chaos, travels drunken, in a kind of madness of the spirit, along the edge of the abyss, sings drunkenly and fervently, just as Dmitri Karamazov sang. Though offended, the bourgeois laughs at these songs; the saint and the prophet listen to them with tears."

Vienna London
Unreal

A woman drew her long black hair out tight
And fiddled whisper music on those strings
And bats with baby faces in the violet light   380
Whistled, and beat their wings
And crawled head downward down a blackened wall
And upside down in air were towers
Tolling reminiscent bells, that kept the hours
And voices singing out of empty cisterns and exhausted wells.

In this decayed hole among the mountains
In the faint moonlight, the grass is singing
Over the tumbled graves, about the chapel[68]
There is the empty chapel, only the wind's home.
It has no windows, and the door swings,   390
Dry bones can harm no one.
Only a cock stood on the rooftree
Co co rico co co rico
In a flash of lightning. Then a damp gust
Bringing rain

the prince who will bring salvation (margin note)

Ganga[69] was sunken, and the limp leaves
Waited for rain, while the black clouds
Gathered far distant, over Himavant.[70]
The jungle crouched, humped in silence.
Then spoke the thunder   400
D A
Datta:[71] what have we given?
My friend, blood shaking my heart
The awful daring of a moment's surrender
Which an age of prudence can never retract
By this, and this only, we have existed
Which is not to be found in our obituaries
Or in memories draped by the beneficent spider[72]
Or under seals broken by the lean solicitor
In our empty rooms   410
D A
Dayadhvam: I have heard the key
Turn in the door once and turn once only[73]
We think of the key, each in his prison
Thinking of the key, each confirms a prison

give, sympathize, control (margin note)

[68] The chapel suggests both the Chapel Perilous, in which the questing knight must undergo an ordeal before achieving a vision of the Grail, and the decadent modern church.
[69] The Ganges River.   [70] The Himalaya Mountains.   [71] TSE, 1. 402.   [72] TSE, 1. 408.
[73] Eliot cites lines from Dante which read, in English: "And I heard being locked below the door of the horrible tower" (TSE, 1. 412).

Only at nightfall, aethereal rumours
Revive for a moment a broken Coriolanus[74]
DA
Damyata: The boat responded
Gaily, to the hand expert with sail and oar   420
The sea was calm, your heart would have responded

Gaily, when invited, beating obedient
To controlling hands

                I sat upon the shore
Fishing, with the arid plain behind me[75]
Shall I at least set my lands in order?
London Bridge is falling down falling down falling down
Poi s'ascose nel foco che gli affina[76]
Quando fiam uti chelidon[77] — O swallow swallow
Le Prince d'Aquitaine à la tour abolie[78]   430
These fragments I have shored against my ruins
Why then Ile fit you. Hieronymo's mad againe.[79]
Datta. Dayadhvam. Damyata.
       Shantih   shantih   shantih[80]

we are not ready
for the lesson

1922

Notes on "The Waste Land"

Not only the title, but the plan and a good deal of the incidental symbolism of the poem were suggested by Miss Jessie L. Weston's book on the Grail legend: *From Ritual to Romance* (Cambridge). Indeed, so deeply am I indebted, Miss Weston's book will elucidate the difficulties of the poem much better than my notes can do; and I recommend it (apart from the great interest of the book itself) to any who think such elucidation of the poem worth the trouble. To another work of anthropology I am indebted in general, one which has influenced our generation profoundly; I mean *The Golden Bough*; I have used especially the two volumes *Adonis, Attis, Osiris.* Anyone who is acquainted with these works will immediately recognise in the poem certain references to vegetation ceremonies.

---

[74] The Roman general of the 5th century B.C., protagonist of Shakespeare's *Coriolanus.*
[75] TSE, 1. 425.
[76] "Then he hid himself in the flame that refines them." Eliot quotes this and three preceding lines from Dante's *Purgatorio* (TSE, 1. 428). In the first three, the spirit of the Provençal poet Arnaut Daniel addresses the poet: "Now I pray you, by the goodness that guides you to the top of this staircase, be mindful in due season of my pain."
[77] "When shall I be like the swallow?" Eliot cites the anonymous Latin poem *Pervigilium Veneris* (ca. 2nd century A.D.), which celebrates love and springtime (TSE, 1. 429).
[78] "The Prince of Aquitaine at the ruined tower" (TSE, 1. 430).
[79] TSE, 1. 432.   [80] TSE, 1. 434.

I. The Burial of the Dead

Line 20. Cf. Ezekiel II, i.

23. Cf. Ecclesiastes XII, v.

31. V. Tristan und Isolde, I, verses 5 – 8.

42. Id. III, verse 24.

46. I am not familiar with the exact constitution of the Tarot pack of cards, from which I have obviously departed to suit my own convenience. The Hanged Man, a member of the traditional pack, fits my purpose in two ways: because he is associated in my mind with the Hanged God of Frazer, and because I associate him with the hooded figure in the passage of the disciples to Emmaus in Part V. The Phoenician Sailor and the Merchant appear later; also the "crowds of people," and Death by Water is executed in Part IV. The Man with Three Staves (an authentic member of the Tarot pack) I associate, quite arbitrarily, with the Fisher King himself.

60. Cf. Baudelaire:

"Fourmillante cité, cité pleine de rêves,

"Où le spectre en plein jour raccroche le passant."

63. Cf. Inferno III, 55 – 57:

"si lunga tratta

di gente, ch'io non avrei mai creduto

che morte tanta n'avesse disfatta."

64. Cf. Inferno IV, 25 – 27:

"Quivi, secondo che per ascoltare,

"non avea pianto, ma' che di sospiri,

"che l'aura eterna facevan tremare."

68. A phenomenon which I have often noticed.

74. Cf. the Dirge in Webster's *White Devil.*

76. V. Baudelaire, Preface to *Fleurs du Mal.*

II. A Game of Chess

77. Cf. *Antony and Cleopatra*, II, ii, l. 190.

92. Laquearia. V. *Aeneid*, I, 726:

dependent lychni laquearibus aureis incensi, et noctem flammis funalia vincunt.

98. Sylvan scene. V. Milton, *Paradise Lost*, IV, 140.

99. V. Ovid, *Metamorphoses*, VI, Philomela.

100. Cf. Part III, l. 204.

115. Cf. Part III, l. 195.

118. Cf. Webster: "Is the wind in that door still?"

126. Cf. Part I, l. 37, 48.

138. Cf. the game of chess in Middleton's *Women beware Women.*

III. The Fire Sermon

176. V. Spenser, *Prothalamion.*

192. Cf. *The Tempest*, I, ii.

196. Cf. Marvell, *To His Coy Mistress.*

197. Cf. Day, *Parliament of Bees*:

"When of the sudden, listening, you shall hear,
"A noise of horns and hunting, which shall bring
"Actaeon to Diana in the spring,
"Where all shall see her naked skin . . ."

199. I do not know the origin of the ballad from which these lines are taken: it was reported to me from Sydney, Australia.

202. V. Verlaine, *Parsifal.*

210. The currants were quoted at a price "carriage and insurance free to London"; and the Bill of Lading etc. were to be handed to the buyer upon payment of the sight draft.

218. Tiresias, although a mere spectator and not indeed a "character," is yet the most important personage in the poem, uniting all the rest. Just as the one-eyed merchant, seller of currants, melts into the Phoenician Sailor, and the latter is not wholly distinct from Ferdinand Prince of Naples, so all the women are one woman, and the two sexes meet in Tiresias. What Tiresias *sees*, in fact, is the substance of the poem. The whole passage from Ovid is of great anthropological interest:

'. . . Cum Iunone iocos et maior vestra profecto est
Quam, quae contingit maribus,' dixisse, 'voluptas.'
Illa negat; placuit quae sit sententia docti
Quaerere Tiresiae: venus huic erat utraque nota.
Nam duo magnorum viridi coeuntia silva
Corpora serpentum baculi violaverat ictu
Deque viro factus, mirabile, femina septem
Egerat autumnos; octavo rursus eosdem
Vidit et 'est vestrae si tanta potentia plagae,'
Dixit 'ut auctoris sortem in contraria mutet,
Nunc quoque vos feriam!' percussis anguibus isdem
Forma prior rediit genetivaque venit imago.
Arbiter hic igitur sumptus de lite iocosa
Dicta Iovis firmat; gravius Saturnia iusto
Nec pro materia fertur doluisse suique
Iudicis aeterna damnavit lumina nocte,
At pater omnipotens (neque enim licet inrita cuiquam
Facta dei fecisse deo) pro lumine adempto
Scire futura dedit poenamque levavit honore.

221. This may not appear as exact as Sappho's lines, but I had in mind the "longshore" or "dory" fisherman, who returns at nightfall.

253. V. Goldsmith, the song in *The Vicar of Wakefield.*

257. V. *The Tempest*, as above.

264. The interior of St. Magnus Martyr is to my mind one of the finest among Wren's interiors. See *The Proposed Demolition of Nineteen City Churches:* (P. S. King & Son, Ltd.).

266. The Song of the (three) Thames-daughters begins here. From line 292 to 306 inclusive they speak in turn. V. *Götterdämmerung*, III, i: the Rhine-daughters.

279. V. Froude, *Elizabeth*, Vol. I, ch. iv, letter of De Quadra to Philip of Spain:

"In the afternoon we were in a barge, watching the games on the river. (The queen) was alone with Lord Robert and myself on the poop, when they began to talk nonsense, and went so far that Lord Robert at last said, as I was on the spot there was no reason why they should not be married if the queen pleased."

293. Cf. *Purgatorio*, V, 133:

"Ricorditi di me, che son la Pia;
"Siena mi fe', disfecemi Maremma."

307. V. St. Augustine's *Confessions:* "to Carthage then I came, where a cauldron of unholy loves sang all about mine ears."

308. The complete text of the Buddha's Fire Sermon (which corresponds in importance to the Sermon on the Mount) from which these words are taken, will be found translated in the late Henry Clarke Warren's *Buddhism in Translation* (Harvard Oriental Series). Mr. Warren was one of the great pioneers of Buddhist studies in the Occident.

309. From St. Augustine's *Confessions* again. The collocation of these two representatives of eastern and western asceticism, as the culmination of this part of the poem, is not an accident.

V.   What the Thunder Said

In the first part of Part V three themes are employed: the journey to Emmaus, the approach to the Chapel Perilous (see Miss Weston's book) and the present decay of eastern Europe.

357. This is *Turdus aonalaschkae pallasii*, the hermit-thrush which I have heard in Quebec Province. Chapman says (*Handbook of Birds of Eastern North America*) "it is most at home in secluded woodland and thickety retreats. . . . Its notes are not remarkable for variety or volume, but in purity and sweetness of tone and exquisite modulation they are unequalled." Its "water-dripping song" is justly celebrated.

360. The following lines were stimulated by the account of one of the Antarctic expeditions (I forget which, but I think one of Shackleton's): it was related that the party of explorers, at the extremity of their strength, had the constant delusion that there was *one more member* than could actually be counted.

367–77. Cf. Hermann Hesse, *Blick ins Chaos*: "Schon ist halb Europa, schon ist zumindest der halbe Osten Europas auf dem Wege zum Chaos, fährt betrunken im heiligem Wahn am Abgrund entlang und singt dazu, singt betrunken und hymnisch wie Dmitri Karamasoff sang. Ueber diese Lieder lacht der Bürger beleidigt, der Heilige und Seher hört sie mit Tränen."

402. "Datta, dayadhvam, damyata" (Give, sympathise, control). The fable of the meaning of the Thunder is found in the *Brihadara-nyaka—Upanishad*, 5, 1. A translation is found in Deussen's *Sechzig Upanishads des Veda*, p. 489.

408. Cf. Webster, *The White Devil*, V, vi:
". . . they'll remarry
Ere the worm pierce your winding-sheet, ere the spider
Make a thin curtain for your epitaphs."

412. Cf. *Inferno*, XXXIII, 46:
"ed io sentii chiavar l'uscio di sotto
all'orribile torre."
Also F. H. Bradley, *Appearance and Reality*, p. 346.
"My external sensations are no less private to myself than are my thoughts or my feelings. In either case my experience falls within my own circle, a circle closed on the outside; and, with all its elements alike, every sphere is opaque to the others which surround it. . . . In brief, regarded as an existence which appears in a soul, the whole world for each is peculiar and private to that soul."

425. V. Weston: *From Ritual to Romance;* chapter on the Fisher King.

428. V. *Purgatorio*, XXVI, 148.
"Ara vos prec per aquella valor
que vos guida al som de l'escalina,
'sovegna vos a temps de ma dolor.'
Poi s'ascose nel foco che gli affina."

429. V. *Pervigilium Veneris*. Cf. Philomela in Parts II and III.

430. V. Gerard de Nerval, Sonnet *El Desdichado*.

432. V. Kyd's *Spanish Tragedy*.

434. Shantih. Repeated as here, a formal ending to an Upanishad. "The Peace which passeth understanding" is our equivalent to this word.

Journey of the Magi

[handwritten annotation:]
- difficulty of finding religion/faith
-the realization/revalation wanes
- difficulty of spiritual change

'A cold coming we had of it,
Just the worst time of the year
For a journey, and such a long journey:
The ways deep and the weather sharp,

The very dead of winter.'[1]
And the camels galled, sore-footed, refractory,
Lying down in the melting snow.
There were times we regretted
The summer palaces on slopes, the terraces,
And the silken girls bringing sherbet.   10
Then the camel men cursing and grumbling
And running away, and wanting their liquor and women,
And the night-fires going out, and the lack of shelters,
And the cities hostile and the towns unfriendly
And the villages dirty and charging high prices:
A hard time we had of it.
At the end we preferred to travel all night,
Sleeping in snatches,
With the voices singing in our ears, saying
That this was all folly.   20

    Then at dawn we came down to a temperate valley,
Wet, below the snow line, smelling of vegetation;
With a running stream and a water-mill beating the darkness,
And three trees on the low sky,[2]
And an old white horse galloped away in the meadow.
Then we came to a tavern with vine-leaves over the lintel,
Six hands at an open door dicing for pieces of silver,
And feet kicking the empty wine-skins.[3]
But there was no information, and so we continued   30
And arrived at evening, not a moment too soon
Finding the place; it was (you may say) satisfactory.

    All this was a long time ago, I remember,
And I would do it again, but set down
This set down
This: were we led all that way for
Birth or Death? There was a Birth, certainly,
We had evidence and no doubt. I had seen birth and death,
But had thought they were different; this Birth was
Hard and bitter agony for us, like Death, our death.   40
We returned to our places, these Kingdoms,
But no longer at ease here, in the old dispensation,
With an alien people clutching their gods.
I should be glad of another death.

1927

---

[1] A close rendering of a passage from a sermon by Lancelot Andrewes (1555 – 1626) which Eliot had praised for its prose style in his essay "Lancelot Andrewes" (1926). See Eliot's *Selected Essays*, new ed. (New York, 1960), p. 307.

[2] A foreshadowing of the crucifixion.

[3] Grover Smith has suggested that this one sentence may contain allusions "to the Communion (through the tavern 'bush'), to the paschal lamb whose blood was smeared on the lintels of Israel, to the blood money of Judas, to the contumely suffered by Christ before the Crucifixion, to the soldiers casting lots at the foot of the Cross, and, perhaps, to the pilgrims at the open tomb in the garden" (*T. S. Eliot's Poems and Plays* [Chicago, 1956], p. 124).

Burnt Norton[1]

τοῦ λόγου δ'ἐόντος ξυνοῦ ζώουσιν οἱ πολλοί
ὡς ἰδίαν ἔχοντες φρόνησιν.
                                I. p. 77. Fr. 2.
ὁδὸς ἄνω κάτω μία καὶ ὠυτή.
                                I. p. 89. Fr. 60.
Diels: *Die Fragmente der Vorsokratiker* (Herakleitos).[2]

1

Time present and time past
Are both perhaps present in time future,
And time future contained in time past.
If all time is eternally present
All time is unredeemable.
What might have been is an abstraction
Remaining a perpetual possibility
Only in a world of speculation.
What might have been and what has been
Point to one end, which is always present.   10
Footfalls echo in the memory
Down the passage which we did not take
Towards the door we never opened
Into the rose-garden.[3] My words echo
Thus, in your mind.
                        But to what purpose
Disturbing the dust on a bowl of rose-leaves
I do not know.
                Other echoes
Inhabit the garden. Shall we follow?   20
Quick, said the bird, find them, find them,
Round the corner. Through the first gate,

---

[1] "Burnt Norton," the earliest of the *Four Quartets* (1943), was first published in *Collected Poems 1909–1935* (1936). The title of each of the four poems (the others are "East Coker," "The Dry Salvages," and "Little Gidding") designates a place which had personal or historical associations for Eliot. Burnt Norton is the name of a manor house near Chipping Camden, in Gloucestershire, where he had vacationed one summer. Each of the Quartets is organized in the five-part pattern Eliot had developed in *The Waste Land*, but without the radical fragmentation of the earlier poem. The rebirth pattern persists, however, since each of the poems is a parallel extended meditation on the relation of time and eternity (and of past and present time) and on the difficulties of the modern quester for salvation who aspires to attain the mystical goal of the vision of the "still point of the turning world," or turning wheel of time. The effort to integrate the four poems into a single formal pattern (which Eliot explained by comparison with the musical form of Beethoven's late quartets) is appropriate to the poet's attempt to resist time in favor of a unified mystical vision and to emphasize the spatial rather than temporal qualities of his own work.
[2] The two Greek epigraphs from Hermann Diels's edition of Heraclitus (Berlin, 1909) may be translated: "Although the *Word* (*logos*) is universal, most people live according to their individual understanding"; "The way up and the way down, one and the same."
[3] The rose garden, which suggests sexual as well as spiritual awareness, is basically a symbol of the goal of mystical vision toward which the poet strives.

Into our first world, shall we follow
The deception of the thrush? Into our first world.
There they were, dignified, invisible,
Moving without pressure, over the dead leaves,
In the autumn heat, through the vibrant air,
And the bird called, in response to
The unheard music hidden in the shrubbery,
And the unseen eyebeam crossed,[4] for the roses   30
Had the look of flowers that are looked at.
There they were as our guests, accepted and accepting.
So we moved, and they, in a formal pattern,
Along the empty alley, into the box circle,
To look down into the drained pool.
Dry the pool, dry concrete, brown edged,
And the pool was filled with water out of sunlight,[5]
And the lotos rose, quietly, quietly,
The surface glittered out of heart of light,
And they were behind us, reflected in the pool.   40
Then a cloud passed, and the pool was empty.
Go, said the bird, for the leaves were full of children,
Hidden excitedly, containing laughter.
Go, go, go, said the bird: human kind
Cannot bear very much reality.
Time past and time future
What might have been and what has been
Point to one end, which is always present.

2

Garlic and sapphires in the mud[6]
Clot the bedded axle-tree.   50
The trilling wire in the blood
Sings below inveterate scars
And reconciles forgotten wars.
The dance along the artery
The circulation of the lymph
Are figured in the drift of stars
Ascend to summer in the tree
We move above the moving tree
In light upon the figured leaf
And hear upon the sodden floor   60
Below, the boarhound and the boar
Pursue their pattern as before
But reconciled among the stars.

---

[4] Probably an echo of the "eye-beams twisted" of John Donne's poem "The Ecstasy."
[5] The filling pool and the rising lotus suggest the influx of mystical consciousness.
[6] An echo of Stéphane Mallarmé's line "Tonnerre et rubis aux moyeux" ("Thunder and rubies at the hubs") in his sonnet "M'introduire dans ton histoire."

At the still point of the turning world.[7] Neither flesh nor
    fleshless;
Neither from nor towards; at the still point, there the dance is,
But neither arrest nor movement. And do not call it fixity,
Where past and future are gathered. Neither movement from nor
    towards,
Neither ascent nor decline. Except for the point, the still point,
There would be no dance, and there is only the dance.   70
I can only say, *there* we have been: but I cannot say where.
And I cannot say, how long, for that is to place it in time.

    The inner freedom from the practical desire,
The release from action and suffering, release from the inner
And the outer compulsion, yet surrounded
By a grace of sense, a white light still and moving,[8]
Erhebung[9] without motion, concentration
Without elimination, both a new world
And the old made explicit, understood
In the completion of its partial ecstasy,   80
The resolution of its partial horror.
Yet the enchainment of past and future
Woven in the weakness of the changing body,
Protects mankind from heaven and damnation
Which flesh cannot endure.
                  Time past and time future
Allow but a little consciousness.
To be conscious is not to be in time
But only in time can the moment in the rose-garden,
The moment in the arbour where the rain beat,   90
The moment in the draughty church at smokefall
Be remembered; involved with past and future.
Only through time time is conquered.

3

Here is a place of disaffection
Time before and time after
In a dim light: neither daylight
Investing form with lucid stillness
Turning shadow into transient beauty
With slow rotation suggesting permanence
Nor darkness to purify the soul   100
Emptying the sensual with deprivation
Cleansing affection from the temporal.
Neither plenitude nor vacancy. Only a flicker
Over the strained time-ridden faces
Distracted from distraction by distraction

---

[7] See note 1 above.   [8] Most specifically the light of grace or revelation.   [9] Exaltation.

Filled with fancies and empty of meaning
Tumid apathy with no concentration
Men and bits of paper, whirled by the cold wind
That blows before and after time,
Wind in and out of unwholesome lungs   110
Time before and time after.
Eructation of unhealthy souls
Into the faded air, the torpid
Driven on the wind that sweeps the gloomy hills of London,
Hampstead and Clerkenwell, Campden and Putney,
Highgate, Primrose and Ludgate. Not here
Not here the darkness, in this twittering world.[10]

      Descend lower, descend only   120
Into the world of perpetual solitude,[11]
World not world, but that which is not world,
Internal darkness, deprivation
And destitution of all property,
Desiccation of the world of sense,
Evacuation of the world of fancy,
Inoperancy of the world of spirit;
This is the one way, and the other
Is the same, not in movement
But abstention from movement; while the world moves   130
In appetency, on its metalled ways
Of time past and time future.

4

Time and the bell have buried the day,
The black cloud carries the sun away.
Will the sunflower turn to us, will the clematis
Stray down, bend to us; tendril and spray
Clutch and cling?
Chill
Fingers of yew be curled
Down on us? After the kingfisher's wing[12]   140
Has answered light to light, and is silent, the light is still
At the still point of the turning world.

5

Words move, music moves
Only in time; but that which is only living
Can only die. Words, after speech, reach

[10] The phrase identifies the "real" world of time with the diminished world of the dead in Homer's conception of Hades.
[11] The spiritual descent into the "dark night of the soul," a necessary precondition, according to St. John of the Cross, of the mystic union with God.
[12] Reminiscent of the Fisher King and of Christ; the "fragmentary blue" of the kingfisher's wing is the symbol of a hoped-for revelation.

Into the silence. Only by the form, the pattern,
Can words or music reach
The stillness, as a Chinese jar still
Moves perpetually in its stillness.[13]
Not the stillness of the violin, while the note lasts,   150
Not that only, but the co-existence,
Or say that the end precedes the beginning,
And the end and the beginning were always there
Before the beginning and after the end.
And all is always now. Words strain,
Crack and sometimes break, under the burden,
Under the tension, slip, slide, perish,
Decay with imprecision, will not stay in place,
Will not stay still. Shrieking voices   160
Scolding, mocking, or merely chattering,
Always assail them. The Word in the desert
Is most attacked by voices of temptation,[14]
The crying shadow in the funeral dance,
The loud lament of the disconsolate chimera.

      The detail of the pattern is movement,
As in the figure of the ten stairs.[15]
Desire itself is movement
Not in itself desirable;
Love is itself unmoving,
Only the cause and end of movement,   170
Timeless, and undesiring
Except in the aspect of time
Caught in the form of limitation
Between un-being and being.
Sudden in a shaft of sunlight
Even while the dust moves
There rises the hidden laughter
Of children in the foliage
Quick now, here, now, always—
Ridiculous the waste sad time   180
Stretching before and after.

1936

Tradition and the Individual Talent [1]

      In English writing we seldom speak of tradition, though we occasionally apply its name in deploring its absence. We cannot refer to "the

---

[13] The qualities of the "Chinese jar" are reminiscent of those of Keats's "Grecian Urn."
[14] An allusion to the temptation of Christ in the wilderness (*Luke* 4:1–4).
[15] The figure of the "ten stairs" or ladder steps is from St. John of the Cross (*The Dark Night of the Soul*, II, xvii-xix).
[1] This influential early essay, first collected in *The Sacred Wood* (1920), sets forth Eliot's "impersonal theory of poetry."

tradition" or to "a tradition"; at most, we employ the adjective in saying that the poetry of So-and-so is "traditional" or even "too traditional." Seldom, perhaps, does the word appear except in a phrase of censure. If otherwise, it is vaguely approbative, with the implication, as to the work approved, of some pleasing archaeological reconstruction. You can hardly make the word agreeable to English ears without this comfortable reference to the reassuring science of archaeology.

Certainly the word is not likely to appear in our appreciations of living or dead writers. Every nation, every race, has not only its own creative, but its own critical turn of mind; and is even more oblivious of the shortcomings and limitations of its critical habits than of those of its creative genius. We know, or think we know, from the enormous mass of critical writing that has appeared in the French language the critical method or habit of the French; we only conclude (we are such unconscious people) that the French are "more critical" than we, and sometimes even plume ourselves a little with the fact, as if the French were the less spontaneous. Perhaps they are; but we might remind ourselves that criticism is as inevitable as breathing, and that we should be none the worse for articulating what passes in our minds when we read a book and feel an emotion about it, for criticizing our own minds in their work of criticism. One of the facts that might come to light in this process is our tendency to insist, when we praise a poet, upon those aspects of his work in which he least resembles any one else. In these aspects or parts of his work we pretend to find what is individual, what is the peculiar essence of the man. We dwell with satisfaction upon the poet's difference from his predecessors, especially his immediate predecessors; we endeavour to find something that can be isolated in order to be enjoyed. Whereas if we approach a poet without this prejudice we shall often find that not only the best, but the most individual parts of his work may be those in which the dead poets, his ancestors, assert their immortality most vigorously. And I do not mean the impressionable period of adolescence, but the period of full maturity.

Yet if the only form of tradition, of handing down, consisted in following the ways of the immediate generation before us in a blind or timid adherence to its successes, "tradition" should positively be discouraged. We have seen many such simple currents soon lost in the sand; and novelty is better than repetition. Tradition is a matter of much wider significance. It cannot be inherited, and if you want it you must obtain it by great labour. It involves, in the first place, the historical sense, which we may call nearly indispensable to any one who would continue to be a poet beyond his twenty-fifth year;[2] and the historical sense involves a perception, not only of the pastness of the past, but of its presence; the historical sense compels a man to write not

---

[2] By implication, the English Romantic poets are largely disposed of by this statement.

merely with his own generation in his bones, but with a feeling that the whole of the literature of Europe from Homer and within it the whole of the literature of his own country has a simultaneous existence and composes a simultaneous order. This historical sense, which is a sense of the timeless as well as of the temporal and of the timeless and of the temporal together, is what makes a writer traditional. And it is at the same time what makes a writer most acutely conscious of his place in time, of his own contemporaneity.

No poet, no artist of any art, has his complete meaning alone. His significance, his appreciation is the appreciation of his relation to the dead poets and artists. You cannot value him alone; you must set him, for contrast and comparison, among the dead. I mean this as a principle of aesthetic, not merely historical, criticism. The necessity that he shall conform, that he shall cohere, is not onesided; what happens when a new work of art is created is something that happens simultaneously to all the works of art which preceded it. The existing monuments form an ideal order among themselves, which is modified by the introduction of the new (the really new) work of art among them. The existing order is complete before the new work arrives; for order to persist after the supervention of novelty, the *whole* existing order must be, if ever so slightly, altered; and so the relations, proportions, values of each work of art toward the whole are readjusted; and this is conformity between the old and the new. Whoever has approved this idea of order, of the form of European, of English literature will not find it preposterous that the past should be altered by the present as much as the present is directed by the past. And the poet who is aware of this will be aware of great difficulties and responsibilities.

In a peculiar sense he will be aware also that he must inevitably be judged by the standards of the past. I say judged, not amputated, by them; not judged to be as good as, or worse or better than, the dead; and certainly not judged by the canons of dead critics. It is a judgment, a comparison, in which two things are measured by each other. To conform merely would be for the new work not really to conform at all; it would not be new, and would therefore not be a work of art. And we do not quite say that the new is more valuable because it fits in; but its fitting in is a test of its value—a test, it is true, which can only be slowly and cautiously applied, for we are none of us infallible judges of conformity. We say: it appears to conform, and is perhaps individual, or it appears individual, and may conform; but we are hardly likely to find that it is one and not the other.

To proceed to a more intelligible exposition of the relation of the poet to the past: he can neither take the past as a lump, an indiscriminate bolus, nor can he form himself wholly on one or two private admirations, nor can he form himself wholly upon one preferred period. The first course is inadmissible, the second is an important experience of youth, and the third is a pleasant and highly desirable supplement. The poet must be very conscious of the main current, which does not at all flow invariably through the most distinguished reputations. He must be quite aware of the obvious fact that art never improves, but that the material of art is never quite the same. He must be aware that the mind of Europe—the mind of his own country—a mind which he learns in time to be much more important than his own private mind—is a mind which changes, and that this change is a development which abandons nothing *en route*, which does not superannuate either Shakespeare, or Homer, or the rock drawing of the Magdalenian draughtsmen.[3] That this development, refinement perhaps, complication certainly, is not, from the point of view of the artist, any improvement. Perhaps not even an improvement from the point of view of the psychologist or not to the extent which we imagine; perhaps only in the end based upon a complication in economics and machinery. But the difference between the present and the past is that the conscious present is an awareness of the past in a way and to an extent which the past's awareness of itself cannot show.

Some one said: "The dead writers are remote from us because we *know* so much more than they did." Precisely, and they are that which we know.

I am alive to a usual objection to what is clearly part of my programme for the *métier*[4] of poetry. The objection is that the doctrine requires a ridiculous amount of erudition (pedantry), a claim which can be rejected by appeal to the lives of poets in any pantheon. It will even be affirmed that much learning deadens or perverts poetic sensibility. While, however, we persist in believing that a poet ought to know as much as will not encroach upon his necessary receptivity and necessary laziness, it is not desirable to confine knowledge to whatever can be put into a useful shape for examinations, drawing-rooms, or the still more pretentious modes of publicity. Some can absorb knowledge, the more tardy must sweat for it. Shakespeare acquired more essential history from Plutarch than most men could from the whole British Museum. What is to be insisted upon is that the poet must develop or procure the consciousness of the past and that he should continue to develop this consciousness throughout his career.

What happens is a continual surrender of himself as he is at the moment to something which is more valuable. The progress of an artist is a continual self-sacrifice, a continual extinction of personality.

There remains to define this process of depersonalization and its relation to the sense of tradition. It is in this depersonalization that art may be said to approach the condition of science. I, therefore, invite you to consider, as a suggestive analogy, the action which takes place

---

[3] A reference to the paleolithic cave drawings found in France.
[4] Craft.

_{1.} learning acquired by reading and study. scholarship   = pedantry. arbitrary adherence to rules and forms   3 Plutarch - Greek biographer and moralist—46-120 AD ?

when a bit of finely filiated platinum is introduced into a chamber containing oxygen and sulphur dioxide.

2

Honest criticism and sensitive appreciation are directed not upon the poet but upon the poetry. If we attend to the confused cries of the newspaper critics and the *susurrus*[5] of popular repetition that follows, we shall hear the names of poets in great numbers; if we seek not Blue-book knowledge but the enjoyment of poetry, and ask for a poem, we shall seldom find it. I have tried to point out the importance of the relation of the poem to other poems by other authors, and suggested the conception of poetry as a living whole of all the poetry that has ever been written. The other aspect of this Impersonal theory of poetry is the relation of the poem to its author. And I hinted, by an analogy, that the mind of the mature poet differs from that of the immature one not precisely in any valuation of "personality," not being necessarily more interesting, or having "more to say," but rather by being a more finely perfected medium in which special, or very varied, feelings are at liberty to enter into new combinations.

The analogy was that of the catalyst. When the two gases previously mentioned are mixed in the presence of a filament of platinum, they form sulphurous acid. This combination takes place only if the platinum is present; nevertheless the newly formed acid contains no trace of platinum, and the platinum itself is apparently unaffected; has remained inert, neutral, and unchanged. The mind of the poet is the shred of platinum. It may partly or exclusively operate upon the experience of the man himself; but, the more perfect the artist, the more completely separate in him will be the man who suffers and the mind which creates; the more perfectly will the mind digest and transmute the passions which are its material.

The experience, you will notice, the elements which enter the presence of the transforming catalyst, are of two kinds: emotions and feelings. The effect of a work of art upon the person who enjoys it is an experience different in kind from any experience not of art. It may be formed out of one emotion, or may be a combination of several; and various feelings, inhering for the writer in particular words or phrases or images, may be added to compose the final result. Or great poetry may be made without the direct use of any emotion whatever: composed out of feelings solely. Canto XV of the *Inferno* (Brunetto Latini) is a working up of the emotion evident in the situation; but the effect, though single as that of any work of art, is obtained by considerable complexity of detail. The last quatrain gives an image, a feeling attaching to an image, which "came," which did not develop simply out of what precedes, but which was probably in suspension in the poet's

[5] Murmuring.

mind until the proper combination arrived for it to add itself to. The poet's mind is in fact a receptacle for seizing and storing up numberless feelings, phrases, images, which remain there until all the particles which can unite to form a new compound are present together.

If you compare several representative passages of the greatest poetry you see how great is the variety of types of combination, and also how completely any semi-ethical criterion of "sublimity"[1] misses the mark. For it is not the "greatness," the intensity, of the emotions, the components, but the intensity of the artistic process, the pressure, so to speak, under which the fusion takes place, that counts. The episode of Paolo and Francesca[6] employs a definite emotion, but the intensity of the poetry is something quite different from whatever intensity in the supposed experience it may give the impression of. It is no more intense, furthermore, than Canto XXVI, the voyage of Ulysses, which has not the direct dependence upon an emotion. Great variety is possible in the process of transmutation of emotion: the murder of Agamemnon,[7] or the agony of Othello, gives an artistic effect apparently closer to a possible original than the scenes from Dante. In the *Agamemnon*, the artistic emotion approximates to the emotion of an actual spectator; in *Othello* to the emotion of the protagonist himself. But the difference between art and the event is always absolute; the combination which is the murder of Agamemnon is probably as complex as that which is the voyage of Ulysses. In either case there has been a fusion of elements. The ode of Keats contains a number of feelings which have nothing particular to do with the nightingale, but which the nightingale, partly, perhaps, because of its attractive name, and partly because of its reputation, served to bring together.

The point of view which I am struggling to attack is perhaps related to the metaphysical theory of the substantial unity of the soul: for my meaning is, that the poet has, not a "personality" to express, but a particular medium, which is only a medium and not a personality, in which impressions and experiences combine in peculiar and unexpected ways.[8] Impressions and experiences which are important for the man may take no place in the poetry, and those which become important in the poetry may play quite a negligible part in the man, the personality.

I will quote a passage which is unfamiliar enough to be regarded with fresh attention in the light — or darkness — of these observations:

> And now methinks I could e'en chide myself
> For doating on her beauty, though her death
> Shall be revenged after no common action.

---

[6] In Dante's *Inferno* (Canto V).

[7] This event in Aeschylus' *Agamemnon* is also introduced in Eliot's "Sweeney Among the Nightingales" (see above).

[8] A rejection of the Romantic idea of art as self-expression in favor of the modern emphasis on the medium and on the autonomy of the art object.

1. noble, majestic, sublime

> Does the silkworm expend her yellow labours
> For thee? For thee does she undo herself?
> Are lordships sold to maintain ladyships
> For the poor benefit of a bewildering minute?
> Why does yon fellow falsify highways,
> And put his life between the judge's lips,
> To refine such a thing—keeps horse and men
> To beat their valours for her? . . .[9]

In this passage (as is evident if it is taken in its context) there is a combination of positive and negative emotions: an intensely strong attraction toward beauty and an equally intense fascination by the ugliness which is contrasted with it and which destroys it. This balance of contrasted emotion is in the dramatic situation to which the speech is pertinent, but that situation alone is inadequate to it. This is, so to speak, the structural emotion, provided by the drama. But the whole effect, the dominant tone, is due to the fact that a number of floating feelings, having an affinity to this emotion by no means superficially evident, have combined with it to give us a new art emotion.

It is not in his personal emotions, the emotions provoked by particular events in his life, that the poet is in any way remarkable or interesting. His particular emotions may be simple, or crude, or flat. The emotion in his poetry will be a very complex thing, but not with the complexity of the emotions of people who have very complex or unusual emotions in life. One error, in fact, of eccentricity in poetry is to seek for new human emotions to express; and in this search for novelty in the wrong place it discovers the perverse. The business of the poet is not to find new emotions, but to use the ordinary ones and, in working them up into poetry, to express feelings which are not in actual emotions at all. And emotions which he has never experienced will serve his turn as well as those familiar to him. Consequently, we must believe that "emotion recollected in tranquillity" is an inexact formula.[10] For it is neither emotion, nor recollection, nor, without distortion of meaning, tranquillity. It is a concentration, and a new thing resulting from the concentration, of a very great number of experiences which to the practical and active person would not seem to be experiences at all; it is a concentration which does not happen consciously or of deliberation. These experiences are not "recollected," and they finally unite in an atmosphere which is "tranquil" only in that it is a passive attending upon the event. Of course this is not quite the whole story. There is a great deal, in the writing of poetry, which must be conscious and deliberate. In fact, the bad poet is usually unconscious where he ought to be conscious, and conscious where he ought to be

---

[9] Cyril Tourneur, *The Revenger's Tragedy* (1607), (III, v, 71–81).
[10] Wordsworth's definition of poetry in his preface to *Lyrical Ballads* (2nd ed., 1800).

unconscious. Both errors tend to make him "personal." Poetry is not a turning loose of emotion, but an escape from emotion; it is not the expression of personality, but an escape from personality. But, of course, only those who have personality and emotions know what it means to want to escape from these things.

3

ὁ δὲ νοῦς ἴσως θειότερόν τι χαί ἀπαθές ἐστιν.[11]

This essay proposes to halt at the frontier of metaphysics or mysticism, and confine itself to such practical conclusions as can be applied by the responsible person interested in poetry. To divert interest from the poet to the poetry is a laudable aim: for it would conduce to a juster estimation of actual poetry, good and bad. There are many people who appreciate the expression of sincere emotion in verse, and there is a smaller number of people who can appreciate technical excellence. But very few know when there is an expression of *significant* emotion, emotion which has its life in the poem and not in the history of the poet. The emotion of art is impersonal. And the poet cannot reach this impersonality without surrendering himself wholly to the work to be done. And he is not likely to know what is to be done unless he lives in what is not merely the present, but the present moment of the past, unless he is conscious, not of what is dead, but of what is already living.

1920

---

[11] "Mind is, no doubt, something more divine and impassible" (Aristotle, *On the Soul*, Ch. 4).

Theodore Dreiser   *1871 – 1945*

Revolutionary in outlook rather than technique, Theodore Dreiser worked to undermine established orthodoxies and conventions and to make possible a greater freedom for the American writer. Born into a large German-American immigrant family in Terre Haute, Indiana, Dreiser was affected by a conflict of temperament (later reflected in his work) between his strict Roman Catholic father and his loving, "pagan" mother, to whom he was closely attached. The shaky social and economic situation of the family, which drifted from one small midwestern town to another, helped to confirm in the boy a yearning for wealth and luxury that his circumstances could not satisfy. Dreiser came early to a sense of the helplessness of the individual as a "wisp" in the stream of life—a fatalism reinforced by his later reading in mechanistic philosophy. Like many of his midwestern contemporaries, the small town youth was drawn to Chicago, the prairie metropolis. After a succession of odd jobs and one year at Indiana University, he became a newspaperman in Chicago, St. Louis, Pittsburgh, and finally New York City, where he worked successfully as a magazine editor before establishing himself as a writer of fiction.

In his first novel, *Sister Carrie* (printed but withheld from publication in 1900; reissued 1912), the rise to success as an actress of his humble heroine, Carrie Meeber, is paralleled by the decline and disintegration of Hurstwood, the prosperous saloon manager who had tricked her into a false marriage. In Dreiser's view, neither character was responsible for his actions or fate, which were the result of impersonal outer circumstances and irresistible inner desires. This environmental and biological determinism remained a basic assumption in most of Dreiser's subsequent writing. Following *Jennie Gerhardt* (1911), his first successful novel, Dreiser began an ambitious trilogy based on the life of the traction magnate Charles T. Yerkes, who appears in *The Financier* (1912), *The Titan* (1914), and the posthumously published final volume, *The Stoic* (1947), as the materialistic, amoral Frank Algernon Cowperwood. In *The "Genius"* (1915), a long, interesting though repetitive autobiographical novel, the hero, Eugene Witla, is a painter rather than a writer. Dreiser continued his bent for documentary naturalism when he based his best-known novel, *An American Tragedy* (1925), upon a celebrated upstate New York murder case. In portraying his hero, Clyde Griffiths, as the victim of a conflict between his unrealizable dreams of wealth and love and his repressed situation in a class-stratified society, Dreiser worked, in the manner of a Clarence Darrow, to shift responsibility for a murder from the perpetrator to his social environment.

During the depression years, Dreiser was deeply disturbed by the suffering and deprivation of the masses. In the nonfictional works, *Tragic America* (1931) and *America Is Worth Saving* (1941), he expressed his mingled misgivings and hopes for a possible improvement through socialism. Late in life he joined the Communist Party as a symbolic affirmation of his hopes even though the Marxist ideology and discipline were alien to his own outlook and temperament. Not long before his death he also developed an interest in religious experience. His posthumous novel *The Bulwark* (1946), with its Quaker hero Solon Barnes, acknowledges the sustaining power of spiritual values even in the modern world. But what is lacking in all Dreiser's fiction (though not in his social criticism) is any suggestion of the possibility of humanistic values or of mutual moral responsibility as an alternative to the cynical determinism that pervades most of his work or to the religious mysticism which he at last — almost — came to accept.

Dreiser's style is often clumsy and his diction flat. He tends to be repetitive rather than selective in the use of detail. And yet (to use one of his favorite phrases) his contribution is a major one. There is a granitic solidity and authenticity in his documentary accounts (one could almost say case histories) of those aspects of American life that came under his unsparing and gloomy gaze. There is also a virtue in his indictment of much of the falseness and hypocrisy that he saw about him.

Two collections of Dreiser's stories are *Free and Other Stories* (1918) and *Chains* (1927). *Moods, Cadenced and Declaimed* (1926; rev. 1928) is a book of poems. His plays, which were not successful, are gathered in *Plays of the Natural and Supernatural* (1916) and *The Hand of the Potter* (1918). *Hey Rub-a-Dub-Dub* (1920) is a collection of philosophical essays. Autobiographical works include *A Traveler at Forty* (1913); *A Hoosier Holiday* (1916); *A Book About Myself* (1922), reissued as *Newspaper Days* (1931); and *Dawn* (1931).

Dreiser's correspondence has been collected in *Letters of Theodore Dreiser: A Selection*, ed. R. H. Elias, 3 vols. (Philadelphia, 1959). Early critical biographies are R. H. Elias, *Theodore Dreiser, Apostle of Nature* (New York, 1949) and F. O. Matthiessen, *Theodore Dreiser* (New York, 1951). Helen Dreiser, the author's widow, has provided a personal account in *My Life with Dreiser* (Cleveland, 1951). The most thorough and fully documented biographical study, one most damaging to Dreiser's character, is W. A. Swanberg, *Dreiser* (New York, 1965).

The text of "The Second Choice" is that of *Free and Other Stories*

(New York, 1918). "I have lived now to my fortieth year. . ." is from *Hey Rub-a-Dub-Dub* (New York, 1920).

The Second Choice

Shirley dear:

You don't want the letters. There are only six of them, anyhow, and think, they're all I have of you to cheer me on my travels. What good would they be to you — little bits of notes telling me you're sure to meet me — but me — think of me! If I send them to you, you'll tear them up, whereas if you leave them with me I can dab them with musk and ambergris and keep them in a little silver box, always beside me.

Ah, Shirley dear, you really don't know how sweet I think you are, how dear! There isn't a thing we have ever done together that isn't as clear in my mind as this great big skyscraper over the way here in Pittsburgh, and far more pleasing. In fact, my thoughts of you are the most precious and delicious things I have, Shirley.

But I'm too young to marry now. You know that, Shirley, don't you? I haven't placed myself in any way yet, and I'm so restless that I don't know whether I ever will, really. Only yesterday, old Roxbaum — that's my new employer here — came to me and wanted to know if I would like an assistant overseership on one of his coffee plantations in Java, said there would not be much money in it for a year or two, a bare living, but later there would be more — and I jumped at it. Just the thought of Java and going there did that, although I knew I could make more staying right here. Can't you see how it is with me, Shirl? I'm too restless and too young. I couldn't take care of you right, and you wouldn't like me after a while if I didn't.

But ah, Shirley sweet, I think the dearest things of you! There isn't an hour, it seems, but some little bit of you comes back — a dear, sweet bit — the night we sat on the grass in Tregore Park and counted the stars through the trees; that first evening at Sparrows Point when we missed the last train and had to walk to Langley. Remember the tree-toads, Shirl? And then that warm April Sunday in Atholby woods! Ah, Shirl, you don't want the six notes! Let me keep them. But think of me, will you, sweet, wherever you go and whatever you do? I'll always think of you, and wish that you had met a better, saner man than me, and that I really could have married you and been all you wanted me to be. By-by, sweet. I may start for Java within the month. If so, and you would want them, I'll send you some cards from there — if they have any.

Your worthless,
Arthur

She sat and turned the letter in her hand, dumb with despair. It was the very last letter she would ever get from him. Of that she was certain. He was gone now, once and for all. She had written him only once, not making an open plea but asking him to return her letters, and then there had come this tender but evasive reply, saying nothing of a possible return but desiring to keep her letters for old times' sake—the happy hours they had spent together.

The happy hours! Oh, yes, yes, yes—the happy hours!

In her memory now, as she sat here in her home after the day's work, meditating on all that had been in the few short months since he had come and gone, was a world of color and light—a color and a light so transfiguring as to seem celestial, but now, alas, wholly dissipated. It had contained so much of all she had desired—love, romance, amusement, laughter. He had been so gay and thoughtless, or headstrong, so youthfully romantic, and with such a love of play and change and to be saying and doing anything and everything. Arthur could dance in a gay way, whistle, sing after a fashion, play. He could play cards and do tricks, and he had such a superior air, so genial and brisk, with a kind of innate courtesy in it and yet an intolerance for slowness and stodginess or anything dull or dingy, such as characterized——But here her thoughts fled from him. She refused to think of any one but Arthur.

Sitting in her little bedroom now, off the parlor on the ground floor in her home in Bethune Street, and looking out over the Kessels' yard, and beyond that—there being no fences in Bethune Street—over the "yards" or lawns of the Pollards, Bakers, Cryders, and others, she thought of how dull it must all have seemed to him, with his fine imaginative mind and experiences, his love of change and gayety, his atmosphere of something better than she had ever known. How little she had been fitted, perhaps, by beauty or temperament to overcome this—the something—dullness in her work or her home, which possibly had driven him away. For, although many had admired her to date, and she was young and pretty in her simple way and constantly receiving suggestions that her beauty was disturbing to some, still, he had not cared for her—he had gone.

And now, as she meditated, it seemed that this scene, and all that it stood for—her parents, her work, her daily shuttling to and fro between the drug company for which she worked and this street and house—was typical of her life and what she was destined to endure always. Some girls were so much more fortunate. They had fine clothes, fine homes, a world of pleasure and opportunity in which to move. They did not have to scrimp and save and work to pay their own way. And yet she had always been compelled to do it, but had never complained until now—or until he came, and after. Bethune Street, with its commonplace front yards and houses nearly all alike, and this house, so like the others, room for room and porch for porch, and her parents, too, really like all the others, had seemed good enough, quite satisfactory, indeed, until then. But now, now!

Here, in their kitchen, was her mother, a thin, pale, but kindly woman, peeling potatoes and washing lettuce, and putting a bit of steak or a chop or a piece of liver in a frying-pan day after day, morning and evening, month after month, year after year. And next door was Mrs. Kessel doing the same thing. And next door Mrs. Cryder. And next door Mrs. Pollard. But, until now, she had not thought it so bad. But now—now—oh! And on all the porches or lawns all along this street were the husbands and fathers, mostly middle-aged or old men like her father, reading their papers or cutting the grass before dinner, or smoking and meditating afterward. Her father was out in front now, a stooped, forbearing, meditative soul, who had rarely anything to say— leaving it all to his wife, her mother, but who was fond of her in his dull, quiet way. He was a pattern-maker by trade, and had come into possession of this small, ordinary home via years of toil and saving, her mother helping him. They had no particular religion, as he often said, thinking reasonably human conduct a sufficient passport to heaven, but they had gone occasionally to the Methodist Church over in Nicholas Street, and she had once joined it. But of late she had not gone, weaned away by the other commonplace pleasures of her world.

And then in the midst of it, the dull drift of things, as she now saw them to be, he had come—Arthur Bristow—young, energetic, good-looking, ambitious, dreamful, and instanter, and with her never knowing quite how, the whole thing had been changed. He had appeared so swiftly—out of nothing, as it were.

Previous to him had been Barton Williams, stout, phlegmatic, good-natured, well-meaning, who was, or had been before Arthur came, asking her to marry him, and whom she allowed to half assume that she would. She had liked him in a feeble, albeit, as she thought, tender way, thinking him the kind, according to the logic of her neighborhood, who would make her a good husband, and, until Arthur appeared on the scene, had really intended to marry him. It was not really a love-match, as she saw now, but she thought it was, which was much the same thing, perhaps. But, as she now recalled, when Arthur came, how the scales fell from her eyes! In a trice, as it were, nearly, there was a new heaven and a new earth. Arthur had arrived, and with him a sense of something different.

Mabel Gove had asked her to come over to her house in West-leigh, the adjoining suburb, for Thanksgiving eve and day, and without a thought of anything, and because Barton was busy handling a part of the work in the despatcher's office of the Great Eastern and could not see her, she had gone. And then, to her surprise and strange, almost ineffable delight, the moment she had seen him, he was there—Arthur, with his slim, straight figure and dark hair and eyes and clean-cut features, as clean and attractive as those of a coin. And as he had looked at her and smiled and narrated humorous bits of things that had happened to him, something had come over her—a spell—and after dinner they had all gone round to Edith Barringer's to dance, and there as she had danced with him, somehow, without any seeming boldness on his part, he had taken possession of her, as it were, drawn her close, and told her she had beautiful eyes and hair and such a delicately rounded chin, and that he thought she danced gracefully and was sweet. She had nearly fainted with delight.

"Do you like me?" he had asked in one place in the dance, and, in spite of herself, she had looked up into his eyes, and from that moment she was almost mad over him, could think of nothing else but his hair and eyes and his smile and his graceful figure.

Mabel Gove had seen it all, in spite of her determination that no one should, and on their going to bed later, back at Mabel's home, she had whispered:

"Ah, Shirley, I saw. You like Arthur, don't you?"

"I think he's very nice," Shirley recalled replying, for Mabel knew of her affair with Barton and liked him, "but I'm not crazy over him." And for this bit of treason she had sighed in her dreams nearly all night.

And the next day, true to a request and a promise made by him, Arthur had called again at Mabel's to take her and Mabel to a "movie" which was not so far away, and from there they had gone to an ice-cream parlor, and during it all, when Mabel was not lookiing, he had squeezed her arm and hand and kissed her neck, and she had held her breath, and her heart had seemed to stop.

"And now you're going to let me come out to your place to see you, aren't you?" he had whispered.

And she had replied, "Wednesday evening," and then written the address on a little piece of paper and given it to him.

But now it was all gone, gone!

This house, which now looked so dreary—how romantic it had seemed that first night *he* called—the front room with its commonplace furniture, and later in the spring, the veranda, with its vines just sprouting, and the moon in May. Oh, the moon in May, and June and July, when he was here! How she had lied to Barton to make evenings for Arthur, and occasionally to Arthur to keep him from contact with Barton. She had not even mentioned Barton to Arthur because—because—well, because Arthur was so much better, and somehow (she admitted it to herself now) she had not been sure that Arthur would care for her long, if at all, and then—well, and then, to be quite frank, Barton might be good enough. She did not exactly hate him because she had found Arthur—not at all. She still liked him in a way—he was so kind and faithful, so very dull and straightforward and thoughtful of her, which Arthur was certainly not. Before Arthur had appeared, as she well remembered, Barton had seemed to be plenty good enough—in fact, all that she desired in a pleasant, companionable way, calling for her, taking her places, bringing her flowers and candy, which Arthur rarely did, and for that, if nothing more, she could not help continuing to like him and to feel sorry for him, and, besides, as she had admitted to herself before, if Arthur left her—* * *Weren't his parents better off than hers—and hadn't he a good position for such a man as he—one hundred and fifty dollars a month and the certainty of more later on? A little while before meeting Arthur, she had thought this very good, enough for two to live on at least, and she had thought some of trying it at some time or other—but now—now——

And that first night he had called—how well she remembered it—how it had transfigured the parlor next this in which she was now, filling it with something it had never had before, and the porch outside, too, for that matter, with its gaunt, leafless vine, and this street, too, even—dull, commonplace Bethune Street. There had been a flurry of snow during the afternoon while she was working at the store, and the ground was white with it. All the neighboring homes seemed to look sweeter and happier and more inviting than ever they had as she came past them, with their lights peeping from under curtains and drawn shades. She had hurried into hers and lighted the big red-shaded parlor lamp, her one artistic treasure, as she thought, and put it near the piano, between it and the window, and arranged the chairs, and then bustled to the task of making herself as pleasing as she might. For him she had gotten out her one best filmy house dress and done up her hair in the fashion she thought most becoming—and that he had not seen before—and powdered her cheeks and nose and darkened her eyelashes, as some of the girls at the store did, and put on her new gray satin slippers, and then, being so arrayed, waited nervously, unable to eat anything or to think of anything but him.

And at last, just when she had begun to think he might not be coming, he had appeared with that arch smile and a "Hello! It's here you live, is it? I was wondering. George, but you're twice as sweet as I thought you were, aren't you?" And then, in the little entryway, behind the closed door, he had held her and kissed her on the mouth a dozen times while she pretended to push against his coat and struggle and say that her parents might hear.

And, oh, the room afterward, with him in it in the red glow of the lamp, and with his pale handsome face made handsomer thereby, as she thought! He had made her sit near him and had held her hands and told her about his work and his dreams—all that he expected to do in the future—and then she had found herself wishing intensely to share just such a life—his life—anything that he might wish to do; only, she kept wondering, with a slight pain, whether he would want her to—he was so young, dreamful, ambitious, much younger and more dreamful than herself, although, in reality, he was several years older.

And then followed that glorious period from December to this late September, in which everything which was worth happening in love had happened. Oh, those wondrous days the following spring, when, with the first burst of buds and leaves, he had taken her one Sunday to Atholby, where all the great woods were, and they had hunted spring beauties in the grass, and sat on a slope and looked at the river below and watched some boys fixing up a sailboat and setting forth in it quite as she wished she and Arthur might be doing—going somewhere together—far, far away from all commonplace things and life! And then he had slipped his arm about her and kissed her cheek and neck, and tweaked her ear and smoothed her hair—and oh, there on the grass, with the spring flowers about her and a canopy of small green leaves above, the perfection of love had come—love so wonderful that the mere thought of it made her eyes brim now! And then had been days, Saturday afternoons and Sundays, at Atholby and Sparrows Point, where the great beach was, and in lovely Tregore Park, a mile or two from her home, where they could go of an evening and sit in or near the pavilion and have ice-cream and dance or watch the dancers. Oh, the stars, the winds, the summer breath of those days! Ah, me! Ah, me!

Naturally, her parents had wondered from the first about her and Arthur, and her and Barton, since Barton had already assumed a proprietary interest in her and she had seemed to like him. But then she was an only child and a pet, and used to presuming on that, and they could not think of saying anything to her. After all, she was young and pretty and was entitled to change her mind; only, only—she had had to indulge in a career of lying and subterfuge in connection with Barton, since Arthur was headstrong and wanted every evening that he chose—to call for her at the store and keep her down-town to dinner and a show.

Arthur had never been like Barton, shy, phlegmatic, obedient, waiting long and patiently for each little favor, but, instead, masterful and eager, rifling her of kisses and caresses and every delight of love, and teasing and playing with her as a cat would a mouse. She could never resist him. He demanded of her her time and her affection without let or hindrance. He was not exactly selfish or cruel, as some might have been, but gay and unthinking at times, unconsciously so, and yet loving and tender at others—nearly always so. But always he would talk of things in the future as if they really did not include her—and this troubled her greatly—of places he might go, things he might do, which, somehow, he seemed to think or assume that she could not or would not do with him. He was always going to Australia sometime, he thought, in a business way, or to South Africa, or possibly to India. He never seemed to have any fixed clear future for himself in mind.

A dreadful sense of helplessness and of impending disaster came over her at these times, of being involved in some predicament over which she had no control, and which would lead her on to some sad end. Arthur, although plainly in love, as she thought, and apparently delighted with her, might not always love her. She began, timidly at first (and always, for that matter), to ask him pretty, seeking questions about himself and her, whether their future was certain to be together, whether he really wanted her—loved her—whether he might not want to marry some one else or just her, and whether she wouldn't look nice in a pearl satin wedding-dress with a long creamy veil and satin slippers and a bouquet of bridal-wreath. She had been so slowly but surely saving to that end, even before he came, in connection with Barton; only, after *he* came, all thought of the import of it had been transferred to him. But now, also, she was beginning to ask herself sadly, "Would it ever be?" He was so airy, so inconsequential, so ready to say: "Yes, yes," and "Sure, sure! That's right! Yes, indeedy; you bet! Say, kiddie, but you'll look sweet!" but, somehow, it had always seemed as if this whole thing were a glorious interlude and that it could not last. Arthur was too gay and ethereal and too little settled in his own mind. His ideas of travel and living in different cities, finally winding up in New York or San Francisco, but never with her exactly until she asked him, was too ominous, although he always reassured her gaily: "Of course! Of course!" But somehow she could never believe it really, and it made her intensely sad at times, horribly gloomy. So often she wanted to cry, and she could scarcely tell why.

And then, because of her intense affection for him, she had finally quarreled with Barton, or nearly that, if one could say that one ever really quarreled with him. It had been because of a certain Thursday evening a few weeks before about which she had disappointed him. In a fit of generosity, knowing that Arthur was coming Wednesday, and because Barton had stopped in at the store to see her, she had told him that he might come, having regretted it afterward, so enamored was she of Arthur. And then when Wednesday came, Arthur had changed his mind, telling her he would come Friday instead, but on Thursday evening he had stopped in at the store and asked her to go to Sparrows Point, with the result that she had no time to notify Barton. He had gone to the house and sat with her parents until ten-thirty, and then, a few days later, although she had written him offering an excuse, had called at the store to complain slightly.

"Do you think you did just right, Shirley? You might have sent word, mightn't you? Who was it—the new fellow you won't tell me about?"

Shirley flared on the instant.

"Supposing it was? What's it to you? I don't belong to you yet, do I? I told you there wasn't any one, and I wish you'd let me alone about that. I couldn't help it last Thursday—that's all—and I don't want you to be fussing with me—that's all. If you don't want to, you needn't come any more, anyhow."

"Don't say that, Shirley," pleaded Barton. "You don't mean that. I won't bother you, though, if you don't want me any more."

And because Shirley sulked, not knowing what else to do, he had gone and she had not seen him since.

And then sometime later when she had thus broken with Barton, avoiding the railway station where he worked, Arthur had failed to come at his appointed time, sending no word until the next day, when a note came to the store saying that he had been out of town for his firm over Sunday and had not been able to notify her, but that he would call Tuesday. It was an awful blow. At the time, Shirley had a vision of what was to follow. It seemed for the moment as if the whole world had suddenly been reduced to ashes, that there was nothing but black charred cinders anywhere—she felt that about all life. Yet it all came to her clearly then that this was but the beginning of just such days and just such excuses, and that soon, soon, he would come no more. He was beginning to be tired of her and soon he would not even make excuses. She felt it, and it froze and terrified her.

And then, soon after, the indifference which she feared did follow—almost created by her own thoughts, as it were. First, it was a meeting he had to attend somewhere one Wednesday night when he was to have come for her. Then he was going out of town again, over Sunday. Then he was going away for a whole week—it was absolutely unavoidable, he said, his commercial duties were increasing—and once he had casually remarked that nothing could stand in the way where she was concerned—never! She did not think of reproaching him with this; she was too proud. If he was going, he must go. She would not be willing to say to herself that she had ever attempted to hold any man. But, just the same, she was agonized by the thought. When he was with her, he seemed tender enough; only, at times, his eyes wandered and he seemed slightly bored. Other girls, particularly pretty ones, seemed to interest him as much as she did.

And the agony of the long days when he did not come any more for a week or two at a time! The waiting, the brooding, the wondering, at the store and here in her home—in the former place making mistakes at times because she could not get her mind off him and being reminded of them, and here at her own home at nights, being so absent-minded that her parents remarked on it. She felt sure that her parents must be noticing that Arthur was not coming any more, or as much as he had —for she pretended to be going out with him, going to Mabel Gove's instead—and that Barton had deserted her too, he having been driven off by her indifference, never to come any more, perhaps, unless she sought him out.

And then it was that the thought of saving her own face by taking up with Barton once more occurred to her, of using him and his affections and faithfulness and dulness, if you will, to cover up her own dilemma. Only, this ruse was not to be tried until she had written Arthur this one letter—a pretext merely to see if there was a single ray of hope, a letter to be written in a gentle-enough way and asking for the return of the few notes she had written him. She had not seen him now in nearly a month, and the last time she had, he had said he might soon be compelled to leave her awhile—to go to Pittsburgh to work. And it was his reply to this that she now held in her hand—from Pittsburgh! It was frightful! The future without him!

But Barton would never know really what had transpired, if she went back to him. In spite of all her delicious hours with Arthur, she could call him back, she felt sure. She had never really entirely dropped him, and he knew it. He had bored her dreadfully on occasion, arriving on off days when Arthur was not about, with flowers or candy, or both, and sitting on the porch steps and talking of the railroad business and of the whereabouts and doings of some of their old friends. It was shameful, she had thought at times, to see a man so patient, so hopeful, so good-natured as Barton, deceived in this way, and by her, who was so miserable over another. Her parents must see and know, she had thought at these times, but still, what else was she to do?

"I'm a bad girl," she kept telling herself. "I'm all wrong. What right have I to offer Barton what is left?" But still, somehow, she realized that Barton, if she chose to favor him, would only be too grateful for even the leavings of others where she was concerned, and that even yet, if she but deigned to crook a finger, she could have him. He was so simple, so good-natured, so stolid and matter of fact, so different to Arthur whom (she could not help smiling at the thought of it) she was loving now about as Barton loved her—slavishly, hopelessly.

And then, as the days passed and Arthur did not write any more—just this one brief note—she at first grieved horribly, and then in a fit of numb despair attempted, bravely enough from one point of view, to adjust herself to the new situation. Why should she despair? Why die of agony where there were plenty who would still sigh for her—Barton among others? She was young, pretty, very—many told her so. She could, if she chose, achieve a vivacity which she did not feel. Why should she brook this unkindness without a thought of retaliation? Why shouldn't she enter upon a gay and heartless career, indulging in a dozen flirtations at once—dancing and killing all thoughts of Arthur in a round of frivolities? There were many who beckoned to her. She stood at her counter in the drug store on many a day and brooded over this, but at the thought of which one to begin with, she faltered. After her late love, all were so tame, for the present anyhow.

And then—and then—always there was Barton, the humble or

faithful, to whom she had been so unkind and whom she had used and whom she still really liked. So often self-reproaching thoughts in connection with him crept over her. He must have known, must have seen how badly she was using him all this while, and yet he had not failed to come and come, until she had actually quarreled with him, and any one would have seen that it was literally hopeless. She could not help remembering, especially now in her pain, that he adored her. He was not calling on her now at all—by her indifference she had finally driven him away—but a word, a word— She waited for days, weeks, hoping against hope, and then——

The office of Barton's superior in the Great Eastern terminal had always made him an easy object for her blandishments, coming and going, as she frequently did, via this very station. He was in the office of the assistant train-despatcher on the ground floor, where passing to and from the local, which, at times, was quicker than a street-car, she could easily see him by peering in; only, she had carefully avoided him for nearly a year. If she chose now, and would call for a message-blank at the adjacent telegraph-window which was a part of his room, and raised her voice as she often had in the past, he could scarcely fail to hear, if he did not see her. And if he did, he would rise and come over—of that she was sure, for he never could resist her. It had been a wile of hers in the old days to do this or to make her presence felt by idling outside. After a month of brooding, she felt that she must act —her position as a deserted girl was too much. She could not stand it any longer really—the eyes of her mother, for one.

It was six-fifteen one evening when, coming out of the store in which she worked, she turned her step disconsolately homeward. Her heart was heavy, her face rather pale and drawn. She had stopped in the store's retiring-room before coming out to add to her charms as much as possible by a little powder and rouge and to smooth her hair. It would not take much to reallure her former sweetheart, she felt sure —and yet it might not be so easy after all. Suppose he had found another? But she could not believe that. It had scarcely been long enough since he had last attempted to see her, and he was really so very, very fond of her and so faithful. He was too slow and certain in his choosing—he had been so with her. Still, who knows? With this thought, she went forward in the evening, feeling for the first time the shame and pain that comes of deception, the agony of having to relinquish an ideal and the feeling of despair that comes to those who find themselves in the position of suppliants, stooping to something which in better days and better fortune they would not know. Arthur was the cause of this.

When she reached the station, the crowd that usually filled it at this hour was swarming. There were so many pairs like Arthur and herself laughing and hurrying away or so she felt. First glancing in the small mirror of a weighing scale to see if she were still of her former charm, she stopped thoughtfully at a little flower stand which stood outside, and for a few pennies purchased a tiny bunch of violets. She then went inside and stood near the window, peering first furtively to see if he were present. He was. Bent over his work, a green shade over his eyes, she could see his stolid, genial figure at a table. Stepping back a moment to ponder, she finally went forward and, in a clear voice, asked,

"May I have a blank, please?"

The infatuation of the discarded Barton was such that it brought him instantly to his feet. In his stodgy, stocky way he rose, his eyes glowing with a friendly hope, his mouth wreathed in smiles, and came over. At the sight of her, pale, but pretty—paler and prettier, really, than he had ever seen her—he thrilled dumbly.

"How are you, Shirley?" he asked sweetly, as he drew near, his eyes searching her face hopefully. He had not seen her for so long that he was intensely hungry, and her paler beauty appealed to him more than ever. Why wouldn't she have him? he was asking himself. Why wouldn't his persistent love yet win her? Perhaps it might. "I haven't seen you in a month of Sundays, it seems. How are the folks?"

"They're all right, Bart," she smiled archly, "and so am I. How have you been? It has been a long time since I've seen you. I've been wondering how you were. Have you been all right? I was just going to send a message."

As he had approached, Shirley had pretended at first not to see him, a moment later to affect surprise, although she was really suppressing a heavy sigh. The sight of him, after Arthur, was not reassuring. Could she really interest herself in him any more? Could she?

"Sure, sure," he replied genially; "I'm always all right. You couldn't kill me, you know. Not going away, are you, Shirl?" he queried interestedly.

"No; I'm just telegraphing to Mabel. She promised to meet me to-morrow, and I want to be sure she will."

"You don't come past here as often as you did, Shirley," he complained tenderly. "At least, I don't seem to see you so often," he added with a smile. "It isn't anything I have done, is it?" he queried, and then, when she protested quickly, added: "What's the trouble, Shirl? Haven't been sick, have you?"

She affected all her old gaiety and ease, feeling as though she would like to cry.

"Oh, no," she returned; "I've been all right. I've been going through the other door, I suppose, or coming in and going out on the Langdon Avenue car." (This was true, because she had been wanting to avoid him.) "I've been in such a hurry, most nights, that I haven't had time to stop, Bart. You know how late the store keeps us at times."

He remembered, too, that in the old days she had made time to stop or meet him occasionally.

"Yes, I know," he said tactfully. "But you haven't been to any of our old card-parties either of late, have you? At least, I haven't seen you. I've gone to two or three, thinking you might be there."

That was another thing Arthur had done—broken up her interest in these old store and neighborhood parties and a banjo-and-mandolin club to which she had once belonged. They had all seemed so pleasing and amusing in the old days—but now—**** In those days Bart had been her usual companion when his work permitted.

"No," she replied evasively, but with a forced air of pleasant remembrance; "I have often thought of how much fun we had at those, though. It was a shame to drop them. You haven't seen Harry Stull or Trina Task recently, have you?" she inquired, more to be saying something than for any interest she felt.

He shook his head negatively, then added:

"Yes, I did, too; here in the waiting-room a few nights ago. They were coming down-town to a theater, I suppose."

His face fell slightly as he recalled how it had been their custom to do this, and what their one quarrel had been about. Shirley noticed it. She felt the least bit sorry for him, but much more for herself, coming back so disconsolately to all this.

"Well, you're looking as pretty as ever, Shirley," he continued, noting that she had not written the telegram and that there was something wistful in her glance. "Prettier, I think," and she smiled sadly. Every word that she tolerated from him was as so much gold to him, so much of dead ashes to her. "You wouldn't like to come down some evening this week and see 'The Mouse-Trap,' would you? We haven't been to a theater together in I don't know when." His eyes sought hers in a hopeful, doglike way.

So—she could have him again—that was the pity of it! To have what she really did not want, did not care for! At the least nod now he would come, and this very devotion made it all but worthless, and so sad. She ought to marry him now for certain, if she began in this way, and could in a month's time if she chose, but oh, oh—could she? For the moment she decided that she could not, would not. If he had only repulsed her—told her to go—ignored her—but no; it was her fate to be loved by him in this moving, pleading way, and hers not to love him as she wished to love—to be loved. Plainly, he needed some one like her, whereas she, she——. She turned a little sick, a sense of the sacrilege of gaiety at this time creeping into her voice, and exclaimed:

"No, no!" Then seeing his face change, a heavy sadness come over it, "Not this week, anyhow, I mean" ("Not so soon," she had almost said). "I have several engagements this week and I'm not feeling well. But"—seeing his face change, and the thought of her own state returning—"you might come out to the house some evening instead, and then we can go some other time."

His face brightened intensely. It was wonderful how he longed to be with her, how the least favor from her comforted and lifted him up. She could see also now, however, how little it meant to her, how little it could ever mean, even if to him it was heaven. The old relationship would have to be resumed in toto, once and for all, but did she want it that way now that she was feeling so miserable about this other affair? As she meditated, these various moods racing to and fro in her mind, Barton seemed to notice, and now it occurred to him that perhaps he had not pursued her enough—was too easily put off. She probably did like him yet. This evening, her present visit, seemed to prove it.

"Sure, sure!" he agreed. "I'd like that. I'll come out Sunday, if you say. We can go any time to the play. I'm sorry, Shirley, if you're not feeling well. I've thought of you a lot these days. I'll come out Wednesday, if you don't mind."

She smiled a wan smile. It was all so much easier than she had expected—her triumph—and so ashenlike in consequence, a flavor of dead-sea fruit and defeat about it all, that it was pathetic. How could she, after Arthur? How could he, really?

"Make it Sunday," she pleaded, naming the farthest day off, and then hurried out.

Her faithful lover gazed after her, while she suffered an intense nausea. To think—to think—it should all be coming to this! She had not used her telegraph-blank, and now had forgotten all about it. It was not the simple trickery that discouraged her, but her own future which could find no better outlet than this, could not rise above it apparently, or that she had no heart to make it rise above it. Why couldn't she interest herself in some one different to Barton? Why did she have to return to him? Why not wait and meet some other—ignore him as before? But no, no; nothing mattered now—no one—it might as well be Barton really as any one, and she would at least make him happy and at the same time solve her own problem. She went out into the trainshed and climbed into her train. Slowly, after the usual pushing and jostling of a crowd, it drew out toward Latonia, that suburban region in which her home lay. As she rode, she thought.

"What have I just done? What am I doing?" she kept asking herself as the clacking wheels on the rails fell into a rhythmic dance and the houses of the brown, dry, endless city fled past in a maze. "Severing myself decisively from the past—the happy past—for supposing, once I am married, Arthur should return and want me again—suppose! Suppose!"

Below at one place, under a shed, were some market-gardeners disposing of the last remnants of their day's wares—a sickly, dull life, she thought. Here was Rutgers Avenue, with its line of red street-cars, many wagons and tracks and counter-streams of automobiles—how often had she passed it morning and evening in a shuttle-like way, and how often would, unless she got married! And here, now, was the river flowing smoothly between its banks lined with coal-pockets and wharves—away, away to the huge deep sea which she and Arthur had enjoyed so much. Oh, to be in a small boat and drift out, out into the endless, restless, pathless deep! Somehow the sight of this water, to-night and every night, brought back those evenings in the open with Arthur at Sparrows Point, the long line of dancers in Eckert's Pavilion, the woods at Atholby, the park, with the dancers in the pavilion—she choked back a sob. Once Arthur had come this way with her on just such an evening as this, pressing her hand and saying how wonderful she was. Oh, Arthur! Arthur! And now Barton was to take his old place again—forever, no doubt. She could not trifle with her life longer in this foolish way, or his. What was the use? But think of it!

Yes, it must be—forever now, she told herself. She must marry. Time would be slipping by and she would become too old. It was her only future—marriage. It was the only future she had ever contemplated really, a home, children, the love of some man whom she could love as she loved Arthur. Ah, what a happy home that would have been for her! But now, now——

But there must be no turning back now, either. There was no other way. If Arthur ever came back—but fear not, he wouldn't! She had risked so much and lost—lost him. Her little venture into true love had been such a failure. Before Arthur had come all had been well enough. Barton, stout and simple and frank and direct, had in some way—how, she could scarcely realize now—offered sufficient of a future. But now, now! He had enough money, she knew, to build a cottage for the two of them. He had told her so. He would do his best always to make her happy, she was sure of that. They could live in about the state her parents were living in—or a little better, not much—and would never want. No doubt there would be children, because he craved them—several of them—and that would take up her time, long years of it—the sad, gray years! But then Arthur, whose children she would have thrilled to bear, would be no more, a mere memory—think of that!—and Barton, the dull, the commonplace, would have achieved his finest dream—and why?

Because love was a failure for her—that was why—and in her life there could be no more true love. She would never love any one again as she had Arthur. It could not be, she was sure of it. He was too fascinating, too wonderful. Always, always, wherever she might be, whoever she might marry, he would be coming back, intruding between her and any possible love, receiving any possible kiss. It would be Arthur she would be loving or kissing. She dabbed at her eyes with a tiny handkerchief, turned her face close to the window and stared out, and then as the environs of Latonia came into view, wondered (so deep is romance): What if Arthur should come back at some time—or now! Supposing he should be here at the station now, accidentally or on purpose, to welcome her, to soothe her weary heart. He had met her here before. How she would fly to him, lay her head on his shoulder, forget forever that Barton ever was, that they had ever separated for an hour. Oh, Arthur! Arthur!

But no, no; here was Latonia—here the viaduct over her train, the long business street and the cars marked "Center" and "Langdon Avenue" running back into the great city. A few blocks away in tree-shaded Bethune Street, duller and plainer than ever, was her parents' cottage and the routine of that old life which was now, she felt, more fully fastened upon her than ever before—the lawn-mowers, the lawns, the front porches all alike. Now would come the going to and fro of Barton to business as her father and she now went to business, her keeping house, cooking, washing, ironing, sewing for Barton as her mother now did these things for her father and herself. And she would not be in love really, as she wanted to be. Oh, dreadful! She could never escape it really, now that she could endure it less, scarcely for another hour. And yet she must, must, for the sake of—for the sake of—she closed her eyes and dreamed.

She walked up the street under the trees, past the houses and lawns all alike to her own, and found her father on their veranda reading the evening paper. She sighed at the sight.

"Back, daughter?" he called pleasantly.

"Yes."

"Your mother is wondering if you would like steak or liver for dinner. Better tell her."

"Oh, it doesn't matter."

She hurried into her bedroom, threw down her hat and gloves, and herself on the bed to rest silently, and groaned in her soul. To think that it had all come to this!—Never to see him any more!—To see only Barton, and marry him and live in such a street, have four or five children, forget all her youthful companionships—and all to save her face before her parents, and her future. Why must it be? Should it be, really? She choked and stifled. After a little time her mother, hearing her come in, came to the door—thin, practical, affectionate, conventional.

"What's wrong, honey? Aren't you feeling well to-night? Have you a headache? Let me feel."

Her thin cool fingers crept over her temples and hair. She suggested something to eat or a headache powder right away.

"I'm all right, mother. I'm just not feeling well now. Don't bother. I'll get up soon. Please don't."

"Would you rather have liver or steak to-night, dear?"

"Oh, anything—nothing—please don't bother—steak will do—anything"—if only she could get rid of her and be at rest!

Her mother looked at her and shook her head sympathetically, then retreated quietly, saying no more. Lying so, she thought and thought—grinding, destroying thoughts about the beauty of the past, the darkness of the future—until able to endure them no longer she got up and, looking distractedly out of the window into the yard and the house next door, stared at her future fixedly. What should she do? What should she really do? There was Mrs. Kessel in her kitchen getting her dinner as usual, just as her own mother was now, and Mr. Kessel out on the front porch in his shirt-sleeves reading the evening paper. Beyond was Mr. Pollard in his yard, cutting the grass. All along Bethune Street were such houses and such people—simple, commonplace souls all—clerks, managers, fairly successful craftsmen, like her father and Barton, excellent in their way but not like Arthur the beloved, the lost—and here was she, perforce, or by decision of necessity, soon to be one of them, in some such street as this no doubt, forever and—. For the moment it choked and stifled her.

She decided that she would not. No, no, no! There must be some other way—many ways. She did not have to do this unless she really wished to—would not—only—. Then going to the mirror she looked at her face and smoothed her hair.

"But what's the use?" she asked of herself wearily and resignedly after a time. "Why should I cry? Why shouldn't I marry Barton? I don't amount to anything, anyhow. Arthur wouldn't have me. I wanted him, and I am compelled to take some one else—or no one—what difference does it really make who? My dreams are too high, that's all. I wanted Arthur, and he wouldn't have me. I don't want Barton, and he crawls at my feet. I'm a failure, that's what's the matter with me."

And then, turning up her sleeves and removing a fichu which stood out too prominently from her breast, she went into the kitchen and, looking about for an apron, observed:

"Can't I help? Where's the tablecloth?" and finding it among napkins and silverware in a drawer in the adjoining room, proceeded to set the table.

1918

From *Hey, Rub-A-Dub-Dub!*

(Taken from the notes of the late John Paradiso)[1]

I have lived now to my fortieth year, and have seen a good deal

---

[1] The circumstances, experiences, and viewpoint of the fictional John Paradiso are those of the actual Theodore Dreiser.

of life. Just now, because of a stretch of poverty, I am living across the river from New York, in New Jersey, in sight of a splendid tower, the Woolworth Building on the lower end of Manhattan, which lifts its defiant spear of clay into the very maw of heaven. And although I am by no means as far from it as is Fifth Avenue, still I am a dweller in one of the shabbiest, most forlorn neighborhoods which the great metropolis affords. About me dwell principally Poles and Hungarians, who palaver in a lingo of which I know nothing and who live as I would despise to live, poor as I am. For, after all, in my hall-bedroom, which commands the river over the lumberyard, there is some attempt at intellectual adornment, whereas outside and around me there is little more than dull and to a certain extent aggrieved drudgery.

Not so very far from me is a church, a great yellow structure which lifts its walls out of a ruck of cheap frame houses, and those muddy, unpaved streets which are the pride of Jersey City and Hoboken. Here, if I will, I can hear splendid masses intoned, see bright altars and stained glass windows and people going to confession and burning votive candles before images. And if I go of a Sunday, which I rarely do, I can hear regularly that there is a Christ who died for men, and that He was the son of the living God who liveth and reigneth world without end.

I have no quarrel with this doctrine. I can hear it in a hundred thousand churches throughout the world. But I am one of those curious persons who cannot make up their minds about anything. I read and read, almost everything that I can lay hands on—history, politics, philosophy, art. But I find that one history contradicts another, one philosopher drives out another. Essayists, in the main, point out flaws and paradoxes in the current conception of things; novelists, dramatists and biographers spread tales of endless disasters, or silly illusions concerning life, duty, love, opportunity and the like. And I sit here and read and read, when I have time, wondering.

For, friends, I am a scrivener by trade—or try to be. Betimes, trying to make up my mind what to say about life, I am a motorman on a street-car at three dollars and twenty cents a day. I have been a handy man in a junk shop, and wagon driver, anything you will, so long as thereby I could keep body and soul together. I am not handsome, and therefore not attractive to women probably—at any rate I appear not to be—and in consequence am very much alone. Indeed, I am a great coward when it comes to women. Their least frown or mood of indifference frightens me and makes me turn inward to myself, where dwell innumerable beautiful women who smile and nod and hang on my arm and tell me they love me. Indeed, they whisper of scenes so beautiful and so comforting that I know they are not, and never could be, true. And so, in my best moments, I sit at my table and try to write stories which no doubt equally necessitous editors find wholly unavailable.

scrivener - public clerk

The things which keep me thinking and thinking are, first, my social and financial state; second, the difference between my point of view and that of thousands of other respectable citizens, who, being able to make up their minds, seem to find me queer, dull, recessive, or at any rate unsuited to their tastes and pleasures. I look at them, and while I say, "Well, thank heaven I am not like that," still I immediately ask myself, "Am I not all wrong? Should I not be happier if I, too, were like John Spitovesky, or Jacob Feilchenfeld, or Vaclav Melka?" — some of my present neighbors. For Spitovesky, to grow a little personal, is a small dusty man who has a tobacco store around the corner, and who would, I earnestly believe, run if he were threatened with a bath. He smokes his own three-for-fives (Flor de Sissel Grass), and deposits much of the ashes between his waistcoat and his gray striped cotton shirt. His hair, sticking bushily out over his ears, looks as though it were heavily peppered with golden snuff.

"Mr. Spitovesky," I said to him one day not long since, "have you been reading anything about the Colorado mining troubles?"

"I never read de papers," he said with a shrug of his shoulder.

"No? Not at all?" I pursued.

"Dere is nodding in dem — lies mosdly. Somedimes I look ad de baseball news in sommer."

"Oh, I see," I said hopelessly. Then, apropos of nothing, or because I was curious as to my neighbors, "Are you a Catholic?"

"I doaned belong to no church. I doaned mix in no politics, neider. Some hof de men aboud here get excited aboud politics; I got no time. I 'tend to mine store."

Seeing him stand for hours against his doorpost, or sitting out front smoking while his darksome little wife peels potatoes or sews or fusses with the children, I could never understand his "I got no time."

In a related sense there are my friends Jacob Feilchenfeld and Vaclav Melka, whom I sometimes envy because they are so different. The former, the butcher to whom I run for chops and pigs' feet for my landlady, Mrs. Wscrinkuus; the latter the keeper of a spirituous emporium whose windows read "Vynas, Scnapas." Jacob, like every other honest butcher worthy the name, is broad and beefy. He turns on me a friendly eye as he inquires, "About so thick?" or suggests that he has some nice fresh liver or beef tongue, things which he knows Mrs. Wscrinkuus likes. I can sum up Mr. Feilchenfeld's philosophy of life when I report that to every intellectual advance I make he exclaims in a friendly enough way, "I dunno," or "I ain't never heard about dot."

My pride in a sturdy, passive acceptance of things, however, is nearly realized in Vaclav Melka, the happy dispenser of "Vynas, Scnapas," He also is frequently to be found leaning in his doorway in summer, business being not too brisk during the daytime, surveying the world with a reflective eye. He is dark, stocky, black-haired, black-eyed, a good Pole with a head like a wooden peg, almost flat at the top, and driven firmly albeit not ungracefully into his shoulders. He has a wife who is a slattern and nearly a slave, and three children who seem to take no noticeable harm from this saloon life. Leaning in coatless ease against his sticky bar of an evening, he has laid down the law concerning morals and ethics, thus: no lying or stealing — among friends; no brawling or assaults or murdering for any save tremendous reasons of passion; no truckling to priests or sisters who should mind their own business.

"Did you ever read a book, Melka?" I once asked him. It was apropos of a discussion as to a local brawl.

"Once. It was about a feller wot killed a woman. Mostly I ain't got no time to read. Once I was a bath-rubber, and I had time then, but that was long ago. Books ain't nutting for me."

Melka states, however, that he was a fool to come here. "A feller wanted me to take dis saloon, and here I am. I make a living. If my wife died I would go back to my old job, I think." He does not want his wife to die, I am sure. It does not make that much difference.

But over the river from all this is another picture which disturbs me even more than my present surroundings, because, as seen from here, it is seemingly beautiful and inviting. Its tall walls are those of a fabled city. I can almost hear the tinkle of endless wealth in banks, the honks of automobiles, the fanfare of a great constructive trade life. At night all its myriad lights seem to wink at me and exclaim, "Why so incompetent? Why so idle, so poor? Why live in such a wretched neighborhood? Why not cross over and join the great gay throng, make a successful way for yourself? Why sit aside from this great game of materiality and pretend to ignore it or to feel superior?"

And as I sit and think, so it seems to me. But, alas, I haven't the least faculty for making money, not the least. Plainly beyond are all these wonderful things which are being done and made by men with that kind of ability which I appear to lack. I have no material, constructive sense. I can only think and write, in a way. I see these vast institutions (there are great warehouses on this side, too) filled to overflowing apparently with the financially interested and capable, but I — I have not the least idea how to do anything likewise. Yet I am not lazy. I toil over my stories or bounce out of bed and hurry to my work of a morning. But I have never earned more than thirty-five dollars a week in my whole life. No, I am not brilliant financially.

But the thing that troubles me most is the constant palaver going on in the papers and everywhere concerning right, truth, duty, justice, mercy and the like, things which I do not find expressed very clearly in my own motives nor in the motives of those immediately about me; and also the apparently earnest belief on the part of ever so many editors, authors, social reformers, et cetera, that every person, however weak or

dull-appearing externally, contains within himself the seed or the mechanism for producing endless energy and ability, providing he can only
be made to realize that he has it. In other words we are all Napoleons,
only we don't know it. We are lazy Napoleons, idle Hannibals, wasteful
and indifferent John D. Rockefellers. Turn the pages of any magazine — are there not advertisements of and treatises on How To Be
Successful, with the authors thereof offering to impart their knowledge
of how so to be for a comparative song?

Well, I am not one who can believe that. In my very humble
estimation people are not so. They are, in the main, as I see it, weak
and limited, exceedingly so, like Vaclav Melka or Mrs. Wscrinkuus,
and to fill their humble brains with notions of an impossible supremacy,
if it could be done, would be to send them forth to breast the ocean in a
cockleshell. And, yet, here on my table, borrowed from the local library
for purposes of idle or critical examination, is a silly book entitled
"Take It!" — "It" meaning *"the world!"*; and another "It's
Yours!" — the "It" in this case meaning that same great world! All you
have to do is to decide so to do — and to try! Am I a fool to smile at this
very stout doctrine, to doubt whether you can get more than four quarts
out of any four-quart measure, if so much?

But to return to this same matter of right, truth, justice, mercy, so
freely advertised in these days and so clearly defined, apparently, in
every one's mind as open paths by which they may proceed. In the
main, it seems to me that people are not concerned about right, or truth,
or justice, or mercy, or duty, as abstract principles or working rules, nor
do I believe that the average man knows clearly or even semi-clearly
what is meant by the words. His only relation to them, so far as I can
see, is that he finds them used in a certain reckless, thoughtless way to
represent some method of adjustment by which he would like to think
he is protected from assault or saved from misery, and so uses them
himself. His concern for them as related to the other individual is that
the other individual should not infringe on him, and I am now speaking
of the common unsuccessful mass as well as of the successful.

Mrs. Wscrinkuus, poor woman, is stingy and slightly suspicious,
although she goes to church Sundays and believes that Christ's Sermon
on the Mount is the living truth. She does not want any one to be mean
to her; she does not do anything mean to other people, largely because
she has no particular taste or capacity in that direction. Supposing I
should advise her to "Take It!" assure her that "It" was hers by right
of capability! What would become of *right, truth, justice, mercy* in that
case?

Or, once more, let us take Jacob Feilchenfeld and John Spitovesky, who care for no man beyond their trade and whose attitude
toward right, truth, mercy, justice is as above. Suppose I should tell
them to take "It," or assure them that "It" was theirs? Of what import

would the message be? Vaclav Melka does favors only in return for favors. He does not like priests because they are always taking up collections. If you told him to take "It" he would proceed to take something away from the very good priests first of all. Everywhere I find the common man imbued with this feeling for self-protection and self-advancement. *Truth* is something that must be told to *him*; *justice* is what *he* deserves—although if it costs him nothing he will gladly see it extended to the other fellow.

But do not think for one moment because I say this that I think myself better or more deserving or wiser than any of these. As I said before, I do not understand life, although I like it; I may even say that I like this sharp, grasping scheme of things, and find that it works well. Plainly it produces all the fine spectacles I see. If it had not been for a certain hard, seeking ambition in Mr. Woolworth to get up and be superior to his fellows, where would his splendid tower have come from? It is only because I cannot understand why people cling so fatuously to the idea that there is some fixed idyllic scheme or moral order handed down from on high, which is tender and charitable, punishes so-called evil and always rewards so-called good, that I write this. If it punishes evil, it is not all of the evil that I see. If it rewards good, then much of the good that I admire goes wholly unrewarded, on this earth at least.

But to return. The Catholics believe that Christ died on the Cross for them, and that unless the Buddhists, Shintoists, Mohammedans, et cetera, reform or find Christ they will be lost. Three hundred million Mohammedans believe quite otherwise. Two hundred and fifty million Buddhists believe something else. The Christian Scientists and Hicksites[2] believe still differently. Then there are historians who doubt the authenticity of Christ (Gibbon: Vol. I, Chapters 15, 16).[3] Where is a moral order which puts a false interpretation on history as in the case of sectarian literature (lists furnished on application), or allows fetiches to flourish like the grass of the new year?

I will admit that in cases such as lying, stealing and the like there is always a so-called moral thing to do or say when these so-called moral principles or beatitudes are inveighed against. You have ridden on a street-car; pay your fare. You have received five dollars from a given man; return it. You have had endless favors from a given individual; do not malign him. Such are the obvious and commonplace things with which these great words are concerned; and in these prima facie cases these so-called principles work well enough.

But take a case where temperament or body-needs or appetites

[2] The Hicksites are followers of Elias Hicks (1748–1830), a liberal Quaker leader who preached the doctrine of the "Inward Light."

[3] The reference is to the negative criticism of Christianity in Edward Gibbon's *History of the Decline and Fall of the Roman Empire* (1776–1788).

fly in the face of man-made order, where a great spirit-thirst stands out against a life-made conviction. Here is a man-made law, and here is dire necessity. On which side is Right? On which side God?

(1) A girl falls in love with a boy to whom the father takes an instant dislike. The father is not better than the lover, just different. The girl and boy are aflame (no chemical law of their invention, mind you), and when the father opposes them they wed secretly. Result, rage. A weak temperament on the part of the father (no invention of his own) causes him to drink. On sight, in liquor, he kills the youth. The law says he must be hung unless justified. A lie on the part of the girl defaming the lover-husband will save the father. On which side now do right, truth, justice, mercy stand?

(2) A man has a great trade idea. He sees where by combining fourteen companies he can reduce cost of manufacture and sell a very necessary product to the public at a reduced rate, the while he makes himself rich. In the matter of principle and procedure (right, truth, justice, etc.), since his competitors will not sell out, he is confronted by the following propositions: (a) forming a joint stock company and permitting them all to share in the profits; (b) giving them the idea, asking nothing, and allowing them to form a company of their own, so helping humanity; (c) making a secret combination with four or five and underselling the others and so compel them to sell or quit; (d) doing nothing, letting time and chance work and the public wait. Now it so happens that the second and fourth are the only things that can be done without opposition. He is a man of brains and ideals. What are his rights, duties, privileges? Where do justice, mercy, truth, fit in here, and how?

(3) A man's son has committed a crime. The man realizes that owing to deficiencies of his own he has never been able to give the boy a right training or a fair chance. The law demands that he give up his son, even though he loves him dearly and feels himself responsible. Where do right, justice, mercy work here, and can they be made harmonious and consonant?

These are but three of fifty instances out of the current papers which I daily read. I have cited them to show how topsy-turvy the world seems to me, how impossible of a fixed explanation or rule. Scarcely any two individuals but will be at variance on these propositions. Yet the religionists, the moralists, the editorial writers preach a faith and an obvious line of duty which they label grandiosely "right" or "true," "just" or "merciful." My observation and experience lead me to believe that there is scarcely a so-called "sane," right, merciful, true, just, solution to anything. I know that many will cry in answer "Look at all this great world! Look at all the interesting things made, the beautiful things, the pleasures provided. Are not these the intelligent directive product of a superior governing being, who is kind and merciful into the bargain and who has our interests at heart? Can you doubt, when you observe the exact laws that govern in mathematics, chemistry, physics, that there is an intelligent, kindly ruling power, truthful, merciful, etc?" My answer is: I can and do, for these things can be used as readily against right, truth, justice, mercy, as we understand those things, as they can for or with them. If you don't believe this, and are anti-German or anti-Japanese, or anti-anything else, see how those or any other so-called inimical powers can use all these magnificent forces or arts in its behalf and against the powers of light and worth such as you understand and approve of. And when justice and mercy are tacked on as attributes of this intelligence there is no possible appeal to *human* reason.

"But only look," some one is sure to cry, "at some of the beautiful, wonderful, helpful things which Divine Providence, or Life, or Force, or Energy has provided now and here for man! Railroads; telegraphy; the telephone; theaters; gas; electricity; clothing of all sorts; newspapers; books; hotels; stores; fire departments; hospitals; plumbing; the pleasures of love and sex; music." An admirable list, truly, and all provided by one struggling genius or another or by the slow, cataclysmic processes of nature: fires, deaths and painful births. Aside from the fact that all of these things can be and are used for *evil* as well as *good* purposes (trust oppression, enemy wars and the like), still it might as well be supplemented by such things as jails, detectives, penitentiaries, courts of law — good or evil things, as you choose to look at them. All of these things are good in the hands of good people, evil in the hands of the evil, and nature seems not to care which group uses them. A hospital will aid a scoundrel as readily as a good man, and vice versa.

Common dust swept into our atmosphere makes our beautiful sunsets and blue sky. Sidereal space, as we know it, is said to be one welter of strangely flowing streams of rock and dust, a wretched mass made attractive only by some vast compulsory coalition into a star. Stars clash and blaze, and the whole great complicated system seems one erosive, chaffering, bickering effort, with here and there a tendency to stillness and petrifaction. This world as we know it, the human race and the accompanying welter of animals and insects, do they not, aside from momentary phases of delight and beauty, often strike you as dull, aimless, cruel, useless? Are not the processes by which they are produced or those by which they live (the Chicago slaughter-houses, for instance), stark, relentless, brutal, shameful even? — life living on life, the preying of one on another, the compulsory aging of all, the hungers, thirsts, destroying losses and pains. . . .

But I was talking of Jersey City and my difficulty in adjusting myself to the life about me, thinking as I do. Yet such facts as I can gather only confound me the more. Take the daily papers which I have been reading to beguile my loneliness, and note that:

(1) Two old people who lived near me, after working hard for years to supply themselves with a competence, were ruined by the failure of a bank and were therefore forced to seek work. Not finding it, they were compelled to make a choice between subsisting on charity and dying. Desiring to be as agreeable to the world as possible and not to be a burden to it, they chose death by gas, locking the doors of their bare little home, stuffing paper and clothing into chinks and under doors and windows, and turning on the gas, seated side-by-side and hand-in-hand. Naturally the end came quickly enough, for Divine Mind has no objection to ordinary illuminating gas killing any one. It did not inform any one of their predicament. Impartial gas choked them as quickly as it would have lighted the room, and yet at the same time, according to the same papers, in this very same world——

(2) The sixteen-year-old son of a multi-millionaire real estate holder was left over fifty million dollars by his fond father, who did not know what else to do with it, the same son having not as yet exhibited any capacity for handling the money wisely or having done anything to deserve it save be the son of the aforesaid father.

(3) A somewhat bored group of Newport millionairesses give a dinner for the pet dogs of their equally wealthy friends, one particular dog or doggess being host or hostess.

(4) A Staten Island brewer worth twenty millions died of heart failure, induced by undue joy over the fact that he had been elected snare drummer of a shriners' lodge, after spending thousands upon thousands in organizing a band of his own and developing sufficient influence to cause a shriners' organization to tolerate him.

(5) A millionaire politician and horse-racer erected a fifteen-thousand-dollar monument to a horse.

(6) An uneducated darkey, trying to make his way North, climbed upon the carriage trucks of a Pullman attached to a fast express and was swept North into a blizzard, where he was finally found dying of exhaustion, and did die—arms and legs frozen—a victim of an effort to better his condition.

Puzzle: locate Divine Mind, Light, Wisdom, Truth, Justice, Mercy in these items.

By these same papers, covering several months or more, I saw where:

(1) Several people died waiting in line on bundle day for bundles of cast-off clothing given by those who could not use the clothes any longer—not such people as you and I, perhaps, but those who were sick, or old, or weak.

(2) Mr. Ford, manufacturer of automobiles, was convinced that he could reform any criminal or bad character by giving him or her plenty of work to do at good wages and with the prospect of advance-

ment; also that he was earning too much and wished to divide with his fellow man.[4]

(3) August Belmont and J. P. Morgan, Jr.,[5] noting this item, concluded that they could not do anything for any one, intellectually, financially or otherwise.

(4) An attendant in an Odd Fellows Home, having tired of some old patients, chloroformed them all—a purely pagan event and not possible in an enlightened age and a Christian country.

(5) A priest, having murdered a girl and confessed to it, no way was found to electrocute him because of his cloth. Men whose services and aid he contemned insisted that he must be proved insane and not be electrocuted, though he did not agree with them.

(6) A young soldier and his bride, but one day married, walk out to buy furniture for their new home; a street fight in which three toughs assail each other with pistols breaks out and before they can take to cover a stray bullet instantly kills the soldier-husband. Subsequently the bride becomes morbid and goes insane.

(7) In nearly all the countries of the late great war a day of prayer for Divine intervention was indulged in, but prayer having been made and not answered the combatants proceeded to make more and worse war—Divine prohibition of combat, according to the Christian dogma, being no bar nor of any avail.

(8) A well-known Western financier and promoter of strong religious and moralistic leanings, having projected and built a well-known railroad and made it immensely prosperous by reducing the rates to the people of his region, was thereupon set upon by other financiers who wished to secure his property for little or nothing, and being attacked by false charges brought by a suborned stockholder and his road thrown into the hands of a receiver by a compliant judge, was so injured financially thereby as never to be able to recover his property. And those who attacked him justified themselves on the ground that he was a "rate-cutter" and so a disturbing element—a disturber of the peace and profits of other railroads adjacent and elsewhere. His dying statement (years later) was that American history would yet justify him and that God governed for good, if one could wait long enough!

(9) One man was given one year for a cold, brutal manslaughter in New York, whereas a whole family of colored people in the South was strung up and riddled with bullets for so little as that one of them

---

[4] Henry Ford (1863–1947), the American capitalist whose fortune was based on the success of the popular "Model-T" Ford, attracted national attention in January, 1914, by announcing a large-scale profit-sharing plan for his employees.

[5] August Belmont, Jr. (1853–1924) and John Pierpont Morgan, Jr. (1867–1943) were well-known American financiers.

fought with a deputy sheriff; while a woman who had shot another woman through a window because of jealousy (aroused by her husband's assumed attentions to said woman) was acquitted and then went on the stage, the general sentiment being that "one could not electrocute a woman."

(10) The principal charities aid society of New York had spent and was spending one hundred and fifty thousand dollars per year on running expenses, and something over ninety thousand dollars in actual relief work, though it was explained that the hundred and fifty thousand brought about much reference of worthy cases to other agencies and private charities, a thing which could not otherwise have been done.

(11) It is immoral, un-Christian and illegitimate to have a child without a husband, yet when six hundred thousand men are withdrawn from England to fight the Germans and twenty thousand virgins become war-brides it is proposed to legalize the children on the ground that it is nevertheless moral to preserve the nation from extinction.

(12) A doctor may advise against child-birth when that experience would endanger a woman or threaten her permanent disability, but if he gives information or furnishes contraceptal means which would prevent the trying situation he is guilty of a misdemeanor, subject to fine and the ruin of his career.

(13) The president of one of the largest street railway corporations in the world finds it wrong to fail to rise and give your seat to a woman, but right to run so few cars as to make available seats for only one-third of the traffic; wrong not to take extreme precaution in stepping off or on a car or crossing the tracks, but right to leave the cars without heat, the windows and floors dirty and the doors broken, making anger, delay and haste contribute to inattention and unfairness; wrong to read a newspaper wide open, to cross your legs or protrude your feet too far, thereby inconveniencing your fellow-passenger, but right to mulct the city, composed of these same passengers, of millions via stolen franchises, watered stock, avoided taxes, the refusal of transfers at principal intersections, to say nothing of the prevention of fair competition via the jitney bus and other means which would relieve traffic pressure, and all with no excuse save that the corporation desires the money; and a tame public endures it with a little ineffectual murmuring.

(14) A man has been found in a Western penitentiary who had been there for twenty years and who had been sent there because of erroneous circumstantial evidence, the real offender having confessed on his death-bed.

(15) A certain landlord in New York compelled a certain family to move, because, not they, but some of their visitors, wore shabby, hence undesirable, clothes, thus lowering the social and material tone of the apartment house in question and causing their distant but still

watchful fellow-tenants much distress of mind in being compelled to live in such an atmosphere. This was a Riverside Drive apartment.

But need I cite more, really?

It is because of these things that I sit in my hall-bedroom, a great panorama of beauty spread out before me, and in attempting to write of this thing, life, find myself confused. I do not know how to work right, truth, justice, mercy, etc., into these things, nor am I sure that life would be as fascinating without them, as driving or forceful. The scenes that I look upon here and everywhere are beautiful enough, sun, moon and stars swinging in their courses, seemingly mathematically and with great art or charm. I am willing to assume that their courses are calculated and intelligent, but no more and no further. And the river at this moment is begemmed with thousands of lights—a truly artistic and poetic spectacle and one not to be gainsaid. By day it is gray, or blue, or green, wondrous shades by turns; by night a jewel world. Gulls wheel over it; tugs strain cheerily to and fro, emitting gorgeous plumes of smoke. Snows, rains, warmths, colds come in endless variety, the endless fillip which gives force and color to our days.

Still I am confused. For, on the one hand, here is Vaclav Melka, who does not care much for this alleged charm; nor John Spitovesky; nor Jacob Feilchenfeld; nor many, many others like them. On the other hand, myself and many others like me, sitting and meditating on it, are so spellbound that we have scarcely any thought wherewith to earn a living. Life seems to prove but one thing to me, and that is that the various statements concerning right, truth, justice, mercy are palaver merely, an earnest and necessitous attempt, perhaps, at balance and equation where all things are so very much unbalanced, paradoxical and contradictory—the small-change names for a thing or things of which we have not yet caught the meaning. History teaches me little save that nothing is really dependable or assured, but all inexplicable and all shot through with a great desire on the part of many to do or say something by which they may escape the unutterable confusion of time and the feebleness of earthly memory. Current action, it appears, demonstrates much the same thing. Kings and emperors have risen and gone. Generals and captains have warred and departed. Philosophers have dreamed, poets have written; and I, mussing around among religions, philosophies, fiction and facts, can find nothing wherewith to solve my vaulting egoism, no light, and no way to be anything more than the humblest servitor.

Among so much that is tempestuous and glittering I merely occasionally scrub and make bright my room. I look out at the river flowing by now, after hundreds of millions of years of loneliness where there was nothing but silence and waste (past so much now that is vivid, colorful, human), and say to myself: Well, where there is so much order and love of order in every one and everywhere there must be some great elemental spirit holding for order of sorts, at any rate. Stars do not swing in given orbits for nothing surely, or at least I might have faith to that extent. But when I step out and encounter, as I daily do, lust and greed, plotting and trapping, and envy and all uncharitableness, including murder—all severely condemned by the social code, the Bible and a thousand wise saws and laws—and also see, as I daily do, vast schemes of chicane grinding the faces of the poor, and wars brutally involving the death of millions whose lives are precious to them because of the love of power on the part of some one or many, I am not so sure. Illusions hold too many; lust and greed, vast and bleary-eyed, dominate too many more. Ignorance, vast and almost unconquerable, hugs and licks its chains in reverence. Brute strength sits empurpled and laughs a throaty laugh.

Yet here is the great river—that is beautiful; and Mr. Woolworth's tower, a strange attempt on the part of man to seem more than he is; and a thousand other evidences of hopes and dreams, all too frail perhaps against the endless drag toward nothingness, but still lovely and comforting. And yet here also is Vaclav Melka, who wants to be a bath-rubber again! John Spitovesky, who doesn't care; Jacob Feilchenfeld, who never heard; and millions of others like them, and I—I think and grow confused, and earn nineteen-twenty a week or less—never more, apparently.

Come to think of it, is it not a wonder, holding such impossible views as I do, that I earn anything at all?

1920

Gertrude Stein   *1874 – 1946*

Gertrude Stein, who hoped to be remembered as the "grandmother of the modern movement," was born in Allegheny, Pennsylvania. After graduation from Radcliffe College, where William James was one of her favorite teachers, she studied medicine at Johns Hopkins, specializing in the investigation of the structure of the brain. She failed to graduate because she refused to take required examinations. Medical study, she had decided, was boring. She traveled abroad and by 1903 was settled in Paris, which was to remain her home. In 1907 she was joined by Alice B. Toklas, her life-long secretary and companion. The salon she established in her apartment brought together the most distinguished artists of the time, including such figures as the young painter Pablo Picasso, whose works she collected, and the poet Guillaume Apollinaire. In the years following the first World War, their numbers were swelled by expatriates who flocked into Paris. Among these was Ernest Hemingway, to whom Miss Stein addressed the remark that Hemingway used as an epigraph to *The Sun Also Rises* (1926): "You are all a lost generation."

Gertrude Stein's experimental modern techniques—like Ezra Pound's—predated the war. They can be seen in her first books, *Three Lives* (1909) and *The Making of Americans*, a book about her family written in the period 1906–1908 which was not published until 1925. In both she made use of simple idiomatic language and incremental repetition of phrases to give the impression of a prolonged present identified with the spontaneous flow of consciousness. It is likely that one of the early inspirations for her method was William James's conception of the stream of consciousness, although she was more immediately indebted to abstractionist tendencies in the other arts: the multidimensional vision of cubism and the rejection of traditional ideas of harmony and unity in music. She was also interested in the new art of cinema and thought of her "characterizations by repetition" as being like the merging sequential frames of motion picture film. In *Tender Buttons* (1914) she attempted to write poems unencumbered by conventional grammar and syntax, which she (like E. E. Cummings) regarded as an impediment to the free movement of feeling. In her effort to achieve a flowing style more expressive of sensations and feelings than of ideas, she influenced emerging postwar writers, especially her close contemporary Sherwood Anderson, and the younger Ernest Hemingway.

The Autobiography of Alice B. Toklas—which despite its title is Gertrude Stein's own autobiography, told as though by her friend—is a mine of factual information and personal gossip about the international world of arts and letters. The author's indirect method had distinct advantages: besides freeing her of responsibility for her personal judgments of other people, it enabled her to praise herself more fully than would be seemly in a first person narration.

Among numerous other works, *Lectures in America* (1935) presents Miss Stein's theory of composition; *Lucy Church Amiably* (1930) and *Ida* (1941) are unconventional novels; *Four Saints in Three Acts* (1934) is an opera with music by Virgil Thomson. Nonfictional works include *Matisse, Picasso, and Gertrude Stein, with two Shorter Stories* (1933), *Portraits and Prayers* (1934), and *Paris France* (1940). *Wars I Have Seen* (1945) and *Brewsie and Willie* (1946) reflect the author's experiences in the first World War, the German occupation of France during the second war, and the liberation.

Among posthumously published works are *Last Operas and Plays*, ed. Carl Van Vechten (New York, 1949), *The Yale Edition of the Unpublished Writings of Gertrude Stein*, ed. Carl Van Vechten, 8 vols. (New Haven, 1951–58), *and Writings and Lectures, 1911–1945*, ed. Elizabeth Sprigge (London, 1967). A helpful brief introduction is F. J. Hoffman, *Gertrude Stein* (Minneapolis, 1961). Other biographical and critical works include Elizabeth Sprigge, *Gertrude Stein, Her Life and Work* (New York, 1957), Alice B. Toklas, *What Is Remembered* (New York, 1963), and Allegra Stewart, *Gertrude Stein and the Present* (Cambridge, Mass., 1967).The standard bibliographies are R. B. Haas and Donald Gallup, *A Catalogue of the Published and Unpublished Writings of Gertrude Stein* (New Haven, 1941), and Julian Sawyer, *Gertrude Stein, A Bibliography* (New York, 1941).

The text of "Melanctha and Jeff" is that of *Three Lives* (Norfolk, Conn., 1933). "Pound and Eliot" and "Hemingway, Ford, Anderson, Fitzgerald, and Hemingway" are from *The Autobiography of Alice B. Toklas* (New York, 1933). The text of "Portraits and Repetition" is that of *Lectures in America* (New York, 1935).

Melanctha and Jeff

Dr. Campbell sat there very quiet, with only a little thinking and sometimes a beginning feeling, and he was alone until it began to be morning, and then he went, and Melanctha helped him, and he made 'Mis' Herbert more easy in her dying. 'Mis' Herbert lingered on till about ten o'clock the next morning, and then slowly and without much pain she died away. Jeff Campbell staid till the last moment, with Melanctha, to make her mother's dying easy for her. When it was over he sent in the colored woman from next door to help Melanctha fix things, and then he went away to take care of his other patients. He came back very soon to Melanctha. He helped her to have a funeral for her mother. Melanctha then went to live with the good natured woman, who had been her neighbor. Melanctha still saw Jeff Campbell very often. Things began to be very strong between them.

Melanctha now never wandered, unless she was with Jeff Campbell. Sometimes she and he wandered a good deal together. Jeff Campbell had not got over his way of talking to her all the time about all the things he was always thinking. Melanctha never talked much, now, when they were together. Sometimes Jeff Campbell teased her about her not talking to him. "I certainly did think Melanctha you was a great talker from the way Jane Harden and everybody said things to me, and from the way I heard you talk so much when I first met you. Tell me true Melanctha, why don't you talk more now to me, perhaps it is I talk so much I don't give you any chance to say things to me, or perhaps it is you hear me talk so much you don't think so much now of a whole lot of talking. Tell me honest Melanctha, why don't you talk more to me." "You know very well Jeff Campbell," said Melanctha. "You certainly do know very well Jeff, you don't think really much, of my talking. You think a whole lot more about everything than I do Jeff, and you don't care much what I got to say about it. You know that's true what I am saying Jeff, if you want to be real honest, the way you always are when I like you so much." Jeff laughed and looked fondly at her. "I don't say ever I know, you ain't right, when you say things like that to me, Melanctha. You see you always like to be talking just what you think everybody wants to be hearing from you, and when you are like that, Melanctha, honest, I certainly don't care very much to hear you, but sometimes you say something that is what you are really thinking, and then I like a whole lot to hear you talking." Melanctha smiled, with her strong sweetness, on him, and she felt her power very deeply. "I certainly never do talk very much when I like anybody really, Jeff. You see, Jeff, it ain't much use to talk about what a woman is really feeling in her. You see all that, Jeff, better, by and by, when you get to really feeling. You won't be so ready then always with your talking. You see, Jeff, if it don't come true what I am saying." "I don't ever say you ain't always right, Melanctha," said Jeff Campbell. "Perhaps what I call my thinking ain't really so very understanding. I don't say, no never now any more, you ain't right, Melanctha, when you really say things to me. Perhaps I see it all to be very different when I come to really see what you mean by what you are always saying to me." "You is very sweet and good to me always, Jeff Campbell," said Melanctha. "'Deed I certainly am not good to you, Melanctha. Don't I bother you all the time with my talking, but I really do like you a whole lot, Melanctha." "And I like you, Jeff Campbell, and you certainly are mother, and father, and brother, and sister, and child and everything, always to me. I can't say much about how good you been to me, Jeff Campbell, I never knew any man who was good and didn't do things ugly, before I met you to take care of me, Jeff Campbell. Good-by, Jeff, come see me to-morrow, when you get through with your working." "Sure Melanctha, you know that already," said Jeff Campbell, and then he went away and left her.

These months had been an uncertain time for Jeff Campbell. He never knew how much he really knew about Melanctha. He saw her now for long times and very often. He was beginning always more and more to like her. But he did not seem to himself to know very much about her. He was beginning to feel he could almost trust the goodness in her. But then, always, really, he was not very sure about her. Melanctha always had ways that made him feel uncertain with her, and yet he was so near, in his feeling for her. He now never thought about all this in real words any more. He was always letting it fight itself out in him. He was now never taking any part in this fighting that was always going on inside him.

Jeff always loved now to be with Melanctha and yet he always hated to go to her. Somehow he was always afraid when he was to go to her, and yet he had made himself very certain that here he would not be a coward. He never felt any of this being afraid, when he was with her. Then they always were very true, and near to one another. But always when he was going to her, Jeff would like anything that could happen that would keep him a little longer from her.

It was a very uncertain time, all these months, for Jeff Campbell. He did not know very well what it was that he really wanted. He was very certain that he did not know very well what it was that Melanctha wanted. Jeff Campbell had always all his life loved to be with people, and he had loved all his life always to be thinking, but he was still only a great boy, was Jeff Campbell, and he had never before had any of this funny kind of feeling. Now, this evening, when he was free to go and see Melanctha, he talked to anybody he could find who would detain him, and so it was very late when at last he came to the house where Melanctha was waiting to receive him.

Jeff came in to where Melanctha was waiting for him, and he took off his hat and heavy coat, and then drew up a chair and sat down by the fire. It was very cold that night, and Jeff sat there, and rubbed his hands and tried to warm them. He had only said "How do you do" to Melanctha, he had not yet begun to talk to her. Melanctha sat there, by the fire, very quiet. The heat gave a pretty pink glow to her pale yellow and attractive face. Melanctha sat in a low chair, her hands, with their long, fluttering fingers, always ready to show her strong feeling, were lying quiet in her lap. Melanctha was very tired with her waiting for Jeff Campbell. She sat there very quiet and just watching. Jeff was a robust, dark, healthy, cheery negro. His hands were firm and kindly and unimpassioned. He touched women always with his big hands, like a brother. He always had a warm broad glow, like southern sunshine. He never had anything mysterious in him. He was open, he was pleasant, he was cheery and always he wanted, as Melanctha once had wanted, always now he too wanted really to understand.

Jeff sat there this evening in his chair and was silent a long time, warming himself with the pleasant fire. He did not look at Melanctha who was watching. He sat there and just looked into the fire. At first his dark, open face was smiling, and he was rubbing the back of his black-brown hand over his mouth to help him in his smiling. Then he was thinking, and he frowned and rubbed his head hard, to help him in his thinking. Then he smiled again, but now his smiling was not very pleasant. His smile was now wavering on the edge of scorning. His smile changed more and more, and then he had a look as if he were deeply down, all disgusted. Now his face was darker, and he was bitter in his smiling, and he began, without looking from the fire, to talk to Melanctha, who was now very tense with her watching.

"Melanctha Herbert," began Jeff Campbell, "I certainly after all this time I know you, I certainly do know little, real about you. You see, Melanctha, it's like this way with me"; Jeff was frowning, with his thinking and looking very hard into the fire, "You see it's just this way, with me now, Melanctha. Sometimes you seem like one kind of a girl to me, and sometimes you are like a girl that is all different to me, and the two kinds of girls is certainly very different to each other, and I can't see any way they seem to have much to do, to be together in you. They certainly don't seem to be made much like as if they could have anything really to do with each other. Sometimes you are a girl to me I certainly never would be trusting, and you got a laugh then so hard, it just rattles, and you got ways so bad, I can't believe you mean them hardly, and yet all that I just been saying is certainly you one way I often see you, and it's what your mother and Jane Harden always found you, and it's what makes me hate so, to come near you. And then certainly sometimes, Melanctha, you certainly is all a different creature, and sometimes then there comes out in you what is certainly a thing, like a real beauty. I certainly, Melanctha, never can tell just how it is that it comes so lovely. Seems to me when it comes it's got a real sweetness, that is more wonderful than a pure flower, and a gentleness, that is more tender than the sunshine, and a kindness, that makes one feel like summer, and then a way to know, that makes everything all over, and all that, and it does certainly seem to be real for the little while it's lasting, for the little while that I can surely see it, and it gives me to feel like I certainly had got real religion. And then when I got

rich with such a feeling, comes all that other girl, and then that seems
more likely that that is really you what's honest, and then I certainly do
get awful afraid to come to you, and I certainly never do feel I could be
very trusting with you. And then I certainly don't know anything at all
about you, and I certainly don't know which is a real Melanctha Herbert, and I certainly don't feel no longer, I ever want to talk to you. Tell
me honest, Melanctha, which is the way that is you really, when you
are alone, and real, and all honest. Tell me, Melanctha, for I certainly
do want to know it."

Melanctha did not make him any answer, and Jeff, without looking at her, after a little while, went on with his talking. "And then,
Melanctha, sometimes you certainly do seem sort of cruel, and not to
care about people being hurt or in trouble, something so hard about you
it makes me sometimes real nervous, sometimes somehow like you
always, like your being, with 'Mis' Herbert. You sure did do everything
that any woman could, Melanctha, I certainly never did see anybody
do things any better, and yet, I don't know how to say just what I
mean, Melanctha, but there was something awful hard about your
feeling, so different from the way I'm always used to see good people
feeling, and so it was the way Jane Harden and 'Mis' Herbert talked
when they felt strong to talk about you, and yet, Melanctha, somehow I
feel so really near to you, and you certainly have got an awful wonderful, strong kind of sweetness. I certainly would like to know for sure,
Melanctha, whether I got really anything to be afraid for. I certainly did
think once, Melanctha, I knew something about all kinds of women. I
certainly know now really, how I don't know anything sure at all about
you, Melanctha, though I been with you so long, and so many times for
whole hours with you, and I like so awful much to be with you, and I
can always say anything I am thinking to you. I certainly do awful wish,
Melanctha, I really was more understanding. I certainly do that same,
Melanctha."

Jeff stopped now and looked harder than before into the fire. His
face changed from his thinking back into that look that was so like as if
he was all through and through him, disgusted with what he had been
thinking. He sat there a long time, very quiet, and then slowly, somehow, it came strongly to him that Melanctha Herbert, there beside him,
was trembling and feeling it all to be very bitter. "Why, Melanctha,"
cried Jeff Campbell, and he got up and put his arm around her like a
brother. "I stood it just so long as I could bear it, Jeff," sobbed Melanctha, and then she gave herself away, to her misery, "I was awful
ready, Jeff, to let you say anything you liked that gave you any pleasure.
You could say all about me what you wanted, Jeff, and I would try to
stand it, so as you would be sure to be liking it, Jeff, but you was too
cruel to me. When you do that kind of seeing how much you can make
a woman suffer, you ought to give her a little rest, once sometimes, Jeff.

They can't any of us stand it so for always, Jeff. I certainly did stand it just as long as I could, so you would like it, but I,—oh Jeff, you went on too long to-night Jeff. I couldn't stand it not a minute longer the way you was doing of it, Jeff. When you want to be seeing how the way a woman is really made of, Jeff, you shouldn't never be so cruel, never to be thinking how much she can stand, the strong way you always do it, Jeff." "Why, Melanctha," cried Jeff Campbell, in his horror, and then he was very tender to her, and like a good, strong, gentle brother in his soothing of her, "Why Melanctha dear, I certainly don't now see what it is you mean by what you was just saying to me. Why Melanctha, you poor little girl, you certainly never did believe I ever knew I was giving you real suffering. Why, Melanctha, how could you ever like me if you thought I ever could be so like a red Indian?" "I didn't just know, Jeff," and Melanctha nestled to him, "I certainly never did know just what it was you wanted to be doing with me, but I certainly wanted you should do anything you liked, you wanted, to make me more understanding for you. I tried awful hard to stand it, Jeff, so as you could do anything you wanted with me." "Good Lord and Jesus Christ, Melanctha!" cried Jeff Campbell. "I certainly never can know anything about you real, Melanctha, you poor little girl," and Jeff drew her closer to him, "But I certainly do admire and trust you a whole lot now, Melanctha. I certainly do, for I certainly never did think I was hurting you at all, Melanctha, by the things I always been saying to you. Melanctha, you poor little, sweet, trembling baby now, be good, Melanctha. I certainly can't ever tell you how awful sorry I am to hurt you so, Melanctha. I do anything I can to show you how I never did mean to hurt you, Melanctha." "I know, I know," murmured Melanctha, clinging to him. "I know you are a good man, Jeff. I always know that, no matter how much you can hurt me." "I sure don't see how you can think so, Melanctha, if you certainly did think I was trying so hard just to hurt you." "Hush, you are only a great big boy, Jeff Campbell, and you don't know nothing yet about real hurting," said Melanctha, smiling up through her crying, at him. "You see, Jeff, I never knew anybody I could know real well and yet keep on always respecting, till I came to know you real well, Jeff." "I sure don't understand that very well, Melanctha. I ain't a bit better than just lots of others of the colored people. You certainly have been unlucky with the kind you met before me, that's all, Melanctha. I certainly ain't very good, Melanctha." "Hush, Jeff, you don't know nothing at all about what you are," said Melanctha. "Perhaps you are right, Melanctha. I don't say ever any more, you ain't right, when you say things to me, Melanctha," and Jefferson sighed, and then he smiled, and then they were quiet a long time together, and then after some more kindness, it was late, and then Jeff left her.

Jeff Campbell, all these months, had never told his good mother anything about Melanctha Herbert. Somehow he always kept his seeing her so much now, to himself. Melanctha too had never had any of her other friends meet him. They always acted together, these two, as if their being so much together was a secret, but really there was no one who would have made it any harder for them. Jeff Campbell did not really know how it had happened that they were so secret. He did not know if it was what Melanctha wanted. Jeff had never spoken to her at all about it. It just seemed as if it were well understood between them that nobody should know that they were so much together. It was as if it were agreed between them, that they should be alone by themselves always, and so they would work out together what they meant by what they were always saying to each other.

Jefferson often spoke to Melanctha about his good mother. He never said anything about whether Melanctha would want to meet her. Jefferson never quite understood why all this had happened so, in secret. He never really knew what it was that Melanctha really wanted. In all these ways he just, by his nature did, what he sort of felt Melanctha wanted. And so they continued to be alone and much together, and now it had come to be the spring time, and now they had all out-doors to wander.

They had many days now when they were very happy. Jeff every day found that he really liked Melanctha better. Now surely he was beginning to have real, deep feeling in him. And still he loved to talk himself out to Melanctha, and he loved to tell her how good it all was to him, and how he always loved to be with her, and to tell her always all about it. One day, now Jeff arranged, that Sunday they would go out and have a happy, long day in the bright fields, and they would be all day just alone together. The day before, Jeff was called in to see Jane Harden.

Jane Harden was very sick almost all day and Jeff Campbell did everything he could to make her better. After a while Jane became more easy and then she began to talk to Jeff about Melanctha. Jane did not know how much Jeff was now seeing of Melanctha. Jane these days never saw Melanctha. Jane began to talk of the time when she first knew Melanctha. Jane began to tell how in these days Melanctha had very little understanding. She was young then and she had a good mind. Jane Harden never would say Melanctha never had a good mind, but in those days Melanctha certainly had not been very understanding. Jane began to explain to Jeff Campbell how in every way, she Jane, had taught Melanctha. Jane then began to explain how eager Melanctha always had been for all that kind of learning. Jane Harden began to tell how they had wandered. Jane began to tell how Melanctha once had loved her, Jane Harden. Jane began to tell Jeff of all the bad ways Melanctha had used with her. Jane began to tell all she knew of the way Melanctha had gone on, after she had left her. Jane began to tell all about the different men, white ones and blacks, Melanctha never was particular about things like that, Jane Harden said in passing, not that Melanctha was a bad one, and she had a good mind, Jane Harden never would say that she hadn't, but Melanctha always liked to use all the understanding ways that Jane had taught her, and so she wanted to know everything, always, that they knew how to teach her.

Jane was beginning to make Jeff Campbell see much clearer. Jane Harden did not know what it was that she was really doing with all this talking. Jane did not know what Jeff was feeling. Jane was always honest when she was talking, and now it just happened she had started talking about her old times with Melanctha Herbert. Jeff understood very well that it was all true what Jane was saying. Jeff Campbell was beginning now to see very clearly. He was beginning to feel very sick inside him. He knew now many things Melanctha had not yet taught him. He felt very sick and his heart was very heavy, and Melanctha certainly did seem very ugly to him. Jeff was at last beginning to know what it was to have deep feeling. He took care a little longer of Jane Harden, and then he went to his other patients, and then he went home to his room, and he sat down and at last he had stopped thinking. He was very sick and his heart was very heavy in him. He was very tired and all the world was very dreary to him, and he knew very well now at last, he was really feeling. He knew it now from the way it hurt him. He knew very well that now at last he was beginning to really have understanding. The next day he had arranged to spend, long and happy, all alone in the spring fields with Melanctha, wandering. He wrote her a note and said he could not go, he had a sick patient and would have to stay home with him. For three days after, he made no sign to Melanctha. He was very sick all these days, and his heart was very heavy in him, and he knew very well that now at last he had learned what it was to have deep feeling.

At last one day he got a letter from Melanctha. "I certainly don't rightly understand what you are doing now to me Jeff Campbell," wrote Melanctha Herbert. "I certainly don't rightly understand Jeff Campbell why you ain't all these days been near me, but I certainly do suppose it's just another one of the queer kind of ways you have to be good, and repenting of yourself all of a sudden. I certainly don't say to you Jeff Campbell I admire very much the way you take to be good Jeff Campbell. I am sorry Dr. Campbell, but I certainly am afraid I can't stand it no more from you the way you have been just acting. I certainly can't stand it any more the way you act when you have been as if you thought I was always good enough for anybody to have with them, and then you act as if I was a bad one and you always just despise me. I certainly am afraid Dr. Campbell I can't stand it any more like that. I certainly can't stand it any more the way you are always changing. I certainly am afraid Dr. Campbell you ain't man enough to deserve to have anybody care so much to be always with you. I certainly am awful afraid Dr. Campbell I don't ever any more want to really see you. Good-by Dr. Campbell I wish you always to be real happy."

Jeff Campbell sat in his room, very quiet, a long time, after he got through reading this letter. He sat very still and first he was very angry. As if he, too, did not know very badly what it was to suffer keenly. As if he had not been very strong to stay with Melanctha when he never knew what it was that she really wanted. He knew he was very right to be angry, he knew he really had not been a coward. He knew Melanctha had done many things it was very hard for him to forgive her. He knew very well he had done his best to be kind, and to trust her, and to be loyal to her, and now; — and then Jeff suddenly remembered how one night Melanctha had been so strong to suffer, and he felt come back to him the sweetness in her, and then Jeff knew that really, he always forgave her, and that really, it all was that he was so sorry he had hurt her, and he wanted to go straight away and be a comfort to her. Jeff knew very well, that what Jane Harden had told him about Melanctha and her bad ways, had been a true story, and yet he wanted very badly to be with Melanctha. Perhaps she could teach him to really understand it better. Perhaps she could teach him how it could be all true, and yet how he could be right to believe in her and to trust her.

Jeff sat down and began his answer to her. "Dear Melanctha," Jeff wrote to her. "I certainly don't think you got it all just right in the letter, I just been reading, that you just wrote me. I certainly don't think you are just fair or very understanding to all I have to suffer to keep straight on to really always to believe in you and trust you. I certainly don't think you always are fair to remember right how hard it is for a man, who thinks like I was always thinking, not to think you do things very bad very often. I certainly don't think, Melanctha, I ain't right when I was so angry when I got your letter to me. I know very well, Melanctha, that with you, I never have been a coward. I find it very hard, and I never said it any different, it is hard to me to be understanding, and to know really what it is you wanted, and what it is you are meaning by what you are always saying to me. I don't say ever, it ain't very hard for you to be standing that I ain't very quick to be following whichever way that you are always leading. You know very well, Melanctha, it hurts me very bad and way inside me when I have to hurt you, but I always got to be real honest with you. There ain't no other way for me to be, with you, and I know very well it hurts me too, a whole lot, when I can't follow so quick as you would have me. I don't like to be a coward to you, Melanctha, and I don't like to say what I ain't meaning to you. And if you don't want me to do things honest, Melanctha, why I can't ever talk to you, and you are right when you say, you never again want to see me, but if you got any real sense of what I always been feeling with you, and if you got any right sense, Melanctha, of how hard I been trying to think and to feel right for you,

I will be very glad to come and see you, and to begin again with you. I don't say anything now, Melanctha, about how bad I been this week, since I saw you, Melanctha. It don't ever do any good to talk such things over. All I know is I do my best, Melanctha, to you, and I don't say, no, never, I can do any different than just to be honest and come as fast as I think it's right for me to be going in the ways you teach me to be really understanding. So don't talk any more foolishness, Melanctha, about my always changing. I don't change, never, and I got to do what I think is right and honest to me, and I never told you any different, and you always knew it very well that I always would do just so. If you like me to come and see you to-morrow, and go out with you, I will be very glad to, Melanctha. Let me know right away, what it is you want me to be doing for you, Melanctha.

Very truly yours,
Jefferson Campbell

"Please come to me, Jeff." Melanctha wrote back for her answer. Jeff went very slowly to Melanctha, glad as he was, still to be going to her. Melanctha came, very quick, to meet him, when she saw him from where she had been watching for him. They went into the house together. They were very glad to be together. They were very good to one another.

"I certainly did think, Melanctha, this time almost really, you never did want me to come to you at all any more to see you," said Jeff Campbell to her, when they had begun again with their talking to each other. "You certainly did make me think, perhaps really this time, Melanctha, it was all over, my being with you ever, and I was very mad, and very sorry, too, Melanctha."

"Well you certainly was very bad to me, Jeff Campbell," said Melanctha, fondly.

"I certainly never do say any more you ain't always right, Melanctha," Jeff answered and he was very ready now with cheerful laughing, "I certainly never do say that any more, Melanctha, if I know it, but still, really, Melanctha, honest, I think perhaps I wasn't real bad to you any more than you just needed from me."

Jeff held Melanctha in his arms and kissed her. He sighed then and was very silent with her. "Well, Melanctha," he said at last, with some more laughing, "well, Melanctha, any way you can't say ever it ain't, if we are ever friends good and really, you can't say, no, never, but that we certainly have worked right hard to get both of us together for it, so we shall sure deserve it then, if we can ever really get it." "We certainly have worked real hard, Jeff, I can't say that ain't all right the way you say it," said Melanctha. "I certainly never can deny it, Jeff, when I feel so worn with all the trouble you been making for me, you bad boy, Jeff," and then Melanctha smiled and then she sighed, and then she was very silent with him.

At last Jeff was to go away. They stood there on the steps for a long time trying to say good-by to each other. At last Jeff made himself really say it. At last he made himself, that he went down the steps and went away.

On the next Sunday they arranged, they were to have the long happy day of wandering that they had lost last time by Jane Harden's talking. Not that Melanctha Herbert had heard yet of Jane Harden's talking.

Jeff saw Melanctha every day now. Jeff was a little uncertain all this time inside him, for he had never yet told to Melanctha what it was that had so nearly made him really want to leave her. Jeff knew that for him, it was not right he should not tell her. He knew they could only have real peace between them when he had been honest, and had really told her. On this long Sunday Jeff was certain that he would really tell her.

They were very happy all that day in their wandering. They had taken things along to eat together. They sat in the bright fields and they were happy, they wandered in the woods and they were happy. Jeff always loved in this way to wander. Jeff always loved to watch everything as it was growing, and he loved all the colors in the trees and on the ground, and the little, new, bright colored bugs he found in the moist ground and in the grass he loved to lie on and in which he was always so busy searching. Jeff loved everything that moved and that was still, and that had color, and beauty, and real being.

Jeff loved very much this day while they were wandering. He almost forgot that he had any trouble with him still inside him. Jeff loved to be there with Melanctha Herbert. She was always so sympathetic to him for the way she listened to everything he found and told her, the way she felt his joy in all this being, the way she never said she wanted anything different from the way they had it. It was certainly a busy and a happy day, this their first long day of really wandering.

Later they were tired, and Melanctha sat down on the ground, and Jeff threw himself his full length beside her. Jeff lay there, very quiet, and then he pressed her hand and kissed it and murmured to her, "You certainly are very good to me, Melanctha." Melanctha felt it very deep and did not answer. Jeff lay there a long time, looking up above him. He was counting all the little leaves he saw above him. He was following all the little clouds with his eyes as they sailed past him. He watched all the birds that flew high beyond him, and all the time Jeff knew he must tell to Melanctha what it was he knew now, that which Jane Harden, just a week ago, had told him. He knew very well that for him it was certain that he had to say it. It was hard, but for Jeff Campbell the only way to lose it was to say it, the only way to know Melanctha really, was to tell her all the struggle he had made to know her, to tell her so she could help him to understand his trouble better, to help him so that never again he could have any way to doubt her.

Jeff lay there a long time, very quiet, always looking up above him, and yet feeling very close now to Melanctha. At last he turned a little toward her, took her hands closer in his to make him feel it stronger, and then very slowly, for the words came very hard for him, slowly he began his talk to her.

"Melanctha," began Jeff, very slowly, "Melanctha, it ain't right I shouldn't tell you why I went away last week and almost never got the chance again to see you. Jane Harden was sick, and I went in to take care of her. She began to tell everything she ever knew about you. She didn't know how well now I know you. I didn't tell her not to go on talking. I listened while she told me everything about you. I certainly found it very hard with what she told me. I know she was talking truth in everything she said about you. I knew you had been free in your ways, Melanctha, I knew you like to get excitement the way I always hate to see the colored people take it. I didn't know, till I heard Jane Harden say it, you had done things so bad, Melanctha. When Jane Harden told me, I got very sick, Melanctha. I couldn't bear hardly, to think, perhaps I was just another like them to you, Melanctha. I was wrong not to trust you perhaps, Melanctha, but it did make things very ugly to me. I try to be honest to you, Melanctha, the way you say you really want it from me."

Melanctha drew her hands from Jeff Campbell. She sat there, and there was deep scorn in her anger.

"If you wasn't all through just selfish and nothing else, Jeff Campbell, you would take care you wouldn't have to tell me things like this, Jeff Campbell."

Jeff was silent a little, and he waited before he gave his answer. It was not the power of Melanctha's words that held him, for, for them, he had his answer, it was the power of the mood that filled Melanctha, and for that he had no answer. At last he broke through this awe, with his slow fighting resolution, and he began to give his answer.

"I don't say ever, Melanctha," he began, "it wouldn't have been more right for me to stop Jane Harden in her talking and to come to you to have you tell me what you were when I never knew you. I don't say it, no never to you, that that would not have been the right way for me to do, Melanctha. But I certainly am without any kind of doubting, I certainly do know for sure, I had a good right to know about what you were and your ways and your trying to use your understanding, every kind of way you could to get your learning. I certainly did have a right to know things like that about you, Melanctha. I don't say it ever, Melanctha, and I say it very often, I don't say ever I shouldn't have stopped Jane Harden in her talking and come to you and asked you yourself to tell me all about it, but I guess I wanted to keep myself from how much it would hurt me more, to have you yourself say it to me. Perhaps it was I wanted to keep you from having it hurt you so much more, having you to have to tell it to me. I don't know, I don't say it was to help you from being hurt most, or to help me. Perhaps I was a coward to let Jane Harden tell me 'stead of coming straight to you, to have you tell me, but I certainly am sure, Melanctha, I certainly had a right to know such things about you. I don't say it ever, ever, Melanctha, I hadn't the just right to know those things about you." Melanctha laughed her harsh laugh. "You needn't have been under no kind of worry, Jeff Campbell, about whether you should have asked me. You could have asked, it wouldn't have hurt nothing. I certainly never would have told you nothing." "I am not so sure of that, Melanctha," said Jeff Campbell. "I certainly do think you would have told me. I certainly do think I could make you feel it right to tell me. I certainly do think all I did wrong was to let Jane Harden tell me. I certainly do know I never did wrong, to learn what she told me. I certainly know very well, Melanctha, if I had come here to you, you would have told it all to me, Melanctha."

He was silent, and this struggle lay there, strong, between them. It was a struggle, sure to be going on always between them. It was a struggle that was as sure always to be going on between them, as their minds and hearts always were to have different ways of working.

At last Melanctha took his hand, leaned over him and kissed him. "I sure am very fond of you, Jeff Campbell," Melanctha whispered to him.

Now for a little time there was not any kind of trouble between Jeff Campbell and Melanctha Herbert. They were always together now for long times, and very often. They got much joy now, both of them, from being all the time together.

It was summer now, and they had warm sunshine to wander. It was summer now, and Jeff Campbell had more time to wander, for colored people never get sick so much in summer. It was summer now, and there was a lovely silence everywhere, and all the noises, too, that they heard around them were lovely ones, and added to the joy, in these warm days, they loved so much to be together.

They talked some to each other in these days, did Jeff Campbell and Melanctha Herbert, but always in these days their talking more and more was like it always is with real lovers. Jeff did not talk so much now about what he before always had been thinking. Sometimes Jeff would be, as if he was just waking from himself to be with Melanctha, and then he would find he had been really all the long time with her, and he had really never needed to be doing any thinking.

It was sometimes pure joy Jeff would be talking to Melanctha, in these warm days he loved so much to wander with her. Sometimes Jeff would lose all himself in a strong feeling. Very often now, and always with more joy in his feeling, he would find himself, he did not know how or what it was he had been thinking. And Melanctha always loved very well to make him feel it. She always now laughed a little at him, and went back a little in him to his before, always thinking, and she teased him with his always now being so good with her in his feeling, and then she would so well and freely, and with her pure, strong ways of reaching, she would give him all the love she knew now very well, how much he always wanted to be sure he really had it.

And Jeff took it straight now, and he loved it, and he felt, strong, the joy of all this being, and it swelled out full inside him, and he poured it all out back to her in freedom, in tender kindness, and in joy, and in gentle brother fondling. And Melanctha loved him for it always, her Jeff Campbell now, who never did things ugly, for her, like all the men she always knew before always had been doing to her. And they loved it always, more and more, together, with this new feeling they had now, in these long summer days so warm; they, always together now, just these two so dear, more and more to each other always, and the summer evenings when they wandered, and the noises in the full streets, and the music of the organs, and the dancing, and the warm smell of the people, and of dogs and of the horses, and all the joy of the strong, sweet pungent, dirty, moist, warm negro southern summer.

Every day now, Jeff seemed to be coming nearer, to be really loving. Every day now, Melanctha poured it all out to him, with more freedom. Every day now, they seemed to be having more and more, both together, of this strong, right feeling. More and more every day now they seemed to know more really, what it was each other one was always feeling. More and more now every day Jeff found in himself, he felt more trusting. More and more every day now, he did not think anything in words about what he was always doing. Every day now more and more Melanctha would let out to Jeff her real, strong feeling.

One day there had been much joy between them, more than they ever yet had had with their new feeling. All the day they had lost themselves in warm wandering. Now they were lying there and resting, with a green, bright, light-flecked world around them.

What was it that now really happened to them? What was it that Melanctha did, that made everything get all ugly for them? What was it that Melanctha felt then, that made Jeff remember all the feeling he had had in him when Jane Harden told him how Melanctha had learned to be so very understanding? Jeff did not know how it was that it had happened to him. It was all green, and warm, and very lovely to him, and now Melanctha somehow had made it all so ugly for him. What was it Melanctha was now doing with him? What was it he used to be thinking was the right way for him and all the colored people to be always trying to make it right, the way they should be always living? Why was Melanctha Herbert now all so ugly for him?

Melanctha Herbert somehow had made him feel deeply just then, what very more it was that she wanted from him. Jeff Campbell now felt in him what everybody always had needed to make them really understanding, to him. Jeff felt a strong disgust inside him; not for Melanctha herself, to him, not for himself really, in him, not for what it was that everybody wanted, in them; he only had disgust because he never could know really in him, what it was he wanted, to be really right in understanding, for him, he only had disgust because he never could know really what it was really right to him to be always doing, in the things he had before believed in, the things he before had believed in for himself and for all the colored people, the living regular, and the never wanting to be always having new things, just to keep on, always being in excitements. All the old thinking now came up very strong inside him. He sort of turned away then, and threw Melanctha from him.

Jeff never, even now, knew what it was that moved him. He never, even now, was ever sure, he really knew what Melanctha was, when she was real herself, and honest. He thought he knew, and then there came to him some moment, just like this one, when she really woke him up to be strong in him. Then he really knew he could know nothing. He knew then, he never could know what it was she really wanted with him. He knew then he never could know really what it was he felt inside him. It was all so mixed up inside him. All he knew was he wanted very badly Melanctha should be there beside him, and he wanted very badly, too, always to throw her from him. What was it really that Melanctha wanted with him? What was it really, he, Jeff Campbell, wanted she should give him? "I certainly did think now," Jeff Campbell groaned inside him, "I certainly did think now I really was knowing all right, what I wanted. I certainly did really think now I was knowing how to be trusting with Melanctha. I certainly did think it was like that now with me sure, after all I've been through all this time with her. And now I certainly do know I don't know anything that's very real about her. Oh the good Lord help and keep me!" and Jeff groaned hard inside him, and he buried his face deep in the green grass underneath him, and Melanctha Herbert was very silent there beside him.

1909

From *The Autobiography of Alice B. Toklas*[1]

Pound and Eliot

We met Ezra Pound at Grace Lounsbery's house, he came home

---

[1] Although written as though by Miss Toklas (1877–1967), her longtime secretary and companion, the book is Gertrude Stein's autobiography.

to dinner with us and he stayed and he talked about japanese prints among other things. Gertrude Stein liked him but did not find him amusing. She said he was a village explainer, excellent if you were a village, but if you were not, not. Ezra also talked about T. S. Eliot. It was the first time any one had talked about T. S. at the house. Pretty soon everybody talked about T. S. Kitty Buss talked about him and much later Hemingway talked about him as the Major. Considerably later Lady Rothermere talked about him and invited Gertrude Stein to come and meet him. They were founding the Criterion.[2] We had met Lady Rothermere through Muriel Draper whom we had seen again for the first time after many years. Gertrude Stein was not particularly anxious to go to Lady Rothermere's and meet T. S. Eliot, but we all insisted she should, and she gave a doubtful yes. I had no evening dress to wear for this occasion and started to make one. The bell rang and in walked Lady Rothermere and T. S.

Eliot and Gertrude Stein had a solemn conversation, mostly about split infinitives and other grammatical solecisms and why Gertrude Stein used them. Finally Lady Rothermere and Eliot rose to go and Eliot said that if he printed anything of Gertrude Stein's in the Criterion it would have to be her very latest thing. They left and Gertrude Stein said, don't bother to finish your dress, now we don't have to go, and she began to write a portrait of T. S. Eliot and called it the fifteenth of November, that being this day and so there could be no doubt but that it was her latest thing. It was all about wool is wool and silk is silk or wool is woollen and silk is silken. She sent it to T. S. Eliot and he accepted it but naturally he did not print it.

Then began a long correspondence, not between Gertrude Stein and T. S. Eliot, but between T. S. Eliot's secretary and myself. We each addressed the other as Sir, I signing myself A. B. Toklas and she signing initials. It was only considerably afterwards that I found out that his secretary was not a young man. I don't know whether she ever found out that I was not.

In spite of all this correspondence nothing happened and Gertrude Stein mischievously told the story to all the english people coming to the house and at that moment there were a great many english coming in and out. At any rate finally there was a note, it was now early spring, from the Criterion asking would Miss Stein mind if her contribution appeared in the October number. She replied that nothing could be more suitable than the fifteenth of November on the fifteenth of October.

Once more a long silence and then this time came proof of the article. We were surprised but returned the proof promptly. Apparently a young man had sent it without authority because very shortly came an

---

[2] *The Criterion* (1922–39), the London literary quarterly edited by T. S. Eliot.

apologetic letter saying that there had been a mistake, the article was not to be printed just yet. This was also told to the passing english with the result that after all it was printed. Thereafter it was reprinted in the Georgian Stories.[3] Gertrude Stein was delighted when later she was told that Eliot had said in Cambridge that the work of Gertrude Stein was very fine but not for us.

But to come back to Ezra. Ezra did come back and he came back with the editor of The Dial.[4] This time it was worse than japanese prints, it was much more violent. In his surprise at the violence Ezra fell out of Gertrude Stein's favourite little armchair, the one I have since tapestried with Picasso designs, and Gertrude Stein was furious. Finally Ezra and the editor of The Dial left, nobody too well pleased. Gertrude Stein did not want to see Ezra again. Ezra did not quite see why. He met Gertrude Stein one day near the Luxembourg gardens and said, but I do want to come to see you. I am so sorry, answered Gertrude Stein, but Miss Toklas has a bad tooth and beside we are busy picking wild flowers. All of which was literally true, like all of Gertrude Stein's literature, but it upset Ezra, and we never saw him again.

Hemingway, Ford, Anderson, Fitzgerald, and Hemingway

The first thing that happened when we were back in Paris was Hemingway with a letter of introduction from Sherwood Anderson.

I remember very well the impression I had of Hemingway that first afternoon. He was an extraordinarily good-looking young man, twenty-three years old. It was not long after that that everybody was twenty-six. It became the period of being twenty-six. During the next two or three years all the young men were twenty-six years old. It was the right age apparently for that time and place. There were one or two under twenty, for example George Lynes but they did not count as Gertrude Stein carefully explained to them. If they were young men they were twenty-six. Later on, much later on they were twenty-one and twenty-two.

So Hemingway was twenty-three, rather foreign looking, with passionately interested, rather than interesting eyes. He sat in front of Gertrude Stein and listened and looked.

They talked then, and more and more, a great deal together. He asked her to come and spend an evening in their apartment and look at his work. Hemingway had then and has always a very good instinct for finding apartments in strange but pleasing localities and good femmes de ménage and good food. This his first apartment was just off the place

---

[3] *Georgian Stories*, 5 vols. (London, 1922, 1924–27).
[4] Probably Scofield Thayer, who became editor of *The Dial* (1880–1929) in 1920.

du Tertre. We spent the evening there and he and Gertrude Stein went over all the writing he had done up to that time. He had begun the novel that it was inevitable he would begin and there were the little poems afterwards printed by McAlmon[5] in the Contact Edition. Gertrude Stein rather liked the poems, they were direct, Kiplingesque, but the novel she found wanting. There is a great deal of description in this, she said, and not particularly good description. Begin over again and concentrate, she said.

Hemingway was at this time Paris correspondent for a canadian newspaper.[6] He was obliged there to express what he called the canadian viewpoint.

He and Gertrude Stein used to walk together and talk together a great deal. One day she said to him, look here, you say you and your wife have a little money between you. Is it enough to live on if you live quietly. Yes, he said. Well, she said, then do it. If you keep on doing newspaper work you will never see things, you will only see words and that will not do, that is of course if you intend to be a writer. Hemingway said he undoubtedly intended to be a writer. He and his wife went away on a trip and shortly after Hemingway turned up alone. He came to the house about ten o'clock in the morning and he stayed, he stayed for lunch, he stayed all afternoon, he stayed for dinner and he stayed until about ten o'clock at night and then all of a sudden he announced that his wife was enceinte and then with great bitterness, and I, I am too young to be a father. We consoled him as best we could and sent him on his way.

When they came back Hemingway said that he had made up his mind. They would go back to America and he would work hard for a year and with what he would earn and what they had they would settle down and he would give up newspaper work and make himself a writer. They went away and well within the prescribed year they came back with a new born baby. Newspaper work was over.

The first thing to do when they came back was as they thought to get the baby baptised. They wanted Gertrude Stein and myself to be god-mothers and an english war comrade of Hemingway was to be god-father. We were all born of different religions and most of us were not practising any, so it was rather difficult to know in what church the baby could be baptised. We spent a great deal of time that winter, all of us, discussing the matter. Finally it was decided that it should be baptised episcopalian and episcopalian it was. Just how it was managed with the assortment of god-parents I am sure I do not know, but it was baptised in the episcopalian chapel.

Writer or painter god-parents are notoriously unreliable. That is, there is certain before long to be a cooling of friendship. I know several

---

[5] Robert McAlmon (1895–1956), expatriate American author and publisher.
[6] The Toronto *Star*.

cases of this, poor Paulot Picasso's god-parents have wandered out of sight and just as naturally it is a long time since any of us have seen or heard of our Hemingway god-child.

However in the beginning we were active god-parents, I particularly. I embroidered a little chair and I knitted a gay coloured garment for the god-child. In the meantime the god-child's father was very earnestly at work making himself a writer.

Gertrude Stein never corrects any detail of anybody's writing, she sticks strictly to general principles, the way of seeing what the writer chooses to see, and the relation between that vision and the way it gets down. When the vision is not complete the words are flat, it is very simple, there can be no mistake about it, so she insists. It was at this time that Hemingway began the short things that afterwards were printed in a volume called In Our Time.[7]

One day Hemingway came in very excited about Ford Madox Ford and the Transatlantic.[8] Ford Madox Ford had started the Transatlantic some months before. A good many years before, indeed before the war, we had met Ford Madox Ford who was at that time Ford Madox Hueffer. He was married to Violet Hunt and Violet Hunt and Gertrude Stein were next to each other at the tea table and talked a great deal together. I was next to Ford Madox Hueffer and I liked him very much and I liked his stories of Mistral and Tarascon and I liked his having been followed about in that land of the french royalist, on account of his resemblance to the Bourbon claimant. I had never seen the Bourbon claimant but Ford at that time undoubtedly might have been a Bourbon.

We had heard that Ford was in Paris, but we had not happened to meet. Gertrude Stein had however seen copies of the Transatlantic and found it interesting but had thought nothing further about it.

Hemingway came in then very excited and said that Ford wanted something of Gertrude Stein's for the next number and he, Hemingway, wanted The Making of Americans to be run in it as a serial and he had to have the first fifty pages at once. Gertrude Stein was of course quite overcome with her excitement at this idea, but there was no copy of the manuscript except the one that we had had bound. That makes no difference, said Hemingway, I will copy it. And he and I between us did copy it and it was printed in the next number of the Transatlantic. So for the first time a piece of the monumental work which was the beginning, really the beginning of modern writing, was printed, and we were very happy. Later on when things were difficult between Gertrude Stein and Hemingway, she always remembered with gratitude that after all it was Hemingway who first caused to be printed a piece of The Making

---

[7] Fifteen short stories, with vignettes as interchapters, published in New York in 1925. The earlier *in our time* (Paris, 1924) contains only the vignettes.

[8] Hemingway served as editorial assistant to Ford Madox Ford (1873–1939), the English novelist, who established the short-lived *transatlantic review* in Paris in 1924.

of Americans. She always says, yes sure I have a weakness for Hemingway. After all he was the first of the young men to knock at my door and he did make Ford print the first piece of The Making of Americans.[9]

I myself have not so much confidence that Hemingway did do this. I have never known what the story is but I have always been certain that there was some other story behind it all. That is the way I feel about it.[10]

Gertrude Stein and Sherwood Anderson are very funny on the subject of Hemingway. The last time that Sherwood was in Paris they often talked about him. Hemingway had been formed by the two of them and they were both a little proud and a little ashamed of the work of their minds. Hemingway had at one moment, when he had repudiated Sherwood Anderson and all his works, written him a letter in the name of american literature which he, Hemingway, in company with his contemporaries was about to save, telling Sherwood just what he, Hemingway, thought about Sherwood's work, and, that thinking, was in no sense complimentary. When Sherwood came to Paris Hemingway naturally was afraid. Sherwood as naturally was not.

As I say he and Gertrude Stein were endlessly amusing on the subject. They admitted that Hemingway was yellow, he is, Gertrude Stein insisted, just like the flat-boat men on the Mississippi river as described by Mark Twain. But what a book, they both agreed, would be the real story of Hemingway, not those he writes but the confessions of the real Ernest Hemingway. It would be for another audience than the audience Hemingway now has but it would be very wonderful. And then they both agreed that they have a weakness for Hemingway because he is such a good pupil. He is a rotten pupil, I protested. You don't understand, they both said, it is so flattering to have a pupil who does it without understanding it, in other words he takes training and anybody who takes training is a favourite pupil. They both admit it to be a weakness. Gertrude Stein added further, you see he is like Derain.[11] You remember Monsieur de Tuille said, when I did not understand why Derain was having the success he was having that it was because he looks like a modern and he smells of the museums. And that is Hemingway, he looks like a modern and he smells of the museums. But what a story that of the real Hem, and one he should tell himself but alas he never will. After all, as he himself once murmured, there is the career, the career.

But to come back to the events that were happening.

Hemingway did it all. He copied the manuscript and corrected

---

[9] The novel was published as a book in 1925.
[10] For Hemingway's dubious dealings in this matter, see B. J. Poli, *Ford Madox Ford and the Transatlantic Review* (Syracuse, N. Y., 1967), pp. 70–72. Gertrude Stein's technique of using Miss Toklas as a mouthpiece permits her to express her own viewpoint deviously.
[11] André Derain (1880–1954), French postimpressionist painter.

the proof. Correcting proofs is, as I said before, like dusting, you learn the values of the thing as no reading suffices to teach it to you. In correcting these proofs Hemingway learned a great deal and he admired all that he learned. It was at this time that he wrote to Gertrude Stein saying that it was she who had done the work in writing The Making of Americans and he and all his had but to devote their lives to seeing that it was published.

He had hopes of being able to accomplish this. Some one, I think by the name of Sterne, said that he could place it with a publisher. Gertrude Stein and Hemingway believed that he could, but soon Hemingway reported that Sterne had entered into his period of unreliability. That was the end of that.

In the meantime and sometime before this Mina Loy[12] had brought McAlmon to the house and he came from time to time and he brought his wife and brought William Carlos Williams. And finally he wanted to print The Making of Americans in the Contact Edition and finally he did. I will come to that.

In the meantime McAlmon had printed the three poems and ten stories of Hemingway and William Bird[13] had printed In Our Time and Hemingway was getting to be known. He was coming to know Dos Passos and Fitzgerald and Bromfield and George Antheil and everybody else and Harold Loeb was once more in Paris. Hemingway had become a writer. He was also a shadow-boxer, thanks to Sherwood, and he heard about bull-fighting from me. I have always loved spanish dancing and spanish bull-fighting and I loved to show the photographs of bull-fighters and bull-fighting. I also loved to show the photograph where Gertrude Stein and I were in the front row and had our picture taken there accidentally. In these days Hemingway was teaching some young chap how to box. The boy did not know how, but by accident he knocked Hemingway out. I believe this sometimes happens. At any rate in these days Hemingway although a sportsman was easily tired. He used to get quite worn out walking from his house to ours. But then he had been worn by the war. Even now he is, as Hélène says all men are, fragile. Recently a robust friend of his said to Gertrude Stein, Ernest is very fragile, whenever he does anything sporting something breaks, his arm, his leg, or his head.

In those early days Hemingway liked all his contemporaries except Cummings. He accused Cummings of having copied everything, not from anybody but from somebody. Gertrude Stein who had been much impressed by The Enormous Room[14] said that Cummings did not copy, he was the natural heir of the New England tradition with its

<hr />

[12] Expatriate American poet and friend of Ezra Pound's.
[13] A journalist who established his private Three Mountains Press in Paris in 1921.
[14] E. E. Cummings' poetic autobiographical novel (1922) of his experience in a French prison camp in the first World War.

aridity and its sterility, but also with its individuality. They disagreed about this. They also disagreed about Sherwood Anderson. Gertrude Stein contended that Sherwood Anderson had a genius for using the sentence to convey a direct emotion, this was in the great american tradition, and that really except Sherwood there was no one in America who could write a clear and passionate sentence. Hemingway did not believe this, he did not like Sherwood's taste. Taste has nothing to do with sentences, contended Gertrude Stein. She also added that Fitzgerald was the only one of the younger writers who wrote naturally in sentences.

Gertrude Stein and Fitzgerald are very peculiar in their relation to each other. Gertrude Stein had been very much impressed by This Side of Paradise.[15] She read it when it came out and before she knew any of the young american writers. She said of it that it was this book that really created for the public the new generation. She has never changed her opinion about this. She thinks this equally true of The Great Gatsby.[16] She thinks Fitzgerald will be read when many of his well known contemporaries are forgotten. Fitzgerald always says that he thinks Gertrude Stein says these things just to annoy him by making him think that she means them, and he adds in his favourite way, and her doing it is the cruellest thing I ever heard. They always however have a very good time when they meet. And the last time they met they had a good time with themselves and Hemingway.

Then there was McAlmon. McAlmon had one quality that appealed to Gertrude Stein, abundance, he could go on writing, but she complained that it was dull.

There was also Glenway Wescott[17] but Glenway Wescott at no time interested Gertrude Stein. He has a certain syrup but it does not pour.

So then Hemingway's career was begun. For a little while we saw less of him and then he began to come again. He used to recount to Gertrude Stein the conversations that he afterwards used in The Sun Also Rises and they talked endlessly about the character of Harold Loeb.[18] At this time Hemingway was preparing his volume of short stories to submit to publishers in America. One evening after we had not seen him for a while he turned up with Shipman.[19] Shipman was an amusing boy who was to inherit a few thousand dollars when he came of age. He was not of age. He was to buy the Transatlantic Review when he came of age, so Hemingway said. He was to support a surrealist review when he came of age, André Masson said. He was to buy

---

[15] F. Scott Fitzgerald's first novel (1920).
[16] Published in 1925.   [17] American novelist (b. 1901).
[18] American writer and editor of *Broom* (1921 – 24).
[19] Evan Shipman, an American poet.

a house in the country when he came of age, Josette Gris said. As a matter of fact when he came of age nobody who had known him then seemed to know what he did do with his inheritance. Hemingway brought him with him to the house to talk about buying the Transatlantic and incidentally he brought the manuscript he intended sending to America. He handed it to Gertrude Stein. He had added to his stories a little story of meditations and in these he said that The Enormous Room was the greatest book he had ever read. It was then that Gertrude Stein said, Hemingway, remarks are not literature.

After this we did not see Hemingway for quite a while and then we went to see some one, just after The Making of Americans was printed, and Hemingway who was there came up to Gertrude Stein and began to explain why he would not be able to write a review of the book. Just then a heavy hand fell on his shoulder and Ford Madox Ford said, young man it is I who wish to speak to Gertrude Stein. Ford then said to her, I wish to ask your permission to dedicate my new book to you. May I. Gertrude Stein and I were both awfully pleased and touched.

For some years after this Gertrude Stein and Hemingway did not meet. And then we heard that he was back in Paris and telling a number of people how much he wanted to see her. Don't you come home with Hemingway on your arm, I used to say when she went out for a walk. Sure enough one day she did come back bringing him with her.

They sat and talked a long time. Finally I heard her say, Hemingway, after all you are ninety percent Rotarian. Can't you, he said, make it eighty percent. No, said she regretfully, I can't. After all, as she always says, he did, and I may say, he does have moments of disinterestedness.

After that they met quite often. Gertrude Stein always says she likes to see him, he is so wonderful. And if he could only tell his own story. In their last conversation she accused him of having killed a great many of his rivals and put them under the sod. I never, said Hemingway, seriously killed anybody but one man and he was a bad man and, he deserved it, but if I killed anybody else I did it unknowingly, and so I am not responsible.

It was Ford who once said of Hemingway, he comes and sits at my feet and praises me. It makes me nervous. Hemingway also said once, I turn my flame which is a small one down and down and then suddenly there is a big explosion. If there were nothing but explosions my work would be so exciting nobody could bear it.

However, whatever I say, Gertrude Stein always says, yes I know but I have a weakness for Hemingway.

1933

From *Portraits and Repetition*

There is another thing that one has to think about, that is about thinking clearly and about confusion. That is something about which I have almost as much to say as I have about anything.

The difference between thinking clearly and confusion is the same difference that there is between repetition and insistence. A great many think that they know repetition when they see or hear it but do they. A great many think that they know confusion when they know or see it or hear it, but do they. A thing that seems very clear, seems very clear but is it. A thing that seems to be exactly the same thing may seem to be a repetition but is it. All this can be very exciting, and it had a great deal to do with portrait writing.

As I say a thing that is very clear may easily not be clear at all, a thing that may be confused may be very clear. But everybody knows that. Yes anybody knows that. It is like the necessity of knowing one's father and one's mother one's grandmothers and one's grandfathers, but is it necessary and if it is can it be no less easily forgotten.

As I say the American thing is the vitality of movement, so that there need be nothing against which the movement shows as movement. And if this vitality is lively enough is there in that clarity any confusion is there in that clarity any repetition. I myself do not think so. But I am inclined to believe that there is really no difference between clarity and confusion, just think of any life that is alive, is there really any difference between clarity and confusion. Now I am quite certain that there is really if anything is alive no difference between clarity and confusion. When I first began writing portraits of any one I was not so sure, not so certain of this thing that there is no difference between clarity and confusion. I was however almost certain then when I began writing portraits that if anything is alive there is no such thing as repetition. I do not know that I have ever changed my mind about that. At any rate I did then begin the writing of portraits and I will tell you now all there is to tell about all that. I had of course written about every kind of men and women in The Making of Americans[1] but in writing portraits I wanted not to write about any one doing or even saying anything, I found this a difficult enough thing to begin.

I remember very well what happened. As I say I had the habit of conceiving myself as completely talking and listening, listening was talking and talking was listening and in so doing I conceived what I at that time called the rhythm of anybody's personality. If listening was talking and talking was listening then and at the same time any little movement any little expression was a resemblance, and a resemblance

[1] See above.

was something that presupposed remembering.

Listening and talking did not presuppose resemblance and as they do not presuppose resemblance, they do not necessitate remembering. Already then as you see there was a complication which was a bother to me in my conception of the rhythm of a personality. I have for so many years tried to get the better of that the better of this bother. The bother was simply that and one may say it is the bother that has always been a bother to anybody for anybody conceiving anything. Dillinger is dead it was even a bother for him.[2]

As I say as I felt the existence of anybody later as I felt the existence of anybody or anything, there was then the listening and talking which I was doing which anybody was doing and there were the little things that made of any one some one resembling some one.

Any one does of course by any little thing by any little way by any little expression, any one does of course resemble some one, and any one can notice this thing notice this resemblance and in so doing they have to remember some one and this is a different thing from listening and talking. In other words the making of a portrait of any one is as they are existing and as they are existing has nothing to do with remembering any one or anything. Do you see my point, but of course yes you do. You do see that there are two things and not one and if one wants to make one portrait of some one and not two you can see that one can be bothered completely bothered by this thing. As I say it is something that has always bothered any one.

Funnily enough the cinema has offered a solution of this thing. By a continuously moving picture of any one there is no memory of any other thing and there is that thing existing, it is in a way if you like one portrait of anything not a number of them. There again you do see what I mean.

Now I in my way wanted to make portraits of any one later in Tender Buttons[3] I also wanted to make portraits of anything as one thing as one portrait and although and that was my trouble in the beginning I felt the thing the person as existing and as everything in that person entered in to make that person little ways and expressions that made resembling, it was necessary for me nevertheless not to realize these things as remembering but to realize the one thing as existing and there they were and I was noticing, well you do see that it was a bother and I was bothering very much bothering about this thing.

In the beginning and I will read you some portraits to show you this I continued to do what I was doing in The Making of Americans, I was doing what the cinema was doing, I was making a continuous

---

[2] John Dillinger (1902 – 1934), Indiana-born bandit, "Public Enemy Number One" before he was gunned down in Chicago by Federal law officers.
[3] A book of poems published in 1914.

succession of the statement of what that person was until I had not many things but one thing. As I read you some of the portraits of that period you will see what I mean.

I of course did not think of it in terms of the cinema, in fact I doubt whether at that time I had ever seen a cinema but, and I cannot repeat this too often any one is of one's period and this our period was undoubtedly the period of the cinema and series production. And each of us in our own way are bound to express what the world in which we are living is doing.

You see then what I was doing in my beginning portrait writing and you also understand what I mean when I say there was no repetition. In a cinema picture no two pictures are exactly alike each one is just that much different from the one before, and so in those early portraits there was as I am sure you will realize as I read them to you also as there was in The Making of Americans no repetition. Each time that I said the somebody whose portrait I was writing was something that something was just that much different from what I had just said that somebody was and little by little in this way a whole portrait came into being, a portrait that was not description and that was made by each time, and I did a great many times, say it, that somebody was something, each time there was a difference just a difference enough so that it could go on and be a present something. Oh yes you all do understand. You understand this. You see that in order to do this there must be no remembering, remembering is repetition, remembering is also confusion. And this too you will presently know all about.

Remembering is repetition anybody can know that. In doing a portrait of any one, the repetition consists in knowing that that one is a kind of a one, that the things he does have been done by others like him that the things he says have been said by others like him, but, and this is the important thing, there is no repetition in hearing and saying the things he hears and says when he is hearing and saying them. And so in doing a portrait of him if it were possible to make that portrait a portrait of him saying and hearing what he says and hears while he is saying and hearing it there is then in so doing neither memory nor repetition no matter how often that which he says and hears is heard and said. This was the discovery I made as I talked and listened more and more and this is what I did when I made portraits of every one I know. I said what I knew as they said and heard what they heard and said until I had completely emptied myself of all they were that is all that they were in being one hearing and saying what they heard and said in every way that they heard and said anything.

And this is the reason why that what I wrote was exciting although those that did not really see what it was thought it was repetition. If it had been repetition it would not have been exciting but it was exciting and it was not repetition. It never is. I never repeat that is while I am writing.

As I say what one repeats is the scene in which one is acting, the days in which one is living, the coming and going which one is doing, anything one is remembering is a repetition, but existing as a human being, that is being listening and hearing is never repetition. It is not repetition if it is that which you are actually doing because naturally each time the emphasis is different just as the cinema has each time a slightly different thing to make it all be moving. And each one of us has to do that, otherwise there is no existing. As Galileo remarked,[4] it does move.

So you see what I mean about those early portraits and the middle part of The Making of Americans. I built them up little by little each time I said it it changed just a little and then when I was completely emptied of knowing that the one of whom I was making a portrait existed I had made a portrait of that one.

To go back to something I said that remembering was the only repetition, also that remembering was the only confusion. And I think you begin to see what I mean by that.

No matter how complicated anything is, if it is not mixed up with remembering there is no confusion, but and that is the trouble with a great many so called intelligent people they mix up remembering with talking and listening, and as a result they have theories about anything but as remembering is repetition and confusion, and being existing that is listening and talking is action and not repetition intelligent people although they talk as if they knew something are really confusing, because they are so to speak keeping two times going at once, the repetition time of remembering and the actual time of talking but, and as they are rarely talking and listening, that is the talking being listening and the listening being talking, although they are clearly saying something they are not clearly creating something, because they are because they always are remembering, they are not at the same time talking and listening. Do you understand. Do you any or all of you understand. Anyway that is the way it is. And you hear it even if you do not say it in the way I say it as I hear it and say it.

I say I never repeat while I am writing because while I am writing I am most completely, and that is if you like being a genius, I am most entirely and completely listening and talking, the two in one and the one in two and that is having completely its own time and it has in it no element of remembering. Therefore there is in it no element of confusion, therefore there is in it no element of repetition. Do you do you do you really understand.

And does it make any difference to you if you do understand. It

⁴ Of the earth.

makes an awful lot of difference to me. It is very exciting to have all this be.

Gradually then I began making portraits. And how did I begin.

When I first began writing although I felt very strongly that something that made that some one be some one was something that I must use as being them, I naturally began to describe them as they were doing anything. In short I wrote a story as a story, that is the way I began, and slowly I realized this confusion, a real confusion, that in writing a story one had to be remembering, and that novels are soothing because so many people one may say everybody can remember almost anything. It is this element of remembering that makes novels so soothing. But and that was the thing that I was gradually finding out listening and talking at the same time that is realizing the existence of living being actually existing did not have in it any element of remembering and so the time of existing was not the same as in the novels that were soothing. As I say all novels are soothing because they make anything happen as they can happen that is by remembering anything. But and I kept wondering as I talked and listened all at once, I wondered is there any way of making what I know come out as I know it, come out not as remembering. I found this very exciting. And I began to make portraits.

I kept on knowing people by resemblances, that was partly memory and it bothered me but I knew I had to do everything and I tried to do that so completely that I would lose it. I made charts and charts of everybody who looked like anybody until I got so that I hardly knew which one I knew on the street and which one looked like them. I did this until at last any one looking like any one else had no importance. It was not a thing that was any longer an important thing, I knew completely how any one looked like any other one and that became then only a practical matter, a thing one might know as what any one was liable to do, but this to me then was no longer interesting. And so I went on with portrait writing.

I cannot tell you although I think I can, that, as I can read any number of soothing novels in fact nothing else soothes me I found it not a thing that it was interesting to do. And I think now you know why it was not an interesting thing to do. We in this period have not lived in remembering, we have lived in moving being necessarily so intense that existing is indeed something, is indeed that thing that we are doing. And so what does it really matter what anybody does. The newspapers are full of what anybody does and anybody knows what anybody does but the thing that is important is the intensity of anybody's existence. Once more I remind you of Dillinger. It was not what he did that was exciting but the excitement of what he was as being exciting that was exciting. There is a world of difference and in it there is essentially no remembering.

And so I am trying to tell you what doing portraits meant to me, I had to find out what it was inside any one, and by any one I mean every one I had to find out inside every one what was in them that was intrinsically exciting and I had to find out not by what they said not by what they did not by how much or how little they resembled any other one but I had to find it out by the intensity of movement that there was inside in any one of them. And of course do not forget, of course I was interested in any one. I am. Of course I am interested in any one. And in any one I must or else I must betake myself to some entirely different occupation and I do not think I will, I must find out what is moving inside them that makes them them, and I must find out how I by the thing moving excitedly inside in me can make a portrait of them.

You can understand why I did it so often, why I did it in so many ways why I say that there is no repetition because, and this is absolutely true, that the exciting thing inside in any one if it is really inside in them is not a remembered thing, if it is really inside in them, it is not a confused thing, it is not a repeated thing. And if I could in any way and I have done it in every way if I could make a portrait of that inside them without any description of what they are doing and what they are saying then I too was neither repeating, nor remembering nor being in a confusion.

You see what I mean by what I say. But I know you do.

Will you see it as clearly when I read you some of the portraits that I have written. Maybe you will but I doubt it. But if you do well then if you do you will see what I have done and do do.

A thing you all know is that in the three novels written in this generation that are the important things written in this generation, there is, in none of them a story. There is none in Proust[5] in The Making of Americans or in Ulysses.[6] And this is what you are now to begin to realize in this description I am giving you of making portraits.

It is of course perfectly natural that autobiographies are being well written and well read. You do see anybody can see that so much happens every day and that anybody literally anybody can read or hear about it told the day that it happens. A great deal happens every day and any day and as I say anybody literally anybody can hear or read everything or anything about anything or everything that happens every day just as it has happened or is happening on that day. You do see what that means. Novels then which tell a story are really then more of the same much more of the same, and of course anybody likes more of the same and so a great many novels are written and a great many novels are read telling more of these stories but you can see you do see that the important things written in this generation do not tell a story.

---

[5] In *À la Recherche du temps perdu* (English title: *Remembrance of Things Past*), the series of novels (1913–27) by Marcel Proust (1871–1922).
[6] The novel by James Joyce (1882–1941), first published in Paris in 1922.

You can see that it is natural enough.

You begin definitely to feel that it had to be that I was to write portraits as I wrote them. I began to write them when I was about in the middle of The Making of Americans, and if you read The Making of Americans you will realize why this was inevitable.

I began writing the portraits of any one by saying what I knew of that one as I talked and listened that one, and each time that I talked and listened that one I said what I knew they were then. This made my early portraits and some that I finally did such as Four Dishonest Ones Told by a Description of What They Do, Matisse and Picasso and a lot of others, did as completely as I then could strictly did this thing. Every time I said what they were I said it so that they were this thing, and each time I said what they were as they were, as I was, naturally more or less but never the same thing each time that I said what they were I said what they were, not that they were different nor that I was different but as it was not the same moment which I said I said it with a difference. So finally I was emptied of saying this thing, and so no longer said what they were.

FOUR DISHONEST ONES.
Told By a Description Of What They Do.[7]

They are what they are. They have not been changing. They are what they are.

Each one is what that one is. Each is what each is. They are not needing to be changing.

One is what she is. She does not need to be changing. She is what she is. She is not changing. She is what she is.

She is not changing. She is knowing nothing of not changing. She is not needing to be changing.

What is she doing. She is working. She is not needing to be changing. She is working very well, she is not needing to be changing. She has been working very hard. She has been suffering. She is not needing to be changing.

She has been living and working, she has been quiet and working, she has been suffering and working, she has been watching and working, she has been waiting, she has been working, she has been waiting and working, she is not needing to be changing.

1935

---

[7] From Gertrude Stein's *Portraits and Prayers* (1934).

Sherwood Anderson   *1876–1941*

Ohio-born Sherwood Anderson passed his early boyhood years in the village of Clyde, the most likely model for the Winesburg of his later stories. Thrown on his own resources while still in his teens, he worked at many odd jobs, on farms and in towns, arriving finally in Chicago, the Mecca of restless young midwesterners of his generation. After brief service in the Spanish-American War (1898) and a year at Wittenberg Academy in Ohio, he returned to Chicago, where he became an advertising writer. In 1906 he went back to Ohio and acquired an interest in a paint factory, which he managed. He prospered, but at the cost of inner conflict. Realizing that his true vocation lay in literature, he broke off his business connections and his first marriage and settled in Chicago, where he began writing in earnest, although he continued for a time to do some work in advertising. Encouraged by the example of other writers of the Chicago "renaissance" like Carl Sandburg, Vachel Lindsay, and Edgar Lee Masters, Anderson published his largely autobiographical first novel, *Windy McPherson's Son* (1916). It was closely followed by a story of the Pennsylvania coal fields, *Marching Men* (1917), and a book of poems, *Mid-American Chants* (1918).

Winesburg, Ohio (1919), the book of stories that gave Anderson a national reputation, remains his master work. The collection is unified by the central figure of George Willard, the boy reporter who absorbs the experiences of village life in preindustrial Ohio and struggles to attain a fuller consciousness in preparation for his life as a writer. The most vividly realized characters, however, are the "grotesques," as Anderson called them, those whose lives have been warped (like Wing Biddlebaum's in "Hands") by the disparity between their emotional needs and a repressive and limited cultural environment, which thwarts individual self-realization or expression. In *Winesburg* this implicit condemnation of the culture is tempered by a warm nostalgia for the relatively secure though limited country village life in the lull between the harsh pioneer struggle to gain a foothold on the land and the coming storm of industrialization. The novel *Poor White* (1920) shows the impact of the coming of industry upon the town of Bidwell, Ohio, and upon its inarticulate hero, Hugh McVey, whose creative nature is suppressed by his servitude to the machine—and who becomes an inventor rather than an artist. Anderson's belief in the repressiveness of machine civilization encouraged a primitivism (widespread in the 1920's) most fully indulged in his novel *Dark Laughter* (1925), which contrasts the free, spontaneous folkways of Negroes with the cramped and cabined life of middle-class white society.

In 1927, Anderson settled in Marion, Virginia, where he edited two newspapers and renewed his contacts with small-town and rural life. His reason for this move is indicated by the title of one of his next books, *Nearer the Grass Roots* (1929). During the 1930's his concern for social problems discouraged his interest in writing. *Perhaps Women* (1931) suggests that some amelioration of the ills of civilization might be achieved through the leadership of women.

Other novels by Anderson are *Many Marriages* (1923), *Beyond Desire* (1932), and *Kit Brandon* (1936). Collections of short fiction, the form in which Anderson reached the height of his power in supple, deceptively simple, idiomatic narration, include, besides *Winesburg, Ohio*, *The Triumph of the Egg* (1921), *Horses and Men* (1923), and *Death in the Woods* (1933). *A Story Teller's Story* (1924) and *Tar: A Midwest Childhood* (1926) are autobiographical.

Sherwood Anderson's Memoirs (New York, 1942) is a posthumous publication. His correspondence most concerned with writing and literary matters has been collected in *Letters*, ed. H. M. Jones and W. B Rideout (Boston, 1953). Helpful introductions to Anderson's work are Brom Weber, *Sherwood Anderson* (Minneapolis, 1964) and R. L. White, ed., *The Achievement of Sherwood Anderson: Essays in Criticism* (Chapel Hill, N. C., 1966). Other critiques include James Schevill, *Sherwood Anderson, His Life and Work* (Denver, 1951), and Rex Burbank, *Sherwood Anderson* (New York, 1964).

The text of the stories given here is that of *Winesburg, Ohio* (New York, 1919).

Hands

Upon the half decayed veranda of a small frame house that stood near the edge of a ravine near the town of Winesburg, Ohio, a fat little old man walked nervously up and down. Across a long field that had been seeded for clover but that had produced only a dense crop of yellow mustard weeds, he could see the public highway along which went a wagon filled with berry pickers returning from the fields. The berry pickers, youths and maidens, laughed and shouted boisterously. A boy clad in a blue shirt leaped from the wagon and attempted to drag after him one of the maidens who screamed and protested shrilly. The feet of the boy in the road kicked up a cloud of dust that floated across the face of the departing sun. Over the long field came a thin girlish voice. "Oh, you Wing Biddlebaum, comb your hair, it's falling into your eyes," commanded the voice to the man, who was bald and whose nervous little hands fiddled about the bare white forehead as though arranging a mass of tangled locks.

Wing Biddlebaum, forever frightened and beset by a ghostly band of doubts, did not think of himself as in any way a part of the life of the town where he had lived for twenty years. Among all the people of Winesburg but one had come close to him. With George Willard, son of Tom Willard, the proprietor of the new Willard House, he had formed something like a friendship. George Willard was the reporter on the *Winesburg Eagle* and sometimes in the evenings he walked out along the highway to Wing Biddlebaum's house. Now as the old man walked up and down on the veranda, his hands moving nervously about, he was hoping that George Willard would come and spend the evening with him. After the wagon containing the berry pickers had passed, he went across the field through the tall mustard weeds and climbing a rail fence peered anxiously along the road to the town. For a moment he stood thus, rubbing his hands together and looking up and down the road, and then, fear overcoming him, ran back to walk again upon the porch on his own house.

In the presence of George Willard, Wing Biddlebaum, who for twenty years had been the town mystery, lost something of his timidity, and his shadowy personality, submerged in a sea of doubts, came forth to look at the world. With the young reporter at his side, he ventured in the light of day into Main Street or strode up and down on the rickety front porch of his own house, talking excitedly. The voice that had been low and trembling became shrill and loud. The bent figure straightened. With a kind of wriggle, like a fish returned to the brook by the fisherman, Biddlebaum the silent began to talk, striving to put into words the ideas that had been accumulated by his mind during long years of silence.

Wing Biddlebaum talked much with his hands. The slender expressive fingers, forever active, forever striving to conceal themselves in his pockets or behind his back, came forth and became the piston rods of his machinery of expression.

The story of Wing Biddlebaum is a story of hands. Their restless activity, like unto the beating of the wings of an imprisoned bird, had given him his name. Some obscure poet of the town had thought of it. The hands alarmed their owner. He wanted to keep them hidden away and looked with amazement at the quiet inexpressive hands of other men who worked beside him in the fields, or passed, driving sleepy teams on country roads.

When he talked to George Willard, Wing Biddlebaum closed his fists and beat with them upon a table or on the walls of his house. The action made him more comfortable. If the desire to talk came to him when the two were walking in the fields, he sought out a stump or the top board of a fence and with his hands pounding busily talked with renewed ease.

The story of Wing Biddlebaum's hands is worth a book in itself. Sympathetically set forth it would tap many strange, beautiful qualities in obscure men. It is a job for a poet. In Winesburg the hands had attracted attention merely because of their activity. With them Wing Biddlebaum had picked as high as a hundred and forty quarts of strawberries in a day. They became his distinguishing feature, the source of his fame. Also they made more grotesque an already grotesque and elusive individuality. Winesburg was proud of the hands of Wing Biddlebaum in the same spirit in which it was proud of Banker White's new stone house and Wesley Moyer's bay stallion, Tony Tip, that had won the two-fifteen trot at the fall races in Cleveland.

As for George Willard, he had many times wanted to ask about the hands. At times an almost overwhelming curiosity had taken hold of him. He felt that there must be a reason for their strange activity and their inclination to keep hidden away and only a growing respect for Wing Biddlebaum kept him from blurting out the questions that were often in his mind.

Once he had been on the point of asking. The two were walking in the fields on a summer afternoon and had stopped to sit upon a grassy bank. All afternoon Wing Biddlebaum had talked as one inspired. By a fence he had stopped and beating like a giant woodpecker upon the top board had shouted at George Willard, condemning his tendency to be too much influenced by the people about him. "You are destroying yourself," he cried. "You have the inclination to be alone and to dream and you are afraid of dreams. You want to be like others in town here. You hear them talk and you try to imitate them."

On the grassy bank Wing Biddlebaum had tried again to drive his point home. His voice became soft and reminiscent, and with a sigh of contentment he launched into a long rambling talk, speaking as one lost in a dream.

Out of the dream Wing Biddlebaum made a picture for George Willard. In the picture men lived again in a kind of pastoral golden age. Across a green open country came clean-limbed young men, some afoot, some mounted upon horses. In crowds the young men came to gather about the feet of an old man who sat beneath a tree in a tiny garden and who talked to them.

Wing Biddlebaum became wholly inspired. For once he forgot the hands. Slowly they stole forth and lay upon George Willard's shoulders. Something new and bold came into the voice that talked. "You must try to forget all you have learned," said the old man. "You must begin to dream. From this time on you must shut your ears to the roaring of the voices."

Pausing in his speech, Wing Biddlebaum looked long and earnestly at George Willard. His eyes glowed. Again he raised the hands to caress the boy and then a look of horror swept over his face.

With a convulsive movement of his body, Wing Biddlebaum sprang to his feet and thrust his hands deep into his trousers pockets. Tears came to his eyes. "I must be getting along home. I can talk no more with you," he said nervously.

Without looking back, the old man had hurried down the hillside and across a meadow, leaving George Willard perplexed and frightened upon the grassy slope. With a shiver of dread the boy arose and went along the road toward town. "I'll not ask him about his hands," he thought, touched by the memory of the terror he had seen in the man's eyes. "There's something wrong, but I don't want to know what it is. His hands have something to do with his fear of me and of everyone."

And George Willard was right. Let us look briefly into the story of the hands. Perhaps our talking of them will arouse the poet who will tell the hidden wonder story of the influence for which the hands were but fluttering pennants of promise.

In his youth Wing Biddlebaum had been a school teacher in a town in Pennsylvania. He was not then known as Wing Biddlebaum, but went by the less euphonic name of Adolph Myers. As Adolph Myers he was much loved by the boys of his school.

Adolph Myers was meant by nature to be a teacher of youth. He was one of those rare, little-understood men who rule by a power so gentle that it passes as a lovable weakness. In their feeling for the boys under their charge such men are not unlike the finer sort of women in their love of men.

And yet that is but crudely stated. It needs the poet there. With the boys of his school, Adolph Myers had walked in the evening or had sat talking until dusk upon the schoolhouse steps lost in a kind of dream. Here and there went his hands, caressing the shoulders of the boys, playing about the tousled heads. As he talked his voice became soft and musical. There was a caress in that also. In a way the voice and the hands, the stroking of the shoulders and the touching of the hair was a part of the schoolmaster's effort to carry a dream into the young minds. By the caress that was in his fingers he expressed himself. He was one of those men in whom the force that creates life is diffused, not centralized. Under the caress of his hands doubt and disbelief went out of the minds of the boys and they began also to dream.

And then the tragedy. A half-witted boy of the school became enamored of the young master. In his bed at night he imagined unspeakable things and in the morning went forth to tell his dreams as facts. Strange, hideous accusations fell from his loose-hung lips.

Through the Pennsylvania town went a shiver. Hidden, shadowy doubts that had been in men's minds concerning Adolph Myers were galvanized into beliefs.

The tragedy did not linger. Trembling lads were jerked out of bed and questioned. "He put his arms about me," said one. "His fingers were always playing in my hair," said another.

One afternoon a man of the town, Henry Bradford, who kept a saloon, came to the schoolhouse door. Calling Adolph Myers into the school yard he began to beat him with his fists. As his hard knuckles beat down into the frightened face of the schoolmaster, his wrath became more and more terrible. Screaming with dismay, the children ran here and there like disturbed insects. "I'll teach you to put your hands on my boy, you beast," roared the saloon keeper, who, tired of beating the master, had begun to kick him about the yard.

Adolph Myers was driven from the Pennsylvania town in the night. With lanterns in their hands a dozen men came to the door of the house where he lived alone and commanded that he dress and come forth. It was raining and one of the men had a rope in his hands. They had intended to hang the schoolmaster, but something in his figure, so small, white, and pitiful, touched their hearts and they let him escape. As he ran away into the darkness they repented of their weakness and ran after him, swearing and throwing sticks and great balls of soft mud at the figure that screamed and ran faster and faster into the darkness.

For twenty years Adolph Myers had lived alone in Winesburg. He was but forty but looked sixty-five. The name of Biddlebaum he got from a box of goods seen at a freight station as he hurried through an eastern Ohio town. He had an aunt in Winesburg, a black-toothed old woman who raised chickens, and with her he lived until she died. He had been ill for a year after the experience in Pennsylvania, and after his recovery worked as a day laborer in the fields, going timidly about and striving to conceal his hands. Although he did not understand what had happened he felt that the hands must be to blame. Again and again the fathers of the boys had talked of the hands. "Keep your hands to yourself," the saloon keeper had roared, dancing with fury in the schoolhouse yard.

Upon the veranda of his house by the ravine, Wing Biddlebaum continued to walk up and down until the sun had disappeared and the road beyond the field was lost in the grey shadows. Going into his house he cut slices of bread and spread honey upon them. When the rumble of the evening train that took away the express cars loaded with the day's harvest of berries had passed and restored the silence of the summer night, he went again to walk upon the veranda. In the darkness he could not see the hands and they became quiet. Although he still hungered for the presence of the boy, who was the medium through which he expressed his love of man, the hunger became again a part of his loneliness and his waiting. Lighting a lamp, Wing Biddlebaum washed the few dishes soiled by his simple meal and, setting up a folding cot by the screen door that led to the porch, prepared to undress for the night. A few stray white bread crumbs lay on the cleanly washed floor by the table; putting the lamp upon a low stool he began to pick up the crumbs, carrying them to his mouth one by one with unbelievable rapidity. In the dense blotch of light beneath the table, the kneeling figure looked like a priest engaged in some service of his church. The nervous expressive fingers, flashing in and out of the light, might well have been mistaken for the fingers of the devotee going swiftly through decade after decade of his rosary.

1919

The Strength of God

The Reverend Curtis Hartman was pastor of the Presbyterian Church of Winesburg, and had been in that position ten years. He was forty years old, and by his nature very silent and reticent. To preach, standing in the pulpit before the people, was always a hardship for him and from Wednesday morning until Saturday evening he thought of nothing but the two sermons that must be preached on Sunday. Early on Sunday morning he went into a little room called a study in the bell tower of the church and prayed. In his prayers there was one note that always predominated. "Give me strength and courage for Thy work, O Lord!" he pleaded, kneeling on the bare floor and bowing his head in the presence of the task that lay before him.

The Reverend Hartman was a tall man with a brown beard. His wife, a stout, nervous woman, was the daughter of a manufacturer of underwear at Cleveland, Ohio. The minister himself was rather a favorite in the town. The elders of the church liked him because he was quiet and unpretentious and Mrs. White, the banker's wife, thought him scholarly and refined.

The Presbyterian Church held itself somewhat aloof from the other churches of Winesburg. It was larger and more imposing and its minister was better paid. He even had a carriage of his own and on summer evenings sometimes drove about town with his wife. Through Main Street and up and down Buckeye Street he went, bowing gravely to the people, while his wife, afire with secret pride, looked at him out of the corners of her eyes and worried lest the horse become frightened and run away.

For a good many years after he came to Winesburg things went well with Curtis Hartman. He was not one to arouse keen enthusiasm among the worshippers in his church but on the other hand he made no enemies. In reality he was much in earnest and sometimes suffered prolonged periods of remorse because he could not go crying the word of God in the highways and byways of the town. He wondered if the flame of the spirit really burned in him and dreamed of a day when a strong sweet new current of power would come like a great wind into his voice and his soul and the people would tremble before the spirit of God made manifest in him. "I am a poor stick and that will never really happen to me," he mused dejectedly, and then a patient smile lit up his features. "Oh well, I suppose I'm doing well enough," he added philosophically.

The room in the bell tower of the church, where on Sunday mornings the minister prayed for an increase in him of the power of God, had but one window. It was long and narrow and swung outward on a hinge like a door. On the window, made of little leaded panes, was a design showing the Christ laying his hand upon the head of a child. One Sunday morning in the summer as he sat by his desk in the room with a large Bible opened before him, and the sheets of his sermon scattered about, the minister was shocked to see, in the upper room of the house next door, a woman lying in her bed and smoking a cigarette while she read a book. Curtis Hartman went on tiptoe to the window and closed it softly. He was horror stricken at the thought of a woman smoking and trembled also to think that his eyes, just raised from the pages of the book of God, had looked upon the bare shoulders and white throat of a woman. With his brain in a whirl he went down into the pulpit and preached a long sermon without once thinking of his gestures or his voice. The sermon attracted unusual attention because of its power and clearness. "I wonder if she is listening, if my voice is carrying a message into her soul," he thought and began to hope that on future Sunday mornings he might be able to say words that would touch and awaken the woman apparently far gone in secret sin.

The house next door to the Presbyterian Church, through the windows of which the minister had seen the sight that had so upset him, was occupied by two women. Aunt Elizabeth Swift, a grey competent-looking widow with money in the Winesburg National Bank, lived there with her daughter Kate Swift, a school teacher. The school teacher was thirty years old and had a neat trim-looking figure. She had few friends and bore a reputation of having a sharp tongue. When he began to think about her, Curtis Hartman remembered that she had been to Europe and had lived for two years in New York City. "Perhaps after all her smoking means nothing," he thought. He began to remember that when he was a student in college and occasionally read novels, good although somewhat worldly women, had smoked through the pages of a book that had once fallen into his hands. With a rush of new determination he worked on his sermons all through the week and forgot, in his zeal to reach the ears and the soul of this new listener, both his embarrassment in the pulpit and the necessity of prayer in the study on Sunday mornings.

Reverend Hartman's experience with women had been somewhat limited. He was the son of a wagon maker from Muncie, Indiana, and had worked his way through college. The daughter of the underwear manufacturer had boarded in a house where he lived during his school days and he had married her after a formal and prolonged courtship, carried on for the most part by the girl herself. On his marriage day the underwear manufacturer had given his daughter five thousand dollars and he promised to leave her at least twice that amount in his will. The minister had thought himself fortunate in marriage and had never permitted himself to think of other women. He did not want to think of other women. What he wanted was to do the work of God quietly and earnestly.

In the soul of the minister a struggle awoke. From wanting to reach the ears of Kate Swift, and through his sermons to delve into her soul, he began to want also to look again at the figure lying white and quiet in the bed. On a Sunday morning when he could not sleep because of his thoughts he arose and went to walk in the streets. When he had gone along Main Street almost to the old Richmond place he stopped and picking up a stone rushed off to the room in the bell tower. With the stone he broke out a corner of the window and then locked the door and sat down at the desk before the open Bible to wait. When the shade of the window to Kate Swift's room was raised he could see, through the hole, directly into her bed, but she was not there. She also had arisen and had gone for a walk and the hand that raised the shade was the hand of Aunt Elizabeth Swift.

The minister almost wept with joy at this deliverance from the carnal desire to "peep" and went back to his own house praising God. In an ill moment he forgot, however, to stop the hole in the window. The piece of glass broken out at the corner of the window just nipped off the bare heel of the boy standing motionless and looking with rapt eyes into the face of the Christ.

Curtis Hartman forgot his sermon on that Sunday morning. He talked to his congregation and in his talk said that it was a mistake for people to think of their minister as a man set aside and intended by nature to lead a blameless life. "Out of my own experience I know that we, who are the ministers of God's word, are beset by the same temptations that assail you," he declared. "I have been tempted and have surrendered to temptation. It is only the hand of God, placed beneath my head, that has raised me up. As he has raised me so also will he raise you. Do not despair. In your hour of sin raise your eyes to the skies and you will be again and again saved."

Resolutely the minister put the thoughts of the woman in the bed out of his mind and began to be something like a lover in the presence of his wife. One evening when they drove out together he turned the horse out of Buckeye Street and in the darkness on Gospel Hill, above Waterworks Pond, put his arm about Sarah Hartman's waist. When he had eaten breakfast in the morning and was ready to retire to his study at the back of his house he went around the table and kissed his wife on the cheek. When thoughts of Kate Swift came into his head, he smiled and raised his eyes to the skies. "Intercede for me, Master," he muttered, "keep me in the narrow path intent on Thy work."

And now began the real struggle in the soul of the brown-bearded minister. By chance he discovered that Kate Swift was in the habit of lying in her bed in the evenings and reading a book. A lamp stood on a table by the side of the bed and the light streamed down upon her white shoulders and bare throat. On the evening when he made the discovery the minister sat at the desk in the study from nine until after eleven and when her light was put out stumbled out of the church to spend two more hours walking and praying in the streets. He did not want to kiss the shoulders and the throat of Kate Swift and had not allowed his mind to dwell on such thoughts. He did not know what he wanted. "I am God's child and he must save me from myself," he cried, in the darkness under the trees as he wandered in the streets. By a tree he stood and looked at the sky that was covered with hurrying clouds. He began to talk to God intimately and closely. "Please, Father, do not forget me. Give me power to go tomorrow and repair the hole in the window. Lift my eyes again to the skies. Stay with me, Thy servant, in his hour of need."

Up and down through the silent streets walked the minister and for days and weeks his soul was troubled. He could not understand the temptation that had come to him nor could he fathom the reason for its coming. In a way he began to blame God, saying to himself that he had tried to keep his feet in the true path and had not run about seeking sin. "Through my days as a young man and all through my life here I have gone quietly about my work," he declared. "Why now should I be tempted? What have I done that this burden should be laid on me?"

Three times during the early fall and winter of that year Curtis Hartman crept out of his house to the room in the bell tower to sit in the darkness looking at the figure of Kate Swift lying in her bed and later went to walk and pray in the streets. He could not understand himself. For weeks he would go along scarcely thinking of the school teacher and telling himself that he had conquered the carnal desire to look at her body. And then something would happen. As he sat in the study of his own house, hard at work on a sermon, he would become nervous and begin to walk up and down the room. "I will go out into the streets," he told himself and even as he let himself in at the church door he persistently denied to himself the cause of his being here. "I will not repair the hole in the window and I will train myself to come here at night and sit in the presence of this woman without raising my eyes. I will not be defeated in this thing. The Lord has devised this temptation as a test of my soul and I will grope my way out of darkness into the light of righteousness."

One night in January when it was bitter cold and snow lay deep on the streets of Winesburg Curtis Hartman paid his last visit to the room in the bell tower of the church. It was past nine o'clock when he left his own house and he set out so hurriedly that he forgot to put on his overshoes. In Main Street no one was abroad but Hop Higgins the night watchman and in the whole town no one was awake but the watchman and young George Willard, who sat in the office of the *Winesburg Eagle* trying to write a story. Along the street to the church went the minister, plowing through the drifts and thinking that this time he would utterly give way to sin. "I want to look at the woman and to think of kissing her shoulders and I am going to let myself think what I choose," he declared bitterly and tears came into his eyes. He began to think that he would get out of the ministry and try some other way of life. "I shall go to some city and get into business," he declared. "If my nature is such that I cannot resist sin, I shall give myself over to sin. At least I shall not be a hypocrite, preaching the word of God with my mind thinking of the shoulders and neck of a woman who does not belong to me."

It was cold in the room of the bell tower of the church on that January night and almost as soon as he came into the room Curtis Hartman knew that if he stayed he would be ill. His feet were wet from tramping in the snow and there was no fire. In the room in the house next door Kate Swift had not yet appeared. With grim determination the man sat down to wait. Sitting in the chair and gripping the edge of the desk on which lay the Bible he stared into the darkness thinking the blackest thoughts of his life. He thought of his wife and for the moment almost hated her. "She has always been ashamed of passion and has cheated me," he thought. "Man has a right to expect living passion and beauty in a woman. He has no right to forget that he is an animal and in me there is something that is Greek. I will throw off the woman of my bosom and seek other women. I will besiege this school teacher. I will fly in the face of all men and if I am a creature of carnal lusts I will live then for my lusts."

The distracted man trembled from head to foot, partly from cold, partly from the struggle in which he was engaged. Hours passed and a fever assailed his body. His throat began to hurt and his teeth chattered. His feet on the study floor felt like two cakes of ice. Still he would not give up. "I will see this woman and will think the thoughts I have never dared to think," he told himself, gripping the edge of the desk and waiting.

Curtis Hartman came near dying from the effects of that night of waiting in the church, and also he found in the thing that happened what he took to be the way of life for him. On other evenings when he had waited he had not been able to see, through the little hole in the glass, any part of the school teacher's room except that occupied by her bed. In the darkness he had waited until the woman suddenly appeared sitting in the bed in her white night-robe. When the light was turned up she propped herself up among the pillows and read a book. Sometimes she smoked one of the cigarettes. Only her bare shoulders and throat were visible.

On the January night, after he had come near dying with cold and after his mind had two or three times actually slipped away into an odd land of fantasy so that he had by an exercise of will power to force himself back into consciousness, Kate Swift appeared. In the room next door a lamp was lighted and the waiting man stared into an empty bed.

Then upon the bed before his eyes a naked woman threw herself. Lying face downward she wept and beat with her fists upon the pillow. With a final outburst of weeping she half arose, and in the presence of the man who had waited to look and to think thoughts the woman of sin began to pray. In the lamplight her figure, slim and strong, looked like the figure of the boy in the presence of the Christ on the leaded window.

Curtis Hartman never remembered how he got out of the church. With a cry he arose, dragging the heavy desk along the floor. The Bible fell, making a great clatter in the silence. When the light in the house next door went out he stumbled down the stairway and into the street. Along the street he went and ran in at the door of the *Winesburg Eagle*. To George Willard, who was tramping up and down in the office undergoing a struggle of his own, he began to talk half incoherently. "The ways of God are beyond human understanding," he cried, running in quickly and closing the door. He began to advance upon the young man, his eyes glowing and his voice ringing with fervor. "I have found the light," he cried. "After ten years in this town, God has manifested himself to me in the body of a woman." His voice dropped and he began to whisper. "I did not understand," he said. "What I took to be a trial of my soul was only a preparation for a new and more beautiful fervor of the spirit. God has appeared to me in the person of Kate Swift, the school teacher, kneeling naked on a bed. Do you know Kate Swift? Although she may not be aware of it, she is an instrument of God, bearing the message of truth."

Reverend Curtis Hartman turned and ran out of the office. At the door he stopped, and after looking up and down the deserted street, turned again to George Willard. "I am delivered. Have no fear." He held up a bleeding fist for the young man to see. "I smashed the glass of the window," he cried. "Now it will have to be wholly replaced. The strength of God was in me and I broke it with my fist."

The Teacher

Snow lay deep in the streets of Winesburg. It had begun to snow about ten o'clock in the morning and a wind sprang up and blew the snow in clouds along Main Street. The frozen mud roads that led into town were fairly smooth and in places ice covered the mud. "There will be good sleighing," said Will Henderson, standing by the bar in Ed Griffith's saloon. Out of the saloon he went and met Sylvester West the druggist stumbling along in the kind of heavy overshoes called arctics. "Snow will bring the people into town on Saturday," said the druggist. The two men stopped and discussed their affairs. Will Henderson, who had on a light overcoat and no overshoes, kicked the heel of his left foot with the toe of the right. "Snow will be good for the wheat," observed the druggist sagely.

Young George Willard, who had nothing to do, was glad because he did not feel like working that day. The weekly paper had been printed and taken to the post office Wednesday evening and the snow began to fall on Thursday. At eight o'clock, after the morning train had passed, he put a pair of skates in his pocket and went up to Waterworks Pond but did not go skating. Past the pond and along a path that followed Wine Creek he went until he came to a grove of beech trees. There he built a fire against the side of a log and sat down at the end of the log to think. When the snow began to fall and the wind to blow he hurried about getting fuel for the fire.

The young reporter was thinking of Kate Swift, who had once been his school teacher. On the evening before he had gone to her house to get a book she wanted him to read and had been alone with her for an hour. For the fourth or fifth time the woman had talked to him with great earnestness and he could not make out what she meant by her talk. He began to believe she might be in love with him and the thought was both pleasing and annoying.

Up from the log he sprang and began to pile sticks on the fire. Looking about to be sure he was alone he talked aloud pretending he was in the presence of the woman. "Oh, you're just letting on, you know you are," he declared. "I am going to find out about you. You wait and see."

The young man got up and went back along the path toward town leaving the fire blazing in the wood. As he went through the streets the skates clanked in his pocket. In his own room in the New Willard House he built a fire in the stove and lay down on top of the bed. He began to have lustful thoughts and pulling down the shade of the window closed his eyes and turned his face to the wall. He took a pillow into his arms and embraced it thinking first of the school teacher, who by her words had stirred something within him, and later of Helen White, the slim daughter of the town banker, with whom he had been for a long time half in love.

By nine o'clock of that evening snow lay deep in the streets and the weather had become bitter cold. It was difficult to walk about. The stores were dark and the people had crawled away to their houses. The evening train from Cleveland was very late but nobody was interested in its arrival. By ten o'clock all but four of the eighteen hundred citizens of the town were in bed.

Hop Higgins, the night watchman, was partially awake. He was lame and carried a heavy stick. On dark nights he carried a lantern. Between nine and ten o'clock he went his rounds. Up and down Main Street he stumbled through the drifts trying the doors of the stores. Then he went into alleyways and tried the back doors. Finding all tight he hurried around the corner to the New Willard House and beat on the door. Through the rest of the night he intended to stay by the stove. "You go to bed. I'll keep the stove going," he said to the boy who slept on a cot in the hotel office.

Hop Higgins sat down by the stove and took off his shoes. When the boy had gone to sleep he began to think of his own affairs. He intended to paint his house in the spring and sat by the stove calculating the cost of paint and labor. That led him into other calculations. The night watchman was sixty years old and wanted to retire. He had been a soldier in the Civil War and drew a small pension. He hoped to find some new method of making a living and aspired to become a professional breeder of ferrets. Already he had four of the strangely shaped savage little creatures, that are used by sportsmen in the pursuit of rabbits, in the cellar of his house. "Now I have one male and three females," he mused. "If I am lucky by spring I shall have twelve or fifteen. In another year I shall be able to begin advertising ferrets for sale in the sporting papers."

The night watchman settled into his chair and his mind became a blank. He did not sleep. By years of practice he had trained himself to sit for hours through the long nights neither asleep nor awake. In the morning he was almost as refreshed as though he had slept.

With Hop Higgins safely stowed away in the chair behind the stove only three people were awake in Winesburg. George Willard was in the office of the *Eagle* pretending to be at work on the writing of a story but in reality continuing the mood of the morning by the fire in the wood. In the bell tower of the Presbyterian Church the Reverend Curtis Hartman was sitting in the darkness preparing himself for a revelation from God, and Kate Swift, the school teacher, was leaving her house for a walk in the storm.

It was past ten o'clock when Kate Swift set out and the walk was unpremeditated. It was as though the man and the boy, by thinking of her, had driven her forth into the wintry streets. Aunt Elizabeth Swift had gone to the county seat concerning some business in connection with mortgages in which she had money invested and would not be back until the next day. By a huge stove, called a base burner, in the living room of the house sat the daughter reading a book. Suddenly she sprang to her feet and, snatching a cloak from a rack by the front door, ran out of the house.

At the age of thirty Kate Swift was not known in Winesburg as a pretty woman. Her complexion was not good and her face was covered with blotches that indicated ill health. Alone in the night in the winter streets she was lovely. Her back was straight, her shoulders square, and her features were as the features of a tiny goddess on a pedestal in a garden in the dim light of a summer evening.

During the afternoon the school teacher had been to see Doctor Welling concerning her health. The doctor had scolded her and had declared she was in danger of losing her hearing. It was foolish for Kate Swift to be abroad in the storm, foolish and perhaps dangerous.

The woman in the streets did not remember the words of the doctor and would not have turned back had she remembered. She was very cold but after walking for five minutes no longer minded the cold. First she went to the end of her own street and then across a pair of hay scales set in the ground before a feed barn and into Trunion Pike. Along Trunion Pike she went to Ned Winters' barn and turning east followed a street of low frame houses that led over Gospel Hill and into Sucker Road that ran down a shallow valley past Ike Smead's chicken farm to Waterworks Pond. As she went along, the bold, excited mood that had driven her out of doors passed and then returned again.

There was something biting and forbidding in the character of Kate Swift. Everyone felt it. In the schoolroom she was silent, cold, and stern, and yet in an odd way very close to her pupils. Once in a long while something seemed to have come over her and she was happy. All of the children in the schoolroom felt the effect of her happiness. For a time they did not work but sat back in their chairs and looked at her.

With hands clasped behind her back the school teacher walked up and down in the schoolroom and talked very rapidly. It did not seem to matter what subject came into her mind. Once she talked to the children of Charles Lamb and made up strange, intimate little stories concerning the life of the dead writer. The stories were told with the air of one who had lived in a house with Charles Lamb and knew all the secrets of his private life. The children were somewhat confused, thinking Charles Lamb must be someone who had once lived in Winesburg.

On another occasion the teacher talked to the children of Benvenuto Cellini. That time they laughed. What a bragging, blustering, brave, lovable fellow she made of the old artist! Concerning him also she invented anecdotes. There was one of a German music teacher who had a room above Cellini's lodgings in the city of Milan that made the boys guffaw. Sugars McNutts, a fat boy with red cheeks, laughed so hard that he became dizzy and fell off his seat and Kate Swift laughed with him. Then suddenly she became again cold and stern.

On the winter night when she walked through the deserted snow-covered streets, a crisis had come into the life of the school teacher. Although no one in Winesburg would have suspected it, her life had been very adventurous. It was still adventurous. Day by day as she worked in the schoolroom or walked in the streets, grief, hope, and desire fought within her. Behind a cold exterior the most extraordinary events transpired in her mind. The people of the town thought of her as a confirmed old maid and because she spoke sharply and went her own way thought her lacking in all the human feeling that did so much to make and mar their own lives. In reality she was the most eagerly passionate soul among them, and more than once, in the five years since she had come back from her travels to settle in Winesburg and become a school teacher, had been compelled to go out of the house and walk half through the night fighting out some battle raging within. Once on a night when it rained she had stayed out six hours and when she came home had a quarrel with Aunt Elizabeth Swift. "I am glad you're not a man," said the mother sharply. "More than once I've waited for your father to come home, not knowing what new mess he had got into. I've had my share of uncertainty and you cannot blame me if I do not want to see the worst side of him reproduced in you."

.   .   .   .   .   .

Kate Swift's mind was ablaze with thoughts of George Willard. In something he had written as a school boy she thought she had recognized the spark of genius and wanted to blow on the spark. One day in the summer she had gone to the *Eagle* office and finding the boy unoccupied had taken him out Main Street to the Fair Ground, where the two sat on a grassy bank and talked. The school teacher tried to bring home to the mind of the boy some conception of the difficulties he would have to face as a writer. "You will have to know life," she declared, and her voice trembled with earnestness. She took hold of George Willard's shoulders and turned him about so that she could look into his eyes. A passer-by might have thought them about to embrace. "If you are to become a writer you'll have to stop fooling with words," she explained. "It would be better to give up the notion of writing until you are better prepared. Now it's time to be living. I don't want to frighten you, but I would like to make you understand the import of what you think of attempting. You must not become a mere peddler of words. The thing to learn is to know what people are thinking about, not what they say."

On the evening before that stormy Thursday night when the Reverend Curtis Hartman sat in the bell tower of the church waiting to look at her body, young Willard had gone to visit the teacher and to borrow a book. It was then the thing happened that confused and puzzled the boy. He had the book under his arm and was preparing to depart. Again Kate Swift talked with great earnestness. Night was coming on and the light in the room grew dim. As he turned to go she spoke his name softly and with an impulsive movement took hold of his hand. Because the reporter was rapidly becoming a man something of his man's appeal, combined with the winsomeness of the boy, stirred the heart of the lonely woman. A passionate desire to have him under-stand the import of life, to learn to interpret it truly and honestly, swept over her. Leaning forward, her lips brushed his cheek. At the same moment he for the first time became aware of the marked beauty of her features. They were both embarrassed, and to relieve her feeling she became harsh and domineering. "What's the use? It will be ten years before you begin to understand what I mean when I talk to you," she cried passionately.

. . . . . .

On the night of the storm and while the minister sat in the church waiting for her, Kate Swift went to the office of the *Winesburg Eagle*, intending to have another talk with the boy. After the long walk in the snow she was cold, lonely, and tired. As she came through Main Street she saw the light from the printshop window shining on the snow and on an impulse opened the door and went in. For an hour she sat by the stove in the office talking of life. She talked with passionate earnest-ness. The impulse that had driven her out into the snow poured itself out into talk. She became inspired as she sometimes did in the presence of the children in school. A great eagerness to open the door of life to the boy, who had been her pupil and who she thought might possess a talent for the understanding of life, had possession of her. So strong was her passion that it became something physical. Again her hands took hold of his shoulders and she turned him about. In the dim light her eyes blazed. She arose and laughed, not sharply as was customary with her, but in a queer, hesitating way. "I must be going," she said. "In a moment, if I stay, I'll be wanting to kiss you."

In the newspaper office a confusion arose. Kate Swift turned and walked to the door. She was a teacher but she was also a woman. As she looked at George Willard, the passionate desire to be loved by a man, that had a thousand times before swept like a storm over her body, took possession of her. In the lamplight George Willard looked no longer a boy, but a man ready to play the part of a man.

The school teacher let George Willard take her into his arms. In the warm little office the air became suddenly heavy and the strength went out of her body. Leaning against a low counter by the door she waited. When he came and put a hand on her shoulder she turned and let her body fall heavily against him. For George Willard the confusion was immediately increased. For a moment he held the body of the

woman tightly against his body and then it stiffened. Two sharp little fists began to beat on his face. When the school teacher had run
away and left him alone, he walked up and down in the office swearing
furiously.

It was into his confusion that the Reverend Curtis Hartman
protruded himself. When he came in George Willard thought the town
had gone mad. Shaking a bleeding fist in the air, the minister proclaimed
the woman George had only a moment before held in his arms an
instrument of God bearing a message of truth.

.   .   .   .   .   .

George blew out the lamp by the window and locking the door of
the printshop went home. Through the hotel office, past Hop Higgins
lost in his dream of the raising of ferrets, he went and up into his own
room. The fire in the stove had gone out and he undressed in the cold.
When he got into bed the sheets were like blankets of dry snow.

George Willard rolled about in the bed on which he had lain in
the afternoon hugging the pillow and thinking thoughts of Kate Swift.
The words of the minister, who he thought had gone suddenly insane,
rang in his ears. His eyes stared about the room. The resentment,
natural to the baffled male, passed and he tried to understand what had
happened. He could not make it out. Over and over he turned the
matter in his mind. Hours passed and he began to think it must be time
for another day to come. At four o'clock he pulled the covers up about
his neck and tried to sleep. When he became drowsy and closed his
eyes, he raised a hand and with it groped about in the darkness. "I have
missed something. I have missed something Kate Swift was trying to
tell me," he muttered sleepily. Then he slept and in all Winesburg he
was the last soul on that winter night to go to sleep.

Sophistication

It was early evening of a day in the late fall and the Winesburg
County Fair had brought crowds of country people into town. The day
had been clear and the night came on warm and pleasant. On the Trunion Pike, where the road after it left town stretched away between
berry fields now covered with dry brown leaves, the dust from passing
wagons arose in clouds. Children, curled into little balls, slept on the
straw scattered on wagon beds. Their hair was full of dust and their
fingers black and sticky. The dust rolled away over the fields and the
departing sun set it ablaze with colors.

In the main street of Winesburg crowds filled the stores and the
sidewalks. Night came on, horses whinnied, the clerks in the stores ran
madly about, children became lost and cried lustily, an American town
worked terribly at the task of amusing itself.

Pushing his way through the crowds in Main Street, young George Willard concealed himself in the stairway leading to Doctor Reefy's office and looked at the people. With feverish eyes he watched the faces drifting past under the store lights. Thoughts kept coming into his head and he did not want to think. He stamped impatiently on the wooden steps and looked sharply about. "Well, is she going to stay with him all day? Have I done all this waiting for nothing?" he muttered.

George Willard, the Ohio village boy, was fast growing into manhood and new thoughts had been coming into his mind. All that day, amid the jam of people at the Fair, he had gone about feeling lonely. He was about to leave Winesburg to go away to some city where he hoped to get work on a city newspaper and he felt grown up. The mood that had taken possession of him was a thing known to men and unknown to boys. He felt old and a little tired. Memories awoke in him. To his mind his new sense of maturity set him apart, made of him a half-tragic figure. He wanted someone to understand the feeling that had taken possession of him after his mother's death.

There is a time in the life of every boy when he for the first time takes the backward view of life. Perhaps that is the moment when he crosses the line into manhood. The boy is walking through the street of his town. He is thinking of the future and of the figure he will cut in the world. Ambitions and regrets awake within him. Suddenly something happens; he stops under a tree and waits as for a voice calling his name. Ghosts of old things creep into his consciousness; the voices outside of himself whisper a message concerning the limitations of life. From being quite sure of himself and his future he becomes not at all sure. If he be an imaginative boy a door is torn open and for the first time he looks out upon the world, seeing, as though they marched in procession before him, the countless figures of men who before his time have come out of nothingness into the world, lived their lives and again disappeared into nothingness. The sadness of sophistication has come to the boy. With a little gasp he sees himself as merely a leaf blown by the wind through the streets of his village. He knows that in spite of all the stout talk of his fellows he must live and die in uncertainty, a thing blown by the winds, a thing destined like corn to wilt in the sun. He shivers and looks eagerly about. The eighteen years he has lived seem but a moment, a breathing space in the long march of humanity. Already he hears death calling. With all his heart he wants to come close to some other human, touch someone with his hands, be touched by the hand of another. If he prefers that the other be a woman, that is because he believes that a woman will be gentle, that she will understand. He wants, most of all, understanding.

When the moment of sophistication came to George Willard his mind turned to Helen White, the Winesburg banker's daughter. Always he had been conscious of the girl growing into womanhood as he grew into manhood. Once on a summer night when he was eighteen, he had walked with her on a country road and in her presence had given way to an impulse to boast, to make himself appear big and significant in her eyes. Now he wanted to see her for another purpose. He wanted to tell her of the new impulses that had come to him. He had tried to make her think of him as a man when he knew nothing of manhood and now he wanted to be with her and to try to make her feel the change he believed had taken place in his nature.

As for Helen White, she also had come to a period of change. What George felt, she in her young woman's way felt also. She was no longer a girl and hungered to reach into the grace and beauty of womanhood. She had come home from Cleveland, where she was attending college, to spend a day at the Fair. She also had begun to have memories. During the day she sat in the grandstand with a young man, one of the instructors from the college, who was a guest of her mother's. The young man was of a pedantic turn of mind and she felt at once he would not do for her purpose. At the Fair she was glad to be seen in his company as he was well dressed and a stranger. She knew that the fact of his presence would create an impression. During the day she was happy, but when night came on she began to grow restless. She wanted to drive the instructor away, to get out of his presence. While they sat together in the grand-stand and while the eyes of former schoolmates were upon them, she paid so much attention to her escort that he grew interested. "A scholar needs money. I should marry a woman with money," he mused.

Helen White was thinking of George Willard even as he wandered gloomily through the crowds thinking of her. She remembered the summer evening when they had walked together and wanted to walk with him again. She thought that the months she had spent in the city, the going to theatres and the seeing of great crowds wandering in lighted thoroughfares, had changed her profoundly. She wanted him to feel and be conscious of the change in her nature.

The summer evening together that had left its mark on the memory of both the young man and woman had, when looked at quite sensibly, been rather stupidly spent. They had walked out of town along a country road. Then they had stopped by a fence near a field of young corn and George had taken off his coat and let it hang on his arm. "Well, I've stayed here in Winesburg—yes—I've not yet gone away but I'm growing up," he had said. "I've been reading books and I've been thinking. I'm going to try to amount to something in life.

"Well," he explained, "that isn't the point. Perhaps I'd better quit talking."

The confused boy put his hand on the girl's arm. His voice trembled. The two started to walk back along the road toward town. In his desperation George boasted, "I'm going to be a big man, the biggest that ever lived here in Winesburg," he declared. "I want you to do something, I don't know what. Perhaps it is none of my business. I want you to try to be different from other women. You see the point. It's none of my business I tell you. I want you to be a beautiful woman. You see what I want."

The boy's voice failed and in silence the two came back into town and went along the street to Helen White's house. At the gate he tried to say something impressive. Speeches he had thought out came into his head, but they seemed utterly pointless. "I thought—I used to think—I had it in my mind you would marry Seth Richmond. Now I know you won't," was all he could find to say as she went through the gate and toward the door of her house.

On the warm fall evening as he stood in the stairway and looked at the crowd drifting through Main Street, George thought of the talk beside the field of young corn and was ashamed of the figure he had made of himself. In the street the people surged up and down like cattle confined in a pen. Buggies and wagons almost filled the narrow thoroughfare. A band played and small boys raced along the sidewalk, diving between the legs of men. Young men with shining red faces walked awkwardly about with girls on their arms. In a room above one of the stores, where a dance was to be held, the fiddlers tuned their instruments. The broken sounds floated down through an open window and out across the murmur of voices and the loud blare of the horns of the band. The medley of sounds got on young Willard's nerves. Everywhere, on all sides, the sense of crowding, moving life closed in about him. He wanted to run away by himself and think. "If she wants to stay with that fellow she may. Why should I care? What difference does it make to me?" he growled and went along Main Street and through Hern's grocery into a side street.

George felt so utterly lonely and dejected that he wanted to weep but pride made him walk rapidly along, swinging his arms. He came to Westley Moyer's livery barn and stopped in the shadows to listen to a group of men who talked of a race Westley's stallion, Tony Tip, had won at the Fair during the afternoon. A crowd had gathered in front of the barn and before the crowd walked Westley, prancing up and down and boasting. He held a whip in his hand and kept tapping the ground. Little puffs of dust arose in the lamplight. "Hell, quit your talking," Westley exclaimed. "I wasn't afraid, I knew I had 'em beat all the time. I wasn't afraid."

Ordinarily George Willard would have been intensely interested in the boasting of Moyer, the horseman. Now it made him angry. He turned and hurried away along the street. "Old windbag," he sputtered. "Why does he want to be bragging? Why don't he shut up?"

George went into a vacant lot and as he hurried along, fell over a pile of rubbish. A nail protruding from an empty barrel tore his trousers. He sat down on the ground and swore. With a pin he mended the torn place and then arose and went on. "I'll go to Helen White's house, that's what I'll do. I'll walk right in. I'll say that I want to see her. I'll walk right in and sit down, that's what I'll do," he declared, climbing over a fence and beginning to run.

. . . . . .

On the veranda of Banker White's house Helen was restless and distraught. The instructor sat between the mother and daughter. His talk wearied the girl. Although he had also been raised in an Ohio town, the instructor began to put on the airs of the city. He wanted to appear cosmopolitan. "I like the chance you have given me to study the background out of which most of our girls come," he declared. "It was good of you, Mrs. White, to have me down for the day." He turned to Helen and laughed. "Your life is still bound up with the life of this town?" he asked. "There are people here in whom you are interested?" To the girl his voice sounded pompous and heavy.

Helen arose and went into the house. At the door leading to a garden at the back she stopped and stood listening. Her mother began to talk, "There is no one here fit to associate with a girl of Helen's breeding," she said.

Helen ran down a flight of stairs at the back of the house and into the garden. In the darkness she stopped and stood trembling. It seemed to her that the world was full of meaningless people saying words. Afire with eagerness she ran through a garden gate and turning a corner by the banker's barn, went into a little side street. "George! Where are you, George?" she cried, filled with nervous excitement. She stopped running, and leaned against a tree to laugh hysterically. Along the dark little street came George Willard, still saying words. "I'm going to walk right into her house. I'll go right in and sit down," he declared as he came up to her. He stopped and stared stupidly. "Come on," he said and took hold of her hand. With hanging heads they walked away along the street under the trees. Dry leaves rustled under foot. Now that he had found her George wondered what he had better do and say.

. . . . . .

At the upper end of the fair ground, in Winesburg, there is a half decayed old grandstand. It has never been painted and the boards are all warped out of shape. The fair ground stands on top of a low hill rising out of the valley of Wine Creek and from the grandstand one can see at night, over a cornfield, the lights of the town reflected against the sky.

George and Helen climbed the hill to the fair ground, coming by the path past Waterworks Pond. The feeling of loneliness and isolation that had come to the young man in the crowded streets of his town was both broken and intensified by the presence of Helen. What he felt was reflected in her.

In youth there are always two forces fighting in people. The warm unthinking little animal struggles against the thing that reflects and remembers, and the older, the more sophisticated thing had possession of George Willard. Sensing his mood, Helen walked beside him filled with respect. When they got to the grandstand they climbed up under the roof and sat down on one of the long bench-like seats.

There is something memorable in the experience to be had by going into a fair ground that stands at the edge of a Middle Western town on a night after the annual fair has been held. The sensation is one never to be forgotten. On all sides are ghosts, not of the dead, but of living people. Here, during the day just passed, have come the people pouring in from the town and the country around. Farmers with their wives and children and all the people from the hundreds of little frame houses have gathered within these board walls. Young girls have laughed and men with beards have talked of the affairs of their lives. The place has been filled to overflowing with life. It has itched and squirmed with life and now it is night and the life has all gone away. The silence is almost terrifying. One conceals oneself standing silently beside the trunk of a tree and what there is of a reflective tendency in his nature is intensified. One shudders at the thought of the meaning-lessness of life while at the same instant, and if the people of the town are his people, one loves life so intensely that tears come into the eyes.

In the darkness under the roof of the grandstand, George Willard sat beside Helen White and felt very keenly his own insignificance in the scheme of existence. Now that he had come out of town where the presence of the people stirring about, busy with a multitude of affairs, had been so irritating the irritation was all gone. The presence of Helen renewed and refreshed him. It was as though her woman's hand was assisting him to make some minute readjustment of the machinery of his life. He began to think of the people in the town where he had always lived with something like reverence. He had reverence for Helen. He wanted to love and to be loved by her, but he did not want at the moment to be confused by her womanhood. In the darkness he took hold of her hand and when she crept close put a hand on her shoulder. A wind began to blow and he shivered. With all his strength he tried to hold and to understand the mood that had come upon him. In that high place in the darkness the two oddly sensitive human atoms held each other tightly and waited. In the mind of each was the same thought. "I have come to this lonely place and here is this other," was the sub-stance of the thing felt.

In Winesburg the crowded day had run itself out into the long night of the late fall. Farm horses jogged away along lonely country roads pulling their portion of weary people. Clerks began to bring samples of goods in off the sidewalks and lock the doors of stores. In the Opera House a crowd had gathered to see a show and further down Main Street the fiddlers, their instruments tuned, sweated and worked to keep the feet of youth flying over a dance floor.

In the darkness in the grandstand Helen White and George Willard remained silent. Now and then the spell that held them was broken and they turned and tried in the dim light to see into each others eyes. They kissed but that impulse did not last. At the upper end of the fair ground a half dozen men worked over horses that had raced during the afternoon. The men had built a fire and were heating kettles of water. Only their legs could be seen as they passed back and forth in the light. When the wind blew the little flames of the fire danced crazily about.

George and Helen arose and walked away into the darkness. They went along a path past a field of corn that had not yet been cut. The wind whispered among the dry corn blades. For a moment during the walk back into town the spell that held them was broken. When they had come to the crest of Waterworks Hill they stopped by a tree and George again put his hands on the girl's shoulders. She embraced him eagerly and then again they drew quickly back from that impulse. They stopped kissing and stood a little apart. Mutual respect grew big in them. They were both embarrassed and to relieve their embarrassment dropped into the animalism of youth. They laughed and began to pull and haul at each other. In some way chastened and purified by the mood they had been in they became, not man and woman, not boy and girl, but excited little animals.

It was so they went down the hill. In the darkness they played like two splendid young things in a young world. Once, running swiftly forward, Helen tripped George and he fell. He squirmed and shouted. Shaking with laughter, he rolled down the hill. Helen ran after him. For just a moment she stopped in the darkness. There is no way of knowing what woman's thoughts went through her mind but, when the bottom of the hill was reached and she came up to the boy, she took his arm and walked beside him in dignified silence. For some reason they could not have explained they had both got from their silent evening together the thing needed. Man or boy, woman or girl, they had for a moment taken hold of the thing that makes the mature life of men and women in the modern world possible.

1919

Fiction Between the Wars

The most distinguished fiction of the years between the wars was written by men and women born in the 1890's who came of age in the decade of the First World War. In their early work most of them drew upon their experiences of the war years, whether at home or abroad. Much of their fiction reflects the spirit of disillusionment and alienation that T. S. Eliot had expressed in *The Waste Land* (1922). As the twenties gave way to the thirties, the individualism and the introspective temper of the postwar decade was supplanted by the growing social consciousness of the Depression years. The wounded hero of Hemingway's fiction, like the hollow man of Eliot's poetry, was replaced by the proletarian hero, or, in the collective novel, by a group or cast of characters who represent a cross section of society in the work of novelists like John Dos Passos and John Steinbeck.

In both decades, American fiction reveals a high level of craftsmanship, in keeping with the modernist emphasis on technique, and an impulse toward bold and often brilliant experimentation in form. In no other period of American literature have there been so many distinguished stylists in fiction. The work of F. Scott Fitzgerald and Katherine Anne Porter is especially revealing of unusual sensibility and distinction in language. Influenced

Hell Hole by John Sloane Courtesy of the Boston Public Library by the spontaneous conversational styles developed by Gertrude Stein and Sherwood Anderson, Ernest Hemingway developed a sensitive understated prose suited to the mood and outlook of his generation. Other writers, like Faulkner, experimented in unorthodox narrative methods approximating the multidimensional techniques of modern painting and sculpture. In the 1930's, still further innovations were developed by writers of collectivist novels to interrelate the treatment of individual and social concerns. The postwar tradition of surrealism, which had flourished in Europe, was exploited by Nathanael West in his brilliant satiric novels of the 1930's.

In choice of subject and setting, the writers of this period moved in two divergent directions. On the one hand, the war and its aftermath encouraged internationalism, as Hemingway, Fitzgerald, and others drew upon their experience of the war and of life in Europe, especially in Paris, to write cosmopolitan novels and stories. Among other members of the same generation there was a strong tendency toward regionalism, especially for Southerners like William Faulkner, Katherine Anne Porter, Thomas Wolfe, and the somewhat younger R. P. Warren. Recognizing that the sources of the problems of the South lay in the past, they incorporated in their work a probing of cultural roots (much like Nathaniel Hawthorne's earlier exploration of his Puritan heritage) in an effort to ascertain the relation of their present experience to the traditions of what Katherine Anne Porter called "the Old Order." Among the problems with which they were concerned, one of the most important (and one with implications reaching beyond regional boundaries) was that of the relation of the races and the status of the Negro in American society.

Besides figuring as subjects for fiction, black Americans were at the same time finding their voices as modern writers. There was a flowering of Negro writing, centered in New York, that began in the postwar decade. Even before writers like Countee Cullen and Langston Hughes won recognition for their poetry in the mid twenties, Jean Toomer broke ground for the movement in fiction with his *Cane* (1923), a book that influenced later writing about the Negro by both white and black authors. One of the most distinguished of these was Richard Wright, who followed the migrant route northward up the Mississippi Valley to Chicago and then east to New York, to write *Native Son* (1940) and *Black Boy* (1945), the two books singled out by LeRoi Jones as "the most completely valid social novels and social criticisms of South and North, non-urban and urban Negro life."

Ernest Hemingway   *1898—1961*

Ernest Hemingway was born the son of a physician in Oak Park, Illinois. Boyhood summers were spent hunting and fishing in northern Michigan, the setting of many of his later stories. After graduation from high school and rejection by the army because of an eye injury, he worked briefly as a cub reporter on the Kansas City *Star*. In 1918, he volunteered for the Red Cross ambulance service, went overseas, arranged a transfer to the Italian infantry, and was severely wounded in a mortar barrage near Fossalta di Piave. For Hemingway, war and such other primitive activities as big game hunting, bull-fighting, and prize fighting were to supply metaphors for a fictional world in which the individual's lot is existential loneliness and fear in the face of violence. After the war, he served as a foreign reporter and Graeco-Turkish war correspondent for the Toronto *Star*. Settling in Paris, where he got to know Ezra Pound, Gertrude Stein, and other literary expatriates. he began writing the stories that were to win him recognition as the spokesman of a generation. His early collections, *Three Stories and Ten Poems* (1923) and *In Our Time* (1925), contained stories, often drawn from boyhood experience, like "Up in Michigan," "Indian Camp," "My Old Man," and "Big Two-Hearted River." Insecurity, violence, and a necessary stoicism and tense acceptance are recurrent themes of narratives written in a conversational, understated, highly-selective style for which Hemingway was indebted to a considerable extent to Gertrude Stein and Sherwood Anderson. Hemingway characteristically repaid his debt to Anderson, whom he considered guilty of sentimentality, by writing a tasteless and forced satirical novel, *The Torrents of Spring* (1926), aimed most directly at Anderson's *Dark Laughter*. But the same year also saw the publication of his best, most tightly-crafted novel, *The Sun Also Rises* (1926), in which the sexually incapacitated hero, Jake Barnes, is a witness to the disorderly and futile lives of members of his own postwar generation. *A Farewell to Arms* (1929), which portrays the actuality rather than the aftermath of war, is a romantic story of the idyllic love, in the midst of destruction, of the American hero, Lieutenant Frederic Henry, for an English nurse who dies attempting to bear his child. Both novels are typical of Hemingway's viewpoint in their emphasis on sterility and on the impossibility of man's efforts to realize his dreams in the face of a destructive natural order. They also express a cosmic disappointment in the realization that there is nothing by way of a supernatural reality beyond the life of existential suffering. There is still, however, the responsibility of the superior individual to face the world of nothingness with courage and dignity and self-discipline. A ritualistic personal code, which has close affinities with the primitive disciplines of the hunt and the bullfight, thus takes the place of a lost religious ritual. For Hemingway as an artist, the practice of writing was also a necessary discipline by which one might impose some order on an essentially meaningless world.

During the 1930's, when he was living mostly in Key West, Hemingway wrote *Death in the Afternoon* (1932) and *The Green Hills of Africa* (1935), nonfictional works devoted to the arts of the bull-ring and the safari. *To Have and Have Not* (1937), a mediocre novel, shows the stirring of a new social consciousness. This was to be focused on the Loyalist cause in the Spanish Civil War, which Hemingway covered as a correspondent and which supplied fresh subjects for his writing. *The Fifth Column and the First Forty-nine Stories* (1938) includes several of his finest later stories. In *For Whom the Bell Tolls* (1940), his longest novel, the integrity of the hero, Robert Jordan, is given a dimension lacking in Hemingway's earlier war stories through his dedication to the Loyalist cause, even though he sees that cause betrayed in the conduct of the war. World War II provided the subject of his poorest novel, *Across the River and Into the Trees* (1950).

The best work of Hemingway's later years, when he was living in Cuba, was the novella *The Old Man and the Sea* (1952). Despite its too overt symbolism, this story of the endurance of the Cuban fisherman Santiago won great praise, and in 1954 Hemingway was belatedly awarded the Nobel Prize for "forceful and style-making mastery of the art of modern narration" — an eminently just, if somewhat awkward, pronouncement. Seriously ill and unable to write in his last years, Hemingway shot himself to death in his Ketchum, Idaho, home in 1961.

The posthumously published book of reminiscences of the youthful postwar years in Paris, *A Moveable Feast* (1964), is marred by Hemingway's ungenerous and malicious treatment of former friends and benefactors, like Ezra Pound, F. Scott Fitzgerald, Gertrude Stein, and Ford Madox Ford. Earlier collections of stories include *Men Without Women* (1927), *Winner Take Nothing* (1933), and *Men at War* (1942).

A helpful general introduction to Hemingway's work is R. P. Weeks, ed., *Hemingway: A Collection of Critical Essays* (Englewood Cliffs, N. J., 1962). The authorized biography is in preparation by Carlos Baker, who has already produced an informative critical biography in *Hemingway: The Writer as Artist* (Princeton, 1952; rev. 1956). Other more specialized critiques include C. A. Fenton, *The Apprenticeship of Ernest Hemingway: The Early Years* (New York, 1958) and Philip Young, *Ernest Hemingway: A Reconsideration*, revised ed. (University Park, Pa., 1966), a psychological analysis of Hemingway's life and work. The most complete bibliography is Audre Hanneman's thorough and accurately titled work, *Ernest Hemingway: A Comprehensive Bibliography* (Princeton, 1967).

The text of "Big Two-Hearted River" is that of *The Fifth Column and the First Forty-nine Stories* (New York, 1938).

Big Two-Hearted River

1

The train went on up the track out of sight, around one of the hills of burnt timber. Nick sat down on the bundle of canvas and bedding the baggage man had pitched out of the door of the baggage car. There was no town, nothing but the rails and the burned-over country. The thirteen saloons that had lined the one street of Seney had not left a trace. The foundations of the Mansion House hotel stuck up above the ground. The stone was chipped and split by the fire. It was all that was left of the town of Seney. Even the surface had been burned off the ground.

Nick looked at the burned-over stretch of hillside, where he had expected to find the scattered houses of the town and then walked down the railroad track to the bridge over the river. The river was there. It swirled against the log spiles of the bridge. Nick looked down into the clear, brown water, colored from the pebbly bottom, and watched the trout keeping themselves steady in the current with wavering fins. As he watched them they changed their positions by quick angles, only to hold steady in the fast water again. Nick watched them a long time.

He watched them holding themselves with their noses into the current, many trout in deep, fast moving water, slightly distorted as he watched far down through the glassy convex surface of the pool, its surface pushing and swelling smooth against the resistance of the log-driven piles of the bridge. At the bottom of the pool were the big trout. Nick did not see them at first. Then he saw them at the bottom of the pool, big trout looking to hold themselves on the gravel bottom in a varying mist of gravel and sand, raised in spurts by the current.

Nick looked down into the pool from the bridge. It was a hot day. A kingfisher flew up the stream. It was a long time since Nick had looked into a stream and seen trout. They were very satisfactory. As the shadow of the kingfisher moved up the stream, a big trout shot upstream in a long angle, only his shadow marking the angle, then lost his shadow as he came through the surface of the water, caught the sun, and then, as he went back into the stream under the surface, his shadow seemed to float down the stream with the current, unresisting, to his post under the bridge where he tightened facing up into the current.

Nick's heart tightened as the trout moved. He felt all the old feeling.

He turned and looked down the stream. It stretched away, pebbly-bottomed with shallows and big boulders and a deep pool as it curved away around the foot of a bluff.

Nick walked back up the ties to where his pack lay in the cinders beside the railway track. He was happy. He adjusted the pack harness around the bundle, pulling straps tight, slung the pack on his back, got his arms through the shoulder straps and took some of the pull off his shoulders by leaning his forehead against the wide band of the tump-line. Still, it was too heavy. It was much too heavy. He had his leather rod-case in his hand and leaning forward to keep the weight of the pack high on his shoulders he walked along the road that paralleled the railway track, leaving the burned town behind in the heat, and then turned off around a hill with a high, fire-scarred hill on either side onto a road that went back into the country. He walked along the road feeling the ache from the pull of the heavy pack. The road climbed steadily. It was hard work walking up-hill. His muscles ached and the day was hot, but Nick felt happy. He felt he had left everything behind, the need for thinking, the need to write, other needs. It was all back of him.

From the time he had gotten down off the train and the baggage man had thrown his pack out of the open car door things had been different. Seney was burned, the country was burned over and changed, but it did not matter. It could not all be burned. He knew that. He hiked along the road, sweating in the sun, climbing to cross the range of hills that separated the railway from the pine plains.

The road ran on, dipping occasionally, but always climbing. Nick went on up. Finally the road after going parallel to the burnt hillside reached the top. Nick leaned back against a stump and slipped out of the pack harness. Ahead of him, as far as he could see, was the pine plain. The burned country stopped off at the left with the range of hills. On ahead islands of dark pine trees rose out of the plain. Far off to the left was the line of the river. Nick followed it with his eye and caught glints of the water in the sun.

There was nothing but the pine plain ahead of him, until the far blue hills that marked the Lake Superior height of land. He could hardly see them, faint and far away in the heat-light over the plain. If he looked too steadily they were gone. But if he only half-looked they were there, the far-off hills of the height of land.

Nick sat down against the charred stump and smoked a cigarette. His pack balanced on the top of the stump, harness holding ready, a hollow molded in it from his back. Nick sat smoking, looking out over the country. He did not need to get his map out. He knew where he was from the position of the river.

As he smoked, his legs stretched out in front of him, he noticed a grasshopper walk along the ground and up onto his woolen sock. The grasshopper was black. As he had walked along the road, climbing, he had started many grasshoppers from the dust. They were all black. They were not the big grasshoppers with yellow and black or red and black wings whirring out from their black wing sheathing as they fly up. These were just ordinary hoppers, but all a sooty black in color. Nick had wondered about them as he walked, without really thinking about them. Now, as he watched the black hopper that was nibbling at the wool of his sock with its fourway lip, he realized that they had all turned black from living in the burned-over land. He realized that the fire must have come the year before, but the grasshoppers were all black now. He wondered how long they would stay that way.

Carefully he reached his hand down and took hold of the hopper by the wings. He turned him up, all his legs walking in the air, and looked at his jointed belly. Yes, it was black too, iridescent where the back and head were dusty.

"Go on, hopper," Nick said, speaking out loud for the first time. "Fly away somewhere."

He tossed the grasshopper up into the air and watched him sail away to a charcoal stump across the road.

Nick stood up. He leaned his back against the weight of his pack where it rested upright on the stump and got his arms through the shoulder straps. He stood with the pack on his back on the brow of the hill looking out across the country, toward the distant river and then struck down the hillside away from the road. Underfoot the ground was good walking. Two hundred yards down the hillside the fire line stopped. Then it was sweet fern, growing ankle high, to walk through, and clumps of jack pines; a long undulating country with frequent rises and descents, sandy underfoot and the country alive again.

Nick kept his direction by the sun. He knew where he wanted to strike the river and he kept on through the pine plain, mounting small rises to see other rises ahead of him and sometimes from the top of a rise a great solid island of pines off to his right or his left. He broke off some sprigs of the heathery sweet fern, and put them under his pack straps. The chafing crushed it and he smelled it as he walked.

He was tired and very hot, walking across the uneven, shadeless pine plain. At any time he knew he could strike the river by turning off to his left. It could not be more than a mile away. But he kept on toward the north to hit the river as far upstream as he could go in one day's walking.

For some time as he walked Nick had been in sight of one of the big islands of pine standing out above the rolling high ground he was crossing. He dipped down and then as he came slowly up to the crest of the ridge he turned and made toward the pine trees.

There was no underbrush in the island of pine trees. The trunks of the trees were straight up or slanted toward each other. The trunks were straight and brown without branches. The branches were high above. Some interlocked to make a solid shadow on the brown forest floor. Around the grove of trees was a bare space. It was brown and soft underfoot as Nick walked on it. This was the over-lapping of the pine needle floor, extending out beyond the width of the high branches. The trees had grown tall and the branches moved high, leaving in the sun this bare space they had once covered with shadow. Sharp at the edge of this extension of the forest floor commenced the sweet fern.

Nick slipped off his pack and lay down in the shade. He lay on his back and looked up into the pine trees. His neck and back and the small of his back rested as he stretched. The earth felt good against his back. He looked up at the sky, through the branches, and then shut his eyes. He opened them and looked up again. There was a wind high up in the branches. He shut his eyes again and went to sleep.

Nick woke stiff and cramped. The sun was nearly down. His pack was heavy and the straps painful as he lifted it on. He leaned over with the pack on and picked up the leather rod-case and started out from the pine trees across the sweet fern swale, toward the river. He knew it could not be more than a mile.

He came down a hillside covered with stumps into a meadow. At the edge of the meadow flowed the river. Nick was glad to get to the river. He walked upstream through the meadow. His trousers were soaked with the dew as he walked. After the hot day, the dew had come quickly and heavily. The river made no sound. It was too fast and smooth. At the edge of the meadow, before he mounted to a piece of high ground to make camp, Nick looked down the river at the trout rising. They were rising to insects come from the swamp on the other side of the stream when the sun went down. The trout jumped out of water to take them. While Nick walked through the little stretch of meadow alongside the stream, trout had jumped high out of water. Now as he looked down the river, the insects must be settling on the surface, for the trout were feeding steadily all down the stream. As far down the long stretch as he could see, the trout were rising, making circles all down the surface of the water, as though it were starting to rain.

The ground rose, wooded and sandy, to overlook the meadow, the stretch of river and the swamp. Nick dropped his pack and rod-case and looked for a level piece of ground. He was very hungry and he wanted to make his camp before he cooked. Between two jack pines, the ground was quite level. He took the ax out of the pack and chopped out two projecting roots. That leveled a piece of ground large enough to sleep on. He smoothed out the sandy soil with his hand and pulled all the sweet fern bushes by their roots. His hands smelled good from the sweet fern. He smoothed the uprooted earth. He did not want anything making lumps under the blankets. When he had the ground smooth, he spread his three blankets. One he folded double, next to the ground. The other two he spread on top.

With the ax he slit off a bright slab of pine from one of the stumps and split it into pegs for the tent. He wanted them long and solid to hold in the ground. With the tent unpacked and spread on the ground, the pack, leaning against a jackpine, looked much smaller. Nick tied the rope that served the tent for a ridge-pole to the trunk of one of the pine trees and pulled the tent up off the ground with the other end of the rope and tied it to the other pine. The tent hung on the rope like a canvas blanket on a clothesline. Nick poked a pole he had cut up under the back peak of the canvas and then made it a tent by pegging out the sides. He pegged the sides out taut and drove the pegs deep, hitting them down into the ground with the flat of the ax until the rope loops were buried and the canvas was drum tight.

Across the open mouth of the tent Nick fixed cheesecloth to keep out mosquitoes. He crawled inside under the mosquito bar with various things from the pack to put at the head of the bed under the slant of the canvas. Inside the tent the light came through the brown canvas. It smelled pleasantly of canvas. Already there was something mysterious and homelike. Nick was happy as he crawled inside the tent. He had not been unhappy all day. This was different though. Now things were done. There had been this to do. Now it was done. It had been a hard trip. He was very tired. That was done. He had made his camp. He was settled. Nothing could touch him. It was a good place to camp. He was there, in the good place. He was in his home where he had made it. Now he was hungry.

He came out, crawling under the cheesecloth. It was quite dark outside. It was lighter in the tent.

Nick went over to the pack and found, with his fingers, a long nail in a paper sack of nails, in the bottom of the pack. He drove it into the pine tree, holding it close and hitting it gently with the flat of the ax. He hung the pack up on the nail. All his supplies were in the pack. They were off the ground and sheltered now.

Nick was hungry. He did not believe he had ever been hungrier. He opened and emptied a can of pork and beans and a can of spaghetti into the frying pan.

"I've got a right to eat this kind of stuff, if I'm willing to carry it," Nick said. His voice sounded strange in the darkening woods. He did not speak again.

He started a fire with some chunks of pine he got with the ax from a stump. Over the fire he stuck a wire grill, pushing the four legs down into the ground with his boot. Nick put the frying pan on the grill over the flames. He was hungrier. The beans and spaghetti warmed.

Nick stirred them and mixed them together. They began to bubble, making little bubbles that rose with difficulty to the surface. There was a good smell. Nick got out a bottle of tomato catchup and cut four slices of bread. The little bubbles were coming faster now. Nick sat down beside the fire and lifted the frying pan off. He poured about half the contents out into the tin plate. It spread slowly on the plate. Nick knew it was too hot. He poured on some tomato catchup. He knew the beans and spaghetti were still too hot. He looked at the fire, then at the tent, he was not going to spoil it all by burning his tongue. For years he had never enjoyed fried bananas because he had never been able to wait for them to cool. His tongue was very sensitive. He was very hungry. Across the river in the swamp, in the almost dark, he saw a mist rising. He looked at the tent once more. All right. He took a full spoonful from the plate.

"Chrise," Nick said, "Geezus Chrise," he said happily.

He ate the whole plateful before he remembered the bread. Nick finished the second plateful with the bread, mopping the plate shiny. He had not eaten since a cup of coffee and a ham sandwich in the station restaurant at St. Ignace. It had been a very fine experience. He had been that hungry before, but had not been able to satisfy it. He could have made camp hours before if he had wanted to. There were plenty of good places to camp on the river. But this was good.

Nick tucked two big chips of pine under the grill. The fire flared up. He had forgotten to get water for the coffee. Out of the pack he got a folding canvas bucket and walked down the hill, across the edge of the meadow, to the stream. The other bank was in the white mist. The grass was wet and cold as he knelt on the bank and dipped the canvas bucket into the stream. It bellied and pulled hard in the current. The water was ice cold. Nick rinsed the bucket and carried it full up to the camp. Up away from the stream it was not so cold.

Nick drove another big nail and hung up the bucket full of water. He dipped the coffee pot half full, put some more chips under the grill onto the fire and put the pot on. He could not remember which way he made coffee. He could remember an argument about it with Hopkins, but not which side he had taken. He decided to bring it to a boil. He remembered now that was Hopkins's way. He had once argued about everything with Hopkins. While he waited for the coffee to boil, he opened a small can of apricots. He liked to open cans. He emptied the can of apricots out into a tin cup. While he watched the coffee on the fire, he drank the juice syrup of the apricots, carefully at first to keep from spilling, then meditatively, sucking the apricots down. They were better than fresh apricots.

The coffee boiled as he watched. The lid came up and coffee and grounds ran down the side of the pot. Nick took it off the grill. It was a triumph for Hopkins. He put sugar in the empty apricot cup and poured some of the coffee out to cool. It was too hot to pour and he used his hat to hold the handle of the coffee pot. He would not let it steep in the pot at all. Not the first cup. It should be straight Hopkins all the way. Hop deserved that. He was a very serious coffee maker. He was the most serious man Nick had ever known. Not heavy, serious. That was a long time ago. Hopkins spoke without moving his lips. He had played polo. He made millions of dollars in Texas. He had borrowed carfare to go to Chicago, when the wire came that his first big well had come in. He could have wired for money. That would have been too slow. They called Hop's girl the Blonde Venus. Hop did not mind because she was not his real girl. Hopkins said very confidently that none of them would make fun of his real girl. He was right. Hopkins went away when the telegram came. That was on the Black River. It took eight days for the telegram to reach him. Hopkins gave away his .22 caliber Colt automatic pistol to Nick. He gave his camera to Bill. It was to remember him always by. They were all going fishing again next summer. The Hop Head was rich. He would get a yacht and they would all cruise along the north shore of Lake Superior. He was excited but serious. They said good-bye and all felt bad. It broke up the trip. They never saw Hopkins again. That was a long time ago on the Black River.

Nick drank the coffee, the coffee according to Hopkins. The coffee was bitter. Nick laughed. It made a good ending to the story. His mind was starting to work. He knew he could choke it because he was tired enough. He spilled the coffee out of the pot and shook the grounds loose into the fire. He lit a cigarette and went inside the tent. He took off his shoes and trousers, sitting on the blankets, rolled the shoes up inside the trousers for a pillow and got in between the blankets.

Out through the front of the tent he watched the glow of the fire, when the night wind blew on it. It was a quiet night. The swamp was perfectly quiet. Nick stretched under the blanket comfortably. A mosquito hummed close to his ear. Nick sat up and lit a match. The mosquito was on the canvas, over his head. Nick moved the match quickly up to it. The mosquito made a satisfactory hiss in the flame. The match went out. Nick lay down again under the blanket. He turned on his side and shut his eyes. He was sleepy. He felt sleep coming. He curled up under the blanket and went to sleep.

2

In the morning the sun was up and the tent was starting to get hot. Nick crawled out under the mosquito netting stretched across the mouth of the tent, to look at the morning. The grass was wet on his hands as he came out. He held his trousers and his shoes in his hands. The sun was just up over the hill. There was the meadow, the river and the swamp. There were birch trees in the green of the swamp on the other side of the river.

The river was clear and smoothly fast in the early morning. Down about two hundred yards were three logs all the way across the stream. They made the water smooth and deep above them. As Nick watched, a mink crossed the river on the logs and went into the swamp. Nick was excited. He was excited by the early morning and the river. He was really too hurried to eat breakfast, but he knew he must: He built a little fire and put on the coffee pot.

While the water was heating in the pot he took an empty bottle and went down over the edge of the high ground to the meadow. The meadow was wet with dew and Nick wanted to catch grasshoppers for bait before the sun dried the grass. He found plenty of good grasshoppers. They were at the base of the grass stems. Sometimes they clung to a grass stem. They were cold and wet with the dew, and could not jump until the sun warmed them. Nick picked them up, taking only the medium-sized brown ones, and put them into the bottle. He turned over a log and just under the shelter of the edge were several hundred hoppers. It was a grasshopper lodging house. Nick put about fifty of the medium browns into the bottle. While he was picking up the hoppers the others warmed in the sun and commenced to hop away. They flew when they hopped. At first they made one flight and stayed stiff when they landed, as though they were dead.

Nick knew that by the time he was through with breakfast they would be as lively as ever. Without dew in the grass it would take him all day to catch a bottle full of good grasshoppers and he would have to crush many of them, slamming at them with his hat. He washed his hands at the stream. He was excited to be near it. Then he walked up to the tent. The hoppers were already jumping stiffly in the grass. In the bottle, warmed by the sun, they were jumping in a mass. Nick put in a pine stick as a cork. It plugged the mouth of the bottle enough, so the hoppers could not get out and left plenty of air passage.

He had rolled the log back and knew he could get grasshoppers there every morning.

Nick laid the bottle full of jumping grasshoppers against a pine trunk. Rapidly he mixed some buckwheat flour with water and stirred it smooth, one cup of flour, one cup of water. He put a handful of coffee in the pot and dipped a lump of grease out of a can and slid it sputtering across the hot skillet. On the smoking skillet he poured smoothly the buckwheat batter. It spread like lava, the grease spitting sharply. Around the edges the buckwheat cake began to firm, then brown, then crisp. The surface was bubbling slowly to porousness. Nick pushed under the browned under surface with a fresh pine chip. He shook the skillet sideways and the cake was loose on the surface. I won't try and flop it, he thought. He slid the chip of clean wood all the way under the cake, and flopped it over onto its face. It sputtered in the pan.

When it was cooked Nick regreased the skillet. He used all the batter. It made another big flapjack and a smaller one.

Nick ate a big flapjack and a smaller one, covered with apple butter. He put apple butter on the third cake, folded it over twice, wrapped it in oiled paper and put it in his shirt pocket. He put the apple butter jar back in the pack and cut bread for two sandwiches.

In the pack he found a big onion. He sliced it in two and peeled the silky outer skin. Then he cut one half into slices and made onion sandwiches. He wrapped them in oiled paper and buttoned them in the other pocket of his khaki shirt. He turned the skillet upside down on the grill, drank the coffee, sweetened and yellow brown with the condensed milk in it, and tidied up the camp. It was a good camp.

Nick took his fly rod out of the leather rod-case, jointed it, and shoved the rod-case back into the tent. He put on the reel and threaded the line through the guides. He had to hold it from hand to hand, as he threaded it, or it would slip back through its own weight. It was a heavy, double tapered fly line. Nick had paid eight dollars for it a long time ago. It was made heavy to lift back in the air and come forward flat and heavy and straight to make it possible to cast a fly which has no weight. Nick opened the aluminum leader box. The leaders were coiled between the damp flannel pads. Nick had wet the pads at the water cooler on the train up to St. Ignace. In the damp pads the gut leaders had softened and Nick unrolled one and tied it by a loop at the end to the heavy fly line. He fastened a hook on the end of the leader. It was a small hook; very thin and springy.

Nick took it from his hook book, sitting with the rod across his lap. He tested the knot and the spring of the rod by pulling the line taut. It was a good feeling. He was careful not to let the hook bite into his finger.

He started down to the stream, holding his rod, the bottle of grasshoppers hung from his neck by a thong tied in half hitches around the neck of the bottle. His landing net hung by a hook from his belt. Over his shoulder was a long flour sack tied at each corner into an ear. The cord went over his shoulder. The sack flapped against his legs.

Nick felt awkward and professionally happy with all his equipment hanging from him. The grasshopper bottle swung against his chest. In his shirt the breast pockets bulged against him with the lunch and his fly book.

He stepped into the stream. It was a shock. His trousers clung tight to his legs. His shoes felt the gravel. The water was a rising cold shock.

Rushing, the current sucked against his legs. Where he stepped in, the water was over his knees. He waded with the current. The gravel slid under his shoes. He looked down at the swirl of water below each leg and tipped up the bottle to get a grasshopper.

The first grasshopper gave a jump in the neck of the bottle and went out into the water. He was sucked under in the whirl by Nick's right leg and came to the surface a little way down stream. He floated rapidly, kicking. In a quick circle, breaking the smooth surface of the water, he disappeared. A trout had taken him.

Another hopper poked his face out of the bottle. His antennae wavered. He was getting his front legs out of the bottle to jump. Nick took him by the head and held him while he threaded the slim hook under his chin, down through his thorax and into the last segments of his abdomen. The grasshopper took hold of the hook with his front feet, spitting tobacco juice on it. Nick dropped him into the water.

Holding the rod in his right hand he let out line against the pull of the grasshopper in the current. He stripped off line from the reel with his left hand and let it run free. He could see the hopper in the little waves of the current. It went out of sight.

There was a tug on the line. Nick pulled against the taut line. It was his first strike. Holding the now living rod across the current, he brought in the line with his left hand. The rod bent in jerks, the trout pumping against the current. Nick knew it was a small one. He lifted the rod straight up in the air. It bowed with the pull.

He saw the trout in the water jerking with his head and body against the shifting tangent of the line in the stream.

Nick took the line in his left hand and pulled the trout, thumping tiredly against the current, to the surface. His back was mottled the clear, water-over-gravel color, his side flashing in the sun. The rod under his right arm, Nick stooped, dipping his right hand into the current. He held the trout, never still, with his moist right hand, while he unhooked the barb from his mouth, then dropped him back into the stream.

He hung unsteadily in the current, then settled to the bottom beside a stone. Nick reached down his hand to touch him, his arm to the elbow under water. The trout was steady in the moving stream, resting on the gravel, beside a stone. As Nick's fingers touched him, touched his smooth, cool, underwater feeling he was gone, gone in a shadow across the bottom of the stream.

He's all right, Nick thought. He was only tired.

He had wet his hand before he touched the trout, so he would not disturb the delicate mucus that covered him. If a trout was touched with a dry hand, a white fungus attacked the unprotected spot. Years before when he had fished crowded streams, with fly fishermen ahead of him and behind him, Nick had again and again come on dead trout, furry with white fungus, drifted against a rock, or floating belly up in some pool. Nick did not like to fish with other men on the river. Unless they were of your party, they spoiled it.

He wallowed down the stream, above his knees in the current, through the fifty yards of shallow water above the pile of logs that crossed the stream. He did not rebait his hook and held it in his hand as he waded. He was certain he could catch small trout in the shallows, but he did not want them. There would be no big trout in the shallows this time of day.

Now the water deepened up his thighs sharply and coldly. Ahead was the smooth dammed-back flood of water above the logs. The water was smooth and dark; on the left, the lower edge of the meadow; on the right the swamp.

Nick leaned back against the current and took a hopper from the bottle. He threaded the hopper on the hook and spat on him for good luck. Then he pulled several yards of line from the reel and tossed the hopper out ahead onto the fast, dark water. It floated down towards the logs, then the weight of the line pulled the bait under the surface. Nick held the rod in his right hand, letting the line run out through his fingers.

There was a long tug. Nick struck and the rod came alive and dangerous, bent double, the line tightening, coming out of water, tightening, all in a heavy, dangerous, steady pull. Nick felt the moment when the leader would break if the strain increased and let the line go.

The reel ratcheted into a mechanical shriek as the line was out in a rush. Too fast. Nick could not check it, the line rushing out, the reel note rising as the line ran out.

With the core of the reel showing, his heart feeling stopped with the excitement, leaning back against the current that mounted icily his thighs, Nick thumbed the reel hard with his left hand. It was awkward getting his thumb inside the fly reel frame.

As he put on pressure the line tightened into sudden hardness and beyond the logs a huge trout went high out of water. As he jumped, Nick lowered the tip of the rod. But he felt, as he dropped the tip to ease the strain, the moment when the strain was too great; the hardness too tight. Of course, the leader had broken. There was no mistaking the feeling when all spring left the line and it became dry and hard. Then it went slack.

His mouth dry, his heart down, Nick reeled in. He had never seen so big a trout. There was a heaviness, a power not to be held, and then the bulk of him, as he jumped. He looked as broad as a salmon.

Nick's hand was shaky. He reeled in slowly. The thrill had been too much. He felt, vaguely, a little sick, as though it would be better to sit down.

The leader had broken where the hook was tied to it. Nick took it in his hand. He thought of the trout somewhere on the bottom, holding himself steady over the gravel, far down below the light, under the logs, with the hook in his jaw. Nick knew the trout's teeth would cut through the snell of the hook. The hook would imbed itself in his jaw. He'd bet the trout was angry. Anything that size would be angry. That was a trout. He had been solidly hooked. Solid as a rock. He felt like a rock, too, before he started off. By God, he was a big one. By God, he was the biggest one I ever heard of.

Nick climbed out onto the meadow and stood, water running down his trousers and out of his shoes, his shoes squelchy. He went over and sat on the logs. He did not want to rush his sensations any.

He wriggled his toes in the water, in his shoes, and got out a cigarette from his breast pocket. He lit it and tossed the match into the fast water below the logs. A tiny trout rose at the match, as it swung around in the fast current. Nick laughed. He would finish the cigarette.

He sat on the logs, smoking, drying in the sun, the sun warm on his back, the river shallow ahead entering the woods, curving into the woods, shallows, light glittering, big water-smooth rocks, cedars along the bank and white birches, the logs warm in the sun, smooth to sit on, without bark, gray to the touch; slowly the feeling of disappointment left him. It went away slowly, the feeling of disappointment that came sharply after the thrill that made his shoulders ache. It was all right now. His rod lying out on the logs, Nick tied a new hook on the leader, pulling the gut tight until it grimped into itself in a hard knot.

He baited up, then picked up the rod and walked to the far end of the logs to get into the water, where it was not too deep. Under and beyond the logs was a deep pool. Nick walked around the shallow shelf near the swamp shore until he came out on the shallow bed of the stream.

On the left, where the meadow ended and the woods began, a great elm tree was uprooted. Gone over in a storm, it lay back into the woods, its roots clotted with dirt, grass growing in them, rising a solid bank beside the stream. The river cut to the edge of the uprooted tree. From where Nick stood he could see deep channels, like ruts, cut in the shallow bed of the stream by the flow of the current. Pebbly where he stood and pebbly and full of boulders beyond; where it curved near the tree roots, the bed of the stream was marly and between the ruts of deep water green weed fronds swung in the current.

Nick swung the rod back over his shoulder and forward, and the line, curving forward, laid the grasshopper down on one of the deep channels in the weeds. A trout struck and Nick hooked him.

Holding the rod far out toward the uprooted tree and sloshing backward in the current, Nick worked the trout, plunging, the rod bending alive, out of the danger of the weeds into the open river. Holding the rod, pumping alive against the current, Nick brought the trout in. He rushed, but always came, the spring of the rod yielding to the rushes, sometimes jerking under water, but always bringing him in. Nick eased downstream with the rushes. The rod above his head he led the trout over the net, then lifted.

The trout hung heavy in the net, mottled trout back and silver sides in the meshes. Nick unhooked him; heavy sides, good to hold, big undershot jaw, and slipped him, heaving and big sliding, into the long sack that hung from his shoulders in the water.

Nick spread the mouth of the sack against the current and it filled, heavy with water. He held it up, the bottom in the stream, and the water poured through the sides. Inside at the bottom was the big trout, alive in the water.

Nick moved downstream. The sack out ahead of him sunk heavy in the water, pulling from his shoulders.

It was getting hot, the sun hot on the back of his neck.

Nick had one good trout. He did not care about getting many trout. Now the stream was shallow and wide. There were trees along both banks. The trees of the left bank made short shadows on the current in the forenoon sun. Nick knew there were trout in each shadow. In the afternoon, after the sun had crossed toward the hills, the trout would be in the cool shadows on the other side of the stream.

The very biggest ones would lie up close to the bank. You could always pick them up there on the Black. When the sun was down they all moved out into the current. Just when the sun made the water blinding in the glare before it went down, you were liable to strike a big trout anywhere in the current. It was almost impossible to fish then, the surface of the water was blinding as a mirror in the sun. Of course, you could fish upstream, but in a stream like the Black, or this, you had to wallow against the current and in a deep place, the water piled up on you. It was no fun to fish upstream with this much current.

Nick moved along through the shallow stretch watching the banks for deep holes. A beech tree grew close beside the river, so that the branches hung down into the water. The stream went back in under the leaves. There were always trout in a place like that.

Nick did not care about fishing that hole. He was sure he would get hooked in the branches.

It looked deep though. He dropped the grasshopper so the current took it under water, back in under the overhanging branch. The line pulled hard and Nick struck. The trout threshed heavily, half out of water in the leaves and branches. The line was caught. Nick pulled hard and the trout was off. He reeled in and holding the hook in his hand, walked down the stream.

Ahead, close to the left bank, was a big log. Nick saw it was hollow; pointing up river the current entered it smoothly, only a little ripple spread each side of the log. The water was deepening. The top of the hollow log was gray and dry. It was partly in the shadow.

Nick took the cork out of the grasshopper bottle and a hopper clung to it. He picked him off, hooked him and tossed him out. He held the rod far out so that the hopper on the water moved into the current flowing into the hollow log. Nick lowered the rod and the hopper floated in. There was a heavy strike. Nick swung the rod against the pull.

It felt as though he were hooked into the log itself, except for the live feeling.

He tried to force the fish out into the current. It came, heavily.

The line went slack and Nick thought the trout was gone. Then he saw him, very near, in the current, shaking his head, trying to get the hook out. His mouth was clamped shut. He was fighting the hook in the clear flowing current.

Looping in the line with his left hand, Nick swung the rod to make the line taut and tried to lead the trout toward the net, but he was gone, out of sight, the line pumping. Nick fought him against the current, letting him thump in the water against the spring of the rod. He shifted the rod to his left hand, worked the trout upstream, holding his weight, fighting on the rod, and then let him down into the net. He lifted him clear of the water, a heavy half circle in the net, the net dripping, unhooked him and slid him into the sack.

He spread the mouth of the sack and looked down in at the two big trout alive in the water.

Through the deepening water, Nick waded over to the hollow log. He took the sack off, over his head, the trout flopping as it came out of water, and hung it so the trout were deep in the water. Then he pulled himself up on the log and sat, the water from his trousers and boots running down into the stream. He laid his rod down, moved along to the shady end of the log and took the sandwiches out of his pocket. He dipped the sandwiches in the cold water. The current carried away the crumbs. He ate the sandwiches and dipped his hat full of water to drink, the water running out through his hat just ahead of his drinking.

It was cool in the shade, sitting on the log. He took a cigarette out and struck a match to light it. The match sunk into the gray wood, making a tiny furrow. Nick leaned over the side of the log, found a hard place and lit the match. He sat smoking and watching the river.

Ahead the river narrowed and went into a swamp. The river became smooth and deep and the swamp looked solid with cedar trees, their trunks close together, their branches solid. It would not be possible to walk through a swamp like that. The branches grew so low. You would have to keep almost level with the ground to move at all. You could not crash through the branches. That must be why the animals that lived in swamps were built the way they were, Nick thought.

He wished he had brought something to read. He felt like reading. He did not feel like going on into the swamp. He looked down the river. A big cedar slanted all the way across the stream. Beyond that the river went into the swamp.

Nick did not want to go in there now. He felt a reaction against deep wading with the water deepening up under his armpits, to hook big trout in places impossible to land them. In the swamp the banks were bare, the big cedars came together overhead, the sun did not come through, except in patches; in the fast deep water, in the half light, the fishing would be tragic. In the swamp fishing was a tragic adventure. Nick did not want it. He did not want to go down the stream any further today.

He took out his knife, opened it and stuck it in the log. Then he pulled up the sack, reached into it and brought out one of the trout. Holding him near the tail, hard to hold, alive, in his hand, he whacked him against the log. The trout quivered, rigid. Nick laid him on the log in the shade and broke the neck of the other fish the same way. He laid them side by side on the log. They were fine trout.

Nick cleaned them, slitting them from the vent to the tip of the jaw. All the insides and the gills and tongue came out in one piece. They were both males; long gray-white strips of milt, smooth and clean. All the insides clean and compact, coming out all together. Nick tossed the offal ashore for the minks to find.

He washed the trout in the stream. When he held them back up in the water they looked like live fish. Their color was not gone yet. He washed his hands and dried them on the log. Then he laid the trout on the sack spread out on the log, rolled them up in it, tied the bundle and put it in the landing net. His knife was still standing, blade stuck in the log. He cleaned it on the wood and put it in his pocket.

Nick stood up on the log, holding his rod, the landing net hanging heavy, then stepped into the water and splashed ashore. He climbed the bank and cut up into the woods, toward the high ground. He was going back to camp. He looked back. The river just showed through the trees. There were plenty of days coming when he could fish the swamp.

1925

F. Scott Fitzgerald   *1896–1940*

Chronicler of the "jazz age" and a distinguished stylist, Francis Scott Key Fitzgerald was born in St. Paul, Minnesota. After attending public schools and a Catholic preparatory school in New Jersey, he entered Princeton University in 1913. More interested in dramatics and a gay social life than in his studies, he wrote Triangle Club shows in collaboration with his friend Edmund Wilson. After an interrupted academic career, he left Princeton in 1917. During the war he received a commission as second lieutenant in the Army and was sent south to Camp Sheridan, where he fell in love with Zelda Sayre, the daughter of an Alabama judge. Back in civilian life after the war, but unable to marry until he attained financial security, Fitzgerald worked in advertising in New York until the publication of his first novel, *This Side of Paradise* (1920). Based largely on his life at Princeton, the book told the story of the lives and loves of its romantic, egoistic hero, Amory Blaine. The novel captured the imagination of young readers and helped to create a ready market for the many stories of modern youth Fitzgerald was to write during the 1920's. It also made it possible for him to marry Zelda and embark upon a honeymoon that was to extend itself into decade-long champagne and cocktail party that carried the celebrants of youth and beauty and success from the suburbs of New York to Paris and the French Riviera. What is remarkable is that the youthful author, while living the life of an international playboy, was able to achieve so high a level of quality in the many stories he wrote—and also that he was able to see the darker side as well as the glitter of the life in which he was involved. Besides the inferior second novel, *The Beautiful and Damned* (1922), short stories written during these years were collected in *Flappers and Philosophers* (1920), *Tales of the Jazz Age* (1922), and *All the Sad Young Men* (1926), with its stories of the blighted lives of youthful heroes like Dexter Green of

"Winter Dreams." At the midpoint of the decade, Fitzgerald published his finest novel. *The Great Gatsby* (1925) tells the story of its hero's obsessional love for beautiful and wealthy Daisy Buchanan. Economically written in impressionistic, often poetic prose, the novel reveals Fitzgerald's sensitivity to the moral isolation and the destructiveness as well as the glamor of the life of the American rich. In contrast to the corrupt Buchanans and their like, the hero Jay Gatsby, though he becomes a gangster in his effort to attain his dream, is treated sympathetically, as "worth the whole damn bunch put together," for his generosity and his idealism, misguided though it is.

Fitzgerald's popularity and his success ended with the decade of the twenties, as the crash of 1929 and the ensuing depression shook the foundations of modern Babylon. During the 1930's his productivity declined as his personal life was darkened by Zelda's insanity and his own illness and alcoholism. The somberness of the stories of *Taps at Reveille* (1935) reflects the new mood of regret and disillusionment. The failure of *Tender Is the Night* (1934), Fitzgerald's most ambitious novel, is symptomatic of its author's plight. Because it dealt with the life of the idle rich in an international setting it was received coldly by most critics, who from a liberal or radical viewpoint, were concerned primarily with pressing social and economic problems. They failed to take note of the fact that this novel of the thirties, in addition to other virtues, represented an indictment of American capitalistic culture as powerful as any set forth in the proletarian fiction of the decade.

Recognizing his altered circumstances, Fitzgerald went to Los Angeles in 1937 and spent the short remainder of his life as a screen writer—at the same time continuing his own work. The semiautobiographical Pat Hobby stories are a product of these years. When he died suddenly of a heart attack in 1940, he was working on *The Last Tycoon*, a novel of Hollywood that showed him to be still a master of his craft. Although his books were out of print and the public had largely written him off as a has-been, he was working courageously to justify himself as a writer. He died without knowing how high a place he had earned.

Posthumously published works include *The Last Tycoon: An Unfinished* Novel, ed. Edmund Wilson (New York, 1941); *The Crack-Up,* ed. Edmund Wilson (Norfolk, Conn., 1945); *The Stories of F. Scott Fitzgerald,* ed. Malcolm Cowley (New York, 1951); *Afternoon of an Author,* ed. Arthur Mizener (Princeton, 1957), and *The Letters of F. Scott Fitzgerald*, ed. Andrew Turnbull (New York, 1963). A helpful critical introduction is Alfred Kazin, ed., *F. Scott Fitzgerald: The Man and His Work* (Cleveland, 1951). Biographical and critical studies include Arthur Mizener, *The Far Side of Paradise: A Biography of F. Scott Fitzgerald* (Boston, 1951); Sheila Graham, *Beloved Infidel* (New York, 1958); H. D..Piper, *F. Scott Fitzgerald: A Critical Portrait* (New York, 1965); Richard Lehan, *F. Scott Fitzgerald and the Craft of Fiction* (Carbondale, Ill., 1966); and Robert Sklar, *F. Scott Fitzgerald: The Last Laocoön* (New York, 1967). A comprehensive bibliography is J. R. Bryher, *The Critical Reputation of F. Scott Fitzgerald* (New York, 1967).

The text "Winter Dreams" is that of *The Stories of F. Scott Fitzgerald*, ed. Malcolm Cowley (New York, 1951).

Winter Dreams

1

Some of the caddies were poor as sin and lived in one-room houses with a neurasthenic cow in the front yard, but Dexter Green's father owned the second best grocery-store in Black Bear—the best one was "The Hub," patronized by the wealthy people from Sherry Island—and Dexter caddied only for pocket-money.

In the fall when the days became crisp and gray, and the long Minnesota winter shut down like the white lid of a box, Dexter's skis moved over the snow that hid the fairways of the golf course. At these times the country gave him a feeling of profound melancholy—it offended him that the links should lie in enforced fallowness, haunted by ragged sparrows for the long season. It was dreary, too, that on the tees where the gay colors fluttered in summer there were now only the desolate sand-boxes knee-deep in crusted ice. When he crossed the hills the wind blew cold as misery, and if the sun was out he tramped with his eyes squinted up against the hard dimensionless glare.

In April the winter ceased abruptly. The snow ran down into Black Bear Lake scarcely tarrying for the early golfers to brave the season with red and black balls. Without elation, without an interval of moist glory, the cold was gone.

Dexter knew that there was something dismal about this Northern spring, just as he knew there was something gorgeous about the fall. Fall made him clinch his hands and tremble and repeat idiotic sentences to himself, and make brisk abrupt gestures of command to imaginary audiences and armies. October filled him with hope which November raised to a sort of ecstatic triumph, and in this mood the fleeting brilliant impressions of the summer at Sherry Island were ready grist to his mill. He became a golf champion and defeated Mr. T. A. Hedrick in a marvellous match played a hundred times over the fairways of his imagination, a match each detail of which he changed about untiringly—sometimes he won with almost laughable ease, sometimes he came up magnificently from behind. Again, stepping from a Pierce-Arrow automobile, like Mr. Mortimer Jones, he strolled frigidly into the lounge of the Sherry Island Golf Club—or perhaps, surrounded by an admiring crowd, he gave an exhibition of fancy diving from the spring-board of the club raft. . . . Among those who watched him in open-mouthed wonder was Mr. Mortimer Jones.

And one day it came to pass that Mr. Jones—himself and not his ghost—came up to Dexter with tears in his eyes and said that Dexter was the— —best caddy in the club, and wouldn't he decide not to quit if Mr. Jones made it worth his while, because every other— —caddy in the club lost one ball a hole for him—regularly——

"No, sir," said Dexter decisively, "I don't want to caddy any more." Then, after a pause: "I'm too old."

"You're not more than fourteen. Why the devil did you decide just this morning that you wanted to quit? You promised that next week you'd go over to the state tournament with me."

"I decided I was too old."

Dexter handed in his "A Class" badge, collected what money was due him from the caddy master, and walked home to Black Bear Village.

"The best — —caddy I ever saw," shouted Mr. Mortimer Jones over a drink that afternoon. "Never lost a ball! Willing! Intelligent! Quiet! Honest! Grateful!"

The little girl who had done this was eleven — beautifully ugly as little girls are apt to be who are destined after a few years to be inexpressibly lovely and bring no end of misery to a great number of men. The spark, however, was perceptible. There was a general ungodliness in the way her lips twisted down at the corners when she smiled, and in the — Heaven help us! — in the almost passionate quality of her eyes. Vitality is born early in such women. It was utterly in evidence now, shining through her thin frame in a sort of glow.

She had come eagerly out on the course at nine o'clock with a white linen nurse and five small new golf-clubs in a white canvas bag which the nurse was carrying. When Dexter first saw her she was standing by the caddy house, rather ill at ease and trying to conceal the fact by engaging her nurse in an obviously unnatural conversation graced by startling and irrelevant grimaces from herself.

"Well, it's certainly a nice day, Hilda," Dexter heard her say. She drew down the corners of her mouth, smiled, and glanced furtively around, her eyes in transit falling for an instant on Dexter.

Then to the nurse:

"Well, I guess there aren't very many people out here this morning, are there?"

The smile again — radiant, blatantly artificial — convincing.

"I don't know what we're supposed to do now," said the nurse, looking nowhere in particular.

"Oh, that's all right. I'll fix it up."

Dexter stood perfectly still, his mouth slightly ajar. He knew that if he moved forward a step his stare would be in her line of vision — if he moved backward he would lose his full view of her face. For a moment he had not realized how young she was. Now he remembered having seen her several times the year before — in bloomers.

Suddenly, involuntarily, he laughed, a short abrupt laugh — then, startled by himself, he turned and began to walk quickly away.

"Boy!"

Dexter stopped.

"Boy —— "

Beyond question he was addressed. Not only that, but he was treated to that absurd smile, that preposterous smile—the memory of which at least a dozen men were to carry into middle age.

"Boy, do you know where the golf teacher is?"

"He's giving a lesson."

"Well, do you know where the caddy-master is?"

"He isn't here yet this morning."

"Oh." For a moment this baffled her. She stood alternately on her right and left foot.

"We'd like to get a caddy," said the nurse. "Mrs. Mortimer Jones sent us out to play golf, and we don't know how without we get a caddy."

Here she was stopped by an ominous glance from Miss Jones, followed immediately by the smile.

"There aren't any caddies here except me," said Dexter to the nurse, "and I got to stay here in charge until the caddy-master gets here."

"Oh."

Miss Jones and her retinue now withdrew, and at a proper distance from Dexter became involved in a heated conversation, which was concluded by Miss Jones taking one of the clubs and hitting it on the ground with violence. For further emphasis she raised it again and was about to bring it down smartly upon the nurse's bosom, when the nurse seized the club and twisted it from her hands.

"You damn little mean old *thing!*" cried Miss Jones wildly.

Another argument ensued. Realizing that the elements of the comedy were implied in the scene, Dexter several times began to laugh, but each time restrained the laugh before it reached audibility. He could not resist the monstrous conviction that the little girl was justified in beating the nurse.

The situation was resolved by the fortuitous appearance of the caddy-master, who was appealed to immediately by the nurse.

"Miss Jones is to have a little caddy, and this one says he can't go."

"Mr. McKenna said I was to wait here till you came," said Dexter quickly.

"Well, he's here now." Miss Jones smiled cheerfully at the caddy-master. Then she dropped her bag and set off at a haughty mince toward the first tee.

"Well?" The caddy-master turned to Dexter. "What you standing there like a dummy for? Go pick up the young lady's clubs."

"I don't think I'll go out to-day," said Dexter.

"You don't——"

"I think I'll quit."

The enormity of his decision frightened him. He was a favorite caddy, and the thirty dollars a month he earned through the summer were not to be made elsewhere around the lake. But he had received a strong emotional shock, and his perturbation required a violent and immediate outlet.

It is not so simple as that, either. As so frequently would be the case in the future, Dexter was unconsciously dictated to by his winter dreams.

2

Now, of course, the quality and the seasonability of these winter dreams varied, but the stuff of them remained. They persuaded Dexter several years later to pass up a business course at the State university—his father, prospering now, would have paid his way—for the precarious advantage of attending an older and more famous university in the East, where he was bothered by his scanty funds. But do not get the impression, because his winter dreams happened to be concerned at first with musings on the rich, that there was anything merely snobbish in the boy. He wanted not association with glittering things and glittering people—he wanted the glittering things themselves. Often he reached out for the best without knowing why he wanted it—and sometimes he ran up against the mysterious denials and prohibitions in which life indulges. It is with one of those denials and not with his career as a whole that this story deals.

He made money. It was rather amazing. After college he went to the city from which Black Bear Lake draws its wealthy patrons. When he was only twenty-three and had been there not quite two years, there were already people who liked to say: "Now *there's* a boy—" All about him rich men's sons were peddling bonds precariously, or investing patrimonies precariously, or plodding through the two dozen volumes of the "George Washington Commercial Course," but Dexter borrowed a thousand dollars on his college degree and his confident mouth, and bought a partnership in a laundry.

It was a small laundry when he went into it, but Dexter made a specialty of learning how the English washed fine woolen golfstockings without shrinking them, and within a year he was catering to the trade that wore knickerbockers. Men were insisting that their Shetland hose and sweaters go to his laundry, just as they had insisted on a caddy who could find golf-balls. A little later he was doing their wives' lingerie as well—and running five branches in different parts of the city. Before he was twenty-seven he owned the largest string of laundries in his section of the country. It was then that he sold out and went to New York. But the part of his story that concerns us goes back to the days when he was making his first big success.

When he was twenty-three Mr. Hart—one of the gray-haired men who like to say "Now there's a boy"—gave him a guest card to the

Sherry Island Golf Club for a week-end. So he signed his name one day on the register, and that afternoon played golf in a foursome with Mr. Hart and Mr. Sandwood and Mr. T. A. Hedrick. He did not consider it necessary to remark that he had once carried Mr. Hart's bag over this same links, and that he knew every trap and gully with his eyes shut — but he found himself glancing at the four caddies who trailed them, trying to catch a gleam or gesture that would remind him of himself, that would lessen the gap which lay between his present and his past.

It was a curious day, slashed abruptly with fleeting, familiar impressions. One minute he had the sense of being a trespasser — in the next he was impressed by the tremendous superiority he felt toward Mr. T. A. Hedrick, who was a bore and not even a good golfer any more.

Then, because of a ball Mr. Hart lost near the fifteenth green, an enormous thing happened. While they were searching the stiff grasses of the rough there was a clear call of "Fore!" from behind a hill in their rear. And as they all turned abruptly from their search a bright new ball sliced abruptly over the hill and caught Mr. T. A. Hedrick in the abdomen.

"By Gad!" cried Mr. T. A. Hedrick, "they ought to put some of these crazy women off the course. It's getting to be outrageous."

A head and a voice came up together over the hill:

"Do you mind if we go through?"

"You hit me in the stomach!" declared Mr. Hedrick wildly.

"Did I?" The girl approached the group of men. "I'm sorry. I yelled 'Fore!'"

Her glance fell casually on each of the men — then scanned the fairway for her ball.

"Did I bounce into the rough?"

It was impossible to determine whether this question was ingenuous or malicious. In a moment, however, she left no doubt, for as her partner came up over the hill she called cheerfully:

"Here I am! I'd have gone on the green except that I hit something."

As she took her stance for a short mashie shot, Dexter looked at her closely. She wore a blue gingham dress, rimmed at throat and shoulders with a white edging that accentuated her tan. The quality of exaggeration, of thinness, which had made her passionate eyes and down-turning mouth absurd at eleven, was gone now. She was arrestingly beautiful. The color in her cheeks was centred like the color in a picture — it was not a "high" color, but a sort of fluctuating and feverish warmth, so shaded that it seemed at any moment it would recede and disappear. This color and the mobility of her mouth gave a continual impression of flux, of intense life, of passionate vitality — balanced only partially by the sad luxury of her eyes.

She swung her mashie impatiently and without interest, pitching the ball into a sand-pit on the other side of the green. With a quick, insincere smile and a careless "Thank you!" she went on after it.

"That Judy Jones!" remarked Mr. Hedrick on the next tee, as they waited—some moments—for her to play on ahead. "All she needs is to be turned up and spanked for six months and then to be married off to an old-fashioned cavalry captain."

"My God, she's good-looking!" said Mr. Sandwood, who was just over thirty.

"Good-looking!" cried Mr. Hedrick contemptuously, "she always looks as if she wanted to be kissed! Turning those big cow-eyes on every calf in town!"

It was doubtful if Mr. Hedrick intended a reference to the maternal instinct.

"She'd play pretty good golf if she'd try," said Mr. Sandwood.

"She has no form," said Mr. Hedrick solemnly.

"She has a nice figure," said Mr. Sandwood.

"Better thank the Lord she doesn't drive a swifter ball," said Mr. Hart, winking at Dexter.

Later in the afternoon the sun went down with a riotous swirl of gold and varying blues and scarlets, and left the dry, rustling night of Western summer. Dexter watched from the veranda of the Golf Club, watched the even overlap of the waters in the little wind, silver molasses under the harvest-moon. Then the moon held a finger to her lips and the lake became a clear pool, pale and quiet. Dexter put on his bathing-suit and swam out to the farthest raft, where he stretched dripping on the wet canvas of the springboard.

There was a fish jumping and a star shining and the lights around the lake were gleaming. Over on a dark peninsula a piano was playing the songs of last summer and of summers before that—songs from "Chin-Chin" and "The Count of Luxemburg" and "The Chocolate Soldier"—and because the sound of a piano over a stretch of water had always seemed beautiful to Dexter he lay perfectly quiet and listened.

The tune the piano was playing at that moment had been gay and new five years before when Dexter was a sophomore at college. They had played it at a prom once when he could not afford the luxury of proms, and he had stood outside the gymnasium and listened. The sound of the tune precipitated in him a sort of ecstasy and it was with that ecstasy he viewed what happened to him now. It was a mood of intense appreciation, a sense that, for once, he was magnificently attuned to life and that everything about him was radiating a brightness and a glamour he might never know again.

A low, pale oblong detached itself suddenly from the darkness of the Island, spitting forth the reverberate sound of a racing motorboat. Two white streamers of cleft water rolled themselves out behind it and almost immediately the boat was beside him, drowning out the hot tinkle of the piano in the drone of its spray. Dexter raising himself on his arms was aware of a figure standing at the wheel, of two dark eyes regarding him over the lengthening space of water—then the boat had gone by and was sweeping in an immense and purposeless circle of spray round and round in the middle of the lake. With equal eccentricity one of the circles flattened out and headed back toward the raft.

"Who's that?" she called, shutting off her motor. She was so near now that Dexter could see her bathing-suit, which consisted apparently of pink rompers.

The nose of the boat bumped the raft, and as the latter tilted rakishly he was precipitated toward her. With different degrees of interest they recognized each other.

"Aren't you one of those men we played through this afternoon?" she. demanded.

He was.

"Well, do you know how to drive a motor-boat? Because if you do I wish you'd drive this one so I can ride on the surf-board behind. My name is Judy Jones"—she favored him with an absurd smirk —rather, what tried to be a smirk, for, twist her mouth as she might, it was not grotesque, it was merely beautiful—"and I live in a house over there on the Island, and in that house there is a man waiting for me. When he drove up at the door I drove out of the dock because he says I'm his ideal."

There was a fish jumping and a star shining and the lights around the lake were gleaming. Dexter sat beside Judy Jones and she explained how her boat was driven. Then she was in the water, swimming to the floating surf-board with a sinuous crawl. Watching her was without effort to the eye, watching a branch waving or a sea-gull flying. Her arms, burned to butternut, moved sinuously among the dull platinum ripples, elbow appearing first, casting the forearm back with a cadence of falling water, then reaching out and down, stabbing a path ahead.

They moved out into the lake; turning, Dexter saw that she was kneeling on the low rear of the now uptilted surf-board.

"Go faster," she called, "fast as it'll go."

Obediently he jammed the lever forward and the white spray mounted at the bow. When he looked around again the girl was standing up on the rushing board, her arms spread wide, her eyes lifted toward the moon.

"It's awful cold," she shouted. "What's your name?"

He told her.

"Well, why don't you come to dinner to-morrow night?"

His heart turned over like the fly-wheel of the boat, and, for the second time, her casual whim gave a new direction to his life.

3

Next evening while he waited for her to come down-stairs, Dexter peopled the soft deep summer room and the sun-porch that opened from it with the men who had already loved Judy Jones. He knew the sort of men they were—the men who when he first went to college had entered from the great prep schools with graceful clothes and the deep tan of healthy summers. He had seen that, in one sense, he was better than these men. He was newer and stronger. Yet in acknowledging to himself that he wished his children to be like them he was admitting that he was but the rough, strong stuff from which they eternally sprang.

When the time had come for him to wear good clothes, he had known who were the best tailors in America, and the best tailors in America had made him the suit he wore this evening. He had acquired that particular reserve peculiar to his university, that set it off from other universities. He recognized the value to him of such a mannerism and he had adopted it; he knew that to be careless in dress and manner required more confidence than to be careful. But carelessness was for his children. His mother's name had been Krimelich. She was a Bohemian of the peasant class and she had talked broken English to the end of her days. Her son must keep to the set patterns.

At a little after seven Judy Jones came down-stairs. She wore a blue silk afternoon dress, and he was disappointed at first that she had not put on something more elaborate. This feeling was accentuated when, after a brief greeting, she went to the door of a butler's pantry and pushing it open called: "You can serve dinner, Martha." He had rather expected that a butler would announce dinner, that there would be a cocktail. Then he put these thoughts behind him as they sat down side by side on a lounge and looked at each other.

"Father and mother won't be here," she said thoughtfully.

He remembered the last time he had seen her father, and he was glad the parents were not to be here to-night—they might wonder who he was. He had been born in Keeble, a Minnesota village fifty miles farther north, and he always gave Keeble as his home instead of Black Bear Village. Country towns were well enough to come from if they weren't inconveniently in sight and used as footstools by fashionable lakes.

They talked of his university, which she had visited frequently during the past two years, and of the near-by city which supplied Sherry Island with its patrons, and whither Dexter would return next day to his prospering laundries.

During dinner she slipped into a moody depression which gave Dexter a feeling of uneasiness. Whatever petulance she uttered in her throaty voice worried him. Whatever she smiled at—at him, at a chicken liver, at nothing—it disturbed him that her smile could have no root in mirth, or even in amusement. When the scarlet corners of her lips curved down, it was less a smile than an invitation to a kiss.

Then, after dinner, she led him out on the dark sun-porch and deliberately changed the atmosphere.

"Do you mind if I weep a little?" she said.

"I'm afraid I'm boring you," he responded quickly.

"You're not. I like you. But I've just had a terrible afternoon. There was a man I cared about, and this afternoon he told me out of a clear sky that he was poor as a church-mouse. He'd never even hinted it before. Does this sound horribly mundane?"

"Perhaps he was afraid to tell you."

"Suppose he was," she answered. "He didn't start right. You see, if I'd thought of him as poor—well, I've been mad about loads of poor men, and fully intended to marry them all. But in this case, I hadn't thought of him that way, and my interest in him wasn't strong enough to survive the shock. As if a girl calmly informed her fiancé that she was a widow. He might not object to widows, but——"

"Let's start right," she interrupted herself suddenly. "Who are you, anyhow?"

For a moment Dexter hesitated. Then:

"I'm nobody," he announced. "My career is largely a matter of futures."

"Are you poor?"

"No," he said frankly, "I'm probably making more money than any man my age in the Northwest. I know that's an obnoxious remark, but you advised me to start right."

There was a pause. Then she smiled and the corners of her mouth drooped and an almost imperceptible sway brought her closer to him, looking up into his eyes. A lump rose in Dexter's throat, and he waited breathless for the experiment, facing the unpredictable compound that would form mysteriously from the elements of their lips. Then he saw—she communicated her excitement to him, lavishly, deeply, with kisses that were not a promise but a fulfilment. They aroused in him not hunger demanding renewal but surfeit that would demand more surfeit . . . kisses that were like charity, creating want by holding back nothing at all.

It did not take him many hours to decide that he had wanted Judy Jones ever since he was a proud, desirous little boy.

4

It began like that—and continued, with varying shades of intensity, on such a note right up to the dénouement. Dexter surrendered a part of himself to the most direct and unprincipled personality with which he had ever come in contact. Whatever Judy wanted, she went after with the full pressure of her charm. There was no divergence of method, no jockeying for position or premeditation of effects—there was very little mental side to any of her affairs. She simply made men conscious to the highest degree of her physical loveliness. Dexter had no desire to change her. Her deficiencies were knit up with a passionate energy that transcended and justified them.

When, as Judy's head lay against his shoulder that first night, she whispered, "I don't know what's the matter with me. Last night I thought I was in love with a man and to-night I think I'm in love with you —— " —it seemed to him a beautiful and romantic thing to say. It was the exquisite excitability that for the moment he controlled and owned. But a week later he was compelled to view this same quality in a different light. She took him in her roadster to a picnic supper, and after supper she disappeared, likewise in her roadster, with another man. Dexter became enormously upset and was scarcely able to be decently civil to the other people present. When she assured him that she had not kissed the other man, he knew she was lying—yet he was glad that she had taken the trouble to lie to him.

He was, as he found before the summer ended, one of a varying dozen who circulated about her. Each of them had at one time been favored above all others—about half of them still basked in the solace of occasional sentimental revivals. Whenever one showed signs of dropping out through long neglect, she granted him a brief honeyed hour, which encouraged him to tag along for a year or so longer. Judy made these forays upon the helpless and defeated without malice, indeed half unconscious that there was anything mischievous in what she did.

When a new man came to town every one dropped out—dates were automatically cancelled.

The helpless part of trying to do anything about it was that she did it all herself. She was not a girl who could be "won" in the kinetic sense—she was proof against cleverness, she was proof against charm; if any of these assailed her too strongly she would immediately resolve the affair to a physical basis, and under the magic of her physical splendor the strong as well as the brilliant played her game and not their own. She was entertained only by the gratification of her desires and by the direct exercise of her own charm. Perhaps from so much youthful love, so many youthful lovers, she had come, in self-defense, to nourish herself wholly from within.

Succeeding Dexter's first exhilaration came restlessness and dissatisfaction. The helpless ecstasy of losing himself in her was opiate rather than tonic. It was fortunate for his work during the winter that those moments of ecstasy came infrequently. Early in their acquaintance it had seemed for a while that there was a deep and spontaneous mutual attraction—that first August, for example—three days of long evenings on her dusky veranda, of strange wan kisses through the late afternoon, in shadowy alcoves or behind the protecting trellises of the garden arbors, of mornings when she was fresh as a dream and almost shy at meeting him in the clarity of the rising day. There was all the ecstasy of an engagement about it, sharpened by his realization that there was no engagement. It was during those three days that, for the first time, he had asked her to marry him. She said "maybe some day," she said "kiss me," she said "I'd like to marry you," she said "I love you"—she said—nothing.

The three days were interrupted by the arrival of a New York man who visited at her house for half September. To Dexter's agony, rumor engaged them. The man was the son of the president of a great trust company. But at the end of a month it was reported that Judy was yawning. At a dance one night she sat all evening in a motor-boat with a local beau, while the New Yorker searched the club for her frantically. She told the local beau that she was bored with her visitor, and two days later he left. She was seen with him at the station, and it was reported that he looked very mournful indeed.

On this note the summer ended. Dexter was twenty-four, and he found himself increasingly in a position to do as he wished. He joined two clubs in the city and lived at one of them. Though he was by no means an integral part of the stag-lines at these clubs, he managed to be on hand at dances where Judy Jones was likely to appear. He could have gone out socially as much as he liked—he was an eligible young man, now, and popular with down-town fathers. His confessed devotion to Judy Jones had rather solidified his position. But he had no social aspirations and rather despised the dancing men who were always on tap for the Thursday or Saturday parties and who filled in at dinners with the younger married set. Already he was playing with the idea of going East to New York. He wanted to take Judy Jones with him. No disillusion as to the world in which she had grown up could cure his illusion as to her desirability.

Remember that—for only in the light of it can what he did for her be understood.

Eighteen months after he first met Judy Jones he became engaged to another girl. Her name was Irene Scheerer, and her father was one of the men who had always believed in Dexter. Irene was light-haired and sweet and honorable, and a little stout, and she had two suitors whom she pleasantly relinquished when Dexter formally asked her to marry him.

Summer, fall, winter, spring, another summer, another fall—so much he had given of his active life to the incorrigible lips of Judy Jones. She had treated him with interest, with encouragement, with malice, with indifference, with contempt. She had inflicted on him the innumerable little slights and indignities possible in such a case—as if in revenge for having ever cared for him at all. She had beckoned him and yawned at him and beckoned him again and he had responded often with bitterness and narrowed eyes. She had brought him ecstatic happiness and intolerable agony of spirit. She had caused him untold inconvenience and not a little trouble. She had insulted him, and she had ridden over him, and she had played his interest in her against his interest in his work—for fun. She had done everything to him except to criticise him—this she had not done—it seemed to him only because it might have sullied the utter indifference she manifested and sincerely felt toward him.

When autumn had come and gone again it occurred to him that he could not have Judy Jones. He had to beat this into his mind but he convinced himself at last. He lay awake at night for a while and argued it over. He told himself the trouble and the pain she had caused him, he enumerated her glaring deficiencies as a wife. Then he said to himself that he loved her, and after a while he fell asleep. For a week, lest he imagined her husky voice over the telephone or her eyes opposite him at lunch, he worked hard and late, and at night he went to his office and plotted out his years.

At the end of a week he went to a dance and cut in on her once. For almost the first time since they had met he did not ask her to sit out with him or tell her that she was lovely. It hurt him that she did not miss these things—that was all. He was not jealous when he saw that there was a new man to-night. He had been hardened against jealousy long before.

He stayed late at the dance. He sat for an hour with Irene Scheerer and talked about books and about music. He knew very little about either. But he was beginning to be master of his own time now, and he had a rather priggish notion that he—the young and already fabulously successful Dexter Green—should know more about such things.

That was in October, when he was twenty-five. In January, Dexter and Irene became engaged. It was to be announced in June, and they were to be married three months later.

The Minnesota winter prolonged itself interminably, and it was almost May when the winds came soft and the snow ran down into Black Bear Lake at last. For the first time in over a year Dexter was enjoying a certain tranquility of spirit. Judy Jones had been in Florida, and afterward in Hot Springs, and somewhere she had been engaged, and somewhere she had broken it off. At first, when Dexter had definitely given her up, it had made him sad that people still linked them together and asked for news of her, but when he began to be placed at dinner next to Irene Scheerer people didn't ask him about her any more—they told him about her. He ceased to be an authority on her.

May at last. Dexter walked the streets at night when the darkness was damp as rain, wondering that so soon, with so little done, so much of ecstasy had gone from him. May one year back had been marked by Judy's poignant, unforgivable, yet forgiven turbulence — it had been one of those rare times when he fancied she had grown to care for him. That old penny's worth of happiness he had spent for this bushel of content. He knew that Irene would be no more than a curtain spread behind him, a hand moving among gleaming teacups, a voice calling to children . . . fire and loveliness were gone, the magic of nights and the wonder of the varying hours and seasons . . . slender lips, down-turning, dropping to his lips and bearing him up into a heaven of eyes. . . . The thing was deep in him. He was too strong and alive for it to die lightly.

In the middle of May when the weather balanced for a few days on the thin bridge that led to deep summer he turned in one night at Irene's house. Their engagement was to be announced in a week now — no one would be surprised at it. And to-night they would sit together on the lounge at the University Club and look on for an hour at the dancers. It gave him a sense of solidity to go with her — she was so sturdily popular, so intensely "great."

He mounted the steps of the brownstone house and stepped inside.

"Irene," he called.

Mrs. Scheerer came out of the living-room to meet him.

"Dexter," she said, Irene's gone up-stairs with a splitting head-ache. She wanted to go with you but I made her go to bed."

"Nothing serious, I —— "

"Oh, no. She's going to play golf with you in the morning. You can spare her for just one night, can't you Dexter?"

Her smile was kind. She and Dexter liked each other. In the living-room he talked for a moment before he said good-night.

Returning to the University Club, where he had rooms, he stood in the doorway for a moment and watched the dancers. He leaned against the door-post, nodded at a man or two — yawned.

"Hello, darling."

The familiar voice at his elbow startled him. Judy Jones had left a man and crossed the room to him — Judy Jones, a slender enamelled doll in cloth of gold: gold in a band at her head, gold in two slipper points at her dress's hem. The fragile glow of her face seemed to blossom as she smiled at him. A breeze of warmth and light blew through the room. His hands in the pockets of his dinner-jacket tightened spasmodically. He was filled with a sudden excitement.

"When did you get back?" he asked casually.

"Come here and I'll tell you about it."

She turned and he followed her. She had been away — he could have wept at the wonder of her return. She had passed through en-chanted streets, doing things that were like provocative music. All mysterious happenings, all fresh and quickening hopes, had gone away with her, come back with her now.

She turned in the doorway.

"Have you a car here? If you haven't, I have."

"I have a coupé."

In then, with a rustle of golden cloth. He slammed the door. Into so many cars she had stepped—like this—like that—her back against the leather, so—her elbow resting on the door—waiting. She would have been soiled long since had there been anything to soil her—except herself—but this was her own self outpouring.

With an effort he forced himself to start the car and back into the street. This was nothing, he must remember. She had done this before, and he had put her behind him, as he would have crossed a bad account from his books.

He drove slowly down-town and, affecting abstraction, traversed the deserted streets of the business section, peopled here and there where a movie was giving out its crowd or where consumptive or pugilistic youth lounged in front of pool halls. The clink of glasses and the slap of hands on the bars issued from saloons, cloisters of glazed glass and dirty yellow light.

She was watching him closely and the silence was embarrassing, yet in this crisis he could find no casual word with which to profane the hour. At a convenient turning he began to zigzag back toward the University Club.

"Have you missed me?" she asked suddenly.

"Everybody missed you."

He wondered if she knew of Irene Scheerer. She had been back only a day—her absence had been almost contemporaneous with his engagement.

"What a remark!" Judy laughed sadly—without sadness. She looked at him searchingly. He became absorbed in the dashboard.

"You're handsomer than you used to be," she said thoughtfully. "Dexter, you have the most rememberable eyes."

He could have laughed at this, but he did not laugh. It was the sort of thing that was said to sophomores. Yet it stabbed at him.

"I'm awfully tired of everything, darling." She called every one darling, endowing the endearment with careless, individual comraderie. "I wish you'd marry me."

The directness of this confused him. He should have told her now that he was going to marry another girl, but he could not tell her. He could as easily have sworn that he had never loved her.

"I think we'd get along," she continued, on the same note, "un-less probably you've forgotten me and fallen in love with another girl."

Her confidence was obviously enormous. She had said, in effect, that she found such a thing impossible to believe, that if it were true he had merely committed a childish indiscretion — and probably to show off. She would forgive him, because it was not a matter of any moment but rather something to be brushed aside lightly.

"Of course you could never love anybody but me," she continued, "I like the way you love me. Oh, Dexter, have you forgotten last year?"

"No, I haven't forgotten."

"Neither have I!"

Was she sincerely moved — or was she carried along by the wave of her own acting?

"I wish we could be like that again," she said, and he forced himself to answer:

"I don't think we can."

"I suppose not. . . . I hear you're giving Irene Scheerer a violent rush."

There was not the faintest emphasis on the name, yet Dexter was suddenly ashamed.

"Oh, take me home," cried Judy suddenly; "I don't want to go back to that idiotic dance — with those children."

Then, as he turned up the street that led to the residence district, Judy began to cry quietly to herself. He had never seen her cry before.

The dark street lightened, the dwellings of the rich loomed up around them, he stopped his coupé in front of the great white bulk of the Mortimer Joneses' house, somnolent, gorgeous, drenched with the splendor of the damp moonlight. Its solidity startled him. The strong walls, the steel of the girders, the breadth and beam and pomp of it were there only to bring out the contrast with the young beauty beside him. It was sturdy to accentuate her slightness — as if to show what a breeze could be generated by a butterfly's wing.

He sat perfectly quiet, his nerves in wild clamor, afraid that if he moved he would find her irresistibly in his arms. Two tears had rolled down her wet face and trembled on her upper lip.

"I'm more beautiful than anybody else," she said brokenly, "why can't I be happy?" Her moist eyes tore at his stability — her mouth turned slowly downward with an exquisite sadness: "I'd like to marry you if you'll have me, Dexter. I suppose you think I'm not worth having, but I'll be so beautiful for you, Dexter."

A million phrases of anger, pride, passion, hatred, tenderness fought on his lips. Then a perfect wave of emotion washed over him, carrying off with it a sediment of wisdom, of convention, of doubt, of honor. This was his girl who was speaking, his own, his beautiful, his pride.

"Won't you come in?" He heard her draw in her breath sharply.

Waiting.

"All right," his voice was trembling, "I'll come in."

5

It was strange that neither when it was over nor a long time afterward did he regret that night. Looking at it from the perspective of ten years, the fact that Judy's flare for him endured just one month seemed of little importance. Nor did it matter that by his yielding he subjected himself to a deeper agony in the end and gave serious hurt to Irene Scheerer and to Irene's parents, who had befriended him. There was nothing sufficiently pictorial about Irene's grief to stamp itself on his mind.

Dexter was at bottom hard-minded. The attitude of the city on his action was of no importance to him, not because he was going to leave the city, but because any outside attitude on the situation seemed superficial. He was completely indifferent to popular opinion. Nor, when he had seen that it was no use, that he did not possess in himself the power to move fundamentally or to hold Judy Jones, did he bear any malice toward her. He loved her, and he would love her until the day he was too old for loving—but he could not have her. So he tasted the deep pain that is reserved only for the strong, just as he had tasted for a little while the deep happiness.

Even the ultimate falsity of the grounds upon which Judy terminated the engagement that she did not want to "take him away" from Irene—Judy who had wanted nothing else—did not revolt him. He was beyond any revulsion or any amusement.

He went East in February with the intention of selling out his laundries and settling in New York—but the war came to America in March and changed his plans. He returned to the West, handed over the management of the business to his partner, and went into the first officers' training-camp in late April. He was one of those young thousands who greeted the war with a certain amount of relief, welcoming the liberation from webs of tangled emotion.

6

This story is not his biography, remember, although things creep into it which have nothing to do with those dreams he had when he was young. We are almost done with them and with him now. There is only one more incident to be related here, and it happens seven years farther on.

It took place in New York, where he had done well—so well that there were no barriers too high for him. He was thirty-two years old, and, except for one flying trip immediately after the war, he had not been West in seven years. A man named Devlin from Detroit came into his office to see him in a business way, and then and there this incident occurred, and closed out, so to speak, this particular side of his life.

"So you're from the Middle West," said the man Devlin with careless curiosity. "That's funny—I thought men like you were probably born and raised on Wall Street. You know—wife of one of my best friends in Detroit came from your city. I was an usher at the wedding."

Dexter waited with no apprehension of what was coming.

"Judy Simms," said Devlin with no particular interest; "Judy Jones she was once."

"Yes, I knew her." A dull impatience spread over him. He had heard, of course, that she was married—perhaps deliberately he had heard no more.

"Awfully nice girl," brooded Devlin meaninglessly, "I'm sort of sorry for her."

"Why?" Something in Dexter was alert, receptive, at once.

"Oh, Lud Simms has gone to pieces in a way. I don't mean he ill-uses her, but he drinks and runs around——"

"Doesn't she run around?"

"No. Stays at home with her kids."

"Oh."

"She's a little too old for him," said Devlin.

"Too old!" cried Dexter. "Why, man, she's only twenty-seven."

He was possessed with a wild notion of rushing out into the streets and taking a train to Detroit. He rose to his feet spasmodically.

"I guess you're busy," Devlin apologized quickly. "I didn't realize——"

"No, I'm not busy," said Dexter, steadying his voice. "I'm not busy at all. Not busy at all. Did you say she was—twenty-seven? No, I said she was twenty-seven."

"Yes, you did," agreed Devlin dryly.

"Go on, then. Go on."

"What do you mean?"

"About Judy Jones."

Devlin looked at him helplessly.

"Well, that's—I told you all there is to it. He treats her like the devil. Oh, they're not going to get divorced or anything. When he's particularly outrageous she forgives him. In fact, I'm inclined to think she loves him. She was a pretty girl when she first came to Detroit."

A pretty girl! The phrase struck Dexter as ludicrous.

"Isn't she—a pretty girl, any more?"

"Oh, she's all right."

"Look here," said Dexter, sitting down suddenly. "I don't understand. You say she was a 'pretty girl' and now you say she's 'all right.' I don't understand what you mean—Judy Jones wasn't a pretty girl, at all. She was a great beauty. Why, I knew her, I knew her. She was——"

Devlin laughed pleasantly.

"I'm not trying to start a row," he said. "I think Judy's a nice girl and I like her. I can't understand how a man like Lud Simms could fall madly in love with her, but he did." Then he added: "Most of the women like her."

Dexter looked closely at Devlin, thinking wildly that there must be a reason for this, some insensitivity in the man or some private malice.

"Lots of women fade just like *that*," Devlin snapped his fingers. "You must have seen it happen. Perhaps I've forgotten how pretty she was at her wedding. I've seen her so much since then, you see. She has nice eyes."

A sort of dullness settled down upon Dexter. For the first time in his life he felt like getting very drunk. He knew that he was laughing loudly at something Devlin had said, but he did not know what it was or why it was funny. When, in a few minutes, Devlin went he lay down on his lounge and looked out the window at the New York sky-line into which the sun was sinking in dull lovely shades of pink and gold.

He had thought that having nothing else to lose he was invulnerable at last—but he knew that he had just lost something more, as surely as if he had married Judy Jones and seen her fade away before his eyes.

The dream was gone. Something had been taken from him. In a sort of panic he pushed the palms of his hands into his eyes and tried to bring up a picture of the waters lapping on Sherry Island and the moonlit veranda, and gingham on the golf-links and the dry sun and the gold color of her neck's soft down. And her mouth damp to his kisses and her eyes plaintive with melancholy and her freshness like new fine linen in the morning. Why, these things were no longer in the world! They had existed and they existed no longer.

For the first time in years the tears were streaming down his face. But they were for himself now. He did not care about mouth and eyes and moving hands. He wanted to care, and he could not care. For he had gone away and he could never go back any more. The gates were closed, the sun was gone down, and there was no beauty but the gray beauty of steel that withstands all time. Even the grief he could have borne was left behind in the country of illusion, of youth, of the richness of life, where his winter dreams had flourished.

"Long ago," he said, "long ago, there was something in me, but now that thing is gone. Now that thing is gone, that thing is gone. I cannot cry. I cannot care. That thing will come back no more."

1926

Jean Toomer   *1894–1967*

Jean Toomer was born in Washington, D. C., and educated in its public schools. After graduation from high school, he attended the University of Wisconsin (1914–15), taught school briefly in Georgia, and traveled about working at many jobs before gaining recognition as an unusually promising writer with the publication of *Cane* (1923). The book is a collection of intermingled fiction, verse, and drama. A story like "Blood-Burning Moon" successfully combines the qualities of lyric fantasy and chilling realism. In some of the other stories, a tendency toward disembodied fantasy prevails. Because of its poetic lilt and its almost mystical primitivism, *Cane* was warmly praised by such older writers as Sherwood Anderson and Waldo Frank. Encouraged by his reception, Toomer attempted to become a dramatist, but he was unable to find a producer for any of the unusual experimental plays he wrote. Disheartened, he finally turned from writing to other activities, including work sponsored by the Society of Friends for a better understanding among peoples. His only later creative writing was chiefly in the form of aphorisms. His other books include *Essentials* (1931) and *Portage Potential* (1932).

For information on this little-known writer's life and career, see Arna Bontemps, "The Negro Renaissance: Jean Toomer and the Harlem Writers of the 1920's," in *Anger, and Beyond: The Negro Writer in the United States*, ed. Herbert Hill (New York, 1965), and D. T. Turner, "The Failure of a Playwright," *CLA Journal*, X (June, 1967), 308–318.

The text of "Blood-Burning Moon" is that of *Cane* (New York, 1923).

Blood-Burning Moon

1

Up from the skeleton stone walls, up from the rotting floor boards and the solid handhewn beams of oak of the pre-war cotton factory, dusk came. Up from the dusk the full moon came. Glowing like a fired pine-knot, it illumined the great door and soft showered the Negro shanties aligned along the single street of factory town. The full moon in the great door was an omen. Negro women improvised songs against its spell.

Louisa sang as she came over the crest of the hill from the white folks' kitchen. Her skin was the color of oak leaves on young trees in fall. Her breasts, firm and up-pointed like ripe acorns. And her singing had the low murmur of winds in fig trees. Bob Stone, younger son of the people she worked for, loved her. By the way the world reckons things, he had won her. By measure of that warm glow which came into her mind at thought of him, he had won her. Tom Burwell, whom the whole town called Big Boy, also loved her. But working in the fields all day, and far away from her, gave him no chance to show it. Though often enough of evenings he had tried to. Somehow, he never got along. Strong as he was with hands upon the ax or plow, he found it difficult to hold her. Or so he thought. But the fact was that he held her to factory town more firmly than he thought for. His black balanced, and pulled against, the white of Stone, when she thought of them. And her mind was vaguely upon them as she came over the crest of the hill, coming from the white folks' kitchen. As she sang softly at the evil face of the full moon.

A strange stir was in her. Indolently, she tried to fix upon Bob or Tom as the cause of it. To meet Bob in the canebrake, as she was going to do an hour or so later, was nothing new. And Tom's proposal which she felt on its way to her could be indefinitely put off. Separately, there was no unusual significance to either one. But for some reason, they jumbled when her eyes gazed vacantly at the rising moon. And from the jumble came the stir that was strangely within her. Her lips trembled. The slow rhythm of her song grew agitant and restless. Rusty black and tan spotted hounds, lying in the dark corners of porches or prowling around back yards, put their noses in the air and caught its tremor. They began plaintively to yelp and howl. Chickens woke up and cackled. Intermittently, all over the countryside dogs barked and roosters crowed as if heralding a weird dawn or some ungodly awakening. The women sang lustily. Their songs were cotton-wads to stop their ears. Louisa came down into factory town and sank wearily upon the step before her home. The moon was rising towards a thick cloud-bank which soon would hide it.

> Red nigger moon. Sinner!
> Blood-burning moon. Sinner!
> Come out that fact'ry door.

2

Up from the deep dusk of a cleared spot on the edge of the forest a mellow glow arose and spread fan-wise into the low-hanging heavens. And all around the air was heavy with the scent of boiling cane. A large pile of cane-stalks lay like ribboned shadows upon the ground. A mule, harnessed to a pole, trudged lazily round and round the pivot of the grinder. Beneath a swaying oil lamp, a Negro alternately whipped out at the mule, and fed cane-stalks to the grinder. A fat boy waddled pails of fresh ground juice between the grinder and the boiling stove. Steam came from the copper boiling pan. The scent of cane came from the copper pan and drenched the forest and the hill that sloped to factory town, beneath its fragrance. It drenched the men in circle seated around the stove. Some of them chewed at the white pulp of stalks, but there was no need for them to, if all they wanted was to taste the cane. One tasted it in factory town. And from factory town one could see the soft haze thrown by the glowing stove upon the low-hanging heavens.

Old David Georgia stirred the thickening syrup with a long ladle, and ever so often drew it off. Old David Georgia tended his stove and told tales about the white folks, about moonshining and cotton picking, and about sweet nigger gals, to the men who sat there about his stove to listen to him. Tom Burwell chewed cane-stalk and laughed with the others till someone mentioned Louisa. Till someone said something about Louisa and Bob Stone, about the silk stockings she must have gotten from him. Blood ran up Tom's neck hotter than the glow that flooded from the stove. He sprang up. Glared at the men and said, "She's my gal." Will Manning laughed. Tom strode over to him. Yanked him up and knocked him to the ground. Several of Manning's friends got up to fight for him. Tom whipped out a long knife and would have cut them to shreds if they hadnt ducked into the woods. Tom had had enough. He nodded to Old David Georgia and swung down the path to factory town. Just then, the dogs started barking and the roosters began to crow. Tom felt funny. Away from the fight, away from the stove, chill got to him. He shivered. He shuddered when he saw the full moon rising towards the cloud-bank. He who didnt give a godam for the fears of old women. He forced his mind to fasten on Louisa. Bob Stone. Better not be. He turned into the street and saw Louisa sitting before her home. He went towards her, ambling, touched the brim of a marvelously shaped, spotted, felt hat, said he wanted to say something to her, and then found that he didnt know what he had to say, or if he did, that he couldnt say it. He shoved his big fists in his overalls, grinned, and started to move off.

"Youall want me, Tom?"

"Thats what us wants, sho, Louisa."

"Well, here I am—"

"An here I is, but that aint ahelpin none, all th same."

"You wanted to say something? . ."

"I did that, sho. But words is like th spots on dice: no matter how y fumbles em, there's times when they jes wont come. I dunno why. Seems like th love I feels fo yo done stole m tongue. I got it now. Whee! Louisa, honey, I oughtnt tell y, I feel I oughtnt cause yo is young an goes t church an I has had other gals, but Louisa I sho do love y. Lil gal, Ise watched y from them first days when youall sat right here befo yo door befo th well an sang sometimes in a way that like t broke m heart. Ise carried y with me into th fields, day after day, an after that, an I sho can plow when yo is there, an I can pick cotton. Yassur! Come near beatin Barlo yesterday. I sho did. Yassur! An next year if ole Stone'll trust me, I'll have a farm. My own. My bales will buy yo what y gets from white folks now. Silk stockings an purple dresses—course I dont believe what some folks been whisperin as t how y gets them things now. White folks always did do for niggers what they likes. An they jes cant help alikin yo, Louisa. Bob Stone likes y. Course he does. But not th way folks is awhisperin. Does he, hon?"

"I dont know what you mean, Tom."

"Course y dont. Ise already cut two niggers. Had t hon, t tell em so. Niggers always tryin t make somethin out a nothin. An then besides, white folks aint up t them tricks so much nowadays. Godam better not be. Leastawise not with yo. Cause I wouldnt stand f it. Nassur."

"What would you do, Tom?"

"Cut him jes like I cut a nigger."

"No, Tom—"

"I said I would an there aint no mo to it. But that aint th talk f now. Sing, honey Louisa, an while I'm listenin t y I'll be makin love."

Tom took her hand in his. Against the tough thickness of his own, hers felt soft and small. His huge body slipped down to the step beside her. The full moon sank upward into the deep purple of the cloud-bank. An old woman brought a lighted lamp and hung it on the common well whose bulky shadow squatted in the middle of the road, opposite Tom and Louisa. The old woman lifted the well-lid, took hold the chain, and began drawing up the heavy bucket. As she did so, she sang. Figures shifted, restlesslike, between lamp and window in the front rooms of the shanties. Shadows of the figures fought each other on the gray dust of the road. Figures raised the windows and joined the old woman in song. Louisa and Tom, the whole street, singing:

> Red nigger moon. Sinner!
> Blood-burning moon. Sinner!
> Come out that fact'ry door.

3

Bob Stone sauntered from his veranda out into the gloom of fir trees and magnolias. The clear white of his skin paled, and the flush of his cheeks turned purple. As if to balance this outer change, his mind became consciously a white man's. He passed the house with its huge open hearth which, in the days of slavery, was the plantation cookery. He saw Louisa bent over that hearth. He went in as a master should and took her. Direct, honest, bold. None of this sneaking that he had to go through now. The contrast was repulsive to him. His family had lost ground. Hell no, his family still owned the niggers, practically. Damned if they did, or he wouldnt have to duck around so. What would they think if they knew? His mother? His sister? He shouldnt mention them, shouldnt think of them in this connection. There in the dusk he blushed at doing so. Fellows about town were all right, but how about his friends up North? He could see them incredible, repulsed. They didnt know. The thought first made him laugh. Then, with their eyes still upon him, he began to feel embarrassed. He felt the need of explaining things to them. Explain hell. They wouldnt understand, and moreover, who ever heard of a Southerner getting on his knees to any Yankee, or anyone. No sir. He was going to see Louisa to-night, and love her. She was lovely—in her way. Nigger way. What way was that? Damned if he knew. Must know. He'd known her long enough to know. Was there something about niggers that you couldnt know? Listening to them at church didnt tell you anything. Looking at them didnt tell you anything. Talking to them didnt tell you anything—unless it was gossip, unless they wanted to talk. Of course, about farming, and licker, and craps—but those werent nigger. Nigger was something more. How much more? Something to be afraid of, more? Hell no. Who ever heard of being afraid of a nigger? Tom Burwell. Cartwell had told him that Tom went with Louisa after she reached home. No sir. No nigger had ever been with his girl. He'd like to see one try. Some position for him to be in. Him, Bob Stone, of the old Stone family, in a scrap with a nigger over a nigger girl. In the good old days. . . Ha! Those were the days. His family had lost ground. Not so much, though. Enough for him to have to cut through old Lemon's canefield by way of the woods, that he might meet her. She was worth it. Beautiful nigger gal. Why nigger? Why not, just gal? No, it was because she was nigger that he went to her. Sweet. . . The scent of boiling cane came to him. Then he saw the rich glow of the stove. He heard the voices of the men circled around it. He was about to skirt the clearing when he heard his own name mentioned. He stopped. Quivering. Leaning against a tree, he listened.

"Bad nigger. Yassur, he sho is one bad nigger when he gets started."

"Tom Burwell's been on th gang three times fo cuttin men."

"What y think he's agwine t do t Bob Stone?"

"Dunno yet. He aint found out. When he does — Baby!"

"Aint no tellin."

"Young Stone aint no quitter an I ken tell y that. Blood of th old uns in his veins."

"Thats right. He'll scrap, sho."

"Be gettin too hot f niggers round this away."

"Shut up, nigger. Y dont know what y talkin bout."

Bob Stone's ears burned as though he had been holding them over the stove. Sizzling heat welled up within him. His feet felt as if they rested on red-hot coals. They stung him to quick movement. He circled the fringe of the glowing. Not a twig cracked beneath his feet. He reached the path that led to factory town. Plunged furiously down it. Halfway along, a blindness within him veered him aside. He crashed into the bordering canebrake. Cane leaves cut his face and lips. He tasted blood. He threw himself down and dug his fingers in the ground. The earth was cool. Cane-roots took the fever from his hands. After a long while, or so it seemed to him, the thought came to him that it must be time to see Louisa. He got to his feet and walked calmly to their meeting place. No Louisa. Tom Burwell had her. Veins in his forehead bulged and distended. Saliva moistened the dried blood on his lips. He bit down on his lips. He tasted blood. Not his own blood; Tom Burwell's blood. Bob drove through the cane and out again upon the road. A hound swung down the path before him towards factory town. Bob couldn't see it. The dog loped aside to let him pass. Bob's blind rushing made him stumble over it. He fell with a thud that dazed him. The hound yelped. Answering yelps came from all over the countryside. Chickens cackled. Roosters crowed, heralding the bloodshot eyes of southern awakening. Singers in the town were silenced. They shut their windows down. Palpitant between the rooster crows, a chill hush settled upon the huddled forms of Tom and Louisa. A figure rushed from the shadow and stood before them. Tom popped to his feet.

"Whats y want?"

"I'm Bob Stone."

"Yassur — an I'm Tom Burwell. Whats y want?"

Bob lunged at him. Tom side-stepped, caught him by the shoulder, and flung him to the ground. Straddled him.

"Let me up."

"Yassur — but watch yo doins, Bob Stone."

A few dark figures, drawn by the sound of scuffle, stood about them. Bob sprang to his feet.

"Fight like a man, Tom Burwell, an I'll lick y."

Again he lunged. Tom side-stepped and flung him to the ground. Straddled him.

"Get off me, you godam nigger you."

"Yo sho has started somethin now. Get up."

Tom yanked him up and began hammering at him. Each blow sounded as if it smashed into a precious, irreplaceable soft something. Beneath them, Bob staggered back. He reached in his pocket and whipped out a knife.

"Thats my game, sho."

Blue flash, a steel blade slashed across Bob Stone's throat. He had a sweetish sick feeling. Blood began to flow. Then he felt a sharp twitch of pain. He let his knife drop. He slapped one hand against his neck. He pressed the other on top of his head as if to hold it down. He groaned. He turned, and staggered towards the crest of the hill in the direction of white town. Negroes who had seen the fight slunk into their homes and blew the lamps out. Louisa, dazed, hysterical, refused to go indoors. She slipped, crumbled, her body loosely propped against the woodwork of the well. Tom Burwell leaned against it. He seemed rooted there.

Bob reached Broad Street. White men rushed up to him. He collapsed in their arms.

"Tom Burwell. . . ."

White men like ants upon a forage rushed about. Except for the taut hum of their moving, all was silent. Shotguns, revolvers, rope, kerosene, torches. Two high-powered cars with glaring search-lights. They came together. The taut hum rose to a low roar. Then nothing could be heard but the flop of their feet in the thick dust of the road. The moving body of their silence preceded them over the crest of the hill into factory town. It flattened the Negroes beneath it. It rolled to the wall of the factory, where it stopped. Tom knew that they were coming. He couldnt move. And then he saw the search-lights of the two cars glaring down on him. A quick shock went through him. He stiffened. He started to run. A yell went up from the mob. Tom wheeled about and faced them. They poured down on him. They swarmed. A large man with dead-white face and flabby cheeks came to him and almost jabbed a gun-barrel through his guts.

"Hands behind y, nigger."

Tom's wrists were bound. The big man shoved him to the well. Burn him over it, and when the woodwork caved in, his body would drop to the bottom. Two deaths for a godam nigger. Louisa was driven back. The mob pushed in. Its pressure, its momentum was too great. Drag him to the factory. Wood and stakes already there. Tom moved in the direction indicated. But they had to drag him. They reached the great door. Too many to get in there. The mob divided and flowed around the walls to either side. The big man shoved him through the door. The mob pressed in from the sides. Taut humming. No words. A stake was sunk into the ground. Rotting floor boards piled around it. Kerosene poured on the rotting floor boards. Tom bound to the stake.

His breast was bare. Nails scratches let little lines of blood trickle down and mat into the hair. His face, his eyes were set and stony. Except for irregular breathing, one would have thought him already dead. Torches were flung onto the pile. A great flare muffled in black smoke shot upward. The mob yelled. The mob was silent. Now Tom could be seen within the flames. Only his head, erect, lean, like a blackened stone. Stench of burning flesh soaked the air. Tom's eyes popped. His head settled downward. The mob yelled. Its yell echoed against the skeleton stone walls and sounded like a hundred yells. Like a hundred mobs yelling. Its yell thudded against the thick front wall and fell back. Ghost of a yell slipped through the flames and out the great door of the factory. It fluttered like a dying thing down the single street of factory town. Louisa, upon the step before her home, did not hear it, but her eyes opened slowly. They saw the full moon glowing in the great door. The full moon, an evil thing, an omen, soft showering the homes of folks she knew. Where were they, these people? She'd sing, and perhaps they'd come out and join her. Perhaps Tom Burwell would come. At any rate, the full moon in the great door was an omen which she must sing to:

> Red nigger moon. Sinner!
> Blood-burning moon. Sinner!
> Come out that fact'ry door.

1923

William Faulkner *1897–1962*

William Harrison Faulkner, creator and proprietor of Yoknapatawpha County, the scene of his most important novels, was born in New Albany, Mississippi, and grew up in Oxford, the original of his fictional Jefferson. In 1918 he joined the Royal Canadian Air Force, but the war ended before he could see active service. Returning to Oxford, he attended the University of Mississippi for two years. In 1924 he went to New Orleans, where he met Sherwood Anderson, who encouraged his ambition to become a writer. During the same year he published *The Marble Faun*, a book of poems, and began work on his first novels: *Soldier's Pay* (1925), a romantic story of the return from war of a wounded flier, and *Mosquitoes* (1926), a satiric novel. In 1929 he issued two novels that inaugurated the Yoknapatawpha cycle: *Sartoris* and *The Sound and the Fury*. Both deal with the decay of aristocratic "old" families, the Sartorises and the Compsons. *The Sound and the Fury* is especially impressive because of its revolutionary form, consisting of four interrelated parts: three narrated from the viewpoints of individual characters, beginning with the story of the idiot Benjy, and the fourth from the viewpoint of the author.

Parallelling the decline of the old aristocracy was the rise of a new element. In a group of three comic novels—*The Hamlet* (1940), *The Town* (1957), *The Mansion* (1959)—Faulkner portrayed the operations of the unscrupulous, money-minded Snopeses, who represent the emergence of the uncultured, commercial middle class.

The third important group of characters in the Yoknapatawpha stories consists of the displaced and dispossessed Indians and the exploited Negroes. In Faulkner's fiction these characters figure as victims of a materialistic civilization and symbols of the white man's guilt. In a story like

"The Bear," Faulkner mingles the blood of the two races, against the background of the disappearing wilderness, in the character of Sam Fathers, who teaches the white boy Ike McCaslin the code of the hunter. In "Delta Autumn," Ike as an old man looks back on the continuing process of spoliation of the virgin land.

Other novels of Faulkner's early and middle years include *As I Lay Dying* (1930), *Sanctuary* (1931), *Light in August* (1932), *Pylon* (1935), *Absalom, Absalom!* (1936), *The Unvanquished* (1938), *The Wild Palms* (1939), *Intruder in the Dust* (1948), and *Requiem for a Nun* (1951). Later novels are *A Fable* (1954), a Christian allegory in a World War I setting, and *The Reivers* (1962), a nostalgic humorous story published in the year of Faulkner's death. Collections of short fiction are *These Thirteen* (1931), *Dr. Martino and Other Stories* (1934), *Go Down, Moses* (1942), *Knight's Gambit* (1949), *Collected Stories* (1950), and *Big Woods* (1955). Faulkner's literary and social opinions have been recorded in *Faulkner at Nagano* (1956) and *Faulkner in the University* (1959), the product of his residences as a visiting writer in Japan and at the University of Virginia.

A posthumous publication is *Essays, Speeches and Public Letters of William Faulkner*, ed. James Meriwether (New York, 1965). A helpful explanatory introduction to the Yoknapatawpha legend is Malcolm Cowley's introduction to *The Portable Faulkner* (New York, 1946). Other criticism includes F. J. Hoffman and O. W. Vickery, eds., *Three Decades of Faulkner Criticism* (East Lansing, Mich., 1960); W. V. O'Connor, *The Tangled Fire of William Faulkner* (Minneapolis, 1954); and H. H. Waggoner, *William Faulkner: From Jefferson to the World* (Lexington, Ky., 1959). Bibliographical aids are James Meriwether, *William Faulkner: A Check List* (Princeton, 1957); I. L. Sleeth, *William Faulkner: A Bibliography of Criticism* (Denver, 1962); and R. W. Kirk and Marvin Klotz, *Faulkner's People: A Complete Guide and Index to Characters in the Fiction of William Faulkner* (Berkeley, 1963).

The text of "Delta Autumn" is that of *Go Down, Moses* (New York, 1942).

Delta Autumn

Soon now they would enter the Delta.[1] The sensation was familiar to old Isaac McCaslin. It had been renewed like this each last week in November for more than fifty years—the last hill, at the foot of which the rich unbroken alluvial flatness began as the sea began at the base of its cliffs, dissolving away beneath the unhurried November rain as the sea itself would dissolve away.

At first they had come in wagons: the guns, the bedding, the dogs, the food, the whisky, the keen heartlifting anticipation of hunting; the young men who could drive all night and all the following day in the cold rain and pitch a camp in the rain and sleep in the wet blankets and

[1] The Delta is the bottom lands of the actual Tallahatchie River, in the northwest corner of Faulkner's fictional Yoknapatawpha County.

rise at daylight the next morning and hunt. There had been bear then. A man shot a doe or a fawn as quickly as he did a buck, and in the afternoons they shot wild turkey with pistols to test their stalking skill and marksmanship, feeding all but the breast to the dogs. But that time was gone now. Now they were in cars, driving faster and faster each year because the roads were better and they had farther and farther to drive, the territory in which game still existed drawing yearly inward as his life was drawing inward, until now he was the last of those who had once made the journey in wagons without feeling it and now those who accompanied him were the sons and even grandsons of the men who had ridden for twenty-four hours in the rain or sleet behind the steaming mules. They called him "Uncle Ike" now, and he no longer told anyone how near eighty he actually was because he knew as well as they did that he no longer had any business making such expeditions, even by car.

In fact, each time now, on that first night in camp, lying aching and sleepless in the harsh blankets, his blood only faintly warmed by the single thin whisky-and-water which he allowed himself, he would tell himself that this would be his last. But he would stand that trip—he still shot almost as well as he ever had, still killed almost as much of the game he saw as he ever killed; he no longer even knew how many deer had fallen before his gun—and the fierce long heat of the next summer would renew him. Then November would come again, and again in the car with two of the sons of his old companions, whom he had taught not only how to distinguish between the prints left by a buck or a doe but between the sound they made in moving, he would look ahead past the jerking arc of the windshield wiper and see the land flatten suddenly and swoop, dissolving away beneath the rain as the sea itself would dissolve, and he would say, "Well, boys, there it is again."

This time though, he didn't have time to speak. The driver of the car stopped it, slamming it to a skidding halt on the greasy pavement without warning, actually flinging the two passengers forward until they caught themselves with their braced hands against the dash. "What the hell, Roth!" the man in the middle said. "Can't you whistle first when you do that? Hurt you, Uncle Ike?"

"No," the old man said. "What's the matter?" The driver didn't answer. Still leaning forward, the old man looked sharply past the face of the man between them, at the face of his kinsman. It was the youngest face of them all, aquiline, saturnine, a little ruthless, the face of his ancestor too, tempered a little, altered a little, staring sombrely through the streaming windshield across which the twin wipers flicked and flicked.

"I didn't intend to come back in here this time," he said suddenly and harshly.

"You said that back in Jefferson last week," the old man said.

"Then you changed your mind. Have you changed it again? This ain't a very good time to ——"

"Oh, Roth's coming," the man in the middle said. His name was Legate. He seemed to be speaking to no one, as he was looking at neither of them. "If it was just a buck he was coming all this distance for, now. But he's got a doe in here. Of course a old man like Uncle Ike can't be interested in no doe, not one that walks on two legs — when she's standing up, that is. Pretty light-colored, too. The one he was after them nights last fall when he said he was coon-hunting, Uncle Ike. The one I figured maybe he was still running when he was gone all that month last January. But of course a old man like Uncle Ike ain't got no interest in nothing like that." He chortled, still looking at no one, not completely jeering.

"What?" the old man said. "What's that?" But he had not even so much as glanced at Legate. He was still watching his kinsman's face. The eyes behind the spectacles were the blurred eyes of an old man, but they were quite sharp too; eyes which could still see a gunbarrel and what ran beyond it as well as any of them could. He was remembering himself now: how last year, during the final stage by motor boat in to where they camped, a box of food had been lost overboard and how on the next day his kinsman had gone back to the nearest town for supplies and had been gone overnight. And when he did return, something had happened to him. He would go into the woods with his rifle each dawn when the others went, but the old man, watching him, knew that he was not hunting. "All right," he said. "Take me and Will on to shelter where we can wait for the truck, and you can go on back."

"I'm going in," the other said harshly. "Don't worry. Because this will be the last of it."

"The last of deer hunting, or of doe hunting?" Legate said. This time the old man paid no attention to him even by speech. He still watched the young man's savage and brooding face.

"Why?" he said.

"After Hitler gets through with it? Or Smith or Jones or Roosevelt or Willkie or whatever he will call himself in this country?"

"We'll stop him in this country," Legate said. "Even if he calls himself George Washington."

"How?" Edmonds said. "By singing 'God Bless America' in bars at midnight and wearing dime-store flags in our lapels?"

"So that's what's worrying you," the old man said. "I ain't noticed this country being short of defenders yet, when it needed them. You did some of it yourself twenty-odd years ago, before you were a grown man even. This country is a little mite stronger than any one man or group of men, outside of it or even inside of it either. I reckon, when the time comes and some of you have done got tired of hollering we are whipped if we don't go to war and some more are hollering we are whipped if we do, it will cope with one Austrian paperhanger, no matter what he will be calling himself. My pappy and some other better men than any of them you named tried once to tear it in two with a war, and they failed."

"And what have you got left?" the other said. "Half the people without jobs and half the factories closed by strikes. Half the people on public dole that won't work and half that couldn't work even if they would. Too much cotton and corn and hogs, and not enough for people to eat and wear. The country full of people to tell a man how he can't raise his own cotton whether he will or won't, and Sally Rand[2] with a sergeant's stripes and not even the fan couldn't fill the army rolls. Too much not-butter and not even the guns——"

"We got a deer camp—if we ever get to it," Legate said. "Not to mention does."

"It's a good time to mention does," the old man said. "Does and fawns both. The only fighting anywhere that ever had anything of God's blessing on it has been when men fought to protect does and fawns. If it's going to come to fighting, that's a good thing to mention and remember too."

"Haven't you discovered in—how many years more than seventy is it?—that women and children are one thing there's never any scarcity of?" Edmonds said.

"Maybe that's why all I am worrying about right now is that ten miles of river we still have got to run before we can make camp," the old man said. "So let's get on."

They went on. Soon they were going fast again, as Edmonds always drove, consulting neither of them about the speed just as he had given neither of them any warning when he slammed the car to stop. The old man relaxed again. He watched, as he did each recurrent November while more than sixty of them passed, the land which he had seen change. At first there had been only the old towns along the River and the old towns along the hills, from each of which the planters with their gangs of slaves and then of hired laborers had wrested from the impenetrable jungle of waterstanding cane and cypress, gum and holly and oak and ash, cotton patches which, as the years passed, became fields and then plantations. The paths made by deer and bear became roads and then highways, with towns in turn springing up along them and along the rivers Tallahatchie and Sunflower which joined and became the Yazoo, the River of the Dead of the Choctaws—the thick, slow, black, unsunned streams almost without current, which once each year ceased to flow at all and then reversed, spreading, drowning the rich land and subsiding again, leaving it still richer.

Most of that was gone now. Now a man drove two hundred miles

[2] The fan dancer who became a national celebrity at the Chicago Century of Progress Exposition in 1933.

from Jefferson before he found wilderness to hunt in. Now the land lay open from the cradling hills on the East to the rampart of levee on the West, standing horseman-tall with cotton for the world's looms – the rich black land, imponderable and vast, fecund up to the very doorsteps of the Negroes who worked it and of the white men who owned it; which exhausted the hunting life of a dog in one year, the working life of a mule in five and of a man in twenty – the land in which neon flashed past them from the little countless towns, and countless shining this-year's automobiles sped past them on the broad plumb-ruled highways, yet in which the only permanent mark of man's occupation seemed to be the tremendous gins, constructed in sections of sheet iron and in a week's time though they were, since no man, millionaire though he be, would build more than a roof and walls to shelter the camping equipment he lived from, when he knew that once each ten years or so his house would be flooded to the second storey and all within it ruined; – the land across which there came now no scream of panther but instead the long hooting of locomotives: trains of incredible length and drawn by a single engine, since there was no gradient anywhere and no elevation save those raised by forgotten aboriginal hands as refuges from the yearly water and used by their Indian successors to sepulchre their fathers' bones, and all that remained of that old time were the Indian names on the little towns and usually pertaining to water – Aluschaskuna, Tillatoba, Homochitto, Yazoo.

By early afternoon, they were on water. At the last little Indian-named town at the end of pavement they waited until the other car and the two trucks – the one carrying the bedding and tents and food, the other the horses – overtook them. They left the concrete and, after another mile or so, the gravel too. In caravan they ground on through the ceaselessly dissolving afternoon, with skid-chains on the wheels now, lurching and splashing and sliding among the ruts, until presently it seemed to him that the retrograde of his remembering had gained an inverse velocity from their own slow progress, that the land had retreated not in minutes from the last spread of gravel but in years, decades, back toward what it had been when he first knew it: the road they now followed once more the ancient pathway of bear and deer, the diminishing fields they now passed once more scooped punily and terrifically by axe and saw and mule-drawn plow from the wilderness' flank, out of the brooding and immemorial tangle, in place of ruthless mile-wide parallelograms wrought by ditching the dyking machinery.

They reached the river landing and unloaded, the horses to go overland down stream to a point opposite the camp and swim the river, themselves and the bedding and food and dogs and guns in the motor launch. It was himself, though no horseman, no farmer, not even a countryman save by his distant birth and boyhood, who coaxed and soothed the two horses, drawing them by his own single frail hand until, backing, filling, trembling a little, they surged, halted, then sprang scrambling down from the truck, possessing no affinity for them as creatures, beasts, but being merely insulated by his years and time from the corruption of steel and oiled moving parts which tainted the others.

Then, his old hammer double gun which was only twelve years younger than he standing between his knees, he watched even the last puny marks of man — cabin, clearing, the small and irregular fields which a year ago were jungle and in which the skeleton stalks of this year's cotton stood almost as tall and rank as the old cane had stood, as if man had had to marry his planting to the wilderness in order to conquer it — fall away and vanish. The twin banks marched with wilderness as he remembered it — the tangle of brier and cane impenetrable even to sight twenty feet away, the tall tremendous soaring of oak and gum and ash and hickory which had rung to no axe save the hunter's, had echoed to no machinery save the beat of old-time steam boats traversing it or to the snarling of launches like their own of people going into it to dwell for a week or two weeks because it was still wilderness. There was some of it left, although now it was two hundred miles from Jefferson when once it had been thirty. He had watched it, not being conquered, destroyed, so much as retreating since its purpose was served now and its time an outmoded time, retreating southward through this inverted-apex, this ∇-shaped section of earth between hills and River until what was left of it seemed new to be gathered and for the time arrested in one tremendous density of brooding and inscrutable impenetrability at the ultimate funnelling tip.

They reached the site of their last-year's camp with still two hours left of light. "You go on over under that driest tree and set down," Legate told him. "— if you can find it. Me and these other young boys will do this." He did neither. He was not tired yet. That would come later. *Maybe it won't come at all this time*, he thought, as he had thought at this point each November for the last five or six of them. *Maybe I will go out on stand in the morning too;* knowing that he would not, not even if he took the advice and sat down under the driest shelter and did nothing until camp was made and supper cooked. Because it would not be the fatigue. It would be because he would not sleep tonight but would lie instead wakeful and peaceful on the cot amid the tent-filling snoring and the rain's whisper as he always did on the first night in camp; peaceful, without regret or fretting, telling himself that was all right too, who didn't have so many of them left as to waste one sleeping.

In his slicker he directed the unloading of the boat — the tents, the stove, the bedding, the food for themselves and the dogs until there should be meat in camp. He sent two of the Negroes to cut firewood; he had the cook-tent raised and the stove up and a fire going and supper cooking while the big tent was still being staked down. Then in the beginning of dusk he crossed in the boat to where the horses waited, backing and snorting at the water. He took the lead-ropes and with no more weight than that and his voice, he drew them down into the water and held them beside the boat with only their heads above the surface, as though they actually were suspended from his frail and strengthless old man's hands, while the boat recrossed and each horse in turn lay prone in the shallows, panting and trembling, its eyes rolling in the dusk, until the same weightless hand and unraised voice gathered it surging upward, splashing and thrashing up the bank.

Then the meal was ready. The last of light was gone now save the thin stain of it snared somewhere between the river's surface and the rain. He had the single glass of thin whisky-and-water, then, standing in the churned mud beneath the stretched tarpaulin, he said grace over the fried slabs of pork, the hot soft shapeless bread, the canned beans and molasses and coffee in iron plates and cups,—the town food, brought along with them—then covered himself again, the others following. "Eat," he said. "Eat it all up. I don't want a piece of town meat in camp after breakfast tomorrow. Then you boys will hunt. You'll have to. When I first started hunting in this bottom sixty years ago with old General Compson and Major de Spain and Roth's grandfather and Will Legate's too, Major de Spain wouldn't allow but two pieces of foreign grub in his camp. That was one side of pork and one ham of beef. And not to eat for the first supper and breakfast neither. It was to save until along toward the end of camp when everybody was so sick of bear meat and coon and venison that we couldn't even look at it."

"I thought Uncle Ike was going to say the pork and beef was for the dogs," Legate said, chewing. "But that's right; I remember. You just shot the dogs a mess of wild turkey every evening when they got tired of deer guts."

"Times are different now," another said. "There was game here then."

"Yes," the old man said quietly. "There was game here then."

"Besides, they shot does then too," Legate said. "As it is now, we ain't got but one doe hunter in ——"

"And better men hunted it," Edmonds said. He stood at the end of the rough plank table, eating rapidly and steadily as the others ate. But again the old man looked sharply across at the sullen, handsome, brooding face which appeared now darker and more sullen still in the light of the smoky lantern. "Go on. Say it."

"I didn't say that," the old man said. "There are good men everywhere, at all times. Most men are. Some are just unlucky, because most men are a little better than their circumstances give them a chance to be. And I've known some that even the circumstances couldn't stop."

"Well, I wouldn't say—" Legate said.

"So you've lived almost eighty years," Edmonds said, "and that's what you finally learned about the other animals you lived among. I suppose the question to ask you is, where have you been all the time you were dead?"

There was a silence; for the instant even Legate's jaw stopped chewing while he gaped at Edmonds. "Well, by God, Roth—" the third speaker said. But it was the old man who spoke, his voice still peaceful and untroubled and merely grave:

"Maybe so," he said. "But if being what you call alive would have learned me any different, I reckon I'm satisfied, wherever it was I've been."

"Well, I wouldn't say that Roth—" Legate said.

The third speaker was still leaning forward a little over the table, looking at Edmonds. "Meaning that it's only because folks happen to be watching him that a man behaves at all," he said. "Is that it?"

"Yes," Edmonds said. "A man in a blue coat, with a badge on it watching him. Maybe just the badge."

"I deny that," the old man said. "I don't——"

The other two paid no attention to him. Even Legate was listening to them for the moment, his mouth still full of food and still open a little, his knife with another lump of something balanced on the tip of the blade arrested halfway to his mouth. "I'm glad I don't have your opinion of folks," the third speaker said. "I take it you include yourself."

"I see," Edmonds said. "You prefer Uncle Ike's opinion of circumstances. All right. Who makes the circumstances?"

"Luck," the third said. "Chance. Happen-so. I see what you are getting at. But that's just what Uncle Ike said: that now and then, maybe most of the time, man is a little better than the net result of his and his neighbors' doings, when he gets the chance to be."

This time Legate swallowed first. He was not to be stopped this time. "Well, I wouldn't say that Roth Edmonds can hunt one doe every day and night for two weeks and was a poor hunter or a unlucky one neither. A man that still have the same doe left to hunt on again next year——"

"Have some meat," the man next to him said.

"—ain't so unlucky—What?" Legate said.

"Have some meat." The other offered the dish.

"I got some," Legate said.

"Have some more," the third speaker said. "You and Roth Edmonds both. Have a heap of it. Clapping your jaws together that way with nothing to break the shock." Someone chortled. Then they all laughed, with relief, the tension broken. But the old man was speaking, even into the laughter, in that peaceful and still untroubled voice:

"I still believe. I see proof everywhere. I grant that man made a heap of his circumstances, him and his living neighbors between them. He even inherited some of them already made, already almost ruined even. A while ago Henry Wyatt there said how there used to be more game here. There was. So much that we even killed does. I seem to remember Will Legate mentioning that too—" Someone laughed, a single guffaw, stillborn. It ceased and they all listened, gravely, looking down at their plates. Edmonds was drinking his coffee, sullen, brooding, inattentive.

"Some folks still kill does," Wyatt said. "There won't be just one buck hanging in this bottom tomorrow night without any head to fit it."

"I didn't say all men," the old man said. "I said most men. And not just because there is a man with a badge to watch us. We probably won't even see him unless maybe he will stop here about noon tomorrow and eat dinner with us and check our licenses——"

"We don't kill does because if we did kill does in a few years there wouldn't even be any bucks left to kill, Uncle Ike," Wyatt said.

"According to Roth yonder, that's one thing we won't never have to worry about," the old man said. "He said on the way here this morning that does and fawns—I believe he said women and children—are two things this world ain't ever lacked. But that ain't all of it," he said. "That's just the mind's reason a man has to give himself because the heart don't always have time to bother with thinking up words that fit together. God created man and He created the world for him to live in and I reckon He created the kind of world He would have wanted to live in if He had been a man—the ground to walk on, the big woods, the trees and the water, and the game to live in it. And maybe He didn't put the desire to hunt and kill game in man but I reckon He knew it was going to be there, that man was going to teach it to himself, since he wasn't quite God himself yet——"

"When will he be?" Wyatt said.

"I think that every man and woman, at the instant when it don't even matter whether they marry or not, I think that whether they marry then or afterward or don't never, at that instant the two of them together were God."

"Then there are some Gods in this world I wouldn't want to touch, and with a damn long stick," Edmonds said. He set his coffee cup down and looked at Wyatt. "And that includes myself, if that's what you want to know. I'm going to bed." He was gone. There was a general movement among the others. But it ceased and they stood again about the table, not looking at the old man, apparently held there yet by his quiet and peaceful voice as the heads of the swimming horses had been held above the water by his weightless hand. The three Negroes —the cook and his helper and old Isham—were sitting quietly in the entrance of the kitchen tent, listening too, the three faces dark and motionless and musing.

"He put them both here: man, and the game he would follow and kill, foreknowing it. I believe He said, 'So be it.' I reckon He even foreknew the end. But He said, 'I will give him his chance. I will give him warning and foreknowledge too, along with the desire to follow and the power to slay. The woods and fields he ravages and the game he devastates will be the consequence and signature of his crime and guilt, and his punishment.'—Bed time," he said. His voice and inflection did not change at all. "Breakfast at four o'clock, Isham. We want meat on the ground by sunup time."

There was a good fire in the sheet-iron heater; the tent was warm and was beginning to dry out, except for the mud underfoot. Edmonds was already rolled into his blankets, motionless, his face to the wall. Isham had made up his bed too—the strong, battered iron cot, the stained mattress which was not quite soft enough, the worn, often-washed blankets which as the years passed were less and less warm enough. But the tent was warm; presently, when the kitchen was cleaned up and readied for breakfast, the young Negro would come in to lie down before the heater, where he could be roused to put fresh wood into it from time to time. And then, he knew now he would not sleep tonight anyway; he no longer needed to tell himself that perhaps he would. But it was all right now. The day was ended now and night faced him, but alarmless, empty of fret. *Maybe I came for this,* he thought: *Not to hunt, but for this. I would come anyway, even if only to go back home tomorrow.* Wearing only his bagging woolen underwear, his spectacles folded away in the worn case beneath the pillow where he could reach them readily and his lean body fitted easily into the old worn groove of mattress and blankets, he lay on his back, his hands crossed on his breast and his eyes closed while the others undressed and went to bed and the last of the sporadic talking died into snoring. Then he opened his eyes and lay peaceful and quiet as a child, looking up at the motionless belly of rain-murmured canvas upon which the glow of the heater was dying slowly away and would fade still further until the young Negro, lying on two planks before it, would sit up and stoke it and lie back down again.

They had a house once. That was sixty years ago, when the Big Bottom was only thirty miles from Jefferson and old Major de Spain, who had been his father's cavalry commander in '61 and '2 and '3 and '4, and his cousin (his older brother; his father too) had taken him into the woods for the first time. Old Sam Fathers was alive then, born in slavery, son of a Negro slave and a Chickasaw chief, who had taught him how to shoot, not only when to shoot but when not to; such a November dawn as tomorrow would be and the old man led him straight to the great cypress and he had known the buck would pass exactly there because there was something running in Sam Fathers' veins which ran in the veins of the buck too, and they stood there against the tremendous trunk, the old man of seventy and the boy of twelve, and there was nothing save the dawn until suddenly the buck was there, smoke-colored out of nothing, magnificent with speed: and Sam Fathers said, 'Now. Shoot quick and shoot slow:' and the gun levelled rapidly without haste and crashed and he walked to the buck lying still intact and still in the shape of that magnificent speed and bled it with Sam's knife and Sam dipped his hands into the hot blood and marked his face forever while he stood trying not to tremble, humbly and with pride too though the boy of twelve had been unable to phrase it then: *I slew you; my bearing must not shame your quitting life. My conduct forever onward must become your death;* marking him for that and for more than that: that day and himself and McCaslin juxtaposed, not against the wilderness but against the tamed land, the old wrong and shame itself, in repudiation and denial at least of the land and the wrong and shame, even if he couldn't cure the wrong and eradicate the shame, who at fourteen when he learned of it had believed he could do both when he became competent, and when at twenty-one he became competent he knew that he could do neither but at least he could repudiate the wrong and shame, at least in principle, and at least the land itself in fact, for his son at least: and did, thought he had: then (married then) in a rented cubicle in a back-street stock-traders' boardinghouse, the first and last time he ever saw her naked body, himself and his wife juxtaposed in their turn against that same land, that same wrong and shame from whose regret and grief he would at least save and free his son and, saving and freeing his son, lost him.

They had the house then. That roof, the two weeks of each November which they spent under it, had become his home. Although since that time they had lived during the two fall weeks in tents and not always in the same place two years in succession and now his companions where the sons and even the grandsons of them with whom he had lived in the house, and for almost fifty years now the house itself had not even existed, the conviction, the sense and feeling of home, had been merely transferred into the canvas. He owned a house in Jefferson, a good house though small, where he had had a wife and lived with her and lost her, ay, lost her even though he had lost her in the rented cubicle before he and his old clever dipsomaniac partner had finished the house for them to move into it: but lost her, because she loved him. But women hope for so much. They never live too long to still believe that anything within the scope of their passionate wanting is likewise within the range of their passionate hope: and it was still kept for him by his dead wife's widowed niece and her children, and he was comfortable in it, his wants and needs and even the small trying harmless crochets of an old man looked after by blood at least related to the blood which he had elected out of all the earth to cherish. But he spent the time within those walls waiting for November, because even this tent with its muddy floor and the bed which was not wide enough nor soft enough nor even warm enough, was his home and these men, some of whom he only saw during these two November weeks and not one of whom even bore any name he used to know — De Spain and Compson and Ewell and Hogganbeck — were more his kin than any. Because this was his land——

The shadow of the youngest Negro loomed. It soared, blotting the heater's dying glow from the ceiling, the wood billets thumping into the iron maw until the glow, the flame, leaped high and bright across the canvas. But the Negro's shadow still remained, by its length and breadth, standing, since it covered most of the ceiling, until after a moment he raised himself on one elbow to look. It was not the Negro, it was his kinsman; when he spoke the other turned sharp against the red firelight the sullen and ruthless profile.

"Nothing," Edmonds said. "Go on back to sleep."

"Since Will Legate mentioned it," McCaslin said, "I remember you had some trouble sleeping in here last fall too. Only you called it coon-hunting then. Or was it Will Legate called it that?" The other didn't answer. Then he turned and went back to his bed. McCaslin, still propped on his elbow, watched until the other's shadow sank down the wall and vanished, became one with the mass of sleeping shadows. "That's right," he said. "Try to get some sleep. We must have meat in camp tomorrow. You can do all the setting up you want to after that." He lay down again, his hands crossed again on his breast, watching the glow of the heater on the canvas ceiling. It was steady again now, the fresh wood accepted, being assimilated; soon it would begin to fade again, taking with it the last echo of that sudden upflare of a young man's passion and unrest. Let him lie awake for a little while, he thought; He will lie still some day for a long time without even dissatisfaction to disturb him. And lying awake here, in these surroundings, would soothe him if anything could, if anything could soothe a man just forty years old. Yes, he thought; Forty years old or thirty, or even the trembling and sleepless ardor of a boy; already the tent, the rain-murmured canvas globe, was once more filled with it. He lay on his back, his eyes closed, his breathing quiet and peaceful as a child's, listening to it — that silence which was never silence but was myriad. He could almost see it, tremendous, primeval, looming, musing downward upon this puny evanescent clutter of human sojourn which after a single brief week would vanish and in another week would be completely healed, traceless in the unmarked solitude. Because it was his land, although he had never owned a foot of it. He had never wanted to, not even after he saw plain its ultimate doom, watching it retreat year by year before the onslaught of axe and saw and log-lines and then dynamite and tractor plows, because it belonged to no man. It belonged to all; they had only to use it well, humbly and with pride. Then suddenly he knew why he had never wanted to own any of it, arrest at least that much of what people called progress, measure his longevity at least against that much of its ultimate fate. It was because there was just exactly enough of it. He seemed to see the two of them—himself and the wilderness—as coevals, his own span as a hunter, a woodsman, not contemporary with his first breath but transmitted to him, assumed by him gladly, humbly, with joy and pride, from that old Major de Spain and that old Sam Fathers who had taught him to hunt, the two spans running out together, not toward oblivion, nothingness, but into a dimension free of both time and space, where once more the untreed land warped and wrung to mathematical squares of rank cotton for the frantic old-world people to turn into shells to shoot at one another, would find ample room for both—the names, the faces of the old men he had known and loved and for a little while outlived, moving again among the shades of the tall unaxed trees and sightless brakes where the wild strong immortal game ran forever before the tireless belling immortal hounds, falling and rising phoenixlike to the soundless guns.

He had been asleep. The lantern was lighted now. Outside in the darkness the oldest Negro, Isham, was beating a spoon against the bottom of a tin pan and crying, "Raise up and get yo foa clock coffy. Raise up and get yo foa clock coffy," and the tent was full of low talk and of men dressing, and Legate's voice, repeating: "Get out of here now and let Uncle Ike sleep. If you wake him up, he'll go out with us. And he ain't got any business in the woods this morning."

So he didn't move. He lay with his eyes closed, his breathing gentle and peaceful, and heard them one by one leave the tent. He listened to the breakfast sounds from the table beneath the tarpaulin and heard them depart—the horses, the dogs, the last voice until it died away and there was only the sounds of the Negroes clearing breakfast away. After a while he might possibly even hear the first faint clear cry of the first hound ring through the wet woods from where the buck had bedded, then he would go back to sleep again—The tent-flap swung in and fell. Something jarred sharply against the end of the cot and a hand grasped his knee through the blanket before he could open his eyes. It was Edmonds, carrying a shotgun in place of his rifle. He spoke in a harsh, rapid voice:

"Sorry to wake you. There will be a ——"

"I was awake," McCaslin said. "Are you going to shoot that shotgun today?"

"You just told me last night you want meat," Edmonds said. "There will be a ——"

"Since when did you start having trouble getting meat with your rifle?"

"All right," the other said, with that harsh, restrained, furious impatience. Then McCaslin saw in his hand a thick oblong: an envelope. "There will be a message here some time this morning, looking for me. Maybe it won't come. If it does, give the messenger this and tell h— say I said No."

"A what?" McCaslin said. "Tell who?" He half rose onto his
elbow as Edmonds jerked the envelope onto the blanket, already turning toward the entrance, the envelope striking solid and heavy and
without noise and already sliding from the bed until McCaslin caught it,
divining by feel through the paper as instantaneously and conclusively
as if he had opened the envelope and looked, the thick sheaf of banknotes. "Wait," he said. "Wait:"— more than the blood kinsman, more
even than the senior in years, so that the other paused, the canvas lifted,
looking back, and McCaslin saw that outside it was already day.
"Tell her No," he said. "Tell her." They stared at one another— the old
face, wan, sleep-raddled above the tumbled bed, the dark and sullen
younger one at once furious and cold. "Will Legate was right. This is
what you called coon-hunting. And now this." He didn't raise the envelope. He made no motion, no gesture to indicate it. "What did you
promise her that you haven't the courage to face her and retract?"

"Nothing!" the other said. "Nothing! This is all of it. Tell her I
said No." He was gone. The tent flap lifted on an in-waft of faint light
and the constant murmur of rain, and fell again, leaving the old man still
half-raised onto one elbow, the envelope clutched in the other shaking
hand. Afterward it seemed to him that he had begun to hear the approaching boat almost immediately, before the other could have got out
of sight even. It seemed to him that there had been no interval whatever:
the tent flap falling on the same out-waft of faint and rain-filled light
like the suspiration and expiration of the same breath and then in the
next second lifted again— the mounting snarl of the outboard engine,
increasing, nearer and nearer and louder and louder then cut short off,
ceasing with the absolute instantaneity of a blown-out candle, into the
lap and plop of water under the bows as the skiff slid in to the bank,
the youngest Negro, the youth, raising the tent flap beyond which for
that instant he saw the boat— a small skiff with a Negro man sitting in the
stern beside the upslanted motor— then the woman entering, in a man's
hat and a man's slicker and rubber boots, carrying the blanket-swaddled
bundle on one arm and holding the edge of the unbuttoned raincoat
over it with the other hand: and bringing something else, something in-
tangible, an effluvium which he knew he would recognize in a moment
because Isham had already told him, warned him, by sending the young
Negro to the tent to announce the visitor instead of coming himself, the
flap falling at last on the young Negro and they were alone— the face
indistinct and as yet only young and with dark eyes, queerly colorless
but not ill and not that of a country woman despite the garments she
wore, looking down at him where he sat upright on the cot now, clutching the envelope, the soiled undergarment bagging about him and the
twisted blankets huddled about his hips.

"Is this his?" he cried. "Don't lie to me!"

"Yes," she said. "He's gone."

"Yes. He's gone. You won't jump him here. Not this time. I don't reckon even you expected that. He left you this. Here." He fumbled at the envelope. It was not to pick it up, because it was still in his hand; he had never put it down. It was as if he had to fumble somehow to co-ordinate physically his heretofore obedient hand with what his brain was commanding of it, as if he had never performed such an action before, extending the envelope at last, saying again, "Here. Take it. Take it:" until he became aware of her eyes, or not the eyes so much as the look, the regard fixed now on his face with that immersed contemplation, that bottomless and intent candor, of a child. If she had ever seen either the envelope or his movement to extend it, she did not show it.

"You're Uncle Isaac," she said.

"Yes," he said. "But never mind that. Here. Take it. He said to tell you No." She looked at the envelope, then she took it. It was sealed and bore no superscription. Nevertheless, even after she glanced at the front of it he watched her hold it in the one free hand and tear the corner off with her teeth and manage to rip it open and tilt the neat sheaf of bound notes onto the blanket without even glancing at them and look into the empty envelope and take the edge between her teeth and tear it completely open before she crumpled and dropped it.

"That's just money," she said.

"What did you expect? What else did you expect? You have known him long enough or at least often enough to have got that child, and you don't know him any better than that?"

"Not very often. Not very long. Just that week here last fall, and in January he sent for me and we went west, to New Mexico. We were there six weeks, where I could at least sleep in the same apartment where I cooked for him and looked after his clothes ——"

"But not marriage," he said. "Not marriage. He didn't promise you that. Don't lie to me. He didn't have to."

"No. He didn't have to. I didn't ask him to. I knew what I was doing. I knew that to begin with, long before honor, I imagine he called it, told him the time had come to tell me in so many words what his code, I suppose he would call it, would forbid him forever to do. And we agreed. Then we agreed again before he left New Mexico, to make sure. That that would be all of it. I believed him. No, I don't mean that; I mean I believed myself. I wasn't even listening to him any more by then because by that time it had been a long time since he had had anything else to tell me for me to have to hear. By then I wasn't even listening enough to ask him to please stop talking. I was listening to myself. And I believed it. I must have believed it. I don't see how I could have helped but believe it, because he was gone then as we had agreed and he didn't write as we had agreed, just the money came to the bank in Vicksburg in my name but coming from nobody as we had agreed. So I must have believed it. I even wrote him last month to make sure again and the letter came back unopened and I was sure. So I left the hospital and rented myself a room to live in until the deer season opened so I could make sure myself and I was waiting beside the road yesterday when your car passed and he saw me and so I was sure."

"Then what do you want?" he said. "What do you want? What do you expect?"

"Yes," she said. And while he glared at her, his white hair awry from the pillow and his eyes, lacking the spectacles to focus them, blurred and irisless and apparently pupilless, he saw again that grave, intent, speculative and detached fixity like a child watching him. "His great great— Wait a minute—great great *great* grandfather was your grandfather. McCaslin. Only it got to be Edmonds. Only it got to be more than that. Your cousin McCaslin was there that day when your father and Uncle Buddy won Tennie from Mr. Beauchamp for the one that had no name but Terrel so you called him Tomey's Terrel, to marry. But after that it got to be Edmonds." She regarded him, almost peacefully, with that unwinking and heatless fixity—the dark, wide, bottomless eyes in the face's dead and toneless pallor which to the old man looked anything but dead, but young and incredibly and even ineradicably alive—as though she were not only not looking at anything, she was not even speaking to anyone but herself. "I would have made a man of him. He's not a man yet. You spoiled him. You, and Uncle Lucas and Aunt Mollie. But mostly you."

"Me?" he said. "Me?"

"Yes. When you gave to his grandfather that land which didn't belong to him, not even half of it, by will or even law."

"And never mind that too," he said. "Never mind that too. You," he said. "You sound like you have been to college even. You sound almost like a Northerner even, not like the draggle-tailed women of these Delta peckerwoods. Yet you meet a man on the street one afternoon just because a box of groceries happened to fall out of a boat. And a month later you go off with him and live with him until he got a child on you: and then, by your own statement, you sat there while he took his hat and said goodbye and walked out. Even a Delta peckerwood would look after even a draggle-tail better than that. Haven't you got any folks at all?"

"Yes," she said. "I was living with one of them. My aunt, in Vicksburg. I came to live with her two years ago when my father died; we lived in Indianapolis then. But I got a job, teaching school here in Aluschaskuna, because my aunt was a widow, with a big family, taking in washing to sup——"

"Took in what?" he said. "Took in washing?" He sprang, still seated even, flinging himself backward onto one arm, awry-haired, glaring. Now he understood what it was she had brought into the tent with her, what old Isham had already told him by sending the youth to bring her in to him — the pale lips, the skin pallid and dead-looking yet not ill, the dark and tragic and foreknowing eyes. *Maybe in a thousand or two thousand years in America,* he thought. *But not now! Not now!* He cried, not loud, in a voice of amazement, pity, and outrage: "You're a nigger!"

"Yes," she said. "James Beauchamp—you called him Tennie's Jim though he had a name—was my grandfather. I said you were Uncle Isaac."[3]

"And he knows?"

"No," she said. "What good would that have done?"

"But you did," he cried. "But you did. Then what do you expect here?"

"Nothing."

"Then why did you come here? You said you were waiting in Aluschaskuna yesterday and he saw you. Why did you come this morning?"

"I'm going back North. Back home. My cousin brought me up the day before yesterday in his boat. He's going to take me on to Leland to get the train."

"Then go," he said. Then he cried again in that thin not loud and grieving voice: "Get out of here! I can do nothing for you! Can't nobody do nothing for you!" She moved; she was not looking at him again, toward the entrance. "Wait," he said. She paused again, obediently still, turning. He took up the sheaf of banknotes and laid it on the blanket at the foot of the cot and drew his hand back beneath the blanket. "There," he said.

Now she looked at the money, for the first time, one brief blank glance, then away again. "I don't need it. He gave me money last winter. Besides the money he sent to Vicksburg. Provided. Honor and code too. That was all arranged."

"Take it," he said. His voice began to rise again, but he stopped it. "Take it out of my tent." She came back to the cot and took up the money; whereupon once more he said, "Wait:" although she had not turned, still stooping, and he put out his hand. But, sitting, he could not complete the reach until she moved her hand, the single hand which held the money, until he touched it. He didn't grasp it, he merely touched it—the gnarled, bloodless, bone-light bone-dry old man's fingers touching for a second the smooth young flesh where the strong old blood ran after its long lost journey back to home. "Tennie's Jim," he said. "Tennie's Jim." He drew the hand back beneath the blanket

---

[3] Ike and Roth Edmonds and the girl who has born Roth's child are all descendants of Ike's grandfather, L.Q.C. McCaslin — Ike and Roth through the grandfather's white wife, the girl through his black mistress.

again: he said harshly now: "It's a boy, I reckon. They usually are, except that one that was its own mother too."

"Yes," she said. "It's a boy." She stood for a moment longer, looking at him. Just for an instant her free hand moved as though she were about to lift the edge of the raincoat away from the child's face. But she did not. She turned again when once more he said Wait and moved beneath the blanket.

"Turn your back," he said. "I am going to get up. I ain't got my pants on." Then he could not get up. He sat in the huddled blanket, shaking, while again she turned and looked down at him in dark interrogation. "There," he said harshly, in the thin and shaking old man's voice. "On the nail there. The tent-pole."

"What?" she said.

"The horn!" he said harshly. "The horn." She went and got it, thrust the money into the slicker's side pocket as if it were a rag, a soiled handkerchief, and lifted down the horn, the one which General Compson had left him in his will, covered with the unbroken skin from a buck's shank and bound with silver.

"What?" she said.

"It's his. Take it."

"Oh," she said. "Yes. Thank you."

"Yes," he said, harshly, rapidly, but not so harsh now and soon not harsh at all but just rapid, urgent, until he knew that his voice was running away with him and he had neither intended it nor could stop it: "That's right. Go back North, Marry: a man in your own race. That's the only salvation for you—for a while yet, maybe a long while yet. We will have to wait. Marry a black man. You are young, handsome, almost white; you could find a black man who would see in you what it was you saw in him, who would ask nothing of you and expect less and get even still less than that, if it's revenge you want. Then you will forget all this, forget it ever happened, that he ever existed—" until he could stop it at last and did, sitting there in his huddle of blankets during the instant when, without moving at all, she blazed silently down at him. Then that was gone too. She stood in the gleaming and still dripping slicker, looking quietly down at him from under the sodden hat.

"Old man," she said, "have you lived so long and forgotten so much that you don't remember anything you ever knew or felt or even heard about love?"

Then she was gone too. The waft of light and the murmur of the constant rain flowed into the tent and then out again as the flap fell. Lying back once more, trembling, panting, the blanket huddled to his chin and his hands crossed on his breast, he listened to the pop and snarl, the mounting then fading whine of the motor until it died away and once again the tent held only silence and the sound of rain. And cold too: he lay shaking faintly and steadily in it, rigid save for the shaking. This Delta, he thought: This Delta. *This land which man has deswamped and denuded and derivered in two generations so that white men can own plantations and commute every night to Memphis and black men own plantations and ride in Jim Crow cars to Chicago to live in millionaires' mansions on Lake Shore Drive, where white men rent farms and live like niggers and niggers crop on shares and live like animals; where cotton is planted and grows man-tall in the very cracks of the sidewalks, and usury and mortgage and bankruptcy and measureless wealth, Chinese and African and Aryan and Jew, all breed and spawn together until no man has time to say which one is which nor cares . . .* No wonder the ruined woods I used to know don't cry for retribution! he thought: The people who have destroyed it will accomplish its revenge.

The tent flap jerked rapidly in and fell. He did not move save to turn his head and open his eyes. It was Legate. He went quickly to Edmonds' bed and stooped, rummaging hurriedly among the still-tumbled blankets.

"What is it?" he said.

"Looking for Roth's knife," Legate said. "I come back to get a horse. We got a deer on the ground." He rose, the knife in his hand, and hurried toward the entrance.

"Who killed it?" McCaslin said. "Was it Roth?"

"Yes," Legate said, raising the flap.

"Wait," McCaslin said. He moved, suddenly, onto his elbow. "What was it?" Legate paused for an instant beneath the lifted flap. He did not look back.

"Just a deer, Uncle Ike," he said impatiently. "Nothing extra." He was gone; again the flap fell behind him, wafting out of the tent again the faint light and the constant and grieving rain. McCaslin lay back down, the blanket once more drawn to his chin, his crossed hands once more weightless on his breast in the empty tent.

"It was a doe," he said.

1942

Katherine Anne Porter   1890 –

Katherine Anne Porter, whose reputation as a distinguished writer is based on a relatively slight body of work, was born in Indian Creek, Texas. Descended from old Southern stock, she was educated in private and convent schools before going to New York City in 1920. In the years following she also lived at various times in Mexico and in Germany and France. Although she had begun writing stories as a young girl, her standards were high, and it was not until the 1920's, when she was in her thirties, that she began publishing her work in literary magazines. Her first collection of six stories, *Flowering Judas* (1930), was reissued in an enlarged edition in 1935. Much of her work has been done in the form of the novella: *Hacienda* (1934) has as its subject the making of a film in Mexico by the Russian director Eisenstein; *Noon Wine* (1937), which may prove to be her masterpiece, sensitively presents and probes the moral predicament of a South Texas farmer whose act of involuntary murder becomes the focus of a conflict between justification and guilt. In *Pale Horse, Pale Rider* (1939), Miss Porter reissued *Noon Wine* with two other novellas. Both *Old Mortality* and the title story deal with the growth and search for identity of the autobiographical heroine Miranda. In *Pale Horse, Pale Rider*, which has a strong thematic affinity with Hemingway's *Farewell to Arms,* Miranda loses, in an influenza epidemic, the young soldier with whom she had fallen in love.

Among her other work, *No Safe Harbor* (1941) is a novella; *The Leaning Tower* (1944), a collection of later stories; and *The Days Before* (1952), a gathering of essays. The ambitious novel on which Miss Porter had worked many years, *The Ship of Fools* (1962), tells the interrelated stories of a representative collection of ship passengers, many of them German, sailing from Mexico to Germany in 1931, on the brink of that country's descent into Nazism. Although the novel was a popular success, it lacks the intensity and the organic unity of Miss Porter's novellas and short stories. *The Collected Stories of Katherine Anne Porter* appeared in 1965.

A critique and a critical biography of Miss Porter are W. L. Nance, *Katherine Anne Porter and the Art of Rejection* (Chapel Hill, N.C., 1964), and George Hendrick, *Katherine Anne Porter* (New York, 1965). The fullest bibliography is Edward Schwartz, *Katherine Anne Porter: A Critical Bibliography* (New York, 1957).

The text of *Noon Wine* is that of *Pale Horse, Pale Rider* (New York, 1939).

Noon Wine

Time: *1896–1905*
Place: *Small South Texas Farm*

The two grubby small boys with tow-colored hair who were digging among the ragweed in the front yard sat back on their heels and said, "Hello," when the tall bony man with straw-colored hair turned in at their gate. He did not pause at the gate; it had swung back, conveniently half open, long ago, and was now sunk so firmly on its broken hinges no one thought of trying to close it. He did not even glance at the small boys, much less give them good-day. He just clumped down his big square dusty shoes one after the other steadily, like a man following a plow, as if he knew the place well and knew where he was going and what he would find there. Rounding the right-hand corner of the house under the row of chinaberry trees, he walked up to the side porch where Mr. Thompson was pushing a big swing churn back and forth.

Mr. Thompson was a tough weather-beaten man with stiff black hair and a week's growth of black whiskers. He was a noisy proud man who held his neck so straight his whole face stood level with his Adam's apple, and the whiskers continued down his neck and disappeared into a black thatch under his open collar. The churn rumbled and swished like the belly of a trotting horse, and Mr. Thompson seemed somehow to be driving a horse with one hand, reining it in and urging it forward; and every now and then he turned halfway around and squirted a tremendous spit of tobacco juice out over the steps. The door stones were brown and gleaming with fresh tobacco juice. Mr. Thompson had been churning quite a while and he was tired of it. He was just fetching a mouthful of juice to squirt again when the stranger came around the corner and stopped. Mr. Thompson saw a narrow-chested man with blue eyes so pale they were almost white, looking and not looking at him from a long gaunt face, under white eyebrows. Mr. Thompson judged him to be another of these Irishmen, by his long upper lip.

"Howdy do, sir," said Mr. Thompson politely, swinging his churn.

"I need work," said the man, clearly enough but with some kind of foreign accent Mr. Thompson couldn't place. It wasn't Cajun and it wasn't Nigger and it wasn't Dutch, so it had him stumped. "You need a man here?"

Mr. Thompson gave the churn a great shove and it swung back and forth several times on its own momentum. He sat on the steps, shot his quid into the grass, and said, "Set down. Maybe we can make a deal. I been kinda lookin' round for somebody. I had two niggers but they got into a cutting scrape up the creek last week, one of 'em dead now and the other in the hoosegow at Cold Springs. Neither one of 'em worth killing, come right down to it. So it looks like I'd better get somebody. Where'd you work last?"

"North Dakota," said the man, folding himself down on the other end of the steps, but not as if he were tired. He folded up and settled down as if it would be a long time before he got up again. He never had looked at Mr. Thompson, but there wasn't anything sneaking in his eye, either. He didn't seem to be looking anywhere else. His eyes sat in his head and let things pass by them. They didn't seem to be expecting to see anything worth looking at. Mr. Thompson waited a long time for the man to say something more, but he had gone into a brown study.

"North Dakota," said Mr. Thompson, trying to remember where that was. "That's a right smart distance off, seems to me."

"I can do everything on farm," said the man; "cheap. I need work."

Mr. Thompson settled himself to get down to business. "My name's Thompson, Mr. Royal Earle Thompson," he said.

"I'm Mr. Helton," said the man, "Mr. Olaf Helton." He did not move.

"Well, now," said Mr. Thompson in his most carrying voice, "I guess we'd better talk turkey."

When Mr. Thompson expected to drive a bargain he always grew very hearty and jovial. There was nothing wrong with him except that he hated like the devil to pay wages. He said so himself. "You furnish grub and a shack," he said, "and then you got to pay 'em besides. It ain't right. Besides the wear and tear on your implements," he said, "they just let everything go to rack and ruin." So he began to laugh and shout his way through the deal.

"Now, what I want to know is, how much you fixing to gouge outa me?" he brayed, slapping his knee. After he had kept it up as long as he could, he quieted down, feeling a little sheepish, and cut himself a chew. Mr. Helton was staring out somewhere between the barn and the orchard, and seemed to be sleeping with his eyes open.

"I'm good worker," said Mr. Helton as from the tomb. "I get dollar a day."

Mr. Thompson was so shocked he forgot to start laughing again at the top of his voice until it was nearly too late to do any good. "Haw,

haw," he bawled. "Why, for a dollar a day I'd hire out myself. What kinda work is it where they pay you a dollar a day?"

"Wheatfields, North Dakota," said Mr. Helton, not even smiling.

Mr. Thompson stopped laughing. "Well, this ain't any wheatfield by a long shot. This is more of a dairy farm," he said, feeling apologetic. "My wife, she was set on a dairy, she seemed to like working around with cows and calves, so I humored her. But it was a mistake," he said. "I got nearly everything to do, anyhow. My wife ain't very strong. She's sick today, that's a fact. She's been porely for the last few days. We plant a little feed, and a corn patch, and there's the orchard, and a few pigs and chickens, but our main hold is the cows. Now just speakin' as one man to another, there ain't any money in it. Now I can't give you no dollar a day because ackshally I don't make that much out of it. No, sir, we get along on a lot less than a dollar a day, I'd say, if we figger up everything in the long run. Now, I paid seven dollars a month to the two niggers, three-fifty each, and grub, but what I say is, one middlin'-good white man ekals a whole passel of niggers any day in the week, so I'll give you seven dollars and you eat at the table with us, and you'll be treated like a white man, as the feller says — "

"That's all right," said Mr. Helton. "I take it."

"Well, now I guess we'll call it a deal, hey?" Mr. Thompson jumped up as if he had remembered important business. "Now, you just take hold of that churn and give it a few swings, will you, while I ride to town on a coupla little errands. I ain't been able to leave the place all week. I guess you know what to do with butter after you get it, don't you?"

"I know," said Mr. Helton without turning his head. "I know butter business." He had a strange drawling voice, and even when he spoke only two words his voice waved slowly up and down and the emphasis was in the wrong place. Mr. Thompson wondered what kind of foreigner Mr. Helton could be.

"Now just where did you say you worked last?" he asked, as if he expected Mr. Helton to contradict himself.

"North Dakota," said Mr. Helton.

"Well, one place is good as another once you get used to it," said Mr. Thompson, amply. "You're a forriner, ain't you?"

"I'm a Swede," said Mr. Helton, beginning to swing the churn.

Mr. Thompson let forth a booming laugh, as if this was the best joke on somebody he'd ever heard. "Well, I'll be damned," he said at the top of his voice. "A Swede: well, now, I'm afraid you'll get pretty lonesome around here. I never seen any Swedes in this neck of the woods."

"That's all right," said Mr. Helton. He went on swinging the churn as if he had been working on the place for years.

"In fact, I might as well tell you, you're practically the first Swede I ever laid eyes on."

"That's all right," said Mr. Helton.

Mr. Thompson went into the front room where Mrs. Thompson was lying down, with the green shades drawn. She had a bowl of water by her on the table and a wet cloth over her eyes. She took the cloth off at the sound of Mr. Thompson's boots and said, "What's all the noise out there? Who is it?"

"Got a feller out there says he's a Swede, Ellie," said Mr. Thompson; "says he knows how to make butter."

"I hope it turns out to be the truth," said Mrs. Thompson. "Looks like my head never will get any better."

"Don't you worry," said Mr. Thompson. "You fret too much. Now I'm gointa ride into town and get a little order of groceries."

"Don't you linger, now, Mr. Thompson," said Mrs. Thompson. "Don't go to the hotel." She meant the saloon; the proprietor also had rooms for rent upstairs.

"Just a coupla little toddies," said Mr. Thompson, laughing loudly, "never hurt anybody."

"I never took a dram in my life," said Mrs. Thompson, "and what's more I never will."

"I wasn't talking about the womenfolks," said Mr. Thompson.

The sound of the swinging churn rocked Mrs. Thompson first into a gentle doze, then a deep drowse from which she waked suddenly knowing that the swinging had stopped a good while ago. She sat up shading her weak eyes from the flat strips of late summer sunlight between the sill and the lowered shades. There she was, thank God, still alive, with supper to cook but no churning on hand, and her head still bewildered, but easy. Slowly she realized she had been hearing a new sound even in her sleep. Somebody was playing a tune on the harmonica, not merely shrilling up and down making a sickening noise, but really playing a pretty tune, merry and sad.

She went out through the kitchen, stepped off the porch, and stood facing the east, shading her eyes. When her vision cleared and settled, she saw a long, pale-haired man in blue jeans sitting in the doorway of the hired man's shack, tilted back in a kitchen chair, blowing away at the harmonica with his eyes shut. Mrs. Thompson's heart fluttered and sank. Heavens, he looked lazy and worthless, he did, now. First a lot of no-count fiddling darkies and then a no-count white man. It was just like Mr. Thompson to take on that kind. She did wish he would be more considerate, and take a little trouble with his business. She wanted to believe in her husband, and there were too many times when she couldn't. She wanted to believe that tomorrow, or at least the day after, life, such a battle at best, was going to be better.

She walked past the shack without glancing aside, stepping carefully, bent at the waist because of the nagging pain in her side, and went to the springhouse, trying to harden her mind to speak very plainly to that new hired man if he had not done his work.

The milk house was only another shack of weatherbeaten boards nailed together hastily years before because they needed a milk house; it was meant to be temporary, and it was; already shapeless, leaning this way and that over a perpetual cool trickle of water that fell from a little grot, almost choked with pallid ferns. No one else in the whole countryside had such a spring on his land. Mr. and Mrs. Thompson felt they had a fortune in that spring, if ever they got around to doing anything with it.

Rickety wooden shelves clung at hazard in the square around the small pool where the larger pails of milk and butter stood, fresh and sweet in the cold water. One hand supporting her flat, pained side, the other shading her eyes, Mrs. Thompson leaned over and peered into the pails. The cream had been skimmed and set aside, there was a rich roll of butter, the wooden molds and shallow pans had been scrubbed and scalded for the first time in who knows when, the barrel was full of buttermilk ready for the pigs and the weanling calves, the hard packed-dirt floor had been swept smooth. Mrs. Thompson straightened up again, smiling tenderly. She had been ready to scold him, a poor man who needed a job, who had just come there and who might not have been expected to do things properly at first. There was nothing she could do to make up for the injustice she had done him in her thoughts but to tell him how she appreciated his good clean work, finished already, in no time at all. She ventured near the door of the shack with her careful steps; Mr. Helton opened his eyes, stopped playing, and brought his chair down straight, but did not look at her, or get up. She was a little frail woman with long thick brown hair in a braid, a suffering patient mouth and diseased eyes which cried easily. She wove her fingers into an eyeshade, thumbs on temples, and, winking her tearful lids, said with a polite little manner, "Howdy do, sir. I'm Miz Thompson, and I wanted to tell you I think you did real well in the milk house. It's always been a hard place to keep."

He said, "That's all right," in a slow voice, without moving.

Mrs. Thompson waited a moment. "That's a pretty tune you're playing. Most folks don't seem to get much music out of a harmonica."

Mr. Helton sat humped over, long legs sprawling, his spine in a bow, running his thumb over the square mouth-stops; except for his moving hand he might have been asleep. The harmonica was a big shiny new one, and Mrs. Thompson, her gaze wandering about, counted five others, all good and expensive, standing in a row on the shelf beside his cot. "He must carry them around in his jumper pocket," she thought, and noted there was not a sign of any other possession lying about. "I see you're mighty fond of music," she said. "We used to have an old accordion, and Mr. Thompson could play it right smart, but the little boys broke it up."

Mr. Helton stood up rather suddenly, the chair clattered under him, his knees straightened though his shoulders did not, and he looked at the floor as if he were listening carefully. "You know how little boys are," said Mrs. Thompson. "You'd better set them harmonicas on a high shelf or they'll be after them. They're great hands for getting into things. I try to learn 'em, but it don't do much good."

Mr. Helton, in one wide gesture of his long arms, swept his harmonicas up against his chest, and from there transferred them in a row to the ledge where the roof joined to the wall. He pushed them back almost out of sight.

"That'll do, maybe," said Mrs. Thompson. "Now I wonder," she said, turning and closing her eyes helplessly against the stronger western light, "I wonder what became of them little tads. I can't keep up with them." She had a way of speaking about her children as if they were rather troublesome nephews on a prolonged visit.

"Down by the creek," said Mr. Helton, in his hollow voice. Mrs. Thompson, pausing confusedly, decided he had answered her question. He stood in silent patience, not exactly waiting for her to go, perhaps, but pretty plainly not waiting for anything else. Mrs. Thompson was perfectly accustomed to all kinds of men full of all kinds of cranky ways. The point was, to find out just how Mr. Helton's crankiness was different from any other man's, and then get used to it, and let him feel at home. Her father had been cranky, her brothers and uncles had all been set in their ways and none of them alike; and every hired man she'd ever seen had quirks and crotchets of his own. Now here was Mr. Helton, who was a Swede, who wouldn't talk, and who played the harmonica besides.

"They'll be needing something to eat," said Mrs. Thompson in a vague friendly way, "pretty soon. Now I wonder what I ought to be thinking about for supper? Now what do you like to eat, Mr. Helton? We always have plenty of good butter and milk and cream, that's a blessing. Mr. Thompson says we ought to sell all of it, but I say my family comes first." Her little face went all out of shape in a pained blind smile.

"I eat anything," said Mr. Helton, his words wandering up and down.

He *can't* talk, for one thing, thought Mrs. Thompson; it's a shame to keep at him when he don't know the language good. She took a slow step away from the shack, looking back over her shoulder. "We usually have cornbread except on Sundays," she told him. "I suppose in your part of the country you don't get much good cornbread."

Not a word from Mr. Helton. She saw from her eye-corner that he had sat down again, looking at his harmonica, chair tilted. She hoped he would remember it was getting near milking time. As she moved away, he started playing again, the same tune.

Milking time came and went. Mrs. Thompson saw Mr. Helton going back and forth between the cow barn and the milk house. He swung along in an easy lope, shoulders bent, head hanging, the big buckets balancing like a pair of scales at the ends of his bony arms. Mr. Thompson rode in from town sitting straighter than usual, chin in, a towsack full of supplies swung behind the saddle. After a trip to the barn he came into the kitchen full of good will, and gave Mrs. Thompson a hearty smack on the check after dusting her face off with his tough whiskers. He had been to the hotel, that was plain. "Took a look around the premises, Ellie," he shouted. "That Swede sure is grinding out the labor. But he is the closest mouthed feller I ever met up with in all my days. Looks like he's scared he'll crack his jaw if he opens his front teeth."

Mrs. Thompson was stirring up a big bowl of buttermilk cornbread. "You smell like a toper, Mr. Thompson," she said with perfect dignity. "I wish you'd get one of the little boys to bring me in an extra load of firewood. I'm thinking about baking a batch of cookies tomorrow."

Mr. Thompson, all at once smelling the liquor on his own breath, sneaked out, justly rebuked, and brought in the firewood himself. Arthur and Herbert, grubby from thatched head to toes, from skin to shirt, came stamping in yelling for supper. "Go wash your faces and comb your hair," said Mrs. Thompson, automatically. They retired to the porch. Each one put his hand under the pump and wet his forelock, combed it down with his fingers, and returned at once to the kitchen, where all the fair prospects of life were centered. Mrs. Thompson set an extra plate and commanded Arthur, the eldest, eight years old, to call Mr. Helton for supper.

Arthur, without moving from the spot, bawled like a bull calf, "Saaaaaay, Helllllton, suuuuuupper's ready!" and added in a lower voice, "You big Swede!"

"Listen to me," said Mrs. Thompson, "that's no way to act. Now you go out there and ask him decent, or I'll get your daddy to give you a good licking."

Mr. Helton loomed, long and gloomy, in the doorway. "Sit right there," boomed Mr. Thompson, waving his arm. Mr. Helton swung his square shoes across the kitchen in two steps, slumped onto the bench and sat. Mr. Thompson occupied his chair at the head of the table, the two boys scrambled into place opposite Mr. Helton, and Mrs. Thompson sat at the end nearest the stove. Mrs. Thompson clasped her hands, bowed her head and said aloud hastily, "Lord, for all these and Thy other blessings we thank Thee in Jesus' name, amen," trying to finish before Herbert's rusty little paw reached the nearest dish. Otherwise she would be duty-bound to send him away from the table, and growing children need their meals. Mr. Thompson and Arthur always waited, but Herbert, aged six, was too young to take training yet.

Mr. and Mrs. Thompson tried to engage Mr. Helton in conversation, but it was a failure. They tried first the weather, and then the crops, and then the cows, but Mr. Helton simply did not reply. Mr. Thompson then told something funny he had seen in town. It was about some of the other old grangers at the hotel, friends of his, giving beer to a goat, and the goat's subsequent behavior. Mr. Helton did not seem to hear. Mrs. Thompson laughed dutifully, but she didn't think it was very funny. She had heard it often before, though Mr. Thompson, each time he told it, pretended it had happened that self-same day. It must have happened years ago if it ever happened at all, and it had never been a story that Mrs. Thompson thought suitable for mixed company. The whole thing came of Mr. Thompson's weakness for a dram too much now and then, though he voted for local option at every election. She passed the food to Mr. Helton, who took a helping of everything, but not much, not enough to keep him up to his full powers if he expected to go on working the way he had started.

At last, he took a fair-sized piece of cornbread, wiped his plate up as clean as if it had been licked by a hound dog, stuffed his mouth full, and, still chewing, slid off the bench and started for the door.

"Good night, Mr. Helton," said Mrs. Thompson, and the other Thompsons took it up in a scattered chorus. "Good night, Mr. Helton!"

"Good night," said Mr. Helton's wavering voice grudgingly from the darkness.

"Gude not," said Arthur, imitating Mr. Helton.

"Gude not," said Herbert, the copy-cat.

"You don't do it right," said Arthur. "Now listen to me. Guuuuuude naht," and he ran a hollow scale in a luxury of successful impersonation. Herbert almost went into a fit with joy.

"Now you *stop* that," said Mrs. Thompson. "He can't help the way he talks. You ought to be ashamed of yourselves, both of you, making fun of a poor stranger like that. How'd you like to be a stranger in a strange land?"

"I'd like it," said Arthur. "I think it would be fun."

"They're both regular heathens, Ellie," said Mr. Thompson. "Just plain ignoramuses." He turned the face of awful fatherhood upon his young. "You're both going to get sent to school next year, and that'll knock some sense into you."

"I'm going to git sent to the 'formatory when I'm old enough," piped up Herbert. "That's where I'm goin'."

"Oh, you are, are you?" asked Mr. Thompson. "Who says so?"

"The Sunday School Supintendant," said Herbert, a bright boy showing off.

"You see?" said Mr. Thompson, staring at his wife. "What did I tell you?" He became a hurricane of wrath. "Get to bed, you two," he roared until his Adam's apple shuddered. "Get now before I take the hide off you!" They got, and shortly from their attic bedroom the sounds of scuffling and snorting and giggling and growling filled the house and shook the kitchen ceiling.

Mrs. Thompson held her head and said in a small uncertain voice, "It's no use picking on them when they're so young and tender. I can't stand it."

"My goodness, Ellie," said Mr. Thompson, "we've got to raise 'em. We can't just let 'em grow up hog wild."

She went on in another tone. "That Mr. Helton seems all right, even if he can't be made to talk. Wonder how he comes to be so far from home."

"Like I said, he isn't no whamper-jaw," said Mr. Thompson, "but he sure knows how to lay out the work. I guess that's the main thing around here. Country's full of fellers trampin' round looking for work."

Mrs. Thompson was gathering up the dishes. She now gathered up Mr. Thompson's plate from under his chin. "To tell you the honest truth," she remarked, "I think it's a mighty good change to have a man round the place who knows how to work and keep his mouth shut. Means he'll keep out of our business. Not that we've got anything to hide, but it's convenient."

"That's a fact," said Mr. Thompson. "Haw, haw," he shouted suddenly. "Means you can do all the talking, huh?"

"The only thing," went on Mrs. Thompson, "is this: he don't eat hearty enough to suit me. I like to see a man set down and relish a good meal. My granma used to say it was no use putting dependence on a man who won't set down and make out his dinner. I hope it won't be that way this time."

"Tell *you* the truth, Ellie," said Mr. Thompson, picking his teeth with a fork and leaning back in the best of good humors, "I always thought your granma was a ter'ble ole fool. She'd just say the first thing that popped into her head and called it God's wisdom."

"My granma wasn't anybody's fool. Nine times out of ten she knew what she was talking about. I always say, the first thing you think is the best thing you can say."

"Well," said Mr. Thompson, going into another shout, "you're so reefined about that goat story, you just try speaking out in mixed comp'ny sometime! You just try it. S'pose you happened to be thinking about a hen and a rooster, hey? I reckon you'd shock the Babtist preacher!" He gave her a good pinch on her thin little rump. "No more meat on you than a rabbit," he said, fondly. "Now I like 'em cornfed."

Mrs. Thompson looked at him open-eyed and blushed. She could see better by lamplight. "Why, Mr. Thompson, sometimes I think you're the evilest-minded man that ever lived." She took a handful of hair on the crown of his head and gave it a good, slow pull. "That's to show you how it feels, pinching so hard when you're supposed to be playing," she said, gently.

In spite of his situation in life, Mr. Thompson had never been able to outgrow his deep conviction that running a dairy and chasing after chickens was woman's work. He was fond of saying that he could plow a furrow, cut sorghum, shuck corn, handle a team, build a corn crib, as well as any man. Buying and selling, too, were man's work. Twice a week he drove the spring wagon to market with the fresh butter, a few eggs, fruits in their proper season, sold them, pocketed the change, and spent it as seemed best, being careful not to dig into Mrs. Thompson's pin money.

But from the first the cows worried him, coming up regularly twice a day to be milked, standing there reproaching him with their smug female faces. Calves worried him, fighting the rope and strangling themselves until their eyes bulged, trying to get at the teat. Wresling with a calf unmanned him, like having to change a baby's diaper. Milk worried him, coming bitter sometimes, drying up, turning sour. Hens worried him, cackling, clucking, hatching out when you least expected it and leading their broods into the barnyard where the horses could step on them; dying of roup and wryneck and getting plagues of chicken lice; laying eggs all over God's creation so that half of them were spoiled before a man could find them, in spite of a rack of nests Mrs. Thompson had set out for them in the feed room. Hens were a blasted nuisance.

Slopping hogs was hired man's work, in Mr. Thompson's opinion. Killing hogs was a job for the boss, but scraping them and cutting them up was for the hired man again; and again woman's proper work was dressing meat, smoking, pickling, and making lard and sausage. All his carefully limited fields of activity were related somehow to Mr. Thompson's feeling for the appearance of things, his own appearance in the sight of God and man. "It don't *look* right," was his final reason for not doing anything he did not wish to do.

It was his dignity and his reputation that he cared about, and there were only a few kinds of work manly enough for Mr. Thompson to undertake with his own hands. Mrs. Thompson, to whom so many forms of work would have been becoming, had simply gone down on him early. He saw, after a while, how short-sighted it had been of him to expect much from Mrs. Thompson; he had fallen in love with her delicate waist and lace-trimmed petticoats and big blue eyes, and, though all those charms had disappeared, she had in the meantime become Ellie to him, not at all the same person as Miss Ellen Bridges, popular Sunday School teacher in the Mountain City First Baptist Church, but his dear wife, Ellie, who was not strong. Deprived as he was, however, of the main support in life which a man might expect in marriage, he had almost without knowing it resigned himself to failure. Head erect, a prompt payer of taxes, yearly subscriber to the preacher's salary, land owner and father of a family, employer, a hearty good fellow among men, Mr. Thompson knew, without putting it into words, that he had been going steadily down hill. God amighty, it did look like somebody around the place might take a rake in hand now and then and clear up the clutter around the barn and the kitchen steps. The wagon shed was so full of broken-down machinery and ragged harness and old wagon wheels and battered milk pails and rotting lumber you could hardly drive in there any more. Not a soul on the place would raise a hand to it, and as for him, he had all he could do with his regular work. He would sometimes in the slack season sit for hours worrying about it, squirting tobacco on the ragweeds growing in a thicket against the wood pile, wondering what a fellow could do, handicapped as he was. He looked forward to the boys growing up soon; he was going to put them through the mill just as his own father had done with him when he was a boy; they were going to learn how to take hold and run the place right. He wasn't going to overdo it, but those two boys were going to earn their salt, or he'd know why. Great big lubbers sitting around whittling! Mr. Thompson sometimes grew quite enraged with them, when imagining their possible future, big lubbers sitting around whittling or thinking about fishing trips. Well, he'd put a stop to that, mighty damn quick.

As the seasons passed, and Mr. Helton took hold more and more, Mr. Thompson began to relax in his mind a little. There seemed to be nothing the fellow couldn't do, all in the day's work and as a matter of course. He got up at five o'clock in the morning, boiled his own coffee and fried his own bacon and was out in the cow lot before Mr. Thompson had even begun to yawn, stretch, groan, roar and thump around looking for his jeans. He milked the cows, kept the milk house, and churned the butter; rounded the hens up and somehow persuaded them to lay in the nests, not under the house and behind the haystacks; he fed them regularly and they hatched out until you couldn't set a foot down for them. Little by little the piles of trash around the barns and house disappeared. He carried buttermilk and corn to the hogs, and curried cockleburs out of the horses' manes. He was gentle with the calves, if a little grim with the cows and hens; judging by his conduct, Mr. Helton had never heard of the difference between man's and woman's work on a farm.

In the second year, he showed Mr. Thompson the picture of a

cheese press in a mail order catalogue, and said, "This is a good thing. You buy this, I make cheese." The press was bought and Mr. Helton did make cheese, and it was sold, along with the increased butter and the crates of eggs. Sometimes Mr. Thompson felt a little contemptuous of Mr. Helton's ways. It did seem kind of picayune for a man to go around picking up half a dozen ears of corn that had fallen off the wagon on the way from the field, gathering up fallen fruit to feed to the pigs, storing up old nails and stray parts of machinery, spending good time stamping a fancy pattern on the butter before it went to market. Mr. Thompson, sitting up high on the spring-wagon seat, with the decorated butter in a five-gallon lard can wrapped in wet towsack, driving to town, chirruping to the horses and snapping the reins over their backs, sometimes thought that Mr. Helton was a pretty meeching sort of fellow; but he never gave way to these feelings, he knew a good thing when he had it. It was a fact the hogs were in better shape and sold for more money. It was a fact that Mr. Thompson stopped buying feed, Mr. Helton managed the crops so well. When beef- and hog-slaughtering time came, Mr. Helton knew how to save the scraps that Mr. Thompson had thrown away, and wasn't above scraping guts and filling them with sausages that he made by his own methods. In all, Mr. Thompson had no grounds for complaint. In the third year, he raised Mr. Helton's wages, though Mr. Helton had not asked for a raise. The fourth year, when Mr. Thompson was not only out of debt but had a little cash in the bank, he raised Mr. Helton's wages again, two dollars and a half a month each time.

"The man's worth it, Ellie," said Mr. Thompson, in a glow of self-justification for his extravagance. "He's made this place pay, and I want him to know I appreciate it."

Mr. Helton's silence, the pallor of his eyebrows and hair, his long, glum jaw and eyes that refused to see anything, even the work under his hands, had grown perfectly familiar to the Thompsons. At first, Mrs. Thompson complained a little. "It's like sitting down at the table with a disembodied spirit," she said. "You'd think he'd find something to say, sooner or later."

"Let him alone," said Mr. Thompson. "When he gets ready to talk, he'll talk."

The years passed, and Mr. Helton never got ready to talk. After his work was finished for the day, he would come up from the barn or the milk house or the chicken house, swinging his lantern, his big shoes clumping like pony hoofs on the hard path. They, sitting in the kitchen in the winter, or on the back porch in summer, would hear him drag out his wooden chair, hear the creak of it tilted back, and then for a little while he would play his single tune on one or another of his harmonicas. The harmonicas were in different keys, some lower and sweeter than the others, but the same changeless tune went on, a strange tune, with sudden turns in it, night after night, and sometimes even in the afternoons when Mr. Helton sat down to catch his breath. At first the Thompsons liked it very much, and always stopped to listen. Later there came a time when they were fairly sick of it, and began to wish to each other that he would learn a new one. At last they did not hear it any more, it was as natural as the sound of the wind rising in the evenings, or the cows lowing, or their own voices.

Mrs. Thompson pondered now and then over Mr. Helton's soul. He didn't seem to be a church-goer, and worked straight through Sunday as if it were any common day of the week. "I think we ought to invite him to go to hear Dr. Martin," she told Mr. Thompson. "It isn't very Christian of us not to ask him. He's not a forward kind of man. He'd wait to be asked."

"Let him alone," said Mr. Thompson. "The way I look at it, his religion is every man's own business. Besides, he ain't got any Sunday clothes. He wouldn't want to go to church in them jeans and jumpers of his. I don't know what he does with his money. He certainly don't spend it foolishly."

Still, once the notion got into her head, Mrs. Thompson could not rest until she invited Mr. Helton to go to church with the family next Sunday. He was pitching hay into neat little piles in the field back of the orchard. Mrs. Thompson put on smoked glasses and a sunbonnet and walked all the way down there to speak to him. He stopped and leaned on his pitchfork, listening, and for a moment Mrs. Thompson was almost frightened at his face. The pale eyes seemed to glare past her, the eyebrows frowned, the long jaw hardened. "I got work," he said bluntly, and lifting his pitchfork he turned from her and began to toss the hay. Mrs. Thompson, her feelings hurt, walked back thinking that by now she should be used to Mr. Helton's ways, but it did seem like a man, even a foreigner, could be just a little polite when you gave him a Christian invitation. "He's not polite, that's the only thing I've got against him," she said to Mr. Thompson. "He just can't seem to behave like other people. You'd think he had a grudge against the world," she said. "I sometimes don't know what to make of it."

In the second year something had happened that made Mrs. Thompson uneasy, the kind of thing she could not put into words, hardly into thoughts, and if she had tried to explain to Mr. Thompson it would have sounded worse than it was, or not bad enough. It was that kind of queer thing that seems to be giving a warning, and yet, nearly always nothing comes of it. It was on a hot, still spring day, and Mrs. Thompson had been down to the garden patch to pull some new carrots and green onions and string beans for dinner. As she worked, sunbonnet low over her eyes, putting each kind of vegetable in a pile by itself in her basket, she noticed how neatly Mr. Helton weeded, and how rich the soil was. He had spread it all over with manure from the barns, and worked it in, in the fall, and the vegetables were coming up fine and full. She walked back under the nubbly little fig trees where the unpruned branches leaned almost to the ground, and the thick leaves made a cool screen. Mrs. Thompson was always looking for shade to save her eyes. So she, looking idly about, saw through the screen a sight that struck her as very strange. If it had been a noisy spectacle, it would have been quite natural. It was the silence that struck her. Mr. Helton was shaking Arthur by the shoulders, ferociously, his face most terribly fixed and pale. Arthur's head snapped back and forth and he had not stiffened in resistance, as he did when Mrs. Thompson tried to shake him. His eyes were rather frightened, but surprised, too, probably more surprised than anything else. Herbert stood by meekly, watching. Mr. Helton dropped Arthur, and seized Herbert, and shook him with the same methodical ferocity, the same face of hatred. Herbert's mouth crumpled as if he would cry, but he made no sound. Mr. Helton let him go, turned and strode into the shack, and the little boys ran, as if for their lives, without a word. They disappeared around the corner to the front of the house.

Mrs. Thompson took time to set her basket on the kitchen table, to push her sunbonnet back on her head and draw it forward again, to look in the stove and make certain the fire was going, before she followed the boys. They were sitting huddled together under a clump of chinaberry trees in plain sight of her bedroom window, as if it were a safe place they had discovered.

"What are you doing?" asked Mrs. Thompson.

They looked hang-dog from under their foreheads and Arthur mumbled, "Nothin'."

"Nothing *now*, you mean," said Mrs. Thompson, severely. "Well, I have plenty for you to do. Come right in here this minute and help me fix vegetables. This minute."

They scrambled up very eagerly and followed her close. Mrs. Thompson tried to imagine what they had been up to; she did not like the notion of Mr. Helton taking it on himself to correct her little boys, but she was afraid to ask them for reasons. They might tell her a lie, and she would have to overtake them in it, and whip them. Or she would have to pretend to believe them, and they would get in the habit of lying. Or they might tell her the truth, and it would be something she would have to whip them for. The very thought of it gave her a headache. She supposed she might ask Mr. Helton, but it was not her place to ask. She would wait and tell Mr. Thompson, and let him get at the bottom of it. While her mind ran on, she kept the little boys hopping. "Cut those carrot tops closer, Herbert, you're just being careless. Arthur, stop breaking up the beans so little. They're little enough already. Herbert, you go get an armload of wood. Arthur, you take these onions and wash them under the pump. Herbert, as soon as you're done here, you get a broom and sweep out this kitchen. Arthur, you get a shovel and take up the ashes. Stop picking your nose, Herbert. How often must I tell you? Arthur, you go look in the top drawer of my bureau, left-hand side, and bring me the vaseline for Herbert's nose. Herbert, come here to me. . . ."

They galloped through their chores, their animal spirits rose with activity, and shortly they were out in the front yard again, engaged in a wrestling match. They sprawled and fought, scrambled, clutched, rose and fell shouting, as aimlessly, noisily, monotonously as two puppies. They imitated various animals, not a human sound from them, and their dirty faces were streaked with sweat. Mrs. Thompson, sitting at her window, watched them with baffled pride and tenderness, they were so sturdy and healthy and growing so fast; but uneasily, too, with her pained little smile and the tears rolling from her eyelids that clinched themselves against the sunlight. They were so idle and careless, as if they had no future in this world, and no immortal souls to save, and oh, what had they been up to that Mr. Helton had shaken them, with his face positively dangerous?

In the evening before supper, without a word to Mr. Thompson of the curious fear the sight had caused her, she told him that Mr. Helton had shaken the little boys for some reason. He stepped out to the shack and spoke to Mr. Helton. In five minutes he was back, glaring at his young. "He says them brats been fooling with his harmonicas, Ellie, blowing in them and getting them all dirty and full of spit and they don't play good."

"Did he say all that?" asked Mrs. Thompson. "It doesn't seem possible."

"Well, that's what he meant, anyhow," said Mr. Thompson. "He didn't say it just that way. But he acted pretty worked up about it."

"That's a shame," said Mrs. Thompson, "a perfect shame. Now we've got to do something so they'll remember they mustn't go into Mr. Helton's things."

"I'll tan their hides for them," said Mr. Thompson. "I'll take a calf rope to them if they don't look out."

"Maybe you'd better leave the whipping to me," said Mrs. Thompson. "You haven't got a light enough hand for children."

"That's just what's the matter with them now," shouted Mr. Thompson, "rotten spoiled and they'll wind up in the penitentiary. You don't half whip 'em. Just little love taps. My pa used to knock me down with a stick of stove wood or anything else that came handy."

"Well, that's not saying it's right," said Mrs. Thompson. "I don't hold with that way of raising children. It makes them run away from home. I've seen too much of it."

'I'll break every bone in 'em," said Mr. Thompson, simmering down, "if they don't mind you better and stop being so bull-headed."

"Leave the table and wash your face and hands," Mrs. Thompson commanded the boys, suddenly. They slunk out and dabbled at the pump and slunk in again, trying to make themselves small. They had learned long ago that their mother always made them wash when there was trouble ahead. They looked at their plates. Mr. Thompson opened up on them.

"Well, now, what you got to say for yourselves about going into Mr. Helton's shack and ruining his harmonicas?"

The two little boys wilted, their faces drooped into the grieved hopeless lines of children's faces when they are brought to the terrible bar of blind adult justice; their eyes telegraphed each other in panic, "Now we're really going to catch a licking"; in despair, they dropped their buttered cornbread on their plates, their hands lagged on the edge of the table.

"I ought to break your ribs," said Mr. Thompson, "and I'm a good mind to do it."

"Yes, sir," whispered Arthur, faintly.

"Yes, sir," said Herbert, his lip trembling.

"Now, papa," said Mrs. Thompson in a warning tone. The children did not glance at her. They had no faith in her good will. She had betrayed them in the first place. There was no trusting her. Now she might save them and she might not. No use depending on her.

"Well, you ought to get a good thrashing. You deserve it, don't you, Arthur?"

Arthur hung his head. "Yes, sir."

"And the next time I catch either of you hanging around Mr. Helton's shack, I'm going to take the hide off *both* of you, you hear me, Herbert?"

Herbert mumbled and choked, scattering his cornbread. "Yes, sir."

"Well, now sit up and eat your supper and not another word out of you," said Mr. Thompson, beginning on his own food. The little boys perked up somewhat and started chewing, but every time they looked around they met their parents' eyes, regarding them steadily. There was no telling when they would think of something new. The boys ate warily, trying not to be seen or heard, the cornbread sticking, the buttermilk gurgling, as it went down their gullets.

"And something else, Mr. Thompson," said Mrs. Thompson after a pause. "Tell Mr. Helton he's to come straight to us when they bother him, and not to trouble shaking them himself. Tell him we'll look after that."

"They're so mean," answered Mr. Thompson, staring at them. "It's a wonder he don't just kill 'em off and be done with it." But there was something in the tone that told Arthur and Herbert that nothing more worth worrying about was going to happen this time. Heaving deep sighs, they sat up, reaching for the food nearest them.

"Listen," said Mrs. Thompson, suddenly. The little boys stopped eating. "Mr. Helton hasn't come for his supper. Arthur, go and tell Mr. Helton he's late for supper. Tell him nice, now."

Arthur, miserably depressed, slid out of his place and made for the door, without a word.

There were no miracles of fortune to be brought to pass on a small dairy farm. The Thompsons did not grow rich, but they kept out of the poor house, as Mr. Thompson was fond of saying, meaning he had got a little foothold in spite of Ellie's poor health, and unexpected weather, and strange declines in market prices, and his own mysterious handicaps which weighed him down. Mr. Helton was the hope and the prop of the family, and all the Thompsons became fond of him, or at any rate they ceased to regard him as in any way peculiar, and looked upon him, from a distance they did not know how to bridge, as a good man and a good friend. Mr. Helton went his way, worked, played his tune. Nine years passed. The boys grew up and learned to work. They could not remember the time when Ole Helton hadn't been there: a grouchy cuss, Brother Bones; Mr. Helton, the dairymaid; that Big Swede. If he had heard them, he might have been annoyed at some of the names they called him. But he did not hear them, and besides they meant no harm — or at least such harm as existed was all there, in the names; the boys referred to their father as the Old Man, or the Old Geezer, but not to his face. They lived through by main strength all the grimy, secret, oblique phases of growing up and got past the crisis safely if anyone does. Their parents could see they were good solid boys with hearts of gold in spite of their rough ways. Mr. Thompson was relieved to find that, without knowing how he had done it, he had succeeded in raising a set of boys who were not trifling whittlers. They were such good boys Mr. Thompson began to believe they were born that way, and that he had never spoken a harsh word to them in their lives, much less thrashed them. Herbert and Arthur never disputed his word.

Mr. Helton, his hair wet with sweat, plastered to his dripping forehead, his jumper streaked dark and light blue and clinging to his ribs, was chopping a little firewood. He chopped slowly, struck the ax into the end of the chopping log, and piled the wood up neatly. He then disappeared round the house into his shack, which shared with the wood pile a good shade from a row of mulberry trees. Mr. Thompson was lolling in a swing chair on the front porch, a place he had never liked. The chair was new, and Mrs. Thompson had wanted it on the front porch, though the side porch was the place for it, being cooler; and Mr. Thompson wanted to sit in the chair, so there he was. As soon as the new wore off of it, and Ellie's pride in it was exhausted, he would move it round to the side porch. Meantime the August heat was almost unbearable, the air so thick you could poke a hole in it. The dust was inches thick on everything, though Mr. Helton sprinkled the whole yard regularly every night. He even shot the hose upward and washed the tree tops and the roof of the house. They had laid waterpipes to the kitchen and an outside faucet. Mr. Thompson must have dozed, for he opened his eyes and shut his mouth just in time to save his face before a stranger who had driven up to the front gate. Mr. Thompson stood up, put on his hat, pulled up his jeans, and watched while the stranger tied his team, attached to a light spring wagon, to the hitching post. Mr. Thompson recognized the team and wagon. They were from a livery stable in Buda. While the stranger was opening the gate, a strong gate that Mr. Helton had built and set firmly on its hinges several years back, Mr. Thompson strolled down the path to greet him and find out what in God's world a man's business might be that would bring him out at this time of day, in all this dust and welter.

He wasn't exactly a fat man. He was more like a man who had been fat recently. His skin was baggy and his clothes were too big for him, and he somehow looked like a man who should be fat, ordinarily, but who might have just got over a spell of sickness. Mr. Thompson didn't take to his looks at all, he couldn't say why.

The stranger took off his hat. He said in a loud hearty voice, "Is this Mr. Thompson, Mr. Royal Earle Thompson?"

"That's my name," said Mr. Thompson, almost quietly, he was so taken aback by the free manner of the stranger.

"My name is Hatch," said the stranger, "Mr. Homer T. Hatch, and I've come to see you about buying a horse."

"I reckon you've been misdirected," said Mr. Thompson. "I haven't got a horse for sale. Usually if I've got anything like that to sell," he said, "I tell the neighbors and tack up a little sign on the gate."

The fat man opened his mouth and roared with joy, showing rabbit teeth brown as shoeleather. Mr. Thompson saw nothing to laugh at, for once. The stranger shouted, "That's just an old joke of mine." He caught one of his hands in the other and shook hands with himself heartily. "I always say something like that when I'm calling on a stranger, because I've noticed that when a feller says he's come to buy something nobody takes him for a suspicious character. You see? Haw, haw, haw."

His joviality made Mr. Thompson nervous, because the expression in the man's eyes didn't match the sounds he was making. "Haw, haw," laughed Mr. Thompson obligingly, still not seeing the joke. "Well, that's all wasted on me because I never take any man for a suspicious character 'til he shows hisself to be one. Says or does something," he explained. "Until that happens, one man's as good as another, so far's *I'm* concerned."

"Well," said the stranger, suddenly very sober and sensible, "I ain't come neither to buy nor sell. Fact is, I want to see you about something that's of interest to us both. Yes, sir, I'd like to have a little talk with you, and it won't cost you a cent."

"I guess that's fair enough," said Mr. Thompson, reluctantly. "Come on around the house where there's a little shade."

They went round and seated themselves on two stumps under a chinaberry tree.

"Yes, sir, Homer T. Hatch is my name and America is my nation," said the stranger. "I reckon you must know the name? I used to have a cousin named Jameson Hatch lived up the country a ways."

"Don't think I know the name," said Mr. Thompson. "There's some Hatchers settled somewhere around Mountain City."

"Don't know the old Hatch family," cried the man in deep concern. He seemed to be pitying Mr. Thompson's ignorance. "Why, we came over from Georgia fifty years ago. Been here long yourself?"

"Just all my whole life," said Mr. Thompson, beginning to feel peevish. "And my pa and my grampap before me. Yes, sir, we've been right here all along. Anybody wants to find a Thompson knows where to look for him. My grampap immigrated in 1836."

"From Ireland, I reckon?" said the stranger.

"From Pennsylvania," said Mr. Thompson. "Now what makes you think we came from Ireland?"

The stranger opened his mouth and began to shout with merriment, and he shook hands with himself as if he hadn't met himself for a long time. "Well, what I always says is, a feller's got to come from *somewhere*, ain't he?"

While they were talking, Mr. Thompson kept glancing at the face near him. He certainly did remind Mr. Thompson of somebody, or maybe he really had seen the man himself somewhere. He couldn't just place the features. Mr. Thompson finally decided it was just that all rabbit-teethed men looked alike.

"That's right," acknowledged Mr. Thompson, rather sourly, "but what I always say is, Thompsons have been settled here for so long it don't make much difference any more *where* they come from. Now a course, this is the slack season, and we're all just laying round a little, but nevertheless we've all got our chores to do, and I don't want to hurry you, and so if you've come to see me on business maybe we'd better get down to it."

"As I said, it's not in a way, and again in a way it is," said the fat man. "Now I'm looking for a man named Helton, Mr. Olaf Eric Helton, from North Dakota, and I was told up around the country a ways that I might find him here, and I wouldn't mind having a little talk with him. No, siree, I sure wouldn't mind, if it's all the same to you."

"I never knew his middle name," said Mr. Thompson, "but Mr. Helton is right here, and been here now for going on nine years. He's a mighty steady man, and you can tell anybody I said so."

"I'm glad to hear that," said Mr. Homer T. Hatch. "I like to hear of a feller mending his ways and settling down. Now when I knew Mr. Helton he was pretty wild, yes, sir, wild is what he was, he didn't know his own mind atall. Well, now, it's going to be a great pleasure to me to meet up with an old friend and find him all settled down and doing well by hisself."

"We've all got to be young once," said Mr. Thompson. "It's like the measles, it breaks out all over you, and you're a nuisance to yourself and everybody else, but it don't last, and it usually don't leave no ill effects." He was so pleased with this notion he forgot and broke into a guffaw. The stranger folded his arms over his stomach and went into a kind of fit, roaring until he had tears in his eyes. Mr. Thompson stopped shouting and eyed the stranger uneasily. Now he liked a good laugh as well as any man, but there ought to be a little moderation. Now this feller laughed like a perfect lunatic, that was a fact. And he wasn't laughing because he really thought things were funny, either. He was laughing for reasons of his own. Mr. Thompson fell into a moody silence, and waited until Mr. Hatch settled down a little.

Mr. Hatch got out a very dirty blue cotton bandanna and wiped his eyes. "That joke just about caught me where I live," he said, almost apologetically. "Now I wish I could think up things as funny as that to say. It's a gift. It's . . ."

"If you want to speak to Mr. Helton, I'll go and round him up," said Mr. Thompson, making motions as if he might get up. "He may be in the milk house and he may be setting in his shack this time of day." It was drawing towards five o'clock. "It's right around the corner," he said.

"Oh, well, there ain't no special hurry," said Mr. Hatch. "I've been wanting to speak to him for a good long spell now and I guess a few minutes more won't make no difference. I just more wanted to locate him, like. That's all."

Mr. Thompson stopped beginning to stand up, and unbuttoned one more button of his shirt, and said, "Well, he's here, and he's this kind of man, that if he had any business with you he'd like to get it over. He don't dawdle, that's one thing you can say for him."

Mr. Hatch appeared to sulk a little at these words. He wiped his face with the bandanna and opened his mouth to speak, when round the house there came the music of Mr. Helton's harmonica. Mr. Thompson raised a finger. "There he is," said Mr. Thompson. "Now's your time."

Mr. Hatch cocked an ear towards the east side of the house and listened for a few seconds, a very strange expression on his face.

"I know that tune like I know the palm of my own hand," said Mr. Thompson, "but I never heard Mr. Helton say what it was."

"That's a kind of Scandahoovian song," said Mr. Hatch. "Where

I come from they sing it a lot. In North Dakota, they sing it. It says something about starting out in the morning feeling so good you can't hardly stand it, so you drink up all your likker before noon. All the likker, y' understand, that you was saving for the noon lay-off. The words ain't much, but it's a pretty tune. It's a kind of drinking song." He sat there drooping a little, and Mr. Thompson didn't like his expression. It was a satisfied expression, but it was more like the cat that et the canary.

"So far as I know," said Mr. Thompson, "he ain't touched a drop since he's been on the place, and that's nine years this coming September. Yes, sir, nine years, so far as I know, he ain't wetted his whistle once. And that's more than I can say for myself," he said, meekly proud.

"Yes, that's a drinking song," said Mr. Hatch. "I used to play 'Little Brown Jug' on the fiddle when I was younger than I am now," he went on, "but this Helton, he just keeps it up. He just sits and plays it by himself."

"He's been playing it off and on for nine years right here on the place," said Mr. Thompson, feeling a little proprietary.

"And he was certainly singing it as well, fifteen years before that, in North Dakota," said Mr. Hatch. "He used to sit up in a straitjacket, practically, when he was in the asylum—"

"What's that you say?" said Mr. Thompson. "What's that?"

"Shucks, I didn't mean to tell you," said Mr. Hatch, a faint leer of regret in his drooping eyelids. "Shucks, that just slipped out. Funny, now I'd made up my mind I wouldn' say a word, because it would just make a lot of excitement, and what I say is, if a man has lived harmless and quiet for nine years it don't matter if he *is* loony, does it? So long's he keeps quiet and don't do nobody harm."

"You mean they had him in a straitjacket?" asked Mr. Thompson, uneasily. "In a lunatic asylum?"

"They sure did," said Mr. Hatch. "That's right where they had him, from time to time."

"They put my Aunt Ida in one of them things in the State asylum," said Mr. Thompson. "She got vi'lent, and they put her in one of these jackets with long sleeves and tied her to an iron ring in the wall, and Aunt Ida got so wild she broke a blood vessel and when they went to look after her she was dead. I'd think one of them things was dangerous."

"Mr. Helton used to sing his drinking song when he was in a straitjacket," said Mr. Hatch. "Nothing ever bothered him, except if you tried to make him talk. That bothered him, and he'd get vi'lent, like your Aunt Ida. He'd get vi'lent and then they'd put him in the jacket and go off and leave him, and he'd lay there perfickly contented, so far's you could see, singing his song. Then one night he just disappeared.

Left, you might say, just went, and nobody ever saw hide or hair of him again. And then I come along and find him here," said Mr. Hatch, "all settled down and playing the same song."

"He never acted crazy to me," said Mr. Thompson. "He always acted like a sensible man, to me. He never got married, for one thing, and he works like a horse, and I bet he's got the first cent I paid him when he landed here, and he don't drink, and he never says a word, much less swear, and he don't waste time runnin' around Saturday nights, and if he's crazy," said Mr. Thompson, "why, I think I'll go crazy myself for a change."

"Haw, ha," said Mr. Hatch, "heh, he, that's good! Ha, ha, ha, I hadn't thought of it jes like that. Yeah, that's right! Let's all go crazy and get rid of our wives and save our money, hey?" He smiled unpleasantly, showing his little rabbit teeth.

Mr. Thompson felt he was being misunderstood. He turned around and motioned toward the open window back of the honeysuckle trellis. "Let's move off down here a little," he said. "I oughta thought of that before." His visitor bothered Mr. Thompson. He had a way of taking the words out of Mr. Thompson's mouth, turning them around and mixing them up until Mr. Thompson didn't know himself what he had said. "My wife's not very strong," said Mr. Thompson. "She's been kind of invalid now goin' on fourteen years. It's mighty tough on a poor man, havin' sickness in the family. She had four operations," he said proudly, "one right after the other, but they didn't do any good. For five years handrunnin', I just turned every nickel I made over to the doctors. Upshot is, she's a mighty delicate woman."

"My old woman," said Mr. Homer T. Hatch, "had a back like a mule, yes, sir. That woman could have moved the barn with her bare hands if she'd ever took the notion. I used to say, it was a good thing she didn't know her own stren'th. She's dead now, though. That kind wear out quicker than the puny ones. I never had much use for a woman always complainin'. I'd get rid of her mighty quick, yes, sir, mighty quick. It's just as you say: a dead loss, keepin' one of 'em up."

This was not at all what Mr. Thompson had heard himself say; he had been trying to explain that a wife as expensive as his was a credit to a man. "She's a mighty reasonable woman," said Mr. Thompson, feeling baffled, "but I wouldn't answer for what she'd say or do if she found out we'd had a lunatic on the place all this time." They had moved away from the window; Mr. Thompson took Mr. Hatch the front way, because if he went the back way they would have to pass Mr. Helton's shack. For some reason he didn't want the stranger to see or talk to Mr. Helton. It was strange, but that was the way Mr. Thompson felt.

Mr. Thompson sat down again, on the chopping log, offering his guest another tree stump. "Now, I mighta got upset myself at such a thing, once," said Mr. Thompson, "but now I *deefy* anything to get me lathered up." He cut himself an enormous plug of tobacco with his horn-handled pocketknife, and offered it to Mr. Hatch, who then produced his own plug and, opening a huge bowie knife with a long blade sharply whetted, cut off a large wad and put it in his mouth. They then compared plugs and both of them were astonished to see how different men's ideas of good chewing tobacco were.

"Now, for instance," said Mr. Hatch, "mine is lighter colored. That's because, for one thing, there ain't any sweetenin' in this plug. I like it dry, natural leaf, medium strong."

"A little sweetenin' don't do no harm so far as I'm concerned," said Mr. Thompson, "but it's got to be mighty little. But with me, now, I want a strong leaf, I want it heavy-cured, as the feller says. There's a man near here, named Williams, Mr. John Morgan Williams, who chews a plug—well, sir, it's black as your hat and soft as melted tar. It fairly drips with molasses, jus' plain molasses, and it chews like licorice. Now, I don't call that a good chew."

"One man's meat," said Mr. Hatch, "is another man's poison. Now, such a chew would simply gag me. I couldn't begin to put it in my mouth."

"Well," said Mr. Thompson, a tinge of apology in his voice, "I jus' barely tasted it myself, you might say. Just took a little piece in my mouth and spit it out again."

"I'm dead sure I couldn't even get that far," said Mr. Hatch. "I like a dry natural chew without any artificial flavorin' of any kind."

Mr. Thompson began to feel that Mr. Hatch was trying to make out he had the best judgment in tobacco, and was going to keep up the argument until he proved it. He began to feel seriously annoyed with the fat man. After all, who was he and where did he come from? Who was he to go around telling other people what kind of tobacco to chew?

"Artificial flavorin'," Mr. Hatch went on, doggedly, "is jes put in to cover up a cheap leaf and make a man think he's gettin' somethin' more than he *is* gettin'. Even a little sweetenin' is a sign of a cheap leaf, you can mark my words."

"I've always paid a fair price for my plug," said Mr. Thompson, stiffly. "I'm not a rich man and I don't go round settin' myself up for one, but I'll say this, when it comes to such things as tobacco, I buy the best on the market."

"Sweetenin', even a little," began Mr. Hatch, shifting his plug and squirting tobacco juice at a dry-looking little rose bush that was having a hard enough time as it was, standing all day in the blazing sun, its roots clenched in the baked earth, "is the sign of—"

"About this Mr. Helton, now," said Mr. Thompson, determinedly, "I don't see no reason to hold it against a man because he went loony once or twice in his lifetime and so I don't expect to take no steps about it. Not a step. I've got nothin' against the man, he's always treated me fair. They's things and people," he went on, "'nough to drive any man loony. The wonder to me is, more men don't wind up in straitjackets, the way things are going these days and times."

"That's right," said Mr. Hatch, promptly, entirely too promptly, as if he were turning Mr. Thompson's meaning back on him. "You took the words right out of my mouth. There ain't every man in a straitjacket that ought to be there. Ha, ha, you're right all right. You got the idea."

Mr. Thompson sat silent and chewed steadily and stared at a spot on the ground about six feet away and felt a slow muffled resentment climbing from somewhere deep down in him, climbing and spreading all through him. What was this fellow driving at? What was he trying to say? It wasn't so much his words, but his looks and his way of talking: that droopy look in the eye, that tone of voice, as if he was trying to mortify Mr. Thompson about something. Mr. Thompson didn't like it, but he couldn't get hold of it either. He wanted to turn around and shove the fellow off the stump, but it wouldn't look reasonable. Suppose something happened to the fellow when he fell off the stump, just for instance, if he fell on the ax and cut himself, and then someone should ask Mr. Thompson why he shoved him, and what could a man say? It would look mighty funny, it would sound mighty strange to say, Well, him and me fell out over a plug of tobacco. He might just shove him anyhow and then tell people he was a fat man not used to the heat and while he was talking he got dizzy and fell off by himself, or something like that, and it wouldn't be the truth either, because it wasn't the heat and it wasn't the tobacco. Mr. Thompson made up his mind to get the fellow off the place pretty quick, without seeming to be anxious, and watch him sharp till he was out of sight. It doesn't pay to be friendly with strangers from another part of the country. They're always up to something, or they'd stay at home where they belong.

"And they's some people," said Mr. Hatch, "would jus' as soon have a loonatic around their house as not, they can't see no difference between them and anybody else. I always say, if that's the way a man feels, don't care who he associates with, why, why, that's his business, not mine. I don't wanta have a thing to do with it. Now back home in North Dakota, we don't feel that way. I'd like to a seen anybody hiring a loonatic there, aspecially after what he done."

"I didn't understand your home was North Dakota," said Mr. Thompson. "I thought you said Georgia."

"I've got a married sister in North Dakota," said Mr. Hatch, "married a Swede, but a white man if ever I saw one. So I say *we* because we got into a little business together out that way. And it seems like home, kind of."

"What did he do?" asked Mr. Thompson, feeling very uneasy again.

"Oh, nothin' to speak of," said Mr. Hatch, jovially, "jus' went loony one day in the hayfield and shoved a pitchfork right square through his brother, when they was makin' hay. They was goin' to execute him, but they found out he had went crazy with the heat, as the feller says, and so they put him in the asylum. That's all he done. Nothin' to get lathered up about, ha, ha, ha!" he said, and taking out his sharp knife he began to slice off a chew as carefully as if he were cutting cake.

"Well," said Mr. Thompson, "I don't deny that's news. Yes, sir, news. But I still say somethin' must have drove him to it. Some men make you feel like giving 'em a good killing just by lookin' at you. His brother may a been a mean ornery cuss."

"Brother was going to get married," said Mr. Hatch; "used to go courtin' his girl nights. Borrowed Mr. Helton's harmonica to give her a serenade one evenin', and lost it. Brand new harmonica."

"He thinks a heap of his harmonicas," said Mr. Thompson. "Only money he ever spends, now and then he buys hisself a new one. Must have a dozen in that shack, all kinds and sizes."

"Brother wouldn't buy him a new one," said Mr. Hatch, "so Mr. Helton just ups, as I says, and runs his pitchfork through his brother. Now you know he musta been crazy to get all worked up over a little thing like that."

"Sounds like it," said Mr. Thompson, reluctant to agree in anything with this intrusive and disagreeable fellow. He kept thinking he couldn't remember when he had taken such a dislike to a man on first sight.

"Seems to me you'd get pretty sick of hearin' the same tune year in, year out," said Mr. Hatch.

"Well, sometimes I think it wouldn't do no harm if he learned a new one," said Mr. Thompson, "but he don't, so there's nothin' to be done about it. It's a pretty good tune, though."

"One of the Scandahoovians told me what it meant, that's how I come to know," said Mr. Hatch. "Especially that part about getting so gay you jus' go ahead and drink up all the likker you got on hand before noon. It seems like up in them Swede countries a man carries a bottle of wine around with him as a matter of course, at least that's the way I understood it. Those fellers will tell you anything, though—" He broke off and spat.

The idea of drinking any kind of liquor in this heat made Mr. Thompson dizzy. The idea of anybody feeling good on a day like this, for instance, made him tired. He felt he was really suffering from the heat. The fat man looked as if he had grown to the stump; he slumped there in his damp, dark clothes too big for him, his belly slack in his pants, his wide black felt hat pushed off his narrow forehead red with prickly heat. A bottle of good cold beer, now, would be a help, thought Mr. Thompson, remembering the four bottles sitting deep in the pool at the springhouse, and his dry tongue squirmed in his mouth. He wasn't going to offer this man anything, though, not even a drop of water. He wasn't even going to chew any more tobacco with him. He shot out his quid suddenly, and wiped his mouth on the back of his hand, and studied the head near him attentively. The man was no good, and he was there for no good, but what was he up to? Mr. Thompson made up his mind he'd give him a little more time to get his business, whatever it was, with Mr. Helton over, and then if he didn't get off the place he'd kick him off.

Mr. Hatch, as if he suspected Mr. Thompson's thoughts, turned his eyes, wicked and pig-like, on Mr. Thompson. "Fact is," he said, as if he had made up his mind about something, "I might need your help in the little matter I've got on hand, but it won't cost you any trouble. Now, this Mr. Helton here, like I tell you, he's a dangerous escaped loonatic, you might say. Now fact is, in the last twelve years or so I musta rounded up twenty-odd escaped loonatics, besides a couple of escaped convicts that I just run into by accident, like. I don't make a business of it, but if there's a reward, and there usually is a reward, of course, I get it. It amounts to a tidy little sum in the long run, but that ain't the main question. Fact is, I'm for law and order, I don't like to see lawbreakers and loonatics at large. It ain't the place for them. Now I reckon you're bound to agree with me on that, aren't you?"

Mr. Thompson said, "Well, circumstances alters cases, as the feller says. Now, what I know of Mr. Helton, he ain't dangerous, as I told you." Something serious was going to happen, Mr. Thompson could see that. He stopped thinking about it. He'd just let this fellow shoot off his head and then see what could be done about it. Without thinking he got out his knife and plug and started to cut a chew, then remembered himself and put them back in his pocket.

"The law," said Mr. Hatch, "is solidly behind me. Now this Mr. Helton, he's been one of my toughest cases. He's kept my record from being practically one hundred per cent. I knew him before he went loony, and I know the fam'ly, so I undertook to help out rounding him up. Well, sir, he was gone slick as a whistle, for all we knew the man was as good as dead long while ago. Now we never might have caught up with him, but do you know what he did? Well, sir, about two weeks ago his old mother gets a letter from him, and in that letter, what do you reckon she found? Well, it was a check on that little bank in town for eight hundred and fifty dollars, just like that; the letter wasn't nothing much, just said he was sending her a few little savings, she might need something, but there it was, name, postmark, date, everything. The old woman practically lost her mind with joy. She's gettin' childish, and it looked like she kinda forgot that her only living son killed his brother and went loony. Mr. Helton said he was getting along all right, and for her not to tell nobody. Well, natchally, she couldn't keep it to herself, with that check to cash and everything. So that's how I come to know." His feelings got the better of him. "You coulda knocked me down with a feather." He shook hands with himself and rocked, wagging his head, going "Heh, heh," in his throat. Mr. Thompson felt the corners of his mouth turning down. Why, the dirty low-down hound, sneaking around spying into other people's business like that. Collecting blood money, that's what it was! Let him talk!

"Yea, well, that musta been a surprise all right," he said, trying to hold his voice even. "I'd say a surprise."

"Well, siree," said Mr. Hatch, "the more I got to thinking about it, the more I just come to the conclusion that I'd better look into the matter a little, and so I talked to the old woman. She's pretty decrepit, now, half blind and all, but she was all for taking the first train out and going to see her son. I put it up to her square—how she was too feeble for the trip, and all. So, just as a favor to her, I told her for my expenses I'd come down and see Mr. Helton and bring her back all the news about him. She gave me a new shirt she made herself by hand, and a big Swedish kind of cake to bring to him, but I musta mislaid them along the road somewhere. It don't reely matter, though, he prob'ly ain't in any state of mind to appreciate 'em."

Mr. Thompson sat up and turning round on the log looked at Mr. Hatch and asked as quietly as he could, "And now what are you aiming to do? That's the question."

Mr. Hatch slouched up to his feet and shook himself. "Well, I come all prepared for a little scuffle," he said. "I got the handcuffs," he said, "but I don't want no violence if I can help it. I didn't want to say nothing around the countryside, making an uproar. I figured the two of us could overpower him." He reached into his big inside pocket and pulled them out. Handcuffs, for God's sake, thought Mr. Thompson. Coming round on a peaceable afternoon worrying a man, and making trouble, and fishing handcuffs out of his pocket on a decent family homestead, as if it was all in the day's work.

Mr. Thompson, his head buzzing, got up too. "Well," he said, roundly, "I want to tell you I think you've got a mighty sorry job on hand, you sure must be hard up for something to do, and now I want to give you a good piece of advice. You just drop the idea that you're going to come here and make trouble for Mr. Helton, and the quicker you drive that hired rig away from my front gate the better I'll be satisfied."

Mr. Hatch put one handcuff in his outside pocket, the other dangling down. He pulled his hat down over his eyes, and reminded Mr.

Thompson of a sheriff, somehow. He didn't seem in the least nervous, and didn't take up Mr. Thompson's words. He said, "Now listen just a minute, it ain't reasonable to suppose that a man like yourself is going to stand in the way of getting an escaped loonatic back to the asylum where he belongs. Now I know it's enough to throw you off, coming sudden like this, but fact is I counted on your being a respectable man and helping me out to see that justice is done. Now a course, if you won't help, I'll have to look around for help somewheres else. It won't look very good to your neighbors that you was harbring an escaped loonatic who killed his own brother, and then you refused to give him up. It will look mighty funny."

Mr. Thompson knew almost before he heard the words that it would look funny. It would put him in a mighty awkward position. He said, "But I've been trying to tell you all along that the man ain't loony now. He's been perfectly harmless for nine years. He's — he's — "

Mr. Thompson couldn't think how to describe how it was with Mr. Helton. "Why, he's been like one of the family," he said, "the best standby a man ever had." Mr. Thompson tried to see his way out. It was a fact Mr. Helton might go loony again any minute, and now this fellow talking around the country would put Mr. Thompson in a fix. It was a terrible position. He couldn't think of any way out. "You're crazy," Mr. Thompson roared suddenly, "you're the crazy one around here, you're crazier than he ever was! You get off this place or I'll handcuff you and turn you over to the law. You're trespassing," shouted Mr. Thompson. "Get out of here before I knock you down!"

He took a step towards the fat man, who backed off, shrinking, "Try it, try it, go ahead!" and then something happened that Mr. Thompson tried hard afterwards to piece together in his mind, and in fact it never did come straight. He saw the fat man with his long bowie knife in his hand, he saw Mr. Helton come round the corner on the run, his long jaw dropped, his arms swinging, his eyes wild. Mr. Helton came in between them, fists doubled up, then stopped short, glaring at the fat man, his big frame seemed to collapse, he trembled like a shied horse; and then the fat man drove at him, knife in one hand, handcuffs in the other. Mr. Thompson saw it coming, he saw the blade going into Mr. Helton's stomach, he knew he had the ax out of the log in his own hands, felt his arms go up over his head and bring the ax down on Mr. Hatch's head as if he were stunning a beef.

Mrs. Thompson had been listening uneasily for some time to the voices going on, one of them strange to her, but she was too tired at first to get up and come out to see what was going on. The confused shouting that rose so suddenly brought her up to her feet and out across the front porch without her slippers, hair half-braided. Shading her eyes, she saw first Mr. Helton, running all stooped over through the orchard, running like a man with dogs after him; and Mr. Thompson supporting himself on the ax handle was leaning over shaking by the shoulder a man Mrs. Thompson had never seen, who lay doubled up with the top of his head smashed and the blood running away in a greasy-looking puddle. Mr. Thompson without taking his hand from the man's shoulder, said in a thick voice, "He killed Mr. Helton, he killed him, I saw him do it. I had to knock him out," he called loudly, "but he won't come to."

Mrs. Thompson said in a faint scream, "Why, yonder goes Mr. Helton," and she pointed. Mr. Thompson pulled himself up and looked where she pointed. Mrs. Thompson sat down slowly against the side of the house and began to slide forward on her face; she felt as if she were drowning, she couldn't rise to the top somehow, and her only thought was she was glad the boys were not there, they were out, fishing at Halifax, oh, God, she was glad the boys were not there.

Mr. and Mrs. Thompson drove up to their barn about sunset. Mr. Thompson handed the reins to his wife, got out to open the big door, and Mrs. Thompson guided old Jim in under the roof. The buggy was gray with dust and age, Mrs. Thompson's face was gray with dust and weariness, and Mr. Thompson's face, as he stood at the horse's head and began unhitching, was gray except for the dark blue of his freshly shaven jaws and chin, gray and blue and caved in, but patient, like a dead man's face.

Mrs. Thompson stepped down to the hard packed manure of the barn floor, and shook out her light flower-sprigged dress. She wore her smoked glasses, and her wide shady leghorn hat with the wreath of exhausted pink and blue forget-me-nots hid her forehead, fixed in a knot of distress.

The horse hung his head, raised a huge sigh and flexed his stiffened legs. Mr. Thompson's words came up muffled and hollow. "Poor ole Jim," he said, clearing his throat, "he looks pretty sunk in the ribs. I guess he's had a hard week." He lifted the harness up in one piece, slid it off and Jim walked out of the shafts halting a little. "Well, this is the last time," Mr. Thompson said, still talking to Jim. "Now you can get a good rest."

Mrs. Thompson closed her eyes behind her smoked glasses. The last time, and high time, and they should never have gone at all. She did not need her glasses any more, now the good darkness was coming down again, but her eyes ran full of tears steadily, though she was not crying, and she felt better with the glasses, safer, hidden away behind them. She took out her handkerchief with her hands shaking as they had been shaking ever since *that day*, and blew her nose. She said, "I see the boys have lighted the lamps. I hope they've started the stove going."

She stepped along the rough path holding her thin dress and

starched petticoats around her, feeling her way between the sharp small stones, leaving the barn because she could hardly bear to be near Mr. Thompson, advancing slowly towards the house because she dreaded going there. Life was all one dread, the faces of her neighbors, of her boys, of her husband, the face of the whole world, the shape of her own house in the darkness, the very smell of the grass and the trees were horrible to her. There was no place to go, only one thing to do, bear it somehow — but how? She asked herself that question often. How was she going to keep on living now? Why had she lived at all? She wished now she had died one of those times when she had been so sick, instead of living on for this.

The boys were in the kitchen; Herbert was looking at the funny pictures from last Sunday's newspapers, the Katzenjammer Kids and Happy Hooligan. His chin was in his hands and his elbows on the table, and he was really reading and looking at the pictures, but his face was unhappy. Arthur was building the fire, adding kindling a stick at a time, watching it catch and blaze. His face was heavier and darker than Herbert's, but he was a little sullen by nature; Mrs. Thompson thought, he takes things harder, too. Arthur said, "Hello, Momma," and went on with his work. Herbert swept the papers together and moved over on the bench. They were big boys — fifteen and seventeen, and Arthur as tall as his father. Mrs. Thompson sat down beside Herbert, taking off her hat. She said, "I guess you're hungry. We were late today. We went the Log Hollow road, it's rougher than ever." Her pale mouth drooped with a sad fold on either side.

"I guess you saw the Mannings, then," said Herbert.

"Yes, and the Fergusons, and the Allbrights, and that new family McClellan."

"Anybody say anything?" asked Herbert.

"Nothing much, you know how it's been all along, some of them keeps saying, yes, they know it was a clear case and a fair trial and they say how glad they are your papa came out so well, and all that, some of 'em do, anyhow, but it looks like they don't really take sides with him. I'm about wore out," she said, the tears rolling again from under her dark glasses. "I don't know what good it does, but your papa can't seem to rest unless he's telling how it happened. I don't know."

"I don't think it does any good, not a speck," said Arthur, moving away from the stove. "It just keeps the whole question stirred up in people's minds. Everybody will go round telling what he heard, and the whole thing is going to get worse mixed up than ever. It just makes matters worse. I wish you could get Papa to stop driving round the country talking like that."

"Your papa knows best," said Mrs. Thompson. "You oughtn't to criticize him. He's got enough to put up with without that."

Arthur said nothing, his jaw stubborn. Mr. Thompson came in, his eyes hollowed out and dead-looking, his thick hands gray white and seamed from washing them clean every day before he started out to see the neighbors to tell them his side of the story. He was wearing his Sunday clothes, a thick pepper-and-salt-colored suit with a black string tie.

Mrs. Thompson stood up, her head swimming. "Now you-all get out of the kitchen, it's too hot in here and I need room. I'll get us a little bite of supper, if you'll just get out and give me some room."

They went as if they were glad to go, the boys outside, Mr. Thompson into his bedroom. She heard him groaning to himself as he took off his shoes, and heard the bed creak as he lay down. Mrs. Thompson opened the icebox and felt the sweet coldness flow out of it; she had never expected to have an icebox, much less did she hope to afford to keep it filled with ice. It still seemed like a miracle, after two or three years. There was the food, cold and clean, all ready to be warmed over. She would never have had that icebox if Mr. Helton hadn't happened along one day, just by the strangest luck; so saving, and so managing, so good, thought Mrs. Thompson, her heart swelling until she feared she would faint again, standing there with the door open and leaning her head upon it. She simply could not bear to remember Mr. Helton, with his long sad face and silent ways, who had always been so quiet and harmless, who had worked so hard and helped Mr. Thompson so much, running through the hot fields and woods, being hunted like a mad dog, everybody turning out with ropes and guns and sticks to catch and tie him. Oh, God, said Mrs. Thompson in a long dry moan, kneeling before the icebox and fumbling inside for the dishes, even if they did pile mattresses all over the jail floor and against the walls, and five men there to hold him to keep him from hurting himself any more, he was already hurt too badly, he couldn't have lived anyway. Mr. Barbee, the sheriff, told her about it. He said, well, they didn't aim to harm him but they had to catch him, he was crazy as a loon; he picked up rocks and tried to brain every man that got near him. He had two harmonicas in his jumper pocket, said the sheriff, but they fell out in the scuffle, and Mr. Helton tried to pick 'em up again, and that's when they finally got him. "They *had* to be rough, Miz Thompson, he fought like a wildcat." Yes, thought Mrs. Thompson again with the same bitterness, of course, they had to be rough. They always have to be rough. Mr. Thompson can't argue with a man and get him off the place peaceably; no, she thought, standing up and shutting the icebox, he has to kill somebody, he has to be a murderer and ruin his boys' lives and cause Mr. Helton to be killed like a mad dog.

Her thoughts stopped with a little soundless explosion, cleared and began again. The rest of Mr. Helton's harmonicas were still in the shack, his tune ran in Mrs. Thompson's head at certain times of the day. She missed it in the evenings. It seemed so strange she had never known the name of that song, nor what it meant, until after Mr. Helton was gone. Mrs. Thompson, trembling in the knees, took a drink of water at the sink and poured the red beans into the baking dish, and began to roll the pieces of chicken in flour to fry them. There was a time, she said to herself, when I thought I had neighbors and friends, there was a time when we could hold up our heads, there was a time when my husband hadn't killed a man and I could tell the truth to anybody about anything.

Mr. Thompson, turning on his bed, figured that he had done all he could, he'd just try to let the matter rest from now on. His lawyer, Mr. Burleigh, had told him right at the beginning, "Now you keep calm and collected. You've got a fine case, even if you haven't got witnesses. Your wife must sit in court, she'll be a powerful argument with the jury. You just plead not guilty and I'll do the rest. The trial is going to be a mere formality, you haven't got a thing to worry about. You'll be clean out of this before you know it." And to make talk Mr. Burleigh had got to telling about all the men he knew around the country who for one reason or another had been forced to kill somebody, always in self-defense, and there just wasn't anything to it at all. He even told about how his own father in the old days had shot and killed a man just for setting foot inside his gate when he told him not to. "Sure, I shot the scoundrel," said Mr. Burleigh's father, "in self-defense; I *told* him I'd shoot him if he set his foot in my yard, and he did, and I did." There had been bad blood between them for years, Mr. Burleigh said, and his father had waited a long time to catch the other fellow in the wrong, and when he did he certainly made the most of his opportunity.

"But Mr. Hatch, as I told you," Mr. Thompson had said, "made a pass at Mr. Helton with his bowie knife. That's why I took a hand."

"All the better," said Mr. Burleigh. "That stranger hadn't any right coming to your house on such an errand. Why, hell," said Mr. Burleigh, "that wasn't even manslaughter you committed. So now you just hold your horses and keep your shirt on. And don't say one word without I tell you."

Wasn't even manslaughter. Mr. Thompson had to cover Mr. Hatch with a piece of wagon canvas and ride to town to tell the sheriff. It had been hard on Ellie. When they got back, the sheriff and the coroner and two deputies, they found her sitting beside the road, on a low bridge over a gulley, about half a mile from the place. He had taken her up behind his saddle and got her back to the house. He had already told the sheriff that his wife had witnessed the whole business, and now he had time, getting her to her room and in bed, to tell her what to say if they asked anything. He had left out the part about Mr. Helton being crazy all along, but it came out at the trial. By Mr. Burleigh's advice Mr. Thompson had pretended to be perfectly ignorant; Mr. Hatch hadn't said a word about that. Mr. Thompson pretended to believe that

Mr. Hatch had just come looking for Mr. Helton to settle old scores, and the two members of Mr. Hatch's family who had come down to try to get Mr. Thompson convicted didn't get anywhere at all. It hadn't been much of a trial, Mr. Burleigh saw to that. He had charged a reasonable fee, and Mr. Thompson had paid him and felt grateful, but after it was over Mr. Burleigh didn't seem pleased to see him when he got to dropping into the office to talk it over, telling him things that had slipped his mind at first: trying to explain what an ornery low hound Mr. Hatch had been, anyhow. Mr. Burleigh seemed to have lost his interest; he looked sour and upset when he saw Mr. Thompson at the door. Mr. Thompson kept saying to himself that he'd got off, all right, just as Mr. Burleigh had predicted, but, but—and it was right there that Mr. Thompson's mind stuck, squirming like an angleworm on a fishhook: he had killed Mr. Hatch, and he was a murderer. That was the truth about himself that Mr. Thompson couldn't grasp, even when he said the word to himself. Why, he had not even once *thought* of killing anybody, much less Mr. Hatch, and if Mr. Helton hadn't come out so unexpectedly, hearing the row, why, then—but then, Mr. Helton had come on the run that way to help him. What he couldn't understand was what happened next. He had seen Mr. Hatch go after Mr. Helton with the knife, he had seen the point, blade up, go into Mr. Helton's stomach and slice up like you slice a hog, but when they finally caught Mr. Helton there wasn't a knife scratch on him. Mr. Thompson knew he had the ax in his own hands and felt himself lifting it, but he couldn't remember hitting Mr. Hatch. He couldn't remember it. He couldn't. He remembered only that he had been determined to stop Mr. Hatch from cutting Mr. Helton. If he was given a chance he could explain the whole matter. At the trial they hadn't let him talk. They just asked questions and he answered yes or no, and they never did get to the core of the matter. Since the trial, now, every day for a week he had washed and shaved and put on his best clothes and had taken Ellie with him to tell every neighbor he had that he never killed Mr. Hatch on purpose, and what good did it do? Nobody believed him. Even when he turned to Ellie and said, "You was there, you saw it, didn't you?" and Ellie spoke up, saying, "Yes, that's the truth. Mr. Thompson was trying to save Mr. Helton's life," and he added, "If you don't believe me, you can believe my wife. She won't lie," Mr. Thompson saw something in all their faces that disheartened him, made him feel empty and tired out. They didn't believe he was not a murderer.

Even Ellie never said anything to comfort him. He hoped she would say finally, "I remember now, Mr. Thompson, I really did come round the corner in time to see everything. It's not a lie, Mr. Thompson. Don't you worry." But as they drove together in silence, with the days still hot and dry, shortening for fall, day after day, the buggy jolting in the ruts, she said nothing; they grew to dread the sight of another house, and the people in it: all houses looked alike now, and the people — old neighbors or new — had the same expression when Mr. Thompson told them why he had come and began his story. Their eyes looked as if someone had pinched the eyeball at the back; they shriveled and the light went out of them. Some of them sat with fixed tight smiles trying to be friendly. "Yes, Mr. Thompson, we know how you must feel. It must be terrible for you, Mrs. Thompson. Yes, you know, I've about come to the point where I believe in such a thing as killing in self-defense. Why, certainly, we believe you, Mr. Thompson, why shouldn't we believe you? Didn't you have a perfectly fair and aboveboard trial? Well, now, natchally, Mr. Thompson, we think you done right."

Mr. Thompson was satisfied they didn't think so. Sometimes the air around him was so thick with their blame he fought and pushed with his fists, and the sweat broke out all over him, he shouted his story in a dust-choked voice, he would fairly bellow at last: "My wife, here, you know her, she was there, she saw and heard it all, if you don't believe me, ask her, she won't lie!" and Mrs. Thompson, with her hands knotted together, aching, her chin trembling, would never fail to say: "Yes, that's right, that's the truth — "

The last straw had been laid on today, Mr. Thompson decided. Tom Allbright, an old beau of Ellie's, why, he had squired Ellie around a whole summer, had come out to meet them when they drove up, and standing there bareheaded had stopped them from getting out. He had looked past them with an embarrassed frown on his face, telling them his wife's sister was there with a raft of young ones, and the house was pretty full and everything upset, or he'd ask them to come in. "We've been thinking of trying to get up to your place one of these days," said Mr. Allbright, moving away trying to look busy, "We've been mighty occupied up here of late." So they had to say, "Well, we just happened to be driving this way," and go on. "The Allbrights," said Mrs. Thompson, "always was fair-weather friends." "They look out for number one, that's a fact," said Mr. Thompson. But it was cold comfort to them both.

Finally Mrs. Thompson had given up. "Let's go home," she said. "Old Jim's tired and thirsty, and we've gone far enough."

Mr. Thompson said, "Well, while we're out this way, we might as well stop at the McClellans'." They drove in, and asked a little cotton-haired boy if his mamma and papa were at home. Mr. Thompson wanted to see them. The little boy stood gazing with his mouth open, then galloped into the house shouting, "Mommer, Popper, come out hyah. That man that kilt Mr. Hatch has come ter see yer!"

The man came out in his sock feet, with one gallus up, the other broken and dangling, and said, "Light down, Mr. Thompson, and come in. The ole woman's washing, but she'll git here." Mrs. Thompson, feeling her way, stepped down and sat in a broken rocking chair on the porch that sagged under her feet. The woman of the house, barefooted, in a calico wrapper, sat on the edge of the porch, her fat sallow face full of curiosity. Mr. Thompson began, "Well, as I reckon you happen to know, I've had some strange troubles lately, and, as the feller says, it's not the kind of trouble that happens to a man every day in the year, and there's some things I don't want no misunderstanding about in the neighbors' minds, so—" He halted and stumbled forward, and the two listening faces took on a mean look, a greedy, despising look, a look that said plain as day, "My, you must be a purty sorry feller to come round worrying about what *we* think, *we* know you wouldn't be here if you had anybody else to turn to—my, I wouldn't lower myself that much, myself." Mr. Thompson was ashamed of himself, he was suddenly in a rage, he'd like to knock their dirty skunk heads together, the low-down white trash—but he held himself down and went on to the end. "My wife will tell you," he said, and this was the hardest place, because Ellie always without moving a muscle seemed to stiffen as if somebody had threatened to hit her; "ask my wife, she won't lie."

"It's true, I saw it—"

"Well, now," said the man, drily, scratching his ribs inside his shirt, "that sholy is too bad. Well, now, I kaint see what we've got to do with all this here, however. I kaint see no good reason for us to git mixed up in these murder matters, I shore kaint. Whichever way you look at it, it ain't none of my business. However, it's mighty nice of you-all to come around and give us the straight of it, fur we've heerd some mighty queer yarns about it, mighty queer, I golly you couldn't hardly make head ner tail of it."

"Evvybody goin' round shootin' they heads off," said the woman. "Now we don't hold with killin'; the Bible says—"

"Shet yer trap," said the man, "and keep it shet 'r I'll shet it fer yer. Now it shore looks like to me—"

"We mustn't linger," said Mrs. Thompson, unclasping her hands. "We've lingered too long now. It's getting late, and we've far to go." Mr. Thompson took the hint and followed her. The man and the woman lolled against their rickety porch poles and watched them go.

Now lying on his bed, Mr. Thompson knew the end had come. Now, this minute, lying in the bed where he had slept with Ellie for eighteen years; under this roof where he had laid the shingles when he was waiting to get married; there as he was with his whiskers already sprouting since his shave that morning; with his fingers feeling his bony chin, Mr. Thompson felt he was a dead man. He was dead to his other life, he had got to the end of something without knowing why, and he had to make a fresh start, he did not know how. Something different was going to begin, he didn't know what. It was in some way not his business. He didn't feel he was going to have much to do with it. He got up, aching, hollow, and went out to the kitchen where Mrs. Thompson was just taking up the supper.

"Call the boys," said Mrs. Thompson. They had been down to the barn, and Arthur put out the lantern before hanging it on a nail near the door. Mr. Thompson didn't like their silence. They had hardly said a word about anything to him since that day. They seemed to avoid him, they ran the place together as if he wasn't there, and attended to everything without asking him for any advice. "What you boys been up to?" he asked, trying to be hearty. "Finishing your chores?"

"No, sir," said Arthur, "there ain't much to do. Just greasing some axles." Herbert said nothing. Mrs. Thompson bowed her head: "For these and all Thy blessings. . . . Amen," she whispered weakly, and the Thompsons sat there with their eyes down and their faces sorrowful, as if they were at a funeral.

Every time he shut his eyes, trying to sleep, Mr. Thompson's mind started up and began to run like a rabbit. It jumped from one thing to another, trying to pick up a trail here or there that would straighten out what had happened that day he killed Mr. Hatch. Try as he might, Mr. Thompson's mind would not go anywhere that it had not already been, he could not see anything but what he had seen once, and he knew that was not right. If he had not seen straight that first time, then everything about his killing Mr. Hatch was wrong from start to finish, and there was nothing more to be done about it, he might just as well give up. It still seemed to him that he had done, maybe not the right thing, but the only thing he could do, that day, but had he? *Did he have to kill Mr. Hatch?* He had never seen a man he hated more, the minute he laid eyes on him. He knew in his bones the fellow was there for trouble. What seemed so funny now was this: Why hadn't he just told Mr. Hatch to get out before he ever even got in?

Mrs. Thompson, her arms crossed on her breast, was lying beside him, perfectly still, but she seemed awake, somehow. "Asleep, Ellie?"

After all, he might have got rid of him peaceably, or maybe he might have had to overpower him and put those handcuffs on him and turn him over to the sheriff for disturbing the peace. The most they could have done was to lock Mr. Hatch up while he cooled off for a few days, or fine him a little something. He would try to think of things he might have said to Mr. Hatch. Why, let's see, I could just have said, Now look here, Mr. Hatch, I want to talk to you as man to man. But his brain would go empty. What could he have said or done? But if he *could* have done anything else almost except kill Mr. Hatch, then nothing would have happened to Mr. Helton. Mr. Thompson hardly ever thought of Mr. Helton. His mind just skipped over him and went on. If he stopped to think about Mr. Helton he'd never in God's world get anywhere. He tried to imagine how it might all have been, this very night even, if Mr. Helton were still safe and sound out in his shack playing his tune about feeling so good in the morning, drinking up all the wine so you'd feel even better; and Mr. Hatch safe in jail somewhere, mad as hops, maybe, but out of harm's way and ready to listen to reason and to repent of his meanness, the dirty, yellow-livered hound coming around persecuting an innocent man and ruining a whole family that never harmed him! Mr. Thompson felt the veins of his forehead start up, his fists clutched as if they seized an ax handle, the sweat broke out on him, he bounded up from the bed with a yell smothered in his throat, and Ellie started up after him, crying out, "Oh, oh, don't! Don't! Don't!" as if she were having a nightmare. He stood shaking until his bones rattled in him, crying hoarsely, "Light the lamp, light the lamp, Ellie."

Instead, Mrs. Thompson gave a shrill weak scream, almost the same scream he had heard on that day she came around the house when he was standing there with the ax in his hand. He could not see her in the dark, but she was on the bed, rolling violently. He felt for her in horror, and his groping hands found her arms, up, and her own hands pulling her hair straight out from her head, her neck strained back, and the tight screams strangling her. He shouted out for Arthur, for Herbert. "Your mother!" he bawled, his voice cracking. As he held Mrs. Thompson's arms, the boys came tumbling in, Arthur with the lamp above his head. By this light Mr. Thompson saw Mrs. Thompson's eyes, wide open, staring dreadfully at him, the tears pouring. She sat up at sight of the boys, and held out one arm towards them, the hand wagging in a crazy circle, then dropped on her back again, and suddenly went limp. Arthur set the lamp on the table and turned on Mr. Thompson. "She's scared," he said, "she's scared to death." His face was in a knot of rage, his fists were doubled up, he faced his father as if he meant to strike him. Mr. Thompson's jaw fell, he was so surprised he stepped back from the bed. Herbert went to the other side. They stood on each side of Mrs. Thompson and watched Mr. Thompson as if he were a dangerous wild beast. "What did you do to her?" shouted Arthur, in a grown man's voice. "You touch her again and I'll blow your heart out!" Herbert was pale and his cheek twitched, but he was on Arthur's side; he would do what he could to help Arthur.

Mr. Thompson had no fight left in him. His knees bent as he stood, his chest collapsed. "Why, Arthur," he said, his words crumbling and his breath coming short. "She's fainted again. Get the ammonia." Arthur did not move. Herbert brought the bottle, and handed it, shrinking, to his father.

Mr. Thompson held it under Mrs. Thompson's nose. He poured a little in the palm of his hand and rubbed it on her forehead. She gasped and opened her eyes and turned her head away from him. Herbert began a doleful hopeless sniffling. "Mamma," he kept saying, "Mamma, don't die."

"I'm all right," Mrs. Thompson said. "Now don't you worry around. Now Herbert, you mustn't do that. I'm all right." She closed her eyes. Mr. Thompson began pulling on his best pants; he put on his socks and shoes. The boys sat on each side of the bed, watching Mrs. Thompson's face. Mr. Thompson put on his shirt and coat. He said, "I reckon I'll ride over and get the doctor. Don't look like all this fainting is a good sign. Now you just keep watch until I get back." They listened, but said nothing. He said, "Don't you get any notions in your head. I never did your mother any harm in my life, on purpose." He went out, and, looking back, saw Herbert staring at him from under his brows, like a stranger. "You'll know how to look after her," said Mr. Thompson.

Mr. Thompson went through the kitchen. There he lighted the lantern, took a thin pad of scratch paper and a stub pencil from the shelf where the boys kept their schoolbooks. He swung the lantern on his arm and reached into the cupboard where he kept the guns. The shotgun was there to his hand, primed and ready, a man never knows when he may need a shotgun. He went out of the house without looking around, or looking back when he had left it, passed his barn without seeing it, and struck out to the farthest end of his fields, which ran for half a mile to the east. So many blows had been struck at Mr. Thompson and from so many directions he couldn't stop any more to find out where he was hit. He walked on, over plowed ground and over meadow, going through barbed wire fences cautiously, putting his gun through first; he could almost see in the dark, now his eyes were used to it. Finally he came to the last fence; here he sat down, back against a post, lantern at his side, and, with the pad on his knee, moistened the stub pencil and began to write:

"Before Almighty God, the great judge of all before who I am about to appear, I do hereby solemnly swear that I did not take the life of Mr. Homer T. Hatch on purpose. It was done in defense of Mr. Helton. I did not aim to hit him with the ax but only to keep him off Mr. Helton. He aimed a blow at Mr. Helton who was not looking for it. It was my belief at the time that Mr. Hatch would of taken the life of Mr. Helton if I did not interfere. I have told all this to the judge and the jury and they let me off but nobody believes it. This is the only way I can prove I am not a cold blooded murderer like everybody seems to think. If I had been in Mr. Helton's place he would of done the same for me. I still think I done the only thing there was to do. My wife—"

Mr. Thompson stopped here to think a while. He wet the pencil point with the tip of his tongue and marked out the last two words. He sat a while blacking out the words until he had made a neat oblong patch where they had been, and started again:

"It was Mr. Homer T. Hatch who came to do wrong to a harmless man. He caused all this trouble and he deserved to die but I am sorry it was me who had to kill him."

He licked the point of his pencil again, and signed his full name carefully, folded the paper and put it in his outside pocket. Taking off his right shoe and sock, he set the butt of the shotgun along the ground with the twin barrels pointed towards his head. It was very awkward. He thought about this a little, leaning his head against the gun mouth. He was trembling and his head was drumming until he was deaf and blind, but he lay down flat on the earth on his side, drew the barrel under his chin and fumbled for the trigger with his great toe. That way he could work it.

1937

Thomas Wolfe   *1900–1938*

A writer of tremendous power, Thomas Wolfe never attained formal control of the flood of narrative fiction he poured out during his short life. Romantic, egoistic, and uncannily sensitive to the sights, sounds, and smells of the Southern environment against which he strove to define himself, Wolfe was autobiographical in everything he wrote. The central characters of his novels are the members of his family and his close associates, thinly disguised, as *he* saw their lives, from the time of his precocious infancy. Wolfe grew up in Asheville, North Carolina, the Altamont of his fiction, where his father was a stonecutter, and attended the University of North Carolina. There he became especially interested in the theater, for which he wrote two plays, and in literature. After graduating in 1920, he enrolled at Harvard to study in the "47 Workshop" of George Pierce Baker. He took his M.A. in 1922 and went to New York, hoping to become a playwright. Failing to gain any foothold in the world of the theater, he obtained a position as an English instructor at New York University and began writing a prose narrative that grew to gigantic proportions. With the indispensable assistance of the great editor Maxwell Perkins, who served as his literary midwife, the young writer was delivered of his gargantuan first novel, Look Homeward, Angel (1929), which covered the boyhood years, in Altamont, of its hero Eugene Gant. Its immediate success made it possible for Wolfe to travel abroad on a Guggenheim Fellowship and to devote full time to his writing. *Of Time and the River* (1935), his second novel, continues the life of its hero through study at Harvard and teaching in New York to the beginning of his writing career. *From Death to Morning* (1935), a collection of stories, appeared in the same year. Although Wolfe continued to write voluminously, the only remaining publication to appear before his death from brain disease in 1938 was *The Story of a Novel* (1936), his account of the writing of *Look Homeward, Angel*.

Two novels left in manuscript were *The Web and the Rock* (1939) and

You Can't Go Home Again (1940). These books are a partial repetition and continuation of the life story of the autobiographical protagonist of *Look Homeward, Angel* and *Of Time and the River*. In writing them, Wolfe had striven for greater objectivity by giving his hero a new name, George Webber (for "weaver"), and physical attributes quite different from Eugene Gant's and his own, but the effort was not successful. Of the four novels, the first two are the more impressive because of their sustained narrative drive and lyric power, especially in *Look Homeward, Angel*, which compellingly evokes the growth in consciousness and sensibility of its gifted hero. Of the later novels, *You Can't Go Home Again* is the more interesting because of its revelation of a new social and political consciousness in Wolfe, who had been shocked by the rise of Nazism in the Germany he had come to love as a visitor. The novel ends with a subdued but firm statement of belief in the future of American democracy. In this respect, as well as in his cataloguing of multifarious aspects of American life, Thomas Wolfe stands in the tradition of Whitman. In his eyes, as in those of his predecessor, America was a poem, and his vocation was the struggle to find a language commensurate with his American experience.

The Hills Beyond (1941) includes an unfinished novel and a collection of stories. Of these, "The Lost Boy" tells the moving story of the death of Eugene Gant's brother Grover—also treated as a briefer episode in *Look Homeward, Angel*. Other posthumous publications include two plays—*Gentlemen of the Press* (1942) and *Mannerhouse* (1948)—and *A Western Journal* (1951), an account of a trip Wolfe made to the western states not long before his death.

Standard editions include *Thomas Wolfe's Letters to His Mother*, ed. J. S. Terry (New York, 1943); *The Correspondence of Thomas Wolfe and Homer Andrew Watt*, ed. Oscar Cargill and T. C. Pollock (New York, 1954), and *The Letters of Thomas Wolfe*, ed. Elizabeth Nowell (New York, 1956). T. C. Pollock and Oscar Cargill, eds., *Thomas Wolfe at Washington Square* (New York, 1954), is a collection of essays documenting Wolfe's life as a teacher at New York University. A helpful introduction is L. F. Field, ed., *Thomas Wolfe: Three Decades of Criticism* (New York, 1968). Among numerous other critical and biographical works are Elizabeth Nowell, *Thomas Wolfe* (New York, 1960), and R. S. Kennedy, *The Window of Memory: The Literary Career of Thomas Wolfe* (Chapel Hill, N. C., 1962). A bibliography is E. D. Johnson, *Of Time and Thomas Wolfe: A Bibliography with a Character Index of His Works* (New York, 1959).

The text of "The Lost Boy" is that of *The Hills Beyond* (New York, 1941).

The Lost Boy

I

Light came and went and came again, the booming strokes of three o'clock beat out across the town in thronging bronze from the courthouse bell, light winds of April blew the fountain out in rainbow sheets, until the plume returned and pulsed, as Grover turned into the Square.[1] He was a child, dark-eyed and grave, birthmarked upon his neck—a berry of warm brown—and with a gentle face, too quiet and too listening for his years. The scuffed boy's shoes, the thick-ribbed stockings gartered at the knees, the short knee pants cut straight with three small useless buttons at the side, the sailor blouse, the old cap battered out of shape, perched sideways up on top of the raven head, the old soiled canvas bag slung from the shoulder, empty now, but waiting for the crisp sheets of the afternoon—these friendly, shabby garments, shaped by Grover, uttered him. He turned and passed along the north side of the Square and in that moment saw the union of Forever and of Now.

Light came and went and came again, the great plume of the fountain pulsed and winds of April sheeted it across the Square in a rainbow gossamer of spray. The fire department horses drummed on the floors with wooden stomp, most casually, and with dry whiskings of their clean, coarse tails. The street cars ground into the Square from every portion of the compass and halted briefly like wound toys in their familiar quarter-hourly formula. A dray, hauled by a boneyard nag, rattled across the cobbles on the other side before his father's shop. The courthouse bell boomed out its solemn warning of immediate three, and everything was just the same as it had always been.

He saw that haggis of vexed shapes with quiet eyes—that hodge-podge of ill-sorted architectures that made up the Square, and he did not feel lost. For "Here," thought Grover, "here is the Square as it has always been—and papa's shop, the fire department and the City Hall, the fountain pulsing with its plume, the street cars coming in and halting at the quarter hour, the hardware store on the corner there, the row of old brick buildings on this side of the street, the people passing and the light that comes and changes and that always will come back again, and everything that comes and goes and changes in the Square, and yet will be the same again. And here," the boy thought, "is Grover with his paper bag. Here is old Grover, almost twelve years old. Here is the month of April, 1904. Here is the courthouse bell and three o'clock. Here is Grover on the Square that never changes. Here is Grover, caught upon this point of time."

It seemed to him that the Square, itself the accidental masonry of many years, the chance agglomeration of time and of disrupted strivings, was the center of the universe. It was for him, in his soul's picture, the earth's pivot, the granite core of changelessness, the eternal place

---

[1] The story is a fictionalized autobiographical account of the death in St. Louis of the brother called Grover in *Look Homeward, Angel* (1929), in which the same event is presented as a brief episode in Chapter 5. The other characters—Helen, Eugene, the mother and father—are the Gants of the novel, and the story opens on the familiar square of the fictional Altamont (Asheville, N. C.) where the shop of old Gant, the stone-cutter, stands.

where all things came and passed, and yet abode forever and would never change.

He passed the old shack on the corner—the wooden fire-trap where S. Goldberg ran his wiener stand. Then he passed the Singer place next door, with its gleaming display of new machines. He saw them and admired them, but he felt no joy. They brought back to him the busy hum of housework and of women sewing, the intricacy of stitch and weave, the mystery of style and pattern, the memory of women bending over flashing needles, the pedaled tread, the busy whir. It was women's work: it filled him with unknown associations of dullness and of vague depression. And always, also, with a moment's twinge of horror, for his dark eye would always travel toward that needle stitching up and down so fast the eye could never follow it. And then he would remember how his mother once had told him she had driven the needle through her finger, and always, when he passed this place, he would remember it and for a moment crane his neck and turn his head away.

He passed on then, but had to stop again next door before the music store. He always had to stop by places that had shining perfect things in them. He loved hardware stores and windows full of accurate geometric tools. He loved windows full of hammers, saws, and planing boards. He liked windows full of strong new rakes and hoes, with unworn handles, of white perfect wood, stamped hard and vivid with the maker's seal. He loved to see such things as these in the windows of hardware stores. And he would fairly gloat upon them and think that some day he would own a set himself.

Also, he always stopped before the music and piano store. It was a splendid store. And in the window was a small white dog upon his haunches, with head cocked gravely to one side, a small white dog that never moved, that never barked, that listened attentively at the flaring funnel of a horn to hear "His Master's Voice"[2]—a horn forever silent, and a voice that never spoke. And within were many rich and shining shapes of great pianos, an air of splendor and of wealth.

And now, indeed, he *was* caught, held suspended. A waft of air, warm, chocolate-laden, filled his nostrils. He tried to pass the white front of the little eight-foot shop; he paused, struggling with conscience; he could not go on. It was the little candy shop run by old Crocker and his wife. And Grover could not pass.

"Old stingy Crockers!" he thought scornfully. "I'll not go there any more. But—" as the maddening fragrance of rich cooking chocolate touched him once again—"I'll just look in the window and see what they've got." He paused a moment, looking with his dark and quiet

---

[2] The well-known trademark of the Victor Talking Machine Co. would have been familiar to the younger brother Eugene (the author's representative) rather than to Grover, who died in 1904, the year in which it was patented.

eyes into the window of the little candy shop. The window, spotlessly clean, was filled with trays of fresh-made candy. His eyes rested on a tray of chocolate drops. Unconsciously he licked his lips. Put one of them upon your tongue and it just melted there, like honeydew. And then the trays full of rich homemade fudge. He gazed longingly at the deep body of the chocolate fudge, reflectively at maple walnut, more critically, yet with longing, at the mints, the nougatines, and all the other dainties.

"Old stingy Crockers!" Grover muttered once again, and turned to go. "I wouldn't go in *there* again."

And yet he did not go away. "Old stingy Crockers" they might be; still, they did make the best candy in town, the best, in fact, that he had ever tasted.

He looked through the window back into the little shop and saw Mrs. Crocker there. A customer had gone in and had made a purchase, and as Grover looked he saw Mrs. Crocker, with her little wrenny face, her pinched features, lean over and peer primly at the scales. She had a piece of fudge in her clean, bony, little fingers, and as Grover looked, she broke it, primly, in her little bony hands. She dropped a morsel down into the scales. They weighted down alarmingly, and her thin lips tightened. She snatched the piece of fudge out of the scales and broke it carefully once again. This time the scales wavered, went down very slowly, and came back again. Mrs. Crocker carefully put the reclaimed piece of fudge back in the tray, dumped the remainder in a paper bag, folded it and gave it to the customer, counted the money carefully and doled it out into the till, the pennies in one place, the nickels in another.

Grover stood there, looking scornfully. "Old stingy Crocker — afraid that she might give a crumb away!"

He grunted scornfully and again he turned to go. But now Mr. Crocker came out from the little partitioned place where they made all their candy, bearing a tray of fresh-made fudge in his skinny hands. Old Man Crocker rocked along the counter to the front and put it down. He really rocked along. He was a cripple. And like his wife, he was a wrenny, wizened little creature, with bony hands, thin lips, a pinched and meager face. One leg was inches shorter than the other, and on this leg there was an enormous thick-soled boot, with a kind of wooden, rocker-like arrangement, six inches high at least, to make up for the deficiency. On this wooden cradle Mr. Crocker rocked along, with a prim and apprehensive little smile, as if he were afraid he was going to lose something.

"Old stingy Crocker!" muttered Grover. "Humph! He wouldn't give you anything!"

And yet — he did not go away. He hung there curiously, peering through the window, with his dark and gentle face now focused and intent, alert and curious, flattening his nose against the glass. Unconsciously he scratched the thick-ribbed fabric of one stockinged leg with the scuffed and worn toe of his old shoe. The fresh, warm odor of the new-made fudge was delicious. It was a little maddening. Half consciously he began to fumble in one trouser pocket, and pulled out his purse, a shabby worn old black one with a twisted clasp. He opened it and prowled about inside.

What he found was not inspiring—a nickel and two pennies and—he had forgotten them—the stamps. He took the stamps out and unfolded them. There were five twos, eight ones, all that remained of the dollar-sixty-cents' worth which Reed, the pharmacist, had given him for running errands a week or two before.

"Old Crocker," Grover thought, and looked somberly at the grotesque little form as it rocked back into the shop again, around the counter, and up the other side. "Well—" again he looked indefinitely at the stamps in his hand—"he's had all the rest of them. He might as well take these."

So, soothing conscience with this sop of scorn, he went into the shop and stood looking at the trays in the glass case and finally decided. Pointing with a slightly grimy finger at the fresh-made tray of chocolate fudge, he said, "I'll take fifteen cents' worth of this, Mr. Crocker." He paused a moment, fighting with embarrassment, then he lifted his dark face and said quietly, "And please, I'll have to give you stamps again."

Mr. Crocker made no answer. He did not look at Grover. He pressed his lips together primly. He went rocking away and got the candy scoop, came back, slid open the door of the glass case, put fudge into the scoop, and, rocking to the scales, began to weigh the candy out. Grover watched him as he peered and squinted, he watched him purse and press his lips together, he saw him take a piece of fudge and break it in two parts. And then old Crocker broke two parts in two again. He weighed, he squinted, and he hovered, until it seemed to Grover that by calling *Mrs.* Crocker stingy he had been guilty of a rank injustice. But finally, to his vast relief, the job was over, the scales hung there, quivering apprehensively, upon the very hair-line of nervous balance, as if even the scales were afraid that one more move from Old Man Crocker and they would be undone.

Mr. Crocker took the candy then and dumped it in a paper bag and, rocking back along the counter toward the boy, he dryly said: "Where are the stamps?" Grover gave them to him. Mr. Crocker relinquished his clawlike hold upon the bag and set it down upon the counter. Grover took the bag and dropped it in his canvas sack, and then remembered. "Mr. Crocker—" again he felt the old embarrassment that was almost like strong pain—"I gave you too much," Grover said. "There were eighteen cents in stamps. You—you can just give me three ones back."

Mr. Crocker did not answer. He was busy with his bony little hands, unfolding the stamps and flattening them out on top of the glass counter. When he had done so, he peered at them sharply for a moment, thrusting his scrawny neck forward and running his eye up and down, like a bookkeeper who totes up rows of figures.

When he had finished, he said tartly: "I don't like this kind of business. If you want candy, you should have the money for it. I'm not a post office. The next time you come in here and want anything, you'll have to pay me money for it."

Hot anger rose in Grover's throat. His olive face suffused with angry color. His tarry eyes got black and bright. He was on the verge of saying: "Then why did you take my other stamps? Why do you tell me now, when you have taken all the stamps I had, that you don't want them?"

But he was a boy, a boy of eleven years, a quiet, gentle, gravely thoughtful boy, and he had been taught how to respect his elders. So he just stood there looking with his tar-black eyes. Old Man Crocker, pursing at the mouth a little, without meeting Grover's gaze, took the stamps up in his thin, parched fingers and, turning, rocked away with them down to the till.

He took the twos and folded them and laid them in one rounded scallop, then took the ones and folded them and put them in the one next to it. Then he closed the till and started to rock off, down toward the other end. Grover, his face now quiet and grave, kept looking at him, but Mr. Crocker did not look at Grover. Instead he began to take some stamped cardboard shapes and fold them into boxes.

In a moment Grover said, "Mr. Crocker, will you give me the three ones, please?"

Mr. Crocker did not answer. He kept folding boxes, and he compressed his thin lips quickly as he did so. But Mrs. Crocker, back turned to her spouse, also folding boxes with her birdlike hands, muttered tartly: "Hm! *I'd* give him nothing!"

Mr. Crocker looked up, looked at Grover, said, "What are you waiting for?"

"Will you give me the three ones, please?" Grover said.

"I'll give you nothing," Mr. Crocker said.

He left his work and came rocking forward along the counter. "Now you get out of here! Don't you come in here with any more of those stamps," said Mr. Crocker.

"I should like to know where he gets them — that's what *I* should like to know," said Mrs. Crocker.

She did not look up as she said these words. She inclined her head a little to the side, in Mr. Crocker's direction, and continued to fold the boxes with her bony fingers.

"You get out of here!" said Mr. Crocker. "And don't you come

back here with any stamps. . . . Where did you get those stamps?" he
said.

"That's just what *I've* been thinking," Mrs. Crocker said. "*I've*
been thinking all along."

"You've been coming in here for the last two weeks with those
stamps," said Mr. Crocker. "I don't like the look of it. Where did you
get those stamps?" he said.

"That's what *I've* been thinking," said Mrs. Crocker, for a second
time.

Grover had got white underneath his olive skin. His eyes had lost
their luster. They looked like dull, stunned balls of tar. "From Mr.
Reed," he said. "I got the stamps from Mr. Reed." Then he burst out
desperately: "Mr. Crocker—Mr. Reed will tell you how I got the
stamps. I did some work for Mr. Reed, he gave me those stamps two
weeks ago."

"Mr. Reed," said Mrs. Crocker acidly. She did not turn her head.
"I call it mighty funny."

"Mr. Crocker," Grover said, "if you'll just let me have three
ones—"

"You get out of here!" cried Mr. Crocker, and he began rocking
forward toward Grover. "Now don't you come in here again, boy!
There's something funny about this whole business! I don't like the
look of it," said Mr. Crocker. "If you can't pay as other people do, then
I don't want your trade."

"Mr. Crocker," Grover said again, and underneath the olive skin
his face was gray, "if you'll just let me have those three—"

"You get out of here!" Mr. Crocker cried, rocking down toward
the counter's end. "If you don't get out, boy—"

"*I'd* call a policeman, that's what I'd do," Mrs. Crocker said.

Mr. Crocker rocked around the lower end of the counter. He
came rocking up to Grover. "You get out," he said.

He took the boy and pushed him with his bony little hands, and
Grover was sick and gray down to the hollow pit of his stomach.

"You've got to give me those three ones," he said.

"You get out of here!" shrilled Mr. Crocker. He seized the
screen door, pulled it open, and pushed Grover out. "Don't you come
back in here," he said, pausing for a moment, and working thinly at the
lips. He turned and rocked back in the shop again. The screen door
slammed behind him. Grover stood there on the pavement. And light
came and went and came again into the Square.

The boy stood there, and a wagon rattled past. There were some
people passing by, but Grover did not notice them. He stood there
blindly, in the watches of the sun, feeling this was Time, this was the
center of the universe, the granite core of changelessness, and feeling,
this is Grover, this the Square, this is Now.

But something had gone out of day. He felt the overwhelming, soul-sickening guilt that all the children, all the good men of the earth, have felt since Time began. And even anger had died down, had been drowned out, in this swelling tide of guilt, and "This is the Square"—thought Grover as before—"This is Now. There is my father's shop. And all of it is as it has always been—save I."

And the Square reeled drunkenly around him, light went in blind gray motes before his eyes, the fountain sheeted out to rainbow iridescence and returned to its proud, pulsing plume again. But all the brightness had gone out of day, and "Here is the Square, and here is permanence, and here is Time—and all of it the same as it has always been, save I."

The scuffed boots of the lost boy moved and stumbled blindly. The numb feet crossed the pavement—reached the cobbled street, reached the plotted central square—the grass plots, and the flower beds, so soon to be packed with red geraniums.

"I want to be alone," thought Grover, "where I cannot go near him. . . . Oh God, I hope he never hears, that no one ever tells him—"

The plume blew out, the iridescent sheet of spray blew over him. He passed through, found the other side and crossed the street, and— "Oh God, if papa ever hears!" thought Grover, as his numb feet started up the steps into his father's shop.

He found and felt the steps—the width and thickness of old lumber twenty feet in length. He saw it all—the iron columns on his father's porch, painted with the dull anomalous black-green that all such columns in this land and weather come to; two angels, fly-specked, and the waiting stones. Beyond and all around, in the stonecutter's shop, cold shapes of white and marble, rounded stone, the languid angel with strong marble hands of love.

He went on down the aisle, the white shapes stood around him. He went on to the back of the workroom. This he knew—the little cast-iron stove in the left-hand corner, caked, brown, heat-blistered, and the elbow of the long stack running out across the shop; the high and dirty window looking down across the Market Square toward Niggertown; the rude old shelves, plank-boarded, thick, the wood not smooth but pulpy, like the strong hair of an animal; upon the shelves the chisels of all sizes and a layer of stone dust; an emery wheel with pump tread; and a door that let out on the alleyway, yet the alleyway twelve feet below. Here in the room, two trestles of this coarse spiked wood upon which rested gravestones, and at one, his father at work.

The boy looked, saw the name was Creasman: saw the carved analysis of John, the symmetry of the s, the fine sentiment that was being polished off beneath the name and date: "John Creasman, November 7, 1903."

Gant looked up. He was a man of fifty-three, gaunt-visaged,

mustache cropped, immensely long and tall and gaunt. He wore good dark clothes—heavy, massive—save he had no coat. He worked in shirt-sleeves with his vest on, a strong watch chain stretching across his vest, wing collar and black tie, Adam's apple, bony forehead, bony nose, light eyes, gray-green, undeep and cold, and, somehow, lonely-looking, a striped apron going up around his shoulders, and starched cuffs. And in one hand a tremendous rounded wooden mallet like a butcher's bole; and in his other hand, a strong cold chisel.

"How are you, son?"

He did not look up as he spoke. He spoke quietly, absently. He worked upon the chisel and the wooden mallet, as a jeweler might work on a watch, except that in the man and in the wooden mallet there was power too.

"What is it, son?" he said.

He moved around the table from the head, started up on "J" once again.

"Papa, I never stole the stamps," said Grover.

Gant put down the mallet, laid the chisel down. He came around the trestle.

"What?" he said.

As Grover winked his tar-black eyes, they brightened, the hot tears shot out. "I never stole the stamps," he said.

"Hey? What is this?" his father said. "What stamps?"

"That Mr. Reed gave me, when the other boy was sick and I worked there for three days. . . . And Old Man Crocker," Grover said, "he took all the stamps. And I told him Mr. Reed had given them to me. And now he owes me three ones—and Old Man Crocker says he don't believe that they were mine. He says—he says—that I must have taken them somewhere," Grover blurted out.

"The stamps that Reed gave you—hey?" the stonecutter said. "The stamps you had—" He wet his thumb upon his lips, threw back his head and slowly swung his gaze around the ceiling, then turned and strode quickly from his workshop out into the storeroom.

Almost at once he came back again, and as he passed the old gray painted-board partition of his office he cleared his throat and wet his thumb and said, "Now, I tell you——"

Then he turned and strode up toward the front again and cleared his throat and said, "I tell you now—" He wheeled about and started back, and as he came along the aisle between the marshaled rows of gravestones he said beneath his breath, "By God, now——"

He took Grover by the hand and they went out flying. Down the aisle they went by all the gravestones, past the fly-specked angels waiting there, and down the wooden steps and across the Square. The fountain pulsed, the plume blew out in sheeted iridescence, and it swept across them; an old gray horse, with a peaceful look about his torn lips, swucked up the cool mountain water from the trough as Grover and his father went across the Square, but they did not notice it.

They crossed swiftly to the other side in a direct line to the candy shop. Gant was still dressed in his long striped apron, and he was still holding Grover by the hand. He opened the screen door and stepped inside.

"Give him the stamps," Gant said.

Mr. Crocker came rocking forward behind the counter, with the prim and careful look that now was somewhat like a smile. "It was just—" he said.

"Give him the stamps," Gant said, and threw some coins down on the counter.

Mr. Crocker rocked away and got the stamps. He came rocking back. "I just didn't know—" he said.

The stonecutter took the stamps and gave them to the boy. And Mr. Crocker took the coins.

"It was just that—" Mr. Crocker began again, and smiled.

Gant cleared his throat: "You never were a father," he said. "You never knew the feelings of a father, or understood the feelings of a child; and that is why you acted as you did. But a judgment is upon you. God has cursed you. He has afflicted you. He has made you lame and childless as you are—and lame and childless, miserable as you are, you will go to your grave and be forgotten!"

And Crocker's wife kept kneading her bony little hands and said, imploringly, "Oh, no—oh don't say that, please don't say that."

The stonecutter, the breath still hoarse in him, left the store, still holding the boy tightly by the hand. Light came again into the day.

"Well, son," he said, and laid his hand on the boy's back. "Well, son," he said, "now don't you mind."

They walked across the Square, the sheeted spray of iridescent light swept out on them, the horse swizzled at the water-trough, and "Well, son," the stonecutter said.

And the old horse sloped down, ringing with his hoofs upon the cobblestones.

"Well, son," said the stonecutter once again, "be a good boy."

And he trod his own steps then with his great stride and went back again into his shop.

The lost boy stood upon the Square, hard by the porch of his father's shop.

"This is Time," thought Grover. "Here is the Square, here is my father's shop, and here am I."

And light came and went and came again—but now not quite the same as it had done before. The boy saw the pattern of familiar shapes and knew that they were just the same as they had always been. But something had gone out of day, and something had come in again. Out of the vision of those quiet eyes some brightness had gone, and into their vision had come some deeper color. He could not say, he did not know through what transforming shadows life had passed within that quarter hour. He only knew that something had been lost—something forever gained.

Just then a buggy curved out through the Square, and fastened to the rear end was a poster, and it said "St. Louis" and "Excursion" and "The Fair."

2

The Mother

As we went down through Indiana—you were too young, child, to remember it—but I always think of all of you the way you looked that morning, when we went down through Indiana, going to the Fair. All of the apple trees were coming out, and it was April; it was the beginning of spring in southern Indiana and everything was getting green. Of course we don't have farms at home like those in Indiana. The childern had never seen such farms as those, and I reckon, kidlike, they had to take it in.

So all of them kept running up and down the aisle—well, no, except for you and Grover. *You* were too young, Eugene. You were just three, I kept you with me. As for Grover—well, I'm going to tell you about that.

But the rest of them kept running up and down the aisle and from one window to another. They kept calling out and hollering to each other every time they saw something new. They kept trying to look out on all sides, in every way at once, as if they wished they had eyes at the back of their heads. It was the first time any of them had ever been in Indiana, and I reckon that it all seemed strange and new.

And so it seemed they couldn't get enough. It seemed they never could be still. They kept running up and down and back and forth, hollering and shouting to each other, until—"I'll vow! You childern! I never saw the beat of you!" I said. "The way that you keep running up and down and back and forth and never can be quiet for a minute beats all I ever saw," I said.

You see, they were excited about going to St. Louis, and so curious over everything they saw. They couldn't help it, and they wanted to see everything. But—"I'll vow!" I said. "If you childern don't sit down and rest you'll be worn to a frazzle before we ever get to see St. Louis and the Fair!"

Except for Grover! He—no, sir! not him. Now, boy, I want to tell you—I've raised the lot of you—and if I do say so, there wasn't a numbskull in the lot. But *Grover*! Well, you've all grown up now, all of you have gone away, and none of you are childern any more. . . . And of course, I hope that, as the fellow says, you have reached the dignity of man's estate. I suppose you have the judgment of grown men. . . . But *Grover*! *Grover* had it even then!

Oh, even as a child, you know—at a time when I was almost afraid to trust the rest of you out of my sight—I could depend on Grover. He could go anywhere, I could send him anywhere, and I'd always know he'd get back safe, and do exactly what I told him to!

Why, I didn't even have to tell him. You could send that child to market and tell him what you wanted, and he'd come home with *twice* as much as you could get yourself for the same money!

Now you know, I've always been considered a good trader. But *Grover*!—why, it got so finally that I wouldn't even tell him. Your papa said to me: "You'd be better off if you'd just tell him what you want and leave the rest to him. For," your papa says, "damned if I don't believe he's a better trader than you are. He gets more for the money than anyone I ever saw."

Well, I had to admit it, you know. I had to own up then. Grover, even as a child, was a far better trader than I was. . . . Why, yes, they told it on him all over town, you know. They said all of the market men, all of the farmers, knew him. They'd begin to laugh when they saw him coming—they'd say: "Look out! Here's Grover! Here's one trader you're not going to fool!"

And they were right! *That* child! I'd say, "Grover, suppose you run uptown and see if they've got anything good to *eat* today"—and I'd just wink at him, you know, but he'd know what I meant. I wouldn't let on that I *wanted* anything exactly, but I'd say, "Now it just occurs to me that some good fresh stuff may be coming in from the country, so suppose you take this dollar and just see what you can do with it."

Well, sir, that was all that was needed. The minute you told that child that you depended on his judgment, he'd have gone to the ends of the earth for you—and, let me tell you something, he wouldn't *miss*, either!

His eyes would get as black as coals—oh! the way that child would look at you, the intelligence and sense in his expression. He'd say: "Yes, *ma'am*! Now don't you worry, mama. You leave it all to me—and I'll do *good*!" said Grover.

And he'd be off like a streak of lightning and—oh Lord! As your father said to me, "I've been living in this town for almost thirty years," he said—"I've seen it grow up from a crossroads village, and I thought I knew everything there was to know about it—but that child—" your papa says—"he knows places that I never heard of!" . . . Oh, he'd go right down there to that place below your papa's shop where the draymen and the country people used to park their wagons—or he'd go down there to those old lots on Concord Street where the farmers used to keep their wagons. And, child that he was, he'd go right in among them, sir—*Grover* would!—go right in and barter with them like a grown man!

And he'd come home with things he'd bought that would make your eyes stick out. . . . Here he comes one time with another boy, dragging a great bushel basket full of ripe termaters between them. "Why, Grover!" I says. "How on earth are we ever going to use them? Why they'll go bad on us before we're half way through with them." "Well, mama," he says, "I know—" oh, just as solemn as a judge —"but they were the last the man had," he says, "and he wanted to go home, and so I got them for ten cents," he says. "They were so cheap," said Grover, "I thought it was a shame to let 'em go, and I figgered that what we couldn't eat—why," says Grover, "you could *put up!*" Well, the way he said it—so earnest and so serious—I had to laugh. "But I'll vow!" I said. "If you don't beat all!" . . . But that was *Grover!*—the way he was in *those* days! As everyone said, boy that he was, he had the sense and judgment of a grown man. . . . Child, child, I've seen you all grow up, and all of you were bright enough. There were no half-wits in *my* family. But for all-round intelligence, judgment, and general ability, Grover surpassed the whole crowd. I've never seen his equal, and everyone who knew him as a child will say the same.

So that's what I tell them now when they ask me about all of you. I have to tell the truth. I always said that *you* were smart enough, Eugene—but when they come around and brag to me about you, and about how you have got on and have a kind of name—I don't let on, you know. I just sit there and let them talk. I don't brag on you—if *they* want to brag on you, that's *their* business. I never bragged on one of my own childern in my life. When father raised us up, we were all brought up to believe that it was not good breeding to brag about your kin. "If the others want to do it," father said, "well, let *them* do it. Don't ever let on by a word or sign that you know what they are talking about. Just let *them* do the talking, and say nothing."

So when they come around and tell me all about the things *you've* done—I don't let on to them, I never say a word. Why yes!—why, here, you know—oh, along about a month or so ago, this feller comes—a well-dressed man, you know—he looked intelligent, a good substantial sort of person. He said he came from New Jersey, or somewhere up in that part of the country, and he began to ask me all sorts of questions—what you were like when you were a boy, and all such stuff as that.

I just pretended to study it all over and then I said, "Well, yes"—real serious-like, you know—"well, yes—I reckon I ought to know a little something about him. Eugene was my child, just the same as all the others were. I brought him up just the way I brought up all the others. And," I says—oh, just as solemn as you please—"he wasn't a *bad* sort of a boy. Why," I says, "up to the time that he was twelve years old he was just about the same as any other boy—a good, average, normal sort of fellow."

"Oh," he says. "But didn't you notice something? Wasn't there something kind of strange?" he says—"something different from what you noticed in the other childern?"

I didn't let on, you know—I just took it all in and looked as solemn as an owl—I just pretended to study it all over, just as serious as you please.

"Why no," I says, real slow-like, after I'd studied it all over. "As I remember it, he was a good, ordinary, normal sort of boy, just like all the others."

"Yes," he says—oh, all excited-like, you know— "But didn't you notice how brilliant he was? Eugene must have been more brilliant than the rest!"

"Well, now," I says, and pretended to study that all over too. "Now let me see. . . . Yes," I says—I just looked him in the eye, as solemn as you please—"he did pretty well. . . . Well, yes," I says, "I guess he was a fairly bright sort of a boy. I never had no complaints to make of him on that score. He was bright enough," I says. "The only trouble with him was that he was lazy."

"Lazy!" he says—oh, you should have seen the look upon his face, you know—he jumped like someone had stuck a pin in him. "Lazy!" he says. "Why, you don't mean to tell me——"

"Yes," I says—oh, I never cracked a smile—"I was telling him the same thing myself the last time that I saw him. I told him it was a mighty lucky thing for him that he had the gift of gab. Of course, he went off to college and read a lot of books, and I reckon that's where he got his flow of language they say he has. But as I said to him the last time that I saw him: 'Now look a-here,' I said. 'If you can earn your living doing a light, easy class of work like this you do,' I says, 'you're mighty lucky, because none of the rest of your people,' I says, 'had any such luck as that. They had to work hard for a living.'"

Oh, I told him, you know. I came right out with it. I made no bones about it. And I tell you what—I wish you could have seen his face. It was a study.

"Well," he says, at last, "you've got to admit this, haven't you —he was the brightest boy you had, now wasn't he?"

I just looked at him a moment. I had to tell the truth. I couldn't fool him any longer. "No," I says. "He was a good, bright boy—I got no complaint to make about him on that score—but the brightest boy I had, the one that surpassed all the rest of them in sense, and understanding, and in judgment—the best boy I had—the smartest boy I ever saw—was—well, it wasn't Eugene," I said. "It was another one."

He looked at me a moment, then he said, "Which boy was that?"

Well, I just looked at him, and smiled. I shook my head, you know. I wouldn't tell him. "I never brag about my own," I said. "You'll have to find out for yourself."

But—I'll have to tell *you*—and you know yourself, I brought the whole crowd up, I knew you all. And you can take my word for it—the best one of the lot was—*Grover!*

And when I think of Grover as he was along about that time, I always see him sitting there, so grave and earnest-like, with his nose pressed to the window, as we went down through Indiana in the morning, to the Fair.

All through that morning we were going down along beside the Wabash River—the Wabash River flows through Indiana, it is the river that they wrote the song about—so all that morning we were going down along the river. And I sat with all you childern gathered about me as we went down through Indiana, going to St. Louis, to the Fair.

And Grover sat there, so still and earnest-like, looking out the window, and he didn't move. He sat there like a man. He was just eleven and a half years old, but he had more sense, more judgment, and more understanding than any child I ever saw.

So here he sat beside this gentleman and looked out the window. I never knew the man—I never asked his name—but I tell you what! He was certainly a fine-looking, well-dressed, good, substantial sort of man, and I could see that he had taken a great liking to Grover. And Grover sat there looking out, and then turned to this gentleman, as grave and earnest as a grown-up man, and says "What kind of crops grow here, sir?" Well, this gentleman threw his head back and just hah-hahed. "Well, I'll see if I can tell you," says this gentleman, and then, you know, he talked to him, they talked together, and Grover took it all in, as solemn as you please, and asked this gentleman every sort of question—what the trees were, what was growing there, how big the farms were—all sorts of questions, which this gentleman would answer, until I said: "Why, I'll vow, Grover! You shouldn't ask so many questions. You'll bother the very life out of this gentleman."

The gentleman threw his head back and laughed right out. "Now you leave that boy alone. He's all right," he said. "He doesn't bother me a bit, and if I know the answers to his questions I will answer him. And if I don't know, why, then, I'll tell him so. But he's *all right*," he said, and put his arm round Grover's shoulders. "You leave him alone. He doesn't bother me a bit."

And I can still remember how he looked that morning, with his black eyes, his black hair, and with the birthmark on his neck—so grave, so serious, so earnest-like—as he sat by the train window and watched the apple trees, the farms, the barns, the houses, and the orchards, taking it all in, I reckon, because it was strange and new to him.

It was so long ago, but when I think of it, it all comes back, as if it happened yesterday. Now all of you have either died or grown up and gone away, and nothing is the same as it was then. But all of you were there with me that morning and I guess I should remember how the others looked, but somehow I don't. Yet I can still see Grover just the way he was, the way he looked that morning when we went down through Indiana, by the river, to the Fair.

3

The Sister

Can you remember, Eugene, how Grover used to look? I mean the birthmark, the black eyes, the olive skin. The birthmark always showed because of those open sailor blouses kids used to wear. But I guess you must have been too young when Grover died. . . . I was looking at that old photograph the other day. You know the one I mean — that picture showing mama and papa and all of us children before the house on Woodson Street. *You* weren't there, Eugene. *You* didn't get in. *You* hadn't arrived when that was taken. . . . You remember how mad you used to get when we'd tell you that you were only a dishrag hanging out in Heaven when something happened?

You were the baby. That's what you get for being the baby. You don't get in the picture, do you? . . . I was looking at that old picture just the other day. There we were. And, my God, what is it all about? I mean, when you see the way we were — Daisy and Ben and Grover, Steve and all of us — and then how everyone either dies or grows up and goes away — and then — look at us now! Do you ever get to feeling funny? You know what I mean — do you ever get to feeling *queer* — when you try to figure these things out? You've been to college and you ought to know the answer — and I wish you'd tell me if you know.

My Lord, when I think sometimes of the way I used to be — the dreams I used to have. Playing the piano, practicing seven hours a day, thinking that some day I would be a great pianist. Taking singing lessons from Aunt Nell because I felt that some day I was going to have a great career in opera. . . . Can you beat it now? Can you imagine it? *Me!* In grand opera! . . . Now I want to ask you. I'd like to know.

My Lord! When I go uptown and walk down the street and see all these funny-looking little boys and girls hanging around the drug store — do you suppose any of them have ambitions the way we did? Do you suppose any of these funny-looking little girls are thinking about a big career in opera? . . . Didn't you ever see that picture of us? I was looking at it just the other day. It was made before the old house down on Woodson Street, with papa standing there in his swallow-tail, and mama there beside him—and Grover, and Ben, and Steve, and Daisy, and myself, with our feet upon our bicycles. Luke, poor kid, was only four or five. *He* didn't have a bicycle like us. But there he was. And there were all of us together.

Well, there I was, and my poor old skinny legs and long white dress, and two pigtails hanging down my back. And all the funny-looking clothes we wore, with the doo-lolley business on them. . . . But I guess you can't remember. You weren't born.

But, well, we were a right nice-looking set of people, if I do say so. And there was "86" the way it used to be, with the front porch, the grape vines, and the flower beds before the house—and "Miss Eliza" standing there by papa, with a watch charm pinned upon her waist. . . . I shouldn't laugh, but "Miss Eliza"—well, mama was a pretty woman then. Do you know what I mean? "Miss Eliza" was a right good-looking woman, and papa in his swallow-tail was a good-looking man. Do you remember how he used to get dressed up on Sunday? And how grand we thought he was? And how he let me take his money out and count it? And how rich we all thought he was? And how wonderful that dinkey little shop on the Square looked to us? . . . Can you beat it, now? Why we thought that papa was the biggest man in town and—oh, you can't tell me! You can't tell me! He had his faults, but papa was a wonderful man. You know he was!

And there was Steve and Ben and Grover, Daisy, Luke, and me lined up there before the house with one foot on our bicycles. And I got to thinking back about it all. It all came back.

Do you remember anything about St. Louis? You were only three or four years old then, but you must remember something. . . . Do you remember how you used to bawl when I would scrub you? How you'd bawl for Grover? Poor kid, you used to yell for Grover every time I'd get you in the tub. . . . He was a sweet kid and he was crazy about you—he almost brought you up.

That year Grover was working at the Inside Inn out on the Fair Grounds. Do you remember the old Inside Inn? That big old wooden thing inside the Fair? And how I used to take you there to wait for Grover when he got through working? And old fat Billy Pelham at the newsstand—how he always used to give you a stick of chewing gum?

They were all crazy about Grover. Everybody liked him. . . . And how proud Grover was of you! Don't you remember how he used to show you off? How he used to take you around and make you talk to Billy Pelham? And Mr. Curtis at the desk? And how Grover would try to make you talk and get you to say "Grover"? And you couldn't say it—you couldn't pronounce the "r." You'd say "Gova." Have you forgotten that? You shouldn't forget *that*, because—you were a *cute* kid, then — Ho-ho-ho-ho-ho — I don't know where it's gone to, but you were a big hit in those days. . . . I tell you, boy, you were Somebody back in those days.

And I was thinking of it all the other day when I was looking at that photograph. How we used to go and meet Grover there, and how he'd take us to the Midway. Do you remember the Midway? The Snake-Eater and the Living Skeleton, the Fat Woman and the Chute-the-chute, the Scenic Railway and the Ferris Wheel? How you bawled the night we took you up on the Ferris Wheel? You yelled your head off — I tried to laugh it off, but I tell you, I was scared myself. Back in those days, that was Something. And how Grover laughed at us and told us there was no danger. . . . My lord! poor little Grover. He wasn't quite twelve years old at the time, but he seemed so grown up to us. I was two years older, but I thought he knew it all.

It was always that way with him. Looking back now, it sometimes seems that it was Grover who brought us up. He was always looking after us, telling us what to do, bringing us something — some ice cream or some candy, something he had bought out of the poor little money he'd gotten at the Inn.

Then I got to thinking of the afternoon we sneaked away from home. Mama had gone out somewhere. And Grover and I got on the street car and went downtown. And my Lord, we thought that we were going Somewhere. In those days, that was what we called a *trip*. A ride in the street car was something to write home about in those days. . . . I hear that it's all built up around there now.

So we got on the car and rode the whole way down into the business section of St. Louis. We got out on Washington Street and walked up and down. And I tell you, boy, we thought that that was Something. Grover took me into a drug store and set me up to soda water. Then we came out and walked around some more, down to the Union Station and clear over to the river. And both of us half scared to death at what we'd done and wondering what mama would say if she found out.

We stayed down there till it was getting dark, and we passed by a lunchroom — an old one-armed joint with one-armed chairs and people sitting on stools and eating at the counter. We read all the signs to see what they had to eat and how much it cost, and I guess nothing on the menu was more than fifteen cents, but it couldn't have looked grander to us if it had been Delmonico's. So we stood there with our noses pressed against the window, looking in. Two skinny little kids, both of us scared half to death, getting the thrill of a lifetime out of it. You know what I mean? And smelling everything with all our might and thinking how good it all smelled. . . . Then Grover turned to me and whispered: "Come on, Helen. Let's go in. It says fifteen cents for pork and beans. And I've got the money," Grover said. "I've got sixty cents."

I was so scared I couldn't speak. I'd never been in a place like that before. But I kept thinking, "Oh Lord, if mama should find out!" I felt as if we were committing some big crime. . . . Don't you know how it is when you're a kid? It was the thrill of a lifetime. . . . I couldn't resist. So we both went in and sat down on those high stools before the counter and ordered pork and beans and a cup of coffee. I suppose we were too frightened at what we'd done really to enjoy anything. We just gobbled it all up in a hurry, and gulped our coffee down. And I don't know whether it was the excitement—I guess the poor kid was already sick when we came in there and didn't know it. But I turned and looked at him, and he was white as death. . . . And when I asked him what was the matter, he wouldn't tell me. He was too proud. He said he was all right, but I could see that he was sick as a dog. . . . So he paid the bill. It came to forty cents—I'll never forget *that* as long as I live. . . . And sure enough, we no more than got out the door—he hardly had time to reach the curb—before it all came up.

And the poor kid was so scared and so ashamed. And what scared him so was not that he had gotten sick, but that he had spent all that money and it had come to nothing. And mama would find out. . . . Poor kid, he just stood there looking at me and he whispered: "Oh Helen, don't tell mama. She'll be mad if she finds out." Then we hurried home, and he was still white as a sheet when we got there.

Mama was waiting for us. She looked at us—you know how "Miss Eliza" looks at you when she thinks you've been doing something that you shouldn't. Mama said, "Why, where on earth have you two children been?" I guess she was all set to lay us out. Then she took one look at Grover's face. That was enough for her. She said, "Why, child, what in the world!" She was white as a sheet herself. . . . And all that Grover said was—"Mama, I feel sick."

He was sick as a dog. He fell over on the bed, and we undressed him and mama put her hand upon his forehead and came out in the hall—she was so white you could have made a black mark on her face with chalk—and whispered to me, "Go get the doctor quick, he's burning up."

And I went chasing up the street, my pigtails flying, to Dr. Packer's house. I brought him back with me. When he came out of Grover's room he told mama what to do but I don't know if she even heard him.

Her face was white as a sheet. She looked at me and looked right through me. She never saw me. And oh, my Lord, I'll never forget the way she looked, the way my heart stopped and came up in my throat. I was only a skinny little kid of fourteen. But she looked as if she was dying right before my eyes. And I knew that if anything happened to him, she'd never get over it if she lived to be a hundred.

Poor old mama. You know, he always was her eyeballs—you know that, don't you?—not the rest of us!—no, sir! I know what I'm talking about. It always has been Grover—she always thought more of him than she did of any of the others. And—poor kid!—he was a sweet kid. I can still see him lying there, and remember how sick he was, and how scared I was! I don't know why I was so scared. All we'd done had been to sneak away from home and go into a lunchroom—but I felt guilty about the whole thing, as if it was my fault.

It all came back to me the other day when I was looking at that picture, and I thought, my God, we were two kids together, and I was only two years older than Grover was, and now I'm forty-six. . . . Can you believe it? Can you figure it out—the way we grow up and change and go away? . . . And my Lord, Grover seemed so grown-up to me. He was such a quiet kid—I guess that's why he seemed older than the rest of us.

I wonder what Grover would say now if he could see that picture. All my hopes and dreams and big ambitions have come to nothing, and it's all so long ago, as if it happened in another world. Then it comes back, as if it happened yesterday. . . . Sometimes I lie awake at night and think of all the people who have come and gone, and how everything is different from the way we thought that it would be. Then I go out on the street next day and see the faces of the people that I pass. . . . Don't they look strange to you? Don't you see something funny in people's eyes, as if all of them were puzzled about something? As if they were wondering what had happened to them since they were kids? Wondering what it is that they have lost? . . . Now am I crazy, or do you know what I mean? You've been to college, Gene, and I want you to tell me if you know the answer. Now do they look that way to you? I never noticed that look in people's eyes when I was a kid —did you?

My God, I wish I knew the answer to these things. I'd like to find out what is wrong—what has changed since then—and if we have the same queer look in our eyes, too. Does it happen to us all, to everyone? . . . Grover and Ben, Steve, Daisy, Luke, and me—all standing there before that house on Woodson Street in Altamont—there we are, and you see the way we were—and how it all gets lost. What is it, anyway, that people lose?

How is it that nothing turns out the way we thought it would be? It all gets lost until it seems that it has never happened—that it is something we dreamed somewhere. . . . You see what I mean? . . . It seems that it must be something we heard somewhere—that it happened to someone else. And then it all comes back again.

And suddenly you remember just how it was, and see again those two funny, frightened, skinny little kids with their noses pressed against

the dirty window of that lunchroom thirty years ago. You remember the
way it felt, the way it smelled, even the strange smell in the old pantry in
that house we lived in then. And the steps before the house, the way
the rooms looked. And those two little boys in sailor suits who used to
ride up and down before the house on tricycles. . . . And the birthmark
on Grover's neck. . . . The Inside Inn. : . . St. Louis, and the Fair.

It all comes back as if it happened yesterday. And then it goes
away again, and seems farther off and stranger than if it happened in a
dream.

4

The Brother

"*This* is King's Highway," the man said.

And then Eugene looked and saw that it was just a street. There
were some big new buildings, a large hotel, some restaurants and
"bar-grill" places of the modern kind, the livid monotone of neon lights,
the ceaseless traffic of motor cars — all this was new, but it was just a
street. And he knew that it had always been just a street, and nothing
more — but somehow — well, he stood there looking at it, wondering
what else he had expected to find.

The man kept looking at him with inquiry in his eyes, and Eugene
asked him if the Fair had not been out this way.

"Sure, the Fair was out beyond here," the man said. "Out where
the park is now. But this street you're looking for — don't you remember
the name of it or nothing?" the man said.

Eugene said he thought the name of the street was Edgemont, but
that he wasn't sure. Anyhow it was something like that. And he said the
house was on the corner of that street and of another street.

Then the man said: "What was that other street?"

Eugene said he did not know, but that King's Highway was a
block or so away, and that an interurban line ran past about half a block
from where he once had lived.

"What line was this?" the man said, and stared at him.

"The interurban line," Eugene said.

Then the man stared at him again, and finally, "I don't know no
interurban line," he said.

Eugene said it was a line that ran behind some houses, and that
there were board fences there and grass beside the tracks. But somehow he could not say that it was summer in those days and that you
could smell the ties, a wooden, tarry smell, and feel a kind of absence in
the afternoon after the car had gone. He only said the interurban line
was back behind somewhere between the backyards of some houses

and some old board fences, and that King's Highway was a block or two away.

He did not say that King's Highway had not been a street in those days but a kind of road that wound from magic out of some dim and haunted land, and that along the way it had got mixed in with Tom the Piper's son, with hot cross buns, with all the light that came and went, and with coming down through Indiana in the morning, and the smell of engine smoke, the Union Station, and most of all with voices lost and far and long ago that said "King's Highway."

He did not say these things about King's Highway because he looked about him and he saw what King's Highway was. All he could say was that the street was near King's Highway, and was on the corner, and that the interurban trolley line was close to there. He said it was a stone house, and that there were stone steps before it, and a strip of grass. He said he thought the house had had a turret at one corner, he could not be sure.

The man looked at him again, and said, "This is King's Highway, but I never heard of any street like that."

Eugene left him then, and went on till he found the place. And so at last he turned into the street, finding the place where the two corners met, the huddled block, the turret, and the steps, and paused a moment, looking back, as if the street were Time.

For a moment he stood there, waiting—for a word, and for a door to open, for the child to come. He waited, but no words were spoken; no one came.

Yet all of it was just as it had always been, except that the steps were lower, the porch less high, the strip of grass less wide, than he had thought. All the rest of it was as he had known it would be. A graystone front, three-storied, with a slant slate roof, the side red brick and win-dowed, still with the old arched entrance in the center for the doctor's use.

There was a tree in front, and a lamp post; and behind and to the side, more trees than he had known there would be. And all the slatey turret gables, all the slatey window gables, going into points, and the two arched windows, in strong stone, in the front room.

It was all so strong, so solid, and so ugly—and all so enduring and so good, the way he had remembered it, except he did not smell the tar, the hot and caulky dryness of the old cracked ties, the boards of back-yard fences and the coarse and sultry grass, and absence in the after-noon when the street car had gone, and the twins, sharp-visaged in their sailor suits, pumping with furious shrillness on tricycles up and down before the house, and the feel of the hot afternoon, and the sense that everyone was absent at the Fair.

Except for this, it all was just the same; except for this and for

King's Highway, which was now a street; except for this, and for the child that did not come.

It was a hot day. Darkness had come. The heat rose up and hung and sweltered like a sodden blanket in St. Louis. It was wet heat, and one knew that there would be no relief or coolness in the night. And when one tried to think of the time when the heat would go away, one said: "It cannot last. It's bound to go away," as we always say it in America. But one did not believe it when he said it. The heat soaked down and men sweltered in it; the faces of the people were pale and greasy with the heat. And in their faces was a patient wretchedness, and one felt the kind of desolation that one feels at the end of a hot day in a great city in America—when one's home is far away, across the continent, and he thinks of all that distance, all that heat, and feels, "Oh God! but it's a big country!"

And he feels nothing but absence, absence, and the desolation of America, the loneliness and sadness of the high, hot skies, and evening coming on across the Middle West, across the sweltering and heat-sunken land, across all the lonely little towns, the farms, the fields, the oven swelter of Ohio, Kansas, Iowa, and Indiana at the close of day, and voices, casual in the heat, voices at the little stations, quiet, casual, somehow faded into that enormous vacancy and weariness of heat, of space, and of the immense, the sorrowful, the most high and awful skies.

Then he hears the engine and the wheel again, the wailing whistle and the bell, the sound of shifting in the sweltering yard, and walks the street, and walks the street, beneath the clusters of hard lights, and by the people with sagged faces, and is drowned in desolation and in no belief.

He feels the way one feels when one comes back, and knows that he should not have come, and when he sees that, after all, King's Highway is—a street; and St. Louis—the enchanted name—a big, hot, common town upon the river, sweltering in wet, dreary heat, and not quite South, and nothing else enough to make it better.

It had not been like this before. He could remember how it would get hot, and how good the heat was, and how he would lie out in the backyard on an airing mattress, and how the mattress would get hot and dry and smell like a hot mattress full of sun, and how the sun would make him want to sleep, and how, sometimes, he would go down into the basement to feel coolness, and how the cellar smelled as cellars always smell—a cool, stale smell, the smell of cobwebs and of grimy bottles. And he could remember, when you opened the door upstairs, the smell of the cellar would come up to you—cool, musty, stale and dank and dark—and how the thought of the dark cellar always filled him with a kind of numb excitement, a kind of visceral expectancy.

He could remember how it got hot in the afternoons, and how he would feel a sense of absence and vague sadness in the afternoons, when everyone had gone away. The house would seem so lonely, and sometimes he would sit inside, on the second step of the hall stairs, and listen to the sound of silence and of absence in the afternoon. He could smell the oil upon the floor and on the stairs, and see the sliding doors with their brown varnish and the beady chains across the door, and thrust his hands among the beady chains, and gather them together in his arms, and let them clash, and swish with light beady swishings all around him. He could feel darkness, absence, varnished darkness, and stained light within the house, through the stained glass of the window on the stairs, through the small stained glasses by the door, stained light and absence, silence and the smell of floor oil and vague sadness in the house on a hot mid-afternoon. And all these things themselves would have a kind of life: would seem to wait attentively, to be most living and most still.

He would sit there and listen. He could hear the girl next door practice her piano lessons in the afternoon, and hear the street car coming by between the backyard fences, half a block away, and smell the dry and sultry smell of backyard fences, the smell of coarse hot grasses by the car tracks in the afternoon, the smell of tar, of dry caulked ties, the smell of bright worn flanges, and feel the loneliness of back-yards in the afternoon and the sense of absence when the car was gone.

Then he would long for evening and return, the slant of light, and feet along the street, the sharp-faced twins in sailor suits upon their tricycles, the smell of supper and the sound of voices in the house again, and Grover coming from the Fair.

That is how it was when he came into the street, and found the place where the two corners met, and turned at last to see if Time was there. He passed the house: some lights were burning, the door was open, and a woman sat upon the porch. And presently he turned, came back, and stopped before the house again. The corner light fell blank upon the house. He stood looking at it, and put his foot upon the step.

Then he said to the woman who was sitting on the porch: "This house—excuse me—but could you tell me, please, who lives here in this house?"

He knew his words were strange and hollow, and he had not said what he wished to say. She stared at him a moment, puzzled.

Then she said: "I live here. Who are you looking for?"

He said, "Why, I am looking for——"

And then he stopped, because he knew he could not tell her what it was that he was looking for.

"There used to be a house——" he said.

The woman was now staring at him hard.

He said, "I think I used to live here."

She said nothing.

In a moment he continued, "I used to live here in this house," he said, "when I was a little boy."

She was silent, looking at him, then she said: "Oh. Are you sure this was the house? Do you remember the address?"

"I have forgotten the address," he said, "but it was Edgemont Street, and it was on the corner. And I know this is the house."

"This isn't Edgemont Street," the woman said. "The name is Bates."

"Well, then, they changed the name of the street," he said, "but this is the same house. It hasn't changed."

She was silent a moment, then she nodded: "Yes. They did change the name of the street. I remember when I was a child they called it something else," she said. "But that was a long time ago. When was it that you lived here?"

"In 1904."

Again she was silent, looking at him. Then presently: "Oh. That was the year of the Fair. You were here then?"

"Yes." He now spoke rapidly, with more confidence. "My mother had the house, and we were here for seven months. And the house belonged to Dr. Packer," he went on. "We rented it from him."

"Yes," the woman said, and nodded, "this was Dr. Packer's house. He's dead now, he's been dead for many years. But this was the Packer house, all right."

"That entrance on the side," he said, "where the steps go up, that was for Dr. Packer's patients. That was the entrance to his office."

"Oh," the woman said, "I didn't know that. I've often wondered what it was. I didn't know what it was for."

"And this big room in front here," he continued, "that was the office. And there were sliding doors, and next to it, a kind of alcove for his patients — "

"Yes, the alcove is still there, only all of it has been made into one room now — and I never knew just what the alcove was for."

"And there were sliding doors on this side, too, that opened on the hall — and a stairway going up upon this side. And halfway up the stairway, at the landing, a little window of colored glass — and across the sliding doors here in the hall, a kind of curtain made of strings of beads."

She nodded, smiling. "Yes, it's just the same — we still have the sliding doors and the stained glass window on the stairs. There's no bead curtain any more," she said, "but I remember when people had them. I know what you mean."

"When we were here," he said, "we used the doctor's office for a parlor — except later on — the last month or two — and then we used it for — a bedroom."

"It is a bedroom now," she said. "I run the house—I rent rooms—all of the rooms upstairs are rented—but I have two brothers and they sleep in this front room."

Both of them were silent for a moment, then Eugene said, "My brother stayed there too."

"In the front room?" the woman said.

He answered, "Yes."

She paused, then said: "Won't you come in? I don't believe it's changed much. Would you like to see?"

He thanked her and said he would, and he went up the steps. She opened the screen door to let him in.

Inside it was just the same—the stairs, the hallway, the sliding doors, the window of stained glass upon the stairs. And all of it was just the same, except for absence, the stained light of absence in the afternoon, and the child who once had sat there, waiting on the stairs.

It was all the same except that as a child he had sat there feeling things were *Somewhere*—and now he *knew*. He had sat there feeling that a vast and sultry river was somewhere—and now he knew! He had sat there wondering what King's Highway was, where it began, and where it ended—now he knew! He had sat there haunted by the magic word "downtown"—now he knew!—and by the street car, after it had gone—and by all things that came and went and came again, like the cloud shadows passing in a wood, that never could be captured.

And he felt that if he could only sit there on the stairs once more, in solitude and absence in the afternoon, he would be able to get it back again. Then would he be able to remember all that he had seen and been—the brief sum of himself, the universe of his four years, with all the light of Time upon it—that universe which was so short to measure, and yet so far, so endless, to remember. Then would he be able to see his own small face again, pooled in the dark mirror of the hall, and peer once more into the grave eyes of the child that he had been, and discover there in his quiet three-years' self the lone integrity of "I," knowing: "Here is the House, and here House listening; here is Absence, Absence in the afternoon; and here in this House, this Absence, is my core, my kernel—here am I!"

But as he thought it, he knew that even if he could sit here alone and get it back again, it would be gone as soon as seized, just as it had been then—first coming like the vast and drowsy rumors of the distant and enchanted Fair, then fading like cloud shadows on a hill, going like faces in a dream—coming, going, coming, possessed and held but never captured, like lost voices in the mountains long ago—and like the dark eyes and quiet face of the dark, lost boy, his brother, who, in the mysterious rhythms of his life and work, used to come into this house, then go, and then return again.

The woman took Eugene back into the house and through the

hall. He told her of the pantry, told her where it was and pointed to the place, but now it was no longer there. And he told her of the backyard, and of the old board fence around the yard. But the old board fence was gone. And he told her of the carriage house, and told her it was painted red. But now there was a small garage. And the backyard was still there, but smaller than he thought, and now there was a tree.

"I did not know there was a tree," he said. "I do not remember any tree."

"Perhaps it was not there," she said. "A tree could grow in thirty years." And then they came back through the house again and paused at the sliding doors.

"And could I see this room?" he said.

She slid the doors back. They slid open smoothly, with a rolling heaviness, as they used to do. And then he saw the room again. It was the same. There was a window at the side, the two arched windows at the front, the alcove and the sliding doors, the fireplace with the tiles of mottled green, the mantel of dark mission wood, the mantel posts, a dresser and a bed, just where the dresser and the bed had been so long ago.

"Is this the room?" the woman said. "It hasn't changed?"

He told her that it was the same.

"And your brother slept here where my brothers sleep?"

"This is his room," he said.

They were silent. He turned to go, and said, "Well, thank you. I appreciate your showing me."

She said that she was glad and that it was no trouble. "And when you see your family, you can tell them that you saw the house," she said. "My name is Mrs. Bell. You can tell your mother that a Mrs. Bell has the house now. And when you see your brother, you can tell him that you saw the room he slept in, and that you found it just the same."

He told her then that his brother was dead.

The woman was silent for a moment. Then she looked at him and said: "He died here, didn't he? In this room?"

He told her that it was so.

"Well, then," she said, "I knew it. I don't know how. But when you told me he was here, I knew it."

He said nothing. In a moment the woman said, "What did he die of?"

"Typhoid."

She looked shocked and troubled, and said involuntarily, "My two brothers — "

"That was a long time ago," he said. "I don't think you need to worry now."

"Oh, I wasn't thinking about that," she said. "It was just hearing that a little boy—your brother—was—was in this room that my two brothers sleep in now——"

"Well, maybe I shouldn't have told you then. But he was a good boy—and if you'd known him you wouldn't mind."

She said nothing, and he added quickly: "Besides, he didn't stay here long. This wasn't really his room—but the night he came back with my sister he was so sick—they didn't move him."

"Oh," the woman said, "I see." And then: "Are you going to tell your mother you were here?"

"I don't think so."

"I—I wonder how she feels about this room."

"I don't know. She never speaks of it."

"Oh. . . . How old was he?"

"He was twelve."

"You must have been pretty young yourself."

"I was not quite four."

"And—you just wanted to see the room, didn't you? That's why you came back."

"Yes."

"Well—" indefinitely—"I guess you've seen it now."

"Yes, thank you."

"I guess you don't remember much about him, do you? I shouldn't think you would."

"No, not much."

The years dropped off like fallen leaves: the face came back again—the soft dark oval, the dark eyes, the soft brown berry on the neck, the raven hair, all bending down, approaching—the whole appearing to him ghost-wise, intent and instant.

"Now say it—*Grover*!"

"Gova."

"No—not Gova—*Grover*! . . . Say it!"

"Gova."

"Ah-h—you didn't say it. You said Gova. *Grover*—now say it!"

"Gova."

"Look, I tell you what I'll do if you say it right. Would you like to go down to King's Highway? Would you like Grover to set you up? All right, then. If you say Grover and say it right, I'll take you to King's Highway and set you up to ice cream. Now say it right—*Grover*!"

"Gova."

"Ah-h, you-u. You're the craziest little old boy I ever did see. Can't you even say Grover?"

"Gova."

"Ah-h, you-u. Old Tongue-Tie, that's what you are. . . . Well, come on, then, I'll set you up anyway."

It all came back, and faded, and was lost again. Eugene turned to go, and thanked the woman and said good-bye.

"Well, then, good-bye," the woman said, and they shook hands. "I'm glad if I could show you. I'm glad if—" She did not finish, and at length she said: "Well, then, that was a long time ago. You'll find everything changed now, I guess. It's all built up around here now—and way out beyond here, out beyond where the Fair Grounds used to be. I guess you'll find it changed."

They had nothing more to say. They just stood there for a moment on the steps, and then shook hands once more.

"Well, good-bye."

And again he was in the street, and found the place where the corners met, and for the last time turned to see where Time had gone.

And he knew that he would never come again, and that lost magic would not come again. Lost now was all of it—the street, the heat, King's Highway, and Tom the Piper's son, all mixed in with the vast and drowsy murmur of the Fair, and with the sense of absence in the afternoon, and the house that waited, and the child that dreamed. And out of the enchanted wood, that thicket of man's memory, Eugene knew that the dark eye and the quiet face of his friend and brother—poor child, life's stranger, and life's exile, lost like all of us, a cipher in blind mazes, long ago—the lost boy was gone forever, and would not return.

1941

John Dos Passos   *1896 –*

Although John Dos Passos has enjoyed a career as a writer extending over half a century, his reputation is largely staked on his three-volume collective novel *USA*, written during the 1930's. John Roderigo Dos Passos was born in Chicago in 1896 and educated at schools in the United States and abroad before he entered Harvard. After graduating in 1916, he went to Spain as a student of architecture but soon volunteered as a driver in the French ambulance service. After America's entry into the war, he enlisted as a private in the Army medical corps. Turning to journalism after the Armistice, he became a foreign correspondent. His first two novels, based on his war experience, were *One Man's Initiation* (1920; reissued as *First Encounter* in 1945) and *Three Soldiers* (1921). The latter, which treats the impact of war on three young Americans of contrasting backgrounds, can be seen as a first step toward the collective novel. A more decisive move in the same direction was taken in *Manhattan Transfer* (1925), which portrays the partially interrelated lives of a group of representative citizens of the complex metropolis from a disillusioned viewpoint. In *Streets of Night* (1923), a sensitive, aesthetic young hero is subjected to the destructive influences of the philistine world. Dos Passos' aestheticism, which had also been apparent in his earlier writing, is a strain which continued to exist side by side with the deepening radicalism of his social and political views.

This radicalism, expressed as a condemnation of capitalism and a sympathy for Marxism and proletarian causes, furnished the motive power of the three novels—*The 42nd Parallel* (1930), *1919* (1932), *The Big Money* (1936)—reissued together as *USA* (1937). As a collective novel the trilogy depicts the course of American society through the first three decades of the century by tracing the lives of a large cast of characters defined in terms of their environmental conditioning. To provide a fuller social and personal context for his story, Dos Passos developed three experimental devices dispersed as interchapters throughout the book. These include: (1) brief "biographies," or poetic profiles, of influential historical figures, often characterized as either culture heroes (like Eugene Debs, Joe Hill, Frank Lloyd Wright) or villains (Henry Ford, J. P. Morgan); (2) "newsreels" made up of scraps of headlines, popular songs, speeches, and other quotations that suggest the (usually turbulent) cultural climate at various stages of the story; and (3) impressionistic "camera eye" sections which reveal the author's subjective feelings during the successive periods covered by his fictional narration. Much of the interest and complexity of *USA* as a whole is supplied by these features, which exerted an influence on the techniques of later writers like John Steinbeck and Norman Mailer. One virtue of these shorter pieces is that any one can stand by itself as an interesting work, apart from its relation to the larger story.

With such developments as the Spanish Civil War and the outbreak of World War II, Dos Passos' viewpoint shifted suddenly from revolutionary radicalism to a conservatism motivated largely by a fear of collectivism. A more recent but less experimental trilogy, *District of Columbia* (1952), consists of three novels—*Adventures of a Young Man* (1939), *Number One* (1943), and *The Grand Design* (1948)—directed largely against the targets of demagoguery and New Deal bureaucracy. Dos Passos has also written nonfictional works like *The Ground We Stand On* (1941) and *The Head* and *Heart of Thomas Jefferson* (1963), dedicated to the principles of democratic republicanism. Among other works of the postwar years are two novels: *Most Likely to Succeed* (1954), a satire of Communist "intellectuals," and *Midcentury* (1961), a story of present-day America that praises the principle of free enterprise.

In the years since the war, Dos Passos' work has been neglected by English and American critics. The first book-length study, by a French critic, is Georges-Albert Astre, *Thèmes et structures dans l'oeuvre de John Dos Passos* (Paris, 1956). A critique in English is J. H. Wrenn, *John Dos Passos* (New York, 1962), which contains a bibliography.

The text of the selections given here is that of *USA* (New York, 1937).

From *The 42nd Parallel*

U.S.A.

The young man walks fast by himself through the crowd that thins into the night streets; feet are tired from hours of walking; eyes greedy for warm curve of faces, answering flicker of eyes, the set of a head, the lift of a shoulder, the way hands spread and clench; blood tingles with wants; mind is a beehive of hopes buzzing and stinging; muscles ache for the knowledge of jobs, for the roadmender's pick and shovel work, the fisherman's knack with a hook when he hauls on the slithery net from the rail of the lurching trawler, the swing of the bridgeman's arm as he slings down the whitehot rivet, the engineer's slow grip wise on the throttle, the dirtfarmer's use of his whole body when, whoaing the mules, he yanks the plow from the furrow. The young man walks by himself searching through the crowd with greedy eyes, greedy ears taut to hear, by himself, alone.

The streets are empty. People have packed into subways, climbed into streetcars and buses; in the stations they've scampered for suburban trains; they've filtered into lodgings and tenements, gone up in elevators into apartmenthouses. In a showwindow two sallow windowdressers in their shirtsleeves are bringing out a dummy girl in a red evening dress, at a corner welders in masks lean into sheets of blue flame repairing a cartrack, a few drunk bums shamble along, a sad streetwalker fidgets under an arclight. From the river comes the deep rumbling whistle of a steamboat leaving dock. A tug hoots far away.

The young man walks by himself, fast but not fast enough, far but not far enough (faces slide out of sight, talk trails into tattered scraps, footsteps tap fainter in alleys); he must catch the last subway, the streetcar, the bus, run up the gangplanks of all the steamboats, register at all the hotels, work in the cities, answer the wantads, learn the trades, take up the jobs, live in all the boardinghouses, sleep in all the beds. One bed is not enough, one job is not enough, one life is not enough. At night, head swimming with wants, he walks by himself alone.

No job, no woman, no house, no city.

Only the ears busy to catch the speech are not alone; the ears are caught tight, linked tight by the tendrils of phrased words, the turn of a joke, the singsong fade of a story, the gruff fall of a sentence; linking tendrils of speech twine through the city blocks, spread over pavements, grow out along broad parked avenues, speed with the trucks leaving on their long night runs over roaring highways, whisper down sandy byroads past wornout farms, joining up cities and fillingstations, roundhouses, steamboats, planes groping along airways; words call out on mountain pastures, drift slow down rivers widening to the sea and the hushed beaches.

It was not in the long walks through jostling crowds at night that he was less alone, or in the training camp at Allentown, or in the day on the docks at Seattle, or in the empty reek of Washington City hot boyhood summer nights, or in the meal on Market Street, or in the swim off the red rocks at San Diego, or in the bed full of fleas in New Orleans, or in the cold razorwind off the lake, or in the gray faces trembling in the grind of gears in the street under Michigan Avenue, or in the smokers of limited expresstrains, or walking across county, or riding up the dry mountain canyons, or the night without a sleepingbag among frozen beartracks in the Yellowstone, or canoeing Sundays on the Quinnipiac;

but in his mother's words telling about longago, in his father's telling about when I was a boy, in the kidding stories of uncles, in the lies the kids told at school, the hired man's yarns, the tall tales the doughboys told after taps;

it was the speech that clung to the ears, the link that tingled in the blood; U.S.A.

U.S.A is the slice of a continent. U.S.A. is a group of holding companies, some aggregations of trade unions, a set of laws bound in calf, a radio network, a chain of moving picture theatres, a column of stock-quotations rubbed out and written in by a Western Union boy on a blackboard, a publiclibrary full of old newspapers and dogeared historybooks with protests scrawled on the margins in pencil. U.S.A. is the world's greatest rivervalley fringed with mountains and hills, U.S.A. is a set of bigmouthed officials with too many bankaccounts. U.S.A. is a lot of men buried in their uniforms in Arlington Cemetery. U.S.A. is the letters at the end of an address when you are away from home. But mostly U.S.A is the speech of the people.

1930

Lover of Mankind

Debs[1] was a railroad man, born in a weatherboarded shack at Terre Haute.

He was one of ten children.

His father had come to America in a sailingship in '49,

an Alsatian from Colmar; not much of a moneymaker, fond of music and reading,

he gave his children a chance to finish public school and that was about all he could do.

At fifteen Gene Debs was already working as a machinist on the Indianapolis and Terre Haute Railway.

He worked as locomotive fireman,

clerked in a store

joined the local of the Brotherhood of Locomotive Firemen, was elected secretary, traveled all over the country as organizer.

He was a tall shamblefooted man, had a sort of gusty rhetoric that set on fire the railroad workers in their pineboarded halls

made them want the world he wanted,

a world brothers might own

where everybody would split even:

I am not a labor leader. I don't want you to follow me or anyone else. If you are looking for a Moses to lead you out of the capitalist wilderness you will stay right where you are. I would not lead you into this promised land if I could, because if I could lead you in, someone else would lead you out.

That was how he talked to freighthandlers and gandywalkers, to firemen and switchmen and engineers, telling them it wasn't enough to

---

[1] Eugene Victor Debs (1855–1926), labor leader and Socialist candidate for the presidency in five campaigns over the years 1900–1920.

organize the railroadmen, that all workers must be organized, that all workers must be organized in the workers' cooperative commonwealth.

Locomotive fireman on many a long night's run,

under the smoke a fire burned him up, burned in gusty words that beat in pineboarded halls; he wanted his brothers to be free men.

That was what he saw in the crowd that met him at the Old Wells Street Depot when he came out of jail after the Pullman strike,[2]

those were the men that chalked up nine hundred thousand votes for him in nineteen twelve and scared the frockcoats and the tophats and diamonded hostesses at Saratoga Springs, Bar Harbor, Lake Geneva with the bogy of a socialist president.

But where were Gene Debs' brothers in nineteen eighteen when Woodrow Wilson had him locked up in Atlanta for speaking against war,

where were the big men fond of whisky and fond of each other, gentle rambling tellers of stories over bars in small towns in the Middle West,

quiet men who wanted a house with a porch to putter around and a fat wife to cook for them, a few drinks and cigars, a garden to dig in, cronies to chew the rag with

and wanted to work for it
and others to work for it;

where were the locomotive firemen and engineers when they hustled him off to Atlanta Penitentiary?

And they brought him back to die in Terre Haute
to sit on his porch in a rocker with a cigar in his mouth,
beside him American Beauty roses his wife fixed in a bowl;

and the people of Terre Haute and the people in Indiana and the people of the Middle West were fond of him and afraid of him and thought of him as an old kindly uncle who loved them, and wanted to be with him and to have him give them candy,

but they were afraid of him as if he had contracted a social disease, syphilis or leprosy, and thought it was too bad,

but on account of the flag
and prosperity
and making the world safe for democracy,
they were afraid to be with him,
or to think much about him for fear they might believe him;
for he said:

While there is a lower class I am of it, while there is a criminal class I am of it, while there is a soul in prison I am not free.

1930

[2] In Chicago in 1904.

From *1919*

Joe Hill

A young Swede named Hillstrom went to sea, got himself calloused hands on sailingships and tramps, learned English in the focastle
of the steamers that make the run from Stockholm to Hull, dreamed
the Swede's dream of the west;

when he got to America they gave him a job polishing cuspidors
in a Bowery saloon.

He moved west to Chicago and worked in a machineshop.

He moved west and followed the harvest, hung around employment agencies, paid out many a dollar for a job in a construction camp,
walked out many a mile when the grub was too bum, or the boss too
tough, or too many bugs in the bunkhouse;

read Marx and the I.W.W.[1] Preamble and dreamed about forming
the structure of the new society within the shell of the old.

He was in California for the S.P.[2] strike (*Casey Jones, two locomotives, Casey Jones*), used to play the concertina outside the bunkhouse door, after supper, evenings (*Longhaired preachers come out
every night*), had a knack for setting rebel words to tunes (*And the
union makes us strong*).

Along the coast in cookshacks flophouses jungles wobblies ho-
boes bindlestiffs began singing Joe Hill's songs. They sang 'em in the
county jails of the State of Washington, Oregon, California, Nevada,
Idaho, in the bullpens in Montana and Arizona, sang 'em in Walla
Walla, San Quentin and Leavenworth,

forming the structure of the new society within the jails of the old.

At Bingham, Utah, Joe Hill organized the workers of the Utah
Construction Company in the One Big Union, won a new wagescale,
shorter hours, better grub. (The angel Moroni[3] didn't like labororgan-
izers any better than the Southern Pacific did.)

The angel Moroni moved the hearts of the Mormons to decide it
was Joe Hill shot a grocer named Morrison. The Swedish consul and
President Wilson tried to get him a new trial but the angel Moroni
moved the hearts of the supreme court of the State of Utah to sustain
the verdict of guilty. He was in jail a year, went on making up songs. In
November 1915 he was stood up against the wall in the jail yard in Salt
Lake City.

"Don't mourn for me organize," was the last word he sent out to
the workingstiffs of the I.W.W. Joe Hill stood up against the wall of the

---

[1] International Workers of the World. Members of this labor organization, founded in 1905,
were nicknamed "Wobblies."

[2] The Southern Pacific Railroad.

[3] Joseph Smith (1805–1844), the Mormon prophet, identified the angel Moroni as the
source of the scriptures he published as *The Book of Mormon* (1830).

jail yard, looked into the muzzles of the guns and gave the word to fire.

They put him in a black suit, put a stiff collar around his neck and a bow tie, shipped him to Chicago for a bangup funeral, and photographed his handsome stony mask staring into the future.

The first of May they scattered his ashes to the wind.

1932

The Body of an American

Whereasthe   Congressoftheunitedstates   byaconcurrentresolutionadoptedon   the4thdayofmarch   lastauthorizedthe   Secretaryofwar   to   cause   to   be   brought   to   theunitedstatesthe   body   of   an   Americanwhowasamemberoftheamericanexpeditionaryforcesineurope   wholosthislifeduringtheworldwarandwhoseidentityhasnotbeenestablished   for   burial   inthememorialamphitheatreofthe   nationalcemeteryatarlingtonvirginia

In the tarpaper morgue at Chalons-sur-Marne in the reek of chloride of lime and the dead, they picked out the pine box that held all that was left of

enie menie minie moe plenty other pine boxes stacked up there containing what they'd scraped up of Richard Roe

and other person or persons unknown. Only one can go. How did they pick John Doe?

Make sure he aint a dinge, boys,

make sure he aint a guinea or a kike,

how can you tell a guy's a hundredpercent when all you've got's a gunnysack full of bones, bronze buttons stamped with the screaming eagle and a pair of roll puttees?

. . . and the gagging chloride and the puky dirtstench of the yearold dead . . .

The day withal was too meaningful and tragic for applause. Silence, tears, songs and prayer, muffled drums and soft music were the instrumentalities today of national approbation.

John Doe was born (thudding din of blood in love into the shuddering soar of a man and a woman alone indeed together lurching into

and ninemonths sick drowse waking into scared agony and the pain and blood and mess of birth). John Doe was born

and raised in Brooklyn, in Memphis, near the lakefront in Cleveland, Ohio, in the stench of the stockyards in Chi, on Beacon Hill, in an old brick house in Alexandria Virginia, on Telegraph Hill, in a halftimbered Tudor cottage in Portland the city of roses,

in the Lying-In Hospital old Morgan endowed on Stuyvesant Square,

across the railroad tracks, out near the country club, in a shack cabin tenement apartmenthouse exclusive residential suburb;

scion of one of the best families in the social register, won first prize in the baby parade at Coronado Beach, was marbles champion of the Little Rock grammarschools, crack basketballplayer at the Booneville High, quarterback at the State Reformatory, having saved the sheriff's kid from drowning in the Little Missouri River was invited to Washington to be photographed shaking hands with the President on the White House steps; —

though this was a time of mourning, such an assemblage necessarily has about it a touch of color. In the boxes are seen the court uniforms of foreign diplomats, the gold braid of our own and foreign fleets and armies, the black of the conventional morning dress of American statesmen, the varicolored furs and outdoor wrapping garments of mothers and sisters come to mourn, the drab and blue of soldiers and sailors, the glitter of musical instruments and the white and black of a vested choir

—busboy harveststiff hogcaller boyscout champeen cornshucker of Western Kansas bellhop at the United States Hotel at Saratoga Springs office boy callboy fruiter telephone lineman longshoreman lumberjack plumber's helper,

worked for an exterminating company in Union City, filled pipes in an opium joint in Trenton, N.J.

Y.M.C.A. secretary, express agent, truckdriver, fordmechanic, sold books in Denver Colorado: Madam would you be willing to help a young man work his way through college?

President Harding, with a reverence seemingly more significant because of his high temporal station, concluded his speech:

We are met today to pay the impersonal tribute;
the name of him whose body lies before us took flight with his imperishable soul . . .
as a typical soldier of this representative democracy he fought and died believing in the indisputable justice of his country's cause . . .

by raising his right hand and asking the thousands within the sound of his voice to join in the prayer:

Our Father which art in heaven hallowed be thy name . . .

Naked he went into the army;

they weighed you, measured you, looked for flat feet, squeezed your penis to see if you had clap, looked up your anus to see if you had piles, counted your teeth, made you cough, listened to your heart and lungs, made you read the letters on the card, charted your urine and your intelligence,

gave you a service record for a future (imperishable soul)

and an identification tag stamped with your serial number to hang around your neck, issued O D regulation equipment, a condiment can and a copy of the articles of war.

Atten'SHUN suck in your gut you c————r wipe that smile off your face eyes right wattja tink dis is a choirch-social? For-war-D'ARCH.

John Doe
and Richard Roe and other person or persons unknown
drilled hiked, manual of arms, ate slum, learned to salute, to soldier, to loaf in the latrines, forbidden to smoke on deck, overseas guard duty, forty men and eight horses, shortarm inspection and the ping of shrapnel and the shrill bullets combing the air and the sorehead woodpeckers the machineguns mud cooties gasmasks and the itch.
Say feller tell me how I can get back to my outfit.

John Doe had a head
for twentyodd years intensely the nerves of the eyes the ears the palate the tongue the fingers the toes the armpits, the nerves warmfeeling under the skin charged the coiled brain with hurt sweet warm cold mine must dont sayings print headlines:
Thou shalt not the multiplication table long division, Now is the time for all good men knocks but once at a young man's door, It's a great life if Ish gebibbel, The first five years'll be the Safety First, Suppose a hun tried to rape your my country right or wrong, Catch 'em young, What he dont know wont treat 'em rough, Tell 'em nothin, He got what was coming to him he got his, This is a white man's country, Kick the bucket, Gone west, If you dont like it you can croaked him
Say buddy cant you tell me how I can get back to my outfit?

Cant help jumpin when them things go off, give me the trots them things do. I lost my identification tag swimmin in the Marne, roughousin with a guy while we was waitin to be deloused, in bed with a girl named Jeanne (Love moving picture wet French postcard dream began with saltpeter in the coffee and ended at the propho station);—
Say soldier for chrissake cant you tell me how I can get back to my outfit?
John Doe's

heart pumped blood:
alive thudding silence of blood in your ears
down in the clearing in the Oregon forest where the punkins were punkincolor pouring into the blood through the eyes and the fallcolored trees and the bronze hoopers were hopping through the dry grass, where tiny striped snails hung on the underside of the blades and the flies hummed, wasps droned, bumblebees buzzed, and the woods smelt of wine and mushrooms and apples, homey smell of fall pouring into the blood,

and I dropped the tin hat and the sweaty pack and lay flat with the dogday sun licking my throat and adamsapple and the tight skin over the breastbone.

The shell had his number on it.

The blood ran into the ground.

The service record dropped out of the filing cabinet when the quartermaster sergeant got blotto that time they had to pack up and leave the billets in a hurry.
The identification tag was in the bottom of the Marne.

The blood ran into the ground, the brains oozed out of the cracked skull and were licked up by the trenchrats, the belly swelled and raised a generation of bluebottle flies,
    and the incorruptible skeleton,
    and the scraps of dried viscera and skin bundled in khaki

    they took to Chalon-sur-Marne
    and laid it out neat in a pine coffin
    and took it home to God's Country on a battleship
    and buried it in a sarcophagus in the Memorial Amphitheatre in the Arlington National Cemetery
    and draped the Old Glory over it
    and the bugler played taps
    and Mr. Harding prayed to God and the diplomats and the generals and the admirals and the brasshats and the politicians and the handsomely dressed ladies out of the society column of the *Washington Post* stood up solemn
    and thought how beautiful sad Old Glory God's Country it was to have the bugler play taps and the three volleys made their ears ring.

    Where his chest ought to have been they pinned
    the Congressional Medal, the D.S.C., the Medaille Militaire, the Belgian Croix de Guerre, the Italian gold medal, the Vitutea Militara sent by Queen Marie of Rumania, the Czechoslovak war cross, the Virtuti Militari of the Poles, a wreath sent by Hamilton Fish, Jr., of New York, and a little wampum presented by a deputation of Arizona redskins in warpaint and feathers. All the Washingtonians brought flowers.

Woodrow Wilson brought a bouquet of poppies.

1932

From *The Big Money*
Architect

A muggy day in late spring in eighteen eighty-seven a tall young-ster of eighteen[1] with fine eyes and a handsome arrogant way of carrying his head arrived in Chicago with seven dollars left in his pocket from buying his ticket from Madison with some cash he'd got by pawn-ing Plutarch's *Lives*, a Gibbon's *Decline and Fall of the Roman Empire* and an old furcollared coat.

Before leaving home to make himself a career in an architect's office (there was no architecture course at Wisconsin to clutter his mind with stale Beaux Arts drawings); the youngster had seen the dome of the new State Capitol in Madison collapse on account of bad rubblework in the piers, some thieving contractors' skimping materials to save the politicians their rakeoff, and perhaps a trifling but deadly error in the architect's plans;

he never forgot the roar of burst masonry, the flying plaster, the soaring dustcloud, the mashed bodies of the dead and dying being carried out, set faces livid with plasterdust.

Walking round downtown Chicago, crossing and recrossing the bridges over the Chicago River in the jingle and clatter of traffic, the rattle of vans and loaded wagons and the stamping of big drayhorses and the hooting of towboats with barges and the rumbling whistle of lakesteamers waiting for the draw,

he thought of the great continent stretching a thousand miles east and south and north, three thousand miles west, and everywhere, at mineheads, on the shores of newlydredged harbors, along watercourses, at the intersections of railroads, sprouting

shacks roundhouses tipples grainelevators stores warehouses tenements, great houses for the wealthy set in broad treeshaded lawns, domed statehouses on hills, hotels churches operahouses auditoriums.

He walked with long eager steps

towards the untrammeled future opening in every direction for a young man who'd keep his hands to his work and his wits sharp to invent.

The same day he landed a job in an architect's office.

Frank Lloyd Wright was the grandson of a Welsh hatter and preacher who'd settled in a rich Wisconsin valley, Spring Valley, and raised a big family of farmers and preachers and schoolteachers there. Wright's father was a preacher too, a restless illadjusted Newenglander who studied medicine, preached in a Baptist church in Weymouth, Massachusetts, and then as a Unitarian in the middle west, taught

[1] Frank Lloyd Wright (1869–1959).

music, read Sanskrit and finally walked out on his family.

Young Wright was born on his grandfather's farm, went to school in Weymouth and Madison, worked summers on a farm of his uncle's in Wisconsin.

His training in architecture was the reading of Viollet le Duc, the apostle of the thirteenth century and of the pure structural mathematics of gothic stone-masonry, and the seven years he worked with Louis Sullivan in the office of Adler and Sullivan in Chicago. (It was Louis Sullivan who, after Richardson, invented whatever was invented in nineteenthcentury architecture in America).

When Frank Lloyd Wright left Sullivan he had already launched a distinctive style, prairie architecture. In Oak Park he built broad suburban dwellings for rich men that were the first buildings to break the hold on American builders' minds of centuries of pastward routine, of the wornout capital and plinth and pediment dragged through the centuries from the Acropolis, and the jaded traditional stencils of Roman masonry, the halfobliterated Palladian copybooks.

Frank Lloyd Wright was cutting out a new avenue that led towards the swift constructions in glassbricks and steel

foreshadowed today.

Delightedly he reached out for the new materials, steel in tension, glass, concrete, the million new metals and alloys.

The son and grandson of preachers, he became a preacher in blueprints,

projecting constructions in the American future instead of the European past.

Inventor of plans,

plotter of tomorrow's girderwork phrases,

he preaches to the young men coming of age in the time of oppression, cooped up by the plasterboard partitions of finance routine, their lives and plans made poor by feudal levies of parasite money standing astride every process to shake down progress for the cutting of coupons:

> *The properly citified citizen has become a broker, dealing chiefly in human frailties or the ideas and inventions of others, a puller of levers, a presser of buttons of vicarious power, his by way of machine craft . . . and over beside him and beneath him, even in his heart as he sleeps, is the taximeter of rent, in some form to goad this anxious consumer's unceasing struggle for or against more or less merciful or merciless money increment.*

To the young men who spend their days and nights drafting the plans for new *rented aggregates of rented cells upended on hard pavements,*

he preaches
the horizons of his boyhood,
a future that is not the rise of a few points in a hundred selected

stocks, or an increase in carloadings, or a multiplication of credit in the bank or a rise in the rate on callmoney,

but a new clean construction, from the ground up, based on uses and needs,

towards the American future instead of towards the painsmeared past of Europe and Asia. Usonia he calls the broad teeming band of this new nation across the enormous continent between Atlantic and Pacific. He preaches a project for Usonia:

It is easy to realize how the complexity of crude utilitarian construction in the mechanical infancy of our growth, like the crude scaffolding for some noble building, did violence to the landscape. . . . The crude purpose of pioneering days has been accomplished. The scaffolding may be taken down and the true work, the culture of a civilization, may appear.

Like the life of many a preacher, prophet, exhorter, Frank Lloyd Wright's life has been stormy. He has raised children, had rows with wives, overstepped boundaries, got into difficulties with the law, divorcecourts, bankruptcy, always the yellow press yapping at his heels, his misfortunes yelled out in headlines in the evening papers: affairs with women, the nightmare horror of the burning of his house in Wisconsin.

By a curious irony

the building that is most completely his is the Imperial Hotel in Tokyo that was one of the few structures to come unharmed through the earthquake of 1923 (the day the cable came telling him that the building had stood saving so many hundreds of lives he writes was one of his happiest days)

and it was reading in German that most Americans first learned of his work.

His life has been full of arrogant projects unaccomplished. (How often does the preacher hear, his voice echo back hollow from the empty hall, the draftsman watch the dust fuzz over the carefullycontrived plans, the architect see the rolledup blueprints curl yellowing and brittle in the filingcabinet.)

Twice he's rebuilt the house where he works in his grandfather's valley in Wisconsin after fires and disasters that would have smashed most men forever.

He works in Wisconsin,

an erect spare whitehaired man, his sons are architects, apprentices from all over the world come to work with him,

drafting the new city (he calls it Broadacre City).

Near and Far are beaten (to imagine the new city you must blot out every ingrained habit of the past, build a nation from the ground up with the new tools). For the architect there are only uses:

the incredible multiplication of functions, strength and tension in metal,

the dynamo, the electric coil, radio, the photoelectric cell, the

internalcombustion motor,
   glass
   concrete;
   and needs. (Tell us, doctors of philosophy, what are the needs of a man. At least a man needs to be notjailed notafraid nothungry notcold not without love, not a worker for a power he has never seen
   that cares nothing for the uses and needs of a man or a woman or a child.)
   Building a building is building the lives of the workers and dwellers in the building.
   The buildings determine civilization as the cells in the honeycomb the functions of bees.
   Perhaps in spite of himself the arrogant draftsman, the dilettante in concrete, the bohemian artist for wealthy ladies desiring to pay for prominence with the startling elaboration of their homes has been forced by the logic of uses and needs, by the lifelong struggle against the dragging undertow of money in mortmain,
   to draft plans that demand for their fulfillment a new life;
   only in freedom can we build the Usonian city. His plans are coming to life. His blueprints, as once Walt Whitman's words, stir the young men: —
   Frank Lloyd Wright,
   patriarch of the new building,
   not without honor except in his own country.

                                                               1936

Newsreel LXVIII

WALL STREET STUNNED[1]

*This is not Thirty-eight but it's old Ninety-seven
You must put her in Center on time*

MARKET SURE TO RECOVER FROM SLUMP

Decline in Contracts

POLICE TURN MACHINE GUNS ON COLORADO MINE STRIKERS
KILL 5 WOUND 40

   sympathizers appeared on the scene just as thousands of office workers were pouring out of the buildings at the lunch hour. As they raised their placard high and started an indefinite march from one side

[1] The headline refers to the stockmarket crash of October 24, 1929.

to the other, they were jeered and hooted not only by the office workers but also by workmen on a building under construction

NEW METHODS OF SELLING SEEN

Rescue Crews Try to Upend Ill-fated Craft While Waiting For Pontoons

> *He looked 'round an' said to his black greasy fireman*
> *Jus' shovel in a little more coal*
> *And when we cross that White Oak Mountain*
> *You can watch your Ninety-seven roll*

I find your column interesting and need advice. I have saved four thousand dollars which I want to invest for a better income. Do you think I might buy stocks?

POLICE KILLER FLICKS CIGARETTE AS HE GOES TREMBLING TO DOOM

PLAY AGENCIES IN RING OF SLAVE GIRL MARTS

Maker of Love Disbarred as Lawyer

> *Oh the right wing clothesmakers*
> *And the Socialist fakers*
> *They make by the workers . . .*
> *Double cross*

> *They preach Social-ism*
> *But practice Fasc-ism*
> *To keep capitalism*
> *By the boss*

MOSCOW CONGRESS OUSTS OPPOSITION

> *It's a mighty rough road from Lynchburg to Danville*
> *An' a line on a three mile grade*
> *It was on that grade he lost his average*
> *An' you see what a jump he made*

MILL THUGS IN MURDER RAID

here is the most dangerous example of how at the decisive moment the bourgeois ideology liquidates class solidarity and turns a

military intervention for economic expansion

friend of the workingclass of yesterday into a most miserable propagandist for imperialism today

RED PICKETS FINED FOR PROTEST HERE

We leave our home in the morning
We kiss our children goodby

OFFICIALS STILL HOPE FOR RESCUE OF MEN

He was goin' downgrade makin' ninety miles an hour
When his whistle broke into a scream
He was found in the wreck with his hand on the throttle
An' was scalded to death with the steam.[2]

RADICALS FIGHT WITH CHAIRS AT UNITY MEETING

PATROLMEN PROTECT REDS

U.S. CHAMBER OF COMMERCE URGES CONFIDENCE

REAL VALUES UNHARMED

While we slave for the bosses
Our children scream an' cry
But when we draw our money
Our grocery bills to pay

PRESIDENT SEES PROSPERITY NEAR

Not a cent to spend for clothing
Not a cent to lay away

STEAMROLLER IN ACTION AGAINST MILITANTS

MINERS BATTLE SCABS

But we cannot buy for our children
Our wages are too low
Now listen to me you workers
Both you women and men

---

[2] The third of three and a half stanzas from the ballad "Casey Jones" included in this newsreel. The wreck of old "Ninety-seven" is suggestive of the wreck of the nation's economic machine.

Let us win for them the victory
I'm sure it ain't no sin

CARILLON PEALS IN SINGING TOWER

the President declared it was impossible to view the increased advantages for the many without smiling at those who a short time ago expressed so much fear lest our country might come under the control of a few individuals of great wealth

HAPPY CROWDS THRONG CEREMONY

on a tiny island nestling like a green jewel in the lake that mirrors the singing tower, the President today participated in the dedication of a bird sanctuary and its pealing carillon, fulfilling the dream of an immigrant boy[3]

1936

The Camera Eye (49)[1]

walking from Plymouth to North Plymouth through the raw air of Massachusetts Bay at each step a small cold squudge through the sole of one shoe

looking out past the grey framehouses under the robinsegg April sky across the white dories anchored in the bottleclear shallows across the yellow sandbars and the slaty bay ruffling to blue to the eastward.

this is where the immigrants landed the roundheads the sackers of castles the kingkillers haters of oppression this is where they stood in a cluster after landing from the crowded ship that stank of bilge   on the beach that belonged to no one   between the ocean that belonged to no one and the enormous forest that belonged to no one that stretched over the hills where the deertracks were up the green rivervalleys where the redskins grew their tall corn in patches forever into the incredible west

for threehundred years the immigrants toiled into the west
and now today

walking from Plymouth to North Plymouth suddenly round a bend in the road beyond a little pond and yellowtwigged willows hazy with green you see the Cordage   huge sheds and buildings company-

---

[3] Edward W. Bok (1863–1930).
[1] The function of the Camera Eye is to present the subjective view of the author, focused in this instance on Plymouth both as the foundation stone of America and a symbol of freedom from oppression and as a background for the Sacco-Vanzetti case, viewed as a betrayal of freedom.

houses all the same size all grimed the same color a great square chimney long roofs sharp ranked squares and oblongs cutting off the sea the Plymouth Cordage   this is where another immigrant worked hater of oppression who wanted a world unfenced   when they fired him from the cordage he peddled fish[2]   the immigrants in the dark framehouses knew him   bought his fish listened to his talk following his cart around from door to door   you ask them   What was he like?   why are they scared to talk of Bart scared because they knew him scared eyes narrowing black with fright?   a barber the man in the little grocerystore the woman he boarded with   in scared voices they ask Why won't they believe? We knew him We seen him every day Why won't they believe that day we buy the eels?[3]

only the boy isn't scared

pencil scrawls in my notebook the scraps of recollection the broken halfphrases the effort to intersect word with word to dovetail clause with clause to rebuild out of mangled memories unshakably (Oh Pontius Pilate) the truth

the boy walks shyly browneyed beside me to the station talks about how Bart helped him with his homework wants to get ahead why should it hurt him to have known Bart? wants to go to Boston University   we shake hands   don't let them scare you

accustomed the smokingcar   accustomed the jumble of faces rumble cozily homelike towards Boston through the gathering dark how can I make them feel how our fathers our uncles haters of oppression came to this coast   how say   Don't let them scare you how make them feel who are your oppressors America

rebuild the ruined words worn slimy in the mouths of lawyers districtattorneys collegepresidents judges   without the old words the immigrants haters of oppression brought to Plymouth how can you know who are your betrayers America

or that this fishpeddler you have in Charlestown Jail is one of your founders Massachusetts?

1936

Vag

The young man waits at the edge of the concrete, with one hand he grips a rubbed suitcase of phony leather, the other hand almost making a fist, thumb up

that moves in ever so slight an arc when a car slithers past, a

---

[2] Bartolomeo Vanzetti (1888–1927).

[3] The townspeople support Vanzetti's assertion that he had been peddling fish in Plymouth on April 15, 1920, the day of the murder and robbery at the shoe factory in South Braintree, Mass.

truck roars clatters; the wind of cars passing ruffles his hair, slaps grit in his face.

Head swims, hunger has twisted the belly tight,

he has skinned a heel through the torn sock, feet ache in the broken shoes, under the threadbare suit carefully brushed off with the hand, the torn drawers have a crummy feel, the feel of having slept in your clothes; in the nostrils lingers the staleness of discouraged carcasses crowded into a transient camp, the carbolic stench of the jail, on the taut cheeks the shamed flush from the boring eyes of cops and deputies, railroadbulls (they eat three squares a day, they are buttoned into wellmade clothes, they have wives to sleep with, kids to play with after supper, they work for the big men who buy their way, they stick their chests out with the sureness of power behind their backs). Git the hell out, scram. Know what's good for you, you'll make yourself scarce. Gittin' tough, eh? Think you kin take it, eh?

The punch in the jaw, the slam on the head with the nightstick, the wrist grabbed and twisted behind the back, the big knee brought up sharp into the crotch,

the walk out of town with sore feet to stand and wait at the edge of the hissing speeding string of cars where the reek of ether and lead and gas melts into the silent grassy smell of the earth.

Eyes black with want seek out the eyes of the drivers, a hitch, a hundred miles down the road.

Overhead in the blue a plane drones. Eyes follow the silver Douglas that flashes once in the sun and bores its smooth way out of sight into the blue.

(The transcontinental passengers sit pretty, big men with bankaccounts, highlypaid jobs, who are saluted by doormen; telephonegirls say goodmorning to them. Last night after a fine dinner, drinks with friends, they left Newark. Roar of climbing motors slanting up into the inky haze. Lights drop away. An hour staring along a silvery wing at a big lonesome moon hurrying west through curdling scum. Beacons flash in a line across Ohio.

At Cleveland the plane drops banking in a smooth spiral, the string of lights along the lake swings in a circle. Climbing roar of the motors again; slumped in the soft seat drowsing through the flat moonlight night.

Chi. A glimpse of the dipper. Another spiral swoop from cool into hot air thick with dust and the reek of burnt prairies.

Beyond the Mississippi dawn creeps up behind through the murk over the great plains. Puddles of mist go white in the Iowa hills, farms, fences, silos, steel glint from a river. The blinking eyes of the beacons reddening into day. Watercourses vein the eroded hills.

Omaha. Great cumulus clouds, from coppery churning to creamy to silvery white, trail brown skirts of rain over the hot plains. Red and yellow badlands, tiny horned shapes of cattle.

Cheyenne. The cool high air smells of sweetgrass.

The tightbaled clouds to westward burst and scatter in tatters over the strawcolored hills. Indigo mountains jut rimrock. The plane breasts a huge crumbling cloudbank and toboggans over bumpy air across green and crimson slopes into the sunny dazzle of Salt Lake.

The transcontinental passenger thinks contracts, profits, vacationtrips, mighty continent between Atlantic and Pacific, power, wires humming dollars, cities jammed, hills empty, the indiantrail leading into the wagonroad, the macadamed pike, the concrete skyway; trains, planes: history the billiondollar speedup,

and in the bumpy air over the desert ranges towards Las Vegas sickens and vomits into the carton container the steak and mushrooms he ate in New York. No matter, silver in the pocket, greenbacks in the wallet, drafts, certified checks, plenty restaurants in L.A.)

The young man waits on the side of the road; the plane has gone; thumb moves in a small arc when a car tears hissing past. Eyes seek the driver's eyes. A hundred miles down the road. Head swims, belly tightens, wants crawl over his skin like ants:

went to school, books said opportunity, ads promised speed, own your home, shine bigger than your neighbor, the radiocrooner whispered girls, ghosts of platinum girls coaxed from the screen, millions in winnings were chalked up on the boards in the offices, paychecks were for hands willing to work, the cleared desk of an executive with three telephones on it;

waits with swimming head, needs knot the belly, idle hands numb, beside the speeding traffic.

A hundred miles down the road.

1936

John Steinbeck 1902–1968

Born in California's Salinas Valley, the setting of his stories of remembered childhood, John Steinbeck attended Stanford University sporadically
while supporting himself by working at many different jobs. After a brief
trip to New York, where he was disappointed in his hope of establishing
himself as a writer, he returned to California. His first novels were not
especially promising: *Cup of Gold* (1929) is a fictional account of the life of
the buccaneer Sir Henry Morgan. *To a God Unknown* (1933), in which a California farmer engages in pagan fertility rites, introduced a strain of nature
mysticism which was to persist in Steinbeck's writing. *Tortilla Flat* (1935),
his first successful book, is a light-spirited, humorous celebration of the
primitive lives and loves of a group of California *paisanos*.

It was not until he began writing about the migrant workers in California in the 1930's that Steinbeck achieved recognition as a serious novelist. *In Dubious Battle* (1936) is the story of a strike among fruit pickers that
was unscrupulously broken by vigilante tactics. The class struggle that
underlay this conflict is more fully explored in *The Grapes of Wrath* (1939),
Steinbeck's finest work. In this story of dispossessed dustbowl farmers, the
epic westward journey of the migrants to California is a latter-day ironic
reenactment of the earlier trek of the pioneers in their covered wagons.
From Steinbeck's proletarian viewpoint, both movements ended in broken
promises and a betrayal of the American dream. (The same disillusionment
colors Steinbeck's account of the earlier westward movement in the story
"The Leader of the People.") Balancing the author's pessimistic analysis of
the exploitative status quo is an expression, largely through Ma Joad and
Tom and Casey, of faith in the endurance and the cause of the common
people. Although the novel is basically a realistic narrative, Steinbeck
makes use of the device (probably suggested by Dos Passos' *USA*) of
interchapters, like those on the used-car lot and the California land grab, to
supply a broader social and historical context for his story of the Joads and

their companions. Among Steinbeck's other books of the thirties are the novella *Of Mice and Men* (1937), which was converted into a successful play; *The Red Pony* (1937); and *The Long Valley* (1938), a collection of stories that includes "The Leader of the People."

Steinbeck's publications of the 1940's and the postwar years include travel narratives and war reporting as well as fiction. *The Moon Is Down* (1942) is a short novel about the Norwegian resistance to Germany in World War II. In *Cannery Row* (1945) and its sequel, *Sweet Thursday* (1954), Steinbeck attempts with a different set of characters to recapture the debonair primitivism of *Tortilla Flat*, but with little success. In addition to *East of Eden (1952) and The Winter of Our Discontent* (1961), his two most ambitious recent novels, publications of these later years include *The Wayward Bus* (1947), *Burning Bright* (1950), *The Short Reign of Pippin IV* (1957), and *Travels with Charley in Search of America* (1962).

A critical introduction to Steinbeck's work is E. W. Tedlock and C. V. Wicker, eds. *Steinbeck and His Critics, A Record of Twenty-five Years* (Albuquerque, N. M., 1957). Other critiques include H. T. Moore, *The Novels of John Steinbeck* (Chicago, 1939), and Warren French, *John Steinbeck* (New York, 1961). A recent bibliography is Tetsumaro Hayashi, *John Steinbeck: A Concise Bibliography (1930–65)*, (Metuchen, N. J., 1967).

The text of "A Leader of the People" is that of *The Long Valley* (1938). The other selections presented here are from *The Grapes of Wrath* (New York, 1939).

The Leader of the People

On Saturday afternoon Billy Buck, the ranch-hand, raked together the last of the old year's haystack and pitched small forkfuls over the wire fence to a few mildly interested cattle. High in the air small clouds like puffs of cannon smoke were driven eastward by the March wind. The wind could be heard whishing in the brush on the ridge crests, but no breath of it penetrated down into the ranch-cup.

The little boy, Jody, emerged from the house eating a thick piece of buttered bread. He saw Billy working on the last of the haystack. Jody tramped down scuffing his shoes in a way he had been told was destructive to good shoe-leather. A flock of white pigeons flew out of the black cypress tree as Jody passed, and circled the tree and landed again. A half-grown tortoise-shell cat leaped from the bunkhouse porch, galloped on stiff legs across the road, whirled and galloped back again. Jody picked up a stone to help the game along, but he was too late, for the cat was under the porch before the stone could be discharged. He threw the stone into the cypress tree and started the white pigeons on another whirling flight.

Arriving at the used-up haystack, the boy leaned against the barbed wire fence. "Will that be all of it, do you think?" he asked.

The middle-aged ranch-hand stopped his careful raking and stuck his fork into the ground. He took off his black hat and smoothed down his hair. "Nothing left of it that isn't soggy from ground moisture," he said. He replaced his hat and rubbed his dry leathery hands together.

"Ought to be plenty mice," Jody suggested.

"Lousy with them," said Billy. "Just crawling with mice."

"Well, maybe, when you get all through, I could call the dogs and hunt the mice."

"Sure, I guess you could," said Billy Buck. He lifted a forkful of the damp ground-hay and threw it into the air. Instantly three mice leaped out and burrowed frantically under the hay again.

Jody sighed with satisfaction. Those plump, sleek, arrogant mice were doomed. For eight months they had lived and multiplied in the haystack. They had been immune from cats, from traps, from poison and from Jody. They had grown smug in their security, overbearing and fat. Now the time of disaster had come; they would not survive another day.

Billy looked up at the top of the hills that surrounded the ranch. "Maybe you better ask your father before you do it," he suggested.

"Well, where is he? I'll ask him now."

"He rode up to the ridge ranch after dinner. He'll be back pretty soon."

Jody slumped against the fence post. "I don't think he'd care."

As Billy went back to his work he said ominously, "You'd better ask him anyway. You know how he is."

Jody did know. His father, Carl Tiflin, insisted upon giving permission for anything that was done on the ranch, whether it was important or not. Jody sagged farther against the post until he was sitting on the ground. He looked up at the little puffs of wind-driven cloud. "Is it like to rain, Billy?"

"It might. The wind's good for it, but not strong enough."

"Well, I hope it don't rain until after I kill those damn mice." He looked over his shoulder to see whether Billy had noticed the mature profanity. Billy worked on without comment.

Jody turned back and looked at the side-hill where the road from the outside world came down. The hill was washed with lean March sunshine. Silver thistles, blue lupins and a few poppies bloomed among the sage bushes. Halfway up the hill Jody could see Doubletree Mutt, the black dog, digging in a squirrel hole. He paddled for a while and then paused to kick bursts of dirt out between his hind legs, and he dug with an earnestness which belied the knowledge he must have had that no dog had ever caught a squirrel by digging in a hole.

Suddenly, while Jody watched, the black dog stiffened, and backed out of the hole and looked up the hill toward the cleft in the ridge where the road came through. Jody looked up too. For a moment

Carl Tiflin on horseback stood out against the pale sky and then he moved down the road toward the house. He carried something white in his hand.

The boy started to his feet. "He's got a letter," Jody cried. He trotted away toward the ranch house, for the letter would probably be read aloud and he wanted to be there. He reached the house before his father did, and ran in. He heard Carl dismount from his creaking saddle and slap the horse on the side to send it to the barn where Billy would unsaddle it and turn it out.

Jody ran into the kitchen. "We got a letter!" he cried.

His mother looked up from a pan of beans. "Who has?"

"Father has. I saw it in his hand."

Carl strode into the kitchen then, and Jody's mother asked, "Who's the letter from, Carl?"

He frowned quickly. "How did you know there was a letter?"

She nodded her head in the boy's direction. "Big-Britches Jody told me."

Jody was embarrassed.

His father looked down at him contemptuously. "He *is* getting to be a Big-Britches," Carl said. "He's minding everybody's business but his own. Got his big nose into everything."

Mrs. Tiflin relented a little. "Well, he hasn't enough to keep him busy. Who's the letter from?"

Carl still frowned on Jody. "I'll keep him busy if he isn't careful." He held out a sealed letter. "I guess it's from your father."

Mrs. Tiflin took a hairpin from her head and slit open the flap. Her lips pursed judiciously. Jody saw her eyes snap back and forth over the lines. "He says," she translated, "he says he's going to drive out Saturday to stay for a little while. Why, this is Saturday. The letter must have been delayed." She looked at the postmark. "This was mailed day before yesterday. It should have been here yesterday." She looked up questioningly at her husband, and then her face darkened angrily. "Now what have you got that look on you for? He doesn't come often."

Carl turned his eyes away from her anger. He could be stern with her most of the time, but when occasionally her temper arose, he could not combat it.

"What's the matter with you?" she demanded again.

In his explanation there was a tone of apology Jody himself might have used. "It's just that he talks," Carl said lamely. "Just talks."

"Well, what of it? You talk yourself."

"Sure I do. But your father only talks about one thing."

"Indians!" Jody broke in excitedly. "Indians and crossing the plains!"

Carl turned fiercely on him. "You get out, Mr. Big-Britches! Go on, now! Get out!"

Jody went miserably out the back door and closed the screen with elaborate quietness. Under the kitchen window his shamed, downcast eyes fell upon a curiously shaped stone, a stone of such fascination that he squatted down and picked it up and turned it over in his hands.

The voices came clearly to him through the open kitchen window. "Jody's damn well right," he heard his father say. "Just Indians and crossing the plains. I've heard that story about how the horses got driven off about a thousand times. He just goes on and on, and he never changes a word in the things he tells."

When Mrs. Tiflin answered her tone was so changed that Jody, outside the window, looked up from his study of the stone. Her voice had become soft and explanatory. Jody knew how her face would have changed to match the tone. She said quietly, "Look at it this way, Carl. That was the big thing in my father's life. He led a wagon train clear across the plains to the coast, and when it was finished, his life was done. It was a big thing to do, but it didn't last long enough. Look!" she continued, "it's as though he was born to do that, and after he finished it, there wasn't anything more for him to do but think about it and talk about it. If there'd been any farther west to go, he'd have gone. He's told me so himself. But at last there was the ocean. He lives right by the ocean where he had to stop."

She had caught Carl, caught him and entangled him in her soft tone.

"I've seen him," he agreed quietly. "He goes down and stares off west over the ocean." His voice sharpened a little. "And then he goes up to the Horseshoe Club in Pacific Grove, and he tells people how the Indians drove off the horses."

She tried to catch him again. "Well, it's everything to him. You might be patient with him and pretend to listen."

Carl turned impatiently away. "Well, if it gets too bad, I can always go down to the bunkhouse and sit with Billy," he said irritably. He walked through the house and slammed the front door after him.

Jody ran to his chores. He dumped the grain to the chickens without chasing any of them. He gathered the eggs from the nests. He trotted into the house with the wood and interlaced it so carefully in the wood-box that two armloads seemed to fill it to overflowing.

His mother had finished the beans by now. She stirred up the fire and brushed off the stove-top with a turkey wing. Jody peered cautiously at her to see whether any rancor toward him remained. "Is he coming today?" Jody asked.

"That's what his letter said."

"Maybe I better walk up the road to meet him."

Mrs. Tiflin clanged the stove-lid shut. "That would be nice," she said. "He'd probably like to be met."

"I guess I'll just do it then."

Outside, Jody whistled shrilly to the dogs. "Come on up the hill," he commanded. The two dogs waved their tails and ran ahead. Along the roadside the sage had tender new tips. Jody tore off some pieces and rubbed them on his hands until the air was filled with the sharp wild smell. With a rush the dogs leaped from the road and yapped into the brush after a rabbit. That was the last Jody saw of them, for when they failed to catch the rabbit, they went back home.

Jody plodded on up the hill toward the ridge top. When he reached the little cleft where the road came through, the afternoon wind struck him and blew up his hair and ruffled his shirt. He looked down on the little hills and ridges below and then out at the huge green Salinas Valley. He could see the white town of Salinas far out in the flat and the flash of its windows under the waning sun. Directly below him, in an oak tree, a crow congress had convened. The tree was black with crows all cawing at once.

Then Jody's eyes followed the wagon road down from the ridge where he stood, and lost it behind a hill, and picked it up again on the other side. On that distant stretch he saw a cart slowly pulled by a bay horse. It disappeared behind the hill. Jody sat down on the ground and watched the place where the cart would reappear again. The wind sang on the hilltops and the puff-ball clouds hurried eastward.

Then the cart came into sight and stopped. A man dressed in black dismounted from the seat and walked to the horse's head. Although it was so far away, Jody knew he had unhooked the check-rein, for the horse's head dropped forward. The horse moved on, and the man walked slowly up the hill beside it. Jody gave a glad cry and ran down the road toward them. The squirrels bumped along off the road, and a road-runner flirted its tail and raced over the edge of the hill and sailed out like a glider.

Jody tried to leap into the middle of his shadow at every step. A stone rolled under his foot and he went down. Around a little bend he raced, and there, a short distance ahead, were his grandfather and the cart. The boy dropped from his unseemly running and approached at a dignified walk.

The horse plodded stumble-footedly up the hill and the old man walked beside it. In the lowering sun their giant shadows flickered darkly behind them. The grandfather was dressed in a black broadcloth suit and he wore kid congress gaiters and a black tie on a short, hard collar. He carried his black slouch hat in his hand. His white beard was cropped close and his white eyebrows overhung his eyes like mustaches. The blue eyes were sternly merry. About the whole face and figure there was a granite dignity, so that every motion seemed an impossible thing. Once at rest, it seemed the old man would be stone, would never move again. His steps were slow and certain. Once made, no step could ever be retraced; once headed in a direction, the path would never bend nor the pace increase nor slow.

When Jody appeared around the bend, Grandfather waved his hat slowly in welcome, and he called, "Why, Jody! Come down to meet me, have you?"

Jody sidled near and turned and matched his step to the old man's step and stiffened his body and dragged his heels a little. "Yes, sir," he said. "We got your letter only today."

"Should have been here yesterday," said Grandfather. "It certainly should. How are all the folks?"

"They're fine, sir." He hesitated and then suggested shyly, "Would you like to come on a mouse hunt tomorrow, sir?"

"Mouse hunt, Jody?" Grandfather chuckled. "Have the people of this generation come down to hunting mice? They aren't very strong, the new people, but I hardly thought mice would be game for them."

"No, sir. It's just play. The haystack's gone. I'm going to drive out the mice to the dogs. And you can watch, or even beat the hay a little."

The stern, merry eyes turned down on him. "I see. You don't eat them, then. You haven't come to that yet."

Jody explained, "The dogs eat them, sir. It wouldn't be much like hunting Indians, I guess."

"No, not much—but then later, when the troops were hunting Indians and shooting children and burning teepees, it wasn't much different from your mouse hunt."

They topped the rise and started down into the ranch-cup, and they lost the sun from their shoulders. "You've grown," Grandfather said. "Nearly an inch, I should say."

"More," Jody boasted. "Where they mark me on the door, I'm up more than an inch since Thanksgiving even."

Grandfather's rich throaty voice said, "Maybe you're getting too much water and turning to pith and stalk. Wait until you head out, and then we'll see."

Jody looked quickly into the old man's face to see whether his feelings should be hurt, but there was no will to injure, no punishing nor putting-in-your-place light in the keen blue eyes. "We might kill a pig," Jody suggested.

"Oh, no! I couldn't let you do that. You're just humoring me. It isn't the time and you know it."

"You know Riley, the big boar, sir?"

"Yes. I remember Riley well."

"Well, Riley ate a hole into that same haystack, and it fell down on him and smothered him."

"Pigs do that when they can," said Grandfather.

"Riley was a nice pig, for a boar, sir. I rode him sometimes, and he didn't mind."

A door slammed at the house below them, and they saw Jody's mother standing on the porch waving her apron in welcome. And they saw Carl Tiflin walking up from the barn to be at the house for the arrival.

The sun had disappeared from the hills by now. The blue smoke from the house chimney hung in flat layers in the purpling ranch-cup. The puff-ball clouds, dropped by the falling wind, hung listlessly in the sky.

Billy Buck came out of the bunkhouse and flung a wash basin of soapy water on the ground. He had been shaving in mid-week, for Billy held Grandfather in reverence, and Grandfather said that Billy was one of the few men of the new generation who had not gone soft. Although Billy was in middle age, Grandfather considered him a boy. Now Billy was hurrying toward the house too.

When Jody and Grandfather arrived, the three were waiting for them in front of the yard gate.

Carl said, "Hello, sir. We've been looking for you."

Mrs. Tiflin kissed Grandfather on the side of his beard, and stood still while his big hand patted her shoulder. Billy shook hands solemnly, grinning under his straw moustache. "I'll put up your horse," said Billy, and he led the rig away.

Grandfather watched him go, and then, turning back to the group, he said as he had said a hundred times before, "There's a good boy. I knew his father, old Mule-tail Buck. I never knew why they called him Mule-tail except he packed mules."

Mrs. Tiflin turned and led the way into the house. "How long are you going to stay, Father? Your letter didn't say."

"Well, I don't know. I thought I'd stay about two weeks. But I never stay as long as I think I'm going to."

In a short while they were sitting at the white oilcloth table eating their supper. The lamp with the tin reflector hung over the table. Outside the dining-room windows the big moths battered softly against the glass.

Grandfather cut his steak into tiny pieces and chewed slowly. "I'm hungry," he said. "Driving out here got my appetite up. It's like when we were crossing. We all got so hungry every night we could hardly wait to let the meat get done. I could eat about five pounds of buffalo meat every night."

"It's moving around does it," said Billy. "My father was a government packer. I helped him when I was a kid. Just the two of us could about clean up a deer's ham."

"I knew your father, Billy," said Grandfather. "A fine man he was. They called him Mule-tail Buck. I don't know why except he packed mules."

"That was it," Billy agreed. "He packed mules."

Grandfather put down his knife and fork and looked around the table. "I remember one time we ran out of meat—" His voice dropped to a curious low sing-song, drooped into a tonal groove the story had worn for itself. "There was no buffalo, no antelope, not even rabbits. The hunters couldn't even shoot a coyote. That was the time for the leader to be on the watch. I was the leader, and I kept my eyes open. Know why? Well, just the minute the people began to get hungry they'd start slaughtering the team oxen. Do you believe that? I've heard of parties that just ate up their draft cattle. Started from the middle and worked toward the ends. Finally they'd eat the lead pair, and then the wheelers. The leader of a party had to keep them from doing that."

In some manner a big moth got into the room and circled the hanging kerosene lamp. Billy got up and tried to clap it between his hands. Carl struck with a cupped palm and caught the moth and broke it. He walked to the window and dropped it out.

"As I was saying," Grandfather began again, but Carl interrupted him. "You'd better eat some more meat. All the rest of us are ready for our pudding."

Jody saw a flash of anger in his mother's eyes. Grandfather picked up his knife and fork. "I'm pretty hungry, all right," he said. "I'll tell you about that later."

When supper was over, when the family and Billy Buck sat in front of the fireplace in the other room, Jody anxiously watched Grandfather. He saw the signs he knew. The bearded head leaned forward; the eyes lost their sternness and looked wonderingly into the fire; the big lean fingers laced themselves on the black knees. "I wonder," he began, "I just wonder whether I ever told you how those thieving Piutes drove off thirty-five of our horses."

"I think you did," Carl interrupted. "Wasn't it just before you went up into the Tahoe country?"

Grandfather turned quickly toward his son-in-law. "That's right. I guess I must have told you that story."

"Lots of times," Carl said cruelly, and he avoided his wife's eyes. But he felt the angry eyes on him, and he said, "'Course I'd like to hear it again."

Grandfather looked back at the fire. His fingers unlaced and laced again. Jody knew how he felt, how his insides were collapsed and empty. Hadn't Jody been called a Big-Britches that very afternoon? He arose to heroism and opened himself to the term Big-Britches again. "Tell about Indians," he said softly.

Grandfather's eyes grew stern again. "Boys always want to hear about Indians. It was a job for men, but boys want to hear about it.

Well, let's see. Did I ever tell you how I wanted each wagon to carry a long iron plate?"

Everyone but Jody remained silent. Jody said, "No. You didn't."

"Well, when the Indians attacked, we always put the wagons in a circle and fought from between the wheels. I thought that if every wagon carried a long plate with rifle holes, the men could stand the plates on the outside of the wheels when the wagons were in the circle and they would be protected. It would save lives and that would make up for the extra weight of the iron. But of course the party wouldn't do it. No party had done it before and they couldn't see why they should go to the expense. They lived to regret it, too."

Jody looked at his mother, and knew from her expression that she was not listening at all. Carl picked at a callus on his thumb and Billy Buck watched a spider crawling up the wall.

Grandfather's tone dropped into its narrative groove again. Jody knew in advance exactly what words would fall. The story droned on, speeded up for the attack, grew sad over the wounds, struck a dirge at the burials on the great plains. Jody sat quietly watching Grandfather. The stern blue eyes were detached. He looked as though he were not very interested in the story himself.

When it was finished, when the pause had been politely respected as the frontier of the story, Billy Buck stood up and stretched and hitched his trousers. "I guess I'll turn in," he said. Then he faced Grandfather. "I've got an old powder horn and a cap and ball pistol down to the bunkhouse. Did I ever show them to you?"

Grandfather nodded slowly. "Yes, I think you did, Billy. Reminds me of a pistol I had when I was leading the people across." Billy stood politely until the little story was done, and then he said, "Good night," and went out of the house.

Carl Tiflin tried to turn the conversation then. "How's the country between here and Monterey? I've heard it's pretty dry."

"It is dry," said Grandfather. "There's not a drop of water in the Laguna Seca. But it's a long pull from '87. The whole country was powder then, and in '61 I believe all the coyotes starved to death. We had fifteen inches of rain this year."

"Yes, but it all came too early. We could do with some now." Carl's eye fell on Jody. "Hadn't you better be getting to bed?"

Jody stood up obediently. "Can I kill the mice in the old haystack, sir?"

"Mice? Oh! Sure, kill them all off. Billy said there isn't any good hay left."

Jody exchanged a secret and satisfying look with Grandfather. "I'll kill every one tomorrow," he promised.

Jody lay in his bed and thought of the impossible world of Indians and buffaloes, a world that had ceased to be forever. He wished he could have been living in the heroic time, but he knew he was not of heroic timber. No one living now, save possibly Billy Buck, was worthy to do the things that had been done. A race of giants had lived then, fearless men, men of a staunchness unknown in this day. Jody thought of the wide plains and of the wagons moving across like centipedes. He thought of Grandfather on a huge white horse, marshaling the people. Across his mind marched the great phantoms, and they marched off the earth and they were gone.

He came back to the ranch for a moment, then. He heard the dull rushing sound that space and silence make. He heard one of the dogs, out in the doghouse, scratching a flea and bumping his elbow against the floor with every stroke. Then the wind arose again and the black cypress groaned and Jody went to sleep.

He was up half an hour before the triangle sounded for breakfast. His mother was rattling the stove to make the flames roar when Jody went through the kitchen. "You're up early," she said. "Where are you going?"

"Out to get a good stick. We're going to kill the mice today."

"Who is 'we'?"

"Why, Grandfather and I."

"So you've got him in it. You always like to have someone in with you in case there's blame to share."

"I'll be right back," said Jody. "I just want to have a good stick ready for after breakfast."

He closed the screen door after him and went out into the cool blue morning. The birds were noisy in the dawn and the ranch cats came down from the hill like blunt snakes. They had been hunting gophers in the dark, and although the four cats were full of gopher meat, they sat in a semi-circle at the back door and mewed piteously for milk. Doubletree Mutt and Smasher moved sniffing along the edge of the brush, performing the duty with rigid ceremony, but when Jody whistled, their heads jerked up and their tails waved. They plunged down to him, wriggling their skins and yawning. Jody patted their heads seriously, and moved on to the weathered scrap pile. He selected an old broom handle and a short piece of inch-square scrap wood. From his pocket he took a shoelace and tied the ends of the sticks loosely together to make a flail. He whistled his new weapon through the air and struck the ground experimentally, while the dogs leaped aside and whined with apprehension.

Jody turned and started down past the house toward the old haystack ground to look over the field of slaughter, but Billy Buck, sitting patiently on the back steps, called to him, "You better come back. It's only a couple of minutes till breakfast."

Jody changed his course and moved toward the house. He leaned his flail against the steps. "That's to drive the mice out," he said. "I'll bet they're fat. I'll bet they don't know what's going to happen to them today."

"No, nor you either," Billy remarked philosophically, "nor me, nor anyone."

Jody was staggered by this thought. He knew it was true. His imagination twitched away from the mouse hunt. Then his mother came out on the back porch and struck the triangle, and all thoughts fell in a heap.

Grandfather hadn't appeared at the table when they sat down. Billy nodded at his empty chair. "He's all right? He isn't sick?"

"He takes a long time to dress," said Mrs. Tiflin. "He combs his whiskers and rubs up his shoes and brushes his clothes."

Carl scattered sugar on his mush. "A man that's led a wagon train across the plains has got to be pretty careful how he dresses."

Mrs. Tiflin turned on him. "Don't do that, Carl! Please don't!" There was more of threat than of request in her tone. And the threat irritated Carl.

"Well, how many times do I have to listen to the story of the iron plates, and the thirty-five horses? That time's done. Why can't he forget it, now it's done?" He grew angrier while he talked, and his voice rose. "Why does he have to tell them over and over? He came across the plains. All right! Now it's finished. Nobody wants to hear about it over and over."

The door into the kitchen closed softly. The four at the table sat frozen. Carl laid his mush spoon on the table and touched his chin with his fingers.

Then the kitchen door opened and Grandfather walked in. His mouth smiled tightly and his eyes were squinted. "Good morning," he said, and he sat down and looked at his mush dish.

Carl could not leave it there. "Did—did you hear what I said?"

Grandfather jerked a little nod.

"I don't know what got into me, sir. I didn't mean it. I was just being funny."

Jody glanced in shame at his mother, and he saw that she was looking at Carl, and that she wasn't breathing. It was an awful thing that he was doing. He was tearing himself to pieces to talk like that. It was a terrible thing to him to retract a word, but to retract it in shame was infinitely worse.

Grandfather looked sidewise. "I'm trying to get right side up," he said gently. "I'm not being mad. I don't mind what you said, but it might be true, and I would mind that."

"It isn't true," said Carl. "I'm not feeling well this morning. I'm sorry I said it."

"Don't be sorry, Carl. An old man doesn't see things sometimes.

Maybe you're right. The crossing is finished. Maybe it should be forgotten, now it's done."

Carl got up from the table. "I've had enough to eat. I'm going to
work. Take your time, Billy!" He walked quickly out of the dining-
room. Billy gulped the rest of his food and followed soon after. But
Jody could not leave his chair.

"Won't you tell any more stories?" Jody asked.

"Why, sure I'll tell them, but only when — I'm sure people want to
hear them."

"I like to hear them, sir."

"Oh! Of course you do, but you're a little boy. It was a job for
men, but only little boys like to hear about it."

Jody got up from his place. "I'll wait outside for you, sir. I've got
a good stick for those mice."

He waited by the gate until the old man came out on the porch.
"Let's go down and kill the mice now," Jody called.

"I think I'll just sit in the sun, Jody. You go kill the mice."

"You can use my stick if you like."

"No, I'll just sit here a while."

Jody turned disconsolately away, and walked down toward the
old haystack. He tried to whip up his enthusiasm with thoughts of the
fat juicy mice. He beat the ground with his flail. The dogs coaxed and
whined about him, but he could not go. Back at the house he could see
Grandfather sitting on the porch, looking small and thin and black.

Jody gave up and went to sit on the steps at the old man's feet.

"Back already? Did you kill the mice?"

"No, sir. I'll kill them some other day."

The morning flies buzzed close to the ground and the ants dashed
about in front of the steps. The heavy smell of sage slipped down the
hill. The porch boards grew warm in the sunshine.

Jody hardly knew when Grandfather started to talk. "I shouldn't
stay here, feeling the way I do." He examined his strong old hands. "I
feel as though the crossing wasn't worth doing." His eyes moved up the
side-hill and stopped on a motionless hawk perched on a dead limb. "I
tell those old stories, but they're not what I want to tell. I only know
how I want people to feel when I tell them.

"It wasn't Indians that were important, nor adventures, nor even
getting out here. It was a whole bunch of people made into one big
crawling beast. And I was the head. It was westering and westering.
Every man wanted something for himself, but the big beast that was all
of them wanted only westering. I was the leader, but if I hadn't been
there, someone else would have been the head. The thing had to have a
head.

"Under the little bushes the shadows were black at white noonday. When we saw the mountains at last, we cried—all of us. But it wasn't getting here that mattered, it was movement and westering.

"We carried life out here and set it down the way those ants carry eggs. And I was the leader. The westering was as big as God, and the slow steps that made the movement piled up and piled up until the continent was crossed.

"Then we came down to the sea, and it was done." He stopped and wiped his eyes until the rims were red. "That's what I should be telling instead of stories."

When Jody spoke, Grandfather started and looked down at him. "Maybe I could lead the people some day," Jody said.

The old man smiled. "There's no place to go. There's the ocean to stop you. There's a line of old men along the shore hating the ocean because it stopped them."

"In boats I might, sir."

"No place to go, Jody. Every place is taken. But that's not the worst—no, not the worst. Westering has died out of the people. Westering isn't a hunger any more. It's all done. Your father is right. It is finished." He laced his fingers on his knee and looked at them.

Jody felt very sad. "If you'd like a glass of lemonade I could make it for you."

Grandfather was about to refuse, and then he saw Jody's face. "That would be nice," he said. "Yes, it would be nice to drink a lemonade."

Jody ran into the kitchen where his mother was wiping the last of the breakfast dishes. "Can I have a lemon to make a lemonade for Grandfather?"

His mother mimicked—"And another lemon to make a lemonade for you."

"No, ma'am. I don't want one."

"Jody! You're sick!" Then she stopped suddenly. "Take a lemon out of the cooler," she said softly. "Here, I'll reach the squeezer down to you."

1938

The Used Car Lot [1]

In the towns, on the edges of the towns, in fields, in vacant lots, the used-car yards, the wreckers' yards, the garages with blazoned signs—Used Cars, Good Used Cars. Cheap transportation, three trailers. '27 Ford, clean. Checked cars, guaranteed cars. Free radio. Car with 100 gallons of gas free. Come in and look. Used Cars. No overhead.

A lot and a house large enough for a desk and chair and a blue

---

[1] Chapter 7, *The Grapes of Wrath* (New York, 1939). The present title is the editors'.

book. Sheaf of contracts, dog-eared, held with paper clips, and a neat pile of unused contracts. Pen—keep it full, keep it working. A sale's been lost 'cause a pen didn't work.

Those sons-of-bitches over there ain't buying. Every yard gets 'em. They're lookers. Spend all their time looking. Don't want to buy no cars; take up your time. Don't give a damn for your time. Over there, them two people—no, with the kids. Get 'em in a car. Start 'em at two hundred and work down. They look good for one and a quarter. Get 'em rolling. Get 'em out in a jalopy. Sock it to 'em! They took our time.

Owners with rolled-up sleeves. Salesmen, neat, deadly, small intent eyes watching for weaknesses.

Watch the woman's face. If the woman likes it we can screw the old man. Start' em on that Cad.' Then you can work 'em down to that '26 Buick. 'F you start on the Buick, they'll go for a Ford. Roll up your sleeves an' get to work. This ain't gonna last forever. Show 'em that Nash while I get the slow leak pumped up on that '25 Dodge. I'll give you a Hymie when I'm ready.

What you want is transportation, ain't it? No baloney for you. Sure the upholstery is shot. Seat cushions ain't turning no wheels over.

Cars lined up, noses forward, rusty noses, flat tires. Parked close together.

Like to get in to see that one? Sure, no trouble. I'll pull her out of the line.

Get 'em under obligation. Make 'em take up your time. Don't let 'em forget they're takin' your time. People are nice, mostly. They hate to put you out. Make 'em put you out, an' then sock it to 'em.

Cars lined up, Model T's, high and snotty, creaking wheel, worn bands. Buicks, Nashes, De Sotos.

Yes, sir. '22 Dodge. Best goddamn car Dodge ever made. Never wear out. Low compression. High compression got lots a sap for a while, but the metal ain't made that'll hold it for long. Plymouths, Rocknes, Stars.

Jesus, where'd that Apperson come from, the Ark? And a Chalmers and a Chandler—ain't made 'em for years. We ain't sellin' cars—rolling junk. Goddamn it, I got to get jalopies. I don't want nothing for more'n twenty-five, thirty bucks. Sell 'em for fifty, seventy-five. That's a good profit. Christ, what cut do you make on a new car? Get jalopies. I can sell 'em fast as I get 'em. Nothing over two hundred fifty. Jim, corral that old bastard on the sidewalk. Don't know his ass from a hole in the ground. Try him on that Apperson. Say, where is that Apperson? Sold? If we don't get some jalopies we got nothing to sell.

Flags, red and white, white and blue—all along the curb. Used Cars. Good Used Cars.

Today's bargain—up on the platform. Never sell it. Makes folks come in, though. If we sold that bargain at that price we'd hardly make a dime. Tell 'em it's jus' sold. Take out that yard battery before you make delivery. Put in that dumb cell. Christ, what they want for six bits? Roll up your sleeves — pitch in. This ain't gonna last. If I had enough jalopies I'd retire in six months.

Listen, Jim, I heard that Chevvy's rear end. Sounds like bustin' bottles. Squirt in a couple quarts of sawdust. Put some in the gears, too. We got to move that lemon for thirty-five dollars. Bastard cheated me on that one. I offer ten an' he jerks me to fifteen, an' then the son-of-a-bitch took the tools out. God Almighty! I wisht I had five hundred jalopies. This ain't gonna last. He don't like the tires? Tell 'im they got ten thousand in 'em, knock off a buck an' a half.

Piles of rusty ruins against the fence, rows of wrecks in back, fenders, grease-black wrecks, blocks lying on the ground and a pig weed growing up through the cylinders. Brake rods, exhausts, piled like snakes. Grease, gasoline.

See if you can't find a spark plug that ain't cracked. Christ, if I had fifty trailers at under a hundred I'd clean up. What the hell is he kickin' about? We sell 'em, but we don't push 'em home for him. That's good! Don't push 'em home. Get that one in the Monthly, I bet. You don't think he's a prospect? Well, kick 'im out. We got too much to do to bother with a guy that can't make up his mind. Take the right front tire off the Graham. Turn that mended side down. The rest looks swell. Got tread an' everything.

Sure! There's fifty thousan' in that ol' heap yet. Keep plenty oil in. So long. Good luck.

Lookin' for a car? What did you have in mind? See anything attracts you? I'm dry. How about a little snort a good stuff? Come on, while your wife's lookin' at that La Salle. You don't want no La Salle. Bearings shot. Uses too much oil. Got a Lincoln '24. There's a car. Run forever. Make her into a truck.

Hot sun on rusted metal. Oil on the ground. People are wandering in, bewildered, needing a car.

Wipe your feet. Don't lean on that car, it's dirty. How do you buy a car? What does it cost? Watch the children, now. I wonder how much for this one? We'll ask. It don't cost money to ask. We can ask, can't we? Can't pay a nickel over seventy-five, or there won't be enough to get to California.

God, if I could only get a hundred jalopies. I don't care if they run or not.

Tires, used, bruised tires, stacked in tall cylinders; tubes, red, gray, hanging like sausages.

Tire patch? Radiator cleaner? Spark intensifier? Drop this little pill in your gas tank and get ten extra miles to the gallon. Just paint it on — you got a new surface for fifty cents. Wipers, fan belts, gaskets?

Maybe it's the valve. Get a new valve stem. What can you lose for a nickel?

All right, Joe. You soften 'em up an' shoot 'em in here. I'll close 'em, I'll deal 'em or I'll kill 'em. Don't send in no bums. I want deals.

Yes, sir, step in. You got a buy there. Yes, sir! At eighty bucks you got a buy.

I can't go no higher than fifty. The fella outside says fifty.

Fifty. Fifty? He's nuts. Paid seventy-eight fifty for that little number. Joe, you crazy fool, you tryin' to bust us? Have to can that guy. I might take sixty. Now look here, mister, I ain't got all day. I'm a business man but I ain't out to stick nobody. Got anything to trade?

Got a pair of mules I'll trade.

Mules! Hey, Joe, hear this? This guy wants to trade mules. Didn't nobody tell you this is the machine age? They don't use mules for nothing but glue no more.

Fine big mules — five and seven years old. Maybe we better look around.

Look around! You come in when we're busy, an' take up our time an' then walk out! Joe, did you know you was talkin' to pikers?

I ain't a piker. I got to get a car. We're goin' to California. I got to get a car.

Well, I'm a sucker. Joe says I'm a sucker. Says if I don't quit givin' my shirt away I'll starve to death. Tell you what I'll do — I can get five bucks apiece for them mules for dog feed.

I wouldn't want them to go for dog feed.

Well, maybe I can get ten or seven maybe. Tell you what we'll do. We'll take your mules for twenty. Wagon goes with 'em, don't it? An' you put up fifty, an' you can sign a contract to send the rest at ten dollars a month.

But you said eighty.

Didn't you never hear about carrying charges and insurance? That just boosts her a little. You'll get her all paid up in four-five months. Sign your name right here. We'll take care of ever'thing.

Well, I don't know —

Now, look here, I'm givin' you my shirt, an' you took all this time. I might a made three sales while I been talkin' to you. I'm disgusted. Yeah, sign right there. All right, sir. Joe, fill up the tank for this gentleman. We'll give him gas.

Jesus, Joe, that was a hot one! What'd we give for that jalopy? Thirty bucks — thirty-five wasn't it? I got that team, an' if I can't get seventy-five for that team, I ain't a business man. An' I got fifty cash an' a contract for forty more. Oh, I know they're not all honest, but it'll surprise you how many kick through with the rest. One guy come through with a hundred two years after I wrote him off. I bet you this guy sends the money. Christ, if I could only get five hundred jalopies!

Roll up your sleeves, Joe. Go out an' soften 'em, an' send 'em in to me. You get twenty on that last deal. You ain't doing bad.

Limp flags in the afternoon sun. Today's Bargain. '29 Ford pickup, runs good.

What do you want for fifty bucks — a Zephyr?

Horsehair curling out of seat cushions, fenders battered and hammered back. Bumpers torn loose and hanging. Fancy Ford roadster with little colored lights at fender guide, at radiator cap, and three behind. Mud aprons, and a big die on the gear-shift lever. Pretty girl on tire cover, painted in color and named Cora. Afternoon sun on the dusty windshields.

Christ, I ain't had time to go out an' eat! Joe, send a kid for a hamburger.

Spattering roar of ancient engines.

There's a dumb-bunny lookin' at that Chrysler. Find out if he got any jack in his jeans. Some a these farm boys is sneaky. Soften 'em up an' roll 'em in to me, Joe. You're doin' good.

Sure, we sold it. Guarantee? We guaranteed it to be an automobile. We didn't guarantee to wet-nurse it. Now listen here, you — you bought a car, an' now you're squawkin'. I don't give a damn if you don't make payments. We ain't got your paper. We turn that over to the finance company. They'll get after you, not us. We don't hold no paper. Yeah? Well you jus' get tough an' I'll call a cop. No, we did not switch the tires. Run 'im outa here, Joe. He bought a car, an' now he ain't satisfied. How'd you think if I bought a steak an' et half an' try to bring it back? We're runnin' a business, not a charity ward. Can ya imagine that guy, Joe? Say — looka there! Got a Elk's tooth! Run over there. Let 'em glance over that '36 Pontiac. Yeah.

Square noses, round noses, rusty noses, shovel noses, and the long curves of streamlines, and the flat surfaces before streamlining. Bargains Today. Old monsters with deep upholstery — you can cut her into a truck easy. Two-wheel trailers, axles rusty in the hard afternoon sun. Used Cars. Good Used Cars. Clean, runs good. Don't pump oil.

Christ, look at 'er! Somebody took nice care of 'er.

Cadillacs, La Salles, Buicks, Plymouths, Packards, Chevies, Fords, Pontiacs. Row on row, headlights glinting in the afternoon sun. Good Used Cars.

Soften 'em up, Joe. Jesus, I wisht I had a thousand jalopies! Get 'em ready to deal, an' I'll close 'em.

Goin' to California? Here's jus' what you need. Looks shot, but they's thousan's of miles in her.

Lined up side by side. Good Used Cars. Bargains. Clean, runs good.

1939

The Land Grab[1]

Once California belonged to Mexico and its land to Mexicans; and a horde of tattered feverish Americans poured in. And such was their hunger for land that they took the land — stole Sutter's land, Guerrero's land,[2] took the grants and broke them up and growled and quarreled over them, those frantic hungry men; and they guarded with guns the land they had stolen. They put up houses and barns, they turned the earth and planted crops. And these things were possession, and possession was ownership.

The Mexicans were weak and fled. They could not resist, because they wanted nothing in the world as frantically as the Americans wanted land.

Then, with time, the squatters were no longer squatters, but owners; and their children grew up and had children on the land. And the hunger was gone from them, the feral hunger, the gnawing, tearing hunger for land, for water and earth and the good sky over it, for the green thrusting grass, for the swelling roots. They had these things so completely that they did not know about them any more. They had no more the stomach-tearing lust for a rich acre and a shining blade to plow it, for seed and a windmill beating its wings in the air. They arose in the dark no more to hear the sleepy birds' first chittering, and the morning wind around the house while they waited for the first light to go out to the dear acres. These things were lost, and crops were reckoned in dollars, and land was valued by principal plus interest, and crops were bought and sold before they were planted. Then crop failure, drought, and flood were no longer little deaths within life, but simple losses of money. And all their love was thinned with money, and all their fierceness dribbled away in interest until they were no longer farmers at all, but little shopkeepers of crops, little manufacturers who must sell before they can make. Then those farmers who were not good shopkeepers lost their land to good shopkeepers. No matter how clever, how loving a man might be with earth and growing things, he could not survive if he were not also a good shopkeeper. And as time went on, the business men had the farms, and the farms grew larger, but there were fewer of them.

Now farming became industry, and the owners followed Rome, although they did not know it. They imported slaves, although they did not call them slaves: Chinese, Japanese, Mexicans, Filipinos. They live

---

[1] Chapter 19 of *The Grapes of Wrath;* the present title is the editors'.
[2] John Augustus Sutter (1803 – 1880), the founder of the colony of Nueva Helvetia at the junction of the American and Sacramento rivers. After the discovery of gold on his land on January 24, 1848, it was ruined by squatters, and Sutter ended in bankruptcy. Francisco Guerrero, Mexican Sub-prefect in Yerba Buena before the United States annexation in 1848, vainly attempted to discourage the settlement and purchase of land by "foreigners."

on rice and beans, the business men said. They don't need much. They wouldn't know what to do with good wages. Why, look how they live. Why, look what they eat. And if they get funny—deport them.

And all the time the farms grew larger and the owners fewer. And there were pitifully few farmers on the land any more. And the imported serfs were beaten and frightened and starved until some went home again, and some grew fierce and were killed or driven from the country. And the farms grew larger and the owners fewer.

And the crops changed. Fruit trees took the place of grain fields, and vegetables to feed the world spread out on the bottoms: lettuce, cauliflower, artichokes, potatoes—stoop crops. A man may stand to use a scythe, a plow, a pitchfork; but he must crawl like a bug between the rows of lettuce, he must bend his back and pull his long bag between the cotton rows, he must go on his knees like a penitent across a cauliflower patch.

And it came about that owners no longer worked on their farms. They farmed on paper; and they forgot the land, the smell, the feel of it, and remembered only that they owned it, remembered only what they gained and lost by it. And some of the farms grew so large that one man could not even conceive of them any more, so large that it took batteries of bookkeepers to keep track of interest and gain and loss; chemists to test the soil, to replenish; straw bosses to see that the stooping men were moving along the rows as swiftly as the material of their bodies could stand. Then such a farmer really became a storekeeper, and kept a store. He paid the men, and sold them food, and took the money back. And after a while he did not pay the men at all, and saved bookkeeping. These farms gave food on credit. A man might work and feed himself; and when the work was done, he might find that he owed money to the company. And the owners not only did not work the farms any more, many of them had never seen the farms they owned.

And then the dispossessed were drawn west—from Kansas, Oklahoma, Texas, New Mexico; from Nevada and Arkansas families, tribes, dusted out, tractored out. Carloads, caravans, homeless and hungry; twenty thousand and fifty thousand and a hundred thousand and two hundred thousand. They streamed over the mountains, hungry and restless—restless as ants, scurrying to find work to do—to lift, to push, to pull, to pick, to cut—anything, any burden to bear, for food. The kids are hungry. We got no place to live. Like ants scurrying for work, for food, and most of all for land.

We ain't foreign. Seven generations back Americans, and beyond that Irish, Scotch, English, German. One of our folks in the Revolution, an' they was lots of our folks in the Civil War—both sides. Americans.

They were hungry, and they were fierce. And they had hoped to find a home, and they found only hatred. Okies—the owners hated them because the owners knew they were soft and the Okies strong, that they were fed and the Okies hungry; and perhaps the owners had heard from their grandfathers how easy it is to steal land from a soft man if you are fierce and hungry and armed. The owners hated them. And in the towns, the storekeepers hated them because they had no money to spend. There is no shorter path to a storekeeper's contempt, and all his admirations are exactly opposite. The town men, little bankers, hated Okies because there was nothing to gain from them. They had nothing. And the laboring people hated Okies because a hungry man must work, and if he must work, if he has to work, the wage payer automatically gives him less for his work; and then no one can get more.

And the dispossessed, the migrants, flowed into California, two hundred and fifty thousand, and three hundred thousand. Behind them new tractors were going on the land and the tenants were being forced off. And new waves were on the way, new waves of the dispossessed and the homeless, hardened, intent, and dangerous.

And while the Californians wanted many things, accumulation, social success, amusement, luxury, and a curious banking security, the new barbarians wanted only two things—land and food; and to them' the two were one. And whereas the wants of the Californians were nebulous and undefined, the wants of the Okies were beside the roads, lying there to be seen and coveted: the good fields with water to be dug for, the good green fields, earth to crumble experimentally in the hand, grass to smell, oaten stalks to chew until the sharp sweetness was in the throat. A man might look at a fallow field and know, and see in his mind that his own bending back and his own straining arms would bring the cabbages into the light, and the golden eating corn, the turnips and carrots.

And a homeless hungry man, driving the roads with his wife beside him and his thin children in the back seat, could look at the fallow fields which might produce food but not profit, and that man could know how a fallow field is a sin and the unused land a crime against the thin children. And such a man drove along the roads and knew temptation at every field, and knew the lust to take these fields and make them grow strength for his children and a little comfort for his wife. The temptation was before him always. The fields goaded him, and the company ditches with good water flowing were a goad to him.

And in the south he saw the golden oranges hanging on the trees, the little golden oranges on the dark green trees; and guards with shotguns patrolling the lines so a man might not pick an orange for a thin child, oranges to be dumped if the price was low.

He drove his old car into a town. He scoured the farms for work. Where can we sleep the night?

Well, there's Hooverville[3] on the edge of the river. There's a

---

[3] A temporary shantytown of the displaced and unemployed, named after the Depression presidency (1929–1933) of Herbert Hoover (1874–1964).

whole raft of Okies there.

He drove his old car to Hooverville. He never asked again, for there was a Hooverville on the edge of every town.

The rag town lay close to water; and the houses were tents, and weed-thatched enclosures, paper houses, a great junk pile. The man drove his family in and became a citizen of Hooverville—always they were called Hooverville. The man put up his own tent as near to water as he could get; or if he had no tent, he went to the city dump and brought back cartons and built a house of corrugated paper. And when the rains came the house melted and washed away. He settled in Hooverville and he scoured the countryside for work, and the little money he had went for gasoline to look for work. In the evening the men gathered and talked together. Squatting on their hams they talked of the land they had seen.

There's thirty thousan' acres, out west of here. Layin' there. Jesus, what I could do with that, with five acres of that! Why, hell, I'd have ever'thing to eat.

Notice one thing? They ain't no vegetables nor chickens nor pigs at the farms. They raise one thing—cotton, say, or peaches, or lettuce. 'Nother place'll be all chickens. They buy the stuff they could raise in the dooryard.

Jesus, what I could do with a couple pigs!

Well, it ain't yourn, an' it ain't gonna be yourn.

What we gonna do? The kids can't grow up this way.

In the camps the word would come whispering, There's work at Shafter. And the cars would be loaded in the night, the highways crowded—a gold rush for work. At Shafter the people would pile up, five times too many to do the work. A gold rush for work. They stole away in the night, frantic for work. And along the roads lay the temptations, the fields that could bear food.

That's owned. That ain't our'n.

Well, maybe we could get a little piece of her. Maybe—a little piece. Right down there—a patch. Jimson weed now. Christ, I could git enough potatoes off'n that little patch to feed my whole family!

It ain't our'n. It got to have Jimson weeds.

Now and then a man tried; crept on the land and cleared a piece, trying like a thief to steal a little richness from the earth. Secret gardens hidden in the weeds. A package of carrot seeds and a few turnips. Planted potato skins, crept out in the evening secretly to hoe in the stolen earth.

Leave the weeds around the edge—then nobody can see what we're a-doin'. Leave some weeds, big tall ones, in the middle.

Secret gardening in the evenings, and water carried in a rusty can.

And then one day a deputy sheriff: Well, what you think you're doin'?

I ain't doin' no harm.

I had my eye on you. This ain't your land. You're trespassing.

The land ain't plowed, an' I ain't hurtin' it none.

You goddamned squatters. Pretty soon you'd think you owned it. You'd be sore as hell. Think you owned it. Get off now.

Well, hell.

And the little green carrot tops were kicked off and the turnip greens trampled. And then the Jimson weed moved back in. But the cop was right. A crop raised — why, that makes ownership. Land hoed and the carrots eaten — a man might fight for land he's taken food from. Get him off quick! He'll think he owns it. He might even die fighting for the little plot among the Jimson weeds.

Did ya see his face when we kicked them turnips out? Why, he'd kill a fella soon's he'd look at him. We got to keep these here people down or they'll take the country. They'll take the country.

Outlanders, foreigners.

Sure, they talk the same language, but they ain't the same. Look how they live. Think any of us folks'd live like that? Hell, no!

In the evenings, squatting and talking. And an excited man: Whyn't twenty of us take a piece of lan'? We got guns. Take it an' say, "Put us off if you can." Whyn't we do that?

They'd jus' shoot us like rats.

Well, which'd you ruther be, dead or here? Under groun' or in a house all made of gunny sacks? Which'd you ruther for your kids, dead now or dead in two years with what they call malnutrition? Know what we et all week? Biled nettles an' fried dough! Know where we got the flour for the dough? Swep' the floor of a boxcar.

Talking in the camps, and the deputies, fat-assed men with guns slung on fat hips, swaggering through the camps: Give 'em somepin to think about. Got to keep 'em in line or Christ only knows what they'll do! Why, Jesus, they're as dangerous as niggers in the South! If they ever get together there ain't nothin' that'll stop 'em.

Quote: In Lawrenceville a deputy sheriff evicted a squatter, and the squatter resisted, making it necessary for the officer to use force. The eleven-year-old son of the squatter shot and killed the deputy with a .22 rifle.

Rattlesnakes! Don't take chances with 'em, an' if they argue, shoot first. If a kid'll kill a cop, what'll the men do? Thing is, get tougher'n they are. Treat 'em rough. Scare 'em.

What if they won't scare? What if they stand up and take it and shoot back? These men were armed when they were children. A gun is an extension of themselves. What if they won't scare? What if some time an army of them marches on the land as the Lombards did in Italy, as the Germans did on Gaul and the Turks did on Byzantium? They were land-hungry, ill-armed hordes too, and the legions could not stop them. Slaughter and terror did not stop them. How can you frighten a man whose hunger is not only in his own cramped stomach but in the wretched bellies of his children? You can't scare him — he has known a fear beyond every other.

In Hooverville the men talking: Grampa took his lan' from the Injuns.

Now, this ain't right. We're a-talkin' here. This here you're talkin' about is stealin'. I ain't no thief.

No? You stole a bottle of milk from a porch night before last. An' you stole some copper wire and sold it for a piece of meat.

Yeah, but the kids was hungry.

It's stealin', though.

Know how the Fairfiel' ranch was got? I'll tell ya. It was all gov'ment lan', an' could be took up.⁴ Ol' Fairfiel', he went into San Francisco to the bars, an' he got him three hunderd stew bums. Them bums took up the lan'. Fairfiel' kep' 'em in food an' whisky, an' then when they'd proved the lan', ol' Fairfiel' took it from 'em. He used to say the lan' cost him a pint of rotgut an acre. Would you say that was stealin'?

Well, it wasn't right, but he never went to jail for it.

No, he never went to jail for it. An' the fella that put a boat in a wagon an' made his report like it was all under water 'cause he went in a boat — he never went to jail neither. An' the fellas that bribed congressmen and the legislatures never went to jail neither.

All over the State, jabbering in the Hoovervilles.

And then the raids — the swoop of armed deputies on the squatters' camps. Get out. Department of Health orders. This camp is a menace to health.

Where we gonna go?

That's none of our business. We got orders to get you out of here. In half an hour we set fire to the camp.

They's typhoid down the line. You want ta spread it all over?

We got orders to get you out of here. Now get! In half an hour we burn the camp.

In half an hour the smoke of paper houses, of weed-thatched huts, rising to the sky, and the people in their cars rolling over the highways, looking for another Hooverville.

And in Kansas and Arkansas, in Oklahoma and Texas and New Mexico, the tractors moved in and pushed the tenants out.

Three hundred thousand in California and more coming. And in California the roads full of frantic people running like ants to pull, to push, to lift, to work. For every manload to lift, five pairs of arms

---

⁴ Under the Homestead Law (1862), which provided a quarter-section of public land (160 acres) to a man who would live on the land five years and improve it.

extended to lift it; for every stomachful of food available, five mouths open.

And the great owners, who must lose their land in an upheaval, the great owners with access to history, with eyes to read history and to know the great fact: when property accumulates in too few hands it is taken away. And that companion fact: when a majority of the people are hungry and cold they will take by force what they need. And the little screaming fact that sounds through all history: repression works only to strengthen and knit the repressed. The great owners ignored the three cries of history. The land fell into fewer hands, the number of the dispossessed increased, and every effort of the great owners was directed at repression. The money was spent for arms, for gas to protect the great holdings, and spies were sent to catch the murmuring of revolt so that it might be stamped out. The changing economy was ignored, plans for the change ignored; and only means to destroy revolt were considered, while the causes of revolt went on.

The tractors which throw men out of work, the belt lines which carry loads, the machines which produce, all were increased; and more and more families scampered on the highways, looking for crumbs from the great holdings, lusting after the land beside the roads. The great owners formed associations for protection and they met to discuss ways to intimidate, to kill, to gas. And always they were in fear of a principle—three hundred thousand—if they ever move under a leader—the end. Three hundred thousand, hungry and miserable; if they ever know themselves, the land will be theirs and all the gas, all the rifles in the world won't stop them. And the great owners, who had become through their holdings both more and less than men, ran to their destruction, and used every means that in the long run would destroy them. Every little means, every violence, every raid on a Hooverville, every deputy swaggering through a ragged camp put off the day a little and cemented the inevitability of the day.

The men squatted on their hams, sharp-faced men, lean from hunger and hard from resisting it, sullen eyes and hard jaws. And the rich land was around them.

D'ja hear about the kid in that fourth tent down?

No, I jus' come in.

Well, that kid's been a-cryin' in his sleep an' a-rollin' in his sleep. Them folks thought he got worms. So they give him a blaster, an' he died. It was what they call black-tongue the kid had. Comes from not gettin' good things to eat.

Poor little fella.

Yeah, but them foks can't bury him. Got to go to the county stone orchard.

And hands went into pockets and little coins came out. In front of the tent a little heap of silver grew. And the family found it there.

Our people are good people; our people are kind people. Pray God some day kind people won't all be poor. Pray God some day a kid can eat.

And the associations of owners knew that some day the praying would stop.

And there's the end.

1939

Dance Night at Weedpatch[1]

On Saturday morning the wash tubs were crowded. The women washed dresses, pink ginghams and flowered cottons, and they hung them in the sun and stretched the cloth to smooth it. When afternoon came the whole camp quickened and the people grew excited. The children caught the fever and were more noisy than usual. About mid-afternoon child bathing began, and as each child was caught, subdued, and washed, the noise on the playground gradually subsided. Before five, the children were scrubbed and warned about getting dirty again; and they walked about, stiff in clean clothes, miserable with carefulness.

At the big open-air dance platform a committee was busy. Every bit of electric wire had been requisitioned. The city dump had been visited for wire, every tool box had contributed friction tape. And now the patched, spliced wire was strung out to the dance floor, with bottle necks as insulators. This night the floor would be lighted for the first time. By six o'clock the men were back from work or from looking for work, and a new wave of bathing started. By seven, dinners were over, men had on their best clothes: freshly washed overalls, clean blue shirts, sometimes the decent blacks. The girls were ready in their print dresses, stretched and clean, their hair braided and ribboned. The worried women watched the families and cleaned up the evening dishes. On the platform the string band practiced, surrounded by a double wall of children. The people were intent and excited.

In the tent of Ezra Huston, chairman, the Central Committee of five men went into meeting. Huston, a tall spare man, wind-blackened, with eyes like little blades, spoke to his committee, one man from each sanitary unit.

"It's goddamn lucky we got the word they was gonna try to bust up the dance!" he said.

The tubby little representative from Unit Three spoke up. "I think we oughta squash the hell out of 'em, an' show 'em."

"No," said Huston. "That's what they want. No, sir. If they can

---

[1] Chapter 24 of *The Grapes of Wrath*; the present title is the editors'.

git a fight goin', then they can run in the cops an' say we ain't orderly. They tried it before—other places." He turned to the sad dark boy from Unit Two. "Got the fellas together to go roun' the fences an' see nobody sneaks in?"

The sad boy nodded. "Yeah! Twelve. Tol' 'em not to hit nobody. Jes' push 'em out ag'in."

Huston said, "Will you go out an' find Willie Eaton? He's chairman a the entertainment, ain't he?"

"Yeah."

"Well, tell 'im we wanta see 'im."

The boy went out, and he returned in a moment with a stringy Texas man. Willie Eaton had a long fragile jaw and dust-colored hair. His arms and legs were long and loose, and he had the gray sunburned eyes of the Panhandle. He stood in the tent, grinning, and his hands pivoted restlessly on his wrists.

Huston said, "You heard about tonight?"

Willie grinned. "Yeah!"

"Did anything 'bout it?"

"Yeah!"

"Tell what you done."

Willie Eaton grinned happily. "Well, sir, ordinary ent'tainment committee is five. I got twenty more—all good strong boys. They're a-gonna be a-dancin' an' a-keepin' their eyes open an' their ears open. First sign—any talk or argament, they close in tight. Worked her out purty nice. Can't even see nothing. Kinda move out, an' the fella will go out with 'em."

"Tell 'em they ain't to hurt the fellas."

Willie laughed gleefully. "I tol' 'em," he said.

"Well, tell 'em so they know."

"They know. Got five men out to the gate lookin' over the folks that comes in. Try to spot 'em 'fore they git started."

Huston stood up. His steel-colored eyes were stern. "Now you look here, Willie. We don't want them fellas hurt. They's gonna be deputies out by the front gate. If you blood 'em up, why—them deputies'll git you."

"Got that there figgered out," said Willie. "Take 'em out the back way, into the fiel'. Some a the boys'll see they git on their way."

"Well, it soun's awright," Huston said worriedly. "But don't you let nothing happen, Willie. You're responsible. Don' you hurt them fellas. Don' you use no stick nor no knife or arn, or nothing like that."

"No, sir," said Willie. "We won't mark 'em."

Huston was suspicious. "I wisht I knowed I could trus' you, Willie. If you got to sock 'em, sock 'em where they won't bleed."

"Yes, sir!" said Willie.

"You sure of the fellas you picked?"

"Yes, sir."

"Awright. An' if she gits outa han', I'll be in the right-han' corner, this way on the dance floor."

Willie saluted in mockery and went out.

Huston said, "I dunno. I jes' hope Willie's boys don't kill nobody. What the hell the deputies want to hurt the camp for? Why can't they let us be?"

The sad boy from Unit Two said, "I lived out at Sunlan' Lan' an' Cattle Company's place. Honest to God, they got a cop for ever' ten people. Got one water faucet for 'bout two hundred people."

The tubby man said, "Jesus, God, Jeremy. You ain't got to tell me. I was there. They got a block of shacks—thirty-five of 'em in a row, an' fifteen deep. An' they got ten crappers for the whole shebang. An', Christ, you could smell 'em a mile. One of them deputies give me the lowdown. We was settin' around', an' he says. 'Them goddamn gov'ment camps,' he says. 'Give people hot water, an' they gonna want hot water. Give 'em flush toilets, an' they gonna want 'em.' He says. 'You give them goddamn Okies stuff like that an' they'll want 'em.' An' he says, 'They hol' red meetin's in them gov'ment camps. All figgerin' how to git on relief,' he says."

Huston asked, "Didn' nobody sock him?"

"No. They was a little fella, an' he says, 'What you mean, relief?'

"'I mean relief—what us taxpayers puts in an' you goddamn Okies takes out.'

"'We pay sales tax an' gas tax an' tobacco tax,' this little guy says. An' he says, 'Farmers get four cents a cotton poun' from the gov'ment—ain't that relief?' An' he says, 'Railroads an' shippin' companies draws subsidies—ain't that relief?'

"'They're doin' stuff got to be done,' this deputy says.

"'Well,' the little guy says, 'how'd your goddamn crops get picked if it wasn't for us?'" The tubby man looked around.

"What'd the deputy say?" Huston asked.

"Well, the deputy got mad. An' he says, 'You goddamn reds is all the time stirrin' up trouble,' he says. 'You better come along with me.' So he takes this little guy in, an' they give him sixty days in jail for vagrancy."

"How'd they do that if he had a job?" asked Timothy Wallace.

The tubby man laughed. "You know better'n that," he said. "You know a vagrant is anybody a cop don't like. An' that's why they hate this here camp. No cops can get in. This here's United States, not California."

Huston sighed. "Wisht we could stay here. Got to be goin' 'fore long. I like this here. Folks gits along nice; an', God Awmighty, why can't they let us do it 'stead of keepin' us miserable an' puttin' us in jail?

I swear to God they gonna push us into fightin' if they don't quit aworryin' us." Then he calmed his voice. "We jes' got to keep peaceful," he reminded himself. "The committee got no right to fly off'n the handle."

The tubby man from Unit Three said, "Anybody that thinks this committee got all cheese an' crackers ought to jes' try her. They was a fight in my unit today—women. Got to callin' names, an' then got to throwin' garbage. Ladies' Committee couldn' handle it, an' they come to me. Want me to bring the fight in this here committee. I tol' 'em they got to handle women trouble theirselves. This here committee ain't gonna mess with no garbage fights."

Huston nodded. "You done good," he said.

And now the dusk was falling, and as the darkness deepened the practicing of the string band seemed to grow louder. The lights flashed on and two men inspected the patched wire to the dance floor. The children crowded thickly about the musicians. A boy with a guitar sang the "Down Home Blues," chording delicately for himself, and on his second chorus three harmonicas and a fiddle joined him. From the tents the people streamed toward the platform, men in their clean blue denim and women in their ginghams. They came near to the platform and then stood quietly waiting, their faces bright and intent under the light.

Around the reservation there was a high wire fence, and along the fence, at intervals of fifty feet, the guards sat in the grass and waited.

Now the cars of the guests began to arrive, small farmers and their families, migrants from other camps. And as each guest came through the gate he mentioned the name of the camper who had invited him.

The string band took a reel tune up and played loudly, for they were not practicing any more. In front of their tents the Jesus-lovers sat and watched, their faces hard and contemptuous. They did not speak to one another, they watched for sin, and their faces condemned the whole proceeding.

At the Joad tent Ruthie and Winfield had bolted what little dinner they had, and then they started for the platform. Ma called them back, held up their faces with a hand under each chin, and looked into their nostrils, pulled their ears and looked inside, and sent them to the sanitary unit to wash their hands once more. They dodged around the back of the building and bolted for the platform, to stand among the children, close-packed about the band.

Al finished his dinner and spent half an hour shaving with Tom's razor. Al had a tight-fitting wool suit and a striped shirt, and he bathed and washed and combed his straight hair back. And when the washroom was vacant for a moment, he smiled engagingly at himself in the mirror, and he turned and tried to see himself in profile when he smiled. He slipped his purple arm-bands on and put on his tight coat. And he rubbed up his yellow shoes with a piece of toilet paper. A late bather came in, and Al hurried out and walked recklessly toward the platform, his eye peeled for girls. Near the dance floor he saw a pretty blond girl sitting in front of a tent. He sidled near and threw open his coat to show his shirt.

"Gonna dance tonight?" he asked.

The girl looked away and did not answer.

"Can't a fella pass a word with you? How 'bout you an me dancin'?" And he said nonchalantly, "I can waltz."

The girl raised her eyes shyly, and she said, "That ain't nothin' — anybody can waltz."

"Not like me," said Al. The music surged, and he tapped one foot in time. "Come on," he said.

A very fat woman poked her head out of the tent and scowled at him. "You git along," she said fiercely. "This here girl's spoke for. She's a-gonna be married, an' her man's a-comin' for her."

Al winked rakishly at the girl, and he tripped on, striking his feet to the music and swaying his shoulders and swinging his arms. And the girl looked after him intently.

Pa put down his plate and stood up. "Come on, John," he said; and he explained to Ma, "We're a-gonna talk to some fellas about gettin' work." And Pa and Uncle John walked toward the manager's house.

Tom worked a piece of store bread into the stew gravy on his plate and ate the bread. He handed his plate to Ma, and she put it in the bucket of hot water and washed it and handed it to Rose of Sharon to wipe. "Ain't you goin' to the dance?" Ma asked.

"Sure," said Tom. "I'm on a committee. We're gonna entertain some fellas."

"Already on a committee?" Ma said. "I guess it's 'cause you got work."

Rose of Sharon turned to put the dish away. Tom pointed at her. "My God, she's a-gettin' big," he said.

Rose of Sharon blushed and took another dish from Ma. "Sure she is," Ma said.

"An' she's gettin' prettier," said Tom.

The girl blushed more deeply and hung her head. "You stop it," she said, softly.

"'Course she is," said Ma. "Girl with a baby always gets prettier."

Tom laughed. "If she keeps a-swellin' like this, she gonna need a wheelbarra to carry it."

"Now you stop," Rose of Sharon said, and she went inside the tent, out of sight.

Ma chuckled, "You shouldn' ought to worry her."

"She likes it," said Tom.

"I know she likes it, but it worries her, too. And she's a-mournin' for Connie."

"Well, she might's well give him up. He's prob'ly studyin' to be President of the United States by now."

"Don't worry her," Ma said. "She ain't got no easy row to hoe."

Willie Eaton moved near, and he grinned and said, "You Tom Joad?"

"Yeah."

"Well, I'm Chairman the Entertainment Committee. We gonna need you. Fella tol' me 'bout you."

"Sure, I'll play with you," said Tom. "This here's Ma."

"Howdy," said Willie.

"Glad to meet ya."

Willie said, "Gonna put you on the gate to start, an' then on the floor. Want ya to look over the guys when they come in, an' try to spot 'em. You'll be with another fella. Then later I want ya to dance an' watch."

"Yeah! I can do that awright," said Tom.

Ma said apprehensively, "They ain't no trouble?"

"No, ma'am," Willie said. "They ain't gonna be no trouble."

"None at all," said Tom. "Well, I'll come 'long. See you at the dance, Ma." The two young men walked quickly away toward the main gate.

Ma piled the washed dishes on a box. "Come on out," she called, and when there was no answer, "Rosasharn, you come out."

The girl stepped from the tent, and she went on with the dish-wiping.

"Tom was on'y jollyin' ya."

"I know. I didn't mind; on'y I hate to have folks look at me."

"Ain't no way to he'p that. Folks gonna look. But it makes folks happy to see a girl in a fambly way—makes folks sort of giggly an' happy. Ain't you a-goin' to the dance?"

"I was—but I don' know. I wisht Connie was here." Her voice rose. "Ma, I wisht he was here. I can't hardly stan' it."

Ma looked closely at her. "I know," she said. "But, Rosa-sharn—don't shame your folks."

"I don' aim to, Ma."

"Well, don't you shame us. We got too much on us now, without no shame."

The girl's lip quivered. "I—I ain' goin' to the dance. I couldn'—Ma—he'p me!" She sat down and buried her head in her arms.

Ma wiped her hands on the dish towel and she squatted down in front of her daughter, and she put her two hands on Rose of Sharon's hair. "You're a good girl," she said. "You always was a good girl. I'll

take care a you. Don't you fret." She put an interest in her tone.
"Know what you an' me's gonna do? We're a-goin' to that dance, an'
we're a-gonna set there an' watch. If anybody says to come dance
— why, I'll say you ain't strong enough. I'll say you're poorly. An' you
can hear the music an' all like that."

Rose of Sharon raised her head. "You won't let me dance?"

"No, I won't."

"An' don' let nobody touch me."

"No, I won't."

The girl sighed. She said desperately, "I don' know what I'm
a-gonna do, Ma. I jus' don' know. I don' know."

Ma patted her knee. "Look," she said. "Look here at me. I'm
a-gonna tell ya. In a little while it ain't gonna be so bad. In a little while.
An' that's true. Now come on. We'll go get washed up, an' we'll put on
our nice dress an' we'll set by the dance." She led Rose of Sharon
toward the sanitary unit.

Pa and Uncle John squatted with a group of men by the porch of
the office. "We nearly got work today," Pa said. "We was jus' a few
minutes late. They awready got two fellas. An', well, sir, it was a funny
thing. They's a straw boss there, an' he says, 'We jus' got some two-bit
men. 'Course we could use twenty-cent men. We can use a lot a
twenty-cent men. You go to your camp an' say we'll put a lot a fellas on
for twenty cents.'"

The squatting men moved nervously. A broad-shouldered man,
his face completely in the shadow of a black hat, spatted his knee with
his palm. "I know it, goddamn it!" he cried. "An' they'll git men.
They'll git hungry men. You can't feed your fam'ly on twenty cents an
hour, but you'll take anything. They got you goin' an' comin'. They jes'
auction a job off. Jesus Christ, pretty soon they're gonna make us pay
to work."

"We would of took her," Pa said. "We ain't had no job. We sure
would a took her, but they was them guys in there, an' the way they
looked, we was scairt to take her."

Black Hat said, "Get crazy thinkin'! I been workin' for a fella, an'
he can't pick his crop. Cost more jes' to pick her than he can git for her,
an' he don' know what to do."

"Seems to me—" Pa stopped. The circle was silent for him.
"Well—I jus' thought, if a fella had a acre. Well, my woman she could
raise a little truck an' a couple pigs an' some chickens. An' us men
could get out an' find work, an' then go back. Kids could maybe go to
school. Never seen sech schools as out here."

"Our kids ain't happy in them schools," Black Hat said.

"Why not? They're pretty nice, them schools."

"Well, a raggedy kid with no shoes, an' them other kids with
socks on, an' nice pants, an' them a-yellin' 'Okie.' My boy went to

school. Had a fight evr' day. Done good, too. Tough little bastard.
Ever' day he got to fight. Come home with his clothes tore an' his nose
bloody. An' his ma'd whale him. Made her stop that. No need
ever'body beatin' the hell outa him, poor little fella. Jesus! He give
some a them kids a goin'-over, though—them nice-pants sons-a-bitches.
I dunno. I dunno."

Pa demanded, "Well, what the hell am I gonna do? We're outa
money. One of my boys got a short job, but that won't feed us. I'm
a-gonna go an' take twenty cents. I got to."

Black Hat raised his head, and his bristled chin showed in the
light, and his stringy neck where the whiskers lay flat like fur. "Yeah!"
he said bitterly. "You'll do that. An' I'm a two-bit man. You'll take my
job for twenty cents. An' then I'll git hungry an' I'll take my job back
for fifteen. Yeah! You go right on an' do her."

"Well, what the hell can I do?" Pa demanded. "I can't starve so's
you can get two bits."

Black Hat dipped his head again, and his chin went into the
shadow. "I dunno," he said. "I jes' dunno. It's bad enough to work
twelve hours a day an' come out jes' a little bit hungry, but we got to
figure all a time, too. My kid ain't gettin' enough to eat. I can't think all
the time, goddamn it! It drives a man crazy." The circle of men shifted
their feet nervously.

Tom stood at the gate and watched the people coming in to the
dance. A floodlight shone down into their faces. Willie Eaton said, "Jes'
keep your eyes open. I'm sendin' Jule Vitela over. He's half Cherokee.
Nice fella. Keep your eyes open. An' see if you can pick out the ones."

"O.K.," said Tom. He watched the farm families come in, the
girls with braided hair and the boys polished for the dance. Jule came
and stood beside him.

"I'm with you," he said.

Tom looked at the hawk nose and the high brown cheek bones
and the slender receding chin. "They says you're half Injun. You look
all Injun to me."

"No," said Jule. "Jes' half. Wisht I was a full-blood. I'd have my
lan' on the reservation. Them full-bloods got it pretty nice, some of
'em."

"Look a them people," Tom said.

The guests were moving in through the gateway, families from the
farms, migrants from the ditch camps. Children straining to be free and
quiet parents holding them back.

Jule said, "These here dances done funny things. Our people got
nothing, but jes' because they can ast their frien's to come here to the
dance, sets 'em up an' makes 'em proud. An' the folks respects 'em
'count of these here dances. Fella got a little place where I was a-workin'.

He come to a dance here. I ast him myself, an' he come. Says we got the only decent dance in the country, where a man can take his girls an' his wife. Hey! Look."

Three young men were coming through the gate — young working men in jeans. They walked close together. The guard at the gate questioned them, and they answered and passed through.

"Look at 'em careful," Jule said. He moved to the guard. "Who ast them three?" he asked.

"Fella named Jackson, Unit Four."

Jule came back to Tom. "I think them's our fellas."

"How ya know?"

"I dunno how. Jes' got a feelin'. They're kinda scared. Foller 'em an' tell Willie to look 'em over, an' tell Willie to check with Jackson, Unit Four. Get him to see if they're all right. I'll stay here."

Tom strolled after the three young men. They moved toward the dance floor and took their positions quietly on the edge of the crowd. Tom saw Willie near the band and signaled him.

"What cha want?" Willie asked.

"Them three — see — there?"

"Yeah."

"They say a fella name' Jackson, Unit Four, ast 'em."

Willie craned his neck and saw Huston and called him over. "Them three fellas," he said. "We better get Jackson, Unit Four, an' see if he ast 'em."

Huston turned on his heel and walked away; and in a few moments he was back with a lean and bony Kansan. "This here's Jackson," Huston said. "Look, Jackson, see them three young fellas — ?"

"Yeah."

"Well, did you ast 'em?"

"No."

"Ever see 'em before?"

Jackson peered at them. "Sure. Worked at Gregorio's with 'em."

"So they knowed your name."

"Sure. I worked right beside 'em."

"Awright," Huston said. "Don't you go near 'em. We ain't gonna th'ow 'em out if they're nice. Thanks, Mr. Jackson."

"Good work," he said to Tom. "I guess them's the fellas."

"Jule picked 'em out," said Tom.

"Hell, no wonder," said Willie. "His Injun blood smelled 'em. Well, I'll point 'em out to the boys."

A sixteen-year-old boy came running through the crowd. He stopped, panting, in front of Huston. "Mista Huston," he said. "I been like you said. They's a car with six men parked down by the euc'lyptus trees, an' they's one with four men up that north-side road. I ast 'em for a match. They got guns. I seen 'em."

Huston's eyes grew hard and cruel. "Willie," he said, "you sure you got ever'thing ready?"

Willie grinned happily. "Sure have, Mr. Huston. Ain't gonna be no trouble."

"Well, don't hurt 'em. 'Member now. If you kin, quiet an' nice, I kinda like to see 'em. Be in my tent."

"I'll see what we kin do," said Willie.

Dancing had not formally started, but now Willie climbed onto the platform. "Choose up your squares," he called. The music stopped. Boys and girls, young men and women, ran about until eight squares were ready on the big floor, ready and waiting. The girls held their hands in front of them and squirmed their fingers. The boys tapped their feet restlessly. Around the floor the old folks sat, smiling slightly, holding the children back from the floor. And in the distance the Jesus-lovers sat with hard condemning faces and watched the sin.

Ma and Rose of Sharon sat on a bench and watched. And as each boy asked Rose of Sharon as partner, Ma said, "No, she ain't well." And Rose of Sharon blushed and her eyes were bright.

The caller stepped to the middle of the floor and held up his hands. "All ready? Then let her go!"

The music snarled out "Chicken Reel," shrill and clear, fiddle skirling, harmonicas nasal and sharp, and the guitars booming on the bass strings. The caller named the turns, the squares moved. And they danced forward and back, hands 'round, swing your lady. The caller, in a frenzy, tapped his feet, strutted back and forth, went through the figures as he called them.

"Swing your ladies an' a dol ce do. Join han's roun' an' away we go." The music rose and fell, and the moving shoes beating in time on the platform sounded like drums. "Swing to the right an' a swing to lef'; break, now — break — back to — back," the caller sang the high vibrant monotone. Now the girls' hair lost the careful combing. Now perspiration stood out on the foreheads of the boys. Now the experts showed the tricky inter-steps. And the old people on the edge of the floor took up the rhythm, patted their hands softly, and tapped their feet; and they smiled gently and then caught one another's eyes and nodded.

Ma leaned her head close to Rose of Sharon's ear. "Maybe you wouldn' think it, but your Pa was as nice a dancer as I ever seen, when he was young." And Ma smiled. "Makes me think of ol' times," she said. And on the faces of the watchers the smiles were of old times.

"Up near Muskogee twenty years ago, they was a blin' man with a fiddle ——"

"I seen a fella oncet could slap his heels four times in one jump."

"Swedes up in Dakota — know what they do sometimes? Put pepper on the floor. Gits up the ladies' skirts an' makes 'em purty lively — lively as a filly in season. Swedes do that sometimes."

In the distance, the Jesus-lovers watched their restive children. "Look on sin," they said. "Them folks is ridin' to hell on a poker. It's a shame the godly got to see it." And their children were silent and nervous.

"One more roun' an' then a little res'," the caller chanted. "Hit her hard, 'cause we're gonna stop soon." And the girls were damp and flushed, and they danced with open mouths and serious reverent faces, and the boys flung back their long hair and pranced, pointed their toes, and clicked their heels. In and out the squares moved, crossing, backing, whirling, and the music shrilled.

Then suddenly it stopped. The dancers stood still, panting with fatigue. And the children broke from restraint, dashed on the floor, chased one another madly, ran, slid, stole caps, and pulled hair. The dancers sat down, fanning themselves with their hands. The members of the band got up and stretched themselves and sat down again. And the guitar players worked softly over their strings.

Now Willie called, "Choose again for another square, if you can." The dancers scrambled to their feet and new dancers plunged forward for partners. Tom stood near the three young men. He saw them force their way through, out on the floor, toward one of the forming squares. He waved his hand at Willie, and Willie spoke to the fiddler. The fiddler squawked his bow across the strings. Twenty young men lounged slowly across the floor. The three reached the square. And one of them said, "I'll dance with this here."

A blond boy looked up in astonishment. "She's my partner."

"Listen, you little son-of-a-bitch——"

Off in the darkness a shrill whistle sounded. The three were walled in now. And each one felt the grip of hands. And then the wall of men moved slowly off the platform.

Willie yelped, "Le's go!" The music shrilled out, the caller intoned the figures, the feet thudded on the platform.

A touring car drove to the entrance. The driver called, "Open up. We hear you got a riot."

The guard kept his position. "We got no riot. Listen to that music. Who are you?"

"Deputy sheriffs."

"Got a warrant?"

"We don't need a warrant if there's a riot."

"Well, we got no riots here," said the gate guard.

The men in the car listened to the music and the sound of the caller, and then the car pulled slowly away and parked in a crossroad and waited.

In the moving squad each of the three young men was pinioned, and a hand was over each mouth. When they reached the darkness the group opened up.

Tom said, "That sure was did nice." He held both arms of his victim from behind.

Willie ran over to them from the dance floor. "Nice work," he said. "On'y need six now. Huston wants to see these here fellers."

Huston himself emerged from the darkness. "These the ones?"

"Sure," said Jule. "Went right up an' started it. But they didn' even swing once."

"Let's look at 'em." The prisoners were swung around to face him. Their heads were down. Huston put a flashlight beam in each sullen face. "What did you wanta do it for?" he asked. There was no answer. "Who the hell tol' you to do it?"

"Goddarn it, we didn' do nothing. We was jes' gonna dance."

"No, you wasn't," Jule said. "You was gonna sock that kid."

Tom said, "Mr. Huston, jus' when these here fellas moved in, somebody give a whistle."

"Yeah, I know! The cops come right to the gate." He turned back. "We ain't gonna hurt you. Now who tol' you to come bus' up our dance?" He waited for a reply. "You're our own folks," Huston said sadly. "You belong with us. How'd you happen to come? We know all about it," he added.

"Well, goddamn it, a fella got to eat."

"Well, who sent you? Who paid you to come?"

"We ain't been paid."

"An' you ain't gonna be. No fight, no pay. Ain't that right?"

One of the pinioned men said. "Do what you want. We ain't gonna tell nothing."

Huston's head sank down for a moment, and then he said softly, "O.K. Don't tell. But looka here. Don't knife your own folks. We're tryin' to get along, havin' fun an' keepin' order. Don't tear all that down. Jes' think about it. You're jes' harmin' yourself.

"Awright, boys, put 'em over the back fence. An' don't hurt 'em. They don't know what they're doin'."

The squad moved slowly toward the rear of the camp, and Huston looked after them.

Jule said, "Le's jes' take one good kick at 'em."

"No, you don't!" Willie cried. "I said we wouldn'."

"Jes' one nice little kick," Jule pleaded. "Jes' loft 'em over the fence."

"No, sir," Willie insisted.

"Listen, you," he said, "we're lettin' you off this time. But you take back the word. If'n ever this here happens again, we'll jes' natcherally kick the hell outa whoever comes; we'll bust ever' bone in their body. Now you tell your boys that. Huston says you're our kinda folks—maybe. I'd hate to think it."

They neared the fence. Two of the seated guards stood up and moved over. "Got some fellas goin' home early," said Willie. The three men climbed over the fence and disappeared into the darkness.

And the squad moved quickly back toward the dance floor. And the music of "Ol' Dan Tucker" skirled and whined from the string band.

Over near the office the men still squatted and talked, and the shrill music came to them.

Pa said, "They's change a-comin'. I don' know what. Maybe we won't live to see her. But she's a-comin'. They's a res'less feelin'. Fella can't figger nothin' out, he's so nervous."

And Black Hat lifted his head up again, and the light fell on his bristly whiskers. He gathered some little rocks from the ground and shot them like marbles, with his thumb. "I don' know. She's a-comin' awright, like you say. Fella tol' me what happened in Akron, Ohio. Rubber companies. They got mountain people in 'cause they'd work cheap. An' these here mountain people up an' joined the union. Well, sir, hell jes' popped. All them storekeepers and legioners an' people like that, they get drillin' an' yellin', 'Red!' An' they're gonna run the union right outa Akron. Preachers git a-preachin' about it, an' papers a-yowlin', an' they's pick handles put out by the rubber companies, an' they're a – buyin' gas. Jesus, you'd think them mountain boys was reg'lar devils!" He stopped and found some more rocks to shoot. "Well, sir – it was las' March, an' one Sunday five thousan' of them mountain men had a turkey shoot outside a town. Five thousan' of 'em jes' marched through town with their rifles. An' they had their turkey shoot, an' then they marched back. An' that's all they done. Well, sir, they ain't been no trouble sence then. These here citizens committees give back the pick handles, an' the storekeepers keep their stores, an' nobody been clubbed nor tarred an' feathered, an' nobody been killed." There was a long silence, and then Black Hat said, "They're gettin' purty mean out here. Burned that camp an' beat up folks. I been thinkin'. All our folks got guns. I been thinkin' maybe we ought to git up a turkey shootin' club an' have meetin's ever' Sunday."

The men looked up at him, and then down at the ground, and their feet moved restlessly and they shifted their weight from one leg to the other.

1939

Nathanael West   *1903-1940*

The satiric novelist Nathanael West was born Nathan Wallenstein Weinstein in New York City in 1903. After graduation from Brown University in 1924, he spent two years in Paris as a member of the expatriate colony. Returning to New York, West earned his living as a hotel clerk while beginning the first of the four short novels that constitute his life work. His extreme pessimism and his ironic manipulation of his grotesque and often caricature-like characters shocked many early readers, as did his apparent irreverence and disregard for convention. In these qualities, and in the sense of utter alienation that pervades the novels, his writing can best be understood as the expression of a revolted modern sensibility which uses ironic fantasy to depict the irrationality and delusion that prevail in the "real" world. Yet there is also in his best work a compassion for human suffering and a manner of expression remarkable for its compression, wit, and vivid, often metaphysical metaphor. West's style can also be forced and precious, as it often is in his first book, *The Dream Life of Balso Snell* (1931), which, influenced by the traditions of Dadaism and Surrealism, is a scatological¹ anti-intellectual attack on literature and the unworthy motives of its producers.

In his next and best novel, *Miss Lonelyhearts* (1933), the central character is the writer (male) of a newspaper column for the lovelorn who comes to see that the grotesque and often illiterate letters that had at first amused him are actually humble and profound pleas for understanding and spiritual guidance. Miss Lonelyhearts shares in the desperation of his society, and his effort to find some solution, and finally to revitalize the "Christ myth," ends in a violent unredemptive death. In its sterile urban setting and its quest theme the novel has affinities with *The Waste Land* of T. S. Eliot, which West admired. Despite its sordid and often repellent details, *Miss Lonelyhearts* is a serious, important book in which West confronts the fact of moral isolation and suffering while he rejects specious

plausible but not genuine

¹ the study of feces or fossil excrement   **or** excrement, excretion, or literature   the study or obsession with

solutions that have been put forward as ways of escaping the human predicament.

A Cool Million (1934), West's third novel, is a contrived and too-clever debunking of the American myth of success according to the Horatio Alger formula. A move to California, where he became a screen writer and an observer of the Hollywood dream factory, provided West with fresh subjects of satire for his last novel. In *The Day of the Locust* (1939), he anatomizes a culture by examining the twisted lives and self-deceptions of an array of representative Hollywood types. As in *Miss Lonelyhearts*, there is an implied protest against the essential meaninglessness (actually valuelessness) of modern life as West saw it. But the conclusion of *The Day of the Locust* goes beyond the earlier novel of despair by focusing on the social implications of a collective frustration and rage that seek release through mob violence.

In 1940, West, together with his wife Eileen (of Ruth McKenney's *My Sister Eileen*), was killed in an auto crash in California.

The standard edition of West's fiction is *The Complete Works of Nathanael West*, ed. Alan Ross (New York, 1957). A helpful brief introduction is S. E. Hyman, *Nathanael West* (Minneapolis, 1962). Two book-length critiques are J.F. Light, *Nathanael West: An Interpretive Study* (Evanston, Ill., 1961), and Victor Comerchero, *Nathanael West: The Ironic Prophet* (Syracuse, 1964).

The text of the selection from *Miss Lonelyhearts* is that of *The Complete Works of Nathanael West* (New York, 1957).

for March 5

✳ From *Miss Lonelyhearts*

Miss Lonelyhearts, help me, help me

The Miss Lonelyhearts of The New York *Post-Dispatch* (Are-you-in-trouble? — Do-you-need-advice? — Write-to-Miss-Lonelyhearts-and-she-will-help-you) sat at his desk and stared at a piece of white card-board. On it a prayer had been printed by Shrike, the feature editor.

> *"Soul of Miss L, glorify me.*
> *Body of Miss L, nourish me*
> *Blood of Miss L, intoxicate me.*
> *Tears of Miss L, wash me.*
> *Oh good Miss L, excuse my plea,*
> *And hide me in your heart,*
> *And defend me from mine enemies.*
> *Help me, Miss L, help me, help me.*
> *In sæcula sæculorum. Amen."*

Although the deadline was less than a quarter of an hour away, he was still working on his leader. He had gone as far as: "Life *is* worth while, for it is full of dreams and peace, gentleness and ecstasy, and faith that burns like a clear white flame on a grim dark altar." But he found it impossible to continue. The letters were no longer funny. He could not go on finding the same joke funny thirty times a day for months on end. And on most days he received more than thirty letters, all of them alike, stamped from the dough of suffering with a heart-shaped cookie knife.

On his desk were piled those he had received this morning. He started through them again, searching for some clue to a sincere answer.

Dear Miss Lonelyhearts—

I am in such pain I dont know what to do sometimes I think I will kill myself my kidneys hurt so much. My husband thinks no woman can be a good catholic and not have children irregardless of the pain. I was married honorable from our church but I never knew what married life meant as I never was told about man and wife. My grandmother never told me and she was the only mother I had but made a big mistake by not telling me as it dont pay to be inocent and is only a big disapointment. I have 7 children in 12 yrs and ever since the last 2 I have been so sick. I was operatored on twice and my husband promised no more children on the doctors advice as he said I might die but when I got back from the hospital he broke his promise and now I am going to have a baby and I dont think I can stand it my kidneys hurt so much. I am so sick and scared because I cant have an abortion on account of being a catholic and my husband so religious. I cry all the time it hurts so much and I dont know what to do.

> *Yours respectfully,*
> *Sick-of-it-all*

Miss Lonelyhearts threw the letter into an open drawer and lit a cigarette.

Dear Miss Lonelyhearts—

I am sixteen years old now and I dont know what to do and would appreciate it if you could tell me what to do. When I was a little girl it was not so bad because I got used to the kids on the block makeing fun of me, but now I would like to have boy friends like the other girls and go out on Saturday nites, but no boy will take me because I was born without a nose—although I am a good dancer and have a nice shape and my father buys me pretty clothes.

I sit and look at myself all day and cry. I have a big hole in the middle of my face that scares people even myself so I cant blame the boys for not wanting to take me out. My mother loves me, but she crys terrible when she looks at me.

What did I do to deserve such a terrible bad fate? Even if I did do some bad things I didnt do any before I was a year old and I was born this way. I asked Papa and he says he doesnt know, but that maybe I did something in the other world before I was born or that maybe I was being punished for his sins. I dont believe that because he is a very nice man. Ought I commit suicide?

> *Sincerely yours,*
> *Desperate*

The cigarette was imperfect and refused to draw. Miss Lonely-hearts took it out of his mouth and stared at it furiously. He fought himself quiet, then lit another one.

Dear Miss Lonelyhearts—
    I am writing to you for my little sister Gracie because something awfull hapened to her and I am afraid to tell mother about it. I am 15 years old and Gracie is 13 and we live in Brooklyn. Gracie is deaf and dumb and biger than me but not very smart on account of being deaf and dumb. She plays on the roof of our house and dont go to school except to deaf and dumb school twice a week on tuesdays and thursdays. Mother makes her play on the roof because we dont want her to get run over as she aint very smart. Last week a man came on the roof and did something dirty to her. She told me about it and I dont know what to do as I am afraid to tell mother on account of her being liable to beat Gracie up. I am afraid that Gracie is going to have a baby and I listened to her stomack last night for a long time to see if I could hear the baby but I couldn't. If I tell mother she will beat Gracie up awfull because I am the only one who loves her and last time when she tore her dress they loked her in the closet for 2 days and if the boys on the blok hear about it they will say dirty things like they did on Peewee Conors sister the time she got caught in the lots. So please what would you do if the same hapened in your family.

Yours truly,
Harold S.

    He stopped reading. Christ was the answer, but, if he did not want to get sick, he had to stay away from the Christ business. Besides, Christ was Shrike's particular joke. "Soul of Miss L, glorify me. Body of Miss L, save me. Blood of . . ." He turned to his typewriter.

    Although his cheap clothes had too much style, he still looked like the son of a Baptist minister. A beard would become him, would accent his Old-Testament look. But even without a beard no one could fail to recognize the New England puritan. His forehead was high and narrow. His nose was long and fleshless. His bony chin was shaped and cleft like a hoof. On seeing him for the first time, Shrike had smiled and said, "The Susan Chesters, the Beatrice Fairfaxes and the Miss Lonelyhearts are the priests of twentieth-century America."

    A copy boy came up to tell him that Shrike wanted to know if the stuff was ready. He bent over the typewriter and began pounding its keys.

    But before he had written a dozen words, Shrike leaned over his shoulder. "The same old stuff," Shrike said. "Why don't you give them something new and hopeful? Tell them about art. Here, I'll dictate:

    "*Art Is a Way Out.*

    "Do not let life overwhelm you. When the old paths are choked with the débris of failure, look for newer and fresher paths. Art is just such a path. Art is distilled from suffering. As Mr. Polnikoff exclaimed through his fine Russian beard, when, at the age of eighty-six, he gave up his business to learn Chinese, 'We are, as yet, only at the beginning. . . .'

    "*Art Is One of Life's Richest Offerings.*

"For those who have not the talent to create, there is appreciation. For those . . .

"Go on from there."

Miss Lonelyhearts on a field trip

It was cold and damp in the city room the next day, and Miss Lonelyhearts sat at his desk with his hands in his pockets and his legs pressed together. A desert, he was thinking, not of sand, but of rust and body dirt, surrounded by a back-yard fence on which are posters describing the events of the day. Mother slays five with ax, slays seven, slays nine. . . . Babe slams two, slams three. . . . Inside the fence Desperate, Broken-hearted, Disillusioned-with-tubercular-husband and the rest were gravely forming the letters MISS LONELYHEARTS out of white-washed clam shells, as if decorating the lawn of a rural depot.

He failed to notice Goldsmith's waddling approach until a heavy arm dropped on his neck like the arm of a deadfall. He freed himself with a grunt. His anger amused Goldsmith, who smiled, bunching his fat cheeks like twin rolls of smooth pink toilet paper.

"Well, how's the drunkard?" Goldsmith asked, imitating Shrike.

Miss Lonelyhearts knew that Goldsmith had written the column for him yesterday, so he hid his annoyance to be grateful.

"No trouble at all," Goldsmith said. "It was a pleasure to read your mail." He took a pink envelope out of his pocket and threw it on the desk "From an admirer." He winked, letting a thick gray lid down slowly and luxuriously over a moist, rolling eye.

Miss Lonelyhearts picked up the letter.

Dear Miss Lonelyhearts—

I am not very good at writing so I wonder if I could have a talk with you. I am only 32 years old but have had a lot of trouble in my life and am unhappily married to a cripple. I need some good advice bad but cant state my case in a letter as I am not good at letters and it would take an expert to state my case. I know your a man and am glad as I dont trust women. You were pointed out to me in Delehantys as a man who does the advice in the paper and the minute I saw you I said you can help me. You had on a blue suit and a gray hat when I came in with my husband who is a cripple.

I don't feel so bad about asking to see you personal because I feel almost like I knew you. So please call me up at Burgess 7-7323 which is my number as I need your advice bad about my married life.

An admirer,

Fay Doyle

He threw the letter into the waste-paper basket with a great show of distaste.

Goldsmith laughed at him. "How now, Dostoievski?" he said. "That's no way to act. Instead of pulling the Russian by recommending suicide, you ought to get the lady with child and increase the potential circulation of the paper."

To drive him away, Miss Lonelyhearts made believe that he was busy. He went over to his typewriter and started pounding out his column.

"Life, for most of us, seems a terrible struggle of pain and heartbreak, without hope or joy. Oh, my dear readers, it only seems so. Every man, no matter how poor or humble, can teach himself to use his senses. See the cloud-flecked sky, the foam-decked sea. . . . Smell the sweet pine and heady privet. . . . Feel of velvet and of satin. . . . As the popular song goes, 'The best things in life are free.' Life is . . ."

He could not go on with it and turned again to the imagined desert where Desperate, Broken-hearted and the others were still building his name. They had run out of sea shells and were using faded photographs, soiled fans, time-tables, playing cards, broken toys, imitation jewelry—junk that memory had made precious, far more precious than anything the sea might yield.

He killed his great understanding heart by laughing, then reached into the waste-paper basket for Mrs. Doyle's letter. Like a pink tent, he set it over the desert. Against the dark mahogany desk top, the cheap paper took on rich flesh tones. He thought of Mrs. Doyle as a tent, hair-covered and veined, and of himself as the skeleton in a water closet, the skull and cross-bones on a scholar's bookplate. When he made the skeleton enter the flesh tent, it flowered at every joint.

But despite these thoughts, he remained as dry and cold as a polished bone and sat trying to discover a moral reason for not calling Mrs. Doyle. If he could only believe in Christ, then adultery would be a sin, then everything would be simple and the letters extremely easy to answer.

The completeness of his failure drove him to the telephone. He left the city room and went into the hall to use the pay station from which all private calls had to be made. The walls of the booth were covered with obscene drawings. He fastened his eyes on two disembodied genitals and gave the operator Burgess 7-7323.

"Is Mrs. Doyle in?"

"Hello, who is it?"

"I want to speak to Mrs. Doyle," he said. "Is this Mrs. Doyle?"

"Yes, that's me." Her voice was hard with fright.

"This is Miss Lonelyhearts."

"Miss who?"

"Miss Lonelyhearts, Miss Lonelyhearts, the man who does the column."

He was about to hang up, when she cooed, "Oh, hello. . . ."

"You said I should call."

"Oh, yes . . . what?"

He guessed that she wanted him to do the talking. "When can you see me?"

"Now." She was still cooing and he could almost feel her warm, moisture-laden breath through the earpiece.

"Where?"

"You say."

"I'll tell you what," he said. "Meet me in the park, near the obelisk, in about an hour."

He went back to his desk and finished his column, then started for the park. He sat down on a bench near the obelisk to wait for Mrs. Doyle. Still thinking of tents, he examined the sky and saw that it was canvas-colored and ill-stretched. He examined it like a stupid detective who is searching for a clue to his own exhaustion. When he found nothing, he turned his trained eye on the skyscrapers that menaced the little park from all sides. In their tons of forced rock and tortured steel, he discovered what he thought was a clue.

Americans have dissipated their racial energy in an orgy of stone breaking. In their few years they have broken more stones than did centuries of Egyptians. And they have done their work hysterically, desperately, almost as if they knew that the stones would some day break them.

The detective saw a big woman enter the park and start in his direction. He made a quick catalogue: legs like Indian clubs, breasts like balloons and a brow like a pigeon. Despite her short plaid skirt, red sweater, rabbit-skin jacket and knitted tam-o'-shanter, she looked like a police captain.

He waited for her to speak first.

"Miss Lonelyhearts? Oh, hello . . ."

"Mrs. Doyle?" He stood up and took her arm. It felt like a thigh.

"Where are we going?" she asked, as he began to lead her off.

"For a drink."

"I can't go to Delehanty's. They know me."

"We'll go to my place."

"Ought I?"

He did not have to answer, for she was already on her way. As he followed her up the stairs to his apartment, he watched the action of her massive hams; they were like two enormous grindstones.

He made some highballs and sat down beside her on the bed.

"You must know an awful lot about women from your job," she said with a sigh, putting her hand on his knee.

He had always been the pursuer, but now found a strange pleasure in having the rôles reversed. He drew back when she reached for a kiss. She caught his head and kissed him on his mouth. At first it ticked like a watch, then the tick softened and thickened into a heart throb. It beat louder and more rapidly each second, until he thought that it was going to explode and pulled away with a rude jerk.

"Don't," she begged.

"Don't what?"

"Oh, darling, turn out the light."

He smoked a cigarette, standing in the dark and listening to her undress. She made sea sounds; something flapped like a sail; there was the creak of ropes; then he heard the wave-against-a-wharf smack of rubber on flesh. Her call for him to hurry was a sea-moan, and when he lay beside her, she heaved, tidal, moon-driven.

Some fifteen minutes later, he crawled out of bed like an exhausted swimmer leaving the surf, and dropped down into a large armchair near the window. She went into the bathroom, then came back and sat in his lap.

"I'm ashamed of myself," she said. "You must think I'm a bad woman."

He shook his head no.

"My husband isn't much. He's a cripple like I wrote you, and much older than me." She laughed. "He's all dried up. He hasn't been a husband to me for years. You know, Lucy, my kid, isn't his."

He saw that she expected him to be astonished and did his best to lift his eyebrows.

"It's a long story," she said. "It was on account of Lucy that I had to marry him. I'll bet you must have wondered how it was I came to marry a cripple. It's a long story."

Her voice was as hypnotic as a tom-tom, and as monotonous. Already his mind and body were half asleep.

"It's a long, long story, and that's why I couldn't write it in a letter. I got into trouble when the Doyles lived above us on Center Street. I used to be kind to him and go to the movies with him because he was a cripple, although I was one of the most popular girls on the block. So when I got into trouble, I didn't know what to do and asked him for the money for an abortion. But he didn't have the money, so we got married instead. It all came through my trusting a dirty dago. I thought he was a gent, but when I asked him to marry me, why he spurned me from the door and wouldn't even give me money for an abortion. He said if he gave me the money that would mean it was his fault and I would have something on him. Did you ever hear of such a skunk?"

"No," he said. The life out of which she spoke was even heavier than her body. It was as if a gigantic, living Miss Lonelyhearts letter in the shape of a paper weight had been placed on his brain.

"After the baby was born, I wrote the skunk, but he never wrote back, and about two years ago, I got to thinking how unfair it was for Lucy to have to depend on a cripple and not come into her rights. So I looked his name up in the telephone book and took Lucy to see him. As I told him then, not that I wanted anything for myself, but just that I wanted Lucy to get what was coming to her. Well, after keeping us waiting in the hall over an hour—I was boiling mad, I can tell you, thinking of the wrong he had done me and my child—we were taken into the parlor by the butler. Very quiet and lady-like, because money ain't everything and he's no more a gent than I'm a lady, the dirty wop—I told him he ought to do something for Lucy see'n' he's her father. Well, he had the nerve to say that he had never seen me before and that if I didn't stop bothering him, he'd have me run in. That got me riled and I lit into the bastard and gave him a piece of my mind. A woman came in while we were arguing that I figured was his wife, so I hollered, 'He's the father of my child, he's the father of my child.' When they went to the 'phone to call a cop, I picked up the kid and beat it.

"And now comes the funniest part of the whole thing. My husband is a queer guy and he always makes believe that he is the father of the kid and even talks to me about *our* child. Well, when we got home, Lucy kept asking me why I said a strange man was her papa. She wanted to know if Doyle wasn't really her papa. I must of been crazy because I told her that she should remember that her real papa was a man named Tony Benelli and that he had wronged me. I told her a lot of other crap like that—too much movies I guess. Well, when Doyle got home the first thing Lucy says to him is that he ain't her papa. That got him sore and he wanted to know what I had told her. I didn't like his high falutin' ways and said, 'The truth,' I guess too that I was kinda sick of see'n him moon over her. He went for me and hit me one on the cheek. I wouldn't let no man get away with that so I socked back and he swung at me with his stick but missed and fell on the floor and started to cry. The kid was on the floor crying too and that set me off because the next thing I know I'm on the floor bawling too."

She waited for him to comment, but he remained silent until she nudged him into speech with her elbow. "Your husband probably loves you and the kid," he said.

"Maybe so, but I was a pretty girl and could of had my pick. What girl wants to spend her life with a shrimp of a cripple?"

"You're still pretty," he said without knowing why, except that he was frightened.

She rewarded him with a kiss, then dragged him to the bed.

Miss Lonelyhearts in the dismal swamp

Soon after Mrs. Doyle left, Miss Lonelyhearts became physically sick and was unable to leave his room. The first two days of his illness were blotted out by sleep, but on the third day, his imagination began again to work.

He found himself in the window of a pawnshop full of fur coats, diamond rings, watches, shotguns, fishing tackle, mandolins. All these things were the paraphernalia of suffering. A tortured high light twisted on the blade of a gift knife, a battered horn grunted with pain.

He sat in the window thinking. Man has a tropism for order. Keys in one pocket, change in another. Mandolins are tuned G D A E. The physical world has a tropism for disorder, entropy. Man against Nature . . . the battle of the centuries. Keys yearn to mix with change. Mandolins strive to get out of tune. Every order has within it the germ of destruction. All order is doomed, yet the battle is worth while.

A trumpet, marked to sell for $2.49, gave the call to battle and Miss Lonelyhearts plunged into the fray. First he formed a phallus of old watches and rubber boots, then a heart of umbrellas and trout flies, then a diamond of musical instruments and derby hats, after these a circle, triangle, square, swastika. But nothing proved definitive and he began to make a gigantic cross. When the cross became too large for the pawnshop, he moved it to the shore of the ocean. There every wave added to his stock faster than he could lengthen its arms. His labors were enormous. He staggered from the last wave line to his work, loaded down with marine refuse — bottles, shells, chunks of cork, fish heads, pieces of net.

Drunk with exhaustion, he finally fell asleep. When he awoke, he felt very weak, yet calm.

There was a timid knock on the door. It was open and Betty tiptoed into the room with her arms full of bundles. He made believe that he was asleep.

"Hello," he said suddenly.

Startled, she turned to explain. "I heard you were sick, so I brought some hot soup and other stuff."

He was too tired to be annoyed by her wide-eyed little mother act and let her feed him with a spoon. When he had finished eating, she opened the window and freshened the bed. As soon as the room was in order, she started to leave, but he called her back.

"Don't go, Betty."

She pulled a chair to the side of his bed and sat there without speaking.

"I'm sorry about what happened the other day," he said. "I guess I was sick."

She showed that she accepted his apology by helping him to excuse himself. "It's the Miss Lonelyhearts job. Why don't you give it up?"

"And do what?"

"Work in an advertising agency, or something."

"You don't understand, Betty, I can't quit. And even if I were to quit, it wouldn't make any difference. I wouldn't be able to forget the letters, no matter what I did."

"Maybe I don't understand," she said, "but I think you're making a fool of yourself."

tropism — the tendency to move or turn in response to an external stimulus.

entropy — the theoretical measure of energy which cannot be transformed into mechanical work in a thermodynamic system.

"Perhaps I can make you understand. Let's start from the beginning. A man is hired to give advice to the readers of a newspaper. The job is a circulation stunt and the whole staff considers it a joke. He welcomes the job, for it might lead to a gossip column, and anyway he's tired of being a leg man. He too considers the job a joke, but after several months at it, the joke begins to escape him. He sees that the majority of the letters are profoundly humble pleas for moral and spiritual advice, that they are inarticulate expressions of genuine suffering. He also discovers that his correspondents take him seriously. For the first time in his life, he is forced to examine the values by which he lives. This examination shows him that he is the victim of the joke and not its perpetrator."

Although he had spoken soberly, he saw that Betty still thought him a fool. He closed his eyes.

"You're tired," she said. "I'll go."

"No, I'm not tired. I'm just tired of talking, you talk a while."

She told him about her childhood on a farm and of her love for animals, about country sounds and country smells and of how fresh and clean everything in the country is. She said that he ought to live there and that if he did, he would find that all his troubles were city troubles.

While she was talking, Shrike burst into the room. He was drunk and immediately set up a great shout, as though he believed that Miss Lonelyhearts was too near death to hear distinctly. Betty left without saying good-by.

Shrike had evidently caught some of her farm talk, for he said: "My friend, I agree with Betty, you're an escapist. But I do not agree that the soil is the proper method for you to use."

Miss Lonelyhearts turned his face to the wall and pulled up the covers. But Shrike was unescapable. He raised his voice and talked through the blankets into the back of Miss Lonelyhearts' head.

"There are other methods, and for your edification I shall describe them. But first let us do the escape to the soil, as recommended by Betty:

"You are fed up with the city and its teeming millions. The ways and means of men, as getting and lending and spending, you lay waste your inner world, are too much with you. The bus takes too long, while the subway is always crowded. So what do you do? So you buy a farm and walk behind your horse's moist behind, no collar or tie, plowing your broad swift acres. As you turn up the rich black soil, the wind carries the smell of pine and dung across the fields and the rhythm of an old, old work enters your soul. To this rhythm, you sow and weep and chivy your kine, not kin or kind, between the pregnant rows of corn and taters. Your step becomes the heavy sexual step of a dance-drunk Indian and you tread the seed down into the female earth. You plant, not dragon's teeth, but beans and greens. . . .

"Well, what do you say, my friend, shall it be the soil?"

Miss Lonelyhearts did not answer. He was thinking of how Shrike had accelerated his sickness by teaching him to handle his one escape, Christ, with a thick glove of words.

"I take your silence to mean that you have decided against the soil. I agree with you. Such a life is too dull and laborious. Let us now consider the South Seas:

"You live in a thatch hut with the daughter of the king, a slim young maiden in whose eyes is an ancient wisdom. Her breasts are golden speckled pears, her belly a melon, and her odor is like nothing so much as a jungle fern. In the evening, on the blue lagoon, under the silvery moon, to your love you croon in the soft sylabelew and vocabelew of her langorour tongorour. Your body is golden brown like hers, and tourists have need of the indignant finger of the missionary to point you out. They envy you your breech clout and carefree laugh and little brown bride and fingers instead of forks. But you don't return their envy, and when a beautiful society girl comes to your hut in the night, seeking to learn the secret of your happiness, you send her back to her yacht that hangs on the horizon like a nervous racehorse. And so you dream away the days, fishing, hunting, dancing, swimming, kissing, and picking flowers to twine in your hair. . . .

"Well, my friend, what do you think of the South Seas?"

Miss Lonelyhearts tried to stop him by making believe that he was asleep. But Shrike was not fooled.

"Again silence," he said, "and again you are right. The South Seas are played out and there's little use in imitating Gauguin. But don't be discouraged, we have only scratched the surface of our subject. Let us now examine Hedonism, or take the cash and let the credit go. . . .

"You dedicate your life to the pursuit of pleasure. No overindulgence, mind you, but knowing that your body is a pleasure machine, you treat it carefully in order to get the most out of it. Golf as well as booze, Philadelphia Jack O'Brien and his chestweights as well as Spanish dancers. Nor do you neglect the pleasures of the mind. You fornicate under pictures by Matisse and Picasso, you drink from Renaissance glassware, and often you spend an evening beside the fireplace with Proust and an apple. Alas, after much good fun, the day comes when you realize that soon you must die. You keep a stiff upper lip and decide to give a last party. You invite all your old mistresses, trainers, artists and boon companions. The guests are dressed in black, the waiters are coons, the table is a coffin carved for you by Eric Gill. You serve caviar and blackberries and licorice candy and coffee without cream. After the dancing girls have finished, you get to your feet and call for silence in order to explain your philosophy of life. 'Life,' you say, 'is a club where they won't stand for squawks, where they deal you only one hand and you must sit in. So even if the cards are cold and marked by the hand of fate, play up, play up like a gentleman and a sport. Get tanked, grab what's on the buffet, use the girls upstairs, but remember, when you throw box cars, take the curtain like a dead game sport, don't squawk.' . . .

"I won't even ask you what you think of such an escape. You haven't the money, nor are you stupid enough to manage it. But we come now to one that should suit you much better. . . .

"Art! Be an artist or a writer. When you are cold, warm yourself before the flaming tints of Titian, when you are hungry, nourish yourself with great spiritual foods by listening to the noble periods of Bach, the harmonies of Brahms and the thunder of Beethoven. Do you think there is anything in the fact that their names all begin with B? But don't take a chance, smoke a 3 B pipe, and remember these immortal lines: *When to the suddenness of melody the echo parting falls the failing day.* What a rhythm! Tell them to keep their society whores and pressed duck with oranges. For you *l'art vivant*, the living art, as you call it. Tell them that you know that your shoes are broken and that there are pimples on your face, yes, and that you have buck teeth and a club foot, but that you don't care, for to-morrow they are playing Beethoven's last quartets in Carnegie Hall and at home you have Shakespeare's plays in one volume."

After art, Shrike described suicide and drugs. When he had finished with them, he came to what he said was the goal of his lecture.

"My friend, I know of course that neither the soil, nor the South Seas, nor Hedonism, nor art, nor suicide, nor drugs, can mean anything to us. We are not men who swallow camels only to strain at stools. God alone is our escape. The church is our only hope, the First Church of Christ Dentist, where He is worshiped as Preventer of Decay. The church whose symbol is the trinity new-style: Father, Son and Wire-haired Fox Terrier. . . . And so, my good friend, let me dictate a letter to Christ for you:

Dear Miss Lonelyhearts of Miss Lonelyhearts —

I am twenty-six years old and in the newspaper game. Life for me is a desert empty of comfort. I cannot find pleasure in food, drink, or women — nor do the arts give me joy any longer. The Leopard of Discontent walks the streets of my city; the Lion of Discouragement crouches outside the walls of my citadel. All is desolation and a vexation of the spirit. I feel like hell. How can I believe, how can I have faith in this day and age? Is it true that the greatest scientists believe again in you?

I read your column and like it very much. There you once wrote: 'When the salt has lost its savour, who shall savour it again?' Is the answer: 'None but the Saviour?'[3]

Thanking you very much for a quick reply, I remain yours truly,

A Regular Subscriber"

[3] "Ye are the salt of the earth: but if the salt have lost his savour, wherewith shall it be salted?" (*Matthew* v:13).

- - - - - - -

Miss Lonelyhearts and the cripple

Miss Lonelyhearts dodged Betty because she made him feel ridiculous. He was still trying to cling to his humility, and the farther he got below self-laughter, the easier it was for him to practice it. When Betty telephoned, he refused to answer and after he had twice failed to call her back, she left him alone.

One day, about a week after he had returned from the country, Goldsmith asked him out for a drink. When he accepted, he made himself so humble that Goldsmith was frightened and almost suggested a doctor.

They found Shrike in Delehanty's and joined him at the bar. Goldsmith tried to whisper something to him about Miss Lonelyhearts' condition, but he was drunk and refused to listen. He caught only part of what Goldsmith was trying to say.

"I must differ with you, my good Goldsmith," Shrike said. "Don't call sick those who have faith. They are the well. It is you who are sick."

Goldsmith did not reply and Shrike turned to Miss Lonelyhearts. "Come, tell us, brother, how it was that you first came to believe. Was it music in a church, or the death of a loved one, or mayhap, some wise old priest?"

The familiar jokes no longer had any effect on Miss Lonelyhearts. He smiled at Shrike as the saints are supposed to have smiled at those about to martyr them.

"Ah, but how stupid of me," Shrike continued. "It was the letters, of course. Did I myself not say that the Miss Lonelyhearts are the priests of twentieth-century America?"

Goldsmith laughed, and Shrike, in order to keep him laughing, used an old trick; he appeared to be offended. "Goldsmith, you are the nasty product of this unbelieving age. You cannot believe, you can only laugh. You take everything with a bag of salt and forget that salt is the enemy of fire as well as of ice. Be warned, the salt you use is not Attic salt, it is coarse butcher's salt. It doesn't preserve; it kills."

The bartender who was standing close by, broke in to address Miss Lonelyhearts. "Pardon me, sir, but there's a gent here named Doyle who wants to meet you. He says you know his wife."

Before Miss Lonelyhearts could reply, he beckoned to someone standing at the other end of the bar. The signal was answered by a little cripple, who immediately started in their direction. He used a cane and dragged one of his feet behind him in a box-shaped shoe with a four-inch sole. As he hobbled along, he made many waste motions, like those of a partially destroyed insect.

The bartender introduced the cripple as Mr. Peter Doyle. Doyle was very excited and shook hands twice all around, then with a wave that was meant to be sporting, called for a round of drinks.

Before lifting his glass, Shrike carefully inspected the cripple. When he had finished, he winked at Miss Lonelyhearts and said, "Here's to humanity." He patted Doyle on the back. "Mankind, mankind . . ." he sighed, wagging his head sadly. "What is man that . . ."

The bartender broke in again on behalf of his friend and tried to change the conversation to familiar ground. "Mr. Doyle inspects meters for the gas company."

"And an excellent job it must be," Shrike said. "He should be able to give us the benefit of a different viewpoint. We newspapermen are limited in many ways and I like to hear both sides of a case."

Doyle had been staring at Miss Lonelyhearts as though searching for something, but he now turned to Shrike and tried to be agreeable. "You know what people say, Mr. Shrike?"

"No, my good man, what is it that people say?"

"Everybody's got a frigidaire nowadays, and they say that we meter inspectors take the place of the iceman in the stories." He tried, rather diffidently, to leer.

"What!" Shrike roared at him. "I can see, sir, that you are not the man for us. You can know nothing about humanity; you are humanity. I leave you to Miss Lonelyhearts." He called to Goldsmith and stalked away.

The cripple was confused and angry. "Your friend is a nut," he said. Miss Lonelyhearts was still smiling, but the character of his smile had changed. It had become full of sympathy and a little sad.

The new smile was for Doyle and he knew it. He smiled back gratefully.

"Oh, I forgot," Doyle said, "the wife asked me, if I bumped into you, to ask you to our house to eat. That's why I made Jake introduce us."

Miss Lonelyhearts was busy with his smile and accepted without thinking of the evening he had spent with Mrs. Doyle. The cripple felt honored and shook hands for a third time. It was evidently his only social gesture.

After a few more drinks, when Doyle said that he was tired, Miss Lonelyhearts suggested that they go into the back room. They found a table and sat opposite each other.

The cripple had a very strange face. His eyes failed to balance; his mouth was not under his nose; his forehead was square and bony; and his round chin was like a forehead in miniature. He looked like one of those composite photographs used by screen magazines in guessing contests.

They sat staring at each other until the strain of wordless communication began to excite them both. Doyle made vague, needless adjustments to his clothing. Miss Lonelyhearts found it very difficult to keep his smile steady.

When the cripple finally labored into speech, Miss Lonelyhearts was unable to understand him. He listened hard for a few minutes and realized that Doyle was making no attempt to be understood. He was giving birth to groups of words that lived inside of him as things, a jumble of the retorts he had meant to make when insulted and the private curses against fate that experience had taught him to swallow.

Like a priest, Miss Lonelyhearts turned his face slightly away. He watched the play of the cripple's hands. At first they conveyed nothing but excitement, then gradually they became pictorial. They lagged behind to illustrate a matter with which he was already finished, or ran ahead to illustrate something he had not yet begun to talk about. As he grew more articulate, his hands stopped trying to aid his speech and began to dart in and out of his clothing. One of them suddenly emerged from a pocket of his coat, dragging some sheets of letter paper. He forced these on Miss Lonelyhearts.

Dear Miss Lonelyhearts—

I am kind of ashamed to write you because a man like me dont take stock in things like that but my wife told me you were a man and not some dopey woman so I thought I would write to you after reading your answer to Disillu-sioned. I am a cripple 41 yrs of age which I have been all my life and I have never let myself get blue until lately when I have been feeling lousy all the time on account of not getting anywhere and asking myself what is it all for. You have a education so I figured may be you no. What I want to no is why I go around pulling my leg up and down stairs reading meters for the gas company for a stinking $22.50 per while the bosses ride around in swell cars living off the fat of the land. Dont think I am a greasy red. I read where they shoot cripples in Russia because they cant work but I can work better than any park bum and support a wife and child to. But thats not what I am writing you about. What I want to no is what is it all for my pulling my god damed leg along the streets and down in stinking cellars with it all the time hurting fit to burst so that near quitting time I am crazy with pain and when I get home all I hear is money money which aint no home for a man like me. What I want to no is what in hell is the use day after day with a foot like mine when you have to go around pulling and scrambling for a lousy three squares with a toothache in it that comes from useing the foot so much. The doctor told me I ought to rest it for six months but who will pay me when I am resting it. But that aint what I mean either because you might tell me to change my job and where could I get another one I am lucky to have one at all. It aint the job that I am complaining about but what I want to no is what is the whole stinking business for.

Please write me an answer not in the paper because my wife reads your stuff and I dont want her to no I wrote to you because I always said the papers is crap but I figured maybe you no something about it because you have read a lot of books and I never even finished high.

Yours truly,
Peter Doyle

While Miss Lonelyhearts was puzzling out the crabbed writing, Doyle's damp hand accidentally touched his under the table. He jerked away, but then drove his hand back and forced it to clasp the cripple's. After finishing the letter, he did not let go, but pressed it firmly with all the love he could manage. At first the cripple covered his embarrassment by disguising the meaning of the clasp with a handshake, but he soon gave in to it and they sat silently, hand in hand.

Miss Lonelyhearts pays a visit

They left the speakeasy together, both very drunk and very busy: Doyle with the wrongs he had suffered and Miss Lonelyhearts with the triumphant thing that his humility had become.

They took a cab. As they entered the street in which Doyle lived, he began to curse his wife and his crippled foot. He called on Christ to blast them both.

Miss Lonelyhearts was very happy and inside of his head he was also calling on Christ. But his call was not a curse, it was the shape of his joy.

When the cab drew up to the curb, Miss Lonelyhearts helped his companion out and led him into the house. They made a great deal of noise with the front door and Mrs. Doyle came into the hall. At the sight of her the cripple started to curse again.

She greeted Miss Lonelyhearts, then took hold of her husband and shook the breath out of him. When he was quiet, she dragged him into their apartment. Miss Lonelyhearts followed and as he passed her in the dark foyer, she goosed him and laughed.

After washing their hands, they sat down to eat. Mrs. Doyle had had her supper earlier in the evening and she waited on them. The first thing she put on the table was a quart bottle of guinea red.

When they had reached their coffee, she sat down next to Miss Lonelyhearts. He could feel her knee pressing his under the table, but he paid no attention to her and only broke his beatific smile to drink. The heavy food had dulled him and he was trying desperately to feel again what he had felt while holding hands with the cripple in the speakeasy.

She put her thigh under his, but when he still failed to respond, she got up abruptly and went into the parlor. They followed a few minutes later and found her mixing ginger-ale highballs.

They all drank silently. Doyle looked sleepy and his wife was just beginning to get drunk. Miss Lonelyhearts made no attempt to be sociable. He was busy trying to find a message. When he did speak it would have to be in the form of a message.

After the third highball, Mrs. Doyle began to wink quite openly at Miss Lonelyhearts, but he still refused to pay any attention to her. The cripple, however, was greatly disturbed by her signals. He began to fidget and mumble under his breath.

The vague noises he was making annoyed Mrs. Doyle. "What in hell are you talking about?" she demanded.

The cripple started a sigh that ended in a groan and then, as though ashamed of himself, said, "Ain't I the pimp, to bring home a guy for my wife?" He darted a quick look at Miss Lonelyhearts and laughed apologetically.

Mrs. Doyle was furious. She rolled a newspaper into a club and struck her husband on the mouth with it. He surprised her by playing the fool. He growled like a dog and caught the paper in his teeth. When she let go of her end, he dropped to his hands and knees and continued the imitation on the floor.

Miss Lonelyhearts tried to get the cripple to stand up and bent to lift him; but, as he did so, Doyle tore open Miss Lonelyhearts' fly, then rolled over on his back, laughing wildly.

His wife kicked him and turned away with a snort of contempt.

The cripple soon laughed himself out, and they all returned to their seats. Doyle and his wife sat staring at each other, while Miss Lonelyhearts again began to search for a message.

The silence bothered Mrs. Doyle. When she could stand it no longer, she went to the sideboard to make another round of drinks. But the bottle was empty. She asked her husband to go to the corner drug store for some gin. He refused with a single, curt nod of his head.

She tried to argue with him. He ignored her and she lost her temper. "Get some gin!" she yelled. "Get some gin, you bastard!"

Miss Lonelyhearts stood up. He had not yet found his message, but he had to say something. "Please don't fight," he pleaded. "He loves you, Mrs. Doyle; that's why he acts like that. Be kind to him."

She grunted with annoyance and left the room. They could hear her slamming things around in the kitchen.

Miss Lonelyhearts went over to the cripple and smiled at him with the same smile he had used in the speakeasy. The cripple returned the smile and stuck out his hand. Miss Lonelyhearts clasped it, and they stood this way, smiling and holding hands, until Mrs. Doyle re-entered the room.

"What a sweet pair of fairies you guys are," she said.

The cripple pulled his hand away and made as though to strike his wife. Miss Lonelyhearts realized that now was the time to give his message. It was now or never.

"You have a big, strong body, Mrs. Doyle. Holding your husband in your arms, you can warm him and give him life. You can take the chill out of his bones. He drags his days out in areaways and cellars, carrying a heavy load of weariness and pain. You can substitute a dream of yourself for this load. A buoyant dream that will be like a dynamo in him. You can do this by letting him conquer you in your bed. He will repay you by flowering and becoming ardent over you. . . .''

She was too astonished to laugh, and the cripple turned his face away as though embarrassed.

With the first few words Miss Lonelyhearts had known that he would be ridiculous. By avoiding God, he had failed to tap the force in his heart and had merely written a column for his paper.

He tried again by becoming hysterical. "Christ is love," he screamed at them. It was a stage scream, but he kept on. "Christ is the black fruit that hangs on the crosstree. Man was lost by eating of the forbidden fruit. He shall be saved by eating of the bidden fruit. The black Christ-fruit, the love fruit . . .''

This time he had failed still more miserably. He had substituted the rhetoric of Shrike for that of Miss Lonelyhearts. He felt like an empty bottle, shiny and sterile.

He closed his eyes. When he heard the cripple say, "I love you, I love you," he opened them and saw him kissing his wife. He knew that the cripple was doing this, not because of the things he had said, but out of loyalty.

"All right, you nut," she said, queening it over her husband. "I forgive you, but go to the drug store for some gin."

Without looking at Miss Lonelyhearts, the cripple took his hat and left. When he had gone Mrs. Doyle smiled. "You were a scream with your fly open," she said. "I thought I'd die laughing."

He did not answer.

"Boy, is he jealous," she went on. "All I have to do is point to some big guy and say, 'Gee, I'd love to have him love me up.' It drives him nuts."

Her voice was low and thick and it was plain that she was trying to excite him. When she went to the radio to tune in on a jazz orchestra, she waved her behind at him like a flag.

He said that he was too tired to dance. After doing a few obscene steps in front of him, she sat down in his lap. He tried to fend her off, but she kept pressing her open mouth against his and when he turned away, she nuzzled his cheek. He felt like an empty bottle that is being slowly filled with warm, dirty water.

When she opened the neck of her dress and tried to force his head between her breasts, he parted his knees with a quick jerk that spilled her to the floor. She tried to pull him down on top of her. He struck out blindly and hit her in the face. She screamed and he hit her again and again. He kept hitting her until she stopped trying to hold him, then he ran out of the house.

- - - - - -

Miss Lonelyhearts has a religious experience

After a long night and morning, towards noon, Miss Lonelyhearts welcomed the arrival of fever. It promised heat and mentally un-motivated violence. The promise was soon fulfilled; the rock became a furnace.

He fastened his eyes on the Christ that hung on the wall opposite his bed. As he stared at it, it became a bright fly, spinning with quick grace on a background of blood velvet sprinkled with tiny nerve stars.

Everything else in the room was dead—chairs, table, pencils, clothes, books. He thought of this black world of things as a fish. And he was right, for it suddenly rose to the bright bait on the wall. It rose with a splash of music and he saw its shining silver belly.

Christ is life and light.

"Christ! Christ!" This shout echoed through the innermost cells of his body.

He moved his head to a cooler spot on the pillow and the vein in his forehead became less swollen. He felt clean and fresh. His heart was a rose and in his skull another rose bloomed.

The room was full of grace. A sweet, clean grace, not washed clean, but clean as the innersides of the inner petals of a newly forced rosebud.

Delight was also in the room. It was like a gentle wind, and his nerves rippled under it like small blue flowers in a pasture.

He was conscious of two rhythms that were slowly becoming one. When they became one, his identification with God was complete. His heart was the one heart, the heart of God. And his brain was likewise God's.

God said, "Will you accept it, now?"

And he replied, "I accept, I accept."

He immediately began to plan a new life and his future conduct as Miss Lonelyhearts. He submitted drafts of his column to God and God approved them. God approved his every thought.

Suddenly the door bell rang. He climbed out of bed and went into the hall to see who was coming. It was Doyle, the cripple, and he was slowly working his way up the stairs.

God had sent him so that Miss Lonelyhearts could perform a miracle and be certain of his conversion. It was a sign. He would embrace the cripple and the cripple would be made whole again, even as he, a spiritual cripple, had been made whole.

He rushed down the stairs to meet Doyle with his arms spread for the miracle.

Doyle was carrying something wrapped in a newspaper. When he saw Miss Lonelyhearts, he put his hand inside the package and stopped. He shouted some kind of a warning, but Miss Lonelyhearts continued his charge. He did not understand the cripple's shout and heard it as a cry for help from Desperate, Harold S., Catholic-mother, Broken-hearted, Broad-shoulders, Sick-of-it-all, Disillusioned-with-tubercular-husband. He was running to succor them with love.

The cripple turned to escape, but he was too slow and Miss Lonelyhearts caught him.

While they were struggling, Betty came in through the street door. She called to them to stop and started up the stairs. The cripple saw her cutting off his escape and tried to get rid of the package. He pulled his hand out. The gun inside the package exploded and Miss Lonelyhearts fell, dragging the cripple with him. They both rolled part of the way down the stairs.

1933

Robert Penn Warren   *1905 –*

Native Kentuckian Robert Penn Warren attended Vanderbilt University in Nashville, Tennessee, where he studied under John Crowe Ransom and helped edit *The Fugitive*, the little magazine (1922–25) conducted by Ransom and other Southerners who were to form the nucleus of the later group of New Critics. Graduating in 1925, Warren took an M.A. degree at the University of California. After further study at Yale and at Oxford University, where he was a Rhodes Scholar, he began a university teaching career that involved positions at Louisiana State University, the University of Minnesota, and Yale University. At Louisiana he was closely associated with Cleanth Brooks, with whom he co-edited *Understanding Poetry* (1938), the influential textbook that helped to revolutionize the college teaching of literature by focusing attention on the problem of close textual analysis. The two men were also co-editors of *The Southern Review* during its final year of publication (1941–42).

Warren's first books were *John Brown: The Making of a Martyr* (1929), an unsympathetic biography, and *Thirty-Six Poems* (1935). From the time of publication of his first novel, *Night Rider* (1939), the story of a conflict between Kentucky tobacco growers and manufacturers, he devoted his energies largely to the writing of fiction. His second novel, *At Heaven's Gate* (1943), was followed by his most successful and best-known work, *All the King's Men* (1946). Focused on the career of the political demagogue Willie Stark (whose character is based on that of Louisiana's Huey Long), the novel examines and rejects the extremes of pure idealism and pragmatic expediency in favor of the view reached by the narrator Jack Burden, who comes to recognize both the inescapability of human corruption and a concomitant moral responsibility to live and act in the world of history. A Puritan-like preoccupation with corruption and guilt, combined with an emphasis on violence, dominates Warren's later novels of the South, which often employ rhetoric and sensational detail reminiscent of the tradition of Gothic fiction.

These novels include *World Enough and Time* (1950), *Band of Angels* (1955), *The Cave* (1959), and *Wilderness* (1961). His most recent novel, *The Flood* (1964), deals with the psychological reactions of a group of Tennesseans whose town must be sacrificed to make way for a dam.

Warren's short stories have been collected in *The Circus in the Attic* (1947). One of the best of these, "Blackberry Winter," is a reminiscence of a boyhood experience that foreshadows the youthful hero's impending alienation from the Southern family tradition in which he had been reared. Among Warren's later volumes of poems and verse narratives are *Selected Poems, 1923–1943* (1944), *Brother to Dragons* (1953), *Promises: Poems, 1954–1956* (1957), and *You, Emperors, and Others: Poems 1957–1960* (1960). Warren has also written on the race problem in *Who Speaks for the Negro?* (1965).

A useful introduction to Warren's work is J. L. Longley, ed., *Robert Penn Warren: A Collection of Critical Essays* (New York, 1965). Two longer critiques are Leonard Casper, *Robert Penn Warren: The Dark and Bloody Ground* (Seattle, 1960), and C. H. Bohner, *Robert Penn Warren* (New York, 1964).

The text of "Blackberry Winter" is that of *The Circus in the Attic* (New York, 1947).

Blackberry Winter

It was getting into June and past eight o'clock in the morning, but there was a fire—even if it wasn't a big fire, just a fire of chunks—on the hearth of the big stone fireplace in the living room. I was standing on the hearth, almost into the chimney, hunched over the fire, working my bare toes slowly on the warm stone. I relished the heat which made the skin of my bare legs warp and creep and tingle, even as I called to my mother, who was somewhere back in the dining room or kitchen, and said: "But it's June, I don't have to put them on!"

"You put them on if you are going out," she called.

I tried to assess the degree of authority and conviction in the tone, but at that distance it was hard to decide. I tried to analyze the tone, and then I thought what a fool I had been to start out the back door and let her see that I was barefoot. If I had gone out the front door or the side door she would never have known, not till dinner time anyway, and by then the day would have been half gone and I would have been all over the farm to see what the storm had done and down to the creek to see the flood. But it had never crossed my mind that they would try to stop you from going barefoot in June, no matter if there had been a gully-washer and a cold spell.

Nobody had ever tried to stop me in June as long as I could remember, and when you are nine years old, what you remember seems forever; for you remember everything and everything is important and stands big and full and fills up Time and is so solid that you can walk around and around it like a tree and look at it. You are aware that time

passes, that there is a movement in time, but that is not what Time is.
Time is not a movement, a flowing, a wind then, but is, rather, a kind of
climate in which things are, and when a thing happens it begins to live
and keeps on living and stands solid in Time like the tree that you can
walk around. And if there is a movement, the movement is not Time
itself, any more than a breeze is climate, and all the breeze does is to
shake a little the leaves on the tree which is alive and solid. When you
are nine, you know that there are things that you don't know, but you
know that when you know something you know it. You know how a
thing has been and you know that you can go barefoot in June. You do
not understand that voice from back in the kitchen which says that you
cannot go barefoot outdoors and run to see what has happened and rub
your feet over the wet shivery grass and make the perfect mark of your
foot in the smooth, creamy, red mud and then muse upon it as though
you had suddenly come upon that single mark on the glistening auroral
beach of the world. You have never seen a beach, but you have read
the book and how the footprint was there.

The voice had said what it had said, and I looked savagely at the
black stockings and the strong, scuffed brown shoes which I had
brought from my closet as far as the hearth rug. I called once more,
"But it's June," and waited.

"It's June," the voice replied from far away, "but it's blackberry
winter."

I had lifted my head to reply to that, to make one more test of
what was in that tone, when I happened to see the man.

The fireplace in the living room was at the end; for the stone
chimney was built, as in so many of the farmhouses in Tennessee, at the
end of a gable, and there was a window on each side of the chimney.
Out of the window on the north side of the fireplace I could see the
man. When I saw the man I did not call out what I had intended, but,
engrossed by the strangeness of the sight, watched him, still far off,
come along the path by the edge of the woods.

What was strange was that there should be a man there at all.
That path went along the yard fence, between the fence and the woods
which came right down to the yard, and then on back past the chicken
runs and on by the woods until it was lost to sight where the woods
bulged out and cut off the back field. There the path disappeared into
the woods. It led on back, I knew, through the woods and to the
swamp, skirted the swamp where the big trees gave way to sycamores
and water oaks and willows and tangled cane, and then led on to the
river. Nobody ever went back there except people who wanted to gig
frogs in the swamp or to fish in the river or to hunt in the woods, and
those people, if they didn't have a standing permission from my father,
always stopped to ask permission to cross the farm. But the man whom
I now saw wasn't, I could tell even at that distance, a sportsman. And

what would a sportsman have been doing down there after a storm? Besides, he was coming from the river, and nobody had gone down there that morning. I knew that for a fact, because if anybody had passed, certainly if a stranger had passed, the dogs would have made a racket and would have been out on him. But this man was coming up from the river and had come up through the woods. I suddenly had a vision of him moving up the grassy path in the woods, in the green twilight under the big trees, not making any sound on the path, while now and then, like drops off the eaves, a big drop of water would fall from a leaf or bough and strike a stiff oak leaf lower down with a small, hollow sound like a drop of water hitting tin. That sound, in the silence of the woods, would be very significant.

When you are a boy and stand in the stillness of woods, which can be so still that your heart almost stops beating and makes you want to stand there in the green twilight until you feel your very feet sinking into and clutching the earth like roots and your body breathing slow through its pores like the leaves — when you stand there and wait for the next drop to drop with its small, flat sound to a lower leaf, that sound seems to measure out something, to put an end to something, to begin something, and you cannot wait for it to happen and are afraid it will not happen, and then when it has happened, you are waiting again, almost afraid.

But the man whom I saw coming through the woods in my mind's eye did not pause and wait, growing into the ground and breathing with the enormous, soundless breathing of the leaves. Instead, I saw him moving in the green twilight inside my head as he was moving at that very moment along the path by the edge of the woods, coming toward the house. He was moving steadily, but not fast, with his shoulders hunched a little and his head thrust forward, like a man who has come a long way and has a long way to go. I shut my eyes for a couple of seconds, thinking that when I opened them he would not be there at all. There was no place for him to have come from, and there was no reason for him to come where he was coming, toward our house. But I opened my eyes, and there he was, and he was coming steadily along the side of the woods. He was not yet even with the back chicken yard.

"Mama," I called.

"You put them on," the voice said.

"There's a man coming," I called, "out back."

She did not reply to that, and I guessed that she had gone to the kitchen window to look. She would be looking at the man and wondering who he was and what he wanted, the way you always do in the country, and if I went back there now she would not notice right off whether or not I was barefoot. So I went back to the kitchen.

She was standing by the window. "I don't recognize him," she said, not looking around at me.

"Where could he be coming from?" I asked.

"I don't know," she said.

"What would he be doing down at the river? At night? In the storm?"

She studied the figure out the window, then said, "Oh, I reckon maybe he cut across from the Dunbar place."

That was, I realized, a perfectly rational explanation. He had not been down at the river in the storm, at night. He had come over this morning. You could cut across from the Dunbar place if you didn't mind breaking through a lot of elder and sassafras and blackberry bushes which had about taken over the old cross path, which nobody ever used any more. That satisfied me for a moment, but only for a moment. "Mama," I asked, "what would he be doing over at the Dunbar place last night?"

Then she looked at me, and I knew I had made a mistake, for she was looking at my bare feet. "You haven't got your shoes on," she said.

But I was saved by the dogs. That instant there was a bark which I recognized as Sam, the collie, and then a heavier, churning kind of bark which was Bully, and I saw a streak of white as Bully tore round the corner of the back porch and headed out for the man. Bully was a big, bone-white bull dog, the kind of dog that they used to call a farm bull dog but that you don't see any more, heavy chested and heavy headed, but with pretty long legs. He could take a fence as light as a hound. He had just cleared the white paling fence toward the woods when my mother ran out to the back porch and began calling, "Here you, Bully! Here you!"

Bully stopped in the path, waiting for the man, but he gave a few more of those deep, gargling, savage barks that reminded you of something down a stone-lined well. The red clay mud, I saw, was splashed up over his white chest and looked exciting, like blood.

The man, however, had not stopped walking even when Bully took the fence and started at him. He had kept right on coming. All he had done was to switch a little paper parcel which he carried from the right hand to the left, and then reach into his pants pocket to get something. Then I saw the glitter and knew that he had a knife in his hand, probably the kind of mean knife just made for devilment and nothing else, with a blade as long as the blade of a frog-sticker, which will snap out ready when you press a button in the handle. That knife must have had a button in the handle, or else how could he have had the blade out glittering so quick and with just one hand?

Pulling his knife against the dogs was a funny thing to do, for Bully was a big, powerful brute and fast, and Sam was all right. If those dogs had meant business, they might have knocked him down and ripped him before he got a stroke in. He ought to have picked up a heavy stick, something to take a swipe at them with and something which they could see and respect when they came at him. But he apparently did not know much about dogs. He just held the knife blade close against the right leg, low down, and kept on moving down the path.

Then my mother had called, and Bully had stopped. So the man let the blade of the knife snap back into the handle, and dropped it into his pocket, and kept on coming. Many women would have been afraid with the strange man who they knew had that knife in his pocket. That is, if they were alone in the house with nobody but a nine-year-old boy. And my mother was alone, for my father had gone off, and Dellie, the cook, was down at her cabin because she wasn't feeling well. But my mother wasn't afraid. She wasn't a big woman, but she was clear and brisk about everything she did and looked everybody and everything right in the eye from her own blue eyes in her tanned face. She had been the first woman in the county to ride a horse astride (that was back when she was a girl and long before I was born), and I have seen her snatch up a pump gun and go out and knock a chicken hawk out of the air like a busted skeet when he came over her chicken yard. She was a steady and self-reliant woman, and when I think of her now after all the years she has been dead, I think of her brown hands, not big, but somewhat square for a woman's hands, with square-cut nails. They looked, as a matter of fact, more like a young boy's hands than a grown woman's. But back then it never crossed my mind that she would ever be dead.

She stood on the back porch and watched the man enter the back gate, where the dogs (Bully had leaped back into the yard) were dancing and muttering and giving sidelong glances back to my mother to see if she meant what she had said. The man walked right by the dogs, almost brushing them, and didn't pay them any attention. I could see now that he wore old khaki pants, and a dark wool coat with stripes in it, and a gray felt hat. He had on a gray shirt with blue stripes in it, and no tie. But I could see a tie, blue and reddish, sticking in his side coat-pocket. Everything was wrong about what he wore. He ought to have been wearing blue jeans or overalls, and a straw hat or an old black felt hat, and the coat, granting that he might have been wearing a wool coat and not a jumper, ought not to have had those stripes. Those clothes, despite the fact that they were old enough and dirty enough for any tramp, didn't belong there in our back yard, coming down the path, in Middle Tennessee, miles away from any big town, and even a mile off the pike.

When he got almost to the steps, without having said anything, my mother, very matter-of-factly, said, "Good morning."

"Good morning," he said, and stopped and looked her over. He did not take off his hat, and under the brim you could see the perfectly unmemorable face, which wasn't old and wasn't young, or thick or thin. It was grayish and covered with about three days of stubble. The eyes were a kind of nondescript, muddy hazel, or something like that, rather bloodshot. His teeth, when he opened his mouth, showed yellow and uneven. A couple of them had been knocked out. You knew that they had been knocked out, because there was a scar, not very old, there on the lower lip just beneath the gap.

"Are you hunting work?" my mother asked him.

"Yes," he said — not "yes, mam" — and still did not take off his hat.

"I don't know about my husband, for he isn't here," she said, and didn't mind a bit telling the tramp, or whoever he was, with the mean knife in his pocket, that no man was around, "but I can give you a few things to do. The storm has drowned a lot of my chicks. Three coops of them. You can gather them up and bury them. Bury them deep so the dogs won't get at them. In the woods. And fix the coops the wind blew over. And down yonder beyond that pen by the edge of the woods are some drowned poults. They got out and I couldn't get them in. Even after it started to rain hard. Poults haven't got any sense."

"What are them things — poults?" he demanded, and spat on the brick walk. He rubbed his foot over the spot, and I saw that he wore a black, pointed-toe low shoe, all cracked and broken. It was a crazy kind of shoe to be wearing in the country.

"Oh, they're young turkeys," my mother was saying. "And they haven't got any sense. I oughtn't to try to raise them around here with so many chickens, anyway. They don't thrive near chickens, even in separate pens. And I won't give up my chickens." Then she stopped herself and resumed briskly on the note of business. "When you finish that, you can fix my flower beds. A lot of trash and mud and gravel has washed down. Maybe you can save some of my flowers if you are careful."

"Flowers," the man said, in a low, impersonal voice which seemed to have a wealth of meaning, but a meaning which I could not fathom. As I think back on it, it probably was not pure contempt. Rather, it was a kind of impersonal and distant marveling that he should be on the verge of grubbing in a flower bed. He said the word, and then looked off across the yard.

"Yes, flowers," my mother replied with some asperity, as though she would have nothing said or implied against flowers. "And they were very fine this year." Then she stopped and looked at the man. "Are you hungry?" she demanded.

"Yeah," he said.

"I'll fix you something," she said, "before you get started." She turned to me. "Show him where he can wash up," she commanded, and went into the house.

I took the man to the end of the porch where a pump was and where a couple of wash pans sat on a low shelf for people to use before they went into the house. I stood there while he laid down his little parcel wrapped in newspaper and took off his hat and looked around for a nail to hang it on. He poured the water and plunged his hands into it. They were big hands, and strong looking, but they did not have the creases and the earth-color of the hands of men who work outdoors. But they were dirty, with black dirt ground into the skin and under the nails. After he had washed his hands, he poured another basin of water and washed his face. He dried his face, and with the towel still dangling in his grasp, stepped over to the mirror on the house wall. He rubbed one hand over the stubble on his face. Then he carefully inspected his face, turning first one side and then the other, and stepped back and settled his striped coat down on his shoulders. He had the movements of a man who has just dressed up to go to church or a party—the way he settled his coat and smoothed it and scanned himself in the mirror.

Then he caught my glance on him. He glared at me for an instant out of the bloodshot eyes, then demanded in a low, harsh voice, "What you looking at?"

"Nothing," I managed to say, and stepped back a step from him.

He flung the towel down, crumpled, on the shelf, and went toward the kitchen door and entered without knocking.

My mother said something to him which I could not catch. I started to go in again, then thought about my bare feet, and decided to go back of the chicken yard, where the man would have to come to pick up the dead chicks. I hung around behind the chicken house until he came out.

He moved across the chicken yard with a fastidious, not quite finicking motion, looking down at the curdled mud flecked with bits of chicken-droppings. The mud curled up over the soles of his black shoes. I stood back from him some six feet and watched him pick up the first of the drowned chicks. He held it up by one foot and inspected it.

There is nothing deader looking than a drowned chick. The feet curl in that feeble, empty way which back when I was a boy, even if I was a country boy who did not mind hog-killing or frog-gigging, made me feel hollow in the stomach. Instead of looking plump and fluffy, the body is stringy and limp with the fluff plastered to it, and the neck is long and loose like a little string of rag. And the eyes have that bluish membrane over them which makes you think of a very old man who is sick about to die.

The man stood there and inspected the chick. Then he looked all around as though he didn't know what to do with it.

"There's a great big old basket in the shed," I said, and pointed to the shed attached to the chicken house.

He inspected me as though he had just discovered my presence, and moved toward the shed.

"There's a spade there, too," I added.

He got the basket and began to pick up the other chicks, picking each one up slowly by a foot and then flinging it into the basket with a nasty, snapping motion. Now and then he would look at me out of the blood-shot eyes. Every time he seemed on the verge of saying something, but he did not. Perhaps he was building up to say something to me, but I did not wait that long. His way of looking at me made me so uncomfortable that I left the chicken yard.

Besides, I had just remembered that the creek was in flood, over the bridge, and that people were down there watching it. So I cut across the farm toward the creek. When I got to the big tobacco field I saw that it had not suffered much. The land lay right and not many tobacco plants had washed out of the ground. But I knew that a lot of tobacco round the country had been washed right out. My father had said so at breakfast.

My father was down at the bridge. When I came out of the gap in the osage hedge into the road, I saw him sitting on his mare over the heads of the other men who were standing around, admiring the flood. The creek was big here, even in low water; for only a couple of miles away it ran into the river, and when a real flood came, the red water got over the pike where it dipped down to the bridge, which was an iron bridge, and high over the floor and even the side railings of the bridge. Only the upper iron work would show, with the water boiling and frothing red and white around it. That creek rose so fast and so heavy because a few miles back it came down out of the hills, where the gorges filled up with water in no time when a rain came. The creek ran in a deep bed with limestone bluffs along both sides until it got within three quarters of a mile of the bridge, and when it came out from between those bluffs in flood it was boiling and hissing and steaming like water from a fire hose.

Whenever there was a flood, people from half the county would come down to see the sight. After a gully-washer there would not be any work to do anyway. If it didn't ruin your crop, you couldn't plow and you felt like taking a holiday to celebrate. If it did ruin your crop, there wasn't anything to do except to try to take your mind off the mortgage, if you were rich enough to have a mortgage, and if you couldn't afford a mortgage you needed something to take your mind off how hungry you would be by Christmas. So people would come down to the bridge and look at the flood. It made something different from the run of days.

There would not be much talking after the first few minutes of trying to guess how high the water was this time. The men and kids just stood around, or sat their horses or mules, as the case might be, or stood up in the wagon beds. They looked at the strangeness of the flood for an hour or two, and then somebody would say that he had better be getting on home to dinner and would start walking down the gray, puddled limestone pike, or would touch heel to his mount and start off.

Everybody always knew what it would be like when he got down to the bridge, but people always came. It was like church or a funeral. They always came, that is, if it was summer and the flood unexpected. Nobody ever came down in winter to see high water.

When I came out of the gap in the bodock[1] hedge, I saw the crowd, perhaps fifteen or twenty men and a lot of kids, and saw my father sitting his mare, Nellie Gray. He was a tall, limber man and carried himself well. I was always proud to see him sit a horse, he was so quiet and straight, and when I stepped through the gap of the hedge that morning, the first thing that happened was, I remember, the warm feeling I always had when I saw him up on a horse, just sitting. I did not go toward him, but skirted the crowd on the far side, to get a look at the creek. For one thing, I was not sure what he would say about the fact that I was barefoot. But the first thing I knew, I heard his voice calling, "Seth!"

I went toward him, moving apologetically past the men, who bent their large, red or thin, sallow faces above me. I knew some of the men, and knew their names, but because those I knew were there in a crowd, mixed with the strange faces, they seemed foreign to me, and not friendly. I did not look up at my father until I was almost within touching distance of his heel. Then I looked up and tried to read his face, to see if he was angry about my being barefoot. Before I could decide anything from that impassive, high-boned face, he had leaned over and reached a hand to me. "Grab on," he commanded.

I grabbed on and gave a little jump, and he said, "Up-see-daisy!" and whisked me, light as a feather, up to the pommel of his McClellan saddle.[2]

"You can see better up here," he said, slid back on the cantle a little to make me more comfortable, and then, looking over my head at the swollen, tumbling water, seemed to forget all about me. But his right hand was laid on my side, just above my thigh, to steady me.

I was sitting there as quiet as I could, feeling the faint stir of my father's chest against my shoulders as it rose and fell with his breath, when I saw the cow. At first, looking up the creek, I thought it was just another big piece of driftwood steaming down the creek in the ruck of water, but all at once a pretty good-size boy who had climbed part way up a telephone pole by the pike so that he could see better yelled out, "Golly-damn, look at that-air cow!"

Everybody looked. It was a cow all right, but it might just as well have been driftwood; for it was dead as a chunk, rolling and roiling down the creek, appearing and disappearing, feet up or head up, it didn't matter which.

The cow started up the talk again. Somebody wondered whether

---

[1] Osage orange (a corruption of *bois d'arc*).
[2] A type of military saddle named for General George B. McClellan (1826–1885).

it would hit one of the clear places under the top girder of the bridge
and get through or whether it would get tangled in the drift and trash
that had piled against the upright girders and braces. Somebody remembered how about ten years before so much driftwood had piled up on
the bridge that it was knocked off its foundations. Then the cow hit. It
hit the edge of the drift against one of the girders, and hung there. For a
few seconds it seemed as though it might tear loose, but then we saw
that it was really caught. It bobbed and heaved on its side there in a
slow, grinding, uneasy fashion. It had a yoke around its neck, the kind
made out of a forked limb to keep a jumper behind fence.

"She shore jumped one fence," one of the men said.

And another: "Well, she done jumped her last one, fer a fack."

Then they began to wonder about whose cow it might be. They
decided it must belong to Milt Alley. They said that he had a cow that
was a jumper, and kept her in a fenced-in piece of ground up the creek.
I had never seen Milt Alley, but I knew who he was. He was a squatter
and lived up the hills a way, on a shirt-tail patch of set-on-edge land, in
a cabin. He was pore white trash. He had lots of children. I had seen
the children at school, when they came. They were thin-faced, with
straight, sticky-looking, dough-colored hair, and they smelled something
like old sour buttermilk, not because they drank so much buttermilk but
because that is the sort of smell which children out of those cabins tend
to have. The big Alley boy drew dirty pictures and showed them to the
little boys at school.

That was Milt Alley's cow. It looked like the kind of cow he
would have, a scrawny, old, sway-backed cow, with a yoke around her
neck. I wondered if Milt Alley had another cow.

"Poppa," I said, "do you think Milt Alley has got another cow?"

"You say 'Mr. Alley,'" my father said quietly.

"Do you think he has?"

"No telling," my father said.

Then a big gangly boy, about fifteen, who was sitting on a scraggly
little old mule with a piece of croker sack thrown across the sawtooth
spine, and who had been staring at the cow, suddenly said to nobody in
particular, "Reckin anybody ever et drownt cow?"

He was the kind of boy who might just as well as not have been
the son of Milt Alley, with his faded and patched overalls ragged at the
bottom of the pants and the mud-stiff brogans hanging off his skinny,
bare ankles at the level of the mule's belly. He had said what he did,
and then looked embarrassed and sullen when all the eyes swung at
him. He hadn't meant to say it, I am pretty sure now. He would have
been too proud to say it, just as Milt Alley would have been too proud.
He had just been thinking out loud, and the words had popped out.

There was an old man standing there on the pike, an old man with
a white beard. "Son," he said to the embarrassed and sullen boy on the

mule, "you live long enough and you'll find a man will eat anything when the time comes."

"Time gonna come fer some folks this year," another man said.

"Son," the old man said, "in my time I et things a man don't like to think on. I was a sojer and I rode with Gin'l Forrest,[3] and them things we et when the time come. I tell you. I et meat what got up and run when you taken out yore knife to cut a slice to put on the fire. You had to knock it down with a carbeen butt, it was so active. That-air meat would jump like a bullfrog, it was so full of skippers."

But nobody was listening to the old man. The boy on the mule turned his sullen sharp face from him, dug a heel into the side of the mule and went off up the pike with a motion which made you think that any second you would hear mule bones clashing inside that lank and scrofulous hide.

"Cy Dundee's boy," a man said, and nodded toward the figure going up the pike on the mule.

"Reckin Cy Dundee's young-uns seen times they'd settle fer drownt cow," another man said.

The old man with the beard peered at them both from his weak, slow eyes, first at one and then at the other. "Live long enough," he said, "and a man will settle fer what he kin git."

Then there was silence again, with the people looking at the red, foam-flecked water.

My father lifted the bridle rein in his left hand, and the mare turned and walked around the group and up the pike. We rode on up to our big gate, where my father dismounted to open it and let me myself ride Nellie Gray through. When he got to the lane that led off from the drive about two hundred yards from our house, my father said, "Grab on." I grabbed on, and he let me down to the ground. "I'm going to ride down and look at my corn," he said. "You go on." He took the lane, and I stood there on the drive and watched him ride off. He was wearing cowhide boots and an old hunting coat, and I thought that that made him look very military, like a picture. That and the way he rode.

I did not go to the house. Instead, I went by the vegetable garden and crossed behind the stables, and headed down for Dellie's cabin. I wanted to go down and play with Jebb, who was Dellie's little boy about two years older than I was. Besides, I was cold. I shivered as I walked, and I had gooseflesh. The mud which crawled up between my toes with every step I took was like ice. Dellie would have a fire, but she wouldn't make me put on shoes and stockings.

Dellie's cabin was of logs, with one side, because it was on a slope, set on limestone chunks, with a little porch attached to it, and had a little whitewashed fence around it and a gate with plow-points on

---

[3] The Confederate cavalry general, Nathan B. Forrest (1821–1877).

a wire to clink when somebody came in, and had two big white oaks in the yard and some flowers and a nice privy in the back with some honeysuckle growing over it. Dellie and Old Jebb, who was Jebb's father and who lived with Dellie and had lived with her for twenty-five years even if they never had got married, were careful to keep everything nice around their cabin. They had the name all over the community for being clean and clever Negroes. Dellie and Jebb were what they used to call "white-folks' niggers." There was a big difference between their cabin and the other two cabins farther down where the other tenants lived. My father kept the other cabins weatherproof, but he couldn't undertake to go down and pick up after the litter they strewed. They didn't take the trouble to have a vegetable patch like Dellie and Jebb or to make preserves from wild plum, and jelly from crab apple the way Dellie did. They were shiftless, and my father was always threatening to get shed of them. But he never did. When they finally left, they just up and left on their own, for no reason, to go and be shiftless somewhere else. Then some more came. But meanwhile they lived down there, Matt Rawson and his family, and Sid Turner and his, and I played with their children all over the farm when they weren't working. But when I wasn't around they were mean sometimes to Little Jebb. That was because the other tenants down there were jealous of Dellie and Jebb.

I was so cold that I ran the last fifty yards to Dellie's gate. As soon as I had entered the yard, I saw that the storm had been hard on Dellie's flowers. The yard was, as I have said, on a slight slope, and the water running across had gutted the flower beds and washed out all the good black woods-earth which Dellie had brought in. What little grass there was in the yard was plastered sparsely down on the ground, the way the drainage water had left it. It reminded me of the way the fluff was plastered down on the skin of the drowned chicks that the strange man had been picking up, up in my mother's chicken yard.

I took a few steps up the path to the cabin, and then I saw that the drainage water had washed a lot of trash and filth out from under Dellie's house. Up toward the porch, the ground was not clean any more. Old pieces of rag, two or three rusted cans, pieces of rotten rope, some hunks of old dog dung, broken glass, old paper, and all sorts of things like that had washed out from under Dellie's house to foul her clean yard. It looked just as bad as the yards of the other cabins, or worse. It was worse, as a matter of fact, because it was a surprise. I had never thought of all that filth being under Dellie's house. It was not anything against Dellie that the stuff had been under the cabin. Trash will get under any house. But I did not think of that when I saw the foulness which had washed out on the ground which Dellie sometimes used to sweep with a twig broom to make nice and clean.

I picked my way past the filth, being careful not to get my bare feet on it, and mounted to Dellie's door. When I knocked, I heard her voice telling me to come in.

It was dark inside the cabin, after the daylight, but I could make out Dellie piled up in bed under a quilt, and Little Jebb crouched by the hearth, where a low fire simmered. "Howdy," I said to Dellie, "how you feeling?"

Her big eyes, the whites surprising and glaring in the black face, fixed on me as I stood there, but she did not reply. It did not look like Dellie, or act like Dellie, who would grumble and bustle around our kitchen, talking to herself, scolding me or Little Jebb, clanking pans, making all sorts of unnecessary noises and mutterings like an old-fashioned black steam thrasher engine when it has got up an extra head of steam and keeps popping the governor and rumbling and shaking on its wheels. But now Dellie just lay up there on the bed, under the patchwork quilt, and turned the black face, which I scarcely recognized, and the glaring white eyes to me.

"How you feeling?" I repeated.

"I'se sick," the voice said croakingly out of the strange black face which was not attached to Dellie's big, squat body, but stuck out from under a pile of tangled bedclothes. Then the voice added: "Mighty sick."

"I'm sorry," I managed to say.

The eyes remained fixed on me for a moment, then they left me and the head rolled back on the pillow. "Sorry," the voice said, in a flat way which wasn't question or statement of anything. It was just the empty word put into the air with no meaning or expression, to float off like a feather or a puff of smoke, while the big eyes, with the whites like the peeled white of hard-boiled eggs, stared at the ceiling.

"Dellie," I said after a minute, "there's a tramp up at the house. He's got a knife."

She was not listening. She closed her eyes.

I tiptoed over to the hearth where Jebb was and crouched beside him. We began to talk in low voices. I was asking him to get out his train and play train. Old Jebb had put spool wheels on three cigar boxes and put wire links between the boxes to make a train for Jebb. The box that was the locomotive had the top closed and a length of broom stick for a smoke stack. Jebb didn't want to get the train out, but I told him I would go home if he didn't. So he got out the train, and the colored rocks, and fossils of crinoid stems, and other junk he used for the load, and we began to push it around, talking the way we thought trainmen talked, making a chuck-chucking sound under the breath for the noise of the locomotive and now and then uttering low, cautious toots for the whistle. We got so interested in playing train that the toots got louder.

Then, before he thought, Jebb gave a good, loud *toot-toot*, blowing for a crossing.

"Come here," the voice said from the bed.

Jebb got up slow from his hands and knees, giving me a sudden, naked, inimical look.

"Come here!" the voice said.

Jebb went to the bed. Dellie propped herself weakly up on one arm, muttering, "Come closer."

Jebb stood closer.

"Last thing I do, I'm gonna do it," Dellie said. "Done tole you to be quiet."

Then she slapped him. It was an awful slap, more awful for the kind of weakness which it came from and brought to focus. I had seen her slap Jebb before, but the slapping had always been the kind of easy slap you would expect from a good-natured, grumbling Negro woman like Dellie. But this was different. It was awful. It was so awful that Jebb didn't make a sound. The tears just popped out and ran down his face, and his breath came sharp, like gasps.

Dellie fell back. "Cain't even be sick," she said to the ceiling. "Git sick and they won't even let you lay. They tromp all over you. Cain't even be sick." Then she closed her eyes.

I went out of the room. I almost ran getting to the door, and I did run across the porch and down the steps and across the yard, not caring whether or not I stepped on the filth which had washed out from under the cabin. I ran almost all the way home. Then I thought about my mother catching me with the bare feet. So I went down to the stables.

I heard a noise in the crib, and opened the door. There was Big Jebb, sitting on an old nail keg, shelling corn into a bushel basket. I went in, pulling the door shut behind me, and crouched on the floor near him. I crouched there for a couple of minutes before either of us spoke, and watched him shelling the corn.

He had very big hands, knotted and grayish at the joints, with calloused palms which seemed to be streaked with rust with the rust coming up between the fingers to show from the back. His hands were so strong and tough that he could take a big ear of corn and rip the grains right off the cob with the palm of his hand, all in one motion, like a machine. "Work long as me," he would say, "and the good Lawd'll give you a hand lak cass-ion won't nuthin' hurt." And his hands did look like cast iron, old cast iron streaked with rust.

He was an old man, up in his seventies, thirty years or more older than Dellie, but he was strong as a bull. He was a squat sort of man, heavy in the shoulders, with remarkably long arms, the kind of build they say the river natives have on the Congo from paddling so much in their boats. He had a round bullet-head, set on powerful shoulders. His skin was very black, and the thin hair on his head was now grizzled like tufts of old cotton batting. He had small eyes and a flat nose, not big, and the kindest and wisest old face in the world, the blunt, sad, wise face of an old animal peering tolerantly out on the goings-on of the merely human creatures before him. He was a good man, and I loved him next to my mother and father. I crouched there on the floor of the crib and watched him shell corn with the rusty cast-iron hands, while he looked down at me out of the little eyes set in the blunt face.

"Dellie says she's might sick," I said.

"Yeah," he said.

"What's she sick from?"

"Woman-mizry," he said.

"What's woman-mizry?"

"Hit comes on 'em," he said. "Hit just comes on 'em when the time comes."

"What is it?"

"Hit is the change," he said. "Hit is the change of life and time."

"What changes?"

"You too young to know."

"Tell me."

"Time come and you find out everthing."

I knew that there was no use in asking him any more. When I asked him things and he said that, I always knew that he would not tell me. So I continued to crouch there and watch him. Now that I had sat there a little while, I was cold again.

"What you shiver fer?" he asked me.

"I'm cold. I'm cold because it's blackberry winter," I said.

"Maybe 'tis and maybe 'tain't," he said.

"My mother says it is."

"Ain't sayen Miss Sallie doan know and ain't sayen she do. But folks doan know everthing."

"Why isn't it blackberry winter?"

"Too late fer blackberry winter. Blackberries done bloomed."

"She said it was."

"Blackberry winter just a leetle cold spell. Hit come and then hit go away, and hit is growed summer of a sudden lak a gunshot. Ain't no tellen hit will go way this time."

"It's June," I said.

"June," he replied with great contempt. "That what folks say. What June mean? Maybe hit is come cold to stay."

"Why?"

"Cause this-here old yearth is tahrd. Hit is tahrd and ain't gonna perduce. Lawd let hit come rain one time forty days and forty nights, 'cause He wus tahrd of sinful folks. Maybe this-here old yearth say to the Lawd, Lawd, I done plum tahrd, Lawd, lemme rest. And Lawd say, Yearth, you done yore best, you give 'em cawn and you give 'em taters, and all they think on is they gut, and, Yearth, you kin take a rest."

"What will happen?"

"Folks will eat up everthing. The yearth won't perduce no more. Folks cut down all the trees and burn 'em cause they cold, and the yearth won't grow no more. I been tellen 'em. I been tellen folks. Sayen, maybe this year, hit is the time. But they doan listen to me, how the yearth is tahrd. Maybe this year they find out."

"Will everything die?"

"Everthing and everbody, hit will be so."

"This year?"

"Ain't no tellen. Maybe this year."

"My mother said it is blackberry winter," I said confidently, and got up.

"Ain't sayen nothin' agin Miss Sallie," he said.

I went to the door of the crib. I was really cold now. Running, I had got up a sweat and now I was worse.

I hung on the door, looking at Jebb, who was shelling corn again.

"There's a tramp came to the house," I said. I had almost forgotten the tramp.

"Yeah."

"He came by the back way. What was he doing down there in the storm?"

"They comes and they goes," he said, "and ain't no tellen."

"He had a mean knife."

"The good ones and the bad ones, they comes and they goes. Storm or sun, light or dark. They is folks and they comes and they goes lak folks."

I hung on the door, shivering.

He studied me a moment, then said, "You git on to the house. You ketch yore death. Then what yore mammy say?"

I hesitated.

"You git," he said.

When I came to the back yard, I saw that my father was standing by the back porch and the tramp was walking toward him. They began talking before I reached them, but I got there just as my father was saying, "I'm sorry, but I haven't got any work. I got all the hands on the place I need now. I won't need any extra until wheat thrashing."

The stranger made no reply, just looked at my father.

My father took out his leather coin purse, and got out a half-dollar. He held it toward the man. "This is for half a day," he said.

The man looked at the coin, and then at my father, making no motion to take the money. But that was the right amount. A dollar a day was what you paid them back in 1910. And the man hadn't even worked half a day.

Then the man reached out and took the coin. He dropped it into the right side pocket of his coat. Then he said, very slowly and without feeling: "I didn't want to work on your —— farm."

He used the word which they would have frailed[4] me to death for using.

I looked at my father's face and it was streaked white under the sunburn. Then he said, "Get off this place. Get off this place or I won't be responsible."

The man dropped his right hand into his pants pocket. It was the pocket where he kept the knife. I was just about to yell to my father about the knife when the hand came back out with nothing in it. The man gave a kind of twisted grin, showing where the teeth had been knocked out above the new scar. I thought that instant how maybe he had tried before to pull a knife on somebody else and had got his teeth knocked out.

So now he just gave that twisted, sickish grin out of the unmemorable, grayish face, and then spat on the brick path. The glob landed just about six inches from the toe of my father's right boot. My father looked down at it, and so did I. I thought that if the glob had hit my father's boot something would have happened. I looked down and saw the bright glob, and on one side of it my father's strong cowhide boots, with the brass eyelets and the leather thongs, heavy boots splashed with good red mud and set solid on the bricks, and on the other side the pointed-toe, broken, black shoes, on which the mud looked so sad and out of place. Then I saw one of the black shoes move a little, just a twitch first, then a real step backward.

The man moved in a quarter circle to the end of the porch, with my father's steady gaze upon him all the while. At the end of the porch, the man reached up to the shelf where the wash pans were to get his little newspaper-wrapped parcel. Then he disappeared around the corner of the house and my father mounted the porch and went into the kitchen without a word.

I followed around the house to see what the man would do. I wasn't afraid of him now, no matter if he did have the knife. When I got around in front, I saw him going out the yard gate and starting up the drive toward the pike. So I ran to catch up with him. He was sixty yards or so up the drive before I caught up.

I did not walk right up even with him at first, but trailed him, the way a kid will, about seven or eight feet behind, now and then running two or three steps in order to hold my place against his longer stride. When I first came up behind him, he turned to give me a look, just a meaningless look, and then fixed his eyes up the drive and kept on walking.

When we had got around the bend in the drive which cut the

---

[4] Whipped (a dialect variant of *flailed*).

house from sight, and were going along by the edge of the woods, I decided to come up even with him. I ran a few steps, and was by his side, or almost, but some feet off to the right. I walked along in this position for a while, and he never noticed me. I walked along until we got within sight of the big gate that let on the pike.

Then I said: "Where did you come from?"

He looked at me then with a look which seemed almost surprised that I was there. Then he said, "It ain't none of yore business."

We went on another fifty feet.

Then I said, "Where are you going?"

He stopped, studied me dispassionately for a moment, then suddenly took a step toward me and leaned his face down at me. The lips jerked back, but not in any grin, to show where the teeth were knocked out and to make the scar on the lower lip come white with the tension.

He said: "Stop following me. You don't stop following me and I cut yore throat, you little son-of-a-bitch."

Then he went on to the gate, and up the pike.

That was thirty-five years ago. Since that time my father and mother have died. I was still a boy, but a big boy, when my father got cut on the blade of a mowing machine and died of lockjaw. My mother sold the place and went to town to live with her sister. But she never took hold after my father's death, and she died within three years, right in middle life. My aunt always said, "Sallie just died of a broken heart, she was so devoted." Dellie is dead, too, but she died, I heard, quite a long time after we sold the farm.

As for Little Jebb, he grew up to be a mean and ficey Negro. He killed another Negro in a fight and got sent to the penitentiary, where he is yet, the last I heard tell. He probably grew up to be mean and ficey from just being picked on so much by the children of the other tenants, who were jealous of Jebb and Dellie for being thrifty and clever and being white-folks' niggers.

Old Jebb lived forever. I saw him ten years ago and he was about a hundred then, and not looking much different. He was living in town then, on relief—that was back in the Depression—when I went to see him. He said to me: "Too strong to die. When I was a young feller just comen on and seen how things wuz, I prayed the Lawd. I said, Oh, Lawd, gimme strength and meke me strong fer to do and to in-dure. The Lawd hearkened to my prayer. He give me strength. I was in-duren proud fer being strong and me much man. The Lawd give me my prayer and my strength. But now He done gone off and fergot me and left me alone with my strength. A man doan know what to pray fer, and him mortal."

Jebb is probably living yet, as far as I know.

That is what has happened since the morning when the tramp

leaned his face down at me and showed his teeth and said: "Stop following me. You don't stop following me and I cut yore throat, you little son-of-a-bitch." That was what he said, for me not to follow him. But I did follow him, all the years.

1947

Richard Wright   *1909–1960*

Born in Mississippi, the son of a mill worker and a country school teacher, Richard Wright spent his boyhood in Memphis, Tennessee. He learned at an early age the hard lesson of what it meant to be a Negro and poor. Through hard work and self-discipline, he supported and educated himself. At the age of fifteen he left home and traveled about the country working at whatever menial job he could find. At nineteen he arrived in Chicago, where he stayed for several years. During the 1930's he joined the Communist Party but left it in the 1940's—writing later of his disillusionment in *The God That Failed* (1950). Moving to New York, he found a newspaper job and began writing the stories of Negro life in the South that made up his first book, *Uncle Tom's Children* (1938; rev. 1940). His first novel, *Native Son* (1940), won both critical acclaim and best sellerdom. It is a powerful psychological study of a Negro boy, Bigger Thomas, who grows up in the Chicago slums and commits a murder which is the consequence of his reactions to the pressures of his environment and not of a wish to kill. In this respect there is a similarity between Wright's viewpoint and Theodore Dreiser's in *An American Tragedy* (1925). An important difference is that Wright was a protestor who hoped that the conditions suffered by his Negro hero might be changed, while Dreiser remained a fatalistic observer. *Native Son* was made into a successful drama, and in 1950 Wright played the lead role in a film he made of it in Argentina. After publishing *Native Son,* Wright collaborated on *Twelve Million Black Voices* (1941), a photographic history of the American Negro, and wrote *Black Boy* (1945), an autobiographical account of his childhood and early youth.

After World War II, Wright made his home in Paris. His later books include two novels—*The Outsider* (1953) and *The Long Dream* (1958)—and several nonfictional works: *Black Power* (1954), an account of a trip to Africa; *The Color Curtain* (1956), the report of a conference of Asian and African nations; and *Pagan Spain* (1957), a disillusioned view of that country. Posthumous publications are *Lawd Today* (1963), a very early, previously unpublished novel, and *Eight Men* (1961), a collection of stories. Of these, "The Man Who Went to Chicago," based on Wright's early years in that city, is an accounting of the many frustrations and indignities suffered by an intelligent young black American in his efforts to find a place in a white-dominated society.

The text of "The Man Who Went to Chicago" is that of *Eight Men* (New York, 1961).

The Man Who Went to Chicago

When I rose in the morning the temperature had dropped below zero. The house was as cold to me as the Southern streets had been in winter. I dressed, doubling my clothing. I ate in a restaurant, caught a streetcar, and rode south, rode until I could see no more black faces on the sidewalks. I had now crossed the boundary line of the Black Belt and had entered the territory where jobs were perhaps to be had from white folks. I walked the streets and looked into shop windows until I saw a sign in a delicatessen: PORTER WANTED.

I went in and a stout white woman came to me.

"Vat do you vant?" she asked.

The voice jarred me. She's Jewish, I thought, remembering with shame the obscenities I used to shout at Jewish storekeepers in Arkansas.

"I thought maybe you needed a porter," I said.

"Meester 'Offman, he eesn't here yet," she said. "Vill you vait?"

"Yes, ma'am."

"Seet down."

"No, ma'am, I'll wait outside."

"But eet's cold out zhere," she said.

"That's all right," I said.

She shrugged. I went to the sidewalk. I waited for a half an hour in the bitter cold, regretting that I had not remained in the warm store, but unable to go back inside. A bald, stoutish white man went into the store and pulled off his coat. Yes, he was the boss man . . .

"Zo you vant a job?" he asked.

"Yes, sir," I answered, guessing at the meaning of his words.

"Vhere you vork before?"

"In Memphis, Tennessee."

"My brudder-in-law vorked in Tennessee vonce," he said.

I was hired. The work was easy, but I found to my dismay that I could not understand a third of what was said to me. My slow Southern ears were baffled by their clouded, thick accents. One morning Mrs. Hoffman asked me to go to a neighboring store — it was owned by a cousin of hers — and get a can of chicken *à la* king. I had never heard the phrase before and I asked her to repeat it.

"Don't you know nosing?" she demanded of me.

"If you would write it down for me, I'd know what to get," I ventured timidly.

"I can't vite!" she shouted in a sudden fury. "Vat kinda boy iss you?"

I memorized the separate sounds that she had uttered and went to the neighboring store.

"Mrs. Hoffman wants a can Cheek Keeng Awr Lar Keeng," I said slowly, hoping he would not think I was being offensive.

"All vite," he said, after staring at me a moment.

He put a can into a paper bag and gave it to me; outside in the street I opened the bag and read the label: Chicken *à la* King. I cursed, disgusted with myself. I knew those words. It had been her thick accent that had thrown me off. Yet I was not angry with her for speaking broken English; my English, too, was broken. But why could she not have taken more patience? Only one answer came to my mind. I was black and she did not care. Or so I thought . . . I was persisting in reading my present environment in the light of my old one. I reasoned thus: though English was my native tongue and America my native land, she, an alien, could operate a store and earn a living in a neighborhood where I could not even live. I reasoned further that she was aware of this and was trying to protect her position against me.

It was not until I had left the delicatessen job that I saw how grossly I had misread the motives and attitudes of Mr. Hoffman and his wife. I had not yet learned anything that would have helped me to thread my way through these perplexing racial relations. Accepting my environment at its face value, trapped by my own emotions, I kept asking myself what had black people done to bring this crazy world upon them?

The fact of the separation of white and black was clear to me; it was its effect upon the personalities of people that stumped and dismayed me. I did not feel that I was a threat to anybody; yet, as soon as I had grown old enough to think, I had learned that my entire personality, my aspirations, had long ago been discounted; that, in a measure, the very meaning of the words I spoke could not be fully understood.

And when I contemplated the area of No Man's Land into which the Negro mind in America had been shunted I wondered if there had ever been in all human history a more corroding and devastating attack upon the personalities of men than the idea of racial discrimination. In order to escape the racial attack that went to the roots of my life, I would have gladly accepted any way of life but the one in which I found myself. I would have agreed to live under a system of feudal oppression, not because I preferred feudalism but because I felt that feudalism made use of a limited part of a man, defined man, his rank, his function in society. I would have consented to live under the most rigid type of dictatorship, for I felt that dictatorships, too, defined the use of men, however degrading that use might be.

While working as a porter in Memphis I had often stood aghast as a friend of mine had offered himself to be kicked by the white men; but now, while working in Chicago, I was learning that perhaps even a kick was better than uncertainty . . . I had elected, in my fevered search for honorable adjustment to the American scene, not to submit and in doing so I had embraced the daily horror of anxiety, of tension, of eternal disquiet. I could now sympathize with—though I could never bring myself to approve—those tortured blacks who had given up and had gone to their white tormentors and had said: "Kick me, if that's all there is for me; kick me and let me feel at home, let me have peace!"

Color-hate defined the place of black life as below that of white life; and the black man, responding to the same dreams as the white man, strove to bury within his heart his awareness of this difference because it made him lonely and afraid. Hated by whites and being an organic part of the culture that hated him, the black man grew in turn to hate in himself that which others hated in him. But pride would make him hate his self-hate, for he would not want whites to know that he was so thoroughly conquered by them that his total life was conditioned by their attitude; but in the act of hiding his self-hate, he could not help but hate those who evoked his self-hate in him. So each part of his day would be consumed in a war with himself, a good part of his energy would be spent in keeping control of his unruly emotions, emotions which he had not wished to have, but could not help having. Held at bay by the hate of others, preoccupied with his own feelings, he was continuously at war with reality. He became inefficient, less able to see and judge the objective world. And when he reached that state, the white people looked at him and laughed and said:

"Look, didn't I tell you niggers were that way?"

To solve this tangle of balked emotion, I loaded the empty part of the ship of my personality with fantasies of ambition to keep it from toppling over into the sea of senselessness. Like any other American, I dreamed of going into business and making money; I dreamed of working for a firm that would allow me to advance until I reached an important position; I even dreamed of organizing secret groups of blacks to fight all whites . . . And if the blacks would not agree to organize, then they would have to be fought. I would end up again with self-hate, but it was now a self-hate that was projected outward upon other blacks. Yet

I knew—with that part of my mind that the whites had given me—that none of my dreams were possible. Then I would hate myself for allowing my mind to dwell upon the unattainable. Thus the circle would complete itself.

Slowly I began to forge in the depths of my mind a mechanism that repressed all the dreams and desires that the Chicago streets, the newspapers, the movies were evoking in me. I was going through a second childhood; a new sense of the limit of the possible was being born in me. What could I dream of that had the barest possibility of coming true? I could think of nothing. And, slowly, it was upon exactly that nothingness that my mind began to dwell, that constant sense of wanting without having, of being hated without reason. A dim notion of what life meant to a Negro in America was coming to consciousness in me, not in terms of external events, lynchings, Jim Crowism, and the endless brutalities, but in terms of crossed-up feeling, of emotional tension. I sensed that Negro life was a sprawling land of unconscious suffering, and there were but few Negroes who knew the meaning of their lives, who could tell their story.

Word reached me that an examination for postal clerk was impending and at once I filed an application and waited. As the date for the examination drew near, I was faced with another problem. How could I get a free day without losing my job? In the South it would have been an unwise policy for a Negro to have gone to his white boss and ask for time to take an examination for another job. It would have implied that the Negro did not like to work for the white boss, that he felt he was not receiving just consideration and, inasmuch as most jobs that Negroes held in the South involved a personal, paternalistic relationship, he would have been risking an argument that might have led to violence.

I now began to speculate about what kind of man Mr. Hoffman was, and I found that I did not know him; that is, I did not know his basic attitude toward Negroes. If I asked him, would he be sympathetic enough to allow me time off with pay? I needed the money. Perhaps he would say: "Go home and stay home if you don't like this job!" I was not sure of him. I decided, therefore, that I had better not risk it. I would forfeit the money and stay away without telling him.

The examination was scheduled to take place on a Monday; I had been working steadily and I would be too tired to do my best if I took the examination without benefit of rest. I decided to stay away from the shop Saturday, Sunday, and Monday. But what could I tell Mr. Hoffman? Yes, I would tell him that I had been ill. No, that was too thin. I would tell him that my mother had died in Memphis and that I had gone down to bury her. That lie might work.

I took the examination and when I came to the store on Tuesday, Mr. Hoffman was astonished, of course.

"I didn't sink you vould ever come back," he said.

"I'm awfully sorry, Mr. Hoffman."

"Vat happened?"

"My mother died in Memphis and I had to go down and bury her," I lied.

He looked at me, then shook his head.

"Rich, you lie," he said.

"I'm not lying," I lied stoutly.

"You vanted to do somesink, zo you zayed ervay," he said, shrugging.

"No, sir. I'm telling you the truth," I piled another lie upon the first one.

"No. you lie. You disappoint me," he said.

"Well, all I can do is tell you the truth," I lied indignantly.

"Vy didn't you use the phone?"

"I didn't think of it," I told a fresh lie.

"Rich, if your mudder die, you vould tell me," he said.

"I didn't have time. Had to catch the train," I lied yet again.

"Vhere did you get the money?"

"My aunt gave it to me," I said, disgusted that I had to lie and lie again.

"I don't vant a boy vat tells lies," he said.

"I don't lie," I lied passionately to protect my lies.

Mrs. Hoffman joined in and both of them hammered at me.

"Ve know. You come from ze Zouth. You feel you can't tell us ze truth. But ve don't bother you. Ve don't feel like people in ze Zouth. Ve treat you nice, don't ve?" they asked.

"Yes, ma'am," I mumbled.

"Zen vy lie?"

"I'm not lying," I lied with all my strength.

I became angry because I knew that they knew that I was lying. I had lied to protect myself, and then I had to lie to protect my lie. I had met so many white faces that would have violently disapproved of my taking the examination that I could not have risked telling Mr. Hoffman the truth. But how could I tell him that I had lied because I was so unsure of myself? Lying was bad, but revealing my own sense of insecurity would have been worse. It would have been shameful, and I did not like to feel ashamed.

Their attitudes had proved utterly amazing. They were taking time out from their duties in the store to talk to me, and I had never encountered anything like that from whites before. A Southern white man would have said: "Get to hell out of here!" or "All right, nigger. Get to work." But no white people had ever stood their ground and probed at me, questioned me at such length. It dawned upon me that they were trying to treat me as an equal, which made it even more impossible for me ever to tell them that I had lied, why I had lied. I felt that if I confessed I would be giving them a moral advantage over me that would have been unbearable.

"All vight, zay and vork," Mr. Hoffman said. "I know you're lying, but I don't care, Rich."

I wanted to quit. He had insulted me. But I liked him in spite of myself. Yes, I had done wrong; but how on earth could I have known the kind of people I was working for? Perhaps Mr. Hoffman would have gladly consented for me to take the examination; but my hopes had been far weaker than my powerful fears.

Working with them from day to day and knowing that they knew I had lied from fear crushed me. I knew that they pitied me and pitied the fear in me. I resolved to quit and risk hunger rather than stay with them. I left the job that following Saturday, not telling them that I would not be back, not possessing the heart to say good-by. I just wanted to go quickly and have them forget that I had ever worked for them.

After an idle week, I got a job as a dishwasher in a North Side cafe that had just opened. My boss, a white woman, directed me in unpacking barrels of dishes, setting up new tables, painting, and so on. I had charge of serving breakfast; in the late afternoon I carted trays of food to patrons in the hotel who did not want to come down to eat. My wages were fifteen dollars a week; the hours were long, but I ate my meals on the job.

The cook was an elderly Finnish woman with a sharp, bony face. There were several white waitresses. I was the only Negro in the café. The waitresses were a hard, brisk lot, and I was keenly aware of how their attitudes contrasted with those of Southern white girls. They had not been taught to keep a gulf between me and themselves; they were relatively free of the heritage of racial hate.

One morning as I was making coffee, Cora came forward with a tray loaded with food and squeezed against me to draw a cup of coffee.

"Pardon me, Richard," she said.

"Oh, that's all right," I said in an even tone.

But I was aware that she was a white girl and that her body was pressed closely against mine, an incident that had never happened to me before in my life, an incident charged with the memory of dread. But she was not conscious of my blackness or of what her actions would have meant in the South. And had I not been born in the South, her trivial act would have been as unnoticed by me as it was by her. As she stood close to me, I could not help thinking that if a Southern white girl had wanted to draw a cup of coffee, she would have commanded me to step aside so that she might not come in contact with me. The work of the hot and busy kitchen would have had to cease for the moment so that I could have taken my tainted body far enough away to allow the

Southern white girl a chance to get a cup of coffee. There lay a deep, emotional safety in knowing that the white girl who was now leaning carelessly against me was not thinking of me, had no deep, vague, irrational fright that made her feel that I was a creature to be avoided at all costs.

One summer morning a white girl came late to work and rushed into the pantry where I was busy. She went into the women's room and changed her clothes; I heard the door open and a second later I was surprised to hear her voice:

"Richard, quick! Tie my apron!"

She was standing with her back to me and the strings of her apron dangled loose. There was a moment of indecision on my part, then I took the two loose strings and carried them around her body and brought them again to her back and tied them in a clumsy knot.

"Thanks a million," she said, grasping my hand for a split second, and was gone.

I continued my work, filled with all the possible meanings that that tiny, simple, human event could have meant to any Negro in the South where I had spent most of my hungry days.

I did not feel any admiration or any hate for the girls. My attitude was one of abiding and friendly wonder. For the most part I was silent with them, though I knew that I had a firmer grasp of life than most of them. As I worked I listened to their talk and perceived its puzzled, wandering, superficial fumbling with the problems and facts of life. There were many things they wondered about that I could have explained to them, but I never dared.

During my lunch hour, which I spent on a bench in a near-by park, the waitresses would come and sit beside me, talking at random, laughing, joking, smoking cigarettes. I learned about their tawdry dreams, their simple hopes, their home lives, their fear of feeling anything deeply, their sex problems, their husbands. They were an eager, restless, talkative, ignorant bunch, but casually kind and impersonal for all that. They knew nothing of hate and fear, and strove instinctively to avoid all passion.

I often wondered what they were trying to get out of life, but I never stumbled upon a clue, and I doubt if they themselves had any notion. They lived on the surface of their days; their smiles were surface smiles, and their tears were surface tears. Negroes lived a truer and deeper life than they, but I wished that Negroes, too, could live as thoughtlessly, serenely, as they. The girls never talked of their feelings; none of them possessed the insight or the emotional equipment to understand themselves or others. How far apart in culture we stood! All my life I had done nothing but feel and cultivate my feelings; all their lives they had done nothing but strive for petty goals, the trivial material prizes of American life. We shared a common tongue, but my language was a different language from theirs.

It was in the psychological distance that separated the races that the deepest meaning of the problem of the Negro lay for me. For these poor, ignorant white girls to have understood my life would have meant nothing short of a vast revolution in theirs. And I was convinced that what they needed to make them complete and grown-up in their living was the inclusion in their personalities of a knowledge of lives such as I lived and suffered containedly.

As I, in memory, think back now upon those girls and their lives I feel that for white America to understand the significance of the problem of the Negro will take a bigger and tougher America than any we have yet known. I feel that America's past is too shallow, her national character too superficially optimistic, her very morality too suffused with color hate for her to accomplish so vast and complex a task. Culturally the Negro represents a paradox: Though he is an organic part of the nation, he is excluded by the entire tide and direction of American culture. Frankly, it is felt to be right to exclude him, and it is felt to be wrong to admit him freely. Therefore if, within the confines of its present culture, the nation ever seeks to purge itself of its color hate, it will find itself at war with itself, convulsed by a spasm of emotional and moral confusion. If the nation ever finds itself examining its real relation to the Negro, it will find itself doing infinitely more than that; for the anti-Negro attitude of whites represents but a tiny part — though a symbolically significant one — of the moral attitude of the nation. Our too-young and too-new America, lusty because it is lonely, aggressive because it is afraid, insists upon seeing the world in terms of good and bad, the holy and the evil, the high and the low, the white and the black; our America is frightened by fact, by history, by processes, by necessity. It hugs the easy way of damning those whom it cannot understand, of excluding those who look different; and it salves its conscience with a self-draped cloak of righteousness. Am I damning my native land? No; for I, too, share these faults of character! And I really do not think that America, adolescent and cocksure, a stranger to suffering and travail, an enemy of passion and sacrifice, is ready to probe into its most fundamental beliefs.

I knew that not race alone, not color alone, but the daily values that gave meaning to life stood between me and those white girls with whom I worked. Their constant outwardlooking, their mania for radios, cars, and a thousand other trinkets, made them dream and fix their eyes upon the trash of life, made it impossible for them to learn a language that could have taught them to speak of what was in theirs or others' hearts. The words of their souls were the syllables of popular songs.

The essence of the irony of the plight of the Negro in America, to me, is that he is doomed to live in isolation, while those who condemn him seek the basest goals of any people on the face of the earth. Perhaps it would be possible for the Negro to become reconciled to his plight if he could be made to believe that his sufferings were for some remote, high, sacrificial end; but sharing the culture that condemns him, and seeing that a lust for trash is what blinds the nation to his claims, is what sets storms to rolling in his soul.

Though I had fled the pressure of the South, my outward conduct had not changed. I had been schooled to present an unalteringly smiling face and I continued to do so despite the fact that my environment allowed more open expression. I hid my feelings and avoided all relationships with whites that might cause me to reveal them.

Tillie, the Finnish cook, was a tall, ageless, red-faced, rawboned woman with long snow-white hair, which she balled in a knot at the nape of her neck. She cooked expertly and was superbly efficient. One morning as I passed the sizzling stove, I thought I heard Tillie cough and spit, but I saw nothing; her face, obscured by steam, was bent over a big pot. My senses told me that Tillie had coughed and spat into that pot, but my heart told me that no human being could possibly be so filthy. I decided to watch her. An hour or so later I heard Tillie clear her throat with a grunt, saw her cough and spit into the boiling soup. I held my breath; I did not want to believe what I had seen.

Should I tell the boss lady? Would she believe me? I watched Tillie for another day to make sure that she was spitting into the food. She was; there was no doubt of it. But who would believe me if I told them what was happening? I was the only black person in the café. Perhaps they would think that I hated the cook. I stopped eating my meals there and bided my time.

The business of the café was growing rapidly and a Negro girl was hired to make salads. I went to her at once.

"Look, can I trust you?" I asked.

"What are you talking about?" she asked.

"I want you to say nothing, but watch that cook."

"For what?"

"Now, don't get scared. Just watch the cook."

She looked at me as though she thought I was crazy; and, frankly, I felt that perhaps I ought not to say anything to anybody.

"What do you mean?" she demanded.

"All right," I said. "I'll tell you. That cook spits in the food."

"What are you saying?" she asked aloud.

"Keep quiet," I said.

"Spitting?" she asked me in a whisper. "Why would she do that?"

"I don't know. But watch her."

She walked away from me with a funny look in her eyes. But half an hour later she came rushing to me, looking ill, sinking into a chair.

"Oh, God, I feel awful!"

"Did you see it?"

"She *is* spitting in the food!"

"What ought we do?" I asked.

"Tell the lady," she said.

"She wouldn't believe me," I said.

She widened her eyes as she understood. We were black and the cook was white.

"But I can't work here if she's going to do that," she said.

"Then you tell her," I said.

"She wouldn't believe me either," she said.

She rose and ran to the women's room. When she returned she stared at me. We were two Negroes and we were silently asking ourselves if the white boss lady would believe us if we told her that her expert white cook was spitting in the food all day long as it cooked on the stove.

"I don't know," she wailed, in a whisper, and walked away.

I thought of telling the waitresses about the cook, but I could not get up enough nerve. Many of the girls were friendly with Tillie. Yet I could not let the cook spit in the food all day. That was wrong by any human standard of conduct. I washed dishes, thinking, wondering; I served breakfast, thinking, wondering; I served meals in the apartments of patrons upstairs, thinking, wondering. Each time I picked up a tray of food I felt like retching. Finally the Negro salad girl came to me and handed me her purse and hat.

"I'm going to tell her and quit, goddamn," she said.

"I'll quit too, if she doesn't fire her," I said.

"Oh, she won't believe me," she wailed, in agony.

"You tell her. You're a woman. She might believe you."

Her eyes welled with tears and she sat for a long time; then she rose and went abruptly into the dining room. I went to the door and peered. Yes, she was at the desk, talking to the boss lady. She returned to the kitchen and went into the pantry; I followed her.

"Did you tell her?" I asked.

"Yes."

"What did she say?"

"She said I was crazy."

"Oh, God!" I said.

"She just looked at me with those gray eyes of hers," the girl said. "Why would Tillie do that?"

"I don't know," I said.

The boss lady came to the door and called the girl; both of them went into the dining room. Tillie came over to me; a hard cold look was in her eyes.

"What's happening here?" she asked.

"I don't know," I said, wanting to slap her across the mouth.

She muttered something and went back to the stove, coughed,

and spat into a bubbling pot. I left the kitchen and went into the back areaway to breathe. The boss lady came out.

"Richard," she said.

Her face was pale. I was smoking a cigarette and I did not look at her.

"Is this true?"

"Yes, ma'am."

"It couldn't be. Do you know what you're saying?"

"Just watch her," I said.

"I don't know," she moaned.

She looked crushed. She went back into the dining room, but I saw her watching the cook through the doors. I watched both of them, the boss lady and the cook, praying that the cook would spit again. She did. The boss lady came into the kitchen and stared at Tillie, but she did not utter a word. She burst into tears and ran back into the dining room.

"What's happening here?" Tillie demanded.

No one answered. The boss lady came out and tossed Tillie her hat, coat, and money.

"Now, get out of here, you dirty dog!" she said.

Tillie stared, then slowly picked up her hat, coat, and the money; she stood a moment, wiped sweat from her forehead with her hand, then spat—this time on the floor. She left.

Nobody was ever able to fathom why Tillie liked to spit into the food.

Brooding over Tillie, I recalled the time when the boss man in Mississippi had come to me and had tossed my wages to me and said:

"Get out, nigger! I don't like your looks."

And I wondered if a Negro who did not smile and grin was as morally loathsome to whites as a cook who spat into the food.

The following summer I was called for temporary duty in the post office, and the work lasted into the winter. Aunt Cleo succumbed to a severe cardiac condition and, hard on the heels of her illness, my brother developed stomach ulcers. To rush my worries to a climax, my mother also became ill. I felt that I was maintaining a private hospital. Finally, the postoffice work ceased altogether and I haunted the city for jobs. But when I went into the streets in the morning I saw sights that killed my hope for the rest of the day. Unemployed men loitered in doorways with blank looks in their eyes, sat dejectedly on front steps in shabby clothing, congregated in sullen groups on street corners, and filled all the empty benches in the parks of Chicago's South Side.

Luck of a sort came when a distant cousin of mine, who was a superintendent for a Negro burial society, offered me a position on his staff as an agent. The thought of selling insurance policies to ignorant Negroes disgusted me.

"Well, if you don't sell them, somebody else will," my cousin told me. "You've got to eat, haven't you?"

During that year I worked for several burial and insurance societies that operated among Negroes, and I received a new kind of education. I found that the burial societies, with some exceptions, were mostly "rackets." Some of them conducted their business legitimately, but there were many that exploited the ignorance of their black customers.

I was paid under a system that netted me fifteen dollars for every dollar's worth of new premiums that I placed upon the company's books, and for every dollar's worth of old premiums that lapsed I was penalized fifteen dollars. In addition, I was paid a commission of ten percent on total premiums collected, but during the Depression it was extremely difficult to persuade a black family to buy a policy carrying even a dime premium. I considered myself lucky if, after subtracting lapses from new business, there remained fifteen dollars that I could call my own.

This "gambling" method of remuneration was practiced by some of the burial companies because of the tremendous "turnover" in policyholders, and the companies had to have a constant stream of new business to keep afloat. Whenever a black family moved or suffered a slight reverse in fortune, it usually let its policy lapse and later bought another policy from some other company.

Each day now I saw how the Negro in Chicago lived, for I visited hundreds of dingy flats filled with rickety furniture and ill-clad children. Most of the policyholders were illiterate and did not know that their policies carried clauses severely restricting their benefit payments, and, as an insurance agent, it was not my duty to tell them.

After tramping the streets and pounding on doors to collect premiums, I was dry, strained, too tired to read or write. I hungered for relief and, as a salesman of insurance to many young black girls, I found it. There were many comely black housewives who, trying desperately to keep up their insurance payments, were willing to make bargains to escape paying a ten-cent premium. I had a long, tortured affair with one girl by paying her ten-cent premium each week. She was an illiterate black child with a baby whose father she did not know. During the entire period of my relationship with her, she had but one demand to make of me: she wanted me to take her to a circus. Just what significance circuses had for her, I was never able to learn.

After I had been with her one morning—in exchange for the dime premium—I sat on the sofa in the front room and began to read a book I had with me. She came over shyly.

"Lemme see that," she said.

"What?" I asked.

"That book," she said.

I gave her the book; she looked at it intently. I saw that she was holding it upside down.

"What's in here you keep reading?" she asked.

"Can't you really read?" I asked.

"Naw," she giggled. "You know I can't read."

"You can read *some*," I said.

"Naw," she said.

I stared at her and wondered just what a life like hers meant in the scheme of things, and I came to the conclusion that it meant absolutely nothing. And neither did my life mean anything.

"How come you looking at me that way for?"

"Nothing."

"You don't talk much."

"There isn't much to say."

"I wished Jim was here," she sighed.

"Who's Jim?" I asked, jealous. I knew that she had other men, but I resented her mentioning them in my presence.

"Just a friend," she said.

I hated her then, then hated myself for coming to her.

"Do you like Jim better than you like me?" I asked.

"Naw. Jim just likes to talk."

"Then why do you be with me, if you like Jim better?" I asked, trying to make an issue and feeling a wave of disgust because I wanted to.

"You all right," she said, giggling. "I like you."

"I could kill you," I said.

"What?" she exclaimed.

"Nothing," I said, ashamed.

"Kill me, you said? You crazy, man," she said.

"Maybe I am," I muttered, angry that I was sitting beside a human being to whom I could not talk, angry with myself for coming to her, hating my wild and restless loneliness.

"You oughta go home and sleep," she said. "You tired."

"What do you ever think about?" I demanded harshly.

"Lotta things."

"What, for example?"

"You," she said, smiling.

"You know I mean just one dime to you each week," I said.

"Naw, I thinka lotta you."

"Then what do you think?"

"'Bout how you talk when you talk. I wished I could talk like you," she said seriously.

"Why?" I taunted her.

"When you gonna take me to a circus?" she demanded suddenly.

"You ought to be in a circus," I said.

"I'd like it," she said, her eyes shining.

I wanted to laugh, but her words sounded so sincere that I could not.

"There's no circus in town," I said.

"I bet there is and you won't tell me 'cause you don't wanna take me," she said, pouting.

"But there's no circus in town, I tell you!"

"When will one come?"

"I don't know."

"Can't you read it in the papers?" she asked.

"There's nothing in the papers about a circus."

"There is," she said. "If I could read, I'd find it."

I laughed, and she was hurt.

There *is* a circus in town," she said stoutly.

"There's no circus in town," I said. "But if you want to learn to read, then I'll teach you."

She nestled at my side, giggling.

"See that word?" I said, pointing.

"Yeah."

"That's an 'and,'" I said.

She doubled, giggling.

"What's the matter?" I asked.

She rolled on the floor, giggling.

"What's so funny?" I demanded.

"You," she giggled. "You so funny."

I rose.

"The hell with you," I said.

"Don't you go and cuss me now," she said. "I don't cuss you."

"I'm sorry," I said.

I got my hat and went to the door.

"I'll see you next week?" she asked.

"Maybe," I said.

When I was on the sidewalk, she called to me from a window.

"You promised to take me to a circus, remember?"

"Yes." I walked close to the window. "What is it you like about a circus?"

"The animals," she said simply.

I felt that there was a hidden meaning, perhaps, in what she had said, but I could not find it. She laughed and slammed the window shut.

Each time I left her I resolved not to visit her again. I could not talk to her; I merely listened to her passionate desire to see a circus. She was not calculating; if she liked a man, she just liked him. Sex relations were the only relations she had ever had; no others were possible with her, so limited was her intelligence.

Most of the other agents also had their bought girls and they were extremely anxious to keep other agents from tampering with them. One day a new section of the South Side was given to me as a part of my collection area, and the agent from whom the territory had been taken suddenly became very friendly with me.

"Say, Wright," he asked, "did you collect from Ewing on Champlain Avenue yet?"

"Yes," I answered, after consulting my book.

"How did you like her?" he asked, staring at me.

"She's a good-looking number," I said.

"You had anything to do with her yet?" he asked.

"No, but I'd like to," I said laughing.

"Look," he said. "I'm a friend of yours."

"Since when?" I countered.

"No, I'm really a friend," he said.

"What's on your mind?"

"Listen, that gal's sick," he said seriously.

"What do you mean?"

"She's got the clap," he said. "Keep away from her. She'll lay with anybody."

"Gee, I'm glad you told me," I said.

"You had your eye on her, didn't you?" he asked.

"Yes, I did," I said.

"Leave her alone," he said. "She'll get you down."

That night I told my cousin what the agent had said about Miss Ewing. My cousin laughed.

"That gal's all right," he said. "That agent's been fooling around with her. He told you she had a disease so that you'd be scared to bother her. He was protecting her from you."

That was the way the black women were regarded by the black agents. Some of the agents were vicious; if they had claims to pay to a sick black woman and if the woman was able to have sex relations with them, they would insist upon it, using the claims money as a bribe. If the woman refused, they would report to the office that the woman was a malingerer. The average black woman would submit because she needed the money badly.

As an insurance agent, it was necessary for me to take part in one swindle. It appears that the burial society had originally issued a policy that was—from their point of view—too liberal in its provisions, and the officials decided to exchange the policies then in the hands of their clients for other policies carrying stricter clauses. Of course, this had to be done in a manner that would not allow the policyholder to know that his policy was being switched—that he was being swindled. I did not like it, but there was only one thing I could do to keep from being a party to it: I could quit and starve. But I did not feel that being honest was worth the price of starvation.

The swindle worked in this way. In my visits to the homes of the policyholders to collect premiums, I was accompanied by the superintendent who claimed to the policyholder that he was making a routine inspection. The policyholder, usually an illiterate black woman, would dig up her policy from the bottom of a trunk or chest and hand it to the superintendent. Meanwhile I would be marking the woman's premium book, an act which would distract her from what the superintendent was doing. The superintendent would exchange the old policy for a new one which was identical in color, serial number, and beneficiary, but which carried smaller payments. It was dirty work and I wondered how I could stop it. And when I could think of no safe way I would curse myself and the victims and forget about it. (The black owners of the burial societies were leaders in the Negro communities and were respected by whites.)

When I reached the relief station, I felt that I was making a public confession of my hunger. I sat waiting for hours, resentful of the mass of hungry people about me. My turn finally came and I was questioned by a middle-class Negro woman who asked me for a short history of my life. As I waited, I became aware of something happening in the room. The black men and women were mumbling quietly among themselves; they had not known one another before they had come here, but now their timidity and shame were wearing off and they were exchanging experiences. Before this they had lived as individuals, each somewhat afraid of the other, each seeking his own pleasure, each stanch in that degree of Americanism that had been allowed him. But now life had tossed them together, and they were learning to know the sentiments of their neighbors for the first time; their talking was enabling them to sense the collectivity of their lives, and some of their fear was passing.

Did the relief officials realize what was happening? No. If they had, they would have stopped it. But they saw their "clients" through the eyes of their profession, saw only what their "science" allowed them to see. As I listened to the talk, I could see black minds shedding many illusions. These people now knew that the past had betrayed them, had cast them out; but they did not know what the future would be like, did not know what they wanted. Yes, some of the things that the Communists said were true; they maintained that there came times in history when a ruling class could no longer rule. And now I sat looking at the beginnings of anarchy. To permit the birth of this new consciousness in these people was proof that those who ruled did not quite know what they were doing, assuming that they were trying to save themselves and their class. Had they understood what was happening, they would never have allowed millions of perplexed and defeated people to sit together for long hours and talk, for out of their talk was rising a new realization of life. And once this new conception of themselves had formed, no power on earth could alter it.

I left the relief station with the promise that food would be sent to me, but I also left with a knowledge that the relief officials had not wanted to give to me. I had felt the possibility of creating a new under-standing of life in the minds of people rejected by the society in which they lived, people to whom the Chicago *Tribune* referred contemp-tuously as the "idle" ones, as though these people had deliberately sought their present state of helplessness.

Who would give these people a meaningful way of life? Commu-nist theory defined these people as the molders of the future of man-kind, but the Communist speeches I had heard in the park had mocked that definition. These people, of course, were not ready for a revolu-tion; they had not abandoned their past lives by choice, but because they simply could not live the old way any longer. Now, what new faith would they embrace? The day I begged bread from the city officials was the day that showed me I was not alone in my loneliness; society had cast millions of others with me. But how could I be with them? How many understood what was happening? My mind swam with questions that I could not answer.

I was slowly beginning to comprehend the meaning of my envi-ronment; a sense of direction was beginning to emerge from the condi-tions of my life. I began to feel something more powerful than I could express. My speech and manner changed. My cynicism slid from me. I grew open and questioning. I wanted to know.

If I were a member of the class that rules, I would post men in all the neighborhoods of the nation, not to spy upon or club rebellious workers, not to break strikes or disrupt unions, but to ferret out those who no longer respond to the system under which they live. I would make it known that the real danger does not stem from those who seek to grab their share of wealth through force, or from those who try to defend their property through violence, for both of these groups, by their affirmative acts, support the values of the system under which they live. The millions that I would fear are those who do not dream of the prizes that the nation holds forth, for it is in them, though they may not know it, that a revolution has taken place and is biding its time to translate itself into a new and strange way of life.

I feel that the Negroes' relation to America is symbolically peculiar, and from the Negroes' ultimate reactions to their trapped state a lesson can be learned about America's future. Negroes are told in a language they cannot possibly misunderstand that their native land is not their own; and when, acting upon impulses which they share with whites, they try to assert a claim to their birthright, whites retaliate with terror, never pausing to consider the consequences should the Negroes give up completely. The whites never dream that they would face a situation far more terrifying if they were confronted by Negroes who made no claims at all than by those who are buoyed up by social ag-gressiveness. My knowledge of how Negroes react to their plight makes me declare that no man can possibly be individually guilty of treason, that an insurgent act is but a man's desperate answer to those who twist his environment so that he cannot fully share the spirit of his native land. Treason is a crime of the State.]

Christmas came and I was once more called to the post office for temporary work. This time I met many young white men and we discussed world happenings, the vast armies of unemployed, the rising tide of radical action. I now detected a change in the attitudes of the whites I met; their privations were making them regard Negroes with new eyes, and, for the first time, I was invited to their homes.

When the work in the post office ended, I was assigned by the relief system as an orderly to a medical research institute in one of the largest and wealthiest hospitals in Chicago. I cleaned operating rooms, dog, rat, mice, cat, and rabbit pans, and fed guinea pigs. Four of us Negroes worked there and we occupied an underworld position, remembering that we must restrict ourselves—when not engaged upon some task—to the basement corridors, so that we would not mingle with white nurses, doctors, or visitors.

The sharp line of racial division drawn by the hospital authorities came to me the first morning when I walked along an underground corridor and saw two long lines of women coming toward me. A line of white girls marched past, clad in starched uniforms that gleamed white; their faces were alert, their step quick, their bodies lean and shapely, their shoulders erect, their faces lit with the light of purpose. And after them came a line of black girls, old, fat, dressed in ragged gingham, walking loosely, carrying tin cans of soap powder, rags, mops, brooms . . . I wondered what law of the universe kept them from being mixed? The sun would not have stopped shining had there been a few black girls in the first line, and the earth would not have stopped whirling on its axis had there been a few white girls in the second line. But the two lines I saw graded social status in purely racial terms.

Of the three Negroes who worked with me; one was a boy about my own age, Bill, who was either sleepy or drunk most of the time. Bill straightened his hair and I suspected that he kept a bottle hidden somewhere in the piles of hay which we fed to the guinea pigs. He did not like me and I did not like him, though I tried harder than he to conceal my dislike. We had nothing in common except that we were both black and lost. While I contained my frustration, he drank to drown his. Often I tried to talk to him, tried in simple words to convey to him some of my ideas, and he would listen in sullen silence. Then one day he came to me with an angry look on his face.

"I got it," he said.

"You've got what?" I asked.

"This old race problem you keep talking about," he said.

"What about it?"

"Well, it's this way," he explained seriously. "Let the government give every man a gun and five bullets, then let us all start over again. Make it just like it was in the beginning. The ones who come out on top, white or black, let them rule."

His simplicity terrified me. I had never met a Negro who was so irredeemably brutalized. I stopped pumping my ideas into Bill's brain for fear that the fumes of alcohol might send him reeling toward some fantastic fate.

The two other Negroes were elderly and had been employed in the institute for fifteen years or more. One was Brand, a short, black, morose bachelor; the other was Cooke, a tall, yellow, spectacled fellow who spent his spare time keeping track of world events through the Chicago *Tribune*. Brand and Cooke hated each other for a reason that I was never able to determine, and they spent a good part of each day quarreling.

When I began working at the institute, I recalled my adolescent dream of wanting to be a medical research worker. Daily I saw young Jewish boys and girls receiving instruction in chemistry and medicine that the average black boy or girl could never receive. When I was alone, I wandered and poked my fingers into strange chemicals. watched intricate machines trace red and black lines on ruled paper. At times I paused and stared at the walls of the rooms, at the floors, at the wide desks at which the white doctors sat; and I realized—with a feeling that I could never quite get used to—that I was looking at the world of another race.

My interest in what was happening in the institute amused the three other Negroes with whom I worked. They had no curiosity about "white folks' things," while I wanted to know if the dogs being treated for diabetes were getting well; if the rats and mice in which cancer had been induced showed any signs of responding to treatment. I wanted to know the principle that lay behind the Aschheim-Zondek tests that were made with rabbits, the Wassermann tests that were made with guinea pigs. But when I asked a timid question I found that even Jewish doctors had learned to imitate the sadistic method of humbling a Negro that the others had cultivated.

"If you know too much, boy, your brains might explode," a doctor said one day.

Each Saturday morning I assisted a young Jewish doctor in slitting the vocal cords of a fresh batch of dogs from the city pound. The object was to devocalize the dogs so that their howls would not disturb the patients in the other parts of the hospital. I held each dog as the doctor injected Nembutal into its veins to make it unconscious; then I held the dog's jaws open as the doctor inserted the scalpel and severed the vocal cords. Later, when the dogs came to, they would lift their heads to the ceiling and gape in a soundless wail. The sight became lodged in my imagination as a symbol of silent suffering.

To me Nembutal was a powerful and mysterious liquid, but when I asked questions about its properties I could not obtain a single intelligent answer. The doctor simply ignored me with:

"Come on. Bring me the next dog. I haven't got all day."

One Saturday morning, after I had held the dogs for their vocal cords to be slit, the doctor left the Nembutal on a bench. I picked it up, uncorked it, and smelled it. It was odorless. Suddenly Brand ran to me with a stricken face.

"What're you doing?" he asked.

"I was smelling this stuff to see if it had any odor," I said.

"Did you really smell it?" he asked me.

"Yes."

"Oh, God!" he exclaimed.

"What's the matter?" I asked.

"You shouldn't've done that!" he shouted.

"Why?"

He grabbed my arm and jerked me across the room.

"Come on!" he yelled, snatching open the door.

"What's the matter?" I asked.

"I gotta get you to a doctor 'fore it's too late," he gasped.

Had my foolish curiosity made me inhale something dangerous?

"But — Is it poisonous?"

"Run, boy!" he said, pulling me. "You'll fall dead."

Filled with fear, with Brand pulling my arm, I rushed out of the room, raced across a rear areaway, into another room, then down a long corridor. I wanted to ask Brand what symptoms I must expect, but we were running too fast. Brand finally stopped, gasping for breath. My heart beat wildly and my blood pounded in my head. Brand then dropped to the concrete floor, stretched out on his back, and yelled with laughter, shaking all over. He beat his fists against the concrete; he moaned, giggled, he kicked.

I tried to master my outrage, wondering if some of the white doctors had told him to play the joke. He rose and wiped tears from his eyes, still laughing. I walked away from him. He knew that I was angry and he followed me.

"Don't get mad," he gasped through his laughter.

"Go to hell," I said.

"I couldn't help it," he giggled. "You looked at me like you'd believe anything I said. Man, you was scared."

He leaned against the wall, laughing again, stomping his feet. I was angry, for I felt that he would spread the story. I knew that Bill and Cooke never ventured beyond the safe bounds of Negro living, and they would never blunder into anything like this. And if they heard about this, they would laugh for months.

"Brand, if you mention this, I'll kill you," I swore.

"You ain't mad?" he asked, laughing, staring at me through tears. Sniffling. Brand walked ahead of me. I followed him back into the room that housed the dogs. All day, while at some task, he would pause and giggle, then smother the giggling with his hand, looking at me out of the corner of his eyes, shaking his head. He laughed at me for a week. I kept my temper and let him amuse himself. I finally found out the properties of Nembutal by consulting medical books; but I never told Brand.

One summer morning, just as I began work, a young Jewish boy came to me with a stop watch in his hand.

"Dr. —— wants me to time you when you clean a room," he said. "We're trying to make the institute more efficient."

"I'm doing my work, and getting through on time," I said.

"This is the boss's order," he said.

"Why don't you work for a change?" I blurted, angry.

"Now, look," he said. "*This* is my work. Now *you* work."

I got a mop and pail, sprayed a room with disinfectant, and scrubbed at coagulated blood and hardened dog, rat, and rabbit feces. The normal temperature of a room was ninety, but, as the sun beat down upon the skylights, the temperature rose above a hundred. Stripped to my waist, I slung the mop, moving steadily like a machine, hearing the boy press the button on the stop watch as I finished cleaning a room.

"Well, how is it?" I asked.

"It took you seventeen minutes to clean that last room," he said. "That ought to be the time for each room."

"But that room was not very dirty," I said.

"You have seventeen rooms to clean," he went on as though I had not spoken. "Seventeen times seventeen make four hours and forty-nine minutes." He wrote upon a little pad. "After lunch, clean the five flights of stone stairs. I timed a boy who scrubbed one step and multiplied that time by the number of steps. You ought to be through by six."

"Suppose I want relief?" I asked.

"You'll manage," he said and left.

Never had I felt so much the slave as when I scoured those stone steps each afternoon. Working against time, I would wet five steps, sprinkle soap powder, and then a white doctor or a nurse would come along and, instead of avoiding the soapy steps, would walk on them and track the dirty water onto the steps that I had already cleaned. To obviate this, I cleaned but two steps at a time, a distance over which a ten-year-old child could step. But it did no good. The white people still plopped their feet down into the dirty water and muddied the other clean steps. If I ever really hotly hated unthinking whites, it was then.

Not once during my entire stay at the institute did a single white person show enough courtesy to avoid a wet step. I would be on my knees, scrubbing, sweating, pouring out what limited energy my body could wring from my meager diet, and I would hear feet approaching. I would pause and curse with tense lips:

"These sonofabitches are going to dirty these steps again, goddamn their souls to hell!"

Sometimes a sadistically observant white man would notice that he had tracked dirty water up the steps, and he would look back down at me and smile and say:

"Boy, we sure keep you busy, don't we?"

And I would not be able to answer.

The feud that went on between Brand and Cooke continued. Although they were working daily in a building where scientific history was being made, the light of curiosity was never in their eyes. They were conditioned to their racial "place," had learned to see only a part of the whites and the white world; and the whites, too, had learned to see only a part of the lives of the blacks and their world.

Perhaps Brand and Cooke, lacking interests that could absorb them, fuming like children over trifles, simply invented their hate of each other in order to have something to feel deeply about. Or perhaps there was in them a vague tension stemming from their chronically frustrating way of life, a pain whose cause they did not know; and, like those devocalized dogs, they would whirl and snap at the air when their old pain struck them. Anyway, they argued about the weather, sports, sex, war, race, politics, and religion; neither of them knew much about the subjects they debated, but it seemed that the less they knew the better they could argue.

The tug of war between the two elderly men reached a climax one winter day at noon. It was incredibly cold and an icy gale swept up and down the Chicago streets with blizzard force. The door of the animal-filled room was locked, for we always insisted that we be allowed one hour in which to eat and rest. Bill and I were sitting on wooden boxes, eating our lunches out of paper bags. Brand was washing his hands at the sink. Cooke was sitting on a rickety stool, munching an apple and reading the Chicago *Tribune*.

Now and then a devocalized dog lifted his nose to the ceiling and howled soundlessly. The room was filled with many rows of high steel tiers. Perched upon each of these tiers were layers of steel cages containing the dogs, rats, mice, rabbits, and guinea pigs. Each cage was labeled in some indecipherable scientific jargon. Along the walls of the room were long charts with zigzagging red and black lines that traced the success or failure of some experiment. The lonely piping of guinea pigs floated unheeded about us. Hay rustled as a rabbit leaped restlessly about in its pen. A rat scampered around in its steel prison. Cooke tapped the newspaper for attention.

"It says here," Cooke mumbled through a mouthful of apple, "that this is the coldest day since 1888."

Bill and I sat unconcerned. Brand chuckled softly.

"What in hell you laughing about?" Cooke demanded of Brand.

"You can't believe what that damn *Tribune* says," Brand said.

"How come I can't?" Cooke demanded. "It's the world's greatest newspaper."

Brand did not reply; he shook his head pityingly and chuckled again.

"Stop that damn laughing at me!" Cooke said angrily.

"I laugh as much as I wanna," Brand said. "You don't know what you talking about. The *Herald-Examiner* says it's the coldest day since 1873."

But the *Trib* oughta know," Cooke countered. "It's older'n that *Examiner*."

"That damn *Trib* don't know nothing!" Brand drowned out Cooke's voice.

"How in hell you know?" Cooke asked with rising anger.

The argument waxed until Cooke shouted that if Brand did not shut up he was going to "cut his black throat."

Brand whirled from the sink, his hands dripping soapy water, his eyes blazing.

"Take that back," Brand said.

"I take nothing back! What you wanna do about it?" Cooke taunted.

The two elderly Negroes glared at each other. I wondered if the quarrel was really serious, or if it would turn out harmlessly as so many others had done.

Suddenly Cooke dropped the Chicago *Tribune* and pulled a long knife from his pocket; his thumb pressed a button and a gleaming steel blade leaped out. Brand stepped back quickly and seized an ice pick that was stuck in a wooden board above the sink.

"Put that knife down," Brand said.

"Stay 'way from me, or I'll cut your throat," Cooke warned.

Brand lunged with the ice pick. Cooke dodged out of range. They circled each other like fighters in a prize ring. The cancerous and tubercular rats and mice leaped about in their cages. The guinea pigs whistled in fright. The diabetic dogs bared their teeth and barked soundlessly in our direction. The Aschheim-Zondek rabbits flopped their ears and tried to hide in the corners of their pens. Cooke now crouched and sprang forward with the knife. Bill and I jumped to our feet, speechless with surprise. Brand retreated. The eyes of both men were hard and unblinking; they were breathing deeply.

"Say, cut it out!" I called in alarm.

"Them damn fools is really fighting," Bill said in amazement.

Slashing at each other, Brand and Cooke surged up and down the aisles of steel tiers. Suddenly Brand uttered a bellow and charged into Cooke and swept him violently backward. Cooke grasped Brand's hand to keep the ice pick from sinking into his chest. Brand broke free and charged Cooke again, sweeping him into an animal-filled steel tier. The tier balanced itself on its edge for an indecisive moment, then toppled.

Like kingpins, one steel tier lammed into another, then they all crashed to the floor with a sound as of the roof falling. The whole aspect of the room altered quicker than the eye could follow. Brand and Cooke stood stock-still, their eyes fastened upon each other, their pointed weapons raised; but they were dimly aware of the havoc that churned about them.

The steel tiers lay jumbled; the doors of the cages swung open. Rats and mice and dogs and rabbits moved over the floor in wild panic. The Wassermann guinea pigs were squealing as though judgment day had come. Here and there an animal had been crushéd beneath a cage.

All four of us looked at one another. We knew what this meant. We might lose our jobs. We were already regarded as black dunces; and if the doctors saw this mess they would take it as final proof. Bill rushed to the door to make sure that it was locked. I glanced at the clock and saw that it was 12:30. We had one half-hour of grace.

"Come on," Bill said uneasily. "We got to get this place cleaned."

Brand and Cooke stared at each other, both doubting.

"Give me your knife, Cooke," I said.

"Naw! Take Brand's ice pick *first*," Cooke said.

"The hell you say!" Brand said. "Take his knife *first!*"

A knock sounded at the door.

"Sssssh," Bill said.

We waited. We heard footsteps going away. We'll all lose our jobs, I thought.

Persuading the fighters to surrender their weapons was a difficult task, but at last it was done and we could begin to set things right. Slowly Brand stooped and tugged at one end of a steel tier. Cooke stooped to help him. Both men seemed to be acting in a dream. Soon, however, all four of us were working frantically, watching the clock.

As we labored we conspired to keep the fight a secret; we agreed to tell the doctors — if any should ask — that we had not been in the room during our lunch hour; we felt that that lie would explain why no one had unlocked the door when the knock had come.

We righted the tiers and replaced the cages; then we were faced with the impossible task of sorting the cancerous rats and mice, the diabetic dogs, the Aschheim-Zondek rabbits, and the Wassermann guinea pigs. Whether we kept our jobs or not depended upon how shrewdly we could cover up all evidence of the fight. It was pure guesswork, but we had to try to put the animals back into the correct cages. We knew that certain rats or mice went into certain cages, but we did not know *what* rat or mouse went into *what* cage. We did not know a tubercular mouse from a cancerous mouse—the white doctors had made sure that we would not know. They had never taken time to answer a single question; though we worked in the institute, we were as remote from the meaning of the experiments as if we lived in the moon. The doctors had laughed at what they felt was our childlike interest in the fate of the animals.

First we sorted the dogs; that was fairly easy, for we could remember the size and color of most of them. But the rats and mice and guinea pigs baffled us completely.

We put our heads together and pondered, down in the underworld of the great scientific institute. It was a strange scientific conference; the fate of the entire medical research institute rested in our ignorant, black hands.

We remembered the number of rats, mice, or guinea pigs—we had to handle them several times a day—that went into a given cage, and we supplied the number helter-skelter from those animals that we could catch running loose on the floor. We discovered that many rats, mice, and guinea pigs were missing—they had been killed in the scuffle. We solved that problem by taking healthy stock from other cages and putting them into cages with sick animals. We repeated this process until we were certain that, numerically at least, all the animals with which the doctors were experimenting were accounted for.

The rabbits came last. We broke the rabbits down into two general groups; those that had fur on their bellies and those that did not. We knew that all those rabbits that had shaven bellies—our scientific knowledge adequately covered this point because it was our job to shave the rabbits—were undergoing the Aschheim-Zondek tests. But in what pen did a given rabbit belong? We did not know. I solved the problem very simply. I counted the shaven rabbits; they numbered seventeen. I counted the pens labeled "Aschheim-Zondek," then proceeded to drop a shaven rabbit into each pen at random. And again we were numerically successful. At least white America had taught us how to count . . .

Lastly we carefully wrapped all the dead animals in newspapers and hid their bodies in a garbage can.

At a few minutes to one the room was in order; that is, the kind of order that we four Negroes could figure out. I unlocked the door and we sat waiting, whispering, vowing secrecy, wondering what the reaction of the doctors would be.

Finally a doctor came, gray-haired, white-coated, spectacled, efficient, serious, taciturn, bearing a tray upon which sat a bottle of mysterious fluid and a hypodermic needle.

"My rats, please."

Cooke shuffled forward to serve him. We held our breath. Cooke got the cage which he knew the doctor always called for at that hour and brought it forward. One by one, Cooke took out the rats and held them as the doctor solemnly injected the mysterious fluid under their skins.

"Thank you, Cooke," the doctor murmured.

"Not at all, sir," Cooke mumbled with a suppressed gasp.

When the doctor had gone we looked at one another, hardly daring to believe that our secret would be kept. We were so anxious that we did not know whether to curse or laugh. Another doctor came.

"Give me A-Z rabbit number 14."

"Yes, sir," I said.

I brought him the rabbit and he took it upstairs to the operating room. We waited for repercussions. None came.

All that afternoon the doctors came and went. I would run into the room—stealing a few seconds from my step-scrubbing—and ask what progress was being made and would learn that the doctors had detected nothing. At quitting time we felt triumphant.

"They won't ever know," Cooke boasted in a whisper.

I saw Brand stiffen. I knew that he was aching to dispute Cooke's optimism, but the memory of the fight he had just had was so fresh in his mind that he could not speak.

Another day went by and nothing happened. Then another day. The doctors examined the animals and wrote in their little black books, in their big black books, and continued to trace red and black lines upon the charts.

A week passed and we felt out of danger. Not one question had been asked.

Of course, we four black men were much too modest to make our contribution known, but we often wondered what went on in the laboratories after that secret disaster. Was some scientific hypothesis, well on its way to validation and ultimate public use, discarded because of unexpected findings on that cold winter day? Was some tested principle given a new and strange refinement because of fresh, remarkable evidence? Did some brooding research worker—those who held stop watches and slopped their feet carelessly in the water of the steps. I tried so hard to keep clean—get a wild, if brief, glimpse of a new scientific truth? Well, we never heard . . .

I brooded upon whether I should have gone to the director's office and told him what had happened, but each time I thought of it I remembered that the director had been the man who had ordered the boy to stand over me while I was working and time my movements with a stop watch. He did not regard me as a human being. I did not share his world. I earned thirteen dollars a week and I had to support four people with it, and should I risk that thirteen dollars by acting idealistically? Brand and Cooke would have hated me and would have eventually driven me from the job had I "told" on them. The hospital kept us four Negroes as though we were close kin to the animals we tended, huddled together down in the underworld corridors of the hospital, separated by a vast psychological distance from the significant processes of the rest of the hospital—just as America had kept us locked in the dark underworld of American life for three hundred years—and we had made our own code of ethics, values, loyalty.

1961

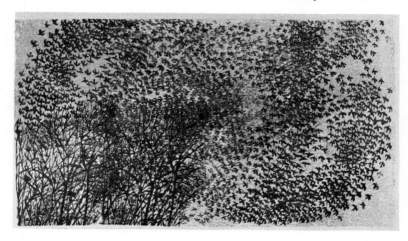

The New Poetry

The modern verse revolution instigated by Ezra Pound and the Imagists led to a renaissance in American poetry during the 1920's and 1930's. In keeping with the temper of the early revolutionaries, the dominant mood of American poets in the years between the wars was experimentalist and individualistic. Besides the forerunners Pound and Eliot, outstanding poets among the moderns included Wallace Stevens, William Carlos Williams, Marianne Moore, and E. E. Cummings—each of whom developed a distinctive and highly original style. Although some, like Wallace Stevens, were influenced by the French Symbolist poets, as Eliot had been, none succumbed to the mood and manner of *The Waste Land,* as many lesser poets of the period did. Instead, their work reveals fresh and distinctive attitudes and techniques, including the exotic aestheticism of Stevens' work, the vital immediacy of Williams' objectivist poems, the eccentric but carefully ordered compositions of Marianne Moore, and the pyrotechnics of Cummings' more experimental poems. Despite a tendency toward conventional metrics in some of the poems of Stevens and Cummings, the most distinctive work of the modern poets succeeds in fulfilling the organic requirement established by the Romantics and reaffirmed by the Imagists: the demand that the form of the work is determined by the poet's perception.

One remarkable feature of the new poetry is the extent of the influence

Migration VI, *original woodcut by Antonio Frasconi.*
Courtesy of the Weyhe Gallery, New York.

of Walt Whitman, the giant of nineteenth century poets and the founder of the modern free verse movement. Pound acknowledged his debt when he addressed Whitman in his poem "A Pact" and said, "It was you that broke the new wood, / Now is a time for carving." Other writers of modern epics or culture poems who looked back to Whitman and identified their efforts with his were Hart Crane in *The Bridge* and William Carlos Williams in *Paterson.* In his early Chicago poems, Sandburg combined the methods of Whitman and the Imagists; in his later long poem *The People, Yes,* he became what Whitman thought of himself as being, a spokesman for the inarticulate masses. The same role was assumed, but in a more disillusioned spirit, by Edward Lee Masters in *Spoon River Anthology.* Disillusion carried to the point of cynicism marks the poetry of Robinson Jeffers, but it should be recognized that he also accepted the older poet's conception of the poet as bard and prophet and cast his gloomy speculations on the plight of Western man in Whitmanesque verses. If it is true, as Whitman proclaimed at the end of his 1855 preface to *Leaves of Grass,* that "the proof of a poet is that his country absorbs him as affectionately as he absorbs it," then Whitman has met his own test in the present century.

A more conservative formal tradition also existed, though it was less conspicuous. Eliot's close contemporary John Crowe Ransom, the leader of the Southern Fugitive poets in the 1920's and of the later New Critics, was a traditionalist who preferred to work within the limits of established metrical patterns. Like such other New Critics as Cleanth Brooks and Allen Tate, Ransom prescribed and wrote a poetry of tension marked by irony, wit, and paradox. Although not in the main stream of the poetry produced by his contemporaries, Ransom's conventionally-ordered metaphysical poetry became an influence on the work of younger poets of the "middle generation."

Wallace Stevens   *1879–1955*

Born in Pennsylvania and educated at Harvard (1897–1900) and the New York University Law School, Wallace Stevens simultaneously pursued two careers: one as a successful and increasingly influential modern poet, the other as a successful executive of a Hartford, Connecticut, insurance company. It was not until 1923, when he was in his forties, that Stevens felt ready to issue the first collection of his poems under the title *Harmonium* (2nd ed., 1931). Subsequent volumes included *Ideas of Order* (1935), *Owl's Clover* (1936), *The Man with the Blue Guitar* (1937), *Parts of a World* (1942; 1951), *Notes Toward a Supreme Fiction* (1942), *Transport to Summer* (1947), *The Auroras of Autumn* (1950), and *Collected Poems* (1954). Like his younger contemporary Eliot, Stevens was deeply influenced by French Symbolist poetry. But his work, unlike Eliot's, shows little if any interest in English or other European poetry. From the beginning Stevens' finely crafted poems were distinguished by irony, wit, musicality, and a flair for colorful and exotic imagery. Typically his verse defines the role of the poet as that of a comedian and illusionist devoted to the imaginative enhancement of the "quotidian" or commonplace life. But Stevens' sensuous and sometimes gaudy language is also the expression of a persistent, and serious, metaphysical concern. The whole body of his work represents a continuing struggle with the problem of the relation of reality and illusion and of the relation of the reality of the imagination to the reality of experience. Like Coleridge, but without his supernaturalism, Stevens regards the imagination as a "necessary angel" which can provide man with values and principles of order through the "supreme fictions" of poetry. Stevens' speculations on the imagination and the nature of poetry can be found in his prose essays gathered under the title *The Necessary Angel* (1951) and in the "Adagia" and prose essays of *Opus Posthumous* (1957).

The standard editions of Stevens' poetry and prose are *The Collected Poems of Wallace Stevens* (New York, 1954); *Opus Posthumous*, ed. S. F.

Morse (New York, 1957); *The Necessary Angel: Essays on Reality and the Imagination* (New York, 1951); and *Letters of Wallace Stevens,* ed. Holly Stevens (New York, 1966). A helpful brief introduction to Stevens' work is Frank Kermode, *Wallace Stevens* (New York, 1961). Representative collections of criticism include Marie Boroff, ed., *Wallace Stevens: A Collection of Critical Essays* (Englewood Cliffs, N. J., 1963), and R. H. Pearce and J. H. Miller, eds., *The Act of the Mind: Essays on the Poetry of Wallace Stevens* (Baltimore, 1966). Frank Doggett's *Stevens' Poetry of Thought* (Baltimore, 1966) is one of several recent book-length critiques of the poet's work. Bibliographical aids include S. F. Morse, *Wallace Stevens: A Preliminary Checklist of His Published Writings, 1898–1954* (New Haven, Conn., 1954), and T. F. Walsh, ed., *A Concordance to the Poetry of Wallace Stevens* (University Park, Pa., 1954).

    The text of all but one of the poems presented here is that of *The Collected Poems of Wallace Stevens* (New York, 1954); "Of Mere Being" is from *Opus Posthumous* (New York, 1957). The text of "About One of Marianne Moore's Poems" is that of *The Necessary Angel* (New York, 1951).

astericks are "musts" for next week

✱ *The Emperor of Ice-Cream*

Call the roller of big cigars,
The muscular one, and bid him whip
In kitchen cups concupiscent curds.
Let the wenches dawdle in such dress
As they are used to wear, and let the boys
Bring flowers in last month's newspapers.
Let be be finale of seem.
The only emperor is the emperor of <u>ice-cream</u>.

melts

Take from the dresser of deal
Lacking the three glass knobs, that sheet
On which she embroidered fantails once
And spread it so as to cover her face.
If her horny feet protrude, they come
To show how cold she is, and dumb.
Let the lamp affix its beam.
The only emperor is the emperor of ice-cream.

frankness about death
the temporary, the here and now—
this is the formula for a funeral
could be in a whore-house

✱concupiscent-strongly desirous, especially, sexually desirous;   *1923* *lustful*
     ✱ think of Caravagio's "Death of Virgin"

Peter Quince¹ at the Clavier

1

Just as my fingers on these keys
Make music, so the selfsame sounds
On my spirit make a music, too.

¹ The name is taken from Shakespeare's *A Midsummer-Night's Dream,* in which Peter Quince the carpenter acts as stage manager of the "Pyramus and Thisbe" interlude.

Music is feeling, then, not sound;
And thus it is that what I feel,
Here in this room, desiring you,

Thinking of your blue-shadowed silk,
Is music. It is like the strain
Waked in the elders by Susanna.[2]

Of a green evening, clear and warm,   10
She bathed in her still garden, while
The red-eyed elders watching, felt

The basses of their beings throb
In witching chords, and their thin blood
Pulse pizzicati of Hosanna.

2

In the green water, clear and warm,
Susanna lay.
She searched
The touch of springs,
And found   20
Concealed imaginings.
She sighed,
For so much melody.

Upon the bank, she stood
In the cool
Of spent emotions.
She felt, among the leaves,
The dew
Of old devotions.

She walked upon the grass,   30
Still quavering.
The winds were like her maids,
On timid feet,
Fetching her woven scarves,
Yet wavering.

A breath upon her hand
Muted the night.
She turned—
A cymbal crashed,
And roaring horns.   40

---

[2] For the story of Susanna and the Elders, see the Old Testament apocryphal book, *The History of Susanna.*

3

Soon, with a noise like tambourines,
Came her attendant Byzantines.

They wondered why Susanna cried
Against the elders by her side;

And as they whispered, the refrain
Was like a willow swept by rain.

Anon, their lamps' uplifted flame
Revealed Susanna and her shame.

And then, the simpering Byzantines
Fled, with a noise like tambourines.   50

4

Beauty is momentary in the mind—
The fitful tracing of a portal;
But in the flesh it is immortal.
The body dies; the body's beauty lives.
So evenings die, in their green going,
A wave, interminably flowing.
So gardens die, their meek breath scenting
The cowl of winter, done repenting.
So maidens die, to the auroral
Celebration of a maiden's choral.   60
Susanna's music touched the bawdy strings
Of those white elders; but, escaping,
Left only Death's ironic scraping.
Now, in its immortality, it plays
On the clear viol of her memory,
And makes a constant sacrament of praise.

1923

✳ *Sunday Morning*

1

Complacencies of the peignoir, and late
Coffee and oranges in a sunny chair,
And the green freedom of a cockatoo
Upon a rug mingle to dissipate
The holy hush of <u>ancient sacrifice</u>.
She dreams a little, and she feels the dark
Encroachment of that old catastrophe,
As a calm darkens among water-lights.

peignoir— negligee

The pungent oranges and bright, green wings
Seem things in some procession of the dead,   10
Winding across wide water, without sound.
The day is like wide water, without sound,
Stilled for the passing of her dreaming feet   *portrait of*
Over the seas, to silent <u>Palestine</u>,   *the new madonna*
Dominion of the blood and sepulchre.

2

Why should she give her bounty to the dead?
What is <u>divinity</u> if it can come
Only in silent shadows and in dreams?
Shall she not find in comforts of the sun,   *be here now*
In pungent fruit and bright, green wings, or else   20
In any balm or beauty of the earth,
Things to be cherished like the thought of heaven?
Divinity must live within herself:
Passions of rain, or moods in falling snow;
Grievings in loneliness, or unsubdued
Elations when the forest blooms; gusty
Emotions on wet roads on autumn nights;
All pleasures and all pains, remembering
The bough of summer and the winter branch.
These are the measures destined for her soul.   30

3

Jove in the clouds had his inhuman birth.   *the creation*
No mother suckled him, no sweet land gave
Large-mannered motions to his mythy mind
He moved among us, as a muttering king,
Magnificent, would move among his hinds,
Until our blood, commingling, virginal,
With heaven, brought such requital to desire
The very hinds discerned it, in a star.
Shall our blood fail? Or shall it come to be
The blood of paradise? And shall the earth   40
Seem all of paradise that we shall know?
The sky will be much friendlier then than now,
A part of labor and a part of pain,   *fall from grace*
And next in glory to enduring love,
Not this dividing and indifferent blue.

4

She says, "<u>I am content when wakened birds</u>,
Before they fly, test the reality   *birds/innocence*
Of misty fields, by their sweet questionings;
But when the birds are gone, and their warm fields
Return no more, where, then, is paradise?"   50

There is not any haunt of prophecy,
Nor any old chimera of the grave,
Neither the golden underground, nor isle
Melodious, where spirits gat them home,
Nor visionary south, nor cloudy palm
Remote on heaven's hill, that has endured
As April's green endures; or will endure
Like her remembrance of awakened birds,
Or her desire for June and evening, tipped
By the consummation of the swallow's wings.   60

nothing inspires like the promise of Life

desire for Experience —

5

She says, "But in contentment I still feel
The need of some imperishable bliss."
Death is the mother of beauty; hence from her,
Alone, shall come fulfilment to our dreams
And our desires. Although she strews the leaves
Of sure obliteration on our paths,
The path sick sorrow took, the many paths
Where triumph rang its brassy phrase, or love
Whispered a little out of tenderness,
She makes the willow shiver in the sun   70
For maidens who were wont to sit and gaze
Upon the grass, relinquished to their feet.
She causes boys to pile new plums and pears
On disregarded plate. The maidens taste
And stray impassioned in the littering leaves.

we seek happiness

6

Is there no change of death in paradise?
Does ripe fruit never fall? Or do the boughs
Hang always heavy in that perfect sky,
Unchanging, yet so like our perishing earth,
With rivers like our own that seek for seas   80
They never find, the same receding shores
That never touch with inarticulate pang?
Why set the pear upon those river-banks
Or spice the shores with odors of the plum?
Alas, that they should wear our colors there,
The silken weavings of our afternoons,
And pick the strings of our insipid lutes!
Death is the mother of beauty, mystical,
Within whose burning bosom we devise
Our earthly mothers waiting, sleeplessly.   90

7

Supple and turbulent, a ring of men
Shall chant in orgy on a summer morn

chimera - fire breathing monster / foolish fancy   gat - archaic past tense of get

Their boisterous devotion to the sun,
Not as a god, but as a god might be,
Naked among them, like a savage source.   *eloquence of primitive*
Their chant shall be a chant of paradise,   *religion, ritual*
Out of their blood, returning to the sky;
And in their chant shall enter, voice by voice,
The windy lake wherein their lord delights,
The trees, like serafin, and echoing hills,   100
That choir among themselves long afterward.
They shall know well the heavenly fellowship
Of men that perish and of summer morn.
And whence they came and whither they shall go
The dew upon their feet shall manifest.

8

She hears, upon that water without sound,
A voice that cries, "The tomb in Palestine
Is not the porch of spirits lingering.
It is the grave of Jesus, where he lay."   *Jesus is dead*
We live in an old chaos of the sun,   110
Or old dependency of day and night,   *man/nature/death*
Or island solitude, unsponsored, free,
Of that wide water, inescapable.
Deer walk upon our mountains, and the quail
Whistle about us their spontaneous cries;
Sweet berries ripen in the wilderness;
And, in the isolation of the sky,
At evening, casual flocks of pigeons make   *holy spirit*
Ambiguous undulations as they sink,
Downward to darkness, on extended wings.   120

1923

To the One of Fictive Music

Sister and mother and diviner love,
And of the sisterhood of the living dead
Most near, most clear, and of the clearest bloom,
And of the fragrant mothers the most dear
And queen, and of diviner love the day
And flame and summer and sweet fire, no thread
Of cloudy silver sprinkles in your gown
Its venom of renown, and on your head
No crown is simpler than the simple hair.

Now, of the music summoned by the birth   10
That separates us from the wind and sea,
Yet leaves us in them, until earth becomes,
By being so much of the things we are,
Gross effigy and simulacrum, none

Gives motion to perfection more serene
Than yours, out of our imperfections wrought,
Most rare, or even of more kindred air
In the laborious weaving that you wear.

For so retentive of themselves are men
That music is intensest which proclaims   20
The near, the clear, and vaunts the clearest bloom,
And of all vigils musing the obscure,
That apprehends the most which sees and names,
As in your name, an image that is sure,
Among the arrant spices of the sun,
O bough and bush and scented vine, in whom
We give ourselves our likest issuance.

Yet not too like, yet not so like to be
Too near, too clear, saving a little to endow
Our feigning with the strange unlike, whence springs   30
The difference that heavenly pity brings.
For this, musician, in your girdle fixed
Bear other perfumes. On your pale head wear
A band entwining, set with fatal stones.
Unreal, give back to us what once you gave:
The imagination that we spurned and crave.

                                                          1923

Anecdote of the Jar

I placed a jar in Tennessee,
And round it was, upon a hill.
It made the slovenly wilderness
Surround that hill.

The wilderness rose up to it,
And sprawled around, no longer wild.
The jar was round upon the ground
And tall and of a port in air.

It took dominion everywhere.
The jar was gray and bare.
It did not give of bird or bush,
Like nothing else in Tennessee.

                                                          1923

 ## Sea Surface Full of Clouds

1

In that November off Tehuantepec,
The slopping of the sea grew still one night

And in the morning summer hued the deck

And made one think of rosy chocolate
And gilt umbrellas. Paradisal green
Gave suavity to the perplexed machine

Of ocean, which like limpid water lay.
Who, then, in that ambrosial latitude
Out of the light evolved the moving blooms,

Who, then, evolved the sea-blooms from the clouds   10
Diffusing balm in that Pacific calm?
C'était mon enfant, mon bijou, mon âme.[1]

The sea-clouds whitened far below the calm
And moved, as blooms move, in the swimming green
And in its watery radiance, while the hue

Of heaven in an antique reflection rolled
Round those flotillas. And sometimes the sea
Poured brilliant iris on the glistening blue.

2

In that November off Tehuantepec
The slopping of the sea grew still one night.   20
At breakfast jelly yellow streaked the deck

And made one think of chop-house chocolate
And sham umbrellas. And a sham-like green
Capped summer-seeming on the tense machine

Of ocean, which in sinister flatness lay.
Who, then, beheld the rising of the clouds
That strode submerged in that malevolent sheen,

Who saw the mortal massives of the blooms
Of water moving on the water-floor?
C'était mon frère du ciel, ma vie, mon or.[2]   30

The gongs rang loudly as the windy booms
Hoo-hooed it in the darkened ocean-blooms.
The gongs grew still. And then blue heaven spread

Its crystalline pendentives on the sea
And the macabre of the water-glooms
In an enormous undulation fled.

[1] "It was my child, my darling, my soul."
[2] "It was my heavenly brother, my life, my gold."

3

In that November off Tehuantepec,
The slopping of the sea grew still one night
And a pale silver patterned on the deck

And made one think of porcelain chocolate   40
And pied umbrellas. An uncertain green,
Piano-polished, held the tranced machine

Of ocean, as a prelude holds and holds.
Who, seeing silver petals of white blooms
Unfolding in the water, feeling sure

Of the milk within the saltiest spurge, heard, then,
The sea unfolding in the sunken clouds?
Oh! C'était mon extase et mon amour.[3]

So deeply sunken were they that the shrouds,
The shrouding shadows, made the petals black   50
Until the rolling heaven made them blue,

A blue beyond the rainy hyacinth,
And smiting the crevasses of the leaves
Deluged the ocean with a sapphire blue.

4

In that November off Tehuantepec
The night-long slopping of the sea grew still.
A mallow morning dozed upon the deck

And made one think of musky chocolate
And frail umbrellas. A too-fluent green
Suggested malice in the dry machine   60

Of ocean, pondering dank stratagem.
Who then beheld the figures of the clouds
Like blooms secluded in the thick marine?

Like blooms? Like damasks that were shaken off
From the loosed girdles in the spangling must.
C'était ma foi, la nonchalance divine.[4]

The nakedness would rise and suddenly turn
Salt masks of beard and mouths of bellowing,
Would— But more suddenly the heaven rolled

---

[3] "It was my ecstasy and my love."   [4] "It was my faith, a divine carelessness."

Its bluest sea-clouds in the thinking green,   70
And the nakedness became the broadest blooms,
Mile-mallows that a mallow sun cajoled.

5

In that November off Tehuantepec
Night stilled the slopping of the sea. The day
Came, bowing and voluble, upon the deck,

Good clown. . . . One thought of Chinese chocolate
And large umbrellas. And a motley green
Followed the drift of the obese machine

Of ocean, perfected in indolence.
What pistache one, ingenious and droll,   80
Beheld the sovereign clouds as jugglery

And the sea as turquoise-turbaned Sambo, neat
At tossing saucers — cloudy-conjuring sea?
C'était mon esprit bâtard, l'ignominie.[5]

The sovereign clouds came clustering. The conch
Of loyal conjuration trumped. The wind
Of green blooms turning crisped the motley hue

To clearing opalescence. Then the sea
And heaven rolled as one and from the two
Came fresh transfigurings of freshest blue.   90

1931

The Idea of Order at Key West

She sang beyond the genius of the sea.
The water never formed to mind or voice,
Like a body wholly body, fluttering
Its empty sleeves; and yet its mimic motion
Made constant cry, caused constantly a cry,
That was not ours although we understood,
Inhuman, of the veritable ocean.

The sea was not a mask. No more was she.
The song and water were not medleyed sound
Even if what she sang was what she heard,
Since what she sang was uttered word by word.
It may be that in all her phrases stirred   10

---

[5] "It was my bastard spirit, my shame."

○ veritable—true, real accurate

The grinding water and the gasping wind;
But it was she and not the sea we heard.

For she was the maker of the song she sang.
The ever-hooded, tragic-gestured sea
Was merely a place by which she walked to sing.
Whose spirit is this? we said, because we knew
It was the spirit that we sought and knew
That we should ask this often as she sang.

If it was only the dark voice of the sea   20
That rose, or even colored by many waves;
If it was only the outer voice of sky
And cloud, of the sunken coral water-walled,
However clear, it would have been deep air,
The heaving speech of air, a summer sound
Repeated in a summer without end
And sound alone. But it was more than that,
More even than her voice, and ours, among
The meaningless plungings of water and the wind,
Theatrical distances, bronze shadows heaped   30
On high horizons, mountainous atmospheres
Of sky and sea.
                  It was her voice that made
The sky acutest at its vanishing.
She measured to the hour its solitude.
She was the single artificer of the world
In which she sang. And when she sang, the sea,
Whatever self it had, became the self
That was her song, for she was the maker. Then we,
As we beheld her striding there alone,   40
Knew that there never was a world for her
Except the one she sang and, singing, made.

Ramon Fernandez,[1] tell me, if you know,
Why, when the singing ended and we turned
Toward the town, tell why the glassy lights,
The lights in the fishing boats at anchor there,
As the night descended, tilting in the air,
Mastered the night and portioned out the sea,
Fixing emblazoned zones and fiery poles,
Arranging, deepening, enchanting night.   50

Oh! Blessed rage for order, pale Ramon,
The maker's rage to order words of the sea,
Words of the fragrant portals, dimly-starred,

---

[1] The name Ramon Fernandez was invented by Stevens for use in this poem although it is also the name of a French literary critic (1894–1944).

And of ourselves and of our origins,
In ghostlier demarcations, keener sounds.

1935

The Glass of Water

That the glass would melt in heat,
That the water would freeze in cold,
Shows that this object is merely a state,
One of many, between two poles. So,
In the metaphysical, there are these poles.

Here in the centre stands the glass. Light
Is the lion that comes down to drink. There
And in that state, the glass is a pool.
Ruddy are his eyes and ruddy are his claws
When light comes down to wet his frothy jaws   10

And in the water winding weeds move round.
And there and in another state—the refractions,
The *metaphysica*, the plastic parts of poems
Crash in the mind—But, fat Jocundus, worrying
About what stands here in the centre, not the glass,

But in the centre of our lives, this time, this day,
It is a state, this spring among the politicians
Playing cards. In a village of the indigenes,
One would have still to discover. Among the dogs and dung,
One would continue to contend with one's ideas.   20

1942

Prologues to What is Possible

1

There was an ease of mind that was like being alone in a boat at
        sea,
A boat carried forward by waves resembling the bright backs of
        rowers,
Gripping their oars, as if they were sure of the way to their
        destination,
Bending over and pulling themselves erect on the wooden handles,
Wet with water and sparkling in the one-ness of their motion.

The boat was built of stones that had lost their weight and being
        no longer heavy
Had left in them only a brilliance, of unaccustomed origin,
So that he that stood up in the boat leaning and looking before
        him
Did not pass like someone voyaging out of and beyond the
        familiar.

[handwritten margin note: ①demarcations—① the act of setting or marking a boundry, ② a limit or boundry]

He belonged to the far-foreign departure of his vessel and was
    part of it,   10
Part of the speculum of fire on its prow, its symbol, whatever it
    was,
Part of the glass-like sides on which it glided over the salt-stained
    water,
As he traveled alone, like a man lured on by a syllable without
    any meaning,
A syllable of which he felt, with an appointed sureness,
That it contained the meaning into which he wanted to enter,
A meaning which, as he entered it, would shatter the boat and
    leave the oarsmen quiet
As at a point of central arrival, an instant moment, much or little,
Removed from any shore, from any man or woman, and needing
    none.

    2

The metaphor stirred his fear. The object with which he was
    compared
Was beyond his recognizing. By this he knew that likeness of him
    extended   20
Only a little way, and not beyond, unless between himself
And things beyond resemblance there was this and that intended
    to be recognized,
The this and that in the enclosures of hypotheses
On which men speculated in summer when they were half asleep.

What self, for example, did he contain that had not yet been
    loosed,
Snarling in him for discovery as his attentions spread,
As if all his hereditary lights were suddenly increased
By an access of color, a new and unobserved, slight dithering,
The smallest lamp, which added its puissant flick, to which he
    gave
A name and privilege over the ordinary of his commonplace —   30

A flick which added to what was real and its vocabulary,
The way some first thing coming into Northern trees
Adds to them the whole vocabulary of the South,
The way the earliest single light in the evening sky, in spring,
Creates a fresh universe out of nothingness by adding itself,
The way a look or a touch reveals its unexpected magnitudes.
                                            1954

Of Mere Being

The palm at the end of the mind,
Beyond the last thought, rises
In the bronze distance,

A gold-feathered bird
Sings in the palm, without human meaning,
Without human feeling, a foreign song.

You know then that it is not the reason
That makes us happy or unhappy.
The bird sings. Its feathers shine.

The palm stands on the edge of space.
The wind moves slowly in the branches.
The bird's fire-fangled feathers dangle down.

1957

About One of Marianne Moore's Poems

My purpose is to bring together one of Miss Moore's poems and a paper, "On Poetic Truth," by H. D. Lewis. The poem, "He 'Digesteth Harde Yron,'" has just been reprinted in the *Partisan Reader*. The paper is to be found in the July number (1946) of *Philosophy, the Journal of the British Institute of Philosophy* (Macmillan, London).

1

Mr. Lewis begins by saying that poetry has to do with reality in its most individual aspect. An isolated fact, cut loose from the universe, has no significance for the poet. It derives its significance from the reality to which it belongs. To see things in their true perspective, we require to draw very extensively upon experiences that are past. All that we see and hear is given a meaning in this way. There is in reality an aspect of individuality at which every form of rational explanation stops short. Now, in his *Euphues*, Lyly repeats the following bit of folk-lore:

> *Let them both remember that the Estridge*
> *digesteth harde yron to preserve his health.*

The "Estridge," then, is the subject of Miss Moore's poem. In the second stanza she says:

> *This bird watches his chicks with*
> *a maternal concentration, after*
> *he has sat on the eggs*
> *at night six weeks, his legs*
> *their only weapon of defense.*

The *Encyclopaedia Britannica* says of the ostrich:

[1] See Moore, "He 'Digesteth Harde Yron.'"

Extremely fleet of foot, when brought to bay the ostrich uses its strong legs with
great effect. Several hens combine to lay their eggs in one nest, and on these the
cock sits by night, while the females relieve one another by day.

Somehow, there is a difference between Miss Moore's bird and the bird
of the *Encyclopaedia*. This difference grows when she describes her
bird as

> The friend
> of hippotigers and wild
> asses, it is as
> though schooled by them he was
>
> the best of the unflying
> pegasi.

The difference signalizes a transition from one reality to another. It is
the reality of Miss Moore that is the individual reality. That of the
Encyclopaedia is the reality of isolated fact. Miss Moore's reality is
significant. An aesthetic integration is a reality.

Nowhere in the poem does she speak directly of the subject of
the poem by its name. She calls it "the camel-sparrow" and "the large
sparrow Xenophon saw walking by a stream," "the bird," "quad-
ruped-like bird" and

> alert gargantuan
> little-winged, magnificently
> speedy running-bird.

This, too, marks a difference. To confront fact in its total bleakness is
for any poet a completely baffling experience. Reality is not the thing
but the aspect of the thing. At first reading, this poem has an extraordinarily factual appearance. But it is, after all, an abstraction. Mr. Lewis
says that for Plato the only reality that mattered is exemplified best for
us in the principles of mathematics. The aim of our lives should be to
draw ourselves away as much as possible from the unsubstantial,
fluctuating facts of the world about us and establish some communion
with the objects which are apprehended by thought and not sense. This
was the source of Plato's asceticism. To the extent that Miss Moore
finds only allusion tolerable she shares that asceticism. While she
shares it she does so only as it may be necessary for her to do so in
order to establish a particular reality or, better, a reality of her own
particulars: the "overt" reality of Mr. Lewis. Take, for example, her
particulars of the bird's egg. She says:

> The egg piously shown
> as Leda's very own

> *from which Castor and Pollux hatched,*
> *was an ostrich-egg.*

Again she speaks of

> *jewel-*
> *gorgeous ugly egg-shell*
>   *goblet.*

It is obvious from these few quotations that Miss Moore has already found an individual reality in the ostrich and again in its egg. After all, it is the subject in poetry that releases the energy of the poet.

Mr. Lewis says that poetry has to do with matter that is foreign and alien. It is never familiar to us in the way in which Plato wished the conquests of the mind to be familiar. On the contrary its function, the need which it meets and which has to be met in some way in every age that is not to become decadent or barbarous, is precisely this contact with reality as it impinges upon us from outside, the sense that we can touch and feel a solid reality which does not wholly dissolve itself into the conceptions of our own minds. It is the individual and particular that does this. No fact is a bare fact, no individual fact is a universe in itself. Is not Miss Moore creating or finding and revealing some such reality in the stanza that follows?

> *Six hundred ostrich-brains served*
> *at one banquet, the ostrich-plume-tipped tent*
>   *and desert spear . . .*
>   *eight pairs of ostriches*
> *in harness, dramatize a*
>   *meaning always missed*
>   *by the externalist.*

Here the sparrow-camel is all pomp and ceremony, a part of justice of which it was not only the symbol, as Miss Moore says, but also the source of its panoply and the delicacy of its feasts; that is to say, a part of unprecedented experience.

Miss Moore's finical phraseology is an element in her procedure. These lines illustrate this:

> *Although the sepyornis*
> *or roc that lives in Madagascar, and*
>   *the moa are extinct*

and

> *Heroism is exhausting.*

But what irrevocably detaches her from the *Encyclopaedia* is the irony of the following:

How
could he, prized for plumes and eggs and young, used
even as a riding-
beast, respect men hiding
actorlike in ostrich-skins, with
the right hand making the neck move
as if alive and
from a bag the left hand

strewing grain, that ostriches
might be decoyed and killed!

and the delighted observation of the following:

whose comic duckling head on its
great neck, revolves with compass-
needle nervousness,
when he stands guard, in S-

like foragings as he is
preening the down on his leaden-skinned back.

The gist of the poem is that the camel-sparrow has escaped the greed that has led to the extinction of other birds linked to it in size, by its solicitude for its own welfare and that of its chicks. Considering the great purposes that poetry must serve, the interest of the poem is not in its meaning but in this, that it illustrates the achieving of an individual reality. Mr. Lewis has some very agreeable things to say about meaning. He says that the extraction of a meaning from a poem and appraisement of it by rational standards of truth have mainly been due to enthusiasm for moral or religious truth. He protests against the abstraction of this content from the whole and appraisement of it by other than aesthetic standards. The "something said" is important, but it is important for the poem only in so far as the saying of that particular something in a special way is a revelation of reality. He says:

If I am right, the essence of art is insight of a special kind into reality.

Moreover, if he is right, the question as to Miss Moore's poem is not in respect to its meaning but in respect to its potency as a work of art. Does it make us so aware of the reality with which it is concerned, because of the poignancy and penetration of the poet, that it forces something upon our consciousness? The reality so imposed need not be a great reality.

Of course, if it does, it serves our purpose quite as certainly as a less modest poem would serve it. It is here, Mr. Lewis concludes, that the affinity of art and religion is most evident today. He says that both have to mediate for us a reality not ourselves and that this is what the poet does and that the supreme virtue here is humility, for the humble are they that move about the world with the lure of the real in their hearts.

2

Life, not the artist, creates or reveals reality: time and experience in the poet, in the painter. During this last September, I visited the old Zeller[2] house in the Tulpehocken, in Pennsylvania. This family of religious refugees came to this country in 1709, lived for some fifteen or twenty years in the Scoharie region in New York and then went down the Susquehanna to the valley in which the house was built. Over the door there is an architectural cartouche of the cross with palm-branches below, placed there, no doubt, to indicate that the house and those that lived in it were consecrated to the glory of God. From this doorway they faced the hills that were part of the frame of their valley, the familiar shelter in which they spent their laborious lives, happy in the faith and worship in which they rejoiced. Their reality consisted of both the visible and the invisible. On another occasion, a man went with me to visit Christ Church near Stouchsburg. This stout old Lutheran felt about his church very much as the Irish are said to feel about God. Kate O'Brien says that in Ireland God is a member of the family. The man told me that last spring a scovy duck had built her nest in the chimney of the church. When, finally, her brood was hatched, the duck-lings came out of a stove in one of the rooms in the basement of the church. There were six of them and they are alive today on the sexton's farm. When the committee of the church in charge of the building was making its plans last spring, this true lover of his church agreed to paint the fence around the adjoining graveyard. In part, this fence consisted of cast-iron spears. He painted the spear-head silver and the staves black, one by one, week after week, until the job was done. Yet obviously this man's reality is the church-building but as a fellow-existence, of a sort.

.   .   .   .   .   .

As we drove along the road, we met one of the Lutheran's friends, who had been leader of the choir in Trinity Tulpehocken Reformed Church for more than a generation. He had wrapped his throat up in flannel because, he said, one of his tendons was sore. At choir-practice the night before, the hymns for the Sunday service had been selected. He was on his way to the church to put the numbers in the rack. When he had done this, he went with us to the old graveyard of this church. This was an enclosure of about an acre, possibly a little more. The wall was of limestone about four feet high, weatherbeaten,

---

[2] The maiden name of Stevens' mother was Zeller.

barren, bald. In the graveyard were possibly eight or ten sheep, the color of the wall and of many of the gravestones and even of some of the tufts of grass, bleached and silvery in the hard sunlight. The droppings of the sheep fertilized the soil. There were a few cedars here and there but these only accentuated the sense of abandonment and destitution, the sense that, after all, the vast mausoleum of human memory is emptier than one had supposed. Near by stood the manse, also of limestone, apparently vacant, the upper part of each window white with the half-drawn blind, the lower part black with the vacantness of the place. Although the two elderly men were in a way a diversion from the solitude, there could not be any effective diversion from the reality that time and experience had created here, the desolation that penetrated one like something final. Later, when I had returned to New York, I went to the exhibition of books in the Morgan Library held by the American Institute of Graphic Arts. The brilliant pages from Poland, France, Finland and so on, books of tales, of poetry, of folk-lore, were as if the barren reality that I had just experienced had suddenly taken color, become alive and from a single thing become many things and people, vivid, active, intently trying out a thousand characters and illuminations.

3

It is true that Mr. Lewis contemplates a reality adequate to the profound necessities of life today. But it is no less true that it is easier to try to recognize it or something like it or the possible beginnings of it than to achieve it on that scale. Thus, the field in poetry is as great as it is in anything else. Nothing illustrates this better and nothing illustrates the importance of poetry better than this possibility that within it there may yet be found a reality adequate to the profound necessities of life today or for that matter any day. Miss Moore's poem is an instance of method and is not an example beyond the scale intended by her. She may well say:

Que ce n'est pas grand merveille de voir que l'Ostruche digère le fer, veu que les poulles n'en font pas moins.[3]

For she is not a proud spirit. It may be that proud spirits love only the lion or the elephant with his howdah. Miss Moore, however, loves all animals, fierce or mild, ancient or modern. When she observes them she is transported into the presence of a recognizable reality, because, as it happens, she has the faculty of digesting the "harde yron" of appearance.

1951

---

[3] "That it is not a great marvel to see that the ostrich digests iron, seeing that chickens do no less."

William Carlos Williams *1883–1963*

In 1883 William Carlos Williams was born in Rutherford, New Jersey, the son of an English father and a Puerto Rican mother. He grew up in Rutherford with a strong sense of his own Americanism and a deep attachment to his local environment—qualities reflected in his later poetry. After attending Horace Mann High School in New York City, he entered the Medical School of the University of Pennsylvania. While there he formed a life-long friendship with Ezra Pound, then an undergraduate and became acquainted with Hilda Doolittle, later to be known as H.D., and Charles Demuth, the semi-abstract painter. He was also working on a long, never-to-be-published Keatsian poem. After receiving his M.D. in 1906, he interned in New York City for three years and studied pediatrics in Leipzig before settling down to the practice of medicine and poetry in Rutherford, a few miles from Paterson. Williams' first book, *Poems* (1909), privately printed in Rutherford, was followed by *The Tempers* (1913), published in London under arrangements made by Ezra Pound, and *Al Que Quiere! A Book of Poems* (1917), the volume which shows him emerging as a successful master of free verse forms. Although Williams, like Pound, had begun by writing conventionally, he early shifted to the freer forms championed by the Imagists. But his own "objectivism" (the term he preferred) is not to be understood as simply an effort to copy or "represent" a preexisting object in nature. Rather, the "object" is the poem itself, the verbal construct which the poet has created, or "invented," in a form organically determined by the nature of his perception. The poet's concern, therefore, is with the reality and the integrity of the aesthetic object he has contrived rather than with the reality of whatever natural occurrence may have occasioned it. This distinctively modern poetic theory places a value upon the poetic image as a unique reality rather than as a "symbol" of some preexisting reality. This anti-symbolistic attitude dominates much of the poetry of Williams' early and middle years even though symbolism and even the poetry of statement are inevitably present in many of his poems. His poetry is also distinguished by freshness and originality of viewpoint and by excellence of diction—of words carefully selected from living speech, or, in one of his favorite phrases, the "American idiom."

During these years, Williams attempted to promote his own ideas about poetry by editing, first with Robert McAlmon and then with Nathanael West, the magazine *Contact* (1920–23; 1932). He also contributed generously to a multitude of other little magazines and published many volumes of poems. Among these are *Kora in Hell* (1920), *Sour Grapes* (1921), *Spring and All* (1923), *Collected Poems 1921–1931* (1934), the misleadingly-titled *Complete Collected Poems of William Carlos Williams 1906–1938* (1938), and *The Wedge* (1944). In *The Clouds* (1948) and *The Pink Church* (1949), which celebrate the free poetic imagination and the institution ("church") of art, Williams was turning to the more symbolic mode of expression that prevails in *Paterson* and other late poems.

Paterson, first published in four parts (1946, 1948, 1949, 1951) and expanded by the addition of *Paterson, Book Five* (1958), represents Williams' ambitious effort to write an epic or culture poem, comparable to *The Waste Land* of Eliot or *The Cantos* of Pound. It is typical of Williams, however, that he made use of native American and especially local materials in his attempt to define poetically himself and his culture. "Paterson" represents not only the poet himself and the New Jersey city he has known but the city of man, imaginatively conceived, in all its trivial actualities and limitless possibilities. Besides *Paterson,* Williams' later volumes of poetry include *The Desert Music and Other Poems* (1954), *Journey to Love* (1955), and *Pictures from Brueghel and Other Poems* (1962).

Williams also wrote extensively in prose. His stories are collected in *The Knife of the Times and Other Stories* (1932), *Life Along the Passaic River* (1938), *Make Light of It* (1950), and *The Farmers' Daughters* (1961). Among longer narratives and novels are *The Great American Novel* (1923), *In the American Grain* (1925), *A Voyage to Pagany* (1928), *White Mule* (1937), *In the Money* (1940), and *The Build-Up* (1952). Plays he wrote are collected in *Many Loves and Other Plays* (1961). Autobiographical writings include *The Autobiography of William Carlos Williams* (1951), *I Wanted to Write a Poem: The Autobiography of the Works of a Poet,* ed. Edith Heal (1958), and *Yes, Mrs. Williams: A Personal Record of My Mother* (1959).

When Williams died in 1963, his achievement was just beginning to be appreciated. In recent years, which have seen his influence extended, a younger generation of poets has responded eagerly to his democratic sensibility, his essentially modern (rather than modernist) science-conditioned outlook, and the freshness and originality of all his poetry.

Standard editions of Williams' writings include *The Collected Earlier Poems* (New York, 1951); *The Collected Later Poems*, rev. ed. (New York, 1963); *Pictures from Brueghel and Other Poems* (New York, 1963); *Paterson* (New York, 1963); *Selected Essays* (New York, 1954); and *The Selected Letters,* ed.) J. C. Thirlwall (New York, 1957).

A helpful brief introduction to Williams' work is J. H. Miller, ed., *William Carlos Williams: A Collection of Critical Essays* (Englewood Cliffs, N.J., 1966). Book-length studies are Vivienne Koch, *William Carlos Williams*

(Norfolk, Conn., 1950), and L.W. Wagner, *The Poems of William Carlos Williams: A Critical Study* (Middletown, Conn., 1964).

The text of the first twelve poems given here is that of *The Collected Earlier Poems* (New York, 1951). "A Sort of a Song" and the two poems following are from *The Collected Later Poems*, rev. ed. (New York, 1963). The "Coda" of "Asphodel, That Greeny Flower" is from *Pictures from Brueghel* (New York, 1962). "The Descent" and "A Poem by Sappho" are from *Paterson* (New York, 1963).

To Mark Anthony in Heaven[1]

This quiet morning light
reflected, how many times
from grass and trees and clouds
enters my north room
touching the walls with
grass and clouds and trees.
Anthony,
trees and grass and clouds.
Why did you follow
that beloved body   10
with your ships at Actium?
I hope it was because
you knew her inch by inch
from slanting feet upward
to the roots of her hair
and down again and that
you saw her
above the battle's fury —
clouds and trees and grass —

For then you are   20
listening in heaven.

1913

Portrait of a Lady

Your thighs are appletrees
whose blossoms touch the sky.
Which sky? The sky
where Watteau hung a lady's
slipper. Your knees
are a southern breeze — or
a gust of snow. Agh! what
sort of man was Fragonard?
— as if that answered

[1] Unless otherwise indicated the text of this and following poems is that of *The Collected Earlier Poems of William Carlos Williams* (New York, 1951).

anything. Ah, yes — below   10
the knees, since the tune
drops that way, it is
one of those white summer days,
the tall grass of your ankles
flickers upon the shore —
Which shore? —
the sand clings to my lips —
Which shore?
Agh, petals maybe. How
should I know?   20
Which shore? Which shore?
I said petals from an appletree.

                                                         1913

Tract

I will teach you my townspeople
how to perform a funeral
for you have it over a troop
of artists —
unless one should scour the world —
you have the ground sense necessary.

See! the hearse leads.
I begin with a design for a hearse.
For Christ's sake not black —
nor white either — and not polished!
Let it be weathered — like a farm wagon —   10
with gilt wheels (this could be
applied fresh at small expense)
or no wheels at all:
a rough dray to drag over the ground.

Knock the glass out!
My God — glass, my townspeople!
For what purpose? Is it for the dead
to look out or for us to see
how well he is housed or to see   20
the flowers or the lack of them —
or what?
To keep the rain and snow from him?
He will have a heavier rain soon:
pebbles and dirt and what not.
Let there be no glass —
and no upholstery, phew!
and no little brass rollers
and small easy wheels on the bottom —
my townspeople what are you thinking of?   30
A rough plain hearse then

with gilt wheels and no top at all.
On this the coffin lies
by its own weight.

       No wreaths please—
especially no hot house flowers.
Some common memento is better,
something he prized and is known by:
his old clothes—a few books perhaps—
God knows what! You realize   40
how we are about these things
my townspeople—
something will be found—anything
even flowers if he had come to that.
So much for the hearse.

For heaven's sake though see to the driver!
Take off the silk hat! In fact
that's no place at all for him—
up there unceremoniously
dragging our friend out to his own dignity!   50
Bring him down—bring him down!
Low and inconspicuous! I'd not have him ride
on the wagon at all—damn him—
the undertaker's understrapper!
Let him hold the reins
and walk at the side
and inconspicuously too!

Then briefly as to yourselves:
Walk behind—as they do in France,
seventh class, or if you ride   60
Hell take curtains! Go with some show
of inconvenience; sit openly—
to the weather as to grief.
Or do you think you can shut grief in?
What—from us? We who have perhaps
nothing to lose? Share with us
share with us—it will be money
in your pockets.
       Go now
I think you are ready.   70

           1917

The Botticellian Trees

The alphabet of
the trees

is fading in the
song of the leaves

the crossing
bars of the thin

letters that spelled
winter

and the cold
have been illumined   10

with
pointed green

by the rain and sun —
The strict simple

principles of
straight branches

are being modified
by pinched-out

ifs of color, devout
conditions   20

the smiles of love —
    . . . . . .

until the stript
sentences

move as a woman's
limbs under cloth

and praise from secrecy
quick with desire

love's ascendancy
in summer —

In summer the song   30
sings itself

above the muffled words —   *1934*

The Widow's Lament in Springtime

Sorrow is my own yard
where the new grass
flames as it has flamed
often before but not
with the cold fire
that closes round me this year.
Thirtyfive years
I lived with my husband.
The plumtree is white today
with masses of flowers.   10
Masses of flowers
load the cherry branches
and color some bushes
yellow and some red
but the grief in my heart
is stronger than they
for though they were my joy
formerly, today I notice them
and turned away forgetting.
Today my son told me   20
that in the meadows,
at the edge of the heavy woods
in the distance, he saw
trees of white flowers.
I feel that I would like
to go there
and fall into those flowers
and sink into the marsh near them.

                                        1921

From *Spring and All*

1

Spring and All

By the road to the contagious hospital
under the surge of the blue
mottled clouds driven from the
northeast—a cold wind. Beyond, the
waste of broad, muddy fields
brown with dried weeds, standing and fallen

patches of standing water
the scattering of tall trees

All along the road the reddish
purplish, forked, upstanding, twiggy   10
stuff of bushes and small trees
with dead, brown leaves under them
leafless vines —

Lifeless in appearance, sluggish
dazed spring approaches —

They enter the new world naked,
cold, uncertain of all
save that they enter. All about them
the cold, familiar wind —

Now the grass, tomorrow   20
the stiff curl of wildcarrot leaf
One by one objects are defined —
It quickens: clarity, outline of leaf

But now the stark dignity of
entrance — Still, the profound change
has come upon them: rooted, they
grip down and begin to awaken

                                                        1923

18

To Elsie

The pure products of America
go crazy —
mountain folk from Kentucky

or the ribbed north end of
Jersey
with its isolate lakes and

valleys, its deaf-mutes, thieves
old names
and promiscuity between

devil-may-care men who have taken   10
to railroading
out of sheer lust of adventure —

and young slatterns, bathed
in filth
from Monday to Saturday

to be tricked out that night

with gauds
from imaginations which have no

peasant traditions to give them
character
but flutter and flaunt   20

sheer rags — succumbing without
emotion
save numbed terror

under some hedge of choke-cherry
or viburnum —
which they cannot express —

Unless it be that marriage
perhaps
with a dash of Indian blood   30

will throw up a girl so desolate
so hemmed round
with disease or murder

that she'll be rescued by an
agent —
reared by the state and

sent out at fifteen to work in
some hard-pressed
house in the suburbs —

some doctor's family, some Elsie —   40
voluptuous water
expressing with broken

brain the truth about us —
her great
ungainly hips and flopping breasts

addressed to cheap
jewelry
and rich young men with fine eyes

as if the earth under our feet
were   50
an excrement of some sky

and we degraded prisoners
destined
to hunger until we eat filth

while the imagination strains
after deer
going by fields of goldenrod in

the stifling heat of September
Somehow
it seems to destroy us   60

It is only in isolate flecks that
something
is given off

No one
to witness
and adjust, no one to drive the car

1923

21

The Red Wheelbarrow

so much depends
upon

a red wheel
barrow

glazed with rain
water

beside the white
chickens.

1923

Nantucket

Flowers through the window.
lavender and yellow

changed by white curtains —
Smell of cleanliness —

Sunshine of late afternoon —
On the glass tray

a glass pitcher, the tumbler
turned down, by which

a key is lying—And the
immaculate white bed

1934

The Yachts

contend in a sea which the land partly encloses
shielding them from the too-heavy blows
of an ungoverned ocean which when it chooses

tortures the biggest hulls, the best man knows
to pit against its beatings, and sinks them pitilessly.
Mothlike in mists, scintillant in the minute

brilliance of cloudless days, with broad bellying sails
they glide to the wind tossing green water
from their sharp prows while over them the crew crawls

ant-like, solicitously grooming them, releasing,   10
making fast as they turn, lean far over and having
caught the wind again, side by side, head for the mark.

In a well guarded arena of open water surrounded by
lesser and greater craft which, sycophant, lumbering
and flittering follow them, they appear youthful, rare

as the light of a happy eye, live with the grace
of all that in the mind is feckless, free and
naturally to be desired. Now the sea which holds them

is moody, lapping their glossy sides, as if feeling
for some slightest flaw but fails completely.   20
Today no race. Then the wind comes again. The yachts

move, jockeying for a start, the signal is set and they
are off. Now the waves strike at them but they are too
well made, they slip through, though they take in canvas.

Arms with hands grasping seek to clutch at the prows.
Bodies thrown recklessly in the way are cut aside.
It is a sea of faces about them in agony, in despair

until the horror of the race dawns staggering the mind,
the whole sea become an entanglement of watery bodies
lost to the world bearing what they cannot hold. Broken,   30

beaten, desolate, reaching from the dead to be taken up
they cry out, failing, failing! their cries rising
in waves still as the skillful yachts pass over.   1935

St. Francis Einstein of the Daffodils

*On the first visit of Professor Einstein to
the United States in the spring of 1921.*

"Sweet land"
at last!
out of the sea—
the Venusremembering wavelets
rippling with laughter—
freedom
for the daffodils!
—in a tearing wind
that shakes
the tufted orchards—   10
Einstein, tall as a violet
in the lattice-arbor corner
is tall as
a blossomy peartree

O Samos, Samos
dead and buried. Lesbia
a black cat in the freshturned
garden. All dead.
All flesh they sung
is rotten   20
Sing of it no longer—

Side by side young and old
take the sun together—
maples, green and red
yellowbells
and the vermilion quinceflower
together—

The peartree
with fœtid blossoms
sways its high topbranches   30
with contrary motions
and there are both pinkflowered
and coralflowered peachtrees
in the bare chickenyard
of the old negro
with white hair who hides
poisoned fish-heads
here and there
where stray cats find them—
find them   40

Spring days
swift and mutable

winds blowing four ways
hot and cold
shaking the flowers—

Now the northeast wind
moving in fogs leaves the grass
cold and dripping. The night
is dark. But in the night
the southeast wind approaches.   50
The owner of the orchard
lies in bed
with open windows
and throws off his covers
one by one

1936

The Poor

It's the anarchy of poverty
delights me, the old
yellow wooden house indented
among the new brick tenements

Or a cast-iron balcony
with panels showing oak branches
in full leaf. It fits
the dress of the children

reflecting every stage and
custom of necessity—   10
Chimneys, roofs, fences of
wood and metal in an unfenced

age and enclosing next to
nothing at all: the old man
in a sweater and soft black
hat who sweeps the sidewalk—

his own ten feet of it
in a wind that fitfully
turning his corner has
overwhelmed the entire city   20

1938

A Sort of a Song [1]

Let the snake wait under
his weed

[1] Unless otherwise indicated, the text of this and the following poems is that of *The Collected Later Poems of William Carlos Williams*, revised ed. (New York, 1963).

·and the writing
be of words, slow and quick, sharp
to strike, quiet to wait,
sleepless.

—through metaphor to reconcile
the people and the stones.
Compose. (No ideas
but in things) Invent!
✷ Saxifrage is my flower that splits
the rocks.

✷small delicate flowers   *1944*

Burning the Christmas Greens

Their time past, pulled down
cracked and flung to the fire
—go up in a roar

All recognition lost, burnt clean
clean in the flame, the green
dispersed, a living red,
flame red, red as blood wakes
on the ash—

and ebbs to a steady burning
the rekindled bed become   10
a landscape of flame

At the winter's midnight
we went to the trees, the coarse
holly, the balsam and
the hemlock for their green

At the thick of the dark
the moment of the cold's
deepest plunge we brought branches
cut from the green trees

to fill our need, and over   20
doorways, about paper Christmas
bells covered with tinfoil
and fastened by red ribbons

we stuck the green prongs
in the windows hung
woven wreaths and above pictures
the living green. On the

mantle we built a green forest
and among those hemlock
sprays put a herd of small   30
white deer as if they

were walking there. All this!
and it seemed gentle and good
to us. Their time past,
relief! The room bare. We

stuffed the dead grate
with them upon the half burnt out
log's smoldering eye, opening
red and closing under them

and we stood there looking down.   40
Green is a solace
a promise of peace, a fort
against the cold (though we

did not say so) a challenge
above the snow's
hard shell. Green (we might
have said) that, where

small birds hide and dodge
and lift their plaintive
rallying cries, blocks for them   50
and knocks down

the unseeing bullets of
the storm. Green spruce boughs
pulled down by a weight of
snow — Transformed!

Violence leaped and appeared.
Recreant! roared to life
as the flame rose through and
our eyes recoiled from it.

In the jagged flames green   60
to red, instant and alive. Green!
those sure abutments . . . Gone!
lost to mind

and quick in the contracting
tunnel of the grate
appeared a world! Black
mountains, black and red — as

yet uncolored—and ash white,
an infant landscape of shimmering
ash and flame and we, in   70
that instant, lost,

breathless to be witnesses,
as if we stood
ourselves refreshed among
the shining fauna of that fire.

1944

Raleigh Was Right[1]

We cannot go to the country
for the country will bring us no peace
What can the small violets tell us
that grow on furry stems in
the long grass among lance shaped leaves?

Though you praise us
and call to mind the poets
who sung of our loveliness   10
it was long ago!
long ago! when country people
would plow and sow with
flowering minds and pockets at ease—
if ever this were true.

Not now. Love itself a flower
with roots in a parched ground.
Empty pockets make empty heads.
Cure it if you can but   20
do not believe that we can live
today in the country
for the country will bring us no peace.

1944

From *Paterson, Book II*
THE DESCENT[1]

The descent beckons
            as the ascent beckoned
                        Memory is a kind

---

[1] The title alludes to Sir Walter Raleigh's disillusioned "Her Reply" in answer to Christopher
Marlowe's "The Passionate Shepherd to His Love." Both poems appear in *The Oxford Book
of English Verse*, ed. A. T. Quiller-Couch (Oxford, 1907), pp. 173–175.
[1] The text is that of *Paterson* (New York, 1951).

of accomplishment
        a sort of renewal
              even
an initiation, since the spaces it opens are new places
        inhabited by hordes
              heretofore unrealized,
of new kinds —   10
        since their movements
              are towards new objectives
(even though formerly they were abandoned)

No defeat is made up entirely of defeat — since
the world it opens is always a place
        formerly
              unsuspected. A
world lost,
        a world unsuspected
              beckons to new places   20
and no whiteness (lost) is so white as the memory
of whiteness

With evening, love wakens
        though its shadows
              which are alive by reason
of the sun shining —
        grow sleepy now and drop away
              from desire   30

Love without shadows stirs now
        beginning to waken
              as night
advances.

The descent
        made up of despairs
              and without accomplishment
realizes a new awakening :
              which is a reversal
of despair.   40
        For what we cannot accomplish, what
is denied to love,
        what we have lost in the anticipation —
              a descent follows,
endless and indestructible

                                        1948

From *Asphodel, That Greeny Flower* [1]

CODA

Inseparable from the fire   1
      its light
           takes precedence over it.
Then follows
      what we have dreaded—
           but it can never
overcome what has gone before.
      In the huge gap
           between the flash
and the thunderstroke   10
      spring has come in
           or a deep snow fallen.
Call it old age.
      In that stretch
           we have lived to see
a colt kick up his heels.
      Do not hasten
           laugh and play
in an eternity
      the heat will not overtake the light.
           That's sure.   20
That gelds the bomb,
      permitting
           that the mind contain it.
This is that interval,
      that sweetest interval,
           when love will blossom,
come early, come late
      and give itself to the lover.
Only the imagination is real!   30
      I have declared it
           time without end.
If a man die
      it is because death
           has first
possessed his imagination.
      But if he refuse death—
           no greater evil
can befall him
      unless it be the death of love   40
           meet him
in full career.
      Then indeed
           for him
the light has gone out.

[1] The text of this poem, which first appeared in Williams' *Journey to Love* (1955), is that of *Pictures from Brueghel* (New York, 1962).

But love and the imagination
          are of a piece,
                    swift as the light
to avoid destruction.
          So we come to watch time's flight   50
                    as we might watch
summer lightning
          or fireflies, secure,
                    by grace of the imagination,
safe in its care.
          For if
                    the light itself
has escaped,
          the whole edifice opposed to it
                    goes down.   60
Light, the imagination
          and love,
                    in our age,
by natural law,
          which we worship,
                    maintain
all of a piece
          their dominance.
So let us love
          confident as is the light   70
                    in its struggle with darkness
that there is as much to say
          and more
                    for the one side
and that not the darker
          which John Donne
                    for instance
among many men
          presents to us.
                    In the controversy   80
touching the younger
          and the older Tolstoi,
                    Villon, St. Anthony, Kung,
Rimbaud, Buddha
          and Abraham Lincoln
                    the palm goes
always to the light;
          Who most shall advance the light —
                    call it what you may!
The light   90
          for all time shall outspeed
                    the thunder crack.
Medieval pageantry
          is human and we enjoy
                    the rumor of it

as in our world we enjoy
            the reading of Chaucer,
                        likewise
a priest's raiment
            (or that of a savage chieftain).   100
                        It is all
a celebration of the light.
            All the pomp and ceremony
                        of weddings,
"Sweet Thames, run softly
            till I end
                        my song," — [2]
are of an equal sort.
For our wedding, too,
            the light was wakened   110
                        and shone. The light!
the light stood before us
            waiting!
                        I thought the world
stood still.
            At the altar
                        so intent was I
before my vows,
            so moved by your presence
                        a girl so pale   120
and ready to faint
            that I pitied
                        and wanted to protect you.
As I think of it now,
            after a lifetime,
                        it is as if
a sweet-scented flower
            were poised
                        and for me did open.
Asphodel   130
            has no odor
                        save to the imagination
but it too
            celebrates the light.
                        It is late
but an odor
            as from our wedding
                        has revived for me
and begun again to penetrate
            into all crevices   140
                        of my world.

1955

---

[2] For Eliot's much different use of the same refrain from Edmund Spenser's "Prothalam-ion," see above, *The Waste Land,* Part 3.

From *Paterson, Book V*

A POEM BY SAPPHO[1]

Peer of the gods is that man, who
face to face, sits listening
to your sweet speech and lovely
    laughter.

It is this that rouses a tumult
in my breast. At mere sight of you
my voice falters, my tongue
    is broken.

Straightway, a delicate fire runs in
my limbs; my eyes
are blinded and my ears
    thunder.

Sweat pours out: a trembling hunts
me down. I grow paler
than dry grass and lack little
    of dying.

1957

---

[1] The text of this translation into American English by Williams, which first appeared in *Poems in Folio* (San Francisco, 1957), is that of *Paterson, Book Five* (New York, 1958).

Marianne Moore   *1887–1972*

Marianne Craig Moore, whose original and meticulously crafted poems have won her a distinguished position among modern poets, was born in Kirkwood, Missouri, in 1887. After graduating from Bryn Mawr College in 1909, she studied "business" and became a teacher of commercial subjects at the Carlisle Indian School in Pennsylvania (1910–15). In 1915, her first poems appeared in *Poetry* and *The Egoist*. In 1920 she settled firmly in New York City, where she at first held a position as a branch librarian. The recognition received by her first volume, *Poems* (1921), and even more by her second, *Observations* (1924), which won the *Dial* award, led to a position as an editor of that distinguished literary journal from 1925 until its demise in 1929.

Miss Moore's poems are distinguished by freshness of observation and originality of response. In form they are unconventional and experimental, but usually not entirely in the tradition of "free" verse because the poet is concerned with observing principles of unity and symmetry in her metrical patterns. In place of conventional rhyme and meter, she typically makes use of lines that observe a regular measure or count of syllables. Thus, although any one stanza of a poem like "The Fish" may seem to be eccentric, it will be found to consist of a pattern of syllabically-ordered verses that corresponds to the pattern of the other stanzas of the poem. The same principle cannot of course apply to a one-stanza poem like "The Snail," but this, like all her poems, observes an organic principle of form in which "compression is the first grace of style" and the snail itself is an image of the aesthetic virtues the poet must strive for. Miss Moore has elsewhere commented that in poetry "metaphor substitutes compactness for confusion," an elegant aphorism that her own work verifies. The detached rationalism of many of Miss Moore's unique "observations" is tempered by the humane sympathies revealed in a poem like "He 'Digesteth

Harde Yron,'" in which the virtues of the ostrich are a reproach to his human hunters. Another poet's appreciation of the qualities of Miss Moore's verse can be read in Wallace Stevens' essay "About One of Marianne Moore's Poems."

Miss Moore's *Collected Poems* (1951) won the Pulitzer Prize, the National Book Award, and the Bollingen Award. The poems contained in it and subsequent volumes including *Like a Bulwark* (1956), *O To Be a Dragon* (1959), and *Tell Me, Tell Me* (1966) have been gathered in *The Complete Poems of Marianne Moore* (1967). Other works include *The Fables of La Fontaine* (1954), a translation, and *Predilections* (1955), a collection of critical essays.

A Marianne Moore Reader (New York, 1961) is a representative selection of Miss Moore's work. The standard edition of her poems is *The Complete Poems of Marianne Moore* (New York, 1967). A helpful brief introduction is Jean Garrigue, *Marianne Moore* (Minneapolis, 1965). A book-length critique is B. F. Engel, *Marianne Moore* (New York, 1964). A full bibliography is E. P. Sheehy and K. A. Lohf, *The Achievement of Marianne Moore: A Bibliography, 1907–1957* (New York, 1958).

The text of "Poetry" is that of *Collected Poems* (New York, 1951); the other poems presented here are from *The Complete Poems of Marianne Moore* (New York, 1967).

The Fish

wade
through black jade.
     Of the crow-blue mussel shells, one keeps
     adjusting the ash-heaps;
          opening and shutting itself like

an
injured fan.
     The barnacles which encrust the side
     of the wave, cannot hide
          there for the submerged shafts of the

sun,
split like spun
     glass, move themselves with spotlight swiftness
     into the crevices —
          in and out, illuminating

the
turquoise sea

of bodies. The water drives a wedge
of iron through the iron edge
  of the cliff; whereupon the stars,

pink
rice-grains, ink-
  bespattered jelly fish, crabs like green
  lilies, and submarine
    toadstools, slide each on the other.

All
external
  marks of abuse are present on this
  defiant edifice—
    all the physical features of

ac-
cident—lack
  of cornice, dynamite grooves, burns, and
  hatchet strokes, these things stand
    out on it; the chasm side is

dead.
Repeated
  evidence has proved that it can live
  on what can not revive
    its youth. The sea grows old in it.

[handwritten: sea/rock]
[handwritten: life-change in]
[handwritten: stability-permanence]

1921

[handwritten: Cornice - horizontal moulding projecting along the top of a wall, building, etc.]

Poetry[1]

I, too, dislike it: there are things that are important beyond all
    this fiddle.
  Reading it, however, with a perfect contempt for it, one
    discovers in
  it after all, a place for the genuine.
    Hands that can grasp, eyes
    that can dilate, hair that can rise
      if it must, these things are important not because
      a
high-sounding interpretation can be put upon them but because
    they are
  useful. When they become so derivative as to become

[1] The text of this poem is that of *Collected Poems* (New York, 1951). In *The Complete Poems* (1967), in which the reader is advised that "Omissions are not accidents," the poem has been reduced to a selection from its original opening lines: "I, too, dislike it./Reading it, however, with a perfect contempt for it, one dis-/covers in/it, after all, a place for the genuine."

unintelligible,
the same thing may be said for all of us, that we
    do not admire what
    we cannot understand: the bat
        holding on upside down or in quest of some-
            thing to

eat, elephants pushing, a wild horse taking a roll, a tireless wolf
                under
    a tree, the immovable critic twitching his skin like a horse
            that feels a flea, the base-
ball fan, the statistician—
        nor is it valid
            to discriminate against 'business documents and

school-books'; all these phenomena are important. One must
                make a distinction
    however: when dragged into prominence by half poets,
                the result is not poetry,
    nor till the poets among us can be
        'literalists of
        the imagination'—above
            insolence and triviality and can present

for inspection, 'imaginary gardens with real toads in them', shall
                we have
    it. In the meantime, if you demand on the one hand,
    the raw material of poetry in
        all its rawness and
        that which is on the other hand
            genuine, you are interested in poetry.

1921

To A Snail

If "compression is the first grace of style,"
you have it. Contractility is a virtue
as modesty is a virtue.
It is not the acquisition of any one thing
that is able to adorn,
or the incidental quality that occurs
as a concomitant of something well said,
that we value in style,
but the principle that is hid:
in the absence of feet, "a method of conclusions";
"a knowledge of principles,"
in the curious phenomenon of your occipital horn.   *1935*

head-occipital bone - skull bone

He "Digesteth Harde Yron" [1]

Although the aepyornis
　　or roc that lived in Madagascar, and
the moa are extinct,
the camel-sparrow, linked
　　with them in size—the large sparrow
Xenophon saw walking by a stream—was and is
a symbol of justice.

　　This bird watches his chicks with
　　a maternal concentration—and he's
been mothering the eggs
at night six weeks—his legs
　　their only weapon of defense.
He is swifter than a horse; he has a foot hard
as a hoof; the leopard

　　is not more suspicious. How
　　could he, prized for plumes and eggs and young,
used even as a riding-beast, respect men
　　hiding actor-like in ostrich skins, with the right hand
making the neck move as if alive
and from a bag the left hand

　　strewing grain, that ostriches
　　might be decoyed and killed! Yes, this is he
whose plume was anciently
the plume of justice; he
　　whose comic duckling head on its
great neck revolves with compass-needle nervousness
when he stands guard,

　　in S-like foragings as he is
　　preening the down on his leaden-skinned back.
The egg piously shown
as Leda's very own
　　from which Castor and Pollux hatched,
was an ostrich egg. And what could have been more fit
for the Chinese lawn it

　　grazed on as a gift to an
　　emperor who admired strange birds, than this
one who builds his mud-made
nest in dust yet will wade
　　in lake or sea till only the head shows.
　　．　　．　　．　　．　　．　　．

[1] For Wallace Stevens' essay on this poem, see above.

Wallace Stevens 3357

Six hundred ostrich brains served
    at one banquet, the ostrich-plume-tipped tent
and desert spear, jewel-
gorgeous ugly egg-shell
    goblets, eight pairs of ostriches
in harness, dramatize a meaning
always missed by the externalist.

    The power of the visible
    is the invisible; as even where
no tree of freedom grows,
so-called brute courage knows.
    Heroism is exhausting, yet
it contradicts a greed that did not wisely spare
the harmless solitaire

    or great auk in its grandeur;
    unsolicitude having swallowed up
all giant birds but an alert gargantuan
    little-winged, magnificently speedy running-bird.
This one remaining rebel
is the sparrow-camel.

                               1941

Archibald MacLeish   *1892–1973*

Born in a suburb of Chicago in 1892, Archibald MacLeish attended Hotchkiss School and Yale University (B.A., 1915). Further study at the Harvard Law School was interrupted by service in the Army (1917–18). When he returned to Harvard after the war, he had already published a book of poems, *Tower of Ivory* (1917). After taking his LL.B. degree (1919), MacLeish practiced law in Boston until 1923, when, recognizing that poetry was his chief interest, he went to France, where he lived as a literary expatriate for five years. The work of MacLeish's early period, which ended with *The Hamlet of A. MacLeish* (1928), reflects the prevailing tone of postwar disillusionment that the poetry of Eliot and Pound had helped to establish. A poem like "Ars Poetica," in *Streets in the Moon* (1926), also shows MacLeish's acceptance of the principles of modern poetic theory, especially the stress upon sensuous immediacy, as set forth in the tenets of Imagism, which called for the "direct treatment of the 'thing.'" Other publications of these years include *The Happy Marriage* (1924), *The Pot of Earth* (1925), and *Nobodaddy*, (1926), a verse drama.

MacLeish's poetry of the 1930's, written after his return to America in 1928, reveals a new social and historical consciousness. His ambitious epic of the Mexican conquest, *Conquistador* (1932), is somewhat less typical of his work of this period than the poems of *New Found Land* (1930), which contains "You, Andrew Marvell," and *Frescoes for Mr. Rockefeller's City* (1933). In these works particularly MacLeish is concerned with the returned expatriate's problem of defining himself as an American in contemporary terms and increasingly, as in *Frescoes*, with protesting the exploitation of the masses by the capitalistic betrayers of the American dream. In keeping with his proletarian sympathies, the poet brings his language closer to the vernacular of the common people than he had in his earlier work. As the decade advanced, MacLeish came to feel that it was the responsibility of the poet to be actively engaged in current affairs and to influence public opinion. In *Panic* (1935), a verse drama, and in verse radio plays like *The Fall of the City* (1937) and *Air Raid* (1938), he expresses his views on capitalism, totalitarianism, and modern war. *America Was Promises* (1939) reiterates the theme of betrayal but also urges action ("The promises are those who take them") to redeem America's potential.

With the emergence of the totalitarian threat of the late thirties, as World War II erupted, MacLeish shifted to the view that a patriotic support of the Government was the duty of the writer. In 1940, shortly after he was named Librarian of Congress (1939–44), he published *The Irresponsibles*, a prose tract censuring American intellectuals and writers for their presumed lack of active commitment to the cause of democracy. During the year 1944–45 he served as Assistant Secretary of State, the highest public office ever held by an American man of letters. The long poem *Actfive* (1948) reveals a resurgence of postwar disillusionment, only this time, thirty years and another war later, tempered by a humanist existential faith in man's capacity to "endure and love" despite his knowledge of the void.

Among MacLeish's more important later works are *Collected Poems 1917–1952* (1952) and the highly successful verse drama *J. B.* (1958), a contemporary treatment of the story of Job. Among additional prose works are *A Time to Speak* (1941), *A Time to Act* (1943), *Poetry and Opinion: The Pisan Cantos of Ezra Pound* (1950), *Poetry and Experience* (1960), and *The Dialogues of Archibald MacLeish and Mark Van Doren*, ed. W. V. Bush (1962). Recent collections of verse include *Songs for Eve* (1954) and *"The Wild Old Wicked Man" and Other Poems* (1968).

MacLeish is a skillful and sensitive poet who is at his best, perhaps, in the elegiac vein of "You, Andrew Marvell" and other lyrics of his earlier years. Because he has always been extremely responsive to the dominant attitudes and currents of opinion of his times, his work also has interest as a barometer of the intellectual climate of the five troubled decades he has witnessed and recorded as an engaged observer.

There is no biography of MacLeish or book-length study of his work.

The text of the poems given here is that of *Collected Poems 1917–1952* (1952).

L'an trentiesme de mon eage[1]

And I have come upon this place
By lost ways, by a nod, by words,
By faces, by an old man's face
At Morlaix lifted to the birds,

By hands upon the tablecloth
At Aldebori's, by the thin
Child's hands that opened to the moth
And let the flutter of the moonlight in,

[1] "The thirtieth year of my age." For Pound's use of the same quotation from "The Testament" of François Villon, see above.

By hands, by voices, by the voice
Of Mrs. Whitman on the stair,   10
By Margaret's "If we had the choice
To choose or not—" through her thick hair,

By voices, by the creak and fall
Of footsteps on the upper floor,
By silence waiting in the hall
Between the doorbell and the door,

By words, by voices, a lost way—
And here above the chimney stack
The unknown constellations sway—
And by what way shall I go back?   20

1926

Ars Poetica[1]

A poem should be palpable and mute
As a globed fruit,

Dumb
As old medallions to the thumb,

Silent as the sleeve-worn stone
Of casement ledges where the moss has grown—

A poem should be wordless
As the flight of birds.

*

A poem should be motionless in time
As the moon climbs,   10

Leaving, as the moon releases
Twig by twig the night-entangled trees,

Leaving, as the moon behind the winter leaves,
Memory by memory the mind—

A poem should be motionless in time
As the moon climbs.

*

A poem should be equal to:
Not true.

[1] "The art of poetry." The title is that of the famous epistle of Horace (65–8 B.C.).

For all the history of grief
An empty doorway and a maple leaf.   20

For love
The leaning grasses and two lights above the sea—

A poem should not mean ✗
But be.

                                                              1926

You, Andrew Marvell [1]

And here face down beneath the sun
And here upon earth's noonward height
To feel the always coming on
The always rising of the night:

To feel creep up the curving east
The earthy chill of dusk and slow
Upon those under lands the vast
And ever climbing shadow grow

And strange at Ecbatan the trees
Take leaf by leaf the evening strange
The flooding dark about their knees
The mountains over Persia change   10

And now at Kermanshah the gate
Dark empty and the withered grass
And through the twilight now the late
Few travelers in the westward pass

And Baghdad darken and the bridge
Across the silent river gone
And through Arabia the edge
Of evening widen and steal on   20

And deepen on Palmyra's street
The wheel rut in the ruined stone
And Lebanon fade out and Crete
High through the clouds and overblown

And over Sicily the air
Still flashing with the landward gulls

---

[1] The allusion is to Marvell's well-known poem "To His Coy Mistress," and especially to its most familiar lines: "But at my back I always hear / Time's winged chariot hurrying near."

And loom and slowly disappear
The sails above the shadowy hulls

And Spain go under and the shore
Of Africa the gilded sand   30
And evening vanish and no more
The low pale light across that land

Nor now the long light on the sea:

And here face downward in the sun
To feel how swift how secretly
The shadow of the night comes on . . .

1930

From *Frescoes for Mr. Rockefeller's City*
LANDSCAPE AS A NUDE

She lies on her left side her flank golden:
Her hair is burned black with the strong sun.
The scent of her hair is of rain in the dust on her shoulders:
She has brown breasts and the mouth of no other country.

Ah she is beautiful here in the sun where she lies:
She is not like the soft girls naked in vineyards
Nor the soft naked girls of the English islands
Where the rain comes in with the surf on an east wind:

Hers is the west wind and the sunlight: the west
Wind is the long clean wind of the continents—   10
The wind turning with earth, the wind descending
Steadily out of the evening and following on.

The wind here where she lies is west; the trees
Oak ironwood cottonwood hickory: standing in
Great groves they roll on the wind as the sea would.
The grasses of Iowa Illinois Indiana

Run with the plunge of the wind as a wave tumbling.

Under her knees there is no green lawn of the Florentines:
Under her dusty knees is the corn stubble:
Her belly is flecked with the flickering light of the corn.   20

She lies on her left side her flank golden:
Her hair is burned black with the strong sun.
The scent of her hair is of dust and of smoke on her shoulders:
She has brown breasts and the mouth of no other country.

1933

Epilogue to *Actfive*

The scene dissolves. The closet world
Collapses in enormous night.
The garden where the marble Gods
Kept music and the player Kings
Is gone and gone the golden light,
The careful lawns, the ordered trees,
Where man upon the waste of time
Enclosed his small eternities.
All this has vanished. In its stead,
Minute upon an immense plain   10
Where vultures huddle and the soft
And torpid rats recoil and crawl,
Gorged with a food that has no name,
And voices in the dark of air
Cry out Despair and fall and fail —
Minute upon an immense plain
The mortal flesh and mortal bone
Are left among the stones to play
The man beneath the moon alone: —
And know the part they have to bear   20
And know the void vast night above
And know the night below and dare
Endure and love.

1948

E. E. Cummings   *1894 – 1962*

Edward Estlin Cummings, whose rebellion against typographical conventions has given his work an unmistakable signature, grew up in Cambridge, Massachusetts, where his admired father, a Congregational preacher, had been a member of the English faculty at Harvard. Cummings attended Harvard, specializing in Greek and Latin. He took his B.A. degree in 1915 and his M.A. in 1916. In 1917 he went to France as a volunteer ambulance driver with the French army. Arrested on a mistaken charge of treasonable correspondence, he was imprisoned for several months in a French concentration camp — an experience that provided the subject of his poetic novel *The Enormous Room* (1922). After the war, Cummings returned to Paris to study painting, an art he practiced concurrently with poetry for the rest of his life. By the end of the decade of the twenties he had returned to New York and settled into the Greenwich Village apartment that was to remain his home.

Cummings' first book of poems, *Tulips and Chimneys* (1923), established the attitudes and the style of expression that were characteristic of all his later work. Cumming's rejection of formal typography and syntax (the "logic" of language) was a romantic rejection of rationality and its limiting conventions in favor of a celebration of the life of spontaneous feeling and passion of which Spring was the "omnipotent goddess." He preferred the lower-case "i," which designated the natural, unsophisticated self, to the "I" which represented the rational censorious ego; and he thought of the spontaneous natural self as the originator of the poems of e. e. cummings. In his choice of poetic forms Cummings was not entirely a revolutionary, however. In addition to many distinctively original poems in the free, organic forms favored by modern poetic theory, there are many quite conventional poems — often in sing-song rhymed quatrains — in which the only "modern" feature is his unconventional typography. He also retained a fondness for the sonnet (in either its traditional or a modified form) based on his early reading of the romantic poets, especially Wordsworth and Keats. Although Cummings was preeminently a praiseful poet of love and the beauties of nature, he was also an extremely skillful and witty satirist who resisted any and all efforts to curb or repress the freedom and dignity of the individual. Among the many targets of his satire are middle-class conventionality, business, materialism, war, and political regimentation.

Collections of Cummings' poems include *&* (1925), *XLI POEMS* (1925), *is 5* (1926), *W* [*ViVa*] (1931), *no thanks* (1935), *Collected Poems* (1938), *50 POEMS* (1940), *1 × 1* (1944), and *XAIPE* (1950). These, together with *Tulips and Chimneys*, were brought together in *Poems 1923–1954* (1954). Subsequent volumes of poetry include *95 poems* (1958) and the posthumous *73 poems* (1963). Among other works, *Him* (1927) is an expressionist drama. *CIOPW* (1933) is a collection of drawings and paintings, with verse notes, in charcoal, ink, oil, pencil, and watercolor. *Eimi* (1933) is an impressionistic travel journal that records the disillusioning experience of a trip to Russia. *Tom* (1935) is a satirical ballet, and *Santa Claus* (1946) is a poetic morality play. The autobiographial *i: six nonlectures* (1953) is a lyrical tribute to the poet's childhood environment and to the Romantic poets who had inspired him.

The standard edition of Cummings' poetry is *Poems 1923–1954* (New York, 1954), supplemented by *95 poems* (New York, 1958) and *73 poems* (New York, 1963). Biographical and critical works on Cummings include Charles Norman, *The Magic-Maker: E. E. Cummings* (New York, 1958), a factual biography; Norman Friedman, E. E. Cummings: *The Art of His Poetry* (Baltimore, 1960), and e. e. cummings: *The Growth of a Writer* (Carbondale, Ill., 1964); B. A. Marks, *E. E. Cummings* (New York, 1964), and R. E. Wegner, *The Poetry and Prose of E. E. Cummings* (New York, 1965). Bibliographical aids include Paul Lauter, *E. E. Cummings: Index to First Lines and Bibliography of Works by and about the Poet* (Denver, 1955), and G. J. Firmage, *E. E. Cummings: A Bibliography* (Middletown, Conn., 1964).

The text of the poems given here is that of *Poems 1923–1954* (New York, 1954).

O sweet spontaneous
earth how often have
the
doting

     fingers of
prurient philosophers pinched
and
poked

thee
, has the naughty thumb   10
of science prodded
thy

beauty   how
often have religions taken
thee upon their scraggy knees
squeezing and

buffeting thee that thou mightest conceive
gods
        (but
true   20

to the incomparable
couch of death thy
rhythmic
lover

        thou answerest

them only with

                spring)

                                                                1923

    spring omnipotent goddess thou dost
* inveigle into crossing sidewalks the
    unwary june-bug and the frivolous angleworm
    thou dost persuade to serenade his
    lady the musical tom-cat, thou stuffest
    the parks with overgrown pimply
* cavaliers and gumchewing giggly
    girls and not content
    Spring, with this
    thou hangest canary-birds in parlor windows   10

    spring slattern of seasons you
    have dirty legs and a muddy
    petticoat, drowsy is your
    mouth your eyes are sticky
    with dreams and you have
    a sloppy body
    from being brought to bed of crocuses
    When you sing in your whiskey-voice
                                the grass

    rises on the head of the earth   20
    and all the trees are put on edge

    spring,
    of the jostle of

inveigle- to read on   cavalier- gallant gentleman   slattern - untidy woman,
with deception   ladys escort

thy breasts and the slobber
of your thighs
i am so very
          glad that the soul inside me Hollers
for thou comest and your hands
are the snow
and thy fingers are the rain,   30
and i hear
the screetch of dissonant
flowers, and most of all
i hear your stepping
                    freakish feet
                    feet incorrigible⚹
ragging the world,

                                                   1923

          incorrigible—cannot be corrected,
                    or reformed

the Cambridge ladies who live in furnished souls
are unbeautiful and have comfortable minds
(also, with the church's protestant blessings
daughters, unscented shapeless spirited)
they believe in Christ and Longfellow, both dead,
are invariably interested in so many things—
at the present writing one still finds
delighted fingers knitting for the is it Poles?
perhaps. While permanent faces coyly bandy
scandal of Mrs. N and Professor D   10
. . . . the Cambridge ladies do not care, above
Cambridge if sometimes in its box of
sky lavender and cornerless, the
moon rattles like a fragment of angry candy

                                                   1923

Spring is like a perhaps hand
(which comes carefully
out of Nowhere)arranging
a window, into which people look (while
people stare
arranging and changing placing
carefully there a strange
thing and a known thing here)and

changing everything carefully

spring is like a perhaps
Hand in a window   10
(carefully to

and fro moving New and
Old things, while
people stare carefully
moving a perhaps
fraction of flower here placing
an inch of air there)and

without breaking anything.

1925

Humanity i love you
because you would rather black the boots of
success than enquire whose soul dangles from his
watch-chain which would be embarrassing for both
　　　　　inquire
parties and because you
unflinchingly applaud all
songs containing the words country home and
mother when sung at the old howard[1]

Humanity i love you because
when you're hard up you pawn your   10
intelligence to buy a drink and when
you're flush pride keeps

you from the pawn shop and
because you are continually committing
nuisances but more
especially in your own house

Humanity i love you because you
are perpetually putting the secret of
life in your pants and forgetting
it's there and sitting down   20

on it
and because you are
forever making poems in the lap
of death Humanity

i hate you

1925

come, gaze with me upon this dome
of many coloured glass, and see

---

[1] A well-known burlesque theater in Boston, the Old Howard was for many years a popular
haunt of college students and visiting sailors.

his mother's pride, his father's joy,
unto whom duty whispers low

"thou must!" and who replies "I can!"
— yon clean upstanding well dressed boy
that with his peers full oft hath quaffed
the wine of life and found it sweet —

a tear within his stern blue eye,
upon his firm white lips a smile,   10
one thought alone: to do or die
for God for country and for Yale

above his blond determined head
the sacred flag of truth unfurled,
in the bright heyday of his youth
the upper class American

unsullied stands, before the world:
with manly heart and conscience free,
upon the front steps of her home
by the high minded pure young girl   20

much kissed, by loving relatives
well fed, and fully photographed
the son of man goes forth to war
with trumpets clap and syphilis

                                          1926

my sweet old etcetera
aunt lucy during the recent

war could and what
is more did tell you just
what everybody was fighting

for,
my sister
isabel created hundreds
(and
hundreds)of socks not to   10
mention shirts fleaproof earwarmers

etcetera wristers etcetera, my
mother hoped that

i would die etcetera
bravely of course my father used

to become hoarse talking about how it was
a privilege and if only he
could meanwhile my

self etcetera lay quietly
in the deep mud et   20

cetera
(dreaming,
et
   cetera, of
Your smile
eyes knees and of your Etcetera)

                                        1926

since feeling is first
who pays any attention
to the syntax of things
will never wholly kiss you;

wholly to be a fool
while Spring is in the world
my blood approves,
and kisses are a better fate
than wisdom
lady i swear by all flowers. Don't cry   10
— the best gesture of my brain is less than
your eyelids' flutter which says

we are for each other: then
laugh, leaning back in my arms
for life's not a paragraph

And death i think is no parenthesis

                                        1926

my father moved through dooms of love
through sames of am through haves of give,
singing each morning out of each night
my father moved through depths of height

this motionless forgetful where
turned at his glance to shining here;
that if(so timid air is firm)
under his eyes would stir and squirm

newly as from unburied which
floats the first who,his april touch
drove sleeping selves to swarm their fates
woke dreamers to their ghostly roots

and should some why completely weep
my father's fingers brought her sleep:
vainly no smallest voice might cry
for he could feel the mountains grow.

Lifting the valleys of the sea
my father moved through griefs of joy;
praising a forehead called the moon
singing desire into begin

joy was his song and joy so pure
a heart of star by him could steer
and pure so now and now so yes
the wrists of twilight would rejoice

keen as midsummer's keen beyond
conceiving mind of sun will stand,
so strictly(over utmost him
so hugely)stood my father's dream

his flesh was flesh his blood was blood:
no hungry man but wished him food;
no cripple wouldn't creep one mile
uphill to only see him smile.

Scorning the pomp of must and shall
my father moved through dooms of feel;
his anger was as right as rain
his pity was as green as grain

septembering arms of year extend
less humbly wealth to foe and friend
than he to foolish and to wise
offered immeasurable is

proudly and(by octobering flame
beckoned)as earth will downward climb,
so naked for immortal work
his shoulders marched against the dark

his sorrow was as true as bread:
no liar looked him in the head;
if every friend became his foe
he'd laugh and build a world with snow.

My father moved through theys of we,
singing each new leaf out of each tree   50
(and every child was sure that spring
danced when she heard my father sing)

then let men kill which cannot share,
let blood and flesh be mud and mire,
scheming imagine,passion willed,
freedom a drug that's bought and sold

giving to steal and cruel kind,
a heart to fear,to doubt a mind,
to differ a disease of same,
conform the pinnacle of am   60

though dull were all we taste as bright,
bitter all utterly things sweet,
maggoty minus and dumb death
all we inherit,all bequeath

and nothing quite so least as truth
—i say though hate were why men breathe—
because my father lived his soul
love is the whole and more than all

                                                            1940

plato told

him:he couldn't
believe it(jesus

told him;he
wouldn't believe
it)lao

tsze[1]
certainly told
him,and general
(yes   10

mam)
sherman;[2]
and even
(believe it
or

---

[1] The Chinese philosopher Lao-tse (604–531 B.C.) was the founder of Taoism.
[2] An allusion to the "War is hell" pronouncement attributed to General William T. Sherman of Civil War fame.

not)you
told him:i told
him;we told him
(he didn't believe it,no

sir)it took
a nipponized bit of
the old sixth

avenue
el;in the top of his head:to tell[3]

him

1944

pity this busy monster,manunkind,

not. Progress is a comfortable disease:
your victim(death and life safely beyond)

plays with the bigness of his littleness
— electrons deify one razorblade
into a mountainrange;lenses extend

unwish through curving wherewhen till unwish
returns on its unself.
          A world of made
is not a world of born — pity poor flesh

and trees,poor stars and stones,but never this
fine specimen of hypermagical

ultraomnipotence. We doctors know

a hopeless case if — listen:there's a hell
of a good universe next door;let's go

1944

yes is a pleasant country:
if's wintry
(my lovely)
let's open the year

both is the very weather
(not either)

---

[3] An allusion to the Japanese purchase of American scrap metal for the manufacture of war materials.

my treasure,
when violets appear

love is a deeper season
than reason;   10
my sweet one
(and april's where we're)

1944

Robinson Jeffers   *(1887–1962)*

Robinson Jeffers, the most pessimistic of modern poets, was born in Pittsburgh, Pennsylvania, in 1887. He traveled widely with his family, which moved to California in 1903. He graduated from Occidental College two years later, at the age of eighteen. After taking an M.A. degree in literature at the University of Southern California, he studied first medicine and then forestry before settling down to write poetry in a stone house and tower he built at Carmel on the California coast. His first two undistinguished volumes—*Flagons and Apples* (1912) and *Californians* (1916)—were followed by *Tamar and Other Poems* (1924). Besides the title piece, this collection contained another long poem entitled "The Tower Beyond," Jeffers' version of the story of Orestes and Electra. A deep disillusionment with man led Jeffers to prefer the fatalistic tragic vision of the Greeks to the gospel of progress of later Western culture. Regarding civilization as a "transient sickness," Jeffers was of the opinion that "humanity is needless." Considering nature purer than man, he idealized the hawk as a symbol of naturalistic virtues that man might do well to emulate. Viewing with horror the evils and destructiveness of modern civilization, which seemed to be preparing its own doom, he looked forward with gloomy satisfaction to the age, foreshadowed in "November Surf," when nature would purge itself of the filth of human existence. In his unrelieved antihumanism Jeffers shared in but pushed to a darker extreme the Spenglerian pessimism of the period in which he began to write. His poems are cast in Whitmanesque long lines integrated by the familiar devices of parallelism, alliteration, and assonance—although these are employed for a bardic prophecy Whitman could hardly have anticipated.

Jeffers' other volumes of poetry include *Roan Stallion, Tamar, and Other Poems* (1925), *The Women at Point Sur* (1927), *Cawdor and Other Poems* (1928), *Dear Judas and Other Poems* (1929), *Apology for Bad*

Dreams (1930), *Descent to the Dead* (1931), *Thurso's Landing* (1932), *Give Your Heart to the Hawks* (1933), *Solstice and Other Poems* (1935), *Such Counsels You Gave to Me* (1937), *The Selected Poetry of Robinson Jeffers* (1938), *Two Consolations* (1940), and *Be Angry at the Sun* (1941). Later works include *Medea* (1946), a highly successful modern adaptation of Euripides' drama; *The Double Axe and Other Poems* (1948); *Hungerford and Other Poems* (1954); *The Cretan Woman* (1954); and a posthumous volume, *The Beginning and the End* (1963).

There is no collected edition of Jeffers' poems. Book-length studies include L. C. Powell, *Robinson Jeffers: The Man and His Work*, rev. ed. (Pasadena, Calif., 1940); Radcliffe Squires, *The Loyalties of Robinson Jeffers* (Ann Arbor, Mich., 1956); and M. C. Monjian, *Robinson Jeffers: A Study in Inhumanism* (Pittsburgh, 1958).

The text of "Credo" is that of *Roan Stallion, Tamar, and Other Poems* (New York, 1925); "Original Sin" is from *The Double Axe and Other Poems* (New York, 1948). The other poems given here are from *The Selected Poetry of Robinson Jeffers* (New York, 1938).

Credo[1]   Roan Stallion, Tamar, and Other Poems

My friend from Asia has powers and magic, he plucks a blue leaf
    from the young blue-gum
And gazing upon it, gathering and quieting
The God in his mind, creates an ocean more real than the ocean,
    the salt, the actual
Appalling presence, the power of the waters.
He believes that nothing is real except as we make it. I humbler
    have found in my blood
Bred west of Caucasus a harder mysticism.
Multitude stands in my mind but I think that the ocean in the
    bone vault is only   10
The bone vault's ocean: out there is the ocean's;
The water is the water, the cliff is the rock, come shocks and
    flashes of reality. The mind
Passes, the eye closes, the spirit is a passage;
The beauty of things was born before eyes and sufficient to itself;
    the heart-breaking beauty
Will remain when there is no heart to break for it.

brain ⟶ (margin note)

1924

Shine, Perishing Republic[1]   same as above

While this America settles in the mould of its vulgarity, heavily
    thickening to empire,

[1] The text of this poem is that of *Roan Stallion, Tamar, and Other Poems* (New York, 1925).
[1] Unless otherwise indicated, the text of this and following poems is that of *The Selected Poetry of Robinson Jeffers* (New York, 1938).

And protest, only a bubble in the molten mass, pops and sighs
    out, and the mass hardens,

I sadly smiling remember that the flower fades to make fruit, the
    fruit rots to make earth.
Out of the mother; and through the spring exultances, ripeness
    and decadence; and home to the mother.

You making haste haste on decay: not blameworthy; life is good,
    be it stubbornly long or suddenly
A mortal splendor: meteors are not needed less than mountains: 10
    shine, perishing republic.

But for my children, I would have them keep their distance from
    the thickening center; corruption
Never has been compulsory, when the cities lie at the monster's
    feet there are left the mountains.

And boys, be in nothing so moderate as in love of man, a clever
    servant, insufferable master.
There is the trap that catches noblest spirits, that caught — they
    say — God, when he walked on earth.

1925   20

/Hurt Hawks   Cawdor and other Poems

1

The broken pillar of the wing jags from the clotted shoulder,
The wing trails like a banner in defeat,
No more to use the sky forever but live with famine
And pain a few days: cat nor coyote
Will shorten the week of waiting for death, there is game without
    talons.
He stands under the oak-bush and waits
The lame feet of salvation; at night he remembers freedom
And flies in a dream, the dawns ruin it.
He is strong and pain is worse to the strong, incapacity is
    worse.   10
The curs of the day come and torment him
At distance, no one but death the redeemer will humble that head,
The intrepid readiness, the terrible eyes.
The wild God of the world is sometimes merciful to those
That ask mercy, not often to the arrogant.
You do not know him, you communal people, or you have for-
    gotten him;
Intemperate and savage, the hawk remembers him;
Beautiful and wild, the hawks, and men that are dying, remember
    him.

2

⇨ I'd sooner, except the penalties, kill a man than a hawk; but the
    great redtail   20
Had nothing left but unable misery
From the bone too shattered for mending, the wing that trailed
    under his talons when he moved.
We had fed him six weeks, I gave him freedom,
He wandered over the foreland hill and returned in the evening,
    asking for death,
Not like a beggar, still eyed with the old
Implacable arrogance. I gave him the lead gift in the twilight.
    What fell was relaxed,
Owl-downy, soft feminine feathers; but what   30
Soared: the fierce rush: the night-herons by the flooded river
    cried fear at its rising
Before it was quite unsheathed from reality.

                                                                  1928

November Surf

Some lucky day each November great waves awake and are
    drawn
Like smoking mountains bright from the west
And come and cover the cliff with white violent cleanness: then
    suddenly
The old granite forgets half a year's filth:
The orange-peel, eggshells, papers, pieces of clothing, the clots
Of dung in corners of the rock, and used
Sheaths that make light love safe in the evenings: all the drop-
    pings of the summer
Idlers washed off in a winter ecstasy: 10
I think this cumbered continent envies its cliff then. . . . But all
    seasons
The earth, in her childlike prophetic sleep,
Keeps dreaming of the bath of a storm that prepares up the long
    coast
Of the future to scour more than her sea-lines:
The cities gone down, the people fewer and the hawks more
    numerous,
The rivers mouth to source pure; when the two-footed
Mammal, being someways one of the nobler animals, regains   20
The dignity of room, the value of rareness.

                                                                  1932

The Purse-Seine   Such Counsels You Gave Me

Our sardine fishermen work at night in the dark of the moon;
    daylight or moonlight

They could not tell where to spread the net, unable to see the
  phosphorescence of the shoals of fish.
They work northward from Monterey, coasting Santa Cruz; off
  New Year's Point or off Pigeon Point
The look-out man will see some lakes of milk-color light on the
  seas's night-purple; he points, and the helmsman
Turns the dark prow, the motorboat circles the gleaming shoal
  and drifts out her seine-net. They close the circle   10
And purse the bottom of the net, then with great labor haul it in.

                                                        I cannot tell you
How beautiful the scene is, and a little terrible, then, when the
  crowded fish
Know they are caught, and wildly beat from one wall to the other
  of their closing destiny the phosphorescent
Water to a pool of flame, each beautiful slender body sheeted
  with flame, like a live rocket
A comet's tail wake of clear yellow flame; while outside the
  narrowing   20
Floats and cordage of the net great sea-lions come up to watch,
  sighing in the dark; the vast walls of night
Stand erect to the stars.

                    Lately I was looking from a night mountain-top
On a wide city, the colored splendor, galaxies of light: how could
  I help but recall the seine-net
Gathering the luminous fish? I cannot tell you how beautiful the
  city appeared, and a little terrible.
I thought, We have geared the machines and locked all together
  into interdependence; we have built the great cities; now   30
There is no escape. We have gathered vast populations incapable
  of free survival, insulated
From the strong earth, each person in himself helpless, on all
  dependent. The circle is closed, and the net
Is being hauled in. They hardly feel the cords drawing, yet they
  shine already. The inevitable mass-disasters
Will not come in our time nor in our children's, but we and our
  children
Must watch the net draw narrower, government take all powers — or revolution, and the new government   40
Take more than all, add to kept bodies kept souls — or anarchy,
  the mass-disasters.

                                    These things are Progress;
Do you marvel our verse is troubled or frowning, while it keeps its
  reason? Or it lets go, lets the mood flow
In the manner of the recent young men into mere hysteria, splin-
  tered gleams, crackled laughter. But they are quite wrong.
There is no reason for amazement: surely one always knew that
  cultures decay, and life's end is death.
                                                            1937

Original Sin[1]

The man-brained and man-handed ground-ape, physically
The most repulsive of all hot-blooded animals
Up to that time of the world: they had dug a pitfall
And caught a mammoth, but how could their sticks and stones
Reach the life in that hide? They danced around the pit, shrieking
With ape excitement, flinging sharp flints in vain, and the stench
    of their bodies
Stained the white air of dawn; but presently one of them
Remembered the yellow dancer, wood-eating fire
That guards the cave-mouth: he ran and fetched him, and others   10
Gathered sticks at the wood's edge; they made a blaze
And pushed it into the pit, and they fed it high, around the mired
    sides
Of their huge prey. They watched the long hairy trunk
Waver over the stifle-trumpeting pain,
And they were happy.

                  Meanwhile the intense color and
    nobility of sunrise,
Rose and gold and amber, flowed up the sky. Wet rocks were
    shining, a little wind   20
Stirred the leaves of the forest and the marsh flag-flowers; the soft
    valley between the low hills
Became as beautiful as the sky; while in its midst, hour after
    hour, the happy hunters
Roasted their living meat slowly to death.

                      These are the people.
This is the human dawn. As for me, I would rather
Be a worm in a wild apple than a son of man.
But we are what we are, and we might remember
Not to hate any person, for all are vicious;   30
And be not astonished at any evil, all are deserved;
And not fear death; it is the only way to be cleansed.

                        1948

[1] The text of this poem is that of *The Double Axe* (New York, 1948).

Hart Crane   *1899–1932*

Although he published only two slim volumes during his short and troubled life, Hart Crane holds a place in the first rank of American poets of this century. Harold Hart Crane was born in northern Ohio in 1899 and grew up in Cleveland, where his father was a candy manufacturer. Conflicts arising from his relations with his father and from the breakup of his parents' marriage contributed to the psychological insecurity and sexual inversion that were to disorder his life. His schooling was at best irregular, but he traveled widely in youth, developing a special affection for the Isle of Pines, Cuba, and for Paris and New York City. Determined to become a poet, he settled in New York in 1923, supporting himself by writing advertising copy. He read other poets, especially T. S. Eliot and the metaphysical and symbolist poets whose influence Eliot had helped to establish through his criticism. He also read and admired Walt Whitman.

White Buildings (1926), Crane' first book of verse, displays a remarkable talent and potential. Although the poet's shifting images and strained brilliant metaphors reveal the symbolist and metaphysical influences to which he had responded, the poems have a distinction of phrasing and a lyric intensity.

Crane's most ambitious work is *The Bridge* (1930), which represents his effort (inspired largely by disapproval of the pessimism of *The Waste Land*) to write an affirmative American epic. Crane hoped that the work might express a faith in American culture based on a vision, inherited from Whitman, of the mystical unity of material and spiritual reality. The central symbol of the poem is Brooklyn Bridge, introduced as "the harp and altar, of the fury fused," the product of the combined creative genius of the engineer and the artist, which, like Whitman's Brooklyn Ferry, represents the synthesis of past and present, science and faith, time and eternity, man and god. Within the larger work, the bridge is linked with the aspiration of the Old World through the voyage of Columbus and with the body of the

American continent through the merging images of the subway train, the railroad, and the river, which lead to an identification, through the dance, with the fertility myths of the primitive past and beyond them to the final apocalyptic vision in which are fused the mystical dreams of West and East, of Atlantis and Cathay. Crane did not succeed in his effort to impose a transcendentalist unity upon his materials (it is doubtful that a truly modern poet could). He had even lost confidence in his conception before the poem was finished. But *The Bridge* remains an impressive achievement, including, as it does, individual poems that in imaginative and lyric power can stand beside any in the language.   -

Crane's next project was to have been an epic poem of Mexico, based on the life of Cortez. But he was not able to get the work under way. On April 24, 1932, while sailing from Vera Cruz bound for New York on the *S. S. Orizaba*, he jumped from the deck of the ship into the Caribbean Sea.

The Collected Poems of Hart Crane, ed. Waldo Frank (New York, 1933), includes *White Buildings* and *The Bridge*, together with previously unpublished poems. The standard edition of Crane's work is *The Complete Poems and Selected Letters and Prose of Hart Crane*, ed. Brom Weber (New York, 1966). Correspondence is collected in *The Letters of Hart Crane, 1916–1932*, ed. Brom Weber (New York, 1952; Berkeley and Los Angeles, 1965).

A helpful brief introduction is M. K. Spears, *Hart Crane* (Minneapolis, 1965). Critical biographies include Philip Horton, *Hart Crane: The Life of an American Poet* (New York, 1937; 1957), and Brom Weber, *Hart Crane: A Biographical and Critical Study* (New York, 1948). Among recent critiques are L. S. Dembo, *Hart Crane's Sanskrit Charge: A Study of* The Bridge (Ithaca, N. Y., 1960); R. W. B. Lewis, *The Poetry of Hart Crane: A Critical Study* (Princeton, 1967); and H. A. Leibowitz, *Hart Crane: An Introduction to the Poetry* (New York, 1968).

The text of the poems given here is that of *The Complete Poems and Selected Letters and Prose of Hart Crane*, ed. Brom Weber (New York, 1966).

Black Tambourine

The interests of a black man in a cellar
Mark tardy judgment on the world's closed door.
Gnats toss in the shadow of a bottle,
And a roach spans a crevice in the floor.

Æsop, driven to pondering, found
Heaven with the tortoise and the hare;
Fox brush and sow ear top his grave
And mingling incantations on the air.

The black man, forlorn in the cellar,
Wanders in some mid-kingdom, dark, that lies,

10

Between his tambourine, stuck on the wall,
And, in Africa, a carcass quick with flies.

1926

Chaplinesque

We make our meek adjustments,
Contented with such random consolations
As the wind deposits
In slithered and too ample pockets.

For we can still love the world, who find
A famished kitten on the step, and know
Recesses for it from the fury of the street,
Or warm torn elbow coverts.

We will sidestep, and to the final smirk
Dally the doom of that inevitable thumb   10
That slowly chafes its puckered index toward us,
Facing the dull squint with what innocence
And what surprise!

And yet these fine collapses are not lies
More than the pirouettes of any pliant cane;   15
Our obsequies are, in a way, no enterprise.
We can evade you, and all else but the heart:
What blame to us if the heart live on.

The game enforces smirks; but we have seen
The moon in lonely alleys make   20
A grail of laughter of an empty ash can,
And through all sound of gaiety and quest
Have heard a kitten in the wilderness.

1926

Voyages II

And yet this great wink of eternity,
Of rimless floods, unfettered leewardings,
Samite sheeted and processioned where
Her undinal vast belly moonward bends,
Laughing the wrapt inflections of our love;

Take this Sea, whose diapason knells
On scrolls of silver snowy sentences,
The sceptred terror of whose sessions rends
As her demeanors motion well or ill,
All but the pieties of lovers' hands.   10

And onward, as bells off San Salvador
Salute the crocus lustres of the stars,
In these poinsettia meadows of her tides, —
Adagios of islands, O my Prodigal,
Complete the dark confessions her veins spell.

Mark how her turning shoulders wind the hours,
And hasten while her penniless rich palms
Pass superscription of bent foam and wave, —
Hasten, while they are true, — sleep, death, desire,
Close round one instant in one floating flower.   20

Bind us in time, O Seasons clear, and awe.
O minstrel galleons of Carib fire,
Bequeath us to no earthly shore until
Is answered in the vortex of our grave
The seal's wide spindrift gaze toward paradise.

                                                        1926

From *The Bridge*

To Brooklyn Bridge

How many dawns, chill from his rippling rest
The seagull's wings shall dip and pivot him,
Shedding white rings of tumult, building high
Over the chained bay waters Liberty —

Then, with inviolate curve, forsake our eyes
As apparitional as sails that cross
Some page of figures to be filed away;
— Till elevators drop us from our day . . .

I think of cinemas, panoramic sleights
With multitudes bent toward some flashing scene   10
Never disclosed, but hastened to again,
Foretold to other eyes on the same screen;

And Thee, across the harbor, silver-paced
As though the sun took step of thee, yet left
Some motion ever unspent in thy stride, —
Implicitly thy freedom staying thee!

Out of some subway scuttle, cell or loft
A bedlamite speeds to thy parapets,
Tilting there momently, shrill shirt ballooning,
A jest falls from the speechless caravan.   20

Down Wall, from girder into street noon leaks,
A rip-tooth of the sky's acetylene;

All afternoon the cloud-flown derricks turn . . .
Thy cables breathe the North Atlantic still.

And obscure as that heaven of the Jews,
Thy guerdon . . . Accolade thou dost bestow
Of anonymity time cannot raise:
Vibrant reprieve and pardon thou dost show.

O harp and altar, of the fury fused,
(How could mere toil align thy choiring strings!)   30
Terrific threshold of the prophet's pledge,
Prayer of pariah, and the lover's cry,—

Again the traffic lights that skim thy swift
Unfractioned idiom, immaculate sigh of stars,
Beading thy path—condense eternity:
And we have seen night lifted in thine arms.

Under thy shadow by the piers I waited;
Only in darkness is thy shadow clear.
The City's fiery parcels all undone,
Already snow submerges an iron year . . .   40

O Sleepless as the river under thee,
Vaulting the sea, the prairies' dreaming sod,
Unto us lowliest sometime sweep, descend
And of the curveship lend a myth to God.

1930

The Dance

The swift red flesh, a winter king—   [*Then you shall*
Who squired the glacier woman down the sky?   *see her truly—*
She ran the neighing canyons all the spring;   *your blood*
She spouted arms; she rose with maize—to die.   *remembering*
                                                             its first
                                                             invasion of her
And in the autumn drouth, whose burnished hands   *secrecy, its*
With mineral wariness found out the stone   *first encounters*
Where prayers, forgotten, streamed the mesa sands?   *with her kin*
He holds the twilight's dim, perpetual throne.   *her chieftain*
                                                             lover . . . his
                                                             shade that
                                                             haunts the
Mythical brows we saw retiring—loth,   *lakes and hills*]
Disturbed and destined, into denser green.   10
Greeting they sped us, on the arrow's oath:
Now lie incorrigibly what years between. . .

There was a bed of leaves, and broken play;
There was a veil upon you, Pocahontas, bride—

O Princess whose brown lap was virgin May;
And bridal flanks and eyes hid tawny pride.

I left the village for dogwood. By the canoe
Tugging below the mill-race, I could see
Your hair's keen crescent running, and the blue
First moth of evening take wing stealthily.   20

What laughing chains the water wove and threw!
I learned to catch the trout's moon whisper; I
Drifted how many hours I never knew,
But, watching, saw that fleet young crescent die,—

And one star, swinging, take its place, alone,
Cupped in the larches of the mountain pass—
Until, immortally, it bled into the dawn.
I left my sleek boat nibbling margin grass. . .

I took the portage climb, then chose
A further valley-shed; I could not stop.   30
Feet nozzled wat'ry webs of upper flows;
One white veil gusted from the very top.

O Appalachian Spring! I gained the ledge;
Steep, inaccessible smile that eastward bends
And northward reaches in that violet wedge
Of Adirondacks!—wisped of azure wands,

Over how many bluffs, tarns, streams I sped!
—And knew myself within some boding shade:—
Grey tepees tufting the blue knolls ahead,
Smoke swirling through the yellow chestnut glade. . .   40

A distant cloud, a thunder-bud—it grew,
That blanket of the skies: the padded foot
Within,—I heard it; 'til its rhythm drew,
—Siphoned the black pool from the heart's hot root!

A cyclone threshes in the turbine crest,
Swooping in eagle feathers down your back;
Know, Maquokeeta,[1] greeting; know death's best;
—Fall, Sachem, strictly as the tamarack!

A birch kneels. All her whistling fingers fly.
The oak grove circles in a crash of leaves;   50

---

[1] In this context, the Indian name suggests a Dionysian fertility god who dies by fire but is reborn.

The long moan of a dance is in the sky.
Dance, Maquokeeta: Pocahontas grieves. . .

And every tendon scurries toward the twangs
Of lightning deltaed down your saber hair.
Now snaps the flint in every tooth; red fangs
And splay tongues thinly busy the blue air. . .

Dance, Maquokeeta! snake that lives before,
That casts his pelt, and lives beyond! Sprout, horn!
Spark, tooth! Medicine-man, relent, restore —
Lie to us, — dance us back the tribal morn!   60

Spears and assemblies: black drums thrusting on —
O yelling battlements, — I, too, was liege
To rainbows currying each pulsant bone:
Surpassed the circumstance, danced out the siege!

And buzzard-circleted, screamed from the stake;
I could not pick the arrows from my side.
Wrapped in that fire, I saw more escorts wake —
Flickering, sprint up the hill groins like a tide.

I heard the hush of lava wrestling your arms,
And stag teeth foam about the raven throat;   70
Flame cataracts of heaven in seething swarms
Fed down your anklets to the sunset's moat.

O, like the lizard in the furious noon,
That drops his legs and colors in the sun,
— And laughs, pure serpent, Time itself, and moon
Of his own fate, I saw thy change begun!

And saw thee dive to kiss that destiny
Like one white meteor, sacrosanct and blent
At last with all that's consummate and free
There, where the first and last gods keep thy tent.   80
       .   .   .   .   .   .

Thewed of the levin, thunder-shod and lean,
Lo, through what infinite seasons dost thou gaze —
Across what bivouacs of thine angered slain,
And see'st thy bride immortal in the maize!

Totem and fire-gall, slumbering pyramid —
Though other calendars now stack the sky,
Thy freedom is her largesse, Prince, and hid
On paths thou knewest best to claim her by.

High unto Labrador the sun strikes free
Her speechless dream of snow, and stirred again,   90
She is the torrent and the singing tree;
And she is virgin to the last of men. . .

West, west and south! winds over Cumberland
And winds across the Ilano grass resume
Her hair's warm sibilance. Her breasts are fanned
O stream by slope and vineyard — into bloom!

And when the caribou slant down for salt
Do arrows thirst and leap? Do antlers shine
Alert, star-triggered in the listening vault
Of dusk? — And are her perfect brows to thine?   100

We danced, O Brave, we danced beyond their farms,
In cobalt desert closures made our vows. . .
Now is the strong prayer folded in thine arms,
The serpent with the eagle[2] in the boughs.

1930

Southern Cross

I wanted you, nameless Woman of the South,
No wraith, but utterly — as still more alone
The Southern Cross takes night
And lifts her girdles from her, one by one —
High, cool,
        wide from the slowly smoldering fire
Of lower heavens, —
          vaporous scars!
Eve! Magdalene!
        or Mary, you?   10

Whatever call — falls vainly on the wave.
O simian Venus, homeless Eve,
Unwedded, stumbling gardenless to grieve
Windswept guitars on lonely decks forever;
Finally to answer all within one grave!

And this long wake of phosphor,
               iridescent
Furrow of all our travel — trailed derision!
Eyes crumble at its kiss. Its long-drawn spell

[2] The serpent and the eagle are traditional symbols in Southwestern and Mexican Indian culture. Lawrence S. Dembo has suggested that in this image "the eagle of space and the serpent of time" are fused into a single entity. (*Hart Crane's Sanskrit Charge* [Ithaca, N.Y., 1960], p. 76).

Incites a yell. Slid on that backward vision   20
The mind is churned to spittle, whispering hell.

I wanted you . . . The embers of the Cross
Climbed by aslant and huddling aromatically.
It is blood to remember; it is fire
To stammer back . . . It is
God—your namelessness. And the wash—

All night the water combed you with black
Insolence. You crept out simmering, accomplished.
Water rattled that stinging coil, your
Rehearsed hair—docile, alas, from many arms.   30
Yes, Eve—wraith of my unloved seed!

The Cross, a phantom, buckled—dropped below the dawn.
Light drowned the lithic trillions of your spawn.

1930

The Tunnel

*To Find the Western path
Right thro' the Gates of Wrath*
BLAKE

Performance, assortments, résumés—
Up Times Square to Columbus Circle lights
Channel the congresses, nightly sessions,
Refractions of the thousand theatres, faces—
Mysterious kitchens. . . . You shall search them all.
Some day by heart you'll learn each famous sight
And watch the curtain lift in hell's despite;
You'll find the garden in the third act dead,
Finger your knees—and wish yourself in bed
With tabloid crime-sheets perched in easy sight.   10

Then let you reach your hat
and go.
As usual, let you—also
walking down—exclaim
to twelve upward leaving
a subscription praise
for what time slays.

Or can't you quite make up your mind to ride;
A walk is better underneath the L a brisk
Ten blocks or so before? But you find yourself   20
Preparing penguin flexions of the arms,—

As usual you will meet the scuttle yawn:
The subway yawns the quickest promise home.

Be minimum, then, to swim the hiving swarms
Out of the Square, the Circle burning bright —
Avoid the glass doors gyring at your right,
Where boxed alone a second, eyes take fright
— Quite unprepared rush naked back to light:
And down beside the turnstile press the coin
Into the slot. The gongs already rattle.   30

                And so
                of cities you bespeak
                subways, rivered under streets
                and rivers. . . . In the car
                the overtone of motion
                underground, the monotone
                of motion is the sound
                of other faces, also underground —

"Let's have a pencil Jimmy — living now
at Floral Park   40
Flatbush — on the Fourth of July —
like a pigeon's muddy dream — potatoes
to dig in the field — travlin the town — too —
night after night — the Culver line — the
girls all shaping up — it used to be — "

Our tongues recant like beaten weather vanes.
This answer lives like verdigris, like hair
Beyond extinction, surcease of the bone;
And repetition freezes — "What

"what do you want? getting weak on the links?   50
fandaddle daddy don't ask for change — IS THIS
FOURTEENTH? it's half past six she said — if
you don't like my gate why did you
swing on it, why *didja*
swing on it
anyhow — "

                And somehow anyhow swing —

The phonographs of hades in the brain
Are tunnels that re-wind themselves, and love
A burnt match skating in a urinal —   60
Somewhere above Fourteenth TAKE THE EXPRESS
To brush some new presentiment of pain —

"But I want service in this office SERVICE
I said—after
the show she cried a little afterwards but—"

Whose head is swinging from the swollen strap?
Whose body smokes along the bitten rails,
Bursts from a smoldering bundle far behind
In back forks of the chasms of the brain,—
Puffs from a riven stump far out behind
In interborough fissures of the mind . . . ?   70

And why do I often meet your visage here,
Your eyes like agate lanterns—on and on
Below the toothpaste and the dandruff ads?
—And did their riding eyes right through your side,
And did their eyes like unwashed platters ride?
And Death, aloft,—gigantically down
Probing through you—toward me, O evermore!
And when they dragged your retching flesh,
Your trembling hands that night through Baltimore—   80
That last night on the ballot rounds, did you
Shaking, did you deny the ticket, Poe?[1]

For Gravesend Manor change at Chambers Street.
The platform hurries along to a dead stop.

The intent escalator lifts a serenade
Stilly
Of shoes, umbrellas, each eye attending its shoe, then
Bolting outright somewhere above where streets
Burst suddenly in rain. . . . The gongs recur:
Elbows and levers, guard and hissing door.   90
Thunder is galvothermic here below. . . . The car
Wheels off. The train rounds, bending to a scream,
Taking the final level for the dive
Under the river—
And somewhat emptier than before,
Demented, for a hitching second, humps; then
Lets go. . . . Toward corners of the floor
Newspapers wing, revolve and wing.
Blank windows gargle signals through the roar.

And does the Dæmon take you home, also,   100
Wop washerwoman, with the bandaged hair?
After the corridors are swept, the cuspidors—
The gaunt sky-barracks cleanly now, and bare,
O Genoese, do you bring mother eyes and hands
Back home to children and to golden hair?

[1] An allusion to the death of Edgar Allan Poe as the presumed victim of an election gang in Baltimore.

Dæmon, demurring and eventful yawn!
Whose hideous laughter is a bellows mirth
— Or the muffled slaughter of a day in birth —
O cruelly to inoculate the brinking dawn   110
With antennæ toward worlds that glow and sink; —
To spoon us out more liquid than the dim
Locution of the eldest star, and pack
The conscience navelled in the plunging wind,
Umbilical to call — and straightway die!

O caught like pennies beneath soot and steam,
Kiss of our agony thou gatherest;
Condensed, thou takest all — shrill ganglia
Impassioned with some song we fail to keep.
And yet, like Lazarus, to feel the slope,   120
The sod and billow breaking, — lifting ground,
— A sound of waters bending astride the sky
Unceasing with some Word that will not die . . . !
        .   .   .   .   .   .

A tugboat, wheezing wreaths of steam,
Lunged past, with one galvanic blare stove up the River.
I counted the echoes assembling, one after one,
Searching, thumbing the midnight on the piers.
Lights, coasting, left the oily tympanum of waters;
The blackness somewhere gouged glass on a sky.   130
And this thy harbor, O my City, I have driven under,
Tossed from the coil of ticking towers. . . . Tomorrow,
And to be. . . . Here by the River that is East —
Here at the waters' edge the hands drop memory;
Shadowless in that abyss they unaccounting lie.
How far away the star has pooled the sea —
Or shall the hands be drawn away, to die?

Kiss of our agony Thou gatherest,
                O Hand of Fire
                        gatherest —   140
                                          1930

O Carib Isle!

The tarantula rattling at the lily's foot
Across the feet of the dead, laid in white sand
Near the coral beach — nor zigzag fiddler crabs
Side-stilting from the path (that shift, subvert
And anagrammatize your name) — No, nothing here
Below the palsy that one eucalyptus lifts
In wrinkled shadows — mourns.

                                        And yet suppose
I count these nacreous frames of tropic death,
Brutal necklaces of shells around each grave   10
Squared off so carefully. Then

To the white sand I may speak a name, fertile
Albeit in a stranger tongue. Tree names, flower names
Deliberate, gainsay death's brittle crypt. Meanwhile
The wind that knots itself in one great death—
Coils and withdraws. So syllables want breath.

But where is the Captain of the doubloon isle
Without a turnstile? Who but catchword crabs
Patrols the dry groins of the underbrush?
What man, or What   20
Is Commissioner of the mildew throughout the ambushed senses?
His Carib mathematics web the eyes' baked lenses!

Under the poinciana, of a noon or afternoon
Let fiery blossoms clot the light, render my ghost
Sieved upward, white and black along the air
Until it meets the blue's comedian host.

Let not the pilgrim see himself again
For slow evisceration bound like those huge terrapin
Each daybreak on the wharf, their brine-caked eyes;
—Spiked, overturned; such thunder in their strain!   30
And clenched beaks coughing for the surge again!

Slagged of the hurricane—I, cast within its flow,
Congeal by afternoons here, satin and vacant.
You have given me the shell, Satan,—carbonic amulet
Sere of the sun exploded in the sea.

                                                    1933

The Broken Tower

The bell-rope that gathers God at dawn
Dispatches me as though I dropped down the knell
Of a spent day—to wander the cathedral lawn
From pit to crucifix, feet chill on steps from hell.

Have you not heard, have you not seen that corps
Of shadows in the tower, whose shoulders sway
Antiphonal carillons launched before
The stars are caught and hived in the sun's ray?

The bells, I say, the bells break down their tower;
And swing I know not where. Their tongues engrave   10

Membrane through marrow, my long-scattered score
Of broken intervals. . . . And I, their sexton slave!

Oval encyclicals in canyons heaping
The impasse high with choir. Banked voices slain!
Pagodas, campaniles with reveilles outleaping—
O terraced echoes prostrate on the plain! . . .

And so it was I entered the broken world
To trace the visionary company of love, its voice
An instant in the wind (I know not whither hurled)
But not for long to hold each desperate choice.   20

My word I poured. But was it cognate, scored
Of that tribunal monarch of the air
Whose thigh embronzes earth, strikes crystal Word
In wounds pledged once to hope—cleft to despair?

The steep encroachments of my blood left me
No answer (could blood hold such a lofty tower
As flings the question true?)—or is it she
Whose sweet mortality stirs latent power?—

And through whose pulse I hear, counting the strokes
My veins recall and add, revived and sure   30
The angelus of wars my chest evokes:
What I hold healed, original now, and pure . . .

And builds, within, a tower that is not stone
(Not stone can jacket heaven)—but slip
Of pebbles—visible wings of silence sown
In azure circles, widening as they dip

The matrix of the heart, lift down the eye
That shrines the quiet lake and swells a tower . . .
The commodious, tall decorum of that sky
Unseals her earth, and lifts love in its shower.   40

1933

Carl Sandburg   *1878–1967*

Charles August Sandburg, the son of Swedish immigrant parents, was born in Galesburg, Illinois, in 1878. Leaving school at thirteen, he became a migratory worker. At the age of twenty, he enlisted in the Army and served briefly in Puerto Rico during the Spanish-American War. Returning, he attended Lombard College in Galesburg but left before graduating to go into newspaper work in Chicago. He went to Wisconsin as an organizer for the Social Democratic Party. In Milwaukee, he served as secretary to the city's first Socialist mayor, Emil Seidel, worked on the editorial staff of Victor Berger's Milwaukee *Leader,* and (most permanently) married Lillian Steichen, the sister of the photographer Edward Steichen. In 1913 he moved to Chicago, where after a few years he came to hold an editorial position (1918–33) on the Chicago *Daily News.* He began publishing poems he had been writing in Harriet Monroe's *Poetry* and other magazines. His first book of verse, *Chicago Poems* (1916), combined the techniques of contemporary Imagism (in a poem like "Fog") with a Whitmanesque faith in the common man. There is also satire, from a proletarian viewpoint, of enemies of the people like the revivalist characterized in "To a Contemporary Bunkshooter." Subsequent volumes include *Cornhuskers* (1918), *Smoke and Steel* (1920), *Slabs of the Sunburnt West* (1922), and *Good Morning, America* (1928). *The People, Yes* (1936), written in the dark years of the Depression, is a collection of poems and folk sayings which express a faith in the persistence of the common people like that which was to animate John Steinbeck's *Grapes of Wrath* (1939). Sandburg also collected ballads and folksongs in *The American Songbag* (1927). *His Complete Poems* (1950) was followed by a shorter late collection, *Honey and Salt* (1963).

Sandburg's most ambitious project in prose was a monumental biography of Abraham Lincoln: *The Prairie Years,* 2 vols. (1926) was followed by *The War Years,* 4 vols. (1939). Among other prose writings are

Steichen the Photographer (1929); *Mary Lincoln, Wife and Widow,* with P. M. Angle (1932); and several books for children: *Rootabaga Stories* (1922), *Rootabaga Pigeons* (1923), and *Potato Face* (1930). *Remembrance Rock* (1948) is a long novel about an American family from the seventeenth century to World War II. *Always the Young Strangers* (1953) is an autobiography of the author's youth.

The standard edition of the poetry is *Complete Poems of Carl Sandburg* (New York, 1950). Books about Sandburg and his work include K. W. Detzer, *Carl Sandburg: A Study in Personality and Background* (New York, 1941); Harry Golden, *Carl Sandburg* (New York, 1961); and Richard Crowder, *Carl Sandburg* (New York, 1964).

The text of the poems given here is that of *Complete Poems of Carl Sandburg* (New York, 1950).

Chicago

Hog Butcher for the World,
Tool Maker, Stacker of Wheat,
Player with Railroads and the Nation's Freight Handler;
Stormy, husky, brawling,
City of the Big Shoulders:

They tell me you are wicked and I believe them, for I have seen
    your painted women under the gas lamps luring the farm
    boys.
And they tell me you are crooked and I answer: Yes, it is true I
    have seen the gunman kill and go free to kill again.
And they tell me you are brutal and my reply is: On the faces of
    women and children I have seen the marks of wanton hunger.
And having answered so I turn once more to those who sneer at
    this my city, and I give them back the sneer and say to
    them:
Come and show me another city with lifted head singing so proud
    to be alive and coarse and strong and cunning.
Flinging magnetic curses amid the toil of piling job on job, here is
    a tall bold slugger set vivid against the little soft cities;
Fierce as a dog with tongue lapping for action, cunning as a
    savage pitted against the wilderness,
          Bareheaded,
          Shoveling,
          Wrecking,
          Planning,
          Building, breaking, rebuilding,
Under the smoke, dust all over his mouth, laughing with white
    teeth,
Under the terrible burden of destiny laughing as a young man
    laughs,

Laughing even as an ignorant fighter laughs who has never lost a
battle,
Bragging and laughing that under his wrist is the pulse, and under
his ribs the heart of the people,
Laughing!
Laughing the stormy, husky, brawling laughter of Youth, half-
naked, sweating, proud to be Hog Butcher, Tool Maker,
Stacker of Wheat, Player with Railroads and Freight Handler to the Nation.

1916

Limited

I am riding on a limited express, one of the crack trains of the
nation.
Hurtling across the prairie into blue haze and dark air go fifteen
all-steel coaches holding a thousand people.
(All the coaches shall be scrap and rust and all the men and
women laughing in the diners and sleepers shall pass to
ashes.)
I ask a man in the smoker where he is going and he answers:
"Omaha."

1916

To a Contemporary Bunkshooter [1]

You come along . . . tearing your shirt . . . yelling about Jesus.
Where do you get that stuff?
What do you know about Jesus?
Jesus had a way of talking soft and outside of a few bankers and
higherups among the con men of Jerusalem everybody liked
to have this Jesus around because he never made any fake
passes and everything he said went and he helped the sick
and gave the people hope.

You come along squirting words at us, shaking your fist and
calling us all dam fools so fierce the froth slobbers over
your lips . . . always blabbing we're all going to hell
straight off and you know all about it.

I've read Jesus' words. I know what he said. You don't throw any
scare into me. I've got your number. I know how much you

[1] The original version of this poem was first published in *The Masses* (September, 1915)
under the title "To Billy Sunday"—a direct reference to the well-known evangelist, William
Ashley Sunday (1862–1935).

know about Jesus.

He never came near clean people or dirty people but they felt
cleaner because he came along. It was your crowd of bankers and business men and lawyers hired the sluggers and
murderers who put Jesus out of the running.

I say the same bunch backing you nailed the nails into the hands
of this Jesus of Nazareth. He had lined up against him the
same crooks and strong-arm men now lined up with you
paying your way.

This Jesus was good to look at, smelled good, listened good. He
threw out something fresh and beautiful from the skin of his
body and the touch of his hands wherever he passed along.

You slimy bunkshooter, you put a smut on every human blossom
in reach of your rotten breath belching about hell-fire and
hiccupping about this Man who lived a clean life in Galilee.

When are you going to quit making the carpenters build emergency hospitals for women and girls driven crazy with
wrecked nerves from your gibberish about Jesus — I put it
to you again: Where do you get that stuff; what do you
know about Jesus?

Go ahead and bust all the chairs you want to. Smash a whole
wagon load of furniture at every performance. Turn sixty
somersaults and stand on your nutty head. If it wasn't for
the way you scare the women and kids I'd feel sorry for
you and pass the hat.

I like to watch a good four-flusher work, but not when he starts
people puking and calling for the doctors.

I like a man that's got nerve and can pull off a great original
performance, but you — you're only a bug-house peddler of
second-hand gospel — you're only shoving out a phoney
imitation of the goods this Jesus wanted free as air and
sunlight.

You tell people living in shanties Jesus is going to fix it up all
right with them by giving them mansions in the skies after
they're dead and the worms have eaten 'em.

You tell $6 a week department store girls all they need is Jesus;
you take a steel trust wop, dead without having lived, gray
and shrunken at forty years of age, and you tell him to look
at Jesus on the cross and he'll be all right.

You tell poor people they don't need any more money on payday
and even if it's fierce to be out of a job, Jesus'll fix that up
all right, all right — all they gotta do is take Jesus the way
you say.

I'm telling you Jesus wouldn't stand for the stuff you're handing
  out. Jesus played it different. The bankers and lawyers of
  Jerusalem got their sluggers and murderers to go after Jesus
  just because Jesus wouldn't play their game. He didn't sit in
  with the big thieves.

I don't want a lot of gab from a bunkshooter in my religion.
I won't take my religion from any man who never works except
  with his mouth and never cherishes any memory except the
  face of the woman on the American silver dollar.

I ask you to come through and show me where you're pouring out
  the blood of your life.
I've been to this suburb of Jerusalem they call Golgotha, where
  they nailed Him, and I know if the story is straight it was
  real blood ran from His hands and the nail-holes, and it was
  real blood spurted in red drops where the spear of the Roman soldier rammed in between the ribs of this Jesus of
  Nazareth.

1916

Fog

The fog comes
on little cat feet.

It sits looking
over harbor and city
on silent haunches
and then moves on.

1916

I Am the People, the Mob

I am the people—the mob—the crowd—the mass.
Do you know that all the great work of the world is done through
  me?
I am the workingman, the inventor, the maker of the world's food
  and clothes.
I am the audience that witnesses history. The Napoleons come
  from me and the Lincolns. They die. And then I send forth
  more Napoleons and Lincolns.
I am the seed ground. I am a prairie that will stand for much
  plowing. Terrible storms pass over me. I forget. The best of   10
  me is sucked out and wasted. I forget. Everything but
  Death comes to me and makes me work and give up what I
  have. And I forget.
Sometimes I growl, shake myself and spatter a few red drops for

history to remember. Then — I forget.

When I, the People, learn to remember, when I, the People, use
the lessons of yesterday and no longer forget who robbed
me last year, who played me for a fool — then there will be
no speaker in all the world say the name: "The People,"
with any fleck of a sneer in his voice or any far-off smile of   20
derision.

The mob — the crowd — the mass — will arrive then.

1916

Cool Tombs

When Abraham Lincoln was shoveled into the tombs, he forgot
the copperheads[1] and the assassin . . . in the dust, in the
cool tombs.

And Ulysses Grant lost all thought of con men and Wall Street,
cash and collateral turned ashes . . . in the dust, in the cool
tombs.

Pocahontas' body, lovely as a poplar, sweet as a red haw in
November or a pawpaw in May, did she wonder? does she
remember? . . . in the dust, in the cool tombs?

Take any streetful of people buying clothes and groceries, cheer-
ing a hero or throwing confetti and blowing tin horns . . .
tell me if the lovers are losers . . . tell me if any get more
than the lovers . . . in the dust . . . in the cool tombs.

1918

Old Timers

I am an ancient reluctant conscript.

On the soup wagons of Xerxes[1] I was a cleaner of pans.

On the march of Miltiades'[2] phalanx I had a haft and head;
I had a bristling gleaming spear-handle.

Red-headed Cæsar[3] picked me for a teamster.
He said, "Go to work, you Tuscan bastard,
Rome calls for a man who can drive horses."

The units of conquest led by Charles the Twelfth,[4]

---

[1] Copperheads were Northerners who sympathized with the South and sometimes obstructed
the war effort.
[1] Xerxes (519?–465 B.C.) was king of Persia (486–465 B.C.).
[2] Miltiades, the Athenian general, defeated the Persians at Marathon in 490 B.C.
[3] Julius Caesar (100–44 B.C.).
[4] Charles XII of Sweden (1682–1718), a warlike king, known as the "Madman of the
North."

The whirling whimsical Napoleonic columns:
They saw me one of the horseshoers.   10

I trimmed the feet of a white horse Bonaparte[5] swept the night
  stars with.

Lincoln said, "Get into the game; your nation takes you."
And I drove a wagon and team and I had my arm shot off
At Spotsylvania Court House.

I am an ancient reluctant conscript.

                                                        1918

From *The People, Yes*

        The people will live on.
The learning and blundering people will live on.
        They will be tricked and sold and again sold
And go back to the nourishing earth for rootholds,
        The people so peculiar in renewal and comeback,
        You can't laugh off their capacity to take it.
The mammoth rests between his cyclonic dramas.

The people so often sleepy, weary, enigmatic,
is a vast huddle with many units saying:
        "I earn my living.   10
        I make enough to get by
        and it takes all my time.
        If I had more time
        I could do more for myself
        and maybe for others.
        I could read and study
        and talk things over
        and find out about things.
        It takes time.
        I wish I had the time."   20

The people is a tragic and comic two-face:
hero and hoodlum: phantom and gorilla twisting to moan with a gargoyle mouth: "They
buy me and sell me . . . it's a game . . .
sometime I'll break loose . . ."

        Once having marched
Over the margins of animal necessity,
Over the grim line of sheer subsistence
        Then man came
To the deeper rituals of his bones,   30

5 Napoleon Bonaparte (1769–1821), emperor of France (1804–1815).

To the lights lighter than any bones,
To the time for thinking things over,
To the dance, the song, the story,
Or the hours given over to dreaming,
    Once having so marched.

Between the finite limitations of the five senses
and the endless yearnings of man for the beyond
the people hold to the humdrum bidding of work and food
while reaching out when it comes their way
for lights beyond the prisms of the five senses,   40
for keepsakes lasting beyond any hunger or death.
    This reaching is alive.
The panderers and liars have violated and smutted it.
    Yet this reaching is alive yet
    for lights and keepsakes.

        The people know the salt of the sea
        and the strength of the winds
        lashing the corners of the earth.
        The people take the earth
        as a tomb of rest and a cradle of hope.   50
        Who else speaks for the Family of Man?
        They are in tune and step
        with constellations of universal law.

        The people is a polychrome,
        a spectrum and a prism
        held in a moving monolith,
        a console organ of changing themes,
        a clavilux of color poems
        wherein the sea offers fog
        and the fog moves off in rain   60
        and the labrador sunset shortens
        to a nocturne of clear stars
        serene over the shot spray
        of northern lights.

        The steel mill sky is alive.
        The fire breaks white and zigzag
        shot on a gun-metal gloaming.
        Man is a long time coming.
        Man will yet win.
        Brother may yet line up with brother: 70

  This old anvil laughs at many broken hammers.
      There are men who can't be bought.

The fireborn are at home in fire.
The stars make no noise.
You can't hinder the wind from blowing.
Time is a great teacher.
Who can live without hope?

In the darkness with a great bundle of grief
    the people march.
In the night, and overhead a shovel of stars for   80
    keeps, the people march:
                    "Where to? what next?"
                                        1936

Edgar Lee Masters   *1868 – 1950*

A prolific and long-lived author, Edgar Lee Masters is known mostly for *Spoon River Anthology*, his unique contribution to midwestern American literature. Born in Garnett, Kansas, in 1868 – 1869 according to his account in *Across Spoon River* (1936) – he spent his boyhood in New Salem and Lewiston, Illinois, small towns not unlike the fictive Spoon River. After attending Knox College in Galesburg, he read law and was admitted to the bar in 1891. In the next year he settled in Chicago as a lawyer and writer. He had already published eleven books before winning recognition and praise for *Spoon River Anthology* (1915). It was followed by a second, enlarged edition in 1916 and by *The New Spoon River* (1924). In the free verse poems of the "anthology," residents of the town graveyard tell the story of their inner lives in pungent, idiomatic language. The collection contrasts the meanness of the later generation of the dead, which usually speaks in disillusioned and defeated terms, with the vigor and joy in life of older pioneer settlers, like Fiddler Jones and Lucinda Matlock. Reinforcing the obvious satire of small town life is a psychological interest provided by the contrasts between outer appearances and covert motives in the interrelated lives of the characters.

Masters moved to New York City, where he continued writing even more prolifically but without repeating the success of the Spoon River collection. Among his later volumes of poetry, *Domesday Book* (1920) and its sequel, *The Fate of the Jury* (1929) have been well regarded. Among many volumes of prose are several biographies: *Lincoln, the Man* (1931), an attack on Lincoln's character; *Vachel Lindsay* (1935); *Walt Whitman* (1937); and *Mark Twain* (1938). Masters also wrote *The Sangamon* (1942) for the "Rivers of America" series.

In the absence of a collected edition, the most representative collec-

tion of Masters' poetry is *Selected Poems* (New York, 1925).
       The text of the poems given here is *Spoon River Anthology,* New Edition (New York, 1944).

The Hill

Where are Elmer, Herman, Bert, Tom and Charley,
The weak of will, the strong of arm, the clown, the boozer, the
        fighter?
All, all, are sleeping on the hill.

One passed in a fever,
One was burned in a mine,
One was killed in a brawl,
One died in a jail,
One fell from a bridge toiling for children and wife —
All, all are sleeping, sleeping, sleeping on the hill.   10

Where are Ella, Kate, Mag, Lizzie and Edith,
The tender heart, the simple soul, the loud, the proud, the happy
        one? —
All, all, are sleeping on the hill.

One died in shameful child-birth,
One of a thwarted love,
One at the hands of a brute in a brothel,
One of a broken pride, in the search for heart's desire,
One after life in far-away London and Paris
Was brought to her little space by Ella and Kate and Mag —   20
All, all are sleeping, sleeping, sleeping on the hill.

Where are Uncle Isaac and Aunt Emily,
And old Towny Kincaid and Sevigne Houghton,
And Major Walker who had talked
With venerable men of the revolution? —
All, all, are sleeping on the hill.

They brought them dead sons from the war,
And daughters whom life had crushed,
And their children fatherless, crying —
All, all are sleeping, sleeping, sleeping on the hill.   30

Where is Old Fiddler Jones
Who played with life all his ninety years,
Braving the sleet with bared breast,
Drinking, rioting, thinking neither of wife nor kin,
Nor gold, nor love, nor heaven?

Lo! he babbles of the fish-frys of long ago,
Of the horse-races of long ago at Clary's Grove,
Of what Abe Lincoln said
One time at Springfield.

1915

Fiddler Jones

The earth keeps some vibration going
There in your heart, and that is you.
And if the people find you can fiddle,
Why, fiddle you must, for all your life.
What do you see, a harvest of clover?
Or a meadow to walk through to the river?
The wind's in the corn; you rub your hands
For beeves hereafter ready for market;
Or else you hear the rustle of skirts
Like the girls when dancing at Little Grove.   10
To Cooney Potter a pillar of dust
Or whirling leaves meant ruinous drouth;
They looked to me like Red-Head Sammy
Stepping it off, to "Toor-a-Loor."
How could I till my forty acres
Not to speak of getting more,
With a medley of horns, bassoons and piccolos
Stirred in my brain by crows and robins
And the creak of a wind-mill—only these?
And I never started to plow in my life   20
That some one did not stop in the road
And take me away to a dance or picnic.
I ended up with forty acres;
I ended up with a broken fiddle—
And a broken laugh, and a thousand memories,
And not a single regret.

1915

Editor Whedon

To be able to see every side of every question;
To be on every side, to be everything, to be nothing long;
To pervert truth, to ride it for a purpose,
To use great feelings and passions of the human family
For base designs, for cunning ends,
To wear a mask like the Greek actors—
Your eight-page paper—behind which you huddle,
Bawling through the megaphone of big type:
"This is I, the giant."
Thereby also living the life of a sneak-thief,   10

Poisoned with the anonymous words
Of your clandestine soul.
To scratch dirt over scandal for money,
And exhume it to the winds for revenge,
Or to sell papers,
Crushing reputations, or bodies, if need be,
To win at any cost, save your own life.
To glory in demoniac power, ditching civilization,
As a paranoiac boy puts a log on the track
And derails the express train.   20
To be an editor, as I was.
Then to lie here close by the river over the place
Where the sewage flows from the village,
And the empty cans and garbage are dumped,
And abortions are hidden.

1915

Anne Rutledge

Out of me unworthy and unknown
The vibrations of deathless music;
"With malice toward none, with charity for all."
Out of me the forgiveness of millions toward millions,
And the beneficent face of a nation
Shining with justice and truth.
I am Anne Rutledge who sleep beneath these weeds,
Beloved in life of Abraham Lincoln,
Wedded to him, not through union,
But through separation.
Bloom forever, O Republic,
From the dust of my bosom!

1915

Lucinda Matlock

I went to the dances at Chandlerville,
And played snap-out at Winchester.
One time we changed partners,
Driving home in the moonlight of middle June,
And then I found Davis.
We were married and lived together for seventy years,
Enjoying, working, raising the twelve children,
Eight of whom we lost
Ere I had reached the age of sixty.
I spun, I wove, I kept the house, I nursed the sick,   10
I made the garden, and for holiday
Rambled over the fields where sang the larks,
And by Spoon River gathering many a shell,

And many a flower and medicinal weed—
Shouting to the wooded hills, singing to the green valleys.
At ninety-six I had lived enough, that is all,
And passed to a sweet repose.
What is this I hear of sorrow and weariness,
Anger, discontent and drooping hopes?
Degenerate sons and daughters,   20
Life is too strong for you—
It takes life to love Life.

1915

Vachel Lindsay   *1879–1931*

Nicholas Vachel Lindsay was born in Springfield, Illinois, in 1879. After attending Hiram College, he studied art in Chicago and New York (1900–05). For several years he lectured on art and on temperance for the Y.M.C.A. during the winters and spent his summers tramping about the country asking for his food and lodging and offering poems in return. Verse he wrote during this period was published in *The Tree of Laughing Bells* (1905) and *Rhymes to Be Traded for Bread* (1912). With the appearance of *General William Booth Enters Into Heaven and Other Poems* (1912) and *The Congo and Other Poems* (1914), he began to establish a reputation as a public reader of poetry which exploited the rhythms and other primitive qualities of religious revival hymns and jazz. Although Lindsay was not influenced by the theory that shaped the new poetry of Eliot, Pound, and their associates (many of his poems are quite conventional), he contributed to the modern movement by opening his poetry to popular and primitive influences. Socially motivated, he wished to bring the gospel of beauty and democratic brotherhood into the limited lives (described by his contemporaries Sherwood Anderson and Edgar Lee Masters) of his audiences through what he called the "higher vaudeville" of his readings. *The Chinese Nightingale and Other Poems* (1917) contains the last of Lindsay's durable work, although he continued to write and publish poetry. Among his prose works are *Adventures While Preaching the Gospel of Beauty* (1914), *A*

Handy Guide for Beggars (1916), and *The Golden Book of Springfield* (1920), a mystical expression of his cult of beauty.

The standard edition of his poetry is *Collected Poems by Vachel Lindsay* (New York, 1923; rev. ed., 1925). Two biographies are E. L. Masters, *Vachel Lindsay* (New York, 1935), and Mark Harris, *City of Discontent: An Interpretive Biography* (Indianapolis, 1952).

The text of the poems given here is that of *Collected Poems by Vachel Lindsay*, rev. ed. (New York, 1925).

General William Booth Enters into Heaven[1]

(To be sung to the tune of "The Blood of the Lamb" with indicated instrument)

1

(Bass drum beaten loudly.)
Booth led boldly with his big bass drum —
(Are you washed in the blood of the Lamb?)
The Saints smiled gravely and they said: "He's come."
(Are you washed in the blood of the Lamb?)
Walking lepers followed, rank on rank,
Lurching bravos from the ditches dank,
Drabs from the alleyways and drug fiends pale —
Minds still passion-ridden, soul-powers frail: —
Vermin-eaten saints with moldy breath,
Unwashed legions with the ways of Death —   10
(Are you washed in the blood of the Lamb?)

(Banjos.)
Every slum had sent its half-a-score
The round world over. (Booth had groaned for more.)
Every banner that the wide world flies
Bloomed with glory and transcendent dyes.
Big-voiced lasses made their banjos bang,
Tranced, fanatical they shrieked and sang: —
"Are you washed in the blood of the Lamb?"
Hallelujah! It was queer to see
Bull-necked convicts with that land make free.   20
Loons with trumpets blowed a blare, blare, blare
On, on upward thro' the golden air!
(Are you washed in the blood of the Lamb?)

2

(Bass drum slower and softer.)
Booth died blind and still by faith he trod,
Eyes still dazzled by the ways of God.
Booth led boldly, and he looked the chief
Eagle countenance in sharp relief,

[1] William Booth (1829–1912), English revivalist and founder of the Salvation Army. "The Blood of the Lamb" is an old revival hymn.

Beard a-flying, air of high command
Unabated in that holy land.

   (Sweet flute music.)
Jesus came from out the court-house door,   30
Stretched his hands above the passing poor.
Booth saw not, but led his queer ones there
Round and round the mighty court-house square.
Then, in an instant all that blear review
Marched on spotless, clad in raiment new.
The lame were straightened, withered limbs uncurled
And blind eyes opened on a new, sweet world.

   (Bass drum louder.)
Drabs and vixens in a flash made whole!
Gone was the weasel-head, the snout, the jowl!
Sages and sibyls now, and athletes clean,   40
Rulers of empires, and of forests green!

   *(Grand chorus of all instruments. Tambourines to the
   foreground.)*
The hosts were sandalled, and their wings were fire!
(Are you washed in the blood of the Lamb?)
But their noise played havoc with the angel-choir.
(Are you washed in the blood of the Lamb?)
Oh, shout Salvation! It was good to see
Kings and Princes by the Lamb set free.
The banjos rattled and the tambourines
Jing-jing-jingled in the hands of Queens.

   (Reverently sung, no instruments.)
And when Booth halted by the curb for prayer   50
He saw his Master thro' the flag-filled air.
Christ came gently with a robe and crown
For Booth the soldier, while the throng knelt down.
He saw King Jesus. They were face to face,
And he knelt a-weeping in that holy place.
Are you washed in the blood of the Lamb?
                                                          1913

Abraham Lincoln Walks at Midnight

(In Springfield, Illinois)

It is portentous, and a thing of state
That here at midnight, in our little town
A mourning figure walks, and will not rest,
Near the old court-house pacing up and down,

Or by his homestead, or in shadowed yards
He lingers where his children used to play,
Or through the market, on the well-worn stones
He stalks until the dawn-stars burn away.

A bronzed, lank man! His suit of ancient black,
A famous high top-hat and plain worn shawl   10
Make him the quaint great figure that men love,
The prairie-lawyer, master of us all.

He cannot sleep upon his hillside now.
He is among us:—as in times before!
And we who toss and lie awake for long
Breathe deep, and start, to see him pass the door.

His head is bowed. He thinks on men and kings.
Yea, when the sick world cries, how can he sleep?
Too many peasants fight, they know not why,
Too many homesteads in black terror weep.   20

The sins of all the war-lords burn his heart.
He sees the dreadnaughts scouring every main.
He carries on his shawl-wrapped shoulders now
The bitterness, the folly and the pain.

He cannot rest until a spirit-dawn
Shall come;—the shining hope of Europe free:
The league of sober folk, the Workers' Earth,
Bringing long peace to Cornland, Alp and Sea.

It breaks his heart that kings must murder still,
That all his hours of travail here for men   30
Seem yet in vain. And who will bring white peace
That he may sleep upon his hill again?

1917

The Congo

A STUDY OF THE NEGRO RACE

(Being a memorial to Ray Eldred,[1] a Disciple missionary of the Congo River)

1

Their Basic Savagery

Fat black bucks in a wine-barrel room,
Barrel-house kings, with feet unstable,
Sagged and reeled and pounded on the table,

[1] This poem, particularly the third section, was suggested by an allusion in a sermon by my pastor, F. W. Burnham, to the heroic life and death of Ray Eldred. Eldred was a missionary of the Disciples of Christ who perished while swimming a treacherous branch of the Congo. See *A Master Builder on the Congo*, by Andrew F. Henesey, published by Fleming H. Revell. (V.L.)

Pounded on the table,
Beat an empty barrel with the handle of a
    broom.   *A deep rolling*
                                                    bass.
Hard as they were able,
Boom, boom, BOOM,
With a silk umbrella and the handle of a broom,
Boomlay, boomlay, boomlay, BOOM.   10
THEN I had religion, THEN I had a vision.
I could not turn from their revel in derision.
THEN I SAW THE CONGO, CREEPING THROUGH   *More deliberate.*
    THE BLACK,   *Solemnly chanted.*
CUTTING THROUGH THE FOREST WITH A
    GOLDEN TRACK.
Then along that riverbank
A thousand miles
Tattooed cannibals danced in files;
Then I heard the boom of the blood-lust song   20
And a thigh-bone beating on a tin-pan gong.   *A rapidly*
And "BLOOD" screamed the whistles and the   *piling climax*
    fifes of the warriors,   *of speed and*
                                                    racket.
"BLOOD" screamed the skull-faced, lean
    witch-doctors,
"Whirl ye the deadly voo-doo rattle,
Harry the uplands,
Steal all the cattle,
Rattle-rattle, rattle-rattle,
Bing.   30
Boomlay, boomlay, boomlay, BOOM,"
A roaring, epic, rag-time tune   *With a philo-*
From the mouth of the Congo   *sophic pause.*
To the Mountains of the Moon.
Death is an Elephant,
Torch-eyed and horrible,   *Shrilly and*
Foam-flanked and terrible.   *with a heavily*
BOOM, steal the pygmies,   *accented metre.*
BOOM, kill the Arabs,
BOOM, kill the white men,   40
Hoo, Hoo, Hoo.
Listen to the yell of Leopold's ghost   *Like the wind*
Burning in Hell for his hand-maimed host.   *in the chimney.*
Hear how the demons chuckle and yell
Cutting his hands off, down in Hell.
Listen to the creepy proclamation,
Blown through the lairs of the forest-nation,
Blown past the white-ants' hill of clay,
Blown past the marsh where the butterflies play: —
"Be careful what you do,   50
Or Mumbo-Jumbo, God of the Congo,   *All the "o"*
And all of the other   *sounds very*

Gods of the Congo,
Mumbo-Jumbo will hoo-doo you,
Mumbo-Jumbo will hoo-doo you,
Mumbo-Jumbo will hoo-doo you."

*golden. Heavy
accents very
heavy. Light
accents very
light. Last line
whispered.*

2

Their Irrepressible High Spirits

Wild crap-shooters with a whoop and a call
Danced the juba in their gambling hall
And laughed fit to kill, and shook the town,
And guyed the policemen and laughed them
    down
With a boomlay, boomlay, boomlay, Boom.
THEN I SAW THE CONGO, CREEPING THROUGH
    THE BLACK,
CUTTING THROUGH THE FOREST WITH A
    GOLDEN TRACK.
A negro fairyland swung into view,
A minstrel river
Where dreams come true.
The ebony palace soared on high
Through the blossoming trees to the evening
    sky.
The inlaid porches and casements shone
With gold and ivory and elephant-bone.
And the black crowd laughed till their sides
    were sore
At the baboon butler in the agate door,
And the well-known tunes of the parrot band
That trilled on the bushes of that magic land.

A troupe of skull-faced witch-men came
Through the agate doorway in suits of flame,
Yea, long-tailed coats with a gold-leaf crust
And hats that were covered with diamond-dust.
And the crowd in the court gave a whoop and a
    call
And danced the juba from wall to wall.
But the witch-men suddenly stilled the throng
With a stern cold glare, and a stern old song: —
"Mumbo-Jumbo will hoo-doo you." . . .
Just then from the doorway, as fat as shotes,
Came the cake-walk princes in their long red
    coats,
Canes with a brilliant lacquer shine,
And tall silk hats that were red as wine.

*Rather shrill
and high.*

60

*Read exactly as
in first section.*

*Lay emphasis
on the delicate
ideas. Keep as
light-footed as
possible.*

70

*With
pomposity.*

80

*With a great
deliberation
and ghostliness.*

*With over-
whelming as-
surance, good
cheer, and
pomp.*

90

And they pranced with their butterfly partners
    there,
Coal-black maidens with pearls in their hair,
Knee-skirts trimmed with the jassamine sweet,
And bells on their ankles and little black-feet.
And the couples railed at the chant and the
    frown
Of the witch-men lean, and laughed them down.
(Oh, rare was the revel, and well worth while
That made those glowering witch-men smile.)

*With growing
speed and
sharply marked
dance-rhythm.*

100

The cake-walk royalty then began
To walk for a cake that was tall as a man
To the tune of "Boomlay, boomlay, Boom,"
While the witch-men laughed, with a sinister
    air,
And sang with the scalawags prancing there:—
"Walk with care, walk with care,
Or Mumbo-Jumbo, God of the Congo,
And all of the other Gods of the Congo,
Mumbo-Jumbo will hoo-doo you.
Beware, beware, walk with care,
Boomlay, boomlay, boomlay, boom.
Boomlay, boomlay, boomlay, boom.
Boomlay, boomlay, boomlay, boom.
Boomlay, boomlay, boomlay,
Boom."
(Oh, rare was the revel, and well worth while
That made those glowering witch-men smile.)

*With a touch
of negro dia-
lect, and
as rapidly as
possible toward
the end.*

110

*Slow philo-
sophic calm.*

120

3

The Hope of Their Religion

A good old negro in the slums of the town
Preached at a sister for her velvet gown.
Howled at a brother for his low-down ways,
His prowling, guzzling, sneak-thief days.
Beat on the Bible till he wore it out
Starting the jubilee revival shout.
And some had visions, as they stood on chairs,
And sang of Jacob, and the golden stairs,
And they all repented, a thousand strong
From their stupor and savagery and sin and
    wrong
And slammed with their hymn books till they
    shook the room
With "glory, glory, glory,"
And "Boom, boom, Boom."

*Heavy bass.
With a literal
imitation of
camp-meeting
racket, and
trance.*

130

THEN I SAW THE CONGO, CREEPING THROUGH
      THE BLACK,
CUTTING THROUGH THE JUNGLE WITH A
      GOLDEN TRACK.
And the gray sky opened like a new-rent veil
And showed the Apostles with their coats of
      mail.

*Exactly as in
the first section.
Begin with
terror and   140
power, end with
joy.*

In bright white steel they were seated round
And their fire-eyes watched where the Congo
      wound.
And the twelve Apostles, from their thrones on
      high

Thrilled all the forest with their heavenly cry:—   150
"Mumbo-Jumbo will die in the jungle;
Never again will he hoo-doo you,
Never again will he hoo-doo you."

*Sung to the
tune of "Hark,
ten thousand
harps and
voices."*

Then along that river, a thousand miles
The vine-snared trees fell down in files.
Pioneer angels cleared the way
For a Congo paradise, for babes at play,
For sacred capitals, for temples clean.
Gone were the skull-faced witch-men lean.
There, where the wild ghost-gods had wailed
A million boats of the angels sailed
With oars of silver, and prows of blue
And silken pennants that the sun shone
      through.

*With growing
deliberation
and joy.*

*In a rather   160
high key—as
delicately as
possible.*

'Twas a land transfigured, 'twas a new creation.
Oh, a singing wind swept the negro nation
And on through the backwoods clearing flew:—
"Mumbo-Jumbo is dead in the jungle.
Never again will he hoo-doo you.
Never again will he hoo-doo you."

*To the tune of
"Hark, ten
thousand harps
and voices."*   170

Redeemed were the forests, the beasts and the
      men,
And only the vulture dared again
By the far, lone mountains of the moon
To cry, in the silence, the Congo tune:—
"Mumbo-Jumbo will hoo-doo you,
Mumbo-Jumbo will hoo-doo you.
Mumbo . . . Jumbo . . . will . . . hoo-doo
      . . . you."

*Dying down
into a pene-
trating,
terrified
whisper.*

1917

John Crowe Ransom   *1888–*

A poet and critic best known as the leader of the New Critics of the 1940's and 1950's, John Crowe Ransom was born in Pulaski, Tennessee, in 1888. He was educated at Vanderbilt University (B. A., 1909) and at Oxford, where he studied as a Rhodes Scholar. Returning to Vanderbilt as a professor of English (1914–37), he edited *The Fugitive* (1922–25), a little magazine devoted chiefly to poetry, and contributed to the Southern agrarian symposium *I'll Take My Stand* (1930). His first undistinguished book of verse, *Poems About God* (1919), was followed by two others, *Chills and Fever* (1924) and *Two Gentlemen in Bonds* (1927), in which the level of performance is high. *Grace After Meat* (London, 1924) is a selection from his first two books. Ransom's carefully crafted poems, which he winnowed for his *Selected Poems* (1945), are marked by metaphysical irony and wit and an extreme aversion to sentiment. Metrically more conventional than the work of Eliot, Pound, or Williams, they exerted a strong influence on the "middle generation" of poets like Robert Lowell and others who grew up as students of the New Critics.

In 1937 Ransom moved to Kenyon College in Ohio, where he founded *The Kenyon Review* (1939–) and devoted his attention chiefly to criticism. Collections of his essays include *God Without Thunder* (1930), which attacks, from a religious viewpoint, modern science-conditioned thought; *The World's Body* (1938), which asserts the superiority of poetic myth over scientific knowledge; and *The New Criticism* (1941), which surveys developments in contemporary literary study and calls for a new "ontological" criticism (to which he was himself contributing). Like the other New Critics with whom he was associated (Allen Tate, Cleanth Brooks, Robert Penn Warren, Yvor Winters), Ransom was interested in focusing the critical act of analysis upon the text of the individual poem, isolated from its environment. Two terms he contributed to the definition of poetic form are *structure* and *texture*. These, together with his idea of the function of criticism, are explained in his essay "Criticism as Pure Speculation." Ransom retired as editor of *The Kenyon Review* in 1961. His later books include *Poems and Essays* (1955) and *Selected Poems* (1963).

Two critiques of Ransom's poetry are K. F. Knight, *The Poetry of John Crowe Ransom: A Study of Diction, Metaphor, and Symbol* (The Hague, 1964), and T. H. Parsons, *John Crowe Ransom* (New York, 1969).

The text of the poems given here is that of *Selected Poems of John Crowe Ransom* (New York, 1963). The selection of "Criticism as Pure Speculation" is taken from Donald A. Stauffer, ed., *The Intent of the Critic* (Princeton, 1941).

Here Lies a Lady

Here lies a lady of beauty and high degree.
Of chills and fever she died, of fever and chills,
The delight of her husband, her aunt, an infant of three,
And of medicos marveling sweetly on her ills.

For either she burned, and her confident eyes would blaze,
And her fingers fly in a manner to puzzle their heads —
What was she making? Why, nothing; she sat in a maze
Of old scraps of laces, snipped into curious shreds —

Or this would pass, and the light of her fire decline
Till she lay discouraged and cold, like a thin stalk white and
     blown,
And would not open her eyes, to kisses, to wine;
The sixth of these states was her last; the cold settled down.

Sweet ladies, long may ye bloom, and toughly I hope ye may
     thole,
But was she not lucky? In flowers and lace and mourning,
In love and great honor we bade God rest her soul
After six little spaces of chill, and six of burning.

1924

Blue Girls

Twirling your blue skirts, travelling the sward
Under the towers of your seminary,
Go listen to your teachers old and contrary
Without believing a word.

Tie the white fillets then about your hair
And think no more of what will come to pass
Than bluebirds that go walking on the grass
And chattering on the air.

Practise your beauty, blue girls, before it fail;
And I will cry with my loud lips and publish
Beauty which all our power shall never establish,
It is so frail.

For I could tell you a story which is true;
I know a lady with a terrible tongue,
Blear eyes fallen from blue,
All her perfections tarnished — yet it is not long
Since she was lovelier than any of you.

                                                            1927

Piazza Piece

— I am a gentleman in a dustcoat trying
To make you hear. Your ears are soft and small
And listen to an old man not at all,
They want the young men's whispering and sighing.
But see the roses on your trellis dying
And hear the spectral singing of the moon;
For I must have my lovely lady soon,
I am a gentleman in a dustcoat trying.

— I am a lady young in beauty waiting
Until my truelove comes, and then we kiss.
But what grey man among the vines is this
Whose words are dry and faint as in a dream?
Back from my trellis, Sir, before I scream!
I am a lady young in beauty waiting.

                                                            1927

From *Criticism as Pure Speculation*

1

A chasm, perhaps an abyss, separates the critic and the esthetician ordinarily, if the books in the library are evidence. But the authority of criticism depends on its coming to terms with esthetics, and the authority of literary esthetics depends on its coming to terms with criticism.

When we inquire into the "intent of the critic," we mean: the intent of the generalized critic, or critic as such. We will concede that any professional critic is familiar with the technical practices of poets so long as these are conventional, and is expert in judging when they perform them badly. We expect a critical discourse to cover that much but we know that more is required. The most famous poets of our time, for example, make wide departures from conventional practices: how are they to be judged? Innovations in poetry, or even conventions when pressed to their logical limits, cause the ordinary critic to despair. They cause the good critic to review his esthetic principles; perhaps to reformulate his esthetic principles. He tries the poem against his best philosophical conception of the peculiar character that a poem should have.

Mr. T. S. Eliot is an extraordinarily sensitive critic. But when he discusses the so-called "metaphysical" poetry, he surprises us by refusing to study the so-called "conceit"[1] which is its reputed basis; he observes instead that the metaphysical poets of the seventeenth century are more like their immediate predecessors than the latter are like the eighteenth and nineteenth century poets, and then he goes into a very broad philosophical comparison between two whole "periods" or types of poetry.[2] I think it has come to be understood that his comparison is unsound; it has not proved workable enough to assist critics who have otherwise borrowed liberally from his critical principles. (It contains the famous dictum about the "sensibility" of the earlier poets, it imputes to them a remarkable ability to "feel their thought," and to have a kind of "experience" in which the feeling cannot be differentiated from the thinking.) Now there is scarcely another critic equal to Eliot at distinguishing the practices of two poets who are closely related. He is supreme as a comparative critic when the relation in question is delicate and subtle; that is, when it is a matter of close perception and not a radical difference in kind. But this line of criticism never goes far enough. In Eliot's own range of criticism the line does not always answer. He is forced by discontinuities in the poetic tradition into sweeping theories that have to do with esthetics, the philosophy of poetry; and his own philosophy probably seems to us insufficient, the philosophy of the literary man.

The intent of the critic may well be, then, first to read his poem sensitively, and make comparative judgments about its technical practice, or, as we might say, to emulate Eliot. Beyond that, it is to read and remark the poem knowingly; that is, with an esthetician's understanding of what a poem generically "is."

Before I venture, with inadequate argument, to describe what I take to be the correct understanding of poetry, I would like to describe two other understandings which, though widely professed, seem to me misunderstandings. First, there is a smart and belletristic theory of poetry which may be called "psychologistic." Then there is an altogether staid and commonplace theory which is moralistic. Of these in their order.

[1] The ingenious and often strained metaphor peculiar to the poetry of John Donne and other 17th century metaphysical poets.

[2] For the argument of Eliot's essay "The Metaphysical Poets" (1921), see *Selected Essays*, New Edition (New York, 1960), pp. 241–250.

2

It could easily be argued about either of these untenable conceptions of poetry that it is an act of despair to which critics resort who cannot find for the discourse of poetry any precise differentia to remove it from the category of science. Psychologistic critics hold that poetry is addressed primarily to the feelings and motor impulses; they remind us frequently of its contrast with the coldness, the unemotionality, of science, which is supposed to address itself to the pure cognitive mind. Mr. Richards came out spectacularly for the doctrine, and furnished it with detail of the greatest ingenuity.[3] He very nearly severed the dependence of poetic effect upon any standard of objective knowledge or belief. But the feelings and impulses which he represented as gratified by the poem were too tiny and numerous to be named. He never identified them; they seemed not so much psychological as infrapsychological. His was an esoteric poetic: it could not be disproved. But neither could it be proved, and I think it is safe at this distance to say that eventually his readers, and Richards himself, lost interest in it as being an improvisation, much too unrelated to the public sense of a poetic experience.

With other critics psychologism of some sort is an old story, and one that will probably never cease to be told. For, now that all of us know about psychology, there must always be persons on hand precisely conditioned to declare that poetry is an emotional discourse indulged in resentment and compensation for science, the bleak cognitive discourse in its purity. It becomes less a form of knowledge than a form of "expression." The critics are willing to surrender the honor of objectivity to science if they may have the luxury of subjectivity for poetry. Science will scarcely object. But one or two things have to be said about that. In every experience, even in science, there is feeling. No discourse can sustain itself without interest, which is feeling. The interest, or the feeling, is like an automatic index to the human value of the proceeding—which would not otherwise proceed. . . .

I do not mean to differ with that judgment at all in remarking that we might very well let the passions and the feelings take care of themselves; it is precisely what we do in our pursuit of science. The thing to attend to is the object to which they attach. As between two similar musical phrases, or between two similar lines of poetry, we may often defy the most proficient psychologist to distinguish the one feeling-response from the other; unless we permit him to say at long last that one is the kind of response that would be made to the first line, and the other is the kind of response that would be made to the second line. But that is to do, after much wasted motion, what I have just suggested: to

---

[3] I. A. Richards' *Principles of Literary Criticism* (London, 1924) set forth a psychological theory of criticism which Richards later abandoned.

attend to the poetic object and let the feelings take care of themselves. It is their business to "respond." There may be a feeling correlative with the minutest alteration in an object, and adequate to it, but we shall hardly know. What we do know is that the feelings are grossly inarticulate if we try to abstract them and take their testimony in their own language. Since it is not the intent of the critic to be inarticulate, his discriminations must be among the objects. We understand this so well intuitively that the critic seems to us in possession of some esoteric knowledge, some magical insight, if he appears to be intelligent elsewhere and yet refers confidently to the "tone" or "quality" or "value" of the feeling he discovers in a given line. Probably he is bluffing. The distinctness resides in the cognitive or "semantical" objects denoted by the words. When Richards bewilders us by reporting affective and motor disturbances that are too tiny for definition, and other critics by reporting disturbances that are too massive and gross, we cannot fail to grow suspicious of this whole way of insight as incompetent.

Eliot has a special version of psychologistic theory which looks extremely fertile, though it is broad and nebulous as his psychologistic terms require it to be. He likes to regard the poem as a structure of emotion and feeling. But the emotion is singular, there being only one emotion per poem, or at least per passage: it is the central emotion or big emotion which attaches to the main theme or situation. The feeling is plural. The emotion combines with many feelings; these are our little responses to the single words and phrases, and he does not think of them as being parts of the central emotion or even related to it. The terminology is greatly at fault, or we should recognize at once, I think, a principle that might prove very valuable. I would not answer for the conduct of a technical philosopher in assessing this theory; he might throw it away, out of patience with its jargon. But a lay philosopher who respects his Eliot and reads with all his sympathy might salvage a good thing from it, though I have not heard of anyone doing so. He would try to escape from the affective terms, and translate Eliot into more intelligible language. Eliot would be saying in effect that a poem has a central logic or situation or "paraphrasable core" to which an appropriate interest doubtless attaches, and that in this respect the poem is like a discourse of science behind which lies the sufficient passion. But he would be saying at the same time, and this is the important thing, that the poem has also a context of lively local details to which other and independent interests attach; and that in this respect it is unlike the discourse of science. For, the detail of scientific discourse intends never to be independent of the thesis (either objectively or affectively) but always functional, and subordinate to the realization of the thesis. To say that is to approach to a structural understanding of poetry, and to the kind of understanding that I wish presently to urge.

3

As for the moralistic understanding of poetry, it is sometimes the specific moralists, men with moral axes to grind, and incidentally men of unassailable public position, who cherish that; they have a "use" for poetry. But not exclusively, for we may find it held also by critics who are more spontaneous and innocent: apparently they fall back upon it because it attributes some special character to poetry, which otherwise refuses to yield up to them a character. The moral interest is so much more frequent in poetry than in science that they decide to offer its moralism as a differentia.

This conception of poetry is of the greatest antiquity—it antedates the evolution of close esthetic philosophy, and persists beside it too. Plato sometimes spoke of poetry in this light—perhaps because it was recommended to him in this light—but nearly always scornfully. In the *Gorgias*, and other dialogues, he represents the poets as moralizing, and that is only what he, in the person of Socrates, is doing at the very moment, and given to doing; but he considers the moralizing of poets as mere "rhetoric," or popular philosophy, and unworthy of the accomplished moralist who is the real or technical philosopher. Plato understood very well that the poet does not conduct a technical or an original discourse like that of the scientist—and the term includes here the moral philosopher—and that close and effective moralizing is scarcely to be had from him. It is not within the poet's power to offer that if his intention is to offer poetry; for the poetry and the morality are so far from being identical that they interfere a little with each other.

Few famous estheticians in the history of philosophy have cared to bother with the moralistic conception; many critics have, in all periods. Just now we have at least two schools of moralistic critics contending for the official possession of poetry. One is the Neo-Humanist, and Mr. Foerster has identified himself with that.[4] The other is the Marxist, and I believe it is represented in some degree and shade by Mr. Wilson, possibly by Mr. Auden.[5] I have myself taken profit from the discussions by both schools, but recently I have taken more—I suppose this is because I was brought up in a scholastic discipline rather like the Neo-Humanist—from the writings of the Marxist critics. One of the differences is that the Neo-Humanists believe in the "respectable" virtues, but the Marxists believe that respectability is the greatest of vices, and equate respectable with "genteel." That is a very striking difference, and I think it is also profound.

But I do not wish to be impertinent; I can respect both these moralities, and appropriate moral values from both. The thing I wish to

[4] Norman Foerster, editor of the symposium *Humanism in America* (New York, 1930).
[5] The American critic Edmund Wilson, who has consistently related literature to its social and historical context. The English poet W. H. Auden was a Marxist sympathizer during the 1930's.

argue is not the comparative merits of the different moralities by which poetry is judged, but their equal inadequacy to the reading of the poet's intention. The moralistic critics wish to isolate and discuss the "ideology" or theme or paraphrase of the poem and not the poem itself. But even to the practitioners themselves, if they are sophisticated, comes sometimes the apprehension that this is moral rather than literary criticism. I have not seen the papers of my colleagues in this discussion, for that was against the rules, but it is reported to me that both Mr. Wilson and Mr. Foerster concede in explicit words that criticism has both the moral and the esthetic branches; Mr. Wilson may call them the "social" and esthetic branches. And they would hold the critical profession responsible for both branches. Under these circumstances the critics cease to be mere moralists and become dualists; that is better. My feeling about such a position would be that the moral criticism we shall have with us always, and have had always, and that it is easy — comparatively speaking — and that what is hard, and needed, and indeed more and more urgent after all the failures of poetic understanding, is a better esthetic criticism. This is the branch which is all but invariably neglected by the wise but morally zealous critics; they tend to forget their dual responsibility. I think I should go so far as to think that, in strictness, the business of the literary critic is exclusively with an esthetic criticism. The business of the moralist will naturally, and properly, be with something else.

If we have the patience to read for a little while in the anthology, paying some respect to the varieties of substance actually in the poems, we cannot logically attribute ethical character by definition to poetry; for that character is not universal in the poems. And if we have any faith in a community of character among the several arts, we are stopped quickly from risking such a definition for art at large. To claim a moral content for most of sculpture, painting, music, or architecture, is to plan something dialectically very round-about and subtle, or else to be so arbitrary as to invite instant exposure. I should think the former alternative is impractical, and the latter, if it is not stupid, is masochistic.

The moralistic critics are likely to retort upon their accusers by accusing them in turn of the vapid doctrine known as Art for Art's Sake. And with frequent justice; but again we are likely to receive the impression that it is just because Art for Art's Sake, the historic doctrine, proved empty, and availed them so little esthetically, like all the other doctrines that came into default, that they have fled to their moralism. Moralism does at least impute to poetry a positive substance, as Art for Art's Sake does not. It asserts an autonomy for art, which is excellent; but autonomy to do what? Only to be itself, and to reduce its interpreters to a tautology? With its English adherents in the 'nineties the doctrine seemed to make only a negative requirement of art, that is, that it should be anti-Victorian as we should say today, a little bit naughty and immoral perhaps, otherwise at least non-moral, or carefully squeezed dry of moral substance. An excellent example of how two doctrines, inadequate equally but in opposite senses, may keep themselves alive by abhorring each other's errors.

It is highly probable that the poem considers an ethical situation, and there is no reason why it should repel this from its consideration. But, if I may say so without being accused of verbal trifling, the poetic consideration of the ethical situation is not the same as the ethical consideration of it. The straight ethical consideration would be prose; it would be an act of interested science, or an act of practical will. The poetic consideration, according to Schopenhauer, is the objectification of this act of will; that is, it is our contemplation and not our exercise of will, and therefore qualitatively a very different experience; knowledge without desire. That doctrine also seems too negative and indeterminate. I will put the point as I see it in another way. It should be a comfort to the moralist that there is ordinarily a moral composure in the poem, as if the poet had long known good and evil, and made his moral choice between them once and for all. Art is post-ethical rather than unethical. In the poem there is an increment of meaning which is neither the ethical content nor opposed to the ethical content. The poetic experience would have to stop for the poet who is developing it, or for the reader who is following it, if the situation which is being poetically treated should turn back into a situation to be morally determined; if, for example, the situation were not a familiar one, and one to which we had habituated our moral wills; for it would rouse the moral will again to action, and make the poetic treatment impossible under its heat. Art is more cool than hot, and a moral fervor is as disastrous to it as a burst of passion itself. We have seen Marxists recently so revolted by Shakespeare's addiction to royal or noble *personae* that they cannot obtain esthetic experience from the plays; all they get is moral agitation. In another art, we know, and doubtless we approve, the scruple of the college authorities in not permitting the "department of fine arts" to direct the collegians in painting in the nude. Doctor Hanns Sachs, successor to Freud, in a recent number of his *American Imago*,[6] gives a story from a French author as follows:

He tells that one evening strolling along the streets of Paris he noticed a row of slot machines which for a small coin showed pictures of women in full or partial undress. He observed the leering interest with which men of all kind and description, well dressed and shabby, boys and old men, enjoyed the peep show. He remarked that they all avoided one of these machines, and wondering what uninteresting pictures it might show, he put his penny in the slot. To his great astonishment the generally shunned picture turned out to be the Venus of Medici. Now he begins to ponder: Why does nobody get excited about her? She

---

[6] A psychoanalytical journal of criticism of literature and the arts, successor to the European *Imago* established by Sigmund Freud.

is decidedly feminine and not less naked than the others which hold such strong fascination for everybody. Finally he finds a satisfactory answer: They fight shy of her because she is beautiful.

And Doctor Sachs, though in his own variety of jargon, makes a number of wise observations about the psychic conditions precedent to the difficult apprehension of beauty. The experience called beauty is beyond the powerful ethical will precisely as it is beyond the animal passion, and indeed these last two are competitive, and coordinate. Under the urgency of either we are incapable of appreciating the statue or understanding the poem.

4

The ostensible substance of the poem may be anything at all which words may signify: an ethical situation, a passion, a train of thought, a flower or landscape, a thing. This substance receives its poetic increment. It might be safer to say it receives some subtle and mysterious alteration under poetic treatment, but I will risk the cruder formula: the ostensible substance is increased by an x, which is an increment. The poem actually continues to contain its ostensible substance, which is not fatally diminished from its prose state: that is its logical core, or paraphrase. The rest of the poem is x, which we are to find.

We feel the working of this simple formula when we approach a poetry with our strictest logic, provided we can find deliverance from certain inhibiting philosophical prepossessions into which we have been conditioned by the critics we have had to read. Here is Lady Macbeth planning a murder with her husband:

> When Duncan is asleep—
> Whereto the rather shall his hard day's journey
> Soundly invite him—his two chamberlains
> Will I with wine and wassail so convince,
> That memory, the warder of the brain,
> Shall be a fume, and the receipt of reason
> A limbec only; when in swinish sleep
> Their drenched natures lie as in a death,
> What cannot you and I perform upon
> The unguarded Duncan? what not put upon
> His spongy officers, who shall bear the guilt
> Of our great quell?[7]

It is easy to produce the prose argument or paraphrase of this speech; it has one upon which we shall all agree. But the passage is more than its argument. Any detail, with this speaker, seems capable of being expanded in some direction which is not that of the argument. For example, Lady Macbeth says she will make the chamberlains drunk so that they

[7] *Macbeth* (I, vii, 61–72).

will not remember their charge, nor keep their wits about them. But it is indifferent to this argument whether memory according to the old psychology is located at the gateway to the brain, whether it is to be disintegrated into fume as of alcohol, and whether the whole receptacle of the mind is to be turned into a still. These are additions to the argument both energetic and irrelevant—though they do not quite stop or obscure the argument. From the point of view of the philosopher they are excursions into particularity. They give, in spite of the argument, which would seem to be perfectly self-sufficient, a sense of the real density and contingency of the world in which arguments and plans have to be pursued. They bring out the private character which the items of an argument can really assume if we look at them. This character spreads out in planes at right angles to the course of the argument, and in effect gives to the discourse another dimension, not present in a perfectly logical prose. We are expected to have sufficient judgment not to let this local character take us too far or keep us too long from the argument.

All this would seem commonplace remark, I am convinced, but for those philosophically timid critics who are afraid to think that the poetic increment is local and irrelevant, and that poetry cannot achieve its own virtue and keep undiminished the virtues of prose at the same time. But I will go a little further in the hope of removing the sense of strangeness in the analysis. I will offer a figurative definition of a poem.

A poem is, so to speak, a democratic state, whereas a prose discourse—mathematical, scientific, ethical, or practical and vernacular—is a totalitarian state. The intention of a democratic state is to perform the work of state as effectively as it can perform it, subject to one reservation of conscience: that it will not despoil its members, the citizens, of the free exercise of their own private and independent characters. But the totalitarian state is interested solely in being effective, and regards the citizens as no citizens at all; that is, regards them as functional members whose existence is totally defined by their allotted contributions to its ends; it has no use for their private characters, and therefore no provision for them. I indicate of course the extreme or polar opposition between two polities without denying that a polity may come to us rather mixed up.

In this trope the operation of the state as a whole represents of course the logical paraphrase or argument of the poem. The private character of the citizens represents the particularity asserted by the parts in the poem. And this last is our x.

For many years I had seen—as what serious observer has not—that a poem as a discourse differentiated itself from prose by its particularity, yet not to the point of sacrificing its logical cogency or universality. But I could get no further. I could not see how real particularity could get into a universal. The object of esthetic studies became for me a kind of discourse, or a kind of natural configuration, which like any other discourse or configuration claimed universality, but which consisted actually, and notoriously, of particularity. The poem was concrete, yet universal, and in spite of Hegel I could not see how the two properties could be identified as forming in a single unit the "concrete universal." It is usual, I believe, for persons at this stage to assert that somehow the apparent diffuseness or particularity in the poem gets itself taken up or "assimilated" into the logic, to produce a marvellous kind of unity called a "higher unity," to which ordinary discourse is not eligible. The belief is that the "idea" or theme proves itself in poetry to be even more dominating than in prose by overcoming much more energetic resistance than usual on the part of the materials, and the resistance, as attested in the local development of detail, is therefore set not to the debit but to the credit of the unifying power of the poetic spirit. A unity of that kind is one which philosophers less audacious and more factual than Hegel would be loath to claim. Critics incline to call it, rather esoterically, an "imaginative" rather than a logical unity, but one supposes they mean a mystical, an ineffable, unity. I for one could neither grasp it nor deny it. I believe that is not an uncommon situation for poetic analysts to find themselves in.

It occurred to me at last that the solution might be very easy if looked for without what the positivists call "metaphysical prepossessions." Suppose the logical substance remained there all the time, and was in no way specially remarkable, while the particularity came in by accretion, so that the poem turned out partly universal, and partly particular, but with respect to different parts. I began to remark the dimensions of a poem, or other work of art. The poem was not a mere moment in time, nor a mere point in space. It was sizeable, like a house. Apparently it had a "plan," or a central frame of logic, but it had also a huge wealth of local detail, which sometimes fitted the plan functionally or served it, and sometimes only subsisted comfortably under it; in either case the house stood up. But it was the political way of thinking which gave me the first analogy which seemed valid. The poem was like a democratic state, in action, and observed both macroscopically and microscopically.

The house occurred also, and provided what seems to be a more negotiable trope under which to construe the poem. A poem is a *logical structure* having a *local texture*. These terms have been actually though not systematically employed in literary criticism. To my imagination they are architectural. The walls of my room are obviously structural; the beams and boards have a function; so does the plaster, which is the visible aspect of the final wall. The plaster might have remained naked, aspiring to no character, and purely functional. But actually it has been painted, receiving color; or it has been papered, receiving color and design, though these have no structural value; and perhaps it has been hung with tapestry, or with paintings, for "decoration." The paint, the paper, the tapestry are texture. It is logically unrelated to structure. But I indicate only a few of the textural possibilities in architecture. There are not fewer of them in poetry.

The intent of the good critic becomes therefore to examine and define the poem with respect to its structure and its texture. If he has nothing to say about its texture he has nothing to say about it specifically as a poem, but is treating it only insofar as it is prose.

I do not mean to say that the good critic will necessarily employ my terms. . . .

1941

Humor and Satire

Humor and satire have been generously diffused in American literature from its seventeenth century beginnings. Even the Puritans relished humor, often in its grimmer and more sardonic forms, in keeping with their low opinion of human nature. Satirical humor was a natural mode for the eighteenth century, the age of reason and wit, when Benjamin Franklin and Hugh Henry Brackenridge employed it for purposes of entertainment and instruction. Renewed by the use of local color and dialect in the nineteenth century, it reached its finest flower in the genius of Mark Twain. In the twentieth century, it provided contrast and relief from the serious and often tragic vision of modern writers like F. Scott Fitzgerald and William Faulkner. In the years since the Second World War, irrationalistic Existentialism stimulated the new vogue of the humor of absurdity, which has flourished in drama and in fiction.

From the time of the Romantic revolution of the early nineteenth century, which broke down the conventional type categories of the Neoclassical tradition, satire has not existed as a distinct genre. But this change has not lessened its importance. Satirical humor has continued to flourish, and writers who have specialized in it have continued to assume the position of self-appointed guardians of moral health. From earliest times the satirist has devoted himself to exposing the follies and vices of his society. Through criticism by ridicule, the satirist makes laughable that which he finds offensive. He is basically a moralist who may or may not have positive alternatives for the irrationalities and evils he attacks. The modern satirist tends to be less didactic than his classical and neoclassical forebears because his pluralistic culture does not supply, to the same extent, universally accepted norms of conduct and value. But he is no less eager to seek out and destroy attitudes and acts that violate his own sense of reason and morality. His tone and technique may range from the lethal irony of Ring Lardner and the devastating sarcasm of H. L. Mencken to the quieter and more genial humor of Langston Hughes and James Thurber. But mildness of manner, as in Langston Hughes's "Simple" sketches, may be as potent as invective in attacking hated injustices.

Ring Lardner   *1885–1933*

Ring Lardner, an unpretentious master of ironic satire, was born Ringgold Wilmer Lardner in Niles, Michigan, in 1885. In 1905 he began his career as a sports writer in South Bend, Indiana. Moving to Chicago, he wrote a popular sports column for the Chicago *Tribune* (1913–19) and began contributing "Jack Keefe" letters about baseball to *The Saturday Evening Post*. These were collected and published in the book that gave him a national reputation as a humorist: *You Know Me, Al; A Busher's Letters* (1916). In this work Lardner made use of the colorful language of baseball to describe the experiences of his narrator, a naive rookie on a professional team. Other publications of his early years include *Bib Ballads* (1915), *Gullible's Travels* (1917), *My Four Weeks in France* (1918), *Treat 'Em Rough* (1918), *Own Your Own Home* (1919), *Regular Fellows I have Met* (1919), *The Real Dope* (1919), *The Young Immigrunts* (1920), *Symptoms of Being 35* (1921), *The Big Town* (1921), *Say It with Oil* (1923), *How to Write Short Stories (with Samples)* (1924).

With the passing of time and the deepening of Lardner's pessimism, the satirical implications that had always lain beneath the surface humor of his stories became more sharply defined. With a Swiftian revulsion he skillfully made use of the American idiom to expose the vanity, meanness, and contemptibility of his common American Yahoos—whether they might be athletes, salesmen, barbers, songwriters, married couples, or young ladies on the make. He had a special gift for the epistolary method, through which he permitted his semiliterate characters, like the correspondents of "Some Like Them Cold," to reveal their essential egoism, shallowness, and moral and emotional bankruptcy. In these respects his work complements that of H. L. Mencken, another pitiless critic of the provincialism of American culture in the 1920's.

Lardner's later publications include *What of It?* (1925), *The Love Nest* and *Other Stories* (1926), and *Round Up* (1929). *The Story of a Wonder Man* (1927) is a burlesque autobiography. Collaborating with George S. Kaufman, Lardner wrote the book for the successful musical comedy *June Moon* (1930). His last book, published in the year of his death, is *Lose with a Smile* (1933).

Ring Lardner's *Best Stories*, ed. William McFee (Garden City, N. Y., 1938), brings together the stories of *The Big Town* (1921) and *Round Up* (1929). *The Collected Short Stories of Ring Lardner* (New York, 1941) is a reprint of *Round Up*. A brief introduction is Otto Friedrich, *Ring Lardner* (Minneapolis, 1965), which contains a bibliography. A book-length study is Donald Elder, *Ring Lardner* (New York, 1956).

The text of "Some Like Them Cold" is that of *Round Up* (New York, 1929).

Some Like Them Cold

N.Y., Aug. 3.

Dear Miss Gillespie: How about our bet now as you bet me I would forget all about you the minute I hit the big town and would never write you a letter. Well girlie it looks like you lose so pay me. Seriously we will call all bets off as I am not the kind that bet on a sure thing and it sure was a sure thing that I would not forget a girlie like you and all that is worrying me is whether it may not be the other way round and you are wondering who this fresh guy is that is writeing you this letter. I bet you are so will try and refreshen your memory.

Well girlie I am the handsome young man that was wondering round the Lasalle st. station Monday and "happened" to sit down beside of a mighty pretty girlie who was waiting to meet her sister from Toledo and the train was late and I am glad of it because if it had not of been that little girlie and I would never of met. So for once I was a lucky guy but still I guess it was time I had some luck as it was certainly tough luck for you and I to both be liveing in Chi all that time and never get together till a half hour before I was leaveing town for good.

Still "better late than never" you know and maybe we can make up for lost time though it looks like we would have to do our makeing up at long distants unless you make good on your threat and come to N.Y. I wish you would do that little thing girlie as it looks like that was the only way we would get a chance to play round together as it looks like they was little or no chance of me comeing back to Chi as my whole future is in the big town. N.Y. is the only spot and specially for a man that expects to make my liveing in the song writeing game as here is the Mecca for that line of work and no matter how good a man may be they don't get no recognition unless they live in N.Y.

Well girlie you asked me to tell you all about my trip. Well I remember you saying that you would give anything to be makeing it yourself but as far as the trip itself was conserned you ought to be thankfull you did not have to make it as you would of sweat your head off. I know I did specially wile going through Ind. Monday P. M. but Monday night was the worst of all trying to sleep and finely I give it up and just layed there with the prespiration rolling off of me though I was laying on top of the covers and nothing on but my underwear.

Yesterday was not so bad as it rained most of the A. M. comeing through N.Y. state and in the P.M. we road along side of the Hudson all P. M. Some river girlie and just looking at it makes a man forget all about the heat and everything else except a certain girlie who I seen for the first time Monday and then only for a half hour but she is the kind of a girlie that a man don't need to see her only once and they would be no danger of forgetting her. There I guess I better lay off that subject or you will think I am a "fresh guy."

Well that is about all to tell you about the trip only they was one amuseing incidence that come off yesterday which I will tell you. Well they was a dame got on the train at Toledo Monday and had the birth opp. mine but I did not see nothing of her that night as I was out smoking till late and she hit the hay early but yesterday A. M. she come in the dinner and sit at the same table with me and tried to make me and it was so raw that the dinge waiter seen it and give me the wink and of course I paid no tension and I waited till she got through so as they would be no danger of her folling me out but she stopped on the way out to get a tooth pick and when I come out she was out on the platform with it so I tried to brush right by but she spoke up and asked me what time it was and I told her and she said she guessed her watch was slow so I said maybe it just seemed slow on acct. of the company it was in.

I don't know if she got what I was driveing at or not but any way she give up trying to make me and got off at Albany. She was a good looker but I have no time for gals that tries to make strangers on a train.

Well if I don't quit you will think I am writeing a book but will expect a long letter in answer to this letter and we will see if you can keep your promise like I have kept mine. Don't dissapoint me girlie as I am all alone in a large city and hearing from you will keep me from getting home sick for old Chi though I never thought so much of the old town till I found out you lived there. Don't think that is kidding girlie as I mean it.

You can address me at this hotel as it looks like I will be here right along as it is on 47th st. right off of old Broadway and handy to everything and am only paying $21 per wk. for my rm. and could of got one for $16 but without bath but am glad to pay the differents as am lost without my bath in the A. M. and sometimes at night too.

Tomorrow I expect to commence fighting the "battle of Broad-way" and will let you know how I come out that is if you answer this letter. In the mean wile girlie au reservoir and don't do nothing I would not do.

Your new friend (?)
Chas. F. Lewis.

Chicago, Ill., Aug. 6.

My Dear Mr. Lewis: Well, that certainly was a "surprise party" getting your letter and you are certainly a "wonder man" to keep your word as I am afraid most men of your sex are gay deceivers but maybe you are "different." Any way it sure was a surprise and will gladly pay the bet if you will just tell me what it was we bet. Hope it was not money as I am a "working girl" but if it was not more than a dollar or two will try to dig it up even if I have to "beg, borrow or steal."

Suppose you will think me a "case" to make a bet and then forget what it was, but you must remember, Mr. Man, that I had just met you and was "dazzled." Joking aside I was rather "fussed" and will tell you why. Well, Mr. Lewis, I suppose you see lots of girls like the one you told me about that you saw on the train who tried to "get acquainted" but I want to assure you that I am not one of those kind and sincerely hope you will believe me when I tell you that you was the first man I ever spoke to meeting them like that and my friends and the people who know me would simply faint if they knew I ever spoke to a man without a "proper introduction."

Believe me, Mr. Lewis, I am not that kind and I don't know now why I did it only that you was so "different" looking if you know what I mean and not at all like the kind of men that usually try to force their attentions on every pretty girl they see. Lots of times I act on impulse and let my feelings run away from me and sometimes I do things on the impulse of the moment which I regret them later on, and that is what I did this time, but hope you won't give me cause to regret it and I know you won't as I know you are not that kind of a man a specially after what you told me about the girl on the train. But any way as I say, I was in a "daze" so can't remember what it was we bet, but will try and pay it if it does not "break" me.

Sis's train got in about ten minutes after yours had gone and when she saw me what do you think was the first thing she said? Well, Mr. Lewis, she said: "Why Mibs (That is a pet name some of my friends have given me) what has happened to you? I never seen you have as much color." So I passed it off with some remark about the heat and changed the subject as I certainly was not going to tell her that I had just been talking to a man who I had never met or she would of dropped dead from the shock. Either that or she would not of believed me as it would be hard for a person who knows me well to imagine me doing a thing like that as I have quite a reputation for "squelching" men who try to act fresh. I don't mean anything personal by that, Mr. Lewis, as am a good judge of character and could tell without you telling me that you are not that kind.

Well, Sis and I have been on the "go" ever since she arrived as I took yesterday and today off so I could show her the "sights" though she says she would be perfectly satisfied to just sit in the apartment and listen to me "rattle on." Am afraid I am a great talker, Mr. Lewis, but Sis says it is as good as a show to hear me talk as I tell things in such a different way as I cannot help from seeing the humorous side of everything and she says she never gets tired of listening to me, but of course she is my sister and thinks the world of me, but she really does laugh like she enjoyed my craziness.

Maybe I told you that I have a tiny little apartment which a girl friend of mine and I have together and it is hardly big enough to turn round in, but still it is "home" and I am a great home girl and hardly ever care to go out evenings except occasionally to the theater or dance. But even if our "nest" is small we are proud of it and Sis complimented us on how cozy it is and how "homey" it looks and she said she did not see how we could afford to have everything so nice and Edith (my girl friend) said: "Mibs deserves all the credit for that. I never knew a girl who could make a little money go a long ways like she can." Well, of course she is my best friend and always saying nice things about me, but I do try and I hope I get results. Have always said that good taste and being careful is a whole lot more important than lots of money though it is nice to have it.

You must write and tell me how you are getting along in the "battle of Broadway" (I laughed when I read that) and whether the publishers like your songs though I know they will. Am crazy to hear them and hear you play the piano as I love good jazz music even better than classical, though I suppose it is terrible to say such a thing. But I usually say just what I think though sometimes I wish afterwards I had not of. But still I believe it is better for a girl to be her own self and natural instead of always acting. But am afraid I will never have a chance to hear you play unless you come back to Chi and pay us a visit as my "threat" to come to New York was just a "threat" and I don't see any hope of ever getting there unless some rich New Yorker should fall in love with me and take me there to live. Fine chance for poor little me, eh Mr. Lewis?

Well, I guess I have "rattled on" long enough and you will think I am writing a book unless I quit and besides, Sis has asked me as a special favor to make her a pie for dinner. Maybe you don't know it, Mr. Man, but I am quite famous for my pie and pastry, but I don't suppose a "genius" is interested in common things like that.

Well, be sure and write soon and tell me what N.Y. is like and all about it and don't forget the little girlie who was "bad" and spoke to a strange man in the station and have been blushing over it ever since.

Your friend (?)
Mabelle Gillespie.

N.Y., Aug. 10.

Dear Girlie: I bet you will think I am a fresh guy commenceing that way but Miss Gillespie is too cold and a man can not do nothing cold in this kind of weather specially in this man's town which is the hottest place I ever been in and I guess maybe the reason why New Yorkers is so bad is because they think they are all ready in H—— and can not go no worse place no matter how they behave themselves. Honest girlie I certainly envy you being where there is a breeze off the old Lake and Chi may be dirty but I never heard of nobody dying because they was dirty but four people died here yesterday on acct. of the heat and I seen two different women flop right on Broadway and had to be taken away in the ambulance and it could not of been because they was dressed too warm because it would be impossible for the women here to leave off any more cloths.

Well have not had much luck yet in the battle of Broadway as all the heads of the big music publishers is out of town on their vacation and the big boys is the only ones I will do business with as it would be silly for a man with the stuff I have got to waste my time on somebody that is just on the staff and have not got the final say. But I did play a couple of my numbers for the people up to Levy's and Goebel's and they went crazy over them in both places. So it looks like all I have to do is wait for the big boys to get back and then play my numbers for them and I will be all set. What I want is to get taken on the staff of one of the big firms as that gives a man the inside and they will plug your numbers more if you are on the staff. In the mean wile have not got nothing to worry me but am just seeing the sights of the big town as have saved up enough money to play round for a wile and any way a man that can play piano like I can don't never have to worry about starveing. Can certainly make the old music box talk girlie and am always good for a $75 or $100 job.

Well have been here a week now and on the go every minute and I thought I would be lonesome down here but no chance of that as I have been treated fine by the people I have met and have sure met a bunch of them. One of the boys liveing in the hotel is a vaudeville actor and he is a member of the Friars club and took me over there to dinner the other night and some way another the bunch got wise that I could play piano so of course I had to sit down and give them some of my numbers and everybody went crazy over them. One of the boys I met there was Paul Sears the song writer but he just writes the lyrics and has wrote a bunch of hits and when he heard some of my melodies he called me over to one side and said he would like to work with me on some numbers. How is that girlie as he is one of the biggest hit writers in N.Y.

N.Y. has got some mighty pretty girlies and I guess it would not be hard to get acquainted with them and in fact several of them has tried to make me since I been here but I always figure that a girl must be something wrong with her if she tries to make a man that she don't know nothing about so I pass them all up. But I did meet a couple of pips that a man here in the hotel went up on Riverside Drive to see them and insisted on me going along and they got on some way that I could make a piano talk so they was nothing but I must play for them so I sit down and played some of my own stuff and they went crazy over it.

One of the girls wanted I should come up and see her again, and I said I might but I think I better keep away as she acted like she wanted to vamp me and I am not the kind that likes to play round with a gal just for their company and dance with them etc. but when I see the right gal that will be a different thing and she won't have to beg me to come and see her as I will camp right on her trail till she says yes. And it won't be none of these N.Y. fly by nights neither. They are all right to look at but a man would be a sucker to get serious with them as they might take you up and next thing you know you would have a wife on your hands that don't know a dish rag from a waffle iron.

Well girlie will quit and call it a day as it is too hot to write any more and I guess I will turn on the cold water and lay in the tub a wile and then turn in. Don't forget to write to

> Your friend,
> Chas. F. Lewis.

Chicago, Ill., Aug. 13.

Dear Mr. Man: Hope you won't think me a "silly Billy" for starting my letter that way but "Mr. Lewis" is so formal and "Charles" is too much the other way and any way I would not dare call a man by their first name after only knowing them only two weeks. Though I may as well confess that Charles is my favorite name for a man and have always been crazy about it as it was my father's name. Poor old dad, he died of cancer three years ago, but left enough insurance so that mother and we girls were well provided for and do not have to do anything to support ourselves though I have been earning my own living for two years to make things easier for mother and also because I simply can't bear to be doing nothing as I feel like a "drone." So I flew away from the "home nest" though mother felt bad about it as I was her favorite and she always said I was such a comfort to her as when I was in the house she never had to worry about how things would go.

But there I go gossiping about my domestic affairs just like you would be interested in them though I don't see how you could be though personly I always like to know all about my friends, but I know men are different so will try and not bore you any longer. Poor Man, I certainly feel sorry for you if New York is as hot as all that. I guess it has been very hot in Chi, too, at least everybody has been complaining about how terrible it is. Suppose you will wonder why I say "I guess" and you will think I ought to know if it is hot. Well, sir, the reason I say "I guess" is because I don't feel the heat like others do or at least I don't let myself feel it. That sounds crazy I know, but don't you think there is a good deal in mental suggestion and not letting yourself feel things? I believe that if a person simply won't allow themselves to be affected by disagreeable things, why such things won't bother them near as much. I know it works with me and that is the reason why I am never cross when things go wrong and "keep smiling" no matter what happens and as far as the heat is concerned, why I just don't let myself feel it and my friends say I don't even look hot no matter if the weather is boiling and Edith, my girl friend, often says that I am like a breeze and it cools her off just to have me come in the room. Poor Edie suffers terribly during the hot weather and says it almost makes her mad at me to see how cool and unruffled I look when everybody else is perspiring and have red faces etc.

I laughed when I read what you said about New York being so hot that people thought it was the "other place." I can appreciate a joke, Mr. Man, and that one did not go "over my head." Am still laughing at some of the things you said in the station though they probably struck me funnier than they would most girls as I always see the funny side and sometimes something is said and I laugh and the others wonder what I am laughing at as they cannot see anything in it themselves, but it is just the way I look at things so of course I cannot explain to them why I laughed and they think I am crazy. But I had rather part with almost anything rather than my sense of humour as it helps me over a great many rough spots.

Sis has gone back home though I would of liked to of kept her here much longer, but she had to go though she said she would of liked nothing better than to stay with me and just listen to me "rattle on." She always says it is just like a show to hear me talk as I always put things in such a funny way and for weeks after she has been visiting me she thinks of some of the things I said and laughs over them. Since she left Edith and I have been pretty quiet though poor Edie wants to be on the "go" all the time and tries to make me go out with her every evening to the pictures and scolds me when I say I had rather stay home and read and calls me a "book worm." Well, it is true that I had rather stay home with a good book than go to some crazy old picture and the last two nights I have been reading myself to sleep with Robert W.

Service's poems.[1] Don't you love Service or don't you care for "high-brow" writings?

Personly there is nothing I love more than to just sit and read a good book or sit and listen to somebody play the piano, I mean if they can really play and I really believe I like popular music better than the classical though I suppose that is a terrible thing to confess, but I love all kinds of music but a specially the piano when it is played by some-body who can really play.

Am glad you have not "fallen" for the "ladies" who have tried to make your acquaintance in New York. You are right in thinking there must be something wrong with girls who try to "pick up" strange men as no girl with self respect would do such a thing and when I say that, Mr. Man, I know you will think it is a funny thing for me to say on account of the way our friendship started, but I mean it and I assure you that was the first time I ever done such a thing in my life and would never of thought of doing it had I not known you were the right kind of a man as I flatter myself that I am a good judge of character and can tell pretty well what a person is like by just looking at them and I assure you I had made up my mind what kind of a man you were before I allowed myself to answer your opening remark. Otherwise I am the last girl in the world that would allow myself to speak to a person without being introduced to them.

When you write again you must tell me all about the girl on Riverside Drive and what she looks like and if you went to see her again and all about her. Suppose you will think I am a little old "curiosity shop" for asking all those questions and will wonder why I want to know. Well, sir, I won't tell you why, so there, but I insist on you answering all the questions and will scold you if you don't. Maybe you will think that the reason why I am so curious is because I am "jeal-ous" of the lady in question. Well, sir, I won't tell you whether I am or not, but will keep you "guessing." Now, don't you wish you knew?

Must close or you will think I am going to "rattle on" forever or maybe you have all ready become disgusted and torn my letter up. If so all I can say is poor little me—she was a nice little girl and meant well, but the man did not appreciate her.

There! Will stop or you will think I am crazy if you do not all ready.

Yours (?)
Mabelle.

N.Y., Aug. 20.

Dear Girlie: Well girlie I suppose you thought I was never going to answer your letter but have been busier than a one armed paper

---

[1] The reference is to the Canadian author (1874–1958) of the immortal "The Shooting of Dan McGrew."

hanger the last week as have been working on a number with Paul
Sears who is one of the best lyric writers in N.Y. and has turned out as
many hits as Berlin or Davis or any of them. And believe me girlie he
has turned out another hit this time that is he and I have done it together. It is all done now and we are just waiting for the best chance to
place it but will not place it nowheres unless we get the right kind of a
deal but maybe will publish it ourselves.

The song is bound to go over big as Sears has wrote a great lyric
and I have give it a great tune or at least every body that has heard it
goes crazy over it and it looks like it would go over bigger than any
song since Mammy and would not be surprised to see it come out the
hit of the year. If it is handled right we will make a bbl. of money and
Sears says it is a cinch we will clean up as much as $25000 apiece
which is pretty fair for one song but this one is not like the most of
them but has got a great lyric and I have wrote a melody that will knock
them out of their seats. I only wish you could hear it girlie and hear it
the way I play it. I had to play it over and over about 50 times at the
Friars last night.

I will copy down the lyric of the chorus so you can see what it is
like and get the idea of the song though of course you can't tell much
about it unless you hear it played and sang. The title of the song is
When They're Like You and here is the chorus:

> "Some like them hot, some like them cold.
> Some like them when they're not too darn old.
> Some like them fat, some like them lean.
> Some like them only at sweet sixteen.
> Some like them dark, some like them light.
> Some like them in the park, late at night.
> Some like them fickle, some like them true,
> But the time I like them is when they're like you."

How is that for a lyric and I only wish I could play my melody for
you as you would go nuts over it but will send you a copy as soon as the
song is published and you can get some of your friends to play it over
for you and I know you will like it though it is a different melody when
I play it or when somebody else plays it.

Well girlie you will see how busy I have been and am libel to keep
right on being busy as we are not going to let the grass grow under our
feet but as soon as we have got this number placed we will get busy on
another one as a couple like that will put me on Easy st. even if they
don't go as big as we expect but even 25 grand is a big bunch of money
and if a man could only turn out one hit a year and make that much out
of it I would be on Easy st. and no more hammering on the old music
box in some cabaret.

Who ever we take the song to we will make them come across with one grand for advance royaltys and that will keep me going till I can turn out another one. So the future looks bright and rosey to yours truly and I am certainly glad I come to the big town though sorry I did not do it a whole lot quicker.

This is a great old town girlie and when you have lived here a wile you wonder how you ever stood for a burg like Chi which is just a hick town along side of this besides being dirty etc. and a man is a sucker to stay there all their life specially a man in my line of work as N.Y. is the Mecca for a man that has got the musical gift. I figure that all the time I spent in Chi I was just wasteing my time and never really started to live till I come down here and I have to laugh when I think of the boys out there that is trying to make a liveing in the song writeing game and most of them starve to death all their life and the first week I am down here I meet a man like Sears and the next thing you know we have turned out a song that will make us a fortune.

Well girlie you asked me to tell you about the girlie up on the Drive that tried to make me and asked me to come and see her again. Well I can assure you you have no reasons to be jealous in that quarter as I have not been back to see her as I figure it is wasteing my time to play round with a dame like she that wants to go out somewheres every night and if you married her she would want a house on 5th ave. with a dozen servants so I have passed her up as that is not my idea of home.

What I want when I get married is a real home where a man can stay home and work and maybe have a few of his friends in once in a wile and entertain them or go to a good musical show once in a wile and have a wife that is in sympathy with you and not nag at you all the wile but be a real help mate. The girlie up on the Drive would run me ragged and have me in the poor house inside of a year even if I was makeing 25 grand out of one song. Besides she wears a make up that you would have to blast to find out what her face looks like. So I have not been back there and don't intend to see her again so what is the use of me telling you about her. And the only other girlie I have met is a sister of Paul Sears who I met up to his house wile we was working on the song but she don't hardly count as she has not got no use for the boys but treats them like dirt and Paul says she is the coldest proposition he ever seen.

Well I don't know no more to write and besides have got a date to go out to Paul's place for dinner and play some of my stuff for him so as he can see if he wants to set words to some more of my melodies. Well don't do nothing I would not do and have as good a time as you can in old Chi and will let you know how we come along with the song.

Chas. F. Lewis.

Chicago, Ill., Aug. 23.

Dear Mr. Man: I am thrilled to death over the song and think the words awfully pretty and am crazy to hear the music which I know must be great. It must be wonderful to have the gift of writing songs and then hear people play and sing them and just think of making $25,000 in such a short time. My, how rich you will be and I certainly congratulate you though am afraid when you are rich and famous you will have no time for insignificant little me or will you be an exception and remember your "old" friends even when you are up in the world? I sincerely hope so.

Will look forward to receiving a copy of the song and will you be sure to put your name on it? I am all ready very conceited just to think that I know a man that writes songs and makes all that money.

Seriously I wish you success with your next song and I laughed when I read your remark about being busier than a one armed paper hanger. I don't see how you think up all those comparisons and crazy things to say. The next time one of the girls asks me to go out with them I am going to tell them I can't go because I am busier than a one armed paper hanger and then they will think I made it up and say: "The girl is clever."

Seriously I am glad you did not go back to see the girl on the Drive and am also glad you don't like girls who makes themselves up so much as I think it is disgusting and would rather go round looking like a ghost than put artificial color on my face. Fortunately I have a complexion that does not need "fixing" but even if my coloring was not what it is I would never think of lowering myself to "fix" it. But I must tell you a joke that happened just the other day when Edith and I were out at lunch and there was another girl in the restaurant whom Edie knew and she introduced her to me and I noticed how this girl kept staring at me and finally she begged my pardon and asked if she could ask me a personal question and I said yes and she asked me if my complexion was really "mine." I assured her it was and she said: "Well, I thought so because I did not think anybody could put it on so artistically. I certainly envy you." Edie and I both laughed.

Well, if that girl envies me my complexion, why I envy you living in New York. Chicago is rather dirty though I don't let that part of it bother me as I bathe and change my clothing so often that the dirt does not have time to "settle." Edie often says she cannot see how I always keep so clean looking and says I always look like I had just stepped out of a band box. She also calls me a fish (jokingly) because I spend so much time in the water. But seriously I do love to bathe and never feel so happy as when I have just "cleaned up" and put on fresh clothing.

Edie has just gone out to see a picture and was cross at me because I would not go with her. I told her I was going to write a letter and she wanted to know to whom and I told her and she said: "You write to him so often that a person would almost think you was in love with him." I just laughed and turned it off, but she does say the most embarrassing things and I would be angry if it was anybody but she that said them.

Seriously I had much rather sit here and write letters or read or just sit and dream than go out to some crazy old picture show except once in awhile I do like to go to the theater and see a good play and a specially a musical play if the music is catchy. But as a rule I am contented to just stay home and feel cozy and lots of evenings Edie and I sit here without saying hardly a word to each other though she would love to talk but she knows I had rather be quiet and she often says it is just like living with a deaf and dumb mute to live with me because I make so little noise round the apartment. I guess I was born to be a home body as I so seldom care to go "gadding."

Though I do love to have company once in awhile, just a few congenial friends whom I can talk to and feel at home with and play cards or have some music. My friends love to drop in here, too, as they say Edie and I always give them such nice things to eat. Though poor Edie has not much to do with it, I am afraid, as she hates anything connected with cooking which is one of the things I love best of anything and I often say that when I begin keeping house in my own home I will insist on doing most of my own work as I would take so much more interest in it than a servant, though I would want somebody to help me a little if I could afford it as I often think a woman that does all her own work is liable to get so tired that she loses interest in the bigger things of life like books and music. Though after all what bigger thing is there than home making a specially for a woman?

I am sitting in the dearest old chair that I bought yesterday at a little store on the North Side. That is my one extravagance, buying furniture and things for the house, but I always say it is economy in the long run as I will always have them and have use for them and when I can pick them up at a bargain I would be silly not to. Though heaven knows I will never be "poor" in regards to furniture and rugs and things like that as mother's house in Toledo is full of lovely things which she says she is going to give to Sis and myself as soon as we have real homes of our own. She is going to give me the first choice as I am her favorite. She has the loveliest old things that you could not buy now for love or money including lovely old rugs and a piano which Sis wanted to have a player attachment put on it but I said it would be an insult to the piano so we did not get one. I am funny about things like that, a specially old furniture and feel towards them like people whom I love.

Poor mother, I am afraid she won't live much longer to enjoy her lovely old things as she has been suffering for years from stomach trouble and the doctor says it has been worse lately instead of better and her heart is weak besides. I am going home to see her a few days this fall as it may be the last time. She is very cheerful and always says she is ready to go now as she has had enough joy out of life and all she would like would be to see her girls settled down in their own homes before she goes.

There I go, talking about my domestic affairs again and I will bet you are bored to death though personly I am never bored when my friends tell me about themselves. But I won't "rattle on" any longer, but will say good night and don't forget to write and tell me how you come out with the song and thanks for sending me the words to it. Will you write a song about me some time? I would be thrilled to death! But I am afraid I am not the kind of girl that inspires men to write songs about them, but am just a quiet "mouse" that loves home and am not giddy enough to be the heroine of a song.

Well, Mr. Man, good night and don't wait so long before writing again to

Yours (?)
Mabelle.

N.Y., Sept. 8.

Dear Girlie: Well girlie have not got your last letter with me so cannot answer what was in it as I have forgotten if there was anything I was supposed to answer and besides have only a little time to write as I have a date to go out on a party with the Sears. We are going to the Georgie White show and afterwards somewheres for supper. Sears is the boy who wrote the lyric to my song and it is him and his sister I am going on the party with. The sister is a cold fish that has no use for men but she is show crazy and insists on Paul takeing her to 3 or 4 of them a week.

Paul wants me to give up my room here and come and live with them as they have plenty of room and I am running a little low on money but don't know if I will do it or not as am afraid I would freeze to death in the same house with a girl like the sister as she is ice cold but she don't hang round the house much as she is always takeing trips or going to shows or somewheres.

So far we have not had no luck with the song. All the publishers we have showed it to has went crazy over it but they won't make the right kind of a deal with us and if they don't loosen up and give us a decent royalty rate we are libel to put the song out ourselves and show them up. The man up to Goebel's told us the song was O. K. and he liked it but it was more of a production number than anything else and ought to go in a show like the Follies but they won't be in N.Y. much longer and what we ought to do is hold it till next spring.

Mean wile I am working on some new numbers and also have taken a position with the orchestra at the Wilton and am going to work there starting next week. They pay good money $60 and it will keep me going.

Well girlie that is about all the news. I believe you said your father was sick and hope he is better and also hope you are getting along O. K. and take care of yourself. When you have nothing else to do write to your friend,

Chas. F. Lewis.

Chicago, Ill., Sept. 11.

Dear Mr. Lewis: Your short note reached me yesterday and must say I was puzzled when I read it. It sounded like you was mad at me though I cannot think of any reason why you should be. If there was something I said in my last letter that offended you I wish you would tell me what it was and I will ask your pardon though I cannot remember anything I could of said that you could take offense at. But if there was something, why I assure you, Mr. Lewis, that I did not mean anything by it. I certainly did not intend to offend you in any way.

Perhaps it is nothing I wrote you, but you are worried on account of the publishers not treating you fair in regards to your song and that is why your letter sounded so distant. If that is the case I hope that by this time matters have rectified themselves and the future looks brighter. But any way, Mr. Lewis, don't allow yourself to worry over business cares as they will all come right in the end and I always think it is silly for people to worry themselves sick over temporary troubles, but the best way is to "keep smiling" and look for the "silver lining" in the cloud. That is the way I always do and no matter what happens, I manage to smile and my girl friend, Edie, calls me Sunny because I always look to the bright side.

Remember also, Mr. Lewis, that $60 is a salary that a great many men would like to be getting and are living on less than that and supporting a wife and family on it. I always say that a person can get along on whatever amount they make if they manage things in the right way.

So if it is business troubles, Mr. Lewis, I say don't worry, but look on the bright side. But if it is something I wrote in my last letter that offended you I wish you would tell me what it was so I can apologize as I assure you I meant nothing and would not say anything to hurt you for the world.

Please let me hear from you soon as I will not feel comfortable until I know I am not to blame for the sudden change.

Sincerely,
Mabelle Gillespie.

N.Y. Sept. 24.

Dear Miss Gillespie: Just a few lines to tell you the big news or at least it is big news to me. I am engaged to be married to Paul Sears' sister and we are going to be married early next month and live in Atlantic City where the orchestra I have been playing with has got an engagement in one of the big cabarets.

I know this will be a surprise to you as it was even a surprise to me as I did not think I would ever have the nerve to ask the girlie the big question as she was always so cold and acted like I was just in the way. But she said she supposed she would have to marry somebody some time and she did not dislike me as much as most of the other men her brother brought round and she would marry me with the understanding that she would not have to be a slave and work round the house and also I would have to take her to a show or somewheres every night and if I could not take her myself she would "run wild" alone. Atlantic City will be O. K. for that as a lot of new shows opens down there and she will be able to see them before they get to the big town. As for her being a slave, I would hate to think of marrying a girl and then have them spend their lives in druggery round the house. We are going to live in a hotel till we find something better but will be in no hurry to start house keeping as we will have to buy all new furniture.

Betsy is some doll when she is all fixed up and believe me she knows how to fix herself up. I don't know what she uses but it is weather proof and I have been out in a rain storm with her and we both got drowned but her face stayed on. I would almost think it was real only she tells me different.

Well girlie I may write to you again once in a wile as Betsy says she don't give a damn if I write to all the girls in the world just so I don't make her read the answers but that is all I can think of to say now except good bye and good luck and may the right man come along soon and he will be a lucky man getting a girl that is such a good cook and got all that furniture etc.

But just let me give you a word of advice before I close and that is don't never speak to strange men who you don't know nothing about as they may get you wrong and think you are trying to make them. It just happened that I knew better so you was lucky in my case but the luck might not last.

> Your friend,
> Chas. F. Lewis.

Chicago, Ill., Sept. 27.

My Dear Mr. Lewis: Thanks for your advice and also thank your fiance for her generosity in allowing you to continue your correspondence with her "rivals," but personly I have no desire to take advantage of that generosity as I have something better to do than read letters from a man like you, a specially as I have a man friend who is not so generous as Miss Sears and would strongly object to my continuing a correspondence with another man. It is at his request that I am writing this note to tell you not to expect to hear from me again.

Allow me to congratulate you on your engagement to Miss Sears and I am sure she is to be congratulated too, though if I met the lady I would be tempted to ask her to tell me her secret, namely how she is going to "run wild" on $60.

Sincerely,
Mabelle Gillespie.

1925

H. L. Mencken   *1880 – 1956*

Most boisterous and robust of the iconoclasts of the 1920's, Henry Louis Mencken was born in 1880 in Baltimore, Maryland, where he continued to maintain his home even after his successful invasion of New York City. After graduating from the Baltimore Polytechnic Institute at the age of sixteen, he decided to become a journalist rather than go to college. In 1906, he obtained a position on the Baltimore *Sun*, establishing a relationship he maintained for many years. In 1908, he became a commuting literary critic of *The Smart Set*, a publication on which George Jean Nathan, the drama critic, became his editorial associate. In 1924 the two men established *The American Mercury*, which Mencken continued to edit until 1934. The magazine was devoted for the most part to a raucous exposé of the "gaudy, gorgeous American scene." The chief targets of Mencken and his cohorts were the complacent stupidity of the American "booboisie"; the tradition of blue-nose Puritanism and its offspring Prohibition; democracy; aestheticism; intellectual pretentiousness, especially among the "professors"; and organized religion. One of the best examples of Mencken's satiric technique is his devastating attack on the late William Jennings Bryan. In "In Memoriam: W. J. B.," Mencken's merciless ridicule is directed against Bryan not as a politician but as a champion of the anti-intellectual, fundamentalist religiosity that Mencken despised. His favorite verbal weapon was not a rapier but a warclub with which he laid about lustily in his attacks on the vices and foibles of his time. Although his humor now seems somewhat heavy and much of his slang is dated, Mencken did a great deal to ventilate the genteel Victorian establishment and create a freer atmosphere for the American writer.

Of Mencken's many books, the most influential in his time were the collections of *Prejudices*, made up of his magazine and newspaper pieces and issued in six "Series" (1919 – 27). He also wrote books on Shaw (1905) and on Nietzsche (1908), whose philosophy he admired. His most ambitious and scholarly work, on a subject he loved, is *The American Language* (1919; revised and supplemented, 1921–45). *Happy Days, 1880–1892* (1940), *Newspaper Days, 1899–1906* (1941), and *Heathen Days, 1890–1936* (1943) are collections of entertaining autobiographical sketches.

A Mencken Chrestomathy (New York, 1949) is the best representative collection of his work. Book-length studies of Mencken and his work are Edgar Kemler, *The Irreverent Mr. Mencken* (Boston, 1950), and William Manchester, *Disturber of the Peace* (New York, 1951).

The text of the selections given here is that of *A Mencken Chrestomathy* (New York, 1949).

American Culture [1]

The capital defect in the culture of These States is the lack of a civilized aristocracy, secure in its position, animated by an intelligent curiosity, skeptical of all facile generalizations, superior to the sentimentality of the mob, and delighting in the battle of ideas for its own sake. The word I use, despite the qualifying adjective, has got itself meanings, of course, that I by no means intend to convey. Any mention of an aristocracy, to a public fed upon democratic fustian, is bound to bring up images of stockbrokers' wives lolling obscenely in opera boxes, or of haughty Englishmen slaughtering whole generations of grouse in an inordinate and incomprehensible manner, or of bogus counts coming over to work their magic upon the daughters of breakfast-food and bathtub kings. This misconception belongs to the general American tradition. Its depth and extent are constantly revealed by the naïve assumption that the so-called fashionable folk of the large cities —chiefly wealthy industrials in the interior-decorator and country-club stage of culture—constitute an aristocracy, and by the scarcely less remarkable assumption that the peerage of England is identical with the gentry—that is, that such men as Lord Northcliffe, Lord Riddel and even Lord Reading were English gentlemen.

Here, as always, the worshiper is the father of the gods, and no less when they are evil than when they are benign. The inferior man must find himself superiors, that he may marvel at his political equality with them, and in the absence of recognizable superiors *de facto* he creates superiors *de jure*.[2] The sublime principle of one man, one vote must be translated into terms of dollars, diamonds, fashionable intelligence; the equality of all men before the law must have clear and dramatic proofs. Sometimes, perhaps, the thing goes further and is more subtle. The inferior man needs an aristocracy to demonstrate, not only his mere equality, but also his actual superiority. The society columns in the newspapers may have some such origin. They may visualize once

---

[1] First printed in the *Yale Review*, June, 1920, pp. 804–17 (H.L.M.).
[2] "In fact" . . . "in accordance with law."

more the accomplished journalist's understanding of the mob mind that he plays upon so skillfully, as upon some immense and cacophonous organ, always going *fortissimo*. What the inferior man and his wife see in the sinister revels of those brummagem first families, I suspect, is often a massive witness to their own higher rectitude — in brief, to their firmer grasp upon the immutable axioms of Christian virtue, the one sound boast of the nether nine-tenths of humanity in every land under the cross.

But this bugaboo aristocracy is actually bogus, and the evidence of its bogusness lies in the fact that it is insecure. One gets into it only onerously, but out of it very easily. Entrance is effected by dint of a long and bitter struggle, and the chief incidents of that struggle are almost intolerable humiliations. The aspirant must school and steel himself to sniffs and sneers; he must see the door slammed upon him a hundred times before ever it is thrown open to him. To get in at all he must show a talent for abasement — and abasement makes him timorous. Worse, that timorousness is not cured when he succeeds at last. On the contrary, it is made even more tremulous, for what he faces within the gates is a scheme of things made up almost wholly of harsh and often unintelligible taboos, and the penalty for violating even the least of them is swift and disastrous. He must exhibit exactly the right social habits, appetites and prejudices, public and private. He must harbor exactly the right enthusiasms and indignations. He must have a hearty taste for exactly the right sports and games. His attitude toward the fine arts must be properly tolerant and yet not a shade too eager. He must read and like exactly the right books, pamphlets and public journals. He must put up at the right hotels when he travels. His wife must patronize the right milliners. He himself must stick to the right haberdashery. He must live in the right neighborhood. He must even embrace the right doctrines of religion. It would ruin him, for all society column purposes, to move to Union Hill, N. J., or to drink coffee from his saucer, or to marry a chambermaid with a gold tooth, or to join the Seventh Day Adventists. Within the boundaries of his curious order he is worse fettered than a monk in a cell. Its obscure conception of propriety, its nebulous notion that this or that is honorable, hampers him in every direction, and very narrowly. What he resigns when he enters, even when he makes his first deprecating knock at the door, is every right to attack the ideas that happen to prevail within. Such as they are, he must accept them without question. And as they shift and change he must shift and change with them, silently and quickly.

Obviously, that order cannot constitute a genuine aristocracy, in any rational sense. A genuine aristocracy is grounded upon very much different principles. Its first and most salient character is its interior security, and the chief visible evidence of that security is the freedom that goes with it — not only freedom in act, the divine right of the aristocrat to do what he damn well pleases, so long as he does not violate the primary guarantees and obligations of his class, but also and more importantly freedom in thought, the liberty to try and err, the right to be his own man. It is the instinct of a true aristocracy, not to punish eccentricity by expulsion, but to throw a mantle of protection about it — to safeguard it from the suspicions and resentments of the lower orders. Those lower orders are inert, timid, inhospitable to ideas, hostile to changes, faithful to a few maudlin superstitions. All progress goes on on the higher levels. It is there that salient personalities, made secure by artificial immunities, may oscillate most widely from the normal track. It is within that entrenched fold, out of reach of the immemorial certainties of the mob, that extraordinary men of the lower orders may find their city of refuge, and breathe a clear air. This, in-deed, is at once the hall-mark and the justification of a genuine aristoc-racy — that it is beyond responsibility to the general masses of men, and hence superior to both their degraded longings and their no less de-graded aversions. It is nothing if it is not autonomous, curious, venture-some, courageous, and everything if it is. It is the custodian of the qualities that make for change and experiment; it is the class that organizes danger to the service of the race; it pays for its high preroga-tives by standing in the forefront of the fray.

No such aristocracy, it must be plain, is now on view in the United States. The makings of one were visible in the Virginia of the Eighteenth Century, but with Jefferson and Washington the promise died. In New England, it seems to me, there was never anything of the sort, either in being or in nascency: there was only a theocracy that degenerated very quickly into a plutocracy on the one hand and a caste of sterile pedants on the other — the passion for God splitting into a lust for dollars and a weakness for mere words. Despite the common notion to the contrary — a notion generated by confusing literacy with intelli-gence — the New England of the great days never showed any genuine enthusiasm for ideas. It began its history as a slaughter-house of ideas, and it is today not easily distinguishable from a cold-storage plant. Its celebrated adventures in mysticism, once apparently so bold and sig-nificant, are now seen to have been little more than an elaborate hocus-pocus — respectable Unitarians shocking the peasantry and scaring the horned cattle in the fields by masquerading in the robes of Rosicru-cians. The notions that it embraced in those austere and far-off days were stale, and when it had finished with them they were dead. So in politics. Since the Civil War it has produced fewer political ideas, as political ideas run in the Republic, than any average county in Kansas or Nebraska. Appomattox seemed to be a victory for New England idealism. It was actually a victory for the New England plutocracy, and that plutocracy has dominated thought above the Housatonic ever since. The sect of professional idealists has so far dwindled that it has ceased to be of any importance, even as an opposition. When the plutocracy is challenged now, it is challenged by the proletariat.

Well, what is on view in New England is on view in all other parts of the nation, sometimes with ameliorations, but usually with the colors merely exaggerated. What one beholds, sweeping the eye over the land, is a culture that, like the national literature, is in three layers—the plutocracy on top, a vast mass of undifferentiated human blanks bossed by demagogues at the bottom, and a forlorn *intelligentsia* gasping out a precarious life between. I need not set out at any length, I hope, the intellectual deficiencies of the plutocracy—its utter failure to show anything even remotely resembling the makings of an aristocracy. It is badly educated, it is stupid, it is full of low-caste superstitions and indignations, it is without decent traditions or informing vision; above all, it is extraordinarily lacking in the most elemental independence and courage. Out of this class comes the grotesque fashionable society of our big towns, already described. It shows all the stigmata of inferiority—moral certainty, cruelty, suspicion of ideas, fear. Never does it function more revealingly than in the recurrent *pogroms* against radicalism, *i.e.*, against humorless persons who, like Andrew Jackson, take the platitudes of democracy seriously. And what is the theory at the bottom of all these proceedings? So far as it can be reduced to comprehensible terms it is much less a theory than a fear—a shivering, idiotic, discreditable fear of a mere banshee—an overpowering, paralyzing dread that some extra-eloquent Red, permitted to emit his balderdash unwhipped, may eventually convert a couple of courageous men, and that the courageous men, filled with indignation against the plutocracy, may take to the highroad, burn down a nail-factory or two, and slit the throat of some virtuous profiteer.

Obviously, it is out of reason to look for any hospitality to ideas in a class so extravagantly fearful of even the most palpably absurd of them. Its philosophy is firmly grounded upon the thesis that the existing order must stand forever free from attack, and not only from attack, but also from mere academic criticism, and its ethics are as firmly grounded upon the thesis that every attempt at any such criticism is a proof of moral turpitude. Within its own ranks, protected by what may be regarded as the privilege of the order, there is nothing to take the place of this criticism. In other countries the plutocracy has often produced men of reflective and analytical habit, eager to rationalize its instincts and to bring it into some sort of relationship to the main streams of human thought. The case of David Ricardo at once comes to mind, and there have been many others: John Bright, Richard Cobden, George Grote.[3] But in the United States no such phenomenon has been visible.

---

[3] David Ricardo (1772–1823), the English economist, son of a Dutch Jew, made his fortune in the London stock exchange. John Bright (1811–1889) and Richard Cobden (1804–1865) were leading representatives of the manufacturing class in British politics. George Grote (1794–1871) was an English banker, politician, and classical historian.

Nor has the plutocracy ever fostered an inquiring spirit among its intellectual valets and footmen, which is to say, among the gentlemen who compose headlines and leading articles for its newspapers. What chiefly distinguishes the daily press of the United States from the press of all other countries pretending to culture is not its lack of truthfulness or even its lack of dignity and honor, for these deficiencies are common to newspapers everywhere, but its incurable fear of ideas, its constant effort to evade the discussion of fundamentals by translating all issues into a few elemental fears, its incessant reduction of all reflection to mere emotion. It is, in the true sense, never well-informed. It is seldom intelligent, save in the arts of the mob-master. It is never courageously honest. Held harshly to a rigid correctness of opinion, it sinks rapidly into formalism and feebleness. Its yellow section is perhaps its best section, for there the only vestige of the old free journalist survives. In the more respectable papers one finds only a timid and petulant animosity to all questioning of the existing order, however urbane and sincere—a pervasive and ill-concealed dread that the mob now heated up against the orthodox hobgoblins may suddenly begin to unearth hobgoblins of its own, and so run amok.

For it is upon the emotions of the mob, of course, that the whole comedy is played. Theoretically, the mob is the repository of all political wisdom and virtue; actually, it is the ultimate source of all political power. Even the plutocracy cannot make war upon it openly, or forget the least of its weaknesses. The business of keeping it in order must be done discreetly, warily, with delicate technique. In the main that business consists in keeping alive its deep-seated fears—of strange faces, of unfamiliar ideas, of unhackneyed gestures, of untested liberties and responsibilities. The one permanent emotion of the inferior man, as of all the simpler mammals, is fear—fear of the unknown, the complex, the inexplicable. What he wants beyond everything else is security. His instincts incline him toward a society so organized that it will protect him at all hazards, and not only against perils to his hide but also against assaults upon his mind—against the need to grapple with unaccustomed problems, to weigh ideas, to think things out for himself, to scrutinize the platitudes upon which his everyday thinking is based.

1920

Ring Lardner [1]

A few years ago a young college professor, eager to make a name for himself, brought out a laborious "critical" edition of "Sam Slick," by Judge Thomas C. Haliburton, eighty-seven years after its first publication. It turned out to be quite unreadable—a dreadful series of archaic jocosities about varieties of *Homo americanus* long perished and forgotten, in a dialect now intelligible only to paleophilologists.

[1] First printed in the *American Mercury*, July, 1924, pp. 376–77 (H.L.M.).

Sometimes I have a fear that the same fate awaits Ring Lardner. The professors of his own days, of course, were quite unaware of him, save perhaps as a low zany to be enjoyed behind the door. They would no more have ventured to whoop him up publicly and officially than their predecessors of 1880 would have ventured to whoop up Mark Twain, or their remoter predecessors of 1837 would have dared to say anything for Haliburton. In such matters the academic mind, being chiefly animated by a fear of sneers, works very slowly. So slowly, indeed, does it work that it usually works too late. By the time Mark Twain got into the text-books for sophomores two-thirds of his compositions had already begun to date; by the time Haliburton was served up as a sandwich between introduction and notes he was long dead. As I say, I suspect sadly that Lardner is doomed to go the same route. His stories, it seems to me, are superbly adroit and amusing; no other American of his generation, sober or gay, wrote better. But I doubt that they last: our grandchildren will wonder what they are about. It is not only, or even mainly, that the dialect that fills them will pass, though that fact is obviously a serious handicap in itself. It is principally that the people they depict will pass, that Lardner's incomparable baseball players, pugs, song-writers, Elks, small-town Rotarians, and golf caddies were flittering figures of a transient civilization, and are doomed to be as puzzling and soporific, in the year 2000, as Haliburton's Yankee clock peddler is today.

The fact — if I may assume it to be a fact — is certain not to be set against Lardner's account; on the contrary, it is, in its way, highly complimentary to him. For he deliberately applied himself, not to the anatomizing of the general human soul, but to the meticulous histological study of a few salient individuals of his time and nation, and he did it with such subtle and penetrating skills that one must belong to his time and nation to follow him. I doubt that anyone who is not familiar with professional ball players, intimately and at first hand, will ever comprehend the full merit of the amazing sketches in "You Know Me, Al";[2] I doubt that anyone who has not given close and deliberate attention to the American vulgate will ever realize how magnificently Lardner handled it. He had more imitators, I suppose, than any other American writer of the first third of the century, but had he any actual rivals? If so, I have yet to hear of them. They all tried to write the speech of the streets as adeptly and as amusingly as he wrote it, and they all fell short of him; the next best was miles and miles behind him. And they were all inferior in observation, in sense of character, in shrewdness and insight. His studies, to be sure, are never very profound; he made no attempt to get at the primary springs of human motive; all his people share the same amiable stupidity, the same

[2] *You Know Me, Al; A Busher's Letters* (1916).

transparent vanity, the same shallow swinishness; they are all human Fords in bad repair, and alike at bottom. But if he thus confined himself to the surface, it yet remains a fact that his investigations on that surface were extraordinarily alert, ingenious and brilliant — that the character he finally set before us, however roughly articulated as to bones, was so astoundingly realistic as to epidermis that the effect is indistinguishable from that of life itself. The old man in "The Golden Honeymoon" is not merely well done: he is perfect. And so is the girl in "Some Like Them Cold."[3] And so, even, is the idiotic Frank X. Farrell in "Alibi Ike" — an extravagant grotesque and yet quite real from glabella to calcaneus.

Lardner knew more about the management of the short story than all of its professors. His stories are built very carefully, and yet they seem to be wholly spontaneous, and even formless. He grasped the primary fact that no conceivable ingenuity can save a story that fails to show a recognizable and interesting character; he knew that a good character sketch is always a good story, no matter what its structure. Perhaps he got less attention than he ought to have got, even among the anti-academic critics, because his people were all lowly boors. For your reviewer of books, like every other sort of American, is always vastly impressed by fashionable pretensions. He belongs to the white collar class of labor, and shares its prejudices. He can't rid himself of the feeling that Edith Wharton, whose people have butlers, was a better novelist than Willa Cather, whose people, in the main, dine in their kitchens. He lingers under the spell of Henry James, whose most humble character, at any rate of the later years, was at least an Englishman, and hence superior. Lardner, so to speak, hit such critics under the belt. He not only filled his stories with people who read the tabloids, said "Shake hands with my friend," and bought diamond rings on the installment plan; he also showed them having a good time in the world, and quite devoid of inferiority complexes. They amused him sardonically, but he did not pity them. A fatal error! The moron, perhaps, has a place in fiction, as in life, but he is not to be treated too easily and casually. It must be shown that he suffers tragically because he cannot abandon the plow to write poetry, or the sample-case to study for opera. Lardner was more realistic. If his typical hero has a secret sorrow it is that he is too old to take up osteopathy and too much in dread of his wife to venture into bookmaking.

In his later years a sharply acrid flavor got into Lardner's buffoonery. His baseball players and fifth-rate pugilists, beginning in his first stories as harmless jackasses, gradually converted themselves into loathsome scoundrels. Turn, for example, to the sketches in the volume called "The Love Nest." The first tells the story of a cinema queen

[3] See above.

married to a magnate of the films. On the surface she seems to be
nothing but a noodle, but underneath there is a sewer; the woman is
such a pig that she makes one shudder. Again, he investigated another
familiar type: the village practical joker. The fellow, in one form or
other, has been laughed at since the days of Aristophanes. But here is a
mercilessly realistic examination of his dunghill humor, and of its
effects upon decent people. A third figure is a successful theatrical
manager: he turns out to have the professional competence of a phre-
nologist and the honor of a highjacker. A fourth is a writer of popular
songs: stealing other men's ideas has become so fixed a habit with him
that he comes to believe that he has an actual right to them. A fourth is
a trained nurse — but I spare you this dreadful nurse. The rest are bores
of the homicidal type. One gets the effect, communing with the whole
gang, of visiting a museum of anatomy. They are as shocking as what
one encounters there — but in every detail they are unmistakably real.

Lardner concealed his new savagery, of course, beneath his old
humor. It did not flag. No man writing among us had greater skill at the
more extravagant varieties of jocosity. He saw startling and revelatory
likeness between immensely disparate things, and he was full of pawky
observations and bizarre comments. Two baseball players are palaver-
ing, and one of them, Young Jake, is boasting of his conquests during
Spring practise below the Potomac. "Down South ain't here!" replies
the other. "Those dames in some of those swamps, they lose their head
when they see a man with shoes on!" The two proceed to the discussion of a third imbecile, guilty of some obscure tort. "Why," inquires
Young Jake, "didn't you break his nose or bust him in the chin?" "His
nose was already broke," replied the other, "and he didn't have no
chin." Such wise cracks seem easy to devise. Broadway diverts itself
by manufacturing them. They constitute the substance of half the town
shows. But in those made by Lardner there is something far more than
mere facile humor: they are all rigidly in character, and they illuminate
that character. Few American novelists, great or small, have had
character more firmly in hand. Lardner did not see situations; he saw
people. And what people! They are all as revolting as so many Methodist bishops, and they are all as thoroughly American.

1926

In Memoriam: W. J. B.

*From Prejudices: Fifth Series, 1926, pp. 64–74. In its first
form this was printed in the Baltimore* Evening Sun, *July 27,
1925, the day after Bryan's death at Dayton, Tenn. I reworked it
for the* American Mercury, *Oct., 1925, pp. 158–60. My adventures as a newspaper correspondent at the Scopes trial are told in
my Newspaper Days; New York, 1943, pp. 214–38.*

Has it been duly marked by historians that William Jennings Bryan's last secular act on this globe of sin was to catch flies? A curious detail, and not without its sardonic overtones. He was the most sedulous fly-catcher in American history, and in many ways the most successful. His quarry, of course, was not *Musca domestica* but *Homo neandertalensis*.[1] For forty years he tracked it with coo and bellow, up and down the rustic backways of the Republic. Wherever the flambeaux of Chautauqua smoked and guttered, and the bilge of idealism ran in the veins, and Baptist pastors dammed the brooks with the sanctified, and men gathered who were weary and heavy laden, and their wives who were full of Peruna and as fecund as the shad (*Alosa sapidissima*), there the indefatigable Jennings set up his traps and spread his bait. He knew every country town in the South and West, and he could crowd the most remote of them to suffocation by simply winding his horn. The city proletariat, transiently flustered by him in 1896, quickly penetrated his buncombe and would have no more of him; the cockney gallery jeered him at every Democratic national convention for twenty-five years. But out where the grass grows high, and the horned cattle dream away the lazy afternoons, and men still fear the powers and principalities of the air—out there between the corn-rows he held his old puissance to the end. There was no need of beaters to drive in his game. The news that he was coming was enough. For miles the flivver dust would choke the roads. And when he rose at the end of the day to discharge his Message there would be such breathless attention, such a rapt and enchanted ecstasy, such a sweet rustle of amens as the world had not known since Johann fell to Herod's ax.[2]

There was something peculiarly fitting in the fact that his last days were spent in a one-horse Tennessee village, beating off the flies and gnats, and that death found him there. The man felt at home in such simple and Christian scenes. He liked people who sweated freely, and were not debauched by the refinements of the toilet. Making his progress up and down the Main street of little Dayton, surrounded by gaping primates from the upland valleys of the Cumberland Range, his coat laid aside, his bare arms and hairy chest shining damply, his bald head sprinkled with dust—so accoutred and on display, he was obviously happy. He liked getting up early in the morning, to the tune of cocks crowing on the dunghill. He liked the heavy, greasy victuals of the farmhouse kitchen. He liked country lawyers, country pastors, all country people. He liked country sounds and country smells.

I believe that this liking was sincere—perhaps the only sincere thing in the man. His nose showed no uneasiness when a hillman in faded overalls and hickory shirt accosted him on the street, and be-

---

[1] "Not the domestic fly but Neanderthal man."
[2] A reference to the story of John the Baptist; see *Matthew* xiv: 2–12.

sought him for light upon some mystery of Holy Writ. The simian gabble of the cross-roads was not gabble to him, but wisdom of an occult and superior sort. In the presence of city folks he was palpably uneasy. Their clothes, I suspect, annoyed him, and he was suspicious of their too delicate manners. He knew all the while that they were laughing at him — if not at his baroque theology, then at least at his alpaca pantaloons. But the yokels never laughed at him. To them he was not the huntsman but the prophet, and toward the end, as he gradually forsook mundane politics for more ghostly concerns, they began to elevate him in their hierarchy. When he died he was the peer of Abraham. His old enemy, Wilson,[3] aspiring to the same white and shining robe, came down with a thump. But Bryan made the grade. His place in Tennessee hagiography is secure. If the village barber saved any of his hair, then it is curing gall-stones down there today.

But what label will he bear in more urbane regions? One, I fear, of a far less flattering kind. Bryan lived too long, and descended too deeply into the mud, to be taken seriously hereafter by fully literate men, even of the kind who write schoolbooks. There was a scattering of sweet words in his funeral notices, but it was no more than a response to conventional sentimentality. The best verdict the most romantic editorial writer could dredge up, save in the humorless South, was to the general effect that his imbecilities were excused by his earnestness — that under his clowning, as under that of the juggler of Notre Dame, there was the zeal of a steadfast soul. But this was apology, not praise; precisely the same thing might be said of Mary Baker G. Eddy.[4] The truth is that even Bryan's sincerity will probably yield to what is called, in other fields, definitive criticism. Was he sincere when he opposed imperialism in the Philippines, or when he fed it with deserving Democrats in Santo Domingo? Was he sincere when he tried to shove the Prohibitionists under the table, or when he seized their banner and began to lead them with loud whoops? Was he sincere when he bellowed against war, or when he dreamed of himself as a tin-soldier in uniform, with a grave reserved at Arlington among the generals? Was he sincere when he fawned over Champ Clark, or when he betrayed Clark?[5] Was he sincere when he pleaded for tolerance in New York, or when he bawled for the faggot and the stake in Tennessee?

This talk of sincerity, I confess, fatigues me. If the fellow was sincere, then so was P. T. Barnum.[6] The word is disgraced and degraded by such uses. He was, in fact, a charlatan, a mountebank, a zany without sense or dignity. His career brought him into contact with the

---

[3] Woodrow Wilson (1856–1924); the reference is to Wilson's failure to gain grass-roots support for his effort to win approval for the Covenant of the League of Nations.
[4] Mary Baker Eddy (1821–1910), founder of the Christian Science Church.
[5] Champ Clark (1850–1921), member of the House of Representatives.
[6] Phineas Taylor Barnum (1810–1891), the great American showman.

first men of his time; he preferred the company of rustic ignoramuses. It was hard to believe, watching him at Dayton, that he had traveled, that he had been received in civilized societies, that he had been a high officer of state. He seemed only a poor clod like those around him, deluded by a childish theology, full of an almost pathological hatred of all learning, all human dignity, all beauty, all fine and noble things. He was a peasant come home to the barnyard. Imagine a gentleman, and you have imagined everything that he was not. What animated him from end to end of his grotesque career was simply ambition — the ambition of a common man to get his hand upon the collar of his superiors, or, failing that, to get his thumb into their eyes. He was born with a roaring voice, and it had the trick of inflaming half-wits. His whole career was devoted to raising those half-wits against their betters, that he himself might shine.

His last battle will be grossly misunderstood if it is thought of as a mere exercise in fanaticism — that is, if Bryan the Fundamentalist Pope is mistaken for one of the bucolic Fundamentalists. There was much more in it than that, as everyone knows who saw him on the field. What moved him, at bottom, was simply hatred of the city men who had laughed at him so long, and brought him at last to so tatterdemalion an estate. He lusted for revenge upon them. He yearned to lead the anthropoid rabble against them, to punish them for their execution upon him by attacking the very vitals of their civilization. He went far beyond the bounds of any merely religious frenzy, however inordinate. When he began denouncing the notion that man is a mammal even some of the hinds at Dayton were agape. And when, brought upon Clarence Darrow's cruel hook,[7] he writhed and tossed in a very fury of malignancy, bawling against the veriest elements of sense and decency like a man frantic — when he came to that tragic climax of his striving there were snickers among the hinds as well as hosannas.

Upon that hook, in truth, Bryan committed suicide, as a legend as well as in the body. He staggered from the rustic court ready to die, and he staggered from it ready to be forgotten, save as a character in a third-rate farce, witless and in poor taste. It was plain to everyone who knew him, when he came to Dayton, that his great days were behind him — that, for all the fury of his hatred, he was now definitely an old man, and headed at last for silence. There was a vague, unpleasant manginess about his appearance; he somehow seemed dirty, though a close glance showed him as carefully shaven as an actor, and clad in immaculate linen. All the hair was gone from the dome of his head, and it had begun to fall out, too, behind his ears, in the obscene manner of Samuel Gompers.[8] The resonance had departed from his voice; what

[7] Clarence S. Darrow (1857–1938), who defended J. T. Scopes for teaching evolution, made Bryan look ridiculous even though Bryan won the case for the prosecution.
[8] Samuel Gompers (1850–1924), founder of the American Federation of Labor.

was once a bugle blast had become reedy and quavering. Who knows that, like Demosthenes,[9] he had a lisp? In the old days, under the magic of his eloquence, no one noticed it. But when he spoke at Dayton it was always audible.

When I first encountered him, on the sidewalk in front of the office of the rustic lawyers who were his associates in the Scopes case, the trial was yet to begin, and so he was still expansive and amiable. I had printed in the *Nation*, a week or so before, an article arguing that the Tennessee anti-evolution law, whatever its wisdom, was at least constitutional—that the yahoos of the State had a clear right to have their progeny taught whatever they chose, and kept secure from whatever knowledge violated their superstitions. The old boy professed to be delighted with the argument, and gave the gaping bystanders to understand that I was a publicist of parts. Not to be outdone, I admired the preposterous country shirt that he wore—sleeveless and with the neck cut very low. We parted in the manner of two ambassadors.

But that was the last touch of amiability that I was destined to see in Bryan. The next day the battle joined and his face became hard. By the end of the week he was simply a walking fever. Hour by hour he grew more bitter. What the Christian Scientists call malicious animal magnetism seemed to radiate from him like heat from a stove. From my place in the courtroom, standing upon a table, I looked directly down upon him, sweating horribly and pumping his palm-leaf fan. His eyes fascinated me; I watched them all day long. They were blazing points of hatred. They glittered like occult and sinister gems. Now and then they wandered to me, and I got my share, for my reports of the trial had come back to Dayton, and he had read them. It was like coming under fire.

Thus he fought his last fight, thirsting savagely for blood. All sense departed from him. He bit right and left, like a dog with rabies. He descended to demagogy so dreadful that his very associates at the trial table blushed. His one yearning was to keep his yokels heated up—to lead his forlorn mob of imbeciles against the foe. That foe, alas, refused to be alarmed. It insisted upon seeing the whole battle as a comedy. Even Darrow, who knew better, occasionally yielded to the prevailing spirit. One day he lured poor Bryan into the folly I have mentioned: his astounding argument against the notion that man is a mammal. I am glad I heard it, for otherwise I'd never believe it. There stood the man who had been thrice a candidate for the Presidency of the Republic—there he stood in the glare of the world, uttering stuff that a boy of eight would laugh at. The artful Darrow led him on: he repeated it, ranted for it, bellowed it in his cracked voice. So he was prepared for the final slaughter. He came into life a hero, a Galahad, in bright and shining armor. He was passing out a poor mountebank.

1926

[9] The famous Athenian orator (ca 385–322 B.C.).

Langston Hughes   *1902–1967*

A man of great compassion, humor, and vitality, Langston Hughes wrote prolifically, in verse and prose, about the experience of being a black man in America. Born James Langston Hughes in Joplin, Missouri, he grew up in Lawrence, Kansas, Lincoln, Illinois, and Cleveland, Ohio, where he was named poet of his Central High School graduating class. After a year at Columbia University, which he found dull, he signed aboard a freighter to see the world. In Africa, which he found interesting, he felt discriminated against because of the lightness of his skin—the result of an admixture of Cherokee Indian blood. In Paris, where he stayed for a year, he earned his living by washing dishes. After returning to the States, he was working as a busboy in a Washington hotel when Vachel Lindsay saw some of his poems, including "Weary Blues," and presented them in his public readings. At Lindsay's advice, Hughes went on to complete his formal education at Lincoln University, from which he graduated in 1929.

Hughes's first book of poems, *Weary Blues* (1926), in which his stripped, laconic lines echo the rhythms of jazz and idiomatic speech, was followed by others including *Fine Clothes to the Jew* (1927), *Dear Lovely Death* (1931), *The Negro Mother* (1931), *Scottsboro Limited* (1932), *The Dream Keeper* (1932), *A New Song* (1938), *Shakespeare in Harlem* (1942), *Freedom's Plow* (1943), *Fields of Wonder* (1947), *One-Way Ticket* (1949), *Montage of a Dream Deferred* (1951), *Selected Poems* (1959), *Ask Your Mama* (1961), and *The Panther and the Lash* (1967).

In his prose, the character Jesse B. Semple, nicknamed Simple, is Hughes's memorable contribution to the literature of race relations. Although Simple speaks wryly and humorously, he is not a clown. The injustices he protests are serious, and the author's satiric thrusts are telling, even though his treatment has been considered too "cool" by recent, more militant critics. Hughes defended his approach, arguing that humor is a weapon of "no mean value against one's foes," and adding that if it had not been for the saving grace of humor the Negro race would have gone under long ago. He entitled one of his later collections of stories *Laughing to Keep from Crying* (1952). Langston Hughes had grace. His Simple sketches have been collected in *Simple Speaks His Mind* (1950), *Simple Takes a Wife* (1953), *The Best of Simple* (1957), and *Simple Stakes a Claim* (1957). Among other volumes of prose are *Not Without Laughter* (1930), a novel, and *The Ways of White Folks* (1934). *The Big Sea* (1940) and *I Wonder as I Wander* (1956) are lively and interesting autobiographies. In his last years Hughes edited *New Negro Poets, U.S.A.* (1964) and wrote *Fight for Freedom* (1962), a book about the National Association for the Advancement of Colored People.

A recent book-length study of Hughes's life and work is James Emanuel, *Langston Hughes* (New York, 1967), which contains a bibliography.

The text of the prose selections is that of *The Best of Simple* (New York, 1957); the poems are from *Selected Poems of Langston Hughes* (New York, 1959).

Simple Prays a Prayer

It was a hot night. Simple was sitting on his landlady's stoop reading a newspaper by streetlight. When he saw me coming, he threw the paper down.

"Good evening," I said.

"Good evening nothing," he answered. "It's too hot to be any good evening. Besides, this paper's full of nothing but atom bombs and bad news, wars and rumors of wars, airplane crashes, murders, fightings, wife-whippings, and killings from the Balkans to Brooklyn. Do you know one thing? If I was a praying man, I would pray a prayer for this world right now."

"What kind of prayer would you pray, friend?"

"I would pray a don't-want-to-have-no-more-wars prayer, and it would go like this: 'Lord,' I would say, I would ask Him, 'Lord, kindly please, take the blood off my hands and off of my brothers' hands, and make us shake hands *clean* and not be afraid. Neither let me nor them have no knives behind our backs, Lord, nor up our sleeves, nor no bombs piled out yonder in a desert. Let's forget about bygones. Too many mens and womens are dead. The fault is mine and theirs, too. So teach us *all* to do right, Lord, *please*, and to get along together with that atom bomb on this earth—because I do not want it to fall on me—nor Thee—nor anybody living. Amen!'"

"I didn't know you could pray like that," I said.

"It ain't much," said Simple, "but that girl friend of mine, Joyce, drug me to church last Sunday where the man was preaching and praying about peace, so I don't see why I shouldn't make myself up a prayer, too. I figure God will listen to me as well as the next one."

"You certainly don't have to be a minister to pray," I said, "and you have composed a good prayer. But now it's up to you to help God bring it into being, since God is created in your image."

"I thought it was the other way around," said Simple.

"However that may be," I said, "according to the Bible, God can bring things about on this earth only through man. You are a man, so you must help God make a good world."

"I am willing to help Him," said Simple, "but I do not know much what to do. The folks who run this world are going to run it in the ground in spite of all, throwing people out of work and then saying, 'Peace, it's wonderful!' Peace ain't wonderful when folks ain't got no job."

"Certainly a good job is essential to one's well-being," I said.

"It is essential to me," said Simple, "if I do not want to live off of Joyce. And I do *not* want to live off of no woman. A woman will take advantage of you, if you live off of her."

"If a woman loves you, she does not mind sharing with you," I said. "Share and share alike."

"Until times get hard!" said Simple. "But when there is not much to share, *loving* is one thing, and *sharing* is another. Often they parts company. I know because I have both loved and shared. As long as I shared *mine*, all was well, but when my wife started sharing, skippy!

"My wife said, 'Baby, when is you going to work?'

"I said, 'When I find a job.'

"She said, 'Well, it better be soon because I'm giving out.'

"And, man, I felt bad. You know how long and how hard it took to get on WPA. Many a good man lost his woman in them dark days when that stuff about 'I can't give you anything but love' didn't go far. Now it looks like love is all I am going to have to share again. Do you reckon depression days is coming back?"

"I don't know," I said. "I am not a sociologist."

"You's colleged," said Simple. "Anyhow, it looks like every time I gets a little start, something happens. I was doing right well pulling down that *fine* defense check all during the war, then all of a sudden the war had to jump up and end!"

"If you wanted the war to continue just on your account, you are certainly looking at things from a selfish viewpoint."

"Selfish!" said Simple. "You may *think* I am selfish when the facts is I *am just hongry* if I didn't have a job. It looks like in peace time nobody works as much or gets paid as much as in a war. Is that clear?"

"Clear, but not right," I said.

"Of course, it's not right to be out of work and hongry," said Simple, "just like it's not right to want to fight. That's why I prayed my prayer. I prayed for white folks, too, even though a lot of them don't believe in religion. If they did, they couldn't act the way they do.

"Last Sunday morning when I was laying in bed drowsing and resting, I turned on the radio on my dresser and got a church—by accident. I was trying to get the Duke on records, but I tuned into the wrong station. I got some white man preaching a sermon. He was talking about peace on earth, good will to men, and all such things, and he said Christ was born to bring this peace he was talking about. He said mankind has sinned! But that we have got to get ready for the Second Coming of Christ—because Christ will be back! That is what started me to wondering."

"Wondering what?" I asked.

"Wondering what all these prejudiced white folks would do if Christ did come back. I always thought Christ believed in folks' treating people right."

"He did," I said.

"Well, if He did," said Simple, "what will all these white folks do who believe in Jim Crow? Jesus said, 'Love one another,' didn't He? But they don't love me, do they?"

"Some do not," I said.

"Jesus said, 'Do unto others as you would have others do unto you.' But they don't do that way unto me, do they?"

"I suppose not," I said.

"You know not," said Simple. "They Jim Crow me and lynch me any time they want to. Suppose I was to do unto them as they does unto me? Suppose I was to lynch and Jim Crow white folks, where would I be? Huh?"

"In jail."

"You can bet your boots I would! But these are *Christian* white folks that does such things to me. At least, they call themselves Christians in my home. They got more churches down South than they got up North. They read more Bibles and sing more hymns. I hope when Christ comes back, He comes back down South. My folks need Him down there to tell them Ku Kluxers where to head in. But I'll bet you if Christ does come back, not only in the South but all over America, there would be such another running and shutting and slamming of white folks' doors in His face as you never saw! And I'll bet the Southerners couldn't get inside their Jim Crow churches fast enough to lock the gates and keep Christ out. Christ said, 'Such as ye do unto the least of these, ye do it unto me.' And Christ *knows* what these white folks have been doing to old colored me all these years."

"Of course, He knows," I said. "When Christ was here on earth, He fought for the poor and the oppressed. But some people called Him an agitator. They cursed Him and reviled Him and sent soldiers to lock Him up. They killed Him on the cross."

"At Calvary," said Simple, "way back in B.C. I know the Bible, too. My Aunt Lucy read it to me. She read how He drove the money-changers out of the Temple. Also how He changed the loaves and fishes into many and fed the poor—which made the rulers in their high places mad because they didn't want the poor to eat. Well, when Christ comes back this time, I hope He comes back *mad* His own self. I hope He drives the Jim Crowers out of their high places, every living last one of them from Washington to Texas! I hope He smites white folks down!"

"You don't mean *all* white folks, do you?"

"No," said Simple. "I hope He lets Mrs. Roosevelt[1] alone."

Simple on Indian Blood

"Anybody can look at me and tell I am part Indian," said Simple.

"I see you almost every day," I said, "and I did not know it until now."

"I have Indian blood but I do not show it much," said Simple. "My uncle's cousin's great-grandma were a Cherokee. I only shows mine when I lose my temper—then my Indian blood boils. I am quick-tempered just like a Indian. If somebody does something to me, I always fights back. In fact, when I get mad, I am the toughest Negro God's got. It's my Indian blood. When I were a young man, I used to play baseball and steal bases just like Jackie. If the empire would rule me out, I would get mad and hit the empire. I had to stop playing. That Indian temper. Nowadays, though, it's mostly womens that riles me up, especially landladies, waitresses, and girl friends. To tell the truth, I believe in a woman keeping her place. Womens is beside themselves these days. They want to rule the roost."

"You have old-fashioned ideas about sex," I said. "In fact, your line of thought is based on outmoded economics."

"What?"

"In the days when women were dependent upon men for a living, you could be the boss. But now women make their own living. Some of them make more money than you do."

"True," said Simple. "During the war they got into that habit. But boss I am still due to be."

"So you think. But you can't always put your authority into effect."

"I can try," said Simple. "I can say, 'Do this!' And if she does something else, I can raise my voice, if not my hand."

---

[1] Eleanor Roosevelt (1884–1962), widow of Franklin D. Roosevelt, widely loved for her liberal humanitarian spirit and concern for the underprivileged.

"You can be sued for raising your voice," I stated, "and arrested for raising your hand."

"And she can be annihilated when I return from being arrested," said Simple. "That's my Indian blood!"

"You must believe in a woman being a squaw."

"She better not look like no squaw," said Simple. "I want a woman to look sharp when she goes out with me. No moccasins. I wants high-heel shoes and nylons, cute legs—and short dresses. But I also do not want her to talk back to me. As I said, I am the man. *Mine* is the word, and she is due to hush."

"Indians customarily expect their women to be quiet," I said.

"I do not expect mine to be *too* quiet," said Simple. "I want 'em to sweet-talk me—'Sweet baby, this,' and 'Baby, that,' and 'Baby, you's right, darling,' when they talk to me."

"In other words, you want them both old-fashioned and modern at the same time," I said. "The convolutions of your hypothesis are sometimes beyond cognizance."

"Cog hell!" said Simple. "I just do not like no old loud back-talking chick. That's the Indian in me. My grandpa on my father's side were like that, too, an Indian. He was married five times and he really ruled his roost."

"There are a mighty lot of Indians up your family tree," I said. "Did your granddad look like one?"

"Only his nose. He was dark brownskin otherwise. In fact, he were black. And the womens! Man! They was crazy about Grandpa. Every time he walked down the street, they stuck their heads out the windows and kept 'em turned South—which was where the beer parlor was."

"So your grandpa was a drinking man, too. That must be whom you take after."

"I also am named after him," said Simple. "Grandpa's name was Jess, too. So I am Jesse B. Semple."

"What does the B stand for?"

"Nothing. I just put it there myself since they didn't give me no initial when I was born. I am really Jess Semple—which the kids changed around into a nickname when I were in school. In fact, they used to tease me when I were small, calling me 'Simple Simon.' But I was right handy with my fists, and after I beat the 'Simon' out of a few of them, they let me alone. But my friends still call me 'Simple.'"

"In reality, you are Jesse Semple," I said, "colored."

"Part Indian," insisted Simple, reaching for his beer.

"Jess is certainly not an Indian name."

"No, it ain't," said Simple, "but we did have a Hiawatha in our family. She died."

"*She?*" I said. "Hiawatha was no *she*."

"She was a *she* in our family. And she had long coal-black hair just like a Creole. You know, I started to marry a Creole one time when I was coach-boy on the L. & N. down to New Orleans. Them Louisiana girls are bee-oou-te-ful! Man, I mean!"

"Why didn't you marry her, fellow?"

"They are more dangerous than a Indian," said Simple, "also I do not want no pretty woman. First thing you know, you fall in love with her—then you got to kill somebody about her. She'll make you so jealous you'll bust! A pretty woman will get a man in trouble. Me and my Indian blood, quick-tempered as I is. No! I do not crave a pretty woman."

"Joyce is certainly not bad-looking," I said. "You hang around her all the time."

"She is far from a Creole. Besides, she appreciates me," said Simple. "Joyce knows I got Indian blood which makes my temper bad. But we take each other as we is. I respect her and she respects me."

"That's the way it should be with the whole world," I said. "Therefore, you and Joyce are setting a fine example in these days of trials and tribulations. Everybody should take each other as they are, white, black, Indians, Creole. Then there would be no prejudice, nations would get along."

"Some folks do not see it like that," said Simple. "For instant, my landlady—and my wife. Isabel could never get along with me. That is why we are not together today."

"I'm not talking personally," I said, "so why bring in your wife?"

"Getting along *starts* with persons, don't it?" asked Simple. "You *must* include my wife. That woman got my Indian blood so riled up one day I thought I would explode."

"I still say, I'm not talking personally."

"Then stop talking," exploded Simple, "because with me it is personal. Facts, I cannot even talk about my wife if I don't get personal. That's how it is if you're part Indian—everything is personal. *Heap much personal.*"

1950

The Weary Blues

Droning a drowsy syncopated tune,
Rocking back and forth to a mellow croon,
    I heard a Negro play.
Down on Lenox Avenue the other night
By the pale dull pallor of an old gas light

He did a lazy sway. . . .
He did a lazy sway. . . .
To the tune o' those Weary Blues.
With his ebony hands on each ivory key
He made that poor piano moan with melody.
    O Blues!
Swaying to and fro on his rickety stool
He played that sad raggy tune like a musical fool.
    Sweet Blues!
Coming from a black man's soul.
    O Blues!
In a deep song voice with a melancholy tone
I heard that Negro sing, that old piano moan—
    "Ain't got nobody in all this world,
    Ain't got nobody but ma self.
    I's gwine to quit ma frownin'
    And put ma troubles on the shelf."
Thump, thump, thump, went his foot on the floor.
He played a few chords then he sang some more—
    "I got the Weary Blues
    And I can't be satisfied.
    Got the Weary Blues
    And can't be satisfied—
    I ain't happy no mo'
    And I wish that I had died."
And far into the night he crooned that tune.
The stars went out and so did the moon.
The singer stopped playing and went to bed
While the Weary Blues echoed through his head.
He slept like a rock or a man that's dead.

1926

American Heartbreak

I am the American heartbreak—
Rock on which Freedom
Stumps its toe—
The great mistake
That Jamestown
Made long ago.

1926

Harlem[1]

What happens to a dream deferred?

    Does it dry up
    like a raisin in the sun?

[1] This poem from *Montage of a Dream Deferred* suggested the title of *Raisin in the Sun*, the play (which was also made into a movie) by Lorraine Hansbury.

Or fester like a sore—
And then run?
Does it stink like rotten meat?
Or crust and sugar over—
like a syrupy sweet?

Maybe it just sags
like a heavy load.

Or does it explode?

1951

James Thurber   *1894–1961*

James Grover Thurber, most distinguished of the humorists associated with *The New Yorker* magazine, was born and raised, in a frequently
hair-raising way, in the Columbus, Ohio, so warmly remembered in his later
autobiographical sketches. After attending Ohio State University, he worked
on newspapers in Columbus and in New York City before joining the staff of
The New Yorker in 1927.

Throughout his life he maintained a close relationship with the
magazine, helping to develop its distinctive style. In its pages appeared not
only his humorous prose, but his unmistakable cartoons, which created a
world inhabited by large misshapen dogs, timid and baffled men, and predatory women. An admirer of Henry James, Thurber was an accomplished if
low-keyed stylist and a master of a quiet, whimsical humor. The dominant
mood of his stories is an ironic resignation to a confused and irrational world.
As a satirist Thurber also often attacks irrationality, violence, and the suppression of individuality from a viewpoint that is essentially liberal and
humane. "The Catbird Seat" is different from many of his other stories in
that its meek, order-loving hero avoids victimization and scores a triumph
of intellect over his amazonian foe.

Among Thurber's many books are *Is Sex Necessary?* (1929), written
in collaboration with E. B. White, and numerous collections, illustrated with
his own drawings, of stories, humorous essays (some autobiographical),
fables, and fantasies. These include *The Owl in the Attic and Other Perplexities* (1931), *The Seal in the Bedroom and Other Predicaments* (1932), *My
Life and Hard Times* (1933), *The Middle-Aged Man on the Flying Trapeze*
(1935), *Let Your Mind Alone* (1937), *Fables for Our Times* (1940; 1956), *My
World—and Welcome to It* (1942), *Men, Women, and Dogs* (1943), *The
Thurber Carnival* (1945), *The Beast in Me and Other Animals* (1949), *Thurber
Country* (1953), *Further Fables for Our Time* (1956), *Alarms and Diversions*
(1957), and *Lanterns and Lances* (1961). He wrote a number of fantasies for

children: *Many Moons* (1943), *The Great Quillow* (1944), *The White Deer* (1945), *The 13 Clocks* (1950), and *The Wonderful O* (1957). *The Last Flower* (1939) is an ironic picture commentary on war. He also wrote, with his old friend Elliott Nugent, the highly successful comedy *The Male Animal* (1940). *The Years with Ross* (1957) is an affectionate chronicle of *The New Yorker* and its founder, Harold Ross.

A book-length study of Thurber and his work is R. E. Morsberger, *James Thurber* (New York, 1964), which includes a bibliography.

The text of "The Catbird Seat" is that of *The Thurber Carnival* (New York, 1945). "The American Literary Scene" is from *The New Yorker* (July 30, 1949), pp. 21–22.

The Catbird Seat

Mr. Martin bought the pack of Camels on Monday night in the most crowded cigar store on Broadway. It was theater time and seven or eight men were buying cigarettes. The clerk didn't even glance at Mr. Martin, who put the pack in his overcoat pocket and went out. If any of the staff at F & S had seen him buy the cigarettes, they would have been astonished, for it was generally known that Mr. Martin did not smoke, and never had. No one saw him.

It was just a week to the day since Mr. Martin had decided to rub out Mrs. Ulgine Barrows. The term "rub out" pleased him because it suggested nothing more than the correction of an error—in this case an error of Mr. Fitweiler. Mr. Martin had spent each night of the past week working out his plan and examining it. As he walked home now he went over it again. For the hundredth time he resented the element of imprecision, the margin of guesswork that entered into the business. The project as he had worked it out was casual and bold, the risks were considerable. Something might go wrong anywhere along the line. And therein lay the cunning of his scheme. No one would ever see in it the cautious, painstaking hand of Erwin Martin, head of the filing department at F & S, of whom Mr. Fitweiler had once said, "Man is fallible but Martin isn't." No one would see his hand, that is, unless it were caught in the act.

Sitting in his apartment, drinking a glass of milk, Mr. Martin reviewed his case against Mrs. Ulgine Barrows, as he had every night for seven nights. He began at the beginning. Her quacking voice and braying laugh had first profaned the halls of F & S on March 7, 1941 (Mr. Martin had a head for dates). Old Roberts, the personnel chief, had introduced her as the newly appointed special adviser to the president of the firm, Mr. Fitweiler. The woman had appalled Mr. Martin instantly, but he hadn't shown it. He had given her his dry hand, a look of studious concentration, and a faint smile. "Well," she had said, looking at the papers on his desk, "are you lifting the oxcart out of the ditch?" As Mr. Martin recalled that moment, over his milk, he squirmed slightly. He must keep his mind on her crimes as a special adviser, not on her peccadillos as a personality. This he found difficult to do, in spite of entering an objection and sustaining it. The faults of the woman as a woman kept chattering on in his mind like an unruly witness. She had, for almost two years now, baited him. In the halls, in the elevator, even in his own office, into which she romped now and then like a circus horse, she was constantly shouting these silly questions at him. "Are you lifting the oxcart out of the ditch? Are you tearing up the pea patch? Are you hollering down the rain barrel? Are you scraping around the bottom of the pickle barrel? Are you sitting in the catbird seat?"

It was Joey Hart, one of Mr. Martin's two assistants, who had explained what the gibberish meant. "She must be a Dodger fan," he had said. "Red Barber announces the Dodger games over the radio and he uses those expressions — picked 'em up down South." Joey had gone on to explain one or two. "Tearing up the pea patch" meant going on a rampage; "sitting in the catbird seat" meant sitting pretty, like a batter with three balls and no strikes on him. Mr. Martin dismissed all this with an effort. It had been annoying, it had driven him near to distraction, but he was too solid a man to be moved to murder by anything so childish. It was fortunate, he reflected as he passed on to the important charges against Mrs. Barrows, that he had stood up under it so well. He had maintained always an outward appearance of polite tolerance. "Why, I even believe you like the woman," Miss Paird, his other assistant, had once said to him. He had simply smiled.

A gavel rapped in Mr. Martin's mind and the case proper was resumed. Mrs. Ulgine Barrows stood charged with willful, blatant, and persistent attempts to destroy the efficiency and system of F & S. It was competent, material, and relevant to review her advent and rise to power. Mr. Martin had got the story from Miss Paird, who seemed always able to find things out. According to her, Mrs. Barrows had met Mr. Fitweiler at a party, where she had rescued him from the embraces of a powerfully built drunken man who had mistaken the president of F & S for a famous retired Middle Western football coach. She had led him to a sofa and somehow worked upon him a monstrous magic. The aging gentleman had jumped to the conclusion there and then that this was a woman of singular attainments, equipped to bring out the best in him and in the firm. A week later he had introduced her into F & S as his special adviser. On that day confusion got its foot in the door. After Miss Tyson, Mr. Brundage, and Mr. Bartlett had been fired and Mr. Munson had taken his hat and stalked out, mailing in his resignation later, old Roberts had been emboldened to speak to Mr. Fitweiler. He mentioned that Mr. Munson's department had been "a little disrupted" and hadn't they perhaps better resume the old system there? Mr.

Fitweiler had said certainly not. He had the greatest faith in Mrs. Barrow's ideas. "They require a little seasoning, a little seasoning, is all," he had added. Mr. Roberts had given it up. Mr. Martin reviewed in detail all the changes wrought by Mrs. Barrows. She had begun chipping at the cornices of the firm's edifice and now she was swinging at the foundation stones with a pickaxe.

Mr. Martin came now, in his summing up, to the afternoon of Monday, November 2, 1942 — just one week ago. On that day, at 3 P.M., Mrs. Barrows had bounced into his office. "Boo!" she had yelled. "Are you scraping around the bottom of the pickle barrel?" Mr. Martin had looked at her from under his green eyeshade, saying nothing. She had begun to wander about the office, taking it in with her great, popping eyes. "Do you really need *all* these filing cabinets?" she had demanded suddenly. Mr. Martin's heart had jumped. "Each of these files," he had said, keeping his voice even, "plays an indispensable part in the system of F & S." She had brayed at him, "Well, don't tear up the pea patch!" and gone to the door. From there she had bawled, "But you sure have got a lot of fine scrap in here!" Mr. Martin could no longer doubt that the finger was on his beloved department. Her pickaxe was on the upswing, poised for the first blow. It had not come yet; he had received no blue memo from the enchanted Mr. Fitweiler bearing nonsensical instructions deriving from the obscene woman. But there was no doubt in Mr. Martin's mind that one would be forthcoming. He must act quickly. Already a precious week had gone by. Mr. Martin stood up in his living room, still holding his milk glass. "Gentlemen of the jury," he said to himself, "I demand the death penalty for this horrible person."

The next day Mr. Martin followed his routine, as usual. He polished his glasses more often and once sharpened an already sharp pencil, but not even Miss Paird noticed. Only once did he catch sight of his victim; she swept past him in the hall with a patronizing "Hi!" At five-thirty he walked home, as usual, and had a glass of milk, as usual. He had never drunk anything stronger in his life — unless you could count ginger ale. The late Sam Schlosser, the S of F & S, had praised Mr. Martin at a staff meeting several years before for his temperate habits. "Our most efficient worker neither drinks nor smokes," he had said. "The results speak for themselves." Mr. Fitweiler had sat by, nodding approval.

Mr. Martin was still thinking about that red-letter day as he walked over to the Schrafft's on Fifth Avenue near Forty-sixth Street. He got there, as he always did, at eight o'clock. He finished his dinner and the financial page of the *Sun* at a quarter to nine, as he always did. It was his custom after dinner to take a walk. This time he walked down Fifth Avenue at a casual pace. His gloved hands felt moist and warm, his forehead cold. He transferred the Camels from his overcoat to a jacket pocket. He wondered, as he did so, if they did not represent an unnecessary note of strain. Mrs. Barrows smoked only Luckies. It was his idea to puff a few puffs on a Camel (after the rubbing-out), stub it out in the ashtray holding her lipstick-stained Luckies, and thus drag a small red herring across the trail. Perhaps it was not a good idea. It would take time. He might even choke, too loudly.

Mr. Martin had never seen the house on West Twelfth Street where Mrs. Barrows lived, but he had a clear enough picture of it. Fortunately, she had bragged to everybody about her ducky first-floor apartment in the perfectly darling three-story redbrick. There would be no doorman or other attendants; just the tenants of the second and third floors. As he walked along, Mr. Martin realized that he would get there before nine-thirty. He had considered walking north on Fifth Avenue from Schrafft's to a point from which it would take him until ten o'clock to reach the house. At that hour people were less likely to be coming in or going out. But the procedure would have made an awkward loop in the straight thread of his casualness, and he had abandoned it. It was impossible to figure when people would be entering or leaving the house, anyway. There was a great risk at any hour. If he ran into anybody, he would simply have to place the rubbing-out of Ulgine Barrows in the inactive file forever. The same thing would hold true if there were someone in her apartment. In that case he would just say that he had been passing by, recognized her charming house and thought to drop in.

It was eighteen minutes after nine when Mr. Martin turned into Twelfth Street. A man passed him, and a man and a woman talking. There was no one within fifty paces when he came to the house, half-way down the block. He was up the steps and in the small vestibule in no time, pressing the bell under the card that said "Mrs. Ulgine Barrows." When the clicking in the lock started, he jumped forward against the door. He got inside fast, closing the door behind him. A bulb in a lantern hung from the hall ceiling on a chain seemed to give a monstrously bright light. There was nobody on the stair, which went up ahead of him along the left wall. A door opened down the hall in the wall on the right. He went toward it swiftly, on tiptoe.

"Well, for God's sake, look who's here!" bawled Mrs. Barrows, and her braying laugh rang out like the report of a shotgun. He rushed past her like a football tackle, bumping her. "Hey, quit shoving!" she said, closing the door behind them. They were in her living room, which seemed to Mr. Martin to be lighted by a hundred lamps. "What's after you?" she said. "You're as jumpy as a goat." He found he was unable to speak. His heart was wheezing in his throat. "I—yes," he finally brought out. She was jabbering and laughing as she started to help him off with his coat. "No, no," he said. "I'll put it here." He took it off and put it on a chair near the door. "Your hat and gloves, too," she said. "You're in a lady's house." He put his hat on top of the coat. Mrs. Barrows seemed larger than he had thought. He kept his gloves on. "I was passing by," he said. "I recognized—is there anyone here?" She laughed louder than ever. "No," she said, "we're all alone. You're as white as a sheet, you funny man. Whatever *has* come over you? I'll mix you a toddy." She started toward a door across the room. "Scotch-and-soda be all right? But say, you don't drink, do you?" She turned and gave him her amused look. Mr. Martin pulled himself together. "Scotch-and-soda will be all right," he heard himself say. He could hear her laughing in the kitchen.

Mr. Martin looked quickly around the living room for the weapon. He had counted on finding one there. There were andirons and a poker and something in a corner that looked like an Indian club. None of them would do. It couldn't be that way. He began to pace around. He came to a desk. On it lay a metal paper knife with an ornate handle. Would it be sharp enough? He reached for it and knocked over a small brass jar. Stamps spilled out of it and it fell to the floor with a clatter. "Hey," Mrs. Barrows yelled from the kitchen, "are you tearing up the pea patch?" Mr. Martin gave a strange laugh. Picking up the knife, he tried its point against his left wrist. It was blunt. It wouldn't do.

When Mrs. Barrows reappeared, carrying two highballs, Mr. Martin, standing there with his gloves on, became acutely conscious of the fantasy he had wrought. Cigarettes in his pocket, a drink prepared for him—it was all too grossly improbable. It was more than that; it was impossible. Somewhere in the back of his mind a vague idea stirred, sprouted. "For heaven's sake, take off those gloves," said Mrs. Barrows. "I always wear them in the house," said Mr. Martin. The idea began to bloom, strange and wonderful. She put the glasses on a coffee table in front of a sofa and sat on the sofa. "Come over here, you odd little man," she said. Mr. Martin went over and sat beside her. It was difficult getting a cigarette out of the pack of Camels, but he managed it. She held a match for him, laughing. "Well," she said, handing him his drink, "this is perfectly marvelous. You with a drink and a cigarette."

Mr. Martin puffed, not too awkwardly, and took a gulp of the highball. "I drink and smoke all the time," he said. He clinked his glass against hers. "Here's nuts to that old windbag, Fitweiler," he said, and gulped again. The stuff tasted awful, but he made no grimace. "Really, Mr. Martin," she said, her voice and posture changing, "you are insulting our employer." Mrs. Barrows was now all special adviser to the president. "I am preparing a bomb," said Mr. Martin, "which will blow the old goat higher than hell." He had only had a little of the drink, which was not strong. It couldn't be that. "Do you take dope or something?" Mrs. Barrows asked coldly. "Heroin," said Mr. Martin.

"I'll be coked to the gills when I bump that old buzzard off." "Mr. Martin!" she shouted, getting to her feet. "That will be all of that. You must go at once." Mr. Martin took another swallow of his drink. He tapped his cigarette out in the ashtray and put the pack of Camels on the coffee table. Then he got up. She stood glaring at him. He walked over and put on his hat and coat. "Not a word about this," he said, and laid an index finger against his lips. All Mrs. Barrows could bring out was "Really!" Mr. Martin put his hand on the doorknob. "I'm sitting in the catbird seat," he said. He stuck his tongue out at her and left. Nobody saw him go.

Mr. Martin got to his apartment, walking, well before eleven. No one saw him go in. He had two glasses of milk after brushing his teeth, and he felt elated. It wasn't tipsiness, because he hadn't been tipsy. Anyway, the walk had worn off all effects of the whisky. He got in bed and read a magazine for a while. He was asleep before midnight.

Mr. Martin got to the office at eight-thirty the next morning, as usual. At a quarter to nine, Ulgine Barrows, who had never before arrived at work before ten, swept into his office. "I'm reporting to Mr. Fitweiler now!" she shouted. "If he turns you over to the police, it's no more than you deserve!" Mr. Martin gave her a look of shocked surprise. "I beg your pardon?" he said. Mrs. Barrows snorted and bounced out of the room, leaving Miss Paird and Joey Hart staring after her. "What's the matter with that old devil now?" asked Miss Paird. "I have no idea," said Mr. Martin, resuming his work. The other two looked at him and then at each other. Miss Paird got up and went out. She walked slowly past the closed door of Mr. Fitweiler's office. Mrs. Barrows was yelling inside, but she was not braying. Miss Paird could not hear what the woman was saying. She went back to her desk.

Forty-five minutes later, Mrs. Barrows left the president's office and went into her own, shutting the door. It wasn't until half an hour later that Mr. Fitweiler sent for Mr. Martin. The head of the filing department, neat, quiet, attentive, stood in front of the old man's desk. Mr. Fitweiler was pale and nervous. He took his glasses off and twiddled them. He made a small, bruffing sound in his throat. "Martin," he said, "you have been with us more than twenty years." "Twenty-two, sir," said Mr. Martin. "In that time," pursued the president, "your work and your—uh—manner have been exemplary." "I trust so, sir," said Mr. Martin. "I have understood, Martin," said Mr. Fitweiler, "that you have never taken a drink or smoked." "That is correct, sir," said Mr. Martin. "Ah, yes." Mr. Fitweiler polished his glasses. "You may describe what you did after leaving the office yesterday, Martin," he said. Mr. Martin allowed less than a second for his bewildered pause. "Certainly, sir," he said. "I walked home. Then I went to Schrafft's for dinner. Afterward I walked home again. I went to bed early, sir, and read a magazine for a while. I was asleep before eleven." "Ah, yes," said Mr. Fitweiler again. He was silent for a moment, searching for the proper words to say to the head of the filing department. "Mrs. Barrows," he said finally, "Mrs. Barrows has worked hard, Martin, very hard. It grieves me to report that she has suffered a severe breakdown. It has taken the form of a persecution complex accompanied by distressing hallucinations." "I am very sorry, sir," said Mr. Martin. "Mrs. Barrows is under the delusion," continued Mr. Fitweiler, "that you visited her last evening and behaved yourself in an—uh—unseemly manner." He raised his hand to silence Mr. Martin's little pained outcry. "It is the nature of these psychological diseases," Mr. Fitweiler said, "to fix upon the least likely and most innocent party as the—uh—source of persecution. These matters are not for the lay mind to grasp, Martin. I've just had my psychiatrist, Dr. Fitch, on the phone. He would not, of course, commit himself, but he made enough generalizations to substantiate my suspicions. I suggested to Mrs. Barrows when she had completed her—uh—story to me this morning, that she visit Dr. Fitch, for I suspected a condition at once. She flew, I regret to say, into a rage, and demanded—uh—requested that I call you on the carpet. You may not know, Martin, but Mrs. Barrows had planned a reorganization of your department—subject to my approval, of course, subject to my approval. This brought you, rather than anyone else, to her mind—but again that is a phenomenon for Dr. Fitch and not for us. So, Martin, I am afraid Mrs. Barrows' usefulness here is at an end." "I am dreadfully sorry, sir," said Mr. Martin.

It was at this point that the door to the office blew open with the suddenness of a gas-main explosion and Mrs. Barrows catapulted through it. "Is the little rat denying it?" she screamed. "He can't get away with that!" Mr. Martin got up and moved discreetly to a point beside Mr. Fitweiler's chair. "You drank and smoked at my apartment," she bawled at Mr. Martin, "and you know it! You called Mr. Fitweiler an old windbag and said you were going to blow him up when you got coked to the gills on your heroin!" She stopped yelling to catch her breath and a new glint came into her popping eyes. "If you weren't such a drab, ordinary little man," she said, "I'd think you'd planned it all. Sticking your tongue out, saying you were sitting in the catbird seat, because you thought no one would believe me when I told it! My God, it's really too perfect!" She brayed loudly and hysterically, and the fury was on her again. She glared at Mr. Fitweiler. "Can't you see how he has tricked us, you old fool? Can't you see his little game?" But Mr. Fitweiler had been surreptitiously pressing all the buttons under the top of his desk and employees of F & S began pouring into the room. "Stockton," said Mr. Fitweiler, "you and Fishbein will take Mrs. Barrows to her home. Mrs. Powell, you will go with them." Stockton, who had played a little football in high school, blocked Mrs. Barrows as she made for Mr. Martin. It took him and Fishbein together to force her out of the door into the hall, crowded with stenographers and office boys. She was still screaming imprecations at Mr. Martin, tangled and contradictory imprecations. The hubbub finally died out down the corridor.

"I regret that this has happened," said Mr. Fitweiler. "I shall ask you to dismiss it from your mind, Martin." "Yes, sir," said Mr. Martin, anticipating his chief's "That will be all" by moving to the door. "I will dismiss it." He went out and shut the door, and his step was light and quick in the hall. When he entered his department he had slowed down to his customary gait, and he walked quietly across the room to the W20 file, wearing a look of studious concentration.

1945

The American Literary Scene[1]
AFTER READING SEVERAL ESSAYS, IN ENGLISH MAGAZINES, ON THE PLIGHT OF THE AMERICAN WRITER AND THE NATURE OF THE AMERICAN MALE

I have but now returned to England, and to my tranquil pen, after spending six interesting, rather, but scarcely restful weeks in America. It had been my purpose in setting out, or perhaps I should say my thought, to look at, but not exactly to examine, in the journalistic sense of the word, what is going on in the field, or fields — they are quite separate — of book and magazine publishing over there. I bore, in my portfolio, letters, pressed upon me by various friends, to Mr. Horace-Lorimer, of the *Saturday Review Post*; a Mr. Bok, whom my distinguished compatriot, Lord Tweedley, had visited in Tamiami, long years since, and who turned out unhappily to be deceased; and to the strenuous Mr. William Rose, who in addition to writing for *New Yorker*, conducts a column of chat about the underworld in the *New York Herald*, known for some amusing American reason as "the Trib."

Mr. Rose was not in when I called at *New Yorker*, a weekly journal of capricious opinion published, with massive drollery, in an enormous hotel of the same name, and I was unable, alas, to present my letter to Mr. Horace-Lorimer, since I could not find him in Boston, and, indeed, no one seemed to have heard of him.

At this point, I am afflicted by the uneasy suspicion that my American readers, if perchance I have any, will condemn this small commentary for its confessed, its flaunted lack of that kind of wearisome research of which Americans, in their desperate and deplorable love of fact, are so intensely avid. I have not "checked," as they would say, a solitary statement herein contained. I proudly, even gaily, protest

[1] The text is that of *The New Yorker* (July 30, 1949), pp. 21–22.

that at no time during my sojourn abroad did I descend to the vulgarity of "taking notes"—to use another Americanism. My prayer for forgiveness, if such I must seek, rises from the heart of a stout conviction that speculation, when cramped by certainties, is eased of its wonder and its warmth. So much, then, for apology.

New Yorker, the journal and hotel, rises, I should imagine, to a height of one thousand feet, and it contains somewhere between two and four thousand rooms, of which, I fancy, a third to a half is given over to the editorial offices. This amazing "plant" labours incessantly to turn out, on each Wednesday, a periodical that contains surely not more than twenty thousand words of letterpress.

One should not be led to assume that *New Yorker* is the most commodious plant in the city of New York. The American Broadcasting System, owned by Time-Holiday, Ltd., I believe someone said, is housed in Rockefeller's Plaza, a gigantic world of steel and granite, somewhat north of my hotel, that once accommodated the entire population of Kansas City. The ABS employs one hundred and fifty thousand persons, or perhaps a hundred thousand more than *New Yorker*. The Staff of that weekly is made up exclusively of wealthy residents of the city, curiously devoted to its prodigious commerce and shipping, its eccentric millionaires and their wives, and its several legends—the metropolis, of course, has no traditions.

It has several times been pointed out, I expect, that *New Yorker* letterpress sounds as if it were the work of one man. This comes delightfully close to being true. The letterpress is, in reality, written by three men: Mr. Alexander Wolcott, our own Mr. John Collier, and Mr. William Rose himself. Mr. Rose actually has two styles of writing, the exasperatingly lucid and understandable prose of *New Yorker*, in which one may never find comfort for even a moment in a weirdly managed construction or a charmingly uncorrected error of printing, and the sort of hard-hitting bully-boy mannerism he affects in his underworld gossip. On the side, it is interesting to note, Mr. Rose manufactures hundreds of kinds of tinned goods, which are marketed under the trade label of "White Rose."

I was appalled to learn, at a cocktail party (which degenerated, as not infrequently happens, into an alcoholic rout), that the Rose weekly, after employing America's most distinguished novelist, Truman Capote, had let him go, out of hand. My informant, a Mr. Busby or Bixby—it was infernally noisy at the party—told me that the magazine's controlling stock is held by a syndicate of Southern bankers, or bakers, who had conceived the fantastic notion that Mr. Truman's novel, "Other Rooms, Other Voices," was a deliberate assault on the virtue of Southern womanhood. He was given the sack, without ado or farewell, and New York publishers are now madly bidding against one another for the rights to his future work. This bidding is an odd and graceless procedure, in which the rival publishers outdo one another in wining and dining the prospective author. They are not above buying him expensive cars and other costly presents, and advance royalties in the amount of fifty thousand dollars are by no means unknown.

Publishers all occupy skyscraper penthouses, or "random houses," and although I was never actually in one of them, I can see them clearly as if I had been. The publishers dictate ideas for novels to the writers, supplying them with titles and, in some instances, writing the books themselves. The American custom of seducing one's best friend's wife, and later killing oneself while on a "spree," out of fear that one is actually in love with one's best friend, is the basic theme most recently insisted upon by the publishers. It is good to be able to report that a small but sturdy group of male American writers (there has been no woman novelist since Miss Cather's death) stubbornly and courageously refuse to be enslaved or chivvied about. This little band consists of Ernest Hemingway, Elliott-Paul, the Dreiser brothers, Henry Miller, Faulkner, Upton Sinclair, Earl Stanley Gardner, and possibly a few others. The chances of this slender list being appreciably lengthened are far from good. A great many young American writers, having made sizable fortunes before the age of thirty, have retired, and pass their time drinking and attending the boxing matches.

Drinking, in the American literary set, has reached unbelievable heights, or depths, depending upon one's view. I think Spender, in his *Horizon* essay, went a bit far in intimating that many older authors have surrendered themselves completely to alcoholism. That word connotes, indeed it specifically defines, a form of almost incurable disease, whose most distinctive characteristic is the inability to stop, after one has started. I am sure that I got about as much as Spender, but it is obvious that he is able to sit up later than I am. Since all the American writers I met, of every age, were still carrying on at evening parties after I had left, it is impossible for me to estimate fairly how many of them eventually stopped and how many were unable to stop. I was informed that one American writer sat for seven days in an actors' club without going home, or ceasing his tippling, but this was told me by a gentleman well into his own fourth day and "unfolding" rapidly, and its credibility is perhaps negligible. It is safe to say that quantitative literary drinking in America is well beyond any and every mark that we English writers might fear, or hope, to achieve. American writers speak, quite openly and freely, of "drinking their luncheon" and of being "poured onto trains." The latest expressions for being intoxicated are "buzzed," "punch drunk," and "mugged."

The social intercourse of the American writer is realized, almost exclusively, in public houses or private homes and flats, between the hours of 5 P. M. and 4 A. M. the following day. When the writers meet in a public house, there is little conversation, the eleven hours of confined but distant intimacy being given over to a gambling game known as "matches." I think as much as forty thousand dollars may change hands in one night. The superficial observer might regard these nocturnal meetings as a sign of gregariousness, but they are, in reality, gloomily planned assemblages of separate lonelinesses. Friendship in America is indicated and proved by a steady flow of insult and contumely between friends, who smilingly accuse each other of insanity, depravity, spiritual damnation, duplicity, conspiracy, and the stealing of flowers from the graves of mothers.

Some American writers who have known each other for years have never met in the daytime or when both were sober. The coming together of writers in the home or flat of one of their number is invariably a signal for trouble to start. There is no discussion, to speak of, but controversy rages shortly after all are seated in the living, or "rumpus," room. A controversy usually rises out of a fiercely stated prejudice, hatred, or admiration by the host or one of his guests. A novelist or essayist is likely to get to his feet, on his twentieth or twenty-first highball, and announce that he is "the greatest goddam writer in the world" or that one of his friends is. This is instantly challenged by one or more candidates for the special distinction of greatest goddam writer in the world. The commonest terms of opprobrium during these bitter debates are: interior decorator, poet, chef, florist, and milliner, since Americans believe that a talent in any of these directions is *prima-facie* evidence of a lack of virility, or at the very least a dearth of the true go-getter spirit.

The foreign writer who is fortunate enough to be present at one of those rare evening parties at which there is discussion instead of argument is likely to be at a loss, nonetheless, since the conversation holds tenaciously to such highly specialized subjects as the Buick, the Pontiac, the Cadillac, the Saint Louis Cardinals, the Cincinnati Communists, money, clothes, success, ladies of questionable discretion, and heels (both goddam and round).

I had wished to make some small exploration of Hollywood, home of the millionaire cinema writers, whose life span is so shockingly brief. (I understand that they are taken directly from the studio to the cemetery, such is the pace even of death in California.) I must confess, however, that my farthest west in America was an hotel in the Eighth Avenue, a region of New York City charmingly named the Devil's Kitchen. The trip to this hotel marked the end of my American adventure. Others will follow me to those violent shores, just as, in the past, others have preceded me, from Mrs. Trollope to Geoffrey Gorer and Evelyn Waugh. The American writer will always be a richly rewarding subject for study.

He does not, to be sure, like to be studied, but he loves to be listened to, and thus the path of the foreign observer is made comparatively easy. It is well to remember that he resents all and every criticism of himself, his colleagues, or anything else, and he is likely to regard whatever you may say as "goddam patronizing." The American writer is constitutionally unable to "take it," but there is always the danger that he may turn on one, and "dish it up." In such event, it is advisable to apologize and to "powder out" before objects are thrown. Of course, if one has nothing to apologize for, one does not want meekly to "put up and shut up."

It is rather difficult, I see, to formulate a code of behaviour for the Englishman in America that is at once judicious and honourable. I shall continue to think about it.

1949

Middle Generation Poets

The poets of the middle generation were born in the first and second decades of the century, when the modern movement in the arts was just beginning. As beneficiaries of the revolution, they incorporated in their work many of the conventions of their elders, especially in symbolism and in attitude. But most of them reacted against the experimentalism and radical individualism of Pound, Williams, Cummings, and Marianne Moore. They worked instead, often with great competence, within metrically regular forms.

They also did not attempt the kind of ambitious culture poem or epic written by Ezra Pound, T. S. Eliot, William Carlos Williams, and Hart Crane. Eschewing broad social problems (except for those suggested by their involvement in World War II), they turned instead to the treatment of personal feelings and experience. Within these limits, upon their chosen ground, they wrote with authority and skill as poetic craftsmen of a high order.

Much of their work reflects the pervasive influence of T. S. Eliot, who dominated modern poetry during their formative years. Karl Shapiro's early poems express an attitude of irony and worldly disillusionment reminiscent of Eliot's earlier work. Robert Lowell was much impressed by Eliot's religious poetry. Many of Lowell's poems treat problems of religious salvation through the kind of metaphysical imagery admired by Eliot within the metri-

The River by Stow Wengenroth, lithograph, 1936 courtesy of the Boston Public Library.

cally regular forms favored by John Crowe Ransom and most of the New Critics.

In the years since the Second World War, as yet another generation has risen to carry forward the free verse tradition of Pound and Williams, some of the members of the middle generation have shifted to the use of freer poetic forms.

Theodore Roethke   *1908–1963*

Born in Saginaw, Michigan, where his father was a florist, Theodore Roethke was educated at the University of Michigan (B.A., 1929; M.A., 1936). He began teaching in colleges and universities while learning his craft as a poet. From 1947 until his death, he was a member of the Department of English of the University of Washington. The imagery of vegetable growth that dominates the poems of his first collection, *Open House* (1941), is the result of his boyhood experiences in his father's greenhouse. An impulse toward nature mysticism reminiscent of Emerson, Thoreau and Whitman remained a tendency in Roethke's work. A reconciliation of past and present is also evident in the metrical form of his poems, in which he adapts basically traditional patterns of rhyme and meter with freedom and flexibility. His later poetry, up to the time of his sudden death in 1963, reveals an openness to experience and a continuing growth in power.

His other books include *The Lost Son and Other Poems* (1948), *Praise to the End!* (1951), *The Waking: Poems 1933–1953* (1953), *Words for the Wind: The Collected Verse of Theodore Roethke* (1958), and *I Am! Says the Lamb* (1961). Among posthumous publications are *The Far Field* (1964) and *The Collected Poems* (1965). *On the Poet and His Craft: Selected Prose*, ed. R. J. Mills (1965), is a gathering of essays and lectures. Roethke's correspondence has been gathered in *Selected Letters, 1908–1963*, ed. R. J. Mills (1968).

Brief introductions to Roethke's life and work are R. J. Mills, *Theodore Roethke* (Minneapolis, 1963), and Karl Malkoff, *Theodore Roethke: An Introduction to the Poetry* (New York, 1966). For other critiques, see Arnold Stein, ed., *Theodore Roethke: Essays on the Poetry* (Seattle, 1965).

The text of the poems given here is that of *The Collected Poems of Theodore Roethke* (New York, 1965).

Open House

My secrets cry aloud.
I have no need for tongue.
My heart keeps open house,
My doors are widely swung.
An epic of the eyes
My love, with no disguise.

My truths are all foreknown,
This anguish self-revealed.
I'm naked to the bone,
With nakedness my shield.   10
Myself is what I wear:
I keep the spirit spare.

The anger will endure,
The deed will speak the truth
In language strict and pure.
I stop the lying mouth:
Rage warps my clearest cry
To witless agony.

1941

Root Cellar

Nothing would sleep in that cellar, dank as a ditch,
Bulbs broke out of boxes hunting for chinks in the dark,
Shoots dangled and drooped,
Lolling obscenely from mildewed crates,
Hung down long yellow evil necks, like tropical snakes.
And what a congress of stinks!—
Roots ripe as old bait,
Pulpy stems, rank, silo-rich,
Leaf-mold, manure, lime, piled against slippery planks.
Nothing would give up life:
Even the dirt kept breathing a small breath.

1948

Elegy for Jane

(My student, thrown by a horse)

I remember the neckcurls, limp and damp as tendrils;
And her quick look, a sidelong pickerel smile;
And how, once startled into talk, the light syllables leaped for her,
And she balanced in the delight of her thought,
A wren, happy, tail into the wind,

Her song trembling the twigs and small branches.
The shade sang with her;
The leaves, their whispers turned to kissing;
And the mold sang in the bleached valleys under the rose.

Oh, when she was sad, she cast herself down into such a pure   10
    depth,
Even a father could not find her:
Scraping her cheek against straw;
Stirring the clearest water.

My sparrow, you are not here,
Waiting like a fern, making a spiny shadow.
The sides of wet stones cannot console me,
Nor the moss, wound with the last light.

If only I could nudge you from this sleep,   20
My maimed darling, my skittery pigeon.
Over this damp grave I speak the words of my love:
I, with no rights in this matter,
Neither father nor lover.

1953

Four for Sir John Davies[1]

1. The Dance

Is that dance slowing in the mind of man
That made him think the universe could hum?
The great wheel turns its axle when it can;
I need a place to sing, and dancing-room,
And I have made a promise to my ears
I'll sing and whistle romping with the bears.

For they are all my friends: I saw one slide
Down a steep hillside on a cake of ice,—
Or was that in a book? I think with pride:
A caged bear rarely does the same thing twice   10
In the same way: O watch his body sway!—
This animal remembering to be gay.

I tried to fling my shadow at the moon,
The while my blood leaped with a wordless song.
Though dancing needs a master, I had none
To teach my toes to listen to my tongue.
But what I learned there, dancing all alone,
Was not the joyless motion of a stone.

[1] In "Orchestra" (1596), a poem in seven-line stanzas by Sir John Davies (1569–1626), natural phenomena are reduced to an ordered motion or "dancing."

I take this cadence from a man named Yeats;
I take it, and I give it back again: 20
For other tunes and other wanton beats
Have tossed my heart and fiddled through my brain.
Yes, I was dancing-mad, and how
That came to be the bears and Yeats would know.

2. The Partner

Between such animal and human heat
I find myself perplexed. What is desire?—
The impulse to make someone else complete?
That woman would set sodden straw on fire.
Was I the servant of a sovereign wish,
Or ladle rattling in an empty dish?   30

We played a measure with commingled feet:
The lively dead had taught us to be fond.
Who can embrace the body of his fate?
Light altered light along the living ground.
She kissed me close, and then did something else.
My marrow beat as wildly as my pulse.

I'd say it to my horse: we live beyond
Our outer skin. Who's whistling up my sleeve?
I see a heron prancing in his pond;
I know a dance the elephants believe.   40
The living all assemble! What's the cue?—
Do what the clumsy partner wants to do!

Things loll and loiter. Who condones the lost?
This joy outleaps the dog. Who cares? Who cares?
I gave her kisses back, and woke a ghost.
O what lewd music crept into our ears!
The body and the soul know how to play
In that dark world where gods have lost their way.

3. The Wraith

Incomprehensible gaiety and dread   50
Attended what we did. Behind, before,
Lay all the lonely pastures of the dead;
The spirit and the flesh cried out for more.
We two, together, on a darkening day
Took arms against our own obscurity.

Did each become the other in that play?
She laughed me out, and then she laughed me in;

In the deep middle of ourselves we lay;
When glory failed, we danced upon a pin.
The valley rocked beneath the granite hill;
Our souls looked forth, and the great day stood still.   60

There was a body, and it cast a spell,—
God pity those but wanton to the knees,—
The flesh can make the spirit visible;
We woke to find the moonlight on our toes.
In the rich weather of a dappled wood
We played with dark and light as children should.

What shape leaped forward at the sensual cry?—
Sea-beast or bird flung toward the ravaged shore?
Did space shake off an angel with a sigh?
We rose to meet the moon, and saw no more.   70
It was and was not she, a shape alone,
Impaled on light, and whirling slowly down.

4. The Vigil

Dante attained the purgatorial hill,
Trembled at hidden virtue without flaw,
Shook with a mighty power beyond his will,—
Did Beatrice deny what Dante saw?
All lovers live by longing, and endure:
Summon a vision and declare it pure.

Though everything's astonishment at last,
Who leaps to heaven at a single bound?   80
The links were soft between us; still, we kissed;
We undid chaos to a curious sound:
The waves broke easy, cried to me in white;
Her look was morning in the dying light.

The visible obscures. But who knows when?
Things have their thought: they are the shards of me;
I thought that once, and thought comes round again;
Rapt, we leaned forth with what we could not see.
We danced to shining; mocked before the black
And shapeless night that made no answer back.   90

The world is for the living. Who are they?
We dared the dark to reach the white and warm.
She was the wind when wind was in my way;
Alive at noon, I perished in her form.
Who rise from flesh to spirit know the fall:
The word outleaps the world, and light is all.

1953

In a Dark Time

In a dark time, the eye begins to see,
I meet my shadow in the deepening shade;
I hear my echo in the echoing wood—
A lord of nature weeping to a tree.
I live between the heron and the wren,
Beasts of the hill and serpents of the den.

What's madness but nobility of soul
At odds with circumstance? The day's on fire!
I know the purity of pure despair,
My shadow pinned against a sweating wall.   10
That place among the rocks—is it a cave,
Or winding path? The edge is what I have.

A steady storm of correspondences!
A night flowing with birds, a ragged moon,
And in broad day the midnight come again!
A man goes far to find out what he is—
Death of the self in a long, tearless night,
All natural shapes blazing unnatural light.

Dark, dark my light, and darker my desire.
My soul, like some heat-maddened summer fly,   20
Keeps buzzing at the sill. Which I is *I*?
A fallen man, I climb out of my fear.
The mind enters itself, and God the mind,
And one is One, free in the tearing wind.

                                    1964

Richard Eberhart   *1904—*

Minnesota-born Richard Eberhart was educated at Dartmouth College (B.A., 1926), Cambridge University (M.A., 1933), and Harvard. His subsequent career as a college and university teacher was interrupted by World War II, when he served in the Navy as an instructor of aircraft gunnery, and by a brief postwar excursion into business and manufacturing. Since 1956 he has been a professor of English and poet in residence at Dartmouth. From the appearance of his first volume, *A Bravery of Earth* (1930), his poems have been distinguished by intensity of perception and economy and precision of language. In one of his best-known poems, Eberhart has described his function as a poet as the painful effort to see and express the beauty of experience "in a hard intellectual light."

His other books include *Reading the Spirit* (1937), *Song and Idea* (1942), *Poems, New and Selected* (1944), *Burr Oaks* (1947), *Brotherhood of Men* (1949), *An Herb Basket* (1950), *Selected Poems* (1951), *Undercliff* (1953), *Great Praises* (1957), *Collected Poems: 1930–1960* (1960), *The Quarry* (1964), and *Richard Eberhart: Selected Poems 1930–1965* (1965). Published drama includes *The Visionary Farms* (1952) and *Collected Verse Plays* (1962).

A brief introduction to Eberhart's work is R. J. Mills, *Richard Eberhart* (Minneapolis, 1966).

The text of the poems given here is that of *Richard Eberhart: Selected Poems 1930–1965* (New York, 1965).

'In a Hard Intellectual Light'

In a hard intellectual light
I will kill all delight,
And I will build a citadel✔
Too beautiful to tell

✔citadel- a fortified place, stronghold

O too austere to tell
And far too beautiful to see,
Whose evident distance
I will call the best of me.

And this light of intellect
Will shine on all my desires,   10
It will my flesh protect
And flare my bold constant fires,

For the hard intellectual light
Will lay the flesh with nails.
And it will keep the world bright
And closed the body's soft jails.

And from this fair edifice
I shall see, as my eyes blaze,
The moral grandeur of man
Animating all his days.   20

And peace will marry purpose,
And purity married to grace
Will make the human absolute
As sweet as the human face.

Until my hard vision blears,
And Poverty and Death return
In organ music like the years,
Making the spirit leap, and burn

For the hard intellectual light
That kills all delight   30
And brings the solemn, inward pain
Of truth into the heart again.

                                        1936

The Groundhog

In June, amid the golden fields,
I saw a groundhog lying dead.
Dead lay he; my senses shook,
And mind outshot our naked frailty.
There lowly in the vigorous summer
His form began its senseless change,
And made my senses waver dim
Seeing nature ferocious in him.
Inspecting close his maggots' might
And seething cauldron of his being,   10
Half with loathing, half with a strange love,

austere - severe, stern, harsh, rigorous

I poked him with an angry stick.
The fever arose, became a flame
And Vigour circumscribed the skies,
Immense energy in the sun,
And through my frame a sunless trembling.
My stick had done nor good nor harm.
Then stood I silent in the day
Watching the object, as before;
And kept my reverence for knowledge   20
Trying for control, to be still,
To quell the passion of the blood;
Until I had bent down on my knees
Praying for joy in the sight of decay.
And so I left; and I returned
In Autumn strict of eye, to see
The sap gone out of the groundhog,
But the bony sodden hulk remained.
But the year had lost its meaning,
And in intellectual chains   30
I lost both love and loathing,
Mured up in the wall of wisdom.
Another summer took the fields again
Massive and burning, full of life,
But when I chanced upon the spot
There was only a little hair left,
And bones bleaching in the sunlight
Beautiful as architecture;
I watched them like a geometer,
And cut a walking stick from a birch.   40
It has been three years, now.
There is no sign of the groundhog.
I stood there in the whirling summer,
My hand capped a withered heart,
And thought of China and of Greece,
Of Alexander in his tent;
Of Montaigne in his tower,
Of Saint Theresa in her wild lament.

1936

'I Went to See Irving Babbitt'

I went to see Irving Babbitt
In the Eighteenth Century clean and neat
When he opened his mouth to speak French
I fell clean off my seat.

---

[1] Irving Babbitt (1865–1933), Harvard professor of French literature, leader of the
anti-modernist, anti-democratic movement in criticism known as the New Humanism.

He spoke it not fair and fetisly[2]
But harshly laboured it like a Yankee
Even as my nubian Swahili
Is sweet and pleasant to me.

And when we went out of the critical door
Crying for more, crying for more   10
I saw the hater of mechanical America
Bulge through the Square in a critical Ford.

Harvard is a good place, Harvard is the best,
Among the immemorial elms you'll come to rest
Strolling the Yard, the only proper yardstick,
Warbling your native foot-notes mild.

1940

New Hampshire, February

Nature had made them hide in crevices,
Two wasps so cold they looked like bark.
Why I do not know, but I took them
And I put them
In a metal pan, both day and dark.

Like God touching his finger to Adam
I felt, and thought of Michaelangelo,
For whenever I breathed on them,
The slightest breath,
They leaped, and preened as if to go.   10

My breath controlled them always quite.
More sensitive than electric sparks
They came into life
Or they withdrew to ice,
While I watched, suspending remarks.

Then one in a blind career got out,
And fell to the kitchen floor. I
Crushed him with my cold ski boot,
By accident. The other
Had not the wit to try or die.   20

And so the other is still my pet.
The moral of this is plain.
But I will shirk it.
You will not like it. And
God does not live to explain.

1947

[2] An echo of Chaucer's description of his prioress (in the Prologue to the *Canterbury Tales*): "And Frenssh she spak ful faire and fetisly, / After the scole of Stratford atte Bowe."

The Fury of Aerial Bombardment

You would think the fury of aerial bombardment
Would rouse God to relent; the infinite spaces
Are still silent. He looks on shock-pried faces.
History, even, does not know what is meant.

You would feel that after so many centuries
God would give man to repent; yet he can kill
As Cain could, but with multitudinous will,
No farther advanced than in his ancient furies.

Was man made stupid to see his own stupidity?
Is God by definition indifferent, beyond us all?   10
Is the eternal truth man's fighting soul
Wherein the Beast ravens in its own avidity?

Of Van Wettering I speak, and Averill,
Names on a list, whose faces I do not recall
But they are gone to early death, who late in school
Distinguished the belt feed lever from the belt holding pawl.

Eberhart was a gunner instructor –   1947
those who learned first, died first

The Human Being Is a Lonely Creature

It is borne in upon me that pain
Is essential. The bones refuse to act.
→ Recalcitrancy is life's fine flower.   *stubbornly defiant*
The human being is a lonely creature.

Fear is of the essence. You do not fear?
I say you lie. Fear is the truth of time.
If it is not now, it will come hereafter.
Death is waiting for the human creature.

Praise to harmony and love.
They are best, all else is false.   10
Yet even in love and harmony
The human being is a lonely creature.

The old sloughed off, the new new-born,
What fate and what high hazards join
As life tries out the soul's enterprise.
Time is waiting for the human creature.

pawl–mechanical device
which allows motion
in one direction

Life is daring all our human stature.
Death looks, and waits for each bright eye.
Love and harmony are our best nurture.
The human being is a lonely creature.   20

1953

avidity– eagerness, greed   *ravens–to devour greedily/search greedily for prey*

Karl Shapiro   *1913—*

Karl Jay Shapiro was born in Baltimore and studied at the University
of Virginia and Johns Hopkins University. From 1941 to 1945 he served in
the Army with an extended tour of duty in the South Pacific. He first gained
wide recognition for two volumes of verse written while he was in service:
V-Letter and Other Poems (1944) and *Essay on Rime* (1945). They were
followed by *Trial of a Poet* (1947). The often satiric poems of this early
period, which ended with *Poems 1940–1953* (1953), were written from an
ironic and disillusioned viewpoint reminiscent of T. S. Eliot and other
modern poets of the *Waste Land* era, although Shapiro was more conservative in his choice of metrical forms than his elders had been.

After the war, Shapiro edited *Poetry*, the magazine of verse, for six
years (1950–56) and then became a professor of English at the University of
Nebraska, where he edited the little magazine *The Prairie Schooner*.
During this period his poetic output declined, and the verse he did publish
lacked the ironic edge of his earlier work. In *Poems of a Jew* (1958), Shapiro
explores the meaning of his heritage and in the process rejects the model of
Eliot for that of Walt Whitman. In all his later writing, in both verse and
prose, Shapiro has strongly repudiated the "intellectual" verse of the
moderns in favor of a poetry of Whitmanesque cosmic vision. In keeping
with his change of attitude, Shapiro has also shifted to a freer form of
expression. In *The Bourgeois Poet* (1958), he has attempted to write prose
poems in which the conventions of rhyme and meter are entirely ignored.

Other volumes of Shapiro's poetry include *Poems* (1935), *Person,
Place and Thing* (1942), *The Place of Love* (1942), and *Selected Poems* (1968).
The essays of *Beyond Criticism* (1953) and *In Defense of Ignorance* (1960)
set forth his anti-intellectual critical position.

The text of the poems given here is that of *Poems 1940–1953* (New
York, 1953).

Drug Store

I do remember an apothecary,
And hereabouts 'a dwells[1]

It baffles the foreigner like an idiom,
And he is right to adopt it as a form
Less serious than the living-room or bar;
          For it disestablishes the cafe,
Is a collective, and on basic country.

Not that it praises hygiene and corrupts
The ice-cream parlor and the tobacconist's
Is it a center; but that the attractive symbols
          Watch over puberty and leer
Like rubber bottles waiting for sick-use.   10

Youth comes to jingle nickels and crack wise;
The baseball scores are his, the magazines
Devoted to lust, the jazz, the Coca-Cola,
          The lending-library of love's latest.
He is the customer; he is heroized.

And every nook and cranny of the flesh
Is spoken to by packages with wiles.
"Buy me, buy me," they whimper and cajole;
          The hectic range of lipsticks pouts,
Revealing the wicked and the simple mouth.   20

With scarcely any evasion in their eye
They smoke, undress their girls, exact a stance;
But only for a moment. The clock goes round;
          Crude fellowships are made and lost;
They slump in booths like rags, not even drunk.

                                        1942

University

To hurt the Negro and avoid the Jew
Is the curriculum. In mid-September
The entering boys, identified by hats,
Wander in a maze of mannered brick
          Where boxwood and magnolia brood
          And columns with imperious stance
          Like rows of ante-bellum girls
          Eye them, outlanders.

overbearing, arrogant

---

[1] Shakespeare, *Romeo and Juliet* (V, i, 37–38).

In whited cells, on lawns equipped for peace,
Under the arch, and lofty banister,   10
Equals shake hands, unequals blankly pass;
The exemplary weather whispers, "Quiet, quiet"
    And visitors on tiptoe leave
    For the raw North, the unfinished West,
    As the young, detecting an advantage,
        Practice a face.

Where, on their separate hill, the colleges,
Like manor houses of an older law,
Gaze down embankments on a land in fee,
The Deans, dry spinsters over family plate,   20
    Ring out the English name like coin,
    Humor the snob and lure the lout.
    Within the precincts of this world
        Poise is a club.

But on the neighboring range, misty and high,
The past is absolute: some luckless race
Dull with inbreeding and conformity
Wears out its heart, and comes barefoot and bad
    For charity or jail. The scholar
    Sanctions their obsolete disease;   30
    The gentleman revolts with shame
        At his ancestor.

And the true nobleman, once a democrat,
Sleeps on his private mountain.[1] He was one
Whose thought was shapely and whose dream was broad;
This school he held his art and epitaph.
    But now it takes from him his name,
    Falls open like a dishonest look,
    And shows us, rotted and endowed,
        Its senile pleasure.   40
                  1942

Elegy for a Dead Soldier

1

A white sheet on the tail-gate of a truck
Becomes an altar; two small candlesticks
Sputter at each side of the crucifix
Laid round with flowers brighter than the blood,
Red as the red of our apocalypse,
Hibiscus that a marching man will pluck

---

[1] Monticello, the home and resting place of Thomas Jefferson (1743 – 1826).

To stick into his rifle or his hat,
And great blue morning-glories pale as lips
That shall no longer taste or kiss or swear.
The wind begins a low magnificat,   10
The chaplain chats, the palmtrees swirl their hair,
The columns come together through the mud.

2

We too are ashes as we watch and hear
The psalm, the sorrow, and the simple praise
Of one whose promised thoughts of other days
Were such as ours, but now wholly destroyed,
The service record of his youth wiped out,
His dream dispersed by shot, must disappear.
What can we feel but wonder at a loss
That seems to point at nothing but the doubt   20
Which flirts our sense of luck into the ditch?
Reader of Paul who prays beside this fosse, — *ditch or mote*
Shall we believe our eyes or legends rich
With glory and rebirth beyond the void?

3

For this comrade is dead, dead in the war,
A young man out of millions yet to live,
One cut away from all that war can give,
Freedom of self and peace to wander free.
Who mourns in all this sober multitude
Who did not feel the bite of it before   30
The bullet found its aim? This worthy flesh,
This boy laid in a coffin and reviewed—
Who has not wrapped himself in this same flag,
Heard the light fall of dirt, his wound still fresh,
Felt his eyes closed, and heard the distant brag
Of the last volley of humanity?

4

By chance I saw him die, stretched on the ground,
A tattooed arm lifted to take the blood
Of someone else sealed in a tin. I stood
During the last delirium that stays   40
The intelligence a tiny moment more,
And then the strangulation, the last sound.
The end was sudden, like a foolish play,
A stupid fool slamming a foolish door,
The absurd catastrophe, half-prearranged,
And all the decisive things still left to say.
So we disbanded, angrier and unchanged,
Sick with the utter silence of dispraise.

5

We ask for no statistics of the killed,
For nothing political impinges on   50
This single casualty, or all those gone,
Missing or healing, sinking or dispersed,
Hundreds of thousands counted, millions lost.
More than an accident and less than willed
Is every fall, and this one like the rest.
However others calculate the cost,
To us the final aggregate is *one*,
One with a name, one transferred to the blest;
And though another stoops and takes the gun,
We cannot add the second to the first.   60

6

I would not speak for him who could not speak
Unless my fear were true: he was not wronged,
He knew to which decision he belonged
But let it choose itself. Ripe in instinct,
Neither the victim nor the volunteer,
He followed, and the leaders could not seek
Beyond the followers. Much of this he knew;
The journey was a detour that would steer
Into the Lincoln Highway of a land
Remorselessly improved, excited, new,   70
And that was what he wanted. He had planned
To earn and drive. He and the world had winked.

7

No history deceived him, for he knew
Little of times and armies not his own;
He never felt that peace was but a loan,
Had never questioned the idea of gain.
Beyond the headlines once or twice he saw
The gathering of a power by the few
But could not tell their names; he cast his vote,
Distrusting all the elected but not law.   80
He laughed at socialism; *on mourrait
Pour les industriels?*[1] He shed his coat
And not for brotherhood, but for his pay.
To him the red flag marked the sewer main.

8

Above all else he loathed the homily,
The slogan and the ad. He paid his bill

---

[1] "Would one die for the industrialists?"

But not for Congressmen at Bunker Hill.
Ideals were few and those there were not made
For conversation. He belonged to church
But never spoke of God. The Christmas tree,   90
The Easter egg, baptism, he observed,
Never denied the preacher on his perch,
And would not sign Resolved That or Whereas.
Softness he had and hours and nights reserved
For thinking, dressing, dancing to the jazz.
His laugh was real, his manners were home made.

9

Of all men poverty pursued him least;
He was ashamed of all the down and out,
Spurned the panhandler like an uneasy doubt,
And saw the unemployed as a vague mass   100
Incapable of hunger or revolt.
He hated other races, south or east,
And shoved them to the margin of his mind.
He could recall the justice of the Colt,
Take interest in a gang-war like a game.
His ancestry was somewhere far behind
And left him only his peculiar name.
Doors opened, and he recognized no class.

10

His children would have known a heritage,
Just or unjust, the richest in the world,   110
The quantum of all art and science curled
In the horn of plenty, bursting from the horn,
A people bathed in honey, Paris come,
Vienna transferred with the highest wage,
A World's Fair spread to Phoenix, Jacksonville,
Earth's capitol, the new Byzantium,
Kingdom of man—who knows? Hollow or firm,
No man can ever prophesy until
Out of our death some undiscovered germ,
Whole toleration or pure peace is born.   120

11

The time to mourn is short that best becomes
The military dead. We lift and fold the flag,
Lay bare the coffin with its written tag,
And march away. Behind, four others wait
To lift the box, the heaviest of loads.
The anesthetic afternoon benumbs,
Sickens our senses, forces back our talk.
We know that others on tomorrow's roads

Will fall, ourselves perhaps, the man beside,
Over the world the threatened, all who walk: 130
And could we mark the grave of him who died
We would write this beneath his name and date:

Epitaph

Underneath this wooden cross there lies
A Christian killed in battle. You who read,
Remember that this stranger died in pain;
And passing here, if you can lift your eyes
Upon a peace kept by a human creed,
Know that one soldier has not died in vain.

1944

The Conscientious Objector

The gates clanged and they walked you into jail
More tense than felons but relieved to find
The hostile world shut out, the flags that dripped
From every mother's windowpane, obscene
The bloodlust sweating from the public heart,
The dog authority slavering at your throat.
A sense of quiet, of pulling down the blind
Possessed you. Punishment you felt was clean.

The decks, the catwalks, and the narrow light
Composed a ship. This was a mutinous crew   10
Troubling the captains for plain decencies,
A *Mayflower* brim with pilgrims headed out
To establish new theocracies to west,
A Noah's ark coasting the topmost seas
Ten miles above the sodomites and fish.
These inmates loved the only living doves.

Like all men hunted from the world you made
A good community, voyaging the storm
To no safe Plymouth or green Ararat;
Trouble or calm, the men with Bibles prayed,   20
The gaunt politicals construed our hate.
The opposite of all armies, you were best
Opposing uniformity and yourselves;
Prison and personality were your fate.

You suffered not so physically but knew
Maltreatment, hunger, ennui of the mind.
Well might the soldier kissing the hot beach

ennui- dissatisfaction resulting from inactivity

Erupting in his face damn all your kind.
Yet you who saved neither yourselves nor us
Are equally with those who shed the blood
The heroes of our cause. Your conscience is
What we come back to in the armistice.

30

1947

Robert Lowell 1917—

Robert Traill Spence Lowell was born in Boston and educated at Harvard and Kenyon College. At Kenyon he studied under John Crowe Ransom and was converted to Roman Catholicism in the year of his graduation (1940). During World War II he served time in prison as a conscientious objector. He won praise for his first volume of poems, *Land of Unlikeness* (1944), and a Pulitzer Prize for his second, *Lord Weary's Castle* (1946; 1947). Two further volumes—*Poems: 1938–1949* (1950) and *The Mills of the Kavanaughs* (1951)—complete the work of his early period. In these poems, which reflect the combined influences of Eliot and Ransom, Lowell employs devices of paradox and metaphysical metaphor to develop, within the regular metrical forms favored by the New Critics, themes of personal religious conflict and cultural decay. The poems of *Life Studies* (1959) show an abrupt shift in technique as Lowell turned, like many younger poets of the time, from regular metrical patterns to the freer forms inspired by the work of Ezra Pound and William Carlos Williams. In these later poems, which explore the unhappy family relationships that disturbed his childhood and youth, Lowell continues with even greater emphasis a tendency toward intimate psychological and moral self-analysis. For this reason he has been identified with a tradition of contemporary "confessional" poetry.

Lowell's other books include two volumes of free translations—*Imitations* (1961) and *Phaedra* (1961)—and two later collections of poems: *For the Union Dead* (1964) and *Near the Ocean* (1967).

Critiques of Lowell's poetry include H. B. Staples, *Robert Lowell: The First Twenty Years* (New York, 1962), and Jerome Mazzaro, *The Poetic Themes of Robert Lowell* (Ann Arbor, Mich., 1965).

The text of the first three poems is that of *Poems: 1938–1949* (London, 1950). "Ford Madox Ford" and "Skunk Hour" are from *Life Studies* (New York, 1959). The text of "For the Union Dead" is that of the volume of the same name (New York, 1964).

Christmas Eve Under Hooker's Statue[1]

Tonight a blackout. Twenty years ago
I hung my stocking on the tree, and hell's
Serpent entwined the apple in the toe
To sting the child with knowledge. Hooker's heels
Kicking at nothing in the shifting snow,
A cannon and a cairn of cannon balls
Rusting before the blackened Statehouse, know
How the long horn of plenty broke like glass
In Hooker's gauntlets. Once I came from Mass;

Now storm-clouds shelter Christmas, once again   10
Mars meets his fruitless star with open arms,
His heavy sabre flashes with the rime,
The war-god's bronzed and empty forehead forms
Anonymous machinery from raw men;
The cannon on the Common[2] cannot stun
The blundering butcher as he rides on Time—
The barrel clinks with holly. I am cold:
I ask for bread, my father gives me mould;

His stocking is full of stones, Santa in red
Is crowned with wizened berries. Man of war,   20
Where is the summer's garden? In its bed
The ancient speckled serpent will appear,
And black-eyed susan with her frizzled head.
When Chancellorsville[3] mowed down the volunteer,
"All wars are boyish," Herman Melville said;[4]
But we are old, our fields are running wild:
Till Christ again turn wanderer and child.

                                        1944

Children of Light

Our fathers wrung their bread from stocks and stones
And fenced their gardens with the Redman's bones;
Embarking from the Nether Land of Holland,

---

[1] The statue before the statehouse in Boston of General Joseph ("Fighting Joe") Hooker (1814–1879).
[2] Boston Common.
[3] The Battle of Chancellorsville (May 2–4, 1863), in which Hooker was defeated by the Confederates under Lee and Stonewall Jackson.
[4] "All wars are boyish, and are fought by boys," a quotation from Melville's poem "The March Into Virginia," from *Battle Pieces* (1866).

Pilgrims unhouseled by Geneva's night,[1]
They planted here the Serpent's seeds of light;
And here the pivoting searchlights probe to shock
The riotous glass houses built on rock,
And candles gutter by an empty altar,
And light is where the landless blood of Cain
Is burning, burning the unburied grain.

1944

Mr. Edwards and the Spider [2]

I saw the spiders marching through the air,
Swimming from tree to tree that mildewed day
    In latter August when the hay
      Came creaking to the barn. But where
        The wind is westerly,
Where gnarled November makes the spiders fly
Into the apparitions of the sky,
    They purpose nothing but their ease and die
Urgently beating east to sunrise and the sea;

    What are we in the hands of the great God?   10
It was in vain you set up thorn and briar
    In battle array against the fire
      And treason crackling in your blood;
        For the wild thorns grow tame
And will do nothing to oppose the flame;
    Your lacerations tell the losing game
You play against a sickness past your cure.
How will the hands be strong? How will the heart endure?

    A very little thing, a little worm,
Or hourglass-blazoned spider, it is said,   20
    Can kill a tiger. Will the dead
      Hold up his mirror and affirm
        To the four winds the smell
And flash of his authority? It's well
    If God who holds you to the pit of hell,
Much as one holds a spider, will destroy,
Baffle and dissipate your soul. As a small boy

    On Windsor Marsh, I saw the spider die
When thrown into the bowels of fierce fire:
    There's no long struggle, no desire   30

[1] A reference to the pessimistic theology of John Calvin (1509–1564) of Geneva, which the English Puritans accepted.
[2] The title and poem point back both to Jonathan Edwards' youthful observations of the migration of spiders and to his later harsh Calvinist sermon "Sinners in the Hands of an Angry God."

To get up on its feet and fly —
    It stretches out its feet
And dies. This is the sinner's last retreat;
Yes, and no strength exerted on the heat
    Then sinews the abolished will, when sick
And full of burning, it will whistle on a brick.

    But who can plumb the sinking of that soul?
    Josiah Hawley, picture yourself cast
        Into a brick-kiln where the blast
        Fans your quick vitals to a coal —   40
            If measured by a glass,
    How long would it seem burning! Let there pass
    A minute, ten, ten trillion; but the blaze
    Is infinite eternal: this is death,
To die and know it. This is the Black Widow, death.

                                            1946

Ford Madox Ford[1]

The lobbed ball plops, then dribbles to the cup. . . .
(a birdie Fordie!) But it nearly killed
the ministers. Lloyd George was holding up
the flag. He gabbled, "Hop-toad, hop-toad, hop-toad!
Hueffer[2] has used a niblick on the green;
it's filthy art, Sir, filthy art!"
You answered, "What is art to me and thee?
Will a blacksmith teach a midwife how to bear?"
That cut the puffing statesman down to size,
Ford. You said, "Otherwise,   10
I would have been general of a division." Ah Ford!
Was it war, the sport of kings, that your *Good Soldier*,[3]
the best French novel in the language, taught
those Georgian Whig magnificoes at Oxford,
at Oxford decimated on the Somme?
Ford, five times black-balled for promotion,
then mustard gassed voiceless some seven miles
behind the lines at Nancy or Belleau Wood:
you emerged in your "worn uniform,
gilt dragons on the revers of the tunic,"   20
a Jonah — O divorced, divorced
from the whale-fat of post-war London! Boomed,
cut, plucked and booted! In Provence, New York . . .
marrying, blowing . . . nearly dying
at Boulder, when the altitude
pressed the world on your heart,

[1] For Gertrude Stein's references to the English novelist Ford Madox Ford, veteran of World War I, and later a resident of Provence and New York City, see above.
[2] Born Ford Madox Hueffer, the novelist changed his name to Ford after World War I.
[3] Ford's novel, *The Good Soldier* (1915)

and your audience, almost football-size,
shrank to a dozen, while you stood
mumbling, with fish-blue-eyes,
and mouth pushed out   30
fish-fashion, as if you gagged for air. . . .
Sandman! Your face, a childish *O*. The sun
is pernod-yellow and it gilds the heirs
of all the ages there on Washington
and Stuyvesant, your Lilliputian squares,
where writing turned your pockets inside out.
But master, mammoth mumbler, tell me why
the bales of your left-over novels buy
less than a bandage for your gouty foot.
Wheel-horse, O unforgetting elephant,   40
I hear you huffing at your old Brevoort,[4]
Timon and Falstaff, while you heap the board
for publishers. Fiction! I'm selling short
your lies that made the great your equals. Ford,
you were a kind man and you died in want.

                                        1959

Skunk Hour

For Elizabeth Bishop[1]

Nautilus Island's hermit
heiress still lives through winter in her Spartan cottage;
her sheep still graze above the sea.
Her son's a bishop. Her farmer   *the dying aristocracy*
is first selectman in our village;
she's in her dotage.

Thirsting for
the hierarchic privacy
of Queen Victoria's century,   *two*
she buys up all   *study of culture's*   10
the eyesores facing her shore,   *the rich-island-*
and lets them fall.   *the small town,*
                                             airs, affectations
The season's ill—
we've lost our summer millionaire,
who seemed to leap from an L. L. Bean[2]
catalogue. His nine-knot yawl
was auctioned off to lobstermen.
A red fox stain covers Blue Hill.[3]

[4] A well-known New York hotel. The earlier linking of Washington Square and "the heirs of all the ages" (ll. 33–34) is a reminder of the earlier New York novelist, Henry James (1843–1916), whom Ford had known and admired in England.
[1] American poet (b. 1911).
[2] The well-known outdoorsmen's mail-order house in Freeport, Maine.
[3] Name of a hill and a town on the coast of Maine.

And now our fairy
decorator brightens his shop for fall;   *— delusion*   20
his fishnet's filled with orange cork,
orange, his cobbler's bench and awl;
there is no money in his work,
he'd rather marry.

One dark night,
my Tudor Ford climbed the hill's skull;   *St. John's dark*
I watched for love-cars. Lights turned down,   *night*
they lay together, hull to hull,
where the graveyard shelves on the town. . . .
My mind's not right.   30

A car radio bleats,
"Love, O careless Love. . . ." I hear
my ill-spirit sob in each blood cell,
as if my hand were at its throat. . . .
I myself am hell;
nobody's here—   *Satan's language in*
          "Paradise Lost"

only skunks, that search
in the moonlight for a bite to eat.
They march on their soles up Main Street:
white stripes, moonstruck eyes' red fire   40
under the chalk-dry and spar spire
of the Trinitarian Church.

I stand on top
of our back steps and breathe the rich air—
a mother skunk with her column of kittens swills the garbage pail.
She jabs her wedge-head in a cup
of sour cream, drops her ostrich tail,
and will not scare.

          1959

For the Union Dead [1]

"Relinquunt omnia servare rem publicam." [2]

The old South Boston Aquarium stands
in a Sahara of snow now. Its broken windows are boarded.
The bronze weathervane cod has lost half its scales.
The airy tanks are dry.

Once my nose crawled like a snail on the glass;
my hand tingled

[1] First published in *Life Studies* (1959) under the title "Colonel Shaw and the Massachusetts 54th."
[2] "They give up everything to save the Republic."

to burst the bubbles
drifting from the noses of the cowed, compliant fish.

My hand draws back. I often sigh still
for the dark downward and vegetating kingdom   10
of the fish and reptile. One morning last March,
I pressed against the new barbed and galvanized

fence on the Boston Common. Behind their cage,
yellow dinosaur steamshovels were grunting
as they cropped up tons of mush and grass
to gouge their underworld garage.

Parking spaces luxuriate like civic
sandpiles in the heart of Boston.
A girdle of orange, Puritan-pumpkin colored girders
braces the tingling Statehouse,   20

shaking over the excavations, as it faces Colonel Shaw
and his bell-cheeked Negro infantry
on St. Gaudens' shaking Civil War relief,[3]
propped by a plank splint against the garage's earthquake.

Two months after marching through Boston,
half the regiment was dead;
at the dedication,
William James[4] could almost hear the bronze Negroes breathe.

Their monument sticks like a fishbone
in the city's throat.   30
Its Colonel is as lean
as a compass-needle.

He has an angry wrenlike vigilance,
a greyhound's gentle tautness;
he seems to wince at pleasure,
and suffocate for privacy.

He is out of bounds now. He rejoices in man's lovely,
peculiar power to choose life and die—
when he leads his black soldiers to death,
he cannot bend his back.   40

On a thousand small town New England greens,
the old white churches hold their air
of sparse, sincere rebellion; frayed flags
quilt the graveyards of the Grand Army of the Republic.

---

[3] For other reference to the sculptor August St. Gaudens (1848–1907), see Henry Adams.
[4] The philosopher and psychologist (1842–1910), brother to Henry James.

The stone statues of the abstract Union Soldier
grow slimmer and younger each year—
wasp-waisted, they doze over muskets
and muse through their sideburns . . .

Shaw's father wanted no monument
except the ditch,   50
where his son's body was thrown
and lost with his "niggers."

The ditch is nearer.
There are no statues for the last war here;
on Boylston Street, a commercial photograph
shows Hiroshima boiling

over a Mosler Safe, the "Rock of Ages"
that survived the blast. Space is nearer.
When I crouch to my television set,
the drained faces of Negro school-children rise like balloons.   60

Colonel Shaw
is riding on his bubble,
he waits
for the blesséd break.

The Aquarium is gone. Everywhere,
giant finned cars nose forward like fish;
a savage servility
slides by on grease.

                                        1959

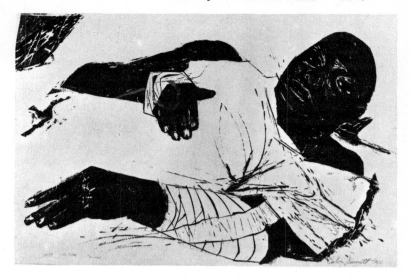

Fiction of the Postwar Years

The fiction published in the years since World War II is remarkable for the range of its interests and viewpoints. Although none of the younger writers has gained the stature of Hemingway, Fitzgerald, or Faulkner, their work reveals a high level of achievement and a variety of new trends.

As in every period of transition—in this case from the modern to an as yet not clearly defined post-modern period—there has been an inter-action of tradition and innovation. This process can be seen at work in the war novel, a type of modern fiction established by veterans of World War I in the 1920's and renewed by the veterans of World War II. Among the many novels inspired by the Second War, the most distinguished early example is Norman Mailer's *The Naked and the Dead* (1948), which combines the pessimistic naturalism of the war fiction of the 1920's with the collectivist interests of the 1930's. Like the writers of the Depression years, Mailer expresses a fear of the fascism that threatens an industrial society, and he almost, but not quite, creates a proletarian hero in Red Valsen to counter (ineffectually) native fascist types like Sergeant Croft and General Cummings.

A more recent and equally interesting war novel is Joseph Heller's comic masterpiece, *Catch-22* (1961). With a hatred of authoritarianism equal to Mailer's, Heller makes use of paradox and existential absurdity to attack the illogic and inhumanity of modern war and the modern society it represents. He succeeds in exploiting a contemporary interest in comedy which is alien to the earlier modern writer's preoccupation with the tragic vision.

Vote Victim by Calvin Burnett, serigraph in color, 1956. Courtesy of the Boston Public Library

The tradition of modern Southern regionalism that bourgeoned in the 1920's and 1930's has been carried forward by many writers, including Eudora Welty, Truman Capote, and Flannery O'Connor. Their stories and novels perpetuate the themes of decadence and violence established in the Southern Gothic tradition, but usually without the countervailing magnanimity and even heroic dignity that Faulkner gave to his more admirable characters.

The renaissance in Negro literature that began with Jean Toomer in the early 1920's gained a new momentum in the postwar years. Among Negro writers, two of the most accomplished are Ralph Ellison and James Baldwin. Baldwin's most interesting fiction is based on his youthful experience of growing up in Harlem in a revivalistic religious atmosphere in which piety and the ever-present threat of violence existed side by side. Ellison's *The Invisible Man* (1952) is a story of a young Negro's search for individuality that attains a universal significance as the claims of race are finally transcended by considerations of humanity.

A development paralleling the growth of Negro literature is the emergence, since the war, of the Jewish author and Jewish protagonist in contemporary American fiction. Many writers have dealt intelligently, interestingly, often amusingly, with the problem of Jewishness in a white Anglo-Saxon Protestant society that had in earlier periods been the exclusive breeding ground of American artists and intellectuals. The situation of the Jewish intellectual is one that Saul Bellow has treated with great skill and understanding in *Herzog* (1964), an important book also because it points to new possibilities for American writers in the development of the novel of ideas, a type of fiction heretofore more typical of Europe than the United States.

The diversity of regional, racial, and religious interests that have marked postwar fiction is in keeping with the turbulence and unrest in American society as contending groups struggle for a fuller participation in the social and political process. The apparent confusion of voices among these groups may seem to threaten chaos and anarchy, but collectively they also represent a dynamic society with a tremendous capacity for change and growth.

Norman Mailer   *1923–*

Born in Long Branch, New Jersey, Norman Mailer grew up in Brooklyn and went to Harvard University. After graduating in 1943, he served with the Army in the Pacific Theater, part of the time with a reconnaissance unit in the Philippine Islands. His first and most successful novel, *The Naked and the Dead* (1948), tells the story of a reconnaissance platoon in the invasion of a Japanese-held island. Since the platoon represents a cross-section of American society, the novel is in the tradition of the collective novel of John Dos Passos and John Steinbeck, but without the spirit of protest and proletarian affirmation of their novels of the 1930's. Like these writers, Mailer makes use of interchapters—biographical "time machines"—which explain the natures of his soldier characters in terms of their social backgrounds. In his time machine on General Cummings, Mailer portrays the development of a fascist personality under the conditions of modern American life. *The Naked and the Dead* was followed by *Barbary Shore* (1951) and *The Deer Park* (1955).

Although Mailer has continued to be concerned with social and political problems from a strongly anticonservative viewpoint, the focus of his later work has shifted from a relatively objective analysis of American culture to a strongly subjective preoccupation with existential self-identification in a world of violence and irrationality. His later books include *The White Negro* (1958), *Advertisements for Myself* (1959), *Deaths for the Ladies and Other Disasters* (1962), *The Presidential Papers of Norman Mailer* (1963), and *An American Dream* (1965), and *Why Are We in Vietnam: A Novel* (1967).

The text of "General Cummings: A Peculiarly American Statement" is that of *The Naked and the Dead* (New York, 1948).

General Cummings: A Peculiarly American Statement[1]

At first glance he did not look unlike other general officers. A little over medium height, well fleshed, with a rather handsome suntanned face and graying hair, but there were differences. His expression when he smiled was very close to the ruddy complacent and hard appearance of any number of American senators and businessmen, but the tough good-guy aura never quite remained. There was a certain vacancy in his face . . . there was the appearance and yet it was not there. Hearn[2] always felt as if the smiling face were numb.

The town has existed for a long time in this part of the Midwest, more than seventy years by 1910, but it has not been a city very long. "Why, not so long ago," they will say, "I can remember when this here town was nothin' much more than a post office and the school house, the Old Presbyterian church and the Main Hotel. Old Ike Cummings had the general store then, and for a while we had a feller barbered hair, but he didn't last long, moved on some'er else. And then," with a slow evaluating wink, "they was a town whoor used to do business in the county."

And of course when Cyrus Cummings (named after the older McCormick)[3] went to New York on those banking trips, he didn't waste his time. "I tell you," the people will say, "they had to bring that factory here. Cy Cummings didn't give his help to McKinley for nothing back in 'ninety-six; he's a Yankee trader. He might not a had much of a bank in those days but when he called in all the farmer debts the week before election this here became a McKinley county. Cy is even smarter than old Ike, an' you remember when Ike had the general store nobody traded him a horse with a canker." And the old man on the vanishing cracker barrel fluffs some spittle into his corded stale handkerchief. "Course," with a grin, "I ain't sayin' that anyone in town loves Cy more than is proper, but the town . . ." (with another grin) "I mean, the city, sure as hell owes him a lot, be it in gratitude or hard dollar bills."

The town is set in the middle of the great American plain. There are a few knolls or rills bordering it, one of the insignificant accidents of land in the long flat face of the Midwest, and you can find quite a few trees on the lee side of the railroad tracks. The streets are broad and the elm and oak bloom in summer, soften the harsh crabbed outlines of the

---

[1] In this "Time Machine," or biographical interchapter in *The Naked and the Dead*, the author "documents" the development of the fascist personality of one of his major characters.

[2] Robert Hearn, a lieutenant and aide to General Cummings.

[3] Cyrus McCormick (1809–1884), inventor and manufacturer of farm machinery.

Queen Anne houses, throw interesting shadows into the angles of the gable windows and truncated dormer roofs. Center Street has only a few buildings left with false façades, and there are lots of stores now, so many farmers in town on Saturday afternoons that they are beginning to pave it with cobblestones so the horses won't bog in the mud.

For the richest man in town, Cy Cummings's house is not too different. The Cummingses built it thirty years ago at a time when it stood all alone on the edge of town and you walked to your thighs in mud to reach it in early fall and spring. But the town has encompassed it now and there is not much Cy Cummings can do in the way of improvements.

The worst of the changes you can blame on his wife. The folks who know them say it's her fault, a fancy eastern woman with Culture. Cy's a hard man, but he isn't a fancy one, and that new front door with all the windowpanes on the bias is something French. She's mentioned the name at church meeting, Newvelle something. And Cy Cummings has even turned High Episcopal for her, was instrumental in getting the 'Piscopal church built.

Odd family, people will tell you, funny kids.

In the parlor with the portraits on the wall, the brown murky landscapes in golden scalloped frames, the dark draperies, the brown furniture, the fireplace—in the parlor the family is sitting around.

That feller Debs[4] is making trouble again, Cy Cummings says. (A sharp-featured face with a partially bald head, silver-rimmed glasses.)

Yes, dear? The wife turns to her sewing, embroiders another golden stitch on the buttocks of the Cupid in the center of the doily. (A pretty woman, flutters a little, with the long dress, the impressive bosom of the period.) Well, why does he make trouble?

Aaahr, Cy snorts, the basic disgust for a woman's remark.

Hang 'em, Ike Cummings says, with the old man's quaver. In the war (the Civil War) we used to take 'em up, set 'em on a mare, and spank her rump, and watch them kick their heels a little.

Cy rustles his paper. Don't need to hang 'em. He looks at his hands, laughs dourly. Edward go to sleep yet?

She looks up, answers quickly, nervously, I think so, that is he said he was. He and Matthew said they were going to sleep. (Matthew Arnold Cummings is the younger one.)

I'll take a look.

In the boys' bedroom, Matthew is asleep, and Edward, age seven, is sitting in a corner, sewing snips of thread into a scrap of cloth.

The father steps toward him, throws his shadow across the boy's face. What are you doing, boy?

---

[4] For John Dos Passos' biography of the Socialist leader, Eugene V. Debs, see above.

The child looks up petrified. Sewin'. Ma said it was okay.

Give it to me. And the scraps, the thread, are hurled into the wastebasket. Come up, 'Lizabeth.

He hears the argument raging about him, conducted in hoarse passionate whispers as a sop to his sleeping brother. I won't have him actin' like a goddam woman, you're to stop feedin' him all these books, all this womanish . . . claptrap. (The baseball bat and glove are gathering dust in the attic.)

But I didn't . . . I didn't tell him a thing.

You didn't tell him to sew?

Please, Cyrus, let him alone. The slap reddens his cheek from the ear to the mouth. The boy sits on the floor, the tears dropping in his lap.

And you're to act like a man from now on, do you understand?

Only when they have gone, too many things twist in his comprehension. The mother had given him the thread, told him to do it quietly.

The sermon ends in church. We are all children of the Lord Jesus and God, instruments of His compassion, committed unto earth to enact the instruments of His goodness, to sow the seeds of brotherhood and good works.

A fine sermon, the mother says.

Yeahp.

Was he right? Edward asks.

Certainly, Cyrus says, only you got to take it with a grain of caution. Life's a hard thing and nobody gives you nothing. You do it alone. Every man's hand is against you, that's what you also find out.

Then he was wrong, Father.

I didn't say that. He's right and I'm right, and it's just in religion you act one way, and in business, which is a lesser thing, well, you go about things in another way. It's still Christian.

The mother caresses his shoulder. It was a wonderful sermon, Edward.

Nearly everybody in this town hates me, Cyrus says. They hate you too, Edward, you might as well learn it early, ain't nothing they hate like a success, and you're sure gonna be one, if they don't like you they can still lick your boots.

The mother and the son pack up the paints and easel, start back in the chilly spring afternoon from their jaunt outside the town, sketching the meager hills on the plain.

Have a good time, Eddie dear? Her voice has a new trill in it now, a new warmth when they are alone.

Loved it, Ma.

When I was a little girl, I always used to dream I'd have a little boy and I'd go out with him and paint, just like this. Come on, I'll teach you a funny song while we go back.

What is Boston like? he asks.

Oh, it's a big city, it's dirty, coooold, everybody's always dressed up.

Like Pa?

She laughs doubtfully. Yes, like Pa. Now, don't you say anything to him about what we did this afternoon. . . . Was it wrong?

No, now you just march right on home with me, and don't say a word to him, it's a secret.

He hates her suddenly, and is quiet, moody, as they walk back to the town. That night he tells his father, listens with a kind of delicious glee and fright to the quarrel that follows.

I'm going to tell you that that boy is all your fault, you indulge him, you bring out the worst in him, you never could get over leaving Boston, now, could you, we're really not fine enough out here for you.

Cyrus, please.

I'll be damned, I'm going to send him to military school, he's old enough to shift for himself, at nine years old a boy has to start thinking how to act like a man.

Ike Cummings nods. Military school's all right, that boy likes to listen to things about the war.

What is partially behind it all is the conversation Cyrus has had with the town doctor. The fabulous beard, the hard shrewd eyes have twinkled at him, got a little of their own back. Well, now, Mr. Cummings, there ain't a damn thing can be done now, it's over my head, if he were a little older I'd say take the boy over to Sally's and let him get some jism in his system.

The basic good-bye at the age of ten, the railroad train, the farewell to the muddy roads at the periphery of town, the gaunt family houses, the smell of his father's bank, and the laundry on the lines.

Good-bye, Son, and do all right for yourself, do you hear?

He has accepted the father's decision without any feeling, but now he shudders almost imperceptibly at the hand on his shoulder.

Good-bye, Ma. She is weeping, and he feels a mild contempt, an almost lost compassion.

Good-bye, and he goes, plummets into the monastery and becomes lost in the routine of the school, in polishing his buttons and making his bed.

There are changes in him. He has never been friendly with other boys, but now he is cold rather than shy. The water colors, the books like *Little Lord Fauntleroy* and *Ivanhoe* and *Oliver Twist* are far less important; he never misses them. Through the years there he gets the best marks in his class, becomes a minor athlete, No. 3 man on the tennis team. Like his father, he is respected if he is not loved.

And the crushes of course: he stands by his bunk at Saturday morning inspection, rigidly upright, clicking his heels as the colonel headmaster comes by. The suite of officer-teachers pass, and he waits numbly for the cadet colonel, a tall dark-haired youth.

Cummings, the cadet colonel says.

Yes, sir.

Your web belt has verdigris in the eyelets.

Yes, sir. And he watches him go, shuttling between anguish and a troubled excitement because he has been noticed. A subterranean phenomenon, for he takes no part in the special activities pertinent to a boys' private school, is almost conspicuous by his avoidance.

Nine years of it, the ascetic barracks, and the communal sleeping, the uniform-fears, the equipment-fears, the marching-tensions, and the meaningless vacations. He sees his parents for six weeks each summer, finds them strange, feels distant toward his brother. Mrs. Cyrus Cummings bores him now with her nostalgia.

Remember, Eddie, when we went out to the hill and painted?

Yes, Mother.

He graduates as cadet colonel.

At home he makes a little stir in his uniform. The people know he is going to West Point, and he is pointed out to the young girls, to whom he is polite and indifferent. He is handsome now, not too tall, but his build is respectable, and his face has an intelligent scrubbed look.

Cyrus talks to him. Well, Son, you're ready for West Point, eh?

Yes, sir, I expect so.

Mmm. Glad you went to military school?

Tried to do the best I could, sir.

Cyrus nods. West Point pleases him. He has decided long ago that little Matthew Arnold can carry on the bank, and this strange stiff son in the uniform is best away from home. Good idea sending you there, Cyrus says.

Why . . . His mind is blank, but a powerful anxiety stirs along his spine. His palms are always wet when he talks to his father. Why, yes, sir (knowing somehow that this is what Cyrus wants to hear). Yes, sir. I hope to do well at the Point, sir.

You will if you're a son of mine. (Laughing heartily in the consummation-of-business-deal heartiness, he claps him on the back.)

Again . . . Yes, sir. And he withdraws, the basic reaction.

He meets the girl he is to marry in the summer after his second year at West Point. He has not been home in two years because there have been no vacations long enough for him to make the trip, but he has not missed the town. When this vacation comes he goes to Boston to visit his mother's relatives.

The city delights him; the manners of his relatives come as a revelation after the crude probing speech of the town. He is very polite at first, very reticent, aware that until he learns the blunders he must not make he cannot talk freely. But there are stirrings. He walks the streets of Beacon Hill, ascending eagerly along the narrow sidewalks to the State House where he stands motionless, watching the light-play on the Charles, a half mile below him. The brass knockers, the dull black knockers intrigue him; he stares at all the narrow doors, touches his hat to the old ladies in black who smile pleasantly, a trifle doubtfully, at his cadet's uniform.

This is what I like.

I'm very fond of Boston, he says a few weeks later to his cousin Margaret. They have become confidants.

Are you? she says. It's getting a little seedy. Father said there are always less and less places where one may go. (Her face is delicately long, pleasantly cold. Despite the length of her nose it turns up at the tip.)

Oh, well, the Irish, he miffs, but he is vaguely uncomfortable in saying it, conscious that his answer is trite.

Uncle Andrew is always complaining that they've taken the government away from us. I heard him say the other night that it's like France now, he was there, you know, the only careers left are in the service (State department) or in uniform, and even there the elements are undependable. (Conscious of an error, she adds quickly) He's very fond of you.

I'm glad.

You know, it's odd, Margaret says, only a few years ago Uncle Andrew was very intolerant about the whole thing. I'll tell you a secret. (She laughs, puts her arm through his.) He always preferred the Navy. He says they have better manners.

Oh. (For a moment he feels lost. All their politeness, their acceptance of him as a relative is seen from the other side of the door. There is the brief moment when he tries to reverse all the things he remembers their saying, examines them from the new approach.)

That doesn't mean anything, Margaret says, we're all such frauds. It's a terrible thing to say, but you know whatever we have in the family is what we accept. I was terribly shocked when I first realized that.

Then I'm all right, he says lightly.

Oh, no, you won't do at all. (She laughs first, and he joins in a little hesitantly.) You're just our second cousin from the West. That isn't done. (Her long face seems merry for a moment.) Seriously, it's just that we've known only Navy up till now. Tom Hopkinson and Thatcher Lloyd, I think you met him at Dennis, well, they're all Navy, and Uncle Andrew knows their fathers so well. But he likes you. I think he had a crush on your mother.

Well, that makes it better. (They laugh again, sit down on a bench and throw pebbles into the Charles River basin.)

You're awfully vivacious, Margaret.

Oh, I'm a fraud too. If you knew me you'd say I was awfully moody.

I bet I wouldn't.

Oh, I wept, you know I completely wept when Minot and I lost our boat class race two years ago. It was just silly. Father wanted us to win it, and I was terrified what he would say. You can't move around here at all, nothing one can do, there's always a reason why it isn't *advisable*. (For an instant her voice is almost bitter.) You're not like us at all, you're serious, you're important. (Her voice lilts again.) Father told me you were second from the top in your class. That's bad manners.

Would the middle third be respectable?

Not for you. You're going to be a general.

I don't believe it. (His voice in these weeks in Boston has assumed the proper tone, become a little higher, a little more lazy. He cannot express the excitement, perhaps the exaltation Boston gives him. Everyone is so perfect here.)

You're just doodling me, he says. (A leprous phrase of the Midwest, he realizes too late, and is unbalanced for a moment.)

Oh, no, I'm convinced you're going to be a great man.

I like you, Margaret.

You should after I praised you like that. (She giggles once more, says ingenuously) I suppose I want you to like me.

At the end of summer when he is leaving she hugs him, whispers in his ear, I wish we were definitely engaged so you could kiss me.

So do I. But it is the first time he has thought of her as a woman to be loved, and he is a little shocked, a little empty. On the train going back, she has lost her disturbing individuality already, remains as the pleasant focus of her family and Boston behind them. He feels an unfamiliar, a satisfying identity with his classmates when he talks about his girl. It's important to have one, he decides.

He is always learning things, understanding already that his mind must work on many levels. There is the thing he thinks of as the truth, the objective situation which his mind must unravel; there is the "deep layer," as he calls it, the mattress resting on the cloud, and he does not care to plumb for the legs; there is, and it is very important, the level where he must do and say things for their effect upon the men with whom he lives and works.

He learns the last dramatically in the hour on Military History and Tactics. (The brown scrubbed room, the blackboards at the front, the benches where the cadets sit in the unquestioned symmetry of ancient patterns, the squares of a chessboard.)

Sir (he gets permission to speak), is it fair to say that Lee was the better general than Grant? I know that their tactics don't compare, but Grant had the knowledge of strategy. What good are tactics, sir, if the . . . the larger mechanics of men and supplies are not developed properly, because the tactics are just the part of the whole? In this conception wasn't Grant the greater man because he tried to take into account the intangibles. He wasn't much good at the buck-and-wing but he could think up the rest of the show. (The class-room roars.)

It has been a triple error. He has been contradictory, rebellious and facetious.

Cummings, you'll make your points in the future more concisely. Yes, sir.

You happen to be wrong. You men will find out that experience is worth a great deal more than theory. It is impossible to account for all your strategy, those things have a way of balancing out as happened at Richmond, as is happening now in the trench warfare in Europe. Tactics is always the determinant. (He writes it on the blackboard.)

And, Cummings . . .

Sir?

Since you will be fortunate if you command a battalion by the end of twenty years, you'll do a sight better to concern yourself with the strategic problems of a platoon (there is muffled laughter at his sarcasm) than with those of an Army. (Seeing the approval in his eyes, the class releases its laughter, singeing Cummings's flesh.)

He hears about it for weeks. Hey, Cummings, how many hours will you need to take Richmond?

They're sending you over, Ed, I hear, as adviser to the French. With the proper concepts the Hindenburg Line may be breached.

He learns so many things from this, understands, besides all else, that he is not liked, will not be liked, and he can't make mistakes, cannot expose himself to the pack. He will have to wait. But he is hurt, cannot restrain himself from writing about it to Margaret. And his contempt thrives in recompense; there is a world of manners about which these men know nothing.

In *The Howitzer*, when he graduates, they have printed "The Strategist" under his record, and then to soften it, for it jars with the mellow sentimental glow of yearbooks, they have added a little ambiguously, "Handsome Is as Handsome Does."

He goes out to an abridged furlough with Margaret, the announcement of their engagement, and the rapid shuttle on the transport to the war in Europe.

In the planning section of GHQ he lives in the remaining wing of a château, occupies the bare whitewashed room that had once belonged to a chambermaid, but he does not know this. The war has caught him up agreeably, altered the deadening routine of forms, the detail work of outlining troop movements. The sound of the artillery is always an enrichment to his work, the bare gnashed ground outside speaks of the importance of his figures.

There is even one night when the entire war stands out for him on the edge of a knife blade, a time when everything balances in his mind.

He goes out with his colonel, an enlisted chauffeur, and two other officers on an inspection of the front. It is picnic style with sandwiches packed away and a hot thermos of coffee. The canned rations are brought along, but there is not likely to be an opportunity of using them. They motor along the back roads to the front, jouncing slowly over the potholes and shellholes, splashing ponderously through the mud. For an hour they move along a vast desolated plain, the drab afternoon sky lighted only by the bursts of artillery, the crude evil flickering of the flares like heat lightning on a sultry evening in summer. A mile from the trenches they come to a low ridge-line barely obscuring the horizon and they halt, march slowly along a communication trench which is filled with a half foot of water from the morning's rain. As they approach the secondary trenches the communication ditch begins to zigzag and becomes deeper. Every hundred yards Cummings steps up on the parapet, and peers cautiously into the gloom of No Man's Land.

In the reserve trenches they halt, and take up their position in a concrete dugout, listening respectfully to the conversation between their colonel and the Regimental Commander of that sector of the line. He too has come up for the attack. An hour before dark the artillery begins a creeping barrage which moves closer and closer to the enemy trenches, finally centers on them for a bombardment which lasts fifteen minutes. German artillery is answering, and every few minutes a mis-directed shell swooshes down near their observation post. The trench mortars have begun to fire and the volume of sound increases, floods everything, until they are shouting at each other.

It's time, there they go, someone bellows.

Cummings puts up his field glasses, looks out the slit in the concrete wall. In the twilight, covered with mud, the men look like silver shadows on a wan silver plain. It is raining again, and they waver forward between a walk and a run, falling on their faces, tottering backward, sliding on their bellies in the leaden-colored muck. The German lines are aroused and furious, return the fire cruelly. Light and sound erupt from them viciously, become so immense that his senses are overwhelmed, finally perceive them only as a background for the advance of the infantry across the plain.

The men move slowly now, leaning forward as if striding into the wind. He is fascinated by the sluggishness of it all, the lethargy with which they advance and fall. There seems no pattern to the attack, no volition to the men; they advance in every direction like floating leaves in a pool disturbed by a stone, and yet there is a cumulative movement forward. The ants in the final sense all go in one direction.

Through the field glasses he watches one soldier run forward, plunge his head toward the mud, stand up and run again. It is like watching a crowd from a high window or separating a puppy from the rest of the wriggling brood in a pet-store window. There is an oddness, an unreality, in realizing that the group is made up of units.

The soldier falls, quivers in the mud, and he switches his glasses to another.

They're at the German trenches, someone shouts.

He looks up hastily, sees a few men jumping over the parapet, their bayonets forward like pole vaulters approaching the bar. They seem to move so leisurely, so few men follow them that he is puzzled. Where are the rest he is about to say when there is a shout from the Regimental Commander. They took it, they're good boys, they took it. He is holding the phone in his hand, shouting orders quickly.

The German artillery is beginning to fall on the newly taken trenches, and columns of men advance slowly through the dusk over the quiet field, circling around the dead men, and filing into the German trenches. It is almost dark, and the sky has assumed a rosy wash in the east where a house is burning. He cannot see through his field glasses any longer, and he puts them down, stares across the field with a silent wonder. It looks primal, unfamiliar, the way he has imagined the surface of the moon might look. In the craters the water glistens, slides away in long rippling shadows from the bodies of the men who have fallen.

What'd you think of it? The Colonel nudges him.

Oh, it was . . . But he cannot find the words. It has been too immense, too shattering. The long dry battles of the textbooks come alive for him, mass themselves in his mind. He can only think of the man who has ordered the attack, and he pictures him with wonder. What . . . courage. The responsibility. (For want of a richer word he picks up the military expression.)

There were all those men, and there had been someone above them, ordering them, changing perhaps forever the fiber of their lives. In the darkness he looks blankly at the field, tantalized by the largest vision that has ever entered his soul.

There were things one could do.

To command all that. He is choked with the intensity of his emotion, the rage, the exaltation, the undefined and mighty hunger.

He returns a captain (temporary), is promoted and demoted in the same order, made first lieutenant (permanent). There is his marriage with Margaret against the subtle opposition of her parents, the brief honeymoon, and they settle down at an Army post, drift in the pleasantly vacant circle of parties and Saturday night dances at the officers' club.

Their lovemaking is fantastic for a time:

He must subdue her, absorb her, rip her apart and consume her.

This motif is concealed for a month or two, clouded over by their mutual inexperience, by the strangeness, the unfamiliarity, but it must come out eventually. And for a half year, almost a year, they have love passages of intense fury, enraged and powerful, which leave him sobbing from exhaustion and frustration on her breast.

Do you love me, are you mine, love me.

Yes yes.

I'll take you apart, I'll eat you, oh, I'll make you mine, I'll make you mine, you bitch.

And surprising profanity, words he is startled to hear himself speak.

Margaret is kindled by it, exalted for a time, sees it as passion, glows and becomes rounded, but only for a time. After a year it is completely naked, apparent to her, that he is alone, that he fights out battles with himself upon her body, and something withers in her. There is all the authority she has left, the family and the Boston streets and the history hanging upon them, and she has left it, to be caught in a more terrifying authority, a greater demand.

This is all of course beneath words, would be unbearable if it were ever said, but their marriage re-forms, assumes a light and hypocritical companionship with a void at the center, and very little lovemaking now, painfully isolated when it occurs. He retreats from her, licks his wounds, and twists in the circle beyond which he cannot break. Their social life becomes far more important.

She busies herself with running her house, keeping a list of the delicate debits and credits of entertainment and visiting. It always takes them two hours to figure out the list for their monthly party.

Once they spend a week wondering if they can invite the General to their house, discuss the elaborate arguments on either side. They conclude it would be in bad taste, might hurt them even if he came, but a few nights later Captain Cummings wrestles with the problem again, wakes up at dawn and knows it is a chance he must take.

They plan it very carefully, picking a weekend when the General has no obligations and it seems as if none will develop. From the General's house orderly, Margaret finds out which foods he likes; at a post dance she talks to the General's wife for twenty minutes, discovers an acquaintance of her father's whom the General knows.

They send out the invitations and the General accepts. There is the nervous preceding week, the tension at the party. The General walks in, stands about at the buffet table, picking not without zeal at the smoked turkey, the shrimp for which she has sent to Boston.

It is finally a success and the General smiles at Cummings mistily, pleased with his eighth Scotch, the puffed and tufted furniture (he had been expecting maple), the sharp sweet bite of the shrimp sauce through the fur of drinking. When he says good-bye he pats Cummings on the shoulder, pinches Margaret's cheek. The tension collapses, the junior officers and their wives begin to sing. But they are too exhausted and the party ends early.

That night when they congratulate each other Cummings is satisfied.

But Margaret ruins it; she has a facility for ruining things now. You know, honestly, Edward, I wonder what the point to it all was, you can't get promoted any faster, and the old fart (she has taken to swearing mildly) will be dead by the time it's a question of recommending you for general's rank.

You have to start your reputation early, he says quickly. He has accepted all these mores, forced himself dutifully into them, but he does not like them to be questioned.

Oh, what a perfectly vague thing to say. You know I'm feeling now as if we were silly to have invited him. It would have been much more fun without him.

Fun? (This hits at the core of him, leaves him actually weak with anger.) *There are more important things than fun.* He feels as if he has closed a door behind him.

You're in danger of becoming a bore.

Let it go, he almost shouts, and she subsides before his rage. But there it is between them, stated again.

I don't know what gets into you, he mutters.

There are other movements, other directions. For a time he moves through the drinking circles of the officers' club, plays poker, and indulges in a few side affairs. But it is a repetition of Margaret with humiliating endings, and in another year or two he keeps to himself, devotes himself to running his outfits.

In that he has talent. He absorbs the problem completely, thinks at night in bed of how best to treat the different men, how to command them most effectively. In the daytime he spends nearly all his time with the company, supervising labor details, conducting continual inspections. His companies are always the best managed on the post; his company street is easily the cleanest and neatest.

On Saturday mornings a squad from each platoon is put to work cutting the weeds from under the barracks.

He has all the patent brass polishers tested, selects the best, and has an order posted that the men can use only that brand.

In the daily latrine inspections he is always one step ahead of the men; one morning he gets down on his hands and knees, lifts the drain plate, and gigs the platoon because there is grease in the pipe.

When he inspects he brings a needle, probes the cracks on the stairs for dust.

In the gymkhana which the post holds every summer his company teams always win. He has them practicing from the first of February.

The company mess floor is scrubbed with boiling water after every meal.

He is always ahead of the men. One big Saturday inspection when a visiting general is expected, he instructs his first sergeant to have the men grease the soles of their extra shoes, which are exhibited at the foot of their bed.

He has been known to strip a rifle on the parade ground and examine the rear of the hammer spring for dirt.

There is always a standing gag in his company that the Old Man is thinking of having the men take off their shoes before they enter the barracks.

The field officers are agreed that Captain Cummings is the best junior officer on the post.

On a visit to her family in Boston, Margaret is questioned.

You're not planning any children yet?

No, I don't think so, she laughs. I'm afraid to. Edward would probably have him scrubbing the bassinette.

Don't you think seven years now is a long time?

Oh, it is, I suppose. I really don't know.

It's not a good idea to wait too long.

Margaret sighs. Men are very odd, positively odd. You always think they're one thing and they turn out to be another.

Her aunt purses her thin mouth. I've always felt, Margaret, that you'd have done better to have married someone we know.

That's an awfully stuffy idea. Edward is going to be a great general. All we need is a war, and I'll feel just like Josephine.

(The shrewd look.) There's no need to be flippant, Margaret. I had expected that marriage in all this time might have made you more . . . womanly. It isn't wise to marry someone about whom you know nothing, and I've always suspected that you married Edward for precisely that reason. (The significant pause.) Ruth, Thatcher's wife, is carrying a third child.

(Margaret is angry.) I wonder if I shall be as dirty as you when I'm as old.

I'm afraid you'll always be *pungent*, my dear.

At the officers' dance on Saturday night, Margaret gets drunk a little more frequently. There are times when an indiscretion is not too far away.

Captain, I see you're all alone, one of the officers' ladies remarks.

Yes, I'm afraid I'm a little too old-fashioned. The war and . . . (Her husband has been commissioned after 1918.) One of my more recurrent regrets is that I never learned to dance well. (His manner, which is to set him off from other professional officers, is beginning in these years.)

Your wife does.

Yes. (At the other end of the officers' club, Margaret is the center of a circle of men. She is laughing loudly now, her hand on the sleeve of a second lieutenant's blouse.) He stares across at her with loathing and disgust.

From Webster's: *hatred*, n., strong aversion or detestation; settled ill will or malevolence.

A thread in most marriages, growing dominant in Cummings's. The cold form of it. No quarrels. No invective.

He is all application now, all study. At night, in the parlor of the succession of post houses in which they live, he reads five or six nights a week. There is all the education he has missed, and he takes giant strides in recouping it. There is philosophy first, and then political science, sociology, psychology, history, even literature and art. He absorbs it all with the fantastic powers of memory and assimilation he can exhibit at times, absorbs it and immediately transmutes it into something else, satisfies the dominant warp of his mind.

It comes out a little in the infrequent intellectual discussions he can find on an Army post. I find Freud rather stimulating, he says. The idea is that man is a worthless bastard, and the only problem is how best to control him.

In 1931 Spengler[5] is particularly congenial. To his company he makes short cautious talks.

I don't have to tell you men how bad things are. Some of you are in the Army for just that reason. But I want to point out that we may have an important function. If you read the papers you see where troops are being called out everywhere. There may be a great many changes, and your duty in such a case will be to obey the orders of the government as they come down through me.

The plans, not quite defined, never put to paper, dissolve at last. By 1934 Major Cummings is far more interested in foreign news.

I tell you that Hitler is not a flash in the pan, he will argue. He has the germ of an idea, and moreover you've got to give him political

[5] Oswald Spengler (1880–1936), whose pessimistic cyclical theory of history appeared in English translation under the title *The Decline of the West* (1926–28).

credit. He plays on the German people with consummate skill. That Siegfried[6] business is fundamental to them.

In 1935 Cummings is remembered for making some innovations at the Infantry School in Fort Benning.

In '36 he is considered the most promising field officer of the year at the War College in Washington. And he makes a little ripple in Washington society, becomes friendly with a few congressmen, meets the most important hostess in town. For a while he is in danger of becoming Military Adviser to Washington Society.

But always he is branching out. The confusions, the cross-impulses are concealed now, buried under the concentration with which he works. On a thirty-day leave in the summer of '37 he pays a visit to his brother-in-law, who is vacationing in Maine. They have become very friendly during Cummings's tour of duty in Washington.

On one of the afternoons in a sailboat:

You know, I've always disagreed with the family, Edward. Through no fault of your own they've never entirely approved of you. I think their backward attitude is a little distressing, but of course you understand it.

I think I do, Minot. (There is this other network of emotions and ambitions which recurs now and then. The ineffable perfection of Boston, which had beckoned him, leaves him always curiously satisfied yet troubled. He has traded on Boston in Washington, he knows cynically, aware of himself, but there is still the attraction and the uncertainty.) His speech sounds florid in his ears. Margaret has been mighty fine about it all.

Wonderful woman, that sister of mine.

Yes.

I think it a shame I didn't know you very well years ago. You really would have fitted into the department. I've watched you develop, Edward; I think, when the occasion demands, you have as much perception and tact, you grasp the core of a situation as quickly as any man I know. It's a pity it's too late now.

I think sometimes I might have been good at it, Cummings agrees. But you know I'll be lieutenant colonel in a year or two, and after that I'm free of seniority. It might be a little impolitic to brag, but I should make colonel within a year after.

Mmm. You don't speak French, do you?

A fair amount. I learned some over there in '17, and I've kept up with it since.

The brother-in-law fingers his chin. You know, Edward, I suppose it's one of the laws of government, but there are always many points of view in a department. I'll tell you, I've been wondering if you couldn't be sent on a little joust to France, in your capacity as an officer of course. Nothing official.

What about, Minot?

Oh, it's nebulous. A few talks here and there. An element in the department is attempting to change our Spain policy. I don't think they're going to succeed but it would be disastrous if they should, be tantamount to handing Gibraltar to the Russians. What worries me is France. So long as they stay on the fence I don't think there's a chance of our trying anything by ourselves.

I'm to keep them on the fence?

Nothing so big as that. I've got some assurances, some financial contracts which might put a little pressure in the proper places. The thing to remember is that everyone in France can be bought, none of them has clean hands.

I wonder if I could get away.

We're sending a military mission to France and Italy. I can work it through the War Department. I'll have quite a briefing to give you, but that should give you no trouble.

I'm very interested, Cummings says. The problems of manipulation . . . He trails off, not finishing the sentence.

The water slaps past, resolves itself again behind the stern, quietly, softly, like a cat grooming its fur. Beyond the catboat the sunlight is scattered over the bay, tinkling upon the water.

We might as well put back, the brother-in-law says.

The shore line is wooded, olive-green, a pristine cove.

I never get over this, he says to Cummings. I still expect to see Indians in the forest. Pure country, Maine.

The office is smaller than he has expected, more leathery, somehow more greasy. The map of France is covered with pencil smudges, and a corner is folded over like a dog-eared book.

I must apologize for this place, the man says. (His accent is negligible, a certain preciseness of speech perhaps.) When you first suggested the nature of our business I thought it perhaps best to meet here, not that there should be anything clandestine, but you would attract attention at the Bourse. There are spies everywhere.

I understand. It's been difficult to see you. The party we know suggested Monsieur de Vernay, but I think he is a little too far away to judge.

You state there are credits?

More than enough. I must emphasize that this is not official. There is a tacit agreement . . .

Tacit? Tacit?

An understanding with Leeway Chemical that they will invest in such French firms as *he* thinks advisable. There is no *chou* involved. (He wonders if the slang is correct.) A legitimate business arrangement, but the profits I think are large enough to benefit Sallevoisseux Frères, and enable you to conduct any *adjustments* which might be necessary.

On s'arrangera.

I would have to know some further details of course on the processes you will employ.

Ah, Major Cummings, I can assure you of the vote of twenty-five members of the Chamber of Deputies.

I think it would be best if it didn't come to a vote. There are other ways.

I do not believe I may disclose my routes of access.

(The core of the situation.) Monsieur Sallevoisseux, a man of your . . . vision can see certainly that an enterprise of the magnitude which Leeway Chemical is proposing would demand something more concrete on your part. The decision to set up a subsidiary in France has been taken for some years; it is a question of who will get it. I have with me, subject to the necessary financial guarantees on your part, the power to consolidate with Sallevoisseux Frères. If you cannot give me more definite assurances I will be obliged unfortunately to deal in other channels which I am investigating at present.

I should regret that, Major Cummings.

I should regret it myself.

Sallevoisseux twists in the chair, stares out the high narrow window at the cobblestones in the street below. The horns of the French automobiles sound high-pitched to Cummings.

There are routes. For example—I will give the assurances, the documents, the introductions afterward—for example, I have friends in Les Cagoulards who can influence certain firms, not Chemical, by virtue of some tasks they have performed for them in the past. These firms in turn could if necessary control the decision of a bloc of seventy-five deputies. (He raises his hand.) I know you prefer it does not come to a vote, but no man may control that for you. I can free the vote of any uncertainty. Many of these deputies can influence members of the Ministry.

He pauses. These politics are complicated.

I understand them.

There are several Radical Socialists high-placed in the Foreign Department whom I may influence. I know from a service that there is information to be bought about them. They will be amiable. There are journalists by the dozen, several men in the Bank of France whose *dossiers intimes* I possess. A block of Socialists is controlled by a labor leader with whom I have an understanding. These routes, all indirect, mount up, create a necessary dispersion. You must realize I am not working alone. I can assure you that nothing will be done for eighteen months; beyond that history is involved, and no man may divert it indefinitely.

They talk for several hours, work out the first terms of the agreement.

As he leaves, Cummings smiles. What we're doing is really in the long run what is best for France and America.

Sallevoisseux smiles also. Of course, Major Cummings. A peculiarly American statement, do you know?

You'll show me the dossiers you possess at hand. Tomorrow, is that right?

D'accord!

A month later, his part in the assignment completed, Cummings moves down to Rome. A telegram reaches him from his brother-in-law.

Preliminary dispositions satisfactory. Very well done. Congratulations.

He talks to an Italian colonel as part of the military mission.

I would like you to see, Signor Maggiore, our work on the problems of dysentery in the successful African campaign. We have discovered a new series of sanitary measures 73% more effective in avoiding the dreadful, the malign propensities of such a disease.

The summer heat is stifling. Despite the lecture by the Italian Colonel he suffers from diarrhea, and is plagued by a severe cold. He spends a miserable week in bed, abysmally tired. A letter follows from his brother-in-law.

I think it's a shame to ruin the understandable elation you must be feeling now after such a neat job in Paris, but there's something I really ought to tell you. Margaret, you know, has been down in Washington with me for the past two weeks, and to put it as kindly as possible, she has been acting very odd. There's a certain abandonment about her which is not proper to her age; I must confess I find it hard to believe she is my sister at times. If it were not for you, I would have told her to leave my house. I'm really awfully disturbed to ruin what must be a vacation in Rome, but I think if you can it might not be a bad idea to be thinking of coming back. Do see Monsignor Truffenio and give him my regards.

This time it is a tired hatred. I just hope she keeps it quiet he swears to himself. He has a nightmare that evening, waking up on a fever-ridden bed. He thinks of his father for the first time in a year or two, remembers his death a few years ago and relives a little of the anxiety it had caused him. After midnight he gets up on an impulse and walks the streets, ending up in an alley where he becomes drunk in a bar.

There is a little man pawing him. Signor Maggiore you come home with me now?

He staggers along dimly aware of what he wants, but he does not find it. In another alley the little man and a confederate jump him, strip his pockets, and leave him to awaken in the harsh glare, the quick stench of the sun on a garbage-filled alley in Rome. He makes it back to his hotel without too many people seeing him, change his clothes, takes a bath, and goes to bed for over a day. He feels as if he is breaking apart.

I must confess, your Reverence, that I have admired the Church for many years. In the immensity of your conception lies your greatness.

The Cardinal bows his head. I am pleased to give you an audience, my son. You have done good work already. I have heard of your labors in Paris against the Antichrist.

I labored for my country. (In this setting the words cause him no embarrassment.)

There is a nobler labor.

I am aware of it, your Reverence . . . There are times when I feel a great weariness.

You may be preparing for an important change.

Sometimes I think so. I've always looked upon your Church with admiration.

He walks through the great courtyard of the Vatican, stares for a long time at the dome of St. Peter's. The ceremony he has just heard has moved him, sent music lapping through his brain.

Maybe I should turn.

But on the boat going back he thinks of other things, reads with quiet satisfaction in the newspaper he has brought on board that Leeway Chemical is opening negotiations with Sallevoisseux Frères.

Man, I'll be glad to get back from frog-land and the wops, one of the officers who has been on the mission says to him.

Yes.

That Italy's a backward country even if they say Musso did a lot for it. You can still keep it. The Catholic countries are the ones who are always backward.

I suppose so.

He thinks clearly for a few minutes. The thing that happened in the Rome alley is a danger sign, and he will have to be very careful from now on. It must never come out again. The Church business is understandable in its light, a highly impractical move at this juncture. *I'll be a colonel soon. I can't risk it turning.*

Cummings sighs. I've learned a lot.

Yeah, me too.

Cummings looks at the water. Slowly his eyes raise, include the horizon. Lieutenant colonel . . . colonel . . . brigadier . . . major general . . . lieutenant general . . . general?

If there's a war soon it'll help.

But afterward. The politicos were even more important. After the war . . .

He must not commit himself politically yet. There would be too many turns. It might be Stalin, it might be Hitler. But the eventual line to power in America would always be anticommunism.

He must keep his eyes open, Cummings decided.

1948

Ralph Ellison   *1914—*

Ralph Waldo Ellison, best known for his novel *Invisible Man*, was born in Oklahoma City and educated at Tuskegee Institute (1933–36). He began writing seriously in 1939 and became associated with the New York Federal Writers' Project. After wartime service in the Merchant Marine (1943–45), he lectured on Negro culture and taught creative writing at several institutions including, since 1957, Bard College. His one novel, *Invisible Man* (1952; rev. ed., 1961) deals with the struggle of an intelligent Negro boy to achieve a sense of identity, first in his Southern environment and then in New York City. He finds his efforts impeded by the tendency of both white and black people to think and see in stereotypes that prevent them from recognizing the real individual, who remains an "invisible" man. Ellison has also published numerous short stories and a book of essays, *Shadow and Act* (1964).

The text of "The Battle Royal" is that of *Invisible Man* (New York, 1952), Chapter 1. The present title is the editors'.

The Battle Royal

It goes a long way back, some twenty years. All my life I had been looking for something, and everywhere I turned someone tried to tell me what it was. I accepted their answers too, though they were often in contradiction and even self-contradictory. I was naïve. I was looking for myself and asking everyone except myself questions which I, and only I, could answer. It took me a long time and much painful boomeranging of my expectations to achieve a realization everyone else appears to have been born with: That I am nobody but myself. But first I had to discover that I am an invisible man!

And yet I am no freak of nature, nor of history. I was in the cards, other things having been equal (or unequal) eighty-five years ago. I am not ashamed of my grandparents for having been slaves. I am only ashamed of myself for having at one time been ashamed. About eighty-five years ago they were told that they were free, united with others in our country in everything pertaining to the common good, and, in everything social, separate like the fingers of the hand. And they believed it. They exulted in it. They stayed in their place, worked hard, and brought up my father to do the same. But my grandfather is the one. He was an odd old guy, my grandfather, and I am told I take after him. It was he who caused the trouble. On his deathbed he called my father to him and said, "Son, after I'm gone I want you to keep up the good fight. I never told you, but our life is a war and I have been a traitor all my born days, a spy in the enemy's country ever since I give up my gun back in the Reconstruction. Live with your head in the lion's mouth. I want you to overcome 'em with yeses, undermine 'em with grins, agree 'em to death and destruction, let 'em swoller you till they vomit or bust wide open." They thought the old man had gone out of his mind. He had been the meekest of men. The younger children were rushed from the room, the shades drawn and the flame of the lamp turned so low that it sputtered on the wick like the old man's breathing. "Learn it to the younguns," he whispered fiercely; then he died.

But my folks were more alarmed over his last words than over his dying. It was as though he had not died at all, his words caused so much anxiety. I was warned emphatically to forget what he had said and, indeed, this is the first time it has been mentioned outside the family circle. It had a tremendous effect upon me, however. I could never be sure of what he meant. Grandfather had been a quiet old man who never made any trouble, yet on his deathbed he had called himself a traitor and a spy, and he had spoken of his meekness as a dangerous activity. It became a constant puzzle which lay unanswered in the back of my mind. And whenever things went well for me I remembered my grandfather and felt guilty and uncomfortable. It was as though I was carrying out his advice in spite of myself. And to make it worse, everyone loved me for it. I was praised by the most lily-white men of the town. I was considered an example of desirable conduct—just as my grandfather had been. And what puzzled me was that the old man had defined it as *treachery*. When I was praised for my conduct I felt a guilt that in some way I was doing something that was really against the wishes of the white folks, that if they had understood they would have desired me to act just the opposite, that I should have been sulky and mean, and that that really would have been what they wanted, even though they were fooled and thought they wanted me to act as I did. It made me afraid that some day they would look upon me as a traitor and I would be lost. Still I was more afraid to act any other way because they didn't like that at all. The old man's words were like a curse. On my graduation day I delivered an oration in which I showed that humility was the secret, indeed, the very essence of progress. (Not that I believed this — how could I, remembering my grandfather? — I only believed that it worked.) It was a great success. Everyone praised me and I was invited to give the speech at a gathering of the town's leading white citizens. It was a triumph for our whole community.

It was in the main ballroom of the leading hotel. When I got there I discovered that it was on the occasion of a smoker, and I was told that since I was to be there anyway I might as well take part in the battle royal to be fought by some of my schoolmates as part of the entertainment. The battle royal came first.

All of the town's big shots were there in their tuxedoes, wolfing down the buffet foods, drinking beer and whiskey and smoking black cigars. It was a large room with a high ceiling. Chairs were arranged in neat rows around three sides of a portable boxing ring. The fourth side was clear, revealing a gleaming space of polished floor. I had some misgivings over the battle royal, by the way. Not from a distaste for fighting, but because I didn't care too much for the other fellows who were to take part. They were tough guys who seemed to have no grandfather's curse worrying their minds. No one could mistake their toughness. And besides, I suspected that fighting a battle royal might detract from the dignity of my speech. In those pre-invisible days I visualized myself as a potential Booker T. Washington.[1] But the other fellows didn't care too much for me either, and there were nine of them. I felt superior to them in my way, and I didn't like the manner in which we were all crowded together into the servants' elevator. Nor did they like my being there. In fact, as the warmly lighted floors flashed past the elevator we had words over the fact that I, by taking part in the fight, had knocked one of their friends out of a night's work.

We were led out of the elevator through a rococo hall into an anteroom and told to get into our fighting togs. Each of us was issued a pair of boxing gloves and ushered out into the big mirrored hall, which we entered looking cautiously about us and whispering, lest we might accidentally be heard above the noise of the room. It was foggy with cigar smoke. And already the whiskey was taking effect. I was shocked to see some of the most important men of the town quite tipsy. They were all there — bankers, lawyers, judges, doctors, fire chiefs, teachers, merchants. Even one of the more fashionable pastors. Something we could not see was going on up front. A clarinet was vibrating sensuously and the men were standing up and moving eagerly forward. We were a small tight group, clustered together, our bare upper bodies touching and shining with anticipatory sweat; while up front the big shots were becoming increasingly excited over something we still could not see.

[1] Negro leader and educator (1859?-1915), founder of Tuskegee Institute.

Suddenly I heard the school superintendent, who had told me to come, yell, "Bring up the shines, gentlemen! Bring up the little shines!"

We were rushed up to the front of the ballroom, where it smelled even more strongly of tobacco and whiskey. Then we were pushed into place. I almost wet my pants. A sea of faces, some hostile, some amused, ringed around us, and in the center, facing us, stood a magnificent blonde — stark naked. There was dead silence. I felt a blast of cold air chill me. I tried to back away, but they were behind me and around me. Some of the boys stood with lowered heads, trembling. I felt a wave of irrational guilt and fear. My teeth chattered, my skin turned to goose flesh, my knees knocked. Yet I was strongly attracted and looked in spite of myself. Had the price of looking been blindness, I would have looked. The hair was yellow like that of a circus kewpie doll, the face heavily powdered and rouged, as though to form an abstract mask, the eyes hollow and smeared a cool blue, the color of a baboon's butt. I felt a desire to spit upon her as my eyes brushed slowly over her body. Her breasts were firm and round as the domes of East Indian temples, and I stood so close as to see the fine skin texture and beads of pearly perspiration glistening like dew around the pink and erected buds of her nipples. I wanted at one and the same time to run from the room, to sink through the floor, or go to her and cover her from my eyes and the eyes of the others with my body; to feel the soft thighs, to caress her and destroy her, to love her and murder her, to hide from her, and yet to stroke where below the small American flag tattooed upon her belly her thighs formed a capital V. I had a notion that of all in the room she saw only me with her impersonal eyes.

And then she began to dance, a slow sensuous movement; the smoke of a hundred cigars clinging to her like the thinnest of veils. She seemed like a fair bird-girl girdled in veils calling to me from the angry surface of some gray and threatening sea. I was transported. Then I became aware of the clarinet playing and the big shots yelling at us. Some threatened us if we looked and others if we did not. On my right I saw one boy faint. And now a man grabbed a silver pitcher from a table and stepped close as he dashed ice water upon him and stood him up and forced two of us to support him as his head hung and moans issued from his thick bluish lips. Another boy began to plead to go home. He was the largest of the group, wearing dark red fighting trunks much too small to conceal the erection which projected from him as though in answer to the insinuating low-registered moaning of the clarinet. He tried to hide himself with his boxing gloves.

And all the while the blonde continued dancing, smiling faintly at the big shots who watched her with fascination, and faintly smiling at our fear. I noticed a certain merchant who followed her hungrily, his lips loose and drooling. He was a large man who wore diamond studs in a shirtfront which swelled with the ample paunch underneath, and each time the blonde swayed her undulating hips he ran his hand through the thin hair of his bald head and, with his arms upheld, his posture clumsy like that of an intoxicated panda, wound his belly in a slow and obscene grind. This creature was completely hypnotized. The music had quickened. As the dancer flung herself about with a detached expression on her face, the men began reaching out to touch her. I could see their beefy fingers sink into the soft flesh. Some of the others tried to stop them and she began to move around the floor in graceful circles, as they gave chase, slipping and sliding over the polished floor. It was mad. chairs went crashing, drinks were spilt, as they ran laughing and howling after her. They caught her just as she reached a door, raised her from the floor, and tossed her as college boys are tossed at a hazing, and above her red, fixed-smiling lips I saw the terror and disgust in her eyes, almost like my own terror and that which I saw in some of the other boys. As I watched, they tossed her twice and her soft breasts seemed to flatten against the air and her legs flung wildly as she spun. Some of the more sober ones helped her to escape. And I started off the floor, heading for the anteroom with the rest of the boys.

Some were still crying and in hysteria. But as we tried to leave we were stopped and ordered to get into the ring. There was nothing to do but what we were told. All ten of us climbed under the ropes and allowed ourselves to be blindfolded with broad bands of white cloth. One of the men seemed to feel a bit sympathetic and tried to cheer us up as we stood with our backs against the ropes. Some of us tried to grin. "See that boy over there?" one of the men said. "I want you to run across at the bell and give it to him right in the belly. If you don't get him, I'm going to get you. I don't like his looks." Each of us was told the same. The blindfolds were put on. Yet even then I had been going over my speech. In my mind each word was as bright as flame. I felt the cloth pressed into place, and frowned so that it would be loosened when I relaxed.

But now I felt a sudden fit of blind terror. I was unused to darkness. It was as though I had suddenly found myself in a dark room filled with poisonous cottonmouths. I could hear the bleary voices yelling insistently for the battle royal to begin.

"Get going in there!"

"Let me at that big nigger!"

I strained to pick up the school superintendent's voice, as though to squeeze some security out of that slightly more familiar sound.

"Let me at those black sonsabitches!" someone yelled.

"No, Jackson, no!" another voice yelled. "Here, somebody, help me hold Jack."

"I want to get at that ginger-colored nigger. Tear him limb from limb," the first voice yelled.

I stood against the ropes trembling. For in those days I was what they called ginger-colored, and he sounded as though he might crunch me between his teeth like a crisp ginger cookie.

Quite a struggle was going on. Chairs were being kicked about and I could hear voices grunting as with a terrific effort. I wanted to see, to see more desperately than ever before. But the blindfold was tight as a thick skin-puckering scab and when I raised my gloved hands to push the layers of white aside a voice yelled, "Oh, no you don't, black bastard! Leave that alone!"

"Ring the bell before Jackson kills him a coon!" someone boomed in the sudden silence. And I heard the bell clang and the sound of the feet scuffling forward.

A glove smacked against my head. I pivoted, striking out stiffly as someone went past, and felt the jar ripple along the length of my arm to my shoulder. Then it seemed as though all nine of the boys had turned upon me at once. Blows pounded me from all sides while I struck out as best I could. So many blows landed upon me that I wondered if I were not the only blindfolded fighter in the ring, or if the man called Jackson hadn't succeeded in getting me after all.

Blindfolded, I could no longer control my motions. I had no dignity. I stumbled about like a baby or a drunken man. The smoke had become thicker and with each new blow it seemed to sear and further restrict my lungs. My saliva became like hot bitter glue. A glove connected with my head, filling my mouth with warm blood. It was everywhere. I could not tell if the moisture I felt upon my body was sweat or blood. A blow landed hard against the nape of my neck. I felt myself going over, my head hitting the floor. Streaks of blue light filled the black world behind the blindfold. I lay prone, pretending that I was knocked out, but felt myself seized by hands and yanked to my feet. "Get going, black boy! Mix it up!" My arms were like lead, my head smarting from blows. I managed to feel my way to the ropes and held on, trying to catch my breath. A glove landed in my mid-section and I went over again, feeling as though the smoke had become a knife jabbed into my guts. Pushed this way and that by the legs milling around me, I finally pulled erect and discovered that I could see the black, sweat-washed forms weaving in the smoky-blue atmosphere like drunken dancers weaving to the rapid drum-like thuds of blows.

Everyone fought hysterically. It was complete anarchy. Everybody fought everybody else. No group fought together for long. Two, three, four, fought one, then turned to fight each other, were themselves attacked. Blows landed below the belt and in the kidney, with the gloves open as well as closed, and with my eye partly opened now there was not so much terror. I moved carefully, avoiding blows, although not too many to attract attention, fighting from group to group. The boys groped about like blind, cautious crabs crouching to protect their mid-sections, their heads pulled in short against their shoulders, their arms stretched nervously before them, with their fists testing the smoke-filled air like the knobbed feelers of hypersensitive snails. In one corner I glimpsed a boy violently punching the air and heard him scream in pain as he smashed his hand against a ring post. For a second I saw him bent over holding his hand, then going down as a blow caught his unprotected head. I played one group against the other, slipping in and throwing a punch then stepping out of range while pushing the others into the melee to take the blows blindly aimed at me. The smoke was agonizing and there were no rounds, no bells at three minute intervals to relieve our exhaustion. The room spun round me, a swirl of lights, smoke, sweating bodies surrounded by tense white faces. I bled from both nose and mouth, the blood spattering upon my chest.

The men kept yelling, "Slug him, black boy! Knock his guts out!"

"Uppercut him! Kill him! Kill that big boy!"

Taking a fake fall, I saw a boy going down heavily beside me as though we were felled by a single blow, saw a sneaker-clad foot shoot into his groin as the two who had knocked him down stumbled upon him. I rolled out of range, feeling a twinge of nausea.

The harder we fought the more threatening the men became. And yet, I had begun to worry about my speech again. How would it go? Would they recognize my ability? What would they give me?

I was fighting automatically when suddenly I noticed that one after another of the boys was leaving the ring. I was surprised, filled with panic, as though I had been left alone with an unknown danger.

Then I understood. The boys had arranged it among themselves. It was the custom for the two men left in the ring to slug it out for the winner's prize. I discovered this too late. When the bell sounded two men in tuxedoes leaped into the ring and removed the blindfold. I found myself facing Tatlock, the biggest of the gang. I felt sick at my stomach. Hardly had the bell stopped ringing in my ears than it clanged again and I saw him moving swiftly toward me. Thinking of nothing else to do I hit him smash on the nose. He kept coming, bringing the rank sharp violence of stale sweat. His face was a black blank of a face, only his eyes alive—with hate of me and aglow with a feverish terror from what had happened to us all. I became anxious. I wanted to deliver my speech and he came at me as though he meant to beat it out of me. I smashed him again and again, taking his blows as they came. Then on a sudden impulse I struck him lightly and as we clinched, I whispered, "Fake like I knocked you out, you can have the prize."

"I'll break your behind," he whispered hoarsely.

"For *them*?"

"For *me*, sonofabitch!"

They were yelling for us to break it up and Tatlock spun me half around with a blow, and as a joggled camera sweeps in a reeling scene, I saw the howling red faces crouching tense beneath the cloud of blue-gray smoke. For a moment the world wavered, unraveled, flowed, then my head cleared and Tatlock bounced before me. That fluttering shadow before my eyes was his jabbing left hand. Then falling forward, my head against his damp shoulder, I whispered,

"I'll make it five dollars more."

"Go to hell!"

But his muscles relaxed a trifle beneath my pressure and I breathed, "Seven?"

"Give it to your ma," he said, ripping me beneath the heart.

And while I still held him I butted him and moved away. I felt myself bombarded with punches. I fought back with hopeless desperation. I wanted to deliver my speech more than anything else in the world, because I felt that only these men could judge truly my ability, and now this stupid clown was ruining my chances. I began fighting carefully now, moving in to punch him and out again with my greater speed. A lucky blow to his chin and I had him going too — until I heard a loud voice yell, "I got my money on the big boy."

Hearing this, I almost dropped my guard. I was confused: Should I try to win against the voice out there? Would not this go against my speech, and was not this a moment for humility, for nonresistance? A blow to my head as I danced about sent my right eye popping like a jack-in-the-box and settled my dilemma. The room went red as I fell. It was a dream fall, my body languid and fastidious as to where to land, until the floor became impatient and smashed up to meet me. A moment later I came to. An hypnotic voice said FIVE emphatically. And I lay there, hazily watching a dark red spot of my own blood shaping itself into a butterfly, glistening and soaking into the soiled gray world of the canvas.

When the voice drawled TEN I was lifted up and dragged to a chair. I sat dazed. My eye pained and swelled with each throb of my pounding heart and I wondered if now I would be allowed to speak. I was wringing wet, my mouth still bleeding. We were grouped along the wall now. The other boys ignored me as they congratulated Tatlock and speculated as to how much they would be paid. One boy whimpered over his smashed hand. Looking up front, I saw attendants in white jackets rolling the portable ring away and placing a small square rug in the vacant space surrounded by chairs. Perhaps, I thought, I will stand on the rug to deliver my speech.

Then the M.C. called to us, "Come on up here boys and get your money."

We ran forward to where the men laughed and talked in their chairs, waiting. Everyone seemed friendly now.

"There it is on the rug," the man said. I saw the rug covered with coins of all dimensions and a few crumpled bills. But what excited me, scattered here and there, were the gold pieces.

"Boys, it's all yours," the man said. "You get all you grab."

"That's right, Sambo," a blond man said, winking at me confidentially.

I trembled with excitement, forgetting my pain. I would get the gold and the bills, I thought. I would use both hands. I would throw my body against the boys nearest me to block them from the gold.

"Get down around the rug now," the man commanded, "and don't anyone touch it until I give the signal."

"This ought to be good," I heard.

As told, we got around the square rug on our knees. Slowly the man raised his freckled hand as we followed it upward with our eyes.

I heard, "These niggers look like they're about to pray!"

Then, "Ready," the man said. "Go!"

I lunged for a yellow coin lying on the blue design of the carpet, touching it and sending a surprised shriek to join those rising around me. I tried frantically to remove my hand but could not let go. A hot, violent force tore through my body, shaking me like a wet rat. The rug was electrified. The hair bristled up on my head as I shook myself free. My muscles jumped, my nerves jangled, writhed. But I saw that this was not stopping the other boys. Laughing in fear and embarrassment, some were holding back and scooping up the coins knocked off by the painful contortions of the others. The men roared above us as we struggled.

"Pick it up, goddamnit, pick it up!" someone called like a bass-voiced parrot. "Go on, get it!"

I crawled rapidly around the floor, picking up the coins, trying to avoid the coppers and to get greenbacks and the gold. Ignoring the shock by laughing, as I brushed the coins off quickly, I discovered that I could contain the electricity—a contradiction, but it works. Then the men began to push us onto the rug. Laughing embarrassedly, we struggled out of their hands and kept after the coins. We were all wet and slippery and hard to hold. Suddenly I saw a boy lifted into the air, glistening with sweat like a circus seal, and dropped, his wet back landing flush upon the charged rug, heard him yell and saw him literally dance upon his back, his elbows beating a frenzied tattoo upon the floor, his muscles twitching like the flesh of a horse stung by many flies. When he finally rolled off, his face was gray and no one stopped him when he ran from the floor amid booming laughter.

"Get the money," the M.C. called. "That's good hard American cash!"

And we snatched and grabbed, snatched and grabbed. I was careful not to come too close to the rug now, and when I felt the hot whiskey breath descend upon me like a cloud of foul air I reached out and grabbed the leg of a chair. It was occupied and I held on desperately.

"Leggo, nigger! Leggo!"

The huge face wavered down to mine as he tried to push me free. But my body was slippery and he was too drunk. It was Mr. Colcord, who owned a chain of movie houses and "entertainment palaces." Each time he grabbed me I slipped out of his hands. It became a real struggle. I feared the rug more than I did the drunk, so I held on, surprising myself for a moment by trying to topple *him* upon the rug. It was such an enormous idea that I found myself actually carrying it out. I tried not to be obvious, yet when I grabbed his leg, trying to tumble him out of the chair, he raised up roaring with laughter, and, looking at me with soberness dead in the eye, kicked me viciously in the chest. The chair leg flew out of my hand and I felt myself going and rolled. It was as though I had rolled through a bed of hot coals. It seemed a whole century would pass before I would roll free, a century in which I was seared through the deepest levels of my body to the fearful breath within me and the breath seared and heated to the point of explosion. It'll all be over in a flash, I thought as I rolled clear. It'll all be over in a flash.

But not yet, the men on the other side were waiting, red faces swollen as though from apoplexy as they bent forward in their chairs. Seeing their fingers coming toward me I rolled away as a fumbled football rolls off the receiver's fingertips, back into the coals. That time I luckily sent the rug sliding out of place and heard the coins ringing against the floor and the boys scuffling to pick them up and the M.C. calling, "All right, boys, that's all. Go get dressed and get your money."

I was limp as a dish rag. My back felt as though it had been beaten with wires.

When we had dressed the M.C. came in and gave us each five dollars, except Tatlock, who got ten for being last in the ring. Then he told us to leave. I was not to get a chance to deliver my speech, I thought. I was going out into the dim alley in despair when I was stopped and told to go back. I returned to the ballroom, where the men were pushing back their chairs and gathering in groups to talk.

The M.C. knocked on a table for quiet. "Gentlemen," he said, "we almost forgot an important part of the program. A most serious part, gentlemen. This boy was brought here to deliver a speech which he made at his graduation yesterday . . ."

"Bravo!"

"I'm told that he is the smartest boy we've got out there in Greenwood. I'm told that he knows more big words than a pocket-sized dictionary."

Much applause and laughter.

"So now, gentlemen, I want you to give him your attention."

There was still laughter as I faced them, my mouth dry, my eye throbbing. I began slowly, but evidently my throat was tense, because they began shouting, "Louder! Louder!"

"We of the younger generation extol the wisdom of that great leader and educator," I shouted, "who first spoke these flaming words of wisdom: 'A ship lost at sea for many days suddenly sighted a friendly vessel. From the mast of the unfortunate vessel was seen a signal: "Water, water; we die of thirst!" The answer from the friendly vessel came back: "Cast down your bucket where you are." The captain of the distressed vessel, at last heeding the injunction, cast down his bucket, and it came up full of fresh sparkling water from the mouth of the Amazon River.' And like him I say, and in his words, 'To those of my race who depend upon bettering their condition in a foreign land, or who underestimate the importance of cultivating friendly relations with the Southern white man, who is his next-door neighbor, I would say: "Cast down your bucket where you are" — cast it down in making friends in every manly way of the people of all races by whom we are surrounded . . .'"

I spoke automatically and with such fervor that I did not realize that the men were still talking and laughing until my dry mouth, filling up with blood from the cut, almost strangled me. I coughed, wanting to stop and go to one of the tall brass, sand-filled spittoons to relieve myself, but a few of the men, especially the superintendent, were listening and I was afraid. So I gulped it down, blood, saliva and all, and continued. (What powers of endurance I had during those days! What enthusiasm! What a belief in the rightness of things!) I spoke even louder in spite of the pain. But still they talked and still they laughed, as though deaf with cotton in dirty ears. So I spoke with greater emotional emphasis. I closed my ears and swallowed blood until I was nauseated. The speech seemed a hundred times as long as before but I could not leave out a single word. All had to be said, each memorized nuance considered, rendered. Nor was that all. Whenever I uttered a word of three or more syllables a group of voices would yell for me to repeat it. I used the phrase "social responsibility" and they yelled:

"What's that word you say, boy?"

"Social responsibility," I said.

"What?"

"Social . . ."

"Louder."

". . . responsibility."

"More!"

"Respon—"

"Repeat!"

"—sibility."

The room filled with the uproar of laughter until, no doubt, distracted by having to gulp down my blood, I made a mistake and yelled a phrase I had often seen denounced in newspaper editorials, heard debated in private.

"Social . . ."

"What?" they yelled.

". . . equality — "

The laughter hung smokelike in the sudden stillness. I opened my eyes, puzzled. Sounds of displeasure filled the room. The M.C. rushed forward. They shouted hostile phrases at me. But I did not understand.

A small dry mustached man in the front row blared out, "Say that slowly, son!"

"What, sir?"

"What you just said!"

"Social responsibility, sir," I said.

"You weren't being smart, were you, boy?" he said, not unkindly.

"No, sir!"

"You sure that about 'equality' was a mistake?"

"Oh, yes, sir, I said. "I was swallowing blood."

"Well, you had better speak more slowly so we can understand. We mean to do right by you, but you've got to know your place at all times. All right, now, go on with your speech."

I was afraid. I wanted to leave but I wanted also to speak and I was afraid they'd snatch me down.

"Thank you, sir," I said, beginning where I had left off, and having them ignore me as before.

Yet when I finished there was a thunderous applause. I was surprised to see the superintendent come forth with a package wrapped in white tissue paper, and, gesturing for quiet, address the men.

"Gentlemen, you see that I did not overpraise this boy. He makes a good speech and some day he'll lead his people in the proper paths. And I don't have to tell you that that is important in these days and times. This is a good, smart boy, and so to encourage him in the right direction, in the name of the Board of Education I wish to present him a prize in the form of this . . ."

He paused, removing the tissue paper and revealing a gleaming calfskin brief case.

". . . in the form of this first-class article from Shad Whitmore's shop."

"Boy," he said, addressing me, "take this prize and keep it well. Consider it a badge of office. Prize it. Keep developing as you are and some day it will be filled with important papers that will help shape the destiny of your people."

I was so moved that I could hardly express my thanks. A rope of bloody saliva forming a shape like an undiscovered continent drooled upon the leather and I wiped it quickly away. I felt an importance that I had never dreamed.

"Open it and see what's inside," I was told.

My fingers a-tremble, I complied, smelling the fresh leather and finding an official-looking document inside. It was a scholarship to the state college for Negroes. My eyes filled with tears and I ran awkwardly off the floor.

I was overjoyed; I did not even mind when I discovered that the gold pieces I had scrambled for were brass pocket tokens advertising a certain make of automobile.

When I reached home everyone was excited. Next day the neighbors came to congratulate me. I even felt safe from grandfather, whose deathbed curse usually spoiled my triumphs. I stood beneath his photograph with my brief case in hand and smiled triumphantly into his stolid black peasant's face. It was a face that fascinated me. The eyes seemed to follow everywhere I went.

That night I dreamed I was at a circus with him and that he refused to laugh at the clowns no matter what they did. Then later he told me to open my brief case and read what was inside and I did, finding an official envelope stamped with the state seal; and inside the envelope I found another and another, endlessly, and I thought I would fall of weariness. "Them's years," he said. "Now open that one." And I did and in it I found an engraved document containing a short message in letters of gold. "Read it," my grandfather said. "Out loud!"

"To Whom It May Concern," I intoned. "Keep This Nigger-Boy Running."

I awoke with the old man's laughter ringing in my ears.

(It was a dream I was to remember and dream again for many years after. But at that time I had no insight into its meaning. First I had to attend college.)

1952

Bernard Malamud   *1914–*

Bernard Malamud was born in Brooklyn of Russian immigrant parents. After graduating from City College (B.A., 1936), he supported himself by teaching night classes while earning his M.A. degree at Columbia University (1942). He has taught at Oregon State University (1949–61) and, since 1961, at Bennington College. His first book, *The Natural* (1952), is a comic novel about a baseball player. His second, *The Assistant* (1957), his most successful and best-known work, is the tragi-comic story of a young Italian-American vagrant who tries to find a place for himself in the family of the Jewish proprietor of a Depression-ridden neighborhood grocery store. For all the bleakness of its world, the novel differs from earlier naturalistic fiction in its affirmation of the capacity for change in its young hero.

Malamud's later novels include *A New Life* (1961) and *The Fixer* (1966). His stories have been collected in *The Magic Barrel* (1958) and *Idiots First* (1963). Of these, "Black Is My Favorite Color" is typical of Malamud's work in its compassionate humor and its subordination of the claims of race or religion to those of humanity.

A biographical and critical treatment is Sidney Richman, *Bernard Malamud* (New York, 1966), which includes a bibliography.

The text of "Black Is My Favorite Color" is that of *Idiots First* (New York, 1963).

Black Is My Favorite Color

Charity Sweetness sits in the toilet eating her two hard-boiled eggs while I'm having my ham sandwich and coffee in the kitchen. That's how it goes only don't get the idea of ghettoes. If there's a ghetto I'm the one that's in it. She's my cleaning woman from Father Divine[1] and comes in once a week to my small three-room apartment on my day off from the liquor store. "Peace," she says to me, "Father reached on down and took me right up in Heaven." She's a small person with a flat body, frizzy hair, and a quiet face that the light shines out of, and Mama had such eyes before she died. The first time Charity Sweetness came in to clean, a little more than a year and a half, I made the mistake to ask her to sit down at the kitchen table with me and eat her lunch. I was still feeling not so hot after Ornita left but I'm the kind of a man—Nat Lime, forty-four, a bachelor with a daily growing bald spot on the back of my head, and I could lose frankly fifteen pounds—who enjoys company so long as he has it. So she cooked up her two hardboiled eggs and sat down and took a small bite out of one of them. But after a minute she stopped chewing and she got up and carried the eggs in a cup in the bathroom, and since then she eats there. I said to her more than once, "Okay, Charity Sweetness, so have it your way, eat the eggs in the kitchen by yourself and I'll eat when you're done," but she smiles absentminded, and eats in the toilet. It's my fate with colored people.

Although black is still my favorite color you wouldn't know it from my luck except in short quantities even though I do all right in the liquor store business in Harlem, on Eighth Avenue between 110th and 111th. I speak with respect. A large part of my life I've had dealings with Negro people, most on a business basis but sometimes for friendly reasons with genuine feeling on both sides. I'm drawn to them. At this time of my life I should have one or two good colored friends but the fault isn't necessarily mine. If they knew what was in my heart towards them, but how can you tell that to anybody nowadays? I've tried more than once but the language of the heart either is a dead language or else nobody understands it the way you speak it. Very few. What I'm saying is, personally for me there's only one human color and that's the color of blood. I like a black person if not because he's black, then because I'm white. It comes to the same thing. If I wasn't white my first choice would be black. I'm satisfied to be white because I have no other choice. Anyway, I got an eye for color. I appreciate. Who wants everybody to be the same? Maybe it's like some kind of a talent. Nat Lime might be a liquor dealer in Harlem, but once in the jungle in New Guinea in the Second War, I got the idea when I shot at a running Jap and missed him, that I had some kind of a talent, though maybe it's the kind where you have a marvelous idea now and then but in the end what do they come to? After all, it's a strange world.

Where Charity Sweetness eats her eggs makes me think about Buster Wilson when we were both boys in the Williamsburg section of

[1] Father Divine (d. 1965), whose real name may have been George Baker or Frederick Devoe, was the (self-proclaimed) divine leader of a religious sect. He maintained homes or "Heavens" in New York and other American cities.

Brooklyn. There was this long block of run-down dirty frame houses in the middle of a not-so-hot white neighborhood full of pushcarts. The Negro houses looked to me like they had been born and died there, dead not long after the beginning of the world. I lived on the next street. My father was a cutter with arthritis in both hands, big red knuckles and swollen fingers so he didn't cut, and my mother was the one who went to work. She sold paper bags from a second-hand pushcart in Ellery Street. We didn't starve but nobody ate chicken unless we were sick or the chicken was. This was my first acquaintance with a lot of black people and I used to poke around on their poor block. I think I thought, brother, if there can be like this, what can't there be? I mean I caught an early idea what life was about. Anyway I met Buster Wilson there. He used to play marbles by himself. I sat on the curb across the street, watching him shoot one marble lefty and the other righty. The hand that won picked up the marbles. It wasn't so much of a game but he didn't ask me to come over. My idea was to be friendly, only he never encouraged, he discouraged. Why did I pick him out for a friend? Maybe because I had no others then, we were new in the neighborhood, from Manhattan. Also I liked his type. Buster did everything alone. He was a skinny kid and his brothers' clothes hung on him like worn-out potato sacks. He was a beanpole boy, about twelve, and I was then ten. His arms and legs were burnt out matchsticks. He always wore a brown wool sweater, one arm half unraveled, the other went down to the wrist. His long and narrow head had a white part cut straight in the short woolly hair, maybe with a ruler there, by his father, a barber but too drunk to stay a barber. In those days though I had little myself I was old enough to know who was better off, and the whole block of colored houses made me feel bad in the daylight. But I went there as much as I could because the street was full of life. In the night it looked different, it's hard to tell a cripple in the dark. Sometimes I was afraid to walk by the houses when they were dark and quiet. I was afraid there were people looking at me that I couldn't see. I liked it better when they had parties at night and everybody had a good time. The musicians played their banjos and saxophones and the houses shook with the music and laughing. The young girls, with their pretty dresses and ribbons in their hair, caught me in my throat when I saw them through the windows.

But with the parties came drinking and fights. Sundays were bad days after the Saturday night parties. I remember once that Buster's father, also long and loose, always wearing a dirty gray Homburg hat, chased another black man in the street with a half-inch chisel. The other one, maybe five feet high, lost his shoe and when they wrestled on the ground he was already bleeding through his suit, a thick red blood smearing the sidewalk. I was frightened by the blood and wanted to pour it back in the man who was bleeding from the chisel. On another time Buster's father was playing in a crap game with two big bouncy red dice, in the back of an alley between two middle houses. Then about six men started fist-fighting there, and they ran out of the alley and hit each other in the street. The neighbors, including children, came out and watched, everybody afraid but nobody moving to do anything. I saw the same thing near my store in Harlem, years later, a big crowd watching two men in the street, their breaths hanging in the air on a winter night murdering each other with switch knives, but nobody moved to call a cop. I didn't either. Anyway, I was just a young kid but I still remember how the cops drove up in a police paddy wagon and broke up the fight by hitting everybody they could hit with big nightsticks. This was in the days before LaGuardia.[2] Most of the fighters were knocked out cold, only one or two got away. Buster's father started to run back in his house but a cop ran after him and cracked him on his Homburg hat with a club, right on the front porch. Then the Negro men were lifted up by the cops, one at the arms and the other at the feet, and they heaved them in the paddy wagon. Buster's father hit the back of the wagon and fell, with his nose spouting very red blood, on top of three other men. I personally couldn't stand it, I was scared of the human race so I ran home, but I remember Buster watching without any expression in his eyes. I stole an extra fifteen cents from my mother's pocketbook and I ran back and asked Buster if he wanted to go to the movies. I would pay. He said yes. This was the first time he talked to me.

So we went more than once to the movies. But we never got to be friends. Maybe because it was a one-way proposition—from me to him. Which includes my invitations to go with me, my (poor mother's) movie money, Hershey chocolate bars, watermelon slices, even my best Nick Carter and Merriwell books that I spent hours picking up in the junk shops, and that he never gave me back. Once he let me go in his house to get a match so we could smoke some butts we found, but it smelled so heavy, so impossible, I died till I got out of there. What I saw in the way of furniture I won't mention—the best was falling apart in pieces. Maybe we went to the movies all together five or six matinees that spring and in the summertime, but when the shows were over he usually walked home by himself.

"Why don't you wait for me, Buster?" I said. "We're both going in the same direction."

But he was walking ahead and didn't hear me. Anyway he didn't answer.

One day when I wasn't expecting it he hit me in the teeth. I felt like crying but not because of the pain. I spit blood and said, "What did you hit me for? What did I do to you?"

"Because you a Jew bastard. Take your Jew movies and your Jew candy and shove them up your Jew ass."

[2] Fiorello LaGuardia (1882–1947), popular mayor of New York (1934–1945).

And he ran away.

I thought to myself how was I to know he didn't like the movies. When I was a man I thought, you can't force it.

Years later, in the prime of my life, I met Mrs. Ornita Harris. She was standing by herself under an open umbrella at the bus stop, cross-town 110th, and I picked up her green glove that she had dropped on the wet sidewalk. It was in the end of November. Before I could ask her was it hers, she grabbed the glove out of my hand, closed her umbrella, and stepped in the bus. I got on right after her.

I was annoyed so I said, "If you'll pardon me, Miss, there's no law that you have to say thanks, but at least don't make a criminal out of me."

"Well, I'm sorry," she said, "but I don't like white men trying to do me favors."

I tipped my hat and that was that. In ten minutes I got off the bus but she was already gone.

Who expected to see her again but I did. She came into my store about a week later for a bottle of scotch.

"I would offer you a discount," I told her, "but I know you don't like a certain kind of a favor and I'm not looking for a slap in the face."

Then she recognized me and got a little embarrassed.

"I'm sorry I misunderstood you that day."

"So mistakes happen."

The result was she took the discount. I gave her a dollar off.

She used to come in about every two weeks for a fifth of Haig and Haig. Sometimes I waited on her, sometimes my helpers, Jimmy or Mason, also colored, but I said to give the discount. They both looked at me but I had nothing to be ashamed. In the spring when she came in we used to talk once in a while. She was a slim woman, dark but not the most dark, about thirty years I would say, also well built, with a com- bination nice legs and a good-size bosom that I like. Her face was pretty, with big eyes and high cheek bones, but lips a little thick and nose a little broad. Sometimes she didn't feel like talking, she paid for the bottle, less discount, and walked out. Her eyes were tired and she didn't look to me like a happy woman.

I found out her husband was once a window cleaner on the big buildings, but one day his safety belt broke and he fell fifteen stories. After the funeral she got a job as a manicurist in a Times Square barber shop. I told her I was a bachelor and lived with my mother in a small three-room apartment on West Eighty-third near Broadway. My mother had cancer, and Ornita said she was very sorry.

One night in July we went out together. How that happened I'm still not so sure. I guess I asked her and she didn't say no. Where do you go out with a Negro woman? We went to the Village. We had a good dinner and walked in Washington Square Park. It was a hot night.

Nobody was surprised when they saw us, nobody looked at us like we were against the law. If they looked maybe they saw my new light-weight suit that I bought yesterday and my shiny bald spot when we walked under a lamp, also how pretty she was for a man of my type. We went in a movie on West Eighth Street. I didn't want to go in but she said she had heard about the picture. We went in like strangers and we came out like strangers. I wondered what was in her mind and I thought to myself, whatever is in there it's not a certain white man that I know. All night long we went together like we were chained. After the movie she wouldn't let me take her back to Harlem. When I put her in a taxi she asked me, "Why did we bother?"

For the steak, I wanted to say. Instead I said, "You're worth the bother."

"Thanks anyway."

Kiddo, I thought to myself after the taxi left, you just found out what's what, now the best thing is forget her.

It's easy to say. In August we went out the second time. That was the night she wore a purple dress and I thought to myself, my God, what colors. Who paints that picture paints a masterpiece. Everybody looked at us but I had pleasure. That night when she took off her dress it was in a furnished room I had the sense to rent a few days before. With my sick mother, I couldn't ask her to come to my apartment, and she didn't want me to go home with her where she lived with her brother's family on West 115th near Lenox Avenue. Under her purple dress she wore a black slip, and when she took that off she had white underwear. When she took off the white underwear she was black again. But I know where the next white was, if you want to call it white. And that was the night I think I fell in love with her, the first time in my life though I have liked one or two nice girls I used to go with when I was a boy. It was a serious proposition. I'm the kind of a man when I think of love I'm thinking of marriage. I guess that's why I am a bachelor.

That same week I had a holdup in my place, two big men—both black—with revolvers. One got excited when I rang open the cash register so he could take the money and he hit me over the ear with his gun. I stayed in the hospital a couple of weeks. Otherwise I was insured. Ornita came to see me. She sat on a chair without talking much. Finally I saw she was uncomfortable so I suggested she ought to go home.

"I'm sorry it happened," she said.

"Don't talk like it's your fault."

When I got out of the hospital my mother was dead. She was a wonderful person. My father died when I was thirteen and all by herself she kept the family alive and together. I sat shive for a week and remembered how she sold paper bags on her pushcart. I remembered her life and what she tried to teach me. Nathan, she said, if you ever forget you are a Jew a goy will remind you. Mama, I said, rest in peace on this subject. But if I do something you don't like, remember, on earth it's harder than where you are. Then when my week of mourning was finished, one night I said, "Ornita, let's get married. We're both honest people and if you love me like I love you it won't be such a bad time. If you don't like New York I'll sell out here and we'll move someplace else. Maybe to San Francisco where nobody knows us. I was there for a week in the Second War and I saw white and colored living together."

"Nat," she answered me, "I like you but I'd be afraid. My husband woulda killed me."

"Your husband is dead."

"Not in my memory."

"In that case I'll wait."

"Do you know what it'd be like—I mean the life we could expect?"

"Ornita," I said, "I'm the kind of a man, if he picks his own way of life he's satisfied."

"What about children? Were you looking forward to half-Jewish polka dots?"

"I was looking forward to children."

"I can't," she said.

Can't is can't. I saw she was afraid and the best thing was not to push. Sometimes when we met she was so nervous that whatever we did she couldn't enjoy it. At the same time I still thought I had a chance. We were together more and more. I got rid of my furnished room and she came to my apartment—I gave away Mama's bed and bought a new one. She stayed with me all day on Sundays. When she wasn't so nervous she was affectionate, and if I know what love is, I had it. We went out a couple of times a week, the same way—usually I met her in Times Square and sent her home in a taxi, but I talked more about marriage and she talked less against it. One night she told me she was still trying to convince herself but she was almost convinced. I took an inventory of my liquor stock so I could put the store up for sale.

Ornita knew what I was doing. One day she quit her job, the next she took it back. She also went away a week to visit her sister in Philadelphia for a little rest. She came back tired but said maybe. Maybe is maybe so I'll wait. The way she said it it was closer to yes. That was the winter two years ago. When she was in Philadelphia I called up a friend of mine from the Army, now a CPA, and told him I would appreciate an invitation for an evening. He knew why. His wife said yes right away. When Ornita came back we went there. The wife made a fine dinner. It wasn't a bad time and they told us to come again. Ornita had a few drinks. She looked relaxed, wonderful. Later, because of a twenty-four hour taxi strike I had to take her home on the subway.

When we got to the 116th Street station she told me to stay on the train, and she would walk the couple of blocks to her house. I didn't like a woman walking alone on the streets at that time of the night. She said she never had any trouble but I insisted nothing doing. I said I would walk to her stoop with her and when she went upstairs I would go back to the subway.

On the way there, on 115th in the middle of the block before Lenox, we were stopped by three men—maybe they were boys. One had a black hat with a half-inch brim, one a green cloth hat, and the third wore a black leather cap. The green hat was wearing a short coat and the other two had long ones. It was under a street light but the leather cap snapped a six-inch switchblade open in the light.

"What you doin' with this white son of a bitch?" he said to Ornita.

"I'm minding my own business," she answered him, "and I wish you would too."

"Boys," I said, "we're all brothers. I'm a reliable merchant in the neighborhood. This young lady is my dear friend. We don't want any trouble. Please let us pass."

"You talk like a Jew landlord," said the green hat. "Fifty a week for a single room."

"No charge fo' the rats," said the half-inch brim.

"Believe me, I'm no landlord. My store is 'Nathan's Liquors' between Hundred Tenth and Eleventh. I also have two colored clerks, Mason and Jimmy, and they will tell you I pay good wages as well as I give discounts to certain customers."

"Shut your mouth, Jewboy," said the leather cap, and he moved the knife back and forth in front of my coat button. "No more black pussy for you."

"Speak with respect about this lady, please."

I got slapped on my mouth.

"That ain't no lady," said the long face with the half-inch brim, "that's black pussy. She deserve to have evvy bit of her hair shave off. How you like to have evvy bit of your hair shave off, black pussy?"

"Please leave me and this gentleman alone or I'm gonna scream long and loud. That's my house three doors down."

They slapped her. I never heard such a scream. Like her husband was falling fifteen stories.

I hit the one that slapped her and the next I knew I was laying in the gutter with a pain in my head. I thought, goodbye, Nat, they'll stab me for sure, but all they did was take my wallet and run in three different directions.

Ornita walked back with me to the subway and she wouldn't let me go home with her again.

"Just get home safely."

She looked terrible. Her face was gray and I still remembered her scream. It was a terrible winter night, very cold February, and it took me an hour and ten minutes to get home. I felt bad for leaving her but what could I do?

We had a date downtown the next night but she didn't show up, the first time.

In the morning I called her in her place of business.

"For God's sake, Ornita, if we got married and moved away we wouldn't have that kind of trouble that we had. We wouldn't come in that neighborhood any more.·

"Yes, we would. I have family there and don't want to move anyplace else. The truth of it is I can't marry you, Nat. I got troubles enough of my own."

"I coulda sworn you love me."

"Maybe I do but I can't marry you."

"For God's sake, why?"

"I got enough trouble of my own."

I went that night in a cab to her brother's house to see her. He was a quiet man with a thin mustache. "She gone," he said, "left for a long visit to some close relatives in the South. She said to tell you she appreciate your intentions but didn't think it will work out."

"Thank you kindly," I said.

Don't ask me how I got home.

Once on Eighth Avenue, a couple of blocks from my store, I saw a blind man with a white cane tapping on the sidewalk. I figured we were going in the same direction so I took his arm.

"I can tell you're white," he said.

A heavy colored woman with a full shopping bag rushed after us. "Never mind," she said, "I know where he live."

She pushed me with her shoulder and I hurt my leg on the fire hydrant.

That's how it is. I give my heart and they kick me in my teeth.

"Charity Sweetness—you hear me?—come out of that goddamn toilet!"

1963

Saul Bellow   *1915—*

Born in Quebec of Russian immigrant parents, Saul Bellow grew up in Chicago, the scene of much of his fiction. He attended the University of Chicago and Northwestern University (B.A., 1937). As a beginning writer he supported himself by working in the editorial department of the *Encyclopaedia Britannica* (1943—46); he has subsequently taught at several universities including the University of Minnesota and University of Chicago. His first novel, *Dangling Man* (1944), which describes the anxieties of a man waiting to be drafted, was followed by *The Victim* (1947), which considers the relations of Jews and Gentiles. *The Adventures of Augie March* (1953) is a successful picaresque novel about a young Jewish hero who becomes involved in many strange predicaments in his effort to find himself and establish his values. *Seize the Day* (1956)—which includes a novella, stories, and a play—was followed by *Henderson the Rain King* (1959), a fantastic novel set in Africa.

Herzog (1964), Bellow's most recent novel, describes the efforts of its middle-aged hero, an intellectual, to achieve stability after a period of emotional and mental turmoil in the course of which he had been betrayed by his wife Madeleine and his friend Valentine Gersbach and estranged from his children, Marco and June. In an attempt to sort out his ideas, Herzog writes many unposted "letters" which enable him to externalize his conflicts and define his values. At the end of the novel Herzog "comes home" to his New England country house, not cured but restored to a measure of self-control and acceptance. Rejecting both his own earlier illusions and certain attitudes he has come to recognize as perversions of intellectualism, Herzog remains confident of the importance of reason, will, and mature love. Although typical of Bellow's concern for the theme of self-discovery, *Herzog* is unusual in American fiction in that it is a novel of ideas, in which the hero feels a compulsion to test his own outlook against the intellectual traditions he has encountered in his study and experience.

Bellow has recently also begun writing for the stage. His play *The Last Analysis* was produced in 1964. *Mosby's Memoirs and Other Stories* (1968) is his most recent book.

Critical studies of Bellow's work include Robert Detweiler, *Saul Bellow: A Critical Essay* (Grand Rapids, Mich., 1967); Irving Malin, ed., *Saul Bellow and the Critics* (New York, 1967); K. M. Opdahl, *The Novels of Saul Bellow: An Introduction* (University Park, Pa., 1967); and Earl Rovit, *Saul Bellow* (Minneapolis, 1967).

The text of "Herzog Comes Home" is that of *Herzog* (New York, 1964).

Herzog Comes Home[1]

1

He reached his country place the following afternoon, after taking a plane to Albany, from there the bus to Pittsfield, and then a cab to Ludeyville. Asphalter had given him some Tuinal the night before. He slept deeply and was feeling perfectly fine, despite his taped sides.

The house was two miles beyond the village, in the hills. Beautiful, sparkling summer weather in the Berkshires, the air light, the streams quick, the woods dense, the green new. As for birds, Herzog's acres seemed to have become a sanctuary. Wrens nested under the ornamental scrolls of the porch. The giant elm was not quite dead, and the orioles lived in it still. Herzog had the driver stop in the mossy roadway, boulder-lined. He couldn't be sure the house was approachable. But no fallen trees blocked the path, and although much of the gravel had washed down in thaws and storms the cab might easily have gotten through. Moses, however, didn't mind the short climb. His chest was securely armored in tape and his legs were light. He had bought some groceries in Ludeyville. If hunters and prowlers had not eaten it, there was a supply of canned goods in the cellar. Two years ago he had put up tomatoes and beans and raspberry preserves, and before leaving for Chicago he had hidden his wine and whisky. The electricity of course was turned off but perhaps the old hand pump could be made to work. There was always cistern water to fall back on. He could cook in the fireplace; there were old hooks and trivets — and here (his heart trembled) the house rose out of weeds, vines, trees, and blossoms. Herzog's folly! Monument to his sincere and loving idiocy, to the unrecognized evils of his character, symbol of his Jewish struggle for a solid footing in White Anglo-Saxon Protestant America ("The land was ours before we were the land's," as that sententious old man declared at the In-

---

[1] The final (9th) chapter of *Herzog*. The present title is the editors'.

auguration).[2] I too have done my share of social climbing, he thought, with hauteur to spare, defying the Wasps, who, because the government gave much of this continent away to the railroads, stopped boiling their own soap circa 1880, took European tours, and began to complain of the Micks and the Spicks and the Sheenies. What a struggle I waged! —left-handed but fierce. But enough of that—here I am. *Hineni!* How marvelously beautiful it is today. He stopped in the overgrown yard, shut his eyes in the sun, against flashes of crimson, and drew in the odors of catalpa-bells, soil, honeysuckle, wild onions, and herbs. Either deer or lovers had lain in this grass near the elm, for it was flattened. He circled the house to see whether it was much damaged. There were no broken windows. All the shutters, hooked from within, were undisturbed. Only a few of the posters he had put up warning that this property was under police protection had been torn down. The garden was a thick mass of thorny canes, roses and berries twisted together. It looked too hopeless—past regretting. He would never have the strength to throw himself into such tasks again, to hammer, paint, patch, splice, prune, spray. He was here only to look things over.

The house was as musty as he had expected. He opened a few windows and shutters in the kitchen. The debris of leaves and pine needles, webs, cocoons, and insect corpses he brushed away. What was needed, immediately, was a fire. He had brought matches. One of the benefits of a riper age was that you became clever about such things —foresightful. Of course he had a bicycle—he could ride to the village to buy what he had forgotten. He had even been smart enough to set the bike on its saddle, to spare the tires. There was not much air in them, but they'd get him down to the Esso station. He carried in a few pine logs, kindling, and started a small blaze first, to make sure of the draft. Birds or squirrels might have nested in the flues. But then he remembered that he had climbed out on the roof to fasten wire mesh over the chimneys—part of his frenzy of efficient toil. He laid on more wood. The old bark dropped away and disclosed the work of insects underneath—grubs, ants, long-legged spiders ran away. He gave them every opportunity to escape. The black, dry branches began to burn with yellow flames. He heaped on more logs, secured them with the andirons, and continued his examination of the house.

The canned food had not been touched. There was fancy-goods bought by Madeleine (always the best of everything), S. S. Pierce terrapin soup, Indian pudding, truffles, olives, and then grimmer-looking victuals bought by Moses himself at Army surplus sales—beans, canned bread, and the like. He made his inventory with a sort of dreamy curiosity about his onetime plan for solitary self-sufficiency —the washer, dryer, the hot-water unit, pure white and gleaming forms into which he had put his dead father's dollars, ugly green, laboriously

[2] Robert Frost at the Inauguration (January, 1961) of President John F. Kennedy.

made, tediously counted, divided in agony among the heirs. Well, well, thought Herzog, he shouldn't have sent me to school to learn about dead emperors. "My name is Ozymandias, king of kings:/Look on my works, ye Mighty, and despair!" But self-sufficiency and solitude, gentleness, it all was so tempting, and had sounded so innocent, it became smiling Herzog so well in the description. It's only later you discover how much viciousness is in these hidden heavens. *Unemployed consciousness,* he wrote in the pantry. *I grew up in a time of widespread unemployment, and never believed there might be work for me. Finally, jobs appeared, but somehow my consciousness remained unemployed. And after all,* he continued beside the fire, *the human intellect is one of the great forces of the universe. It can't safely remain unused. You might almost conclude that the boredom of so many human arrangements (middle-class family life, for instance) has the historical aim of freeing the intellect of newer generations, sending them into science. But a terrible loneliness throughout life is simply the plankton on which Leviathan feeds. . . . Must reconsider. The soul requires intensity. At the same time virtue bores mankind. Read Confucius again. With vast populations, the world must prepare to turn Chinese.*

Herzog's present loneliness did not seem to count because it was so consciously cheerful. He peered through the chink in the lavatory where he used to hide away with his ten-cent volume of Dryden and Pope, reading "I am His Highness' dog at Kew" or "Great wits to madness sure are near allied." There, in the same position as in former years, was the rose that used to give him comfort—as shapely, as red (as nearly "genital" to his imagination) as ever. Some good things do recur. He was a long time peering at it through the meeting of masonry and lumber. The same damp-loving grasshoppers (giant orthoptera) still lived in this closet of masonry and plywood. A struck match revealed them. Among the pipes.

It was odd, the tour he made through his property. In his own room he found the ruins of his scholarly enterprise strewn over the desk and the shelves. The windows were so discolored as to seem stained with iodine, and the honeysuckles outside had almost pulled the screens down. On the sofa he found proof that the place was indeed visited by lovers. Too blind with passion to hunt in darkness for the bedrooms. But they'll get curvature of the spine using Madeleine's horsehair antiques. For some reason it particularly pleased Herzog that his room should be the one chosen by the youth of the village—here among bales of learned notes. He found girls' hairs on the curving armrests, and tried to imagine bodies, faces, odors. Thanks to Ramona he had no need to be greatly envious, but a little envy of the young was quite natural too. On the floor was one of his large cards with a note in which he had written *To do justice to Condorcet* . . . He hadn't the heart to read further and turned it face down on the table. For the present, anyway, Condorcet would have to find another defender. In the dining room were the precious dishes that Tennie wanted, crimson-rimmed bone china, very handsome. He wouldn't need that. The books, muslin-covered, were undisturbed. He lifted the cloth and glanced at them with no special interest. Visiting the little bathroom, he was entertained to see the lavish fittings Madeleine had bought at Sloane's, scalloped silver soap dishes and flashing towel racks too heavy for the plaster, even after they were fastened with toggle bolts. They were drooping now. The shower stall, for Gersbach's convenience — the Gersbachs had had no shower in Barrington — was thoughtfully equipped with a handrail. "If we're going to put it in, let's make it so Valentine can use it," Mady had said. Ah, well — Moses shrugged. A strange odor in the toilet bowl attracted his notice next, and raising the wooden lid he found the small beaked skulls and other remains of birds who had nested there after the water was drained, and then had been entombed by the falling lid. He looked grimly in, his heart aching somewhat at this accident. There must be a broken window in the attic, he inferred from this, and other birds nesting in the house. Indeed, he found owls in his bedroom, perched on the red valances, which they had streaked with droppings. He gave them every opportunity to escape, and, when they were gone, looked for a nest. He found the young owls in the large light fixture over the bed where he and Madeleine had known so much misery and hatred. (Some delight as well.) On the mattress much nest litter had fallen — straws, wool threads, down, bits of flesh (mouse ends) and streaks of excrement. Unwilling to disturb these flat-faced little creatures, Herzog pulled the mattress of his marriage bed into June's room. He opened more windows, and the sun and country air at once entered. He was surprised to feel such contentment . . . contentment? Whom was he kidding, this was joy! For perhaps the first time he felt what it was to be free from Madeleine. Joy! His servitude was ended, and his heart released from its grisly heaviness and encrustation. Her absence, no more than her absence itself, was simply sweetness and lightness of spirit. To her, at 11th and State, it had been happiness to see him in trouble, and to him in Ludeyville it was a delicious joy to have her removed from his flesh, like something that had stabbed his shoulders, his groin, made his arms and his neck lame and cumbersome. *My dear sage and imbecilic Edvig. It may be that the remission of pain is no small part of human happiness. In its primordial and stupider levels, where now and then a closed valve opens again. . . .* Those strange lights, Herzog's brown eyes, so often overlaid with the film or protective chitin of melancholy, the by-product of his laboring brain, shone again.

It cost him some effort to turn over the mattress on the floor of June's old room. He had to move aside some of her cast-off toys and kiddie furniture, a great stuffed blue-eyed tiger, the potty chair, a red snowsuit, perfectly good. He recognized also the grandmother's bikini, shorts, and halters, and, among other oddities, a washrag which Phoebe had stitched with his initials, a birthday present, a possible hint that his ears were not clean. Beaming, he pushed it aside with his foot. A beetle escaped from beneath. Herzog, lying under the open window with the sun in his face, rested on the mattress. Over him the great trees, the spruces in the front yard, showed their beautiful jaggedness and sent down the odor of heated needles and gum.

It was here, until the sun passed from the room, that he began in earnest, from tranquil fullness of heart, to consider another series of letters.

Dear Ramona. Only "Dear"? Come, Moses, open up a little. *Darling Ramona. What an excellent woman you are.* Here he paused to consider whether he should say he was in Ludeyville. In her Mercedes she could drive from New York in three hours, and it was probable that she would. God's blessing on her short but perfect legs, her solid, well-tinted breasts, and her dashing curved teeth and gypsy brows and curls. *La devoradora de hombres.*[3] He decided, however, to date his letter Chicago and ask Lucas to remail it. What he wanted now was peace — peace and clarity. *I hope I didn't upset you by copping out. But I know you're not one of those conventional women it takes a month to appease because of a broken date. I had to see my daughter, and my son. He's at Camp Ayumah, near Catskill. It's turning into a busy summer. Several interesting developments. I hesitate to make too many assertions yet, but at least I can admit what I never stopped asserting anyway, or feeling. The light of truth is never far away, and no human being is too negligible or corrupt to come into it.* I don't see why I shouldn't say that. *But to accept ineffectuality, banishment to personal life, confusion . . .* Why don't you try this out, Herzog, on the owls next door, those naked owlets pimpled with blue. *Since the last question, also the first one, the question of death, offers us the interesting alternatives of disintegrating ourselves by our own wills in proof of our "freedom," or the acknowledging that we owe a human life to this waking spell of existence, regardless of the void. (After all, we have no positive knowledge of that void.)*

Should I say all this to Ramona? Some women think that earnestness is wooing. She'll want a child. She'll want to breed with a man who talks to her like this. *Work. Work. Real, relevant work. . . .* He paused. But Ramona was a willing worker. According to her lights. And she loved her work. He smiled affectionately on his sunlit mattress.

Dear Marco. I've come up to the old homestead to look things over and relax a bit. The place is in pretty good shape, considering. Perhaps you'd like to spend some time here with me, only the two of

[3] "The devourer of men."

us—roughing it—after camp. We'll talk about it Parents' Day. I'm looking forward to that, eagerly. Your little sister whom I saw in Chicago yesterday is very lively and as pretty as ever. She received your postcard.

Do you remember the talks we had about Scott's Antarctic Expedition, and how poor Scott was beaten to the Pole by Amundsen? You seemed interested. This is a thing that always gets me. There was a man in Scott's party who went out and lost himself to give the others a chance to survive. He was ailing, footsore, couldn't keep up any longer, And do you remember how by chance they found a mound of frozen blood, the blood of one of their slaughtered ponies, and how thankful they were to thaw and drink it? The success of Amundsen was due to his use of dogs instead of ponies. The weaker were butchered and fed to the stronger. Otherwise the expedition would have failed. I have often wondered at one thing. Hungry as they were, the dogs would sniff at the flesh of their own and back away. The skin had to be removed before they would eat it.

Maybe you and I could take a trip at Xmas to Canada just to get the feel of genuine cold. I am a Canadian, too, you know. We could visit Ste. Agathe, in the Laurentians. Expect me on the 16th, bright and early.

Dear Luke—Be so kind as to post these enclosures. I hope to hear your depression is over. I think your visions of the aunt being rescued by the fireman and of the broads playing piggy-move-up are signs of psychological resiliency. I predict your recovery. As for me. . . . As for you, thought Herzog, you will not tell him how you feel now, all this overflow! It wouldn't make him happier. Keep it to yourself if you feel exalted. Anyway, he may think you've simply gone off your nut.

But if I am out of my mind, it's all right with me.

My dear Professor Mermelstein. I want to congratulate you on a splendid book. In some matters you scooped me, you know, and I felt like hell about it—hated you one whole day for making a good deal of my work superfluous (Wallace and Darwin?). However, I well know what labor and patience went into such a work—so much digging, learning, synthesizing, and I'm all admiration. When you are ready to print a revised edition—or perhaps another book—it would be a great pleasure to talk over some of these questions. There are parts of my projected book I'll never return to. You may do what you like with those materials. In my earlier book (to which you were kind enough to refer) I devoted one section to Heaven and Hell in apocalyptic Romanticism. I may not have done it to your taste, but you ought not to have over-looked it completely. You ought to have a look at the monograph by that fat natty brute Egbert Shapiro, "From Luther to Lenin, A History of Revolutionary Psychology." His fat cheeks give him a great resem-

blance to Gibbon. *It is a valuable piece of work. I was greatly impressed by the section called Millenarianism and Paranoia. It should not be ignored that modern power-systems do offer a resemblance to this psychosis. A gruesome and crazy book on this has been written by a man named Banowitch. Fairly inhuman, and filled with vile paranoid hypotheses such as that crowds are fundamentally cannibalistic, that people standing secretly terrify the sitting, that smiling teeth are the weapons of hunger, that the tyrant is mad for the sight of (possibly edible?) corpses about him. It seems quite true that the making of corpses has been the most dramatic achievement of modern dictators and their followers (Hitler, Stalin, etc.).* Just to see—Herzog tried this on, experimenting—whether Mermelstein didn't have a vestige of old Stalinism about him. *But this fellow Shapiro is something of an eccentric, and I mention him as an extreme case. How we all love extreme cases and apocalypses, fires, drownings, stranglings, and the rest of it. The bigger our mild, basically ethical, safe middle classes grow the more radical excitement is in demand. Mild or moderate truthfulness or accuracy seems to have no pull at all. Just what we need now!* ("When a dog is drowning, you offer him a cup of water," Papa used to say, bitterly.) *In any case, if you had read that chapter of mine on apocalypse and Romanticism you might have looked a little straighter at that Russian you admire so much—Isvolsky? The man who sees the souls of monads as the legions of the damned, simply atomized and pulverized, a dust storm in Hell; and warns that Lucifer must take charge of collectivized mankind, devoid of spiritual character and true personality. I don't deny this makes some sense, here and there, though I do worry that such ideas, because of the bit of suggestive truth in them, may land us in the same old suffocating churches and synagogues. I was somewhat bothered by borrowings and references which I considered "hit and run," or the use of other writers' serious beliefs as mere metaphors. For instance, I liked the section called "Interpretations of Suffering" and also the one called "Toward a Theory of Boredom." This was an excellent piece of research. But then I thought the treatment you gave Kierkegaard was fairly frivolous. I venture to say Kierkegaard meant that truth has lost its force with us and horrible pain and evil must teach it to us again, the eternal punishments of Hell will have to regain their reality before mankind turns serious once more. I do not see this. Let us set aside the fact that such convictions in the mouths of safe, comfortable people playing at crisis, alienation, apocalypse and desperation, make me sick. We must get it out of our heads that this is a doomed time, that we are waiting for the end, and the rest of it, mere junk from fashionable magazines. Things are grim enough without these shivery games. People frightening one another—a poor sort of moral exercise. But, to get to the main point, the advocacy and praise of suffering take us in the wrong direction and those of us who re-*

*main loyal to civilization must not go for it. You have to have the power
to employ pain, to repent, to be illuminated, you must have the opportunity and even the time. With the religious, the love of suffering is a form
of gratitude to experience or an opportunity to experience evil and
change it into good. They believe the spiritual cycle can and will be
completed in a man's existence and he will somehow make use of his
suffering, if only in the last moments of his life, when the mercy of God
will reward him with a vision of the truth, and he will die transfigured.
But this is a special exercise. More commonly suffering breaks people,
crushes them, and is simply unilluminating. You see how gruesomely
human beings are destroyed by pain, when they have the added torment
of losing their humanity first, so that their death is a total defeat, and
then you write about "modern forms of Orphism" and about "people
who are not afraid of suffering" and throw in other such cocktail-party
expressions. Why not say rather that people of powerful imagination,
given to dreaming deeply and to raising up marvelous and self-sufficient fictions, turn to suffering sometimes to cut into their bliss, as
people pinch themselves to feel awake. I know that my suffering, if I
may speak of it, has often been like that, a more extended form of life, a
striving for true wakefulness and an antidote to illusion, and therefore I
can take no moral credit for it. I am willing without further exercise in
pain to open my heart. And this needs no doctrine or theology of suffering. We love apocalypses too much, and crisis ethics and florid
extremism with its thrilling language. Excuse me, no. I've had all the
monstrosity I want. We've reached an age in the history of mankind
when we can ask about certain persons, "What is this Thing?" No
more of that for me—no, no! I am simply a human being, more or less.
I am even willing to leave the more or less in your hands. You may
decide about me. You have a taste for metaphors. Your otherwise
admirable work is marred by them. I'm sure you can come up with a
grand metaphor for me. But don't forget to say that I will never ex-
pound suffering for anyone or call for Hell to make us serious and
truthful. I even think man's perception of pain may have grown too
refined. But that is another subject for lengthy treatment.*

Very good, Mermelstein. Go, and sin no more. And Herzog,
perhaps somewhat sheepish over this strange diatribe, rose from the
mattress (the sun was moving away) and went downstairs again. He ate
several slices of bread, and baked beans—a cold bean sandwich, and
afterward carried outside his hammock and two lawn chairs.

Thus began his final week of letters. He wandered over his
twenty acres of hillside and woodlot, composing his messages, none of
which he mailed. He was not ready to pedal to the post office and
answer questions in the village about Mrs. Herzog and little June. As
he knew well, the grotesque facts of the entire Herzog scandal had been
overheard on the party line and become the meat and drink of Ludey-

ville's fantasy life. He had never restrained himself on the telephone; he was too agitated. And Madeleine was far too patrician to care what the hicks were overhearing. Anyway, she had been throwing him out. It reflected no discredit on her.

Dear Madeleine—You are a terrific one, you are! Bless you! What a creature! To put on lipstick, after dinner in a restaurant, she would look at her reflection in a knife blade. He recalled this with delight. *And you, Gersbach, you're welcome to Madeleine. Enjoy her—rejoice in her. You will not reach me through her, however. I know you sought me in her flesh. But I am no longer there.*

Dear Sirs, The size and number of the rats in Panama City, when I passed through, truly astonished me. I saw one of them sunning himself beside a swimming pool. And another was looking at me from the wainscoting of a restaurant as I was eating fruit salad. Also, on an electric wire which slanted upward into a banana tree, I saw a whole rat-troupe go back and forth, harvesting. They ran the wire twenty times or more without a single collision. My suggestion is that you put birth-control chemicals in the baits. Poisons will never work (for Malthusian reasons; reduce the population somewhat and it only increases more vigorously). But several years of contraception may eliminate your rat problem.

Dear Herr Nietzsche—My dear sir, May I ask a question from the floor? You speak of the power of the Dionysian spirit to endure the sight of the Terrible, the Questionable, to allow itself the luxury of Destruction, to witness Decomposition, Hideousness, Evil. All this the Dionysian spirit can do because it has the same power of recovery as Nature itself. Some of these expressions, I must tell you, have a very Germanic ring. A phrase like the "luxury of Destruction" is positively Wagnerian, and I know how you came to despise all that sickly Wagnerian idiocy and bombast. Now we've seen enough destruction to test the power of the Dionysian spirit amply, and where are the heroes who have recovered from it? Nature (itself) and I are alone together, in the Berkshires, and this is my chance to understand. I am lying in a hammock, chin on breast, hands clasped, mind jammed with thoughts, agitated, yes, but also cheerful, and I know you value cheerfulness —true cheerfulness, not the seeming sanguinity of Epicureans, nor the strategic buoyancy of the heartbroken. I also know you think that deep pain is ennobling, pain which burns slow, like green wood, and there you have me with you, somewhat. But for this higher education survival is necessary. You must outlive the pain. Herzog! you must stop this quarrelsomeness and baiting of great men. *No, really, Herr Nietzsche, I have great admiration for you. Sympathy. You want to make us able to live with the void. Not lie ourselves into good-naturedness, trust, ordinary middling human considerations, but to question as has never been questioned before, relentlessly, with iron determination, into evil, through evil, past evil, accepting no abject comfort. The most absolute, the most piercing questions. Rejecting mankind as it is, that ordinary, practical, thieving, stinking, unilluminated, sodden rabble, not only the laboring rabble, but even worse the "educated" rabble with its books and concerts and lectures, its liberalism and its romantic theatrical "loves" and "passions" — it all deserves to die, it will die. Okay. Still, your extremists must survive. No survival, no* Amor Fati. *Your immoralists also eat meat. They ride the bus. They are only the most bussick travelers. Humankind lives mainly upon perverted ideas. Perverted, your ideas are no better than those of the Christianity you condemn. Any philosopher who wants to keep his contact with mankind should pervert his own system in advance to see how it will really look a few decades after adoption. I send you greetings from this mere border of grassy temporal light, and wish you happiness, wherever you are. Yours, under the veil of Maya, M.E.H.*

Dear Dr. Morgenfruh. Dead for some time now. *This is Herzog, Moses E.* Discover yourself. *We played billiards in Madison, Wisconsin.* Tell him more. *Until Willie Hoppe arrived to demonstrate, and put us to shame.* The great billiard artist got absolute obedience from those three balls; as if he whispered to them, stroked them a little with his cue, and they would part and kiss again. And old Morgenfruh with his bald head and fine, humorous, curved nose and foreign charm, applauding, getting up all his breath to exclaim "Bravo." Morgenfruh played the piano and made himself weep. Helen played Schumann better but she had less at stake. She frowned at the music as if to show that it was dangerous, but that she could tame it. Morgenfruh, however, groaned, sitting at the keys in his fur coat. Next he sang along, and lastly he cried — it overcame him. He was a splendid old man, only partly fraudulent, and what more can you ask of anyone? *Dear Dr. Morgenfruh, Latest intelligence from the Olduvai Gorge in East Africa gives grounds to suppose that man did not descend from a peaceful arboreal ape, but from a carnivorous, terrestrial type, a beast that hunted in packs and crushed the skulls of prey with a club or femoral bone. It sounds bad, Morgenfruh, for the optimists, for the lenient hopeful view of human nature. The work of Sir Solly Zuckerman on the apes in the London Zoo, of which you spoke so often, has been superseded. Apes in their own habitat are less sexually driven than those in captivity. It must be that captivity, boredom, breeds lustfulness. And it may also be that the territorial instinct is stronger than the sexual. Abide in light, Morgenfruh. I will keep keep you posted from time to time.*

Despite the hours he spent in the open he believed he still looked pale. Perhaps this was because the mirror of the bathroom door into which he stared in the morning reflected the massed green of the trees. No, he did not look well. His excitement must be a great drain on his strength, he thought. And then there was the persistently medicinal smell of the tapes on his chest to remind him that he was not quite well. After the second or third day he stopped sleeping on the second floor. He didn't want to drive the owls out of the house and leave a brood to die in the old fixture with the triple brass chain. It was bad enough to have those tiny skeletons in the toilet bowl. He moved downstairs, taking with him a few useful articles, an old trench coat and rain hat, his boots ordered from Gokey's in St. Paul—marvelous, flexible, handsome snakeproof boots; he had forgotten that he had them. In the storeroom he made other interesting discoveries, photographs of the "happy days," boxes of clothing, Madeleine's letters, bundles of canceled checks, elaborately engraved wedding announcements, and a recipe book belonging to Phoebe Gersbach. The photographs were all of him. Madeleine had left those behind, taking the others. Interesting—her attitude. Among the abandoned dresses were her expensive maternity outfits. The checks were for large sums, and many of these were paid to Cash. Had she secretly been saving? He wouldn't put it past her. The announcements made him laugh. Mr. and Mrs. Pontritter were giving their daughter in marriage to Mr. Moses E Herzog Ph D.

In one of the closets he found a dozen or so Russian books under a stiff painter's drop cloth. Shestov, Rozanov—he rather liked Rozanov, who was, luckily, in English. He read a few pages of *Solitaria*. Then he looked over the paint situation—old brushes, thinners, evaporated, crusted buckets. There were several cans of enamel, and Herzog thought, What if I should paint up the little piano? I could send it out to Chicago, to Junie. The kid is really highly musical. As for Madeleine, she'll have to take it in, the bitch, when it's delivered, paid for. She can't send it back. The green enamel seemed to him exactly right, and he wasted no time but found the most usable brushes and set himself to work, full of eagerness, in the parlor. *Dear Rozanov.* He painted the lid of the piano with absorption; the green was light, beautiful, like summer apples. *A stupendous truth you say, heard from none of the prophets, is that private life is above everything. More universal than religion. Truth is higher than the sun. The soul is passion. "I am the fire that consumeth." It is joy to be choked with thought. A good man can bear to listen to another talk about himself. You can't trust the people who are bored by such talk. God has gilded me all over. I like that, God has gilded me all over.* Very touching, this man, though extremely coarse at times, and stuffed with violent prejudices. The enamel covered well but it would probably need a second coat, and he might not have enough paint for that. Putting down the brush he gave the piano lid time to dry, considering how to get the instrument out of here. He couldn't expect one of the giant interstate vans to climb this hill. He would have to hire Tuttle from the village to come in his pick-up truck. The cost would amount to something like a hundred dollars, but he must do everything possible for the child, and he had no serious problems about money. Will[4] had offered him as much as he needed to get through the summer. *A curious result of the increase of historical consciousness is that people think explanation is a necessity of survival. They have to explain their condition. And if the unexplained life is not worth living, the explained life is unbearable, too. "Synthesize or perish!" Is that the new law? But when you see what strange notions, hallucinations, projections, issue from the human mind you begin to believe in Providence again. To survive these idiocies . . . Anyway the intellectual has been a Separatist. And what kind of synthesis is a Separatist likely to come up with?* Luckily for me, I didn't have the means to get too far away from our common life. I am glad of that. I mean to share with other human beings as far as possible and not destroy my remaining years in the same way. Herzog felt a deep, dizzy eagerness to *begin.*

He had to get water from the cistern; the pump was too rusty; he had primed it and worked the handle but only tired himself. The cistern was full. He raised the iron lid with a pry bar and put down a bucket. It made a good sound, dropping, and you couldn't get softer water anywhere, but it had to be boiled. There was always a chipmunk or two, a rat, dead at the bottom though it looked pure enough when you drew it up, pure, green water.

He went to sit under the trees. *His* trees. He was amused, resting here on his American estate, twenty thousand dollars' worth of country solitude and privacy. He did not feel an owner. As for the twenty grand, the place was certainly not worth more than three or four. Nobody wanted these old-fashioned houses on the fringes of the Berkshires, not the fashionable section where there were music festivals and modern dancing, riding to hounds or other kinds of snobbery. You couldn't even ski on these slopes. No one came here. He had only gentle, dotty old neighbors, Jukes and Kallikaks, rocking themselves to death on their porches, watching television, the nineteenth century quietly dying in this remote green hole. Well, this was his own, his hearth; these were *his* birches, catalpas, horse chestnuts. His rotten dreams of peace. The patrimony of his children—a sunken corner of Massachusetts for Marco, the little piano for June painted a loving green by her solicitous father. That, too, like most other things he would probably botch. But at least he would not die here, as he had once feared. In former summers, when cutting the grass, he would sometimes lean on the mower, overheated, and think, What if I were to die suddenly, of a heart attack? Where will they put me? Maybe I should pick my own spot. Under the spruce? That's too close to the house. Now he reflected that Madeleine would have had him cremated. *And these explanations are unbearable, but they have to be made. In the seventeenth century the passionate search for absolute truth stopped so that mankind might transform the world. Something practical was done with*

4 Herzog's brother, a successful contractor.

thought. The mental became also the real. Relief from the pursuit of absolutes made life pleasant. Only a small class of fanatical intellectuals, professionals, still chased after these absolutes. But our revolutions, including nuclear terror, return the metaphysical dimension to us. All practical activity has reached this culmination: everything may go now, civilization, history, meaning, nature. Everything! Now to recall Mr. Kierkegaard's question . . .

To Dr. Waldemar Zozo: You, Sir, were the Navy psychiatrist who examined me in Norfolk, Va., about 1942, and told me I was unusually immature. I knew that, but professional confirmation caused me deep anguish. In anguish I was not immature. I could call upon ages of experience. I took it all very seriously then. Anyway, I was subsequently discharged for asthma, not childishness. I fell in love with the Atlantic. O the great reticulated, mountain-bottomed sea! *But the sea fog paralyzed my voice, and for a communications officer it was the end. However, in your cubicle, as I sat naked, pale, listened to the sailors at drill in the dust, heard what you told me about my character, felt the Southern heat, it was unsuitable that I should wring my hands. I kept them lying on my thighs.*

From hatred at first, but later because I became objectively interested, I followed your career in the journals. Your article "Existential Unrest in the Unconscious" recently beguiled me. It was really quite a classy piece of work. You don't mind if I speak to you in this way, I hope. I am really in an unusually free condition of mind. "In paths untrodden," as Walt Whitman marvelously put it. "Escaped from the life that exhibits itself . . ." Oh, that's a plague, the life that exhibits itself, a real plague! There comes a time when every ridiculous son of Adam wishes to arise before the rest, with all his quirks and twitches and tics, all the glory of his self-adored ugliness, his grinning teeth, his sharp nose, his madly twisted reason, saying to the rest—in an overflow of narcissism which he interprets as benevolence—"I am here to witness. I am come to be your exemplar." Poor dizzy spook! . . . Escaped, anyway, as Whitman says, from the life that exhibits itself and "talked to by tongues aromatic." . . . But here is a further interesting fact. I recognized you last spring in the Primitive Art Museum on 54th Street. How my feet ached! I had to ask Ramona to sit down. *I said to the lady I had come with, "Isn't that Dr. Waldemar Zozo?" She happened also to know you, and brought me up to date: You were quite rich, a collector of African antiquities, your daughter a folk singer, and much else. I realized sharply how I still loathed you. I thought I had forgiven you, too. Isn't that interesting? Seeing you, your white turtle-necked shirt and dinner jacket, your Edwardian mustache, your damp lips, the back hair trained over your bald spot, your barren paunch, apish buttocks* (chemically old!) *I recognized with joy how I abhorred you. It sprang fresh from my heart after 22 years!*

His mind took one of its odd jumps. He opened a clean page in his grimy notebook, and in the twig-divided shade of a wild cherry, infested with tent caterpillars, he began to make notes for a poem. He was going to try an Insect Iliad for Junie. She couldn't read, but maybe Madeleine would allow Luke Asphalter to take the child to Jackson Park and read the installments to her as he received them. Luke knew a lot of natural history. It would do him good, too. Moses, pale with this heartfelt nonsense, stared at the ground with brown eyes, standing round-shouldered, the notebook held behind him as he thought it over. He could make the Trojans ants. The Argives might be water-skaters. Luke might find them for her along the edge of the lagoon, where those stupid caryatides were posted. The water-skaters, therefore, with long velvet hairs beaded with glittering oxygen. Helen, a beautiful wasp. Old Priam a cicada, sucking sap from the roots and with his trowel-shaped belly plastering the tunnels. And Achilles a stag-beetle with sharp spikes and terrible strength, but doomed to a brief life though half a god. At the edge of the water he cried out to his mother

> *Thus spoke Achilles*
> *And Thetis heard him in the ooze,*
> *Sitting beside her ancient father*
> *In glorious debris, enough for all.*

But this project was quickly abandoned. It wasn't a good idea, really not. For one thing, he wasn't stable enough, he could never keep his mind at it. His state was too strange, this mixture of clairvoyance and spleen, *esprit de l'escalier*,[5] noble inspirations, poetry and non-sense, ideas, hyperesthesia — wandering about like this, hearing forceful but indefinite music within, seeing things, violet fringes about the clearest objects. His mind was like that cistern, soft pure water sealed under the iron lid but not entirely safe to drink. No, he was better occupied painting the piano for the child. Go! let the fiery claw of imagination take up the green brush. Go! But the first coat was not dry yet, and he wandered out to the woods, eating a piece of bread from the package he carried in his trench-coat pocket. He was aware that his brother might now show up at any time. Will had been disturbed by his appearance. It was unmistakable. And I had better look out, thought Herzog, people do get put away, and seem even to intend it. I have wanted to be cared for. I devoutly hoped Emmerich would find me sick. But I have no intention of doing that — I am responsible, responsible to reason. This is simply temporary excitement. Responsible to the children. He walked quietly into the woods, the many leaves, living and fallen, green and tan, going between rotted stumps, moss, fungus disks; he found a hunters' path, also a deer trail. He felt quite well here, and calmer. The silence sustained him, and the brilliant weather, the feeling that he was easily contained by everything about him *Within the hol-*

---

[5] "Spirit of the staircase."

lowness of God, as he noted, *and deaf to the final multiplicity of facts,* as well as, *blind to ultimate distances. Two billion light-years out. Supernovae.*

> *Daily radiance, trodden here*
> *Within the hollowness of God*

To God he jotted several lines.

How my mind has struggled to make coherent sense. I have not been too good at it. But have desired to do your unknowable will, taking it, and you, without symbols. Everything of intensest significance. Especially if divested of me.

Returning once more to practical considerations, he must be very careful with Will and talk to him only in the most concrete terms about concrete matters, like this property, and look as ordinary as possible. If you wear a wise look, he warned himself, you'll be in trouble, and fast. No one can bear such looks any longer, not even your brother. Therefore, watch your face! Certain expressions burn people up, and especially the expression of wisdom, which can lead you straight to the loony bin. You will have earned it!

He lay down near the locust trees. They bloomed with a light, tiny but delicious flower—he was sorry to have missed that. He recognized that with his arms behind him and his legs extended any way, he was lying as he had lain less than a week ago on his dirty little sofa in New York. But was it only a week—five days? Unbelievable! How different he felt! Confident, even happy in his excitement, stable. The bitter cup would come round again, by and by. This rest and well-being were only a momentary difference in the strange lining or variable silk between life and void. *The life you gave me has been curious,* he wanted to say to his mother, *and perhaps the death I must inherit will turn out to be even more profoundly curious. I have sometimes wished it would hurry up, longed for it to come soon. But I am still on the same side of eternity as ever. It's just as well, for I have certain things still to do. And without noise, I hope. Some of my oldest aims seem to have slid away. But I have others. Life on this earth can't be simply a picture.* And terrible forces in me, including the force of admiration or praise, powers, including loving powers, very damaging, making me almost an idiot because I lacked the capacity to manage them. *I may turn out to be not such a terrible hopeless fool as everyone, as you, as I myself suspected.* Meantime, to lay off certain persistent torments. To surrender the hyperactivity of this hyperactive face. But just to put it out instead to the radiance of the sun. *I want to send you, and others, the most loving wish I have in my heart. This is the only way I have to reach out—out where it is incomprehensible. I can only pray toward it. So . . . Peace!*

. . . . . .

For the next two days—or were there three?—Herzog did nothing but send such messages, and write down songs, psalms, and utterances, putting into words what he had often thought but, for the sake of form, or something of the sort, had always suppressed. Once in a while he found himself painting the little piano again, or eating bread and beans in the kitchen, or sleeping in the hammock, and he was always slightly surprised to discover how he had been occupied. He looked at the calendar one morning, and tried to guess the date, counting in silence, or rather groping over nights and days. His beard informed him better than his brain. His bristles felt like four days' growth, and he thought it best to be clean-shaven when Will arrived.

He built a fire and heated a pan of water, lathered his cheeks with brown laundry soap. Clean-shaven, he was extremely pale. His face had become much thinner, too. He had just put down his razor when he heard the smooth noise of an engine at the foot of the drive. He ran into the garden to meet his brother.

Will was alone in his Cadillac. The great car got up the hill slowly, scraping its underbelly on rocks and bending the tall growth of weeds and canes. Will was a masterful driver. He might be short but there was nothing timid about him, and as for the beautiful Italian Plum finish of the Cadillac he was not the sort of man to fret about a few scratches. On level ground, under the elm, the car stood idling. Two Chinese fangs of vapor came from the rear, and William got out, his face lined in the sun. He took in the house, Moses approaching eagerly. What must Will feel? Moses wondered. He must be appalled. What else could he be?

"Will! How are you?" He embraced his brother.

"How are you, Moses. Are you feeling all right?" Will might act as conservative as he pleased. He could never conceal his real emotions from his brother.

"I just shaved. I always look white after shaving, but I feel well. Honest, I do."

"You've lost weight. Maybe ten pounds, since you left Chicago. It's too much," said Will. "How's your rib?"

"Doesn't bother me a bit."

"And the head?"

"Fine. I've been resting. Where's Muriel? I thought she was coming, too."

"She took the plane. I'm going to meet her in Boston."

Will had learned to conduct himself with restraint. A Herzog, he had a good deal to hold down. Moses could remember a time when Willie, too, had been demonstrative, passionate, explosive, given to bursts of rage, flinging objects on the ground. Just a moment—what was it, now, that he had thrown down? A brush! That was it! The broad old Russian shoe brush. Will slammed it to the floor so hard the veneer backing fell off, and beneath were the stitches, ancient waxed thread, maybe even sinew. But that was long ago. Thirty-five years ago, easily. And where had it gone, the wrath of Willie Herzog? my dear brother? Into a certain poise and quiet humor, part decorousness, part (possibly) slavery. The explosions had become implosions, and where light once was darkness came, bit by bit. It didn't matter. The sight of Will stirred Moses' love for him. Will looked tired and wrinkled; he had been on the road a long time, he needed something to eat, and a rest. He had taken this long trip because he was concerned about him, Moses. And how considerate of him not to bring Muriel.

"How was the drive, Will? Are you hungry? Shall I open a can of tuna?"

"You're the one that doesn't seem to have eaten. I had something on the road."

"Well, come, sit down a while." He led him toward the lawn chairs. "It was lovely here when I took care of the grounds."

"So this is the house? No, I don't want to sit, thanks. I'd rather move around. Let's see it."

"Yes, this is the famous house, the house of happiness," said Moses, but he added, "As a matter of fact, I *have* been happy here. None of this ingratitude."

"It seems well built."

"From a builder's viewpoint it's terrific. Imagine what it would cost today. The foundations would hold the Empire State Building. And I'll show you the hard-hewn chestnut beams. Old mortice and tenon. No metal at all."

"It must be hard to heat."

"Not so hard. Electric baseboards."

"I wish I were selling you the current. Make a fortune . . . But it is a beautiful spot, I'll give you that. These trees are fine. How many acres have you got?"

"Forty. But surrounded by abandoned farms. Not a neighbor in two miles."

"Oh . . . Is that good?"

"Very private, I mean."

"What are your taxes?"

"One-eighty-six or so. Never over one-ninety."

"And the mortgage?"

"There's only a small principal. Payments and interest are two hundred and fifty a year."

"Very good," said Will approvingly. "But now tell me, how much money have you put into this place, Mose?"

"I've never totaled it up. Twenty grand, I guess. More than half of it in improvements."

Will nodded. His arms crossed, he gazed upward at the structure with his partly averted face—he too had this hereditary peculiarity. Only his eyes were quietly and firmly shrewd, not dreaming. Moses, however, saw without the slightest difficulty what Will was thinking.

He expressed it to himself in Yiddish. *In drerd aufn deck. The edge of nowhere. Out on the lid of Hell.*

"In itself, it's a fine-looking piece of property. It may turn out to be a pretty reasonable investment at that. Of course, the location *is* a bit peculiar. Ludeyville isn't on the map."

"No, not on the Esso map," Moses conceded. "The state of Massachusetts knows where it is, naturally."

Both brothers smiled slightly, without looking at each other.

"Let's look over the interior," said Will.

Moses gave him a tour of the house, beginning in the kitchen. "It needs an airing."

"It is a bit musty. But handsome. The plaster is in excellent condition."

"You need a cat to police the fieldmice. They winter in here. I'm fond of them but they chew everything. Even book bindings. They seem to love glue. And wax. Paraffin. Candles. Anything like that."

Will showed him great politeness. He did not confront him harshly with fundamentals, as Shura[6] would have done. There was a certain sweet decency in Will. Helen had it, too. Shura would have said, "What a jerk you were to sink so much dough into this old barn." Well, that was simply Shura's way. Moses loved them all, notwithstanding.

"And the water supply?" said Will.

"Gravity-fed, from the spring. We have two old wells, too. One of them was ruined by kerosene. Someone let a whole tankful of kerosene leak out and soak down. But it doesn't matter. The water supply is excellent. The cesspool is well built. Could accommodate twenty people. You wouldn't need orange trees."

"Meaning what?"

"It means that at Versailles Louis Quatorze planted oranges because the excrement of the court made the air foul."

"How nice to have an education," said Will.

"To be pedantic, you mean," said Herzog. He spoke with a great deal of caution, taking special pains to give an impression of completest normalcy. That Will was studying him—Will who had become the most discreet and observant of the Herzogs—was transparently plain. Moses thought he could bear his scrutiny fairly well. His haggard, just-shaven cheeks were against him; as was the whole house (the skeletons in the toilet bowl, the owls in the fixtures, the half-painted piano, the remains of meals, the wife-deserted atmosphere); his "inspired" visit to Chicago was bad, too. Very bad. It must be noticeable, also, that he was in an extraordinary state, eyes dilated with excitement, the very speed of

6 Herzog's other brother; Helen is his sister.

his pulses possibly visible in his large irises. *Why must I be such a throb-hearted character . . . But I am. I am, and you can't teach old dogs. Myself is thus and so, and will continue thus and so. And why fight it? My balance comes from instability. Not organization, or courage, as with other people. It's tough, but that's how it is. On these terms I, too—even I!—apprehend certain things. Perhaps the only way I'm able to do it. Must play the instrument I've got.*

"You've been painting this piano, I see."

"For June," said Herzog. "A present. A surprise."

"What?" Will laughed. "Are you planning to send it from here? Why it'll cost two hundred bucks in freight. And it would have to be fixed up, tuned. Is it such a great piano?"

"Madeleine bought it at auction for twenty-five bucks."

"Take my word for it, Moses, you can buy a nice old piano right in Chicago, at a warehouse sale. Lots of old instruments like this, kicking around."

"Yes . . . ? Only I like this color." This apple, parrot green, the special Ludeyville color. Moses' eyes were fixed upon his work with a certain inspired persistency. He was near a point of open impulsiveness, and some peculiarity might now dart forth. He couldn't allow that to happen. Under no circumstances must he utter a single word that might be interpreted as irrational. Things already looked bad enough. He glanced away from the piano into the clear shade of the garden, and tried to become as clear as *that*. He deferred to his brother's opinion. "Okay. Next trip, I'll get her a piano."

"What you've got here is an excellent summer house." said Will. "A little lonely, but nice. If you can clean it up."

"It can be lovely here. But you know, we might make it a Herzog summer resort. For the family. Everyone put in a little money. Cut the brush. Build a swimming pool."

"Oh, sure. Helen hates travel, you know that. And Shura is just the man to come up here where there are no race horses, or card games, or other tycoons, or broads."

"There are trotter races at the Barrington Fair. . . . No, I guess that's not such a good idea, either. Well, perhaps we could make it into a nursing home. Or move it to another location."

"Not worth it. I've seen mansions wrecked for slum clearance or for new superhighways. This isn't worth dismantling. Can't you rent it out?"

Herzog silently grinned, staring with piercing humor at Will.

"All right, Mose, the only other suggestion is that you put it up for sale. You won't get your money out of it."

"I could go to work and become rich. Make a ton of money, just to keep this house."

"Yes," said Will. "You might." He spoke gently to his brother.

"Odd situation I've gotten into, Will—isn't it?" said Moses. "For me. For us—the Herzogs, I mean. It seems a strange point to arrive at after all the other points. In this lovely green hole . . . You're worried about me, I see."

Will, troubled but controlled, one of the most deeply familiar and longest-loved of human faces, looked at him in a way that could not be mistaken. "Of course I'm worried. Helen too."

"Well, you mustn't be distressed about me. I'm in a peculiar state, but not in a bad one. I'd open my heart to you, Will, if I could find the knob. There's no reason to be upset about me. By God, Will, I'm about to cry! How did that happen? I won't do it. It's only love. Or something that bears down like love. It probably is love. I'm in no shape to buck it. I don't want you to think anything wrong."

"Mose—why should I?" Will spoke in a low voice. "I have something deep-in for you, too. I feel about the way you do. Just because I'm a contractor doesn't mean I can't understand what you mean. I didn't come to do you harm, you know. That's right, Mose, take a chair. You look out on your feet."

Moses sat on the old sofa, which gave off dust as soon as you touched it.

"I'd like to see you less agitated. You must get some food and sleep. Probably a little medical care. A few days in the hospital, taking it easy."

"Will, I'm excited, not sick. I don't want to be treated as though I were sick in the head. I'm grateful that you came." Silently and stubbornly he sat, persisting, putting down his violent, choking craving for tears. His voice was dim.

"Take your time," said Will.

"I . . ." Herzog found his voice again and said distinctly, "I want to be straight about one thing. I'm not turning myself over to you out of weakness, or because I can't make my own way. I don't mind taking it easy in some hospital for a few days. If you and Helen decided that that was what I should do, I see no objection. Clean sheets and a bath and some hot food. Sleep. That's all pleasant. But only a few days. I have to visit Marco at camp on the sixteenth. That's Parents' Day and he's expecting me."

"Fair enough," said Will. "That's no more than right."

"Only a while back, in New York, I had fantasies about being put in the hospital."

"You were only being sensible," said his brother. "What you need is supervised rest. I've thought about it, too, for myself. Once in a while, we all get that way. Now"—he looked at his watch—"I asked my physician to phone a local hospital. In Pittsfield."

As soon as Will had spoken, Moses sat forward on the sofa. He could not find words. He only made a negative sign with his head. At this, Will's face changed, too. He seemed to think he had pronounced the word hospital too abruptly, that he ought to have been more gradual, circumspect.

"No," said Moses, still shaking his head. "No. Definitely."

Now Will was silent, still with the pained air of a man who had made a tactical error. Moses could easily imagine what Will had said to Helen, after he had bailed him out, and what a worried consultation they had had about him. ("What shall we do? Poor Mose—maybe it's all driven him mad. Let's at least get a professional opinion about him.") Helen was great on professional opinions. The veneration with which she said "professional opinion" had always amused Moses. And so they had approached Will's internist to ask if he would, discreetly, arrange something in the Berkshire area. "But I thought we already agreed," said Will.

"No, Will. No hospitals. I know you and Helen are doing what brother and sister should. And I'm tempted to go along. To a man like me, it's a seductive idea. 'Supervised rest.'"

"And why not? If I'd found some improvement in you I might not have brought it up," said Will. "But look at you."

"I know," said Moses. "But just as I begin to be a little rational you want to hand me over to a psychiatrist. It *was* a psychiatrist you and Helen had in mind, wasn't it?"

Will was silent, taking counsel with himself. Then he sighed and said, "What harm could there be in it?"

"Was it any more fantastic for me to have these wives, children, to move to a place like this than for Papa to have been a bootlegger? We never thought he was mad." Moses began to smile. ". . . Do you remember, Will—he had those phony labels printed up: White Horse, Johnnie Walker, Haig and Haig, and we'd sit at the table with the paste-pot, and he'd flash those labels and say, 'Well, children, what should we make today?', and we'd start to cry out and squeak 'White Horse,' 'Teacher's.' And the coal stove was hot. It dropped embers like red teeth in the ash. He had those dark green lovely bottles. They don't make glass like that, in those shapes, any more. My favorite was White Horse."

Will laughed softly.

"Going to the hospital would be fine," said Herzog. "But it would be just the wrong thing to do. It's about time I stopped laboring with this curse—I think, I figure things out. I see exactly what I should avoid. Then, all of a sudden, I'm in bed with that very thing, and making love to it. As with Madeleine. She seems to have filled a special need."

"How do you figure that, Moses?" Will joined him on the sofa, and sat beside him.

"A very special need. I don't know what. She brought ideology into my life. Something to do with catastrophe. After all, it's an ideological age. Maybe she wouldn't make a father of anyone she liked."

Will smiled at Moses' way of putting it. "But what do you intend to do here now?"

"I may as well stay on. I'm not far from Marco's camp. Yes, that's it. If Daisy'll let me, I'll bring him here next month. What I'll do is this, if you'll drive me and my bike into Ludeyville, I'll have the lights and the phone turned on. Tuttle'll come up and mow the place. Maybe Mrs. Tuttle will clean up for me. That's what I'll do." He stood up. "I'll get the water running again, and buy some solid food. Come, Will, give me a lift down to Tuttle's."

"Who is this Tuttle?"

"He runs everything. He's the master spirit of Ludeyville. A tall fellow. He's shy, to look at, but that's only more of his shrewdness. He's the demon of these woods. He can have the lights burning here within an hour. He knows all. He overcharges, but very, very shyly."

.   .   .   .   .   .

Tuttle was standing beside his high, lean, antiquated gas pumps when Will drove up. Thin, wrinkled, the hairs on his corded forearms bleached meal-white, he wore a cotton paint cap and between his false teeth (to help him kick the smoking habit, as he had once explained to Herzog) he kept a plastic toothpick. "I knew you was up in the place, Mr. Herzog," he said. "Welcome back."

"How did you know?"

"I saw the smoke onto your chimney, that's the first of all."

"Yes? And what's the second?"

"Why, a lady's been tryin' to get you on the telephone."

"Who?" said Will.

"A party in Barrington. She left the number."

"Only her number?" said Herzog. "No name?"

"Miss Harmona, or Armona."

"Ramona," said Herzog. "Is she in Barrington?"

"Were you expecting someone?" Will turned to him in the seat.

"No one but you."

Will insisted on knowing more. "Who is she?"

Somewhat unwillingly, and with an evasive look, Moses answered, "A lady—a woman." Then, putting off his reticence—why, after all, should he be nervous about it?—he added, "A woman, a florist, a friend from New York."

"Are you going to return her call?"

"Yes, of course." He observed the white listening face of Mrs. Tuttle in the dark store. "I wonder," he said to Tuttle. ". . . I want to open the house. I have to get the current on. Maybe Mrs. Tuttle will help me clean the place a bit."

"Oh, I think she might."

Mrs. Tuttle wore tennis shoes and, under her dress, the edge of her nightgown showed. Her polished fingernails were tobacco-stained. She had gained much weight in Herzog's absence, and he noted the distortion of her pretty face, the heaviness of her neglected dark hair and the odd distant look in her gray eyes, as if the fat of her body had an opiate effect on her. He knew that she had monitored his conversations with Madeleine on the party line. Probably she had heard all the shameful, terrible things that had been said, listened to the rant and the sobbing. Now he was about to invite her to come to work, to sweep the floors, make his bed. She reached for a filter cigarette, lit it like a man, stared through smoke with tranced gray eyes and said, "Why, I think so, yes. It's my day off from the mortel. I been working as a chambermaid over in the new mortel on the highway."

"Moses!" said Ramona, on the telephone. "You got my message. How lovely you're in your place. Everybody in Barrington says if you want things done in Ludeyville, call Tuttle."

"Hello, Ramona. Didn't my wire from Chicago reach you?"

"Yes, Moses. It was very considerate. But I didn't think you'd stay away long, and I had a feeling about your house in the country. Anyway, I had to visit old friends in Barrington, so I drove up."

"Really?" said Herzog. "What day of the week is this?"

Ramona laughed. "How typical. No wonder women lose their heads over you. It's Saturday. I'm staying with Myra and Eduardo Misseli."

"Oh, the fiddler. I only know him to nod to at the supermarket."

"He's a charming man. Do you know he's studying the art of violin-making? I've been in his shop all morning. And I thought I must have a look at the Herzog estate."

"My brother is with me — Will."

"Oh, splendid," said Ramona, in her lifted voice. "Is he staying with you?"

"No, he's passing through."

"I'd love to meet him. The Misselis are giving a little party for me. After dinner."

Will stood beside the booth, listening. Earnest, worried, his dark eyes discreetly appealed to Moses to make no more mistakes. I can't promise that, thought Moses. I can only tell him that I don't contemplate putting myself in the hands of Ramona or any woman, at this time. Will's gaze held a family look, a brown light as clear as any word.

"No, thank you," said Herzog. "No parties. I'm not up to them. But look, Ramona . . ."

"Should I run up?" said Ramona. "It's silly, being on the phone like this. You're only eight minutes away."

"Well, perhaps," said Herzog. "It occurs to me I have to come down to Barrington anyway, to shop, and to have my phone reconnected."

"Oh, you're planning to stay awhile in Ludeyville?"

"Yes. Marco'll be joining me. Just a moment, Ramona." Herzog put a hand over the instrument and said to Will, "Can you take me into Barrington?" Will of course said yes.

Ramona was waiting, smiling, a few minutes later. She stood beside her black Mercedes in shorts and sandals. She wore a Mexican blouse with coin buttons. Her hair glittered, and she looked flushed. The anxiety of the moment threatened her self-control. "Ramona," said Moses, "this is Will."

"Oh, Mr. Herzog, what a pleasure to meet Moses' brother."

Will, though wary of her, was courteous nevertheless. He had a quiet, tidy social manner. Herzog was grateful to him for the charming reserve of his courtesy to Ramona. Will's glance was sympathetic. He smiled, but not too much. Obviously he found Ramona impressively attractive. "He must have been expecting a dog," thought Herzog.

"Why, Moses," said Ramona, "you've cut yourself shaving. And badly. Your whole jaw is scraped."

"Ah?" He touched himself with vague concern.

"You look so much like your brother, Mr. Herzog. The same fine head, and those soft hazel eyes. You're not staying?"

"I'm on my way to Boston."

"And I simply had to get out of New York. Aren't the Berkshires marvelous? Such green!"

Love-bandit, the tabloids used to print over such dark heads. In the twenties. Indeed, Ramona did look like those figures of sex and swagger. But there was something intensely touching about her, too. She struggled, she fought. She needed extraordinary courage to hold this poise. In this world, to be a woman who took matters into her own hands! And this courage of hers was unsteady. At times it trembled. She pretended to look for something in her purse because her cheek quivered. The perfume of her shoulders reached his nostrils. And, as almost always, he heard the deep, the cosmic, the idiotic masculine response — *quack*. The progenitive, the lustful quacking in the depths. *Quack. Quack.*

"You won't come to the party then?" said Ramona. "And when am I going to see your house?"

"Why, I'm having it cleaned up a little," said Herzog.

"Then can't we . . . Why don't we have dinner together?" she said. "You, too, Mr. Herzog. Moses can tell you that my shrimp remoulade is rather good."

"It's better than that. I never ate better. But Will has to go on, and you're on a holiday, Ramona, we can't have you cooking for three. Why don't you come out and have dinner with me?"

"Oh," said Ramona with a new rise of gaiety. "You want to entertain me?"

"Well, why not? I'll get a couple of swordfish steaks."

Will looked at him with his uncertain smile.

"Wonderful. I'll bring a bottle of wine," said Ramona.

"You'll do nothing of the sort. Come up at six. We'll eat at seven and you can still get back to your party in plenty of time."

Musically (was it a deliberate effect? Moses could not decide), Ramona said to Will, "Then good-by, Mr. Herzog. I hope we shall meet again." Turning to get into her Mercedes, she put her hand momentarily on Moses' shoulder. "I expect a good dinner. . . ."

She wanted Will to be aware of their intimacy, and Moses saw no reason to deny her this. He pressed his face to hers.

"Shall we say good-by here, too?" said Moses as she drove off. "I can take a cab back. I don't want to make you late."

"No, no, I'll run you up to Ludeyville."

"I'll go in here and get my swordfish. Some lemon, too. Butter. Coffee."

They were on the last slope before Ludeyville when Will said, "Am I leaving you in good hands, Mose?"

"Is it safe to go, you mean? I think you can, with confidence. Ramona's not so bad."

"Bad? What do you mean? She's stunning. But so was Madeleine."

"I'm not being left in anyone's hands."

With a mild, soft look of irony, sad and affectionate, Will said, "Amen. But what about this ideology. Doesn't she have some?"

"This will do, here, in front of Tuttle's. They'll take me in the pickup, bike and all. Yes, I think she has some. About sex. She's pretty fanatical about it. But I don't mind that."

"I'll get out and make certain of the directions," said Will.

Tuttle, as they walked slowly past him, told Moses, "I think we'll have that current onto your house in a few minutes."

"Thanks . . . Here, Will, take a little of this arborvitae to chew. It's a very pleasant taste."

"Don't decide anything now. You can't afford any more mistakes."

"I've asked her to dinner. Only that. She goes back to the party at Misseli's — I'm not going with her. Tomorrow is Sunday. She's got a business in New York, and she can't stay. I won't elope with her. Or she with me, as you see it."

"You have a strange influence on people," said Will. "Well, good-by, Mose. Maybe Muriel and I will stop by on our way west."

"You'll find me unmarried."

"If you didn't give a goddamn, it wouldn't matter. You could marry five more wives. But with your intense way of doing everything . . . and your talent for making a fatal choice."

"Will, you can go with an easy mind. I tell you . . . I promise. Nothing like that will happen. Not a chance. Good-by, and thanks. And as for the house . . ."

"I'll be thinking about that. Do you need money?"

"No."

"You're sure? You're telling the truth? Remember, you're talking to your brother."

"I know whom I'm talking to." He took Will by the shoulders and kissed him on the cheek. "Good-by, Will. Take the first right as you leave town. You'll see the turnpike sign."

When Will had gone, Moses waited for Mrs. Tuttle in the seat by the arborvitae, having his first leisurely look at the village. *Everywhere on earth, the model of natural creation seems to be the ocean. The mountains certainly look that way, glossy, plunging, and that haughty blue color. And even these scrappy lawns. What keeps these red brick houses from collapse on these billows is their inner staleness. I smell it yawning through the screens. The odor of souls is a brace to the walls. Otherwise the wrinkling of the hills would make them crumble.*

"You got a gorgeous old place here, Mr. Herzog," said Mrs. Tuttle as they drove in her old car up the hill. "It must've cost you a penny to improve it. It's a shame you don't use it more."

"We've got to get the kitchen cleaned up so I can cook a meal. I'll find you the brooms and pails and such."

He was groping in the dark pantry when the lights went on. Tuttle is a miracle man, he thought. I asked him at about two. It must be four-thirty, five.

Mrs. Tuttle, a cigarette in her mouth, tied her head up in a bandanna. Beneath the hem of her dress the peach nylon of her nightgown nearly touched the floor. In the stone cellar Herzog found the pump switch. At once he heard the water rising, washing into the empty pressure tank. He connected the range. He turned on the refrigerator; it would take a while to get cold. Then it occurred to him to chill the wine in the spring. After that, he took up the scythe to clear the yard, so that Ramona would have a better view of the house. But after he had cut a few swathes his ribs began to ache. He didn't feel well enough for this sort of work. He lay stretched in the lawn chair, facing south. As soon as the sun lost its main strength the hermit thrushes began, and while they sang their sweet fierce music threatening trespassers, the black-birds would begin to gather in flocks for the night, and just toward sunset they would break from these trees in waves, wave after wave, three or four miles in one flight to their waterside nests.

To have Ramona coming troubled him slightly, it was true. But they would eat. She would help him with the dishes, and then he'd see her to her car.

I will do no more to enact the peculiarities of life. This is done well enough without my special assistance.

Now on one side the hills lost the sun and began to put on a more intense blue color; on the other they were still white and green. The birds were very loud.

Anyway, can I pretend I have much choice? I look at myself and see chest, thighs, feet—a head. This strange organization, I know it will die. And inside—something, something, happiness . . . "Thou movest me." That leaves no choice. Something produces intensity, a holy feeling, as oranges produce orange, as grass green, as birds heat. Some hearts put out more love and some less of it, presumably. Does it signify anything? There are those who say this product of hearts is knowledge. "Je sens mon cœur et je connais les hommes." But his mind now detached itself also from its French. *I couldn't say that, for sure. My face too blind, my mind too limited, my instincts too narrow. But this intensity, doesn't it mean anything? Is it an idiot joy that makes this animal, the most peculiar animal of all, exclaim something? And he thinks this reaction a sign, a proof, of eternity? And he has it in his breast? But I have no arguments to make about it. "Thou movest me." "But what do you want, Herzog?" "But that's just it—not a solitary thing. I am pretty well satisfied to be, to be just as it is willed, and for as long as I may remain in occupancy."*

Then he thought he'd light candles at dinner, because Ramona was fond of them. There might be a candle or two in the fuse box. But now it was time to get those bottles from the spring. The labels had washed off, but the glass was well chilled. He took pleasure in the vivid cold of the water.

Coming back from the woods, he picked some flowers for the table. He wondered whether there was a corkscrew in the drawer. Had Madeleine taken it to Chicago? Well, maybe Ramona had a corkscrew in her Mercedes. An unreasonable thought. A nail could be used, if it came to that. Or you could break the neck of the bottle as they did in old movies. Meanwhile, he filled his hat from the rambler vine, the one that clutched the rainpipe. The spines were still too green to hurt much. By the cistern there were yellow day lilies. He took some of these, too, but they wilted instantly. And, back in the darker garden, he looked for peonies; perhaps some had survived. But then it struck him that he might be making a mistake, and he stopped, listening to Mrs. Tuttle's sweeping, the rhythm of bristles. Picking flowers? He was being thoughtful, being lovable. How would it be interpreted? (He smiled slightly.) Still, he need only know his own mind, and the flowers couldn't be used; no, they couldn't be turned against him. So he did not throw them away. He turned his dark face toward the house again. He went around and entered from the front, wondering what further evidence of his sanity, besides refusing to go to the hospital, he could show. Perhaps he'd stop writing letters. Yes, that was what was coming, in fact. The knowledge that he was done with these letters. Whatever had come over him during these last months, the spell, really seemed to be passing, really going. He set down his hat, with the roses and day lilies, on the half-painted piano, and went into his study, carrying the wine bottles in one hand like a pair of Indian clubs. Walking over notes and papers, he lay down on his Recamier couch. As he stretched out, he took a long breath, and then he lay, looking at the mesh of the screen, pulled loose by vines, and listening to the steady scratching of Mrs. Tuttle's broom. He wanted to tell her to sprinkle the floor. She was raising too much dust. In a few minutes he would call down to her, "Damp it down, Mrs. Tuttle. There's water in the sink." But not just yet. At this time he had no messages for anyone. Nothing. Not a single word.

1964

Flannery O'Connor *1925–1964*

Born in Savannah, Georgia, Flannery O'Connor grew up in the small town of Milledgeville. After attending the Women's College of Georgia (B.A., 1945), she studied in the writers' program at the State University of Iowa, where she received the degree of Master of Fine Arts in 1947. She lived for most of her life in Georgia and died in Milledgeville at the age of thirty-nine. In her short stories and novels, which reflect her power of unsentimental observation and her ear for the Southern vernacular, she displays a partiality for grotesque characters and sensational incident. In these respects her two novels, *Wise Blood* (1942) and *The Violent Bear It Away* (1960), both set in the backwoods country of Tennessee, are in the modern Southern Gothic tradition. Her stories, for which she is best known, are collected in *A Good Man is Hard to Find* (1955) and the posthumously-published *Everything that Rises Must Converge* (1965). They often treat a conflict (violently resolved) between illusion and reality in the lives of their central characters. But the absence of physical violence in "The Enduring Chill" does not minimize the impact of self-revelation upon its youthful hero.

A brief introduction to Flannery O'Connor and her work is S. E. Hyman, *Flannery O'Connor* (Minneapolis, 1966). For other critiques, see M. J. Friedman and L. A. Lawson, eds., *The Added Dimension: The Art and Mind of Flannery O'Connor* (New York, 1966).

The text of "The Enduring Chill" is that of *Everything That Rises Must Converge* (New York, 1965).

The Enduring Chill

Asbury's train stopped so that he would get off exactly where his mother was standing waiting to meet him. Her thin spectacled face below him was bright with a wide smile that disappeared as she caught sight of him bracing himself behind the conductor. The smile vanished so suddenly, the shocked look that replaced it was so complete, that he realized for the first time that he must look as ill as he was. The sky was a chill gray and a startling white-gold sun, like some strange potentate from the east, was rising beyond the black woods that surrounded Timberboro. It cast a strange light over the single block of one-story brick and wooden shacks. Asbury felt that he was about to witness a majestic transformation, that the flat of roofs might at any moment turn into the mounting turrets of some exotic temple for a god he didn't know. The illusion lasted only a moment before his attention was drawn back to his mother.

She had given a little cry; she looked aghast. He was pleased that she should see death in his face at once. His mother, at the age of sixty, was going to be introduced to reality and he supposed that if the experience didn't kill her, it would assist her in the process of growing up. He stepped down and greeted her.

"You don't look very well," she said and gave him a long clinical stare.

"I don't feel like talking," he said at once. "I've had a bad trip."

Mrs. Fox observed that his left eye was bloodshot. He was puffy and pale and his hair had receded tragically for a boy of twenty-five. The thin reddish wedge of it left on top bore down in a point that seemed to lengthen his nose and give him an irritable expression that matched his tone of voice when he spoke to her. "It must have been cold up there," she said. "Why don't you take off your coat? It's not cold down here."

"You don't have to tell me what the temperature is!" he said in a high voice. "I'm old enough to know when I want to take my coat off!" The train glided silently away behind him, leaving a view of the twin blocks of dilapidated stores. He gazed after the aluminum speck disappearing into the woods. It seemed to him that his last connections with a larger world were vanishing forever. Then he turned and faced his mother grimly, irked that he had allowed himself, even for an instant, to see an imaginary temple in this collapsing country junction. He had become entirely accustomed to the thought of death, but he had not become accustomed to the thought of death *here*.

He had felt the end coming on for nearly four months. Alone in his freezing flat, huddled under his two blankets and his overcoat and with three thicknesses of the New York *Times* between, he had had a chill one night, followed by a violent sweat that left the sheets soaking and removed all doubt from his mind about his true condition. Before this there had been a gradual slackening of his energy and vague inconsistent aches and headaches. He had been absent so many days from his part-time job in the bookstore that he had lost it. Since then he had been living, or just barely so, on his savings and these, diminishing day by day, had been all he had between him and home. Now there was nothing. He was here.

"Where's the car?" he muttered.

"It's over yonder," his mother said. "And your sister is asleep in the back because I don't like to come out this early by myself. There's no need to wake her up."

"No," he said, "let sleeping dogs lie," and he picked up his two bulging suitcases and started across the road with them.

They were too heavy for him and by the time he reached the car, his mother saw that he was exhausted. He had never come home with two suitcases before. Ever since he had first gone away to college, he had come back every time with nothing but the necessities for a two-week stay and with a wooden resigned expression that said he was prepared to endure the visit for exactly fourteen days. "You've brought more than usual," she observed, but he did not answer.

He opened the car door and hoisted the two bags in beside his sister's upturned feet, giving first the feet—in Girl Scout shoes—and then the rest of her a revolted look of recognition. She was packed into a black suit and had a white rag around her head with metal curlers sticking out from under the edges. Her eyes were closed and her mouth was open. He and she had the same features except that hers were bigger. She was eight years older than he was and was principal of the county elementary school. He shut the door softly so she wouldn't wake up and then went around and got in the front seat and closed his eyes. His mother backed the car into the road and in a few minutes he felt it swerve into the highway. Then he opened his eyes. The road stretched between two open fields of yellow bitterweed.

"Do you think Timberboro has improved?" his mother asked. This was her standard question, meant to be taken literally.

"It's still there, isn't it?" he said in an ugly voice.

"Two of the stores have new fronts," she said. Then with a sudden ferocity, she said, "You did well to come home where you can get a good doctor! I'll take you to Doctor Block this afternoon."

"I am not," he said, trying to keep his voice from shaking, "going to Doctor Block. This afternoon or ever. Don't you think if I'd wanted to go to a doctor I'd have gone up there where they have some good ones? Don't you know they have better doctors in New York?"

"He would take a personal interest in you," she said. "None of those doctors up there would take a personal interest in you."

"I don't want him taking a personal interest in me." Then after a minute, staring out across a blurred purple-looking field, he said, "What's wrong with me is way beyond Block," and his voice trailed off into a frayed sound almost a sob.

He could not, as his friend Goetz had recommended, prepare to see it all as illusion, either what had gone before or the few weeks that were left to him. Goetz was certain that death was nothing at all. Goetz, whose whole face had always been purple-splotched with a million indignations, had returned from six months in Japan as dirty as ever but as bland as the Buddha himself. Goetz took the news of Asbury's approaching end with a calm indifference. Quoting something or other he said, "Although the Bodhisattva leads an infinite number of creatures into nirvana, in reality there are neither any Bodhisattvas to do the leading nor any creatures to be led." However, out of some feeling for his welfare, Goetz had put forth $4.50 to take him to a lecture on Vedanta. It had been a waste of his money. While Goetz had listened enthralled to the dark little man on the platform, Asbury's bored gaze had roved among the audience. It had passed over the heads of several girls in saris, past a Japanese youth, a blue-black man with a fez, and several girls who looked like secretaries. Finally, at the end of the row, it had rested on a lean spectacled figure in black, a priest. The priest's expression was of a polite but strictly reserved interest. Asbury identified his own feelings immediately in the taciturn superior expression. When the lecture was over a few students met in Goetz's flat, the priest among them, but here he was equally reserved. He listened with a marked politeness to the discussion of Asbury's approaching death, but he said little. A girl in a sari remarked that self-fulfillment was out of the question since it meant salvation and the word was meaningless. "Salvation," quoted Goetz, "is the destruction of a simple prejudice, and no one is saved."

"And what do you say to that?" Asbury asked the priest and returned his reserved smile over the heads of the others. The borders of his smile seemed to touch on some icy clarity.

"There is," the priest said, "a real probability of the New Man, assisted, of course" he added brittlely "by the Third Person of the Trinity."

"Ridiculous!" the girl in the sari said, but the priest only brushed her with his smile, which was slightly amused now.

When he got up to leave, he silently handed Asbury a small card on which he had written his name, Ignatius Vogle, S.J., and an address. Perhaps, Asbury thought now, he should have used it for the priest appealed to him as a man of the world, someone who would have understood the unique tragedy of his death, a death whose meaning had been far beyond the twittering group around them. And how much more beyond Block. "What's wrong with me," he repeated, "is way beyond Block."

His mother knew at once what he meant: he meant he was going to have a nervous breakdown. She did not say a word. She did not say that this was precisely what she could have told him would happen. When people think they are smart—even when they are smart—there is nothing anybody else can say to make them see things straight, and with Asbury, the trouble was that in addition to being smart, he had an artistic temperament. She did not know where he had got it from because his father, who was a lawyer and businessman and farmer and politician all rolled into one, had certainly had his feet on the ground; and she had certainly always had hers on it. She had managed after he died to get the two of them through college and beyond; but she had observed that the more education they got, the less they could do. Their father had gone to a one-room schoolhouse through the eighth grade and he could do anything.

She could have told Asbury what would help him. She could have said, "If you would get out in the sunshine, or if you would work for a month in the dairy, you'd be a different person!" but she knew exactly how that suggestion would be received. He would be a nuisance in the dairy but she would let him work in there if he wanted to. She had let him work in there last year when he had come home and was writing the play. He had been writing a play about Negroes (why anybody would want to write a play about Negroes was beyond her) and he had said he wanted to work in the dairy with them and find out what their interests were. Their interests were in doing as little as they could get by with, as she could have told him if anybody could have told him anything. The Negroes had put up with him and he had learned to put the milkers on and once he had washed all the cans and she thought that once he had mixed feed. Then a cow had kicked him and he had not gone back to the barn again. She knew that if he would get in there now, or get out and fix fences, or do any kind of work—real work, not writing—that he might avoid this nervous breakdown. "Whatever happened to that play you were writing about the Negroes?" she asked.

"I am not writing plays," he said. "And get this through your head: I am not working in any dairy. I am not getting out in the sunshine. I'm ill. I have fever and chills and I'm dizzy and all I want you to do is leave me alone."

"Then if you are really ill, you should see Doctor Block."

"And I am not seeing Block," he finished and ground himself down in the seat and stared intensely in front of him.

She turned into their driveway, a red road that ran for a quarter of a mile through the two front pastures. The dry cows were on one side and the milk herd on the other. She slowed the car and then stopped altogether, her attention caught by a cow with a bad quarter. "They haven't been attending to her," she said. "Look at that bag!"

Asbury turned his head abruptly in the opposite direction, but there a small, walleyed Guernsey was watching him steadily as if she sensed some bond between them. "Good God!" he cried in an agonized voice, "can't we go on? It's six o'clock in the morning!"

"Yes, yes," his mother said and started the car quickly.

"What's that cry of deadly pain?" his sister drawled from the back seat. "Oh it's you," she said. "Well well, we have the artist with us again. How utterly utterly." She had a decidedly nasal voice.

He didn't answer her or turn his head. He had learned that much. Never answer her.

"Mary George!" his mother said sharply. "Asbury is sick. Leave him alone."

"What's wrong with him?" Mary George asked.

"There's the house!" his mother said as if they were all blind but her. It rose on the crest of the hill—a white two-story farmhouse with a wide porch and pleasant columns. She always approached it with a feeling of pride and she had said more than once to Asbury, "You have a home here that half those people up there would give their eyeteeth for!"

She had been once to the terrible place he lived in New York. They had gone up five flights of dark stone steps, past open garbage cans on every landing, to arrive finally at two damp rooms and a closet with a toilet in it. "You wouldn't live like this at home," she had muttered.

"No!" he'd said with an ecstatic look, "it wouldn't be possible!"

She supposed the truth was that she simply didn't understand how it felt to be sensitive or how peculiar you were when you were an artist. His sister said he was not an artist and that he had no talent and that that was the trouble with him; but Mary George was not a happy girl herself. Asbury said she posed as an intellectual but that her I.Q. couldn't be over seventy-five, that all she was really interested in was getting a man but that no sensible man would finish a first look at her. She had tried to tell him that Mary George could be very attractive when she put her mind to it and he had said that that much strain on her mind would break her down. If she were in any way attractive, he had said, she wouldn't now be principal of a county elementary school, and Mary George had said that if Asbury had had any talent, he would by now have published something. What had he ever published, she wanted to know, and for that matter, what had he ever written?

Mrs. Fox had pointed out that he was only twenty-five years old and Mary George had said that the age most people published something at was twenty-one, which made him exactly four years overdue. Mrs. Fox was not up on things like that but she suggested that he might be writing a very *long* book. Very long book, her eye, Mary George said, he would do well if he came up with so much as a poem. Mrs. Fox hoped it wasn't going to be just a poem.

She pulled the car into the side drive and a scattering of guineas exploded into the air and sailed screaming around the house. "Home again, home again jiggity jig!" she said.

"Oh God," Asbury groaned.

"The artist arrives at the gas chamber," Mary George said in her nasal voice.

He leaned on the door and got out, and forgetting his bags he moved toward the front of the house as if he were in a daze. His sister got out and stood by the car door, squinting at his bent unsteady figure. As she watched him go up the front steps, her mouth fell slack in her astonished face. "Why," she said, "there *is* something the matter with him. He looks a hundred years old."

"Didn't I tell you so?" her mother hissed. "Now you keep your mouth shut and let him alone."

He went into the house, pausing in the hall only long enough to see his pale broken face glare at him for an instant from the pier mirror. Holding onto the banister, he pulled himself up the steep stairs, across the landing and then up the shorter second flight and into his room, a large open airy room with a faded blue rug and white curtains freshly put up for his arrival. He looked at nothing, but fell face down on his own bed. It was a narrow antique bed with a high ornamental headboard on which was carved a garlanded basket overflowing with wooden fruit.

While he was still in New York, he had written a letter to his mother which filled two notebooks. He did not mean it to be read until after his death. It was such a letter as Kafka had addressed to his father. Asbury's father had died twenty years ago and Asbury considered this a great blessing. The old man, he felt sure, had been one of the courthouse gang, a rural worthy with a dirty finger in every pie and he knew he would not have been able to stomach him. He had read some of his correspondence and had been appalled by its stupidity.

He knew, of course, that his mother would not understand the letter at once. Her literal mind would require some time to discover the significance of it, but he thought she would be able to see that he forgave her for all she had done to him. For that matter, he supposed that she would realize what she had done to him only through the letter. He didn't think she was conscious of it at all. Her self-satisfaction itself was barely conscious, but because of the letter, she might experience a painful realization and this would be the only thing of value he had to leave her.

If reading it would be painful to her, writing it had sometimes been unbearable to him—for in order to face her, he had had to face himself. "I came here to escape the slave's atmosphere of home," he had written, "to find freedom, to liberate my imagination, to take it like a hawk from its cage and set it 'whirling off into the widening gyre' (Yeats) and what did I find? It was incapable of flight. It was some bird you had domesticated, sitting huffy in its pen, refusing to come out!" The next words were underscored twice. "I have no imagination. I have no talent. I can't create. I have nothing but the desire for these things. Why didn't you kill that too? Woman, why did you pinion me?"

Writing this, he had reached the pit of despair and he thought that reading it, she would at least begin to sense his tragedy and her part in it. It was not that she had ever forced her way on him. That had never been necessary. Her way had simply been the air he breathed and when at last he had found other air, he couldn't survive in it. He felt that even if she didn't understand at once, the letter would leave her with an enduring chill and perhaps in time lead her to see herself as she was.

He had destroyed everything else he had ever written—his two lifeless novels, his half-dozen stationary plays, his prosy poems, his sketchy short stories—and kept only the two notebooks that contained the letter. They were in the black suitcase that his sister, huffing and blowing, was now dragging up the second flight of stairs. His mother was carrying the smaller bag and came on ahead. He turned over as she entered the room.

"I'll open this and get out your things," she said, "and you can go right to bed and in a few minutes I'll bring your breakfast."

He sat up and said in a fretful voice, "I don't want any breakfast and I can open my own suitcase. Leave that alone."

His sister arrived in the door, her face full of curiosity, and let the black bag fall with a thud over the doorsill. Then she began to push it across the room with her foot until she was close enough to get a good look at him. "If I looked as bad as you do," she said, "I'd go to the hospital."

Her mother cut her eyes sharply at her and she left. Then Mrs. Fox closed the door and came to the bed and sat down on it beside him. "Now this time I want you to make a long visit and rest," she said.

"This visit," he said, "will be permanent."

"Wonderful!" she cried. "You can have a little studio in your room and in the mornings you can write plays and in the afternoons you can help in the dairy!"

He turned a white wooden face to her. "Close the blinds and let me sleep," he said.

When she was gone, he lay for some time staring at the water stains on the gray walls. Descending from the top molding. long icicle shapes had been etched by leaks and, directly over his bed on the ceiling, another leak had made a fierce bird with spread wings. It had an icicle crosswise in its beak and there were smaller icicles depending from its wings and tail. It had been there since his childhood and had always irritated him and sometimes had frightened him. He had often had the illusion that it was in motion and about to descend mysteriously and set the icicle on his head. He closed his eyes and thought: I won't have to look at it for many more days. And presently he went to sleep.

When he woke up in the afternoon, there was a pink open-mouthed face hanging over him and from two large familiar ears on either side of it the black tubes of Block's stethoscope extended down to his exposed chest. The doctor, seeing he was awake, made a face like a Chinaman, rolled his eyes almost out of his head and cried, "Say AHHHH!"

Block was irresistible to children. For miles around they vomited and went into fevers to have a visit from him. Mrs. Fox was standing behind him, smiling radiantly. "Here's Doctor Block!" she said as if she had captured this angel on the rooftop and brought him in for her little boy.

"Get him out of here," Asbury muttered. He looked at the asinine face from what seemed the bottom of a black hole.

The doctor peered closer, wiggling his ears. Block was bald and had a round face as senseless as a baby's. Nothing about him indicated intelligence except two cold clinical nickel-colored eyes that hung with a motionless curiosity over whatever he looked at. "You sho do look bad, Azzberry," he murmured. He took the stethoscope off and dropped it in his bag.

"I don't know when I've seen anybody your age look as sorry as you do. What you been doing to yourself?"

There was a continuous thud in the back of Asbury's head as if his heart had got trapped in it and was fighting to get out. "I didn't send for you," he said.

Block put his hand on the glaring face and pulled the eyelid down and peered into it. "You must have been on the bum up there," he said. He began to press his hand in the small of Asbury's back. "I went up there once myself," he said, "and saw exactly how little they had and came straight on back home. Open your mouth."

Asbury opened it automatically and the drill-like gaze swung over it and bore down. He snapped it shut and in a wheezing breathless voice he said, "If I'd wanted a doctor, I'd have stayed up there where I could have got a good one!"

"Asbury!" his mother said.

"How long you been having the so' throat?" Block asked.

"She sent for you!" Asbury said. "She can answer the questions."

"Asbury!" his mother said.

Block leaned over his bag and pulled out a rubber tube. He pushed Asbury's sleeve up and tied the tube around his upper arm. Then he took out a syringe and prepared to find the vein, humming a hymn as he pressed the needle in. Asbury lay with a rigid outraged stare while the privacy of his blood was invaded by this idiot. "Slowly Lord but sure," Block sang in a murmuring voice, "Oh slowly Lord but sure." When the syringe was full, he withdrew the needle. "Blood don't lie," he said. He poured it in a bottle and stopped it up and put the bottle in his bag. "Azzberry," he started, "how long . . ."

Asbury sat up and thrust his thudding head forward and said, "I didn't send for you. I'm not answering any questions. You're not my doctor. What's wrong with me is way beyond you."

"Most things are beyond me," Block said. "I ain't found anything yet that I thoroughly understood," and he sighed and got up. His eyes seemed to glitter at Asbury as if from a great distance.

"He wouldn't act so ugly," Mrs. Fox explained, "if he weren't really sick. And *I* want you to come back every day until you get him well."

Asbury's eyes were a fierce glaring violet. "What's wrong with me is way beyond you," he repeated and lay back down and closed his eyes until Block and his mother were gone.

In the next few days, though he grew rapidly worse, his mind functioned with a terrible clarity. On the point of death, he found himself existing in a state of illumination that was totally out of keeping with the kind of talk he had to listen to from his mother. This was largely about cows with names like Daisy and Bessie Button and their intimate functions—their mastitis and their screwworms and their abortions. His mother insisted that in the middle of the day he get out and sit on the porch and "enjoy the view" and as resistance was too much of a struggle, he dragged himself out and sat there in a rigid slouch, his feet wrapped in an afghan and his hands gripped on the chair arms as if he were about to spring forward into the glaring china blue sky. The lawn extended for a quarter of an acre down to a barbed-wire fence that divided it from the front pasture. In the middle of the day the dry cows rested there under a line of sweetgum trees. On the other side of the road were two hills with a pond between and his mother could sit on the porch and watch the herd walk across the dam to the hill on the other side. The whole scene was rimmed by a wall of trees which, at the time of day he was forced to sit there, was a washed-out blue that reminded him sadly of the Negroes' faded overalls.

He listened irritably while his mother detailed the faults of the help. "Those two are not stupid," she said. "They know how to look out for themselves."

"They need to," he muttered, but there was no use to argue with her. Last year he had been writing a play about the Negro and he had wanted to be around them for a while to see how they really felt about their condition, but the two who worked for her had lost all their initiative over the years. They didn't talk. The one called Morgan was light brown, part Indian; the other, older one, Randall, was very black and fat. When they said anything to him, it was as if they were speaking to an invisible body located to the right or left of where he actually was, and after two days working side by side with them, he felt he had not established rapport. He decided to try something bolder than talk and one afternoon as he was standing near Randall, watching him adjust a milker, he had quietly taken out his cigarettes and lit one. The Negro had stopped what he was doing and watched him. He waited until Asbury had taken two draws and then he said, "She don't 'low no smoking in here."

The other one approached and stood there, grinning.

"I know it," Asbury said and after a deliberate pause, he shook the package and held it out, first to Randall, who took one, and then to Morgan, who took one. He had then lit the cigarettes for them himself and the three of them had stood there smoking. There were no sounds but the steady click of the two milking machines and the occasional slap of a cow's tail against her side. It was one of those moments of communion when the difference between black and white is absorbed into nothing.

The next day two cans of milk had been returned from the creamery because it had absorbed the odor of tobacco. He took the blame and told his mother that it was he and not the Negroes who had been smoking. "If you were doing it, they were doing it," she had said. "Don't you think I know those two?" She was incapable of thinking them innocent; but the experience had so exhilarated him that he had been determined to repeat it in some other way.

The next afternoon when he and Randall were in the milk house pouring the fresh milk into the cans, he had picked up the jelly glass the Negroes drank out of and, inspired, had poured himself a glassful of the warm milk and drained it down. Randall had stopped pouring and had remained, half-bent, over the can, watching him. "She don't 'low that," he said. "That *the* thing she don't 'low."

Asbury poured out another glassful and handed it to him.

"She don't 'low it," he repeated.

"Listen," Asbury said hoarsely, "the world is changing. There's no reason I shouldn't drink after you or you after me!"

"She don't 'low noner us to drink noner this here milk," Randall said.

Asbury continued to hold the glass out to him. "You took the cigarette," he said. "Take the milk. It's not going to hurt my mother to lose two or three glasses of milk a day. We've got to think free if we want to live free!"

The other one had come up and was standing in the door.

"Don't want noner that milk," Randall said.

Asbury swung around and held the glass out to Morgan. "Here boy, have a drink of this," he said.

Morgan stared at him; then his face took on a decided look of cunning. "I ain't seen you drink none of it yourself," he said.

Asbury despised milk. The first warm glassful had turned his stomach. He drank half of what he was holding and handed the rest to the Negro, who took it and gazed down inside the glass as if it contained some great mystery; then he set it on the floor by the cooler.

"Don't you like milk?" Asbury asked.

"I likes it but I ain't drinking noner that."

"Why?"

"She don't 'low it," Morgan said.

"My God!" Asbury exploded, "she she she!" He had tried the same thing the next day and the next and the next but he could not get them to drink the milk. A few afternoons later when he was standing outside the milk house about to go in, he heard Morgan ask, "Howcome you let him drink all that milk every day?"

"What he do is him," Randall said. "What I do is me."

"Howcome he talks so ugly about his ma?"

"She ain't whup him enough when he was little," Randall said.

The insufferableness of life at home had overcome him and he had returned to New York two days early. So far as he was concerned he had died there, and the question now was how long he could stand to linger here. He could have hastened his end but suicide would not have been a victory. Death was coming to him legitimately, as a justification, as a gift from life. That was his greatest triumph. Then too, to the fine minds of the neighborhood, a suicide son would indicate a mother who had been a failure, and while this was the case, he felt that it was a public embarrassment he could spare her. What she would learn from the letter would be a private revelation. He had sealed the notebooks in a manila envelope and had written on it: "To be opened only after the death of Asbury Porter Fox." He had put the envelope in the desk drawer in his room and locked it and the key was in his pajama pocket until he could decide on a place to leave it.

When they sat on the porch in the morning, his mother felt that some of the time she should talk about subjects that were of interest to him. The third morning she started in on his writing. "When you get well," she said, "I think it would be nice if you wrote a book about down here. We need another good book like *Gone With the Wind*."

He could feel the muscles in his stomach begin to tighten.

"Put the war in it," she advised. "That always makes a long book."

He put his head back gently as if he were afraid it would crack. After a moment he said, "I am not going to write any book."

"Well," she said, "if you don't feel like writing a book, you could just write poems. They're nice." She realized that what he needed was someone intellectual to talk to, but Mary George was the only intellectual she knew and he would not talk to her. She had thought of Mr. Bush, the retired Methodist minister, but she had not brought this up.

Now she decided to hazard it. "I think I'll ask Dr. Bush to come to see you," she said, raising Mr. Bush's rank. "You'd enjoy him. He collects rare coins."

She was not prepared for the reaction she got. He began to shake all over and give loud spasmodic laughs. He seemed about to choke. After a minute he subsided into a cough. "If you think I need spiritual aid to die," he said, "you're quite mistaken. And certainly not from that ass Bush. My God!"

"I didn't mean that at all," she said. "He has coins dating from the time of Cleopatra."

"Well if you ask him here, I'll tell him to go to hell," he said. "Bush! That beats all!"

"I'm glad something amuses you," she said acidly.

For a time they sat there in silence. Then his mother looked up. He was sitting forward again and smiling at her. His face was brightening more and more as if he had just had an idea that was brilliant. She stared at him. "I'll tell you who I want to come," he said. For the first time since he had come home, his expression was pleasant; though there was also, she thought, a kind of crafty look about him.

"Who do you want to come?" she asked suspiciously.

"I want a priest," he announced.

"A priest?" his mother said in an uncomprehending voice.

"Preferably a Jesuit," he said, brightening more and more. "Yes, by all means a Jesuit. They have them in the city. You can call up and get me one."

"What is the matter with you?" his mother asked.

"Most of them are very well-educated," he said, "but Jesuits are foolproof. A Jesuit would be able to discuss something besides the weather." Already, remembering Ignatius Vogle, S.J., he could picture the priest. This one would be a trifle more worldly perhaps, a trifle more cynical. Protected by their ancient institution, priests could afford to be cynical, to play both ends against the middle. He would talk to a man of culture before he died—even in this desert! Furthermore, nothing would irritate his mother so much. He could not understand why he had not thought of this sooner.

"You're not a member of that church," Mrs. Fox said shortly. "It's twenty miles away. They wouldn't send one." She hoped that this would end the matter.

He sat back absorbed in the idea, determined to force her to make the call since she always did what he wanted if he kept at her. "I'm dying," he said, "and I haven't asked you to do but one thing and you refuse me that."

"You are NOT dying."

"When you realize it," he said, "it'll be too late."

There was another unpleasant silence. Presently his mother said,

"Nowadays doctors don't *let* young people die. They give them some of these new medicines." She began shaking her foot with a nerve-rattling assurance. "People just don't die like they used to," she said.

"Mother," he said, "you ought to be prepared. I think even Block knows and hasn't told you yet." Block, after the first visit, had come in grimly every time, without his jokes and funny faces, and had taken his blood in silence, his nickel-colored eyes unfriendly. He was, by definition, the enemy of death and he looked now as if he knew he was battling the real thing. He had said he wouldn't prescribe until he knew what was wrong and Asbury had laughed in his face. "Mother," he said, "I AM going to die," and he tried to make each word like a hammer blow on top of her head.

She paled slightly but she did not blink. "Do you think for one minute," she said angrily, "that I intend to sit here and let you die?" Her eyes were as hard as two old mountain ranges seen in the distance. He felt the first distinct stroke of doubt.

"Do you?" she asked fiercely.

"I don't think you have anything to do with it," he said in a shaken voice.

"Humph," she said and got up and left the porch as if she could not stand to be around such stupidity an instant longer.

Forgetting the Jesuit, he went rapidly over his symptoms: his fever had increased, interspersed by chills; he barely had the energy to drag himself out on the porch; food was abhorrent to him; and Block had not been able to give her the least satisfaction. Even as he sat there, he felt the beginning of a new chill, as if death were already playfully rattling his bones. He pulled the afghan off his feet and put it around his shoulders and made his way unsteadily up the stairs to bed.

He continued to grow worse. In the next few days he became so much weaker and badgered her so constantly about the Jesuit that finally in desperation she decided to humor his foolishness. She made the call, explaining in a chilly voice that her son was ill, perhaps a little out of his head, and wished to speak to a priest. While she made the call, Asbury hung over the banisters, barefooted, with the afghan around him, and listened. When she hung up he called down to know when the priest was coming.

"Tomorrow sometime," his mother said irritably.

He could tell by the fact that she made the call that her assurance was beginning to shatter. Whenever she let Block in or out, there was much whispering in the downstairs hall. That evening, he heard her and Mary George talking in low voices in the parlor. He thought he heard his name and he got up and tiptoed into the hall and down the first three steps until he could hear the voices distinctly.

"I had to call that priest," his mother was saying. "I'm afraid this is serious. I thought it was just a nervous breakdown but now I think it's something real. Doctor Block thinks it's something real too and whatever it is is worse because he's so run-down."

"Grow up, Mamma," Mary George said, "I've told you and I tell you again: what's wrong with him is purely psychosomatic." There was nothing she was not an expert on.

"No," his mother said, "it's a real disease. The doctor says so." He thought he detected a crack in her voice.

"Block is an idiot," Mary George said. "You've got to face the facts: Asbury can't write so he gets sick. He's going to be an invalid instead of an artist. Do you know what he needs?"

"No," his mother said.

"Two or three shock treatments," Mary George said. "Get that artist business out of his head once and for all."

His mother gave a little cry and he grasped the banister.

"Mark my words," his sister continued, "all he's going to be around here for the next fifty years is a decoration."

He went back to bed. In a sense she was right. He had failed his god, Art, but he had been a faithful servant and Art was sending him Death. He had seen this from the first with a kind of mystical clarity. He went to sleep thinking of the peaceful spot in the family burying ground where he would soon lie, and after a while he saw that his body was being borne slowly toward it while his mother and Mary George watched without interest from their chairs on the porch. As the bier was carried across the dam, they could look up and see the procession reflected upside down in the pond. A lean dark figure in a Roman collar followed it. He had a mysteriously saturnine face in which there was a subtle blend of asceticism and corruption. Asbury was laid in a shallow grave on the hillside and the indistinct mourners, after standing in silence for a while, spread out over the darkening green. The Jesuit retired to a spot beneath a dead tree to smoke and meditate. The moon came up and Asbury was aware of a presence bending over him and a gentle warmth on his cold face. He knew that this was Art come to wake him and he sat up and opened his eyes. Across the hill all the lights were on in his mother's house. The black pond was speckled with little nickel-colored stars. The Jesuit had disappeared. All around him the cows were spread out grazing in the moonlight and one large white one, violently spotted, was softly licking his head as if it were a block of salt. He awoke with a shudder and discovered that his bed was soaking from a night sweat and as he sat shivering in the dark, he realized that the end was not many days distant. He gazed down into the crater of death and fell back dizzy on his pillow.

The next day his mother noted something almost ethereal about his ravaged face. He looked like one of those dying children who must have Christmas early. He sat up in the bed and directed the rearrangement of several chairs and had her remove a picture of a maiden chained to a rock for he knew it would make the Jesuit smile. He had the comfortable rocker taken away and when he finished, the room with its severe wall stains had a certain cell-like quality. He felt it would be attractive to the visitor.

All morning he waited, looking irritably up at the ceiling where the bird with the icicle in its beak seemed poised and waiting too; but the priest did not arrive until late in the afternoon. As soon as his mother opened the door, a loud unintelligible voice began to boom in the downstairs hall. Asbury's heart beat wildly. In a second there was a heavy creaking on the stairs. Then almost at once his mother, her expression constrained, came in followed by a massive old man who plowed straight across the room, picked up a chair by the side of the bed and put it under himself.

"I'm Fahther Finn — from Purrgatory," he said in a hearty voice. He had a large red face, a stiff brush of gray hair and was blind in one eye, but the good eye, blue and clear, was focussed sharply on Asbury. There was a grease spot on his vest. "So you want to talk to a priest?" he said. "Very wise. None of us knows the hour Our Blessed Lord may call us." Then he cocked his good eye up at Asbury's mother and said, "Thank you, you may leave us now."

Mrs. Fox stiffened and did not budge.

"I'd like to talk to Father Finn alone," Asbury said, feeling suddenly that here he had an ally, although he had not expected a priest like this one. His mother gave him a disgusted look and left the room. He knew she would go no farther than just outside the door.

"It's so nice to have you come," Asbury said. "This place is incredibly dreary. There's no one here an intelligent person can talk to. I wonder what you think of Joyce, Father?"

The priest lifted his chair and pushed closer. "You'll have to shout," he said. "Blind in one eye and deaf in one ear."

"What do you think of Joyce?" Asbury said louder.

"Joyce? Joyce who?" asked the priest.

"James Joyce," Asbury said and laughed.

The priest brushed his huge hand in the air as if he were bothered by gnats. "I haven't met him," he said. "Now. Do you say your morning and night prayers?"

Asbury appeared confused. "Joyce was a great writer," he murmured, forgetting to shout.

"You don't eh?" said the priest. "Well you will never learn to be good unless you pray regularly. You cannot love Jesus unless you speak to Him."

"The myth of the dying god has always fascinated me," Asbury shouted, but the priest did not appear to catch it.

"Do you have trouble with purity?" he demanded, and as Asbury paled, he went on without waiting for an answer. "We all do but you must pray to the Holy Ghost for it. Mind, heart and body. Nothing is overcome without prayer. Pray with your family. Do you pray with your family?"

"God forbid," Asbury murmured. "My mother doesn't have time to pray and my sister is an atheist," he shouted.

"A shame!" said the priest. "Then you must pray for them."

"The artist prays by creating," Asbury ventured.

"Not enough!" snapped the priest. "If you do not pray daily, you are neglecting your immortal soul. Do you know your catechism?"

"Certainly not," Asbury muttered.

"Who made you?" the priest asked in a martial tone.

"Different people believe different things about that," Asbury said.

"God made you," the priest said shortly. "Who is God?"

"God is an idea created by man," Asbury said, feeling that he was getting into stride, that two could play at this.

"God is a spirit infinitely perfect," the priest said. "You are a very ignorant boy. Why did God make you?"

"God didn't. . . ."

"God made you to know Him, to love Him, to serve Him in this world and to be happy with Him in the next!" the old priest said in a battering voice. "If you don't apply yourself to the catechism how do you expect to know how to save your immortal soul?"

Asbury saw he had made a mistake and that it was time to get rid of the old fool. "Listen," he said, "I'm not a Roman."

"A poor excuse for not saying your prayers!" the old man snorted.

Asbury slumped slightly in the bed. "I'm dying," he shouted.

"But you're not dead yet!" said the priest, "and how do you expect to meet God face to face when you've never spoken to Him? How do you expect to get what you don't ask for? God does not send the Holy Ghost to those who don't ask for Him. Ask Him to send the Holy Ghost."

"The Holy Ghost?" Asbury said.

"Are you so ignorant you've never heard of the Holy Ghost?" the priest asked.

"Certainly I've heard of the Holy Ghost" Asbury said furiously, "and the Holy Ghost is the last thing I'm looking for!"

"And He may be the last thing you get," the priest said, his one fierce eye inflamed. "Do you want your soul to suffer eternal damnation? Do you want to be deprived of God for all eternity? Do you want to suffer the most terrible pain, greater than fire, the pain of loss? Do you want to suffer the pain of loss for all eternity?"

Asbury moved his arms and legs helplessly as if he were pinned to the bed by the terrible eye.

"How can the Holy Ghost fill your soul when it's full of trash?"

the priest roared. "The Holy Ghost will not come until you see yourself as you are — a lazy ignorant conceited youth!" he said, pounding his fist on the little bedside table.

Mrs. Fox burst in. "Enough of this!" she cried. "How dare you talk that way to a poor sick boy? You're upsetting him. You'll have to go."

"The poor lad doesn't even know his catechism," the priest said, rising. "I should think you would have taught him to say his daily prayers. You have neglected your duty as his mother." He turned back to the bed and said affably, "I'll give you my blessing and after this you must say your daily prayers without fail," whereupon he put his hand on Asbury's head and rumbled something in Latin. "Call me any time," he said, "and we can have another little chat," and then he followed Mrs. Fox's rigid back out. The last thing Asbury heard him say was, "He's a good lad at heart but very ignorant."

When his mother had got rid of the priest she came rapidly up the steps again to say that she had told him so, but when she saw him, pale and drawn and ravaged, sitting up in his bed, staring in front of him with large childish shocked eyes, she did not have the heart and went rapidly out again.

The next morning he was so weak that she made up her mind he must go to the hospital. "I'm not going to any hospital," he kept repeating, turning his thudding head from side to side as if he wanted to work it loose from his body. "I'm not going to any hospital as long as I'm conscious." He was thinking bitterly that once he lost consciousness, she could drag him off to the hospital and fill him full of blood and prolong his misery for days. He was convinced that the end was approaching, that it would be today, and he was tormented now thinking of his useless life. He felt as if he were a shell that had to be filled with something but he did not know what. He began to take note of everything in the room as if for the last time — the ridiculous antique furniture, the pattern in the rug, the silly picture his mother had replaced. He even looked at the fierce bird with the icicle in its beak and felt that it was there for some purpose that he could not divine.

There was something he was searching for, something that he felt he must have, some last significant culminating experience that he must make for himself before he died — make for himself out of his own intelligence. He had always relied on himself and had never been a sniveler after the ineffable.

Once when Mary George was thirteen and he was five, she had lured him with the promise of an unnamed present into a large tent full of people and had dragged him backwards up to the front where a man in a blue suit and red and white tie was standing. "Here," she said in a loud voice. "I'm already saved but you can save him. He's a real stinker and too big for his britches." He had broken her grip and shot out of there like a small cur and later when he had asked for his present, she had said, "You would have got Salvation if you had waited for it but since you acted the way you did, you get nothing!"

As the day wore on, he grew more and more frantic for fear he would die without making some last meaningful experience for himself. His mother sat anxiously by the side of the bed. She had called Block twice and could not get him. He thought even now she had not realized that he was going to die, much less that the end was only hours off.

The light in the room was beginning to have an odd quality, almost as if it were taking on presence. In a darkened form it entered and seemed to wait. Outside it appeared to move no farther than the edge of the faded treeline, which he could see a few inches over the sill of his window. Suddenly he thought of that experience of communion that he had had in the dairy with the Negroes when they had smoked together, and at once he began to tremble with excitement. They would smoke together one last time.

After a moment, turning his head on the pillow, he said, "Mother, I want to tell the Negroes good-bye."

His mother paled. For an instant her face seemed about to fly apart. Then the line of her mouth hardened; her brows drew together. "Good-bye?" she said in a flat voice. "Where are you going?"

For a few seconds he only looked at her. Then he said, "I think you know. Get them. I don't have long."

"This is absurd," she muttered but she got up and hurried out. He heard her try to reach Block again before she went outside. He thought her clinging to Block at a time like this was touching and pathetic. He waited, preparing himself for the encounter as a religious man might prepare himself for the last sacrament. Presently he heard their steps on the stair.

"Here's Randall and Morgan," his mother said, ushering them in. "They've come to tell you hello."

The two of them came in grinning and shuffled to the side of the bed. They stood there, Randall in front and Morgan behind. "You sho do look well," Randall said. "You looks very well."

"You looks well," the other one said. "Yessuh, you looks fine."

"I ain't ever seen you looking so well before," Randall said.

"Yes, doesn't he look well?" his mother said. "I think he looks just fine."

"Yessuh," Randall said, "I speck you ain't even sick."

"Mother," Asbury said in a forced voice. "I'd like to talk to them alone."

His mother stiffened; then she marched out. She walked across the hall and into the room on the other side and sat down. Through the open doors he could see her begin to rock in little short jerks. The two Negroes looked as if their last protection had dropped away.

Asbury's head was so heavy he could not think what he had been going to do. "I'm dying," he said.

Both their grins became gelid. "You looks fine," Randall said.

"I'm going to die," Asbury repeated. Then with relief he remembered that they were going to smoke together. He reached for the package on the table and held it out to Randall, forgetting to shake out the cigarettes.

The Negro took the package and put it in his pocket. "I thank you," he said. "I certainly do prechate it."

Asbury stared as if he had forgotten again. After a second he became aware that the other Negro's face had turned infinitely sad; then he realized that it was not sad but sullen. He fumbled in the drawer of the table and pulled out an unopened package and thrust it at Morgan.

"I thanks you, Mist Asbury," Morgan said, brightening. "You certly does look well."

"I'm about to die," Asbury said irritably.

"You looks fine," Randall said.

"You be up and around in a few days," Morgan predicted. Neither of them seemed to find a suitable place to rest his gaze. Asbury looked wildly across the hall where his mother had her rocker so that her back faced him. It was apparent she had no intention of getting rid of them for him.

"I speck you might have a little cold," Randall said after a time.

"I takes a little turpentine and sugar when I has a cold," Morgan said.

"Shut your mouth," Randall said, turning on him.

"Shut your own mouth," Morgan said. "I know what I takes."

"He don't take what you take," Randall growled.

"Mother!" Asbury called in a shaking voice.

His mother stood up. "Mister Asbury has had company long enough now," she called. "You all can come back tomorrow."

"We be going," Randall said. "You sho do look well."

"You sho does," Morgan said.

They filed out agreeing with each other how well he looked but Asbury's vision became blurred before they reached the hall. For an instant he saw his mother's form as if it were a shadow in the door and then it disappeared after them down the stairs. He heard her call Block again but he heard it without interest. His head was spinning. He knew now there would be no significant experience before he died. There was nothing more to do but give her the key to the drawer where the letter was, and wait for the end.

He sank into a heavy sleep from which he awoke about five o'-clock to see her white face, very small, at the end of a well of darkness. He took the key out of his pajama pocket and handed it to her and mumbled that there was a letter in the desk to be opened when he was gone, but she did not seem to understand. She put the key down on the bedside table and left it there and he returned to his dream in which two large boulders were circling each other inside his head.

He awoke a little after six to hear Block's car stop below in the driveway. The sound was like a summons, bringing him rapidly and with a clear head out of his sleep. He had a sudden terrible foreboding that the fate awaiting him was going to be more shattering than any he could have reckoned on. He lay absolutely motionless, as still as an animal the instant before an earthquake.

Block and his mother talked as they came up the stairs but he did not distinguish their words. The doctor came in making faces; his mother was smiling. "Guess what you've got, Sugarpie!" she cried. Her voice broke in on him with the force of a gunshot.

"Found theter ol' bug, did ol' Block," Block said, sinking down into the chair by the bed. He raised his hands over his head in the gesture of a victorious prize fighter and let them collapse in his lap as if the effort had exhausted him. Then he removed a red bandanna handkerchief that he carried to be funny with and wiped his face thoroughly, having a different expression on it every time it appeared from behind the rag.

"I think you're just as smart as you can be!" Mrs. Fox said. "Asbury," she said, "you have undulant fever. It'll keep coming back but it won't kill you!" Her smile was as bright and intense as a lightbulb without a shade. "I'm so relieved," she said.

Asbury sat up slowly, his face expressionless; then he fell back down again.

Block leaned over him and smiled. "You ain't going to die," he said, with deep satisfaction.

Nothing about Asbury stirred except his eyes. They did not appear to move on the surface but somewhere in their blurred depths there was an almost imperceptible motion as if something were struggling feebly. Block's gaze seemed to reach down like a steel pin and hold whatever it was until the life was out of it. "Undulant fever ain't so bad, Azzberry," he murmured. "It's the same as Bang's in a cow."

The boy gave a low moan and then was quiet.

"He must have drunk some unpasteurized milk up there," his mother said softly and then the two of them tiptoed out as if they thought he were about to go to sleep.

When the sound of their footsteps had faded on the stairs, Asbury sat up again. He turned his head, almost surreptitiously, to the side where the key he had given his mother was lying on the bedside table. His hand shot out and closed over it and returned it to his pocket. He glanced across the room into the small oval-framed dresser mirror. The eyes that stared back at him were the same that had returned his gaze every day from that mirror but it seemed to him that they were paler.

They looked shocked clean as if they had been prepared for some awful vision about to come down on him. He shuddered and turned his head quickly the other way and stared out the window. A blinding red-gold sun moved serenely from under a purple cloud. Below it the treeline was black against the crimson sky. It formed a brittle wall, standing as if it were the frail defense he had set up in his mind to protect him from what was coming. The boy fell back on his pillow and stared at the ceiling. His limbs that had been racked for so many weeks by fever and chill were numb now. The old life in him was exhausted. He awaited the coming of new. It was then that he felt the beginning of a chill, a chill so peculiar, so light, that it was like a warm ripple across a deeper sea of cold. His breath came short. The fierce bird which through the years of his childhood and the days of his illness had been poised over his head, waiting mysteriously, appeared all at once to be in motion. Asbury blanched and the last film of illusion was torn as if by a whirlwind from his eyes. He saw that for the rest of his days, frail, racked, but enduring, he would live in the face of a purifying terror. A feeble cry, a last impossible protest escaped him. But the Holy Ghost, emblazoned in ice instead of fire, continued, implacable, to descend.

1965

James Baldwin   *1924–*

The first-born of nine children of a preacher father, James Baldwin grew up in Harlem in an atmosphere of revivalistic religion. He himself preached, from the age of fourteen to seventeen, when he left home and worked at many jobs before becoming a writer. At twenty-four he went to Europe and lived there for almost ten years before returning to New York in 1957. His successful first novel, *Go Tell It on the Mountain* (1953), is a story of the lives of members of a Harlem church focused on the events of one day, the fourteenth birthday of its autobiographical hero. His next book, *Giovanni's Room* (1956), is a novel set in Paris and dealing with a conflict between homo- and heterosexual love suffered by its hero. In *Another Country* (1962), the central character is a young Negro jazz musician who, finding his sexual and personal relationships corroded by racial prejudice, commits suicide.

Among Baldwin's nonfictional works are two volumes of essays on the problems of race and on the relation of the Negro artist and intellectual to society: *Notes of a Native Son* (1955) and *Nobody Knows My Name* (1961). In *The Fire Next Time* (1963), Baldwin protests the situation of the Negro by discussing his own youthful experiences and his contacts with Black Muslimism. Plays on the race problem include *The Amen Corner* (1964) and *Blues for Mr. Charley* (1964). In *Going to Meet the Man* (1965), a collection of short stories, "The Rockpile" deals with a crucial event in the lives of the characters of *Go Tell It on the Mountain*—told from the viewpoint of John, the same autobiographical central character.

The text of "The Rockpile" is that of *Going to Meet the Man* (New York, 1965).

The Rockpile

Across the street from their house, in an empty lot between two houses, stood the rockpile. It was a strange place to find a mass of natural rock jutting out of the ground; and someone, probably Aunt Florence, had once told them that the rock was there and could not be taken away because without it the subway cars underground would fly apart, killing all the people. This, touching on some natural mystery concerning the surface and the center of the earth, was far too intriguing an explanation to be challenged, and it invested the rockpile, moreover, with such mysterious importance that Roy felt it to be his right, not to say his duty, to play there.

Other boys were to be seen there each afternoon after school and all day Saturday and Sunday. They fought on the rockpile. Sure footed, dangerous, and reckless, they rushed each other and grappled on the heights, sometimes disappearing down the other side in a confusion of dust and screams and upended, flying feet. "It's a wonder they don't kill themselves," their mother said, watching sometimes from the fire escape. "You children stay away from there, you hear me?" Though she said "children," she was looking at Roy, where he sat beside John on the fire escape. "The good Lord knows," she continued, "I don't want you to come home bleeding like a hog every day the Lord sends." Roy shifted impatiently, and continued to stare at the street, as though in this gazing he might somehow acquire wings. John said nothing. He had not really been spoken to: he was afraid of the rockpile and of the boys who played there.

Each Saturday morning John and Roy sat on the fire escape and watched the forbidden street below. Sometimes their mother sat in the room behind them, sewing, or dressing their younger sister, or nursing the baby, Paul. The sun fell across them and across the fire escape with a high, benevolent indifference; below them, men and women, and boys and girls, sinners all, loitered; sometimes one of the church-members passed and saw them and waved. Then, for the moment that they waved decorously back, they were intimidated. They watched the saint, man or woman, until he or she had disappeared from sight. The passage of one of the redeemed made them consider, however vacantly, the wickedness of the street, their own latent wickedness in sitting where they sat; and made them think of their father, who came home early on Saturdays and who would soon be turning this corner and entering the dark hall below them.

But until he came to end their freedom, they sat, watching and longing above the street. At the end of the street nearest their house was the bridge which spanned the Harlem River and led to a city called the Bronx; which was where Aunt Florence lived. Nevertheless, when they saw her coming, she did not come from the bridge, but from the opposite end of the street. This, weakly, to their minds, she explained by saying that she had taken the subway, not wishing to walk, and that, besides, she did not live in *that* section of the Bronx. Knowing that the Bronx was across the river, they did not believe this story ever, but, adopting toward her their father's attitude, assumed that she had just left some sinful place which she dared not name, as, for example, a movie palace.

In the summertime boys swam in the river, diving off the wooden dock, or wading in from the garbage-heavy bank. Once a boy, whose name was Richard, drowned in the river. His mother had not known where he was; she had even come to their house, to ask if he was there. Then, in the evening, at six o'clock, they had heard from the street a woman screaming and wailing; and they ran to the windows and looked out. Down the street came the woman, Richard's mother, screaming, her face raised to the sky and tears running down her face. A woman walked beside her, trying to make her quiet and trying to hold her up. Behind them walked a man, Richard's father, with Richard's body in his arms. There were two white policemen walking in the gutter, who did not seem to know what should be done. Richard's father and Richard were wet, and Richard's body lay across his father's arms like a cotton baby. The woman's screaming filled all the street; cars slowed down and the people in the cars stared; people opened their windows and looked out and came rushing out of doors to stand in the gutter, watching. Then the small procession disappeared within the house which stood beside the rockpile. Then, *"Lord, Lord, Lord!"* cried Elizabeth, their mother, and slammed the window down.

One Saturday, an hour before his father would be coming home, Roy was wounded on the rockpile and brought screaming upstairs. He and John had been sitting on the fire escape and their mother had gone into the kitchen to sip tea with Sister McCandless. By and by Roy became bored and sat beside John in a restless silence; and John began drawing into his schoolbook a newspaper advertisement which featured a new electric locomotive. Some friends of Roy passed beneath the fire escape and called him. Roy began to fidget, yelling down to them through the bars. Then a silence fell. John looked up. Roy stood looking at him.

"I'm going downstairs," he said.

"You better stay where you is, boy. You know Mama don't want you going downstairs."

"I be right *back*. She won't even know I'm gone, less you run and tell her."

"I ain't *got* to tell her. What's going to stop her from coming in here and looking out the window?"

"She's talking," Roy said. He started into the house.

"But Daddy's going to be home soon!"

"I be back before *that*. What you all the time got to be so *scared* for?" He was already in the house and he now turned, leaning on the windowsill, to swear impatiently, "I be back in *five* minutes."

John watched him sourly as he carefully unlocked the door and disappeared. In a moment he saw him on the sidewalk with his friends. He did not dare to go and tell his mother that Roy had left the fire escape because he had practically promised not to. He started to shout, *Remember, you said five minutes!* but one of Roy's friends was looking up at the fire escape. John looked down at his schoolbook: he became engrossed again in the problem of the locomotive.

When he looked up again he did not know how much time had passed, but now there was a gang fight on the rockpile. Dozens of boys fought each other in the harsh sun: clambering up the rocks and battling hand to hand, scuffed shoes sliding on the slippery rock; filling the bright air with curses and jubilant cries. They filled the air, too, with flying weapons: stones, sticks, tin cans, garbage, whatever could be picked up and thrown. John watched in a kind of absent amazement — until he remembered that Roy was still downstairs, and that he was one of the boys on the rockpile. Then he was afraid; he could not see his brother among the figures in the sun; and he stood up, leaning over the fire-escape railing. Then Roy appeared from the other side of the rocks; John saw that his shirt was torn; he was laughing. He moved until he stood at the very top of the rockpile. Then, something, an empty tin can, flew out of the air and hit him on the forehead, just above the eye. Immediately, one side of Roy's face ran with blood, he fell and rolled on his face down the rocks. Then for a moment there was no movement at all, no sound, the sun, arrested, lay on the street and the sidewalk and the arrested boys. Then someone screamed or shouted; boys began to run away, down the street, toward the bridge. The figure on the ground, having caught its breath and felt its own blood, began to shout. John cried, "Mama! Mama!" and ran inside.

"Don't fret, don't fret," panted Sister McCandless as they rushed down the dark, narrow, swaying stairs, "don't fret. Ain't a boy been born don't get his knocks every now and again. *Lord!*" they hurried into the sun. A man had picked Roy up and now walked slowly toward them. One or two boys sat silent on their stoops; at either end of the street there was a group of boys watching. "He ain't hurt bad," the man said, "Wouldn't be making this kind of noise if he was hurt real bad."

Elizabeth, trembling, reached out to take Roy, but Sister McCandless, bigger, calmer, took him from the man and threw him over her shoulder as she once might have handled a sack of cotton. "God bless you," she said to the man, "God bless you, son." Roy was still screaming. Elizabeth stood behind Sister McCandless to stare at his bloody face.

"It's just a flesh wound," the man kept saying, "just broke the skin, that's all." They were moving across the sidewalk, toward the house. John, not now afraid of the staring boys, looked toward the corner to see if his father was yet in sight.

Upstairs, they hushed Roy's crying. They bathed the blood away, to find, just above the left eyebrow, the jagged, superficial scar. "Lord, have mercy," murmured Elizabeth, "another inch and it would've been his eye." And she looked with apprehension toward the clock. "Ain't it the truth," said Sister McCandless, busy with bandages and iodine.

"When did he go downstairs?" his mother asked at last.

Sister McCandless now sat fanning herself in the easy chair, at the head of the sofa where Roy lay, bound and silent. She paused for a moment to look sharply at John. John stood near the window, holding the newspaper advertisement and the drawing he had done.

"We was sitting on the fire escape," he said. "Some boys he knew called him."

"When?"

"He said he'd be back in five minutes."

"Why didn't you tell me he was downstairs?"

He looked at his hands, clasping his notebook, and did not answer.

"Boy," said Sister McCandless, "you hear your mother a-talking to you?"

He looked at his mother. He repeated:

"He said he'd be back in five minutes."

"He said he'd be back in five minutes," said Sister McCandless with scorn, "don't look to me like that's no right answer. You's the man of the house, you supposed to look after your baby brothers and sisters—you ain't supposed to let them run off and get half-killed. But I expect," she added, rising from the chair, dropping the cardboard fan, "your Daddy'll make you tell the truth. Your Ma's way too soft with you."

He did not look at her, but at the fan where it lay in the dark red, depressed seat where she had been. The fan advertised a pomade for the hair and showed a brown woman and her baby, both with glistening hair, smiling happily at each other.

"Honey," said Sister McCandless, "I got to be moving along. Maybe I drop in later tonight. I don't reckon you going to be at Tarry Service tonight?"

Tarry Service was the prayer meeting held every Saturday night at church to strengthen believers and prepare the church for the coming of the Holy Ghost on Sunday.

"I don't reckon," said Elizabeth. She stood up; she and Sister McCandless kissed each other on the cheek. "But you be sure to remember me in your prayers."

"I surely will do that." She paused, with her hand on the door knob, and looked down at Roy and laughed. "Poor little man," she said, "reckon he'll be content to sit on the fire escape *now*."

Elizabeth laughed with her. "It sure ought to be a lesson to him. You don't reckon," she asked nervously, still smiling, "he going to keep that scar, do you?"

"Lord, no," said Sister McCandless, "ain't nothing but a scratch. I declare, Sister Grimes, you worse than a child. Another couple of weeks and you won't be able to *see* no scar. No, you go on about your housework, honey, and thank the Lord it weren't no worse." She opened the door; they heard the sound of feet on the stairs. "I expect that's the Reverend," said Sister McCandless, placidly, "I *bet* he going to raise cain."

"Maybe it's Florence," Elizabeth said. "Sometimes she get here about this time." They stood in the doorway, staring, while the steps reached the landing below and began again climbing to their floor. "No," said Elizabeth then, "that ain't her walk. That's Gabriel."

"Well, I'll just go on," said Sister McCandless, "and kind of prepare his mind." She pressed Elizabeth's hand as she spoke and started into the hall, leaving the door behind her slightly ajar. Elizabeth turned slowly back into the room. Roy did not open his eyes, or move; but she knew that he was not sleeping; he wished to delay until the last possible moment any contact with his father. John put his newspaper and his notebook on the table and stood, leaning on the table, staring at her.

"It wasn't my fault," he said. "I couldn't stop him from going downstairs."

"No," she said, "you ain't got nothing to worry about. You just tell your Daddy the truth."

He looked directly at her, and she turned to the window, staring into the street. What was Sister McCandless saying? Then from her bedroom she heard Delilah's thin wail and she turned, frowning, looking toward the bedroom and toward the still open door. She knew that John was watching her. Delilah continued to wail, she thought, angrily, *Now that girl's getting too big for that,* but she feared that Delilah would awaken Paul and she hurried into the bedroom. She tried to soothe Delilah back to sleep. Then she heard the front door open and close — too loud, Delilah raised her voice, with an exasperated sigh Elizabeth picked the child up. Her child and Gabriel's, her children and Gabriel's: Roy, Delilah, Paul. Only John was nameless and a stranger, living, unalterable testimony to his mother's days in sin.

"What happened?" Gabriel demanded. He stood, enormous, in the center of the room, his black lunchbox dangling from his hand, staring at the sofa where Roy lay. John stood just before him, it seemed to her astonished vision just below him, beneath his fist, his heavy shoe. The child stared at the man in fascination and terror — when a girl down home she had seen rabbits stand so paralyzed before the barking dog. She hurried past Gabriel to the sofa, feeling the weight of Delilah in her arms like the weight of a shield, and stood over Roy, saying:

"Now, ain't a thing to get upset about, Gabriel. This boy sneaked downstairs while I had my back turned and got hisself hurt a little. He's alright now."

Roy, as though in confirmation, now opened his eyes and looked gravely at his father. Gabriel dropped his lunchbox with a clatter and knelt by the sofa.

"How you feel, son? Tell your Daddy what happened?"

Roy opened his mouth to speak and then, relapsing into panic, began to cry. His father held him by the shoulder.

"You don't want to cry. You's Daddy's little man. Tell your Daddy what happened."

"He went downstairs," said Elizabeth, "where he didn't have no business to be, and got to fighting with them bad boys playing on that rockpile. That's what happened and it's a mercy it weren't nothing worse."

He looked up at her. "Can't you let this boy answer me for hisself?"

Ignoring this, she went on, more gently: "He got cut on the forehead, but it ain't nothing to worry about."

"You call a doctor? How you know it ain't nothing to worry about?"

"Is you got money to be throwing away on doctors? No, I ain't called no doctor. Ain't nothing wrong with my eyes that I can't tell whether he's hurt bad or not. He got a fright more'n anything else, and you ought to pray God it teaches him a lesson."

"You got a lot to say *now*," he said, "but I'll have *me* something to say in a minute. I'll be wanting to know when all this happened, what you was doing with your eyes *then*." He turned back to Roy, who had lain quietly sobbing eyes wide open and body held rigid: and who now, at his father's touch, remembered the height, the sharp sliding rock beneath his feet, the sun, the explosion of the sun, his plunge into darkness and his salty blood; and recoiled, beginning to scream, as his father touched his forehead. "Hold still, hold still," crooned his father, shaking, "hold still. Don't cry. Daddy ain't going to hurt you, he just wants to see this bandage, see what they've done to his little man." But Roy continued to scream and would not be still and Gabriel dared not lift the bandage for fear of hurting him more. And he looked at Elizabeth in fury: "Can't you put that child down and help me with this boy? John, take your baby sister from your mother — don't look like neither of you got good sense."

John took Delilah and sat down with her in the easy chair. His mother bent over Roy, and held him still, while his father, carefully — but still Roy screamed — lifted the bandage and stared at the wound. Roy's sobs began to lessen. Gabriel readjusted the bandage. "You see," said Elizabeth, finally, "he ain't nowhere near dead."

"It sure ain't your fault that he ain't dead." He and Elizabeth considered each other for a moment in silence. "He came mightly close to losing an eye. Course, his eyes ain't as big as your'n, so I reckon you don't think it matters so much." At this her face hardened; he smiled. "Lord, have mercy," he said, "you think you ever going to learn to do right? Where was you when all this happened? Who let him go downstairs?"

"Ain't nobody let him go downstairs, he just went. He got a head just like his father, it got to be broken before it'll bow. I was in the kitchen."

"Where was Johnnie?"

"He was in here."

"Where?"

"He was on the fire escape."

"Didn't he know Roy was downstairs?"

"I reckon."

"What you mean, you reckon? He ain't got your big eyes for nothing, does he?" He looked over at John. "Boy, you see your brother go downstairs?"

"Gabriel, ain't no sense in trying to blame Johnnie. You know right well if you have trouble making Roy behave, he ain't going to listen to his brother. He don't hardly listen to me."

"How come you didn't tell your mother Roy was downstairs?"

John said nothing, staring at the blanket which covered Delilah.

"Boy, you hear me? You want me to take a strap to you?"

"No, you ain't," she said. "You ain't going to take no strap to this boy, not today you ain't. Ain't a soul to blame for Roy's lying up there now but you — you because you done spoiled him so that he thinks he can do just anthing and get away with it. I'm here to tell you that ain't no way to raise no child. You don't pray to the Lord to help you do better than you been doing, you going to live to shed bitter tears that the Lord didn't take his soul today." And she was trembling. She moved, unseeing, toward John and took Delilah from his arms. She looked back at Gabriel, who had risen, who stood near the sofa, staring at her. And she found in his face not fury alone, which would not have surprised her; but hatred so deep as to become insupportable in its lack of personality. His eyes were struck alive, unmoving, blind with malevolence — she felt, like the pull of the earth at her feet, his longing to witness her perdition. Again, as though it might be propitiation, she moved the child in her arms. And at this his eyes changed, he looked at Elizabeth, the mother of his children, the helpmeet given by the Lord. Then her eyes clouded; she moved to leave the room; her foot struck the lunchbox lying on the floor.

"John," she said, "pick up your father's lunchbox like a good boy."

She heard, behind her, his scrambling movement as he left the easy chair, the scrape and jangle of the lunchbox as he picked it up, bending his dark head near the toe of his father's heavy shoe.

1965

Joseph Heller   *1923—*

A New Yorker born and bred, Joseph Heller served in the Army Air Force during World War II. Following the war, he attended New York University (B.A., 1948) and Columbia University (M.A., 1949); he also studied at Oxford University as a Fulbright scholar (1949–50). After a brief period of teaching at Pennsylvania State University (1950–52), he entered magazine work and advertising in New York City. *Catch-22* (1961), a highly successful comic novel, established his reputation as a writer. It tells the story of Yossarian, its bombardier hero, and other members of a Mediterranean-island-based squadron who vainly try to resist their ambitious commander's murderous demands for more and more missions by his men before they can be eligible for rotation home. Heller's portrait of Colonel Cathcart displays his technique of juxtaposing contradictory qualities for the purpose of satirizing the irrationality and inhumanity of war and the military establishment.

Heller has also published a less successful antiwar play, *We Bombed in New Haven* (1968).

The text of "Colonel Cathcart" is that of *Catch-22* (New York, 1961).

Colonel Cathcart [1]

Colonel Cathcart was a slick, successful, slipshod, unhappy man of thirty-six who lumbered when he walked and wanted to be a general. He was dashing and dejected, poised and chagrined. He was complacent and insecure, daring in the administrative stratagems he employed to bring himself to the attention of his superiors and craven in his concern that his schemes might all backfire. He was handsome and

---

[1] This character portrait of an insecure, ambitious group commander is Chapter 19 of *Catch-22* (1961).

unattractive, a swashbuckling, beefy, conceited man who was putting on fat and was tormented chronically by prolonged seizures of apprehension. Colonel Cathcart was conceited because he was a full colonel with a combat command at the age of only thirty-six; and Colonel Cathcart was dejected because although he was already thirty-six he was still only a full colonel.

Colonel Cathcart was impervious to absolutes. He could measure his own progress only in relationship to others, and his idea of excellence was to do something at least as well as all the men his own age who were doing the same thing even better. The fact that there were thousands of men his own age and older who had not even attained the rank of major enlivened him with foppish delight in his own remarkable worth; on the other hand, the fact that there were men of his own age and younger who were already generals contaminated him with an agonizing sense of failure and made him gnaw at his fingernails with an unappeasable anxiety that was even more intense than Hungry Joe's.

Colonel Cathcart was a very large, pouting, broad-shouldered man with close-cropped curly dark hair that was graying at the tips and an ornate cigarette holder that he purchased the day before he arrived in Pianosa to take command of his group. He displayed the cigarette holder grandly on every occasion and had learned to manipulate it adroitly. Unwittingly, he had discovered deep within himself a fertile aptitude for smoking with a cigarette holder. As far as he could tell, his was the only cigarette holder in the whole Mediterranean theater of operations, and the thought was both flattering and disquieting. He had no doubts at all that someone as debonair and intellectual as General Peckem approved of his smoking with a cigarette holder, even though the two were in each other's presence rather seldom, which in a way was very lucky, Colonel Cathcart recognized with relief, since General Peckem might not have approved of his cigarette holder at all. When such misgivings assailed Colonel Cathcart, he choked back a sob and wanted to throw the damned thing away, but he was restrained by his unswerving conviction that the cigarette holder never failed to embellish his masculine, martial physique with a high gloss of sophisticated heroism that illuminated him to dazzling advantage among all the other full colonels in the American Army with whom he was in competition. Although how could he be sure?

Colonel Cathcart was indefatigable that way, an industrious, intense, dedicated military tactician who calculated day and night in the service of himself. He was his own sarcophagus, a bold and infallible diplomat who was always berating himself disgustedly for all the chances he had missed and kicking himself regretfully for all the errors he had made. He was tense, irritable, bitter and smug. He was a valorous opportunist who pounced hoggishly upon every opportunity Colonel Korn discovered for him and trembled in damp despair immediately afterward at the possible consequences he might suffer. He collected rumors greedily and treasured gossip. He believed all the news he heard and had faith in none. He was on the alert constantly for every signal, shrewdly sensitive to relationships and situations that did not exist. He was someone in the know who was always striving pathetically to find out what was going on. He was a blustering, intrepid bully who brooded inconsolably over the terrible ineradicable impressions he knew he kept making on people of prominence who were scarcely aware that he was even alive.

Everybody was persecuting him. Colonel Cathcart lived by his wits in an unstable, arithmetical world of black eyes and feathers in his cap, of overwhelming imaginary triumphs and catastrophic imaginary defeats. He oscillated hourly between anguish and exhilaration, multiplying fantastically the grandeur of his victories and exaggerating tragically the seriousness of his defeats. Nobody ever caught him napping. If word reached him that General Dreedle or General Peckem had been seen smiling, frowning, or doing neither, he could not make himself rest until he had found an acceptable interpretation and grumbled mulishly until Colonel Korn persuaded him to relax and take things easy.

Lieutenant Colonel Korn was a loyal, indispensable ally who got on Colonel Cathcart's nerves. Colonel Cathcart pledged eternal gratitude to Colonel Korn for the ingenious moves he devised and was furious with him afterward when he realized they might not work. Colonel Cathcart was greatly indebted to Colonel Korn and did not like him at all. The two were very close. Colonel Cathcart was jealous of Colonel Korn's intelligence and had to remind himself often that Colonel Korn was still only a lieutenant colonel, even though he was almost ten years older than Colonel Cathcart, and that Colonel Korn had obtained his education at a state university. Colonel Cathcart bewailed the miserable fate that had given him for an invaluable assistant someone as common as Colonel Korn. It was degrading to have to depend so thoroughly on a person who had been educated at a state university. If someone did have to become indispensable to him, Colonel Cathcart lamented, it could just as easily have been someone wealthy and well groomed, someone from a better family who was more mature than Colonel Korn and who did not treat Colonel Cathcart's desire to become a general as frivolously as Colonel Cathcart secretly suspected Colonel Korn secretly did.

Colonel Cathcart wanted to be a general so desperately he was willing to try anything, even religion, and he summoned the chaplain to his office late one morning the week after he had raised the number of missions to sixty[2] and pointed abruptly down toward his desk to his

---

[2] The number of bombing missions required (demoralizingly unreasonable in this case) before an airman would be eligible for rotation back to the States.

copy of *The Saturday Evening Post*. The colonel wore his khaki shirt collar wide open, exposing a shadow of tough black bristles of beard on his egg-white neck, and had a spongy hanging underlip. He was a person who never tanned, and he kept out of the sun as much as possible to avoid burning. The colonel was more than a head taller than the chaplain and over twice as broad, and his swollen, overbearing authority made the chaplain feel frail and sickly by contrast.

"Take a look, Chaplain," Colonel Cathcart directed, screwing a cigarette into his holder and seating himself affluently in the swivel chair behind his desk. "Let me know what you think."

The chaplain looked down at the open magazine compliantly and saw an editorial spread dealing with an American bomber group in England whose chaplain said prayers in the briefing room before each mission. The chaplain almost wept with happiness when he realized the colonel was not going to holler at him. The two had hardly spoken since the tumultuous evening Colonel Cathcart had thrown him out of the officers' club at General Dreedle's bidding after Chief White Halfoat had punched Colonel Moodus in the nose. The chaplain's initial fear had been that the colonel intended reprimanding him for having gone back into the officers' club without permission the evening before. He had gone there with Yossarian[3] and Dunbar after the two had come unexpectedly to his tent in the clearing in the woods to ask him to join them. Intimidated as he was by Colonel Cathcart, he nevertheless found it easier to brave his displeasure than to decline the thoughtful invitation of his two new friends, whom he had met on one of his hospital visits just a few weeks before and who had worked so effectively to insulate him against the myriad social vicissitudes involved in his official duty to live on closest terms of familiarity with more than nine hundred unfamiliar officers and enlisted men who thought him an odd duck.

The chaplain glued his eyes to the pages of the magazine. He studied each photograph twice and read the captions intently as he organized his response to the colonel's question into a grammatically complete sentence that he rehearsed and reorganized in his mind a considerable number of times before he was able finally to muster the courage to reply.

"I think that saying prayers before each mission is a very moral and highly laudatory procedure, sir," he offered timidly, and waited.

"Yeah," said the colonel. "But I want to know if you think they'll work here."

"Yes, sir," answered the chaplain after a few moments. "I should think they would."

"Then I'd like to give it a try." The colonel's ponderous, farina-

---

[3] The central character of the novel.

ceous cheeks were tinted suddenly with glowing patches of enthusiasm. He rose to his feet and began walking around excitedly. "Look how much good they've done for these people in England. Here's a picture of a colonel in *The Saturday Evening Post* whose chaplain conducts prayers before each mission. If the prayers work for him, they should work for us. Maybe if we say prayers, they'll put *my* picture in *The Saturday Evening Post*."

The colonel sat down again and smiled distantly in lavish contemplation. The chaplain had no hint of what he was expected to say next. With a pensive expression on his oblong, rather pale face, he allowed his gaze to settle on several of the high bushels filled with red plum tomatoes that stood in rows against each of the walls. He pretended to concentrate on a reply. After a while he realized that he *was* staring at rows and rows of bushels of red plum tomatoes and grew so intrigued by the question of what bushels brimming with red plum tomatoes were doing in a group commander's office that he forgot completely about the discussion of prayer meetings until Colonel Cathcart, in a genial digression, inquired:

"Would you like to buy some, Chaplain? They come right off the farm Colonel Korn and I have up in the hills. I can let you have a bushel wholesale."

"Oh, no, sir. I don't think so."

"That's quite all right," the colonel assured him liberally. "You don't have to. Milo is glad to snap up all we can produce. These were picked only yesterday. Notice how firm and ripe they are, like a young girl's breasts."

The chaplain blushed, and the colonel understood at once that he had made a mistake. He lowered his head in shame, his cumbersome face burning. His fingers felt gross and unwieldy. He hated the chaplain venomously for being a chaplain and making a coarse blunder out of an observation that in any other circumstances, he knew, would have been considered witty and urbane. He tried miserably to recall some means of extricating them both from their devastating embarrassment. He recalled instead that the chaplain was only a captain, and he straightened at once with a shocked and outraged gasp. His cheeks grew tight with fury at the thought that he had just been duped into humiliation by a man who was almost the same age as he was and still only a captain, and he swung upon the chaplain avengingly with a look of such murderous antagonism that the chaplain began to tremble. The colonel punished him sadistically with a long, glowering, malignant, hateful, silent stare.

"We were speaking about something else," he reminded the chaplain cuttingly at last. "We were not speaking about the firm, ripe breasts of beautiful young girls but about something else entirely. We were speaking about conducting religious services in the briefing room before each mission. Is there any reason why we can't?"

"No, sir," the chaplain mumbled.

"Then we'll begin with this afternoon's mission." The colonel's hostility softened gradually as he applied himself to details. "Now, I want you to give a lot of thought to the kind of prayers we're going to say. I don't want anything heavy or sad. I'd like you to keep it light and snappy, something that will send the boys out feeling pretty good. Do you know what I mean? I don't want any of this Kingdom of God or Valley of Death stuff. That's all too negative. What are you making such a sour face for?"

"I'm sorry, sir," the chaplain stammered. "I happened to be thinking of the Twenty-third Psalm just as you said that."

"How does that one go?"

"That's the one you were just referring to, sir. 'The Lord is my shepherd; I—'"

"*That's* the one I was just referring to. It's out. What else have you got?"

"'Save me, O God; for the waters are come in unto—'"

"No waters," the colonel decided, blowing ruggedly into his cigarette holder after flipping the butt down into his combed-brass ash tray. "Why don't we try something musical? How about the harps on the willows?"

"That has the rivers of Babylon in it, sir," the chaplain replied. "'. . . there we sat down, yea, we wept, when we remembered Zion.'"

"Zion? Let's forget about *that* one right now. I'd like to know how that one even got in there. Haven't you got anything humorous that stays away from waters and valleys and God? I'd like to keep away from the subject of religion altogether if we can."

The chaplain was apologetic. "I'm sorry, sir, but just about all the prayers I know *are* rather somber in tone and make at least some passing reference to God."

"Then let's get some new ones. The men are already doing enough bitching about the missions I send them on without our rubbing it in with any sermons about God or death or Paradise. Why can't we take a more positive approach? Why can't we all pray for something good, like a tighter bomb pattern, for example? Couldn't we pray for a tighter bomb pattern?"

"Well, yes, sir, I suppose so," the chaplain answered hesitantly. "You wouldn't even need me if that's all you wanted to do. You could do that yourself."

"I know I could," the colonel responded tartly. "But what do you think you're here for? I could shop for my own food, too, but that's

Milo's job, and that's why he's doing it for every group in the area. Your job is to lead us in prayer, and from now on you're going to lead us in a prayer for a tighter bomb pattern before every mission. Is that clear? I think a tighter bomb pattern is something really worth praying for. It will be a feather in all our caps with General Peckem. General Peckem feels it makes a much nicer aerial photograph when the bombs explode close together."

"General Peckem, sir?"

"That's right, Chaplain," the colonel replied, chuckling paternally at the chaplain's look of puzzlement. "I wouldn't want this to get around, but it looks like General Dreedle is finally on the way out and that General Peckem is slated to replace him. Frankly, I'm not going to be sorry to see that happen. General Peckem is a very good man, and I think we'll all be much better off under him. On the other hand, it might never take place, and we'd still remain under General Dreedle. Frankly, I wouldn't be sorry to see that happen either, because General Dreedle is another very good man, and I think we'll all be much better off under him too. I hope you're going to keep all this under your hat, Chaplain. I wouldn't want either one to get the idea I was throwing my support on the side of the other."

"Yes, sir."

"That's good," the colonel exclaimed, and stood up jovially. "But all this gossip isn't getting us into *The Saturday Evening Post*, eh, Chaplain? Let's see what kind of procedure we can evolve. Incidentally, Chaplain, not a word about this beforehand to Colonel Korn. Understand?"

"Yes, sir."

Colonel Cathcart began tramping back and forth reflectively in the narrow corridors left between his bushels of plum tomatoes and the desk and wooden chairs in the center of the room. "I suppose we'll have to keep you waiting outside until the briefing is over, because all that information is classified. We can slip you in while Major Danby is synchronizing the watches. I don't think there's anything secret about the right time. We'll allocate about a minute and a half for you in the schedule. Will a minute and a half be enough?"

"Yes, sir. If it doesn't include the time necessary to excuse the atheists from the room and admit the enlisted men."

Colonel Cathcart stopped in his tracks. "What atheists?" he bellowed defensively, his whole manner changing in a flash to one of virtuous and belligerent denial. "There are no atheists in my outfit! Atheism is against the law, isn't it?"

"No, sir."

"It isn't?" The colonel was surprised. "Then it's unAmerican, isn't it?"

"I'm not sure, sir," answered the chaplain.

"Well, I am!" the colonel declared. "I'm not going to disrupt our religious services just to accommodate a bunch of lousy atheists. They're getting no special privileges from me. They can stay right where they are and pray with the rest of us. And what's all this about enlisted men? Just how the hell do they get into this act?"

The chaplain felt his face flush. "I'm sorry, sir. I just assumed you would want the enlisted men to be present, since they would be going along on the same mission."

"Well, I don't. They've got a God and a chaplain of their own, haven't they?"

"No, sir."

"What are you talking about? You mean they pray to the same God we do?"

"Yes, sir."

"And He *listens?*"

"I think so, sir."

"Well, I'll be damned," remarked the colonel, and he snorted to himself in quizzical amusement. His spirits drooped suddenly a moment later, and he ran his hand nervously over his short, black, graying curls. "Do you really think it's a good idea to let the enlisted men in?" he asked with concern.

"I should think it only proper, sir."

"I'd like to keep them out," confided the colonel, and began cracking his knuckles savagely as he wandered back and forth. "Oh, don't get me wrong, Chaplain. It isn't that I think the enlisted men are dirty, common and inferior. It's that we just don't have enough room. Frankly, though, I'd just as soon the officers and enlisted men didn't fraternize in the briefing room. They see enough of each other during the mission, it seems to me. Some of my very best friends are enlisted men, you understand, but that's about as close as I care to let them come. Honestly now, Chaplain, you wouldn't want your sister to marry an enlisted man, would you?"

"My sister is an enlisted man, sir," the chaplain replied.

The colonel stopped in his tracks again and eyed the chaplain sharply to make certain he was not being ridiculed. "Just what do you mean by that remark, Chaplain? Are you trying to be funny?"

"Oh, no, sir," the chaplain hastened to explain with a look of excruciating discomfort. "She's a master sergeant in the Marines."

The colonel had never liked the chaplain and now he loathed and distrusted him. He experienced a deep premonition of danger and wondered if the chaplain too were plotting against him, if the chaplain's reticent, unimpressive manner were really just a sinister disguise masking a fiery ambition that, 'way down deep, was crafty and unscrupulous. There was something funny about the chaplain, and the colonel soon detected what it was. The chaplain was standing stiffly at attention, for the colonel had forgotten to put him at ease. Let him stay that way, the colonel decided vindictively, just to show him who was boss and to safeguard himself against any loss of dignity that might devolve from his acknowledging the omission.

Colonel Cathcart was drawn hypnotically toward the window with a massive, dull stare of moody introspection. The enlisted men were always treacherous, he decided. He looked downward in mournful gloom at the skeet-shooting range he had ordered built for the officers on his headquarters staff, and he recalled the mortifying afternoon General Dreedle had tongue-lashed him ruthlessly in front of Colonel Korn and Major Danby and ordered him to throw open the range to all the enlisted men and officers on combat duty. The skeet-shooting range had been a real black eye for him, Colonel Cathcart was forced to conclude. He was positive that General Dreedle had never forgotten it, even though he was positive that General Dreedle didn't even remember it, which was really very unjust, Colonel Cathcart lamented, since the idea of a skeet-shooting range itself should have been a real feather in his cap, even though it had been such a real black eye. Colonel Cathcart was helpless to assess exactly how much ground he had gained or lost with his goddam skeet-shooting range and wished that Colonel Korn were in his office right then to evaluate the entire episode for him still one more time and assuage his fears.

It was all very perplexing, all very discouraging. Colonel Cathcart took the cigarette holder out of his mouth, stood it on end inside the pocket of his shirt, and began gnawing on the fingernails of both hands grievously. Everybody was against him, and he was sick to his soul that Colonel Korn was not with him in this moment of crisis to help him decide what to do about the prayer meetings. He had almost no faith at all in the chaplain, who was still only a captain. "Do you think," he asked, "that keeping the enlisted men out might interfere with our chances of getting results?"

The chaplain hesitated, feeling himself on unfamiliar ground again. "Yes, sir," he replied finally. "I think it's conceivable that such an action could interfere with your chances of having the prayers for a tighter bomb pattern answered."

"I wasn't even thinking about that!" cried the colonel, with his eyes blinking and splashing like puddles. "You mean that God might even decide to punish me by giving us a *looser* bomb pattern?"

"Yes, sir," said the chaplain. "It's conceivable He might."

"The hell with it, then," the colonel asserted in a huff of independence. "I'm not going to set these damned prayer meetings up just to make things *worse* than they are." With a scornful snicker, he settled himself behind his desk, replaced the empty cigarette holder in his mouth and lapsed into parturient silence for a few moments. "Now that

I think about it," he confessed, as much to himself as to the chaplain, "having the men pray to God probably wasn't such a hot idea anyway. The editors of *The Saturday Evening Post* might not have co-operated."

The colonel abandoned his project with remorse, for he had conceived it entirely on his own and had hoped to unveil it as a striking demonstration to everyone that he had no real need for Colonel Korn. Once it was gone, he was glad to be rid of it, for he had been troubled from the start by the danger of instituting the plan without first checking it out with Colonel Korn. He heaved an immense sigh of contentment. He had a much higher opinion of himself now that his idea was abandoned, for he had made a very wise decision, he felt, and, most important, he had made this wise decision without consulting Colonel Korn.

"Will that be all, sir?" asked the chaplain.

"Yeah," said Colonel Cathcart. "Unless you've got something else to suggest."

"No, sir. Only . . ."

The colonel lifted his eyes as though affronted and studied the chaplain with aloof distrust. "Only what, Chaplain?"

"Sir," said the chaplain, "some of the men are very upset since you raised the number of missions to sixty. They've asked me to speak to you about it."

The colonel was silent. The chaplain's face reddened to the roots of his sandy hair as he waited. The colonel kept him squirming a long time with a fixed, uninterested look devoid of all emotion.

"Tell them there's a war going on," he advised finally in a flat voice.

"Thank you, sir, I will," the chaplain replied in a flood of gratitude because the colonel had finally said something. "They were wondering why you couldn't requisition some of the replacement crews that are waiting in Africa to take their places and then let them go home."

"That's an administrative matter," the colonel said. "It's none of their business." He pointed languidly toward the wall. "Help yourself to a plum tomato, Chaplain. Go ahead, it's on me."

"Thank you, sir. Sir—"

"Don't mention it. How do you like living out there in the woods, Chaplain? Is everything hunky dory?"

"Yes, sir."

"That's good. You get in touch with us if you need anything."

"Yes, sir. Thank you, sir. Sir—"

"Thanks for dropping around, Chaplain. I've got some work to do now. You'll let me know if you can think of anything for getting our names into *The Saturday Evening Post*, won't you?"

"Yes, sir, I will." The chaplain braced himself with a prodigious effort of the will and plunged ahead brazenly. "I'm particularly concerned about the condition of one of the bombardiers, sir. Yossarian."

The colonel glanced up quickly with a start of vague recognition. "Who?" he asked in alarm.

"Yossarian, sir."

"Yossarian?"

"Yes, sir. Yossarian. He's in a very bad way, sir. I'm afraid he won't be able to suffer much longer without doing something desperate."

"Is that a fact, Chaplain?"

"Yes, sir. I'm afraid it is."

The colonel thought about it in heavy silence for a few moments. "Tell him to trust in God," he advised finally.

"Thank you, sir," said the chaplain. "I will."

1961

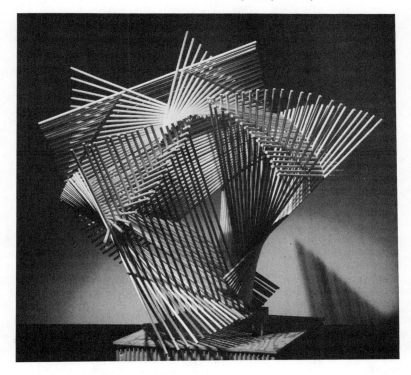

Contemporary Poetry

In the poetry written since the Second World War it is evident, even more than in prose fiction, that the modern period has ended and another, not as yet clearly defined, has begun. It is definitely post-modern in several respects. One indication is the general rejection by postwar poets born in the 1920's and 1930's of the precepts and example of T. S. Eliot, the reigning arbiter of poetic taste during the years between the wars. These younger poets, who have sometimes been called the "third generation," disapprove of Eliot on both social and aesthetic grounds. Besides disliking his social and political conservatism as a defender of the Establishment, most of them disagree with his "classicist" stress upon impersonality and objectivity in poetry.

Their break from the older generation of moderns is not complete. Rejecting Eliot, they have turned to Ezra Pound and William Carlos Williams as representatives of freer and more radical social and aesthetic views. Unlike the more conventional poets of the middle generation, they have responded to the revolutionary spirit of Pound and his early associates and attempted to carry further their theories of organic free verse form.

Dowel Stick Construction by Douglas F. Cowan, '64, Phillips Academy, Andover.

Many have gone beyond the moderns in their social rebellion and in their belief, conditioned by postwar Existentialism, that the poet must be personally committed and "engaged" in his work. Most typically they speak in their own persons rather than indirectly through the medium of a dramatic persona. They have condemned conventional society more sweepingly than their modernist elders who, despite their protests against bourgeois conventions, were more interested in renewing and restoring the established order than in reforming it radically. (Pound is a significant exception.)

The most violent early postwar reaction was expressed by the writers of the Beat movement that flourished in San Francisco, New York, and other urban centers in the 1950's. Completely alienating themselves from middle-class American society, they advocated a withdrawal from reality into an inner world of drug-induced visions, a withdrawal that rendered them politically and socially neuter.

The Beat movement was displaced and superseded by the civil rights movement of the 1960's, which demanded an activist and politically engaged position for the writer, equally remote from the regressive withdrawal of the Beats and the disillusioned alienation of the moderns. Although the rights movement has been beset by many difficulties and problems, it has continued to assume the responsibility and efficacy of political involvement on the part of the writer.

Quite apart from this general shift in social attitudes, most of the younger poets have endorsed the principle of organic form. Stimulated by Charles Olson's essay "Projective Verse,"[1] which stressed the idea of breath-spaced lines, and by William Carlos Williams' remarks on the "variable foot," they have experimented freely in their efforts to achieve more open poetic forms determined by the dynamics of their subjects and their perceptions. In pursuing this end, many of the poets have written verse of considerable distinction. So strong has this trend been in the years since the war that even some of the older middle generation poets have shifted to more experimental forms.

Another contemporary tendency is the effort to renew the language of poetry by freeing it from established symbolic conventions and using non-symbolic imagery in fresh and unexpected ways. In some instances poets have attempted to eliminate referential meaning and to concentrate on other more abstract aspects of form.

Along with these innovations there has been a continuation of the tradition of Whitman. As in every generation of twentieth century poets, a number have supported Whitman's bardic idea of the poet as the voice and conscience of America.

Although in verse as in prose fiction the stirrings of a new era have not as yet produced poets to rival the major figures of the modern period, the continuing process of innovation and change shows a vitality that should sustain and carry forward the great tradition of American literature.

[1] First published in *Poetry New York* (1950) and reprinted in D. M. Allen, ed., *The New American Poetry* (New York, 1960), pp. 386–397.

Denise Levertov   *1923 –*

Outstanding among postwar American poets is Denise Levertov, who was born in England of Welsh and Russian Jewish stock. Privately educated, she worked as a hospital aid and civilian nurse in London during the war. Her first book of poems, *The Double Image*, was published in London in 1946. The next year she married the American writer Mitchell Goodman. When they came to New York to live in 1948, she found the move to America a stimulating experience that "necessitated the finding of new rhythms in which to write, in accordance with new rhythms of life and speech." In this effort she was helped by the example of William Carlos Williams, whose stylistic influence she has acknowledged as indispensable to her development from a "British romantic with almost Victorian background to an American poet of any vitality." As an American poet, her first book of poems, *Here and Now*, was published in San Francisco in 1956.

Miss Levertov has a lyric élan, an economy and distinction in diction and phrasing, and the essential capacity for finding the metrical form most appropriate to her subject. Unlike most transplanted English writers, she has absorbed the rhythms of American life and speech, and she has succeeded in developing a fully realized style of her own. As a modern poet, Miss Levertov is committed to the theory of organic form advocated by Emerson in the nineteenth century and the Imagists in the twentieth. She has described the metrical movement or the "measure" of the poem as "the direct expression of the movement of perception rather than, as in other approaches, the mold into which experience is cast."

Miss Levertov's other books include *Overland to the Islands* (1958), *With Eyes at the Back of Our Heads* (1959), *The Jacob's Ladder* (1962), *O Taste and See* (1964), and *The Sorrow Dance* (1967).

A biography and critique is L. W. Wagner, *Denise Levertov* (New York, 1967), which contains a bibliography.

The text of the first three poems given here is that of *The Jacob's Ladder* (New York, 1961). "September 1961" and "O Taste and See" are from *O Taste and See* (New York, 1964).

Illustrious Ancestors[1]

The Rav
of Northern White Russia declined,
in his youth, to learn
the language of birds, because
the extraneous did not interest him; nevertheless
when he grew old it was found
he understood them anyway, having
listened well, and as it is said, 'prayed
            with the bench and the floor.' He used
what was at hand—as did   10
Angel Jones of Mold, whose meditations
were sewn into coats and britches.
            Well, I would like to make,
thinking some line still taut between me and them,
poems direct as what the birds said,
hard as a floor, sound as a bench,
mysterious as the silence when the tailor
would pause with his needle in the air.

                                                    1958

Come into Animal Presence

Come into animal presence.
No man is so guileless as
the serpent. The lonely white
rabbit on the roof is a star
twitching its ears at the rain.
The llama intricately
folding its hind legs to be seated
not disdains but mildly
disregards human approval.
What joy when the insouciant   10
armadillo glances at us and doesn't
quicken his trotting
across the track into the palm brush.

What is this joy? That no animal
falters, but knows what it must do?
That the snake has no blemish,
that the rabbit inspects his strange surroundings
in white star-silence? The llama
rests in dignity, the armadillo

---

[1] The Rav, or Russian Jewish religious leader, and Angel Jones, the Welsh Christian mystic, were the truly illustrious ancestors of Miss Levertov.

has some intention to pursue in the palm-forest.   20
Those who were sacred have remained so,
holiness does not dissolve, it is a presence
of bronze, only the sight that saw it
faltered and turned from it.
An old joy returns in holy presence.

1961

Matins

1

The authentic! Shadows of it
sweep past in dreams, one could say imprecisely,
evoking the almost-silent
ripping apart of giant
sheets of cellophane. No.
It thrusts up close. Exactly in dreams
it has you off-guard, you
recognize it before you have time.
For a second before waking
the alarm bell is a red conical hat, it   10
takes form.

2

The authentic! I said
rising from the toilet seat.
The radiator in rhythmic knockings
spoke of the rising steam.
The authentic, I said
breaking the handle of my hairbrush as I
brushed my hair in
rhythmic strokes: That's it,
that's joy, it's always   20
a recognition, the known
appearing fully itself, and
more itself than one knew.

3

The new day rises
as heat rises,
knocking in the pipes
with rhythms it seizes for its own
to speak of its invention —
the real, the new-laid
egg whose speckled shell   30
the poet fondles and must break
if he will be nourished.

4

A shadow painted where
yes, a shadow must fall.
The cow's breath
not forgotten in the mist, in the
words. Yes,
verisimilitude draws up
heat in us, zest
to follow through,   40
follow through,
follow
transformations of day
in its turning, in its becoming.

5

Stir the holy grains, set
the bowls on the table and
call the child to eat.

While we eat we think,
as we think an undercurrent
of dream runs through us   50
faster than thought
towards recognition.

Call the child to eat,
send him off, his mouth
tasting of toothpaste, to go down
into the ground, into a roaring train
and to school.

His cheeks are pink
his black eyes hold his dreams, he has left
forgetting his glasses.   60

Follow down the stairs at a clatter
to give them to him and save
his clear sight.

Cold air
comes in at the street door.

6

The authentic! It rolls
just out of reach, beyond
running feet and

stretching fingers, down
the green slope and into
the black waves of the sea.
Speak to me, little horse, beloved,
tell me
how to follow the iron ball,
how to follow through to the country
beneath the waves
to the place where I must kill you and you step out
of your bones and flystrewn meat
tall, smiling, renewed,
formed in your own likeness.

70

80

7

Marvelous Truth, confront us
at every turn,
in every guise, iron ball,
egg, dark horse, shadow,
cloud
of breath on the air,

dwell
in our crowded hearts
our steaming bathrooms, kitchens full of
things to be done, the
ordinary streets.

90

Thrust close your smile
that we know you, terrible joy.

1961

September 1961

This is the year the old ones,
the old great ones
leave us alone on the road.

The road leads to the sea.
We have the words in our pockets,
obscure directions. The old ones

have taken away the light of their presence,
we see it moving away over a hill
off to one side.

They are not dying,
they are withdrawn

10

into a painful privacy

learning to live without words.
E.P. "It looks like dying" — Williams: "I can't
describe to you what has been

happening to me" —
H.D. "unable to speak."[1]
The darkness

twists itself in the wind, the stars
are small, the horizon   20
ringed with confused urban light-haze.

They have told us
the road leads to the sea,
and given

the language into our hands.
We hear
our footsteps each time a truck

has dazzled past us and gone
leaving us new silence.
One can't reach   30

the sea on this endless
road to the sea unless
one turns aside at the end, it seems,

follows
the owl that silently glides above it
aslant, back and forth,

and away into deep woods.

But for us the road
unfurls itself, we count the
words in our pockets, we wonder   40

how it will be without them, we don't
stop walking, we know
there is far to go, sometimes

we think the night wind carries
a smell of the sea . . .

1964

---

[1] The specific comments of the older poets on the approach of death are by Ezra Pound
(1885–1972), William Carlos Williams (1883–1961), and Hilda Doolittle (1886–1961).

O Taste and See

The world is
not with us enough.[1]
O taste and see

the subway Bible poster said,
meaning **The Lord,** meaning
if anything all that lives
to the imagination's tongue,

grief, mercy, language,
tangerine, weather, to
breathe them, bite,
savor, chew, swallow, transform

into our flesh our
deaths, crossing the street, plum, quince,
living in the orchard and being

hungry, and plucking
the fruit.

1964

---

[1] A dissenting variation of Wordsworth's famous sonnet, "The World Is Too Much with Us."

Allen Ginsberg   1926—

Allen Ginsberg, a leader of the postwar "Beat" movement, was born in Paterson, New Jersey, the son of Louis Ginsberg, a poet and teacher. Before completing his studies at Columbia College in 1948, Ginsberg had served in the Merchant Marine and worked at many jobs including dishwashing, welding, and book reviewing. As a member of the Beat group that included Gregory Corso, Lawrence Ferlinghetti, and Jack Kerouac, he combined the writing of visionary poetry with a quest for spiritual illumination in which homosexual experience, hallucinatory drugs, and the prescriptions of Zen Buddhism were valued as inducements. When his first book, *Howl and Other Poems* (1956), appeared, its publisher was tried and acquitted on the charge of issuing obscenity. Because Ginsberg is entirely without inhibitions in his use of language, his poems have a considerable initial impact upon readers or listeners. Time will decide the question of the durability of his work as poetry.

Of the two earlier American poets Ginsberg most admires—William Carlos Williams and Walt Whitman—he is much closer to Whitman in his mystical and sexual inclinations and in his form. Like Whitman's, his rhapsodic (often "frantic") verse is cast in long, grammatically parallel lines that make up huge sentences. But unlike the "barbaric yawp" that Whitman sounded in "Song of Myself" as a hymn of faith, Ginsberg's "Howl" is an expression of outrage at the indignities of life in modern America. Yet for Ginsberg, as for Whitman, there is a belief in a "beatified" life to be attained through mystical experience. For Whitman the vision was that of the Romantic nature mystic. For Ginsberg, as the "*eli, eli*" quoted at the end of the first part of *Howl* suggests, the sought-for vision may be understood as an unorthodox replacement for a traditional faith from which the poet has been alienated. In recent years Ginsberg has spent much of his time traveling and speaking as a prophet and defender of the faith he has assumed. His other books are *Kaddish and Other Poems* (1960), *Empty Mirror* (1960), and *Reality*

Sandwiches (1963). *Yage Letters* (1963) is a collection of Ginsberg's correspondence with William Burroughs.

The text of the selections given here is that of *Howl and Other Poems*
(San Francisco, 1956).

From *Howl*

FOR CARL SOLOMON

Part I

I saw the best minds of my generation destroyed by madness,
    starving hysterical naked,
dragging themselves through the negro streets at dawn looking for
    an angry fix,
angelheaded hipsters burning for the ancient heavenly connection
    to the starry dynamo in the machinery of night,
who poverty and tatters and hollow-eyed and high sat up smoking
    in the supernatural darkness of cold-water flats floating
    across the tops of cities contemplating jazz,
who bared their brains to Heaven under the El and saw Moham-
    medan angels staggering on tenement roofs illuminated,
who passed through universities with radiant cool eyes halluci-
    nating Arkansas and Blake-light tragedy among the scholars
    of war.
who were expelled from the academies for crazy & publishing
    obscene odes on the windows of the skull,
who cowered in unshaven rooms in underwear, burning their
    money in wastebaskets and listening to the Terror through
    the wall,
who got busted in their pubic beards returning through Laredo
    with a belt of marijuana for New York,
who ate fire in paint hotels or drank turpentine in Paradise Alley,
    death, or purgatoried their torsos night after night
with dreams, with drugs, with waking nightmares, alcohol and
    cock and endless balls,
incomparable blind streets of shuddering cloud and lightning in
    the mind leaping toward poles of Canada & Paterson, illu-
    minating all the motionless world of Time between,
Peyote solidities of halls, backyard green tree cemetery dawns,
    wine drunkenness over the rooftops, storefront boroughs of
    teahead joyride neon blinking traffic light, sun and moon
    and tree vibrations in the roaring winter dusks of Brooklyn,
    ashcan rantings and kind king light of mind,
who chained themselves to subways for the endless ride from
    Battery to holy Bronx on benzedrine until the noise of
    wheels and children brought them down shuddering mouth-
    wracked and battered bleak of brain all drained of bril-
    liance in the drear light of Zoo,
who sank all night in submarine light of Bickford's floated out and

sat through the stale beer afternoon in desolate Fugazzi's
listening to the crack of doom on the hydrogen jukebox,
who talked continuously seventy hours from park to pad to bar to
Bellevue to museum to the Brooklyn Bridge,
a lost battalion of platonic conversationalists jumping down the
stoops off fire escapes off windowsills off Empire State out
of the moon,
yacketayakking screaming vomiting whispering facts and memories and anecdotes and eyeball kicks and shocks of hospitals and jails and wars,
whole intellects disgorged in total recall for seven days and nights
with brilliant eyes, meat for the Synagogue cast on the
pavement,
who vanished into nowhere Zen New Jersey leaving a trail of
ambiguous picture postcards of Atlantic City Hall,
suffering Eastern sweats and Tangerian bone-grindings and mi-
graines of China under junk-withdrawal in Newark's bleak
furnished room,
who wandered around and around at midnight in the railroad yard
wondering where to go, and went, leaving no broken hearts,
who lit cigarettes in boxcars boxcars boxcars racketing through
snow toward lonesome farms in grandfather night,
who studied Plotinus Poe St. John of the Cross telepathy and bop
kaballa because the cosmos instinctively vibrated at their
feet in Kansas,
who loned it through the streets of Idaho seeking visionary indian
angels who were visionary indian angels,
who thought they were only mad when Baltimore gleamed in
supernatural ecstasy,
who jumped in limousines with the Chinaman of Oklahoma on
the impulse of winter midnight streetlight smalltown rain,
who lounged hungry and lonesome through Houston seeking jazz
or sex or soup, and followed the brilliant Spaniard to con-
verse about America and Eternity, a hopeless task, and so
took ship to Africa,
who disappeared into the volcanoes of Mexico leaving behind
nothing but the shadow of dungarees and the lava and ash
of poetry scattered in fireplace Chicago,
who reappeared on the West Coast investigating the F.B.I. in
beards and shorts with big pacifist eyes sexy in their dark
skin passing out incomprehensible leaflets,
who burned cigarette holes in their arms protesting the narcotic
tobacco haze of Capitalism,
who distributed Supercommunist pamphlets in Union Square
weeping and undressing while the sirens of Los Alamos
wailed them down, and wailed down Wall, and the Staten
Island ferry also wailed,
who broke down crying in white gymnasiums naked and trembling before the machinery of other skeletons,
who bit detectives in the neck and shrieked with delight in po-

licecars for committing no crime but their own wild cooking
pederasty and intoxication,

who howled on their knees in the subway and were dragged off
the roof waving genitals and manuscripts,

who let themselves be fucked in the ass by saintly motorcyclists,
and screamed with joy,

who blew and were blown by those human seraphim, the sailors,
caresses of Atlantic and Caribbean love,

who balled in the morning in the evenings in rosegardens and the
grass of public parks and cemeteries scattering their semen
freely to whomever come who may,

who hiccupped endlessly trying to giggle but wound up with a
sob behind a partition in a Turkish Bath when the blonde &
naked angel came to pierce them with a sword,

who lost their loveboys to the three old shrews of fate the one
eyed shrew of the heterosexual dollar the one eyed shrew
that winks out of the womb and the one eyed shrew that
does nothing but sit on her ass and snip the intellectual
golden threads of the craftsman's loom,

who copulated ecstatic and insatiate with a bottle of beer a
sweetheart a package of cigarettes a candle and fell off the
bed, and continued along the floor and down the hall and
ended fainting on the wall with a vision of ultimate cunt and
come eluding the last gyzym of consciousness.

who sweetened the snatches of a million girls trembling in the
sunset, and were red eyed in the morning but prepared to
sweeten the snatch of the sunrise, flashing buttocks under
barns and naked in the lake,

who went out whoring through Colorado in myriad stolen night-
cars, N.C., secret hero of these poems, cocksman and
Adonis of Denver—joy to the memory of his innumerable
lays of girls in empty lots & diner backyards, moviehouses,
rickety rows on mountaintops in caves or with gaunt waitresses in familiar roadside lonely petticoat upliftings &
especially secret gas-station solipsisms of johns, & home-
town alleys too,

who faded out in vast sordid movies, were shifted in dreams,
woke on a sudden Manhattan, and picked themselves up
out of basements hungover with heartless Tokay and horrors of Third Avenue iron dreams & stumbled to unemployment offices,

who walked all night with their shoes full of blood on the snow-
bank docks waiting for a door in the East River to open to a
room full of steamheat and opium,

who created great suicidal dramas on the apartment cliff-banks of
the Hudson under the wartime blue floodlight of the moon
& their heads shall be crowned with laurel in oblivion,

who ate the lamb stew of the imagination or digested the crab at
the muddy bottom of the rivers of Bowery,

who wept at the romance of the streets with their pushcarts full of onions and bad music,

who sat in boxes breathing in the darkness under the bridge, and
rose up to build harpsichords in their lofts,

who coughed on the sixth floor of Harlem crowned with flame
under the tubercular sky surrounded by orange crates of
theology,

who scribbled all night rocking and rolling over lofty incantations
which in the yellow morning were stanzas of gibberish,

who cooked rotten animals lung heart feet borsht & tortillas
dreaming of the pure vegetable kingdom,

who plunged themselves under meat trucks looking for an egg,

who threw their watches off the roof to cast their ballot for Eternity outside of Time, & alarm clocks fell on their heads
every day for the next decade,

who cut their wrists three times successively unsuccessfully, gave
up and were forced to open antique stores where they
thought they were growing old and cried,

who were burned alive in their innocent flannel suits on Madison
Avenue amid blasts of leaden verse & the tanked-up clatter
of the iron regiments of fashion & the nitroglycerine shrieks
of the fairies of advertising & the mustard gas of sinister
intelligent editors, or were run down by the drunken taxi-
cabs of Absolute Reality,

who jumped off the Brooklyn Bridge this actually happened and
walked away unknown and forgotten into the ghostly daze
of Chinatown soup alleyways & firetrucks, not even one
free beer,

who sang out of their windows in despair, fell out of the subway
window, jumped in the filthy Passaic, leaped on negroes,
cried all over the street, danced on broken wineglasses
barefoot smashed phonograph records of nostalgic European 1930's German jazz finished the whiskey and threw
up groaning into the bloody toilet, moans in their ears and
the blast of colossal steamwhistles,

who barreled down the highways of the past journeying to each
other's hotrod-Golgotha jail-solitude watch or Birmingham
jazz incarnation,

who drove crosscountry seventytwo hours to find out if I had a
vision or you had a vision or he had a vision to find out
Eternity,

who journeyed to Denver, who died in Denver, who came back
to Denver & waited in vain, who watched over Denver &
brooded & loned in Denver and finally went away to find
out the Time, & now Denver is lonesome for her heroes,

who fell on their knees in hopeless cathedrals praying for each
other's salvation and light and breasts, until the soul illuminated its hair for a second,

who crashed through their minds in jail waiting for impossible
criminals with golden heads and the charm of reality in their

hearts who sang sweet blues to Alcatraz,

who retired to Mexico to cultivate a habit, or Rocky Mount to tender Buddha or Tangiers to boys or Southern Pacific to the black locomotive or Harvard to Narcissus to Woodlawn to the daisychain or grave,

who demanded sanity trials accusing the radio of hypnotism & were left with their insanity & their hands & a hung jury,

who threw potato salad at CCNY lecturers on Dadaism and subsequently presented themselves on the granite steps of the madhouse with shaven heads and harlequin speech of suicide, demanding instantaneous lobotomy,

and who were given instead the concrete void of insulin metrasol electricity hydrotherapy psychotherapy occupational therapy pingpong & amnesia,

who in humorless protest overturned only one symbolic pingpong table, resting briefly in catatonia,

returning years later truly bald except for a wig of blood, and tears and fingers, to the visible madman doom of the wards of the madtowns of the East,

Pilgrim State's Rockland's and Greystone's foetid halls, bickering with the echoes of the soul, rocking and rolling in the midnight solitude-bench dolmen-realms of love, dream of life a nightmare, bodies turned to stone as heavy as the moon,

with mother finally . . . . , and the last fantastic book flung out of the tenement window, and the last door closed at 4 AM and the last telephone slammed at the wall in reply and the last furnished room emptied down to the last piece of mental furniture, a yellow paper rose twisted on a wire hanger in the closet, and even that imaginary, nothing but a hopeful little bit of hallucination —

ah, Carl, while you are not safe I am not safe, and now you're really in the total animal soup of time —

and who therefore ran through the icy streets obsessed with a sudden flash of the alchemy of the use of the ellipse the catalog the meter & the vibrating plane,

who dreamt and made incarnate gaps in Time & Space through images juxtaposed, and trapped the archangel of the soul between 2 visual images and joined the elemental verbs and set the noun and dash of consciousness together jumping with sensation of Pater Omnipotens Aeterna Deus

to recreate the syntax and measure of poor human prose and stand before you speechless and intelligent and shaking with shame, rejected yet confessing out the soul to conform to the rhythm of thought in his naked and endless head,

the madman bum and angel beat in Time, unknown, yet putting down here what might be left to say in time come after death,

and rose reincarnate in the ghostly clothes of jazz in the goldhorn shadow of the band and blew the suffering of America's

naked mind for love into an eli eli lamma lamma sabacthani
saxophone cry that shivered the cities down to the last
radio
with the absolute heart of the poem of life butchered out of their
own bodies good to eat a thousand years.

1956

A Supermarket in California

What thoughts I have of you tonight, Walt Whitman, for I
walked down the sidestreets under the trees with a headache
self-conscious looking at the full moon.

In my hungry fatigue, and shopping for images, I went into
the neon fruit supermarket, dreaming of your enumerations!

What peaches and what penumbras! Whole families shopping at night! Aisles full of husbands! Wives in the avocados,
babies in the tomatoes!—and you, Garcia Lorca, what were you
doing down by the watermelons?

I saw you, Walt Whitman, childless, lonely old grubber,
poking among the meats in the refrigerator and eyeing the grocery
boys.

I heard you asking questions of each: Who killed the pork
chops? What price bananas? Are you my Angel?

I wandered in and out of the brilliant stacks of cans following you, and followed in my imagination by the store detective.

We strode down the open corridors together in our solitary
fancy tasting artichokes, possessing every frozen delicacy, and
never passing the cashier.

Where are we going, Walt Whitman? The doors close in an
hour. Which way does your beard point tonight?

(I touch your book and dream of our odyssey in the supermarket and feel absurd.)

Will we walk all night through solitary streets? The trees
add shade to shade, lights out in the houses, we'll both be lonely.

Will we stroll dreaming of the lost America of love past
blue automobiles in driveways, home to our silent cottage?

Ah, dear father, graybeard, lonely old courage-teacher,
what America did you have when Charon quit poling his ferry
and you got out on a smoking bank and stood watching the boat
disappear on the black waters of Lethe?

1956

Robert Creeley 1926–

Born in Arlington, Massachusetts, Robert Creeley went to Harvard in 1943 but left after a year to serve in the American Field Service in Burma and India. Although he returned to Harvard after the war, he did not take his degree there but finished later at Black Mountain College, where he was associated with Charles Olson as editor of the *Black Mountain Review* (1954–57), which published many of the younger postwar poets. He has an M.A. (1960) from the University of New Mexico, where he has since been in residence as a Lecturer in English. His first book of poems, *Le Fou* (1952), was published by the Golden Goose Press in Columbus, Ohio.

Creeley was strongly influenced by Charles Olson's theory of "projective verse," and the spacing of his laconic short-line poems is the result of his endorsement of Olson's assertion that "the line comes (I swear it) from the breath, from the breathing of the man who writes, at that moment that he writes." In Creeley's understated poems, which often seem to be straining toward, without quite reaching, a full articulation of his independent and somewhat offbeat perceptions, perhaps his most common subject is the complications and perplexities of love.

Creeley's other books of poetry include *The Immoral Proposition* (1953), *The Kind of Act of* (1953), *All That is Lovely in Men* (1955), *If You, Porpoise* (1956), *The Whip* (1957), *A Form of Women* (1959), and *For Love: Poems 1950–1960* (1962). *The Island* (1963) is a novel.

The text of the poems given here is that of *For Love: Poems 1950–1960* (New York, 1962).

The Warning

For love—I would
split open your head and put

a candle in
behind the eyes.

Love is dead in us
if we forget
the virtues of an amulet
and quick surprise.

1957

The Whip

I spent a night turning in bed,
my love was a feather, a flat

sleeping thing. She was
very white

and quiet, and above us on
the roof, there was another woman I

also loved, had
addressed myself to in

a fit she
returned. That   10

encompasses it. But now I was
lonely, I yelled,

but what is that? Ugh,
she said, beside me, she put

her hand on
my back, for which act

I think to say this
wrongly.

1957

The Rain

All night the sound had
come back again,
and again falls
this quiet, persistent rain.

What am I to myself
that must be remembered,

insisted upon
so often? Is it

that never the ease,
even the hardness,
of rain falling   10
will have for me

something other than this,
something not so insistent—
am I to be locked in this
final uneasiness.

Love, if you love me,
lie next to me.
Be for me, like rain,
the getting out   20

of the tiredness, the fatuousness, the semi-
lust of intentional indifference.
Be wet
with a decent happiness.

1962

Donald Justice   1925—

    Born in Florida, Donald Justice attended his home-town University of Miami (B.A., 1945). He later studied at the University of North Carolina (M.A., 1947), Stanford University, and the State University of Iowa (Ph.D., 1954). After nine years at the University of Iowa, he joined the English staff of Syracuse University in 1966. The poems collected in his first book, *The Summer Anniversaries* (1959), were praised for their perceptiveness, precision of language, and mastery of form. In *Night Light* (1967) and in his subsequent

poetry, Justice, who admires the poetry of William Carlos Williams, has
been working toward sparer and more carefully-controlled forms. In these
poems, in which easy symbolism is rejected in favor of rigorously selected
evocative images, Justice is participating in the larger effort of poets of
his generation to "make new" the language they have inherited from the
writers of the modern period. The poems he has written are also an endorsement of Marianne Moore's observation that "compression is the first
grace of style."

The text of "On a Painting by Patient B of the Independence State
Hospital for the Insane" is that of *The Summer Anniversaries* (Middletown,
Conn., 1959). The other poems given here are from *Night Light* (Middletown,
Conn., 1967).

On a Painting by Patient B of the Independence State Hospital for the Insane

1

These seven houses have learned to face one another,
But not at the expected angles. Those silly brown lumps,
That are probably meant for hills and not other houses,
After ages of being themselves, though naturally slow,
Are learning to be exclusive without offending.
The arches and entrances (down to the right out of sight)
Have mastered the lesson of remaining closed.
And even the skies keep a certain understandable distance,
For these are the houses of the very rich.

2

One sees their children playing with leopards, tamed   10
At great cost, or perhaps it is only other children,
For none of these objects is anything more than a spot,
And perhaps there are not any children but only leopards
Playing with leopards, and perhaps there are only the spots.
And the little maids from the windows hanging like tongues,
Calling the children in, admiring the leopards,
Are the dashes a child might represent motion by means of,
Or dazzlement possibly, the brilliance of solid-gold houses.

3

The clouds resemble those empty balloons in cartoons
Which approximate silence. These clouds, if clouds they are   20
(And not the smoke from the seven aspiring chimneys),
The more one studies them the more it appears
They too have expressions. One might almost say
They have their habits, their wrong opinions, that their
Impassivity masks an essentially lovable foolishness,
And they will be given names by those who live ur   : them
Not public like mountains' but private like companions'.

1959

Men at Forty

Men at forty
Learn to close softly
The doors to rooms they will not be
Coming back to.

At rest on a stair landing,
They feel it moving
Beneath them now like the deck of a ship,
Though the swell is gentle.

And deep in mirrors
They rediscover   10
The face of the boy as he practices tying
His father's tie there in secret
And the face of that father,
Still warm with the mystery of lather.
They are more fathers than sons themselves now.
Something is filling them, something

That is like the twilight sound
Of the crickets, immense,
Filling the woods at the foot of the slope
behind their mortgaged houses.   20

1967

The Tourist from Syracuse

> *One of those men who can be a car salesman or a tourist*
> *from Syracuse or a hired assassin.*
>
> John D. MacDonald[1]

You would not recognize me.
Mine is the face which blooms in
The dank mirrors of washrooms
As you grope for the light switch.

My eyes have the expression
Of the cold eyes of statues
Watching their pigeons return
From the feed you have scattered,

And I stand on my corner
With the same marble patience.   10
If I move at all, it is
At the same pace precisely

As the shade of the awning
Under which I stand waiting
And with whose blackness it seems
I am already blended.

[1] In a mystery novel entitled *Murder for the Bride* (D. J.).

I speak seldom, and always
In a murmur as quiet
As that of crowds which surround
The victims of accidents.   20

Shall I confess who I am?
My name is all names and none.
I am the used-car salesman,
The tourist from Syracuse,

The hired assassin, waiting,
I will stand here forever
Like one who has missed his bus —
Familiar, anonymous —

On my usual corner,
The corner at which you turn   30
To approach that place where now
You must not hope to arrive.

                                        1967

James Dickey   *1923—*

A native of Atlanta, Georgia, James Dickey was educated at Clemson
College and Vanderbilt University. After serving in the Air Force in World
War II and the Korean War, he worked for six years in an advertising agency.
He has also taught at colleges and universities including Rice Institute and
the University of Florida. Dickey is an energetic and prolific writer who has
adapted traditional metrical patterns in his apparently free verse poems. In
many, he has worked to develop rhythmic momentum and thrust by writing
in short unrhymed three-stress lines that are basically anapestic in rhythm.
His collections of verse include *Into the Stone* (1960), *Drowning with Others*
(1962), *Helmets* (1964), *Two Poems of the Air* (1964), and *Poems, 1957–1967*

(1967). *The Suspect in Poetry* (1964) and *Babel to Byzantium; Poets and Poetry Now* (1968) are volumes of criticism.

The text of the poems given here is that of *Drowning with Others* (Middletown, Conn., 1962).

The Lifeguard

In a stable of boats I lie still,
From all sleeping children hidden.
The leap of a fish from its shadow
Makes the whole lake instantly tremble.
With my foot on the water, I feel
The moon outside

Take on the utmost of its power.
I rise and go out through the boats.
I set my broad sole upon silver,
On the skin of the sky, on the moonlight,   10
Stepping outward from earth onto water
In quest of the miracle

This village of children believed
That I could perform as I dived
For one who had sunk from my sight.
I saw his cropped haircut go under.
I leapt, and my steep body flashed
Once, in the sun.

Dark drew all the light from my eyes.
Like a man who explores his death   20
By the pull of his slow-moving shoulders,
I hung head down in the cold,
Wide-eyed, contained, and alone
Among the weeds,

And my fingertips turned into stone
From clutching immovable blackness.
Time after time I leapt upward
Exploding in breath, and fell back
From the change in the children's faces
At my defeat.   30

Beneath them I swam to the boathouse
With only my life in my arms
To wait for the lake to shine back
At the risen moon with such power
That my steps on the light of the ripples
Might be sustained.

Beneath me is nothing but brightness
Like the ghost of a snowfield in summer.
As I move toward the center of the lake,
Which is also the center of the moon,   40
I am thinking of how I may be
The savior of one

Who has already died in my care.
The dark trees fade from around me.
The moon's dust hovers together.
I call softly out, and the child's
Voice answers through blinding water.
Patiently, slowly,

He rises, dilating to break
The surface of stone with his forehead.   50
He is one I do not remember
Having ever seen in his life.
The ground I stand on is trembling
Upon his smile.

I wash the black mud from my hands.
On a light given off by the grave
I kneel in the quick of the moon
At the heart of a distant forest
And hold in my arms a child
Of water, water, water.   60

1962

Hunting Civil War Relics at Nimblewill Creek

As he moves the mine detector
A few inches over the ground,
Making it vitally float
Among the ferns and weeds,
I come into this war
Slowly, with my one brother,
Watching his face grow deep
Between the earphones,
For I can tell
If we enter the buried battle   10
Of Nimblewill
Only by his expression.

Softly he wanders, parting
The grass with a dreaming hand.
No dead cry yet takes root
In his clapped ears

Or can be seen in his smile.
But underfoot I feel
The dead regroup,
The burst metals all in place,   20
The battle lines be drawn
Anew to include us
In Nimblewill,
And I carry the shovel and pick

More as if they were
Bright weapons that I bore.
A bird's cry breaks
In two, and into three parts.
We cross the creek; the cry
Shifts into another,   30
Nearer, bird, and is
Like the shout of a shadow —
Lived-with, appallingly close —
Or the soul, pronouncing
"Nimblewill":
Three tones; your being changes.

We climb the bank;
A faint light glows
On my brother's mouth.
I listen, as two birds fight   40
For a single voice, but he
Must be hearing the grave,
In pieces, all singing
To his clamped head.
For he smiles as if
He rose from the dead within
Green Nimblewill
And stood in his grandson's shape.

No shot from the buried war
Shall kill me now,   50
For the dead have waited here
A hundred years to create
Only the look on the face
Of my one brother,
Who stands among them, offering
A metal dish
Afloat in the trembling weeds,
With a long-buried light on his lips
At Nimblewill
And the dead outsinging two birds.   60

I choke the handle
Of the pick, and fall to my knees

To dig wherever he points,
To bring up mess tin or bullet,
To go underground
Still singing, myself,
Without a sound,
Like a man who renounces war,
Or one who shall lift up the past,
Not breathing "Father,"   70
At Nimblewill,
But saying, "Fathers! Fathers!"

                                                                    1962

The Hospital Window

I have just come down from my father.
Higher and higher he lies
Above me in a blue light
Shed by a tinted window.
I drop through six white floors
And then step out onto pavement.

Still feeling my father ascend,
I start to cross the firm street,
My shoulder blades shining with all
The glass the huge building can raise.   10
Now I must turn round and face it,
And know his one pane from the others.

Each window possesses the sun
As though it burned there on a wick.
I wave, like a man catching fire.
All the deep-dyed windowpanes flash,
And, behind them, all the white rooms
They turn to the color of Heaven.

Ceremoniously, gravely, and weakly,
Dozens of pale hands are waving   20
Back, from inside their flames.
Yet one pure pane among these
Is the bright, erased blankness of nothing.
I know that my father is there,

In the shape of his death still living.
The traffic increases around me
Like a madness called down on my head.
The horns blast at me like shotguns,
And drivers lean out, driven crazy—
But now my propped-up father   30

Lifts his arm out of stillness at last.
The light from the window strikes me

And I turn as blue as a soul,
As the moment when I was born.
I am not afraid for my father —
Look! He is grinning; he is not

Afraid for my life, either,
As the wild engines stand at my knees
Shredding their gears and roaring,
And I hold each car in its place   40
For miles, inciting its horn
To blow down the walls of the world

That the dying may float without fear
In the bold blue gaze of my father.
Slowly I move to the sidewalk
With my pin-tingling hand half dead
At the end of my bloodless arm.
I carry it off in amazement,

High, still higher, still waving,
My recognized face fully mortal,   50
Yet not; not at all, in the pale,
Drained, otherworldly, stricken,
Created hue of stained glass.
I have just come down from my father.

1962

Galway Kinnell   *1927 —*

Galway Kinnell was born in Providence, Rhode Island, and grew up in
Pawtucket. After serving in the U.S. Navy (1945–46), he attended Princeton
University (B.A., 1948) and the University of Rochester, where he took an

M.A. degree in 1949. After teaching in several universities in the United States, he lived abroad in the late fifties, teaching at Grenoble in France (1957–59) and the University of Teheran in Iran (1960). His first book of poems, *What a Kingdom It Was* (1960), was published in Boston. Kinnell's free verse, which reflects a freshness of observation and understanding, is distinguished by the skillful use of idiom and by original imagery. The older American poets to whom he seems closest are Walt Whitman and William Carlos Williams. In poems like "The Avenue Bearing the Initial of Christ . . ." and "The River That is East," the reader is aware of the presence of, not only Whitman, but also that other poet of modern New York City, Hart Crane. Kinnell's other books include *Flower Herding on Mount Monadnock* (1964), *Black Light* (1966), and *Body Rags* (1967). He has also published *The Poems of François Villon* (1965), a translation.

The text of the selection from "The Avenue Bearing the Initial of Christ into the New World" is that of *What a Kingdom It Was* (Boston, 1960). "The River That Is East" is from *Flower Herding on Mount Monadnock* (Boston, 1964).

From *The Avenue Bearing the Initial of Christ into the New World*

11

The fishmarket closed, the fishes gone into flesh.
The smelts draped on each other, fat with roe,
The marble cod hacked into chunks on the counter,
Butterfishes mouths still open, still trying to eat,
Porgies with receding jaws hinged apart
In a grimace of dejection, as if like cows
They had died under the sledgehammer, perches
In grass-green armor, spotted squeteagues
In the melting ice meek-faced and croaking no more,
Except in the plip plop plip plip in the bucket,   10
Mud-eating mullets buried in crushed ice,
Tilefishes with scales like chickenfat,
Spanish mackerels, buttercups on the flanks,
Pot-bellied pikes, two-tone flounders
After the long contortion of pushing both eyes
To the brown side that they might look up,
Brown side down, like a mass laying-on of hands,
Or the oath-taking of an army.

The only things alive are the carp
That drift in the black tank in the rear,   20
Kept living for the usual reason, that they have not died,
And perhaps because the last meal was garbage and they might
      begin stinking

On dying, before the customer was halfway home.
They nudge each other, to be netted,
The sweet flesh to be lifted thrashing in the air,
To be slugged, and then to keep on living
While they are opened on the counter.

Fishes do not die exactly, it is more
That they go out of themselves, the visible part
Remains the same, there is little pallor,   30
Only the cataracted eyes which have not shut ever
Must look through the mist which crazed Homer.

These are the vegetables of the deep,
The Sheol-flowers of darkness, swimmers
Of denser darknesses where the sun's rays bend for the last time
And in the sky there burns this shifty jellyfish
That degenerates and flashes and re-forms.

Motes in the eye land is the lid of,
They are plucked out of the green skim milk of the eye.

Fishes are nailed on the wood,   40
The big Jew stands like Christ, nailing them to the wood,
He scrapes the knife up the grain, the scales fly,
He unnails them, reverses them, nails them again,
Scrapes and the scales fly. He lops off the heads,
Shakes out the guts as if they did not belong in the first place,
And they are flesh for the first time in their lives.

Dear Frau_____:

        Your husband, _____, died in the Camp Hospital
on _____. May I express my sincere sympathy on your
bereavement. _____ was admitted to the Hospital on   50
_____ with severe symptoms of exhaustion, complaining
of difficulties in breathing and pains in the chest. Despite competent medication and devoted medical attention, it proved impossible, unfortunately, to keep the patient alive. The deceased
voiced no final requests.

                            Camp Commandant, _____

On 5th Street Bunko Certified Embalmer Catholic
Leans in his doorway drawing on a Natural Bloom Cigar.
He looks up the street. Even the Puerto Ricans are Jews
And the Chinese Laundry closes on Saturday.   60

1960

14

Behind the Power Station on 14th, the held breath
Of light, as God is a held breath, withheld,
Spreads the East River, into which fishes leak:
The brown sink or dissolve,
The white float out in shoals and armadas,
Even the gulls pass them up, pale
Bloated socks of riverwater and rotted seed,
That swirl on the tide, punched back
To the Hell Gate narrows, and on the ebb
Steam seaward, seeding the sea.   10

On the Avenue, through air tinted crimson
By neon over the bars, the rain is falling.
You stood once on Houston, among panhandlers and winos
Who weave the eastern ranges, learning to be free,
To not care, to be knocked flat and to get up clear-headed
Spitting the curses out. "Now be nice,"
The proprietor threatens; "Be nice," he cajoles.
"Fuck you," the bum shouts as he is hoisted again,
"God fuck your mother." (In the empty doorway,
Hunched on the empty crate, the crone gives no sign.)   20

That night a wildcat cab whined crosstown on 7th.
You knew even the traffic lights were made by God,
The red splashes growing dimmer the farther away
You looked, and away up at 14th, a few green stars;
And without sequence, and nearly all at once,
The red lights blinked into green,
And just before there was one complete Avenue of green,
The little green stars in the distance blinked.

It is night, and raining. You look down
Towards Houston in the rain, the living streets,   30
Where instants of transcendence
Drift in oceans of loathing and fear, like lanternfishes,
Or phosphorus flashings in the sea, or the feverish light
Skin is said to give off when the swimmer drowns at night.

From the blind gut Pitt to the East River of Fishes
The Avenue cobbles a swath through the discolored air,
A roadway of refuse from the teeming shores and ghettos
And the Caribbean Paradise, into the new ghetto and new
        paradise,
This God-forsaken Avenue bearing the initial of Christ   40
Through the haste and carelessness of the ages,
The sea standing in heaps, which keeps on collapsing,
Where the drowned suffer a C-change,
And remain the common poor.

Since Providence, for the realization of some unknown purpose,
        has seen fit to leave this dangerous people on the face of the
              earth, and did not destroy it. . .

Listen! the swish of the blood,
The sirens down the bloodpaths of the night,
Bone tapping on the bone, nerve-nets   50
Singing under the breath of sleep —

We scattered over the lonely seaways,
Over the lonely deserts did we run,
In dark lanes and alleys we did hide ourselves . . .

The lungs put out the light of the world as they
The heart beats without windows in its night,
Heave and collapse, the brain turns and rattles
In its own black axlegrease —

                    In the nighttime
Of the blood they are laughing and saying,   60
Our little lane, what a kingdom it was!

                    oi weih, oi weih

                                        1960

The River That Is East

1

Buoys begin clanging like churches
And peter out. Sunk to the gunwhales
In their shapes tugs push upstream.
A carfloat booms down, sweeping past
Illusory suns that blaze in puddles
On the shores where it rained, past the Navy Yard,
Under the Williamsburg Bridge
That hangs facedown from its strings
Over which the Jamaica Local crawls,
Through white-winged gulls which shriek   10
And flap from the water and sideslip in
Over the chaos of illusions, dangling
Limp red hands, and screaming as they touch.

2

A boy swings his legs from the pier,
His days go by, tugs and carfloats go by,
Each prow pushing a whitecap. On his deathbed
Kane remembered the abrupt, missed Grail
Called Rosebud, Gatsby must have thought back
On his days digging clams in Little Girl Bay
In Minnesota, Nick fished in dreamy Michigan,   20
Gant had his memories, Griffeths, those
Who went baying after the immaterial
And whiffed its strange dazzle in a blonde

In a canary convertible, who died
Thinking of the Huck Finns of themselves[1]
On the old afternoons, themselves like this boy
Swinging his legs, who sees the *Ile de France*
Come in, and wonders if in some stateroom
There is not a sick-hearted heiress sitting
Drink in hand, saying to herself his name.   30

3

A man stands on the pier.
He has long since stopped wishing his heart were full
Or his life dear to him.
He watches the snowfall hitting the dirty water.
He thinks: Beautiful. Beautiful.
If I were a gull I would be one with white wings,
I would fly out over the water, explode, and
Be beautiful snow hitting the dirty water.

4

And thou, River of Tomorrow, flowing . . .
We stand on the shore, which is mist beneath us,   40
And regard the onflowing river. Sometimes
It seems the river stops and the shore
Flows into the past. Nevertheless, its leaked promises
Hopping in the bloodstream, we strain for the future,
Sometimes even glimpse it, a vague, scummed thing
We dare not recognize, and peer again
At the cabled shroud out of which it came,
We who have no roots but the shifts of our pain,
No flowering but our own strange lives.

What is this river but the one   50
Which drags the things we love,
Processions of debris like floating lamps,
Towards the radiance in which they go out?

No, it is the River that is East,[2] known once
From a high window in Brooklyn, in agony—river
On which a door locked to the water floats,
A window sash paned with brown water, a whisky crate,
Barrel staves, sun spokes, feathers of the birds,
A breadcrust, a rat, spittle, butts, and peels,
The immaculate stream, heavy, and swinging home again.   60

                                          1964

---

[1] The literary allusions suggest the lure of the American dream and its perversion by materialism.
[2] This phrase, which is also the title of Kinnell's poem, is a quotation from Hart Crane's "The Tunnel" (see above); in this context, coupled with the image of the "high window in Brooklyn," it points back to both Crane and Whitman.

John Ashbery   *1927–*

John Ashbery, who is both an art critic and a poet, was born in Rochester, New York, and educated at Harvard (B.A., 1949) and Columbia University, where he received an M.A. in English (1951). After working in publishing, he went to France in 1955. He lived abroad for several years, mostly in Paris, as an art critic of the Paris *Herald Tribune* and an editor of the quarterly *Art and Literature.* Ashbery's interest in painting and music has influenced his poetry. He has often attempted to approximate the structure of music, which is capable "of carrying an argument through successfully to the finish, though the terms of this argument remain unknown quantities." He has thus worked to renew the language of poetry through a process of abstraction which frees words in a poetic context from their conventional meaning and symbolism and emphasizes other aspects of poetic form. The resulting poems are interesting, even though, since words are words, and thus inherently meaningful, it is difficult if not impossible to exclude patterns of symbolism. In a poem like "Rivers and Mountains," there is, for all its strangeness and obscurity, an unmistakable polarity, reminiscent of much poetry in the romantic tradition, between the attractive and relatively pure imagery of nature and the repellent imagery of a technological and destructive civilization.

Ashbery's books of poetry include *Turandot and Other Poems* (1953), *Some Trees* (1956), *The Poems* (1960), *The Tennis Court Oath* (1962), *Rivers and Mountains* (1965), and *Selected Poems* (London, 1967).

The text of "Rivers and Mountains" is that of the volume of the same title (New York, 1965). The other poems given here are from *Some Trees* (1956).

Glazunoviana

The man with the red hat
And the polar bear, is he here too?
The window giving on shade,
Is that here too?
And all the little helps,
My initials in the sky,
The hay of an arctic summer night?

The bear
Drops dead in sight of the window.
Lovely tribes have just moved to the north.
In the flickering evening the martins grow denser.
Rivers of wings surround us and vast tribulation.

1956

Rivers and Mountains

On the secret map the assassins
Cloistered, the Moon River was marked
Near the eighteen peaks and the city
Of humiliation and defeat — wan ending
Of the trail among dry, papery leaves
Gray-brown quills like thoughts
In the melodious but vast mass of today's
Writing through fields and swamps
Marked, on the map, with little bunches of weeds.
Certainly squirrels lived in the woods   10
But devastation and dull sleep still
Hung over the land, quelled
The rioters turned out of sleep in the peace of prisons
Singing on marble factory walls
Deaf consolation of minor tunes that pack
The air with heavy invisible rods
Pent in some sand valley from
Which only quiet walking ever instructs.
The bird flew over and
Sat — there was nothing else to do.   20
Do not mistake its silence for pride or strength
Or the waterfall for a harbor
Full of light boats that is there
Performing for thousands of people
In clothes some with places to go
Or games. Sometimes over the pillar
Of square stones its impact
Makes a light print.

. . . . .

So going around cities
To get to other places you found   30
It all on paper but the land
Was made of paper processed
To look like ferns, mud or other
Whose sea unrolled its magic
Distances and then rolled them up
Its secret was only a pocket
After all but some corners are darker
Than these moonless nights spent as on a raft
In the seclusion of a melody heard
As though through trees   40
And you can never ignite their touch
Long but there were homes
Flung far out near the asperities
Of a sharp, rocky pinnacle
And other collective places
Shadows of vineyards whose wine
Tasted of the forest floor
Fisheries and oyster beds
Tides under the pole
Seminaries of instruction, public   50
Places for electric light
And the major tax assessment area
Wrinkled on the plan
Of election to public office
Sixty-two years old bath and breakfast
The formal traffic, shadows
To make it not worth joining
After the ox had pulled away the cart.

. . . . .

Your plan was to separate the enemy into two groups
With the razor-edged mountains between.   60
It worked well on paper
But their camp had grown
To be the mountains and the map
Carefully peeled away and not torn
Was the light, a tender but tough bark
On everything. Fortunately the war was solved
In another way by isolating the two sections
Of the enemy's navy so that the mainland
Warded away the big floating ships.
Light bounced off the ends   70
Of the small gray waves to tell
Them in the observatory

About the great drama that was being won
To turn off the machinery
And quietly move among the rustic landscape
Scooping snow off the mountains rinsing
The coarser ones that love had
Slowly risen in the night to overflow
Wetting pillow and petal
Determined to place the letter   80
On the unassassinated president's desk
So that a stamp could reproduce all this
In detail, down to the last autumn leaf
And the affliction of June ride
Slowly out into the sun-blackened landscape.

Chaos   *1965*

Don't ask me to go there again
The white is too painful
Better to forget it
the sleeping river spoke to the awake land

When they first drew the wires
across the field
slowly air settled
on the pools
The blue mirror came to light
Then someone feared the pools
To be armor enough might not someone
draw down the sky
Light emerged
The swimming motion

At last twilight that will not protect the leaves
Death that will not try to scream
Black beaches
That is why I sent you the black postcard that will never deafen

That is why land urges the well
The white is running in its grooves
The river slides under our dreams
but land flows more silently

1956

Some Trees

These are amazing: each
Joining a neighbor, as though speech
Were a still performance.

Arranging by chance

To meet as far this morning
From the world as agreeing
With it, you and I
Are suddenly what the trees try

To tell us we are:
That their merely being there
Means something; that soon
We may touch, love, explain.

And glad not to have invented
Such comeliness, we are surrounded:
A silence already filled with noises,
A canvas on which emerges

A chorus of smiles, a winter morning.
Placed in a puzzling light, and moving,
Our days put on such reticence
These accents seem their own defense.

1956

Kenneth Koch   *1925–*

As a representative of the comic spirit in verse, Kenneth Koch is a rarity among contemporary poets, who have not inclined toward the kind of humor and absurdity that abound in fiction and the drama. Kenneth Koch was born and reared in Cincinnati, Ohio. After wartime service in the Army

(1943–46), he studied at Harvard (A.B., 1948) and Columbia University (M.A., 1953; Ph.D., 1959). He has taught at several institutions, including Rutgers University and Brooklyn College, and is presently a professor of English and comparative literature at Columbia.

Many of Koch's humorous poems, like "Thank You," seem simply nonsensical and facetious, but there is a tendency in some of his work toward critical humor or satire—although it is usually not directed at unmistakable targets. Koch's poems most often seem to be somewhat frivolous attempts at a kind of absurd abstractionism in verse. (In this respect they complement John Ashbery's more serious efforts to create abstract poetic forms.) But regardless of the writer's underlying motives, the kind of irreverent absurdity that prevails in Koch's poems is one way of renewing the language of poetry by purging it of conventional symbolic usages that have become rigid and oppressive.

Koch's books include *Poems* (1953), *KO, or a Season on Earth* (1959), *Permanently* (1960), and *Thank You and Other Poems* (1962). Koch has also written a number of plays that have been produced in off-Broadway theaters. A collection of these is *Bertha & Other Plays* (1966).

The text of the poems given here is that of *Thank You and Other Poems* (New York, 1962).

Variations on a Theme by William Carlos Williams

1

I chopped down the house that you had been saving to live in
    next summer.
I am sorry, but it was morning, and I had nothing to do
and its wooden beams were so inviting.

2

We laughed at the hollyhocks together
and then I sprayed them with lye.
Forgive me. I simply do not know what I am doing.

3

I gave away the money that you had been saving to live on for the
    next ten years.
The man who asked for it was shabby
and the firm March wind on the porch was so juicy and cold.

4

Last evening we went dancing and I broke your leg.
Forgive me. I was clumsy, and
I wanted you here in the wards, where I am the doctor!

1962

Thank You

Oh thank you for giving me the chance
Of being ship's doctor! I am sorry that I shall have to refuse—
But, you see, the most I know of medicine is orange flowers
Tilted in the evening light against a cashmere red
Inside which breasts invent the laws of light
And of night, where cashmere moors itself across the sea.
And thank you for giving me these quintuplets
To rear and make happy . . . My mind was on something else.

Thank you for giving me this battleship to wash,
But I have a rash on my hands and my eyes hurt,   10
And I know so little about cleaning a ship
That I should rather clean an island.
There one knows what one is about—sponge those palm trees,
        sweep up the sand a little, polish those coconuts;
Then take a rest for a while and it's time to trim the grass as well
        as separate it from each other where gummy substances
            have made individual blades stick together, forming
            an ugly bunch;
And then take the dead bark off the trees, and perfume these
        islands a bit with a song. . . . That's easy—but a battle-   20
        ship!
Where does one begin and how does one do? to batten the hatches?
    I would rather clean a million palm trees.

Now here comes an offer of a job for setting up a levee
In Mississippi. No thanks. Here it says *Rape or Worse*. I think
    they must want me to publicize this book.
On the jacket it says "Published in Boothbay Harbor, Maine"
    —what a funny place to publish a book!

I suppose it is some provincial publishing house
Whose provincial pages emit the odor of sails   30
And the freshness of the sea
Breeze. . . . But publicity!

The only thing I could publicize well would be my tooth,
Which I could say came with my mouth and in a most engaging
    manner
With my whole self, my body and including my mind,
Spirits, emotions, spiritual essences, emotional substances, po-
    etry, dreams, and lords
Of my life, everything, all embraceleted with my tooth
In a way that makes one wish to open the windows and scream   40
    "Hi!" to the heavens,
And "Oh, come and take me away before I die in a minute!"

It is possible that the dentist is smiling, that he dreams of extraction
Because he believes that the physical tooth and the spiritual tooth
    are one.

Here is another letter, this one from a textbook advertiser;
He wants me to advertise a book on chopping down trees.
But how could I? I love trees! and I haven't the slightest sympa-
    thy with chopping them down, even though I know
We need their products for wood-fires, some houses, and maple   50
    syrup—
Still I like trees better
In their standing condition, when they sway at the beginning of
    evening . . .
And thank you for the pile of driftwood.
Am I wanted at the sea?

And thank you for the chance to run a small hotel
In an elephant stopover in Zambezi,
But I do not know how to take care of guests, certainly they
    would all leave soon   60
After seeing blue lights out the windows and rust on their iron
    beds—I'd rather own a bird-house in Jamaica:
Those people come in, the birds, they do not care how things are
    kept up . . .
It's true that Zambezi proprietorship would be exciting, with
    people getting off elephants and coming into my hotel,
But as tempting as it is I cannot agree.
And thank you for this offer of the post of referee
For the Danish wrestling championship—I simply do not feel
    qualified . . .   70
But the fresh spring air has been swabbing my mental decks
Until, although prepared for fight, still I sleep on land.
Thank you for the ostriches. I have not yet had time to pluck
    them,
But I am sure they will be delicious, adorning my plate at sunset,
My tremendous plate, and the plate
Of the offers to all my days. But I cannot fasten my exhilaration
    to the sun.

And thank you for the evening of the night on which I fell off my
    horse in the shadows. That was really useful.   80

1962

Sylvia Plath   *1932–1963*

Born in Boston of German and Austrian parents, Sylvia Plath was educated at Smith College. After graduating *summa cum laude* in 1955, she went to England on a scholarship and studied at Cambridge University, where she received an M.A. degree in 1957. Except for a year's visit to the United States, when she taught at Smith College, she lived in England with her husband Ted Hughes, the British poet, and their children until her death by suicide in 1963. The somberness and austerity of the carefully-controlled poems of her first book, *The Colossus* (1960), deepened into the intensity of desperation in the ominously brilliant poems of her second, posthumously-published volume, *Ariel* (1965).

The text of "Point Shirley" is that of *The Colossus*, new ed. (London, 1967). "Ariel" and "Words" are from *Ariel* (London, 1965).

Point Shirley

From Water-Tower Hill to the brick prison
The shingle booms, bickering under
The sea's collapse:
Snowcakes break and welter. This year
The gritted wave leaps
The seawall and drops onto a bier
Of quahog chips,
Leaving a salty mash of ice to whiten

In my grandmother's sand yard. She is dead,
Whose laundry snapped and froze here, who
Kept house against
What the sluttish, rutted sea could do.

Squall waves once danced
Ship timbers in through the cellar window;
A thresh-tailed, lanced
Shark littered in the geranium bed —

Such collusion of mulish elements
She wore her broom straws to the nub.
Twenty years out
Of her hand, the house still hugs in each drab
Stucco socket
The purple egg-stones: from Great Head's knob
To the filled-in Gut
The sea in its cold gizzard ground those rounds.

Nobody wintering now behind
The planked-up windows where she set
Her wheat loaves
And apple cakes to cool. What is it
Survives, grieves
So, over this battered, obstinate spit
Of gravel? The waves'
Spewed relics clicker masses in the wind,

Grey waves the stub-necked eiders ride.
A labour of love, and that labour lost.
Steadily the sea
Eats at Point Shirley. She died blessed,
And I come by
Bones, bones only, pawed and tossed,
A dog-faced sea.
The sun sinks under Boston, bloody red.

I would get from these dry-papped stones
The milk your love instilled in them.
The black ducks dive.
And though your graciousness might stream,
And I contrive,
Grandmother, stones are nothing of home
To that spumiest dove.
Against both bar and tower the black sea runs.

1960

Ariel

Stasis in darkness.
Then the substanceless blue
Pour of tor and distances.

God's lioness,
How one we grow,
Pivot of heels and knees!—The furrow

Splits and passes, sister to
The brown arc
Of the neck I cannot catch,

Nigger-eye
Berries cast dark
Hooks ——

Black sweet blood mouthfuls,
Shadows.
Something else

Hauls me through air ——
Thighs, hair;
Flakes from my heels.

White
Godiva, I unpeel ——
Dead hands, dead stringencies.

And now I
Foam to wheat, a glitter of seas.
The child's cry

Melts in the wall.
And I
Am the arrow,

The dew that flies
Suicidal, at one with the drive
Into the red

Eye, the cauldron of morning.

1965

Words

Axes
After whose stroke the wood rings,
And the echoes!
Echoes travelling
Off from the centre like horses.

The sap
Wells like tears, like the
Water striving
To re-establish its mirror
Over the rock

That drops and turns,
A white skull,
Eaten by weedy greens.
Years later I
Encounter them on the road ——

Words dry and riderless,
The indefatigable hoof-taps.
While
From the bottom of the pool, fixed stars
Govern a life.

1965

LeRoi Jones   *1934—*

A native of Newark, New Jersey, LeRoi Jones attended Rutgers and then Howard University, which he left to enter the Air Force. After serving in Puerto Rico (1954–57), he continued his studies at Columbia University and at the New School for Social Research, where he received an M.A. in German literature. He has subsequently taught at several universities. His first book of poems, *Preface to a Twenty Volume Suicide Note*, was published in New York in 1961. Like most poets of his generation, Jones is committed to the free, organic forms championed by Williams and Pound. "Accentual verse," he believes, "the regular metric of rumbling iambics, is dry as slivers of sand. Nothing happens in that frame anymore. We can get nothing from England. And the diluted formalism of the academy (the formal culture of the U.S.) is anaemic & fraught with incompetence & unreality."

Although Jones has been active in the Negro revolution, the race problem is not so omnipresent an overt theme in his poems as it is in the work of some Negro writers. Awareness of race has, however, affected his outlook in the treatment of other subjects, such as the conflict of identity in "An Agony, as Now." He has been more directly concerned with the social problem of race in his plays, which have been successfully produced as well as published in *Dutchman and the Slave* (1964). He has also written a novel, *The System of Dante's Hell* (1965). His other books include *Blues People: Negro Music in White America* (1963), *The Dead Lecturer* (1964), *Black Music* (1967), and *Home: Social Essays* (London, 1968).

The text of the poems given here is that of *The Dead Lecturer* (New York, 1964).

A contract

FOR THE DESTRUCTION AND REBUILDING OF PATERSON[1]

Flesh, and cars, tar, dug holes beneath stone
a rude hierarchy of money, band saws cross out
music, feeling. Even speech, corrodes.
                              I came here
from where I sat boiling in my veins, cold fear
at the death of men, the death of learning, in
cold fear, at my own. Romantic vests of same death
blank at the corner, blank when they raise their fingers

Criss the hearts, in dark flesh staggered so marvelous
are their lies. So complete, their mastery, of these
stupid niggers. Loud spics kill each other, and will not

make the simple trip to Tiffany's. Will not smash their stainless
heads, against the simpler effrontery of so callous a code as gain.

You are no brothers, dirty woogies, dying under dried rinds, in
        massa's
droopy tuxedos. Cab Calloways of the soul, at the soul's junc-
        ture, a
music, they think will save them from our eyes. (In back of the
        terminal

where the circus will not go. At the backs of crowds, stooped and
        vulgar
breathing hate syllables, unintelligible rapes of all that linger in
our new world. Killed in white fedora hats, they stand so mute at
        what
whiter slaves did to my fathers. They muster silence. They pray
        at the
steps of abstract prisons, to be kings, when all is silence, when all
is stone. When even the stupid fruit of their loins is gold, or
        something
else they cannot eat.

1964

[1] An allusion to William Carlos Williams' poetic Paterson as an image of the city of man in America.

An Agony. As Now.

I am inside someone
who hates me. I look
out from his eyes. Smell
what fouled tunes come in
to his breath. Love his
wretched women.

Slits in the metal, for sun. Where
my eyes sit turning, at the cool air
the glance of light, or hard flesh
rubbed against me, a woman, a man,
without shadow, or voice, or meaning.

This is the enclosure (flesh,
where innocence is a weapon. An
abstraction. Touch. (Not mine.
Or yours, if you are the soul I had
and abandoned when I was blind and had
my enemies carry me as a dead man
(if he is beautiful, or pitied.

It can be pain. (As now, as all his
flesh hurts me.) It can be that. Or
pain. As when she ran from me into
that forest.
          Or pain, the mind
silver spiraled whirled against the
sun, higher than even old men thought
God would be. Or pain. And the other. The
yes. (Inside his books, his fingers. They
are withered yellow flowers and were never
beautiful.) The yes. You will, lost soul, say
'beauty.' Beauty, practiced, as the tree. The
slow river. A white sun in its wet sentences.

Or, the cold men in their gale. Ecstasy. Flesh
or soul. The yes. (Their robes blown. Their bowls
empty. They chant at my heels, not at yours.) Flesh
or soul, as corrupt. Where the answer moves too quickly.
Where the God is a self, after all.)

Cold air blown through narrow blind eyes. Flesh,
white hot metal. Glows as the day with its sun.
It is a human love, I live inside. A bony skeleton
you recognize as words or simple feeling.

But it has no feeling. As the metal, is hot, it is not,
given to love.

It burns the thing
inside it. And that thing
screams.

1964

Sex, like desire.

                 (away from the streets. Flash
into pockets, the fingers' smell, deeply secret.
Each night, another rape. Young boys hide at the tops
of hills, near gas stations and breweries, waiting
to make the hit. It is not even love. Still, they
wait, and make believe
                      they are beautiful.

It could be me, even now. (So slow, I come to see
myself. To be at a point rusted in my dead child's
breast. Where the life is, all the flesh, to make
more than a silhouette, a breathless shadow counting
again, his change.

What is there? Where is it? Who is she? What can I
give myself, trade myself, to make me understand
myself? Nothing is ever finished. Nothing past. Each
act of my life, with me now, till death. Themselves,
the reasons for it. They are stones, in my mouth
and ears. Whole forests on my shoulders.

1964

The dance

                 (held up for me by
an older man. He told me how. Showed
me. Not steps, but the fix
of muscle. A position
for myself: to move.

Duncan[1]
told of dance. His poems
full of what we called
so long for you to be. A
dance. And all his words
ran out of it. That there
was some bright elegance
the sad meat of the body

[1] Robert Duncan (1919 –).

made. Some gesture, that
if we became, for one blank moment,
would turn us
into creatures of rhythm.

I want to be sung. I want
all my bones and meat hummed
against the thick floating
winter sky. I want myself
as dance. As what I am
given love, or time, or space
to feel myself.

The time of thought. The space
of actual movement. (Where they
have taken up the sea, and
keep me against my will.) I said, also,
love, being older or younger
than your world. I am given
to lying, love, call you out
now, given to feeling things
I alone create.

And let me once, create
myself. And let you, whoever
sits now breathing on my words
create a self of your own. One
that will love me.

                                        1964

Acknowledgements

HENRY ADAMS, *The Education of Henry Adams,* copyright © 1946 by Charles F. Adams. Selection reprinted by permission of and arrangement with Houghton Mifflin Company, the authorized publishers.

SHERWOOD ANDERSON, *Winesburg, Ohio,* copyright © 1919 by B. W. Huebsch; renewed 1947 by Eleonor Copenhaver Anderson. Selections reprinted by permission of Harold Ober Associates, Inc.

JOHN ASHBERY, *Rivers and Mountains,* copyright © 1964 by John Ashbery. Poem reprinted by permission of Holt, Rinehart and Winston, Inc. *Some Trees,* copyright © 1956 by John Ashbery. Poems reprinted by permission of John Ashbery, c/o Marvin Josephson Associates, Inc.

JAMES BALDWIN, *Going to Meet the Man,* copyright © 1948, 1951, 1957, 1958, 1960, 1965 by James Baldwin. Selection reprinted by permission of the publisher, The Dial Press, Inc.

SAUL BELLOW, *Herzog,* copyright © 1961, 1963 by Saul Bellow. All rights reserved. Selection reprinted by permission of The Viking Press, Inc.

WILLA CATHER, *Youth and the Bright Medusa,* copyright © 1904, 1932 by Willa Cather. Selection reprinted by permission of Alfred A. Knopf, Inc. *Obscure Destinies,* copyright, 1930 by the Crowell Publishing Company and renewed 1958 by The Executors of The Estate of Willa Cather. Selection reprinted by permission of Alfred A. Knopf, Inc.

HART CRANE, *Complete Poems, Selected Letters and Prose of Hart Crane,* copyright 1953, 1958, 1966 by Liveright Publishing Corporation, and reprinted with their permission.

ROBERT CREELEY, *For Love,* copyright © 1961, 1962, by Robert Creeley. Poems reprinted with the permission of Charles Scribner's Sons.

E. E. CUMMINGS, *Poems 1923-1954,* copyright 1923, 1925, 1931, 1940, 1944, 1950, 1951, 1954, 1959 by E. E. Cummings; copyright © 1926 by Horace Liveright. Poems reprinted by permission of Harcourt, Brace & World, Inc.

JAMES DICKEY, *Drowning With Others.* "The Hospital Window" copyright © 1962 by James Dickey, first published in *Poetry;* "Hunting Civil War Relics. . . " copyright © 1961 by James Dickey; "The Lifeguard" copyright © 1961 by James Dickey, first published in *The New Yorker.* Poems reprinted by permission of Wesleyan University Press.

JOHN DOS PASSOS, *The 42nd Parallel,* first volume of the USA trilogy, copyright 1930, 1958 by John Dos Passos, published by Houghton Mifflin Company. Selections reprinted by permission of John Dos Passos. *Nineteen Nineteen,* second volume of the USA trilogy, copyright 1932, 1960 by John Dos Passos, published by Houghton Mifflin Company. Selections reprinted by permission of John Dos Passos. *The Big Money,* third volume of the USA trilogy, copyright 1936, 1964 by John Dos Passos, published by Houghton Mifflin Company. Selections reprinted by permission of John Dos Passos.

THEODORE DREISER, *Free and Other Stories,* copyright 1918 by Boni and Liveright, copyright 1945 by Theodore Dreiser. Selection reprinted by permission of The World Publishing Company. *Hey Rub-A-Dub-Dub,* copyright 1920 by Boni and Liveright, copyright 1926 by Theodore Dreiser, copyright 1947 by Mrs. Theodore Dreiser. Selections reprinted by permission of The World Publishing Company.

RICHARD EBERHART, *Collected Poems 1930-1960,* copyright © 1960 by Richard Eberhart. Poems reprinted by permission of The Oxford University Press, Inc. and Chatto and Windus Ltd.

T. S. ELIOT, *Complete Poems and Plays* and *Collected Poems 1909-1962,* copyright © 1952 by Harcourt, Brace & World, Inc. Selections reprinted by permission of Harcourt, Brace & World, Inc., and Faber & Faber Ltd. *Selected Essays of T. S. Eliot,* copyright © 1932 by Harcourt, Brace & World, Inc. Selection reprinted by permission of Harcourt, Brace & World Inc. and Faber & Faber Ltd.

RALPH ELLISON, *Invisible Man,* copyright © 1952 by Ralph Ellison. Selection reprinted by permission of Random House, Inc.

WILLIAM FAULKNER, *Go Down Moses,* copyright © 1942 by William Faulkner. Selection reprinted by permission of Random House, Inc.

F. SCOTT FITZGERALD, *All the Sad Young Men,* copyright 1922 by Frances Scott Fitzgerald Lanahan; renewal copyright 1950. Selection reprinted with the permission of Charles Scribner's Sons.

ROBERT FROST, *Complete Poems of Robert Frost,* copyright 1916, 1923, 1928, 1930, 1934, 1939, 1949, © 1967 by Holt, Rinehart and Winston, Inc. Copyright 1936, 1942, 1944, 1951, © 1956, 1958, 1962 by Robert Frost. Copyright © 1964, 1967 by Lesley Frost Ballantine. Poems reprinted by permission of Holt, Rinehart and Winston, Inc.

ALLEN GINSBERG, *Howl, Part I,* copyright © 1956 by Allen Ginsberg. Poem reprinted by permission of City Lights Books. "A Supermarket in California," copyright © 1956 by Allen Ginsberg. Poem reprinted by permission of City Lights Books.

JOSEPH HELLER, *Catch-22,* copyright © 1955, 1961 by Joseph Heller. Selection reprinted by permission of Simon and Schuster, Inc.

ERNEST HEMINGWAY, *In Our Time,* copyright 1925 Charles Scribner's Sons; renewal copyright 1953 Ernest Hemingway. Selection reprinted with the permission of Charles Scribner's Sons.

Bibliography

1. *General Reference Works and Bibliographies*

Adams, J. T., and Coleman, R. V., eds., *Dictionary of American History*. 6 vols. (1940 - 61).

Blanck, Jacob. *Bibliography of American Literature*. In process (1955—).

Cargill, Oscar. *Intellectual America: Ideas on the March* (1941).

Coffman, S. K. *Imagism: A Chapter for the History of Modern Poetry* (1951).

Commager, Henry S. *The American Mind: An Interpretation of American Thought and Character Since the 1880's* (1950).

Curti, Merle. *The Growth of American Thought* (1943).

Dictionary of American Biography. Johnson, Allen, and Malone, Dumas, eds. 20 vols. plus supplements (1928 - 1958).

Ghodes, Clarence. *Bibliographical Guide to the Study of Literature in the United States* (1962).

Hart, J. D. *The Oxford Companion to American Literature* (4th ed., 1965).

Hoffman, F. J.; Allen, Charles; and Ulrich, C. F. *The Little Magazine: A History and Bibliography* (1947).

Jackson, G. P. *White and Negro Spirituals: Their Life Span and Kinship* (1943).

Jones, H. M. *Guide to American Literature and Its Background Since 1890* (1953).

Kunitz, S. J., and Haycraft, Howard, eds., *Twentieth Century Authors* (1942). Supplement (1955).

Larkin, O. W. *Art and Life in America* (revised ed., 1960).

Leary, Lewis, ed., *Articles on American Literature, 1900-1950* (1954).

Ludwig, R. M. ed., *Bibliographical Supplement to Literary History of the United States*, by R. E. Spiller, et al. (1959).

Lynn, Kenneth S., ed., *The Comic Tradition in America* (1958).

Mencken, H. L. *The American Language: An Inquiry into the Development of English in the United States* (1919-1948).

Mott, F. L. *American Journalism: A History of Newspapers in the United States through 250 Years, 1690 to 1940* (revised ed., 1951).

Rosenberg, Bernard, and White, David M. *Mass Culture: The Popular Arts in America* (1957).

Sabin, Joseph, et al. *A Dictionary of Books Relating to America from its Discovery to the Present Time*. 29 vols. (1868-1936).

Schneider, H. W. *History of American Philosophy* (1946).

Spiller, R. E.; Thorp, Willard; Johnson, T. H.; and Canby, H. S. eds., *Literary History of the United States*. 3 vols. (1948) 1 vol. (1953).

Trent, W. P.; Erskine, John; Sherman, S. P.; and Van Doren, Carl, eds., *Cambridge History of American Literature*. 4 vols. (1917-1921).

Welsch, E. K. *The Negro in America: A Research Guide* (1965).

Woodress, James. *Dissertations in American Literature. 1891-1966* (revised ed., 1968)

2. *Historical and Literary Studies*

Aaron, Daniel. *Writers on the Left* (1961).

Ahnebrink, Lars. *The Beginnings of Naturalism in American Fiction* (1950).

Baumbach, Jonathan. *Landscape of Nightmare: Studies in the Contemporary American Novel* (1965).

Beach, Joseph Warren. *American Fiction: 1920-1940* (1941).

Berthott, Warner. *The Ferment of Realism: American Literature, 1884-1919* (1965).

Bogan, Louise. *Achievement in American Poetry, 1900-1950* (1951).

Chase, Richard. *The American Novel and Its Tradition* (1957).

Cowley, Malcolm. *After the Genteel Tradition: American Writers. 1910-1930* (revised ed., 1946).

Downer, Allan. *Fifty Years of American Drama 1900-1950* (1951).
Edel, Leon. *The Psychological Novel, 1900-1950* (1955).
Ehrenpreis, Irvin, ed., *American Poetry* (1965).
Fraiberg, Louis. *Psychoanalysis and American Literary Criticism* (1960).
French, Warren. *The Social Novel at the End of an Era* (1966).
Frohock, W. M. *The Novel of Violence in America* (revised ed., 1957).
Geismar, Maxwell. *American Moderns: From Rebellion to Conformity (1958).*
‐ ‐ ‐ ‐ ‐ ‐ ‐ ‐ ‐. *The Last of the Provincials* (1947).
‐ ‐ ‐ ‐ ‐ ‐ ‐ ‐ ‐. *Rebels and Ancestors, 1890-1915* (1953).
‐ ‐ ‐ ‐ ‐ ‐ ‐ ‐ ‐. *Writers in Crisis: The American Novel Between Two Wars* (1942).
Gregory, Horace, and Zaturenska, Marya. *A History of American Poetry. 1900-1940* (1946).
Gross, Harvey. *Sound and Form in Modern Poetry* (1964).
Gross, S. L., and Hardy, J. E. *Images of the Negro in American Literature* (1966).
Guthrie, Tyrone A. *A New Theater* (1964).
Harrison, J. R. *The Reactionaries: A Study of the Anti-Democratic Intelligentsia* (1967).
Hill, Herbert, ed., *Anger and Beyond: The Negro Writer in the United States* (1966).
Hoffman, Frederick J. *The Twenties: American Writing in the Postwar Decade* (revised ed., 1962).
Howe, Irving. *A World More Attractive: A View of Modern Literature and Politics* (1963).
Hughes, Glenn. *A History of the American Theater, 1700-1950* (1951).
Kazin. Alfred. *On Native Grounds: An Interpretation of Modern American Prose Literature* (1942).
Krutch, J. W. *The American Drama Since 1918: An Informal History* (1939).
Lasch, Christopher. *The New Radicalism, 1899-1962: The Intellectual as a Social Type* (1965).
Leisy, E. E. *The American Historical Novel* (1950).
Manheim, Leonard and Eleanor, eds., *Hidden Patterns: Studies in Psychoanalytic Literary Criticism* (1966).
Marx, Leo. *The Machine in the Garden: Technology and the Pastoral Ideal in America* (1964).
Milne, Gordon. *The American Political Novel* (1966).
O'Connòr, W. V. *An Age of Criticism, 1900-1950* (1952).
Parrington, V. L. *Main Currents in American Thought: An Interpretation of American Literature from the Beginnings to 1920* (1921-1930).
Pearce, R. H. *The Continuity of American Poetry* (1961).
Poirier, Richard. *A World Elsewhere: The Place of Style in American Literature.* (1966).
Quinn, Arthur Hobson. *A History of the American Drama: From the Civil War to the Present Day* (1927; 1936).
Quinn, Sister M. Bernetta. *The Metamorphic Tradition in Modern Poetry* (1955).
Rourke, Constance. *American Humor: A Study of the National Character* (1931).
Sutton, Walter. *Modern American Criticism* (1963).
Spencer, B. T. *The Quest of Nationality: An American Literary Campaign* (1957).
Taylor, W. F. *The Economic Novel in America* (1942).
Walcutt, Charles C. *American Literary Naturalism, a Divided Stream* (1956).
Walker, W. E., and Welker, R. L. *Reality and Myth: Essays in American Literature* (1964).
Weales, Gerard. *American Drama Since World War Two* (1962).
Weber, Brom, ed., *An Anthology of American Humor* (1962).

Index*

*Asterisk indicates that only an excerpt of the
cited work is reprinted here.